We the People

An Introduction to American Politics

SHORTER SECOND EDITION

We the People

An Introduction to American Politics

BENJAMIN GINSBERG

The Johns Hopkins University

THEODORE J. LOWI

Cornell University

MARGARET WEIR

University of California at Berkeley

SHORTER SECOND EDITION

W · W · NORTON & COMPANY · NEW YORK · LONDON

Editor: Stephen Dunn
Project Editor: Traci Nagle
Editorial Assistant & Photo Researcher: Scott McCord
Production Manager: Ruth Dworkin
Text Design: Jack Meserole
Figures: John McAusland
Cover Design: Andrew M. Newman Graphic Design, Inc.
The text of this book is composed in Sabon
with the display set in Myriad.
Composition by TSI Graphics
Manufacturing by Quebecor/Hawkins

Library of Congress Cataloging-in-Publication Data
Ginsberg, Benjamin.
   We the people: an introduction to American politics / Benjamin Ginsberg, Theodore J. Lowi, Margaret Weir. — Shorter 2nd ed.
     p. cm.
   Includes bibliographical references and index.
   ISBN 0-393-97318-2 (pbk.)
   1. United States—Politics and government.   I. Lowi, Theodore J.
II. Weir, Margaret, 1952– .   III. Title.
   JK271.G65 1999b
   320.473—dc21   98-40961

W. W. Norton & Company, Inc., 500 Fifth Avenue, New York, N.Y. 10110
http://www.wwnorton.com

W. W. Norton & Company Ltd., 10 Coptic Street, London WC1A 1PU

1 2 3 4 5 6 7 8 9 0

To
Sandy, Cindy, and Alex Ginsberg
Angele, Anna, and Jason Lowi
Nicholas Ziegler

Contents

PART II

Foundations

6 Civil Rights   194

PART III

Politics

PART IV

Institutions

15   The Federal Courts   576

Appendix   A1

Preface

We the People is a milestone in a collaboration that began between Theodore J. Lowi and Benjamin Ginsberg almost twenty years ago. The first result of that collaboration, *American Government: Freedom and Power,* was first published in 1990. With its most recent edition, we and the publishers feel warranted in expressing satisfaction that its historical/institutional method has been confirmed by its reception among the teachers who have adopted it and the students who have read it.

But unlike political leaders, textbooks should not try to be all things to all people. Endurance is most often ensured by recognition of one's limitations. Lowi and Ginsberg increasingly came to feel that *American Government* needed a sibling to address a number of themes and problems that have become much more central to American politics since *American Government* was conceived in the early 1980s. For a good text should be both timeless and timely: It should present principles whose value goes beyond the immediate events of the day. At the same time, however, it should present students with the principles they need to help elevate their understanding of contemporary events.

We viewed this process as a challenge rather than as a chore. The first step Lowi and Ginsberg took to meet the challenge of developing a new text was to invite a third author to join the enterprise: Margaret Weir, an expert on social policy in the United States and Europe. Weir brought with her a strong background in urban politics as well as the benefit of several years of teaching experience at Harvard and the University of California at Berkeley, where she now teaches.

From the start, the three of us agreed that this younger sibling would be titled *We the People* and would focus on three sets of issues. The first of these is the question of who is and who is not part of the American political community. This question has been the source of enormous conflict throughout American history and has become salient once again as events at home and throughout the world have brightened the light of democracy, exposing for everyone to see the unreasonable restrictions on who are "we the people," how should "we the people" be defined, and what powers, rights, and obligations "we the people" should have. Although the United States has so far experienced comparatively little conflict over the basic institutions and practices of government, and although our institutions have evolved in a roughly democratic direction, the struggle over the scope and inclusiveness of the American political process has often been a bitter one, and neither the struggle nor the bitterness is over.

The original American political community consisted of a rather limited group of white male property holders. Over the ensuing two centuries, "we the people" became a larger and more inclusive body as a result of such forces as the abolitionist movement, the women's suffrage movement, and the civil rights movement. This expansion of the political community was marked by enormous conflicts involving questions of race, gender, social class, and religious identity. Today, these conflicts continue in the form of struggles over such issues as affirmative action, welfare reform, abortion, the gender gap, the political mobilization of religious groups, and the rise and fall of minority voting districts. These themes are raised in Chapter 2 of *We the People* and are explored further throughout the book.

But regardless of our country's spotty record, one American feature has been and remains the envy of the entire world: Expansion of our political community *has* taken place, and it has happened without having to create new institutions, rules, or procedures. Our democracy is no crustacean that has to shed its structure as it grows.

The second set of issues that we focus on concerns American political values. The American nation is defined not only by its form of government but also by a set of shared beliefs and values, the most basic of which are liberty, equality, and democracy. Although these can be located in antiquity, Americans gave them new vitality and credibility in our founding documents—the Declaration of Independence and the Constitution, which transformed ancient and abstract principles into operating structures and rules for the new Republic. Although the path has deviated and wrong turns have been taken, the general direction of America has been one worthy of pride—a pride we authors share with virtually all of the American people. But our job as authors is to recognize the gap between ideals and realities and to treat the gap honestly so that our students come to understand that a good citizen is a critical citizen, one whose obedience is not unconditional. Liberty, equality, and democracy are concepts that link all the chapters of our book. They are also criteria against which to measure and to judge all aspects of governmental and political performance.

Finally, *We the People* addresses a pedagogical question: Why should Americans be engaged with government and politics at all? For the entire first century and more of American history under the Constitution, Americans were relatively heavily involved in political life, as activists or as active spectators. Politics was a kind of entertainment, a defining aspect of community life. Politics in America was interesting even to those who had not yet been made full members of the political community. As the size of all governments, especially the national government, began to grow after World War I, Americans by all appearances still took their politics seriously, and the scope of their interest seemed to expand from campaigns and elections into public policy issues keeping pace with the expansion of government and of government programs.

During the 1960s and 1970s, American students were heavily engaged with politics, many seeing it, quite realistically, as a matter of life and death. Even during the early 1980s, when *American Government: Freedom and Power* was being planned, it was our assumption that political engagement needed guidance—but that it was *there* to be guided. It hardly seemed necessary to explain to students why they should take politics seriously, as observers as well as activists.

But the involvement of the American people in political life has been declining, and students have been increasingly willing to ask why they should be interested in politics at all. We are deeply troubled by this trend and committed this book to its reversal. Our chapters are introduced by discussions that show where students fit into the materials to be addressed by that chapter and why they should take a personal, indeed selfish, interest in the outcomes of government. For example, our discussion of the media opens with the issues of press freedom faced by college newspapers. Our chapter on civil rights begins with an evaluation of affirmative action programs in college admissions. The opening pages of our discussion of federalism deal with interstate differences that affect college students. Our hope is to make politics interesting to students by demonstrating that their interests are at stake—that their forebears were correct in viewing politics as a matter of life and death.

In this Second Edition, we are freshly dedicated to the goal of getting students to see themselves not only as citizens but as citizens in the Greek ideal, where the opposite of citizen was *idiote*. The first major change from the First Edition is an entirely new section toward the end of Chapter 2, focusing on citizen participation. It is a success story of how the one and the few can make a genuine difference through direct political action. Time consuming, yes, but as gratifying as the football or basketball championship, and far more lasting. We recognize at the very outset that politics, like economics, is driven by self-interest, but self-interest includes a commitment to the advancement of one's community as well as to one's purse and property.

This inspired us to use more citizen participation narratives in our teaching, and those successes produced a "Citizen's Role" section at the conclusion of every chapter. In fact, some of the chapters also begin with case studies on the possibilities of one, a few, or many student-citizens influencing a legislature, an agency, a party, a newspaper, and other such centers of power. It should be added here how often political influence comes from the capacity of dedicated citizens to make a nuisance of themselves—badgering members of Congress, in person or by using the magnificent new citizen-friendly technology of fax, e-mail, and Web. From local consumer and environmental groups to pro-choice and pro-life picketers, nuisance value is an important form of influence—and the measure of that influence is the intensity of complaints you hear from its recipients: the legislators and their staffs. But that's a sign of political health. We didn't elect our representatives to a life of comfort and leisure.

On the other hand, we already knew but have become increasingly aware that student-citizens can see through sentimental or moralistic appeals to participate in politics. Students don't have to know much about politics or society to be aware of the inherent limits of individual efficacy in a Big Society like the United States—or, for that matter, a Big City or on a Big Campus. We'd be laughed out of the classroom if we pulled out the old adage that every citizen can be president, or that the views of every citizen are taken into account in the representative process. "The People" is a collective noun; "we, the individuals" don't count for much. But that does not diminish the validity of the message we convey in each and every chapter. First, we demonstrate in every chapter that the one and the few *can* count. Moreover, those who doubt this are engaging in a self-fulfilling prophecy; that is, to be *in*active as a result of a pessimistic view of the capacity of citizens is to confirm to the fullest that citizen action cannot count.

But there is a second dimension to our message about participation that must be taken seriously by even the most pessimistic person. This is that inherent in the definition of citizenship itself is the obligation to be enlightened. Self-interest will get you nowhere unless it is enlightened, by knowledge of who you are, what you want, and how you can go about getting it. This is no less true in political life than it is in economic life. Actually, enlightenment is all the more important to effective citizenship precisely because direct political action is not always a practical alternative. Go back once again to Greek antiquity, where politics *was* talk:

> To classical political theory, speech, not sight, is the most political of the faculties. . . . But political speech—and, especially, *listening* to political speech—is a skill and pleasure that must be learned; it demands an extended span of attention, the capacity for critical reflection, and that art of hearing that lets us separate meaning from its disguises. Always difficult, that command of rhetoric is harder to cultivate in a society as supersonic as ours, and the electronic media actually undermine the arts of speech and hearing.[1]

Each citizen must have a third ear, and must listen with that third ear to become the best citizen, which, we repeat, is a critical citizen. Criticism *is* speech in action.

In this Second Edition we have tried all the harder to design every chapter to the fullest extent of our ability to show why everyone must for their own sakes be interested in politics. We have tried in every way possible to provide the context, the background, and the origin of every political issue on the American political agenda. And we have tried to deal with each institution in a way that gives its place in the system but also provides a sense of how the one and the few citizens can gain access to it. And in this edition we have added what we call a "Greek chorus"—one or more boxes providing student judgments and student perspectives, drawn from case studies, polls, campaigns, and news stories. Some of these perspectives are profound; some may seem silly. As with the Greeks, our student chorus illustrates the range of enlightenment. It also demonstrates the potential of the one and the few and the many when knowledge is added to talk. Knowledge and talk are a prelude to action. Enlightenment without action can make a difference. Action without enlightenment can be dangerous. We continue to hope that our book will itself be accepted as a form of enlightened political action. This Second Edition is our second chance. It is an advancement toward our goal. We promise to keep trying.

ACKNOWLEDGMENTS

Our students at Cornell, Johns Hopkins, Harvard, and Berkeley have been an essential factor in the writing of this book. They have been our most immediate intellectual community, a hospitable one indeed. Another part of our

---

[1]Wilson Carey McWilliams, "The Meaning of the Election," in Gerald Pomper, ed., *The Election of 1988—Reports and Interpretations* (Chatham, NJ: Chatham House Publishers, 1989), p. 183.

community, perhaps a large suburb, is the discipline of political science itself. Our debt to the scholarship of our colleagues is scientifically measurable, probably to several decimal points, in the endnotes of each chapter. Despite many complaints that the field is too scientific or not scientific enough, political science is alive and well in the United States. It is an aspect of democracy itself, and it has grown and changed in response to the developments in government and politics that we have chronicled in our book. If we did a "time line" on the history of political science, it would show a close association with developments in "the American state." Sometimes the discipline has been out of phase and critical; at other times, it has been in phase and perhaps apologetic. But political science has never been at a loss for relevant literature, and without it, our job would have been impossible.

We are especially pleased to acknowledge our debt to the many colleagues who had a direct and active role in criticism and preparation of the manuscript. Our thanks go to

First Edition Reviewers:
Sarah Binder, Brookings Institution
Kathleen Gille, Office of Representative David Bonior
Rodney Hero, University of Colorado at Boulder
Robert Katzmann, Brookings Institution
Kathleen Knight, University of Houston
Robin Kolodny, Temple University
Nancy Kral, Tomball College
Robert C. Lieberman, Columbia University
David A. Marcum, University of Wyoming
Laura R. Winsky Mattei, State University of New York at Buffalo
Marilyn S. Mertens, Midwestern State University
Barbara Suhay, Henry Ford Community College
Carolyn Wong, Stanford University
Julian Zelizer, State University of New York at Albany

Second Edition Reviewers
Lydia Andrade, University of North Texas
John Coleman, University of Wisconsin at Madison
Daphne Eastman, Odessa College
Otto Feinstein, Wayne State University
Elizabeth Flores, Delmar College
James Gimpel, University of Maryland at College Park
Jill Glaathar, Southwest Missouri State University
Shaun Herness, University of Florida
William Lyons, University of Tennessee at Knoxville
Andrew Polsky, Hunter College, City University of New York
Grant Reeher, Syracuse University
Richard Rich, Virginia Polytechnic, and
Bartholomew Sparrow, University of Texas at Austin

We owe a very special thanks to Robert J. Spitzer of the State University of New York at Cortland for preparing the "Policy Debates" and "We the People" essays. Bob's contributions to our writing efforts nearly amount to serving as our co-author and we are especially grateful. We look forward to working with Bob on future projects. In addition, we thank again Michael Harvey of the University of Wisconsin at Milwaukee for preparing the "American Political Culture" essays. By linking concepts to historical events and contemporary debates, these essays help to make this a more lively and interesting book and thus one that students will be more likely to read and remember.

We would also like to thank Paul Gronke of Duke University for authoring the "Politics on the Web" sidebars. Paul also helped develop content for the website accompanying the text. In addition to Paul, Van Wigginton of San Jacinto College and Derek Reveron of the University of Illinois at Chicago contributed enormous amounts of very thoughtful content to the website, in addition to later keeping it as current as this new technology allows for. Finally, we would like to thank Marilyn Mertens of Midwestern State University for her authorship of both the study guide and instructor's manual to accompany the book. Marilyn's teaching experience was a valuable addition to the whole project.

We are also grateful for the talents and hard work of several research assistants, whose contributions can never be adequately compensated. In particular, Mingus Mapps of Cornell and Doug Harris of Johns Hopkins put an enormous amount of thought and time into the figures, tables, and study aids that appear in the text. Mingus also kept a close eye on keeping the book as up-to-date as possible.

We would like to give special thanks to Jacqueline Pastore at Cornell University, who not only prepared portions of the manuscript but also helped to hold the entire project together. We especially thank for her hard work and dedication.

Perhaps above all, we wish to thank those at W. W. Norton. For its two editions, Steve Dunn has helped us shape the book in countless ways and Traci Nagle has helped us refine our arguments and our prose. Norton's editors are the best any of us have ever worked with. In addition to Steve and Traci, we thank Scott McCord for devoting an enormous amount of time to the Second Edition, especially in finding new photos and interviewing dozens of students for the "Students and Politics" sidebars. For our interactive web version of the book, Steve Hoge has been an energetic and visionary editor. John Darger devoted many hours to guaranteeing the book's success. Ruth Dworkin has been dedicated in managing the details of production for both editions. Finally, we wish to thank Roby Harrington, the head of Norton's college department.

We are more than happy, however, to absolve all these contributors from any flaws, errors, and misjudgments that will inevitably be discovered. We wish the book could be free of all production errors, grammatical errors, misspellings, misquotes, missed citations, etc. From that standpoint, a book ought to try to be perfect. But substantively we have not tried to write a flawless book; we have not tried to write a book to please everyone. We have again tried to write an effective book, a book that cannot be taken lightly. Our goal was not to make every reader a political scientist or a political activist. Our goal was to restore politics as a subject matter of vigorous and enjoyable discourse, recapturing it from the bondage of the thirty-second sound bite and the thirty-page technical briefing. Every person can be knowledgeable because everything about politics is accessible. One does not have to be a television anchorperson to profit from political events. One does not have to be a philosopher to argue about the requisites of democracy, a lawyer to dispute constitutional interpretations, an economist to debate a public policy. We would be very proud if our book contributes in a small way to the restoration of the ancient art of political controversy.

BENJAMIN GINSBERG
THEODORE J. LOWI
MARGARET WEIR

SEPTEMBER 1998

We the People

An Introduction to American Politics

SHORTER SECOND EDITION

American Political Life

1

American

Political Culture

ONE of the most striking features of American political life is its openness. Virtually any American citizen who feels strongly about political issues and wants to become involved in the political process can actually do so. The stories of two recent college graduates illustrate this point.

Jim Wilkinson graduated from the University of Texas at Arlington in 1993. During his sophomore year, Jim, a finance major, became convinced that the tax system was unfair and inefficient and needed to be changed. Driven by this conviction, Jim volunteered as an intern in the Arlington, Texas, office of Republican congressional representative Richard Armey, a sharp critic of the current tax structure. Jim worked in Armey's district office for several months, dealing primarily with the problems of people living in Armey's electoral district and learning more about the role and power of a member of Congress. During the summer after his junior year, Jim traveled to Washington, D.C., to work as an unpaid intern in Armey's Capitol Hill office and for Congress's Joint Economic Committee, of which Armey was the senior Republican member.

"That summer changed my life," Wilkinson recalled. "It allowed me to put a face to government." During the course of his internship, Jim worked on education policy and economic policy. He helped to draft a major piece of legislation and, at the same time, had a real chance to act on his conviction that the tax code needed to be overhauled. Jim helped Representative Armey develop a proposal to replace the current tax system with a "flat tax" on all income. Armey's proposal has considerable support among some Republicans and is influencing the current debate over taxation. After graduating from college, Jim became a full-time member of Armey's staff. "I packed up my pickup truck and drove to D.C.," he recalls. Today, Representative Armey holds the powerful position of House majority leader, second in command to the Speaker of the House. Jim Wilkinson serves as Armey's press secretary. Jim says the most important lesson to draw from his political experience is that "in a democracy you have as much right as anyone else to get involved."

Melissa Feld is another recent college graduate working in Congress. While Jim works for the majority leader, Melissa works for the House minority leader, Democratic representative Richard Gephardt of Missouri. In college, Melissa had been vice president of the student government and was very interested in politics. Once in Washington, she worked as a volunteer for several nonprofit groups and looked for ways to become more involved politically. Melissa is adamantly pro-choice and is very concerned with international human rights issues. "The Tiananmen Square massacre was one of the key events that got me into politics," she says. "Here we had students involved in a peaceful demonstration for change and the Chinese government ruthlessly suppressed them. I felt I had to do something."

Her chance to do something came in 1995. Melissa volunteered to work on the Clinton-Gore re-election campaign. Melissa remembers thinking. "This is giving me a chance to get involved in history." As a volunteer, Melissa helped organize rallies, coordinate staff, and, eventually, plan inaugural festivities. During the course of the campaign, Melissa met a member of Representative Gephardt's staff. Through this contact Melissa applied for a staff position with Gephardt. Melissa believed that Gephardt was a staunch proponent of her own views in the areas with which she was most concerned. Working with Gephardt, says Melissa, "I believed I could help make this a better world."

Today, Melissa serves as chief financial officer for Gephardt's re-election committee. One of her primary tasks is making certain that the office is in full compliance with all federal regulations pertaining to fund-raising. She has mastered the intricacies of U.S. election law, federal lobbying laws, and congressional ethics codes.

Although Jim and Melissa are exceptionally talented individuals, their stories are like those of many others. Every year tens of thousands of college students work as interns and staffers in the offices of members of Congress, in state and local legislatures, and in various executive agencies. Like hundreds of thousands before them, these students bring their ideals and passions into the American political arena. They "load up their pickup trucks" and come to Washington or to their state capitals, where they can "get involved in history."

Jim and Melissa are typical in another respect. Jim is a conservative Republican working for one of the most conservative members of Congress. Melissa is a liberal Democrat working for one of the more liberal members of Congress. When students bring their ideals and passions into the political arena, they also bring intense conflicts and disagreements. There are virtually no current political issues on which Jim and Melissa agree. Left in a room together, they could and probably would argue for hours. Yet both work for the same governmental institution and both share a deep commitment to the idea that all citizens have a duty to "get involved" and work to "make this a better world." Ultimately, each also understands that the other's views and intentions are as noble as his or her own and deserve a fair hearing. This is one of the great strengths of American democracy. From differences freely expressed come strength and vitality.

In one important way, however, Jim and Melissa are unusual. These two recent college graduates have chosen to get involved in the political process; most young Americans, however, have chosen not to. And although "getting involved" can mean many different things, it does not necessarily mean a career in politics. Citizen participation is in almost all instances part-time and amateur. Yet even if we measure interest in influencing the political process by whether someone shows up to vote for the president every four years, even then political interest and involvement by Americans is low. College students are no exception to this trend. As we will see in later chapters, political involvement is lowest among eighteen- to twenty-four-year-olds. An annual survey of college freshmen shows that fewer than 20 percent of college students considers "influencing the political structure" to be an important life goal (see Figure 1.1).

What explains Americans' general lack of interest in politics? The relationship between the American people and American government is a complex one that we will explore here and throughout this textbook. There is no doubt that government is a big presence in the lives of all Americans. In today's political

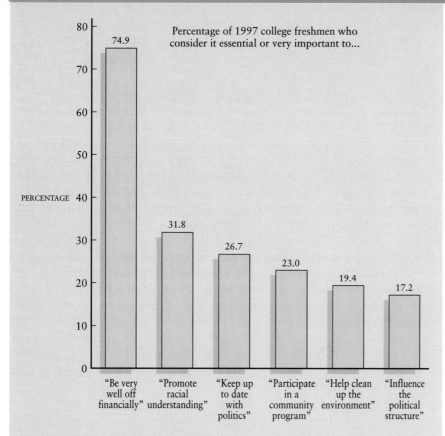

IMPORTANT LIFE GOALS OF COLLEGE FRESHMEN   Figure 1.1

Percentage of 1997 college freshmen who consider it essential or very important to...

Goal	Percentage
"Be very well off financially"	74.9
"Promote racial understanding"	31.8
"Keep up to date with politics"	26.7
"Participate in a community program"	23.0
"Help clean up the environment"	19.4
"Influence the political structure"	17.2

SOURCE: L. J. Sax, A. W. Astin, W. S. Korn, and K. M. Mahoney, *The American Freshman: National Norms for Fall 1997* (Los Angeles: Higher Education Research Institute, UCLA Graduate School of Education, 1997).

Over the past twenty-five years, college freshmen have been consistently uninterested in political participation. The "American Freshman" polls reveal that students are more interested in their own financial well-being, broader social concerns such as the environment, and the communities in which they live than they are the political system.

climate, however, many see this presence as a negative one. Another disturbing trend is that many Americans view government as unresponsive and "out of touch" with their needs. We will assess the causes and consequences of this phenomenon later in this chapter, but let us say for now that apathy and cynicism need not prevail. The view of the pessimist that the American system is unresponsive is not only wrong but is a detestable and harmful view, because it can become a self-fulfilling prophecy.

■ ***In this chapter, we will explore the relationship between the government and the people it governs. First, we will assess what Americans think about their government.*** Although Americans have always been distrustful of governmental power, they rely on government for many of their needs. In recent decades, however, trust in government and the belief that individuals can influence government have both been in decline. These trends have important consequences that we need to examine.

■ **Second, we will explore the principle of democratic citizenship.** We believe that good citizenship begins with political knowledge—knowledge of government, of politics, and of democratic principles. With this knowledge, citizens can identify their interests and take advantage of their opportunities to influence politics.

■ **Next, we will look at the principles of government and politics.** The relationship between a government and its citizens is especially dependent on the form that a government takes. In order to better understand the opportunities that citizens have to influence government, we will look at the alternative forms government can take and the key differences among them. We will also examine the factors that led to the emergence of representative democracy in the United States and elsewhere around the world. In doing so, we will consider one of the most fundamental and enduring problems of democratic politics: the relationship between government and the people it governs.

■ **Finally, we will look at American political culture.** Here, we will examine the political principles that serve as the basis for American government and assess how well government upholds these ideals. We will conclude by suggesting what ordinary citizens can do to make these American political ideals more of a reality.

What Americans Think about Government

▶ Why has trust in government declined considerably in recent decades?

▶ Why is it important that Americans think that they can influence what the government does?

Since the United States was founded, Americans have been reluctant to grant government too much power, and they have often been suspicious of politicians. But over the course of the nation's history, Americans have also turned to government for assistance in times of need and have strongly supported the government in periods of war. These sentiments were reflected in the earliest opinion polls in the 1930s, 1940s, and 1950s, which showed broad public confidence in government. In recent decades, however, the public's view of government has turned more sour. Public trust in government has declined and Americans are now more likely to feel that they can do little to influence government. These developments are important to understand because politically engaged citizens and public confidence in government are vital for the health of a democracy.

TRUST IN GOVERNMENT

The decline in trust in government among Americans is striking. In the early 1960s, three-quarters of Americans said that they trusted government most of the time. By 1994, the proportions had reversed: only one-quarter of Americans expressed trust in government; three-quarters stated that they did not trust government most of the time.[1] Different groups vary somewhat in their levels of trust; African Americans and Latinos generally express more confidence in the federal government than do whites. But even among the groups that are most supportive of government, only one-third express strong trust in government.[2]

The Size and Scope of Government   Why has trust declined so dramatically? One possible reason is that Americans believe government has become too big and too distant. There can be little doubt that government has expanded in scope since this country was founded. In 1789, 1889, and even as recently as 1929, America's national government was limited in size, scope, and influence; most of the important functions of government were provided by the states. In 1933, however, the influence of the government began to expand to meet the crises created by the stock market crash of 1929, the Great Depression, and the run on banks of 1933. Congress passed legislation that brought the government into the businesses of home mortgages, farm mortgages, credit, and relief of personal distress. Whereas in 1933 people had tried to withdraw their money from the banks only to find that their savings had been wiped out, sixty years later most Americans are confident that their money is safe because it is guaranteed by the national government. Today, the national government is an enormous institution with programs and policies reaching into every corner of American life. It oversees the nation's economy; it is the nation's largest employer; it provides citizens with a host of services; it controls the world's most formidable military establishment; and it regulates a wide range of social and commercial activities in which Americans engage. Despite this tremendous expansion of government, there is little indication that the growth of government by itself has caused declining trust. During the times when the government expanded its role the most, public support ran very high.[3]

Another possible reason that Americans distrust government is that they believe that they derive few benefits from government activity, or that it is too intrusive. The influence of government is so pervasive that many people may not realize how much they benefit from government. At the same time, however, they may be all too aware of government regulations.

Americans are completely surrounded by government programs and government controls. Citizens are so dependent upon government today that much of what they have come to take for granted—as, somehow, part of the natural environment—is in fact created by government. For example, a college student who drives her car to school may think that she is engaged in a purely private activity. Yet the simple act of driving an automobile is heavily dependent upon a multitude of government initiatives and is surrounded by a host of governmental rules. The roads upon which the student drives were constructed by a local government, probably with the assistance of some fraction of the more than $20 billion in federal highway funds spent each year. The roads are maintained by municipal, county, and state governments. During the winter, snow is removed from the roads by local governments. Traffic is regulated by local governments. Road signs are placed and maintained by local and state governments. The student holds a driver's license issued by her state government, which has also registered her vehicle and inspected it for safety and compliance with emissions standards. The vehicle itself has been manufactured to meet safety and emissions standards set by the federal government. The contract under which the student purchased the automobile as well as the loan she signed if she borrowed money for the purchase were both governed by commercial sales and banking regulations established by the state and federal governments. The list goes on.

It might be possible for this student to drive to school without all this government assistance and regulation. In principle, roads could be privately owned, traffic unregulated, and neither drivers nor their autos required to meet any standards. Perhaps our student could still reach her destination in such an environment. Certainly, her driving experience would be markedly different from the current one.

The example of this driver could be applied in endless other situations. Government plays a role in everyone's activities and, by the same token, regulates almost everything we do. Figure 1.2 is a diagram of some of the governmental services received by and controls exerted upon any recent college graduate. Some of these governmental activities are federal, while others are the province of state and local governments.

Most Americans want to keep the benefits they receive from government. Although they may resent it in principle, in practice even most conservatives have reconciled themselves to an activist state. Many self-styled "conservatives" differ more with their "liberal" counterparts over the proper character of government than over its ultimate desirability.

Government Performance   As distrust in government has grown, so has public dissatisfaction with the performance of government. Opinion polls clearly show that Americans have not been happy with government performance. In a 1996 poll, 81 percent believed that "government is wasteful and inefficient,"

Most Americans want to keep the benefits they receive from the government. When Congress proposed cutting Medicare funding in 1995, senior citizen groups protested in Washington.

THE ROLE OF GOVERNMENT IN YOUR LIFE Figure 1.2

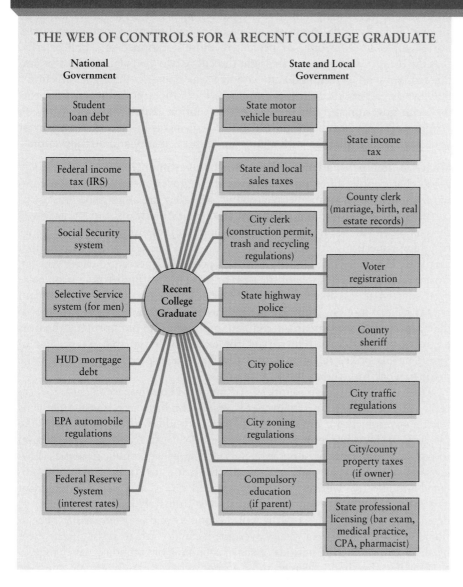

THE WEB OF CONTROLS FOR A RECENT COLLEGE GRADUATE

National Government

- Student loan debt
- Federal income tax (IRS)
- Social Security system
- Selective Service system (for men)
- HUD mortgage debt
- EPA automobile regulations
- Federal Reserve System (interest rates)

Recent College Graduate

State and Local Government

- State motor vehicle bureau
- State income tax
- State and local sales taxes
- County clerk (marriage, birth, real estate records)
- City clerk (construction permit, trash and recycling regulations)
- Voter registration
- State highway police
- County sheriff
- City police
- City traffic regulations
- City zoning regulations
- City/county property taxes (if owner)
- Compulsory education (if parent)
- State professional licensing (bar exam, medical practice, CPA, pharmacist)

Government is a pervasive force in the lives of all Americans, especially at the state and local level. Think of the many ways in which government affects your life every day.

and 79 percent said that "government spends too much money on the wrong things."[4] There is a broad public sense that the government has spent enormous amounts of money on problems that it has done little to solve and that many such problems have only gotten worse. But in many of the areas where the public believes there has been little progress, such as poverty among the elderly and air pollution, government action has in fact had an important positive impact. Some scholars attribute the negative public perceptions of government performance to the news media, which tend to cover public activities in a negative light and at the same time provide sensational coverage of problems. For example, for many years, ABC News ran a nightly feature called "Your Money," which specialized in finding instances of government waste.[5]

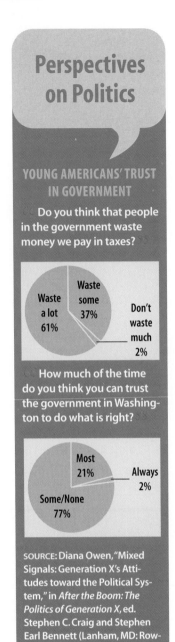

SOURCE: Diana Owen, "Mixed Signals: Generation X's Attitudes toward the Political System," in *After the Boom: The Politics of Generation X,* ed. Stephen C. Craig and Stephen Earl Bennett (Lanham, MD: Rowman and Littlefield, 1997), p. 95.

Public views about government are also strongly affected by the national economy. For much of the early 1990s, public assessments about government performance were highly negative, and public anger with government was at an all-time high. By 1998, however, as the economy improved, opinions shifted. For example, in 1995 only 27 percent of those questioned in a poll believed that the country was going in the right direction; two years later, with a booming economy, 44 percent said the country was going in the right direction.[6] Still, even in a period of prosperity, a majority of those polled seemed dissatisfied with government. And some analysts caution that declining anger with government does not mean more public engagement; in fact, declining anger with government is linked with a growing sense of apathy and disconnection.

What Do Young Americans Think about Government?   We have already noted that people differ in their views about government. The image commonly portrayed of young people today is that they are among the most cynical and most distrustful of government among all Americans. In fact, however, there is little evidence for this view. If we look at measures of trust, the views of young Americans are very similar to those of the rest of the population. Like most Americans, a majority of young people (77 percent) believe you can trust government only some of the time or none of the time. Young people are even somewhat less likely than their older cohorts to say that government wastes a lot of money. And there are indications that a majority of young people believe that government can play an important role in improving the lives of ordinary people. A 1996 survey, for example, found that 52 percent of young people polled felt that "government can help people, and needs to be made to work for average working families."[7]

Does it matter if large numbers of Americans continue to distrust government? For the most part, the answer is yes. As we have seen, most Americans rely on government for a wide range of services and laws that they simply take for granted. But long-term distrust in government can result in public refusal to pay taxes adequate to support such widely approved public activities. Low levels of confidence may also make it difficult for government to attract talented and effective workers to public service.[8] The weakening of government as a result of prolonged levels of distrust may ultimately harm our capacity to defend our national interest in the world economy and may jeopardize our national security. Likewise, a weak government can do little to assist citizens who need help in weathering periods of sharp economic or technological change.

On the other hand, we certainly do not believe that Americans must be completely trusting to make democracy work. After all, Thomas Jefferson said that democracy requires "eternal vigilance" on the part of the people to keep the government in check. Part of our job is to maintain healthy Jeffersonian distrust while fighting against the unhealthy distrust and cynicism that leads people to believe that what they do in political life makes no difference. If you don't trust the government, you should follow Jefferson's lead and become motivated, rather than paralyzed, by your suspicions. Ironically, distrust can be part of healthy citizenship.

POLITICAL EFFICACY

political efficacy

the ability to influence government and politics

Along with growing distrust, another important trend in American views about government has been a declining sense of **political efficacy,** the belief

Time of Day	Schedule
7:00 AM	Wake up. Standard time set by the national government.
7:10 AM	Shower. Water courtesy of local government, either a public entity or a regulated private company. Brush your teeth with toothpaste, with cavity-fighting claims verified by federal agency. Dry your hair with electric dryer, manufactured according to federal government agency guidelines.
7:30 AM	Have a bowl of cereal with milk for breakfast. "Nutrition Facts" on food labels are a federal requirement, pasteurization of milk required by state law, freshness dating on milk based on state and federal standards, recycling the empty cereal box and milk carton required by state or local laws.
8:30 AM	Drive or take public transportation to campus. Air bags and seat belts required by federal and state laws. Roads and bridges paid for by state and local governments, speed and traffic laws set by state and local governments, public transportation subsidized by all levels of government.
8:45 AM	Arrive on campus of large public university. Buildings are 70 percent financed by state taxpayers.
9:00 AM	First class: Chemistry 101. Tuition partially paid by a federal loan (more than half the cost of university instruction is paid for by taxpayers), chemistry lab paid for with grants from the National Science Foundation (a federal agency) and smaller grants from business corporations made possible by federal income tax deductions for charitable contributions.
Noon	Eat lunch. College cafeteria financed by state dormitory authority on land grant from federal Department of Agriculture.
2:00 PM	Second class: American Government 101 (your favorite class!). You may be taking this class because it's required by the state legislature or because it fulfills a university requirement.
4:00 PM	Third class: Computer lab. Free computers, software, and Internet access courtesy of state subsidies plus grants and discounts from IBM and Microsoft, the costs of which are deducted from their corporate income taxes; Internet built in part by federal government. Duplication of software protected by federal copyright laws.
6:00 PM	Eat dinner: hamburger and french fries. Meat inspected by federal agencies for bacteria.
7:00 PM	Work at part-time job at the campus library. Minimum wage set by federal government, books and journals in library paid for by state taxpayers.
10:00 PM	Go to local bar. Purchase and consumption of alcohol regulated by state law and enforced by city police.
11:00 PM	Go home. Street lighting paid for by county and city governments, police patrols by city government.
11:15 PM	Watch TV. Networks regulated by federal government, cable public-access channels required by city law. Weather forecast provided to broadcasters by a federal agency.
Midnight	Put out the garbage before going to bed. Garbage collected by city sanitation department, financed by "user charges."

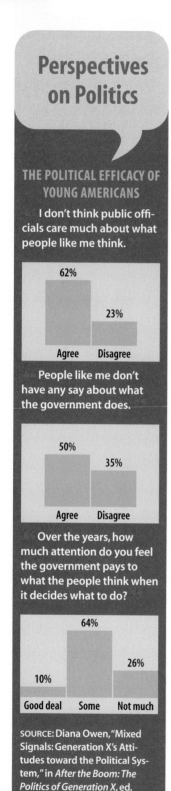

that citizens can affect what government does, that they can take action to make government listen to them. In recent decades, the public belief that government is responsive to ordinary citizens has declined. Today, 66 percent of Americans say that government officials don't care what people think; in 1964, only 36 percent felt so shut out of government. Along with this sense that ordinary people can't get heard is a growing belief—held by 76 percent of the public in 1994—that "government is run by a few big interests looking out only for themselves."[9] These views are widely shared across the age spectrum.

Many young Americans feel that government has ignored their views in particular. They feel that older officials cannot understand the challenges and problems facing the younger generation. For example, 72 percent of young people polled agreed that "our generation has an important voice but no one seems to hear it." But young Americans are not alone in feeling that government doesn't listen to them. In fact, most people of earlier generations feel even more strongly than young Americans that public officials have little interest in what they think.[10] The sense that government is out of touch and the feelings of powerlessness and lack of political efficacy that come with it seem to affect most Americans, regardless of generation.

This widely felt loss of political efficacy is bad news for American democracy. The feeling that you can't affect government decisions can lead to a self-perpetuating cycle of apathy, declining political participation, and withdrawal from political life. Why bother to participate if you believe it makes no difference? Yet, as we will discuss in Chapter 2, the belief that you can be effective is the first step needed to influence government. Not every effort of ordinary citizens to influence government will succeed, but without any such efforts, government decisions will be made by a smaller and smaller circle of powerful people. Such loss of broad popular influence over government actions undermines the key feature of American democracy—government by the people.

★ Citizens and Government

▶ What are the important features of citizenship in America?

We often refer to the ordinary individuals involved in political life as "citizens." *Citizen* and *citizenship* are among the most important—and most frequently misunderstood—terms in politics. What is citizenship?

CITIZENSHIP

Beginning with the ancient Greeks, citizenship has meant membership in one's community. In fact, the Greeks did not even conceive of the individual as a complete person. The complete person was the public person, the *citizen;* noncitizens and private persons were referred to as *idiotés*. Participation in public affairs was virtually the definition of citizenship. Citizenship was never defined as voting. Although voting was not excluded, the essence of citizen participation was talking. As one political philosopher put it, "What counts is argument among the citizens. . . . [T]he citizen who makes the most persuasive argument gets [his or her] way but can't use force, or pull rank, or distribute money; [the citizen] must talk about the issues at hand. . . . Citizens must come into the forum with nothing but their arguments."[11] Involvement in the public debate is the central, quintessential right of citizenship. Following the Greek idea, the First Amendment to the U.S. Constitution makes freedom of speech the primary right of American citizenship. And reading through the Constitution (which is reprinted in the Appendix), you will see that many other rights follow.

Citizens in the United States have a vast array of rights, but what about citizens' obligations to government? From a constitutional standpoint, there are none. The only obligations are those imposed on the government itself. All obligations on citizens are imposed only by law. Citizenship does not entail formal demands on citizens other than to obey the laws passed by the government. But there are less-formal aspects that can be requested of citizens. During certain times in American history, for example, some have suggested that citizenship means unquestioned obedience to the government, or unquestioned patriotism such as saluting the American flag and singing the national anthem, or showing basic trust in government. We disagree with these views because we believe, like Thomas Jefferson, that at times a good citizen is a critical and distrustful citizen. With the goal of eternal vigilance in mind, we prefer another meaning for **citizenship**: enlightened political engagement.[12] To be politically engaged in a meaningful way, citizens require resources, especially political knowledge and information. Democracy functions best when citizens are informed. Using "enlightened political engagement" as our operating definition, there are thus two paths toward "good" citizenship. The first, enlightenment and knowledge, will be the subject of the rest of this chapter. The second, political engagement, will be the subject of Chapter 2, where we will examine the ways in which Americans participate in the American political community.

citizenship

informed and active membership in a political community

CITIZENSHIP AND POLITICAL KNOWLEDGE

To be a citizen in the full sense as understood first by the ancient Greeks requires more than an occasional visit to a polling place. A true citizen must have the knowledge needed to participate in political debate. If you want to be a citizen rather than an *idioté*, it is important that you acquire three forms of political knowledge from this course and this textbook:

1. *Knowledge of government.* Citizens must understand the "rules of the game." From the citizen's perspective, the most important rules concern one's own political rights, which can vary greatly according to the type of government under which one lives. In the United States, these rights are extensive and concrete, and affect every citizen directly.
2. *Knowledge of politics.* We need to understand what is at stake in the political world. This understanding includes the capacity to discern our own interests in the political arena and identify the best means through which to realize them.
3. *Knowledge of democratic principles.* Although politics may divide Americans, democratic ideals hold them together. As citizens, we need to know what forms of political conduct are consistent with democratic

Informed debate is a critical part of citizenship. In 1998, several forums sponsored by the organization Americans Discuss Social Security were held across the United States.

principles. Democracy requires that both government and citizens be aware of and respect the constraints upon their political activities.

Political knowledge means more than having a few opinions to offer the pollster or to guide your decisions in a voting booth. It is important to know the rules and strategies that govern political institutions and the principles upon which they are based, but it is more important to know them in ways that relate to your own interests. Citizens need knowledge in order to identify their interests and know when to act upon them. Knowledgeable citizens are more attentive to and more engaged in politics because they understand how and why politics is relevant to their lives.

FROM KNOWLEDGE TO INTEREST

Sadly, the state of political knowledge in the United States today is dismal. A recent survey that tested the knowledge of the institutions and processes of government in the United States found that 70 percent of the respondents answered correctly fewer than 60 percent of the questions (see Table 1.1). In most colleges and universities, below 60 is a failing grade. But, rather than dwell on the widespread political ignorance of many Americans, we prefer to view this as an opportunity for the readers of this book. Those of you who make the effort to become among the knowledgeable few will be much better prepared to influence the political system regarding the issues and concerns that you care most about. Finally, bear in mind that no citizen has to be alone in the effort to influence government. We will turn to this in more detail in Chapter 2, but an important aspect of political knowledge is knowing who shares your interests.

The rest of this chapter will look at the forms of political knowledge that we believe are most critical for a citizen to possess. In the next section, we will

| **WHO KNOWS WHAT?** | Table 1.1 |

Question	Percentage answering correctly
What is affirmative action?	31
When was the New Deal?	29
How long is a senator's term?	25
Name two First Amendment rights.	20
What is the Food and Drug Administration?	20
Name all three branches of government.	19
What was the New Deal?	15

SOURCE: Michael X. Delli Carpini and Scott Keeter, *What Americans Know about Politics and Why It Matters* (New Haven, CT: Yale University Press, 1996), pp. 58–94.

examine the principles of government and politics. Following that, we will review the democratic principles upon which the United States is based and assess how well American government fulfills these principles. Finally, we will conclude with suggestions of what you and other ordinary citizens can do to become more knowledgeable and more engaged.

★ Government

▶ What are the different forms that a government can take?

▶ How did the principle of limited government develop?

▶ How can people participate in politics and influence what the government does?

Government is the term generally used to describe the formal institutions through which a land and its people are ruled. To govern is to rule. A government may be as simple as a tribal council that meets occasionally to advise the chief, or as complex as the vast establishments, with their forms, rules, and bureaucracies, found in the United States and the countries of Europe. A more complex government is sometimes referred to as "the state." In the history of civilization, governments have not been difficult to establish. There have been thousands of them. The hard part is establishing a government that lasts. Even more difficult is developing a stable government that is compatible with liberty, equality, and democracy.

government

institutions and procedures through which a territory and its people are ruled

FORMS OF GOVERNMENT

Governments vary in their structure, in their size, and in the way they operate. Two questions are of special importance in determining how governments differ: Who governs? And how much government control is permitted?

In some nations, governing is done by a single individual—a king or dictator,

autocracy

a form of government in which a single individual—a king, queen, or dictator—rules

oligarchy

a form of government in which a small group—landowners, military officers, or wealthy merchants—controls most of the governing decisions

democracy

a system of rule that permits citizens to play a significant part in the governmental process, usually through the election of key public officials

constitutional government

a system of rule in which formal and effective limits are placed on the powers of the government

authoritarian government

a system of rule in which the government recognizes no formal limits but may nevertheless be restrained by the power of other social institutions

totalitarian government

a system of rule in which the government recognizes no formal limits on its power and seeks to absorb or eliminate other social institutions that might challenge it

for example. This state of affairs is called **autocracy.** Where a small group—perhaps landowners, military officers, or wealthy merchants—controls most of the governing decisions, that government is said to be an **oligarchy.** If more people participate and have some influence over decision making, that government is a **democracy.**

Governments also vary considerably in terms of how they govern. In the United States and a small number of other nations, governments are limited as to what they are permitted to control (substantive limits), as well as how they go about it (procedural limits). Governments that are so limited are called **constitutional governments,** or liberal governments. In other nations, including many in Europe as well as in South America, Asia, and Africa, though the law imposes few real limits, the government is nevertheless kept in check by other political and social institutions that the government is unable to control and must come to terms with—such as autonomous territories, an organized church, organized business groups, or organized labor unions. Such governments are generally called **authoritarian.** In a third group of nations, including the Soviet Union under Joseph Stalin, Nazi Germany, and perhaps prewar Japan and Italy, governments not only are free of legal limits but also seek to eliminate those organized social groups that might challenge or limit the government's authority. These governments typically attempt to dominate or control every sphere of political, economic, and social life and, as a result, are called **totalitarian** (see Box 1.2).

Americans have the good fortune to live in a nation in which limits are placed on what governments can do and how they can do it. But such constitutional democracies are relatively rare in today's world; it is estimated that only twenty or so of the world's nearly two hundred governments could be included in this category. And constitutional democracies were unheard of before the modern era. Prior to the eighteenth and nineteenth centuries, governments seldom sought—and rarely received—the support of their ordinary subjects. The available evidence strongly suggests that the ordinary people had little love for the government or for the social order. After all, they had no stake in it. They equated government with the police officer, the bailiff, and the tax collector.[13]

Beginning in the seventeenth century, in a handful of Western nations, two important changes began to take place in the character and conduct of government. First, governments began to acknowledge formal limits upon their power. Second, a small number of governments began to provide the ordinary citizen with a formal voice in public affairs—through the vote. Obviously, the desirability of limits on government and the expansion of popular influence were at the heart of the American Revolution in 1776. "No taxation without representation," as we shall see in Chapter 3, was hotly debated from the beginning of the Revolution through the Founding in 1789. But even before the Revolution, a tradition of limiting government and expanding participation in the political process had developed throughout western Europe. Thus, to understand how the relationship between rulers and the ruled was transformed, we must broaden our focus to take into account events in Europe as well as in America. We will have to divide the transformation into its two separate parts. The first is the effort to put limits on government. The second is the effort to expand the influence of the people through access to government and politics.

*M*ost Western democracies have constitutions that actually define the limits and scope of governmental power. But the mere existence of a constitution does not, by itself, define a regime as constitutional. Some governments have constitutions that they ignore. At least until recently, this was the case in such eastern European nations as Romania and Bulgaria. In the true constitutional setting, the actual processes of government follow the forms prescribed by the constitution, and groups in society have sufficient freedom and power to oppose efforts by the government to overstep these limits. The governments in the United States and western Europe provide the best examples.

Authoritarian governments must sometimes be responsive to a small number of powerful social groups and institutions such as the army, but such governments recognize no formal obligations to consult their citizens or to respect limits on their actions. Examples of authoritarian governments in the recent past include Spain under the leadership of General Francisco Franco and Portugal under Prime Minister Antonio Salazar.

Totalitarian governments can be distinguished from both democratic and authoritarian governments by the lack of any distinction between the government and other important social institutions. Indeed, totalitarian governments generally seek to destroy all other social institutions—for example, churches, labor unions, and political parties—that may function as rival sources of power. Examples of totalitarian governments include the Third Reich in Germany under Adolf Hitler in the 1930s and 1940s and the government of the Soviet Union under Joseph Stalin between the 1930s and 1950s.

In recent years, a number of authoritarian regimes in eastern Europe, including the Soviet Union and its satellite states, faced severe economic hardship and popular discontent. After 1989, most of these regimes, including those in Czechoslovakia, Poland, Hungary, East Germany, and the Soviet Union itself, collapsed and were replaced by new, democratically elected governments.

LIMITING GOVERNMENT

The key force behind the imposition of limits on government power was a new social class, the bourgeoisie. Bourgeoisie is a French word for freeman of the city, or *bourg*. Being part of the bourgeoisie later became associated with being "middle class" and with being in commerce or industry. In order to gain a share of control of government, joining or even displacing the kings, aristocrats, and gentry who had dominated government for centuries, the bourgeoisie sought to change existing institutions—especially parliaments—into instruments of real political participation. Parliaments had existed for centuries, but were generally aristocratic institutions. The bourgeoisie embraced parliaments as means by which they could exert the weight of their superior numbers and growing economic advantage against their aristocratic rivals. At the same time, the bourgeoisie sought to place restraints on the capacity of governments to threaten these economic and political interests by placing formal or constitutional limits on governmental power. The three bourgeois (also

In May 1989, demonstrators gathered in Beijing's Tiananmen Square to protest against the totalitarian Chinese government. The protesters chose an American symbol, the Statue of Liberty, as a model for their "Goddess of Democracy." The demonstrations lasted several weeks, but eventually they were brutally suppressed by the Chinese authorities, and many of the protesters were sent to prison.

called liberal) philosophers with the strongest influence on American thinking were John Locke, Adam Smith, and John Stuart Mill (see Box 1.3).

Although motivated primarily by the need to protect and defend their own interests, the bourgeoisie advanced many of the principles that became the central underpinnings of individual liberty for all citizens—freedom of speech, freedom of assembly, freedom of conscience, and freedom from arbitrary search and seizure. It is important to note here that the bourgeoisie generally did not favor democracy as we know it. They were advocates of electoral and representative institutions, but they favored property requirements and other restrictions so as to limit participation to the middle classes. Yet once these institutions of politics and the protection of the right to engage in politics were established, it was difficult to limit them to the bourgeoisie. Time after time, principles first advanced to justify a selfish interest tend to take on a life of their own and to be extended to those for whom the principles were not at first designed.

ACCESS TO GOVERNMENT: THE EXPANSION OF PARTICIPATION

The expansion of participation from the bourgeoisie to ever-larger segments of society took two paths. In some nations, popular participation was expanded by the crown or the aristocracy, which ironically saw common people as potential political allies against the bourgeoisie. Thus in nineteenth-century Prussia,

THE PHILOSOPHICAL BASIS OF LIMITED GOVERNMENT

Box 1.3

*T*hree liberal philosophers had a particularly strong influence on American political thought: John Locke (1632–1704), Adam Smith (1723–90), and John Stuart Mill (1806–73). These three thinkers espoused the liberal philosophy that placed limits on government.

John Locke (below, left) argued for limited government because of his belief that, just as a person had a right to his own body, he had a right to his own labor and the fruits of that labor. From that he argued that people formed a government to protect their property, lives, and liberty, and that this government could not properly act to harm or take away that which it had been created to protect. According to Locke in his *Second Treatise on Government* (1690), government could properly function only with the consent of the governed through their representatives; if the government acted improperly, it would have broken its contract with society and would no longer be a legitimate government. The people would have the right to revolt and the right to form a new government.

Adam Smith (below, center) supported a severely limited government as a protection for the economic freedom of the individual. In his *Wealth of Nations* (1776), he argued for private enterprise as the most efficient means of production, leading to the growth of national wealth and income. He believed that freedom for individual economic and social advancement was possible only in a competitive free market, unhindered by government intervention. Nonetheless, he argued that government must protect the economic freedoms—free trade, free choice of individuals to do what they want, to live where they wish, and to invest and spend as they see fit—by ensuring that the market remains competitive and honest through such governmental actions as the regulation of standard weights and measures, the prevention of the formation of monopolies, and the defense of the community.

John Stuart Mill (below, right) believed that government should be limited so as not to interfere with the self-development of the individual. In order for individuals to fully develop their faculties, Mill believed, they need as large a sphere of freedom as possible, including freedom of thought and discussion. In *On Liberty* (1859), Mill argued that any restrictions on individuals ought to be based on recognized principles rather than on the preferences of the majority. He believed that social control should be exercised only to prevent harm to others. He maintained that when thoughts are suppressed, if they are right, individuals are deprived of truth; if the ideas are wrong, they are deprived of that better understanding of truth that comes out of conflict with error.

for example, it was the emperor and his great minister Otto von Bismarck who expanded popular participation in order to build political support among the lower orders.

In other nations, participation expanded because competing segments of the bourgeoisie sought to gain political advantage by reaching out and mobilizing the support of working- and lower-class groups who craved the opportunity to take part in politics—"lining up the unwashed," as one American historian put it.[14] To be sure, excluded groups often agitated for greater participation. But seldom was such agitation, by itself, enough to secure the right to participate. Usually, expansion of voting rights resulted from a combination of pressure from below and help from above.

This pattern of suffrage expansion by groups hoping to derive some political advantage has been typical in American history. After the Civil War, one of the chief reasons that Republicans moved to enfranchise newly freed slaves was to use the support of the former slaves to maintain Republican control over the defeated Southern states. Similarly, in the early twentieth century, upper-middle-class "Progressives" advocated women's suffrage because they believed that women were likely to support the reforms espoused by the Progressive movement. The expansion of participation and the development of the American political community will be discussed in more detail in Chapter 2.

INFLUENCING THE GOVERNMENT THROUGH PARTICIPATION: POLITICS

Expansion of participation means that more and more people have a legal right to take part in politics. Politics is an important term. In its broadest sense, "politics" refers to conflicts over the character, membership, and policies of any organization to which people belong. As Harold Lasswell, a famous political scientist, once put it, politics is the struggle over "who gets what, when, how."[15] Although politics is a phenomenon that can be found in

In George Caleb Bingham's painting, *The Verdict of the People* (1853–54), a jubilant crowd celebrates the outcome of the political process. While the nineteenth century was marked by high levels of political participation, voting was primarily the domain of white men.

any organization, our concern in this book is more narrow. Here, **politics** will be used to refer only to conflicts and struggles over the leadership, structure, and policies of governments. The goal of politics, as we define it, is to have a share or a say in the composition of the government's leadership, how the government is organized, or what its policies are going to be. Having a share is called **power** or influence.

Politics can take many forms, including everything from sending letters to government officials through voting, lobbying legislators on behalf of particular programs, and participating in protest marches and even violent demonstrations. A system of government that gives citizens a regular opportunity to elect the top government officials is usually called a **representative democracy** or **republic.** A system that permits citizens to vote directly on laws and policies is often called a **direct democracy.** At the national level, America is a representative democracy in which citizens select government officials but do not vote on legislation. Some states, however, have provisions for direct legislation through popular referendum. For example, California voters in 1995 decided to bar undocumented immigrants from receiving some state services.

Groups and organized interests obviously do not vote (although their members do), but they certainly do participate in politics. Their political activities usually consist of such endeavors as providing funds for candidates, lobbying, and trying to influence public opinion. The pattern of struggles among interests is called group politics, or **pluralism.** Americans have always been ambivalent about pluralist politics. Although the right of groups to press their views is the essence of liberty, Americans often fear that organized groups may sometimes exert too much influence, advancing special interests at the expense of larger public interests. We will return to this problem in Chapter 11.

Sometimes, of course, politics does not take place through formal channels at all, but instead involves direct action. **Direct action politics** can include either violent politics or civil disobedience, both of which attempt to shock rulers into behaving more responsibly. Direct action can also be a form of revolutionary politics, which rejects the system entirely and attempts to replace it with a new ruling group and a new set of rules. In recent years in the United States, groups ranging from animal-rights activists through right-to-life advocates have used direct action and even violence to underline their demands. Direct political action is protected by the U.S. Constitution; violence is not. The country's Founders knew that the right to protest is essential to the maintenance of political freedom, even where the ballot box is available.

politics

conflict over the leadership, structure, and policies of governments

power

influence over a government's leadership, organization, or policies

representative democracy/republic

a system of government in which the populace selects representatives, who play a significant role in governmental decision making

direct democracy

a system of rule that permits citizens to vote directly on laws and policies

pluralism

the theory that all interests are and should be free to compete for influence in the government. The outcome of this competition is compromise and moderation

direct-action politics

a form of politics, such as civil disobedience or revolutionary action, that takes place outside formal channels

⭐ American Political Culture: Conflict and Consensus

▶ What are Americans' core political values? What are the meanings of these values?

▶ Does the political system uphold American political values?

▶ How do American political values conflict with one another?

Underlying and framing political life in the United States are agreements and disagreements over basic political values and philosophies. Philosophical positions and values shape citizens' views of the world and define their sense of what is right and wrong, just and unjust, possible and impossible. If Americans shared no philosophical principles or values, they would have difficulty communicating, much less agreeing upon a common system of government and politics. On the other hand, sharing broad values does not guarantee political consensus. We can agree on principles but disagree over their application.

In fact, differing perspectives can help us understand the patterns of conflict and consensus that have marked the development of American politics. Perhaps the dominant interpretation of U.S. history is that of a success story: as the nation developed, different groups gradually gained equal influence in politics and policy. In this story, the American consensus around a set of basic political ideals provided the framework for the political inclusion of all groups. But today this story of progress is questioned from two different sides, highlighting the continuing significance of conflict. Some critics claim that measures such as affirmative action have not promoted political inclusion and instead have condoned reverse discrimination and a segmented society. Far from fulfilling American ideals, they argue, these policies represent a movement away from our most fundamental values. An opposing perspective questions the progress that has been made in promoting equality. Pointing to the disproportionately high rates of poverty among minorities and continuing evidence of discrimination against women and minorities, this side questions whether Americans are serious about equality. Much of the debate over the role of government has been over what government should do and how far it should go to redress the inequalities within our society and political system.

Even though Americans have disagreed over the meaning of such political ideals as equality, they still agree on the importance of these ideals. Within these conflicts, we can identify shared values, beliefs, and attitudes that form our **political culture** and serve to hold the United States and its people together. These values date back to the time of the founding of the union.

The essential documents of the American Founding—the Declaration of Independence and the Constitution—enunciated a set of political principles about the purposes of the new republic. In contrast with many other democracies, in the United States these political ideals did not just remain words on dusty documents. Americans actively embraced the principles of the Founders and made them central to the national identity. Let us look more closely at three of these ideals: liberty, equality, and democracy.

LIBERTY

No ideal is more central to American values than liberty. The Declaration of Independence defined three inalienable rights: "life, liberty and the pursuit of happiness." The preamble of the Constitution likewise identified the need to secure "the blessings of liberty" as one of the key reasons for drawing up the Constitution. For Americans, **liberty** means both personal freedom and economic freedom. Both are closely linked to the idea of **limited government.**

The Bill of Rights above all preserves individual personal liberties and rights. In fact, liberty has come to mean many of the freedoms guaranteed in the Bill of Rights: freedom of speech and writing, the right to assemble freely,

political culture

broadly shared values, beliefs, and attitudes about how the government should function. American political culture emphasizes the values of liberty, equality, and democracy

liberty

freedom from governmental control

limited government

a principle of constitutional government; a government whose powers are defined and limited by a constitution and the right to practice religious beliefs without interference from the government. Over the course of American history, the scope of personal liberties has expanded, as laws have become more tolerant and as individuals have successfully used the courts to challenge restrictions on their individual freedoms. Far fewer restrictions exist today on the press, political speech, and individual moral behavior than in the early years of the nation. Even so, conflicts persist over how personal liberties should be extended and when personal liberties violate community norms. For example, one of the most contentious issues in the last twenty-five years has been that of abortion. Whereas defenders of the right to choose abortion view it is an essential personal freedom for women, opponents view it as murder—something that no society should allow.

In addition to personal freedom, the American concept of liberty means economic freedom. Since the Founding, economic freedom has been linked to capitalism, free markets, and the protection of private property. Free competition, unfettered movement of goods, and the right to enjoy the fruits of one's labor are all essential aspects of economic freedom and American capitalism.[16] In the first century of the Republic, support for capitalism often meant support for the doctrine of laissez-faire. Translated literally as "to leave alone," **laissez-faire capitalism** allowed very little room for the national government to regulate trade or restrict the use of private property, even in the public interest. Americans still strongly support capitalism and economic liberty, but they now also endorse some restrictions on economic freedoms to protect the public. Federal and state governments now deploy a wide array of regulations in the name of public protection. These include health and safety laws, environmental rules, and workplace regulations. Not surprisingly, fierce disagreements often erupt over what the proper scope of government regulation should be. What some people regard as protecting the public, others see as an infringement of their own freedom to run their businesses and use their property as they see fit.

EQUALITY

The Declaration of Independence declares as its first "self-evident" truth that "all men are created equal." As central as it is to the American political creed, however, equality has been a less well defined ideal than liberty because people interpret "equality" in different ways. Few Americans have wholeheartedly embraced full equality of results, but most Americans share the ideal of **equality of opportunity**—that is, the notion that each person should be given a fair chance to go as far as his or her talents will allow. Yet it is hard for Americans to reach agreement about what constitutes equality of opportunity. Must *past* inequalities be remedied in order to ensure equal opportunity in the *present?* Should inequalities in the legal, political, and economic spheres be given the same weight? In contrast to liberty, which requires limits on the role of government, equality implies an *obligation* of the government to the people.[17]

Americans do make clear distinctions between political equality and social or economic equality. **Political equality** means that members of the American political community have the right to participate in politics on equal terms. Beginning from a very restricted definition of political community, which originally included only propertied white men, the United States has moved much closer to an ideal of political equality that can be summed up as "one person,

Patrick Henry delivering his famous "Give me liberty, or give me death" speech. Since the Founding, liberty has been central to the political values of Americans.

laissez-faire capitalism
an economic system in which the means of production and distribution are privately owned and operated for profit with minimal or no government interference

equality of opportunity
a widely shared American ideal that all people should have the freedom to use whatever talents and wealth they have to reach their fullest potential

political equality
the right to participate in politics equally, based on the principle of "one person, one vote"

Residents of rural Wilcox County, Alabama, lining up to vote in 1966. Prior to the passage of the Voting Rights Act of 1965, Wilcox County had no registered black voters.

one vote." Broad support for the ideal of political equality has helped expand the American political community and extend the right to participate to all. Although considerable conflict remains over whether the political system makes it harder for some people to participate and easier for others and about whether the role of money in politics has drowned out the public voice, Americans agree that all citizens should have equal rights to participate and that government should enforce that right.

In part because Americans believe that individuals are free to work as hard as they choose, they have always been less concerned about social or economic inequality. Many Americans regard economic differences as the consequence of individual choices, virtues, or failures. Because of this, Americans tend to be less supportive than most Europeans of government action to ensure equality. Yet when major economic forces, such as the Great Depression of the 1930s, affect many people or when systematic barriers appear to block equality of opportunity, Americans support government action to promote equality. Even then, however, Americans have endorsed only a limited government role designed to help people get back on their feet or to open up opportunity.

DEMOCRACY

popular sovereignty

a principle of democracy in which political authority rests ultimately in the hands of the people

The essence of democracy is the participation of the people in choosing their rulers and the people's ability to influence what those rulers do. In a democracy, political power ultimately comes from the people. The idea of placing power in the hands of the people is known as **popular sovereignty.** In the United States, popular sovereignty and political equality make politicians accountable to the people. Ideally, democracy envisions an engaged citizenry prepared to exercise its power over rulers. As we saw earlier, the United States is a representative democracy, meaning that the people do not rule directly but instead exercise power through elected representatives. Forms of participation in a democracy vary greatly, but voting is a key element of the representative democracy that the American Founders established.

American democracy rests on the principle of **majority rule** with **minority rights.** Majority rule means that the wishes of the majority determine what government does. The House of Representatives—a large body elected directly by the people—was designed in particular to ensure majority rule. But the Founders feared that popular majorities could turn government into a "tyranny of the majority" in which individual liberties would be violated. Concern for individual rights has thus been a part of American democracy from the beginning. The rights enumerated in the Bill of Rights and enforced through the courts provide an important check on the power of the majority.

Democracy also entails the principle of limited government. Concern about the abuse of power was utmost in the minds of the Founders, who had launched a revolution to free themselves from the British government. The idea that government should be limited in its power and authority over citizens found widespread acceptance in the new nation. Even today American political culture reflects a distinctive concern about excessive governmental authority.

DOES THE SYSTEM UPHOLD AMERICAN POLITICAL VALUES?

Clearly, the ideals of liberty, equality, and democracy are open to diverse interpretations. Moreover, the ideals can easily conflict with one another in practice. When we examine American history, we can see that there have been large gaps between these ideals and the practice of American politics. We can also see that some ideals have been prized more than others at different historical moments. But it is also clear that as Americans have engaged in political conflict about who should participate in politics and how political institutions should be organized, they have called upon these ideals to justify their actions. Now let's reexamine these ideals, noting key historical conflicts and current controversies about what they should mean in practice.

Liberty The central historical conflict regarding liberty in the United States was the enslavement of blacks. The facts of slavery and the differential treatment of the races has cast a long shadow over all of American history. In fact, scholars today note that the American definition of freedom has been formed

majority rule/minority rights
the democratic principle that a government follows the preferences of the majority of voters but protects the interests of the minority

The proper scope of governmental regulation of citizens' behavior is the subject of ongoing debate. During 1997 and 1998, the U.S. government took action to ban or limit advertising by tobacco companies, pitting tobacco companies and farmers against health and children's advocates.

in relation to the concept of slavery. The right to control one's labor and the right to receive rewards for that labor have been central elements of our definition of freedom precisely because these freedoms were denied to slaves.[18]

Concerns about the meaning of liberty also arise in connection with government regulation of economic and social activity. Economic regulations imposed to ensure public health and safety are often decried by the affected businesses as infringements on their freedom. For example, in 1994, the Occupational Safety and Health Administration (OSHA) of the national government prepared to issue regulations intended to protect workers from repetitive stress injuries. Such injuries, which affect 700,000 workers a year, are caused by long hours on the assembly line or at the computer. OSHA's regulations would have required employers to provide specified work breaks and proper furniture and other equipment. Although such regulations might have been welcomed by workers, employers viewed them as intrusive and extremely costly. In the face of strong opposition from employers, OSHA backed down and decided not to issue the regulations.[19]

Social regulations prompt similar disputes. Some citizens believe that government should enforce certain standards of behavior or instill particular values in citizens. Examples of such activity abound: welfare rules that once denied benefits to women who were found with a "man in the house," the practice of saying prayers in school, laws that require parents to pay child support for their children even if those children no longer live with them, and laws that require citizens to wear seat belts are just a few examples. Deciding the proper scope of economic and social regulation is a topic of great concern and much conflict among Americans today.

Equality, particularly equal opportunity and equal pay for equal work, has been a primary concern of the women's movement. Here, women's advocates march to the White House to urge the president not to weaken affirmative action programs.

| AMERICAN ATTITUDES ABOUT POLITICAL EQUALITY, 1992 | Table 1.2 |

Statement	Percentage who agree
Our society should do whatever is necessary to make sure that everyone has an equal opportunity to succeed.	95
We have gone too far in pushing equal rights in this country.	53
One of the big problems in this country is that we don't give everyone an equal chance.	71
It is not really that big a problem if some people have more of a chance in life than others.	38
The country would be better off if we worried less about how equal people are.	54
If people were treated more equally in this country, we would have many fewer problems.	84

SOURCE: Based on data from the American National Election Studies conducted by the University of Michigan, Center for Political Studies, and provided by the Inter-University Consortium for Political and Social Research, Ann Arbor, Michigan.

Equality   Because equality is such an elusive concept, many conflicts have arisen over what it should mean in practice. Americans have engaged in three kinds of controversies about the public role in addressing inequality. The first is determining what constitutes equality of access to public institutions. In 1896, the Supreme Court ruled in *Plessy v. Ferguson* that "separate but equal" accommodations for blacks and whites were constitutional. In 1954, in a major legal victory for the civil rights movement, the Supreme Court overturned the separate but equal doctrine in *Brown v. Board of Education* (see Chapter 6). Today, new questions have been raised about what constitutes equal access to public institutions. Some argue that the unequal financing of public schools in cities, suburbs, and rural districts is a violation of the right to equal education. To date, these claims have not been supported by the federal courts, which have rejected the notion that the unequal economic impacts of public policy outcomes are a constitutional matter.[20] Lawsuits arguing a right to "economic equal protection" stalled in 1973 when the Supreme Court ruled that a Texas school-financing law did not violate the Constitution even though the law affected rich and poor students differently.[21]

A second debate concerns the public role in ensuring equality of opportunity in private life. Although Americans generally agree that discrimination should not be tolerated, people disagree over what should be done to ensure equality of opportunity (see Table 1.2). Controversies about affirmative action programs reflect these disputes. Supporters of affirmative action claim that such programs are necessary to compensate for past discrimination in order to obtain true equality of opportunity today. Opponents maintain that affirmative action amounts to reverse discrimination and that a society that espouses true equality should not acknowledge gender or racial differences. The question of the public responsibility for private inequalities is central to gender issues. The

POLITICS ON THE WEB

Many people believe that the Internet is a profound boost to democracy, because it enables anyone and everyone to voice their concerns, frustrations, and aspirations; it gives equal political voice to each person. Already, web sites exist for every conceivable cause, and start-up costs for new web sites are minimal. For these reasons, the Internet will revolutionize politics.

But for real change to occur, the voices on the Internet *must* affect government policy. And so far, it is unclear whether the government is, or can be, listening. There is absolutely no way for a political system, even a democratic one, to address all the opinions that the Internet generates.

The distance between the opportunity for political expression on the Internet and the government's inability to deal with that expression may help perpetuate the cynicism, distrust of government, and, ultimately, apathy about politics that characterizes so many Americans today. If this is the case, then the biggest irony of the Internet is that it was the federal government that built it in the first place.

www.wwnorton.com/wtp2e

traditional view, still held by many today, sees the special responsibilities of women in the family as something that falls outside the range of public concern. Indeed, from this perspective, women's role within families is essential to the functioning of a democratic society. In the past twenty years, especially, these traditional views have come under fire, as advocates for women have argued that women occupy a subordinate place within the family and that such private inequalities *are* a topic of public concern.[22]

A third debate about equality concerns differences in income and wealth. Unlike in other countries, income inequality has not been an enduring topic of political controversy in the United States, which currently has the largest gap in income and wealth between rich and poor citizens of any developed nation. But Americans have generally tolerated great differences among rich and poor citizens, in part because of a pervasive belief that mobility is possible and that economic success is the product of individual effort.[23] At times, however, concern about economic inequalities emerges, often around the issue of fair taxation. Some analysts today warn that the growing division between rich and poor may invigorate a politics of class and polarize political debate along income lines.[24]

Democracy   Despite Americans' deep attachment to the *ideal* of democracy, many questions can be raised about our *practice* of democracy. The first is the restricted definition of the political community during much of American history. The United States was not a full democracy until the 1960s, when African Americans were at last guaranteed the right to vote. Property restrictions on the right to vote were eliminated by 1828; in 1870, the Fifteenth Amendment to the Constitution granted African Americans the vote, although later exclusionary practices denied them that right; in 1920, the Nineteenth Amendment guaranteed women the right to vote; and in 1965, the Voting Rights Act finally secured the right of African Americans to vote.

Just securing the right to vote does not end concerns about democracy, however. The organization of electoral institutions can have a significant impact on access to elections and on who can get elected. During the first two decades of the twentieth century, states and cities enacted many reforms that made it harder to vote, including strict registration requirements and scheduling of elections. The aim was to rid politics of corruption but the consequence was to reduce participation. Other institutional decisions affect which candidates stand the best chance of getting elected (see Chapter 10).

A further consideration about democracy concerns the relationship between economic power and political power. Money has always played an important role in elections and governing in the United States. Many argue that the pervasive influence of money in American electoral campaigns today undermines democracy. With the decline of locally based political parties that depended on party loyalists to turn out the vote, and the rise of political action committees, political consultants, and expensive media campaigns, money has become the central fact of life in American politics. Money often determines who runs for office; it can exert a heavy influence on who wins; and, some argue, money affects what politicians do once they are in office.[25]

A final consideration that must be raised about democracy is the engagement of the citizenry. Low turnout for elections and a pervasive sense of apathy and cynicism characterize American politics today. Many people say that it does not matter if they participate because their votes will not make any difference. This disillusionment and sense of ineffectiveness undermines the vitality of democracy, which in turn reduces the accountability of the rulers to the ruled.

VALUES AND GOVERNMENT

Many of the most important dilemmas of American political life involve conflicts among fundamental political values as those values are put into operation. For example, Americans strongly value both liberty and equality, but often programs designed to promote one may impose restraints upon the other. Thus, affirmative action programs or statutes designed to prevent discrimination against the handicapped, such as the Americans with Disabilities Act, may promote equality but may also infringe upon the liberty of employers to hire whomever they wish. In a similar vein, democratic political processes may sometimes produce results that can challenge both liberty and equality. After all, Adolf Hitler and the Nazis came to power in Germany in the 1930s largely through democratic means. Even in America, political extremists who oppose both liberty and equality have been elected to office. As recently as 1991, a white supremacist, David Duke, was very nearly elected governor of Louisiana.

Conversely, in the name of equality or liberty, courts often hand down verdicts that undo decisions of democratically elected legislatures and even decisions reached in popular referenda. Principles that seem incontrovertible in the abstract become more problematic in operation. In the process of resolving conflicts among core beliefs, America's political principles change and evolve. Even core values should be understood as works in progress rather than immutable facts.

Martin Luther King, Jr., the civil rights leader, shakes the hand of President Lyndon B. Johnson following the signing of the Voting Rights Act of 1965, a milestone in assuring political equality for African Americans.

In principle, conflicts among liberty, equality, and democracy can be reconciled. In practice, however, over time, democracy poses a fundamental threat to liberty. This is so because, over time, democracy promotes strong government, often to promote equality, and, over time, strong government inevitably threatens liberty. And with issues of social policy such as affirmative action, what some see as guaranteeing equality, others view as an infringement of liberty. But as we shall see, in the United States, the institutions of democratic government have been critical in guaranteeing both liberty and equality.

★ The Citizen's Role

This chapter began with the stories of two recent college graduates, Jim Wilkinson and Melissa Feld. Their interests in issues led them to become politically involved and eventually brought them to Washington. Now both occupy positions from which they can work very effectively for the programs and policies they favor.

Jim and Melissa are intelligent, ambitious, and believe passionately in their important, albeit very different, political causes. What made it possible for both these individuals to begin to make their views count in the political process was some knowledge of politics. Jim Wilkinson knew from reading and following the news that Representative Dick Armey shared his own doubts and concerns about the U.S. tax code. Melissa Feld knew from her reading and from her conversations with other politically aware individuals that Representative Dick Gephardt echoed her concern for human rights and abortion rights. Both Jim and Melissa understood the place of Congress in American policy making and had some sense of how to become involved in the congressional policy-making process. In both cases, the key to influence was knowledge.

We have seen that knowledge is the first requisite of democratic citizenship. Armed with a modicum of knowledge, any citizen can find ways to influence the political process. Some may take the path illustrated by Jim Wilkinson or Melissa Feld. Others may pursue the variety of paths described at the conclusion of each chapter of this book. There are many paths to political influence. Each path, however, is effectively blocked by a door that can be unlocked only by those possessing some measure of political knowledge. Furthermore, without an understanding of at least the broad outlines of the political process, political interests, concerns, and passions are largely irrelevant. Only those with some understanding of government and politics can know how to take part in any meaningful way.

Knowledge of politics is not so difficult to obtain. Read the newspaper on a daily basis. Subscribe or visit the library to read a weekly newsmagazine. Watch the evening news and at least one weekly public affairs or discussion program. If you are reading this page, you are taking an important step toward achieving an understanding of politics. From understanding can come the capacity to "make a difference." You thought you were merely completing another homework assignment when, in fact, you are at this moment acquiring political power.

★ Summary

Despite the relative openness of American political life, fewer and fewer Americans are choosing to take part in the political process. Some speculate that Americans' general lack of interest in politics results from their declining trust in government and their decreasing belief that they can influence what government does. As more and more citizens withdraw from political life, democracy suffers.

The citizen's role in political life begins with information and knowledge. A citizen's knowledge should include knowledge of government, of politics, and of democratic principles. Knowledgeable citizens are better able to identify and act upon their political interests. In short, knowledgeable citizens better understand how and why politics and government influences their lives.

The form that a government takes affects citizens because it determines who governs and how much governmental control is permitted. Americans live in a constitutional democracy, where limits are placed on what governments can do and how they can do it. Americans are also given access to government through legal rights to political participation. Through politics, Americans are able to struggle over the leadership, structure, and policies of governments.

Although politics may divide Americans from one another, the core values of American political culture—liberty, equality, and democracy—hold the United States and its people together. Although these values have been important since the time the United States was founded, during much of American history there have been large gaps between these ideals and the practice of American politics. Moreover, liberty, equality, and democracy often conflict with one another in American political life.

FOR FURTHER READING

Craig, Stephen C., and Stephen Earl Bennett, eds. *After the Boom: The Politics of Generation X*. Lanham, MD: Rowman and Littlefield, 1997.

Dahl, Robert. *Democracy and Its Critics*. New Haven, CT: Yale University Press, 1989.

Delli Carpini, Michael X., and Scott Keeter, *What Americans Know about Politics and Why It Matters*. New Haven: Yale University Press, 1996.

Hochschild, Jennifer L. *Facing Up to the American Dream: Race, Class, and the Soul of the Nation*. Princeton, NJ: Princeton University Press, 1995.

Huntington, Samuel P. *American Politics: The Promise of Disharmony*. Cambridge, MA: Harvard University Press, 1981.

Lasswell, Harold. *Politics: Who Gets What, When, How*. New York: Meridian Books, 1958.

McClosky, Herbert, and John Zaller. *The American Ethos: Public Attitudes toward Capitalism and Democracy*. Cambridge, MA: Harvard University Press, 1984.

Nie, Norman H., Jane Junn, and Kenneth Stehlik-Barry. *Education and Democratic Citizenship in America*. Chicago: University of Chicago Press, 1996.

Nye, Joseph S., Jr., Philip D. Zelikow, and David C. King, eds. *Why People Don't Trust Government*. Cambridge, MA: Harvard University Press, 1997.

Putnam, Robert. *Making Democracy Work: Civic Traditions in Modern Italy*. Princeton, NJ: Princeton University Press, 1993.

de Tocqueville, Alexis. *Democracy in America*. Trans. Phillips Bradley. New York: Knopf, Vintage Books, 1945; orig. published 1835.

STUDY OUTLINE

What Americans Think about Government

1. In recent decades, the public's trust in government has declined considerably. Some Americans believe that government has grown too large and that government programs do not benefit them. As public distrust of government has increased, so has public dissatisfaction with the government's performance.
2. Americans today are less likely to think that they can influence what the government does. This view has led to increased apathy and cynicism among the citizenry.

Government

1. Governments vary in their structure, in their size, and in the way they operate.
2. Beginning in the seventeenth century, two important changes began to take place in the governance of some Western nations: governments began to acknowledge formal limits on their power, and governments began to give citizens a formal voice in politics through the vote.
3. Political participation can take many forms: the vote, group activities, and even direct action, such as violence or civil disobedience.

American Political Culture: Conflict and Consensus

1. Three important political values in American politics are liberty, equality, and democracy.
2. At times in American history there have been large gaps between the ideals embodied in Americans' core values and the practice of American government.
3. Many of the important dilemmas of American politics revolve around conflicts over fundamental political values. One such conflict involves the ideals of liberty and democracy. Over time, democracy promotes stronger, more active government, which may threaten liberty.

PRACTICE QUIZ

1. Political efficacy is the belief that
   a) government operates efficiently.
   b) government has grown too large.
   c) government cannot be trusted.
   d) one can influence what government does.

2. The famous political scientist Harold Lasswell defined politics as the struggle over
   a) who gets elected.
   b) who gets what, when, how.
   c) who protests.
   d) who gets to vote.

3. What is the basic difference between autocracy and oligarchy?
   a) the extent to which the average citizen has a say in government affairs
   b) the means of collecting taxes and conscripting soldiers
   c) the number of people who control governing decisions
   d) They are fundamentally the same thing.

4. The bourgeoisie championed
   a) democracy.
   b) "taxation without representation."
   c) limitations on government power.
   d) societal revolution.

5. The principle of political equality can be best summed up as
   a) "equality of results."
   b) "equality of opportunity."
   c) "one person, one vote."
   d) "equality between the sexes."

6. Which of the following is an important principle of American democracy?
   a) popular sovereignty
   b) majority rule/minority rights
   c) limited government
   d) All of the above are important principles of American democracy.

7. Which of the following is not related to the American conception of "liberty"?
   a) freedom of speech
   b) free enterprise
   c) freedom of religion
   d) All of the above are related to liberty.

8. Concerns about the meaning of liberty today focus primarily on
   a) government regulation of economic and social activity.
   b) the separation of church and state.

c) the freedom that immigrants have in coming to the United States.

d) the right to bear arms.

9. Which of the following does not represent a current discrepancy between the ideal and practice of democracy in America?

a) the use of property restrictions for voting in three remaining states

b) the influence of money in electoral politics

c) the low voter turnout in American elections

d) All of the above represent discrepancies between the ideal and practice of democracy in modern America.

10. What is the most dire potential consequence of citizens viewing their government as a servant?

a) Citizens will allow the government to grow to the point where they can no longer control it.

b) Citizens could be served more efficiently by the private sector.

c) The ideals of democracy and equality will eventually conflict.

d) Citizens will no longer be able to do things for themselves.

CRITICAL THINKING QUESTIONS

1. What type of government does the United States have? Is it the most democratic government possible? Do citizens make the decisions of government or do they merely influence them? Describe the ways in which citizens in America participate in politics.

2. Think of some examples that demonstrate the gaps between the ideals of America's core political values and the practice of American politics. Describe how such gaps were reconciled in the past. Identify one current gap between Americans' values and their political practices. How might this discrepancy be reconciled?

KEY TERMS

authoritarian government (p. 16)
autocracy (p. 16)
citizenship (p. 13)
constitutional government (p. 16)
democracy (p. 16)
direct-action politics (p. 21)
direct democracy (p. 21)
equality of opportunity (p. 23)

government (p. 15)
laissez-faire capitalism (p. 23)
liberty (p. 22)
limited government (p. 22)
majority rule/minority rights (p. 25)
oligarchy (p. 16)
pluralism (p. 21)
political culture (p. 22)

political efficacy (p. 10)
political equality (p. 23)
politics (p. 21)
popular sovereignty (p. 24)
power (p. 21)
representative democracy (or republic) (p. 21)
totalitarian government (p. 16)

2

The American

★ **Expanding the American Political Community**

How have racial and ethnic differences, gender, class, and religious affiliation affected the right to participate in the political process throughout America's history?

How successfully have social groups such as white ethnics, African Americans, Latinos, Asian Americans, women, and religious groups realized the right to full political participation?

What tactics did these groups employ to gain full access to the political process?

★ **Participation in the American Political Community**

In what different ways do Americans participate in politics?

What explains levels of participation? Why has participation declined over time?

What roles do social and political institutions play in promoting participation and fulfilling American political values?

Political Community

I N 1971, the Twenty-sixth Amendment to the Constitution enlarged the electorate by nearly 27 million voters when it granted eighteen-, nineteen-, and twenty-year-old Americans the right to vote.[1] This formal expansion of the American political community confirmed what many politicians already knew: young people were an active political force and they had had a wide-ranging impact on politics over the preceding decade. Young people left a lasting imprint on American politics as they took the lead on major issues, including civil rights, antiwar activism, gender discrimination, and the effort to open up political parties to more grassroots influence.

The formal inclusion of young people repeated a process that has occurred over and over again throughout American history. Groups such as women and African Americans, who were in the past formally excluded from the political community, nonetheless found ways to make their views known and to press for full inclusion in the political system. Formally excluded groups and other groups who have felt their views to be insufficiently recognized in politics have won influence through a wide range of activities. They have expressed their views in newspaper editorials and letters, made speeches, circulated and signed petitions, initiated legal challenges in the courts, and protested. Armed with the promises inherent in the American ideals of liberty, equality, and democracy and with their own determination to make the political system respond to them, culturally and socially distinct groups have changed American politics. In so doing they have helped to make the United States one of the most diverse modern democracies. Cultural and socially diversity has made American politics a vibrant and often challenging experience, as groups clash over often very different views about what government should do—and should not do—to live up to our national ideals. Such widespread and varied forms of participation have caused the government to abandon some practices and to institute new policies that reflect changing perspectives of our core values of liberty and equality.

More recently, however, American politics seems to have lost some of its vitality, as growing numbers of citizens have turned away from politics. Participation in most kinds of political activities—with the exception of contributing money—is declining. Instead of a distinctively American optimism, a sense of pessimism pervades our politics. Individuals express a sense of powerlessness, frustration, and disengagement from the political system. Among youth such feelings are especially strong. Many students feel that the political system is not relevant to their lives and that politics will not solve the problems in the world. Only about one in five eighteen- to twenty-year-olds vote, and political organizations that aim to represent the views of young people have a hard time staying afloat.[2] But it is not only among young people that political interest is fading and political organizations are weakening. Many political organizations with long, distinguished histories, such as the National Association for the Advancement of Colored People (NAACP) and the League of Women Voters, have seen their membership numbers fall in recent years. Why is this?

■ *In this chapter we will consider the forms of participation and the kinds of access to the political system that groups of different social backgrounds and cultural beliefs fought for and have subsequently enjoyed.* We will examine the ways that groups with distinctive racial and ethnic, class, gender, and religious backgrounds have used participation to change government policies that mattered to them. We will also see that such identities do not always provide the basis for shared political activity.

■ *Then we will examine patterns of contemporary political participation, discussing the different forms that participation can take and considering the reasons for declining participation in recent decades.* We will see that individual beliefs, such as a sense of efficacy, are important, but that most significant is the failure of our institutions to mobilize people into politics.

■ *We end by considering how citizens can become more involved in politics in order to reinvigorate American democracy and make government reflect their views of liberty and equality.*

Expanding the American Political Community

▶ How have racial and ethnic differences, gender, class, and religious affiliation affected the right to participate in the political process throughout America's history?

▶ How successfully have social groups such as white ethnics, African Americans, Latinos, Asian Americans, women, and religious groups realized the right to full political participation?

▶ What tactics did these groups employ to gain full access to the political process?

American political community

citizens who are eligible to vote and participate in American political life

The original **American political community** restricted membership to white men who owned property. Many of the elite merchants and planters who launched the American Revolution did not envision a broad-based democracy. Instead, they presumed that American democracy would encompass a small, homogeneous group. Ethnically, the earliest members of the American political community were white Anglo-Saxon Protestants (WASPs), who shared a common ancestry and culture. But this narrow membership did not last long.

By the 1830s, property restrictions had been abandoned and in the next decades the pressure to expand the American political community launched the nation on a path that would ultimately lead to the diverse community we have today.

Groups with distinctive social and cultural identities have often played pivotal roles in changing American politics. Conflicts over their inclusion have tested Americans' understanding of liberty, equality, and democracy. Establishing access to the political system for these groups has expanded the definition of the political community and has often provoked important institutional changes as well. Moreover, the ongoing participation of such groups has transformed politics, altering political coalitions and changing political debates. This section will examine the experiences of four kinds of cultural and social groups in American politics: racial and ethnic, class, gender, and religious. It asks to what extent members of these particular groups have recognized common interests and have sought to act politically on those interests. We will pay particular attention to the forms of mobilization these groups used to build political strength and what strategies they employed to gain access to the political system. The story of their fight for political equality and fundamental liberties is a tribute to the creativity and persistence of these groups, but also to the resilience of the American political system.[3]

ETHNICITY AND RACE

Ethnic and racial identities are the most politically significant social identities in the United States. This great diversity has distinguished the United States from most European nations, which for most of modern history have been much more ethnically and racially homogeneous. As we examine the process of political inclusion of different groups, we shall see that American politics encouraged racial and ethnic identification even as it has excluded many groups on the basis of race or national origin.

White Ethnics   The term **"white ethnic"** encompasses a wide range of groups who for most of American history did not identify as a single group. In fact, some of these groups—Italians, for example—were not always identified as "white" when they entered this country.

European immigration was the central fact of American life from the colonial period until the 1920s, when Congress sharply cut off immigration. In peak years nearly a million new immigrants entered the country. The colonists came overwhelmingly from the British Isles, particularly from England; a smattering were German or Dutch. The first postcolonial wave of immigration came in the 1840s, when the Irish began to outnumber all other immigrants; Germans and Scandinavians came in the greatest numbers between 1880 and 1890. Finally, between 1890 and 1910, a huge wave of immigration from eastern and central Europe brought Italians, Slavs, and eastern European Jews to the country.[4] The results of these waves of European immigration are reflected in America today: as Figure 2.1 indicates, whites of European origin comprise 73 percent of the total U.S. population.

Although the American story is often told as one of assimilation, in fact American politics acknowledged and encouraged the maintenance of ethnic identities. The openness of the political system encouraged politicians to recognize ethnic groups and to mobilize them—as a group—into politics.

white ethnics

white immigrants to the United States whose culture differs from that of WASPs

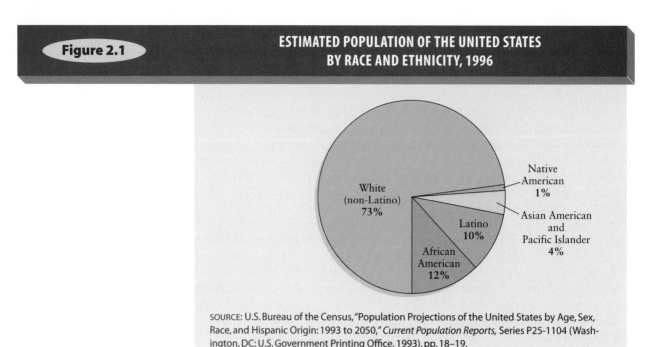

Figure 2.1

**ESTIMATED POPULATION OF THE UNITED STATES
BY RACE AND ETHNICITY, 1996**

White
(non-Latino)
73%

Native
American
1%

Asian American
and
Pacific Islander
4%

Latino
10%

African
American
12%

SOURCE: U.S. Bureau of the Census, "Population Projections of the United States by Age, Sex, Race, and Hispanic Origin: 1993 to 2050," *Current Population Reports,* Series P25-1104 (Washington, DC: U.S. Government Printing Office, 1993), pp. 18–19.

political machines

local party organizations that controlled local politics in the late nineteenth and early twentieth centuries through patronage and control of nominations

For most of American history, citizenship and political equality came to white ethnics without a struggle. Despite the sometimes virulent anti-immigrant sentiment and the eventual restrictions imposed on immigration, the political rights of white immigrants were never in serious peril. They were eligible to become naturalized citizens after five years of residence; rates of naturalization varied from 45.6 percent of all foreign-born residents in 1910 to 67.9 percent by 1950.[5] Many of America's big cities were governed by **political machines,** which were party organizations that controlled local politics by nominating candidates for office and mobilizing voters to elect those candidates. These machines realized that the votes of the newly arrived immigrants could help particular candidates win office and, consequently, saw to it that immigrants quickly became citizens. In New York, the most important political machine, called Tammany Hall, filled out citizenship applications for immigrants and paid the necessary application fees. In the two weeks before elections in New York, Philadelphia, and Baltimore, naturalization rates increased sharply.[6] In addition, many states and territories allowed noncitizens to vote and enjoy other rights of citizenship.

Once immigrants became citizens, their ethnic identifications remained important political guideposts. In cities, political machines appealed to voters along ethnic lines and parceled out patronage on the basis of ethnic group membership. Precinct captains spoke the language of the immigrants and acted as a link to the broader world. Thus, although ethnic neighborhoods were insulated, they were not isolated. Ethnic concerns entered politics around such issues as the prohibition of alcohol, Sunday closing laws (a way to preserve Sunday as a day for religious observance by prohibiting businesses from opening on Sunday), and language instruction in the public schools.

Even after white ethnic groups had become assimilated into a broader American culture—which itself was altered by their inclusion—ethnic appeals remained prominent in political life. This was particularly true in big cities, where the practice of ticket balancing ensured that slates of candidates bore a range of ethnic names. For example, in New York City in 1961, a Republican slate of Lefkowitz, Gilhooley, and Fino faced a Democratic lineup of Wagner, Screvane, and Beame.[7] The presence of Irish (Irish-German in the case of Wagner), Italian, and Jewish names on both tickets reflected the need to cover multiple ethnic bases. In recent years, however, the political significance of ethnic identities has begun to fade. Even in New York City, where ethnicity was once a central concern in politics, white ethnic groups no longer fall into predictable voting blocs.

African Americans   For African Americans, the central fact of political life has been a denial of full citizenship rights for most of American history. By accepting the institution of slavery, the Founders embraced a system fundamentally at odds with the "Blessings of Liberty" promised in the Constitution. Their decision set the stage for two centuries of African American struggles to achieve full citizenship. In the course of these battles, African Americans built organizations and devised political strategies that transformed American politics.

The vast majority of enslaved blacks had few means for organizing to assert themselves. Their hopes for achieving full citizenship rights initially seemed fulfilled when three constitutional amendments were adopted after the Civil War: the Thirteenth Amendment abolished slavery; the Fourteenth Amendment guaranteed equal protection under the law; and the Fifteenth Amendment guaranteed voting rights for blacks. Protected by the presence of federal troops, African American men were able to exercise their political rights immediately after the war. During Reconstruction, blacks were elected to many political offices: two black senators were elected from Mississippi and a total of fourteen African Americans were elected to the House of Representatives between 1869 and 1877. African Americans also held many state-level political offices. As voters and public officials, black citizens found a home in the Republican Party, which had secured the ratification of the three constitutional amendments guaranteeing black rights. After the war, the Republican Party continued to reach out to black voters as a means to build party strength in the South.[8]

This political equality was short-lived, however. The national government withdrew its troops from the South and turned its back on African Americans in 1877. In the Compromise of 1877, southern Democrats agreed to allow the Republican candidate, Rutherford B. Hayes, to become president after a disputed election. In exchange, northern Republicans dropped their support for the civil liberties and political participation of African Americans. After that, southern states erected a tight system of social, political, and economic inequality that made a mockery of the promises in the Constitution. These years marked the beginning of a long process in which African Americans built organizations and devised strategies for asserting their constitutional rights.

One such strategy sought to win political rights through political pressure and litigation. This approach was championed by the NAACP, established by a group of black and white reformers in 1909. Among the NAACP's founders was W. E. B. DuBois, one of the most influential and creative thinkers on racial

W.E.B. DuBois, a founder of the NAACP and a prominent American thinker throughout the twentieth century

We the People

THE AMERICAN AGONY OVER ABOLITION

*N*o issue in the nation's history so deeply divided Americans as that of the abolition of slavery. The importation and subjugation of Africans kidnapped from their native lands was a practice virtually as old as the country itself: the first slaves brought to what became the United States arrived in 1619, a year before the Plymouth colony was established in Massachusetts. White southerners built their agricultural economy (especially cotton production) on a large slave-labor force. By 1840, for example, nearly half of the populations of Alabama and Louisiana consisted of black slaves. Even so, only about a quarter of southern white families owned slaves.

The subjugation of blacks through slavery was so much a part of the southern culture that efforts to restrict or abolish slavery were met with fierce resistance. Despite the manifest cruelties of the slave system, southerners referred to the system by the quaint term "peculiar institution." The label meant little to slavery's opponents, however, and an abolitionist movement grew and spread among north-

erners in the 1830s (although abolitionist sentiment could be traced back to the pre-Revolutionary era). The movement was most closely identified with the writing of William Lloyd Garrison. Slavery had been all but eliminated in the North by this time, but few northerners favored outright abolition. In fact, most whites held attitudes toward blacks that would be considered racist today.

Slavery was important to the South for economic reasons, but the heart of the controversy was moral, not economic. One abolitionist labeled slavery "the blight of this nation, the curse of the North and the curse of the South"; "man cannot, consistently with reason, religion, and the eternal and immutable principles of justice, be the property of man."[1] Southerners responded in increasingly strident terms that not only was slavery not evil, but it was actually beneficial to blacks: "The negro slaves of the South are the happiest, and, in some sense, the freest people in the world," crowed one defender of slavery.[2] According to one historian, "Never before had

Martin Luther King, Jr., addressed the crowd during the 1963 March on Washington, where he delivered his famous "I have a dream" speech.

issues of the twentieth century. Because the northern black vote was so small in the early decades of the twentieth century, the organization primarily relied on the courts to press for black political rights. After the 1920s, the NAACP built a strong membership base, with some strength in the South, which would be critical when the civil rights movement gained momentum in the 1950s.

The great migration of blacks to the North beginning around World War I enlivened a protest strategy. Although protest organizations had existed in the nineteenth century, the continuing migration of blacks to the North made protest an increasingly useful tool. Black labor leader A. Philip Randolph forced the federal government to address racial discrimination in hiring practices during World War II by threatening a massive march on Washington. The federal government also grew more attentive to blacks as their voting strength increased as a result of the northward migration. By the 1940s, the black vote had swung away from Republicans, but the Democratic hold on black votes was by no means absolute.

These strategies—political and legal pressure and protest—all played a part in the modern civil rights movement, which took off in the 1950s. The movement drew on an organizational base and network of communication rooted in black churches, the NAACP, and black colleges.

the justification of human bondage been presented with so much moral fervor."[3]

The abolitionist movement spread primarily through local organizations in the North. Antislavery groups coalesced in New York, Ohio, New Hampshire, Pennsylvania, New Jersey, and Michigan. In addition to forming antislavery societies, the movement spawned two political parties: the Liberty Party, a staunchly antislavery party, and the Free Soil Party, a larger but more moderate third party that sought primarily to restrict the spread of slavery into new western territories. Garrison noted his dismay at the Free Soil Party's more modest and pragmatic approach: "It is a party for keeping Free Soil and not for setting men free."

Some opponents of slavery took matters into their own hands, aiding in the escape of runaway slaves along the Underground Railroad. Even today, private homes and churches scattered throughout the northeast that were used to hide blacks on their trips to Canada attest to the in-

Anti-Slavery Almanac.

volvement of local citizenry. In the South, a similar, if contrary, fervor prompted mobs to break into post offices in order to seize and destroy antislavery literature.

The emotional power of the slavery issue was such that it ruptured the Democratic Party, splitting it into "slave" and "free" factions. It destroyed the other major party of the time, the Whig Party. And it gave rise to a new party, the Republican Party, which would become the last minor political party to become a major political party in the United States. Most important, however, the slavery question precipitated the nation's most bloody conflict, the Civil War. From the ashes of the Civil War came the Thirteenth, Fourteenth, and Fifteenth Amendments, which would redefine civil rights from that day to this.

SOURCE: Merton L. Dillon, *The Abolitionists* (Dekalb, IL: Northern Illinois University Press, 1974).
[1] John M. Blum et al., *The National Experience* (New York: Harcourt, Brace, and World, 1968), p. 266.
[2] Ibid.
[3] Ibid., p. 267.

The nonviolent protest tactics adopted by local clergy members, including Rev. Martin Luther King, Jr., eventually spread across the South and brought national attention to the movement. The clergy organized into a group called the Southern Christian Leadership Conference (SCLC). Students also played a key role. The most important student organization was the Student Nonviolent Coordinating Committee (SNCC). In 1960, four black students sat down at the lunch counter of the Greensboro, North Carolina, Woolworth's department store, which like most southern establishments did not serve African Americans. Their sit-in was the first of many. Through a combination of protest, legal action, and political pressure, the civil rights movement compelled a reluctant federal government to enforce black civil and political rights. The 1964 Civil Rights Act and the 1965 Voting Rights Act were the great legislative victories of the movement; the end of legal segregation and the beginning of black political power were the results.[9]

The victories of the civil rights movement made blacks full citizens and stimulated a tremendous growth in the number of black public officials at all levels of government, as blacks exercised their newfound political rights. Yet despite these successes, racial segregation remains a fact of life in the United States, and new problems have emerged. Most troubling is the persistence of black urban

STUDENTS AND POLITICS

The Woolworth lunch counter sit-in in Greensboro, North Carolina, started a wave of sit-ins throughout the South.

poverty, now coupled with deep social and economic isolation.[10] These conditions raise new questions about African American political participation. One question concerns black political cohesion: Will blacks continue to vote as a bloc, given the sharp economic differences that now divide a large black middle class from an equally large group of deeply impoverished African Americans? A second question concerns the benefits of participation: How can political participation improve the lives of African Americans, especially of the poor?

Public opinion and voting evidence indicate that African Americans continue to vote as a bloc despite their economic differences.[11] Surveys of black voters show that blacks across the income spectrum believe that their fates are linked because of their race. This sense of shared experience and a common fate has united blacks at the polls and in politics.[12] Since the 1960s, blacks have overwhelmingly chosen Democratic candidates and black candidates have sought election under the Democratic banner. In recent years, however, a small number of black Republicans has been elected to the House of Representatives. Evidence that affluent black Americans are less likely than poorer African Americans to support traditional policies that assist the poor suggests that this trend could continue in the future. However, Republican hostility to affirmative action and other programs of racial preference is likely to sharply check any large-scale black migration to the Republican Party.

At the same time, however, the black community and its political leadership has been considerably frustrated about the benefits of loyalty to the Democratic Party. Some analysts argue that the structure of party competition makes it difficult for African Americans to win policy benefits through political participation. Because Republicans have not sought to win the black vote and Democrats take it for granted, neither party is willing to support bold measures to address the mounting problems of poor African Americans.

Thus, concerns about strategy and organization remain very much on the African American political agenda. In the face of unfavorable political and legal outcomes, interest in self-help has grown, as evidenced by the gathering of hundreds of thousands of black men in Washington in 1995 for the Million Man March. Yet many black Americans continue to search for new ways to induce the government to address their distinctive concerns. These questions and problems now confront a new generation of African Americans.

Latinos The labels "Latino" and "Hispanic" encompass a wide range of groups with diverse national origins and distinctive cultural identities. The experiences of these groups in the American political system have often been very different from one another as well. Mexican Americans, Puerto Ricans, Cubans, and Central Americans have used varying strategies and organizational forms to gain access to American politics. As we will see, their struggles for political equality often differed according to when they entered the United States, in what region of the country they lived, and how racial considerations affected white views of whether they could become full citizens.

Mexican Americans are the largest group of Latinos in the United States today; their population is estimated at 14.6 million.[13] The Mexican American experience with political equality has been diverse and changing, because the experiences of Mexican Americans range from a people conquered in the middle of the nineteenth century to immigrants who arrived yesterday. The first Mexican Americans did not immigrate to the United States; the United States came to them when it annexed Texas in 1845 and defeated Mexico in 1848. The land that today makes up the states of New Mexico, California, Nevada, Utah, Colorado, Arizona, and Texas, all once part of Mexico, was added to American territory in those years.

The early political experiences of Mexican Americans were shaped by race and by region. In 1898, Mexican Americans were given formal political rights, including the right to vote. In many places, however, and especially in Texas, Mexican Americans were segregated and prevented from voting through such means as the white primary and the poll tax.[14] Region made a difference too. In contrast to the northeastern and midwestern cities to which most European ethnics immigrated, the Southwest did not have a tradition of ethnic mobilization associated with machine politics. Particularly after the political reforms enacted in the first decades of the twentieth century, city politics in the Southwest was dominated by a small group of Anglo elites. In the countryside, when Mexican Americans participated in politics, it was often as part of a political organization dominated by a large white landowner, or *patron*.

The earliest Mexican American independent political organizations, the League of United Latin American Citizens (LULAC) and the GI Forum, worked to stem discrimination against Mexican Americans in the years after World War II. By the late 1950s, the first Mexican American was elected to Congress, and four others followed in the 1960s. In the late 1960s a new kind of Mexican American political movement was born. Inspired by the black civil rights movement, Mexican American students launched boycotts of high school classes in East Los Angeles, Denver, and San Antonio. Students in colleges and universities across California joined in as well. Among their demands were bilingual education, an end to discrimination, and more cultural recognition. In Crystal City, Texas, which had been dominated by Anglo

Oklahoma representative J. C. Watts, shown here with Speaker of the House Newt Gingrich, is one of only two African American Republican members of Congress. He has said that although Democrats have taken black support for granted, Republicans have tended to write blacks off completely.

politicians despite a population that was overwhelmingly Mexican American, the newly formed La Raza Unida Party took over the city government.[15]

Since that time, Mexican American political strategy has developed along two tracks. One is a traditional ethnic-group path of voter registration and voting along ethnic lines. The second is a legal strategy using the various civil rights laws designed to ensure fair access to the political system. The Mexican American Legal Defense Fund (MALDEF) has played a key role in designing and pursuing the latter strategy. The two strategies are often used to reinforce one another, but at times they come into conflict.

Like that of the Mexicans, the Puerto Rican experience of the United States began with the experience of conquest. Puerto Rico became an unincorporated territory of the United States in 1898, after the Spanish-American War. In 1917, Puerto Ricans were made American citizens, although their island did not become a state. In the 1950s, Puerto Ricans began migrating to the mainland in large numbers, settling mainly in cities on the eastern seaboard—New York in particular.

Although they migrated to cities that had active traditions of ethnic group political participation, Puerto Ricans did not become politically mobilized until the late 1960s. In New York State, the requirement that voters be literate in English barred the majority of Puerto Ricans from registering in the 1950s.[16] By the 1960s, Puerto Ricans had become more politically mobilized and voted predominantly for Democratic candidates. Nevertheless, as one of the poorest ethnic groups in the United States, Puerto Ricans tend to have relatively low rates of political participation.

The Cuban experience with American politics has been quite different from those of Mexicans and Puerto Ricans. The vast majority of Cuban immigrants have come to the United States since the early 1960s as refugees from communist Cuba. In contrast to Puerto Rican and Mexican immigrants, many of the Cubans who came to the United States were middle class. Because they were granted refugee status, they also received federal government assistance in their settlement process. A central feature of Cuban American politics is a resolute anticommunism, which has led Cuban Americans to favor the Republican Party. Cuban political participation has also been shaped by the great concentration of Cubans in southern Florida. This concentration has allowed Cubans to become a major political force in Miami, and in Florida more broadly. The first Cuban American was elected to Congress from Florida in 1989.

Although Mexican Americans, Puerto Ricans, and Cubans make up the majority of Latinos in the United States, in the last decade substantial numbers of Spanish-speaking immigrants and refugees from the Caribbean, Central America, and South America have entered the country. During the 1980s, 23 percent of all legal immigrants to the United States came from these other Latin American countries.[17] These groups have altered the ethnic composition of Latinos in many cities, but they have not yet begun participating in politics in significant numbers.

The experience of Latinos in winning political equality stands between those of African Americans and white immigrants. In some regions of the country, restrictions on participation limited political equality until the 1960s. Even though Latinos have secured formal political equality, as a group Latinos have a relatively low level of political mobilization. Many analysts have called the Hispanic vote "the sleeping giant" because it has not yet realized its poten-

Many Puerto Ricans have lobbied strongly for statehood; the sign reads, "Authentic Puerto Ricans want U.S. citizenship—the 51st state."

A Latino voter registration drive in Texas. Increasing rates of naturalization and voter registration will make the Latino vote a powerful force in American politics.

tial influence. Two important reasons for the low mobilization levels among Latinos are the low rates of voter registration and low rates of naturalization. Only two-thirds of voting-age Latinos are American citizens. Mexican immigrants have the lowest rate of naturalization of all immigrant groups: only 13 percent of legal Mexican immigrants who came to the United States between 1970 and 1979 had become citizens by 1989. (For comparison, the rate for Vietnamese immigrants was 75 percent and for other Asians, 60 percent.)[18] In recent years, Hispanic political organizations have launched campaigns to encourage Latino immigrants to become citizens. They have also sought to register those who *are* citizens to vote, so that they can exercise the rights that come with political equality.

Asian Americans   As with Latinos, Asian Americans are a diverse group with many different national backgrounds. The majority of Asian immigrants have come to the United States in the past thirty years, but people from China began arriving on the West Coast in the 1850s.

The early Asian experience in the United States was shaped by a series of naturalization laws dating back to 1790, the first of which declared that only white aliens were eligible for citizenship. Chinese immigrants had begun arriving in California in the 1850s, drawn by the boom of the Gold Rush, but they were immediately met with hostility. The virulent antagonism toward Chinese immigrants in California led Congress to declare Chinese immigrants ineligible for citizenship in 1870. In 1882, the first Chinese Exclusion Act suspended the entry of Chinese laborers.

At the time of the Exclusion Act, the Chinese community was composed predominantly of single male laborers, with few women and children. The few Chinese children in San Francisco were initially denied entry to the public schools; only after parents of American-born Chinese children pressed legal action were the children allowed to attend public school. Even then, however, they were segregated into a separate Chinese school. American-born Chinese children could not be denied citizenship, however; this right was confirmed by the Supreme Court in 1898, when it ruled in *United States v. Wong Kim Ark* that anyone born in the United States was entitled to full citizenship.[19] Still,

In recent years, Native Americans have used their increasing autonomy to promote economic development on reservations, where deep poverty remains widespread. The biggest moneymaker for reservations has been casino gambling. The Supreme Court paved the way for casino gambling in a 1987 ruling that Indian tribes, as sovereign nations, are exempt from most state gambling regulations. An estimated ninety tribes have opened casinos, which bring in a total income of over $1 billion. Gambling has brought the greatest economic success the tribes have ever seen. They have been able to use the money from gambling to build housing and schools and to establish a base from which to diversify into other forms of economic development. Rather than leasing their lands to non-Indian companies, many tribes are now setting up their own businesses.[27]

IMMIGRATION AND THE AMERICAN POLITICAL COMMUNITY

Immigration raises several questions about our national unity. The first is how many and which immigrants should be allowed in (see the Policy Debate on p. 49). The growing numbers of immigrants have made many Americans uneasy and have prompted calls to restrict immigration. A 1995 poll showed that 65 percent of those questioned believed that immigration levels were too high. When questioned, most Americans pointed to the burden that immigrants place on public services and competition for jobs as the main reasons for limiting immigration.[28] However, some prominent analysts argue that further immigration should be restricted because it changes the racial balance of the country. Peter Brimelow, author of a widely discussed book, argued that "Americans have the right to insist the government stop shifting the racial balance."[29]

A second important issue concerns the rights of noncitizens. The Supreme Court has ruled that illegal immigrants are eligible for education and medical care but can be denied other social benefits; legal immigrants are to be treated much the same as citizens. But growing immigration—including an estimated 300,000 illegal immigrants per year—and mounting economic insecurity have undermined these practices. Groups of voters across the country now strongly support drawing a sharper line between immigrants and citizens. Not surprisingly, the movement to deny benefits to noncitizens began in California, which has been troubled by economic distress and has the highest levels of immigration of any state. In 1994, Californians voted in favor of Proposition 187, denying illegal immigrants all services except emergency medical care. Supporters of the measure hope to discourage illegal immigration and to pressure illegal immigrants already in the country to leave. Opponents contend that denying basic services to illegal immigrants risks creating a subclass of residents in the United States whose lack of education and poor health threaten all Americans.

The question of the rights of legal immigrants poses an even tougher problem. Congress has the power to deny public benefits to this group but doing so would go against long-standing traditions in American political culture. Legal immigrants have traditionally enjoyed most of the rights and obligations (such as paying taxes) of citizens. As constitutional scholar Theodore Bikel points out, the Constitution begins with "We the People of the United States"; likewise the Bill of Rights refers to the rights of *people,* not citizens.[30]

Those who want to retain benefits for legal immigrants and provide some services to illegals worry that we will create a two-tiered society that will hurt

POLICY DEBATE

Should Immigration Be Restricted?

America is a nation of immigrants, yet Americans have always had mixed feelings about who and how many people from other countries should be allowed to become citizens. In the mid-nineteenth century, for example, when millions of Irish immigrants settled in America, their arrival sparked fierce anti-Irish and anti-Catholic sentiment. From 1870 to 1920, more than twenty-six million immigrants came to America. This tide was stemmed by law in 1924. More recently, new tides of Latino and Asian immigrants have spurred pressure to tighten restrictions. In 1996, California passed Proposition 187, which blocked all state assistance to illegal immigrants. In 1997, the federal government imposed new financial support and minimum income requirements on those sponsoring immigrants.

Those who seek to restrict immigration argue that America simply cannot afford to throw open, or even keep open, its gates. Current restrictions do not prevent millions of legal and illegal immigrants from coming to this country. During the 1980s, for example, more than ten million legal and illegal immigrants entered the United States—a record high, eclipsing the nearly nine million immigrants who entered America during the first decade of the twentieth century. A disproportionate number of these newcomers use social services, the educational system, the health care system, and the criminal justice system. The attendant service drain and overall cost places an ever-greater burden on taxpayers, especially in states that receive most new immigrants, including California (whose population has increased by a third in a little more than a decade), Florida, Texas, and New York. Furthermore, immigrants may displace American workers because they are willing to accept lower pay and to work without union protection. The immigrant flood visibly contributes to urban overcrowding and the related problems of energy consumption, waste generation, and environmental degradation. Polls reveal that most Americans favor tougher immigration restrictions.

One remedy, an immigration moratorium, would serve several useful purposes. It would encourage existing immigrant communities to assimilate, a trend that is otherwise impeded by the constant influx of new immigrants. It would allow overburdened public agencies and institutions a chance to improve or rebuild their services. And it would allow for a more measured public dialogue on the future of immigration. Restrictions are a matter of simple necessity, proponents argue, because existing law allows recent immigrants to sponsor family members, who account for a major proportion of the new immigrant population.

Opponents of immigration restriction point out, first, that the stereotypical picture of the illegal, unskilled, crime-prone, welfare-seeking immigrant is a far cry from the actual immigrant population. About three-quarters of all immigrants enter the United States legally. These immigrants are, on average, better-educated and more highly skilled than the average citizens of the countries they leave. While immigrants do provide an important source for manual labor in agriculture and garment work, for example, immigrants also provide critical skills for important industries. California's "Silicon Valley," home to many high-tech industries, relies heavily on skilled immigrant labor. Immigrants also generate jobs. Many Korean immigrants, for example, start small businesses that generate jobs, a significant fact, given that small businesses employ more workers in America than do large businesses.

As for the social service burden imposed by immigrants, this has been exaggerated, according to restriction opponents. According to the 1990 census, 7 percent of foreign-born persons receive social service benefits, compared to 6 percent of native-born citizens and less than 5 percent of illegal immigrants. Much of the opposition to immigration, opponents say, has less to do with economics or crime, and more to do with racial hatred and a generalized fear that new immigrant groups will exert greater political and social influence. But racial and ethnic diversity ought not be feared. Instead, new cultures should be celebrated and embraced precisely for the differences they bring.

Students and Politics

Although California's Proposition 187 passed by a wide margin in a 1994 referendum, many students and faculty members expressed concern that the initiative would unfairly hinder minorities from receiving an equal education. The initiative, which would have forced beneficiaries of public assistance, grants, or medical coverage to provide documentation of their citizenship, contained a clause covering public education: "Commencing with the first term or semester ... each public postsecondary educational institution shall verify the status of each person enrolled...." Some opponents worried that minority students would be singled out for inspection based on their ethnicity. Protest against the initiative was widespread on campuses across the state. Students at California State University, Chico, led by Student Body President Oscar de la Torre, gathered approximately 2,000 signatures protesting the implementation of Proposition 187 at their university.* At Irvine Valley College, faculty and 300 students gathered to protest the law, saying that it played on the public's paranoia about immigrants. "We want to change the way people look at immigration," said student Angel Cervantes, leader of the Four Winds Student Movement, an organization devoted to fighting the proposition. "This is more of a human rights issue than a legal issue."† Students at the rally circulated a petition of noncompliance with the law.

A federal judge declared part of Proposition 187 unconstitutional in 1998, including the clause dealing with higher education.

*"CSU won't enforce Proposition 187," *Orion,* Wednesday, November 30, 1998.
†"Educators, Students Hammer Proposition 187 at 'Teach-In'," *Los Angeles Times,* November 23, 1994.

all Americans if we deny basic services and traditional social benefits to legal immigrants. They fear that establishing such distinctions simply makes immigrants scapegoats for national economic problems and will make integration of immigrants into American society more difficult. One side effect of the movement to restrict the benefits of immigrants may be to move us back to the higher rates of naturalization that characterized earlier waves of immigration. Unlike the political machines of the 1800s, the Immigration and Naturalization Service has traditionally done little to encourage immigrants to become citizens. But in 1996, the Clinton administration launched Citizenship USA, a program to speed up the naturalization process for immigrants, some of whom had been waiting for two years to become citizens. As a result of the program the number of new citizens each year more than doubled. The program drew critics, however, who charged that the citizenship drive was an effort by Democrats to attract immigrant votes. Moreover, congressional investigators found that in the effort to register so many new citizens so fast, improper screening may have allowed unqualified people, including those with criminal backgrounds, to become citizens.[31]

A final issue concerns the assimilation of immigrants into American culture. Many Americans now worry that immigrants are not assimilating into the broader culture. Such fears have given rise to the "English only" movement, which seeks to prevent public services from offering assistance in languages other than English and to allow voter ballots only in English. Fear that immigrants are not assimilating also underlies many calls to restrict immigration. Despite the growing visibility of distinctive immigrant cultures and languages as immigration has increased, there is no evidence that today's immigrants are any less likely to assimilate than those of earlier generations. A 1995 poll found that 59 percent of immigrants questioned believed they should blend into American society even if it means giving up some of their own culture.[32] Evidence suggests that today's second- and third-generation immigrants are in fact learning English and becoming Americanized.[33]

The debate about immigration today reflects both older themes and new concerns. Fears about the ethnic composition of the new immigrants echo sentiments from the nineteenth century, as do efforts to ensure that immigrants are assimilated. Yet changes in the past one hundred years pose new questions about immigration: with the frontier gone and major cities struggling, can we afford to welcome new immigrants, especially those with few resources? What are the implications for American democracy if identifiably different groups have unequal access to public resources?

CLASS

If asked what economic class they belong to, most Americans reply that they are in the middle class. The relative weakness of class in the United States stems in part from the American ideals of equality and individual liberty. But it is also a product of the American political system. For it is not just values but also the experiences—both positive and negative—of workers with the American political system that have prevented class from becoming a significant category of political action in the United States.

A glance at American history shows that there were times when class organization was very important. In the early years of the Republic, workers—mainly skilled artisans—formed political parties in more than sixty cities and towns. They demanded the ten-hour workday, free public schooling, and democratic political reforms. After the Civil War, the Knights of Labor became the first mass organization of the working class. In the 1880s, local elections featured Knights of Labor political tickets in more than two hundred state and local elections. Fueling this political activity was deep discontent with the emergence of big corporations, the factory system, and the degradation of work in general. In addition, deep economic depressions in the 1870s threw people out of work in unprecedented numbers. These conditions lay behind the massive labor strikes in the late nineteenth century. In fact, it is often forgotten that the United States has the most violent labor history of any industrialized nation.

If we look at the demands these workers made, we see that they were very much in tune with the key values of a thriving democracy. In fact, workers often drew on these values to support their positions. For example, workers assailed the emergence of the large corporation as antidemocratic. They defended a shorter working day and adequate wages as essential for workers to exercise the rights and responsibilities of citizenship. They argued that workers needed time to spend with their families and to attend public lectures. Labor organizations at this time had quite a broad notion of who was a member of the working class; for example, anyone except a capitalist or a lawyer could become a member of the Knights of Labor.[34]

The 1886 convention of the Knights of Labor. The organization accepted large numbers of black and female workers as members.

Despite all this working-class activity, workers' parties never managed to last in the United States, and national politics did not organize along class lines. The American Federation of Labor (AFL), the largest labor federation to survive into the twentieth century, turned its back on politics. Instead of formally aligning with a political party, the AFL remained aloof from politics and instead practiced "business unionism"—it would fight for workers' rights but it would not enter the political arena to do so.

The closest Americans have come to having a class-based politics in this century was during the New Deal of the 1930s. President Franklin Roosevelt changed American politics with legislation that assisted workers and their families: work relief, the Social Security Act, and the right to organize labor unions, for instance. Roosevelt used explicit class imagery to retain the political support of working-class voters and spoke of the need to equalize the distribution of wealth in the United States. His policies cemented working-class support for the Democratic Party, and the Republican Party became increasingly identified with business interests. These divisions were by no means absolute, however. The Democratic Party had plenty of supporters in the business community. Furthermore, the southern attachment to the Democratic Party had little to do with class; it was based more on the Democratic Party's refusal to challenge the political and economic inequality of blacks in the South. This loose class alignment characterized American politics until the 1960s, when racial and cultural divisions, along with a growing distrust of all politicians, began to diminish the expression of class in politics.

What are the prospects of reviving a class orientation in politics today? If we simply look at what Americans say about class, it does not look promising. Polls show that 93 percent of all Americans identify themselves as middle class; only 1 percent say they are in the upper class.[35] Nonetheless, some analysts argue that trends in the distribution of income and wealth over the past two decades have laid the groundwork for class politics. Since 1970, while incomes in the United States have remained stagnant, inequality has grown (see Figure 2.2). In fact, the United States has the greatest inequality in income and wealth of any industrial nation.[36] In recent years, Democratic candidates have sought to highlight these realities to revive a politics of class. But, aware of the weakness of class identity in the United States, they embrace only a loose definition of class. For example, Democrats attacked the tax policies of Presidents Ronald Reagan and George Bush as unfair to middle-class Americans. Republicans reject these arguments, however, saying that their policies create economic growth, which benefits all Americans. Thus, Republicans claim, there is a shared interest across classes, not opposing interests. Republicans also charge that class appeals are un-American. For example, President Bush defended himself against Democratic attacks by remarking that class is "for European democracies or something else—it isn't for the United States of America. We are not going to be divided by class."[37]

The recent Democratic efforts reveal the difficulty of trying to organize politics around class. Since most people feel they are in the middle class, Democrats face the challenge of deciding how and where to draw the line between the middle class and the rich. Moreover, the impact of the new inequality has been especially felt by the poor; assisting them requires taxing the upper end of the middle class. Yet upper-middle-class taxpayers participate the most and are the most vocal in American politics. They mounted such vigorous opposition to the in-

INCOME INEQUALITY IN THE UNITED STATES, 1974–94   Figure 2.2

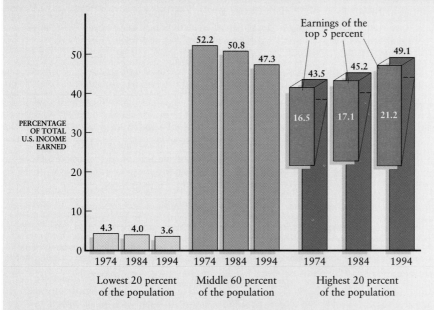

SOURCE: U.S. Bureau of the Census, "Income, Poverty, and Valuation of Noncash Benefits: 1994," *Current Population Reports,* Series P60-189 (Washington, DC: U.S. Government Printing Office, 1996), p. xii.

Over the last two decades, America's lower and middle classes have been growing relatively poorer, while the upper classes have been growing wealthier. In 1994, the top 5 percent of the population took home more than 20 percent of the income in the United States.

come tax increase signed by President Bill Clinton in 1993 that most Americans ended up thinking that their taxes had been raised, when in fact the increase affected only those at the very top of the income distribution.

Democrats also face another problem: to win support from voters on the lower half of the income spectrum, Democrats have to show that they can enact policies that will reduce economic inequality. With an electorate deeply mistrustful of politicians, this is a tall order. Nonetheless, even in times of economic prosperity, public concern about jobs and income suggests that politicians will continue to invoke the themes of class.

GENDER

Until 1920, electoral politics was a decidedly masculine world. Not only were women barred from voting in national politics, but electoral politics was closely tied to such male social institutions as lodges, bars, and clubs. Yet the exclusion of women from this political world did not prevent them from engaging in public life. Instead, women carved out a "separate sphere" for their public activities. Emphasizing female stewardship over the moral realm, women became important voices in social reform well before they won the right to vote.[38]

Women played leading roles in two key groundswells of social reform: the abolitionist movement prior to the Civil War and the movement against political

Shannon Faulkner

In August 1995, after a two-and-a-half-year legal struggle, the Citadel, a state-supported military college in Charleston, South Carolina, was forced by a federal judge to admit a young woman named Shannon Faulkner. Faulkner had originally been admitted to the Citadel in 1993, but when the school discovered that she was a woman (she had had references to her sex deleted from her high school transcript), it rescinded her admission. Faulkner sued on the grounds that the school's male-only policy was unconstitutional. But Faulkner's trailblazing effort came to a stunning end: exhausted by the arduous legal battle and in poor physical shape, Faulkner collapsed from heatstroke within the first hours of training, spent four days in the infirmary, and then announced her withdrawal from the school.

The Citadel, which until 1995 was one of only two male-only, state-supported military colleges in the nation (the other was Virginia Military Institute) prides itself on instilling discipline and loyalty in its cadets—qualities obviously essential to making good soldiers. The Citadel does so by subjecting first-year cadets to a relentless barrage of criticism, lack of privacy, and enforced conformism, all meant to break down their individuality. For those cadets who survive to "Recognition Day" at the end of the year, when they shake hands with their tormentors and can address older students by their first names, the psychological effect can be overwhelming, as a 1989 Citadel graduate, now a lawyer, testified: "I have never experienced anything like that; the feeling of accomplishment is unbelievable. The Citadel made me what I am today."[1]

According to supporters of the all-male policy, the presence of women will erode the intensity of the first-year experience. Faulkner would have enjoyed more privacy than male first-year cadets: a lock on her door, for instance, and private rather than communal showers. Other standards would have differed too: instead of a shaved head, she would have had her hair cut to the standards required for women in the U.S. military. And, in a procedure known as "gender norming," she would not have been subject to the same standards of physical performance as men. In defending their all-male policy,

Citadel officials argued that Faulkner had the opportunity to pursue an equivalent education without being admitted to their school. She could have gotten a degree from the Citadel's nonmilitary night school or she could have attended a military instruction program established by the Citadel at a nearby women's college, Converse College. But Faulkner and her supporters argued that these alternatives did not represent a truly "equal" education. As long as women were not allowed to be cadets, the essence of the Citadel's education, a woman's Citadel degree would not carry the prestige that a man's does. Nor, they said, would a degree from the women's leadership program at Converse College have anything like the value of a Citadel degree.

Faulkner and her supporters forced the Citadel to do what West Point and the other national military academies had already done: admit women on a basis of equality. Rather than celebrate the Citadel's all-male tradition as a source of strength, Faulkner and many others believed it was a source of weakness that made sexist soldiers, not good soldiers. One of Faulkner's lawyers, who watched as cadets boisterously celebrated her withdrawal announcement, said, "I was reminded again of how the Citadel takes these young boys . . . and teaches them antifeminism and teaches them the old-boy network. That's the real illness, not this young woman's stress."[2]

Shannon Faulkner gave up her fight, but other women continued the challenge. In 1996, the Supreme Court ruled that the Virginia Military Institute, also a state-supported, male-only school, could no longer exclude women. The ruling spelled the end of publicly supported single-sex institutions of higher learning. Although many students and alumni remained bitterly opposed to coeducation, the school had little choice. Two days after the Court's decision, the board of the Citadel voted to admit women.

[1] Quoted in Jim Schlosser, "Alumni Believe Citadel Worth It," *Greensboro News & Record,* October 16, 1995, p. A1.
[2] Quoted in Debbi Wilgoren, "The Citadel Reasserts Its All-Male Tradition," *Washington Post,* August 20, 1995, p. A3.

corruption and urban social squalor beginning in the 1880s. Some women pressed for the right to vote immediately after the Civil War, when male ex-slaves won the franchise. Politicians in both parties rejected women's suffrage as disruptive and unrealistic. Barred from voting, women found other means of participating in public life. For one thing, they formed their own clubs; as the nineteenth century ended, the General Federation of Women's Clubs boasted 495 affiliates throughout the country. These clubs provided female fellowship, but they also sought to bring women's distinctive perspectives into the public sphere. Women, they believed, had a special mission to bring morality into public life. Thus, women fought to prohibit alcohol consumption through the Woman's Christian Temperance Union; worked in urban charity organizations; sought to abolish child labor and to establish laws protecting public health; and led movements to reform education and schools in cities across the country.

At the same time, women began organizing to win the right to vote. Women formally started to press for the vote in 1867 when a state referendum to give women the vote in Kansas failed. Scattered efforts over the next decades took organizational form when the National American Woman Suffrage Association (NAWSA) formed in 1890. Many states granted women the right to vote before the national government did; Western states with less-entrenched political systems opened politics to women earliest. When Wyoming became a state in 1890, it was the first state to grant full suffrage to women. Colorado, Utah, and Idaho all followed suit in the next several years. Suffrage organizations grew—NAWSA claimed two million members by 1917—and staged mass meetings, parades, petitions, and protests. NAWSA organized state-by-state efforts to win

Suffragettes on the sidewalk in front of the White House in 1920. That year, after decades of political mobilization and state-level victories, women won a constitutional amendment guaranteeing them the right to vote.

CHRONOLOGY OF THE EQUAL RIGHTS AMENDMENT (ERA)

1923: The ERA, as written by Alice Paul of the National Woman's Party, introduced in Congress.

1950: The ERA passed by the Senate with a rider nullifying equal protection clauses.

1967: The recently formed National Organization for Women (NOW) pledges to make the unaltered amendment a top priority.

1971: ERA approved by the House, 354-24, and the Senate, 84-8; Phyllis Schlafly establishes the National Committee to Stop ERA.

1975: NOW leaders apply for deadline extension; new deadline of June 30, 1982, set.

1982: The ERA stopped, three states short of ratification.

1983: The ERA reintroduced in Congress; House fails to pass the ERA by the required two-thirds majority.

Representative Patsy Mink, a Democrat from Hawaii, speaks during a National Organization for Women rally. Since the 1960s, the women's movement has raised a stronger voice on a number of issues, including gender discrimination and abortion.

gender gap

a distinctive pattern of voting behavior reflecting the differences in views between men and women

the right to vote. A more militant group, the National Woman's Party, staged pickets and got arrested in front of the White House to protest President Wilson's opposition to a constitutional amendment granting women the right to vote. Finally in 1920, the Nineteenth Amendment was ratified, guaranteeing women the right to vote.

The consequences of gaining the vote proved disappointing, however, especially to feminists, who wanted equality between men and women. The earliest advocates of women's rights had favored equality in all spheres of life. By contrast, the mainstream of the suffrage movement stressed "women's special sphere"—the realm of morality, social reform, and family. Politics proved somewhat more amenable to the latter vision because it accorded better with widely held cultural beliefs. The idea of a separate women's sphere also built on institutions and initiatives that had begun before women had the vote. For example, Democrats responded to the women's vote by establishing the Women's Bureau within the Labor Department. Once granted the franchise, however, women did not vote as a group, and many of them did not vote at all. Thus, hopes that women would achieve equality through the vote or that their votes would make some distinctive impact on politics diminished. In this context, the National Woman's Party's legislation for an Equal Rights Amendment stood little chance of success when it was submitted to Congress in 1923. Even legislation premised on women's "special sphere"—such as maternal and child health care reform—was abandoned by the end of the 1920s. Not until the 1960s did a broad movement for women's equality reemerge. The initial impetus for its revival was growing concern about inequality in the world of work.

Armed with new legal tools that outlawed discrimination in employment and wages, women formed a set of organizations dedicated to fight for equality for women in many different spheres. Among the new organizations were the National Organization for Women (NOW), the Women's Equity Action League (WEAL), and the National Women's Political Caucus (NWPC). NOW used protest tactics to combat the unequal treatment of women. It picketed the Equal Employment Opportunity Commission for refusing to ban sex-segregated employment ads and filed charges against the *New York Times* for publishing such ads. WEAL focused on legal action around a wide range of sex discrimination issues, including lawsuits against law and medical schools for discriminatory admissions policies. The NWPC promoted the election of female candidates and the appointment of women to political office.

By the early 1970s, legislative successes were bolstered by important legal victories, the most stunning of which was the 1973 legalization of abortion in *Roe v. Wade.* The movement next turned its efforts to passing an Equal Rights Amendment (ERA), which the National Woman's Party had regularly proposed since 1923. Buoyed by the strength of the new women's movement, success appeared within reach. Congress approved the amendment in 1972 and sent it to the states for ratification. But the ERA fell three states short of the thirty-eight needed for ratification and, by 1982, it was dead.

The failure of the ERA was a defeat for the feminist organizations, but it by no means marked the end of gender politics. Three developments indicate the ongoing significance of gender issues in American politics. First is the emergence of a **gender gap**—a distinctive pattern of male and female voting decisions—in electoral politics. Although proponents of women's suffrage had expected women to make a distinctive impact on politics as soon as they won the vote, not until the 1980s did voting patterns reveal a clear difference between male and female votes. In 1980, men voted heavily for Republican candidate Ronald Reagan; women divided their votes between Reagan and the incumbent Democratic president, Jimmy Carter. Since that election, gender differences have emerged in congressional and state elections, as well. Women tend to vote in higher numbers for Democratic candidates, while Republicans win more male votes. Behind these voting patterns are differing assessments of key policy issues. For one thing, more women than men take liberal positions on political issues; women are more likely than men to oppose military activities and support social spending. For example, 54 percent of women approved of the U.S. decision to send troops to Saudi Arabia in 1991, compared to 78 percent of men. On social spending, these trends reverse: 69 percent of women favor increased spending on Social Security, compared to 57 percent of men; 83 percent of women favor improving the nation's health care, compared to 76 percent of men; 72 percent of women advocate more spending on programs for the homeless, compared to 63 percent of men.[39] It is important to note that these differences do not mean that all women vote more liberally than all men. In fact, the voting differences between women who are homemakers and women who are in the workforce are almost as large as the differences between men and women. The sharpest differences are found between married men and single women, with single women tending to take the most liberal positions.[40]

Students and Politics

California's 1996 battle over Proposition 209, which outlawed affirmative action programs in state and local governments, created a firestorm of debate on campuses across the state. The National Organization for Women (NOW) began several grassroots campaigns to defeat the measure, including at the Claremont Colleges near Los Angeles. Students there made a big effort to get out the vote, organizing marches on the campuses and in the community. A speech by NOW president Patricia Ireland helped spark the movement. Despite the passage of Proposition 209, the students' efforts helped to form the Action Coalition of the Claremont Colleges, a progressive alliance. NOW's intervention and assistance provided a cohesion that had not existed before the election. "The 209 campaign is really what clicked for us," said Amy Drayer, copresident of Scripps NOW. "It is the issue that mobilized our efforts." NOW Action Vice President Rosemary Dempsey agreed: "This kind of organizing doesn't have to focus only on major elections, like the presidential election," she said. "Campus organizing is an effective tool for any kind of issue, particularly issues NOW focuses on, like affirmative action, reproductive rights, and fighting racism."

The second key development in gender politics in recent years is the growing number of women in political office (see Figure 2.3). Journalists dubbed 1992 the "Year of the Woman" because so many women were elected to Congress: women doubled their numbers in the House and tripled them in the Senate. By 1995 women held 10.3 percent of the seats in the House of Representatives and 8 percent in the Senate; 20.1 percent of state legislators in 1995 were women.[41] Organizations supporting female candidates have worked to encourage more women to run for office and have supported them financially. In addition to the bipartisan NWPC, the Women's Campaign Fund and EMILY's List provide pro-choice Democratic women with early campaign financing, which is critical to establishing electoral momentum (the acronym of the latter group stands for Early Money Is Like Yeast). Recent research has shown that the key to increasing the numbers of women in political office is to encourage more women to run for election. Women are disadvantaged as candidates not because they are women but because male candidates are more likely to have the advantage of incumbency.[42] Although women in public office by no means take uniform positions on policy issues, surveys show that, on the whole, women legislators are more supportive of women's rights, health care spending, and children's and family issues.[43]

The third way in which women affect politics today is through the continuing salience of policy issues of special concern to women. Before the women's

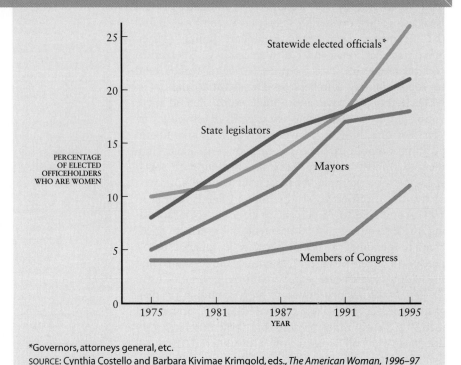

Figure 2.3 — INCREASE IN NUMBER OF WOMEN IN ELECTIVE OFFICE, 1975–95

*Governors, attorneys general, etc.
SOURCE: Cynthia Costello and Barbara Kivimae Krimgold, eds., *The American Woman, 1996–97* (New York: Norton, 1996), p. 338.

Paula Jones, a former Arkansas state employee, filed a civil lawsuit against President Clinton, alleging that he had sexually harassed her when he was governor of Arkansas.

movement, many issues of deep concern to women were simply not on the political agenda. Today, however, issues such as abortion, sexual harassment, and comparable worth, and the concerns of families and children are often central to political debate. In 1991 the issue of sexual harassment burst into public consciousness when University of Oklahoma law professor Anita Hill accused Supreme Court nominee Clarence Thomas of sexual harassment. As Figure 2.4 shows, the number of sexual harassment complaints rose sharply after the hearings. The spectacle of the hearings—in which an all-male Senate Judiciary Committee harshly questioned Hill—also galvanized many women politically. In the words of pollster Celinda Lake, "Anita Hill has become a metaphor for something a lot broader than sexual harassment. She has become a symbol for a system that's failed, that's become distorted and out of touch."[44] The salience of sexual harassment and abortion as political issues contributed to the electoral gains of female candidates in 1992.

Since the 1960s the women's movement has helped to transform the place of women in society and the economy, it has brought unprecedented numbers of women into public office, and it has altered the national political agenda. Although women's opinions diverge widely on many political issues, the emergence of a gender gap in voting and the growing numbers of women in political office ensure that gender issues will continue to influence American politics.

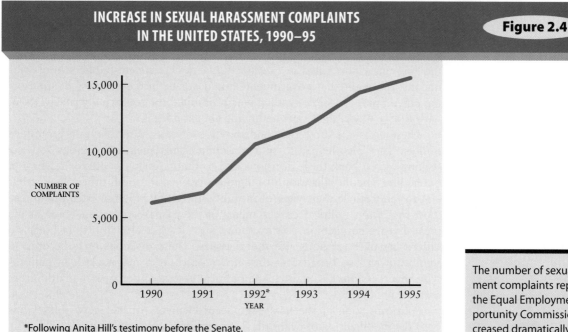

INCREASE IN SEXUAL HARASSMENT COMPLAINTS IN THE UNITED STATES, 1990–95

Figure 2.4

NUMBER OF COMPLAINTS

YEAR

*Following Anita Hill's testimony before the Senate.
SOURCE: Equal Employment Opportunity Commission, Charge Data Systems National Data Base.

The number of sexual harassment complaints reported to the Equal Employment Opportunity Commission has increased dramatically since the early 1990s.

RELIGION

Religion has always played an important role in American politics and public life. Religious freedom was a central tenet of the new nation. The people who first settled the American colonies sought the freedom to practice their religious beliefs. The central role that religion played in their lives made it likely that religious beliefs would spill over into politics and debates about how to organize public life. Thus, despite the formal separation of church and state established by the Constitution, religious groups have regularly entered the political arena, often provoking heated debate about the proper role of government in enforcing moral values and in protecting the personal freedoms of those with different values.

Religion continues to play an important role in American life. For some people, religious groups provide an organizational infrastructure for participating in politics around issues of special group concern. Black churches, for example, were instrumental in the civil rights movement, and black religious leaders continue to play important roles in national and local politics. Jews have also been active as a group in politics, but less through religious bodies than through a variety of social action agencies. Such agencies include the American Jewish Congress, the Anti-Defamation League, and the American Jewish Committee.

For most of American history, religious values have been woven deeply into the fabric of public life. Public school students began the day with prayers or Bible reading; city halls displayed crèches during the Christmas season. Practices that were religiously proscribed—most notably abortion—were also forbidden under law. But over the past thirty-five years, a variety of court decisions greatly reduced this kind of religious influence on public life. In 1962, the Supreme Court ruled in *Engel v. Vitale* that prayer in public schools was unconstitutional—that government should not be in the business of sponsoring official prayers. Bible reading was prohibited the following year. By 1973, with *Roe v. Wade,* the Court had made abortion legal.[45]

These decisions drew the condemnation of many Catholic and Protestant leaders. They also helped to spawn a countermovement of religious activists seeking to roll back these decisions and to find a renewed role for religion in public life. The mobilization of religious organizations and other groups that aim to reintroduce their view of morality into public life has been one of the most significant political developments of the past two decades. Some of the most divisive conflicts in politics today, such as that over abortion, hinge on differences over religious and moral issues. These divisions have become so significant and so broad that they now constitute a major clash of cultures with repercussions throughout the political system and across many different areas of policy.

Politically, one of the most significant elements of this new politics has been the mobilization of evangelical Protestants into a cohesive and politically shrewd organization aligned with the Republican Party. The Moral Majority, the first broad political organization of evangelical Christians, showed its political muscle in the 1980 election, when it aligned with the Republican Party, eventually backing Ronald Reagan for president. Over the next few years, evangelicals strengthened their movement by registering voters and mobilizing them with sophisticated, state-of-the-art political techniques. Their success was evident in the 1984 election, when 80 percent of evangelical Christian voters cast their ballots for Reagan. The 1988 election was a turning point in the political development of the Christian Right. Televangelist Pat Robertson ran for president and, although his candidacy was unsuccessful, his effort laid the groundwork for future political strength. Robertson's supporters gained control of some state Republican parties and won positions of power in others. With this new organizational base and sharply honed political skills, Robertson formed a new organization, the Christian Coalition. This organization has become one of the most important groups in American politics today because of its ability to reach and mobilize a large grassroots base. It is now part of a growing number of loosely connected organizations dedicated to similar goals.[46]

The rise of the Christian Coalition has raised important challenges for both political parties. Republicans, who have benefited enormously from their alliance with this new political base, face the dilemma of retaining the support of the Christian Right without losing more moderate voters. Democrats, in turn, face the challenge of holding on to their liberal base while at the same time acknowledging the widespread fears of social and moral decay so successfully raised by the Christian Right. The sophisticated organization of the Christian Right and the deep divisions among the American people on a range of cultural concerns ensure that such issues will have a prominent place in future politics.

Religious organizations have emerged as a strong influence on voters' choices about issues or candidates. Here, Rev. Rodney Page displays an Interfaith Alliance of Oregon voter's guide.

Participation in the American Political Community

▶ In what different ways do Americans participate in politics?

▶ What explains levels of participation? Why has participation declined over time?

▶ What roles do social and political institutions play in promoting participation and fulfilling American political values?

Political participation makes the ideals of liberty and equality come alive. But by many measures, Americans are participating less and less. For example, in the 1996 presidential election only 49 percent of eligible voters cast ballots, the lowest percentage in a presidential election in more than sixty years. Citizens can, however, participate in ways other than voting. In this section we will examine the different ways that Americans participate in politics. We will look for changes in rates and methods of participation over time and describe the differences in participation among groups. We will then explore the causes for the patterns we observe. Two questions in particular will concern us: Why has participation declined? Why do people with higher levels of education and wealth participate most? Finally, we will consider the role that institutions play in promoting participation in ways that emphasize our values of liberty and equality.

political participation
political activities, such as voting, contacting political officials, volunteering for a campaign, or participating in a protest, whose purpose is to influence government

FORMS OF PARTICIPATION

Voting is one of the most fundamental rights in a democracy, yet it is one that growing numbers of Americans are not exercising. Participation in presidential elections has dropped significantly over the past forty years. In 1960, 64 percent of eligible voters cast ballots; in 1996, less than half of the electorate turned out. Voting in midterm elections is typically lower, on the order of one-third of eligible voters. It took the votes of less than a quarter of the electorate to catapult the Republicans to power in Congress in 1994 because fewer than 39 percent of eligible voters showed up at the polls. Turnout for local elections is usually even lower.[47]

Citizens may still participate in political life even if they do not vote. They can contact political officials, sign petitions, attend public meetings, join organizations, give money to a politician or a political organization, volunteer in a campaign, write a letter to the editor or write an article about an issue, or participate in a protest or rally. Such activities differ from voting because they can communicate much more detailed information to public officials than voting can. Voters may support a candidate for many reasons but their actual votes do not indicate specifically what they like and don't like, nor do they tell officials how intensely voters feel about issues. A vote can convey only a general sense of approval or disapproval. By writing a letter or engaging in other kinds of political participation, people can convey much more specific information, telling public officials exactly what issues they care most about and what their

A "freedom marcher" in 1965. Although the Voting Rights Act of 1965 strengthened the right of African Americans to vote, some have questioned whether this right translated into political power.

| Figure 2.5 | POLITICAL PARTICIPATION: HOW MUCH? ABOUT WHAT? |

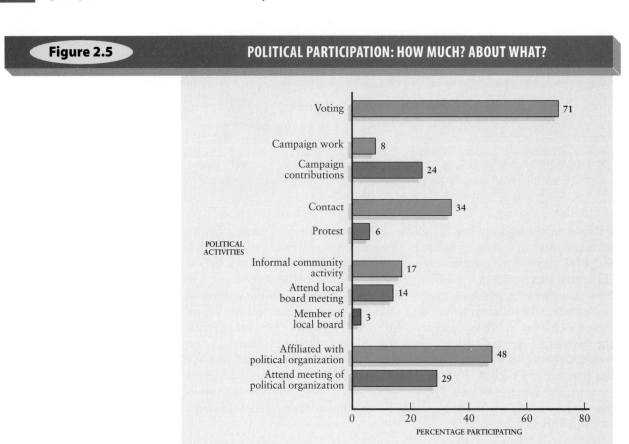

SOURCE: Sidney Verba, Kay Lehman Schlozman, and Henry E. Brady, *Voice and Equality: Civic Voluntarism in American Politics* (Cambridge, MA: Harvard University Press 1995), p. 51.

views on those issues are. For that reason these other political activities are often more satisfying than voting. And citizens who engage in these other activities are more likely to try to influence state and local politics rather than national politics; in voting, people find the national scene more interesting than state and local politics.[48]

But other activities generally require more time, effort, or money than voting does. It is not surprising, then, that far fewer people engage in these forms of political participation than vote. A recent study of participation, for example, found that about a third of those questioned said they had contacted a public official; a quarter reported that they had made a campaign contribution; and fewer than 10 percent said they had been active in a political campaign (see Figure 2.5). Nearly half, however, said they were involved in an organization that took positions on political issues.[49] In contrast to the sharp decline in voting, involvement in these other activities has not fallen off nearly so much and, by some measures, has actually increased. For example, Americans are more likely to contribute money to political organizations and campaigns than in the past, but they are less likely to belong to political organizations.[50]

EXPLAINING POLITICAL PARTICIPATION

Given the decline in voting, concern has mounted that Americans are disengaging from the political system and that participation is skewed toward those with more money. To understand these current patterns we must go back to a basic question: Why do people participate in politics? Simple as it seems, there are different ways to answer this question.

Socioeconomic Status   The first explanation for participation points to the characteristics of individuals. One of the most important and consistent results of surveys about participation is that Americans with higher levels of education, more income, and higher-level occupations—what social scientists call **socioeconomic status**—participate much more in politics than do those with less education and less income. Education level alone is the strongest predictor of most kinds of participation, but income becomes important—not surprisingly—when it comes to making contributions. In addition to education and income, other individual characteristics also affect participation. For example, African Americans and Latinos are less likely to participate than are whites, although when differences in education and income are taken into account, both groups participate at the same or higher levels than do whites. Finally, young people are far less likely to participate in politics than are older people. When eighteen-, nineteen-, and twenty-year-olds won the right to vote in 1971, participation dropped off substantially in the next election. But even more important, the proportion of young people that votes has declined in almost every single election since 1972.[51]

Although they give us a picture of who participates and who does not, explanations based on individual characteristics leave many questions open. One of the biggest questions is why the relationship between education and participation—so strong in surveys—does not seem to hold true over time. As Americans have become more educated, with more people finishing high school and attending college, we would expect to see more people participating in politics. Yet participation has declined, not increased.[52] In the nineteenth century, participation in presidential elections was 20 percent higher than current levels. Moreover, politics was a much more vibrant and encompassing activity: large numbers of people joined in parades, public meetings, and electioneering.[53] This puzzle about declining participation suggests that we need to look beyond the characteristics of individuals to the larger social and political setting to understand changes in patterns of participation over time.

The Social Setting and Civic Engagement   The social setting can affect political participation in a variety of ways. One recent study argued that participation depends on three elements: resources (including time, money, and know-how), **civic engagement** (are you concerned about public issues and do you feel that you can make a difference?), and recruitment (are you asked to participate, especially by someone you know?).[54] Whether a person has resources, feels engaged, and is recruited depends very much on his or her social setting—what his parents are like, who she knows, what associations she belongs to. In the United States, churches are a particularly important social institution in helping to foster political participation. Through their church

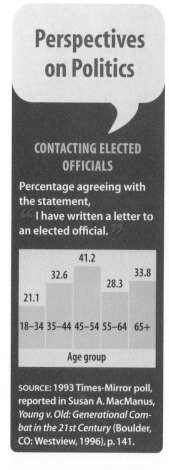

Perspectives on Politics

CONTACTING ELECTED OFFICIALS

Percentage agreeing with the statement, "I have written a letter to an elected official."

Age group	Percentage
18–34	21.1
35–44	32.6
45–54	41.2
55–64	28.3
65+	33.8

SOURCE: 1993 Times-Mirror poll, reported in Susan A. MacManus, *Young v. Old: Generational Combat in the 21st Century* (Boulder, CO: Westview, 1996), p. 141.

socioeconomic status

status in society based on level of education, income, and occupational prestige

civic engagement

a sense of concern among members of the political community about public, social, and political life, expressed through participation in social and political organizations

activities people learn the civic skills that prepare them to participate in the political world more broadly. It is often through church activities that people learn to run meetings, write newsletters, or give speeches and presentations. Churches are also an important setting for meeting people and creating networks for recruitment, since people are more likely to participate if asked by a friend or an acquaintance.

As this model suggests, if fewer people belong to social organizations, they may be less likely to participate in politics. The United States has often been called a nation of joiners because of our readiness to form local associations to address common problems. As early as the 1830s, the Frenchman Alexis de Tocqueville singled out this tendency to form associations as a most distinctive American trait.[55] There is evidence, however, that Americans no longer join organizations as much as they did in the past. This declining membership raises concerns that the civic engagement that ordinary Americans once had is deteriorating. These concerns are magnified by declining levels of social trust, which further contribute to the tendency to pull back from public engagement.[56] There are many possible reasons for the decline in organizational membership and social trust, and consequently in civic engagement. Television, for example, keeps people in their houses and away from meetings or other, more civic, engagements.[57] Crime can also reduce civic engagement by reducing social trust, making people suspicious and unwilling to take part in neighborhood activities.

Another way to explain the decline in civic engagement is to look at how the experiences of different generations might make them more or less oriented toward civic engagement. The generation that came of age during the Great Depression and World War II has been called the "long civic generation" because this group tends to participate in politics and associational life much more than previous or later generations. During the 1930s people looked to government to help them with economic hardships, and in the 1940s, the same generation fought World War II, a popular war in which the entire country pulled together.[58] Later generations have not experienced such popular common causes to bring them together in the public sphere: their wars have been less popular and their great social causes more divisive. In addition, political life has seemed much less inspiring, filled with accusations of wrongdoing and constant investigations into possible scandal. Such a generational perspective makes sense because people form habits and beliefs in their early years that are very important in how they participate later in life. A generational perspective also helps explain why participation has not declined throughout the century, but instead started out low in the early 1900s, rose from the 1930s through the 1960s, and then began to fall once again.

The Political Setting   Arguments about declining public trust and generational effects don't pay enough attention to the political setting in which participation takes place. The organization of politics itself plays a key role in channeling participation in particular directions and in encouraging or discouraging people from participating. Participation depends on whether there are formal obstacles in the political system, what people think political engagement has to offer them, and most important, whether political parties and politicians try to mobilize people into politics.

Some analysts have speculated that the constant scandals surrounding politics, such as that which arose in 1998 over President Clinton and former White House intern Monica Lewinsky, have distanced the public from politics.

Formal obstacles can greatly decrease participation. In the South prior to the 1960s, the widespread use of the **poll tax** and other measures such as the **white primary** essentially deprived black Americans (and many poor whites) of the right to vote during the first part of this century. This system of legal segregation meant that there were few avenues for black Americans in the South to participate in politics. With the removal of these legal barriers in the 1960s, black political participation shot up, with rates of turnout approaching those of southern whites, as early as 1968.[59]

But the removal of formal obstacles is not enough to ensure that people participate, as the example of the National Voter Registration Act passed in 1993 shows. Popularly known as the Motor Voter act, the law aimed to increase participation by making it easier to register to vote. The cumbersome process of registering (and staying registered after moving) has often been singled out as a barrier to participation. The new law aimed to remove this obstacle by allowing people to register when they apply for a driver's license and at other public facilities. Although voter registration increased, turnout did not. An estimated 3.4 million people registered to vote as a result of the Motor Voter act, but turnout in the 1996 election—the first presidential election held after the law went into effect—actually declined by 6 percent from that in 1992.[60] The very limited success of this measure suggests that people need motivation to participate, not simply the removal of barriers.

The political setting can play an important role in motivating people to vote. When elections are closely contested, more people tend to vote. And in political settings where they think their input will make a difference, people are more likely to participate. One study of black political participation, for example, found that blacks were more likely to vote, participate in campaigns, and contact public officials in cities run by a black mayor. Their greater attention to city politics and their belief that city government is more responsive to their concerns helps to spark participation.[61]

poll tax

a tax placed on voters as a precondition to registration, primarily used by southern states before the 1960s to exclude poor African Americans

white primary

primary election in which only white voters are eligible to participate

But the most significant factor affecting participation is whether people are mobilized by parties, candidates, interest groups, and social movements. A recent comprehensive study of the decline in participation in the United States found that fully half of the drop-off could be accounted for by reduced **mobilization** efforts.[62] People are much more likely to participate when someone—preferably someone they know—asks them to get involved. In previous decades that is precisely what political parties, organizations, and social movements did. During the era of face-to-face politics, armies of volunteers mobilized by full-time activists were essential for political victory. With the rise of media campaigns, money has replaced people as the key to political success. Rather than mobilizers of people, political parties have largely become fund-raising and advertising organizations. The experience of a Connecticut woman during the 1996 election is typical. Hoping to participate in the campaign, she sent a check to the Democratic Party and asked how she could volunteer. She subsequently received many more requests to donate money but she was never informed of any other way to become involved.[63] For most people, politics consists of little more than irritating advertisements that take over their television sets around election time.

Interest groups have also reduced their efforts at direct mobilization. Although the number of interest groups has grown dramatically in recent years, the connection that most interest-group members have to these groups often extends no further than their checkbook. Rather than being a means for contact by a friend or an acquaintance to take part in a political activity, belonging to an organization is likely to bring requests through the mail for donations. And, rather than providing a venue for meeting new people and widening your circle of engagement, organizational membership is more likely to land your name on yet another mailing list, generating still more requests for funds. Likewise, past social movements, such as the labor movement in the 1930s and the civil rights movement of the 1960s, played an important role in mobilizing people into politics. As such movements have ebbed, nothing has replaced their mobilizing energy.

PARTICIPATION AND AMERICAN POLITICAL VALUES

Over the course of our history, as we have seen, the American political community has expanded to make our politics more closely match our fundamental values of liberty, equality, and democracy. But more recently, our **political institutions** have ceased to mobilize an active citizenry. Furthermore, our uneven pattern of political participation is at odds with our notions of equality and democracy. These problems highlight the tension among our basic values and raise questions about whether our institutions could help provide a better balance among them. Two questions about institutions are particularly pressing: Is "checkbook democracy" enough? Do our public institutions do enough to bring us together to engage in common problem-solving?

"Checkbook democracy" refers to the new importance of money in politics, both in electoral campaigns and in interest-group activity. Because it has been associated with declining participation and a greater inequality in participation patterns, checkbook politics has been the target of reformers who

mobilization

the process by which large numbers of people are organized for a political activity

political institution

an organization that connects people to politics, such as a political party, or a governmental organization, such as the Congress or the courts

want to limit the role of money in politics. But the Supreme Court greatly limited the scope for reform in an important decision in 1976, when it ruled that individual contributions to candidates were a form of free speech and that it would be a curtailment of liberty to forbid such spending so long as it was not formally connected with a political campaign.[64] Many reformers remain dissatisfied with the Court's decision because they believe that allowing money to play such an important role in politics undermines political equality. Critics also do not think that restricting direct spending on candidates is a significant infringement of liberty.

The other charge against checkbook politics is that it saps the energy from democracy because most members have only very loose connections with the groups who receive their checks. This not only allows interest groups to lobby in Washington with little direct accountability to their membership, it also fails to mobilize people directly and thus does not build the personal connections that promote broad political engagement. Defenders of this style of politics say it does not drain democracy, it only makes it more efficient. In other words, people no longer have to go to meetings; they can simply send a check to the organizations they like and avoid the organizations they dislike.[65] These different views provoke questions about whether we need more direct participation to promote political equality and a vibrant democracy. They also cause us to ask what kinds of changes in social and political institutions would promote more direct participation.

Public institutions can play an important role in helping people understand our values in practice and find acceptable balances among them. Yet there are indications that our institutions are increasingly less able to perform this role. Some people argue that the behavior of American elites—the upper-middle class and the corporate community—has been the driving factor in the weakening of American democracy. Many American elites no longer participate in broad public institutions; instead, they send their children to private schools, obtain their medical care from generous private insurance plans, and hire private police to ensure their security. This "secession of the rich" has had damaging consequences for American democracy because these groups no longer have a stake in what happens in the public sector. Their main interest is in keeping taxes low and protecting themselves from public problems.[66] Yet clearly individuals have the right to participate as they wish and to purchase the services they think they need. But what happens when these individual choices undermine our ability to bring people together to hammer out their differences about what our values should mean in practice?

American political culture has supplied a core set of values that has helped knit together a culturally diverse nation. But the scope and meaning of these values has shifted over the course of history. In the past, these values were applied selectively, and some people were excluded from the definition of the American political community. Today, a more inclusive definition has evolved. Nonetheless, new questions about the role of our institutions in promoting political engagement and broad-based participation have emerged. We now face serious questions about what our values mean in a political system that seems irrelevant to many people and in which higher-income citizens have a disproportionately strong voice. The answers given to these questions today will shape the meaning of the American dream for future generations.

POLITICS ON THE WEB

The Internet could contribute to American democracy by expanding the avenues of political communication and participation available to under-represented segments of the population. Various interest groups representing minority populations, such as the National Association for the Advancement of Colored People, can use the Internet to present information about themselves and their aims, and to recruit members and solicit contributions on-line. Moreover, racial, ethnic, and religious minorities can use the Internet to disseminate their own perspectives on political events, providing a vast array of alternatives to the "mainstream" view.

However, these hopeful predictions rest on a much more equal distribution of Internet access than currently exists in America. Right now, whites use the Internet more than blacks, men more than women, the rich more than the poor, the young more than the old. Only as these disparities lessen will the Internet realize its full potential as an equalizing force in American politics.

www.wwnorton.com/wtp2e

Taking Part in the American Political Community: The Citizen's Role

What can ordinary citizens do to make politics fit their vision of what liberty, equality, and democracy should mean today? Some people answer this question with a defeated cynicism that says not much can be done through the political system. Others express an enthusiasm for participation that is often unrealistic and pays little attention to the question of what constitutes effective participation. Our view of the citizen's role in politics highlights the importance of knowledge, not just about the workings of government but about how politics and policy affect *you*. It also stresses the importance of learning how to be politically effective. What can students do to learn both about how actions of the government affect them and about how to be effective themselves?

The road to knowledge can be a rocky one because it is often hard to know how government is affecting you or how its current policies may affect you in the future. The challenge of identifying your interests among all the different things that government does requires a critical stance toward information. This means being focused enough to sift through the mountain of information easily available today; it also means asking where information is coming from. Is the information really an effort to instill in you one view of the world and to convince you about what your interests are? There is nothing wrong with that, but it is important to know if that is what is going on. For example, the Concord Coalition, which argues that the federal deficit is the biggest problem facing the country, has sought to publicize this particular view among students, arguing that they will be stuck paying off the debt of the country if spending is not dramatically curbed. Yet an alternative view argues that the deficit is not such a big problem and that it is most important to use public resources today to build a productive and educated workforce for the future. From this perspective, cutting spending is a false economy that may actually harm us in the future. To make sense of such divergent views requires a perspective that welcomes debate and looks for connections among issues that may not be apparent at first glance. But the judgment about the right answer is up to the individual.

In Chapter 1, we stressed that most people approach the political system from a perspective of self-interest. This does not mean that they care only about themselves but rather that they want politics to address the things they care about. People may care passionately about things that will not fatten their own wallets but that might push the world a little closer to their vision of how things should be. Most people, in fact, care about both their wallets and their visions of the world. Nor does the premise of self-interest mean that the best way to meet your goals is to act alone. The essence of effective political action is learning how to build **coalitions**. This means that to fulfill your own interests, you need to understand who shares your interests. This can be a straightforward matter, as it was to students protesting hikes in university tuitions in recent years. It can also be more complicated and require learning about the interests of others in order to find common ground. This calls for communication skills: being able to express your own interests so that others can understand them and being able to listen to their views. The ability to locate allies and build cooperative relationships is a key component of political knowledge.

coalition

a group of interests that join together for the purpose of influencing government

Many students do want to be engaged with issues that concern them but they—like many other Americans—simply are not that interested in politics. In a 1997 survey a large majority of freshmen—72 percent—revealed that they had performed volunteer work in the past year, 10 percent more than in 1989. At the same time, however, only about 30 percent said they considered it "very important" to keep up with current events.[67] How does such volunteer activity connect to more political forms of civic engagement? Is it a substitute for politics or does it help people become more politically active? Supporters of "service learning," which engages students in public-service volunteer activities as part of their curriculum, argue that learning firsthand about diverse people and problems prepares students to be better citizens. Some supporters argue that through such volunteer activities, students may be drawn into politics, as they learn about how political decisions affect such issues as care for the elderly, homelessness, or public education. By itself, however, service learning is not likely to help students understand how politics affects their volunteer activities or to draw them into politics. Such connections are often not obvious and it is not easy to see how an individual can affect a political issue. Service learning must be combined with attention to politics and with information about how politics affects a variety of social issues.[68]

As a freshman, University of Pennsylvania student Noah Bilenker arrived on campus with a urge to help the homeless in West Philadelphia. Through his fraternity, he contacted a local soup kitchen and offered to set up tables and clean once each week. "I felt guilty seeing homeless people on the street," he says. "But I was told never to give them money, and with good reason. So I started working with the soup kitchen." As time passed, Bilenker also began to participate in student government, and he realized that the University of Pennsylvania, as the largest employer in Philadelphia, could also serve as a resource to the community in dealing on a much larger scale with some of the problems that he had encountered. During his junior year, Bilenker joined the 40th Street Committee, an organization of students, administration, and faculty that planned ways that the university could aid the surrounding areas, such as helping with soup kitchens. After he graduates, Bilenker plans to continue with both community service and political activism. "I want to continue to do both," he says. "With community [service], you can see a more immediate impact, but politics gives bigger results."[69]

An important lesson of civic education is that it is possible to be effective. At a minimum, effectiveness requires developing basic skills, including how to find information, how to bring people together, how to run meetings, how to speak publicly, and how to express your views in writing. Such skills do not guarantee political success, but it is certain that you cannot be politically successful without them. Political indifference is often simply a habit that stems from a lack of

Students and Politics

Dave Grayson's collegiate political career started modestly. During his first two years at Villanova University in Pennsylvania, he devoted himself to issues on which students had a general consensus, such as reforming meal-plan spending and converting dorms from single-sex to coeducational. After being voted vice president of the student body for his junior year, however, Grayson started to become a major voice for equality on campus; his supporters campaigned hard for several administrative reforms. Concerned that the Scholastic Aptitude Test (SAT) discriminates against minorities, Grayson fought for and gained a policy reform in which the admissions office would reduce its reliance on SAT scores. He also worked with the administration to cede to students some authority for appointing speakers at the college. Many of Grayson's reforms and methods—he threatened to hold a sit-in during the most anticipated basketball game of the year—earned him the enmity of some on campus, and even a few death threats in his senior year. Now he leads a more docile existence working toward his Ph.D. in history, but still manages to find the time to edit a newsletter of multicultural events in the Philadelphia area.

STUDENTS AND POLITICS

political efficacy

the ability to influence government and politics

knowledge about how your interests are affected by politics and from a sense that you can do nothing to affect politics. But **political efficacy** is a self-fulfilling prophecy: if you think you cannot be effective, chances are you will never try. Most research suggests that people active in politics have a high sense of their efficacy. This means they believe they can make a difference—even if they do not win all the time. Most people do not want to be politically active every day of their lives, but it is essential to our political ideals that all citizens be informed and able to act.

Ultimately, if we are to reinvigorate our democracy, we will have to rebuild the organizations and movements that once mobilized people to participate. This means reducing the role of money and bringing people back into politics. This is a long-term project that will require the energies of a new generation of political activists.

★ Summary

Some of the most contentious political issues in the United States today concern conflicts that stem from social differences such as ethnicity and gender. Such struggles reveal the important role that the national government plays in forming and enforcing policies that aim to ensure equality for all groups. Government efforts at guaranteeing equality may create new problems, however, because they often entail restricting the liberties of some citizens. It is through such conflicts that Americans put the core ideals of liberty, equality, and democracy into practice.

The first section of this chapter examined the efforts of groups who had been denied political equality to gain access to the American political system. Throughout much of the country's history, racial and ethnic differences were used as a basis to deny some groups full political equality. White ethnics experienced discrimination, but their rights to political equality were never in serious doubt. For African Americans, the struggle to eliminate slavery and the quest for full political equality after slavery was abolished have constituted the most far-reaching political struggles in all of American history. Over the past decade, the rapidly growing number of new immigrants has raised many new questions about the rights of immigrants and the impact of immigration on American life. Gender differences have also had an important impact on American politics. It took decades of mobilization and a constitutional amendment to grant women the right to vote. For women and racial minorities alike, efforts to achieve political equality did not stop with winning the right to vote. Groups continued to struggle to win political office and to make their voices heard in the political arena.

Class and religion are two other important bases of social difference that were examined in this chapter. Class has never been as important in the American context as it has been elsewhere in the world because Americans believe in individual mobility. Religion, on the other hand, has always played a role in public life in the United States, where religious freedom was a central tenet of the Founders. Today, the mobilization of religious groups has had an important impact on politics.

The last section of the chapter examined patterns of participation in the American political community. Participation can take many forms, including voting, contacting public officials, working on a campaign, organizing and attending meetings, and protesting. Many kinds of participation have declined over the past thirty years, with one big exception: giving money to candidates. An individual's socioeconomic status is the most important characteristic determining whether he or she participates. Social and political institutions also influence political participation. People often get involved in politics and learn political skills through their membership in social organizations, such as churches. The efforts of institutions to mobilize people to participate is especially significant if we wish to understand patterns of participation over time. In recent decades political institutions, such as political parties, and social institutions, such as churches, have done less to mobilize people to participate in politics.

If ordinary citizens are to take a more active role in our democracy, gaining knowledge of how politics and policy affect them is the first important step. Improving their communication skills and learning to build coalitions are other significant ways for people to be effective in the political arena.

FOR FURTHER READING

Dawson, Michael C. *Behind the Mule: Race and Class in African-American Politics.* Princeton, NJ: Princeton University Press, 1994.

Edsall, Thomas B., and Mary D. Edsall. *Chain Reaction: The Impact of Race, Rights, and Taxes on American Politics.* New York: Norton, 1992.

de la Garza, Rodolfo O., Louis DeSipio, F. Chris Garcia, John A. Garcia, and Angelo Falcon. *Latino Voices: Mexican, Puerto Rican, and Cuban Perspectives on American Politics.* Boulder, CO: Westview, 1992.

Hero, Rodney E. *Latinos and the U.S. Political System: Two-Tiered Pluralism.* Philadelphia: Temple University Press, 1992.

Klein, Ethel. *Gender Politics.* Cambridge, MA: Harvard University Press, 1984.

McClain, Paula D., and Joseph Stewart, Jr. *"Can We All Get Along?" Racial and Ethnic Minorities in American Politics.* Boulder, CO: Westview, 1995.

Mansbridge, Jane J. *Why We Lost the ERA.* Chicago: University of Chicago Press, 1986.

Sonenshein, Raphael J. *Politics in Black and White: Race and Power in Los Angeles.* Princeton, NJ: Princeton University Press, 1993.

Takaki, Ronald T. *A Different Mirror: A History of Multicultural America.* Boston: Little, Brown, 1993.

Tate, Katherine. *From Protest to Politics: The New Black Voters in American Elections.* Cambridge, MA: Harvard University Press, 1993.

Verba, Sidney, Kay Lehman Schlozman, and Henry E. Brady. *Voice and Equality: Civic Voluntarism in American Politics.* Cambridge, MA: Harvard University Press, 1996.

STUDY OUTLINE

Expanding the American Political Community

1. Americans hold conflicting perspectives about how to reconcile our core national values of liberty, equality, and democracy with our history of social discrimination and political exclusion.

2. Racial and ethnic identities are the most politically significant social identities in the United States.

3. Although the American story is often told as one of group assimilation, in fact American politics acknowledged and encouraged ethnic identities by providing an incentive for politicians to recognize ethnic groups and mobilize them into politics.

4. For African Americans, the central fact of political life has been a denial of full citizenship rights for most of American history.

5. Several strategies of mobilization emerged to guide African Americans' quest for equality, including political pressure, legal strategies, and protest.

6. The labels "Latino" or "Hispanic" encompass a wide range of groups with diverse national origins, distinc-

tive cultural identities, and disparate political experiences in America.

7. In recent years, Latino political organizations have attempted to mobilize members of their community. This effort, if successful, would tap a "sleeping giant" of political influence.

8. The diversity of national backgrounds among Asian Americans has impeded the development of group-based political power. Furthermore, the geographical dispersion of Asian Americans and their diverse experiences raise questions about whether Asian Americans will ever form a cohesive political bloc.

9. For much of their history, the relationship of Native Americans to the U.S. government has been that of a warring, then a conquered, people.

10. In the 1960s, using protest, litigation, and the assertion of tribal rights, the Native American political movement gained strength, which helped tribes achieve self-government and economic development.

11. The relative weakness of class in the United States stems from the ideals of equality and liberty, as well as from the positive and negative experiences of workers within the American political system.

12. The closest Americans have come to having a class-based politics in this century was during the New Deal.

13. Because most Americans consider themselves to be middle class, mobilizing citizens on class-based appeals is difficult.

14. Although women were barred from electoral politics for much of American history, they were important voices in social reform movements, such as the abolitionist movement and the movements against political corruption and urban squalor.

15. Although women gained the vote in 1920, their political power was still thwarted for decades. Not until the 1960s did a broad movement for women's equality emerge.

16. The ongoing significance of gender issues in American politics is indicated by three trends: the gender gap, the increase in the number of women holding public office, and the continued importance of political issues of special concern to women.

17. Religion has always played an important role in American politics. Despite the formal separation of church and state, religious groups have regularly entered the political arena.

18. A significant element of modern religious politics has been the mobilization of evangelical Protestants into a cohesive and politically active organization aligned with the Republican Party.

Participation in the American Political Community

1. Forms of political participation include voting, contacting political officials, signing petitions, attending public meetings, joining organizations, giving money to a politician or a political organization, volunteering in a campaign, writing a letter to the editor or an article about a political issue, and participating in a protest.

2. Several factors explain political participation. They include socioeconomic status, levels of civic engagement, the political setting, and efforts by social and political institutions to mobilize people. The most significant political factor affecting participation is whether people are mobilized by parties, candidates, interest groups, and social movements.

3. In recent decades, political and social institutions have ceased to mobilize an active citizenry. Declining participation and a greater inequality in participation patterns have been attributed to the new importance of money in politics, both in electoral campaigns and in interest-group activity.

PRACTICE QUIZ

1. Which of the following has (have) been the most politically significant social identities in American politics?
   a) class
   b) race and ethnicity
   c) gender
   d) religion

2. Which of the following statements best describes the impact of Reconstruction on African American political involvement?
   a) It was immediate, but short-lived.
   b) It sustained African American dominance.

   c) It actually hurt African American participation.
   d) It had little impact.

3. Which of the following helps to explain the relatively low level of Latino political participation?
   a) low rates of voter registration
   b) low rates of naturalization
   c) both a and b
   d) neither a nor b

4. What has impeded the group power of Asian Americans?
   a) the corruption of group leaders
   b) a lack of economic resources

c) organized attempts to keep Asian Americans from participating

d) heterogeneity

5. In which of the following eras was class *least* salient in American politics?
   a) the early years of the republic
   b) after the Civil War
   c) during the New Deal
   d) in the 1980s

6. What percentage of Americans identify themselves as upper class?
   a) 1 percent
   b) 5 percent
   c) 10 percent
   d) 18 percent

7. Which of the following helps to explain the ongoing significance of gender issues in American politics?
   a) the similarity of male and female voting trends
   b) the increase in the number of women holding public office
   c) the decline of party politics
   d) the increasing professionalization of state legislatures

8. Which of the following is *not* a form of political participation?
   a) volunteering in a campaign
   b) attending an abortion-rights rally
   c) contributing to the Democratic Party
   d) watching the news on television

9. Of all the factors explaining political participation, which is the most important?
   a) the mobilization of people by social and political institutions
   b) socioeconomic status
   c) civic engagement
   d) level of education

10. Which of the following is an example of a way in which the political setting has served as an obstacle to participation for African Americans?
    a) mobilization and levels of civic engagement
    b) the Civil Rights Acts of 1957 and 1964
    c) poll taxes and white primaries
    d) churches and community centers

CRITICAL THINKING QUESTIONS

1. Trace the development of the "American political community." Describe the evolution of this community in terms of the opportunities for various groups for participation and inclusion in political affairs. Describe one group's struggle for inclusion. What were the obstacles the group's members faced? What strategies did they use to overcome those obstacles? To what extent have they succeeded in their quest for participation and inclusion? How did they succeed?

2. Describe the ways in which the ideals of liberty and equality have come into conflict in terms of the politics of ethnicity, class, gender, and religion. Looking at various laws, court cases, social movements, and political behaviors, describe how liberty has, at times, prevented equality. Might the quest for equality preempt liberty?

KEY TERMS

American political community (p. 36)
civic engagement (p. 63)
coalition (p. 68)
gender gap (p. 56)

mobilization (p. 66)
political efficacy (p. 70)
political institution (p. 66)
political machines (p. 38)
political participation (p. 61)

poll tax (p. 65)
socioeconomic status (p. 63)
white ethnics (p. 37)
white primary (p. 65)

PART II

Foundations

3

The Founding

★ **The First Founding: Interests and Conflicts**

What conflicts were apparent and what interests prevailed during the American Revolution and the drafting of the Articles of Confederation?

★ **The Second Founding: From Compromise to Constitution**

Why were the Articles of Confederation unable to hold the nation together?
In what ways is the United States Constitution a marriage of interest and principle? How did the framers of the Constitution reconcile their competing interests and principles?

★ **The Constitution**

What principles does the Constitution embody? Why did the framers of the Constitution establish the legislative, executive, and judicial branches?
What limits on the national government's power are embodied in the Constitution?

★ **The Fight for Ratification**

What sides did the Federalists and the Antifederalists represent in the fight over ratification?
Over what key principles did the Federalists and the Antifederalists disagree?

★ **The Citizen's Role and the Changing Constitution**

Why is the Constitution difficult to amend?
What purposes do the amendments to the Constitution serve?

★ **Reflections on Liberty, Equality, and Democracy**

Did the framers value liberty, equality, and democracy? Why or why not?

and the Constitution

"NO taxation without representation" were words that stirred a generation of Americans long before they even dreamed of calling themselves Americans rather than Britons. Reacting to new British attempts to extract tax revenues to pay for the troops that were being sent to defend the colonial frontier, protests erupted throughout the colonies against the infamous Stamp Act of 1765. This act created revenue stamps and required that they be affixed to all printed and legal documents, including newspapers, pamphlets, advertisements, notes and bonds, leases, deeds, and licenses. To show their displeasure with the act, the colonists conducted mass meetings, parades, bonfires, and other demonstrations throughout the spring and summer of 1765. In Boston, for example, a stamp agent was hanged and burned in effigy. Later, the home of the lieutenant-governor was sacked, leading to his resignation and that of all of his colonial commission and stamp agents. By November 1765, business proceeded and newspapers were published without the stamp; in March 1766, Parliament repealed the detested law. Through their protest, the nonimportation agreements that the colonists subsequently adopted, and the Stamp Act Congress that met in October 1765, the colonists took the first steps that ultimately would lead to war and a new nation.

The people of every nation tend to glorify their own history and especially their nation's creation. Americans are no exception. To most contemporary Americans, the Revolutionary period represents a heroic struggle by a determined and united group of colonists against British oppression. The Boston Tea Party, the battles of Lexington and Concord, the winter at Valley Forge—these are the events that are emphasized in American history. Similarly, the American Constitution—the document establishing the system of government that ultimately emerged from this struggle—is often seen as an inspired, if not divine, work, expressing timeless principles of democratic government. These views are by no means false. During the Founding era, Americans did struggle against misrule. Moreover, the American Constitution did establish the foundations for more than two hundred years of democratic government.

The story of the Founding and the Constitution is generally presented to students as a fait accompli: the Constitution, which established the best of all possible forms of government, was adopted without much difficulty and its critics and doubters were quickly proven wrong. In reality, though, the constitutional period was precisely the era in American history when *nothing* was a given. Nothing was simple. The proposed new system of government faced considerable opposition. The objections raised by opponents of the proposed constitution—who called themselves Antifederalists—were profound and important. The Antifederalists thought that the state governments

BRITISH TAXES AND COLONIAL INTERESTS

Beginning in the 1750s, the debts and other financial problems faced by the British government forced it to search for new revenue sources. This search rather quickly led to the Crown's North American colonies, which, on the whole, paid remarkably little in taxes to their parent country. The British government reasoned that a sizable fraction of its debt was, in fact, attributable to the expenses it had incurred in defense of the colonies during the recent French and Indian wars, as well as to the continuing protection that British forces were giving the colonists from Indian attacks and that the British navy was providing for colonial shipping. Thus, during the 1760s, England sought to impose new, though relatively modest, taxes upon the colonists.

Like most governments of the period, the British regime had limited ways in which to collect revenues. The income tax, which in the twentieth century has become the single most important source of governmental revenues, had not yet been developed. For the most part, in the mid-eighteenth century, governments relied on tariffs, duties, and other taxes on commerce, and it was to such taxes, including the Stamp Act, that the British turned during the 1760s.

The Stamp Act and other taxes on commerce, such as the Sugar Act of 1764, which taxed sugar, molasses, and other commodities, most heavily affected the two groups in colonial society whose commercial interests and activities were most extensive—the New England merchants and the southern planters. Under the famous slogan "no taxation without representation," the merchants and planters together sought to organize opposition to these new taxes. In the course of the struggle against British tax measures, the planters and merchants broke with their royalist allies and turned to their former adversaries—the shopkeepers, small farmers, laborers, and artisans—for help. With the assistance of these groups, the merchants and planters organized demonstrations and a boycott of British goods that ultimately forced the Crown to rescind most of its new taxes.

From the perspective of the merchants and planters, however, the British government's decision to eliminate most of the hated taxes represented a victorious end to their struggle with the mother country. They were anxious to end the unrest they had helped to arouse, and they supported the British government's efforts to restore order. Indeed, most respectable Bostonians supported the actions of the British soldiers involved in the Boston Massacre. In their subsequent trial, the soldiers were defended by John Adams, a pillar of Boston society and a future president of the United States. Adams asserted that the soldiers' actions were entirely justified, provoked by "a motley rabble of saucy boys, Negroes and mulattos, Irish teagues and outlandish Jack tars." All but two of the soldiers were acquitted.[3]

Despite the efforts of the British government and the better-to-do strata of colonial society, it proved difficult to bring an end to the political strife. The more radical forces representing shopkeepers, artisans, laborers, and small farmers, who had been mobilized and energized by the struggle over taxes, continued to agitate for political and social change within the colonies. These radicals, led by individuals like Samuel Adams, a cousin of John Adams, asserted that British power supported an unjust political and social structure within the colonies, and began to advocate an end to British rule.[4]

In many ways, the British helped provoke the Boston Tea Party by providing the ailing East India Company with a monopoly on the tea trade with the American colonies. But the colonists feared British monopolies would hurt colonial merchants' business; they protested by throwing the East India Company's tea into Boston Harbor.

POLITICAL STRIFE AND THE RADICALIZING OF THE COLONISTS

The political strife within the colonies was the background for the events of 1773–74. In 1773, the British government granted the politically powerful East India Company a monopoly on the export of tea from Britain, eliminating a lucrative form of trade for colonial merchants. To add to the injury, the East India Company sought to sell the tea directly in the colonies instead of working through the colonial merchants. Tea was an extremely important commodity in the 1770s, and these British actions posed a mortal threat to the New England merchants. Together with their southern allies, the merchants once again called upon their radical adversaries for support. The most dramatic result was the Boston Tea Party of 1773, led by Samuel Adams.

This event was of decisive importance in American history. The merchants had hoped to force the British government to rescind the Tea Act, but they did not support any demands beyond this one. They certainly did not seek independence from Britain. Samuel Adams and the other radicals, however, hoped to provoke the British government to take actions that would alienate its colonial supporters and pave the way for a rebellion. This was precisely the purpose of the Boston Tea Party, and it succeeded. By dumping the East India Company's tea into Boston Harbor, Adams and his followers goaded the British into enacting a number of harsh reprisals. Within five months after the incident in Boston, the House of Commons passed a series of acts that closed the port of Boston to commerce, changed the provincial government of Massachusetts, provided for the removal of accused persons to England for trial, and most important, restricted movement to the West—further alienating the southern planters, who depended upon access to new western lands. These acts of retaliation confirmed the worst criticisms of England and helped radicalize Americans. Radicals like Samuel Adams and Christopher Gadsden of South Carolina had been agitating for more violent measures to deal with England. But ultimately they needed Britain's political repression to create widespread support for independence.

Thus, the Boston Tea Party set into motion a cycle of provocation and re-taliation that in 1774 resulted in the convening of the First Continental Con-gress—an assembly of delegates from all parts of the country—that called for a total boycott of British goods and, under the prodding of the radicals, began to consider the possibility of independence from British rule. The eventual re-sult was the Declaration of Independence.

THE DECLARATION OF INDEPENDENCE

In 1776, the Second Continental Congress appointed a committee consisting of Thomas Jefferson of Virginia, Benjamin Franklin of Pennsylvania, Roger Sherman of Connecticut, John Adams of Massachusetts, and Robert Liv-ingston of New York to draft a statement of American independence from British rule. The Declaration of Independence, written by Jefferson and adopted by the Second Continental Congress, was an extraordinary document in both philosophical and political terms. Philosophically, the Declaration was remarkable for its assertion that certain rights, called "unalienable rights"—including life, liberty, and the pursuit of happiness—could not be abridged by governments. In the world of 1776, a world in which some kings still claimed to rule by divine right, this was a dramatic statement. Politically, the Declara-tion was remarkable because, despite the differences of interest that divided the colonists along economic, regional, and philosophical lines, the Declara-tion identified and focused on problems, grievances, aspirations, and princi-ples that might unify the various colonial groups. The Declaration was an attempt to identify and articulate a history and set of principles that might help to forge national unity.[5]

THE ARTICLES OF CONFEDERATION

Articles of Confederation

America's first written constitu-tion; served as the basis for America's national government until 1789

Having declared their independence, the colonies needed to establish a govern-mental structure. In November of 1777, the Continental Congress adopted the **Articles of Confederation and Perpetual Union**—the United States's first writ-ten constitution. Although it was not ratified by all the states until 1781, it was the country's operative constitution for almost twelve years, until March 1789.

The Articles of Confederation was a constitution concerned primarily with limiting the powers of the central government. The central government, first of all, was based entirely in a Congress. Since it was not intended to be a power-ful government, it was given no executive branch. Execution of its laws was to be left to the individual states. Second, the Congress had little power. Its mem-bers were not much more than delegates or messengers from the state legisla-tures. They were chosen by the state legislatures, their salaries were paid out of the state treasuries, and they were subject to immediate recall by state author-ities. In addition, each state, regardless of its size, had only a single vote.

The Congress was given the power to declare war and make peace, to make treaties and alliances, to coin or borrow money, and to regulate trade with the Native Americans. It could also appoint the senior officers of the United States army. But it could not levy taxes or regulate commerce among the states. Moreover, the army officers it appointed had no army to serve in be-cause the nation's armed forces were composed of the state militias. Probably the most unfortunate part of the Articles of Confederation was that the central government could not prevent one state from discriminating against other states in the quest for foreign commerce.

In brief, the relationship between the Congress and the states under the Articles of Confederation was much like the contemporary relationship between the United Nations and its member states, a relationship in which virtually all governmental powers are retained by the states. It was properly called a **confederation** because, as provided under Article II, "each state retains its sovereignty, freedom and independence, and every Power, Jurisdiction and right, which is not by this confederation expressly delegated to the United States, in Congress assembled." Not only was there no executive, there also was no judicial authority and no other means of enforcing the Congress's will. If there was to be any enforcement at all, it would be done for the Congress by the states.[6]

confederation

a system of government in which states retain sovereign authority except for the powers expressly delegated to the national government

★ The Second Founding: From Compromise to Constitution

▶ Why were the Articles of Confederation unable to hold the nation together?

▶ In what ways is the United States Constitution a marriage of interest and principle?

▶ How did the framers of the Constitution reconcile their competing interests and principles?

The Declaration of Independence and the Articles of Confederation were not sufficient to hold the new nation together as an independent and effective nation-state. From almost the moment of armistice with the British in 1783, moves were afoot to reform and strengthen the Articles of Confederation.

INTERNATIONAL STANDING AND BALANCE OF POWER

There was a special concern for the country's international position. Competition among the states for foreign commerce allowed the European powers to play the states off against one another, which created confusion on both sides of the Atlantic. At one point during the winter of 1786–87, John Adams of Massachusetts, a leader in the independence struggle, was sent to negotiate a new treaty with the British, one that would cover disputes left over from the war. The British government responded that, since the United States under the Articles of Confederation was unable to enforce existing treaties, it would negotiate with each of the thirteen states separately.

At the same time, well-to-do Americans—in particular the New England merchants and southern planters—were troubled by the influence that "radical" forces exercised in the Continental Congress and in the governments of several of the states. The colonists' victory in the Revolutionary War had not only meant the end of British rule, but also significantly changed the balance of political power within the new states. As a result of the Revolution, one key segment of the colonial elite—the royal land, office, and patent holders—was

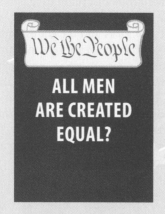

We the People

ALL MEN ARE CREATED EQUAL?

"We hold these truths to be self-evident, that all men are created equal, that they are endowed by their Creator with certain unalienable Rights, that among these are Life, Liberty and the pursuit of Happiness." These noble sentiments, so beautifully expressed in the Declaration of Independence, proclaimed to the world America's devotion to liberty and equality. Yet Americans by no means agreed that liberty and equality did or should apply to all.

To be sure, America lacked the aristocratic class to be found in European nations. As the French writer Hector St. John de Crèvecoeur wrote in 1782, Europe was controlled by "great lords who possess everything, and a herd of people who have nothing." By contrast, America had no "aristocratical families, no courts, no kings, no bishops." Even so, some American revolutionary leaders favored a society where family status and inherited wealth set the few apart from the many. And most agreed that blacks and women were not entitled to the equality of condition expressed in many early documents.

Nearly a quarter of early America's population was bound in servitude through the institutions of slavery and indentured servitude. With rare exceptions, blacks were treated as nothing more than the property of their owners. America's women were normally barred from voting, and were denied equal rights under the law. Even setting these obvious inequities aside—after all, American attitudes toward women and blacks were not so different from those of most Europeans—debate raged in America over the proper scope of popular sovereignty and social equality.

The institution of slavery was hotly debated during the writing of the Declaration of Independence; in fact, a reference to slavery as an evil was removed from a draft of the document at the insistence of southern representatives. Yet Virginia Methodists condemned slavery in 1784. That same year, Connecticut, Massachusetts, Pennsylvania, and Rhode Island all abolished slavery (al-

stripped of its economic and political privileges. In fact, many of these individuals, along with tens of thousands of other colonists who considered themselves loyal British subjects, left for Canada after the British surrender. And while the pre-Revolutionary elite was weakened, the pre-Revolutionary radicals were now better organized than ever before and were the controlling forces in such states as Pennsylvania and Rhode Island, where they pursued economic and political policies that struck terror into the hearts of the pre-Revolutionary political establishment. In Rhode Island, for example, between 1783 and 1785, a legislature dominated by representatives of small farmers, artisans, and shopkeepers had instituted economic policies, including drastic currency inflation, that frightened business and property owners throughout the country. Of course, the central government under the Articles of Confederation was powerless to intervene.

THE ANNAPOLIS CONVENTION

The continuation of international weakness and domestic economic turmoil led many Americans to consider whether their newly adopted form of government might not already require revision. In the fall of 1786, many state leaders accepted an invitation from the Virginia legislature for a conference of repre-

though relatively few slaves lived in the North). Within twenty years, every state north of Delaware had done the same. Many southern blacks took matters into their own hands. For example, more than five thousand slaves left South Carolina with the British army before the Revolutionary War came to an end. Other blacks were able to translate Revolutionary War service into a promise of freedom. In 1800, two blacks plotted a large-scale slave uprising in Richmond, Virginia. Although thwarted, it presaged many future uprisings. And the linkage between American democratic values and the repudiation of slavery eventually became overwhelming.

The prevailing attitude toward women was summarized by a prominent Boston minister, who advised, "Wives submit your selves to your own Husbands, in subjection to them." Prominent women questioned their legal and familial inferiority, as when in 1776 Abigail Adams urged her husband, John, a member of the Continental Congress, to "remember the Ladies, and be more generous to them than your ancestors." John failed to heed his wife's plea. A legal principle called "coverture" limited a wife's

legal rights, including the rights to sue, to make wills and contracts, and even to own property. Another early feminist, Judith Sargent Murray, wrote an essay called "On the Equality of the Sexes," in which she argued for "mutual esteem, mutual friendship, [and] mutual confidence" between husbands and wives. Such beliefs gained wide currency among well-educated women.

By the 1790s, some Christian ministers began to extol the role of women as moral educators. This changing attitude opened the door to educational opportunities for women through religious academies, which by the early 1800s began to produce ever-increasing numbers of women teachers, who in turn spread the cause of women's rights.

The disparity between the high-sounding sentiments of the Declaration of Independence and actual practices in early America was great. Yet Americans were haunted by this contradiction, and the country ultimately abandoned the practices rather than turn their backs on the principles.

SOURCE: Jack P. Greene, ed., *Colonies to Nation, 1763–1789* (New York: Norton, 1975).

sentatives of all the states. Delegates from five states actually attended. This conference, held in Annapolis, Maryland, was the first step toward the second founding. The one positive thing that came out of the Annapolis Convention was a carefully worded resolution calling on the Congress to send commissioners to Philadelphia at a later time "to devise such further provisions as shall appear to them necessary to render the Constitution of the Federal Government adequate to the exigencies of the Union."[7] This resolution was drafted by Alexander Hamilton, a thirty-four-year-old New York lawyer who had played a significant role in the Revolution as George Washington's secretary and who would play a still more significant role in framing the Constitution and forming the new government in the 1790s. But the resolution did not necessarily imply any desire to do more than improve and reform the Articles of Confederation.

SHAYS'S REBELLION

It is quite possible that the Constitutional Convention of 1787 in Philadelphia would never have taken place at all except for a single event that occurred during the winter following the Annapolis Convention: Shays's Rebellion.

Daniel Shays, a former army captain, led a mob of farmers in a rebellion

In the winter of 1787, the Massachusetts legislature levied heavy taxes that hit the poor particularly hard. Daniel Shays led a makeshift army against the federal arsenal at Springfield in protest. Shays's group was easily routed, but they did get the legislature to grant some of their demands.

against the government of Massachusetts. The purpose of the rebellion was to prevent foreclosures on their debt-ridden land by keeping the county courts of western Massachusetts from sitting until after the next election. The state militia dispersed the mob, but for several days Shays and his followers terrified the state government by attempting to capture the federal arsenal at Springfield, provoking an appeal to the Congress to help restore order. Within a few days, the state government regained control and captured fourteen of the rebels (all were eventually pardoned). In 1787, a newly elected Massachusetts legislature granted some of the farmers' demands.

Although the incident ended peacefully, its effects lingered and spread. Washington summed it up: "I am mortified beyond expression that in the moment of our acknowledged independence we should by our conduct verify the predictions of our transatlantic foe, and render ourselves ridiculous and contemptible in the eyes of all Europe."[8]

The Congress under the Confederation had been unable to act decisively in a time of crisis. This provided critics of the Articles of Confederation with precisely the evidence they needed to push Hamilton's Annapolis resolution through the Congress. Thus, the states were asked to send representatives to Philadelphia to discuss constitutional revision. Delegates were eventually sent by every state except Rhode Island.

THE CONSTITUTIONAL CONVENTION

Delegates selected by the state governments convened in Philadelphia in May 1787, with political strife, international embarrassment, national weakness, and local rebellion fixed in their minds. Recognizing that these issues were symptoms of fundamental flaws in the Articles of Confederation, the delegates soon abandoned the plan to revise the Articles and committed themselves to a second founding—a second, and ultimately successful, attempt to create a legitimate and effective national system of government. This effort occupied the convention for the next five months.

A Marriage of Interest and Principle   Scholars have for years disagreed about the motives of the Founders in Philadelphia. Among the most controversial views of the framers' motives is the "economic interpretation" put forward by historian Charles Beard and his disciples.[9] According to Beard's account, America's Founders were a collection of securities speculators and property owners whose only aim was personal enrichment. From this perspective, the Constitution's lofty principles were little more than sophisticated masks behind which the most venal interests sought to enrich themselves.

Contrary to Beard's approach is the view that the framers of the Constitution *were* concerned with philosophical and ethical principles. Indeed, the framers sought to devise a system of government consistent with the dominant philosophical and moral principles of the day. But, in fact, these two views belong together; the Founders' interests were reinforced by their principles. The convention that drafted the American Constitution was chiefly organized by the New England merchants and southern planters. Although the delegates representing these groups did not all hope to profit personally from an increase in the value of their securities, as Beard would have it, they did hope to benefit in the broadest political and economic sense by breaking the power of their radical foes and establishing a system of government more compatible with their long-term economic and political interests. Thus, the framers sought to create a new government capable of promoting commerce and protecting property from radical state legislatures. At the same time, they hoped to fashion a government less susceptible than the existing state and national regimes to populist forces hostile to the interests of the commercial and propertied classes.

The Great Compromise The proponents of a new government fired their opening shot on May 29, 1787, when Edmund Randolph of Virginia offered a resolution that proposed corrections and enlargements in the Articles of Confederation. The proposal, which showed the strong influence of James Madison, was not a simple motion. It provided for virtually every aspect of a new government. Randolph later admitted it was intended to be an alternative draft constitution, and it did in fact serve as the framework for what ultimately became the Constitution. (There is no verbatim record of the debates, but Madison was present during virtually all of the deliberations and kept full notes on them.)[10]

The portion of Randolph's motion that became most controversial was called the **Virginia Plan.** This plan provided for a system of representation in the national legislature based upon the population of each state or the proportion of each state's revenue contribution to the national government, or both. (Randolph also proposed a second branch of the legislature, but it was to be elected by the members of the first branch.) Since the states varied enormously in size and wealth, the Virginia Plan was thought to be heavily biased in favor of the large states.

While the convention was debating the Virginia Plan, additional delegates were arriving in Philadelphia and were beginning to mount opposition to it. Their resolution, introduced by William Paterson of New Jersey and known as the **New Jersey Plan,** did not oppose the Virginia Plan point for point. Instead, it concentrated on specific weaknesses in the Articles of Confederation, in the spirit of revision rather than radical replacement of that document. Supporters of the New Jersey Plan did not seriously question the convention's commitment to replacing the Articles. But their opposition to the Virginia Plan's scheme of representation was sufficient to send its proposals back to committee for reworking into a common document. In particular, delegates from the less-populous states, which included Delaware, New Jersey, Connecticut, and New York, asserted that the more populous states, such as Virginia, Pennsylvania, North Carolina, Massachusetts, and Georgia, would dominate the new government if representation were determined by population. The smaller states argued that each state should be equally represented in the new regime regardless of that state's population.

The issue of representation was one that threatened to wreck the entire constitutional enterprise. Delegates conferred, factions maneuvered, and tempers flared. James Wilson of Pennsylvania told the small-state delegates that if they wanted to disrupt the union they should go ahead. The separation could, he said, "never happen on better grounds." Small-state delegates were equally blunt. Gunning Bedford of Delaware declared that the small states might look elsewhere for friends if they were forced. "The large states," he said, "dare not dissolve the confederation. If they do the small ones will find some foreign ally of more honor and good faith, who will take them by the hand and do them

Virginia Plan

a framework for the Constitution, introduced by Edmund Randolph, which called for representation in the national legislature based upon the population of each state

New Jersey Plan

a framework for the Constitution, introduced by William Paterson, which called for equal state representation in the national legislature regardless of population

justice." These sentiments were widely shared. The union, as Oliver Ellsworth of Connecticut put it, was "on the verge of dissolution, scarcely held together by the strength of a hair."

The outcome of this debate was the Connecticut Compromise, also known as the **Great Compromise.** Under the terms of this compromise, in the first branch of Congress—the House of Representatives—the representatives would be apportioned according to the number of inhabitants in each state. This, of course, was what delegates from the large states had sought. But in the second branch—the Senate—each state would have an equal vote regardless of its size; this provision addressed the concerns of the small states. This compromise was not immediately satisfactory to all the delegates. Indeed, two of the most vocal members of the small-state faction, John Lansing and Robert Yates of New York, were so incensed by the concession that their colleagues had made to the large-state forces that they stormed out of the convention. In the end, however, both sets of forces preferred compromise to the breakup of the Union, and the plan was accepted.

The Question of Slavery: The Three-Fifths Compromise The story so far is too neat, too easy, and too anticlimactic. If it were left here, it would only contribute to American mythology. After all, the notion of a **bicameral** (two-chambered) legislature was very much in the air in 1787. Some of the states had had bicameral legislatures for years. The Philadelphia delegates might well have gone straight to the adoption of two chambers based on two different principles of representation even without the dramatic interplay of conflict and compromise. But a far more fundamental issue had to be confronted before the Great Compromise could take place: the issue of slavery.

Many of the conflicts that emerged during the Constitutional Convention were reflections of the fundamental differences between the slave and the non-slave states—differences that pitted the southern planters and New England merchants against one another. This was the first premonition of a conflict that would almost destroy the Republic in later years. In the midst of debate over large versus small states, Madison observed,

> The great danger to our general government is the great southern and northern interests of the continent, being opposed to each other. Look to the votes in Congress, and most of them stand divided by the geography of the country, not according to the size of the states.[11]

More than 90 percent of the country's slaves resided in five states—Georgia, Maryland, North Carolina, South Carolina, and Virginia—where they accounted for 30 percent of the total population. In some places, slaves outnumbered nonslaves by as much as ten to one. If the Constitution were to embody any principle of national supremacy, some basic decisions would have to be made about the place of slavery in the general scheme. Madison hit on this point on several occasions as different aspects of the Constitution were being discussed. For example, he observed,

> It seemed now to be pretty well understood that the real difference of interests lay, not between the large and small but between the northern and southern states. The institution of slavery and its consequences formed the line of discrimination.

Great Compromise

the agreement reached at the Constitutional Convention of 1787 that gave each state an equal number of senators regardless of its population, but linked representation in the House of Representatives to population

bicameral

having a legislative assembly composed of two chambers or houses

There were five states on the South, eight on the northern side of this line. Should a proportional representation take place it was true, the northern side would still outnumber the other: but not in the same degree, at this time; and every day would tend towards an equilibrium.[12]

Northerners and Southerners eventually reached agreement through the **Three-fifths Compromise.** The seats in the House of Representatives would be apportioned according to a "population" in which five slaves would count as three free persons. The slaves would not be allowed to vote, of course, but the number of representatives would be apportioned accordingly.

The issue of slavery was the most difficult one faced by the framers and nearly destroyed the Union. Although some delegates believed slavery to be morally wrong, an evil and oppressive institution that made a mockery of the ideals and values espoused in the Constitution, morality was not the issue that caused the framers to support or oppose the Three-fifths Compromise. Whatever they thought of the institution of slavery, most delegates from the northern states opposed counting slaves in the distribution of congressional seats. Wilson of Pennsylvania, for example, argued that if slaves were citizens they should be treated and counted like other citizens. If, on the other hand, they were property, then why should not other forms of property be counted toward the apportionment of representatives? But southern delegates made it clear that if the northerners refused to give in, they would never agree to the new government. William R. Davie of North Carolina heatedly said that it was time "to speak out." He asserted that the people of North Carolina would never enter the Union if slaves were not counted as part of the basis for representation. Without such agreement, he asserted ominously, "the business was at an end." Even southerners like Edmund Randolph of Virginia, who conceded that slavery was immoral, insisted upon including slaves in the allocation of congressional seats. This conflict between the southern and northern delegates was so divisive that many came to question the possibility of creating

Three-fifths Compromise

the agreement reached at the Constitutional Convention of 1787 that stipulated that for purposes of the apportionment of congressional seats, every slave would be counted as three-fifths of a person

These cross-sectional views of a slave ship show the crowded conditions that Africans endured on the passage to America. The Constitution explicitly prevented Congress from banning the slave trade until at least 1808. Even though the trade was banned on January 1 of that year, illegal traffic in slaves continued.

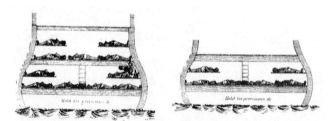

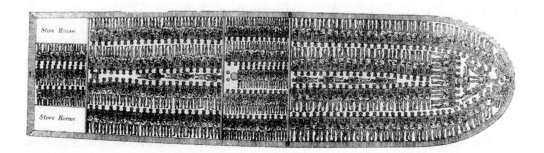

and maintaining a union of the two. Pierce Butler of South Carolina declared that the North and South were as different as Russia and Turkey. Eventually, the North and South compromised on the issue of slavery and representation. Indeed, northerners even agreed to permit a continuation of the odious slave trade to keep the South in the union. But, in due course, Butler proved to be correct, and a bloody war was fought when the disparate interests of the North and the South could no longer be reconciled.

★ The Constitution

▶ What principles does the Constitution embody?

▶ What were the intents of the framers of the Constitution regarding the legislative, executive, and judicial branches?

▶ What limits on the national government's power are embodied in the Constitution?

The political significance of the Great Compromise and the Three-fifths Compromise was to reinforce the unity of the mercantile and planter forces that sought to create a new government. The Great Compromise reassured those who feared that the importance of their own local or regional influence would be reduced by the new governmental framework. The Three-fifths Compromise temporarily defused the rivalry between the merchants and planters. Their unity secured, members of the alliance supporting the establishment of a new government moved to fashion a constitutional framework consistent with their economic and political interests.

In particular, the framers sought a new government that, first, would be strong enough to promote commerce and protect property from radical state legislatures such as Rhode Island's. This became the constitutional basis for

Delegates to the Constitutional Convention gather to sign their names to the Constitution on September 17, 1787.

AMERICAN POLITICAL CULTURE

The Founding in American Culture

In 1923, transport workers in San Pedro Harbor, California, went on strike. The police, cooperating with the workers' employers, arrested hundreds of strikers and detained them in overcrowded jails. At a protest rally for the striking workers and their families, the famous writer Upton Sinclair spoke against the repression of the workers. He began by reading the Bill of Rights. But before he could finish reciting the First Amendment guarantee of "the right of the people peaceably to assemble," the police arrested him. The complaint brought against Sinclair charged him with "discussing, arguing, orating and debating certain thoughts and theories, which . . . were detrimental and in opposition to the orderly conduct of affairs of business, affecting the rights of private property."[1]

The faith Americans have in the Constitution is remarkable, especially when we consider episodes like the arrest of Upton Sinclair for reading the First Amendment in public. How can words on parchment restrain a government from undertaking whatever actions it deems necessary or convenient?

The American faith that the Constitution protects people against tyrannical government is a mixture of reverence, naiveté, and wisdom. It derives in part from a widespread American reverence that the Founders were more like demigods than mortals—that they were wiser, more far-seeing, and more concerned with the good of the nation than the petty politicians of today. "Miracle at Philadelphia," the title of one popular history of the Constitutional Convention, conveys this common impulse to elevate the accomplishments of the Founders above the normal political realm.[2]

Such an attitude, as our look at the Founding reveals, is somewhat naive. The Founders were a disparate group of individuals with varying interests. Many different groups contended for control over the shape of the Constitution. (And many others—women, blacks, and the poor—had no voice in the process at all.) The drafting of the Constitution proceeded not as a majestic exercise in disinterested political wisdom, but as a process of compromise. To treat the Founders as a single, homogeneous group distorts the nature of what they accomplished: a series of brilliant political compromises, rather than the clear articulation of political ideals.

To point this out is not to say that Americans should strip their culture of reverence for the Founding. The American Constitution survives as an amazingly successful expression of political wisdom, of the human effort to balance power and freedom in a lasting political order. And idealizing the Founding is itself an act of wisdom, for it makes it harder for subsequent politicians to turn away from the ideals associated with the Founding. The ideals of representative government, the rule of law, constitutionalism, and the liberties listed in the Bill of Rights serve as effective ongoing checks on the United States government.

In 1838, a young Abraham Lincoln urged his listeners at the Springfield Young Men's Lyceum to "let reverence for the laws" and the Constitution "become the *political religion* of the nation; and let the old and the young, the rich and the poor, the grave and the gay, of all sexes and tongues, and colors and conditions, sacrifice unceasingly upon its altars."[3] Drawing on the ideals of the Founding rather than the reality of its compromise with slavery, and referring specifically to Americans "of all . . . colors and conditions," Lincoln used the Constitution as the basis for an argument against slavery that would become his, and his era's, greatest cause. Such is the noblest end that constitutionalism can achieve.

[1]Quoted in Michael Kammen, *A Machine That Would Go of Itself: The Constitution in American Culture* (New York: Vintage, 1987), p. xv.
[2]Catherine Drinker Bowen, *Miracle at Philadelphia: The Story of the Constitutional Convention, May to September, 1787* (Boston: Little, Brown, 1966).
[3]*The Collected Works of Abraham Lincoln,* ed. Roy P. Basler (New Brunswick, NJ: Rutgers University Press, 1953), vol. 1, p. 112. Emphasis in the original.

checks and balances

mechanisms through which each branch of government is able to participate in and influence the activities of the other branches. Major examples include the presidential veto power over congressional legislation, the power of the Senate to approve presidential appointments, and judicial review of congressional enactments

electoral college

the presidential electors from each state who meet after the popular election to cast ballots for president and vice president

Bill of Rights

the first ten amendments to the U.S. Constitution, ratified in 1791; they ensure certain rights and liberties to the people

separation of powers

the division of governmental power among several institutions that must cooperate in decision making

federalism

a system of government in which power is divided, by a constitution, between a central government and regional governments

national control over commerce and finance, as well as for the establishment of national judicial supremacy and the effort to construct a strong presidency. Second, the framers sought to prevent what they saw as the threat posed by the "excessive democracy" of the state and national governments under the Articles of Confederation. This led to such constitutional principles as bicameralism (division of the Congress into two chambers), **checks and balances,** staggered terms in office, and indirect election (selection of the president by an **electoral college** rather than by voters directly). Third, the framers, lacking the power to force the states or the public at large to accept the new form of government, sought to identify principles that would help to secure support. This became the basis of the constitutional provision for direct popular election of representatives and, subsequently, for the addition of the **Bill of Rights** to the Constitution. Finally, the framers wanted to be certain that the government they created did not pose even more of a threat to its citizens' liberties and property rights than did the radical state legislatures they feared and despised. To prevent the new government from abusing its power, the framers incorporated principles such as the **separation of powers** and **federalism** into the Constitution. Let us assess the major provisions of the Constitution's seven articles (listed in Box 3.1) to see how each relates to these objectives.

THE LEGISLATIVE BRANCH

The Constitution provided in Article I, Sections 1–7, for a Congress consisting of two chambers—a House of Representatives and a Senate. Members of the House of Representatives were given two-year terms in office and were to be elected directly by the people. Members of the Senate were to be appointed by the state legislatures (this was changed in 1913 by the Seventeenth Amendment, which instituted direct election of senators) for six-year terms. These terms were staggered so that the appointments of one-third of the senators would expire every two years. The Constitution assigned somewhat different tasks to the House and Senate. Though the approval of each body was required for the enactment of a law, the Senate alone was given the power to ratify treaties and approve presidential appointments. The House, on the other hand, was given the sole power to originate revenue bills.

The character of the legislative branch was directly related to the framers' major goals. The House of Representatives was designed to be directly responsible to the people in order to encourage popular consent for the new Constitution and to help enhance the power of the new government. At the same time, to guard against "excessive democracy," the power of the House of Representatives was checked by the Senate, whose members were to be appointed by the states for long terms rather than be elected directly by the people. The purpose of this provision, according to Alexander Hamilton, was to avoid "an unqualified complaisance to every sudden breeze of passion, or to every transient impulse which the people may receive."[13] Staggered terms of service in the Senate, moreover, were intended to make that body even more resistant to popular pressure. Since only one-third of the senators would be selected at any given time, the composition of the institution would be protected from changes in popular preferences transmitted by the state legislatures. This would prevent what James Madison called "mutability in the public councils arising from a rapid succession of new members."[14] Thus, the structure of the

THE SEVEN ARTICLES OF THE CONSTITUTION   Box 3.1

1. The Legislative Branch

House: two-year terms, elected directly by the people.

Senate: six-year terms (staggered so that only one-third of the Senate changes in any given election), appointed by state legislature (changed in 1913 to direct election).

Expressed powers of the national government: collecting taxes, borrowing money, regulating commerce, declaring war, and maintaining an army and a navy; all other power belongs to the states, unless deemed otherwise by the elastic ("necessary and proper") clause.

Exclusive powers of the national government: states are expressly forbidden to issue their own paper money, tax imports and exports, regulate trade outside their own borders, and impair the obligation of contracts; these powers are the exclusive domain of the national government.

2. The Executive Branch

Presidency: four-year terms (limited in 1951 to a maximum of two terms), elected indirectly by the electoral college.

Powers: can recognize other countries, negotiate treaties, grant reprieves and pardons, convene Congress in special sessions, and veto congressional enactment.

3. The Judicial Branch

Supreme Court: lifetime terms, appointed by the president with the approval of the Senate.

Powers: include resolving conflicts between federal and state laws, determining whether power belongs to the national government or the states, and settling controversies between citizens of different states.

4. National Unity and Power

Reciprocity among states: establishes that each state must give "full faith and credit" to official acts of other states, and guarantees citizens of any state the "privileges and immunities" of every other state.

5. Amending the Constitution

Procedure: requires approval by two-thirds of Congress and adoption by three-fourths of the states.

6. National Supremacy

The Constitution and national law are the supreme law of the land and cannot be overruled by state law.

7. Ratification

The Constitution became effective when approved by nine states.

---

legislative branch was designed to contribute to governmental power, to promote popular consent for the new government, and at the same time to place limits on the popular political currents that many of the framers saw as a radical threat to the economic and social order.

The issues of power and consent were important throughout the Constitution. Section 8 of Article I specifically listed the powers of Congress, which include the authority to collect taxes, to borrow money, to regulate commerce, to declare war, and to maintain an army and navy. By granting Congress these powers, the framers indicated very clearly that they intended the new government to be far more influential than its predecessor. At the same time, by defining the new government's most important powers as belonging to Congress, the framers sought to promote popular acceptance of this critical change by reassuring citizens that their views would be fully represented whenever the government exercised its new powers.

As a further guarantee to the people that the new government would pose no threat to them, the Constitution implied that any powers not listed were not granted at all. This is the doctrine of **expressed power.** The Constitution grants only those powers specifically expressed in its text. But the framers intended to create an active and powerful government, and so they included the **elastic clause,** sometimes known as the necessary and proper clause, which signified that the enumerated powers were meant to be a source of strength to the national government, not a limitation on it. Each power could be used with the utmost vigor, but no new powers could be seized upon by the national government without a constitutional amendment. In the absence of such an amendment, any power not enumerated was conceived to be "reserved" to the states (or the people).

THE EXECUTIVE BRANCH

The Constitution provided for the establishment of the presidency in Article II. As Alexander Hamilton commented, the presidential article aimed toward "energy in the Executive." It did so in an effort to overcome the natural tendency toward stalemate that was built into the bicameral legislature as well as into the separation of powers among the three branches. The Constitution afforded the president a measure of independence from the people and from the other branches of government—particularly the Congress.

In line with the framers' goal of increased power to the national government, the president was granted the unconditional power to accept ambassadors from other countries; this amounted to the power to "recognize" other countries. The president was also given the power to negotiate treaties, although their acceptance required the approval of the Senate. The president was given the unconditional right to grant reprieves and pardons, except in cases of impeachment. And the president was provided with the power to appoint major departmental personnel, to convene Congress in special session, and to veto congressional enactments. (The veto power is formidable, but it is not absolute, since Congress can override it by a two-thirds vote.)

The framers hoped to create a presidency that would make the federal government rather than the states the agency capable of timely and decisive action to deal with public issues and problems. This was the meaning of the "energy" that Hamilton hoped to impart to the executive branch.[15] At the same time, however, the framers sought to help the president withstand excessively democratic pressures by creating a system of indirect rather than direct election through a separate electoral college.

THE JUDICIAL BRANCH

In establishing the judicial branch in Article III, the Constitution reflected the framers' preoccupations with nationalizing governmental power and checking

expressed powers
specific powers granted to Congress under Article I, Section 8, of the Constitution

elastic clause
Article I, Section 8, of the Constitution (also known as the "necessary and proper" clause), which enumerates the powers of Congress and provides Congress with the authority to make all laws "necessary and proper" to carry them out

radical democratic impulses while guarding against potential interference with liberty and property from the new national government itself.

Under the provisions of Article III, the framers created a court that was to be literally a supreme court of the United States, and not merely the highest court of the national government. The most important expression of this intention was granting the Supreme Court the power to resolve any conflicts that might emerge between federal and state laws. In particular, the Supreme Court was given the right to determine whether a power was exclusive to the national government, concurrent with the states, or exclusive to the states. In addition, the Supreme Court was assigned jurisdiction over controversies between citizens of different states. The long-term significance of this provision was that as the country developed a national economy, it came to rely increasingly on the federal judiciary, rather than on the state courts, for the resolution of disputes.

Judges were given lifetime appointments in order to protect them from popular politics and from interference by the other branches. This, however, did not mean that the judiciary would remain totally impartial to political considerations or to the other branches, for the president was to appoint the judges, and the Senate to approve the appointments. Congress would also have the power to create inferior (lower) courts, to change the jurisdiction of the federal courts, to add or subtract federal judges, and even to change the size of the Supreme Court.

No direct mention is made in the Constitution of **judicial review**—the power of the courts to render the final decision when there is a conflict of interpretation of the Constitution or of laws between the courts and Congress, the courts and the executive branch, or the courts and the states. The Supreme Court eventually assumed the power of judicial review. Its assumption of this power, as we shall see in Chapter 15, was based not on the Constitution itself but on the politics of later decades and the membership of the Court.

NATIONAL UNITY AND POWER

Various provisions in the Constitution addressed the framers' concern with national unity and power, including Article IV's provisions for comity (reciprocity) among states and among citizens of all states. Each state was prohibited from discriminating against the citizens of other states in favor of its own citizens, with the Supreme Court charged with deciding in each case whether a state had discriminated against goods or people from another state. The Constitution restricted the power of the states in favor of ensuring enough power to the national government to give the country a free-flowing national economy.

The framers' concern with national supremacy was also expressed in Article VI, in the **supremacy clause,** which provided that national laws and treaties "shall be the supreme law of the land." This meant that all laws made under the "authority of the United States" would be superior to all laws adopted by any state or any other subdivision, and the states would be expected to respect all treaties made under that authority. The supremacy clause also bound the officials of all state and local as well as federal governments to take an oath of office to support the national Constitution. This meant that every action taken by the United States Congress would have to be applied within each state as though the action were in fact state law.

judicial review

the power of the courts to declare actions of the legislative and executive branches invalid or unconstitutional. The Supreme Court asserted this power in *Marbury v. Madison*

supremacy clause

Article VI of the Constitution, which states that laws passed by the national government and all treaties are the supreme law of the land and superior to all laws adopted by any state or any subdivision

AMENDING THE CONSTITUTION

The Constitution established procedures for its own revision in Article V. Its provisions are so difficult that Americans have availed themselves of the amending process only seventeen times since 1791, when the first ten amendments were adopted. Many other amendments have been proposed in Congress, but fewer than forty of them have even come close to fulfilling the Constitution's requirement of a two-thirds vote in Congress, and only a fraction have gotten anywhere near adoption by three-fourths of the states. Article V also provides that the Constitution can be amended by a constitutional convention. Occasionally, proponents of particular measures, such as a balanced-budget amendment, have called for a constitutional convention to consider their proposals. Whatever the purpose for which it were called, however, such a convention would presumably have the authority to revise America's entire system of government.

RATIFYING THE CONSTITUTION

The rules for the ratification of the Constitution were set forth in Article VII. Nine of the thirteen states would have to ratify, or agree upon, the terms in order for the Constitution to pass.

CONSTITUTIONAL LIMITS ON THE NATIONAL GOVERNMENT'S POWER

As we have indicated, although the framers sought to create a powerful national government, they also wanted to guard against possible misuse of that power. To that end, the framers incorporated two key principles into the Constitution—the separation of powers and federalism. A third set of limitations, in the form of the Bill of Rights, was added to the Constitution to help secure its ratification when opponents of the document charged that it paid insufficient attention to citizens' rights.

The Separation of Powers   No principle of politics was more widely shared at the time of the 1787 founding than the principle that power must be used to balance power. The French political theorist Baron de la Brède et de Montesquieu (1689–1755) believed that this balance was an indispensable defense against tyranny, and his writings, especially his major work, *The Spirit of the Laws,* "were taken as political gospel" at the Philadelphia Convention.[16] The principle of the separation of powers is not stated explicitly in the Constitution, but it is clearly built on Articles I, II, and III, which provide for the following:

1. Three separate and distinct branches of government (see Figure 3.1);
2. Different methods of selecting the top personnel, so that each branch is responsible to a different constituency. This is supposed to produce a "mixed regime," in which the personnel of each department will develop very different interests and outlooks on how to govern, and different groups in society will be assured some access to governmental decision making; and
3. Checks and balances—a system under which each of the branches is given some power over the others. Familiar examples are the presiden-

THE SEPARATION OF POWERS

Figure 3.1

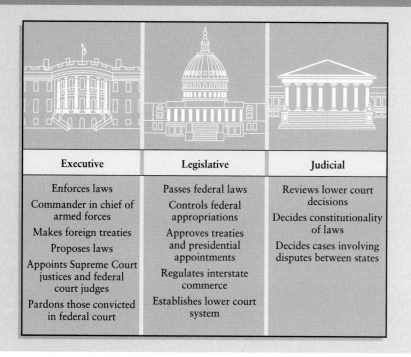

Executive	Legislative	Judicial
Enforces laws	Passes federal laws	Reviews lower court decisions
Commander in chief of armed forces	Controls federal appropriations	Decides constitutionality of laws
Makes foreign treaties	Approves treaties and presidential appointments	Decides cases involving disputes between states
Proposes laws	Regulates interstate commerce	
Appoints Supreme Court justices and federal court judges	Establishes lower court system	
Pardons those convicted in federal court		

The Constitution provides for the separation of powers to ensure that no one branch of American government holds too much power.

tial veto power over legislation, the power of the Senate to approve presidential appointments, and judicial review of acts of Congress (see Figure 3.2).

One clever formulation of the separation of powers is that of a system not of separated powers but of "separated institutions sharing power,"[17] and thus diminishing the chance that power will be misused.

Federalism Compared to the confederation principle of the Articles of Confederation, federalism was a step toward greater centralization of power. The delegates agreed that they needed to place more power at the national level, without completely undermining the power of the state governments. Thus, they devised a system of two sovereigns—the states and the nation—with the hope that competition between the two would be an effective limitation on the power of both.

The Bill of Rights Late in the Philadelphia Convention, a motion was made to include a list of citizens' rights in the Constitution. After a brief debate in which hardly a word was said in its favor and only one speech was made against it, the motion was almost unanimously turned down. Most delegates sincerely believed that since the federal government was already limited to its expressed powers, further protection of citizens was not needed. The delegates argued that the states should adopt bills of rights because their greater powers needed greater limitations. But almost immediately after the Constitution was ratified, there was a movement to adopt a national bill of rights.

Figure 3.2   CHECKS AND BALANCES

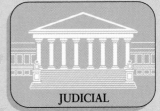

Executive over Legislative
Can veto acts of Congress
Can call Congress into a special session
Carries out, and thereby interprets, laws passed by Congress
Vice president casts tie-breaking vote in the Senate

LEGISLATIVE

Legislative over Judicial
Can change size of federal court system and the number of Supreme Court justices
Can propose constitutional amendments
Can reject Supreme Court nominees
Can impeach and remove federal judges

Legislative over Executive
Can override presidential veto
Can impeach and remove president
Can reject president's appointments and refuse to ratify treaties
Can conduct investigations into president's actions
Can refuse to pass laws or to provide funding that president requests

Judicial over Legislative
Can declare laws unconstitutional
Chief justice presides over Senate during hearing to impeach the president

JUDICIAL

Executive over Judicial
Nominates Supreme Court justices
Nominates federal judges
Can pardon those convicted in federal court
Can refuse to enforce Court decisions

Judicial over Executive
Can declare executive actions unconstitutional
Power to issue warrants
Chief justice presides over impeachment of president

EXECUTIVE

This is why the Bill of Rights, adopted in 1791, comprises the first ten amendments to the Constitution rather than being part of the body of it. We will have a good deal more to say about the Bill of Rights in Chapter 5.

★ The Fight for Ratification

▶ What sides did the Federalists and the Antifederalists represent in the fight over ratification?

▶ Over what key principles did the Federalists and the Antifederalists disagree?

The first hurdle faced by the new Constitution was ratification by state conventions of delegates elected by the people of each state. This struggle for ratification was carried out in thirteen separate campaigns. Each involved

POLICY DEBATE

Religious Freedom and School Prayer

The first two rights enshrined in the First Amendment bar the government from establishing a state religion and from inhibiting the free exercise of religion by individuals. Thus, the government is barred from breaching the "wall of separation" between church and state, so that religious liberty may find full expression. Yet is that wall breached if individuals wish to express their religious beliefs in schools? At first glance, the answer would appear to be yes. In the 1962 case of *Engel v. Vitale,* the Supreme Court barred government-organized and -led religious prayer. Since then, proponents of prayer in school have marshaled much support for a more flexible approach, arguing in part that courts have misunderstood the framers' intent. Proponents have also pushed for a constitutional amendment guaranteeing free religious expression in public schools.

Proponents of prayer in school argue that the Constitution's framers were pious men who were not out to drive religion from schools or other aspects of public life. Thomas Jefferson, for example, who wrote of maintaining a "wall of separation" between church and state, also wrote of the importance of religious training as

an integral part of education. Every congress since the Founding has opened its daily session with a prayer. Supreme Court sessions begin with the words "God save the United States and this Honorable Court." Schoolchildren have prayed in public schools for most of the country's history. By now shunning any form of religious expression at a time when children seem increasingly in need of moral and spiritual guidance, schools are sending the wrong message to the nation's children. Moreover, the absence of school religion implicitly encourages another belief system—secularism. The elimination of all religious teachings elevates a secular ideology that, in the minds of many, amounts to little more than state-sponsored atheism. Thus, some argue, schools that ignore or deny the existence of God

and religion are promoting another belief—that there is no God.

School prayer need not be led by teachers or administrators, nor need it be required. Voluntary prayer led by students would pose no threat to the First Amendment. Instead, it would reflect the proper extension of religious liberty into schools. In short, an enlightened approach to school prayer requires neither a government stamp of approval nor any form of coercion.

Opponents of school prayer argue that both the First Amendment and American respect for individual freedom require that schools avoid any role in religious teaching, instruction, or prayer. They point out the important fact that prayer is not barred from any school, as any student may pray at any time. It is organized prayer, they assert, that must be avoided. Government meddling in religion drove many European settlers to America, and the Founders understood that keeping government out of religious matters was not an expression of hostility to religion, but a simple acknowledgment that both government and religion were better off if the former let the latter alone.

Although most Americans hold some form of religious belief, the range of those beliefs is wide and growing, meaning that any form of religious teaching or prayer is bound to offend the sensibilities of some religious groups. Moreover, the rights of nonbelievers are equal to those of believers. School actions that ostracize, penalize, or stigmatize nonbelievers violate their right to equal treatment and their right not to be subjected to religious teachings in what is a public and secular institution.

The desire to teach moral values in schools is not limited to, or by, religion. Moral and ethical training does not require the infusion of religion. Moral problems related to drugs and sex, for example, already receive considerable attention in public school curricula. Finally, the teaching of religious beliefs is best left to professionals—churches and their clergy—and to families.

Table 3.1	FEDERALISTS VS. ANTIFEDERALISTS	
	Federalists	**Antifederalists**
Who were they?	Property owners, creditors, merchants	Small farmers, frontiersmen, debtors, shopkeepers
What did they believe?	Believed that elites were best fit to govern; feared "excessive democracy"	Believed that government should be closer to the people; feared concentration of power in hands of the elites
What system of government did they favor?	Favored strong national government; believed in "filtration" so that only elites would obtain governmental power	Favored rentention of power by state governments and protection of individual rights
Who were their leaders?	Alexander Hamilton James Madison George Washington	Patrick Henry George Mason Elbridge Gerry George Clinton

Federalists

those who favored a strong national government and supported the constitution proposed at the American Constitutional Convention of 1787

Antifederalists

those who favored strong state governments and a weak national government and who were opponents of the constitution proposed at the American Constitutional Convention of 1787

different people, moved at a different pace, and was influenced by local as well as national considerations. Two sides faced off throughout the states, however; the two sides called themselves Federalists and Antifederalists (see Table 3.1). The **Federalists** (who more accurately should have called themselves "Nationalists" but who took their name to appear to follow in the revolutionary tradition) supported the Constitution and preferred a strong national government. The **Antifederalists** opposed the Constitution and preferred a federal system of government that was decentralized; they took on their name by default, in reaction to their better-organized opponents. The Federalists were united in their support of the Constitution, while the Antifederalists were divided as to what they believed the alternative to the Constitution should be.

During the struggle over ratification of the Constitution, Americans argued about great political issues and principles. How much power should the national government be given? What safeguards were most likely to prevent the abuse of power? What institutional arrangements could best ensure adequate representation for all Americans? Was tyranny to be feared more from the many or from the few?

FEDERALISTS VS. ANTIFEDERALISTS

During the ratification struggle, thousands of essays, speeches, pamphlets, and letters were presented in support of and in opposition to the proposed Constitution. The best-known pieces supporting ratification of the Constitution were the eighty-five essays written, under the name of "Publius," by Alexander

Hamilton, James Madison, and John Jay between the fall of 1787 and the spring of 1788. These **Federalist Papers,** as they are collectively known today, defended the principles of the Constitution and sought to dispel fears of a national authority. The Antifederalists published essays of their own, arguing that the new Constitution betrayed the Revolution and was a step toward monarchy. Among the best of the Antifederalist works were the essays, usually attributed to New York Supreme Court justice Robert Yates, that were written under the name of "Brutus" and published in the *New York Journal* at the same time the Federalist Papers appeared. The Antifederalist view was also ably presented in the pamphlets and letters written by a former delegate to the Continental Congress and future U.S. senator, Richard Henry Lee of Virginia, using the pen name "The Federal Farmer." These essays highlight the major differences of opinion between Federalists and Antifederalists. Federalists appealed to basic principles of government in support of their nationalist vision. Antifederalists cited equally fundamental precepts to support their vision of a looser confederacy of small republics.

Federalist Papers

a series of essays written by James Madison, Alexander Hamilton, and John Jay supporting the ratification of the Constitution

Representation   One major area of contention between the two sides was the question of representation. The Antifederalists asserted that representatives must be "a true picture of the people, . . . [possessing] the knowledge of their circumstances and their wants."[18] This could be achieved, argued the Antifederalists, only in small, relatively homogeneous republics such as the existing states. In their view, the size and extent of the entire nation precluded the construction of a truly representative form of government. As Brutus put it, "Is it practicable for a country so large and so numerous . . . to elect a representation that will speak their sentiments? . . . It certainly is not."[19]

Federalists, for their part, saw no reason that representatives should be precisely like those they represented. In the Federalist view, one of the great advantages of representative government over direct democracy was precisely the possibility that the people would choose as their representatives individuals possessing ability, experience, and talent superior to their own. In Madison's words, rather than serve as a mirror or reflection of society, representatives must be "[those] who possess [the] most wisdom to discern, and [the] most virtue to pursue, the common good of the society."[20]

Although the terms of discussion have changed, this debate over representation continues today. Some argue that representatives must be very close in life experience, race, and ethnic background to their constituents to truly understand the needs and interests of those constituents. This argument is made by contemporary proponents of giving the states more control over social programs. This argument is also made by proponents of "minority districts"—legislative districts whose boundaries are drawn so as to guarantee that minorities will be able to elect their own representative to Congress. Opponents of this practice, which we will explore further in Chapter 10, have argued in court that it is discriminatory and unnecessary; blacks, they say, can be represented by whites and vice versa. Who is correct? It would appear that this question can never be answered to everyone's complete satisfaction.

James Madison, the "father" of the Constitution, was a prominent Federalist.

Tyranny of the Majority   A second important issue dividing Federalists and Antifederalists was the threat of **tyranny**—unjust rule by the group in power. Both opponents and defenders of the Constitution frequently affirmed their

tyranny

oppressive and unjust government that employs cruel and unjust use of power and authority

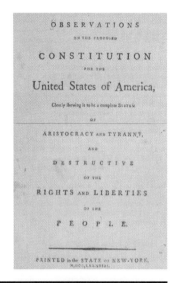

This Antifederalist tract published in 1788 by Mercy Otis Warren of Massachusetts warned of government tyranny and oppression of the rights and liberties of the people.

limited government

a government whose powers are defined and limited by a constitution

fear of tyrannical rule. Each side, however, had a different view of the most likely source of tyranny and, hence, of the way in which the threat was to be forestalled.

From the Antifederalist perspective, the great danger was the tendency of all governments—including republican governments—to become gradually more and more "aristocratic" in character, wherein the small number of individuals in positions of authority would use their stations to gain more and more power over the general citizenry. In essence, the few would use their power to tyrannize the many. For this reason, Antifederalists were sharply critical of those features of the Constitution that divorced governmental institutions from direct responsibility to the people—institutions such as the Senate, the executive, and the federal judiciary. The latter, appointed for life, presented a particular threat: "I wonder if the world ever saw . . . a court of justice invested with such immense powers, and yet placed in a situation so little responsible," protested Brutus.[21]

The Federalists, too, recognized the threat of tyranny, but they believed that the danger particularly associated with republican governments was not aristocracy, but instead, majority tyranny. The Federalists were concerned that a popular majority, "united and actuated by some common impulse of passion, or of interest, adverse to the rights of other citizens," would endeavor to "trample on the rules of justice."[22] From the Federalist perspective, it was precisely those features of the Constitution attacked as potential sources of tyranny by the Antifederalists that actually offered the best hope of averting the threat of oppression. The size and extent of the nation, for instance, was for the Federalists a bulwark against tyranny.

Governmental Power   A third major difference between Federalists and Antifederalists was the issue of governmental power. Both the opponents and proponents of the Constitution agreed on the principle of **limited government.** They differed, however, on the fundamentally important question of how to place limits on governmental action. Antifederalists favored limiting and enumerating the powers granted to the national government in relation both to the states and to the people at large. To them, the powers given the national government ought to be "confined to certain defined national objects."[23] Otherwise, the national government would "swallow up all the power of the state governments."[24] Antifederalists bitterly attacked the supremacy clause and the elastic clause of the Constitution as unlimited and dangerous grants of power to the national government.[25] Antifederalists also demanded that a bill of rights be added to the Constitution to place limits upon the government's exercise of power over the citizenry.

Federalists favored the construction of a government with broad powers. They wanted a government that had the capacity to defend the nation against foreign foes, guard against domestic strife and insurrection, promote commerce, and expand the nation's economy. Antifederalists shared some of these goals but still feared governmental power. Hamilton pointed out, however, that these goals could not be achieved without allowing the government to exercise the necessary power. Federalists acknowledged that every power could be abused but argued that the way to prevent misuse of power was not by depriving the government of the powers needed to achieve national goals. Instead, they argued that the threat of abuse of power would be mitigated by the

Constitution's internal checks and controls. As Madison put it, "the power surrendered by the people is first divided between two distinct governments, and then the portion allotted to each subdivided among distinct and separate departments. Hence, a double security arises to the rights of the people. The different governments will control each other, at the same time that each will be controlled by itself."[26] The Federalists' concern with avoiding unwarranted limits on governmental power led them to oppose a bill of rights, which they saw as nothing more than a set of unnecessary restrictions on the government.

The Federalists acknowledged that abuse of power remained a possibility, but felt that the risk had to be taken because of the goals to be achieved. "The very idea of power included a possibility of doing harm," said the Federalist John Rutledge during the South Carolina ratification debates. "If the gentleman would show the power that could do no harm," Rutledge continued, "he would at once discover it to be a power that could do no good."[27] This aspect of the debate between the Federalists and the Antifederalists, perhaps more than any other, continues to reverberate through American politics. Should the nation limit the federal government's power to tax and spend? Should Congress limit the capacity of federal agencies to issue new regulations? Should the government endeavor to create new rights for minorities, the disabled, and others? What is the proper balance between promoting equality and protecting liberty? Though the details have changed, these are the same great questions that have been debated since the time of the Founding.

REFLECTIONS ON THE FOUNDING

The final product of the Constitutional Convention would have to be considered an extraordinary victory for the groups that had most forcefully called for the creation of a new system of government to replace the Articles of Confederation.

New York was the scene of a great celebration following the ratification of the Constitution. The federal ship *Hamilton* leads this parade.

Antifederalist criticisms forced the Constitution's proponents to accept the addition of a bill of rights designed to limit the powers of the national government. In general, however, it was the Federalist vision of America that triumphed. The Constitution adopted in 1789 created the framework for a powerful national government that for more than two hundred years has defended the nation's interests, promoted its commerce, and maintained national unity. In one notable instance, the national government fought and won a bloody war to prevent the nation from breaking apart. And despite this powerful government, the system of internal checks and balances has functioned reasonably well, as the Federalists predicted, to prevent the national government from tyrannizing its citizens.

Although they were defeated in 1789, the Antifederalists present us with an important picture of a road not taken and of an America that might have been. Would the country have been worse off if it had been governed by a confederacy of small republics linked by a national administration with severely limited powers? Were the Antifederalists correct in predicting that a government given great power in the hope that it might do good would, through "insensible progress," inevitably turn to evil purposes? Two hundred years of government under the federal Constitution are not necessarily enough to definitively answer these questions. Time must tell.

The Citizen's Role and the Changing Constitution

▶ Why is the Constitution difficult to amend?
▶ What purposes do the amendments to the Constitution serve?

The Constitution has endured for more than two centuries as the framework of government. But it has not endured without change. Without change, the Constitution might have become merely a sacred text, stored under glass.

AMENDMENTS: MANY ARE CALLED, FEW ARE CHOSEN

amendment

a change added to a bill, law, or constitution

The need for change was recognized by the framers of the Constitution, and the provisions for **amendment** incorporated into Article V were thought to be "an easy, regular and Constitutional way" to make changes, which would occasionally be necessary because members of Congress "may abuse their power and refuse their consent on that very account . . . to admit to amendments to correct the source of the abuse."[28] Madison made a more balanced defense of the amendment procedure in Article V: "It guards equally against that extreme facility, which would render the Constitution too mutable; and that extreme difficulty, which might perpetuate its discovered faults."[29]

Experience since 1789 raises questions even about Madison's more modest claims. The Constitution has proven to be extremely difficult to amend. In the history of efforts to amend the Constitution, the most appropriate characterization is "many are called, few are chosen." Between 1789 and 1996, more than 11,000 amendments were formally offered in Congress. Of these, Congress officially proposed only 29, and 27 of these were eventually ratified by the states. But the record is even more severe than that. Since 1791, when the first 10 amendments, the Bill of Rights, were added, only 17 amendments have been adopted. And two of them—Prohibition and its repeal—cancel each other out, so that for all practical purposes, only 15 amendments have been added to the Constitution since 1791. Despite vast changes in American society and its economy, only 12 amendments have been adopted since the Civil War amendments in 1868.

Four methods of amendment are provided for in Article V:

1. Passage in House and Senate by two-thirds vote; then ratification by majority vote of the legislatures of three-fourths (thirty-eight) of the states.
2. Passage in House and Senate by two-thirds vote; then ratification by conventions called for the purpose in three-fourths of the states.
3. Passage in a national convention called by Congress in response to petitions by two-thirds of the states; ratification by majority vote of the legislatures of three-fourths of the states.
4. Passage in a national convention, as in (3); then ratification by conventions called for the purpose in three-fourths of the states.

Students and Politics

Few students know that the Bill of Rights as proposed by Madison consisted of twelve amendments, not ten. The states did not ratify two of the proposed amendments, one of which would have prohibited Congress from voting itself a salary raise to take effect before the next election.

That proposed amendment had remained dormant for almost two hundred years when Gregory Watson, a student at the University of Texas at Austin, unearthed it while researching a paper for a political science class. Watson argued that sentiment and viability for the amendment remained, although his professor did not agree; he received a C. Shocked by the poor grade for his hard work, Watson spent the next ten years on a crusade to champion the amendment, including soliciting the support of sympathetic members of Congress and sifting through an immense amount of constitutional scholarship. Finally, despite powerful detractors in the academic and political communities, the measure went before the states, where it gained the necessary number of ratifications to go before Congress, which subsequently voted it the Twenty-seventh Amendment, also known as the Madison/Watson amendment.

SOURCE: "Profile in Constitutional Courage," http://webusers. anet-stl.com/~hvmlr/mf_hon2.html.

(Figure 3.3 illustrates each of these possible methods.) Since no amendment has ever been proposed by national convention, however, methods (3) and (4) have never been employed. And method (2) has only been employed once (the Twenty-first Amendment, which repealed the Eighteenth, or Prohibition, Amendment). Thus, method (1) has been used for all the others.

Now it should be clear why it has been so difficult to amend the Constitution. The requirement of a two-thirds vote in the House and the Senate means that any proposal for an amendment in Congress can be killed by only 34 senators or 136 members of the House. What is more, if the necessary two-thirds vote is obtained, the amendment can still be killed by the refusal or inability of only thirteen state legislatures to ratify it. Since each state has an equal vote regardless of its population, the thirteen holdout states may represent a very small fraction of the total American population.

THE CASE OF THE EQUAL RIGHTS AMENDMENT

The Equal Rights Amendment (ERA) is a case study of a proposed amendment that almost succeeded. In fact, the ERA is one of the very few proposals that

Figure 3.3 FOUR WAYS THE CONSTITUTION CAN BE AMENDED

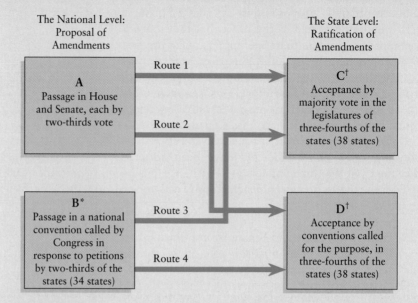

*This method of proposal has never been employed. Thus amendment routes 3 and 4 have never been attempted.
†In each amendment proposal, Congress has the power to choose the method of ratification, the time limit for consideration by the states, and other conditions of ratification.

got the necessary two-thirds vote in Congress yet failed to obtain the ratification of the requisite thirty-eight states.

On October 12, 1971, the U.S. House of Representatives approved the Equal Rights Amendment by the required two-thirds majority; the Senate followed suit on March 22, 1972. The amendment was simple:

Sec. 1. Equality of rights under the law shall not be denied or abridged by the United States or by any State on account of sex.
Sec. 2. The Congress shall have the power to enforce, by appropriate legislation, the provisions of this article.
Sec. 3. This amendment shall take effect two years after the date of ratification.

The congressional resolution provided for the accustomed method of ratification through the state legislatures rather than by state conventions—route (1) rather than route (2) in Figure 3.3—and that it had to be completed within seven years, by March 22, 1979.

Since the amendment was the culmination of nearly a half-century of efforts, and since the women's movement had spread its struggle for several years prior to 1971, the amendment was ratified by twenty-eight state legislatures during the very first year. But opposition forces quickly organized into the "Stop ERA" movement. By the end of 1974, five more states had ratified the amendment, but three states that had ratified it in 1973—Idaho, Nebraska, and Tennessee—had afterwards voted to rescind their ratification. This posed an unprecedented problem: whether a state legislature had the right to rescind its approval. The Supreme Court refused to deal with this question, insisting that it was a political question to be settled by Congress. If the ERA had been ratified by the thirty-eight-state minimum, Congress would have had to decide whether to respect the rescissions or to count them as ratifications.

This point was rendered moot by events. By the end of 1978, thirty-five state legislatures had ratified the ERA—counting the three rescinding legislatures as ratifiers. But even counting them, the three additional state ratifications necessary to reach thirty-eight became increasingly difficult to get. In each of the remaining fifteen states, the amendment had already been rejected at least once. The only hope of the ERA forces was that the 1978 elections would change the composition of some of those state legislatures. Pinning their hopes on that, the ERA forces turned back to Congress and succeeded in getting an extension of the ratification deadline to June 30, 1982. This was an especially significant victory, because it was the first time Congress had extended the time limit since it began placing time restrictions on ratification in 1917. But this victory in Washington failed to impress any of the fifteen holdout legislatures. June 30, 1982, came and went, and the ERA was, for the time being at least, laid to rest. It was beaten by the efforts of Stop ERA and by the emergence of conservatism generally, which had culminated in Ronald Reagan's election as president.[30]

Phyllis Schlafly, leader of the group Stop ERA, argued that the ERA was unnecessary and even harmful to women.

WHICH WERE CHOSEN? AN ANALYSIS OF THE TWENTY-SEVEN

There is more to the amending difficulties than the politics of campaigning and voting. It would appear that only a limited number of changes needed by society can actually be made through the Constitution. Although we shall see that the ERA fits the pattern of successful amendments, most efforts to amend the Constitution have failed because they were simply attempts to use the Constitution as an alternative to legislation for dealing directly with a public problem. A review of the successful amendments will provide two insights: First, it will give us some understanding of the conditions underlying successful amendments; and second, it will reveal a great deal about what constitutionalism means.

The purpose of the ten amendments in the Bill of Rights was basically structural, to give each of the three branches clearer and more restricted boundaries. The First Amendment clarified the jurisdiction of Congress. Although the powers of Congress under Article I, Section 8, would not have justified laws regulating religion, speech, and the like, the First Amendment made this limitation explicit: "Congress shall make no law. . . ." The Second, Third, and Fourth amendments similarly spelled out specific limits on the executive branch. This was seen as a necessity given the abuses of executive power Americans had endured under British rule.

The Fifth, Sixth, Seventh, and Eighth amendments contain some of the most important safeguards for individual citizens against the arbitrary exercise of government power. And these amendments sought to accomplish their goal by defining the judicial branch more concretely and clearly than had been

Gloria Steinem, one of the founders of the National Organization for Women (NOW), helped organize state-by-state campaigns to persuade state legislatures to pass the ERA.

Table 3.2	THE BILL OF RIGHTS: ANALYSIS OF ITS PROVISIONS

Amendment	Purpose
I	*Limits on Congress:* Congress is not to make any law establishing a religion or abridging speech, press, assembly, or petition freedoms.
II, III, IV	*Limits on Executive:* The executive branch is not to infringe on the right of people to keep arms (II), is not to arbitrarily take houses for a militia (III), and is not to engage in the search or seizure of evidence without a court warrant swearing to belief in the probable existence of a crime (IV).
V, VI, VII, VIII	*Limits on Courts:* The courts are not to hold trials for serious offenses without provision for a grand jury (V), a petit (trial) jury (VII), a speedy trial (VI), presentation of charges (VI), confrontation of hostile witnesses (VI), immunity from testimony against oneself (V), and immunity from trial more than once for the same offense (V). Neither bail nor punishment can be excessive (VIII), and no property can be taken without just compensation (V).
IX, X	*Limits on National Government:* All rights not enumerated are reserved to the states or the people.

done in Article III of the Constitution. Table 3.2 analyzes the ten amendments included in the Bill of Rights.

Five of the seventeen amendments adopted since 1791 are directly concerned with the expansion of the electorate and, thus, political equality (see Table 3.3). The Founders were unable to establish a national electorate with uniform voting qualifications. They decided to evade it by providing in the final draft of Article I, Section 2, that eligibility to vote in a national election would be the same as "the Qualification requisite for Elector of the most numerous branch of the state Legislature." Article I, Section 4, added that Congress could alter state regulations as to the "Times, Places, and Manner of holding Elections for Senators and Representatives." Nevertheless, this meant that any important *expansion* of the American electorate would almost certainly require a constitutional amendment.

Six more amendments are also electoral in nature, although they are not concerned directly with voting rights and the expansion of the electorate (see Table 3.4). These six amendments are concerned with the elective offices themselves (the Twentieth, Twenty-second, and Twenty-fifth) or with the relationship between elective offices and the electorate (the Twelfth, Fourteenth, and Seventeenth). One could conclude that one effect was the enhancement of democracy.

Another five amendments have sought to expand or to delimit the powers of the national and state governments (see Table 3.5).[31] The Eleventh Amendment protected the states from suits by private individuals and took away from the federal courts any power to take suits by private individuals of one state (or a foreign country) against another state. The other three amendments

AMENDING THE CONSTITUTION TO EXPAND THE ELECTORATE

Table 3.3

Amendment	Purpose	Year proposed	Year adopted
XV	Extended voting rights to all races	1869	1870
XIX	Extended voting rights to women	1919	1920
XXIII	Extended voting rights to residents of the District of Columbia	1960	1961
XXIV	Extended voting rights to all classes by abolition of poll taxes	1962	1964
XXVI	Extended voting rights to citizens aged 18 and over	1971	1971*

*The Twenty-sixth Amendment holds the record for speed of adoption. It was proposed on March 23, 1971, and adopted on July 5, 1971.

AMENDING THE CONSTITUTION TO CHANGE THE RELATIONSHIP BETWEEN ELECTED OFFICES AND THE ELECTORATE

Table 3.4

Amendment	Purpose	Year proposed	Year adopted
XII	Provided separate ballot for vice president in the electoral college	1803	1804
XIV	(Part 1) Provided a national definition of citizenship*	1866	1868
XVII	Provided direct election of senators	1912	1913
XX	Eliminated "lame duck" session of Congress	1932	1933
XXII	Limited presidential term	1947	1951
XXV	Provided presidential succession in case of disability	1965	1967

*In defining *citizenship,* the Fourteenth Amendment actually provided the constitutional basis for expanding the electorate to include all races, women, and residents of the District of Columbia. Only the "eighteen-year-olds' amendment" should have been necessary, since it changed the definition of citizenship. The fact that additional amendments were required following the Fourteenth suggests that voting is not considered an inherent right of U.S. citizenship. Instead it is viewed as a privilege.

Table 3.5

AMENDING THE CONSTITUTION TO EXPAND OR LIMIT THE POWER OF GOVERNMENT

Amendment	Purpose	Year proposed	Year adopted
XI	Limited jurisdiction of federal courts over suits involving the states	1794	1798
XIII	Eliminated slavery and eliminated the right of states to allow property in persons	1865*	1865
XIV	(Part 2) Applied due process of Bill of Rights to the states	1866	1868
XVI	Established national power to tax incomes	1909	1913
XXVII	Limited Congress's power to raise its own salary	1789	1992

*The Thirteenth Amendment was proposed January 31, 1865, and adopted less than a year later, on December 18, 1865.

in Table 3.5 are obviously designed to reduce state power (Thirteenth), to reduce state power and expand national power (Fourteenth), and to expand national power (Sixteenth). The Twenty-seventh put a limit on Congress's ability to raise its own salary.

The one missing amendment underscores the meaning of the rest: the Eighteenth, or Prohibition, Amendment. This is the only instance in which the country tried to *legislate* by constitutional amendment. In other words, it is the only amendment that was designed to deal directly with some substantive social problem. And it was the only amendment ever to have been repealed. Two other amendments—the Thirteenth, which abolished slavery, and the Sixteenth, which established the power to levy an income tax—can be said to have had the effect of legislation. But the purpose of the Thirteenth was to restrict the power of the states by forever forbidding them to treat any human being as property. As for the Sixteenth, it is certainly true that income tax legislation followed immediately; nevertheless, the amendment concerns itself strictly with establishing the power of Congress to enact such legislation. The legislation came later; and if down the line a majority in Congress had wanted to abolish the income tax, they could also have done this by legislation rather than through the arduous path of a constitutional amendment repealing the income tax.

All of this points to the principle underlying the twenty-five existing amendments: All are concerned with the structure or composition of government. This is consistent with the dictionary, which defines *constitution* as the makeup or composition of something. And it is consistent with the concept of a constitution as "higher law," because the whole point and purpose of a higher law is to establish a framework within which government and the process of making ordinary law can take place. Even those who would have preferred more changes in the Constitution would have to agree that there is great wisdom in this principle. A constitution ought to enable legislation and public policies to take place, but it should not determine what that legislation or those public policies ought to be.

For those whose hopes for change center on the Constitution, it must be emphasized that the amendment route to social change is, and always will be, extremely limited. Through a constitution it is possible to establish a working structure of government, and through a constitution it is possible to establish basic rights of citizens by placing limitations on the powers of that government. Once these things have been accomplished, the real problem is how to extend rights to those people who do not already enjoy them. Of course, the Constitution cannot enforce itself. But it can and does have a real influence on everyday life because a right or an obligation set forth in the Constitution can become a cause of action in the hands of an otherwise powerless person.

Private property is an excellent example. Property is one of the most fundamental and well-established rights in the United States; but it is well established not because it is recognized in so many words in the Constitution, but because legislatures and courts have made it a crime for anyone, including the government, to trespass or to take away property without compensation.

A constitution is good if it produces the cause of action that leads to good legislation, good case law, and appropriate police behavior. A constitution cannot eliminate power. But its principles can be a citizen's dependable defense against the abuse of power.

Students and Politics

The 1996 elections marked the twenty-fifth anniversary of the Twenty-sixth Amendment to the Constitution, which lowered the national voting age from twenty-one to eighteen. Although various political leaders throughout U.S. history had advocated lowering the voting age, and some states (especially in the South) had enfranchised their young citizens, the movement for a national lowering of the voting age did not begin in earnest until the late 1960s. During the Vietnam War, students staged massive protests that occasionally turned violent, including the infamous confrontation between students and the National Guard at Ohio's Kent State University, which left three students dead, and the melee at the Democratic National Convention in Chicago in 1968. In a move to help pacify what seemed like a student rebellion, Congress passed and the states ratified the amendment. Students and congressional leaders argued that those who were conscripted to fight for national interests should have a voice in what those interests were. Furthermore, Congress wished to provide an alternative form of participation to the student protesters. Today, although the turnout of eighteen- to twenty-four-year-old voters remains the lowest of any age group, the 1996 elections saw the highest turnout percentage among voters in that age group since the ratification of the Twenty-sixth Amendment.

Reflections on Liberty, Equality, and Democracy

▶ Did the framers value liberty, equality, and democracy? Why or why not?

The Constitution's framers placed individual liberty ahead of all other political values. Their concern for liberty led many of the framers to distrust both democracy and equality. They feared that democracy could degenerate into a majority tyranny in which the populace, perhaps led by a rabble-rousing demagogue, would trample on liberty. As to equality, the framers were products of their time and place; our contemporary ideas of racial and gender equality would have been foreign to them. The framers were concerned primarily with another manifestation of equality: they feared that those without property or position might be driven by what some called a "leveling spirit" to infringe upon liberty in the name of greater economic or social equality. Indeed, the framers believed that this leveling spirit was most likely to produce demagoguery and majority tyranny. As a result, the basic structure of the Constitution—separated powers, internal checks and balances, and federalism—was designed to safeguard liberty, and the Bill of Rights created further safeguards for liberty. At the same time, however, many of the Constitution's other key provisions, such as indirect election of senators and the president, as well as the appointment of judges for life, were designed to limit democracy and, hence, the threat of majority tyranny.

By championing liberty, however, the framers virtually guaranteed that democracy and even a measure of equality would sooner or later evolve in the United States. For liberty inevitably leads to the growth of political activity and the expansion of political participation. In James Madison's famous phrase, "Liberty is to faction as air is to fire."[32] Where they have liberty, more and more people, groups, and interests will almost inevitably engage in politics and gradually overcome whatever restrictions might have been placed upon participation. This is precisely what happened in the early years of the American Republic. During the Jeffersonian period, political parties formed. During the Jacksonian period, many state suffrage restrictions were removed and popular participation greatly expanded. Over time, liberty is conducive to democracy.

Liberty does not guarantee that everyone will be equal. It does, however, reduce the threat of inequality in one very important way. Historically, the greatest inequalities of wealth, power, and privilege have arisen where governments have used their power to allocate status and opportunity among individuals or groups. From the aristocracies of the early modern period to the *nomenklatura* of twentieth-century despotisms, the most extreme cases of inequality are associated with the most tyrannical regimes. In the United States, however, by promoting a democratic politics, over time liberty unleashed forces that militated against inequality. As a result, over the past two hundred years, groups that have learned to use the political process have achieved important economic and social gains.

When the framers chose liberty as the basis for a constitution, it wasn't such a bad place to start.

Summary

Political conflicts between the colonies and Britain, and among competing groups within the colonies, led to the first founding as expressed by the Declaration of Independence. The first constitution, the Articles of Confederation, was adopted one year later (1777). Under this document, the states retained their sovereignty and the central government had few powers and no means of enforcing its will. The national government's weakness led to the Constitution of 1787, the second founding.

The Constitution's framers sought, first, to fashion a new government sufficiently powerful to promote commerce and protect property from radical state legislatures. Second, the framers sought to bring an end to the "excessive democracy" of the state and national governments under the Articles of Confederation. Third, the framers introduced mechanisms that helped secure popular consent for the new government. Finally, the framers made certain that their new government would not itself pose a threat to liberty and property.

The struggle for the ratification of the Constitution pitted the Antifederalists, who thought the proposed new government would be too powerful, against the Federalists, who supported the Constitution and were able to secure its ratification after a nationwide political debate.

This chapter also sought to gain an appreciation of constitutionalism itself. In addition to describing how the Constitution is formally amended, we analyzed the twenty-seven amendments in order to determine what they had in common, contrasting them with the hundreds of amendments that were offered but never adopted. We found that with the exception of the two Prohibition amendments, all amendments were oriented toward some change in the framework or structure of government. The Prohibition Amendment was the only adopted amendment that sought to legislate by constitutional means.

FOR FURTHER READING

Beard, Charles. *An Economic Interpretation of the Constitution of the United States.* New York: Macmillan, 1913.

Cohler, Anne M. *Montesquieu's Politics and the Spirit of American Constitutionalism.* Lawrence: University Press of Kansas, 1988.

Farrand, Max, ed. *The Records of the Federal Convention of 1787.* 4 vols. New Haven, CT: Yale University Press, 1966.

Hamilton, Alexander, James Madison, and John Jay. *The Federalist Papers.* Edited by Isaac Kramnick. New York: Viking, 1987.

Jensen, Merrill. *The Articles of Confederation.* Madison: University of Wisconsin Press, 1963.

Lipset, Seymour M. *The First New Nation: The United States in Historical and Comparative Perspective.* New York: Basic Books, 1963.

McDonald, Forrest. *The Formation of the American Republic.* New York: Penguin, 1967.

Main, Jackson Turner. *The Social Structure of Revolutionary America.* Princeton, NJ: Princeton University Press, 1965.

Rossiter, Clinton. *1787: Grand Convention.* New York: Macmillan, 1966.

Storing, Herbert, ed. *The Complete Anti-Federalist.* 7 vols. Chicago: University of Chicago Press, 1981.

Wills, Gary. *Explaining America.* New York: Penguin, 1982.

Wood, Gordon S. *The Creation of the American Republic.* New York: Norton, 1982.

STUDY OUTLINE

The First Founding: Interests and Conflicts

1. In an effort to alleviate financial problems, including considerable debt, the British government sought to raise revenue by taxing its North American colonies. This energized New England merchants and southern planters, who then organized colonial resistance.

2. Colonial resistance set into motion a cycle of provocation and reaction that resulted in the First Continental Congress and eventually the Declaration of Independence.

3. The Declaration of Independence was an attempt to identify and articulate a history and set of principles that might help to forge national unity.

4. The colonies established the Articles of Confederation and Perpetual Union. Under the Articles, the central government was based entirely in Congress, yet Congress had little power.

The Second Founding: From Compromise to Constitution

1. Concern over America's precarious position in the international community coupled with domestic concern that "radical forces" had too much influence in Congress and in state governments led to the Annapolis Convention in 1786.

2. Shays's Rebellion in Massachusetts provided critics of

the Articles of Confederation with the evidence they needed to push for constitutional revision.

3. Recognizing fundamental flaws in the Articles, the delegates to the Philadelphia Convention abandoned the plan to revise the Articles and committed themselves to a second founding.

4. Conflict between large and small states over the issue of representation in Congress led to the Great Compromise, which created a bicameral legislature based on two different principles of representation.

5. The Three-fifths Compromise addressed the question of slavery by apportioning the seats in the House of Representatives according to a population in which five slaves would count as three persons.

The Constitution

1. The new government was to be strong enough to defend the nation's interests internationally, promote commerce and protect property, and prevent the threat posed by "excessive democracy."

2. The House of Representatives was designed to be directly responsible to the people in order to encourage popular consent for the Constitution. The Senate was designed to guard against the potential for excessive democracy in the House.

3. The Constitution grants Congress important and influential powers, but any power not specifically enumerated in its text is reserved specifically to the states.

4. The framers hoped to create a presidency with energy—one that would be capable of timely and decisive action to deal with public issues and problems.

5. The establishment of the Supreme Court reflected the framers' preoccupations with nationalizing governmental power and checking radical democratic impulses while guarding against potential interference with liberty and property from the new national government itself.

6. Various provisions in the Constitution addressed the framers' concern with national unity and power. Such provisions included clauses promoting reciprocity among states.

7. Procedures for amending the Constitution are provided in Article V. These procedures are so difficult that

amendments are quite rare in American history.

8. To guard against possible misuse of national government power, the framers incorporated the principles of the separation of powers and federalism, as well as a Bill of Rights, in the Constitution.

9. The separation of powers was based on the principle that power must be used to balance power.

10. Although the framers' move to federalism was a step toward greater centralization of national government power, they retained state power by devising a system of two sovereigns.

11. The Bill of Rights was adopted as the first ten amendments to the Constitution in 1791.

The Fight for Ratification

1. The struggle for ratification was carried out in thirteen separate campaigns—one in each state.

2. The Federalists supported the Constitution and a stronger national government. The Antifederalists, on the other hand, preferred a more decentralized system of government and fought against ratification.

3. Federalists and Antifederalists had differing views regarding issues such as representation and the prevention of tyranny.

4. Antifederalist criticisms helped to shape the Constitution and the national government, but it was the Federalist vision of America that triumphed.

The Citizen's Role and the Changing Constitution

1. Provisions for amending the Constitution, incorporated into Article V, have proven to be difficult criteria to meet. Relatively few amendments have been made to the Constitution.

2. Most of the amendments to the Constitution deal with the structure or composition of the government.

Reflections on Liberty, Equality, and Democracy

1. The Constitution's framers placed individual liberty ahead of all other political values. But by emphasizing liberty, the framers virtually guaranteed that democracy and equality would evolve in the United States.

PRACTICE QUIZ

1. In the Revolutionary struggles, which of the following groups was allied with the New England merchants?
   a) artisans
   b) southern planters
   c) western speculators
   d) laborers

2. How did the British attempt to raise revenue in the North American colonies?
   a) income tax
   b) taxes on commerce
   c) expropriation and government sale of land
   d) government asset sales

3. The first governing document in the United States was
   a) the Declaration of Independence.
   b) the Articles of Confederation and Perpetual Union.
   c) the Constitution.
   d) none of the above.

4. Which state's proposal embodied a principle of representing states in the Congress according to their size and wealth?
   a) Connecticut
   b) Maryland
   c) New Jersey
   d) Virginia

5. Where was the execution of laws conducted under the Articles of Confederation?
   a) the presidency
   b) the Congress
   c) the states
   d) the expanding federal bureaucracy

6. Which of the following was *not* a reason that the Articles of Confederation seemed too weak?
   a) the lack of a single voice in international affairs
   b) the power of radical forces in the Congress
   c) the impending "tyranny of the states"
   d) the power of radical forces in several states

7. What mechanism was instituted in the Congress to guard against "excessive democracy"?
   a) bicameralism
   b) staggered Senate terms
   c) appointment of senators for long terms
   d) all of the above

8. Which of the following best describes the Supreme Court as understood by the Founders?
   a) the highest court of the national government
   b) arbiter of disputes within the Congress
   c) a figurehead commission of elders
   d) a supreme court of the nation and its states

9. Which of the following were the Antifederalists most concerned with?
   a) interstate commerce
   b) the protection of property
   c) the distinction between principles and interests
   d) the potential for tyranny in the central government

10. The draft constitution that was introduced at the start of the Constitutional Convention was authored by
    a) Edmund Randolph.
    b) Thomas Jefferson.
    c) James Madison.
    d) George Clinton.

CRITICAL THINKING QUESTIONS

1. In many ways, the framers of the Constitution created a central government much stronger than the government created by the Articles of Confederation. Still, the framers seem to have taken great care to limit the power of the central government in various ways. Describe the ways in which the central government under the Constitution was stronger than the central government under the Articles. Describe the ways in which the framers limited the national government's power under the Constitution. Why might the framers have placed such limits on the government they had just created?

2. Recount and explain the ideological, geographical, social, and political conflicts both at the time of the American Revolution and at the time of the writing of the United States Constitution. What experiences and interests informed the forces involved in each of these conflicts? How did the framers resolve these conflicts? Were there any conflicts left unresolved?

KEY TERMS

amendment (p. 104)
Antifederalists (p. 100)
Articles of Confederation (p. 82)
bicameral (p. 88)
Bill of Rights (p. 92)
checks and balances (p. 92)
confederation (p. 83)
elastic clause (p. 94)

electoral college (p. 92)
expressed powers (p. 94)
federalism (p. 92)
Federalist Papers (p. 101)
Federalists (p. 100)
Great Compromise (p. 88)
judicial review (p. 95)
limited government (p. 102)

New Jersey Plan (p. 87)
separation of powers (p. 92)
supremacy clause (p. 95)
Three-fifths Compromise (p. 89)
tyranny (p. 101)
Virginia Plan (p. 87)

4

Federalism

STUDENTS AND POLITICS

I F you live in Huntington, West Virginia, you might decide to spend a Saturday night cruising in a friend's new car; in Fargo, North Dakota, the same weekend plans would get you a ticket. And if you decide to take your car out to the highway, in Montana, during the day, you could go as fast as you like, but if you live in New York State, you would risk getting a speeding ticket if you drove over 65 miles per hour.

Driving is just one of the many areas in which where you live affects what you can do and what the government does. If you lose your job in New Hampshire, the highest level of unemployment insurance benefits you can get is $196 per week; in neighboring Massachusetts, you could receive as much as $487 per week. By giving the states power to set benefit levels on such social policies as unemployment insurance and welfare, the American system of federalism allows substantial inequalities to exist across the country. Likewise, what kinds of classes are offered in high schools, the taxes citizens pay for public schools, and the tuition you pay if you attend a state university or college are all affected by where you live. In fact, most of the rules and regulations that Americans face in their daily lives are set by state and local governments.[1]

State and local governments play such important roles in the lives of American citizens because the United States is a federal system in which other levels of government are assigned considerable responsibility. The enduring significance of state and local governments reflects the Founders' mistrust of centralized power and the long-standing preference of Americans for local self-government as the best form of democracy. Such local self-government has meant that personal liberty has varied substantially from state to state. As we saw in Chapter 2, before the 1960s, southern states used their powers of local self-rule to deny basic freedoms to their black citizens. In the two hundred years since the Founding, struggles to realize the ideas of liberty and equality for all citizens have expanded the power of the federal government and reduced the powers of the states. Especially since the New Deal in the 1930s, the national government has played a much more prominent role in protecting liberty and promoting equality. In recent years, however, citizens have become more mistrustful of government, and especially of the national government. Once again we are facing questions about whether the national government is too powerful and whether the institutions of government in Washington should step aside and let the states take on more responsibility. This is an old debate in American politics; it traces back to the Founding, when the Federalists argued in favor of a stronger national government and the Antifederalists opposed them.

The debate about "who should do what" remains one of the most important discussions in American politics. Much is at stake in how authority is divided up among the different levels of government. The debate about how responsibilities should be divided is often informed by conflicting principles and differing evaluations about what each level of government is best suited to do. For example, many people believe that the United States needs national goals and standards to ensure equal opportunities for citizens across the nation; others contend that state and local governments can do a better job at most things because they are closer to the people. For this reason the states have been called "laboratories of democracy": they can experiment with different policies to find measures that best meet the needs and desires of their citizens.

But decisions about who should do what are also highly political. Groups that want government to do more to promote equality frequently prefer a stronger national role. After all, it was the national government that first implemented the civil rights policies in the 1960s and guaranteed civil liberties in all states. Groups that want less government, on the other hand, often favor shifting power to the states or localities. Many conservatives oppose a strong national role because they believe that nationwide regulations infringe on individual liberties. Furthermore, different interest groups argue for placing policy responsibilities at the level of government that they find easiest to influence. And politicians in national, state, and local governments often have quite different views about which level of government should be expected to do what.

Thus, both political principles and interests influence decisions about how power and responsibility should be sorted out across the levels of government. At various points in history, Americans have given different answers to questions about the appropriate role of national, state, and local governments. National power increased as the national government initiated new social and regulatory policies during the New Deal of the 1930s and the Great Society of the 1960s. But in the 1970s and 1980s, states began to claim more authority over these policies. The effort to increase state responsibility and reduce the national role received a boost when the Republicans took over Congress in 1995. With the support of a growing number of Republican governors, congressional Republicans advocated a strategy of devolution, in which the national government would grant the states more authority over a range of policies.

■ *In this chapter, we will first look at how federalism was defined in the Constitution.* The framers sought to limit national power with the creation of a separate layer of government in opposition to it. For the first 150 years of American government, the states were most important in governing the lives of American citizens. Over time, however, the Supreme Court interpreted the principle of federalism in a way that gave the national government more expansive powers.

■ *We will then examine how the federal framework has changed in recent years, especially in the growth of the national government's role.* After the 1930s, the national government began to expand, yet the states maintained most of their traditional powers.

■ *We will then assess how changes in federalism reflect the changes in how Americans perceive liberty, equality, and democracy.* American federalism has always been a work in progress. As federal, state, and local governments change, questions about the relationship between American political values and federalism continue to emerge.

■ *Finally, we will discuss how political participation by citizens at the local, state, and national levels affects the federal system.*

⭐ The Federal Framework

▶ How does federalism limit the power of the national government?

▶ How strong a role have the states traditionally had in the federal framework?

The Constitution has had its most fundamental influence on American life through federalism. **Federalism** can be defined with misleading ease and simplicity as the division of powers and functions between the national government and the state governments. Governments can organize power in a variety of ways. One of the most important distinctions is between unitary and federal governments. In a **unitary system,** the central government makes the important decisions, and lower levels of government have little independent power. In such systems, lower levels of government primarily serve to implement decisions taken by the central government. In France, for example, the central government was once so involved in the smallest details of local activity that the minister of education boasted that by looking at his watch he could tell what all French schoolchildren were learning at that time because the central government set the school curriculum. In a **federal system,** by contrast, the central government shares power or functions with lower levels of government, such as regions or states. Nations with diverse ethnic or language groupings, such as Switzerland and Canada, are most likely to have federal arrangements. In federal systems, lower levels of government often have significant independent power to set policy in some areas, such as education and social programs, and to impose taxes. Yet the specific ways in which power is shared vary greatly: no two federal systems are exactly the same.

federalism
a system of government in which power is divided, by a constitution, between a central government and regional governments

unitary system
a centralized government system in which lower levels of government have little power independent of the national government

federal system
a system of government in which the national government shares power with lower levels of government, such as states

FEDERALISM IN THE CONSTITUTION

The United States was the first nation to adopt federalism as its governing framework. With federalism, the framers sought to limit the national government by creating a second layer of state governments. American federalism recognized two sovereigns in the original Constitution and reinforced the principle in the Bill of Rights by granting a few **"expressed powers"** to the national government and reserving all the rest to the states.

expressed powers
specific powers granted to Congress under Article I, Section 8, of the Constitution

The Powers of the National Government   As we saw in Chapter 3, the "expressed powers" granted to the national government are found in Article I,

implied powers

powers derived from the "necessary and proper" clause of Article I, Section 8, of the Constitution. Such powers are not specifically expressed, but are implied through the expansive interpretation of delegated powers

necessary and proper clause

from Article I, Section 8, of the Constitution, it provides Congress with the authority to make all laws "necessary and proper" to carry out its expressed powers

reserved powers

powers, derived from the Tenth Amendment to the Constitution, that are not specifically delegated to the national government or denied to the states

police power

power reserved to the government to regulate the health, safety, and morals of its citizens

concurrent powers

authority possessed by *both* state and national governments, such as the power to levy taxes

Section 8, of the Constitution. These seventeen powers include the power to collect taxes, to coin money, to declare war, and to regulate commerce (which, as we will see, became a very important power for the national government). Article I, Section 8, also contains another important source of power for the national government: the **implied powers** that enable Congress "to make all Laws which shall be necessary and proper for carrying into Execution the foregoing Powers." Not until several decades after the Founding did the Supreme Court allow Congress to exercise the power granted in this **necessary and proper clause,** but, as we shall see later in this chapter, this doctrine allowed the national government to expand considerably the scope of its authority, although the process was a slow one.

The Powers of State Government   One way in which the framers sought to preserve a strong role for the states was through the Tenth Amendment to the Constitution. The Tenth Amendment states that the powers that the Constitution does not delegate to the national government or prohibit to the states are "reserved to the States respectively, or to the people." The Antifederalists, who feared that a strong central government would encroach on individual liberty, repeatedly pressed for such an amendment as a way of limiting national power. Federalists agreed to the amendment because they did not think it would do much harm, given the powers of the Constitution already granted to the national government. The Tenth Amendment is also called the **reserved powers** amendment because it aims to reserve powers to the states.

The most fundamental power that is retained by the states is that of coercion—the power to develop and enforce criminal codes, to administer health and safety rules, to regulate the family via marriage and divorce laws. The states have the power to regulate individuals' livelihoods; if you're a doctor or a lawyer or a plumber or a barber, you must be licensed by the state. Even more fundamentally, the states had the power to define private property—private property exists because state laws against trespass define who is and is not entitled to use a piece of property. If you own a car, your ownership isn't worth much unless the state is willing to enforce your right to possession by making it a crime for anyone else to drive your car. These are fundamental matters, and the powers of the states regarding these domestic issues are much greater than the powers of the national government, even today.

A state's authority to regulate these fundamental matters is commonly referred to as the **police power** of the state and encompasses the state's power to regulate the health, safety, welfare, and morals of its citizens. Policing is what states do—they coerce you in the name of the community in order to maintain public order. And this was exactly the type of power that the Founders intended the states to exercise.

In some areas, the states share **concurrent powers** with the national government, wherein they retain and share some power to regulate commerce and to affect the currency—for example, by being able to charter banks, grant or deny corporate charters, grant or deny licenses to engage in a business or practice a trade, and regulate the quality of products or the conditions of labor. This issue of concurrent versus exclusive power has come up from time to time in our history, but wherever there is a direct conflict of laws between the federal and the state levels, the issue will most likely be resolved in favor of national supremacy.

State Obligations to One Another   The Constitution also creates obligations among the states. These obligations, spelled out in Article IV, were intended to promote national unity. By requiring the states to recognize actions and decisions taken in other states as legal and proper, the framers aimed to make the states less like independent countries and more like parts of a single nation.

Article IV, Section I, calls for "Full Faith and Credit" among states, meaning that each state is normally expected to honor the "public Acts, Records, and judicial Proceedings" that take place in any other state. So, for example, if a couple is married in Texas—marriage being regulated by state law—Missouri must also recognize that marriage, even though they were not married under Missouri state law.

This **full faith and credit clause** has recently become embroiled in the controversy over gay and lesbian marriage. In 1993, the Hawaii Supreme Court prohibited discrimination against gay and lesbian marriage except in very limited circumstances. Many observers believe that Hawaii will eventually fully legalize gay marriage. This possibility raises the question of whether other states will also have to recognize gay marriage as legal under the full faith and credit clause. Anxious to show its disapproval of gay marriage, Congress passed the Defense of Marriage Act in 1996, which declared that states will *not* have to recognize a same-sex marriage, even if it is legal in one state. The act also said that the federal government will not recognize gay marriage— even if it is legal under state law—and that gay marriage partners will not be eligible for the federal benefits, such as Medicare and Social Security, normally available to spouses.[2]

Because of this controversy, the extent and meaning of the full faith and credit clause is sure to be considered by the Supreme Court. In fact, it is not clear that the clause requires states to recognize gay marriage because the Court's interpretation of the clause in the past has provided exceptions for

full faith and credit clause
provision from Article IV, Section 1 of the Constitution, requiring that the states normally honor the public acts and judicial decisions that take place in another state

Ninia Baehr and Genora Dancel, the plaintiffs in a case to stop Hawaii from denying marriage licenses to gay and lesbian couples, smile after a state judge ruled in their favor. Several states have decided not to recognize same-sex marriages of other states, however.

"public policy" reasons: if states have strong objections to a law they do not have to honor it. In 1997 the Supreme Court took up a case involving the full faith and credit clause. The case concerns a Michigan court order that prevented a former engineer for General Motors Corporation from testifying against the company. The engineer, who left the company on bad terms, later testified in a Missouri court about a car accident in which a woman died when her Chevrolet Blazer caught fire. General Motors challenged his right to testify, arguing that Missouri should give "full faith and credit" to the Michigan ruling. The Supreme Court ruled that the engineer could testify and that the court system in one state cannot hinder other state courts in their "search for the truth."[3]

Article IV, Section 2, known as the "comity clause," also seeks to promote national unity. It provides that citizens enjoying the **"Privileges and Immunities"** of one state should be entitled to similar treatment in other states. What this has come to mean is that a state cannot discriminate against someone from another state or give special privileges to its own residents. For example, in the 1970s, when Alaska passed a law that gave residents preference over nonresidents in obtaining work on the state's oil and gas pipelines, the Supreme Court ruled the law illegal because it discriminated against citizens of other states.[4] This clause also regulates criminal justice among the states by requiring states to return fugitives to the states from which they have fled. Thus, in 1952, when an inmate escaped from an Alabama prison and sought to avoid being returned to Alabama on the grounds that he was being subjected to "cruel and unusual punishment" there, the Supreme Court ruled that he must be returned according to Article IV, Section 2.[5] This example highlights the difference between the obligations among states and those among different countries. Recently, France refused to return an American fugitive because he might be subject to the death penalty, which does not exist in France.[6] The Constitution clearly forbids states from doing something similar.

Local Government and the Constitution   Local government occupies a peculiar but very important place in the American system. In fact, the status of American local government is probably unique in world experience. First, it must be pointed out that local government has no status in the American Constitution. *State* legislatures created local governments, and *state* constitutions and laws permit local governments to take on some of the responsibilities of the state governments. Most states amended their own constitutions to give their larger cities **home rule**—a guarantee of noninterference in various areas of local affairs. But local governments enjoy no such recognition in the Constitution. Local governments have always been mere conveniences of the states.[7]

Local governments became administratively important in the early years of the Republic because the states possessed little administrative capability. They relied on local governments—cities and countries—to implement the laws of the state. Local government was an alternative to a statewide bureaucracy (see Table 4.1).

THE DEVELOPMENT OF FEDERALISM

Tracing the influence of federalism is not simple, but we can make the task easier by breaking it down into three distinct forms. First, federalism sought to

privileges and immunities clause
provision from Article IV, Section 2 of the Constitution, that a state cannot discriminate against someone from another state or give its own residents special privileges

home rule
power delegated by the state to a local unit of government to manage its own affairs

85,006 GOVERNMENTS IN THE UNITED STATES		Table 4.1
Type	**Number**	
National	1	
State	50	
County	3,043	
Municipal	19,279	
Townships	16,656	
School districts	14,422	
Other special districts	31,555	

SOURCE: *Statistical Abstract of the United States, 1996* (Washington, DC: U.S. Government Printing Office, 1996), Table 469.

limit national power by creating two sovereigns—the national government and the state governments. This system was called **dual federalism.** At the time of the Founding, the states had already existed as former colonies and, for nearly thirteen years, as virtually autonomous units under the Articles of Confederation. The Constitution imposed a stronger national government upon the states. But even after the ratification of the Constitution, the states continued to be more important than the national government. For nearly a century and a half, virtually all of the fundamental policies governing the lives of American citizens were made by the state legislatures, not by Congress. The novelty of this arrangement can be appreciated by noting that each of the major European countries at that time had a unitary government: a single national government with national ministries; a national police force; and a single, national code of laws for crimes, commerce, public works, education, and all other areas.

Second, that same federalism specifically restrained the power of the national government over the economy. The Constitution gave the Congress the responsibility to regulate interstate commerce. However, the Supreme Court defined "interstate commerce" in narrow terms that prevented Congress from regulating local economic conditions. The federalist structure of strong states and a weak national government prevailed until 1937, when the Supreme Court redefined "interstate commerce" to permit the national government to regulate local economic conditions.

Third, since federalism freed the states to make so many important policies according to the wishes of their own citizens, states were also free to be different from one another. Federalism allowed a great deal of variation from state to state in the rights enjoyed by citizens, in the roles played by governments, and in definitions of crime and its punishment. During the past half-century, Americans have moved toward greater national uniformity in state laws and in the rights enjoyed by citizens. Nevertheless, as we shall see, federalism continues even today to permit significant differences among the states.

Each of these consequences of federalism will be considered in its turn. The first two—the creating of two sovereigns and the restraining of the economic power of the national government—will be treated in this chapter, along with

dual federalism

the system of government that prevailed in the United States from 1789 to 1937, in which most fundamental governmental powers were shared between the federal and state governments

an assessment of their continuing influence. The third, even though it is an aspect of federalism, will be an important part of the next two chapters, because it relates to the framework of individual liberties and rights.

RESTRAINING NATIONAL POWER WITH DUAL FEDERALISM, 1789–1937

As we have noted, the Constitution created two layers of government: the national government and the state governments. The consequences of this dual federalism are fundamental to the American system of government in theory and in practice; they have meant that states have done most of the fundamental governing. For evidence, look at Table 4.2. It lists the major types of public policies by which Americans were governed for the first century and a half under the Constitution. We call it the "traditional system" because it prevailed for three-quarters of American history and because it closely approximates the intentions of the framers of the Constitution.

Under the traditional system, the national government was quite small by comparison both to the state governments and to the governments of other

Table 4.2

THE FEDERAL SYSTEM: SPECIALIZATION OF GOVERNMENTAL FUNCTIONS IN THE TRADITIONAL SYSTEM (1800–1933)

National government policies (domestic)	State government policies	Local government policies
Internal improvements	Property laws (including slavery)	Adaptation of state laws to local conditions ("variances")
Subsidies	Estate and inheritance laws	Public works
Tariffs	Commerce laws	Contracts for public works
Public lands disposal	Banking and credit laws	Licensing of public accommodations
Patents	Corporate laws	Assessible improvements
Currency	Insurance laws	Basic public services
	Family laws	
	Morality laws	
	Public health laws	
	Education laws	
	General penal laws	
	Eminent domain laws	
	Construction codes	
	Land-use laws	
	Water and mineral laws	
	Criminal procedure laws	
	Electoral and political parties laws	
	Local government laws	
	Civil service laws	
	Occupations and professions laws	

Western nations. Not only was it smaller than most governments of that time, it was actually very narrowly specialized in the functions it performed. The national government built or sponsored the construction of roads, canals, and bridges (internal improvements). It provided cash subsidies to shippers and shipbuilders and distributed free or low-priced public land to encourage western settlement and business ventures. It placed relatively heavy taxes on imported goods (tariffs), not only to raise revenues but to protect "infant industries" from competition from the more advanced European enterprises. It protected patents and provided for a common currency, also to encourage and facilitate enterprises and to expand markets.

What do these functions of the national government reveal? First, virtually all its functions were aimed at assisting commerce. It is quite appropriate to refer to the traditional American system as a "commercial republic." Second, virtually none of the national government's policies directly coerced citizens. The emphasis of governmental programs was on assistance, promotion, and encouragement—the allocation of land or capital where they were insufficiently available for economic development.

Meanwhile, state legislatures were actively involved in economic regulation during the nineteenth century. In the United States, then and now, private property exists only in state laws and state court decisions regarding property, trespass, and real estate. American capitalism took its form from state property and trespass laws, as well as from state laws and court decisions regarding contracts, markets, credit, banking, incorporation, and insurance. Laws concerning slavery were a subdivision of property law in states where slavery existed. The practice of important professions, such as law and medicine, was and is illegal, except as provided for by state law. Marriage, divorce, and the birth or adoption of a child have always been regulated by state law. To educate or not to educate a child has been a decision governed more by state laws than by parents, and not at all by national law. It is important to note also that virtually all criminal laws—regarding everything from trespass to murder—have been state laws. Most of the criminal laws adopted by Congress are concerned with the District of Columbia and other federal territories.

All this (and more, as shown in the middle column of Table 4.2) demonstrates without any question that most of the fundamental governing in the United States was done by the states. The contrast between national and state policies, as shown by Table 4.2, demonstrates the difference in the power vested in each. The list of items in the middle column could actually have been made longer. Moreover, each item on the list is a category of law that fills many volumes of statutes and court decisions.

This contrast between national and state governments is all the more impressive because it is basically what the framers of the Constitution intended. Since the 1930s, the national government has expanded into local and intrastate matters, far beyond what anyone would have foreseen in 1790, 1890,

Students and Politics

In 1984, the national government passed legislation that denied highway funds to states that failed to raise the legal drinking age to twenty-one. The last bastion of eighteen-year-old drinking, Louisiana, capitulated in 1996. Louisiana students reacted swiftly to the legislation. Protests at the state capitol were led by Louisiana State University sophomore Jonathan Doro, who argued that eighteen-year-olds were deemed responsible as adults in every other way, including the obligation to fight in war and the right to vote. Newspapers covered the issue extensively; several national newspapers and a few national television programs ran feature stories on the Louisiana battle. The State Supreme Court ruled the new law violated the state constitution; the state legislature, however, succeeded in passing an amendment to the constitution raising the drinking age to twenty-one. Recent events, such as the death of a Louisiana student due to excessive drinking, have slowed the movement to repeal the amendment.

State laws govern the minimum age for drivers. Shelly Larson, of Bridgewater, South Dakota, testified in favor of increasing the minimum driving age in South Dakota after her fourteen-year-old son, Erich, died after his truck rolled over on a gravel road.

In 1815, President James Madison called for a federally funded program of "internal improvements," which during the first half of the nineteenth century was one of the few policy roles for the national government. By improving transportation through the construction of roads and canals, the government fostered the growth of the market economy.

or even in the 1920s. But this significant expansion of the national government did not alter the basic framework. The national government has become much larger, but the states have continued to be central to the American system of government.

Here lies probably the most important point of all: The fundamental impact of federalism on the way the United States is governed comes not from any particular provision of the Constitution but from the framework itself, which has determined the flow of government functions and, through that, the political development of the country. By allowing state governments to do most of the fundamental governing, the Constitution saved the national government from many policy decisions that might have proven too divisive for a large and very young country. There is no doubt that if the Constitution had provided for a unitary rather than a federal system, the war over slavery would have come in 1789 or 1809 rather than in 1860; and if it had come that early, the South might very well have seceded and established a separate and permanent slaveholding nation.

In helping the national government remain small and aloof from the most divisive issues of the day, federalism contributed significantly to the political stability of the nation, even as the social, economic, and political systems of many of the states and regions of the country were undergoing tremendous, profound, and sometimes violent, change.[8] As we shall see, some important aspects of federalism have changed, but the federal framework has survived two centuries and a devastating civil war.

FEDERALISM AND THE SLOW GROWTH OF THE NATIONAL GOVERNMENT'S POWER

Having created the national government, and recognizing the potential for abuse of power, the states sought through federalism to constrain the national government. The "traditional system" of a weak national government prevailed for over a century despite economic forces favoring its expansion and despite Supreme Court cases giving a pro-national interpretation to Article I, Section 8, of the Constitution.

That article delegates to Congress the power "to regulate commerce with foreign nations, and among the several States and with the Indian tribes." This **commerce clause** was consistently interpreted *in favor* of national power by the Supreme Court for most of the nineteenth century. The first and most important case favoring national power over the economy was *McCulloch v. Maryland.*[9] This case involved the question of whether Congress had the power to charter a national bank, since such an explicit grant of power was nowhere to be found in Article I, Section 8. Chief Justice John Marshall answered that the power could be "implied" from other powers that were expressly delegated to Congress, such as the "powers to lay and collect taxes; to borrow money; to regulate commerce; and to declare and conduct a war."

By allowing Congress to use the necessary and proper clause to interpret its delegated powers expansively, the Supreme Court created the potential for an unprecedented increase in national government power. Marshall also concluded that whenever a state law conflicted with a federal law (as in the case of *McCulloch v. Maryland*), the state law would be deemed invalid since the Constitution states that "the Laws of the United States . . . shall be the supreme Law of the Land." Both parts of this great case are pro-national, yet Congress did not immediately seek to expand the policies of the national government.

Another major case, *Gibbons v. Ogden* in 1824, reinforced this nationalistic interpretation of the Constitution. The important but relatively narrow issue was whether the state of New York could grant a monopoly to Robert Fulton's steamboat company to operate an exclusive service between New York and New Jersey. Chief Justice Marshall argued that New York State did not have the power to grant this particular monopoly. In order to reach this decision, it was necessary for Marshall to define what Article I, Section 8, meant by "commerce among the several states." He insisted that the definition was "comprehensive," extending to "every species of commercial intercourse." He did say that this comprehensiveness was limited "to that commerce which concerns more states than one," giving rise to what later came to be called "interstate commerce." *Gibbons* is important because it established the supremacy of the national government in all matters affecting interstate commerce.[10] But what would remain uncertain during several decades of constitutional discourse was the precise meaning of interstate commerce.

Article I, Section 8, backed by the implied powers decision in *McCulloch* and by the broad definition of "interstate commerce" in *Gibbons*, was a source of power for the national government as long as Congress sought to facilitate commerce through subsidies, services, and land grants. But later in the nineteenth century, when the national government sought to use those powers to *regulate* the economy rather than merely to promote economic development, federalism and the concept of interstate commerce began to operate as restraints on, rather than sources of, national power. Any effort of the national government to regulate commerce in such areas as fraud, the production of impure goods, the use of child labor, or the existence of dangerous working conditions or long hours was declared unconstitutional by the Supreme Court as a violation of the concept of interstate commerce. Such legislation meant

commerce clause

Article I, Section 8, of the Constitution, which delegates to Congress the power "to regulate commerce with foreign nations, and among the several States and with the Indian tribes." This clause was interpreted by the Supreme Court in favor of national power over the economy

that the federal government was entering the factory and the workplace—local areas—and was attempting to regulate goods that had not passed into commerce. To enter these local workplaces was to exercise police power—the power reserved to the states for the protection of the health, safety, and morals of their citizens. No one questioned the power of the national government to regulate businesses that intrinsically involved interstate commerce, such as railroads, gas pipelines, and waterway transportation. But well into the twentieth century, the Supreme Court used the concept of interstate commerce as a barrier against most efforts by Congress to regulate local conditions.

This aspect of federalism was alive and well during an epoch of tremendous economic development, the period between the Civil War and the 1930s. It gave the American economy a freedom from federal government control that closely approximated the ideal of free enterprise. The economy was never entirely free, of course; in fact, entrepreneurs themselves did not want complete freedom from government. They needed law and order. They needed a stable currency. They needed courts and police to enforce contracts and prevent trespass. They needed roads, canals, and railroads. But federalism, as interpreted by the Supreme Court for seventy years after the Civil War, made it possible for business to have its cake and eat it, too. Entrepreneurs enjoyed the benefits of national policies facilitating commerce and were protected by the courts from policies regulating commerce.[11]

All this changed after 1937, when the Supreme Court threw out the old distinction between interstate and intrastate commerce, converting the commerce clause from a source of limitations to a source of power for the national government. The Court began to refuse to review appeals challenging acts of Congress protecting the rights of employees to organize and engage in collective bargaining, regulating the amount of farmland in cultivation, extending low-interest credit to small businesses and farmers, and restricting the activities of corporations dealing in the stock market, and many other laws that contributed to the construction of the "welfare state."[12]

In 1916, the national government passed the Keating-Owen Child Labor Act, which excluded from interstate commerce goods manufactured by children under fourteen. The act was ruled unconstitutional by the Supreme Court on the grounds that the regulation of interstate commerce could not extend to the conditions of labor. The regulation of child labor remained in the hands of state governments until the 1930s.

Republican Party leaders have contended that the national government has grown too powerful at the expense of the states and argue that the Tenth Amendment should restrict the growth of national power.

THE CHANGING ROLE OF THE STATES

As we have seen, the Constitution contained the seeds of a very expansive national government—in the commerce clause. For much of the nineteenth century, federal power remained limited. The Tenth Amendment was used to bolster arguments about **states' rights,** which in their extreme version claimed that the states did not have to submit to national laws when they believed the national government had exceeded its authority. These arguments in favor of states' rights were voiced less often after the Civil War. But the Supreme Court continued to use the Tenth Amendment to strike down laws that it thought exceeded national power, including the Civil Rights Act passed in 1875.

In the early twentieth century, however, the Tenth Amendment appeared to lose its force. Reformers began to press for national regulations to limit the power of large corporations and to preserve the health and welfare of citizens. The Supreme Court approved of some of these laws but it struck others down, including a law combating child labor. The Court stated that the law violated the Tenth Amendment because only states should have the power to regulate conditions of employment. By the late 1930s, however, the Supreme Court had approved such an expansion of federal power that the Tenth Amendment appeared irrelevant. In fact, in 1941, Justice Harlan Fiske Stone declared that the Tenth Amendment was simply a "truism," that it had no real meaning.[13]

Yet the idea that some powers should be reserved to the states did not go away. Indeed, in the 1950s, southern opponents of the civil rights movement revived the idea of states' rights. In 1956, ninety-six southern members of Congress issued a "Southern Manifesto" in which they declared that southern states were not constitutionally bound by Supreme Court decisions outlawing racial segregation. They believed that states' rights should override individual rights to liberty and formal equality. With the triumph of the civil rights movement, the slogan of "states' rights" became tarnished by its association with racial inequality.

states' rights

the principle that the states should oppose the increasing authority of the national government. This principle was most popular in the period before the Civil War

devolution

a policy to remove a program from one level of government by delegating it or passing it down to a lower level of government, such as from the national government to the state and local governments

Recent years have seen a revival of interest in the Tenth Amendment and important Supreme Court decisions limiting federal power. Much of the interest in the Tenth Amendment stems from conservatives who believe that a strong federal government encroaches on individual liberties. They believe such freedoms are better protected by returning more power to the states through the process of **devolution**. In 1996, Republican presidential candidate Bob Dole carried a copy of the Tenth Amendment in his pocket as he campaigned, pulling it out to read at rallies.[14] The Supreme Court's ruling in *United States v. Lopez* in 1995 fueled further interest in the Tenth Amendment. In that case, the Court, stating that Congress had exceeded its authority under the commerce clause, struck down a federal law that barred handguns near schools. This was the first time since the New Deal that the Court had limited congressional powers in this way. The Court further limited the power of the federal government over the states in a 1996 ruling that prevented Native Americans from the Seminole tribe from suing the state of Florida in federal court. A 1988 law had given Indian tribes the right to sue a state in federal court if the state did not negotiate in good faith over issues related to gambling casinos on tribal land. The Supreme Court's ruling appeared to signal a much broader limitation on national power by raising new questions about whether individuals can sue a state if it fails to uphold federal law.[15] It remains to be seen whether these rulings signal a move toward a much more restricted federal government in future Supreme Court decisions, or whether they will simply serve as a reminder that federal power is not infinite.[16]

The expansion of the power of the national government has not left the states powerless. The state governments continue to make most of the fundamental laws; the national government did not expand at the expense of the states. The growth of the national government has been an addition, not a redistribution of power from the states. No better demonstration of the continuing influence of the federal framework can be offered than the fact that the middle column of Table 4.2 is still a fairly accurate characterization of state government today.

★ Who Does What? The Changing Federal Framework

▶ Why did the balance of responsibility shift toward the national government in the 1930s?

▶ What means does the national government use to control the actions of the states?

▶ How has the relationship between the national government and the states evolved over the last several decades?

▶ What methods have been employed to give more control back to the states?

Questions about how to divide responsibilities between the states and the national government first arose more than two hundred years ago, when the framers wrote the Constitution to create a stronger union. But they did not solve the issue of who should do what. There is no "right" answer to that question; each generation of Americans has provided its own answer. In recent years, Americans have grown distrustful of the federal government and have supported giving more responsibility to the states.[17] Even so, they still want the federal government to set standards and promote equality.

Political debates about the division of responsibility often take sides: some people argue for a strong federal role to set national standards, while others say the states should do more. These two goals are not necessarily at odds. The key is to find the right balance. During the first 150 years of American history, that balance favored state power. But the balance began to shift toward Washington in the 1930s. In this section, we will look at how the balance shifted, and then we will consider current efforts to reshape the relationship between the national government and the states.

EXPANSION OF THE NATIONAL GOVERNMENT

The New Deal of the 1930s signaled the rise of a more active national government. The door to increased federal action opened when states proved unable to cope with the demands brought on by the Great Depression. Before the Depression, states and localities took responsibility for addressing the needs of the poor, usually through private charity. But the extent of the need created by the Depression quickly exhausted local and state capacities. By 1932, 25 percent of the workforce was unemployed. The jobless lost their homes and settled into camps all over the country, called "Hoovervilles," after President Herbert Hoover. Elected in 1928, the year before the Depression hit, Hoover steadfastly maintained that there was little the federal government could do to alleviate the misery caused by the Depression. It was a matter for state and local governments, he said.

A "Hooverville" in Seattle, Washington, in 1933. The residents of this Hooverville elected a mayor and city council to govern their "town."

Yet demands mounted for the federal government to take action. In Congress, some Democrats proposed that the federal government finance public works to aid the economy and put people back to work. Other members of Congress introduced legislation to provide federal grants to the states to assist them in their relief efforts. None of these measures passed while Hoover remained in the White House.

When Franklin D. Roosevelt took office in 1933, he energetically threw the federal government into the business of fighting the Depression. He proposed a variety of temporary measures to provide federal relief and work programs. Most of the programs he proposed were to be financed by the federal government but administered by the states. In addition to these temporary measures, Roosevelt presided over the creation of several important federal programs designed to provide future economic security for Americans.

FEDERAL GRANTS

grants-in-aid

programs through which Congress provides money to state and local governments on the condition that the funds be employed for purposes defined by the federal government

For the most part, the new national programs that the Roosevelt administration developed did not directly take power away from the states. Instead, Washington typically redirected states by offering them **grants-in-aid,** whereby Congress appropriates money to state and local governments on the condition that the money be spent for a particular purpose defined by Congress.

The principle of the grant-in-aid can be traced back to the nineteenth-century land grants that the national government made to the states for the improvement of agriculture and farm-related education. Since farms were not in "interstate commerce," it was unclear whether the Constitution permitted the national government to provide direct assistance to agriculture. Grants made to the states, but designated to go to farmers, presented a way of avoiding the question of constitutionality while pursuing what was recognized in Congress as a national goal.

During the 1950s, the national government funded 90 percent of the cost of building more than 42,500 miles of interstate highways. State governments paid for the remaining 10 percent.

THE RISE AND DECLINE OF FEDERAL AID, 1960–97

Figure 4.1

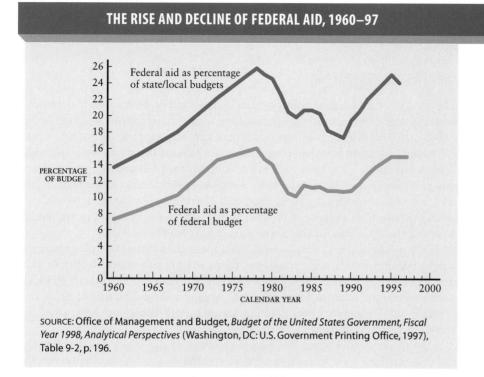

SOURCE: Office of Management and Budget, *Budget of the United States Government, Fiscal Year 1998, Analytical Perspectives* (Washington, DC: U.S. Government Printing Office, 1997), Table 9-2, p. 196.

Franklin Roosevelt's New Deal expanded the range of grants-in-aid into social programs, providing grants to the states for financial assistance to poor children. Congress added new grants after World War II, creating new programs to help states fund activities such as providing school lunches and building highways. Sometimes the national government required state or local governments to match the national contribution dollar for dollar, but in some programs, such as the development of the interstate highway system, the congressional grants provided 90 percent of the cost of the program.

These types of federal grants-in-aid are also called **categorical grants,** because the national government determines the purposes, or categories, for which the money can be used. For the most part, the categorical grants created before the 1960s simply helped the states perform their traditional functions.[18] In the 1960s, however, the national role expanded and the number of categorical grants increased dramatically (see Figure 4.1). For example, during the Eighty-ninth Congress (1965–66) alone, the number of categorical grant-in-aid programs grew from 221 to 379.[19] The grants authorized during the 1960s announced national purposes much more strongly than did earlier grants. Central to that national purpose was the need to provide opportunities to the poor.

Many of the categorical grants enacted during the 1960s were **project grants,** which require state and local governments to submit proposals to federal agencies. In contrast to the older **formula grants,** which used a formula (composed of such elements as need and state and local capacities) to distribute funds, the new project grants made funding available on a competitive basis. Federal agencies would give grants to the proposals they judged to be

categorical grants

congressional grants given to states and localities on the condition that expenditures be limited to a problem or group specified by law

project grants

grant programs in which state and local governments submit proposals to federal agencies and for which funding is provided on a competitive basis

formula grants

grants-in-aid in which a formula is used to determine the amount of federal funds a state or local government will receive

the best. In this way, the national government acquired substantial control over which state and local governments got money, how much they got, and how they spent it.

COOPERATIVE FEDERALISM

The growth of categorical grants created a new kind of federalism. If the traditional system of two sovereigns performing highly different functions could be called dual federalism, historians of federalism suggest that the system since the New Deal could be called **cooperative federalism.** The most important student of the history of American federalism, Morton Grozdins, characterized this as a move from "layer-cake federalism" to "marble-cake federalism,"[20] in which intergovernmental cooperation and sharing have blurred a once-clear distinguishing line, making it difficult to say where the national government ends and the state and local governments begin (see Figure 4.2).

For a while in the 1960s, however, it appeared as if the state governments would become increasingly irrelevant to American federalism. Many of the new federal grants bypassed the states and instead sent money directly to local governments and even to local nonprofit organizations. The theme heard repeatedly in Washington was that the states simply could not be trusted to carry out national purposes.[21]

One of the reasons that Washington distrusted the states was because of the way African American citizens were treated in the South. The southern states' forthright defense of segregation, justified on the grounds of states' rights, helped to tarnish the image of the states as the civil rights movement took hold. The national officials who planned the War on Poverty in the 1960s pointed to the racial exclusion practiced in the southern states as a reason for bypassing state governments. Political scientist James Sundquist described how the "Alabama syndrome" affected the War on Poverty: "In the drafting of the Economic Opportunity Act, an 'Alabama syndrome' developed. Any suggestion within the poverty task force that the states be given a role in the administration of the act was met with the question, 'Do you want to give that kind of power to [Alabama governor] George Wallace?' "[22]

cooperative federalism

a type of federalism existing since the New Deal era in which grants-in-aid have been used strategically to encourage states and localities (without commanding them) to pursue nationally defined goals. Also known as "intergovernmental cooperation"

Figure 4.2

EVOLVING FEDERALISM

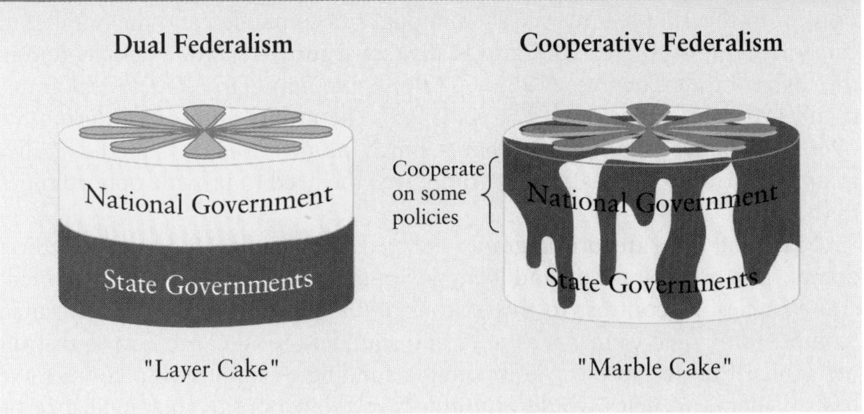

Dual Federalism

National Government

State Governments

"Layer Cake"

Cooperative Federalism

Cooperate on some policies

National Government

State Governments

"Marble Cake"

In marble-cake federalism, national policies, state policies, and local policies overlap in many areas.

AMERICAN POLITICAL CULTURE

The Militia Movement

In American popular culture, militias are synonymous with freedom. In the early history of the United States, the country's defense rested with groups of citizen-soldiers (also called "unorganized" militias), who were generally defined as adult male citizens of fighting age—usually eighteen to forty-five years old—and who were obliged to enroll with the government for military service, serving or training for a few months out of each year. The Revolutionary War was fought in large measure by these citizen-soldiers, who were organized into militias by state governments. America's eventual victory over the British added to the image of militias as the bulwark of American freedom.

The universal militia system effectively ended with the militias' abysmal performance in the War of 1812, where their lack of training and tendency to run in the face of enemy guns culminated in the British sacking of Washington, D.C. Thereafter, America relied for its military needs on select or "organized" militias (small, well-trained volunteer forces that eventually became the National Guard) and standing professional armies filled by enlistment or the draft. Congress revamped the nation's obsolete militia regulations in the early 1900s in order to bring the nation's military, including the militias, under national (as opposed to state) control, based on Congress's constitutional power "to provide for calling forth the Militia" and "organizing, arming, and disciplining, the Militia" (Art. I).

Since that time, however, scattered groups of disaffected citizens have formed their own self-styled "militias." These dissident groups have armed themselves, engaged in military-style maneuvers, and proclaimed the colonial militias as their heritage.

In the early 1990s, fringe groups sprang up in many states. By 1995, such militia groups were said to have been organized in as many as 47 states, comprising perhaps 20,000 members. Public concern over the intentions of these groups heightened with the April 19, 1995, bombing of a federal office building in Oklahoma City. Nearly 170 people died in the blast.

Although militia concerns and motivations vary, they share a profound mistrust of governmental authority and a fear that the American government is poised to turn its authority over to a world government, possibly controlled by the United Nations. (Like earlier militia and paramilitary groups, many of today's "militias" also subscribe to anti-Semitic and racist beliefs.) No evidence supports such allegations, but militia fears were nevertheless fanned by the government's botched attempts to capture extremist Randy Weaver in 1992 and to raid the Branch Davidian compound near Waco, Texas, in 1993.

For all of their claims to the militia tradition, the modern self-styled militias differ from colonial militias in two vital respects. First, the modern militias are organized and operate without government consent or control. By the Constitution's definition, as well as according to federal and state laws, a militia can exist only by or under the regulation and control of a state or national government. Second, the modern militias' very reason for existence is their hostility to the existing American government. While colonial militias fought against British rule, they still fought for a government—namely, the fledgling American government.

Some militia representatives claim that they have a constitutionally protected right to engage in rebellion against the government. Yet no such right exists, for the simple reason that if such a right existed, it would amount to nothing less than government suicide. As legal expert Roscoe Pound noted many years ago, "a legal right of the citizen to wage war on the government is something that cannot be admitted."[1]

SOURCE: Robert J. Spitzer, *The Politics of Gun Control* (Chatham, NJ: Chatham House, 1995).
[1]Quoted in Robert J. Spitzer, *The Politics of Gun Control* (Chatham, NJ: Chatham House, 1995), p. 47.

Governor George Wallace of Alabama stood in defiance as he turned back U.S. Attorney General Nicholas Katzenbach, who was trying to enroll two black students at the University of Alabama at Tuscaloosa in 1963. Wallace, who proclaimed "segregation now, segregation tomorrow, segregation forever," was a vocal advocate of states' rights.

Yet, even though many national policies of the 1960s bypassed the states, other new programs, such as Medicaid—the health program for the poor—relied on state governments for their implementation. In addition, as the national government expanded existing programs run by the states, states had to take on more responsibility. These new responsibilities meant that the states were playing a very important role in the federal system.

REGULATED FEDERALISM AND NATIONAL STANDARDS

The question of who decides what each level of government should do goes to the very heart of what it means to be an American citizen. How different should things be when one crosses a state line? In what policy areas is it acceptable to have state differences and in what areas should states be similar? Supreme Court decisions about the fundamental rights of American citizens provide the most important answers to these questions. Over time, the Court has pushed for greater uniformity across the states. In addition to legal decisions, the national government uses two other tools to create similarities across the states: grants-in-aid and regulations.

Grants-in-aid, as we have seen, are a little like bribes: Congress gives money to state and local governments if they agree to spend it for the purposes Congress specifies. But as Congress began to enact legislation in new areas, such as environmental policy, it also imposed additional regulations on states and localities. Some political scientists call this a move toward **regulated federalism**.[23] The national government began to set standards of conduct or required the states to set standards that met national guidelines. Figure 4.3 shows how much federal regulation grew, especially during the 1970s. The effect of these national standards is that state and local policies in the areas of environmental protection, social services, and education are more uniform from coast to coast than are other nationally funded policies.

Some national standards require the federal government to take over areas of regulation formerly overseen by state or local governments. Such **preemp-**

regulated federalism

a form of federalism in which Congress imposes legislation on states and localities, requiring them to meet national standards

THE CHANGING MIX OF FEDERAL GRANTS AND REGULATIONS, 1951–90   Figure 4.3

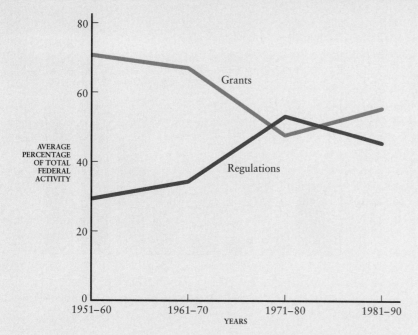

SOURCE: U.S. Advisory Commission on Intergovernmental Relations, *Federal Regulation of State and Local Governments: The Mixed Record of the 1980s* (Washington, DC: Advisory Commission on Intergovernmental Relations, 1993), p. 56.

tion occurs when state and local actions are found to be inconsistent with federal requirements. If this occurs, all regulations in the preempted area must henceforth come from the national government. In many cases, the scope of the federal authority to preempt is decided by the courts. For example, in 1973 the Supreme Court struck down a local ordinance prohibiting jets from taking off from the airport in Burbank, California, between 11 P.M. and 7 A.M. It ruled that the Federal Aeronautics Act granted the Federal Aviation Administration all authority over flight patterns, takeoffs, and landings and that local governments could not impose regulations in this area. As federal regulations increased after the 1970s, Washington increasingly preempted state and local action in many different policy areas.

The growth of national standards has created some new problems and has raised questions about how far federal standardization should go. One problem that emerged in the 1980s was the increase in **unfunded mandates**—regulations or new conditions for receiving grants that impose costs on state and local governments for which they are not reimbursed by the national government. The growth of unfunded mandates was the product of a Democratic Congress, which wanted to achieve liberal social objectives, and a Republican president, who opposed increased social spending. Between 1983 and 1991, Congress mandated standards in many policy areas, including social services and environmental regulations, without providing additional funds to meet

preemption

the principle that allows the national government to override state or local actions in certain policy areas

unfunded mandates

regulations or conditions for receiving grants that impose costs on state and local governments for which they are not reimbursed by the federal government

Figure 4.4   THE RISING COSTS OF UNFUNDED MANDATES, 1984–91

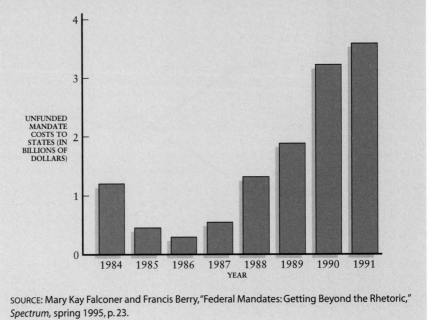

SOURCE: Mary Kay Falconer and Francis Berry, "Federal Mandates: Getting Beyond the Rhetoric," *Spectrum,* spring 1995, p. 23.

those standards. Altogether, Congress enacted twenty-seven laws that imposed new regulations or required states to expand existing programs.[24] For example, in the late 1980s, Congress ordered the states to extend the coverage provided by Medicaid, the medical insurance program for the poor. The aim was to make the program serve more people, particularly poor children, and to expand services. But Congress did not supply additional funding to help states meet these new requirements; the states had to shoulder the increased financial burden themselves.

States and localities quickly began to protest the cost of unfunded mandates. Although it is very hard to determine the exact cost of federal regulations, the Congressional Budget Office estimated that between 1983 and 1990, new federal regulations cost states and localities between $8.9 and $12.7 billion (see Figure 4.4).[25] States complained that mandates took up so much of their budgets that they were not able to set their own priorities.

These burdens became part of a rallying cry to reduce the power of the federal government—a cry that took center stage when a Republican Congress was elected in 1994. One of the first measures the new Congress passed was an act to limit the cost of unfunded mandates. Under the new law, Congress must estimate the cost of any proposal it believes will cost more than $50 million. It must then vote to approve the regulation, acknowledging the expenditure. The effect of this act is likely to be limited; it does not prevent congressional members from passing unfunded mandates, but only makes them think twice before they do. Moreover, the act exempts several areas of regulation. States must still enforce antidiscrimination laws and meet other requirements to receive federal assistance. Only nine of the twenty-seven mandates en-acted between 1981 and 1990 would have been covered by the new law.[26]

NEW FEDERALISM AND STATE CONTROL

In 1970, the mayor of Oakland, California, told Congress that there were twenty-two separate employment and training programs in his city but that few poor residents were being trained for jobs that were available in the local labor market.[27] National programs had proliferated as Congress enacted many small grants, but little effort was made to coordinate or adapt programs to local needs. Today many governors argue for more control over such national grant programs. They complain that national grants do not allow for enough local flexibility and instead take a "one size fits all" approach.[28] These criticisms point to a fundamental problem in American federalism: how to get the best results for the money spent. Do some divisions of responsibility between states and the federal government work better than others? Since the 1970s, as states have become more capable of administering large-scale programs, the idea of solving administrative problems by devolving more responsibility to the states has become popular.

Proponents of more state authority have looked to **block grants** as a way of reducing federal control. Block grants are federal grants that allow the states considerable leeway in spending federal money. President Nixon led the first push for block grants in the early 1970s, as part of his **New Federalism.** Nixon's block grants consolidated programs in the areas of job training, community development, and social services into three large block grants. These grants imposed some conditions on states and localities for how the money should be spent, but not the narrow regulations contained in the categorical grants. In addition, Congress approved a fourth block grant called **revenue sharing.** Revenue sharing provided money to local governments and counties with no strings attached; localities could spend the money as they wished. Reagan's version of new federalism also looked to block grants. Like Nixon, Reagan wanted to reduce the national government's control and return power to the states. In all, Congress created twelve new block grants between 1981 and 1990.[29]

Another way of letting the states do more is by having the national government do less. When Nixon implemented block grants he increased federal spending. But Reagan's block grants cut federal funding by 12 percent. His view was that the states could spend their own funds to make up the difference, if they chose to do so. The Republican Congress elected in 1994 took this strategy even further, supporting block grants as well as substantial cuts in federal programs. The states' governors were divided over how far these changes should go. Some Republican governors, such as John Engler of Michigan, worked with the Congress; they were willing to accept less federal money in exchange for greater state flexibility in administering programs. Other governors

Students and Politics

As the state with the nation's largest student population, California commands the attention of young activists and legislators nationwide in matters of student financial aid. Seeing little representation of students among California lobbyists, University of California at Davis student Scott Lay founded Protect the Promise, an Internet-based organization that connects student leaders throughout California with discussion groups and information about student fees. "We concentrate on financial issues," says Lay. "Lots of groups, like USSA [the United States Students Association] take stands on controversial issues like affirmative action. That can be divisive." Lay often campaigns in nearby Sacramento for Protect the Promise and for another group representing state community college students. The Internet site facilitated a massive campaign to fight student tuition increases. This, combined with Lay's lobbying, convinced the state legislature to pass a tuition decrease. "Most of what we do is not one person's work," he says. "I am augmenting activism and promoting affordable education."

block grants

federal grants-in-aid that allow states considerable discretion in how the funds are spent

New Federalism

attempts by Presidents Nixon and Reagan to return power to the states through block grants

revenue sharing

the process by which one unit of government yields a portion of its tax income to another unit of government, according to an established formula. Revenue sharing typically involves the national government providing money to state governments

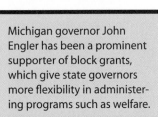

Michigan governor John Engler has been a prominent supporter of block grants, which give state governors more flexibility in administering programs such as welfare.

Cuts in federal funding have had a big impact on universities. These Louisiana State University students are protesting proposed funding cuts.

feared that turning existing programs into block grants with less money would leave the states with too large a financial burden.[30]

But neither block grants nor reduced federal funding have proven to be magic solutions to the problems of federalism. For one thing, there is always a trade-off between accountability, that is, whether the states are using funds for the purposes intended, and flexibility. Accountability and proper use of funds continue to be troublesome issues. Even after block grants were created, Congress reimposed regulations in order to increase the states' accountability. If the objective is to have accountable and efficient government, it is not clear that state bureaucracies are any more efficient or more capable than national agencies. In Mississippi, for example, the state Department of Human Services spent money from the child care block grant for office furniture and designer salt and pepper shakers that cost $37.50 a pair. As one Mississippi state legislator said, "I've seen too many years of good ol' boy politics to know they shouldn't [transfer money to the states] without stricter controls and requirements."[31] Both liberals and conservatives have charged that block grants are a way for politicians to avoid the big, controversial policy questions. Instead of facing problems head-on, these critics say, the federal government uses block grants to kick the problem down to the states.[32]

Reduced federal funding may leave states with problems that they do not have the resources to solve. During the 1980s, many states had to raise taxes in order to make up for some of the cuts in federal funding. (The impact of these cuts can be seen in Table 4.3.) But in the early 1990s, when a recession hit, states had to cut back services because they were short of funds even after raising taxes. How much of a financial burden the states can carry without harming the fundamental services citizens have come to expect from government is a major question now confronting all Americans. One area of state funding that has suffered considerably in the past years is higher education. In 1995, New York's Republican governor, George Pataki, sparked student

City	1977	1992	City	1977	1992
Buffalo	31%	6%	Oakland	39%	6%
Cleveland	29	11	Oklahoma City	39	3
Detroit	31	8	Portland	28	2
Honolulu	30	7	San Antonio	28	3
Louisville	41	8	Tulsa	24	3

FEDERAL AID AS A PERCENTAGE OF GENERAL ANNUAL EXPENDITURE, 1977 AND 1992

Table 4.3

SOURCE: Department of Commerce, *Statistical Abstract of the United States, 1994* (Washington, DC: U.S. Government Printing Office, 1994), pp. 317–18.

protests when he sought deep cuts in state funding for the State University of New York and the City University of New York, while proposing to increase tuition by $1,000 a year.[33]

As states are expected to take on greater responsibility, they will become even more important political arenas, where different interests fight to see their vision of the proper role of government implemented.

IS THERE A RIGHT ANSWER?

Some students of federalism say that states are best at doing some things and the national government is better at doing others. They argue that rather than share responsibility for funding, as many programs now do, each level of government should be fully responsible for the things that it does best.

In 1985, the Robb-Evans Commission, a bipartisan group, proposed a comprehensive approach to the division of responsibility. It argued that the national government should leave all economic development programs to the states and that the national government should take responsibility for programs that serve the poor. The commission built on the ideas of many economists and political scientists who maintain that states and localities should not be in charge of **redistributive programs,** that is, programs that are primarily for the benefit of the poor. These scholars argue that because states and local governments have to compete with one another, they do not have the incentive to spend their money on the needy people in their areas. Instead, they want to keep taxes low and spend money on things that promote economic development.[34] In this situation, states might engage in a "race to the bottom": if one state cuts assistance to the poor, neighboring states will institute similar or deeper cuts both to reduce expenditures and to discourage poorer people from moving into their states. As one New York legislator put it, "The concern we have is that unless we make our welfare system and our tax and regulatory system competitive with the states around us, we will have too many disincentives for business to move here. Welfare is a big part of that."[35]

In 1996, when Congress enacted a major welfare reform law, it followed a different logic. By changing welfare from a combined federal-state program into a block grant to the states, Congress gave the states more responsibility for

redistributive programs

economic policies designed to control the economy through taxing and spending, with the goal of benefiting the poor

Welfare Reform

President Franklin D. Roosevelt's New Deal effort to improve America's social and economic condition established the modern social welfare state, inaugurated with the enactment of the Social Security Act of 1935. This act provided income benefits for retired workers, the disabled, and the unemployed. In the 1960s, social welfare programs were expanded to improve conditions for the nation's poor. In the 1980s, Presidents Ronald Reagan and George Bush won cuts in programs like food stamps, Aid to Families with Dependent Children (AFDC), and job programs. President Bill Clinton also seized on what is now called welfare reform, promising to reorganize and streamline these programs. Congress approved legislation to end AFDC and give the money to the states to run their own welfare programs, limit benefits eligibility to five years, and insist on work requirements for welfare recipients. Yet these and other proposed changes continue to be controversial.

Supporters of welfare reform argue that the federal welfare system has spiraled out of control. Spending on all social welfare programs has topped $300 billion a year in the 1990s, at a time when government resources are shrinking. Despite this vast spending, poverty persists. The United States today supports a self-perpetuating culture of poverty that discourages able-bodied people from working. Welfare tears the fabric of society by producing generations of young people who are ignorant of the work ethic; it encourages unwed motherhood among a rising number of teenagers (three-fourths of all teenage mothers land on welfare within five years); it spawns rising rates of crime. Furthermore, the welfare system is expensive because it is inefficiently run. Too many able-bodied or ineligible people continue to receive government benefits.

Welfare reform seeks not only to weed out those who cheat the system, but to break the cycle of welfare dependency. Proponents of reform argue that the states are in the best position to decide how to handle poverty, since patterns vary widely from state to state. Beyond this, they assert, greater emphasis needs to be placed on the work ethic, so that those who *can* work *do*. "Deadbeat dads," men who fail to support the children they father, should be forced to support their families. The values of family life need to be emphasized to help break the cycle of unmarried teenage motherhood and dependency. Educational opportunities provide a vital route for the poor to acquire the skills they need to lead self-supporting, productive lives. Private charities and the spirit of voluntarism should replace government largesse. A good example of this is the private program Habitat for Humanity, which helps the poor build and occupy their own homes. In short, government welfare may not be ended, but the poor can be aided more cheaply and more effectively through private means.

Opponents of welfare reform argue that a governmental welfare safety net is necessary, and that welfare-related spending levels and problems have been greatly exaggerated. For example, the argument that increases in welfare benefits have encouraged unwed teenage motherhood is not borne out by most studies of the matter. The biggest cause of poverty is economic dislocation and shifts in the nature and demands of the workplace—factors over which individuals have no control. The primary "welfare" programs, including AFDC, food stamps, rent subsidies, and school lunches, comprised only about 5 percent of the 1995 national budget. The most expensive social programs are aimed mostly at the middle class, including Social Security and Medicare, which took up over 30 percent of the 1995 budget. Government spending for AFDC and similar programs has declined by over 40 percent, in real dollars, since the start of the 1980s.

A New Beginning
Welfare to Work

Many of the social and behavioral problems associated with poverty arise from the fact that the government spends far less per capita on its poor than do most other industrialized nations. This keeps the poor at a subsistence level that makes it even more difficult for them to improve their situation. The culture of poverty idea is also greatly exaggerated, as six-sevenths of those who receive AFDC leave the benefits system within five years. Rather than stigmatizing and berating the poor, the government needs to emphasize constructive measures to assist those in need, so that they may get the child care, education, and other support necessary to break out of poverty. Only the federal government can ensure a consistent and fair level of support to those most in need.

programs that serve the poor. One argument in favor of this decision is that states can act as "laboratories of democracy," by experimenting with many different approaches to find one that best meet the needs of their citizens.[36] As states have altered their welfare programs in the wake of the new law, they have indeed designed diverse approaches. For example, Minnesota has adopted an incentive-based approach that offers extra assistance to families that take low-wage jobs. Other states, such as California, have more "sticks" than "carrots" in their new welfare programs. It is still too early to say whether giving the states more responsibility for welfare has been a success. The new programs have been in place for only a short time and they were launched in a time of unusually low unemployment. Advocates of more federal responsibility for welfare fear that when a recession occurs, serious problems will emerge. When state budgets grow tighter, there will be considerable pressure to reduce social spending at the same time that unemployment is growing.

As the case of welfare shows, assessments about "the right way" to divide responsibility in the federal system change over time. The case of speed limits, discussed in the beginning of this chapter, provides another example. Speed limits have traditionally been a state and local responsibility. But in 1973, at the height of the oil shortage, Congress passed legislation to withhold federal highway funds from states that did not adopt a maximum speed limit of 55 miles per hour (mph). The lower speed limit, it was argued, would reduce energy consumption by cars. Although Congress had not formally taken over the authority to set speed limits, the power of its purse was so important that every state adopted the new speed limit. As the energy crisis faded, the national speed limit lost much of its support, even though it was found to have reduced the number of traffic deaths. In 1995, Congress repealed the penalties for higher speed limits, and states once again became free to set their own speed limits. Many states with large rural areas raised their maximum to 75 mph; Montana set unlimited speeds in the rural areas during daylight hours. Early research indicates that numbers of highway deaths have indeed risen in the states that increased the limits.[37] As new evidence becomes available, it will surely provide fuel for the ongoing debate about what are properly the states' responsibilities and what the federal government should do.

Perspectives on Politics

THE EFFICIENCY OF DIFFERENT LEVELS OF GOVERNMENT

Responses of eighteen- to twenty-four-year-olds to the question, " From which level of government do you feel you get the most for your money? "

SOURCE: 1993 U.S. Advisory Commission on Intergovernmental Relations survey, reported in Susan A. MacManus, *Young v. Old: Generational Combat in the 21st Century* (Boulder, CO: Westview, 1996), p. 185.

★ Federalism and American Political Values

▶ How do changes in American federalism reflect different interpretations of liberty, equality, and democracy?

American federalism has changed substantially over the course of our history. The framers would never have dreamed of a federal government with as many powers as ours has today. The changes in American federalism reflect the different ways that we, as a nation, interpret the meanings of liberty, equality, and democracy at different times in our history. They also reflect our changing beliefs about which American institutions can best realize these values. But

Students and Politics

"I was never into politics," says John Potbury describing his youth in Flushing, Michigan. "I just watched some *Nightline* and read the local papers, but never anything in campaigns. . . . I couldn't even identify myself as a Republican or Democrat." A few years later, John's activism had increased significantly. The spark came while in high school, when he and three classmates journeyed to Washington, D.C., to participate in Close Up, a program that brings students from all fifty states together for a week of seminars and behind-the-scenes visits to the legislative, judicial, and executive branches of government. "The air of Washington was really inspiring," he says. "There was so much going on, more than anything I had expected or could imagine from my hometown. I had a new appreciation for the national government." Potbury's Close Up experience prompted him to do more at the local level by winning election to the city council of Flushing, and by working to promote business interests in the area. Today, although he no longer sits on the city council, he divides his time between national Republican Party activities (he worked with the advance teams for Bob Dole's 1996 presidential campaign) and local community service projects, such as bringing professionals into local schools to speak with students about careers. Despite his fascination with the federal government, Potbury still appreciates his time on the city council: "I did things at the local level that *must* be done at the local level."

even today, there is no single consensus on how responsibilities should be organized within the federal system to make our fundamental values come alive. Indeed, a brief look at values and federalism reveals that some of the sharpest tensions among liberty, equality, and democracy are visible in debates over federalism.

The Constitution limited the power of the federal government in order to promote liberty. This decision reflected the framers' suspicions of centralized power, based on their experience with the British Crown. The American suspicion of centralized power lives on today in widespread dislike of "big government," which generally evokes a picture of a bloated federal government. But over the course of our history we have come to realize that the federal government can also be an important guarantor of liberty. As we shall see in Chapter 5, it took enhanced federal power to ensure that local and state governments adhered to the fundamental constitutional freedoms in the Bill of Rights.

One of the most important continuing arguments for a strong federal government is its role in ensuring equality. A key puzzle of federalism is deciding when differences across states represent the proper democratic decisions of the states and when such differences represent inequalities that should not be tolerated. Sometimes a decision to eliminate differences is made on the grounds of equality and individual rights, as in the Civil Rights Act of 1964, which outlawed legal segregation. At other times, a stronger federal role is justified on the grounds of national interest, as in the case of the oil shortage and the institution of a 55 mph speed limit in the 1970s. Advocates of a more limited federal role often point to the value of democracy. Public actions can more easily be tailored to fit distinctive local or state desires if states and localities have more power to make policy. Viewed this way, variation across states can be an expression of democratic will.

In recent years, many Americans have grown disillusioned with the federal government and have supported efforts to give the states more responsibilities. A 1997 poll, for example, found that Americans tended to have the most confidence in governments that were closest to them. Thirty-eight percent expressed "a great deal" of confidence in local government, 32 percent in state government, and 22 percent in the federal government. Nearly two-thirds of those polled believed that shifting some responsibility to states and localities would help achieve excellence in government. But the same survey also revealed reluctance to significantly change the division of responsibilities among the levels of government. When asked what should be done, 54 percent called for improving management and only 32 percent called for passing responsibility to states and localities.[38]

American federalism remains a work in progress. As public problems shift and as local, state, and federal governments change, questions about the relationship between American values and federalism naturally emerge. The different views that people bring to this discussion suggest that concerns about federalism will remain a central issue in American democracy.

The Citizen's Role: Participation at Different Levels of the Federal System

How can citizens contribute to the ongoing design of American federalism? To be effective participants in a federal system, citizens must first understand how responsibilities are divided among the different levels of government. They also need to be aware of how decisions taken at one level of government may affect the possibilities for public action at other levels. In other words, if citizens are to be politically effective they must understand the connections among the levels of the federal system and target their activities where they will be most effective.

One of the striking features of political participation in the United States is the preference for engaging in politics at the state and local levels. One study of political participation found that 92 percent of Americans who participated beyond voting—by campaigning, contacting public officials, or sitting on a governing board, for example—engaged in an activity focused on state and local activity. Fifty-one percent of those questioned engaged only in state and local action, while 41 percent added some form of national participation to their state and local activities.[39] This pattern of participation makes sense because politics at these levels—especially the local level—is more personal and often easier to get involved in. Moreover, many of the things that people care most about are close to home, such as their schools and their neighborhoods.

But to be broadly effective, citizens must be able to engage in political activity at different levels of the federal system. For example, in the 1970s, community groups frustrated in their efforts to revitalize inner-city neighborhoods lobbied Congress to pass the Community Reinvestment Act, which requires banks to invest in the neighborhoods where they do business. With this federal law behind them, community organizations have been much more effective in promoting investment in the 1980s and 1990s. But it is often not easy for groups of citizens to focus their activity at different levels of government as needed. Often they do not have the expertise or the contacts or the information to be effective in a different setting.

In recent years, as states have taken on a greater role in making public policy, it has become more important for citizens to become effective participants in state politics. Moreover, the media coverage of state politics is generally not as deep or informative as coverage of national politics. Citizens need a better knowledge of what states do today and more information about state politics simply as a first step to being effective participants in our federal system.

The federal system makes American democracy a flexible form of government for a large and diverse nation. But citizens must be knowledgeable about how public actions across the federal system are connected and they must be able to act at different levels if federalism is to be an effective and representative form of government.

POLITICS ON THE WEB

As anyone who has ordered clothing from J. Crew can tell you, mail-order shopping has one great advantage: you avoid sales tax. Internet shopping may further erode state sales tax revenues, but increasing computerization of commerce may finally allow states to capture taxes on mail-order purchases.

Who will regulate Internet commerce? The states or the federal government? Although state and federal powers overlap in many areas of commerce, it is most likely that the federal government will have to regulate all aspects of the Internet. States may claim the power to regulate Internet commerce, but, as in the past, they have no power to regulate corporations located in other states. Unlike a factory or a store, it is fast and easy to "relocate" a web site to another city, state, or even country. Only the federal government can set national standards for companies that can easily shift services and production across state lines.

www.wwnorton.com/wtp2e

We the People

COMMUNITY GROUPS

*R*evitalizing poor urban neighborhoods poses difficult challenges for national and local policymakers. As middle-class residents move to the suburbs, the neighborhoods they leave behind often become poorer and more dilapidated. A cycle of decline can set in, making it difficult to provide safe and attractive neighborhoods for low-income residents. By the late 1970s, some urban neighborhoods, such as the South Bronx in New York City, were so littered with abandoned and burned-out buildings that they became national symbols for urban decline.

In the 1980s, however, community-based organizations in many cities took the lead in finding solutions for poor neighborhoods. Guarding against arsonists and working with city governments, such groups have rehabilitated existing housing and, assisted by several federal programs, have built affordable housing for people with low and moderate incomes. Through these activities, community organizations have revived many areas once believed to be hopeless.

Some community development groups grew out of the determination of residents to save their homes. For example, the Banana Kelly Community Improvement Association in the Bronx was formed in 1977, when residents of a curved section of Kelly Street (hence "banana") in the Bronx prevented their building from being demolished and fought for loans to rehabilitate their housing. Adopting the slogan "Don't Move, Improve," the Banana Kelly residents cleaned up their street and patrolled it themselves to make it safer. Small successes multiplied over time as the organization sought to improve nearby housing. By 1995, Banana Kelly managed fifty-two buildings and had real estate holdings estimated to be worth more than $50 million.[1]

Other community development groups are church-based organizations. One such group, East Brooklyn Congregations, was formed in 1978 by a group of ministers in the East New York section of Brooklyn. An area tradition-

Summary

In this chapter, we have examined one of the central principles of American government—federalism. The Constitution divides powers between the national government and the states, but over time national power has grown substantially. Many aspects of expanded federal power stem from struggles to realize the ideals of liberty and equality for all citizens.

The aim of federalism in the Constitution was to limit national power by creating two sovereigns—the national government and the state governments. The Founders hoped that this system of dual federalism would ensure the liberty of citizens by preventing the national government from becoming too powerful. But during the 1930s, American citizens used the democratic system to change the balance between federal and state governments. The failure of the states to provide basic economic security for citizens during the Great Depression led to an expansion of the federal government. Most Americans were supportive of this growing federal power because they believed that economic power had become too concentrated in the hands of big corporations and the

ally populated by poor immigrants and minorities, East New York was littered with abandoned buildings and empty lots by the early 1980s. The East Brooklyn Congregations proposed something quite new to revitalize the community: build low-cost suburban-style housing for low- and moderate-income residents in the city. Called "Nehemiah Homes," after the biblical prophet who rebuilt Jerusalem, the project built 2,300 homes with fences and small yards in a neighborhood once strewn with rubble and abandoned buildings.

Finding the money to finance such projects is not easy and these organizations have had to patch together diverse sources of funds. One important source has been the low-income-housing tax credit, which provides a tax break to corporations that invest in low-income housing. Community development groups have also benefited from the Community Reinvestment Act (CRA), a federal program that requires banks to invest in the neighborhoods in which they do business. During the 1980s, as federal funds for housing declined, community groups became adept at using the CRA to induce banks to finance local development

projects. In addition, community development organizations receive assistance from local public-private partnerships in many cities and from two national organizations, the Local Initiatives Support Corporation and the Enterprise Foundation. These organizations provide loans, grants, and technical assistance for community development.

Despite the many successes of community development organizations, their ability to revitalize poor neighborhoods has been limited. The difficulty in securing funds has limited the scope of their activities and the abilities of community groups vary greatly between different cities and neighborhoods. Moreover, when local community development groups have sought to move beyond housing to economic development, their efforts have been less successful. Access to jobs remains a persistent problem that community development organizations have not been able to address. Nonetheless, successes such as those of Banana Kelly and East Brooklyn Congregations may be the first steps in reclaiming neighborhoods that once seemed beyond hope.

[1]Lis Harris, "Banana Kelly's Toughest Fight," *New Yorker,* July 24, 1995, p. 34.

common person was the loser. Thus, the ideal of equality—in this case, the belief that working people should have a fighting chance to support themselves—overrode fears that a strong federal government would abridge liberties. Expanded federal powers first took the form of grants-in-aid to states. Later, federal regulations became more common.

In recent years, many Americans have come to believe that the pendulum has swung too far in the direction of expanded federal power. A common charge is that the federal government is too big and, as a result, has encroached on fundamental liberties. State and local governments complain that they cannot govern because their powers have been preempted or because they have to use their own funds to fulfill unfunded mandates imposed by the federal government. The move to devolve more powers to the states has been called "New Federalism." Advocates of reduced federal power believe that states can protect liberty without creating unacceptable inequalities. Others continue to believe that a strong central government is essential to ensuring basic equalities. They argue that economic competition among the states means that states cannot ensure equality as well as the federal government can. Such questions about how federalism affects the goals of liberty and equality are not easily settled and will remain a continuing task of American democracy.

FOR FURTHER READING

Anton, Thomas. *American Federalism and Public Policy.* Philadelphia: Temple University Press, 1989.

Bensel, Richard. *Sectionalism and American Political Development: 1880–1980.* Madison: University of Wisconsin Press, 1984.

Bowman, Ann O'M., and Richard Kearny. *The Resurgence of the States.* Englewood Cliffs, NJ: Prentice-Hall, 1986.

Dye, Thomas R. *American Federalism: Competition among Governments.* Lexington, MA: Lexington Books, 1990.

Elazar, Daniel. *American Federalism: A View from the States,* 3rd ed. New York: Harper & Row, 1984.

Grodzins, Morton. *The American System.* Chicago: Rand McNally, 1974.

Kelley, E. Wood. *Policy and Politics in the United States: The Limits of Localism.* Philadelphia: Temple University Press, 1987.

Kettl, Donald. *The Regulation of American Federalism.* Baltimore: Johns Hopkins University Press, 1987.

Peterson, Paul E. *The Price of Federalism.* Washington, DC: Brookings, 1995.

STUDY OUTLINE

The Federal Framework

1. In an effort to limit national power, the framers of the Constitution established a system of dual federalism, wherein both the national and state governments would have sovereignty.
2. Federalism and a restrictive definition of "interstate commerce" limited the national government's control over the economy.
3. Federalism allows a great deal of variation between states.
4. Under the traditional system of federalism, the national government was small and very narrowly specialized in its functions compared with other Western nations. Most of its functions were aimed at promoting commerce.
5. Under the traditional system, states rather than the national government did most of the fundamental governing in the country.
6. The system of federalism limited the expansion of the national government despite economic forces and expansive interpretations of the Constitution in cases such as *McCulloch v. Maryland* and *Gibbons v. Ogden.*
7. For most of U.S. history, the concept of interstate commerce kept the national government from regulating the economy. But in 1937, the Supreme Court converted the commerce clause from a source of limitations to a source of power for the national government.

Who Does What? The Changing Federal Framework

1. The rise of national government activity after the New Deal did not necessarily mean that states lost power directly. Rather, the national government paid states through grants-in-aid to administer federal programs.
2. Some federal programs bypass the states by sending money directly to local governments or local organizations. The states are most important, however; they are integral to federal programs such as Medicaid.
3. As states became more effective, states and state officials sought more influence in national politics. They often lobbied for more state control over federal spending decisions.

Federalism and American Political Values

1. Some of the sharpest tensions among liberty, equality, and democracy are visible in debates over federalism.
2. The Constitution limited the power of the national government as a safeguard for liberty, but over the course of American history, a strong national government has been an important guarantor of liberty.
3. A key puzzle of federalism is deciding when differences across states represent the proper democratic decisions of the states and when such differences represent inequalities that should not be tolerated.

PRACTICE QUIZ

1. Which term describes the sharing of powers between the national government and the state governments?
   a) separation of powers
   b) federalism
   c) checks and balances
   d) shared powers

2. The system of federalism that allowed states to do most of the fundamental governing from 1789 to 1937 was
   a) home rule.
   b) regulated federalism.
   c) dual federalism.
   d) cooperative federalism.

3. Which of the following resulted from the federal system?
   a) It limited the power of the national government in relation to the states.
   b) It restrained the power of the national government over the economy.
   c) It allowed variation among the states.
   d) all of the above

4. The overall effect of the growth of national policies has been
   a) to weaken state government.
   b) to strengthen state government.
   c) to provide uniform laws in the nation.
   d) to make the states more diverse culturally.

5. Which amendment to the Constitution stated that the powers not delegated to the national government or prohibited to the states were "reserved to the states"?
   a) First Amendment
   b) Fifth Amendment
   c) Tenth Amendment
   d) Twenty-sixth Amendment

6. The process of returning more of the responsibilities of governing from the national level to the state level is known as
   a) dual federalism.
   b) devolution.
   c) preemption.
   d) home rule.

7. One of the most powerful tools by which the federal government has attempted to get the states to act in ways that are desired by the federal government is by
   a) providing grants-in-aid.
   b) requiring licensing.
   c) granting home rule.
   d) defending states' rights.

8. The form of regulated federalism that allows the federal government to take over areas of regulation formerly overseen by states or local governments is called
   a) categorical grants.
   b) formula grants.
   c) project grants.
   d) preemption.

9. To what does the term "New Federalism" refer?
   a) the national government's regulation of state action through grants-in-aid
   b) the type of federalism relying on categorical grants
   c) efforts to return more policy-making discretion to the states through the use of block grants
   d) the recent emergence of local governments as important political actors

10. A recent notable example of the process of giving the states more responsibility for administering government programs is
    a) campaign finance reform.
    b) prison reform.
    c) trade reform.
    d) welfare reform.

CRITICAL THINKING QUESTIONS

1. The role of the national government has changed significantly from the Founding era to the present. In what ways and to what extent do you think the framers of the Constitution would recognize modern American federalism? Do you think they would be pleased by the current balance of power between the sovereign national government and the sovereign state governments? In what ways did the system of federalism perform its intended functions? In what ways did it not?

2. Should states be required to implement unfunded mandates? Are Americans better off or worse off as a result of devolution?

KEY TERMS

block grants (p. 139)
categorical grants (p. 133)
commerce clause (p. 127)
concurrent powers (p. 120)
cooperative federalism (p. 134)
devolution (p. 130)
dual federalism (p. 123)
expressed powers (p. 119)
federal system (p. 119)
federalism (p. 119)

formula grants (p. 133)
full faith and credit clause (p. 121)
grants-in-aid (p. 132)
home rule (p. 122)
implied powers (p. 120)
necessary and proper clause (p. 120)
New Federalism (p. 139)
police power (p. 120)
preemption (p. 137)

privileges and immunities clause (p. 122)
project grants (p. 133)
redistributive programs (p. 141)
regulated federalism (p. 136)
reserved powers (p. 120)
revenue sharing (p. 139)
states' rights (p. 129)
unfunded mandates (p. 137)
unitary system (p. 119)

5 Civil Liberties

★ The Bill of Rights: A Charter of Liberties
How does the Bill of Rights provide for individual liberties?
What are the differences between the substantive and procedural restraints contained within the Bill of Rights? What are some examples of each?

★ Nationalizing the Bill of Rights
Does the Bill of Rights put limits only on the national government or does it limit state governments as well?
How and when did the Supreme Court nationalize the Bill of Rights?

★ The First Amendment and Freedom of Religion
How does the First Amendment guarantee the nonestablishment and free exercise of religion?
In what way has the free exercise of religion become a recent political issue?

★ The First Amendment and Freedom of Speech and the Press
What forms of speech are protected by the First Amendment? What forms are not protected?

★ The Second Amendment and the Right to Bear Arms
Is the right to bear arms guaranteed by the Bill of Rights? How is its exercise restricted?

★ Rights of the Criminally Accused
What is due process?
How do the Fourth, Fifth, Sixth, and Eighth Amendments provide for the due process of law?

★ The Right to Privacy
What is the right to privacy? How has it been derived from the Bill of Rights? What forms does the right to privacy take today?

★ The Future of Civil Liberties
What is the likelihood that the Supreme Court will try to reverse the nationalization of the Bill of Rights?

THE first ten amendments of the United States Constitution, together called the **Bill of Rights,** are the basis for the freedoms we enjoy as American citizens. These freedoms include the right to free speech, the right to the free exercise of religion, prohibitions against unreasonable searches and seizures, guarantees of due process of law, and the right to privacy, including a woman's right to have an abortion. Today, we may take the liberties contained within the Bill of Rights for granted. Few citizens of other countries can make such a claim. In fact, few people in recorded history have enjoyed such protections, including American citizens before the 1960s. For more than 170 years after its passage in 1789, the Bill of Rights meant little to most Americans. As we shall see in this chapter, guaranteeing the liberties articulated in the Bill of Rights to all Americans required a long struggle. As new challenges to the Bill of Rights arise, this struggle will likely continue.

As recently as the early 1960s many of the freedoms we enjoy today were not guaranteed. At that time, abortion was illegal everywhere in the United States, criminal suspects in state cases did not have to be informed of their rights, some states required daily Bible readings and prayers in their public schools, and some communities regularly censored reading material that they deemed to be obscene. Since the early 1960s, the Supreme Court has expanded the scope of individual freedoms considerably. But since these liberties are constantly subject to judicial interpretation, their provisions are fragile and need to be vigilantly safeguarded. Nevertheless, the Bill of Rights is available and can make a difference.

In recent years, a new challenge has confronted the Bill of Rights—one that may be of special interest to college students. The controversy involves the persistent and widespread efforts to regulate the Internet. Questions about how much power the national government should have over cyberspace were first answered in 1996, when Congress passed the Communications Decency Act, which prohibited the deliberate transmission of "obscene or indecent . . . or patently offensive" material to persons under eighteen years of age. The constitutionality of the act was immediately challenged by a number of interest groups, ranging from the liberal, pro–free speech American Civil Liberties Union (ACLU); to educational groups like the American Library Association; to groups with an economic interest in an unregulated Internet, such as the American Booksellers Association, Microsoft Corporation, and America Online; to groups with a cultural or lifestyle interest, such as Queer Resources Directory. The case challenging the act, *Reno v. ACLU*, reached the Supreme Court in 1997 and by a unanimous vote, the act was overturned.[1]

Cyberspace has become the new frontier of civil liberties and, as with the crossing of all previous frontiers, a long and difficult process lies ahead: that of

Bill of Rights

the first ten amendments to the Constitution, which guarantee certain rights and liberties to the people

College students have been vocal advocates for free speech on the Internet.

Peacefire's logo has become a symbol for free speech on the Internet.

defending the civil liberties of all citizens by protecting the most obnoxious exercises of freedom. Lines of battle were forming as the Supreme Court was filing out of the courtroom after the *Reno v. ACLU* decision. Conservatives were alarmed over what appeared to them to be a trend of more and bolder on-line pornography, and civil liberties groups were equally alarmed at the prospect that regulations proposed by their opponents would not just protect minors but "create virtual gated communities," where members can screen out "inappropriate" messages.[2]

One such civil liberties group formed in the summer of 1996, when a group of college and high school students from around the nation started Peacefire, an interest group founded "to represent students' and minors' interests in the debate over freedom of speech on the Internet." Today, the group focuses on anticensorship legislation and on curtailing the power of home-censorship programs such as CYBERsitter and Cyber Patrol, which sometimes deny minors access to civil rights pages, including several gay-rights, gun-rights, and environmental-protection sites. Web pages blocked by CYBERsitter have included those of the National Organization for Women, the International Gay and Lesbian Human Rights Commission, and Peacefire itself.

The efforts of Peacefire have raised the ire of CYBERsitter employees, one of whom told the organizers via e-mail, "Get a life! Go hang out at the mall with the other kids or something." Supporters fired back, charging CYBERsitter with barring children from intellectual forums; one parent expressed fears "that today's young people will be greatly victimized, often without even knowing it, by use of [CYBERsitter] software." Amid this firestorm, Peacefire cofounder Bennett Haselton and others continue to monitor potential and actual abuses of minors' civil liberties, including censoring programs and legislation. "Kids do not have enough clout in proportion to their numbers," says Haselton, a senior at Vanderbilt University. Peacefire works to ensure that they do.[3]

Many Americans view companies such as CYBERsitter as infringing on individual liberties. Others argue that parents have the choice not to buy the software in the first place and that they can best regulate their own children's viewing habits. The fundamental liberty at stake is that of free speech, an issue often hotly debated on college campuses. This and the other liberties guaranteed by the Bill of Rights will be the focus of this chapter.

- ■ *In this chapter, our first task is to define the Bill of Rights and establish its relationship to personal liberty.* As we shall see, it is through the Bill of Rights that Americans are protected from government.

- ■ *We then turn to the process by which the Bill of Rights was applied, not only to the national government, but to the state governments, as well.* This nationalizing process has been long and selective in applying only certain provisions of the Bill of Rights.

- ■ *The bulk of this chapter is an analysis of the state of civil liberties today, beginning with the First Amendment and the freedom of religion.* Questions over the meaning of this First Amendment guarantee continue to be a focal point of judicial interpretation of the Bill of Rights.

- ■ *We then turn to the other First Amendment rights regarding the freedoms of speech and of the press.* Although freedom of speech and freedom of the press are critical for a democracy, some forms of speech are only conditionally protected.

- ■ *After briefly reviewing the Second Amendment right to bear arms, we move on to the rights of those accused of a crime.* These rights, contained in the Fourth, Fifth, Sixth, and Eighth Amendments, make up the due process of law, a concept that the Supreme Court continues to reinterpret.

- ■ *We then turn to a right that has become increasingly important in recent decades, the right to privacy.* This right takes many forms and, like the freedoms found directly in the Bill of Rights, has been subject to new judicial interpretations.

- ■ *We conclude by pondering the future of civil liberties in the United States.* As we emphasize throughout this chapter, the Bill of Rights is constantly subject to the interpretations of the Supreme Court. Will the Court try to limit the extent of civil liberties in the near future?

The Bill of Rights: A Charter of Liberties

▶ How does the Bill of Rights provide for individual liberties?

▶ What are the differences between the substantive and procedural restraints contained within the Bill of Rights? What are some examples of each?

When the first Congress under the newly ratified Constitution met in late April of 1789 (having been delayed since March 4 by lack of a quorum because of bad

Table 5.3   INCORPORATION OF THE BILL OF RIGHTS
                                 INTO THE FOURTEENTH AMENDMENT

Selected provisions and amendments	Not "incorporated" until	Key case
Eminent domain (V)	1897	*Chicago, Burlington, and Quincy R.R. v. Chicago*
Freedom of speech (I)	1925	*Gitlow v. New York*
Freedom of press (I)	1931	*Near v. Minnesota*
Free exercise of religion (I)	1934	*Hamilton v. Regents of the University of California*
Freedom of assembly (I)	1939	*Hague v. CIO*
Freedom from unnecessary search and seizure (IV)	1949	*Wolf v. Colorado*
Freedom from warrantless search and seizure (IV) ("exclusionary rule")	1961	*Mapp v. Ohio*
Freedom from cruel and unusual punishment (VIII)	1962	*Robinson v. California*
Right to counsel in any criminal trial (VI)	1963	*Gideon v. Wainwright*
Right against self-incrimination and forced confessions (V)	1964	*Mallory v. Hogan Escobedo v. Illinois*
Right to privacy (III, IV, & V)	1965	*Griswold v. Connecticut*
Right to counsel and to remain silent (VI)	1966	*Miranda v. Arizona*
Right against double jeopardy (V)	1969	*Benton v. Maryland*

persons of trial by jury, to deprive persons of their right not to have to testify against themselves, to deprive accused persons of their right to confront adverse witnesses, and to prosecute accused persons more than once for the same crime.[17] Few states chose to use these kinds of powers, but some states did, and the power to do so was available for any state whose legislative majority or courts so chose.

So, until 1961, only the First Amendment and one clause of the Fifth Amendment had been clearly incorporated into the Fourteenth Amendment as binding on the states as well as on the national government.[18] After that, one by one, most of the important provisions of the Bill of Rights were incorporated into the Fourteenth Amendment and applied to the states. Table 5.3 shows the progress of this revolution in the interpretation of the Constitution.

But the controversy over incorporation lives on. Since liberty requires restraining the power of government, the general status of civil liberties can never be considered fixed and permanent. Every provision in the Bill of Rights is subject to interpretation, and in any dispute involving a clause of the Bill of Rights, interpretations will always be shaped by the interpreter's interest in the outcome. As we shall see, the Court continually reminds everyone that if it has the power to expand the Bill of Rights, it also has the power to contract it.[19]

The best way to examine the Bill of Rights today is the simplest way—to take each of the major provisions one at a time. Some of these provisions are settled areas of law, and others are not. Any one of them can be reinterpreted by the Court at any time.

★ The First Amendment and Freedom of Religion

▶ How does the First Amendment guarantee the nonestablishment and free exercise of religion?

▶ In what way has the free exercise of religion become a recent political issue?

Congress shall make no law respecting an establishment of religion, or prohibiting the free exercise thereof; or abridging the freedom of speech, or of the press; or the right of the people peaceably to assemble, and to petition the Government for a redress of grievances.

The Bill of Rights begins by guaranteeing freedom, and the First Amendment provides for that freedom in two distinct clauses: "Congress shall make no law [1] respecting an establishment of religion, or [2] prohibiting the free exercise thereof." The first clause is called the "establishment clause," and the second is called the "free exercise clause."

SEPARATION BETWEEN CHURCH AND STATE

The **establishment clause** has been interpreted quite strictly to mean that a virtual "wall of separation" exists between church and state. The separation of church and state was especially important to the great numbers of American colonists who had sought refuge from persecution for having rejected membership in state-sponsored churches. The concept of a "wall of separation" was Jefferson's own formulation, and this concept has figured in all of the modern Supreme Court cases arising under the establishment clause.

Despite the absolute sound of the phrase "wall of separation," there is ample room to disagree on how high the wall is or of what materials it is composed. For example, the Court has been consistently strict in cases of school prayer, striking down such practices as Bible reading,[20] nondenominational prayer,[21] and even a moment of silence for meditation.[22] In each of these cases, the Court reasoned that school-sponsored observations, even of an apparently nondenominational character, are highly suggestive of school sponsorship and therefore violate the prohibition against establishment of religion. On the other hand, the Court has been quite permissive (and some would say inconsistent) about the public display of religious symbols, such as city-sponsored Nativity scenes in commercial or municipal areas.[23] And although the Court has

establishment clause

the First Amendment clause that says that "Congress shall make no law respecting an establishment of religion." This law means that a "wall of separation" exists between church and state

School prayer has become a defining issue in the separation of church and state.

Lemon test

a rule articulated in *Lemon v. Kurtz-man* that government action toward religion is permissible if it is secular in purpose, does not lead to "excessive entanglement" with religion, and neither promotes nor inhibits the practice of religion

consistently disapproved of government financial support for religious schools, even when the purpose has been purely educational and secular, the Court has permitted certain direct aid to students of such schools in the form of busing, for example. In 1971, after thirty years of cases involving religious schools, the Court attempted to specify some criteria to guide their decisions and those of lower courts, indicating, for example, in a decision invalidating state payments for the teaching of secular subjects in parochial schools, circumstances under which the Court might allow certain financial assistance. The case was *Lemon v. Kurtzman;* in its decision, the Supreme Court established three criteria to guide future cases, in what came to be called the **Lemon test.** The Court held that government aid to religious schools would be accepted as constitutional if (1) it had a secular purpose, (2) its effect was neither to advance nor to inhibit religion, and (3) it did not entangle government and religious institutions in each other's affairs.[24]

Although these restrictions make the *Lemon* test a hard test to pass, imaginative authorities are finding ways to do so, and the Supreme Court has demonstrated a willingness to let them. For example, in 1995, the Court narrowly ruled that a student religious group at the University of Virginia could not be denied student activities funds merely because it was a religious group espousing a particular viewpoint about a deity. The Court called the denial "viewpoint discrimination" that violated the free speech rights of the group. Dissenting members of the Court argued that since the message was not scholarly discourse but "the evangelists' mission station and the pulpit," any state aid violated the First Amendment's prohibition against the establishment of a religion.[25] This led two years later to a new, more conservative approach to the "separation of church and state." In 1997, the Court explicitly recognized a change in its interpretation of the establishment clause, and then went on to reverse an important 1985 decision that had forbidden the practice of sending public school teachers into parochial schools to provide remedial education to disadvantaged children.[26] In the aftermath of the 1985 case, teachers from the public schools had to hold their classes in vans parked across the street from the parochial schools. This had added greatly to the cost of the remedial education and had led to a request for relief from the 1985 decision. The Court provided that relief in 1997 and went beyond that to assert that such cooperation between public school teachers and parochial schools was not an "entanglement" that amounted to public support (i.e., establishment) of a religion. This case represents quite a change in the prevailing view of the establishment clause.

FREE EXERCISE OF RELIGION

The **free exercise clause** protects the right to believe and to practice whatever religion one chooses; it also protects the right to be a nonbeliever. The precedent-setting case involving free exercise is *West Virginia State Board of Education v. Barnette* (1943), which involved the children of a family of Jehovah's Witnesses who refused to salute and pledge allegiance to the American flag on the grounds that their religious faith did not permit it. Three years earlier, the Court had upheld such a requirement and had permitted schools to expel students for refusing to salute the flag. But the entry of the United States into a war to defend democracy coupled with the ugly treatment to which the Jehovah's Witnesses children had been subjected induced the Court to reverse itself and to endorse the free exercise of religion even when it may be offensive to the beliefs of the majority.[27]

Although the Supreme Court has been fairly consistent and strict in protecting the free exercise of religious belief, it has taken pains to distinguish between religious beliefs and actions based on those beliefs. In one case, for example, two Native Americans had been fired from their jobs for smoking peyote, an illegal drug. They claimed that they had been fired from their jobs illegally because smoking peyote was a religious sacrament protected by the free exercise clause. The Court disagreed with their claim in an important 1990 decision,[28] but Congress supported the claim and it went on to engage in an unusual controversy with the Court, involving the separation of powers as well as the proper application of the separation of church and state. Congress literally reversed the Court's 1990 decision with the enactment of the Religious Freedom Restoration Act of 1993 (RFRA), forbidding any federal agency or state government from restricting a person's free exercise of religion unless the federal agency or state government demonstrates that its action "furthers a compelling government interest" and "is the least restrictive means of furthering that compelling governmental interest." One of the first applications of the RFRA was to a case brought by St. Peter's Catholic Church against the city of Boerne, Texas, which had denied permission to the church to enlarge its building because the building had been declared a historic landmark. The case went to federal court on the argument that the city had violated the church's religious freedom as guaranteed by Congress in RFRA. The Supreme Court declared RFRA unconstitutional, but on grounds rarely utilized, if not unique to this case: Congress had violated the separation of powers principle, infringing on the powers of the judiciary by going so far beyond its lawmaking powers that it ended up actually expanding the scope of religious rights rather than just enforcing them. The Court thereby implied that questions requiring a balancing of religious claims against public policy claims was reserved strictly to the judiciary.[29]

The *City of Boerne* case did settle some matters of constitutional controversy over the religious exercise and the establishment clauses of the First Amendment but left a lot more unsettled. What about polygamy, a practice allowed in the Mormon faith? What about snake worship? Or the refusal of

free exercise clause
the First Amendment clause that protects a citizen's right to believe and practice whatever religion he or she chooses

This Native American holy man performed a "cedar ceremony" outside the Supreme Court prior to the Court's decision against two Native Americans who argued that smoking peyote was a religious sacrament protected by the free exercise clause.

Amish parents to send their children to school beyond eighth grade because exposing their children to "modern values" would undermine their religious commitment? In this last example, the Court decided in favor of the Amish and endorsed a very strong interpretation of the protection of free exercise.[30]

★ The First Amendment and Freedom of Speech and the Press

▶ What forms of speech are protected by the First Amendment? What forms are not protected?

"Congress shall make no law . . . abridging the freedom of speech, or of the press. . . ."

Because democracy depends upon an open political process and because politics is basically talk, freedom of speech and freedom of the press are considered critical. For this reason, they were given a prominence in the Bill of Rights equal to that of freedom of religion. In 1938, freedom of speech (which in all important respects includes freedom of the press) was given extraordinary constitutional status when the Supreme Court established that any legislation that attempts to restrict these fundamental freedoms "is to be subjected to a more exacting judicial scrutiny . . . than are most other types of legislation."[31]

What the Court was saying is that the democratic political process must be protected at almost any cost. This higher standard of judicial review came to be called **strict scrutiny**. Strict scrutiny implies that speech—at least some kinds of speech—will be protected almost absolutely. But as it turns out, only some types of speech are fully protected against restrictions (see Figure 5.1). As we shall see, many forms of speech are less than absolutely protected—even though they are entitled to strict scrutiny. This section will look at these two categories of speech: (1) absolutely protected speech, and (2) conditionally protected speech.

ABSOLUTELY PROTECTED SPEECH

There is one and only one absolute defense against efforts to place limitations on speech, oral or in print: the truth. The truth is protected even when its expression damages the person to whom it applies. And of all forms of speech, political speech is the most consistently protected.

Political Speech   Political speech was the activity of greatest concern to the framers of the Constitution, even though they found it the most difficult provision to observe. Within seven years of the ratification of the Bill of Rights in 1791, Congress adopted the infamous Alien and Sedition Acts, which, among other things, made it a crime to say or publish anything that might tend to defame or bring into disrepute the government of the United States. Quite clearly, the acts' intentions were to criminalize the very conduct given absolute

strict scrutiny

test, used by the Supreme Court in racial discrimination cases and other cases involving civil liberties and civil rights, which places the burden of proof on the government rather than on the challengers to show that the law in question is constitutional

THE PROTECTION OF FREE SPEECH BY THE FIRST AMENDMENT Figure 5.1

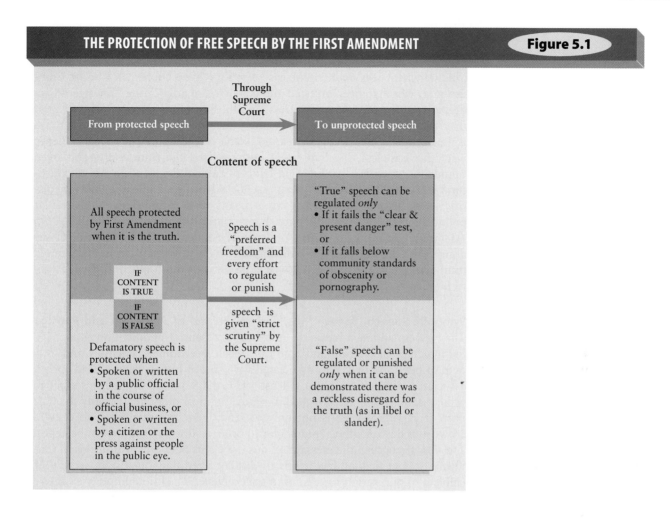

protection by the First Amendment (see also Chapter 9). Fifteen violators—including several newspaper editors—were indicted, and a few were actually convicted before the relevant portions of the acts were allowed to expire.

The first modern free speech case arose immediately after World War I. It involved persons who had been convicted under the federal Espionage Act of 1917 for opposing U.S. involvement in the war. The Supreme Court upheld the Espionage Act and refused to protect the speech rights of the defendants on the grounds that their activities—appeals to draftees to resist the draft—constituted a **"clear and present danger"** to security.[32] This is the first and most famous "test" for when government intervention or censorship could be permitted.

It was only after the 1920s that real progress toward a genuinely effective First Amendment was made. Since then, political speech has been consistently protected by the courts even when it has been deemed "insulting" or "outrageous." Here is the way the Supreme Court put it in one of its most important statements on the subject:

The constitutional guarantees of free speech and free press do not permit a State to forbid or proscribe advocacy of the use of force or of law violation *except where*

"clear and present danger" test

test to determine whether speech is protected or unprotected, based on its capacity to present a "clear and present danger" to society

such advocacy is directed to inciting or producing imminent lawless action and is likely to incite or produce such action [emphasis added].[33]

This statement was made in the case of a Ku Klux Klan leader, Charles Brandenburg, who had been arrested and convicted of advocating "revengent" action against the president, Congress, and the Supreme Court, among others, if they continued "to suppress the white, Caucasian race. . . ." Although Brandenburg was not carrying a weapon, some of the members of his audience were. Nevertheless, the Supreme Court reversed the state courts and freed Brandenburg while also declaring Ohio's Criminal Syndicalism Act unconstitutional because it punished persons who "advocate, or teach the duty, necessity, or propriety [of violence] as a means of accomplishing industrial or political reform . . ."; or who publish materials or "voluntarily assemble . . . to teach or advocate the doctrines of criminal syndicalism." The Supreme Court argued that the statute did not distinguish "mere advocacy" from "incitement to imminent lawless action." It would be difficult to go much further in protecting freedom of speech.

Symbolic Speech, Speech Plus, and the Rights of Assembly and Petition

The First Amendment treats the freedoms of assembly and petition as equal to the freedoms of religion and political speech. Freedom of assembly and freedom of petition are closely associated with speech but go beyond it to speech associated with action. Since at least 1931, the Supreme Court has sought to protect actions that are designed to send a political message. (Usually the purpose of a symbolic act is not only to send a direct message but to draw a crowd—to do something spectacular in order to draw spectators to the action and thus strengthen the message.) Thus the Court held unconstitutional a California statute making it a felony to display a red flag "as a sign, symbol or emblem of opposition to organized government."[34] Although today there are limits on how far one can go with actions that symbolically convey a message, the protection of such action is very broad. Thus, although the Court upheld a federal statute making it a crime to burn draft cards to protest the Vietnam War on the grounds that the government had a compelling interest in preserving draft cards as part of the conduct of the war itself, it considered the wearing of black armbands to school a protected form of assembly for symbolic action.

A more contemporary example is the burning of the American flag as a symbol of protest. In 1984, at a political rally held during the Republican National Convention in Dallas, Texas, a political protester burned an American flag in violation of a Texas statute that prohibited desecration of a venerated object. In a 5-to-4 decision, the Supreme Court declared the Texas law unconstitutional on the grounds that flag burning was expressive conduct protected by the First Amendment.[35] Congress reacted immediately with a proposal for a constitutional amendment reversing the Court's Texas decision, and when the amendment failed to receive the necessary two-thirds majority in the Senate, Congress passed the Flag Protection Act of 1989. Protesters promptly violated this act and their prosecution moved quickly into the federal district court, which declared the new law unconstitutional. The Supreme Court, in another 5-to-4 decision, affirmed the lower court decision.[36] A renewed effort began in Congress to adopt a constitutional amendment that would reverse

Burning the American flag is a constitutionally protected form of symbolic speech.

Antiabortion demonstrators protest outside the Buffalo, N.Y., GYN Womenservices clinic. The Supreme Court has recognized the right of assembly for antiabortion protesters but has allowed the preservation of a "buffer zone" between demonstrators and abortion clinics.

the Supreme Court and place this form of expressive conduct outside the realm of protected speech or assembly.

Closer to the original intent of the assembly and petition clause is the category of **"speech plus"**—following speech with physical activity such as picketing, distributing leaflets, and other forms of peaceful demonstration or assembly. Such assemblies are consistently protected by courts under the First Amendment; state and local laws regulating such activities are closely scrutinized and frequently overturned. But the same assembly on private property is quite another matter and can in many circumstances be regulated. For example, the directors of a shopping center can lawfully prohibit an assembly protesting a war or supporting a ban on abortion. Assemblies in public areas can also be restricted under some circumstances, especially when the assembly or demonstration jeopardizes the health, safety, or rights of others. This condition was the basis of the Supreme Court's decision to uphold a lower court order that restricted the access abortion protesters had to the entrances of abortion clinics.[37]

speech plus

speech accompanied by conduct such as sit-ins, picketing, and demonstrations; protection of this form of speech under the First Amendment is conditional, and restrictions imposed by state or local authorities are acceptable if properly balanced by considerations of public order

CONDITIONALLY PROTECTED SPEECH

At least four forms of speech fall outside the absolute guarantees of the First Amendment and therefore outside the realm of absolute protection. Since they do enjoy some protection, they qualify as "conditionally protected" types of speech: (1) libel and slander, (2) obscenity and pornography, (3) fighting words, and (4) commercial speech. It should be emphasized once again that these four types of speech still enjoy considerable protection by the courts.

Libel and Slander   Some speech is not protected at all. If a written statement is made in "reckless disregard of the truth" and is considered damaging to the victim because it is "malicious, scandalous, and defamatory," it can be

libel

a written statement made in "reckless disregard of the truth" that is considered damaging to a victim because it is "malicious, scandalous, and defamatory"

slander

an oral statement, made in "reckless disregard of the truth," which is considered damaging to the victim because it is "malicious, scandalous, and defamatory"

Larry Flynt, the publisher of *Hustler,* spoke with reporters following the Supreme Court's decision in favor of the magazine.

punished as **libel.** If an oral statement of such nature is made, it can be punished as **slander.**

Today, most libel suits involve freedom of the press, and the realm of free press is enormous. Historically, newspapers were subject to the law of libel, which provided that newspapers that printed false and malicious stories could be compelled to pay damages to those they defamed. In recent years, however, American courts have greatly narrowed the meaning of libel and made it extremely difficult, particularly for politicians or other public figures, to win a libel case against a newspaper. In the important 1964 case of *New York Times v. Sullivan,* the Court held that to be deemed libelous a story about a public official not only had to be untrue, but also had to result from "actual malice" or "reckless disregard" for the truth.[38] In other words, the newspaper had to *deliberately* print false and malicious material. In practice, it is nearly impossible to prove that a paper deliberately printed maliciously false information and, as conservatives discovered in the 1980s, it is especially difficult for a politician or other public figure to win a libel case. Libel suits against CBS News by General William Westmoreland and against *Time* magazine by Israeli general Ariel Sharon, suits that were financed by conservative legal foundations that hoped to embarrass the media, were both defeated in court because they failed to show "actual malice." In the 1991 case of *Masson v. New Yorker Magazine,* this tradition was again affirmed when the Court held that fabricated quotations attributed to a public figure were libelous only if the fabricated account "materially changed" the meaning of what the person actually said.[39] Essentially, the print media have been able to publish anything they want about a public figure.

However, in at least one recent case, the Court has opened up the possibility for public officials to file libel suits against the press. In 1985, the Court held that the press was immune from libel only when the printed material was "a matter of public concern." In other words in future cases a newspaper would have to show that the public official was engaged in activities that were indeed *public.* This new principle has made the press more vulnerable to libel suits, but it still leaves an enormous realm of freedom for the press. For example, Reverend Jerry Falwell, the leader of the Moral Majority, lost his libel suit against *Hustler* magazine even though the magazine had published a cartoon of Falwell showing him having drunken intercourse with his mother in an outhouse. A unanimous Supreme Court rejected a jury verdict in favor of damages for "emotional distress" on the grounds that parodies, no matter how outrageous, are protected because "outrageousness" is too subjective a test and thus would interfere with the free flow of ideas protected by the First Amendment.[40]

Obscenity and Pornography If libel and slander cases can be difficult because of the problem of determining the truth of statements and whether those statements are malicious and damaging, cases involving pornography and obscenity can be even more sticky. It is easy to say that pornography and obscenity fall outside the realm of protected speech, but it is impossible to draw a clear line defining exactly where protection ends and unprotected speech begins. Not until 1957 did the Supreme Court confront this problem, and it did so with a definition of obscenity that may have caused more confusion than it cleared up. Justice William Brennan, in writing the Court's opinion, defined

Pornography and the Internet

The Internet was created in the 1960s as a way for scattered military researchers to communicate with each other via computer. It has now grown into a vast electronic gathering place for hundreds of thousands of people. By its very nature, the Internet is not easy to regulate or restrict. Users roam the "Net" from the anonymity and isolation of their own computers, posting whatever they wish and encountering all kinds of activities and writings: academic forums where researchers from around the world can share ideas and findings; bulletin boards for people who want to talk about any of thousands of topics; diatribes against the government and detailed instructions for making fertilizer-and-fuel-oil bombs; and the rawest kinds of written and visual pornography.

In 1994, Jake Baker, a sophomore at the University of Michigan, wrote a violent sexual fantasy and posted it on the Internet. The story described in vivid detail the capture, rape, torture, and murder of a young woman, a fellow Michigan student whom he identified by name. Others read the posted story; afterwards Mr. Baker and one of his readers in Canada exchanged E-mail about carrying out such an attack. Eventually Mr. Baker was charged with a federal crime: transmitting a threat over state lines by electronic mails. He could have received a prison term of up to five years in jail had he been convicted, but a federal judge dismissed the charge, saying that it would be more appropriate for university officials to discipline Mr. Baker.

Stories such as this have become increasingly familiar in recent years. Are they rare exceptions, or is the Internet dangerously unregulated? How comfortable are we that children can easily access explicit pornographic images and stories over the Internet, or that the anonymity provided by the Internet gives those who wish to the perfect means to befriend and arrange to meet unsuspecting young children? Such concerns have prompted recent calls to regulate the Internet. In the summer of 1995, the Republican majority in the Senate actually passed a bill sponsored by the then–majority leader, Bob Dole, to impose censorship on the Net. Dole proposed outlawing obscenity or sexually explicit material from being posted on computer networks, imposing fines of up to $100,000 on anyone who makes indecent sexual material available to minors via computer, and making the transmission of indecent or harassing messages, such as Jake Baker's, a crime.

Community standards of decency, even within the high-tech "community" of computer networks, are an important value for Republicans. But so is freedom of expression. After Senate Republicans won passage of the bill to regulate the Internet, the Speaker of the House, Newt Gingrich, came out squarely against it: "It is clearly a violation of free speech, and it's a violation of the right of adults to communicate with each other."[1] Gingrich argued that rather than having the government censor the Internet, control should fall to the marketplace, by letting commercial on-line services regulate the material they permit to be posted.

The Internet and its progeny, such as the World Wide Web, are the frontier of modern communication. As technology continues to develop, as costs decline, and as computer literacy spreads, electronic communities and computer communication will surely claim an even greater role in people's lives. And as with all frontier communities, the inhabitants of this community face a challenge in deciding how to police it and what balance of freedom and control to impose upon it. These are political questions, to be settled ultimately by legislatures. But such political questions have their roots in our cultural values. What sort of communities do we wish to live in? How should we choose to balance individual rights against an ordered society?

[1]Edmund L. Andrews, "Gingrich Opposes Smut Rule for Internet," *New York Times*, June 22, 1995, p. A20.

obscenity as speech or writing that appeals to the "prurient interest"—that is, books, magazines, films, etc. whose purpose is to excite lust as this appears "to the average person, applying contemporary community standards. . . ." Even so, Brennan added, the work should be judged obscene only when it is "utterly without redeeming social importance."[41] Brennan's definition, instead of clarifying the Court's view, actually caused more confusion. In 1964, Justice Potter Stewart confessed that, although he found pornography impossible to define, "I know it when I see it."[42]

All attempts by the courts to define pornography and obscenity have proved impractical, because each instance required courts to screen thousands of pages of print material and feet of film alleged to be pornographic. The vague and impractical standards that had been developed meant ultimately that almost nothing could be banned on the grounds that it was pornographic and obscene. An effort was made to strengthen the restrictions in 1973, when the Supreme Court expressed its willingness to define pornography as a work which (1) as a whole, is deemed prurient by the "average person" according to "community standards"; (2) depicts sexual conduct "in a patently offensive way"; and (3) lacks "serious literary, artistic, political, or scientific value." This definition meant that pornography would be determined by local rather than national standards. Thus, a local bookseller might be prosecuted for selling a volume that was a best-seller nationally but that was deemed pornographic locally.[43] This new definition of standards did not help much either, and not long after 1973 the Court began again to review all such community antipornography laws, reversing most of them.

Consequently, today there is a widespread fear that Americans are free to publish any and all variety of intellectual expression, whether there is any "redeeming social value" or not. Yet this area of free speech is far from settled. The search continues for limits to the protection of speech that tends toward the pornographic and obscene. In fact, a surprising new alliance has formed between conservative groups in America and a number of leading feminists.

Demonstrators both for and against the 1996 Communications Decency Act gather outside the Supreme Court. The Court unanimously struck down the act, which would have made it a crime to make "indecent" or "patently offensive" works or pictures available on-line, where they can be accessed by children.

Both mainstream conservatives and the religious Right adamantly believe that virtually nothing of even a barely suggestive and subtle pornographic or obscene nature deserves the protection of the First Amendment. Thus, conservatives are actively supporting state and local antipornography and obscenity legislation and vigorous police enforcement of what they broadly call "standards of decency." Their influence has been felt keenly by top politicians, including 1996 Republican presidential candidate Bob Dole, who publicly condemned the movies and musical output of communications giant Time Warner.[44] Conservatives have joined forces with an impressive number of feminists on the basis of the feminist argument that every pornographic statement is an act of violence against women and should be censored by law. If the Constitution has to be changed or reinterpreted to permit passage of such laws, they support that as well.[45]

A second example of the contemporary battle against obscene speech is that against "cyberporn"—pornography on the Internet. Opponents of this form of expression argue that it should be banned because of the easy access children have to the Internet. Wildly different estimates have been made of the extent and availability of cyberporn, and there are equally vast differences of opinion on the effect of cyberporn on the viewer. Where obscenity and pornography are concerned, Internet technology has simply made the line between free speech and regulated speech impossible to draw. The Supreme Court tried to draw such a line in its 1973 opinion in *Miller v. California,* providing that "contemporary community standards" should be used to determine whether a law restricting pornographic and obscene materials is appropriate. But such a rule can no longer be applied, for the obvious reason that Internet communication is nationwide—and worldwide. It is no longer a matter of what to do about *Playboy* on the shelves of the local newsstand.

The first major effort to regulate the content of the Internet occurred on February 1, 1996, when the 104th Congress passed major telecommunications legislation. Attached to the Telecommunications Act was an amendment, called the Communications Decency Act (CDA), that was designed to regulate the on-line transmission of obscene material. On the same day that President Clinton signed the Telecommunications Act, and the CDA, into law the constitutionality of the CDA was challenged in court by a coalition of interests led by the ACLU. In June a panel of federal judges ruled that the CDA violated the First Amendment to the Constitution. The Department of Justice, citing the need to protect America's children from explicit sexual material on the Internet, appealed the decision to the Supreme Court. In the ensuing case, *Reno v. ACLU,* the Court heard oral arguments on both sides of the issue. In a broad endorsement of free speech on the Internet, the Court struck down the CDA, ruling that it suppressed speech that "adults have a constitutional right to receive." The Court gave several reasons for its decision. First, the CDA's "indecent transmission" and "patently offensive display" were too broad and vague to meet the strict scrutiny of the First Amendment's free speech provisions. Second, the language was too broad and therefore protected children at the price of suppressing speech that adults have a right to send and receive. Governments, as the court argued, may not limit the adult population to messages that are fit for children. "The level of discourse reaching the mailbox simply cannot be limited to that which would be suitable for a sandbox." Moreover, "odds are slim" that a user would enter a sexually

POLITICS ON THE WEB

The Internet is now a crucial forum for battles over civil liberties. The World Wide Web allows any group, regardless of ideology or doctrine, to reach an audience of millions. Because of the low cost of establishing a site, groups that many consider reprehensible are able easily to spread their views all across the country. Whether a neo-Nazi, a pornographer, or a member of an antigovernment militia, anyone can voice his or her beliefs over the Internet. For example, since the 1995 bombing of the federal building in Oklahoma City, the Internet has been blamed for providing bomb-making instruction to those who could not otherwise get such information. This raises a fundamental constitutional issue: Should limitations on free expression exist? If a child can go on the Internet to a site run by a militia group and learn how to make a bomb, whose responsibility is it to protect that child? It is these issues that must be faced by the Congress and the courts and that will ultimately complicate any proposed Internet legislation.
www.wwnorton.com/wtp2e.

explicit site by accident; unlike communications received by radio or television, "the receipt of information on the Internet requires a series of affirmative steps more deliberate and directed than merely turning a dial. A child requires some sophistication and some ability to read to retrieve material and thereby to use the Internet unattended." In other words, factors that permit the regulation of radio or television—such as setting the "time, place and manner" of certain speech—"are not present in cyberspace." The Internet, the Court argued, is not as "invasive" as radio or television because communications do not appear on one's computer screen "unbidden"; and users rarely encounter Internet content "by accident." The implication of the Court's argument is that parents can control what their children receive, and, in any case, software for more effective parental protection of their own children "will soon be widely available."[46]

Although *Reno v. ACLU* is being called the most important First Amendment case to reach the Supreme Court in many years, it is likely that the Court will hear other cases dealing with the Internet in the near future; several states have passed, considered, or are considering legislation to regulate the Internet. In 1995 and 1996, at least eleven states passed legislation regulating on-line content.

fighting words

speech that directly incites damaging conduct

Fighting Words Speech can also lose its protected position when it moves toward the sphere of action. "Expressive speech," for example, is protected until it moves from the symbolic realm to the realm of actual conduct—to direct incitement of damaging conduct with the use of so-called **fighting words.** In 1942, the Supreme Court upheld the arrest and conviction of a man who had violated a state law forbidding the use of offensive language in public. He had called the arresting officer a "goddamned racketeer" and "a damn Fascist." When his case reached the Supreme Court, the arrest was upheld on the grounds that the First Amendment provides no protection for such offensive language because such words "are no essential part of any exposition of ideas."[47] This case was reaffirmed in a much more famous and important case decided at the height of the cold war, when the Supreme Court held that "there is no substantial public interest in permitting certain kinds of utterances: the lewd and obscene, the profane, the libelous, and the insulting or 'fighting' words—those which by their very utterance inflict injury or tend to incite an immediate breach of the peace."[48]

Since that time, however, the Supreme Court has reversed almost every conviction based on arguments that the speaker had used "fighting words." But again, that does not mean that this is an absolutely settled area. In recent years, the increased activism of minority and women's groups has prompted a movement against words that might be construed as offensive to members of a particular group. This movement has come to be called, derisively, "political correctness." In response to

Students and Politics

In 1988, the Supreme Court dealt a major blow to the freedom of public high school journalists in *Hazelwood School District v. Kuhlmeier.* Students and their supporters charged that Hazelwood East High School in suburban St. Louis had censored articles concerning teen pregnancy and the effects of divorce on children, in violation of the writers' First Amendment rights. The Court, in a 5-to-3 decision, ruled that because the newspaper was school-sponsored and thus part of the educational process, it could be regulated by the school district. In his majority opinion, Justice Byron White wrote that three criteria determined the applicability of a publication to be censored: 1) Is it supervised by a faculty member? 2) Was the publication designed to impart particular knowledge or skills to student participants or audiences? and 3) Does the publication use the school's name or resources? Some states, including Arkansas, California, Colorado, Iowa, Kansas, and Massachusetts, have laws that protect the First Amendment rights of such publications, and, in light of *Hazelwood,* many states are considering such legislation.

this movement, many organizations have attempted to impose codes of etiquette that acknowledge these enhanced sensitivities. These efforts to formalize the restraints on the use of certain words in public are causing great concern over their possible infringement of freedom of speech. But how should we determine what words are "fighting words" that fall outside the protections of the freedom of speech?

One category of conditionally protected speech is the free speech of high school students in public schools. In 1986, the Supreme Court backed away from a broad protection of student free-speech rights by upholding the punishment of a high school student for making sexually suggestive speech. The Court opinion held that such speech interfered with the school's goal of teaching students the limits of socially acceptable behavior.[52] Two years later, the Supreme Court took another conservative step and restricted student speech and press rights even further by defining them as part of the educational process not to be treated with the same standard as adult speech in a regular public forum.[53]

In addition, scores of universities have attempted to develop speech codes to suppress utterances deemed to be racial or ethnic slurs. What these universities find, however, is that the codes produce more problems than they solve. The University of Pennsylvania learned this when it first tried to apply its newly written "Harassment Code." Around midnight in January of 1993, Eden Jacobowitz and several other students trying to study yelled from their dorm windows at a noisy group of partying black sorority members: "Shut up, you water buffaloes." Other students also made rude comments, including racial and sexual slurs, but Jacobowitz was the only one who actually came forward and admitted to having yelled. Born in Israel and fluent in Hebrew, Jacobowitz explained that "water buffalo" loosely translated from Hebrew means "rude person." Nevertheless, the University of Pennsylvania brought Jacobowitz before a campus judicial inquiry board and charged him with racial harassment in violation of the new code. The black women at whom he had yelled also brought civil charges of racial harassment against Jacobowitz. Five months after the incident, all charges were dropped—both the civil charges and those brought by the university. After reviewing the matter, Penn officials confessed that the university's harassment code "contained flaws which could not withstand the stress of intense publicity and international attention."[49]

Such concerns are not limited to universities, although universities have probably moved furthest toward efforts to formalize "politically correct" speech guidelines. Similar developments have taken place in large corporations, both public and private, in which many successful complaints and lawsuits have been brought, alleging that the words of employers or their supervisors

Students and Politics

In the early 1990s, colleges around the nation were grappling with the implementation of speech codes: rules of conduct forbidding spoken, written, or broadcast words on race, sex, religion, sexual preference, or national origin that might offend some students. At the University of Massachusetts, Lowell, the editors of the student newspaper, the *Connector,* published a cartoon meant to mock overzealous protesters. One side of the drawing showed an animal rights activist, with the caption, "Some of my best friends are laboratory rats." The other side of the graphic depicted a death penalty advocate, with the legend underneath, "None of his best friends are young, black males." Lowell's administration charged the editors with creating a "hostile environment," assigned them thirty hours of community service, and forced them to resign their positions at the newspaper. The *Connector* took a dim view of the administration's attempt to control speech. "They have had problems in the past with recruiting black students; the administration has been under the gun," said editor Patty Janice. "Attacking us was the easiest way to make it look like they were doing something on the issue." The administration eventually dropped the charges.

Students such as the editors at the *Connector* have led a fight to limit speech codes on college campuses across the nation. Proponents of speech codes consider hostile words to be a form of assault, or "fighting words." Others consider the banning of offensive speech to be a violation of the First Amendment. For now, the events seem to favor those who stand against speech codes.

SOURCE: David G. Savage "Forbidden Words on Campus," *Los Angeles Times,* Tuesday, February 12, 1991, p. A1.

create a "hostile or abusive working environment." These cases arise out of the civil rights laws and will be addressed in more detail in Chapter 6. The Supreme Court has held that "sexual harassment" that creates a "hostile working environment" includes "unwelcome sexual advances, requests for sexual favors, and other *verbal* or physical conduct of a sexual nature" (emphasis added).[50] There is a fundamental free speech issue involved in these regulations of hostile speech. So far, the assumption favoring the regulation of hostile speech in universities and other workplaces is that "some speech must be shut down in the name of free speech because it tends to silence those disparaged by it,"[51] even though a threat of hostile action (usually embodied in "fighting words") is not present. The United States is on something of a collision course between the right to express hostile views and the protection of the sensitivities of minorities and women. The collisions will end up in the courts, but not before a lot more airing in public and balancing efforts by state legislatures and Congress.

The government has taken steps to curb tobacco advertising, including a 1997 ban on all advertising in sporting events. This auto racing crew member wears a shirt that voices the displeasure felt by those in a sport that depends on tobacco advertising.

Commercial Speech   Commercial speech, such as newspaper or television advertisements, does not have full First Amendment protection because it cannot be considered political speech. Initially considered to be entirely outside the protection of the First Amendment, commercial speech has made gains during the twentieth century. Some commercial speech is still unprotected and therefore regulated. For example, the regulation of false and misleading advertising by the Federal Trade Commission is an old and well-established power of the federal government. The Supreme Court long ago approved the constitutionality of laws prohibiting the electronic media from carrying cigarette advertising.[54] The Court has also upheld a state university ban on Tupperware parties in college dormitories.[55] It has also upheld city ordinances prohibiting the posting of all signs on public property (as long as the ban is total, so that there is no hint of censorship).[56] And the Supreme Court, in a heated 5-to-4 decision written by Chief Justice William Rehnquist, upheld Puerto Rico's statute restricting gambling advertising aimed at residents of Puerto Rico.[57]

However, the gains far outweigh the losses in the effort to expand the protection commercial speech enjoys under the First Amendment. "In part, this reflects the growing appreciation that commercial speech is part of the free flow of information necessary for informed choice and democratic participation."[58] For example, the Court in 1975 struck down a state statute making it a misdemeanor to sell or circulate newspapers encouraging abortions; the Court ruled that the statute infringed upon constitutionally protected speech and upon the right of the reader to make informed choices.[59] On a similar basis, the Court reversed its own earlier decisions upholding laws that prohibited dentists and other professionals from advertising their services. For the Court, medical service advertising was a matter of health that could be advanced by the free flow of information.[60] In 1983, the Supreme Court struck down a congressional statute that prohibited the unsolicited mailing of advertisements for contraceptives. And in 1996 the Supreme Court struck down Rhode Island laws and regulations banning the advertisement of liquor prices as a violation of the First Amendment.[61] These instances of commercial speech are significant in themselves, but they are all the more significant because they indicate the breadth and depth of the freedom existing today to direct appeals broadly to a large public, not only to sell goods and services but also to mobilize people for political purposes.

The Second Amendment and the Right to Bear Arms

▶ Is the right to bear arms guaranteed by the Bill of Rights? How is its exercise restricted?

A well regulated Militia, being necessary to the security of a free State, the right of the people to keep and bear Arms, shall not be infringed.

The Second Amendment may seem to some to be the product of a long-ago, quaint era, but it is very much alive in spirit and has emerged as one of America's most pressing contemporary public issues.

The point and purpose of the Second Amendment is the provision for militias; they were to be the backing of the government for the maintenance of local public order. "Militia" was understood at the time of the Founding to be a military or police resource for state governments, and militias were specifically distinguished from armies and troops, which came within the sole constitutional jurisdiction of Congress. Under Article I, Section 8, Congress was given the power

To declare war; . . . To raise and support Armies; . . . To provide and maintain a Navy; . . . To provide for calling forth the Militia to execute the Laws of the Union, suppress Insurrections and repel Invasions; . . . [and] to provide for organizing, arming, and disciplining, the Militia, and for governing such Part of them as may be employed in the Service of the United States, reserving to the States respectively . . . the Authority of training the Militia according to the discipline prescribed by Congress.

Article I, Section 10, made it quite explicit that "no State shall, without the Consent of Congress . . . keep Troops, or Ships of War in time of Peace, . . . or engage in War." The Supreme Court went even further, in the turbulent year of 1939, with the holding that

the Militia which the States were expected to maintain and train is set in contrast with Troops which they were forbidden to keep without the consent of Congress. The sentiment of the time strongly disfavored standing armies; the common view was that adequate defense of country and laws could be secured through the Militia—civilians primarily, soldiers on occasion.[62]

Thus, there seems to be no question that the right of people to bear arms is based upon and associated with participation in a state militia. Nevertheless, individuals do have a constitutional right to bear arms, as is provided in the second half of the amendment. The experience of Americans with colonial military rule pointed the Founders and their supporters to the need of every citizen for some kind of personal self-defense. One of the fundamental requirements of a strong government is that it have a monopoly on the use of force. Broad distribution of guns in the hands of citizens does in fact weaken the government, for better or for worse. When confronted with the issue in those terms, few Americans would be likely to approve of an American government possessing a monopoly on force, with a totally disarmed citizenry. The fundamental right of Americans to own weapons is promoted by one of America's

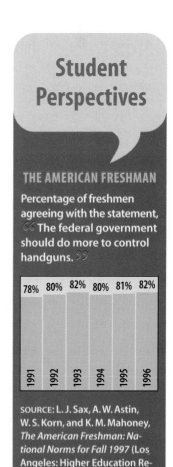

Student Perspectives

THE AMERICAN FRESHMAN

Percentage of freshmen agreeing with the statement, ❝ The federal government should do more to control handguns. ❞

1991	1992	1993	1994	1995	1996
78%	80%	82%	80%	81%	82%

SOURCE: L. J. Sax, A. W. Astin, W. S. Korn, and K. M. Mahoney, *The American Freshman: National Norms for Fall 1997* (Los Angeles: Higher Education Research Institute, UCLA Graduate School of Education, 1997).

The right to bear arms seems unquestionable, although states are allowed to regulate the sale of weapons by requiring a waiting period or a background check on the purchaser.

Former presidential press secretary James Brady salutes the crowd at the Democratic National Convention. Brady supported a congressional bill to establish a waiting period for the purchase of handguns so that background checks could be made on the purchaser. The Supreme Court declared part of the law to be in violation of the Second Amendment.

biggest and most influential contemporary interest groups, the National Rifle Association (NRA).

But the line drawn between owning weapons as part of a militia or army, on the one hand, and as individuals, on the other, raises some complex questions, for which neither the NRA nor its adversaries have good answers. For example, can clear boundaries be drawn around technologies, separating weapons for defense of home and hearth from offensive weapons of massive destructive power? Can a distinction be made between arms necessary for participation in a "well regulated militia" and for individual antipersonnel defense, on the one hand, and weapons used as part of an individual's participation in *private* militias not sponsored or regulated by government, on the other? And, given the absoluteness of the Second Amendment—that "the right of the people to keep and bear Arms, shall not be infringed"—does any government have any authority to draw the boundaries alluded to above?

Part of the answer to these questions can be found in the amendment itself. A "well regulated" militia implies that the state governments *do* have power to regulate the arms as well as the arms bearers. And in Article I, Section 8, clauses 15 and 16, the Constitution seems to be unmistakably clear: Congress is given the power of "calling forth the Militia to execute the Laws of the Union, . . ." and the power "to provide for organizing, arming, and disciplining, the Militia, and for governing such Part of them as may be employed in the Service of the United States. . . ." The Constitution then reinforces the power of the States by granting them the power to appoint the officers and provide for the training of the militia "according to the discipline prescribed by Congress."

Congress tried to exercise its power in 1993 with adoption of the Brady Handgun Violence Prevention Act (Brady Act), as an amendment to the Gun Control Act of 1968. The law took its name from James S. Brady, an aide to President Ronald Reagan who was disabled in the 1981 assassination attempt on the president. Among its provisions was the requirement that state and local law enforcement officials conduct background checks on prospective handgun purchasers. Two local law enforcement officers sued in court, questioning the constitutionality of the Brady Act on the grounds that Congress has no authority to require state and local officials to implement federal laws. Moreover, they claimed that as an "unfunded federal mandate" the law imposed unfair burdens on them and unfair diversions of resources from their other responsibilities to maintain law and order in their communities. The Supreme Court, in a close decision, agreed with the plaintiffs.[63] This case is a small but significant step back toward a pre–New Deal concept of federalism, making a national program of handgun regulation a lot more difficult. But it in no way gives handgun owners a constitutional right to buy, sell, and possess weapons completely free of federal, state, and local regulation.

Thus American citizens unquestionably have a right to bear arms, but the exercise of this right can be regulated by both state and federal law. Within this well-designed domain, however, are no rules for what is wise and what is foolish legislation, or what is appropriate and what is inappropriate regulation. Issues such as these have to be settled through the political process, not by courts—and certainly not by arms, even if Americans do have a right to bear them.[64]

★ Rights of the Criminally Accused

▶ What is due process?
▶ How do the Fourth, Fifth, Sixth, and Eighth Amendments provide for the due process of law?

Except for the First Amendment, most of the battle to apply the Bill of Rights to the states was fought over the various protections granted to individuals who are accused of a crime, who are suspects in the commission of a crime, or who are brought before the court as a witness to a crime. The Fourth, Fifth, Sixth, and Eighth Amendments, taken together, are the essence of the due process of law, even though this fundamental concept does not appear until the very last words of the Fifth Amendment. Even the Supreme Court itself has admitted that "due process of law" cannot be given a precise and final definition or explanation. In lieu of an outright definition, the Court maintains the position it took over a century ago: it prefers to rely on "the gradual process of judicial inclusion and exclusion" to indicate the meaning of "due process."[65]

Because most criminal laws in the United States exist at the state level, most of the questions over due process have concerned state laws as applied by state police, state prosecutors, and state courts. In the next sections we will look at specific cases that illuminate the dynamics of this important constitutional issue. The procedural safeguards that we will discuss may seem remote to most law-abiding citizens, but they help define the limits of government action against the personal liberty of every citizen.

THE RIGHTS OF THE ACCUSED FROM ARREST TO TRIAL

No improper searches and seizures (4th Amendment)
No arrest without probable cause (4th Amendment)
Right to remain silent (5th Amendment)
No self-incrimination during arrest or trial (5th Amendment)
Right to be informed of charges (6th Amendment)
Right to counsel (6th Amendment)
No excessive bail (8th Amendment)
Right to grand jury (5th Amendment)
Right to open trial before a judge (Article 1, Section 9)
Right to speedy and public trial before an impartial jury (6th Amendment)
Evidence obtained by illegal search not admissible during trial (4th Amendment)
Right to confront witnesses (6th Amendment)
No double jeopardy (5th Amendment)
No cruel and unusual punishment (8th Amendment)

The O.J. Simpson trials illustrated the differences between the evidence needed to convict in criminal vs. civil cases. During his criminal trial, Simpson's dramatic difficulty in donning a glove found at the scene of the crime helped to establish "a reasonable doubt" in the jurors' minds. In the later civil case against Simpson, however, the prosecution needed only "the preponderance of the evidence" (a strong probability of guilt) for conviction.

In all court matters involving crime, "the state" is the plaintiff, or the party charging an individual with the crime: *"New York v. Jones," "New Jersey v. Smith,"* or *"The People of the State of California v. Orenthal James Simpson."* The idea of the entire power of a state being arrayed against a defendant is pretty imposing; it seems unequal even if the accused has the resources to hire renowned attorneys for his or her defense—as O. J. Simpson did, for example. Few defendants have the resources that Simpson did, and therefore the requirements of due process are an attempt to equalize the playing field between an accused individual and the all-powerful state.

Many Americans believe that "legal technicalities" are responsible for setting many actual criminals free. In many cases, that is absolutely true. In fact, setting defendants free is the very purpose of the requirements that constitute due process. One of America's traditional and most strongly held juridical values is that "it is far worse to convict an innocent man than to let a guilty man go free."[66] In civil suits, verdicts rest upon "the preponderance of the evidence"; in criminal cases, guilt has to be proven "beyond a reasonable doubt"—a far higher standard. The provisions for due process in the Bill of Rights were added in order to improve the probability that the standard of "reasonable doubt" will be respected.

THE FOURTH AMENDMENT AND SEARCHES AND SEIZURES

> The right of the people to be secure in their persons, houses, papers, and effects, against unreasonable searches and seizures, shall not be violated, and no Warrants shall issue, but upon probable cause, supported by Oath or affirmation, and particularly describing the place to be searched, and the persons or things to be seized.

The purpose of the Fourth Amendment is to guarantee the security of citizens against unreasonable (i.e., improper) searches and seizures. In 1990 the Supreme Court summarized its understanding of the Fourth Amendment brilliantly and succinctly: "A search compromises the individual interest in privacy; a seizure deprives the individual of dominion over his or her person or property."[67]

These high school band members were searched for weapons before a football game in Birmingham, Alabama. A reasonable search?

But how are we to define what is reasonable and what is unreasonable? Generally, in the administration of justice in the United States, the decision about whether a search is reasonable is in the hands of judges and courts. First of all, it is the courts that issue a warrant before a search or arrest can be made. If a court has issued a warrant for a search, that search is considered reasonable. But in some circumstances, the time or opportunity may not be available for a court-issued warrant to be obtained. For example, a police officer has the authority to ask a person on the street to give "credible and reliable" identification and to account for his or her presence. But if that person refuses to cooperate and the officer has to take additional steps to get a response, the Fourth Amendment comes into play. The officer must have "probable cause," or reasonable suspicion that the person may be involved in a crime, to detain him or her for further inquiry. Whether such "probable cause" exists is another decision made by a judge or court.

When a crime has occurred and the investigation of it begins, the police often face a thicket of unknowns, and they are always operating on the verge of trampling valuable evidence or violating the rights of suspects and witnesses. The O. J. Simpson case is illustrative. Without eyewitnesses or videotapes to indicate who had committed two murders, the police had to search for clues. In the hysteria following the public revelation of such a scandal involving an extraordinary celebrity, the murder scene was trampled, potentially valuable evidence was mishandled, accounts of events were inconsistent, and expert reports and lab results from samples of blood, clothing, grass, and soil were inconclusive or uncertain. Should a person's fate hang (pardon the pun) on such evidence?

Often the American public expresses frustration when a jury delivers an acquittal in a case involving a prominent suspect or a seemingly solid presentation of evidence. But, as with freedom of speech and the press, if Americans genuinely support the right to a fair trial, they must also support the acquittal of the accused when the police or the courts fail to adhere to due process.

The 1961 case of *Mapp v. Ohio* illustrates the beauty and the agony of one of the most important procedures that have grown out of the Fourth Amendment—the **exclusionary rule,** which prohibits evidence obtained during an illegal search from being introduced in a trial. Dollree (Dolly) Mapp was "a Cleveland woman of questionable reputation" (by some accounts), the ex-wife of one prominent boxer, and the fiancée of an even more famous one. Acting on a tip that Dolly Mapp was harboring a suspect in a bombing incident, several policemen forcibly entered Ms. Mapp's house claiming they had a warrant to look for the bombing suspect. The police did not find the bombing suspect but did find some materials connected to the local numbers racket (an illegal gambling operation) and a quantity of "obscene materials," in violation of an Ohio law banning possession of such materials. Although the warrant was never produced, the evidence that had been seized was admitted by a court, and Ms. Mapp was charged and convicted for illegal possession of obscene materials.

By the time Ms. Mapp's appeal reached the Supreme Court, the issue of obscene materials had faded into obscurity, and the question before the Court was whether any evidence produced under the circumstances of the search of her home was admissible. The Court's opinion affirmed the exclusionary rule: under the Fourth Amendment (applied to the states through the Fourteenth Amendment), "all evidence obtained by searches and seizures in violation of

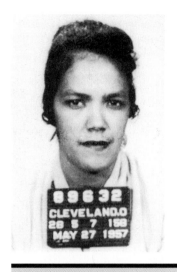

Dollree Mapp's lawsuit against the Cleveland Police Department went to the Supreme Court and nationalized the exclusionary rule.

exclusionary rule

the ability of courts to exclude evidence obtained in violation of the Fourth Amendment

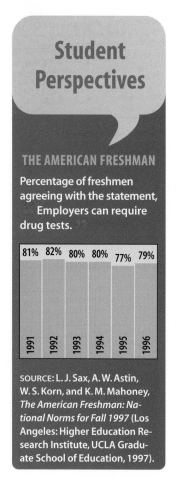

Student Perspectives

THE AMERICAN FRESHMAN

Percentage of freshmen agreeing with the statement, Employers can require drug tests.

1991	1992	1993	1994	1995	1996
81%	82%	80%	80%	77%	79%

SOURCE: L. J. Sax, A. W. Astin, W. S. Korn, and K. M. Mahoney, *The American Freshman: National Norms for Fall 1997* (Los Angeles: Higher Education Research Institute, UCLA Graduate School of Education, 1997).

the Constitution . . . is inadmissible."[68] This means that even people who are clearly guilty of the crime of which they are accused must not be convicted if the only evidence for their conviction was obtained illegally.

The exclusionary rule is the most severe restraint ever imposed by the Constitution and the courts on the behavior of the police. The exclusionary rule is so dramatic a restriction because it rules out precisely the evidence that produces a conviction; it frees those people who are *known* to have committed the crime of which they have been accused. Because it works so dramatically in favor of persons known to have committed a crime, the Court has since softened the application of the rule. In recent years, the federal courts have relied upon a discretionary use of the exclusionary rule, whereby they make a judgment as to the "nature and quality of the intrusion." It is thus difficult to know ahead of time whether a defendant will or will not be protected from an illegal search under the Fourth Amendment.[69]

Another recent issue involving the Fourth Amendment is the controversy over mandatory drug testing. Such tests are most widely used on public employees, and in an important case the Supreme Court has upheld the U.S. Customs Service's drug-testing program for its employees.[70] The same year the Court approved drug and alcohol tests for railroad workers if they were involved in serious accidents.[71] After Court approvals of those two cases in 1989, more than forty federal agencies initiated mandatory employee drug tests. The practice of drug testing was reinforced by a presidential executive order widely touted as the "campaign for a drug-free federal workplace." These growing practices gave rise to public appeals against the general practice of "suspicionless testing" of employees. Regardless of the proven need to limit the spread of drug abuse, working in this manner through public employees seemed patently unconstitutional, in violation of the Fourth Amendment. Another recent case, in which the Court upheld a public school district's policy requiring all students participating in interscholastic sports to submit to random drug tests, surely contributed to the efforts of federal, state, and local agencies to initiate random and suspicionless drug and alcohol testing.[72] But since three and sometimes four justices dissent against these cases, a more balanced and restrained approach may be developed.[73]

THE FIFTH AMENDMENT

> No person shall be held to answer for a capital, or otherwise infamous crime, unless on a presentment or indictment of a Grand Jury, except in cases arising in the land or naval forces, or in the Militia, when in actual service in time of War or public danger; nor shall any person be subject for the same offence to be twice put in jeopardy of life or limb; nor shall be compelled in any criminal case to be a witness against himself, nor be deprived of life, liberty, or property, without due process of law; nor shall private property be taken for public use, without just compensation.

grand jury

jury that determines whether sufficient evidence is available to justify a trial; grand juries do not rule on the accused's guilt or innocence.

Grand Juries   The first clause of the Fifth Amendment, the right to a **grand jury** to determine whether a trial is warranted, is considered "the oldest institution known to the Constitution."[74] Grand juries play an important role in federal criminal cases. However, the provision for a grand jury is the one important civil liberties provision of the Bill of Rights that was not incorporated by the Fourteenth Amendment to apply to state criminal prosecutions. Thus, some states operate without grand juries. In such states, the prosecuting attorney simply files a "bill of information" affirming that there is sufficient evidence available to justify a trial. If the accused person is to be held in custody, the prosecutor must take the available information before a judge to determine that the evidence shows probable cause.

Double Jeopardy "Nor shall any person be subject for the same offence to be twice put in jeopardy of life or limb" is the constitutional protection from **double jeopardy,** or being tried more than once for the same crime. The protection from double jeopardy was at the heart of the *Palko* case in 1937, which, as we saw earlier in this chapter, also established the principle of selective incorporation of the Bill of Rights. In that case, the state of Connecticut had indicted Frank Palko for first-degree murder, but a lower court had found him guilty of only second-degree murder and sentenced him to life in prison. Unhappy with the verdict, the state of Connecticut appealed the conviction to its highest court, won the appeal, got a new trial, and then succeeded in getting Palko convicted of first-degree murder. Palko appealed to the Supreme Court on what seemed an open and shut case of double jeopardy. Yet, although the majority of the Court agreed that this could indeed be considered a case of double jeopardy, they decided that double jeopardy was *not* one of the provisions of the Bill of Rights incorporated in the Fourteenth Amendment as a restriction on the powers of the states. It took more than thirty years for the Court to nationalize the constitutional protection against double jeopardy. Palko was eventually executed for the crime, because he lived in the state of Connecticut rather than in some state whose constitution included a guarantee against double jeopardy.

Self-Incrimination Perhaps the most significant liberty found in the Fifth Amendment, and the one most familiar to many Americans who watch television crime shows, is the guarantee that no citizen "shall be compelled in any criminal case to be a witness against himself. . . ." The most famous case concerning self-incrimination is one of such importance that Chief Justice Earl Warren assessed its results as going "to the very root of our concepts of American criminal jurisprudence."[75] Twenty-three-year-old Ernesto Miranda was sentenced to between twenty and thirty years in prison for the kidnapping and rape of an eighteen-year-old girl. The girl had identified him in a police lineup,

double jeopardy
the Fifth Amendment right providing that a person cannot be tried twice for the same crime

Ernesto Miranda was arrested for kidnapping and rape. At first he denied his guilt, but eventually he confessed to the crimes. Since he was never told that he was not required to answer police questions, his case was appealed on the grounds that his right against self-incrimination had been violated.

Figure 5.2 — **YOUR MIRANDA RIGHTS**

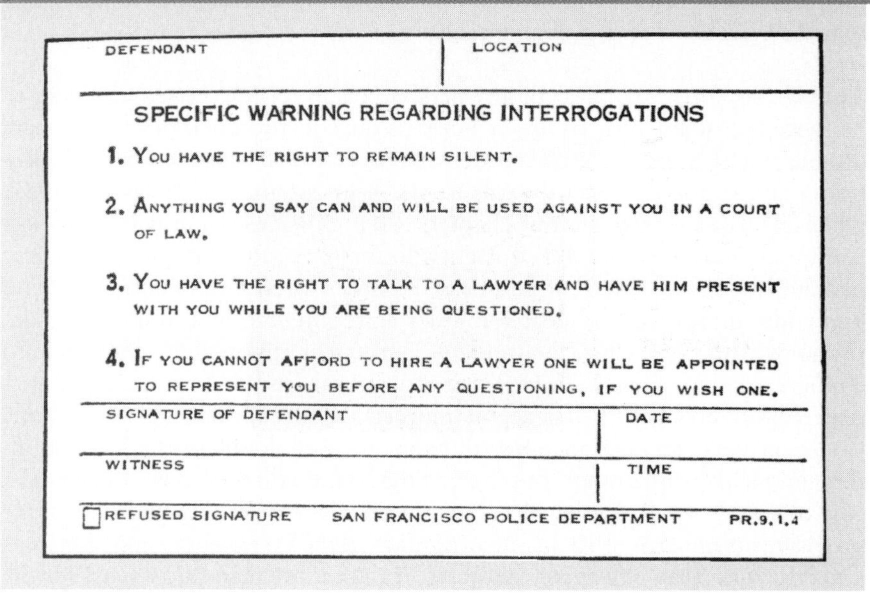

> DEFENDANT   LOCATION
>
> **SPECIFIC WARNING REGARDING INTERROGATIONS**
>
> 1. You have the right to remain silent.
>
> 2. Anything you say can and will be used against you in a court of law.
>
> 3. You have the right to talk to a lawyer and have him present with you while you are being questioned.
>
> 4. If you cannot afford to hire a lawyer one will be appointed to represent you before any questioning, if you wish one.
>
> SIGNATURE OF DEFENDANT   DATE
>
> WITNESS   TIME
>
> ☐ REFUSED SIGNATURE   SAN FRANCISCO POLICE DEPARTMENT   PR.9.1.4

The reading of one's "Miranda rights" is now standard police procedure.

and, after two hours of questioning, Miranda confessed, subsequently signing a statement that his confession had been made voluntarily, without threats or promises of immunity. These confessions were admitted into evidence, served as the basis for Miranda's conviction, and also served as the basis of the appeal of his conviction all the way to the Supreme Court. In one of the most intensely and widely criticized decisions ever handed down by the Supreme Court, Ernesto Miranda's case produced the rules the police must follow before questioning an arrested criminal suspect. The reading of a person's "Miranda rights" (see Figure 5.2) became a standard scene in every police station and on virtually every dramatization of police action on television and in the movies. *Miranda* advanced the civil liberties of accused persons by expanding not only the scope of the Fifth Amendment clause covering coerced confessions and self-incrimination, but also by confirming the right to counsel (discussed later). The Supreme Court under Burger and Rehnquist has considerably softened the *Miranda* restrictions, making the job of the police a little easier, but the **Miranda** rule still stands as a protection against egregious police abuses of arrested persons.

Eminent Domain The other fundamental clause of the Fifth Amendment is the "takings clause," which extends to each citizen a protection against the "taking" of private property "without just compensation." Although this part of the Fifth Amendment is not specifically concerned with protecting persons accused of crimes, it is nevertheless a fundamentally important instance where the government and the citizen are adversaries. The power of any government to take private property for a public use is called **eminent domain**. This power is essential to the very concept of sovereignty. The Fifth Amendment neither invents eminent domain nor takes it away; its purpose is to put limits on that inherent power through procedures that require a showing of a public purpose

Miranda rule

the requirement, articulated by the Supreme Court in Miranda v. Arizona, that persons under arrest must be informed prior to police interrogation of their rights to remain silent and to have the benefit of legal counsel

eminent domain

the right of government to take private property for public use and the provision of fair payment for the taking of someone's property. This provision is now universally observed in all U.S. principalities, but it has not always been meticulously observed.

Take the case of Mr. Berman, who in the 1950s owned and operated a "mom and pop" grocery store in a run-down neighborhood on the southwest side of the District of Columbia. In carrying out a vast urban redevelopment program, the city government of Washington, D.C., took Mr. Berman's property as one of a large number of privately owned lots to be cleared for new housing and business construction. Mr. Berman, and his successors after his death, took the government to court on the grounds that it was an unconstitutional use of eminent domain to take property from one private owner and eventually to turn that property back, in altered form, to another private owner. Berman and his successors lost their case. The Supreme Court's argument was a curious but very important one: the "public interest" can mean virtually anything a legislature says it means. In other words, since the overall slum clearance and redevelopment project was in the public interest, according to the legislature, the eventual transfers of property that were going to take place were justified.[76]

THE SIXTH AMENDMENT AND THE RIGHT TO COUNSEL

In all criminal prosecutions, the accused shall enjoy the right to a speedy and public trial, by an impartial jury of the State and district wherein the crime shall have been committed, which district shall have been ascertained by law, and to be informed of the nature and cause of the accusation; to be confronted with the witnesses against him; to have compulsory process for obtaining witnesses in his favor, and to have the Assistance of Counsel for his defence.

Students and Politics

The right to privacy has become an important issue on college campuses. One controversy at Miami University in Ohio arose in the 1994–95 school year, when student Jennifer Markiewicz, then editor-in-chief of the *Miami Student,* applied under the Ohio Public Records Act for disclosure of students' criminal records kept by the university. The university gave the newspaper the files, minus the names and genders of the accused. The newspaper then filed suit seeking full disclosure. In 1998 the U.S. Department of Education also filed suit, in federal court, to prevent Miami and other universities from releasing the criminal records of students to the media.

This case shows how sensitive the issue is: proponents of disclosure feel that the public has a right to know not only percentages of crimes committed but the context of those crimes, whereas the Department of Education feels that the privacy of the victims, the accused, and the witnesses would be compromised if such information were made public. In this and other examples, college campuses and the media continue to be at the forefront of the battle over privacy.

SOURCE: William H. Honan, "Education Department Sues Universities over Disclosure of Crime Records," *New York Times,* February 12, 1998, p. A12.

Like the exclusionary rule of the Fourth Amendment and the self-incrimination clause of the Fifth Amendment, the "right to counsel" provision of the Sixth Amendment is notable for freeing defendants who seem to the public to be patently guilty as charged. Other provisions of the Sixth Amendment, such as the right to a speedy trial and the right to confront witnesses before an impartial jury, are less controversial in nature.

Gideon v. Wainwright is the perfect case study because it involved a disreputable person who seemed patently guilty of the crime for which he was convicted. In and out of jails for most of his fifty-one years, Clarence Earl Gideon received a five-year sentence for breaking and entering a poolroom in Panama City, Florida. While serving time in jail, Gideon became a fairly well qualified "jailhouse lawyer," made his own appeal on a handwritten petition, and eventually won the landmark ruling on the right to counsel in all felony cases.[77]

The right to counsel has been expanded rather than contracted during the past few decades, when the courts have become more conservative. For example, although at first the right to counsel was met by judges assigning lawyers from the community as a formal public obligation, most states and cities now have created an office of public defender; these state-employed professional defense lawyers typically provide poor defendants with much better legal representation. And, although a defendant does not have the right to choose any private defense attorney, defendants do have the right to appeal a conviction on the grounds that the counsel provided by the state was deficient. Moreover, the right to counsel extends beyond serious crimes to any trial, with or without jury, that holds the possibility of imprisonment. In other words, the Sixth Amendment provides a right that is seriously intended to be implemented.[78]

THE EIGHTH AMENDMENT AND CRUEL AND UNUSUAL PUNISHMENT

The Eighth Amendment prohibits "excessive bail," "excessive fines," and "cruel and unusual punishment." Virtually all the debate over Eighth Amendment issues focuses on the last clause of the amendment: the protection from "cruel and unusual punishment." One of the greatest challenges in interpreting this provision consistently lies in the fact that what is considered "cruel and unusual" varies from culture to culture and from generation to generation. And unfortunately, it also varies by class and race. A sentence of ten years in prison for robbing a liquor store is not considered excessive, yet embezzlement or insider trading involving millions of dollars merits only three years of community service. Are "white-collar" crimes less serious than "working-class" crimes? Consider the 1995 action by Congress to mandate a five-year minimum sentence for offenses involving five or more grams of crack cocaine. The same five-year mandatory sentence for *powdered* cocaine, however, kicks in only when the amount involved is *five hundred* grams or more. As one black member of the House put it, "crack cocaine happens to be used by poor people, mostly black people, because it's cheap. Powdered cocaine happens to be used by wealthy white people."[79]

By far the biggest issue of class and race inconsistency as constituting cruel and unusual punishment arises over the death penalty. In 1972, the Supreme Court overturned several state death penalty laws, not because they were cruel and unusual, but because they were being applied in a capricious manner—i.e., blacks were much more likely than whites to be sentenced to death, and the poor more likely than the rich, and men more likely than women.[80] Very soon after that decision, a majority of states revised their capital punishment provisions to meet the Court's standards.[81] Since 1976, the Court has consistently upheld state laws providing for capital punishment, although the Court also continues to review numerous death penalty appeals each year.

Student Perspectives

THE AMERICAN FRESHMAN

Percentage of freshmen agreeing with the statement, "The death penalty should be abolished."

1991	1992	1993	1994	1995	1996
21%	21%	22%	20%	21%	22%

SOURCE: L. J. Sax, A. W. Astin, W. S. Korn, and K. M. Mahoney, *The American Freshman: National Norms for Fall 1997* (Los Angeles: Higher Education Research Institute, UCLA Graduate School of Education, 1997).

⭐ The Right to Privacy

▶ What is the right to privacy? How has it been derived from the Bill of Rights? What forms does the right to privacy take today?

Some of the people all of the time and all of the people some of the time would just like to be left alone, to have their own private domain into which no

POLICY DEBATE

The Death Penalty

Since the Supreme Court gave a green light to the reenactment of death penalty laws in 1976, most states have embraced capital punishment as a "get-tough" signal to criminals. Between 1976 and 1996, states executed 328 people. Most of those executions occurred in southern states, with Texas leading the way. As of 1997, thirty-eight states had adopted some form of capital punishment, a move approved of by about three-quarters of all Americans.

Despite the fact that virtually all criminal conduct is regulated by the states, Congress has also jumped on the bandwagon, imposing capital punishment for more than fifty federal crimes. Despite the seeming popularity of the death penalty, the debate has become, if anything, more intense. In 1997, for example, the American Bar Association passed a resolution calling for a halt to the death penalty until concerns about its fairness—that is, whether its application violates the principle of equality—and about ensuring due process are addressed.

Many death penalty supporters trumpet its deterrent effects on other would-be criminals. Although studies of capital crimes usually fail to demonstrate any direct deterrent effect, that may be due to the lengthy delays—typically years and even decades—between convictions and executions. A system that eliminates undue delays would surely enhance deterrence. And deterring even one murder or other heinous crime, proponents argue, is more than ample justification for such laws.

Beyond this, the death penalty is seen as a proper expression of retribution, echoed in the biblical phrase "an eye for an eye." People who commit vicious crimes deserve to forfeit their lives in exchange for the suffering they have inflicted. If the world applauded the execution of Nazis after World War II, for example, how could it deny the right of society to execute a serial killer?

Constitutional objections to the death penalty often invoke the Eighth Amendment's protection against punishments that are "cruel and unusual." Yet the death penalty can hardly be considered a violation of

this protection, say supporters, since the death penalty was commonly used in the eighteenth century and was supported by most early American leaders. And while the poor, males, and blacks and Latinos are more likely to find themselves sitting on death row, this fact reflects the painful reality that these categories of individuals are more likely to commit crimes.

Death penalty opponents are quick to point out that the death penalty has not been proven to deter crime, either in the United States or abroad. In fact, America is the only Western nation that still executes criminals. The fact that American states execute criminals debases, rather than elevates, society, by extolling vengeance. If the government is to serve as an example of proper behavior, say foes, it has no business sanctioning killing when incarceration will similarly protect society.

As for the Constitution, most of the Founders surely supported the death penalty. But, foes note, they also countenanced slavery, and lived at a time when society was both less informed about, and more indifferent to, the human condition. Modern Americans' greater civility should be reflected in how it defines individual rights.

Furthermore, according to death penalty foes, execution is expensive—more expensive than life imprisonment—precisely *because* the government must make every effort to ensure that it is not executing an innocent person. Curtailing legal appeals would make the possibility of a mistake too great. And although most Americans do support the death penalty, people also support life without the possibility of parole as an alternative. Race also intrudes in death penalty cases: people of color (who are more likely to face economic deprivation) are disproportionately more likely to be sentenced to death, whereas whites charged with identical crimes are less likely to be given the ultimate punishment. Such disparity of treatment violates the principle of equal protection. And finally, according to opponents, a life sentence may be a worse punishment for criminals than the death penalty.

ABORTION RIGHTS, PRIVACY, AND CIVIL LIBERTIES

In a time when condoms are distributed in some public schools and when birth control and sex education are freely discussed, it seems difficult to believe that the practice of contraception was once illegal in some states. From the 1940s until 1965, the Supreme Court consistently refused to hear legal challenges to laws that barred individuals—even married couples—from purchasing contraceptives.

In 1965, however, the Court ruled in *Griswold v. Connecticut* that a constitutionally based "right to privacy" barred states from preventing married couples from practicing birth control. Although no such right is actually stated in the Bill of Rights, the Court noted that the idea of personal privacy had been recognized in common law for hundreds of years, and could reasonably be considered to arise from the Third Amendment (prohibiting the quartering of troops in people's homes), the Fifth Amendment (protection against self-incrimination), the Ninth Amendment (providing that citizens had other rights beyond those specified rights in the Constitution), and especially the Fourth Amendment (protecting the right of people to be "secure in their persons"). The implication from *Griswold* that people were entitled to privacy rights, as well as reproductive freedom, opened the door to legalized abortion.

In the 1960s, several states enacted liberalized abortion laws as public attention turned for the first time toward this issue. Leaders of the emerging women's movement, physicians, and others concerned with overpopulation and birth control lent their support to the liberalization of abortion laws. California became one of several states to liberalize its laws, a move that resulted in a profound change in practices. In 1968, the state's first year under the liberalized laws, 5,018 abortions were performed. Three years later, that number had jumped to almost 117,000.

one—friends, family, government, church, or employer—has the right to enter without permission.

Many Jehovah's Witnesses felt that way in the 1930s. They risked serious punishment in 1940 by telling their children not to salute the flag or say the "Pledge of Allegiance" in school because of their understanding of the First Commandment's prohibition of the worship of "graven images." They lost their appeal, the children were expelled, and the parents were punished.[82] However, the Supreme Court concluded that the 1940 decision was "wrongly decided."[83] These two cases arose under the freedom of religion provisions of the First Amendment, but they were also the first cases to confront the possibility of another right that is not mentioned anywhere in the Constitution or the Bill of Rights: the right to be left alone. When the Court began to take a more activist role in the mid-1950s and 1960s, the idea of a **right to privacy** was revived. In 1958, the Supreme Court recognized "privacy in one's association" in its decision to prevent the state of Alabama from using the membership list of the National Association for the Advancement of Colored People in the state's investigations.[84]

right to privacy

the right to be let alone, which has been interpreted by the Supreme Court to entail free access to birth control and abortions

Into this changing environment entered the case of *Roe v. Wade,* which sought to challenge Texas's strict abortion law. After two hearings over a period of almost two years, the Supreme Court struck down the Texas law, and therefore similarly strict laws in other states as well. In its decision, the Court relied on the privacy principle. It also ruled that the Fourteenth Amendment did not apply to fetuses; the amendment's guarantees extended only to "all persons born or naturalized in the United States," and no court case had ever recognized a fetus as a person. In addition, the Court cited scientific and medical evidence to lay down a three-tiered approach to abortions. In the first trimester of pregnancy, when over 90 percent of abortions occur, a woman's right to abortion was to be fully protected. In the second trimester, states could enact restrictions only to protect the health and safety of the pregnant woman. In the third trimester, the government may intervene at the point of fetal viability—that is, when the fetus is capable of living outside of the womb.

By extending the umbrella of privacy, this sweeping ruling dramatically changed abortion practices in

America. In addition, it galvanized and nationalized the abortion debate. Groups opposed to abortion, such as the National Right to Life Committee, organized to fight the new liberal standard, while abortion rights groups sought to maintain that protection. In recent years, the legal standard shifted against abortion rights supporters in two key Supreme Court cases. In *Webster v. Reproductive Health Services* (1989), the Court upheld a series of restrictions on abortion practices, but a slim majority of the nine justices still upheld *Roe.* In the 1992 case of *Planned Parenthood of Southeastern Pennsylvania v. Casey,* the Court upheld another series of restrictions, but again, a majority of justices stated strongly that *Roe* should be upheld. With a generation of women now accustomed to having access to abortion, and with over 1.5 million abortions performed in the United States each year, the political pendulum seems to be swinging away from a return to pre-*Roe* days.

SOURCE: Barbara Hinckson Craig and David M. O'Brien, *Abortion and American Politics* (Chatham, NJ: Chatham House, 1993).

The sphere of privacy was drawn in earnest in 1965, when the Court ruled that a Connecticut statute forbidding the use of contraceptives violated the right of marital privacy. Estelle Griswold, the executive director of the Planned Parenthood League of Connecticut, was arrested by the state of Connecticut for providing information, instruction, and medical advice about contraception to married couples. She and her associates were found guilty as accessories to the crime and fined $100 each. The Supreme Court reversed the lower court decisions and declared the Connecticut law unconstitutional because it violated "a right of privacy older than the Bill of Rights—older than our political parties, older than our school system."[85] Justice William O. Douglas, author of the majority decision in the *Griswold* case, argued that this right of privacy is also grounded in the Constitution, because it fits into a "zone of privacy" created by a combination of the Third, Fourth, and Fifth Amendments. A concurring opinion, written by Justice Arthur Goldberg, attempted to strengthen Douglas's argument by adding that "the concept of liberty . . . embraces the right of marital privacy though that right is not mentioned explicitly in the Constitution [and] is supported by numerous decisions of this Court . . .

and *by the language and history of the Ninth Amendment"* (emphasis added).[86]

The right to privacy was confirmed and extended in 1973 in the most important of all privacy decisions, and one of the most important Supreme Court decisions in American history: *Roe v. Wade.* This decision established a woman's right to have an abortion and prohibited states from making abortion a criminal act.[87] The Burger Court's decision in *Roe* took a revolutionary step toward establishing the right to privacy. It is important to emphasize that the preference for privacy rights and for their extension to include the rights of women to control their own bodies was not something invented by the Supreme Court in a vacuum. Most states did not regulate abortions in any fashion until the 1840s, at which time only six of the twenty-six existing states had any regulations governing abortion at all. In addition, many states had begun to ease their abortion restrictions well before the 1973 *Roe* decision, although in recent years a number of states have reinstated some restrictions on abortion (see Figure 5.3).

Like any important principle, once privacy was established as an aspect of civil liberties protected by the Bill of Rights through the Fourteenth Amendment, it took on a life of its own. In a number of important decisions, the Supreme Court and the lower federal courts sought to protect rights that could not be found in the text of the Constitution but could be discovered through the study of the philosophic sources of fundamental rights. Through this line of reasoning, the federal courts sought to protect privacy in the form of sexual autonomy, lifestyle choices, sexual preferences, procreational choice, and various forms of intimate association.

Criticism mounted with every extension of this line of reasoning. The federal courts were accused of creating an uncontrollable expansion of demands for new rights. The Supreme Court, critics argued, had displaced the judgments of legislatures and state courts with its own judgment of what was reasonable, without regard to local popular majorities or specific constitutional provisions. This new "judicial activism," as it came to be called in the 1980s, was the basis for a more strongly critical label for the Court: "the imperial judiciary."[88]

The controversy over judicial power has not diminished. In fact it is intensifying under Chief Justice William Rehnquist, an avowed critic of "judicial activism," especially as it relates to privacy and other new rights, such as the right to be represented in election districts of numerically equal size[89] and the right not to be required to participate in prayers in school.[90] Under Rehnquist, the Court has been moving in a more conservative, de-nationalizing direction.

One of the Court's conservative trends concerns the burning question of abortion rights. In *Webster v. Reproductive Health Services,* the Court narrowly upheld (by a 5-to-4 majority) the constitutionality of restrictions on the use of public medical facilities for abortion.[91] And in the 1992 case of *Planned Parenthood v. Casey,* another 5-to-4 majority of the Court upheld *Roe* but narrowed its scope, refusing to invalidate a Pennsylvania law that significantly limits freedom of choice. The Court's decision defined the right to an abortion as a "limited or qualified" right subject to regulation by the states as long as the regulation does not constitute an "undue burden."[92] As one constitutional authority concluded from this case, "until there is a Freedom of Choice Act, and/or a U.S. Supreme Court able to wean *Roe* from its respirator, state legis-

Student Perspectives

THE AMERICAN FRESHMAN

Percentage of freshmen agreeing with the statement, "Abortion should be legal."

1991	1992	1993	1994	1995	1996
63%	64%	62%	60%	58%	56%

SOURCE: L. J. Sax, A. W. Astin, W. S. Korn, and K. M. Mahoney, *The American Freshman: National Norms for Fall 1997* (Los Angeles: Higher Education Research Institute, UCLA Graduate School of Education, 1997).

ABORTION REGULATION AND DEREGULATION

Figure 5.3

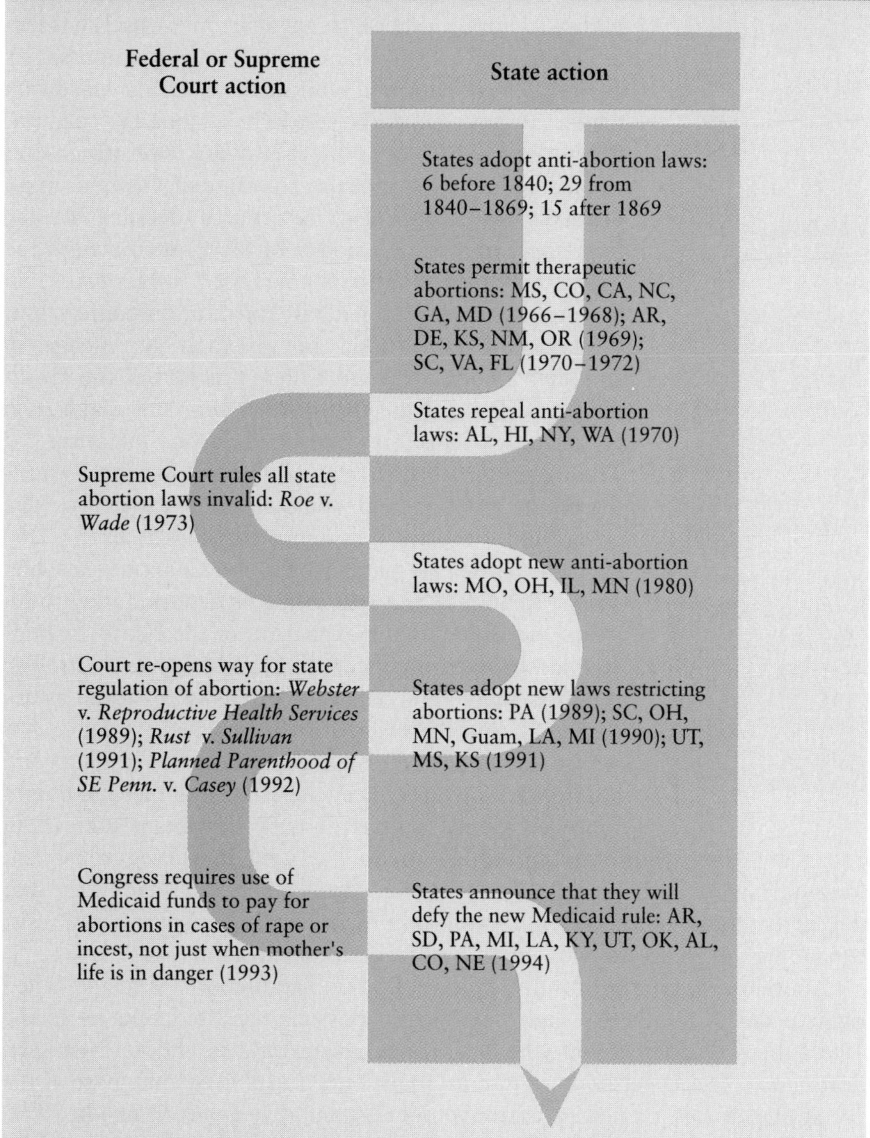

Federal or Supreme Court action	State action
	States adopt anti-abortion laws: 6 before 1840; 29 from 1840–1869; 15 after 1869
	States permit therapeutic abortions: MS, CO, CA, NC, GA, MD (1966–1968); AR, DE, KS, NM, OR (1969); SC, VA, FL (1970–1972)
	States repeal anti-abortion laws: AL, HI, NY, WA (1970)
Supreme Court rules all state abortion laws invalid: *Roe v. Wade* (1973)	
	States adopt new anti-abortion laws: MO, OH, IL, MN (1980)
Court re-opens way for state regulation of abortion: *Webster v. Reproductive Health Services* (1989); *Rust v. Sullivan* (1991); *Planned Parenthood of SE Penn. v. Casey* (1992)	States adopt new laws restricting abortions: PA (1989); SC, OH, MN, Guam, LA, MI (1990); UT, MS, KS (1991)
Congress requires use of Medicaid funds to pay for abortions in cases of rape or incest, not just when mother's life is in danger (1993)	States announce that they will defy the new Medicaid rule: AR, SD, PA, MI, LA, KY, UT, OK, AL, CO, NE (1994)

SOURCES: Raymond Tatalovich and Byron Daynes, *The Politics of Abortion* (New York: Praeger, 1981), p. 18. Copyright © by Praeger Publishers. Used with permission. Updated with data from the *New York Times,* July 4–6, 1989, and the *Los Angeles Times,* March 31, 1994.

latures will have significant discretion over the access that women will have to legalized abortions."[93]

Another possible conservative trend concerns the privacy rights of homosexuals. One morning in Atlanta, Georgia, in the mid-1980s, Michael Hardwick was arrested by a police officer who discovered him in bed with another man. The officer had come to serve a warrant for Hardwick's arrest for failure

Students and Politics

In recent years, the National Right to Life Party has developed college outreach programs. One of the more active chapters has been at the University of Notre Dame, where Catriona Wilkie and others have led activism both in South Bend, Indiana, and on the national level. As a fourteen-year-old, Wilkie was the only minor to testify before the Texas state legislature on a proposed law that would require parental consent for a minor to obtain an abortion. The passionate speakers that day, she says, "made me realize how hard you have to fight; most people would have been scared away." Wilkie's responsibilities at Notre Dame Right to Life include participating in a national march in Washington, fund-raising for the local and national branches, and educating local youth groups and schools about the group's position on abortion. "The strongest voice is always one that is close to their own," she says, referring to her speaking engagements with audiences of her age and younger. "We stay away from slogans and stick to information. People appreciate that."

SOURCE: Catriona Wilkie, interview by author, February 3, 1998.

to appear in court to answer charges of drinking in public. One of Hardwick's unknowing housemates invited the officer to look in Hardwick's room, where he found Hardwick and another man engaging in "consensual sexual behavior." He was then arrested under Georgia's laws against heterosexual and homosexual sodomy. Hardwick filed a lawsuit against the state, challenging the constitutionality of the Georgia law. Hardwick won his case in the federal court of appeals. The state of Georgia, in an unusual move, appealed the court's decision to the Supreme Court. The majority of the Court reversed the lower court decision, holding against Mr. Hardwick, on the grounds that "the federal Constitution confers [no] fundamental right upon homosexuals to engage in sodomy," and that therefore there was no basis to invalidate "the laws of the many states that still make such conduct illegal and have done so for a very long time."[94] The Court majority concluded its opinion with a warning that it ought not and would not use its power to "discover new fundamental rights embedded in the Due Process Clause." In other words, the Court under Chief Justice Rehnquist was expressing its determination to restrict quite severely the expansion of the Ninth Amendment and the development of new substantive rights. The four dissenters argued that the case was not about a fundamental right to engage in homosexual sodomy, but was in fact about "the most comprehensive of rights and the right most valued by civilized men, [namely,] the right to be let alone."[95] It is unlikely that many states will adopt new laws against consensual homosexual activity or will vigorously enforce old laws of such a nature already on their books. But it is equally clear that the current Supreme Court will refrain from reviewing such laws and will resist expanding the Ninth Amendment as a source of new substantive rights.

Another area ripe for future litigation and public discourse is the so-called right to die. A number of highly publicized physician-assisted suicides in the 1990s focused attention on whether people have a right to choose their own death and to receive assistance in carrying it out. Can this become part of the privacy right or is it a new, substantive right? A tentative answer came in 1997, when the Court ruled that a law adopted in the state of Washington establishing a ban on "causing" or "aiding" a suicide did not violate the Fourteenth Amendment or any clauses of the Bill of Rights incorporated in the Fourteenth Amendment.[96] Thus, if a state can constitutionally adopt such a prohibition, there is no constitutional right to suicide or assisted suicide. However, the Court left open the narrower question of "whether a mentally competent person who is experiencing great suffering has a constitutionally cognizable interest in controlling the circumstances of his or her imminent death."[97] "Americans are engaged in an earnest and profound debate about the morality, legality, and practicality of physician-assisted suicide. Our holding permits this debate to continue, as it should in a democratic society."[98] Never before has the Supreme Court more openly invited further litigation on a point.[99]

★ The Future of Civil Liberties

▶ What is the likelihood that the Supreme Court will try to reverse the nation-alization of the Bill of Rights?

The next and final question for this chapter is whether the current Supreme Court, with its conservative majority, will try to reverse the nationalization of the Bill of Rights after a period of more than thirty-five years. Although such a move is possible, it is not certain. First of all, the Rehnquist Court has not actually reversed important decisions made by the Warren or Burger Courts, but instead has given narrower and more restrictive interpretations of earlier Court decisions. For example, in 1997, the Court made it easier for the police to search cars for drugs or other contraband when the cars have been pulled over only for traffic violations. Activists such as Justices Rehnquist, Antonin Scalia, and Clarence Thomas, who would prefer to overturn many of the Court's decisions from the 1960s and 1970s, do not yet command a majority on the Court.

Meanwhile, the resurgence of federalism may play itself out in judicial territory. One certain trend in the Court that is likely to continue is its commitment to giving more discretion to the states, returning some of the power to state legislatures that was taken away during the "nationalization" of the Bill of Rights. But what if the state legislatures begin using their regained powers in ways they had used them before the nationalization of the Bill of Rights? What would be the reaction when states pass laws imposing further criminal restrictions on abortion? Permitting more religious practices in the public schools? Spreading the application of capital punishment to new crimes? Imposing stricter sentences on white-collar crimes? Terminating the use of buses to maintain desegregated schools? On the other hand, there have been times when states were dominated by radical Left rather than radical Right tendencies. If that should occur once again, what would a conservative majority on the Court do? Would the Court be equally respectful of state-level democracy then?

★ The Citizen's Role

The civil liberties that Americans enjoy today have been won by the struggles of ordinary citizens. The Bill of Rights offers Americans who have been denied their civil liberties a remedy through the judicial system. Individuals such as Dolly Mapp, Ernesto Miranda, and Clarence Earl Gideon fought to defend their fundamental liberties, and through their efforts all Americans now possess a more clearly defined and protected right to the due process of law. The most central aspect of a woman's right to privacy started with the difficulties of a poor, high school dropout in Texas. Norma McCorvey was a twenty-one-year-old pregnant, divorced carnival worker with a five-year-old daughter. McCorvey lived regularly on the edge of poverty, and as a high school

BANNED BOOKS

One of the more visible issues of free speech in recent years has been the banning of books in public schools. The following books were the most censored of 1997, with the reasons for which they were banned:

1. *Goosebumps* series, R. L. Stine: horror

2. *The Adventures of Huckleberry Finn,* Mark Twain: racism
3. *I Know Why the Caged Bird Sings,* Maya Angelou: description of rape
4. *It's Perfectly Normal,* Robie Harries: sexual content
5. *The Chocolate War,* Robert Cormier: language and sexual content
6. *Catcher in the Rye,* J. D. Salinger: language
7. *Bridge to Terabithia,* Katherine Paterson: language
8. *Forever,* Judy Blume: sexual content
9. *My Brother Sam Is Dead,* James Lincoln Collier and Christopher Collier: violence, language

SOURCE: American Library Association

dropout, her prospects were poor, all the poorer in Texas, where the carnival had moved, because Texas had prohibited abortion unless necessary to save the mother's life. "I found one doctor who offered to abort me for $500. Only he didn't have a license, and I was scared to turn my body over to him. So there I was—pregnant, . . . alone and stuck."

McCorvey bore her child and gave it up immediately for adoption, but in the process she was introduced to two recent graduates of the University of Texas Law School, Sarah Weddington and Linda Coffey. These three women decided to challenge the Texas abortion statute. In order to avoid any stigma attached to such an emotionally charged case, Norma McCorvey's name was changed to Jane Roe in the court documents. Her case alleged that "she was unmarried and pregnant; that she wished to terminate her pregnancy by an abortion . . . ; [and] that she was unable to get a 'legal' abortion because her life did not appear to be threatened by the continuation of her pregnancy. . . ." The Court's ruling in *Roe v. Wade* subsequently prohibited states from making abortion illegal.[100]

STUDENTS AND POLITICS

In 1995, a student group at the University of Virginia scored a dramatic legal victory before the U.S. Supreme Court. The university had refused to provide support from the student activities fund for *Wide Awake,* a magazine published by a Christian student group. Although other student publications received subsidies from the activities fund, university policy prohibited grants to religious groups. Ronald Rosenberger, a Virginia undergraduate and an editor of the magazine, and his fellow editors filed suit in federal court, charging, among other things, that the university's refusal to fund their magazine because of its religious focus violated their First Amendment right to freedom of speech. A federal district court ruled in favor of the university on the grounds that funding for a religious newspaper by a state university would violate the Constitution's prohibition against government support for religion. Rosenberger and his colleagues appealed, but lost again when the district court's decision was affirmed by the Fourth Circuit Court of Appeals, which said that the Constitution mandated a strict separation of church and state. Undeterred, the student editors appealed the circuit court's decision to the Supreme Court. As we saw earlier in this chapter, the Supreme Court ruled in favor of the student group, holding that the university's policies amounted to state support for some ideas but not others. This, said the Court, represented a fundamental violation of the First Amendment.[101] The *Rosenberger* decision represents a potential loosening of the Court's long-standing opposition to any government support for religious groups or ideas, and it demonstrates how much influence can be exerted by a determined group of students.

In every sense of the word, the American judiciary is the most accessible branch to the least-represented and the least-organized citizens. The judicial branch has the power to give citizenship its full meaning. The sad news in all of this is that citizens, including many of the most educated citizens, have very little appreciation of their own fundamental liberties, which they don't defend unless under threat. Liberty, like art and enterprise, is strengthened, not worn out, by use.

★ Summary

The provisions of the Bill of Rights seek to protect citizens from improper government action. Civil liberties ought to be carefully distinguished from civil rights, which did not become part of the Constitution until the Fourteenth Amendment and its provision for "equal protection of the laws."

During its first century, the Bill of Rights was applicable only to the national government and not to the state governments. The Fourteenth Amendment (1868) seemed to apply the Bill of Rights to the states, but the Supreme Court continued to apply the Bill of Rights as though the Fourteenth Amendment had never been adopted. For sixty years following adoption of the Fourteenth Amendment, only one provision was "incorporated" into the Fourteenth Amendment and applied as a restriction on the state governments: the Fifth Amendment "eminent domain" clause, which was incorporated in 1897. Even as recently as 1961, only the eminent domain clause and the clauses of the First Amendment had been incorporated into the Fourteenth Amendment and applied to the states. After 1961, one by one, most of the provisions of the Bill of Rights were finally incorporated and applied to the states, although a conservative Supreme Court has tried to reverse this trend during the 1980s and 1990s. The status of the First Amendment seems to have been least affected by this conservative trend. Protection of purely political speech remains close to absolute. The categories of conditionally protected speech include "speech-plus," libel and slander, obscenity and pornography, fighting words, and commercial speech. Nevertheless, the realm of free speech in all these areas is still quite broad.

Of the other amendments and clauses in the Bill of Rights, the ones most likely to receive conservative interpretations are the religious clauses of the First Amendment, illegal search and seizure cases arising under the Fourth Amendment, and cases involving the Eighth Amendment cruel and unusual punishment clause.

Where the Bill of Rights will go as the American people approach the end of the century is very unclear.

FOR FURTHER READING

Abraham, Henry J. *Freedom and the Court: Civil Rights and Liberties in the United States.* 6th ed. New York: Oxford University Press, 1994.

Bryner, Gary C., and A. Don Sorensen, eds. *The Bill of Rights: A Bicentennial Assessment.* Albany: State University of New York Press, 1993.

Eisenstein, Zillah. *The Female Body and the Law.* Berkeley: University of California Press, 1988.

Friendly, Fred W. *Minnesota Rag: The Dramatic Story of the Landmark Supreme Court Case that Gave New Meaning to Freedom of the Press.* New York: Vintage, 1982.

Glendon, Mary Ann. *Rights Talk: The Impoverishment of Political Discourse.* New York: Free Press, 1991.

Hentoff, Nat. *The First Freedom: The Tumultuous History of Free Speech in America.* New York: Basic Books, 1994.

Levy, Leonard. *Legacy of Suppression: Freedom of Speech and Press in Early American History.* New York: Harper, 1963.

Lewis, Anthony. *Gideon's Trumpet.* New York: Random House, 1964.

Meyer, Michael J., and William A. Parent. *The Constitution of Rights: Human Dignity and American Values.* Ithaca, NY: Cornell University Press, 1992.

Minow, Martha. *Making All the Difference: Inclusion, Exclusion, and American Law.* Ithaca, NY: Cornell University Press, 1990.

Silverstein, Mark. *Constitutional Faiths.* Ithaca, NY: Cornell University Press, 1984.

Stone, Geoffrey R., Richard A. Epstein, and Cass R. Sunstein, eds. *The Bill of Rights in the Modern State.* Chicago: University of Chicago Press, 1992.

STUDY OUTLINE

The Bill of Rights: A Charter of Liberties

1. Despite the insistence of Alexander Hamilton that a bill of rights was both unnecessary and dangerous, adding a list of explicit rights was the most important item of business for the First Congress in 1789.
2. The Bill of Rights would have been more aptly named the "Bill of Liberties," because it is made up of provisions that protect citizens from improper government action.
3. Civil rights did not become part of the Constitution until 1868 with the adoption of the Fourteenth Amendment, which sought to provide for each citizen "the equal protection of the laws."

Nationalizing the Bill of Rights

1. In 1833, the Supreme Court found that the Bill of Rights limited only the national government and not state governments.
2. Although the language of the Fourteenth Amendment seems to indicate that the protections of the Bill of Rights apply to state governments as well as the national government, for the remainder of the nineteenth century the Supreme Court (with only one exception) made decisions as if the Fourteenth Amendment had never been adopted.
3. As of 1961, only the First Amendment and one clause of the Fifth Amendment had been "selectively incorporated" into the Fourteenth Amendment. After 1961, however, most of the provisions of the Bill of Rights were incorporated into the Fourteenth Amendment and applied to the states.

The First Amendment and Freedom of Religion

1. The religious movement of the 1980s, culminating in the judicial and congressional activities of the 1990s, identi-

fied or created unsettled areas involving the establishment clause and the free exercise clause.

The First Amendment and Freedom of Speech and the Press

1. Although freedom of speech and freedom of the press hold an important place in the Bill of Rights, the extent and nature of certain types of expression are subject to constitutional debate.

The Second Amendment and the Right to Bear Arms

1. Constitutionally, the Second Amendment unquestionably protects citizens' rights to bear arms, but this right can be regulated by both state and federal law.

Rights of the Criminally Accused

1. The purpose of due process is to equalize the playing field between the accused individual and the all-powerful state.

The Right to Privacy

1. In the case of *Griswold v. Connecticut,* the Supreme Court found a right of privacy in the Constitution. This right was confirmed and extended in 1973 in the case of *Roe v. Wade.*

The Future of Civil Liberties

1. Under Chief Justice William Rehnquist, the Court has somewhat restricted civil liberties without actually overturning any of the important decisions from the 1960s and 1970s that established many of the liberties enjoyed today.

PRACTICE QUIZ

1. From 1789 until the 1960s, the Bill of Rights put limits on
   a) the national government only.
   b) the state government only.
   c) both the national and state governments.
   d) neither the national nor the state governments.

2. The amendment that provided the basis for the modern understanding of the government's obligation to protect civil rights was the
   a) First Amendment.
   b) Ninth Amendment.

c) Fourteenth Amendment.
d) Twenty-second Amendment.

3. Which of the following Founders did not support adding a Bill of Rights to the Constitution?
a) George Mason
b) Thomas Jefferson
c) Alexander Hamilton
d) All of the above supported the Bill of Rights.

4. The process by which some of the liberties in the Bill of Rights were applied to the states (or nationalized) is known as
a) selective incorporation.
b) judicial activism.
c) civil liberties.
d) establishment.

5. Which of the following provided that all of the protections contained in the Bill of Rights applied to the states as well as the national government?
a) the Fourteenth Amendment
b) *Palko v. Connecticut*
c) *Gitlow v. New York*
d) none of the above

6. Which of the following protections are not contained in the First Amendment?
a) the establishment clause
b) the free exercise clause
c) freedom of the press
d) All of the above are First Amendment protections.

7. Which of the following describes a written statement made in "reckless disregard of the truth" that is considered damaging to a victim because it is "malicious, scandalous, and defamatory"?
a) slander
b) libel
c) fighting words
d) expressive speech

8. Which chief justice oversaw the softening of *Miranda* restrictions?
a) Earl Warren
b) Warren Burger
c) William Rehnquist
d) Both b and c are correct.

9. In what case was a right to privacy first found in the Constitution?
a) *Griswold v. Connecticut*
b) *Roe v. Wade*
c) *Baker v. Carr*
d) *Planned Parenthood v. Casey*

10. Which famous case deals with Sixth Amendment issues?
a) *Miranda v. Arizona*
b) *Mapp v. Ohio*
c) *Gideon v. Wainwright*
d) *Terry v. Ohio*

CRITICAL THINKING QUESTIONS

1. In many ways it seems that the Bill of Rights is an ambiguous document. Choose one protection offered in the Bill of Rights and explain how it has been interpreted in various ways. What does this say about the role of politics and the Constitution in defining the limits of governmental power? What does it say about the power of the Supreme Court in American politics?

2. Recount the history of the constitutional "right to privacy." How has this right affected American politics since the 1960s? How has this right interacted with the other rights in the Bill of Rights? Read the Third, Fourth, Fifth, and Ninth Amendments. In your opinion, do American citizens have a right to privacy?

KEY TERMS

bills of attainder (p. 154)
Bill of Rights (p. 151)
civil liberties (p. 155)
civil rights (p. 156)
"clear and present danger" test (p. 163)
double jeopardy (p. 179)
due process of law (p. 156)
eminent domain (p. 180)

establishment clause (p. 159)
ex post facto laws (p. 154)
exclusionary rule (p. 177)
fighting words (p. 170)
free exercise clause (p. 161)
grand jury (p. 178)
habeas corpus (p. 154)
Lemon test (p. 160)
libel (p. 166)

Miranda rule (p. 180)
procedural liberties (p. 156)
right to privacy (p. 184)
selective incorporation (p. 157)
slander (p. 166)
speech plus (p.165)
strict scrutiny (p. 162)
substantive liberties (p. 155)

6 Civil Rights

* **Civil Rights**

  What is the legal basis for civil rights?

  How has the equal protection clause historically been enforced?

  What is the critical Supreme Court ruling in the battle for equal protection?

  How has Congress tried to make equal protection a reality?

  In what areas did the civil rights acts seek to provide equal access and protection?

* **The Universalization of Civil Rights**

  What groups were spurred by the provision of the Civil Rights Act of 1964 outlawing discrimination in employment practices based on race, religion, and gender, to seek broader protection under the law?

  What is the politics of the universalization of civil rights?

* **Affirmative Action**

  What is the basis for affirmative action? What forms does it take?

  How does affirmative action contribute to the polarization of the politics of civil rights?

  How does the debate about affirmative action reflect the debate over American political values?

STUDENTS AND POLITICS

IN 1960, four black students from North Carolina A&T made history: the four freshmen sat down at Woolworth's whites-only lunch counter in Greensboro, North Carolina, challenging the policies of segregation that kept blacks and whites in separate public and private accommodations across the South. Day after day the students sat at the counter, ignoring the taunts of onlookers, determined to break the system of segregation. Their actions and those of many other students, clergy members, and ordinary citizens finally did abolish such practices as separate white and black park benches, water fountains, and waiting rooms; the end of segregation meant opening access to public and private institutions on equal terms to all. But the victories of the civil rights movement did not come cheaply: many marchers, freedom riders, and sit-in participants were beaten; some were murdered.

Today, the Greensboro lunch counter is a part of history, on display at the Smithsonian Institution in Washington, D.C. Many goals of the civil rights movement that aroused such controversy in 1960 are now widely accepted as the proper expression of the American commitment to equal rights. But the question of what is meant by "equal rights" is hardly settled. While most Americans reject the idea that government should create equal outcomes for its citizens, they do widely endorse government action to prohibit public and private discrimination and they support the idea of equality of opportunity. However, even this concept is elusive. When past denial of rights creates unequal starting points for some groups, should government take additional steps to ensure equal opportunity? What kinds of groups should be specially protected against discrimination? Should the disabled receive special protection? Should gays and lesbians? Finally, what kinds of steps are acceptable to remedy discrimination, and who should bear the costs? These questions are at the heart of contemporary debates over **civil rights.**

Consider the role of race in university admissions. During the 1970s, in an effort to boost minority enrollment, many universities began to consider an applicant's racial background in their admissions decisions. The University of California (U.C.) system was at the forefront of this process. In 1995, however, the regents of the U.C. system voted to abandon race-based admissions practices. Governor Pete Wilson of California argued that affirmative action trampled on individual rights by admitting unqualified students and denying admission to qualified students. Supporters contended that taking race into account in admissions decisions does not mean accepting unqualified students. Instead, they argued, it means expanding acceptance criteria to include other considerations in addition to grades and test scores. In any event, they argued, merit (defined as test scores) has never been the sole criterion for admission at many universities. Private universities, for example, have long admitted sub-

civil rights

legal or moral claims that citizens are entitled to make upon government

stantial numbers of "legacies"—children of alumni who donate money to the institution—with little attention to grades and test scores. The president of the University of California defended affirmative action in broader public terms: "We are a public institution in the most demographically diverse state in the union. Our affirmative action and other diversity programs more than any other single factor have helped us prepare California for its future. . . ."[1]

What is the proper government action here? How can broad public goals be weighed against individual rights? Is there an individual right to admission to a public university based on test scores and grades? Are twenty-five years of affirmative action sufficient to remedy past inequalities based on race? Why should individuals today be required to pay a price for past discrimination?

In the United States, the history of slavery and legalized racial discrimination against African Americans coexists uneasily with a strong tradition of individual liberty. Indeed, for much of our history Americans have struggled to reconcile such exclusionary racial practices with our notions of individual rights. With the adoption of the Fourteenth Amendment in 1868, civil rights became part of the Constitution, guaranteed to each citizen through "equal protection of the laws." These words launched a century of political movements and legal efforts to press for racial equality. The African American quest for civil rights in turn inspired many other groups, including members of other racial and ethnic groups, women, the disabled, and gays and lesbians, to seek new laws and constitutional guarantees of their civil rights.

■ *First we will review the legal developments and political movements that have expanded the scope of civil rights since the Fourteenth Amendment was adopted in 1868.* In this section, we look at the establishment of legal segregation in the South and the civil rights movement that overthrew it.

■ *Next we will trace the broad impact that civil rights legislation has had on American life.* The Civil Rights Act of 1964 was especially critical in guaranteeing the "equal protection of the laws" set forth in the Fourteenth Amendment almost one hundred years earlier.

■ *We will then explore how other groups, including women, Native Americans, Latinos, the disabled, and gays and lesbians, formed movements to win active protection of their rights as well.* This universalization of civil rights has become the new frontier of the civil rights struggle.

■ *Next we turn to the development of affirmative action and the controversies surrounding it.* The debate over affirmative action has intensified in recent years, revealing the ways in which Americans differ over the meaning of equality.

■ *Finally, we will review the role that citizens play in determining the meaning of civil rights.* As we will see, students have often been in the forefront of the civil rights debate.

★ Civil Rights

▶ What is the legal basis for civil rights?

▶ How has the equal protection clause historically been enforced?

▶ What is the critical Supreme Court ruling in the battle for equal protection?

▶ How has Congress tried to make equal protection a reality?

▶ In what areas did the civil rights acts seek to provide equal access and protection?

Congress passed the Fourteenth Amendment and the states ratified it in the aftermath of the Civil War. Together with the Thirteenth Amendment, which abolished slavery, and the Fifteenth Amendment, which guaranteed voting rights for black men, it seemed to provide a guarantee of civil rights for the newly freed black slaves. But the general language of the Fourteenth Amendment meant that its support for civil rights could be far-reaching. The very simplicity of the **"equal protection clause"** of the Fourteenth Amendment left it open to interpretation:

> No State shall make or enforce any law which shall . . . deny to any person within its jurisdiction the equal protection of the laws.

But in the very first Fourteenth Amendment case to come before the Supreme Court, the majority gave it a distinct meaning:

> . . . it is not difficult to give meaning to this clause ["the equal protection of the laws"]. The existence of laws in the States . . . which discriminated with gross injustice and hardship against [Negroes] as a class, was the evil to be remedied by this clause, and by it such laws are forbidden.[2]

Beyond that, contemporaries of the Fourteenth Amendment understood well that private persons offering conveyances, accommodations, or places of amusement to the public incurred certain public obligations to offer them to one and all—in other words, these are *public* accommodations, such that arbitrary discrimination in their use would amount to denial of equal protection of the laws—unless a government took action to overcome the discrimination.[3] This puts governments under obligation to take positive actions to extend to each citizen the opportunities and resources necessary to their proper enjoyment of freedom. A skeptic once observed that "the law, in its majestic equality, forbids the rich as well as the poor to sleep under bridges, to beg in the streets, and to steal bread."[4] The purpose of civil rights principles and laws is to use government in such a way as to give equality a more substantive meaning than that.

Discrimination refers to the use of any unreasonable and unjust criterion of exclusion. Of course, all laws discriminate, including some people while excluding others; but some forms of discrimination are considered unreasonable. For example, it is considered reasonable to use age as a criterion for legal drinking, excluding all persons younger than twenty-one. But is age a reasonable distinction when seventy (or sixty-five or sixty) is selected as the age for

equal protection clause
provision of the Fourteenth Amendment guaranteeing citizens "the equal protection of the laws." This clause has served as the basis for the civil rights of African Americans, women, and other groups

discrimination
use of any unreasonable and unjust criterion of exclusion

compulsory retirement? In the mid-1970s, Congress answered this question by making old age a new civil right; compulsory retirement at seventy is now an unlawful, unreasonable, discriminatory use of age.

PLESSY V. FERGUSON: "SEPARATE BUT EQUAL"

Following its initial decisions making "equal protection" a civil right, the Supreme Court turned conservative, no more ready to enforce the civil rights aspects of the Fourteenth Amendment than it was to enforce the civil liberties provisions. The Court declared the Civil Rights Act of 1875 unconstitutional on the grounds that the act sought to protect blacks against discrimination by *private* businesses, while the Fourteenth Amendment, according to the Court's interpretation, was intended to protect individuals from discrimination only against actions by *public* officials of state and local governments.

In 1896, the Court went still further, in the infamous case of *Plessy v. Ferguson,* by upholding a Louisiana statute that *required* segregation of the races on trolleys and other public carriers (and by implication in all public facilities, including schools). Plessy, a man defined as "one-eighth black," had violated a Louisiana law that provided for "equal but separate accommodations" on trains and a $25 fine for any white passenger who sat in a car reserved for blacks or any black passenger who sat in a car reserved for whites. The Supreme Court held that the Fourteenth Amendment's "equal protection of the laws" was not violated by racial distinction as long as the facilities were equal, thus establishing the **"separate but equal" rule** that prevailed through the mid-twentieth century. People generally pretended that segregated accommodations were equal as long as some accommodation for blacks existed. The Court said that although "the object of the [Fourteenth] Amendment was undoubtedly to enforce the absolute equality of the two races before the law, . . . it could not have intended to abolish distinctions based on color, or to enforce social, as distinguished from political, equality, or a commingling of the two races upon terms unsatisfactory to either."[5] What the Court was saying in effect was that the use of race as a criterion of exclusion in public matters was not unreasonable.

RACIAL DISCRIMINATION AFTER WORLD WAR II

The shame of discrimination against black military personnel during World War II, plus revelations of Nazi racial atrocities, moved President Harry S. Truman finally to bring the problem to the White House and national attention, with the appointment in 1946 of the President's Commission on Civil Rights. In 1948, the commission submitted its report, *To Secure These Rights,* which laid bare the extent of the problem of racial discrimination and its consequences. The report also revealed the success of experiments with racial integration in the armed forces during World War II to demonstrate to southern society that it had nothing to fear. But the committee recognized that the national government had no clear constitutional authority to pass and implement civil rights legislation. The committee proposed tying civil rights legislation to the commerce power, although it was clear that discrimination was not itself part of the flow of interstate commerce.[6] The committee even suggested using the treaty power as a source of constitutional authority for civil rights legislation.[7]

"separate but equal" rule

doctrine that public accommodations could be segregated by race but still be equal

As for the Supreme Court, it had begun to change its position on racial discrimination before World War II by being stricter about the criterion of equal facilities in the "separate but equal" rule. In 1938, for example, the Court rejected Missouri's policy of paying the tuition of qualified blacks to out-of-state law schools rather than admitting them to the University of Missouri Law School.[8]

After the war, modest progress resumed. In 1950, the Court rejected Texas's claim that its new "law school for Negroes" afforded education equal to that of the all-white University of Texas Law School. Without confronting the "separate but equal" principle itself, the Court's decision anticipated its future civil rights rulings by opening the question of whether *any* segregated facility could be truly equal.[9]

But the Supreme Court, in ordering the admission of blacks to all-white state law schools, did not directly confront the "separate but equal" rule because the Court needed only to recognize the absence of any *equal* law school for blacks. The same was true in 1944, when the Supreme Court struck down the southern practice of "white primaries," which legally excluded blacks from participation in the nominating process. Here the Court simply recognized that primaries could no longer be regarded as the private affairs of the parties but were an integral aspect of the electoral process. This made parties "an agency of the State," and therefore any practice of discrimination against blacks was "state action within the meaning of the Fifteenth Amendment."[10] The most important pre-1954 decision was probably *Shelley v. Kraemer,* in which the Court ruled against the widespread practice of "restrictive covenants," whereby the seller of a home added a clause to the sales contract requiring the buyer to agree not to sell the home later to any non-Caucasian, non-Christian, etc. The Court ruled that although private persons could sign

Separate and *equal?* This 1941 photograph of a school for black students in rural Georgia shows the unequal conditions that African Americans faced in schools and other public accommodations.

Thurgood Marshall (at right), as head of the NAACP's legal staff, led the fight against segregation in cases like that of Autherine Lucy (center), who was denied admission to the University of Alabama because of her race. The NAACP sued to force the university to admit black students. At left is Roy Wilkins, the executive secretary of the NAACP.

A nine-year-old Linda Brown in 1952.

such restrictive covenants, they could not be judicially enforced since the Fourteenth Amendment prohibits any organ of the state, including the courts, from denying equal protection of its laws.[11]

Although none of those pre-1954 cases confronted "separate but equal" and the principle of racial discrimination as such, they were extremely significant to black leaders in the 1940s and gave them encouragement enough to believe that there was at last an opportunity and enough legal precedent to change the constitutional framework itself. Much of this legal work was done by the Legal Defense and Educational Fund of the National Association for the Advancement of Colored People (NAACP). Formed in 1909 to fight discrimination against black people, the NAACP was the most important civil rights organization during the first half of the twentieth century. It set up its Legal Defense Fund to support an ongoing challenge to the legal edifice of segregation. Until the late 1940s, lawyers working for the Legal Defense Fund had concentrated on winning small victories within that framework. Then, in 1948, the Legal Defense Fund upgraded its approach by simultaneously filing suits in different federal districts and through each level of schooling from unequal provision of kindergarten for blacks to unequal sports and science facilities in all-black high schools. After nearly two years of these mostly successful equalization suits, the lawyers decided the time was ripe to confront the "separate but equal" rule head-on, but they felt they needed some heavier artillery to lead the attack. Their choice to lead this attack was African American lawyer Thurgood Marshall, who had been fighting, and often winning, equalization suits since the early 1930s. Marshall was pessimistic about the readiness of the Supreme Court for a full confrontation with segregation itself and the constitutional principle sustaining it. But the unwillingness of Congress after the 1948 election to consider fair employment legislation seems to have convinced Marshall that the courts were the only hope.

The Supreme Court must have come to the same conclusion because, during the four years following 1948, there emerged a clear impression that the Court was willing to take more civil rights cases on appeal. Yet, this was no guarantee that the Court would reverse *on principle* the separate but equal precedent of *Plessy v. Ferguson*. All through 1951 and 1952, as cases were winding slowly through the lower-court litigation maze, intense discussions and disagreements arose among NAACP lawyers as to whether a full-scale assault on *Plessy* was good strategy or whether it might not be better to continue with specific cases alleging unequal treatment and demanding relief with a Court-imposed policy of equalization.[12] But for some lawyers like Marshall, these kinds of victories could amount to a defeat. South Carolina, for example, under the leadership of Governor James F. Byrnes, a former Supreme Court justice, had undertaken a strategy of equalization of school services on a large scale in order to satisfy the *Plessy* rule and to head off or render moot litigation against the principle of separate but equal.

In the fall of 1952, the Court had on its docket cases from Kansas, South Carolina, Virginia, Delaware, and the District of Columbia challenging the constitutionality of school segregation. Of these, the case filed in Kansas became the chosen one. It seemed to be ahead of the pack in its district court, and it had the special advantage of being located in a state outside the Deep South.[13]

Oliver Brown, the father of three girls, lived "across the tracks" in a low-income, racially mixed Topeka neighborhood. Every school-day morning,

Linda Brown took the school bus to the Monroe School for black children about a mile away. In September 1950, Oliver Brown took Linda to the all-white Sumner School, which was closer to home, to enter her into the third grade in defiance of state law and local segregation rules. When they were refused, Brown took his case to the NAACP, and soon thereafter *Brown v. Board of Education* was born. In mid-1953, the Court announced that the several cases on their way up would be reargued within a set of questions having to do with the intent of the Fourteenth Amendment. Almost exactly a year later, the Court responded to those questions in one of the most important decisions in its history.

In deciding the *Brown* case, the Court, to the surprise of many, basically rejected as inconclusive all the learned arguments about the intent and the history of the Fourteenth Amendment and committed itself to considering only the consequences of segregation:

> Does segregation of children in public schools solely on the basis of race, even though the physical facilities and other "tangible" factors may be equal, deprive the children of the minority group of equal educational opportunities? We believe that it does. . . . We conclude that in the field of public education the doctrine of "separate but equal" has no place. Separate educational facilities are inherently unequal.[14]

The *Brown* decision altered the constitutional framework in two fundamental respects. First, after *Brown*, the states no longer had the power to use race as a criterion of discrimination in law. Second, the national government from then on had the power (and eventually the obligation) to intervene with strict regulatory policies against the discriminatory actions of state or local governments, school boards, employers, and many others in the private sector.

CIVIL RIGHTS AFTER *BROWN V. BOARD OF EDUCATION*

Brown v. Board of Education withdrew all constitutional authority to use race as a criterion of exclusion, and it signaled more clearly the Court's determination to use the **strict scrutiny** test in cases related to racial discrimination. This meant that the burden of proof would fall on the government—not on the challengers—to show that the law in question *was* constitutional.[15] Although the use of strict scrutiny in cases relating to racial discrimination would give an advantage to those attacking racial discrimination, the historic decision in *Brown v. Board of Education* was merely a small opening move. First, most states refused to cooperate until sued, and many ingenious schemes were employed to delay obedience (such as paying the tuition for white students to attend newly created "private" academies). Second, even as southern school boards began to cooperate by eliminating their legally enforced (**de jure**) school segregation, there remained extensive actual (**de facto**) school segregation in the North as well as in the South, as a consequence of racially segregated housing that could not be reached by the 1954–55 *Brown* principles. Third, discrimination in employment, public accommodations, juries, voting, and other areas of social and economic activity were not directly touched by *Brown*.

School Desegregation, Phase One Although the District of Columbia and some of the school districts in the border states began to respond almost

---

Brown v. Board of Education
the 1954 Supreme Court decision that struck down the "separate but equal" doctrine as fundamentally unequal. This case eliminated state power to use race as a criterion of discrimination in law and provided the national government with the power to intervene by exercising strict regulatory policies against discriminatory actions

strict scrutiny
test, used by the Supreme Court in racial discrimination cases and other cases involving civil liberties and civil rights, which places the burden of proof on the government rather than on the challengers to show that the law in question is constitutional

de jure
literally, "by law"; legally enforced practices, such as school segregation in the South before the 1960s

de facto
literally, "by fact"; practices that occur even when there is no legal enforcement, such as school segregation in much of the United States today

immediately to court-ordered desegregation, the states of the Deep South responded with a carefully planned delaying tactic commonly called "massive resistance" by the more demagogic southern leaders and "nullification" and "interposition" by the centrists. Either way, southern politicians stood shoulder-to-shoulder to declare that the Supreme Court's decisions and orders were without effect. The legislatures in these states enacted statutes ordering school districts to maintain segregated schools and state superintendents to terminate state funding wherever there was racial mixing in the classroom. Some southern states violated their own long traditions of local school autonomy by centralizing public school authority under the governor or the state board of education and by giving states the power to close the schools and to provide alternative private schooling wherever local school boards might be tending to obey the Supreme Court.

Most of these plans of "massive resistance" were tested in the federal courts and were struck down as unconstitutional.[16] But southern resistance was not confined to legislation. For example, in Arkansas in 1957, Governor Orval Faubus mobilized the Arkansas National Guard to intercede against enforcement of a federal court order to integrate Central High School of Little Rock, and President Eisenhower was forced to deploy U.S. troops and literally place the city under martial law. The Supreme Court considered the Little Rock confrontation so historically important that the opinion it rendered in that case was not only agreed to unanimously but was, unprecedentedly, signed personally by each and every one of the justices.[17] The end of massive resistance, however, became simply the beginning of still another southern strategy, "pupil placement" laws, which authorized school districts to place each pupil in a school according to a whole variety of academic, personal, and psychological considerations, never mentioning race at all. This put the burden of transferring to an all-white school on the nonwhite children and their

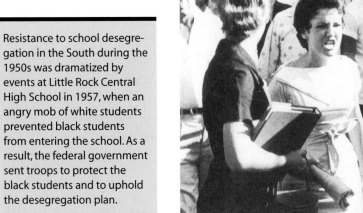

Resistance to school desegregation in the South during the 1950s was dramatized by events at Little Rock Central High School in 1957, when an angry mob of white students prevented black students from entering the school. As a result, the federal government sent troops to protect the black students and to uphold the desegregation plan.

| | PEACEFUL CIVIL RIGHTS DEMONSTRATIONS, 1954–68 | | Table 6.1 |

Year	Total	For Public Accommodations	For Voting
1954	0	0	0
1955	0	0	0
1956	18	6	0
1957	44	9	0
1958	19	8	0
1959	7	11	0
1960	173	127	0
1961	198	122	0
1962	77	44	0
1963	272	140	1
1964	271	93	12
1965	387	21	128
1966	171	15	32
1967	93	3	3
1968	97	2	0

NOTE: This table is drawn from a search of the *New York Times Index* for all references to civil rights demonstrations during the years the table covers. The table should be taken simply as indicative, for the data—news stories in a single paper—are very crude. The classification of the incident as peaceful or violent and the subject area of the demonstration are inferred from the entry in the *Index*, usually the headline from the story. The two subcategories reported here—public accommodations and voting—do not sum to the total because demonstrations dealing with a variety of other issues (e.g., education, employment, police brutality) are included in the total.

SOURCE: Jonathan D. Casper, *The Politics of Civil Liberties* (New York: Harper & Row, 1972), p. 90.

parents, making it almost impossible for a single court order to cover a whole district, let alone a whole state. This delayed desegregation a while longer.[18]

Social Protest and Congressional Action   Ten years after *Brown*, fewer than 1 percent of black school-age children in the Deep South were attending schools with whites.[19] A decade of frustration made it fairly obvious to all observers that adjudication alone would not succeed. The goal of "equal protection" required positive, or affirmative, action by Congress and by administrative agencies. And given massive southern resistance and a generally negative national public opinion toward racial integration, progress would not be made through courts, Congress, or federal agencies without intense, well-organized support. Table 6.1 shows the increase in civil rights demonstrations for voting rights and public accommodations during the fourteen years following *Brown*. It shows that organized civil rights demonstrations began to mount slowly but surely after *Brown v. Board of Education*. By the 1960s, the many organizations that made up the civil rights movement had accumulated experience and built networks capable of launching massive direct-action campaigns against southern segregationists. The Southern Christian Leadership Conference, the Student Nonviolent Coordinating Committee, and many

Hundreds of thousands of demonstrators gathered in the March on Washington in March 1963 to demand civil rights for African Americans.

other organizations had built a movement that stretched across the South. The movement used the media to attract nationwide attention and support. In the massive March on Washington in 1963, the Reverend Martin Luther King, Jr., staked out the movement's moral claims in his famous "I Have a Dream" speech. The image of protesters being beaten, attacked by police dogs, and set upon with fire hoses did much to win broad sympathy for the cause of black civil rights and to discredit state and local governments in the South. In this way, the movement created intense pressure for a reluctant federal government to take more assertive steps to defend black civil rights.

The first modern effort to legislate in the field of civil rights was made in 1957, but the law contained only a federal guarantee of voting rights, without any powers of enforcement, although it did create the Civil Rights Commission to study abuses. Much more important legislation for civil rights followed, especially the Civil Rights Act of 1964. It is important to observe here the mutual dependence of the courts and legislatures—not only do the legislatures need constitutional authority to act, but the courts need legislative and political assistance, through the power of the purse and the power to organize administrative agencies to implement court orders, and through the focusing of political support. Consequently, even as the U.S. Congress finally moved into the field of school desegregation (and other areas of "equal protection"), the courts continued to exercise their powers, not only by placing court orders against recalcitrant school districts, but also by extending and reinterpreting aspects of the "equal protection" clause to support legislative and administrative actions (see Figure 6.1).

CAUSE AND EFFECT IN THE CIVIL RIGHTS MOVEMENT

Figure 6.1

Judicial and Legal Action	Political Action
1954 *Brown v. Board of Education*	
1955 *Brown* II—Implementation of *Brown* I	**1955** Montgomery, Alabama, bus boycott
1956 Federal courts order school integration, especially one ordering Autherine Lucy admitted to University of Alabama, with Governor Wallace officially protesting	
1957 Civil Rights Act creating Civil Rights Commission; President Eisenhower sends paratroops to Little Rock, Arkansas, to enforce integration of Central High School	**1957** Southern Christian Leadership Conference (SCLC) formed, with Martin Luther King, Jr., as president
1960 First substantive Civil Rights Act, primarily voting rights	**1960** Student Nonviolent Coordinating Committee formed to organize protests, sit-ins, freedom rides
1961 Interstate Commerce Commission orders desegregation on all buses and trains, and in terminals	
1961 JFK favors executive action over civil rights legislation	
1963 JFK shifts, supports strong civil rights law; assassination; LBJ asserts strong support for civil rights	**1963** Nonviolent demonstrations in Birmingham, Alabama, lead to King's arrest and his "Letter from the Birmingham Jail"
	1963 March on Washington
1964 Congress passes historic Civil Rights Act covering voting, employment, public accommodations, education	
1965 Voting Rights Act	**1965** King announces drive to register 3 million blacks in the South
1966 War on Poverty in full swing	**Late 1960s** Movement dissipates: part toward litigation, part toward Community Action Programs, part toward war protest, part toward more militant "Black Power" actions

Political action and government action spurred each other to produce dramatic changes in American civil rights policies.

Table 6.2	THE KEY PROVISIONS OF FEDERAL CIVIL RIGHTS LAWS, 1957–91
Civil Rights Act of 1957	Established the Civil Rights Commission to monitor civil rights progress. Elevated the importance of the Civil Rights Division of the Department of Justice, headed by an assistant attorney general. Made it a federal crime to attempt to intimidate a voter or to prevent a person from voting.
Civil Rights Act of 1960	Increased the sanction against obstruction of voting or of court orders enforcing the vote. Established federal power to appoint referees to register voters wherever a "pattern or practice" of discrimination was found by a federal court.
Equal Pay Act of 1963	Banned wage discrimination on the basis of sex in jobs requiring equal skill, effort, and responsibility. Exceptions involved employee pay differentials based on factors other than sex, such as merit or seniority.
Civil Rights Act of 1964	*Voting:* Title I made attainment of a sixth-grade education (in English) a presumption to literacy. *Public accommodations:* Title II barred discrimination in any commercial lodging of more than five rooms for transient guests and in any service station, restaurant, theater, or commercial conveyance. *Public schools:* Title IV empowered the attorney general to sue for desegregation whenever he or she found a segregation complaint meritorious. Title VI authorized the withholding of federal aid from segregated schools. *Private employment:* Title VII outlawed discrimination in a variety of employment practices on the basis of race, religion, and gender (gender added for the first time in an area other than wage discrimination). Established the Equal Employment Opportunity Commission (EEOC) to enforce the law but required it to defer enforcement to state or local agencies for sixty days following each complaint.
Voting Rights Act of 1965	*Voting rights only:* Empowered the attorney general, with the Civil Service Commission, to appoint voting examiners to replace local registrars wherever he or she found fewer than 50 percent of the persons of voting age had voted in the 1964 presidential election and to suspend all literacy tests where they were used as a tool of discrimination.

THE CIVIL RIGHTS ACTS

The right to equal protection of the laws could be established and, to a certain extent, implemented by the courts. But after a decade of very frustrating efforts, the courts and Congress ultimately came to the conclusion that the federal courts alone were not adequate to the task of changing the social rules, and that legislation and administrative action would be needed.

THE KEY PROVISIONS OF FEDERAL CIVIL RIGHTS LAWS, 1957–91 *(continued)*

Table 6.2

Civil Rights Act of 1968	*Open housing:* Made it a crime to refuse to sell or rent a dwelling on the basis of race or religion, if a bona fide offer had been made, or to discriminate in advertising or in the terms and conditions of sale or rental. Administered by the Department of Housing and Urban Development, but the burden of proof is on the complainant, who must seek local remedies first, where they exist.
Amendments of 1970 to 1965 Voting Rights Act	Extended 1965 act and included some districts in northern states.
Equal Employment Opportunity Act of 1972	Increased coverage of the Civil Rights Act of 1964 to include public-sector employees. Gave EEOC authority to bring suit against persons engaging in "patterns or practice" of employment discrimination.
Amendments of 1975 to 1965 Voting Rights Act	Extended 1965 act and broadened antidiscrimination measures to include protection for language minorities (e.g., Latinos, Native Americans).
Amendments of 1978 to 1964 Civil Rights Act	Prohibited discrimination in employment on the basis of pregnancy or related disabilities. Required that pregnancy or related medical conditions be treated as disabilities eligible for medical and liability insurance.
Amendments of 1982 to 1965 Voting Rights Act	Extended 1965 act and strengthened antidiscrimination measures by requiring only proof of *effect* of discrimination, not *intent* to discriminate.
Americans with Disabilities Act of 1990	Extended to people with disabilities protection from discrimination in employment and public accommodations similar to the protection given to women and racial, religious, and ethnic minorities by the 1964 Civil Rights Act. Required that public transportation systems, other public services, and telecommunications systems be accessible to those with disabilities.
Civil Rights Act of 1991	Reversed several Court decisions, beginning with *Wards Cove v. Atonio* (1989), that had made it harder for women and minorities to seek compensation for job discrimination. It put back on the employer the burden of proof to show that a discriminatory policy was a business necessity.

Table 6.2 provides an overview of the efforts made by Congress to use its legislative powers to help make equal protection of the laws a reality. As this table indicates, three civil rights acts were passed during the first decade after the 1954 Supreme Court decision in *Brown v. Board of Education*. But these acts were of only marginal importance. The first two, in 1957 and 1960, established that the Fourteenth Amendment of the Constitution, adopted almost a century earlier, could no longer be disregarded, particularly with regard to

The Civil Rights Act of 1964 helped stop some of the most overt discrimination in public accommodations.

voting. The third, the Equal Pay Act of 1963, was more important, but it was concerned with women, did not touch the question of racial discrimination, and had no enforcement mechanisms.

By far the most important piece of legislation passed by Congress concerning equal opportunity was the Civil Rights Act of 1964. It not only put some teeth in the voting rights provisions of the 1957 and 1960 acts but also went far beyond voting to attack discrimination in public accommodations, segregation in the schools, and at long last, the discriminatory conduct of employers in hiring, promoting, and laying off their employees. Discrimination against women was also included, extending the important 1963 provisions. The 1964 act seemed bold at the time, but it was enacted ten years after the Supreme Court had declared racial discrimination "inherently unequal" under the Fifth and Fourteenth Amendments. And it was enacted long after blacks had demonstrated that discrimination was no longer acceptable. The choice in 1964 was not between congressional action or inaction but between legal action and expanded violence.

Public Accommodations   After the passage of the 1964 Civil Rights Act, public accommodations quickly removed some of the most visible forms of racial discrimination. Signs defining "colored" and "white" rest rooms, water fountains, waiting rooms, and seating arrangements were removed and a host of other practices that relegated black people to separate and inferior arrangements were ended. In addition, the federal government filed more than 400 antidiscrimination suits in federal courts against hotels, restaurants, taverns, gas stations, and other "public accommodations."

Many aspects of legalized racial segregation—such as separate Bibles in the courtroom—seem like ancient history today. But the issue of racial discrimination in public settings is by no means over. In 1993, six African American Secret Service agents filed charges against the Denny's restaurant chain for failing to serve them; white Secret Service agents at a nearby table had received prompt service. Similar charges citing discriminatory service at Denny's restaurants surfaced across the country. Faced with evidence of a pattern of systematic discrimination and numerous lawsuits, Denny's paid $45 million in damages to plaintiffs in Maryland and California in what is said to be the largest settlement ever in a public accommodation case.[20] The Denny's case shows how effective the Civil Rights Act of 1964 can be in challenging racial discrimination. In addition to the settlement, the chain vowed to expand employment and management opportunities for minorities in Denny's restaurants. Other forms of racial discrimination in public accommodations are harder to challenge, however. For example, there is considerable evidence that taxicabs often refuse to pick up black passengers.[21] Such practices may be common, but they are difficult to prove and remedy through the law.

School Desegregation, Phase Two   The 1964 Civil Rights Act also declared discrimination by private employers and state governments (school boards, etc.) illegal, then went further to provide for administrative agencies to help the courts implement these laws. Title IV of the act, for example, authorized the executive branch, through the Justice Department, to implement federal court orders to desegregate schools, and to do so without having to wait for individual parents to bring complaints. Title VI of the act vastly strengthened the role of the executive branch and the credibility of court orders by providing that federal grants-in-aid to state and local governments for education must be withheld from any school system practicing racial segregation. Title VI became the most effective weapon for desegregating schools outside the South, because the situation in northern communities was more subtle and difficult to reach. In the South, the problem was segregation by law coupled with overt resistance to the national government's efforts to change the situation. In contrast, outside the South, segregated facilities were the outcome of hundreds of thousands of housing choices made by individuals and families. Once racial residential patterns emerged, racial homogeneity, property values, and neighborhood schools and churches were defended by realtors, neighborhood organizations, and the like. Thus, in order to eliminate discrimination nationwide, the 1964 Civil Rights Act (1) gave the president through the Office for Civil Rights of the Justice Department the power to withhold federal education grants,[22] and (2) gave the attorney general of the United States the power to initiate suits (rather than having to await complaints) wherever there was a "pattern or practice" of discrimination.[23]

In the decade following the 1964 Civil Rights Act, the Justice Department brought legal action against more than five hundred school districts. During the same period, administrative agencies filed actions against six hundred school districts, threatening to suspend federal aid to education unless real desegregation steps were taken.

Busing   One step taken toward desegregation was busing children from poor urban school districts to wealthier suburban ones. In 1971, the Supreme Court held that state-imposed desegregation could be brought about by busing children across school districts, even where relatively long distances were involved:

> If school authorities fail in their affirmative obligations judicial authority may be invoked. Once a right and a violation have been shown, the scope of a district

In 1993, after the Denny's restaurant chain was charged with racial discrimination, Denny's restaurants were boycotted by protesters such as these from the Labor Black Struggle League.

court's equitable powers to remedy past wrongs is broad. . . . Bus transportation [is] a normal and accepted tool of educational policy.[24]

But the decision went beyond that, adding that under certain limited circumstances even racial quotas could be used as the "starting point in shaping a remedy to correct past constitutional violations," and that pairing or grouping of schools and reorganizing school attendance zones would also be acceptable.

Three years later, however, this principle was severely restricted when the Supreme Court determined that only cities found guilty of deliberate and de jure racial segregation would have to desegregate their schools.[25] This ruling had the effect of exempting most northern states and cities from busing because school segregation in northern cities is generally de facto segregation that follows from segregated housing and from thousands of acts of private discrimination against blacks and other minorities.

Boston provides the best illustration of the agonizing problem of making further progress in civil rights in the schools under the constitutional framework established by these decisions. Boston school authorities were found guilty of deliberately building school facilities and drawing school districts "to increase racial segregation." After vain efforts by Boston school authorities to draw up an acceptable plan to remedy the segregation, federal judge W. Arthur Garrity ordered an elaborate desegregation plan of his own, involving busing between the all-black neighborhood of Roxbury and the nearby white, working-class community of South Boston. Opponents of this plan were organized and eventually took the case to the Supreme Court, where *certiorari* (the Court's device for accepting appeals; see Chapter 15) was denied; this had the effect of approving Judge Garrity's order. The city's schools were so segregated and uncooperative that even the conservative administration of President Richard Nixon had already initiated a punitive cutoff of funds. But many liberals also criticized Judge Garrity's plan as being badly conceived, because it involved two neighboring communities with a history of tension and mutual resentment. The plan worked well at the ele-

Court-ordered busing divided Boston's black and white communities. In 1976, a mob of protesters outside the Boston federal courthouse sought to impale this innocent black bystander, a lawyer on his way to his office. This Pulitzer Prize–winning photograph shows the tension and conflict resulting from the struggle for equal rights for African Americans.

mentary school level but proved so explosive at the high school level that it generated a continuing crisis for the city of Boston and for the whole nation over court-ordered, federally directed desegregation in the North.[26]

Additional progress in the desegregation of schools is likely to be extremely slow unless the Supreme Court decides to permit federal action against de facto segregation and against the varieties of private schools and academies that have sprung up for the purpose of avoiding integration. The prospects for further school integration diminished with a Supreme Court decision handed down on January 15, 1991. The opinion, written for the Court by Chief Justice William Rehnquist, held that lower federal courts could end supervision of local school boards if those boards could show compliance "in good faith" with court orders to desegregate and could show that "vestiges of past discrimination" had been eliminated "to the extent practicable."[27] It is not necessarily easy for a school board to prove that the new standard has been met, but this was the first time since *Brown* and the 1964 Civil Rights Act that the Court had opened the door at all to retreat.

That door was opened further by a 1995 decision in which the Court ruled that the remedies being applied in Kansas City, Missouri, were improper.[28] In accordance with a lower court ruling, the state was pouring additional funding into salaries and remedial programs for Kansas City schools, which had a history of segregation. The aim of the spending was to improve student performance and to attract white students from the suburbs into the city schools. The Supreme Court declared the interdistrict goal improper and reiterated its earlier ruling that states can free themselves of court orders by showing a good faith effort. This decision indicated the Court's new willingness to end desegregation plans even when predominantly minority schools continue to lag significantly behind white suburban schools.

Outlawing Discrimination in Employment   Despite the agonizingly slow progress of school desegregation, there was some progress made in other areas of civil rights during the 1960s and 1970s. Voting rights were established and fairly quickly began to revolutionize southern politics. Service on juries was no longer denied to minorities. But progress in the right to participate in politics and government dramatized the relative lack of progress in the economic domain, and it was in this area that battles over civil rights were increasingly fought.

The federal courts and the Justice Department entered this area through Title VII of the Civil Rights Act of 1964, which outlawed job discrimination by all private and public employers, including governmental agencies (such as fire and police departments), that employed more than fifteen workers. We have already seen (in Chapter 4) that the Supreme Court gave "interstate commerce" such a broad definition that Congress had the constitutional authority to cover discrimination by virtually any local employers.[29] Title VII makes it unlawful to discriminate in employment on the basis of color, religion, sex, or national origin, as well as race.

Title VII delegated some of the powers to enforce fair employment practices to the Justice Department's Civil Rights Division and others to a new agency created in the 1964 act, the Equal Employment Opportunity Commission (EEOC). By executive order, these agencies had the power of the national government to revoke public contracts for goods and services and to refuse to engage in contracts for goods and services with any private company that could not guarantee that its rules for hiring, promotion, and firing were nondiscriminatory. Executive orders in 1965, 1967, and 1969 by Presidents Johnson and Nixon extended and reaffirmed nondiscrimination practices in employment and promotion in the federal government service. And in 1972, President Nixon and a Democratic Congress cooperated to strengthen the EEOC by giving it authority to initiate suits rather than wait for grievances.

But one problem with Title VII was that the complaining party had to show that deliberate discrimination was the cause of the failure to get a job or a training opportunity. Rarely does an employer explicitly admit discrimination on the basis of race, sex, or any other illegal reason. Recognizing the rarity of such an admission, the courts have allowed aggrieved parties (the plaintiffs) to make their case if they can show that an employer's hiring practices had the *effect* of exclusion. A leading case in 1971 involved a "class action" by several black employees in North Carolina attempting to show with statistical evidence that blacks had been relegated to only one department in the Duke Power Company, which involved the least desirable, manual-labor jobs, and that they had been kept out of contention for the better jobs because the employer had added attainment of a high school education and the passing of specially prepared aptitude tests as qualifications for higher jobs. The Supreme Court held that although the statistical evidence did not prove intentional discrimination, and although the requirements were race-neutral in appearance, their effects were sufficient to shift the burden of justification to the employer to show that the requirements were a "business necessity" that bore "a demonstrable relationship to successful performance."[30] The ruling in this case was subsequently applied to other hiring, promotion, and training programs.[31]

Voting Rights   Although 1964 was the *most* important year for civil rights legislation, it was not the only important year. In 1965, Congress significantly strengthened legislation protecting voting rights by barring literacy and other tests as a condition for voting in six southern states,[32] by setting criminal penalties for interference with efforts to vote, and by providing for the replacement of local registrars with federally appointed registrars in counties designated by the attorney general as significantly resistant to registering eligible blacks to vote. The right to vote was further strengthened with ratification in 1964 of the Twenty-fourth Amendment, which abolished the poll tax, and in 1975 with legislation permanently outlawing literacy tests in all fifty states and mandating bilingual ballots or oral assistance for Spanish, Chinese, Japanese, Koreans, Native Americans, and Eskimos.

In the long run, the laws extending and protecting voting rights could prove to be the most effective of all the great civil rights legislation, because the progress in black political participation produced by these acts has altered the shape of American politics. In 1965, in the seven states of the Old Confederacy covered by the Voting Rights Act, 29.3 percent of the eligible black residents were registered to vote, compared to 73.4 percent of the white residents (see Table 6.3). Mississippi was the extreme case, with 6.7 percent black and 69.9 percent white registration. In 1967, a mere two years after implementation of the voting rights laws, 52.1 percent of the eligible blacks in the seven states were registered, comparing favorably to 79.5 percent of the eligible whites, a gap of 27.4 points. By 1972, the gap between black and white registration in the seven states was only 11.2 points, and in Mississippi the gap had been re-

A student volunteer oversees an older woman registering to vote in Mississippi following passage of the Voting Rights Act in 1965. The percentage of African Americans registered to vote in Mississippi increased from about 7 percent in 1965 to more than 62 percent in 1972.

	Before the Act*			After the Act* 1971–72		
	White	**Black**	**Gap†**	**White**	**Black**	**Gap†**
Alabama	69.2%	19.3%	49.9%	80.7%	57.1%	23.6%
Georgia	62.6	27.4	35.2	70.6	67.8	2.8
Louisiana	80.5	31.6	48.9	80.0	59.1	20.9
Mississippi	69.9	6.7	63.2	71.6	62.2	9.4
North Carolina	96.8	46.8	50.0	62.2	46.3	15.9
South Carolina	75.7	37.3	38.4	51.2	48.0	3.2
Virginia	61.1	38.3	22.8	61.2	54.0	7.2
TOTAL	73.4	29.3	44.1	67.8	56.6	11.2

REGISTRATION BY RACE AND STATE IN SOUTHERN STATES COVERED BY THE VOTING RIGHTS ACT

Table 6.3

*Available registration data as of March 1965 and 1971–72.
†The gap is the percentage point difference between white and black registration rates.
SOURCE: U.S. Commission on Civil Rights, *Political Participation* (1968), Appendix VII: Voter Education Project, Attachment to Press Release, October 3, 1972.

duced to 9.4 points. At one time, white leaders in Mississippi attempted to dilute the influence of this growing black vote by **gerrymandering** districts to ensure that no blacks would be elected to Congress. But the black voters changed Mississippi before Mississippi could change them. In 1988, 11 percent of all elected officials in Mississippi were black. This was up one full percentage point from 1987 and closely approximates the size of the national black electorate, which at the time was just over 11 percent of the American voting-age population. Mississippi's blacks had made significant gains (as was true in other Deep South states) as elected state and local representatives, and Mississippi was one of only eight states in the country in which a black judge presided over the highest state court. (Four of the eight were Deep South states.)[33]

Housing   The Civil Rights Act of 1964 did not address housing, but in 1968, Congress passed another civil rights act specifically to outlaw housing discrimination. Called the Fair Housing Act, the law prohibited discrimination in the sale or rental of most housing—eventually covering nearly all the nation's housing. Housing was among the most controversial of discrimination issues because of deeply entrenched patterns of residential segregation across the United States. Such segregation was not simply a product of individual choice. Local housing authorities deliberately segregated public housing, and federal guidelines had sanctioned discrimination in Federal Housing Administration mortgage lending, effectively preventing blacks from joining the exodus to the suburbs in the 1950s and 1960s. Nonetheless, Congress had been reluctant to tackle housing discrimination, fearing the tremendous controversy it could arouse. But, just as the housing legislation was being considered in April 1968, civil rights leader Martin Luther King, Jr., was assassinated; this tragedy brought the measure unexpected support in Congress.

gerrymandering

apportionment of voters in districts in such a way as to give unfair advantage to one racial or ethnic group or political party

Although it pronounced sweeping goals, the Fair Housing Act had little effect on housing segregation because its enforcement mechanisms were so weak. Individuals believing they had been discriminated against had to file suit themselves. The burden was on the individual to prove that housing discrimination had occurred, even though such discrimination is often subtle and difficult to document. Although local fair-housing groups emerged to assist individuals in their court claims, the procedures for proving discrimination proved a formidable barrier to effective change. These procedures were not altered until 1988, when Congress passed the Fair Housing Amendments Act. This new law put more teeth in the enforcement procedures and allowed the Department of Housing and Urban Development (HUD) to initiate legal action in cases of discrimination. With vigorous use, these provisions may prove more successful than past efforts at combating housing discrimination.[34]

Other avenues for challenging residential segregation also had mixed success. HUD tried briefly in the early 1970s to create racially "open communities" by withholding federal funds to suburbs that refused to accept subsidized housing. Confronted with charges of "forced integration" and bitter local protests, however, the administration quickly backed down. Efforts to prohibit discrimination in lending have been somewhat more promising. Several laws passed in the 1970s required banks to report information about their mortgage lending patterns, making it more difficult for them to engage in **redlining,** the practice of refusing to lend to entire neighborhoods. The 1977 Community Reinvestment Act required banks to lend in neighborhoods in which they do business. Through vigorous use of this act, many neighborhood organizations have reached agreements with banks that, as a result, have significantly increased investment in some poor neighborhoods.

redlining

a practice in which banks refuse to make loans to people living in certain geographic locations

The Universalization of Civil Rights

▶ What groups were spurred by the provision of the Civil Rights Act of 1964, outlawing discrimination in employment practices based on race, religion, and gender, to seek broader protection under the law?
▶ What is the politics of the universalization of civil rights?

Even before equal employment laws began to have a positive effect on the economic situation of blacks, something far more dramatic began happening—the universalization of civil rights. The right not to be discriminated against was being successfully claimed by the other groups listed in Title VII of the 1964 Civil Rights Act—those defined by sex, religion, or national origin—and eventually by still other groups defined by age or sexual preference. This universalization of civil rights has become the new frontier of the civil rights struggle, and women have emerged with the greatest prominence in this new struggle. The effort to define and end gender discrimination in employment has led to the historic joining of women's rights to the civil rights cause.

As gender discrimination began to be seen as an important civil rights issue, other groups arose demanding recognition and active protection of their civil rights. Under Title VII, any group or individual can try, and in fact is encouraged to try, to convert goals and grievances into questions of rights and of the deprivation of those rights. A plaintiff must establish only that his or her membership in a group is an unreasonable basis for discrimination—i.e., that it cannot be proven to be a "job-related" or otherwise clearly reasonable and relevant decision. In America today, the list of individuals and groups claiming illegal discrimination is lengthy.

WOMEN AND GENDER DISCRIMINATION

Title VII provided a valuable tool for the growing women's movement in the 1960s and 1970s. In fact, in many ways the law fostered the growth of the women's movement. The first major campaign of the National Organization for Women (NOW) involved picketing the Equal Employment Opportunity Commission for its refusal to ban sex-segregated employment advertisements. NOW also sued the *New York Times* for continuing to publish such ads after the passage of Title VII. Another organization, the Women's Equity Action League (WEAL), pursued legal action on a wide range of sex discrimination issues, filing lawsuits against law schools and medical schools for discriminatory admission policies, for example.

Building on these victories and the growth of the women's movement, feminist activists sought an "Equal Rights Amendment" (ERA) to the Constitution. The proposed amendment was short: its substantive passage stated that "equality of rights under the law shall not be denied or abridged by the United States or by any State on account of sex." The amendment's supporters believed that such a sweeping guarantee of equal rights was a necessary tool for ending all discrimination against women and for making gender roles more equal. Opponents charged that it would be socially disruptive and would introduce changes—such as coed rest rooms—that most Americans did not want. The amendment easily passed Congress in 1972 and won quick approval in many state legislatures, but it fell three states short of the thirty-eight needed to ratify the amendment by the 1982 deadline for its ratification.[35]

In 1993, Teresa Harris won a unanimous Supreme Court decision in her sexual harassment suit against her employer. The Court's decision made it easier for individuals to prove sexual harassment in the workplace.

EQUALITY OF RIGHTS UNDER THE LAW SHALL NOT BE DENIED OR ABRIDGED BY THE UNITED STATES OR BY ANY STATE ON ACCOUNT OF SEX

Even though the Equal Rights Amendment seemed a simple declaration of equal opportunity for women, opposition both inside and outside the women's movement prevented its passage.

Students and Politics

Connecticut College, like an increasing number of colleges in the country, allows its students to establish policy on many issues, including minor legal infractions, sexual harassment, and assault. Dan Thompkins has served on several committees to work with students and faculty in forging policies that are acceptable to all parties. "Lots of what we do is educational," he says. "Conducting forums, things like that—moving beyond the freshman seminars on sexual harassment and date rape into an ongoing dialogue." Thompkins has also served on the college's judiciary board, helping to judge alleged infractions, such as contraband in rooms and vandalism. His experience with his college's decision-making process has translated into an interest in public policy, particularly local politics and issues of civil rights. "I want to remain politically active after school," he says. "Maybe start a local interest group. If I think something needs to happen, and I can do it, why not?"

SOURCE: Dan Thompkins, interview with author, January 27, 1998.

intermediate scrutiny

test, used by the Supreme Court in gender discrimination cases, which places the burden of proof partially on the government and partially on the challengers to show that the law in question is constitutional

Despite the failure of the ERA, gender discrimination expanded dramatically as an area of civil rights law. In the 1970s, the conservative Burger Court (under Chief Justice Warren Burger) helped to establish gender discrimination as a major and highly visible civil rights issue. Although the Burger Court refused to treat gender discrimination as the equivalent of racial discrimination,[36] it did make it easier for plaintiffs to file and win suits on the basis of gender discrimination by applying an "intermediate" level of review to these cases.[37] This **intermediate scrutiny** is midway between traditional rules of evidence, which put the burden of proof on the plaintiff, and the doctrine of strict scrutiny, which requires the defendant to show not only that a particular classification is reasonable but also that there is a need or compelling interest for it. Intermediate scrutiny shifts the burden of proof partially onto the defendant, rather than leaving it entirely on the plaintiff.

One major step was taken in 1992, when the Court decided in *Franklin v. Gwinnett County Public Schools* that violations of Title IX of the 1972 Education Act could be remedied with monetary damages.[38] Title IX forbade gender discrimination in education, but it initially sparked little litigation because of its weak enforcement provisions. The Court's 1992 ruling that monetary damages could be awarded for gender discrimination opened the door for more legal action in the area of education. The greatest impact has been in the areas of sexual harassment—the subject of the *Franklin* case—and in equal treatment of women's athletic programs. The potential for monetary damages has made universities and public schools take the problem of sexual harassment more seriously. Colleges and universities have also started to pay more attention to women's athletic programs. In the two years after the *Franklin* case, complaints to the Education Department's Office for Civil Rights about unequal treatment of women's athletic programs nearly tripled. In several high-profile legal cases, some prominent universities have been ordered to create more women's sports programs; many other colleges and universities have begun to add more women's programs in order to avoid potential litigation.[39] In 1997, the Supreme Court refused to hear a petition by Brown University challenging a lower court ruling that the university establish strict sex equity in its athletic programs. The Court's decision meant that in colleges and universities across the country, varsity athletic positions for men and women must now reflect their overall enrollment numbers.[40]

In 1996, the Supreme Court made another important decision about gender and education by putting an end to all-male schools supported by public funds. It ruled that the policy of the Virginia Military Institute not to admit women was unconstitutional.[41] Along with the Citadel, another all-male military college in South Carolina, VMI had never admitted women in its 157-year history. VMI argued that the unique educational experience it offered—including intense physical training and the harsh treatment of freshmen—would be destroyed if women students were admitted. The Court,

The Violence against Women Act

Each year in the United States, women are the targets of more than half a million sexual assaults, among them 170,000 rapes and 140,000 attempted rapes.[1] This is more than three times the number actually reported to police, a discrepancy that many experts attribute to the reluctance on the part of many women to file formal charges. Everyone agrees that rape and sexual assault represent not just a tragedy for each victim, but a terrible problem for American society. But are rape and other forms of sexual assault also violations of civil rights? Or is the new federal law that defines them as such, the 1994 Violence against Women Act, an excessive broadening of the meaning of "civil rights," one that waters down more traditional understandings of civil rights?

Proponents of the act, prominent among them President Clinton and the National Organization for Women (NOW), argue that rape and sexual assault against women are hate crimes, just as lynching was once a common hate crime against blacks. They argue that just as lynching served to intimidate all blacks in a community, rape and other crimes of violence against individual women serve to intimidate all women. The Violence against Women Act, which gives the victims of sexual assault the right to sue for damages in federal court, draws on federal antilynching laws, which effectively ended the practice by defining it as a violation of civil rights and, consequently, as a violation of federal law.

Skeptics, however, maintain that the Violence against Women Act distorts the notion of "civil rights." They note that lynchings occurred with the wide, if usually tacit, support of whole communities; such wide participation in effect legitimized lynching, turning it from a solitary crime into an act of political oppression. But the situation with rape and other sexual assaults is different, skeptics say. Rape, though it may be statistically too frequent, is never legitimized and supported by a whole community. Thus, skeptics see little basis for finding a political significance in rape. Many of them

assert that proponents of the Violence against Women Act realize this, and are driven by more narrowly political calculations. Such critics charge that the act will erode local jurisdiction over law and order and inundate federal courts with cases.

By early 1995, however, only one case had been brought under the act. It was filed by a young student at Virginia Tech, who claims she was raped during her first month at the school by two members of the school's football team, and that the university did not take her complaint seriously. The woman, Christy Brzonkala (she has chosen to release her name to publicize the case), initially brought a confidential university disciplinary complaint against the two men, but the university dismissed the complaint against one of the men for lack of evidence. The other man, who admitted having sex with the woman but maintained that it had been consensual, received a year's suspension. Just before football season, however, Virginia Tech officials canceled this suspension and cleared him to play. When she heard this, Brzonkala withdrew from the university.

For the two athletes named in the case, who maintain their innocence, and for Virginia Tech, which maintains that it handled the situation properly, the Violence against Women Act represents a form of harassment over matters already resolved. But Christy Brzonkala says that the law is appropriate, because her rape was part of a pattern of misbehavior at Virginia Tech, a pattern in which a female student matters less to the university than a gifted and potentially valuable male athlete. Brzonkala's suit seeks $8.3 million from Virginia Tech and the two young men—a figure chosen because it represents the amount the university's football team received for playing in the 1995 Sugar Bowl.

[1]Data are from the 1995 National Crime Victimization Survey, a federal government survey that each year interviews more than 100,000 Americans aged 12 or older.

College athletics programs have been affected by gender discrimination battles. In recent years, colleges and universities have added more women's sports programs to comply with government orders.

however, ruled that the male-only policy denied "substantial equality" to women. Two days after the Court's ruling, the Citadel announced that it would accept women. VMI considered becoming a private institution in order to remain all-male, but in September 1996, the school board finally voted to admit women. The legal decisions may have removed formal barriers to entry, but the experience of the new female cadets at these schools has not been easy. The first female cadet at the Citadel, Shannon Faulkner, won admission in 1995 under a federal court order but quit after four days. (See the American Political Culture box in Chapter 2.) Although four women were admitted to the Citadel after the Supreme Court decision, two of the four quit several months later. They charged harassment from male students, including attempts to set the female cadets on fire.[42]

Ever since sexual harassment was first declared a form of employment discrimination, employers and many employees have worried about the ambiguity of the issue. When can an employee bring charges and when is the employer liable? In 1998, the Court clarified these questions in an important ruling. It said that if a company has an effective antiharassment policy in place, which the employee fails to use, the company cannot be held liable for sexual harassment. If no policy is in place, the company may be held legally responsible for harassment. In addition, the Court ruled that to pursue a suit on the grounds of sexual harassment, the employee does not have to show that she or he suffered a tangible loss, such as loss of promotion. Most important is whether an effective policy is in place and available to employees.[43]

The development of gender discrimination as an important part of the civil rights struggle has coincided with the rise of women's politics as a discrete movement in American politics. As with the struggle for racial equality, the relationship between changes in government policies and political action suggests that changes in government policies to a great degree produce political action. Today, the existence of a powerful women's movement derives in large measure from the enactment of Title VII of the Civil Rights Act of 1964 and from the Burger Court's vital steps in applying that law to protect women. The recognition of women's civil rights has become an issue that in many ways transcends the usual distinctions of American political debate. In the heavily partisan debate over the federal crime bill enacted in 1994, for instance, the section of the bill that enjoyed the widest support was the Violence Against Women Act, whose most important feature is that it defines gender-biased violent crimes as a matter of civil rights, and creates a civil rights remedy for women who have been the victims of such crimes. Women may now file civil as well as criminal suits against their assailants, which means that they are no longer solely dependent on prosecutors to defend them against violent crime.

LATINOS AND ASIAN AMERICANS

Although the Civil Rights Act of 1964 outlawed discrimination on the basis of national origin, limited English proficiency barred many Asian Americans and Latinos from full participation in American life. Two developments in the 1970s, however, established rights for language minorities. In 1974, the Supreme Court ruled in *Lau v. Nichols,* a suit filed on behalf of Chinese students in San Francisco, that school districts have to provide education for students whose English is limited.[44] It did not mandate bilingual education but it established a duty to provide instruction that the students could understand. A year later, as we saw earlier in this chapter, the 1975 amendments to the Voting Rights Act permanently outlawed literacy tests in all fifty states and mandated bilingual ballots or oral assistance for those who speak Spanish, Chinese, Japanese, Korean, Native American languages, or Eskimo languages.

Asian Americans and Latinos have also been concerned about the impact of immigration laws on their civil rights. Many Asian American and Latino organizations opposed the Immigration Reform and Control Act of 1986 because it imposed sanctions on employers who hire undocumented workers. Such sanctions, they feared, would lead employers to discriminate against Latinos and Asian Americans. These suspicions were confirmed in a 1990 report by the General Accounting Office that found employer sanctions had created a "widespread pattern of discrimination" against Latinos and others who appear foreign.[45] Latinos and Asian Americans have established organizations modeled on the NAACP's Legal Defense Fund, such as the Mexican-American Legal Defense Fund (MALDEF) and the Asian Law Caucus, to monitor and challenge such discrimination. These groups have turned their attention to the rights of legal and illegal immigrants, as anti-immigrant sentiment has grown in recent years.

Students and Politics

In 1992, Amy Cohen sued Brown University over the proposed demotion of women's gymnastics, a team to which Cohen belonged, from an official school-funded sport to a partially funded school club. Also to be cut were women's volleyball, men's golf, and men's water polo. Cohen and her fellow plaintiffs charged the school with violation of Title IX of the Education Amendments of 1972, which states that "no person in the U.S. shall, on the basis of sex, be excluded from participation in, or denied the benefits of, or be subjected to discrimination under any educational program or activity receiving federal aid." The suit claimed that the university had not provided equal opportunities for women to compete in intercollegiate athletics. Though Brown defended its action, saying that 60 percent of those affected by its cuts were male, Federal District Court Judge Raymond J. Pettine agreed with the plaintiffs, forcing Brown to implement a plan of equal athletic opportunity between men and women. *Cohen v. Brown University* was a landmark case in requiring schools to provide opportunities to both female and male athletes.

NATIVE AMERICANS

As a language minority, Native Americans were affected by the 1975 amendments to the Voting Rights Act and the *Lau* decision. The *Lau* decision established the right of Native Americans to be taught in their own languages. This marked quite a change from the boarding schools once run by the Bureau of Indian Affairs, at which members of Indian tribes had been forbidden to speak their own languages. In addition to these language-related issues, Native Americans have sought to expand their rights on the basis of their sovereign status. Since the 1920s and 1930s, Native American tribes have sued the federal government for illegally seizing land, seeking monetary reparations and land as damages. Both types of damages have been awarded in such suits, but only in small amounts. Native American tribes have been more successful in winning federal recognition of their sovereignty. Sovereign status has, in turn, allowed them to exercise greater self-determination. Most significant economically was a 1987 Supreme Court decision that freed Native American tribes from most state regulations prohibiting gambling. The establishment of casino gambling on Native American lands has brought a substantial flow of new income into desperately poor reservations.

In 1998, Casey Martin sued the Professional Golfers' Association (PGA) under the Americans with Disabilities Act of 1990 for the right to use a golf cart in tour events. Martin, who has a degenerative blood disorder in his leg, won the suit.

DISABLED AMERICANS

The concept of rights for the disabled began to emerge in the 1970s as the civil rights model spread to other groups. The seed was planted in a little-noticed provision of the 1973 Rehabilitation Act, which outlawed discrimination against individuals on the basis of disabilities. As in many other cases, the law itself helped give rise to the movement demanding rights for the handicapped.[46] Modeling itself on the NAACP's Legal Defense Fund, the disability movement founded a Disability Rights Education and Defense Fund to press their legal claims. The movement achieved its greatest success with the passage of the Americans with Disabilities Act of 1990, which guarantees equal employment rights and access to public businesses for the disabled. Claims of discrimination in violation of this act are considered by the Equal Employment Opportunity Commission. The impact of the law has been far-reaching, as businesses and public facilities have installed ramps, elevators, and other devices to meet the act's requirements.[47] After its passage, however, concerns about the act's costs began to emerge, as did doubts about whether it truly was assisting people with severe disabilities.

GAYS AND LESBIANS

In less than thirty years, the gay and lesbian movement has become one of the largest civil rights movements in contemporary America. Beginning with street protests in the 1960s, the movement has grown into a well-financed and sophisticated lobby. The Human Rights Campaign Fund is the primary national political action committee (PAC) focused on gay rights; it provides campaign financing and volunteers to work for candidates endorsed by the group. The movement has also formed legal rights organizations, including the Lambda Legal Defense and Education Fund.

Gay and lesbian rights drew national attention in 1993, when President Bill Clinton confronted the question of whether gays should be allowed to serve in the military. As a candidate, Clinton had said he favored lifting the ban on homosexuals in the military. The issue set off a huge controversy in the first months of Clinton's presidency. After nearly a year of deliberation, the administration enunciated a compromise: their "Don't ask, Don't tell" policy. This policy allows gays and lesbians to serve in the military as long as they do not openly proclaim their sexual orientation or engage in homosexual activity. The administration maintained that the ruling would protect gays and lesbians against witch-hunting investigations, but many gay and lesbian advocates expressed disappointment, charging the president with reneging on his campaign promise.

But until 1996, there was no Supreme Court ruling or national legislation explicitly protecting gays and lesbians from discrimination. The first gay rights case that the Court decided, *Bowers v. Hardwick,* ruled against a right to privacy that would protect consensual homosexual activity.[48] After the *Bowers* decision, the gay and lesbian rights movement sought suitable legal cases to test the constitutionality of discrimination against gays and lesbians, much as the black Civil Rights movement did in the late 1940s and 1950s. As one advocate put it, "lesbians and gay men are looking for their *Brown v. Board of Education.*"[49] Among the cases tested were those stemming from local ordinances restricting gay rights (including the right to marry), job discrimination, and family law issues such as adoption and parental rights. In 1996, the Supreme Court, in *Romer v. Evans*, explicitly extended fundamental civil rights protections to gays and lesbians, by declaring unconstitutional a 1992 amendment to the Colorado state constitution that prohibited local governments from passing ordinances to protect gay rights.[50] The decision's forceful language highlighted the connection between gay rights and civil rights as it declared discrimination against gay people unconstitutional.

Despite these Court rulings, gay and lesbian Americans continue to contest other laws that they view as discriminatory. As we saw in Chapter 4, the Hawaiian Supreme Court is likely to declare gay marriage legal in the near future. This victory, however, may well be jeopardized by an amendment to the Hawaiian state constitution, throwing the decision back into the hands of a less-sympathetic state legislature. The favorable rulings of the Hawaiian courts have prompted other states to enact legislation specifically outlawing gay marriage.

Affirmative Action

▶ What is the basis for affirmative action? What forms does it take?

▶ How does affirmative action contribute to the polarization of the politics of civil rights?

▶ How does the debate about affirmative action reflect the debate over American political values?

Not only has the politics of rights spread to increasing numbers of groups in American society since the 1960s, it has also expanded its goal. The relatively narrow goal of equalizing opportunity by eliminating discriminatory barriers developed toward the far broader goal of **affirmative action**—compensatory action to overcome the consequences of past discrimination. An affirmative action policy tends to involve two novel approaches: (1) positive or benign discrimination in which race or some other status is actually taken into account, but for compensatory action rather than mistreatment; and (2) compensatory action to favor members of the disadvantaged group who themselves may never have been the victims of discrimination. Quotas may be but are not necessarily involved in affirmative action policies.

President Lyndon Johnson put the case emotionally in 1965: "You do not take a person who, for years, has been hobbled by chains . . . and then say you are free to compete with all the others, and still just believe that you have been completely fair.[51] Johnson attempted to inaugurate affirmative action by executive orders directing agency heads and personnel officers to pursue vigorously a policy of minority employment in the federal civil service and in companies doing business with the national government. But affirmative action did not become a prominent goal of the national government until the 1970s.

Affirmative action also took the form of efforts by the agencies in the Department of Health, Education, and Welfare to shift their focus from "de-

affirmative action

government policies or programs that seek to redress past injustices against specified groups by making special efforts to provide members of these groups with access to educational and employment opportunities

Student Perspectives

COLLEGE FRESHMEN BACK ADMISSIONS FOR RACE, BUT NOT AFFIRMATIVE ACTION

A 1995 survey of 240,082 students revealed that a large majority supports the use of race as a criterion for college admissions, but fewer are committed to the principle of "affirmative action." Seventy percent of the respondents said that the race of an applicant should be given some special consideration for admissions. On the other hand, about 50 percent thought that "affirmative action" in admissions should be eliminated. This discrepancy reveals both the ambiguity of Americans' views on the topic as well as the political significance of the term "affirmative action."

SOURCE: Tamara Henry, "Freshmen Back Admissions for Race, Not Affirmative Action," *USA Today*, January 8, 1996, p. A1. Data from the UCLA Higher Education Research Institute.

REFERENDUMS ON AFFIRMATIVE ACTION

The courts have not been the only center of action: challenges to affirmative action have also emerged in state and local politics. One of the most significant state actions was the passage of the California Civil Rights Initiative, also known as Proposition 209, in 1996. Proposition 209 outlawed affirmative action programs in the state and local governments of California, thus prohibiting state and local governments from using race or gender preferences in their decisions about hiring, contracting, or university admissions. The political battle over Proposition 209 was heated, and supporters and defenders took to the streets as well as the airwaves to make their cases. When the referendum was held, the measure passed with 54 percent of the vote, including 27 percent of the black vote, 30 percent of the Latino vote, and 45 percent of the Asian American vote.[64] In 1997, the Supreme Court refused to hear a challenge to the new law.

Many observers predicted that the success of California's ban on affirmative action would provoke similar movements in states and localities across the country. But the political factors that contributed to the success of Proposition 209 in California may not exist in many other states. In contrast to California Republican governor Pete Wilson, who strongly opposed affirmative action, other Republican governors, such as New Jersey's Christine Todd Whitman, are strong supporters. Moreover, because public opinion on the issue is very conflicted, the outcome of efforts to roll affirmative action back depends greatly on how the issue is posed to voters. California's Proposition 209 was framed as a civil rights initiative: "the state shall not discriminate against, or grant preferential treatment to, any individual or group on the basis of race, sex, color, ethnicity, or national origin." Different wording can produce quite different outcomes, as a 1997 vote on affirmative action in Houston revealed. There, the ballot initiative asked voters whether they wanted to ban affirmative action in city contracting and hiring, not whether they wanted to end preferential treatment. Fifty-five percent of Houston voters decided in favor of affirmative action.[65]

Affirmative action will continue to be a focus of controversy in coming years, as several other cases challenging affirmative action reach the Supreme Court. There are now several suits similar to the *Hopwood* case working their way through the lower courts, including one against the University of Michigan's affirmative action program. If the Supreme Court decides to hear these cases, the future of affirmative action in universities and colleges will be on the line. Affirmative action is also sure to remain prominent in state and local politics across the country. Efforts to ban affirmative action are under way in a number of states, including Washington, Colorado, Michigan, Massachusetts, Arizona, Arkansas, Ohio, North Dakota, and Oregon.

AFFIRMATIVE ACTION AND AMERICAN POLITICAL VALUES

Affirmative action efforts have contributed to the polarization of the politics of civil rights. At the risk of grievous oversimplification, we can divide the sides by two labels: liberals and conservatives.[66] The conservatives' argument against affirmative action can be reduced to two major points. The first is that rights in the American tradition are *individual* rights, and affirmative action

Affirmative Action

The sweeping civil rights laws enacted in the 1960s officially ended state-sanctioned segregation. They did not, however, end racism, or erase stark inequities between the races in such areas as employment and education. As a consequence, affirmative action policies were enacted to ensure some equality between the races. In the 1978 case of *Regents of the University of California v. Bakke,* the Supreme Court upheld "race-conscious" policies in educational admissions—meaning that race could be used as an admissions criterion—but barred the use of specific, numerical racial quotas. In recent years, a more conservative Supreme Court has chipped away at the scope of such programs—which, incidentally, have become increasingly unpopular among Americans—suggesting that affirmative action programs might be further restricted or eliminated entirely. In 1997, for example, the Court let stand California's Proposition 209, a statewide referendum passed in 1996 that barred the consideration of race or gender in state hiring and school admissions.

Proponents of affirmative action cite the continued need for such programs, especially for African Americans, because of the nation's long history of discrimination and persecution. Racism was institutionalized throughout most of the country's history; indeed, the Constitution specifically recognized, and therefore countenanced, slavery. For example, it rewarded slaveowners with the Three-fifths Compromise, giving slaveowners extra representation in the House of Representatives, a provision excised from the Constitution only after the Civil War. Moreover, few would deny that racism still exists in America. Given these facts, it follows that equal treatment of unequals perpetuates inequality. Programs that give an extra boost to traditionally disadvantaged groups offer the only sure way to overcome structural inequality.

To take the example of university and college admissions, affirmative action opponents argue that admissions decisions should be based on merit, not race. Yet affirmative action does not disregard merit, and in any case, admissions does not operate purely based on merit, however defined, for any college or university. Institutions of higher education rely on such measures as grade point average, board scores, and letters of recommendation. But they also consider such nonmerit factors as region, urban vs. rural background, family relationship to alumni and wealthy donors, athletic ability, or other specialized factors unrelated to the usual definition of merit. The inclusion of race as one of these many admissions criteria is as defensible as any other; moreover, it helps insure a more diverse student body, which in itself is a laudable educational goal. Moreover, such programs do not guarantee educational success, but simply assure that individuals from disadvantaged groups have a chance to succeed, an idea most Americans support. Affirmative action programs have in fact succeeded in providing opportunity to millions who would not otherwise have had the chance.

Opponents of affirmative action argue that such programs, while based on good intentions, do more harm than good. The belief that persons who gain employment or college admission from such programs did not earn their positions stigmatizes those who are supposed to benefit, creating self-doubt among the recipients and mistrust from others. In the realm of education, students admitted to colleges and universities under these special programs have lower graduation rates. Affirmative action also violates the fundamental American value of equality of opportunity. Although all may not possess the same opportunity, the effort expended to provide special advantages to some would be better directed toward making sure that the principles of equal opportunity and merit are followed.

America's history of discrimination, though reprehensible, should not be used as a basis for employment for educational decisions, because it is unreasonable to ask Americans today to pay for the mistakes of their ancestors. Moreover, the track record of affirmative action programs reveals another problem: the groups that have benefited most are middle-class African Americans and women. If anything, preferential programs should focus on *economic* disadvantage, regardless of race, and better education early in life. Good intentions notwithstanding, there are limits to what government social engineering can accomplish, and most Americans favor the abandonment of race-based preference programs.

The Internet has become a battleground for disputes over civil rights. California's battle over affirmative action illustrated the medium's new role, with groups from both sides arguing their case on the Web. The American Civil Liberties Union (ACLU), for example, published a detailed "briefing paper" in favor of continued racial preferences, while the Center for Individual Rights provided arguments against affirmative action legislation, citing Supreme Court decisions in support. Not surprisingly, plenty of less-thoughtful sites also express opinions on this issue. As a result, private groups such as the Anti-Defamation League, as well as law enforcement agencies, monitor the Internet for extremist organizations expressing racist or misogynist opinions. Despite the fact that the Internet provides a forum for neo-Nazis, white supremacists, and conspiracy theorists, the Web makes it easy for all to have their voices heard, and it compels opponents to provide reasons for their opposition.
www.wwnorton.com/wtp2e

violates this concept by concerning itself with "group rights," an idea said to be alien to the American tradition. The second point has to do with quotas. Conservatives would argue that the Constitution is "color-blind," and that any discrimination, even if it is called positive or benign discrimination, ultimately violates the equal protection clause.

The liberal side agrees that rights ultimately come down to individuals, but argues that, since the essence of discrimination is the use of unreasonable and unjust criteria of exclusion to deprive *an entire group* of access to something valuable the society has to offer, then the phenomenon of discrimination itself has to be attacked on a group basis. Liberals can also use Supreme Court history to support their side, because the first definitive interpretation of the Fourteenth Amendment by the Court in 1873 stated explicitly that

> [t]he existence of laws in the state where the newly emancipated Negroes resided, which discriminated with grodss injustice and hardship against them *as a class,* was the evil to be remedied by this clause [emphasis added].[67]

Liberals also have a response to the other conservative argument concerning quotas. The liberal response is that the Supreme Court has already accepted ratios—a form of quota—that are admitted as evidence to prove a "pattern of practice of discrimination" sufficient to reverse the burden of proof—to obligate the employer to show that there was *not* an intent to discriminate. Liberals can also argue that benign quotas often have been used by Americans both to compensate for some bad action in the past or to provide some desired distribution of social characteristics—sometimes called diversity. For example, a long and respected policy in the United States is that of "veteran's preference," on the basis of which the government automatically gives extra consideration in hiring to persons who have served the country in the armed forces. The justification is that ex-soldiers deserve compensation for having made sacrifices for the good of the country. And the goal of social diversity has justified "positive discrimination," especially in higher education, the very institution where conservatives have most adamantly argued against positive quotas for blacks and women. For example, all of the Ivy League schools and many other private colleges and universities regularly and consistently reserve admissions places for some students whose qualifications in a strict academic sense are below those of others who are not admitted. These schools not only recruit students from minority groups, but they set aside places for the children of loyal alumni and of their own faculty, even when, in a pure competition solely and exclusively based on test scores and high school records, many of those same children would not have been admitted. These practices are not conclusive justification in themselves, but they certainly underscore the liberal argument that affirmative or compensatory action for minorities who have been unjustly treated in the past is not alien to American experience.

If we think of the debate about affirmative action in terms of American political values, it is clear that conservatives emphasize liberty, whereas liberals stress equality. Conservatives believe that using government actively to promote equality for minorities and women infringes on the rights of whites. Lawsuits challenging affirmative action often cite this "reverse discrimination" as a justification. Liberals, on the other hand, traditionally have defended affirmative action as the best way to achieve equality. In recent years, however,

AMERICANS' OPINIONS ON CIVIL RIGHTS LAWS | Table 6.4

	Total	Whites	Blacks
Yes	38%	33%	70%
No	58	62	26
No opinion	4	5	4

SOURCE: George Gallup, Jr., *The Gallup Poll: Public Opinion 1993* (Wilmington, DE: Scholarly Resources, 1994), p. 178.

Responses to the question "Do you think new civil rights laws are needed to reduce discrimination against blacks, or not?"

the debate over affirmative action has become more complex and has created divisions among liberals. These divisions stem from growing doubts among some liberals about whether affirmative action can be defended as the best way to achieve equality and about the tensions between affirmative action and democratic values. One recent study of public opinion found that many self-identified liberals were angry about affirmative action.[68] These liberals felt that in the name of equality, affirmative action actually violates norms of fairness and equality of opportunity by giving special advantages to some. Moreover, it is argued, affirmative action is broadly unpopular and is therefore questionable in terms of democratic values. Because our nation has a history of slavery and legalized racial discrimination, and because discrimination continues to exist (although it has declined over time), the question of racial justice, more than any other issue, highlights the difficulty of reconciling our values in practice.

Although the problems of rights in America are agonizing, they can be looked at optimistically. The United States has a long way to go before it constructs a truly just, "equally protected" society. But it also has come very far in a relatively short time. Groups pressing for equality have been able to use government to change a variety of discriminatory practices. The federal government has become an active partner in ensuring civil rights and political equality. All explicit de jure barriers to minorities have been dismantled. Many de facto barriers have also been dismantled, and thousands upon thousands of new opportunities have been opened. Deep and fundamental differences have polarized many Americans (see Table 6.4), but political and governmental institutions have proven themselves capable of maintaining balances between them. This kind of balancing can be done without violence so long as everyone recognizes that policy choices, even about rights, cannot be absolute.

The Citizen's Role

STUDENTS AND POLITICS

Citizens have played the leading role in determining the meaning of civil rights, and students have often been in the forefront of conflicts about civil rights. As we saw in the introduction to this chapter, students played a pivotal role in the Civil Rights movement in the 1960s. When the movement seemed

Many University of California students actively defended affirmative action programs, which came under fire during the 1996 debate over Proposition 209. The initiative, which passed as a statewide referendum, prohibits state or local governments from using race or gender as a basis in hiring, education, or contracting.

to be at an impasse in 1960, students helped to reenergize it with their sit-in at the Woolworth's lunch counter. Sit-ins had been used by labor unions seeking recognition in the 1930s, but it was students who first applied this tactic in civil rights struggles. Likewise, "Freedom Summer," a movement launched in 1964 to register southern blacks to vote, was run by students, four of whom lost their lives registering people to vote that summer.

How have students been involved in civil rights issues in more recent years? Reflecting the conflicting views about what civil rights should mean today, students have been actively involved on both sides of the issue. Students across California were active in the debate about Proposition 209, staging protests and other efforts to persuade voters to reject or support the measure. Since the *Hopwood* decision, students in Texas have held rallies and teach-ins to inform other students about the issues involved. They hope to create a national movement to reinstate affirmative action. Students opposing affirmative action have been less visibly active, but their voices, too, have been heard. For example, the student newspaper at the University of California at Berkeley, *The Californian*, endorsed Proposition 209. Many students on both sides of the issue attended events with speakers presenting arguments for and against affirmative action. Participating in such public events and developing informed opinions is an important kind of political activity.

The range of activities undertaken by supporters of affirmative action raises questions about what is effective political action. On the one hand, protests, such as sit-ins and building takeovers, as occurred after the passage of Proposition 209 and the *Hopwood* decision in Texas, can publicize the views of the protesters. Major newspapers across the country carried accounts of the protests in California. Such protests may spur administrators and politicians to find ways to meet at least some of the goals of affirmative action through different means, since the courts have outlawed current practices. But whether protests can help to change the law or build support for alternatives is an open question. Protests can alienate other students and citizens who may be ambivalent about affirmative action, effectively losing support for the cause. In California, supporters of affirmative action stole copies of the student newspaper that endorsed Proposition 209, making the paper unavailable to readers. Given the commitment to free speech in this country, it is unlikely that such actions generate favorable public opinion, win over new supporters, or put effective pressure on administrators. Decisions about what is effective political action involve thinking hard about the desired outcome and about what actions will help achieve that outcome. These are calculations that every effort to be politically active must make. Often there is no single right answer: effective political action can be learned only by trying many different routes.

Summary

The constitutional basis of civil rights is the "equal protection" clause. This clause imposes a positive obligation on government to advance civil rights, and its original motivation seems to have been to eliminate the gross injustices suffered by "the newly emancipated Negroes . . . as a class." Civil rights call for the expansion of governmental power rather than restraints upon it. This expanded power allows the government to take an active role in promoting equality. But there was little advancement in the interpretation or application of the "equal protection" clause until after World War II. The major breakthrough came in 1954 with *Brown v. Board of Education,* and advancements came in fits and starts during the succeeding ten years.

After 1964, Congress finally supported the federal courts with effective civil rights legislation that outlawed a number of discriminatory practices in the private sector and provided for the withholding of federal grants-in-aid to any local government, school, or private employer as a sanction to help enforce the civil rights laws. From that point, civil rights developed in two ways. First, the definition of civil rights was expanded to include other, nonblack victims of discrimination. Second, the definition of civil rights became increasingly positive; affirmative action has become an official term. Judicial decisions, congressional statutes, and administrative agency actions all have moved beyond the original goal of eliminating discrimination, toward creating new opportunities for minorities and, in some areas, compensating today's minorities for the consequences of discriminatory actions not directly against them but against members of their group in the past. Because compensatory civil rights action has sometimes relied upon quotas, Americans have engaged in intense debate over the constitutionality as well as the desirability of affirmative action, part of a broader debate over American political values. Citizens' involvement in the civil rights movement played a leading role in determining the meaning of civil rights, although recent conflicts over affirmative action have raised questions about what is effective political action.

The story has not ended and is not likely to end. The politics of rights will remain an important part of American political discourse.

FOR FURTHER READING

Baer, Judith A. *Equality under the Constitution: Reclaiming the Fourteenth Amendment.* Ithaca, NY: Cornell University Press, 1983.

Garrow, David J. *Bearing the Cross: Martin Luther King and the Southern Christian Leadership Conference: A Personal Portrait.* New York: Morrow, 1986.

Glendon, Mary Ann. *Rights Talk: The Impoverishment of Political Discourse.* New York: Free Press, 1991.

Greenberg, Jack. *Crusaders in the Courts: How a Dedicated Band of Lawyers Fought for the Civil Rights Revolution.* New York: Basic Books, 1994.

Massey, Douglas S., and Nancy A. Denton. *American Apartheid: Segregation and the Making of the Underclass.* Cambridge, MA: Harvard University Press, 1993.

Nava, Michael. *Created Equal: Why Gay Rights Matter to America.* New York: St. Martin's, 1994.

Rosenberg, Gerald N. *The Hollow Hope: Can Courts Bring About Social Change?* Chicago: University of Chicago Press, 1991.

Thernstrom, Abigail M. *Whose Votes Count? Affirmative Action and Minority Voting Rights.* Cambridge, MA: Harvard University Press, 1987.

STUDY OUTLINE

Civil Rights

1. From 1896 until the end of World War II, the Supreme Court held that the Fourteenth Amendment's equal protection clause was not violated by racial distinction as long as the facilities were equal.

2. After World War II, the Supreme Court began to undermine the separate but equal doctrine, eventually declaring it unconstitutional in *Brown v. Board of Education.*

3. The *Brown* decision marked the beginning of a difficult battle for equal protection in education, employment,

housing, voting, and other areas of social and economic activity.

4. The first phase of school desegregation was met with such massive resistance in the South that, ten years after *Brown,* fewer than 1 percent of black children in the South were attending schools with whites.

5. In 1971, the Supreme Court held that state-imposed desegregation could be brought about by busing children across school districts.

6. Title VII of the Civil Rights Act of 1964 outlawed job discrimination by all private and public employers, including governmental agencies, that employed more than fifteen workers.

7. In 1965, Congress significantly strengthened legislation protecting voting rights by barring literacy and other tests as a condition for voting in southern states. In the long run, the laws extending and protecting voting rights could prove to be the most effective of all civil rights legislation, because increased political participation by minorities has altered the shape of American politics.

The Universalization of Civil Rights

1. The protections won by the African American civil rights movement spilled over to protect other groups as well, including women, Latinos, Asian Americans, Native Americans, disabled Americans, and gays and lesbians.

Affirmative Action

1. By seeking to provide compensatory action to overcome the consequences of past discrimination, affirmative action represents the expansion of the goals of groups championing minority rights.

2. Affirmative action has been a controversial policy. Opponents charge that affirmative action creates group rights and establishes quotas, both of which are inimical to the American tradition. Proponents of affirmative action argue that the long history of group discrimination makes affirmative action necessary and that efforts to compensate for some bad action in the past are well within the federal government's purview. Recent conflicts over affirmative action have raised questions about what is effective political action.

PRACTICE QUIZ

1. When did civil rights become part of the Constitution?
   a) in 1789 at the Founding
   b) with the adoption of the Fourteenth Amendment in 1868
   c) with the adoption of the Nineteenth Amendment in 1920
   d) in the 1954 *Brown v. Board of Education* case

2. Which civil rights case established the "separate but equal" rule?
   a) *Plessy v. Ferguson*
   b) *Brown v. Board of Education*
   c) *Bakke v. Regents of the University of California*
   d) *Adarand Constructors v. Pena*

3. "Massive resistance" refers to efforts by southern states during the late 1950s and early 1960s to
   a) build public housing for poor blacks.
   b) defy federal mandates to desegregate public schools.
   c) give women the right to have an abortion.
   d) bus black students to white schools.

4. Which of the following organizations established a Legal Defense Fund to challenge segregation?
   a) the Association of American Trial Lawyers
   b) the National Association for the Advancement of Colored People
   c) the Student Nonviolent Coordinating Committee
   d) the Southern Christian Leadership Council

5. Which of the following made discrimination by private employers and state governments illegal?
   a) the Fourteenth Amendment
   b) *Brown v. Board of Education*
   c) the 1964 Civil Rights Act
   d) *Bakke v. Board of Regents*

6. In what way does the struggle for gender equality most resemble the struggle for racial equality?
   a) There has been very little political action in realizing the goal.
   b) Changes in government policies to a great degree produced political action.
   c) The Supreme Court has not ruled on the issue.
   d) No legislation has passed adopting the aims of the movement.

7. Which of the following is *not* an example of an area in which women have made progress since the 1970s in guaranteeing certain civil rights?
   a) sexual harassment
   b) integration into all-male publicly supported universities
   c) more equal funding for college women's varsity athletic programs
   d) the passage of the Equal Rights Amendment

8. Which of the following civil rights measures dealt with access to public businesses and accommodations?

a) the 1990 Americans with Disabilities Act
b) the 1964 Civil Rights Act
c) neither a nor b
d) both a and b

9. Which of the following cases represents the *Brown v. Board of Education* case for lesbians and gay men?
a) *Bowers v. Hardwick*
b) *Lau v. Nichols*
c) *Romer v. Evans*

d) There has not been a Supreme Court ruling explicitly protecting gays and lesbians from discrimination.

10. In what case did the Supreme Court find that "rigid quotas" are incompatible with the equal protection clause of the Fourteenth Amendment?
a) *Bakke v. Board of Regents*
b) *Brown v. Board of Education*
c) *United States v. Nixon*
d) *Immigration and Naturalization Service v. Chadha*

CRITICAL THINKING QUESTIONS

1. Supporters of affirmative action argue that it is intended not only to compensate for past discrimination, but also to level an uneven playing field in which discrimination still exists. What do you think? To what extent do we have a society free from discrimination? What is the impact of affirmative action on society today? What alternatives to affirmative action policies exist?

2. Describe the changes in American society between the *Plessy v. Ferguson* and the *Brown v. Board of Education* decisions. Using this as an example, explain how changes in society can lead to changes in civil rights policy or other types of government policy. How might changes in society have predicted the changes in civil rights policy in America since the *Brown* case? How might the changes in civil rights policy have changed American society?

KEY TERMS

affirmative action (p. 221)
Brown v. Board of Education (p. 201)
civil rights (p. 195)
de facto (p. 201)

de jure (p. 201)
discrimination (p. 197)
equal protection clause (p. 197)
gerrymandering (p. 213)
intermediate scrutiny (p. 216)

redlining (p. 214)
"separate but equal" rule (p. 198)
strict scrutiny (p. 201)

PART III

Politics

7

Public Opinion

★ **Political Values**

In what ways do Americans agree on fundamental values but disagree on fundamental issues?

How are political values and beliefs formed? What influences individuals' political beliefs?

What do the differences between liberals and conservatives reveal about American political debate?

★ **How We Form Political Opinions**

What influences the way we form political opinions?

How are political issues marketed and managed by the government, private groups, and the media?

★ **Measuring Public Opinion**

How can public opinion be measured?

What problems arise from public opinion polling?

★ **Public Opinion and Democracy**

How responsive is the government to public opinion?

STUDENTS AND POLITICS

DEMOCRATIC government assumes an informed, interested public. Knowledgeable citizens participate in the political process more than do less-knowledgeable citizens because the former have a better understanding of why politics is relevant to their lives. Political knowledge is also important because it promotes a broader acceptance of democratic values. Thus, political knowledge serves the interests of both the individual and the democracy as a whole. But, as we saw in Chapter 1, many Americans have little political knowledge or interest. In many respects, college students are among the least politically interested and aware of all Americans. A 1996 national survey of more than 300,000 college freshmen, sponsored by the American Council of Education and conducted by the University of California at Los Angeles, found that only about one-fourth of the students surveyed thought "keeping up with political affairs" was important. Only 13 percent said that they frequently discussed political issues. Few students had any interest in civic activism. Less than one-fifth, for example, said that it was important to "participate in programs to help clean up the environment." Less than one-third thought that it was important to "help promote racial understanding." Most students seemed far more concerned with grades, school expenses, and job prospects than with political matters.[1]

It is, of course, perfectly reasonable for individuals to focus more intently on their own immediate concerns than upon national political issues. The former are real and concrete, while the latter seem abstract and distant. Moreover, students can do something about their grades and job prospects, but issues of government and politics often seem utterly beyond their control. As John Muffo, director of academic assessment at Virginia Polytechnic University, said, "There seems to be a growing sense [among students] of, 'Well, there's nothing you can really do about changing politics, so why bother?'"[2]

Nevertheless, if most citizens have no interest in politics and government, how can popular government or the "self-government" so often invoked by the Founders exist? Fortunately, most citizens do have opinions about government and politics and, indeed, may take an interest in the political process when they feel that it affects them. Even apathetic college students can be mobilized to protest, march, and demonstrate to make their opinions known to those in power.

In the spring and fall of 1995, for example, thousands of students at the University of California at Berkeley marched to protest plans by the university's Board of Regents to eliminate affirmative action in the nine-campus University of California system.[3] This was one of the few protests that had taken place on the Berkeley campus since the 1960s, when it was one of the centers of student opposition to the Vietnam War. Public opinion, however, is like the

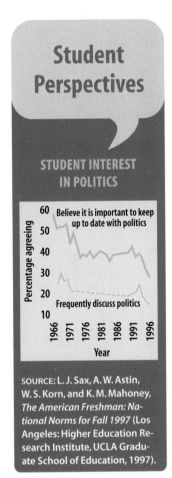

Student Perspectives

STUDENT INTEREST IN POLITICS

SOURCE: L. J. Sax, A. W. Astin, W. S. Korn, and K. M. Mahoney, *The American Freshman: National Norms for Fall 1997* (Los Angeles: Higher Education Research Institute, UCLA Graduate School of Education, 1997).

public opinion

citizens' attitudes about political issues, leaders, institutions, and events

values (or beliefs)

basic principles that shape a person's opinions about political issues and events

political ideology

a cohesive set of beliefs that form a general philosophy about the role of government

attitude (or opinion)

a specific preference on a particular issue

surface of the sea: almost without warning, a calm can give way to powerful storms.

Public opinion is the term used to denote the values and attitudes that people have about issues, events, and personalities. Although the terms are sometimes used interchangeably, it is useful to distinguish between values and beliefs on the one hand, and attitudes or opinions on the other. **Values (or beliefs)** are a person's basic orientations to politics. Values represent deep-rooted goals, aspirations, and ideals that shape an individual's perceptions of political issues and events. Liberty, equality, and democracy are basic political values that most Americans hold. Another useful term for understanding public opinion is *ideology*. **Political ideology** refers to a complex set of beliefs and values that, as a whole, form a general philosophy about government. As we shall see, liberalism and conservatism are important ideologies in America today.

The idea that governmental solutions to problems are inherently inferior to solutions offered by the private sector is a belief held by many Americans. This general belief, in turn, may lead individuals to have negative views of specific government programs even before they know much about them. An **attitude (or opinion)** is a specific view about a particular issue, personality, or event. An individual may have an opinion about Bill Clinton or an attitude toward American policy in Bosnia. The attitude or opinion may have emerged from a broad belief about Democrats or military intervention, but an attitude itself is very specific. Some attitudes may be short-lived.

This chapter will examine the role of public opinion in American politics.

■ *First, we will examine the political values and beliefs that inform how Americans perceive the political process.* After reviewing the most basic American political values, we analyze how values and beliefs are formed and how certain processes and institutions influence their formation. We conclude this introductory section by looking at how a person's set of values and beliefs relates to political ideology.

■ *Second, we turn to the process of how political opinions are formed.* We begin by assessing the relative importance of ideology in this process. We then look at the roles that one's knowledge of politics and influence of political leaders, private groups, and the media have on the formation of political views

■ *Third, we view the science of gathering and measuring public opinion.* The reliability of public opinion is directly related to the way in which it is gathered. Despite the limitations of public opinion polls, they remain an important part of the American political process.

■ *Finally, we conclude with an assessment of the implications of public opinion on American democracy.* Is government responsive to public opinion? Should it be?

★ Political Values

▶ In what ways do Americans agree on fundamental values but disagree on fundamental issues?

▶ How are political values and beliefs formed? What influences individuals' political beliefs?

▶ What do the differences between liberals and conservatives reveal about American political debate?

When we think of opinion, we often think in terms of differences of opinion. The media are fond of reporting and analyzing political differences between blacks and whites, men and women (the so-called gender gap), the young and old, and so on. Certainly, Americans differ on many issues, and often these differences do seem to be associated with race, religion, gender, age, or other social characteristics. Today, Americans seem sharply divided on truly fundamental questions about the role of government in American society, the proper place of religious and moral values in public life, and how best to deal with racial conflicts.

FUNDAMENTAL VALUES

As we review these differences, however, it is important to remember that Americans also agree on a number of matters. Indeed, most Americans share a common set of values, including a belief in the principles—if not always the actual practice—of liberty, equality, and democracy. **Equality of opportunity** has always been an important theme in American society. Americans believe that all individuals should be allowed to seek personal and material success. Moreover, Americans generally believe that such success should be linked to personal effort and ability, rather than to family "connections" or other forms of special privilege. Similarly, Americans have always voiced strong support for the principle of individual **liberty**. They typically support the notion that governmental interference with individuals' lives and property should be kept to the minimum consistent with the general welfare (although in recent years Americans have grown accustomed to greater levels of governmental intervention than would have been deemed appropriate by the founders of liberal theory). And most Americans also believe in **democracy**. They presume that every person should have the opportunity to take part in the nation's governmental and policy-making processes and to have some "say" in determining how they are governed.[4] Figure 7.1 offers some indication of this American consensus on fundamental values: ninety-five percent of Americans who were polled believed in equal opportunity, 89 percent supported free speech without regard to the views being expressed, and 95 percent expressed support for majority rule.

One indication that Americans of all political stripes share these fundamental political values is the content of the acceptance speeches delivered by Bill Clinton and Bob Dole upon receiving their parties' presidential nominations in 1996. Clinton and Dole differed on many specific issues and policies. Yet the political visions they presented reveal an underlying similarity. A major

equality of opportunity

a widely shared American ideal that all people should have the freedom to use whatever talents and wealth they have to reach their fullest potential

liberty

freedom from government control

democracy

a system of rule that permits citizens to play a significant part in the governmental process, usually through the election of key public officials

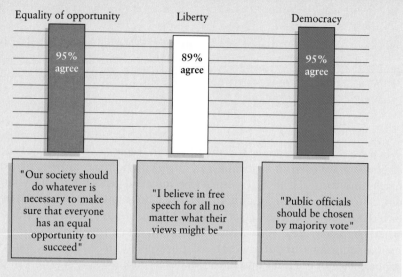

Figure 7.1   **AMERICANS' SUPPORT FOR FUNDAMENTAL VALUES**

SOURCES: 1992 American National Election Studies; Herbert McCloskey and John Zaller, *The American Ethos: Public Attitudes toward Capitalism and Democracy* (Cambridge, MA: Harvard University Press, 1984), p. 25; and Robert S. Erikson, Norman R. Luttbeg, and Kent L. Tedin, *American Public Opinion: Its Origins, Content, and Impact,* 4th ed. (New York: Macmillan, 1991), p. 108.

emphasis of both candidates was equality of opportunity. Clinton referred frequently to opportunity in his speech, even beginning with a poignant story about the importance of equality of opportunity in his own life:

> I never met my father. He was killed in a car wreck on a rainy road three months before I was born. . . . After that my mother had to support us. . . . My mother taught me. She taught me about family and hard work and sacrifice. . . . We must have a government that expands opportunity. . . . We offer our people a new choice based on old values. We offer opportunity. . . . Old fashioned Americans for a new time. Opportunity. Responsibility. Community.

Dole, in his acceptance speech, proclaimed,

> The guiding light of my administration will be that in this country we have no rank order by birth, no claim to favoritism by race, no expectation of judgment other than it be evenhanded. We cannot guarantee the outcome, but we shall guarantee the opportunity.

Thus, however much the two candidates differed on means and specifics, their understandings of the fundamental goals of government were quite similar.

Agreement on fundamental political values, though certainly not absolute, is probably more widespread in the United States than anywhere else in the Western world. During the course of Western political history, competing economic, social, and political groups put forward a variety of radically divergent views, opinions, and political philosophies. America has never been socially or economically homogeneous. But two forces that were extremely powerful and important sources of ideas and beliefs elsewhere in the world were relatively weak or absent in the United States. First, the United States never had the feudal aristocracy that dominated so much of European history. Second, for reasons including America's prosperity and the early availability of political rights, no socialist movements comparable to those that developed in nineteenth-century Europe were ever able to establish themselves in the United States. As a result, during the course of American history, there existed neither an aristocracy to assert the virtues of inequality, special privilege, and a rigid class structure, nor a powerful American communist or socialist party to seriously challenge the desirability of limited government and individualism.[5]

Obviously, the principles that Americans espouse have not always been put into practice. For two hundred years, Americans were able to believe in the principles of equality of opportunity and individual liberty while denying them in practice to generations of African Americans. Yet it is important to note that the strength of the principles ultimately helped to overcome practices that deviated from those principles. Proponents of slavery and, later, of segregation were defeated in the arena of public opinion because their practices differed so sharply from the fundamental principles accepted by most Americans. Ironically, in contemporary politics, Americans' fundamental commitment to equality of opportunity has led to divisions over racial policy. In particular, both proponents and opponents of affirmative action programs cite their belief in equality of opportunity as the justification for their position. Proponents see these programs as necessary to ensure equality of opportunity, while opponents believe that affirmative action is a form of preferential treatment that violates basic American values.[6]

FORMS OF DISAGREEMENT

Agreement on fundamentals by no means implies that Americans do not differ with one another on a wide variety of issues. American political life is characterized by vigorous debate on economic, foreign policy, and social policy issues; race relations; environmental affairs; and a host of other matters. At times, even in America, disagreement on issues becomes so sharp that the proponents of particular points of view have sought to stifle political debate by declaring their opponents' positions to be too repulsive to be legitimately discussed. During the 1950s, for example, some ultraconservatives sought to outlaw the expression of opinions they deemed to be "communistic." Often this label was applied as a way of discrediting what were essentially liberal views. In the 1990s, some groups have sought to discredit conservatives by accusing them of racism, sexism, and homophobia when their views have not agreed with more liberal sentiments. On a number of university campuses, some African American and feminist groups have advocated the adoption of speech codes outlawing expression seen as insulting to individuals on the basis of their race or gender. In general, however, efforts to regulate the expression of opinion in this way have not been very successful in the United States. Americans believe strongly in free speech and prefer the hidden regulatory hand of the market to the heavier regulatory hand of the law. Many of the universities that initially adopted speech codes have been forced to rescind them.[7]

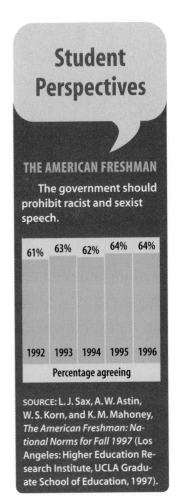

Student Perspectives

THE AMERICAN FRESHMAN

The government should prohibit racist and sexist speech.

61%	63%	62%	64%	64%
1992	1993	1994	1995	1996

Percentage agreeing

SOURCE: L. J. Sax, A. W. Astin, W. S. Korn, and K. M. Mahoney, *The American Freshman: National Norms for Fall 1997* (Los Angeles: Higher Education Research Institute, UCLA Graduate School of Education, 1997).

Gay Marriage

The idea that all Americans are entitled to equal treatment is today a widely accepted principle. More controversial, however, is the matter of how that principle ought to apply to homosexuals. Most Americans embrace a live-and-let-live philosophy regarding homosexuality; at the same time, however, many Americans are uneasy with some highly publicized efforts to define or extend civil rights for gays. This unease is reflected in voters' rejection of some local and state resolutions barring discrimination based on sexual preference.

Central to this debate has been the question of whether states should officially sanction gay marriage. Marriage itself is a private decision, but such a union between two people must also be approved by the state through the issuance of a marriage license if the couple is to receive many of the benefits of marriage, from tax breaks to insurance protection. Complicating this debate is the "full faith and credit" clause of the Constitution (Article IV, Section 1), which says that all states  must honor the public acts of any other state, including marriage licenses. Thus, if gay marriage is recognized in even one state, other states are obliged to recognize its legality, too.

Supporters of gay marriage point out that homosexuality is neither a fad nor a choice, but an involuntary condition. Given this, loving relationships are inevitable, and it is a denial of equality to discriminate against gays because they seek the same bond of marriage as heterosexuals. The objective is not to elevate gay rights above those of other persons, but to end discrimination against gays. Civil marriage for gays would amount to formal public recognition of a homosexual union, making it in principle the same as a heterosexual marriage—that is, a formal recognition of a lifelong emotional commitment of two people to each other—ending the hypocrisy of pretending that a gay union is somehow less loving or less important than a heterosexual one. Such recognition would actually encourage traditional values of fidelity and stability among homosexuals. It would also ease financial, insurance, and other problems, because gay partners could receive health, life insurance, and pension benefits, and it would clarify such matters as inheritance, property, and adoption rights. Some localities have extended such rights through domestic-partnership laws, but these enactments are relatively uncommon and vary in their applicability. Gay marriage would not demean heterosexual marriage; rather, it would help promote the traditional virtues of marriage.

Opponents of gay marriage argue that marriage, as it is traditionally defined by law and religion, does and ought to apply only to heterosexual unions. If state governments officially sanctioned gay marriage, they would, in effect, be endorsing a lifestyle that society simply does not equate with heterosexual marriage. Law reflects society's moral values, and those values do not countenance gay unions. Furthermore, a traditional purpose of marriage is the creation of children, and that cannot occur within the confines of a gay marriage (without the intervention of a third person). Many gay couples would seek to adopt children, but not enough research exists to demonstrate whether children would be harmed by such a situation.

Far from elevating traditional marriage values, state sanctioning of gay marriage would demean heterosexual marriage at a time when that venerable institution is being rocked by high divorce rates, spousal abuse, juvenile delinquency, and more single-parent families. The use of domestic-partnership laws can provide a remedy for problems related to insurance, inheritance, and the like, without taking the more extreme step of officially sanctioning gay marriage. Above all, marriage represents the union of a man and a woman. Efforts to redefine this relationship by incorporating gay unions violate long and deeply held societal principles of right and wrong. One can still support the right of individuals to engage in consensual behavior in private without embracing public recognition of such activity.

Disagreement over abortion rights has been particularly divisive in the United States.

As we shall see later in this chapter, differences of political opinion are often associated with such variables as income, education, and occupation. Similarly, factors such as race, gender, ethnicity, age, religion, and region, which not only influence individuals' interests but also shape their experiences and upbringing, have enormous influence on their beliefs and opinions. For example, individuals whose incomes differ substantially have different views on the desirability of a number of important economic and social programs. In general, the poor—who are the chief beneficiaries of these programs—support them more strongly than do those whose taxes pay for the programs. Similarly, blacks and whites have different views on questions of civil rights and civil liberties—presumably reflecting differences of interest and historical experience. In recent years, many observers have begun to take note of a number of differences between the views expressed by men and those supported by women, especially on foreign policy questions, where women appear to be much more concerned with the dangers of war, and on social welfare issues, where women show more concern than men for the problems of the poor and the unfortunate. Let us see how such differences develop.

HOW POLITICAL VALUES ARE FORMED

The attitudes that individuals hold about political issues and personalities tend to be shaped by their underlying political beliefs and values. For example, an individual who has basically negative feelings about government intervention into America's economy and society would probably be predisposed to oppose the development of new health care and social programs. Similarly, someone who distrusts the military would likely be suspicious of any call for the use of American troops. The processes through which these underlying political beliefs and values are formed are collectively called **political socialization.**

political socialization

the induction of individuals into the political culture; learning the underlying beliefs and values that the political system is based on

FREE SPEECH AND THE VIETNAM WAR

The relative political calm of the 1950s gave way to a turbulent, frenetic, and anti-status quo political environment in the 1960s. This dramatic political change was sparked by a variety of concerns, including poverty, racial discrimination, and, especially, America's growing involvement in the Vietnam War. College campuses became hotbeds of protest and discontent, and the University of California at Berkeley, long known for student agitation, was among the first places to register that discontent. The Berkeley campus was the birthplace of what came to be known as the "free speech movement."

In the early 1960s, politicized Berkeley students launched a series of protests, demonstrations, marches, sit-ins, and other activities intended to draw attention to several causes, including the Civil Rights movement, nuclear disarmament, and the fight against a nationwide anticommunist movement. These protests were held both on and off campus, and followed the nonviolent style used by civil rights activists in the South. The formerly strict campus rules against political activities had been loosened at Berkeley, but students continued to push for greater freedom of expression. In the face of what it saw as improper student organization of social and political protest from the campus, the university administration imposed restrictions on certain on-campus activities, expelled some students, and called in police forces to maintain campus order.

In 1964, student leaders at Berkeley formed the Free Speech Movement. Within a few months, they won their effort to get the university to roll back its restrictions on political speech and other lawful political activities. Yet the movement was less about the particular question of free speech on campus as it was an umbrella organization encompassing a wide array of protest activities. Increasingly mistrustful of authority figures at the university and in the country at large, the Free Speech Movement's adherents sought to extend the classroom into the street and

---

The process of political socialization is important. Probably no nation, and certainly no democracy, could survive if its citizens did not share some fundamental beliefs. If Americans had few common values or perspectives, it would be very difficult for them to reach agreement on particular issues. In contemporary America, some elements of the socialization process tend to produce differences in outlook, whereas others promote similarities. Four of the most important **agencies of socialization** that foster differences in political perspectives are the family, membership in social groups, education, and prevailing political conditions.

No inventory of agencies of socialization can fully explain the development of a given individual's basic political beliefs. In addition to the factors that are important for everyone, forces that are unique to each individual play a role in shaping political orientations. For one person, the character of an early encounter with a member of another racial group can have a lasting impact on that individual's view of the world. For another, a highly salient political event, such as the Vietnam War, can leave an indelible mark on that person's political consciousness. For a third person, some deep-seated personality characteristic, such as paranoia, for example, may strongly influence the formation of political beliefs. Nevertheless, knowing that we cannot fully explain the development of any given individual's political outlook, let us look at some of the most important agencies of socialization that do affect one's beliefs.

agencies of socialization

social institutions, including families and schools, that help to shape individuals' basic political beliefs and values

bring the street into the classroom. By the spring of 1965, as America began to escalate its military involvement in Vietnam, students began to lodge protests against the war and against the military draft that supported it. A new group, Students for a Democratic Society (SDS), epitomized the new political movement that sought to accelerate political and social change in the United States.

As America's involvement in Vietnam increased, so too did student agitation and protest. The antiwar movement spread to many college campuses and became both more vocal and more radicalized. President Lyndon Johnson came under particular attack for his Vietnam policies. Johnson continued to assure the country that the U.S. military was winning the war, but when Americans learned that Johnson had not been honest with the public about what turned out to be a military and political quagmire, American sentiment began to turn against the war. In 1967 and 1968, disaffected students worked intensively to dislodge Johnson by supporting the peace candidacy of Democratic senator Eugene McCarthy. Rising support for McCarthy helped persuade Johnson not to seek re-election in 1968.

The election of Richard Nixon to the presidency in 1968 did not put an end to the war, and antiwar activities intensified across the country. Those activities peaked with Nixon's invasion of Cambodia in 1970, which prompted tumultuous student reaction on campuses everywhere. The student cause was further dramatized when four students at Kent State University in Ohio were shot and killed by National Guard troops during a protest against the invasion of Cambodia.

By 1972, American military involvement had been significantly cut, and a year later, American involvement in Vietnam effectively ended. The eclipsing war also meant an eclipsing student movement. Student activism and protests encompassing such issues as the environment, women's rights, and civil rights continued, but the degree and intensity of student activism seen in the 1960s would not appear again. In the words of Berkeley faculty member Nathan Glazer, the Free Speech Movement "stands at the beginning of the student rebellion in this country."

SOURCE: David Lance Goines, *The Free Speech Movement* (Berkeley, CA: Ten Speed Press, 1993).

INFLUENCES ON OUR POLITICAL VALUES

The Family   Most people acquire their initial orientation to politics from their families. As might be expected, differences in family background tend to produce divergent political outlooks. Although relatively few parents spend much time teaching their children about politics, political conversations occur in most households and children tend to absorb many of their parents' political views, perhaps without realizing it. Studies have suggested, for example, that party preferences are initially acquired at home. Children raised in households in which both parents are Democrats tend to become Democrats themselves, whereas children raised in homes where both parents are Republicans tend to favor the GOP (Grand Old Party, a traditional nickname for the Republican Party).[8] Similarly, children reared in politically liberal households are more likely than not to develop a liberal outlook, whereas children raised in politically conservative settings are prone to see the world through conservative lenses. Obviously, not all children absorb their parents' political views. Two of former president Ronald Reagan's three children, for instance, rejected their parents' conservative values. Moreover, even those children whose views are initially shaped by parental values may change their minds as they mature and experience political life for themselves. Nevertheless, the family is an important initial source of political orientation for everyone.

Political beliefs begin to be formed at an early age, as children are exposed to their parents' political views.

Social Groups   Another important source of divergent political orientations and values are the social groups to which individuals belong. Social groups include those to which individuals belong involuntarily—gender and racial groups, for example—as well as those to which people belong voluntarily—such as political parties, labor unions, and educational and occupational groups. Some social groups have both voluntary and involuntary attributes. For example, individuals are born with a particular social-class background, but as a result of their own efforts people may move up—or down—the class structure.

Membership in social groups can affect political values in a variety of ways. Membership in a particular group can give individuals important experiences and perspectives that shape their view of political and social life. In American society, for example, the experiences of blacks and whites can differ significantly. Blacks are a minority and have been victims of persecution and discrimination throughout American history. Blacks and whites also have different educational and occupational opportunities, often live in separate communities, and may attend separate schools. Such differences tend to produce distinctive political outlooks. For example, in 1995 blacks and whites had very different reactions to the murder trial of former football star O. J. Simpson, who was accused of killing his ex-wife and a friend of hers. Seventy percent of the white Americans surveyed believed that Simpson was guilty, based on the evidence presented by the police and prosecutors. But an identical 70 percent of the black Americans surveyed immediately after the trial believed that the police had fabricated evidence and had sought to convict Simpson of a crime he had not committed; these beliefs were presumably based on blacks' experiences with and perceptions of the criminal justice system.[9]

According to other recent surveys, blacks and whites in the United States differ on a number of issues. For example, among middle-income Americans (defined as those earning between $30,000 and $75,000 per year), 65 percent of black respondents and only 35 percent of white respondents thought racism was a major problem in the United States today. Within this same group of respondents, 63 percent of blacks and only 39 percent of whites thought the federal government should provide more services even at the cost of higher taxes.[10] Other issues show a similar pattern of disagreement, reflecting the differences in experience, background, and interests between blacks and whites in America (see Figure 7.2).

Men and women have important differences of opinion as well. Reflecting differences in social roles, political experience, and occupational patterns, women tend to be less militaristic than men on issues of war and peace, more likely than men to favor measures to protect the environment, and more supportive than men of government social and health care programs (see Table 7.1). Perhaps because of these differences on issues, women are more likely than men to vote for Democratic candidates.[11] This tendency for men's and women's opinions to differ is called the **gender gap.**

gender gap

a distinctive pattern of voting behavior reflecting the differences in views between women and men

DISAGREEMENT AMONG BLACKS AND WHITES — Figure 7.2

The average African American is **"just as well off"** as the average white person in terms of ...
- ...income — Whites 44%, Blacks 0%
- ...jobs — Whites 51%, Blacks 13%

The average African American is **"a lot worse off"** than the average white person in terms of ...
- ...income — Whites 20%, Blacks 53%
- ...jobs — Whites 11%, Blacks 63%

I would rather have the federal government provide more services, even if it costs more in taxes. — Whites 39%, Blacks 63%

Racism is a big problem in our society today. — Whites 35%, Blacks 65%

Past and present discrimination is the major reason for the economic and social ills blacks face. — Whites 30%, Blacks 84%

Affirmative action should be for low-income people, not for persons of a specific race or sex. — Whites 60%, Blacks 44%

SOURCE: Washington Post/Kaiser Family Foundation/Harvard University survey reported in Kevin Merida, "Worry, Frustration Build for Many in Black Middle Class," *Washington Post,* October 9, 1995, p. A1. © 1995 The Washington Post. Reprinted with permission.

African Americans and white Americans have strong differences of opinion on certain issues.

The reactions of these college students to the announcement of the "not guilty" verdict in the trial of O. J. Simpson reveal the gulf of opinion between whites and blacks about Simpson's guilt.

Membership in a social group can affect individuals' political orientations in another way: through the efforts of groups themselves to influence their members. Labor unions, for example, often seek to "educate" their members through meetings, rallies, and literature. These activities are designed to shape union members' understanding of politics and to make them more amenable to supporting the political positions favored by union leaders. Similarly, organization can sharpen the impact of membership in an involuntary group. Women's groups, black groups, religious groups, and the like usually endeavor to structure their members' political views through intensive educational pro-

Table 7.1

DISAGREEMENTS AMONG MEN AND WOMEN ON ISSUES OF WAR AND PEACE

Government action	Percentage approving of action	
	Men	Women
Presence of U.S. troops in Bosnia	44	38
Bombing of military sites in Iraq	86	80
Ending ban on homosexuals in military	34	51
Military operation against Somali warlord	72	60
Going to war against Iraq	72	53
Sending U.S. troops to Saudi Arabia in response to Iraqi invasion of Kuwait	78	54

SOURCE: Gallup Poll, 1991, 1993, 1995.

Talking About Race

He poked and prodded and preached. He wandered the stage with microphone in hand and often challenged his audience: When is voluntary segregation acceptable? What difference does it make for whites and blacks to socialize together? Is it time for government to stop helping people based on race and focus instead on class? The answers were not always as blunt as the questions. But as President Clinton hosted his first town hall meeting on race [on December 4, 1997], he labored to . . . get the nation to explore perhaps its most vexing and volatile social issues.

"What we're trying to do here is drop a pebble in the pond and have it reverberate all across America," Clinton said. "If we can find constructive ways for people to work together, learn together, talk together, be together, that's the best shot we've got . . . to avoid some of the difficult problems we've had in our history."

Never before has a president personally conducted such a public discussion on race in America. For two hours, as a national television audience watched, Clinton and 67 college students, civic leaders and business executives recounted their experiences with people of different colors. From a white man who admitted fearing black men on the street to a biracial youth insulted because his checks are held up at the bank, the talk at times touched on the most sensitive and poignant of human relations. Yet as divisive as race has been in the nation's political arena lately, [the president's] forum produced more anecdotes and entreaties for better relations—one woman urged everyone to follow the Golden Rule—than extended debate about the public-policy issues that remain unsettled in the post–civil rights era. . . .

The town hall meeting, conducted at the University of Akron and broadcast live on C-SPAN, was the first of several Clinton [planned] to hold . . . as part of [a] yearlong campaign for racial reconciliation. To encourage Americans to talk about issues that often are left undiscussed absent a national crisis, the White House organized 96 "watch sites" around the country where groups of people tuned into the Akron forum and then engaged in their own discussions after it was over. . . .

In selecting people to share the stage with Clinton [in Akron], the White House pledged to find a cross section of society and came up with a blend of participants from different racial and ethnic backgrounds. But in addition to students, organizers drew heavily from the local establishment, including a senator, congressman, mayor, university president, school superintendent, city council member, county executive, bank vice president, newspaper publisher and Fortune 500 CEO. . . .

During the program, many shared sometimes painful memories of how they have been treated because of their race. "I've been to banks where I've given them a check to deposit for my mother and . . . they've put holds on them unnecessarily," said McHughson Chambers, a biracial University of Akron student. "When I tell people I'm Puerto Rican, they wonder why I'm not like [actress] Rosie Perez or anybody like that—why don't I speak like her, why don't I look like her," said Anna Arroyo, a pre-med student. An African American woman who did not give her name recalled that a college roommate "broke out in hives when she discovered that I was going to be her roommate and I was black." . . .

Many of the 1,500 local residents who watched the exchange in the campus hall here later said they were encouraged by the dialogue—even if it did not always delve as deeply as they wished into the subtler issues of race. "They touched on a lot of things, but they didn't always dig into them," said Christavus Dominic, a graduate student.

JoAnn Harris, a criminal-justice professor at the university, called the meeting refreshing. "I'm glad he's doing it," she said of Clinton. "But it is almost sinful that we are still talking about and dealing with a problem that has plagued us for so long."

SOURCE: Peter Baker and Michael A. Fletcher, "Explosive Issue Fails to Ignite at Town Hall Meeting on Race," *Washington Post*, December 4, 1997, p. A1. ©1997, The Washington Post. Reprinted with permission.

grams. The importance of such group efforts can be seen from the impact of group membership on political opinion. Women who belong to women's organizations, for example, are likely to differ more from men in their political views than women without such group affiliation.[12] Other analysts have found that African Americans who belong to black organizations are likely to differ more from whites in their political orientations than blacks who lack such affiliations.[13]

In many cases, no particular efforts are required by groups to affect their members' beliefs and opinions. Often, individuals will consciously or unconsciously adapt their views to those of the groups with which they identify. For example, an African American who is dubious about affirmative action is likely to come under considerable peer pressure and internal pressure to modify his or her views. In this and other cases, dissenters are likely gradually to shift their own views to conform to those of the group. Political psychologist Elisabeth Noelle-Neumann has called this process the "spiral of silence."[14]

A third way that membership in social groups can affect political beliefs is through what might be called objective political interests. On many economic issues, for example, the interests of the rich and poor differ significantly. Inevitably, these differences of interest will produce differences of political outlook. James Madison and other framers of the Constitution thought that the inherent gulf between the rich and the poor would always be the most important source of conflict in political life. Certainly today, struggles over tax policy, welfare policy, health care policy, and so forth are fueled by differences of interest between wealthier and poorer Americans. In a similar vein, objective differences of interest between "senior citizens" and younger Americans can lead to very different views on such diverse issues as health care policy, social security, and criminal justice.

It is worth pointing out again that, like the other agencies of socialization, group membership can never fully explain a given individual's political views. One's unique personality and life experiences may produce political views very different from those of the group to which one might nominally belong. This is why some African Americans are conservative Republicans, or why an occasional wealthy industrialist is also a socialist. Group membership is conducive to particular outlooks, but it is not determinative.

Differences in Education   A third important source of differences in political perspectives comes from a person's education. In some respects, of course, schooling is a great equalizer. Governments use public education to try to teach all children a common set of civic values. It is mainly in school that Americans acquire their basic belief in liberty, equality, and democracy. In history classes, students are taught that the Founders fought for the principle of liberty. Through participation in class elections and student government, students are taught the virtues of democracy. In the course of studying such topics as the Constitution, the Civil War, and the civil rights movement, students are taught the importance of equality. These lessons are repeated in every grade in a variety of contexts. No wonder they are such an important element in Americans' beliefs.

At the same time, however, differences in educational attainment are strongly associated with differences in political outlook. In particular, those who attend college are often exposed to philosophies and modes of thought

EDUCATION AND PUBLIC OPINION

Table 7.2

| | Education | | | |
Issues	Drop-out	High school	Some college	College grad.
1. Women and men should have equal roles.	62%	74%	82%	83%
2. The Gulf War was worth it.	48	55	57	61
3. The death penalty should be abolished.	23	17	16	25
4. Government should see to it that people have good jobs and an acceptable standard of living.	43	29	26	27
5. Government should improve the social and economic conditions of African Americans.	25	13	20	31
6. Government should provide fewer services to reduce government spending.	25	28	26	42

SOURCE: The American National Election Studies, 1992 data, provided by the Inter-University Consortium for Political and Social Research, University of Michigan.

The figures show the percentage of respondents in each category agreeing with the statement.

that will forever distinguish them from their friends and neighbors who do not pursue college diplomas. Table 7.2 outlines some general differences of opinion that are found between college graduates and other Americans.

In recent years, conservatives have charged that liberal college professors indoctrinate their students with liberal ideas. College does seem to have some "liberalizing" effect upon students, but, more significantly, college seems to convince students of the importance of political participation and of their own capacity to have an impact on politics and policy. Thus, one of the major differences between college graduates and other Americans can be seen in levels of political participation. College graduates vote, write "letters to the editor," join campaigns, take part in protests, and, generally, make their voices heard. Does this mean that college graduates are turned into dangerous radicals by liberal professors? Quite the contrary: College seems to convince individuals that it is important to involve themselves in the nation's politics. What perspective could be more conservative?

Political Conditions   A fourth set of factors that shape political orientations and values are the conditions under which individuals and groups are recruited into and involved in political life. Although political beliefs are influenced by family background and group membership, the precise content and character of these views is, to a large extent, determined by political circumstances. For example, in the nineteenth century, millions of southern Italian peasants left their homes. Some migrated to cities in northern Italy; others came to cities in the United States. Many of those who moved to northern Italy were recruited by socialist and communist parties and became mainstays of the forces of the Italian Left. At the same time, their cousins and neighbors who migrated to American cities were recruited by urban patronage machines and became mainstays of political conservatism. In both instances, group membership influenced political beliefs. Yet the character of those beliefs varied enormously with the political circumstances in which a given group found itself.

In a similar vein, the views held by members of a particular group can shift drastically over time, as political circumstances change. For example, American white southerners were staunch members of the Democratic Party from the Civil War through the 1960s. As members of this political group, they became key supporters of liberal New Deal and post–New Deal social programs that greatly expanded the size and power of the American national government. Since the 1960s, however, southern whites have shifted in large numbers to the Republican Party. Now they provide a major base of support for efforts to scale back social programs and to sharply reduce the size and power of the national government. The South's move from the Democratic to the Republican camp took place because of white southern opposition to the Democratic Party's racial policies and because of determined Republican efforts to win white southern support. It was not a change in the character of white southerners but a change in the political circumstances in which they found themselves that induced this major shift in political allegiances and outlooks in the South.

The moral of this story is that a group's views cannot be inferred simply from the character of the group. College students are not inherently radical or inherently conservative. Jews are not inherently liberal. Southerners are not inherently conservative. Men are not inherently supportive of the military. Any group's political outlooks and orientations are shaped by the political circumstances in which that group finds itself, and those outlooks can change as circumstances change.

FROM POLITICAL VALUES TO IDEOLOGY

As we have seen, people's beliefs about government can vary widely. But for some individuals, this set of beliefs can fit together into a coherent philosophy about government. This set of underlying orientations, ideas, and beliefs through which we come to understand and interpret politics is called a political ideology. Ideologies take many different forms. Some people may view politics primarily in religious terms. During the course of European political history, for example, Protestantism and Catholicism were often political ideologies as much as they were religious creeds. Each set of beliefs not only included elements of religious practice but also involved ideas about secular authority and political action. Other people may see politics through racial lenses. Nazism was a political ideology that placed race at the center of political life and sought to interpret politics in terms of racial categories.

In America today, people often describe themselves as liberals or conservatives. Liberalism and conservatism are political ideologies that include beliefs about the role of the government, ideas about public policies, and notions about which groups in society should properly exercise power (see Boxes 7.1 and 7.2). These ideologies can be seen as the end results of the process of political socialization that was discussed in the preceding section.

PROFILE OF A LIBERAL: JESSE JACKSON   Box 7.1

dvocates increasing taxes for corporations and for the wealthy. Advocates a "Right to Food Policy" to make available a nutritionally balanced diet for all U.S. citizens.

Advocates the establishment of a national health care program for all citizens.

Advocates higher salaries for teachers, more college grants and loans, and a doubling of the federal education budget.

Favors increasing the minimum wage.

Advocates the use of $500 billion in pension funds to finance public works programs, including the construction of a "national railroad."

Favors foreign assistance programs designed to wipe out hunger and starvation throughout the world.

Advocates dramatic expansion of federal social and urban programs.

Today, the term **liberal** has come to imply support for political and social reform, extensive government intervention in the economy, the expansion of federal social services, and more vigorous efforts on behalf of the poor, minorities, and women, as well as greater concern for consumers and the environment. In social and cultural areas, liberals generally support abortion rights, are concerned with the rights of persons accused of crime, support decriminalization of drug use, and oppose state involvement with religious institutions and religious expression. In international affairs, liberal positions are usually seen as including support for arms control, opposition to the development and testing of nuclear weapons, support for aid to poor nations, opposition to the use of American troops to influence the domestic affairs of developing nations, and support for international organizations such as the United Nations.

liberal

a liberal today generally supports political and social reform; extensive governmental intervention in the economy; the expansion of federal social services; more vigorous efforts on behalf of the poor, minorities, and women; and greater concern for consumers and the environment

PROFILE OF A CONSERVATIVE: PATRICK BUCHANAN   Box 7.2

ants to trim the size of the federal government and transfer power to state and local governments. Wants to diminish government regulation of business.

Favors prayer in the public schools.

Opposes gay rights legislation.

Supports programs that would allow children and parents more flexibility in deciding what school to attend.

Supports strict regulation of pornography.

Favors making most abortions illegal.

Would eliminate some environmental regulations.

Supports harsher treatment of criminals.

Opposes affirmative action programs.

Opposes allowing women to serve in military combat units.

Opposes U.S. participation in international organizations.

Opposes the North American Free Trade Agreement (NAFTA).

conservative

today this term refers to those who generally support the social and economic status quo and are suspicious of efforts to introduce new political formulae and economic arrangements. Conservatives believe that a large and powerful government poses a threat to citizens' freedom

By contrast, the term **conservative** today is used to describe those who generally support the social and economic status quo and are suspicious of efforts to introduce new political formulae and economic arrangements. Conservatives believe strongly that a large and powerful government poses a threat to citizens' freedom. Thus, in the domestic arena, conservatives generally oppose the expansion of governmental activity, asserting that solutions to social and economic problems can be developed in the private sector. Conservatives particularly oppose efforts to impose government regulation on business, pointing out that such regulation is frequently economically inefficient and costly and can ultimately lower the entire nation's standard of living. As to social and cultural positions, many conservatives oppose abortion, support school prayer, are more concerned for the victims than the perpetrators of crimes, oppose school busing, and support traditional family arrangements. In international affairs, conservatism has come to mean support for the maintenance of American military power.

To some extent, contemporary liberalism and conservatism can be seen as differences of emphasis with regard to the fundamental American political values of liberty and equality. For liberals, equality is the most important of the core values. Liberals are willing to tolerate government intervention in such areas as college admissions and business decisions when these seem to result in high levels of race, class, or gender inequality. For conservatives, on the other hand, liberty is the core value. Conservatives oppose most efforts by the government, however well intentioned, to intrude into private life or the marketplace. This simple formula for distinguishing liberalism and conservatism, however, is not always accurate, because political ideologies seldom lend themselves to neat or logical characterizations. Often political observers search for logical connections among the various positions identified with liberalism or with conservatism, and they are disappointed or puzzled when they are unable to find a set of coherent philosophical principles that define and unite the several elements of either of these sets of beliefs. On the liberal side, for example, what is the logical connection between opposition to U.S. government intervention in the affairs of foreign nations and calls for greater intervention in America's economy and society? On the conservative side, what is the logical relationship between opposition to governmental regulation of business and support for a government ban on abortion? Indeed, the latter would seem to be just the sort of regulation of private conduct that conservatives claim to abhor.

Frequently, the relationships among the various elements of liberalism or of conservatism are political rather then logical. One underlying basis of liberal views is that all or most represent criticisms of or attacks on the foreign and domestic policies and cultural values of the business and commercial strata that have been prominent in the United States for the past century. In some measure, the tenets of contemporary conservatism represent this elite's defense of its positions against its enemies, who include organized labor, minority groups, and some intellectuals and professionals. Thus, liberals attack business and commercial elites by advocating more governmental regulation, including consumer protection and environmental regulation, opposing new military weapons programs, and supporting expensive social programs. Conservatives counterattack by asserting that governmental regulation of the economy is ruinous and that new military weapons are needed in a changing

Student Perspectives

THE AMERICAN FRESHMAN

"How would you describe your political orientation?"

Far left	Liberal	Middle of the road	Conservative	Far right
3%	22%	53%	21%	2%

SOURCE: L. J. Sax, A. W. Astin, W. S. Korn, and K. M. Mahoney, *The American Freshman: National Norms for Fall 1997* (Los Angeles: Higher Education Research Institute, UCLA Graduate School of Education, 1997).

AMERICANS' SHIFTING IDEOLOGY, 1973–94

Figure 7.3

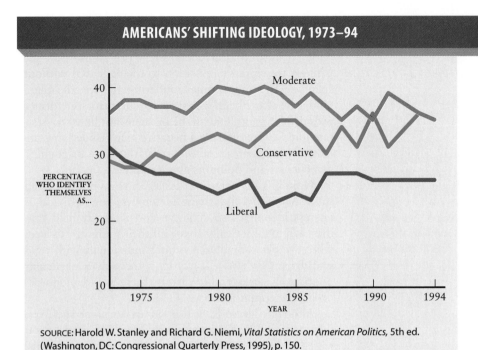

SOURCE: Harold W. Stanley and Richard G. Niemi, *Vital Statistics on American Politics,* 5th ed. (Washington, DC: Congressional Quarterly Press, 1995), p. 150.

world, and they seek to stigmatize their opponents for showing no concern for the rights of "unborn" Americans.

Of course, it is important to note that many people who call themselves liberals or conservatives accept only part of the liberal or conservative ideology. During the 1980s, many political commentators asserted that Americans were becoming increasingly conservative. Indeed, it was partly in response to this view that the Democrats in 1992 selected a presidential candidate, Bill Clinton, drawn from the party's moderate wing. Although it appears that Americans have adopted more conservative outlooks on some issues, their views in most areas have remained largely unchanged or even have become more liberal in recent years. Thus, many individuals who are liberal on social issues are conservative on economic issues. There is nothing illogical about these mixed positions. They simply indicate the relatively open and fluid character of American political debate. As Figure 7.3 indicates, Americans are often apt to shift their ideological preferences.

How We Form Political Opinions

▶ What influences the way we form political opinions?
▶ How are political issues marketed and managed by the government, private groups, and the media?

An individual's opinions on particular issues, events, and personalities emerge as he or she evaluates these phenomena through the lenses of the beliefs and

Students and Politics

In his first year of college, University of Virginia (UVA) student Eric Stetson has already begun to influence one of America's major third parties, the Libertarians, who promote the idea of a minimalist government that allows its citizens maximum freedom. Stetson started an Internet campaign for media recognition of Libertarian candidate Harry Brown in 1996 called "News from Cyberspace," which helped introduce Brown to audiences of *Crossfire* and *Politically Incorrect*. More recently, Stetson has taken an active role in Libertarian issues on the UVA campus, including organizing FreedomFest, a weekend of events celebrating a Jeffersonian idea of freedom. Finally, Stetson and fellow UVA student Byron Smith have started the Libertarian Students of America (www.libertarians.com/students), an organization meant to link campus Libertarian groups in an effort to increase dialogue and influence. According to Stetson, although his ideology would appeal to many Americans, the public must be aware of third parties for Libertarians to have more than a fringe effect, and that means getting the word out. "It's something I love to do and believe in," he says. "We're laying the groundwork for future Libertarians to enter politics."

SOURCE: Eric Stetson, interview with author, February 12, 1998.

orientations that, taken together, comprise his or her political ideology. Thus, if a conservative is confronted with a plan to expand federal social programs, he or she is likely to express opposition to the endeavor without spending too much time pondering the specific plan. Similarly, if a liberal is asked to comment on former president Ronald Reagan, he or she is not likely to hesitate long before offering a negative view. Underlying beliefs and ideologies tend to automatically color people's perceptions and opinions about politics.

Opinions on particular issues, however, are seldom fully shaped by underlying ideologies. Few individuals possess ideologies so cohesive and intensely held that they will automatically shape all their opinions. Indeed, when we occasionally encounter individuals with rigid worldviews, who see everything through a particular political lens, we tend to dismiss them as "ideologues," or lacking common sense.

Although ideologies color our political perspectives, they seldom fully determine our views. This is true for a variety of reasons. First, as noted earlier, most individuals' ideologies contain internal contradictions. Take, for example, a conservative view of the issue of abortion. Should conservatives favor outlawing abortion as an appropriate means of preserving public morality, or should they oppose restrictions on abortion because these represent government intrusions into private life? In this instance, as in many others, ideology can point in different directions.

Second, individuals may have difficulty linking particular issues or personalities to their own underlying beliefs. Some issues defy ideological characterization. Should conservatives support or oppose the proposed elimination of the Department of Commerce? What should liberals think about America's 1994 intervention in Haiti? Each of these policies combines a mix of issues and is too complex to be viewed through simple ideological lenses.

Finally, most people have at least some conflicting underlying attitudes. Most conservatives support *some* federal programs—defense, or tax deductions for businesses, for example—and wish to see them, and hence the government, expanded. Many liberals favor American military intervention in other nations for what they deem to be humanitarian purposes, but generally oppose American military intervention in the affairs of other nations.

Thus, most individuals' attitudes on particular issues do not spring automatically from their ideological predispositions. It is true that most people have underlying beliefs that help to shape their opinions on particular issues, but two other factors are also important: a person's knowledge of political issues, and outside influences on that person's views.

POLITICAL KNOWLEDGE

As we have seen, general political beliefs can guide the formation of opinions on specific issues, but an individual's beliefs and opinions are not always consistent with one another. Studies of political opinion have shown that most people don't hold specific and clearly defined opinions on every political issue. As a result, they are easily influenced by others. What best explains whether citizens are generally consistent in their political views or inconsistent and open to the influence of others? The key is knowledge and information about political issues. In general, knowledgeable citizens are better able to evaluate new information and determine whether it is relevant to and consistent with their beliefs and opinions. As a result, better-informed individuals can recognize their political interests and act consistently on behalf of them.

One of the most obvious and important examples of this proposition is voting. Despite the predisposition of voters to support their own party's candidates (see Chapter 9 for a discussion of party identification), millions of voters are affected by the information they receive about candidates during a campaign. During the 1996 presidential campaign, for instance, voters weighed the arguments of Bill Clinton against those of Bob Dole about who was better fit to run the U.S. economy based on what they (the voters) knew about the country's economic health. Many Republican voters actually supported Bill Clinton because they approved of the economic policies followed during his first term in office. Thus citizens can use information and judgment to overcome their predispositions. Without some political knowledge, citizens would have a difficult time making sense of the complex political world in which they live.

This point brings up two questions, however. First, how much political knowledge is necessary to act as an effective citizen? And second, how is political knowledge distributed throughout the population? In a recent study of political knowledge in the United States, political scientists Michael X. Delli Carpini and Scott Keeter found that the average American exhibits little knowledge of political institutions, processes, leaders, and policy debates. For example, in a 1996 poll, only about half of all Americans could correctly identify Newt Gingrich as the Speaker of the House of Representatives.[15] Does this ignorance of key political facts matter?

Another important concern is the character of those who possess and act upon the political information that they acquire. Political knowledge is not evenly distributed throughout the population. As we saw in Chapters 1 and 2, those with higher education, income, and occupational status and who are members of social or political organizations are more likely to know about and be active in politics. An interest in politics reinforces an individual's sense of **political efficacy** and provides more incentive to acquire additional knowledge and information about politics. Those who don't think they can have an effect on government tend not to be interested in learning about or participating in politics. As a result, individuals with a disproportionate share of income and education also have a disproportionate share of knowledge and influence and are better able to get what they want from government.

political efficacy
the ability to influence government and politics

THE INFLUENCE OF POLITICAL LEADERS, PRIVATE GROUPS, AND THE MEDIA

When individuals attempt to form opinions about particular political issues, events, and personalities, they seldom do so in isolation. Typically, they are confronted—sometimes bombarded—by the efforts of a host of individuals and groups seeking to persuade them to adopt a particular point of view. Someone trying to decide what to think about Bill Clinton, Colin Powell, or Newt Gingrich could hardly avoid an avalanche of opinions expressed

marketplace of ideas

the public forum in which beliefs and
ideas are exchanged and compete

through the media, in meetings, or in conversations with friends. The **marketplace of ideas** is the interplay of opinions and views that takes place as competing forces attempt to persuade as many people as possible to accept a particular position on a particular event. Given constant exposure to the ideas of others, it is virtually impossible for most individuals to resist some modification of their own beliefs. For example, as we saw earlier, African Americans and white Americans disagree on a number of matters. Yet, as political scientists Paul Sniderman and Edward Carmines have shown, considerable cross-racial agreement has evolved on fundamental issues of race and civil rights.[16]

The marketplace of ideas has created a common ground on which the discussion of issues is encouraged, based on common understandings. Despite the many and often sharp divisions that exist in the twentieth century—between liberals and conservatives or different income groups—most Americans see the world through similar lenses. This idea market makes it possible for ideas of all sorts to compete for attention and acceptance.

Few ideas spread spontaneously. Usually, whether they are matters of fashion, science, or politics, ideas must be vigorously promoted to become widely known and accepted. For example, the clothing, sports, and entertainment fads that occasionally seem to appear from nowhere and sweep the country before being replaced by some other new trend are almost always the product of careful marketing campaigns by some commercial interest, rather than spontaneous phenomena. Like their counterparts in fashion, successful—or at least widely held—political ideas are usually the products of carefully orchestrated campaigns by government or by organized groups and interests, rather than the results of spontaneous popular enthusiasm. In general, new ideas are presented in ways that make them seem consistent with, or even logical outgrowths of, Americans' more fundamental beliefs. For example, proponents of affirmative action generally present the policy as a necessary step toward racial equality. Or opponents of a proposed government regulation will vehemently assert that the rule is inconsistent with liberty. Both supporters and opponents of campaign finance reform seek to wrap their arguments in the cloak of democracy.[17]

Three forces that play important roles in shaping opinions are the government, private groups, and the news media.

Government and the Shaping of Public Opinion   All governments attempt, to a greater or lesser extent, to influence, manipulate, or manage their citizens' beliefs. But the extent to which public opinion is actually affected by governmental public relations efforts is probably limited. The government—despite its size and power—is only one source of information and evaluation in the United States. Very often, governmental claims are disputed by the media, by interest groups, and at times by opposing forces within the government itself. Often, too, governmental efforts to manipulate public opinion backfire when the public is made aware of the government's tactics. Thus, in 1971, the United States government's efforts to build popular support for the Vietnam War were hurt when CBS News aired its documentary "The Selling of the Pentagon," which purported to reveal the extent and character of governmental efforts to sway popular sentiment. In this documentary, CBS demonstrated the techniques, including planted news stories and faked film footage, that the government had used to misrepresent its activities in Vietnam. These revelations, of course, undermined popular trust in all governmental claims.

A hallmark of the Clinton administration has been the steady use of techniques like those used in election campaigns to bolster popular enthusiasm for White House initiatives. The president established a political "war room," similar to the one that operated in his campaign headquarters, where representatives from all departments meet daily to discuss and coordinate the president's public relations efforts. Many of the same consultants and pollsters who directed the successful Clinton campaign have been employed in the selling of the president's programs.[18]

Indeed, the Clinton White House has made more sustained and systematic use of public-opinion polling than any previous administration. For example, during his presidency Bill Clinton has relied heavily on the polling firm of Penn & Schoen to help him decide which issues to emphasize and what strategies to adopt. During the 1995–96 budget battle with Congress, the White House commissioned polls almost every night to chart changes in public perceptions about the struggle. Poll data suggested to Clinton that he should present himself as struggling to save Medicare from Republican cuts. Clinton responded by launching a media attack against what he claimed were GOP efforts to hurt the elderly. This proved to be a successful strategy and helped Clinton defeat the Republican budget.[19] The administration, however, has asserted that it uses polls only as a check on its communications strategy.[20]

Of course, at the same time that the Clinton administration has worked diligently to mobilize popular support, its opponents have struggled equally hard to mobilize popular opinion against the White House. A host of public and private interest groups opposed to President Clinton's programs crafted public relations campaigns designed to generate opposition to the president. For example, in 1994, while Clinton campaigned to bolster popular support for his health care reform proposals, groups representing small businesses and segments of the insurance industry, among others, developed their own publicity campaigns that ultimately convinced many Americans that Clinton's initiative posed a threat to their own health care. These opposition campaigns played an important role in the eventual defeat of the president's proposal.

Private Groups and the Shaping of Public Opinion As the story of the health care debate may suggest, political issues and ideas seldom emerge spontaneously from the grass roots. We have already seen how the government tries to shape public opinion. But the ideas that become prominent in political life are also developed and spread by important economic and political groups searching for issues that will advance their causes. One example is the "right-to-life" issue that has inflamed American politics over the past twenty years.

The notion of right-to-life, whose proponents seek to outlaw abortion and overturn the Supreme Court's *Roe v. Wade* decision, was developed and heavily promoted by conservative politicians who saw the issue of abortion as a means of uniting Catholic and Protestant conservatives and linking both groups to the Republican Party. These politicians convinced Catholic and evangelical Protestant leaders that they shared similar views on the question of abortion, and they worked with religious leaders to focus public attention on the negative issues in the abortion debate. To advance their cause, leaders of the movement sponsored well-publicized Senate hearings, where testimony, photographs, and other exhibits were presented to illustrate the violent effects of abortion procedures. At the same time, publicists for the movement produced leaflets, articles, books, and films such as *The Silent Scream* to highlight the agony and pain ostensibly felt by the "unborn" when they were being aborted. All this underscored the movement's claim that abortion was nothing more or less than the murder of millions of innocent human beings. Finally, Catholic and evangelical Protestant religious leaders were organized to denounce abortion from their church pulpits and, increasingly, from their electronic pulpits on the Christian Broadcasting Network (CBN) and the various other television forums available for religious programming. Religious leaders also organized demonstrations, pickets, and disruptions at abortion clinics throughout the nation.[21] Abortion rights remain a potent issue; it even influenced the debate over health care reform.

Among President Clinton's most virulent critics have been leaders of the religious Right who were outraged by his support for abortion and gay rights. Conservative religious leaders have attacked the president's programs and mounted biting personal attacks on both Clinton and his wife, Hillary Rodham Clinton. Other conservative groups not associated with the religious Right also have launched sharp assaults against the president. Nationally syndicated talk-show host Rush Limbaugh, for one, is a constant critic of the administration.

Typically, ideas are marketed most effectively by groups with access to financial resources, public or private institutional support, and sufficient skill or education to select, develop, and draft ideas that will attract interest and support. Thus, the development and promotion of conservative themes and ideas in recent years has been greatly facilitated by the millions of dollars that conservative corporations and business organizations such as the Chamber of Commerce and the Public Affairs Council spend each year on public information and what is now called in corporate circles "issues management." In addition, conservative business leaders have contributed millions of dollars to such conservative institutions as the Heritage Foundation, the Hoover Institution, and the American Enterprise Institute.[22] Many of the ideas that helped those on the right influence political debate were first developed and articulated by scholars associated with institutions such as these.

Although they do not usually have access to financial assets that match those available to their conservative opponents, liberal intellectuals and pro-

Rev. Pat Robertson, founder of the Christian Broadcasting Network and the Christian Coalition. Religion is a dominant influence on the political opinions of many Americans.

fessionals have ample organizational skills, access to the media, and practice in creating, communicating, and using ideas. During the past three decades, the chief vehicle through which liberal intellectuals and professionals have advanced their ideas has been the "public interest group," an institution that relies heavily on voluntary contributions of time, effort, and interest on the part of its members. Through groups like Common Cause, the National Organization for Women, the Sierra Club, Friends of the Earth, and Physicians for Social Responsibility, intellectuals and professionals have been able to use their organizational skills and educational resources to develop and promote ideas.[23] Often, research conducted in universities and in liberal "think tanks" such as the Brookings Institution provides the ideas on which liberal politicians rely. For example, the welfare reform plan introduced by the Clinton administration in 1994 originated with the work of former Harvard professor David Ellwood. Ellwood's academic research led him to the conclusion that the nation's welfare system would be improved if services to the poor were expanded in scope but limited in duration. His idea was adopted by the 1992 Clinton campaign, which was searching for a position on welfare that would appeal to both liberal and conservative Democrats. The Ellwood plan seemed perfect: It promised liberals an immediate expansion of welfare benefits, yet it held out to conservatives the idea that welfare recipients would receive benefits only for a limited period of time. The Clinton welfare reform plan even borrowed phrases from Ellwood's book *Poor Support*.[24]

Students and Politics

Despite being the daughter of a State Department employee, Spellman College student Zarat Akande did not grow up with a career in politics in mind—only a general interest in foreign relations, history, and the Constitution. During her sophomore year, however, school officials convinced Akande to attend the FIRST (Foundation for Individual Responsibility and Social Trust) conference in Philadelphia, a venue to discuss issues important to today's college generation and to form some consensus, both regionally and nationally, from a diverse set of interests, views, and social and geographical backgrounds. FIRST aims eventually to present the younger generation's viewpoints in the form of action plans to the presidential candidates during the elections in the year 2000. "It's not like we're running away from being labeled," says another FIRST participant. "We just want to be labeled differently." As a result of her work in the national discussion group, Akande will help to lead a regional conference in Atlanta. "FIRST is like family," she says. "Everyone listens to everyone's viewpoints with respect and a sense of purpose."

SOURCE: Zarat Akande, interview with author, January 21, 1998.

Journalist and author Joe Queenan has correctly observed that although political ideas can erupt spontaneously, they almost never do. Instead, he says,

> issues are usually manufactured by tenured professors and obscure employees of think tanks. . . . It is inconceivable that the American people, all by themselves, could independently arrive at the conclusion that the depletion of the ozone layer poses a dire threat to our national well-being, or that an immediate, across-the-board cut in the capital-gains tax is the only thing that stands between us and the economic abyss. The American people do not have that kind of sophistication. *They have to have help.*[25]

Whatever their particular ideology or interest, those groups that can muster the most substantial financial, institutional, educational, and organizational resources—or, as we shall see later, access to government power—are also best able to promote their ideas in the marketplace. Obviously, these resources are most readily available to upper-middle- and upper-class groups. As a result, their ideas and concerns are most likely to be discussed and disseminated by books, films, newspapers, magazines, and the electronic media. As we shall see in the next chapter, upper-income groups dominate the marketplace of ideas, not only as producers and promoters, but also as consumers of ideas. In general, and particularly in the political realm, the print and broadcast media and the publishing industry are most responsive to the tastes and views of the more "upscale" segments of the potential audience.

The Media and Public Opinion   The communications media are among the most powerful forces operating in the marketplace of ideas. As we shall see in Chapter 8, the mass media are not simply neutral messengers for ideas developed by others. Instead, the media have an enormous impact on popular attitudes and opinions. Over time, the ways in which the mass media report political events help to shape the underlying attitudes and beliefs from which opinions emerge.[26] For example, for the past thirty years, the national news media have relentlessly investigated personal and official wrongdoing on the part of politicians and public officials. This continual media presentation of corruption in government and venality in politics has undoubtedly fostered the general attitude of cynicism and distrust that exists in the general public.

At the same time, the ways in which media coverage interprets or frames specific events can have a major impact on popular responses and opinions about these events.[27] As we shall see in Chapter 8, the media presented the 1996 budget battle between President Clinton and Republic Speaker of the House Newt Gingrich in a way that served Clinton's interests. By forcing the closing of a number of government agencies, Gingrich hoped that the media would point out how smoothly life could proceed with less government involvement. Instead, the media focused on the hardships the closings inflicted on out-of-work government employees in the months before Christmas. The way in which the media framed the discussion helped turn opinion against Gingrich and handed Clinton an important victory.

★ Measuring Public Opinion

▶ How can public opinion be measured?

▶ What problems arise from public opinion polling?

As recently as fifty years ago, American political leaders gauged public opinion by people's applause and by the presence of crowds at meetings. This direct exposure to the people's views did not necessarily produce accurate knowledge of public opinion. It did, however, give political leaders confidence in their public support—and therefore confidence in their ability to govern by consent.

Abraham Lincoln and Stephen Douglas debated each other seven times in the summer and autumn of 1858, two years before they became presidential nominees. Their debates took place before audiences in parched cornfields and courthouse squares. A century later, the presidential debates, although seen by millions, take place before a few reporters and technicians in television studios that might as well be on the moon. The public's response cannot be experienced directly. This distance between leaders and followers is one of the agonizing problems of modern democracy. The media send information to millions of people, but they are not yet as efficient at getting information back to leaders. Is government by consent possible where the scale of communication is so large and impersonal? In order to compensate for the decline in their ability to experience public opinion for themselves, leaders have turned to science, in particular to the science of opinion polling.

It is no secret that politicians and public officials make extensive use of **public opinion polls** to help them decide whether to run for office, what policies to support, how to vote on important legislation, and what types of appeals to make in their campaigns. President Lyndon Johnson was famous for carrying the latest Gallup and Roper poll results in his pocket, and it is widely believed that he began to withdraw from politics because the polls reported losses in public support. All recent presidents and other major political figures have worked closely with polls and pollsters.

public opinion polls

scientific instruments for measuring public opinion

CONSTRUCTING PUBLIC OPINION FROM SURVEYS

The population in which pollsters are interested is usually quite large. To conduct their polls they first choose a **sample** of the total population. The selection of this sample is important. Above all, it must be representative; the views of those in the sample must accurately and proportionately reflect the views of the whole. To a large extent, the validity of the poll's results depends on the sampling procedure used (see Box 7.3).

sample

a small group selected by researchers to represent the most important characteristics of an entire population

---

METHODS OF MEASURING PUBLIC OPINION — Box 7.3

Interpreting Mass Opinion from Mass Behavior and Mass Attributes

Consumer behavior: predicts that people tend to vote against the party in power during a downturn in the economy

Group demographics: can predict party affiliation and voting by measuring income, race, and type of community (urban or rural)

Getting Public Opinion Directly from the People

Person-to-person: form impressions based on conversations with acquaintances, aides, and associates

Selective polling: form impressions based on interviews with a few representative members of a group or groups

Bellwether districts: form impressions based on an entire community that has a reputation for being a good predictor of the entire nation's attitudes

Constructing Public Opinion from Surveys

Quota sampling: respondents are chosen because they match a general population along several significant dimensions, such as geographic region, sex, age, and race

Probability sampling: respondents are chosen without prior screening, based entirely on a lottery system

Area sampling: respondents are chosen as part of a systematic breakdown of larger homogeneous units into smaller representative areas

Haphazard sampling: respondents are chosen by pure chance with no systematic method

Systematically biased sampling: respondents are chosen with a hidden or undetected bias toward a given demographic group

The second Lincoln-Douglas debate, at Freeport, Illinois, attracted a large local crowd as well as the nation's attention to the debate over slavery.

The degree of reliability in polling is a function of sample size. The same sample is needed to represent a small population as to represent a large population. The typical size of a sample ranges from 450 to 1,500 respondents. This number, however, reflects a trade-off between cost and degree of precision desired. The degree of accuracy that can be achieved with even a small sample can be seen from the polls' success in predicting election outcomes.

Table 7.3 shows how accurate two of the major national polling organizations have been in predicting the outcomes of presidential elections. In only three instances between 1952 and 1996 did the final October poll of a major pollster predict the wrong outcome; and in all three of those instances—Harris in 1968 and Gallup in 1976, as well as Roper in 1960—the actual election was extremely close and the prediction was off by no more than two percentage points.

Even with reliable sampling procedures, problems can occur. Validity can be adversely affected by poor question format, faulty ordering of questions, inappropriate vocabulary, ambiguity of questions, or questions with built-in biases. Often, seemingly minor differences in the wording of a question can convey vastly different meanings to respondents and thus produce quite different response patterns. For example, for many years the University of Chicago's National Opinion Research Center has asked respondents whether they think the federal government is spending too much, too little, or about the right amount of money on "assistance for the poor." Answering the question posed this way, about two-thirds of all respondents seem to believe that the government is spending too little. However, the same survey also asks whether the government spends too much, too little, or about the right amount for "welfare." When the word "welfare" is substituted for "assistance for the poor," about half of all respondents indicate that too much is being spent.[28]

In the early days of a political campaign when voters are asked which candidates they do, or do not, support, the answer they give often has little significance, because the choice is not yet important to them. Their preferences may change many times before the actual election. This is part of the explanation for the phenomenon of the postconvention "bounce" in the popularity of

TWO POLLSTERS AND THEIR RECORDS (1948–96)

Table 7.3

	Harris	Gallup	Actual outcome
1996			
Clinton	51%	52%	49%
Dole	39	41	41
Perot	9	7	8
1992			
Clinton	44%	44%	43%
Bush	38	37	38
Perot	17	14	19
1988			
Bush	51%	53%	54%
Dukakis	47	42	46
1984			
Reagan	56%	59%	59%
Mondale	44	41	41
1980			
Reagan	48%	47%	51%
Carter	43	44	41
Anderson		8	
1976			
Carter	48%	48%	51%
Ford	45	49	48
1972			
Nixon	59%	62%	61%
McGovern	35	38	38
1968			
Nixon	40%	43%	43%
Humphrey	43	42	43
Wallace	13	15	14
1964			
Johnson	62%	64%	61%
Goldwater	33	36	39
1960			
Kennedy	49%	51%	50%
Nixon	41	49	49
1956			
Eisenhower	NA	60%	58%
Stevenson		41	42
1952			
Eisenhower	47%	51%	55%
Stevenson	42	49	44
1948			
Truman	NA	44.5%	49.6%
Dewey		49.5	45.1

All figures except those for 1948 are rounded. NA = Not asked.
SOURCE: Data from the Gallup Poll and the Harris Survey (New York: Chicago Tribune–New York News Syndicate, various press releases 1964–1996). Courtesy of the Gallup Organization and Louis Harris Associates.

presidential candidates, which was observed after the Democratic and Republican national conventions in 1992 and 1996.[29] Respondents' preferences reflected the amount of attention a candidate had received during the conventions rather than strongly held views.

salient interests

attitudes and views that are especially important to the individual holding them

Salient interests are interests that stand out beyond others, that are of more than ordinary concern to respondents in a survey or to voters in the electorate. Politicans, social scientists, journalists, or pollsters who assume something is important to the public, when in fact it is not, are creating an **illusion of saliency.** This illusion can be created and fostered by polls despite careful controls over sampling, interviewing, and data analysis. In fact, the illusion is strengthened by the credibility that science gives survey results.

illusion of saliency

the impression conveyed by polls that something is important to the public when actually it is not

The problem of saliency has become especially acute as a result of the proliferation of media polls. The television networks and major national newspapers all make heavy use of opinion polls. Increasingly, polls are being commissioned by local television stations and local and regional newspapers as well.[30] On the positive side, polls allow journalists to make independent assessments of political realities—assessments not influenced by the partisan claims of politicians.

At the same time, however, media polls can allow journalists to make news when none really exists. Polling diminishes journalists' dependence upon news makers. A poll commissioned by a news agency can provide the basis for a good story even when candidates, politicians, and other news makers refuse to cooperate by engaging in newsworthy activities. Thus, on days when little or nothing is actually taking place in a political campaign, poll results, especially apparent changes in candidate popularity margins, can provide exciting news. Several times during the 1992 presidential campaign, for example, small changes in the relative standing of the Democratic and Republican candidates

In probably the most famous instance of pollsters getting it wrong, Gallup predicted that Thomas E. Dewey would defeat Harry S. Truman in the 1948 presidential election. Truman, pictured here, won easily. The Gallup organization subsequently changed its polling methods.

produced banner headlines around the country. Stories about what the candidates actually did or said often took second place to reporting the "horse race."

Interestingly, because rapid and dramatic shifts in candidate margins tend to take place when voters' preferences are least fully formed, horse-race news is most likely to make the headlines when it is actually least significant.[31] In other words, media interest in poll results is inversely related to the actual salience of voters' opinions and the significance of the polls' findings. However, by influencing perceptions, especially those of major contributors, media polls can influence political realities.

The most noted, but least serious, of polling problems is the **bandwagon effect**, which occurs when polling results influence people to support the candidate marked as the probable victor. Some scholars argue that this bandwagon effect can be offset by an "underdog effect" in favor of the candidate who is trailing in the polls.[32] However, a candidate who demonstrates a lead in the polls usually finds it considerably easier to raise campaign funds than a candidate whose poll standing is poor. With these additional funds, poll leaders can often afford to pay for television time and other campaign activities that will cement their advantage. For example, Bill Clinton's substantial lead in the polls during much of the summer of 1992 helped the Democrats raise far more money than in any previous campaign, primarily from interests hoping to buy access to a future President Clinton. For once, the Democrats were able to outspend the usually better-heeled Republicans. Thus, the *appearance* of a lead, as shown by the polls, helped make Clinton's lead a reality.

In 1996, some major polls were quite wrong in their predictions of the popular vote divisions in both the presidential and congressional races. For example, the *New York Times*/CBS News poll taken two days before the election predicted that Clinton would defeat Dole by a 53 to 35 percent margin (the actual margin was 49 to 41 percent). Similarly, most polls predicted that Democratic House candidates would defeat their GOP rivals by a margin of ten points on a national basis. On election day, however, Republican candidates out-polled the Democrats. The most striking polling error made in 1996 occurred in New Hampshire, where exit polls showed Democratic senatorial candidate Dick Swett defeating Republican senator Bob Smith by a solid 52 to 47 percent. Smith assumed he had lost until early the next morning when actual election results gave him a narrow victory. Some analysts believe that these poll errors are a subtle form of "liberal bias." Since voters often feel that the media have a liberal and Democratic slant, individuals who support the Republicans are slightly more reluctant to confess their true preferences to interviewers. Indications of this phenomenon have appeared in a number of Western democracies whose major media are deemed to be liberal in their political orientation.[33]

In recent years, a new form of bias has been introduced into surveys by the use of a technique called **push polling**. This technique involves asking a respondent a loaded question about a political candidate designed to elicit the response sought by the pollster and, simultaneously, to shape the respondent's perception of the candidate in question. For example, during the 1996 New Hampshire presidential primary, push pollsters employed by the campaign of one of Lamar Alexander's rivals called thousands of voters to ask, "If you knew that Lamar Alexander had raised taxes six times in Tennessee, would you be less inclined or more inclined to support him?"[34] More than

bandwagon effect
a shift in electoral support to the candidate that public opinion polls report as the front-runner

push polling
a polling technique in which the questions are designed to shape the respondent's opinion

POLITICS ON THE WEB

The Internet is an unparalleled source for political information. No other medium has such a variety of political, economic, and social views so readily available. As a *learning tool,* the Internet holds great promise. As a tool for *expression* of public opinion, the Internet presents a more mixed picture. On the one hand, individuals have the ability to articulate their opinions through an on-line democratic debate, where one's ideas can be distributed to millions of computer users worldwide. This is empowering. But on the Internet, no intermediaries evaluate and filter these opinions. Direct democracy becomes mob rule. And those with the most time on their hands to post opinions can easily dominate a discussion, which leads to great difficulties in measuring public opinion via the Internet. The Internet is dominated by white, well-off, educated men—not a representative sample of the population. But despite these limitations, the Internet will continue to grow as a way for individuals to learn about politics.
www.wwnorton.com/wtp2e

one hundred consulting firms across the nation now specialize in push polling.[35] Calling push polling the "political equivalent of a drive-by shooting," Representative Joe Barton (R-Tex.) launched a congressional investigation into the practice.[36] Push polls may be one reason that Americans are becoming increasingly skeptical about the practice of polling and increasingly unwilling to answer pollsters' questions.[37]

PUBLIC OPINION, POLITICAL KNOWLEDGE, AND THE IMPORTANCE OF IGNORANCE

Many people are distressed to find public opinion polls not only unable to discover public opinion, but also unable to avoid producing unintentional distortions of their own. No matter how hard they try, no matter how mature the science of opinion polling becomes, politicians may remain substantially ignorant of public opinion.

Although knowledge is good for its own sake, and knowledge of public opinion may sometimes produce better government, ignorance also has its uses. It can, for example, operate as a restraint on the use of power. Leaders who think they know what the public wants are often autocratic rulers. Leaders who realize that they are always partially in the dark about the public are likely to be more modest in their claims, less strident in their demands, and more uncertain in their uses of power. Their uncertainty may make them more accountable to their constituencies because they will be more likely to continue searching for consent.

One of the most valuable benefits of survey research is actually "negative knowledge"—knowledge that pierces through irresponsible claims about the breadth of opinion or the solidarity of group or mass support. Because this sort of knowledge reveals the complexity and uncertainty of public opinion, it can help make citizens less gullible, group leaders less strident, and politicians less deceitful. This alone gives public opinion research, despite its great limitations, an important place in the future of American politics.[38]

Public Opinion and Democracy

▶ How responsive is the government to public opinion?

In democratic nations, leaders should pay heed to public opinion, and the evidence suggests that indeed they do. There are many instances in which public policy and public opinion do not coincide, but in general the government's actions are consistent with citizens' preferences. One recent study, for example, found that between 1935 and 1979, in about two-thirds of all cases, significant changes in public opinion were followed within one year by changes in government policy consistent with the shift in the popular mood.[39] Other studies have come to similar conclusions about public opinion and government policy at the state level.[40] Some recent studies, however, have suggested that the responsiveness of government to public opinion has been declining, reaching an all-time low during President Clinton's first term. These findings imply that, contrary to popular beliefs, elected leaders don't always pander to the results of public opinion polls, but instead use polling to sell their policy proposals and shape the public's views.[41]

In addition, areas of disagreement always arise between opinion and policy. For example, the majority of Americans favored stricter governmental control of handguns for years before Congress finally adopted the modest restrictions on firearms purchases embodied in the Brady bill and the Violent Crime Control Act, passed in 1993 and 1994, respectively. Similarly, most Americans—blacks as well as whites—oppose school busing to achieve racial balance, yet such busing continues to be used in many parts of the nation. Most Americans are far less concerned with the rights of the accused than the federal courts seem to be. Most Americans oppose U.S. military intervention in other nations' affairs, yet such interventions continue to take place and often win public approval after the fact.

Several factors can contribute to a lack of consistency between opinion and governmental policy. First, the nominal majority on a particular issue may not be as intensely committed to its preference as the adherents of the minority viewpoint. An intensely committed minority may often be more willing to commit its time, energy, efforts, and resources to the affirmation of its opinions than an apathetic, even if large, majority. In the case of firearms, for example, although the proponents of gun control are by a wide margin the majority, most do not regard the issue as one of critical importance to themselves and are not willing to commit much effort to advancing their cause. The opponents of gun control, by contrast, are intensely committed, well organized, and well financed, and as a result are usually able to carry the day.

A second important reason that public policy and public opinion may not coincide has to do with the character and structure of the American system of government. The framers of the American Constitution, as we saw in Chapter 3, sought to create a system of government that was based upon popular consent but that did not invariably and automatically translate shifting popular sentiments into public policies. As a result, the American governmental process includes arrangements such as an appointed judiciary that can produce policy decisions that may run contrary to prevailing popular sentiment—at least for a time.

When all is said and done, however, there can be little doubt that in general the actions of the American government do not remain out of line with popular sentiment for very long. One could take these as signs of a vital and thriving democracy.

★ The Citizen's Role

In a democracy, one central role of the citizen is to be informed and knowledgeable. Many eighteenth- and nineteenth-century political theorists believed that popular government required an informed, aware, and involved citizenry, and wondered whether this condition could be met. The Frenchman, Alexis de Tocqueville, writing in the early nineteenth century, asserted that to participate in democratic politics ordinary citizens needed to be aware of their own interests and understand how those interests might be affected by contemporary issues. De Tocqueville and others have feared that participation by the unenlightened might be worse than no participation at all, since the ignorant could easily be swayed by demagogues to support foolish or even evil causes. Contemporary public opinion research indicates that better-informed citizens are considerably better able than their uninformed counterparts to exert influence in the political arena. Knowledge, indeed, seems to be power.[42]

Fortunately, the most basic element of citizenship is also one of the simplest to achieve. Viewed correctly, reading a daily newspaper is an important political act! Watching a television news or discussion program is an important form of political participation. For some, visiting and comparing the web sites of several candidates is a way of becoming politically involved, albeit in cyberspace.

Those who use newspapers, magazines, television, and the computer to become politically knowledgeable and aware have taken a huge first step toward becoming politically influential. Those who limit their newspaper reading to the sports page and their television viewing to situation comedies are also abdicating the responsibilities and opportunities inherent in democratic citizenship. If a person opts to be indifferent or cynical about politics, his or her decision must be based on an informed indifference or cynicism to be truly meaningful.

★ Summary

Americans disagree on many issues, but they nevertheless share a number of important values, including liberty, equality of opportunity, and democracy. Although factors such as race, education, gender, and social class produce important differences in outlook, Americans probably agree more on fundamental values than do the citizens of most other nations.

Most people acquire their initial orientation to political life from their families. Subsequently, political views are influenced by interests, personal experiences, group memberships, and the conditions under which citizens are first mobilized into politics. Opinions on particular issues may also be influenced by political leaders and the mass media. The media help determine what Americans know about politics.

Most governments, including the U.S. government, endeavor to shape their citizens' political beliefs. In democracies, private groups compete with government to shape opinion.

Public opinion is generally measured by polling. But while polls measure opinion, they also distort it, often imputing salience to issues that citizens care little about or creating the illusion that most people are moderate or centrist in their views.

Over time, the government's policies are strongly affected by public opinion, although there can be lags and divergences, especially when an intense minority confronts a more apathetic majority.

FOR FURTHER READING

Cook, Elizabeth A., Ted G. Jelen, and Clyde Wilcox. *Between Two Absolutes: Public Opinions and the Politics of Abortion*. Boulder, CO: Westview, 1992.

Erikson, Robert S., Norman Luttbeg, and Kent Tedin. *American Public Opinion: Its Origins, Content and Impact*. 5th ed. Boston, MA: Allyn and Bacon, 1994.

Gallup, George. *The Pulse of Democracy*. New York: Simon and Schuster, 1940.

Ginsberg, Benjamin. *The Captive Public: How Mass Opinion Promotes State Power*. New York: Basic Books, 1986.

Herbst, Susan. *Numbered Voices: How Opinion Polling Has Shaped American Politics*. Chicago: University of Chicago Press, 1993.

Key, V. O. *Public Opinion and American Democracy*. New York: Knopf, 1961.

Lippman, Walter. *Public Opinion*. New York: Harcourt, Brace, 1922.

Mayer, William G. *The Changing American Mind: How and Why American Public Opinion Changed between 1960 and 1988*. Ann Arbor: University of Michigan Press, 1992.

Neuman, W. Russell. *The Paradox of Mass Politics: Knowledge and Opinion in the American Electorate*. Cambridge, MA: Harvard University Press, 1986.

Page, Benjamin I., and Robert Y. Shapiro. *The Rational Public: Fifty Years of Trends in Americans' Policy Preferences*. Chicago: University of Chicago Press, 1992.

Rinehart, Sue Tolleson. *Gender Consciousness and Politics*. New York: Routledge, 1992.

Schuman, Howard, Charlotte Steeh, and Lawrence Bobo. *Racial Attitudes in America*. Cambridge, MA: Harvard University Press, 1990.

STUDY OUTLINE

Political Values

1. Although Americans have many political differences, they share a common set of values, including liberty, equality of opportunity, and democracy.
2. Agreement on fundamental political values is probably more widespread in the United States than anywhere else in the Western world.
3. Often for reasons associated with demographics, Americans do differ widely with one another on a variety of issues.
4. Most people acquire their initial orientation to politics from their families.
5. Membership in both voluntary and involuntary social groups can affect an individual's political values through personal experience, the influence of group leaders, and recognition of political interests.
6. One's level of education is an important factor in shaping political beliefs.
7. Conditions under which individuals and groups are recruited into political life also shape political orientations.
8. Many Americans describe themselves as either liberal or conservative in political orientation.

How We Form Political Opinions

1. Although ideologies shape political opinions, they seldom fully determine one's views.

2. Political opinions are influenced by an individual's underlying values, knowledge of political issues, and external forces such as the government, private groups, and the media.

Measuring Public Opinion

1. In order to construct public opinion from surveys, a polling sample must be large and the views of those in the sample must accurately and proportionately reflect the views of the whole.
2. The inability of polls to discover public opinion or to avoid unintentional distortions of political knowledge allows a certain level of ignorance to function as a restraint on the use of political power.

Public Opinion and Democracy

1. Government policies in the United States are generally consistent with popular preferences. There are, however, always some inconsistencies.
2. Disagreements between opinion and policy come about because on some issues, such as gun control, an intensely committed minority can defeat a more apathetic majority. Moreover, the American system of government is not designed to quickly transform changes in opinion into changes in government programs.

PRACTICE QUIZ

1. The term "public opinion" is used to describe
   a) the collected speeches and writings made by a president during his term in office.
   b) the analysis of events broadcast by news reporters during the evening news.
   c) the beliefs and attitudes that people have about issues.
   d) decisions of the Supreme Court.

2. Variables such as income, education, race, gender, and ethnicity
   a) often create differences of political opinion in America.
   b) have consistently been a challenge to America's core political values.
   c) have little impact on political opinions.
   d) help explain why public opinion polls are so unreliable.

3. Which of the following is an agency of socialization?
   a) the family
   b) social groups
   c) education
   d) all of the above

4. When men and women respond differently to issues of public policy, they are demonstrating an example of
   a) liberalism.
   b) educational differences.
   c) the gender gap.
   d) party politics.

5. The process by which Americans learn political beliefs and values is called
   a) brainwashing.
   b) propaganda.
   c) indoctrination.
   d) political socialization.

6. In addition to one's basic political values, what other two factors influence one's political opinions?
   a) ideology and party identification

b) political knowledge and the influence of political leaders, private groups, and the media
   c) the gender gap and the education gap
   d) sample size and the bandwagon effect

7. Which of the following is (are) *not* an important external influence on how political opinions are formed?
   a) the government and political leaders
   b) private interest groups
   c) the media
   d) the Constitution

8. Which of the following is the term used in public opinion polling to denote the small group representing the opinions of the whole population?
   a) control group
   b) sample
   c) micropopulation
   d) respondents

9. When politicians, pollsters, journalists, or social scientists assume something is important to the public when in fact it is not, they are creating
   a) an illusion of saliency.
   b) an illusion of responsibility.
   c) a gender gap.
   d) an elitist issue.

10. A familiar polling problem is the "bandwagon effect," which occurs when
    a) the same results are used over and over again.
    b) polling results influence people to support the candidate marked as the probable victor in a campaign.
    c) polling results influence people to support the candidate who is trailing in a campaign.
    d) background noise makes it difficult for a pollster and a respondent to communicate with one another.

CRITICAL THINKING QUESTIONS

1. In the American system of government, public opinion seems to be an important factor in political and governmental decision making. In what ways does the public, through opinion, control its political leaders? In what ways do political leaders control public opinion? What are the positive and negative consequences of governing by popular opinion?

2. Describe the differences between liberal and conservative ideologies in American politics. Using one social or demographic group as an example, describe some of the factors that may have shaped the ideological orientation of that particular group. What factors may explain inconsistencies in that group's political ideology or issue positions?

KEY TERMS

agencies of socialization (p. 244)
attitude (or opinion) (p. 238)
bandwagon effect (p. 267)
conservative (p. 254)
democracy (p. 239)
equality of opportunity (p. 239)
gender gap (p. 247)

illusion of saliency (p. 266)
liberal (p. 253)
liberty (p. 239)
marketplace of ideas (p. 258)
political efficacy (p. 257)
political ideology (p. 238)
political socialization (p. 243)

public opinion (p. 238)
public opinion polls (p. 263)
push polling (p. 267)
salient interests (p. 266)
sample (p. 263)
values (or beliefs) (p. 238)

8

The Media

- ★ **The Media Industry and Government**

  How has the nationalization of the news media contributed to the nationalization of American politics?

  How is the media regulated by the government? How does this regulation differ between the broadcast media and the print media?

- ★ **News Coverage**

  How are media content, news coverage, and bias affected by the producers, subjects, and consumers of the news?

- ★ **Media Power in American Politics**

  How do the media shape public perceptions of events, issues, and institutions? What are the sources of media power?

- ★ **Media Power and Democracy**

  Are the media too powerful and thus in need of restriction, or are a free media necessary for democracy?

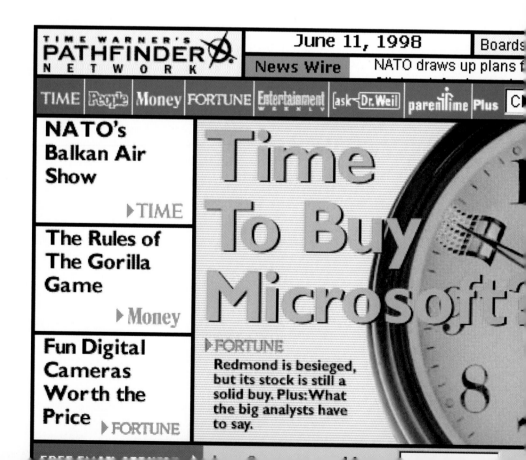

IT is impossible to imagine democratic politics without a vigorous media. The public depends upon the news media to publicize and assess the claims of political candidates. We depend upon the media to examine government policies and programs. We depend upon the media to reveal wrongdoing on the part of government agencies and public officials. Without the information provided by the media, the public could not possibly know enough to play any role in the political process. Freedom of the press definitely belongs in the First Amendment as one of the first principles of democratic government. This freedom gives the media considerable power. Given this substantial freedom, what prevents the media from abusing its power? In a democracy, to whom are the media accountable—to the people?

Virtually all Americans believe in the principle of freedom of the press. Yet it is interesting to see how quickly groups that champion freedom when the press attacks *their enemies* can become advocates of censorship when the press turns and attacks *them*. In recent years, for instance, newspapers on many college campuses have come under attack by groups that object to their coverage. Traditionally, of course, school administrators sought to influence the content of student newspapers. Today, because of court decisions protecting college papers from the actions of school authorities, most college administrations maintain a hands-off policy toward the campus press. In a number of recent cases, however, student groups that differ politically with a campus paper have sought to prevent the paper's publication and distribution, often by stealing thousands of copies of the paper before other students could read it.

For example, in April 1993, a student group at the University of Pennsylvania absconded with 14,000 copies of the student newspaper, the *Daily Pennsylvanian,* after the paper published columns criticizing affirmative action.[1] At Pennsylvania State University, more than 6,000 copies of a conservative student paper, the *Lionhearted,* were stolen after the paper published a cartoon that offended feminist groups. One Penn State professor reportedly defended the thefts, arguing that they were justified because of the paper's "misogynistic" views.[2] At the University of California at Berkeley, more than 6,500 copies of the student-run *Daily Californian* were stolen from news racks in October 1997 after the paper published an editorial criticizing a group called the Coalition to Defend Affirmative Action by Any Means Necessary. This theft was the seventh such incident on the Berkeley campus in less than a year.[3] At Clark University in Worcester, Massachusetts, the editor of the *Wheatbread,* an alternative student newspaper, charged that an administrator had stolen and destroyed 500 copies of an edition of the paper that used obscene language to criticize college officials. University administrators reportedly confirmed that the theft had occurred.[4] At a number of other campuses, including Brandeis,

Cornell, Dartmouth, the University of Wisconsin, Trenton State University, the University of Illinois, and Southeastern Louisiana University (SLU), thousands of copies of student newspapers have been stolen by groups objecting to the views the papers presented. At SLU, the theft of 2,000 copies of the *Lion's Roar* allegedly was perpetrated by an officer of the school's student government who wanted to prevent fellow students from reading an article that criticized his organization. All told, more than 250,000 copies of student newspapers have been stolen on college campuses since 1992.[5]

Attempts to silence or discredit the opposition press have a long history in America. As you will recall from Chapter 5, the infamous Alien and Sedition Acts were enacted by the Federalists in an attempt to silence the Republican press. In more recent times, during the McCarthy era of the 1950s, right-wing politicians used charges of communist infiltration to intimidate the liberal news media. During President Richard Nixon's administration, the White House attacked its critics in the media by threatening to take action to bar the television networks from owning local affiliates, as well as by illegally wire-tapping the phones of government officials suspected of leaking information to the press. In the early 1980s, conservative groups financed a series of libel suits against CBS News, *Time* magazine, and other media organizations, in an attempt to discourage them from publicizing material critical of Reagan administration policies.[6] In 1998, President Clinton's political allies accused the national news media of engaging in tabloid journalism and invading the president's privacy in order to discredit him by publicizing the intimate details of Clinton's sexual relationship with former White House intern Monica Lewinsky. In all these instances, attempts to silence the press failed.

■ ***In this chapter we will examine the place of the media in American politics. First, we will look at the organization and regulation of the American news media.*** The media industry continues to grow larger and more centralized, resulting in little variety in what is reported about national issues. Despite the central importance of freedom of the press in the United States, the media are still subject to some regulation by the government.

■ ***Second, we will discuss the factors that help to determine "what's news."*** The agenda of issues and type of coverage that the media provide are affected most by those who create the news and those who consume the news.

■ ***Third, we will examine the scope of media power in politics.*** What the media report can have far-reaching effects on public perceptions of political events, issues, leaders, and institutions.

■ ***Finally, we will address the question of responsibility: to whom, if anyone, are the media accountable for the use of their formidable power?*** The answer to this question has great implications for American democracy.

The Media Industry and Government

▶ How has the nationalization of the news media contributed to the nationalization of American politics?

▶ How is the media regulated by the government? How does this regulation differ between the broadcast media and the print media?

The American news media are among the world's most vast and most free. Americans literally have thousands of available options to find political reporting. This wide variety of newspapers, newsmagazines, and broadcast media regularly present information that is at odds with the government's claims, as well as editorial opinions sharply critical of high-ranking officials. The freedom to speak one's mind is one of the most cherished of American political values—one that is jealously safeguarded by the media. Yet although thousands of media companies exist across the United States, surprisingly little variety appears in what is reported about national events and issues.

TYPES OF MEDIA

Americans obtain their news from broadcast media (radio, television), print media (newspapers and magazines), and, increasingly, from the Internet. Each of these sources has distinctive characteristics. Television news reaches more Americans than any other single news source (see Figure 8.1). Tens of millions of individuals watch national and local news programs every day. Television news, however, covers relatively few topics and provides little depth of coverage. Television news is more like a series of newspaper headlines connected to pictures. It serves the extremely important function of alerting viewers to issues and events, but provides little else.

Radio news is also essentially a headline service, but without pictures. In the short time—usually five minutes per hour—they devote to news, radio stations announce the day's major events without providing much detail. In major cities, all-news stations provide a bit more coverage of major stories, but for the most part these stations fill the day with repetition rather than detail. All-news stations like Washington, D.C.'s WTOP or New York's WCBS assume that most listeners are in their cars and that, as a result, the people in the audience change markedly throughout the day as listeners reach their destinations. Thus, rather than use their time to flesh out a given set of stories, they repeat the same stories each hour to present them to new listeners. In recent years, radio talk shows have become important sources of commentary and opinion. A number of conservative radio hosts such as Rush Limbaugh have huge audiences and have helped to mobilize support for conservative political causes and candidates. Liberals have been somewhat slower to recognize the potential impact of talk radio.

The most important source of news is the old-fashioned newspaper. Newspapers remain critically important even though they are not the primary news source for most Americans. The print media are important for two reasons. First, as we shall see later in this chapter, the broadcast media rely upon leading newspapers such as the *New York Times* and the *Washington Post* to set

Perspectives on Politics

THE MEDIA AND PRESIDENTIAL CAMPAIGNS

"Where do you get most of your news about the presidential election campaign?"

Legend:
- TV and Newspapers
- TV only
- Newspapers only

Age group	TV and Newspapers	TV only	Newspapers only
18–24	32	51	10
25–29	32	50	12

SOURCE: 1992 Times Mirror Poll, reported in Susan A. MacManus, *Young v. Old: Generational Combat in the 21st Century* (Boulder, CO: Westview, 1996), p. 82.

Figure 8.1　　AMERICANS' PRIMARY MEDIA SOURCES OF NEWS

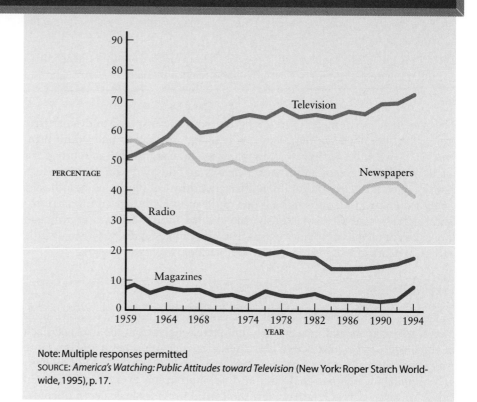

Note: Multiple responses permitted

SOURCE: *America's Watching: Public Attitudes toward Television* (New York: Roper Starch World-wide, 1995), p. 17.

their news agenda. The broadcast media engage in very little actual reporting; they primarily cover stories that have been "broken," or initially reported, by the print media. For example, sensational charges that President Bill Clinton had an affair with a White House intern were reported first by the *Washington Post* and *Newsweek* before being trumpeted around the world by the broadcast media. It is only a slight exaggeration to observe that if an event is not covered in the *New York Times,* it is not likely to appear on the *CBS Evening News.* The print media are also important because they are the prime source of news for educated and influential individuals. The nation's economic, social, and political elites rely upon the detailed coverage provided by the print media to inform and influence their views about important public matters. The print media may have a smaller audience than their cousins in broadcasting, but they have an audience that matters.

A relatively new source of news is the Internet. Every day, several million Americans scan one of many news sites on the Internet for coverage of current events. For the most part, however, the Internet provides electronic versions of coverage offered by print sources. One great advantage of the Internet is that it allows frequent updating. It potentially can combine the depth of coverage of a newspaper with the timeliness of television and radio, and probably will become a major news source in the next decade. As on-line access becomes simpler and faster, the Internet could give Americans access to unprecedented quantities of up-to-the-minute information. If only computers could also give Americans the ability to make good use of that information!

ORGANIZATION AND OWNERSHIP OF THE MEDIA

Media Organization   The United States boasts more than one thousand television stations, approximately eighteen hundred daily newspapers, and more than nine thousand radio stations. The majority of these enterprises (20 percent of which are devoted to news, talk, or public affairs)[7] present a good deal of news and many features with a distinctly local flavor. For example, for many months, viewers of the Syracuse, New York, evening news were informed that the day's "top story" concerned the proposed construction of a local garbage-burning steam plant. Similarly, in Seattle, Washington, viewers were treated to years of discussion about the construction of a domed athletic stadium, and audiences in Baltimore, Maryland, watched and read about struggles over downtown redevelopment. In all these cases, as in literally thousands of others, the local media focused heavily on a matter of particular local concern, providing local viewers, readers, and listeners with considerable information and viewpoints.

Yet, however much variation the American news media offer in terms of local coverage, there is far less diversity in the reporting of national events and issues. More than three-fourths of the daily newspapers in the United States are owned by large media conglomerates such as the Hearst or Gannett corporations; thus the diversity of coverage and editorial opinion in American newspapers is not as broad as it might seem. Most of the national news that is published by local newspapers is provided by one wire service: the Associated Press. More than five hundred of the nation's television stations are affiliated with one of the four networks and carry that network's evening news reports. Dozens of others carry PBS (Public Broadcasting System) news. Several hundred local radio stations also carry network news or National Public Radio news broadcasts. At the same time, although there are only three truly national newspapers, the *Wall Street Journal,* the *Christian Science Monitor,* and *USA Today,* two other papers, the *New York Times* and the *Washington Post,* are read by political leaders and other influential Americans throughout the nation. Such is the influence of these two "elite" newspapers that their news coverage sets the standard for virtually all other news outlets. Stories carried in the *New York Times* or the *Washington Post* influence the content of many other papers as well as of the network news. Note how often this text, like most others, relies upon *New York Times* and *Washington Post* stories as sources for contemporary events.

National news is also carried to millions of Americans by the three major newsmagazines—*Time, Newsweek,* and *U.S. News & World Report.* Thus, even though the number of TV and radio stations and daily newspapers reporting news in the United States is enormous, and local coverage varies greatly from place to place, the number of sources of national news is actually quite small—two wire services, four broadcast networks, public radio and television, two elite newspapers, three newsmagazines, and a scattering of other sources such as the national correspondents of a few large local papers and the small independent radio networks. Beginning in the late 1980s, Cable News Network (CNN) became another major news source for Americans.

POLITICS ON THE WEB

Most mainstream media web sites are simply new conduits for conventional reporters. The most important effect of the Internet has instead occurred through unconventional outlets. The Web has proven itself to be the greatest rumor mill of all time. Alternative news web sites publish unverified stories that the mainstream media will not. Sometimes, however, a rumor becomes too important for the mainstream media to ignore. In early 1998, for example, *Newsweek* had information that President Clinton may have had sexual relations with a White House intern. The source of the information was suspect, however, and the reporter lacked corroborating sources, so *Newsweek* chose not to print the story. The next day, Matt Drudge, a self-styled Internet political maven, scooped *Newsweek* on his web site, "The Drudge Report." Within a day, *Newsweek* had posted a response on its web site, the *Wall Street Journal* had picked up the story, and Monica Lewinsky entered American political lore.
www.wwnorton.com/wtp2e

CNN's live coverage of the Persian Gulf War captivated American television viewers and brought the war into their homes.

The importance of CNN increased dramatically after its spectacular coverage of the Persian Gulf War. At one point, CNN was able to provide live reports of American bombing raids on Baghdad, Iraq, after the major networks' correspondents had been forced to flee to bomb shelters. Even the availability of new electronic media on the Internet has failed to expand news sources. Most national news available on the World Wide Web, for example, consists of electronic versions of the conventional print media.

Media Ownership Since the enactment of the 1996 Telecommunications Act, which opened the way for further consolidation in the media industry, a wave of mergers and consolidations has further reduced the field of independent media across the country. Since that time, among the major news networks, ABC was bought by the Walt Disney corporation, CBS was bought by Westinghouse Electric, and CNN was bought by Time Warner. NBC has been owned by General Electric since 1986. A small number of giant corporations now controls a wide swath of media holdings, including television networks, movie studios, record companies, cable channels and local cable providers, book publishers, magazines, and newspapers. These developments have prompted questions about whether enough competition exists among the media to produce a diverse set of views on political and corporate matters.[8]

NATIONALIZATION OF THE NEWS

Time Warner chairman Gerald Levin announces the 1996 merger of Time Warner and Turner Broadcasting Systems, creating the world's largest media conglomerate.

In general, the national news media cover more or less the same sets of events, present similar information, and emphasize similar issues and problems (see Figure 8.2). Indeed, the national news services watch one another quite carefully. It is very likely that a major story carried by one will soon find its way into the pages or programming of the others. As a result, in the United States a rather centralized national news has developed, through which a relatively similar pic-

THE NATIONALIZATION OF THE NEWS

Figure 8.2

(c) 1996 by the New York Times Company. Reprinted by permission.

ture of events, issues, and problems is presented to the entire nation.[9] The nationalization of the news began at the turn of the century, was accelerated by the development of radio networks in the 1920s and 1930s and by the creation of the television networks after the 1950s, and has been further strengthened by the recent trends toward concentrated ownership. This nationalization of news content has very important consequences for American politics.

Nationalization of the news has contributed greatly to the nationalization of politics and of political perspectives in the United States. Prior to the development of the national media and the nationalization of news coverage, news traveled very slowly. Every region and city saw national issues and problems primarily through a local lens. Concerns and perspectives varied greatly from region to region, city to city, and village to village. Today, in large measure as a result of the nationalization of the media, residents of all parts of the country share a similar picture of the day's events.[10] They may not agree on everything, but most see the world in similar ways.

The exception to this pattern can be found with those Americans whose chief source of news is something other than the "mainstream" national media. Despite the nationalization and homogenization of the news, in some American cities, alternative news coverage is available. Such media markets are known as

Much of the news that is reported in American newspapers grows out of organizational press releases or wire service reports. For example, on August 16, 1996, newspapers across the country reported that estrogen may play a role in preventing Alzheimer's disease. The similarities between the stories suggested that they were all drawn from one or two wire service reports.

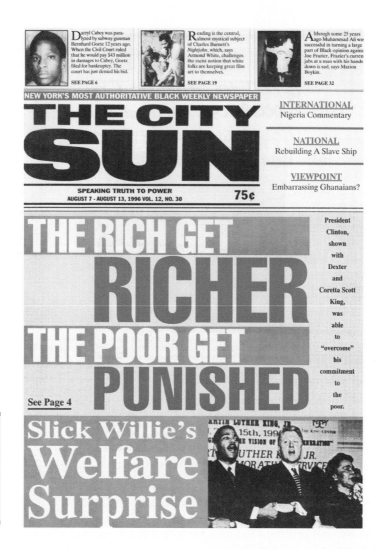

While much of the mainstream media applauded the welfare reform plan of 1996, African American newspapers such as the *City Sun* had a different view.

news enclave

population subgroups that receive most of their political information from sources other than the major national news media

news enclaves. For example, some African Americans rely upon newspapers and radio stations that aim their coverage primarily at black audiences. As a result, these individuals may interpret events differently than white Americans and even other blacks do.[11] The existence of a black-focused media helps to explain why many African Americans and white Americans reacted differently to the 1995 trial of O. J. Simpson in Los Angeles. While national media outlets generally portrayed Simpson as guilty of the murder of his former wife, other media outlets depicted Simpson as a victim of a racist criminal justice system. This latter view came to be held by a large number of African Americans.

In a similar vein, some radio stations and print media are aimed exclusively at religious and social conservatives. These individuals are also likely to develop and retain a perception of the news that is quite different from that of "mainstream" America. For example, the rural Midwesterners who rely upon the ultraconservative People's Radio Network for their news coverage may become concerned about the alleged efforts of the United Nations to subordinate the United States in a world government, a viewpoint unfamiliar to most Americans.

Internet newsgroups are another form of news enclave. Newsgroups are informal and tend to develop around the discussion of a particular set of issues. Individuals post their views for others to read; comments are also posted. In some instances, posted comments are attacked by other members of the community. In general, users seem to seek out and exchange postings with those who share their opinions. On a recent day in 1998, the political topics being discussed in the more than 50,000 postings under the heading alt.politics included such conventional subjects as "Clinton," "corruption," "equality," "media," "libertarianism," and "Democrats and Republicans," as well as racist and neofascist topics that receive little attention from the mass media. While some postings were followed by hostile comments, for the most part responses to postings seemed to come from those who agreed with the position put forth. For example, most of those posting under the heading "libertarianism" seemed to be libertarians, while most of the messages appearing under the heading "white power" put forward racist views.

These and other newsgroups serve as meeting places for the like-minded from all across the nation. Perhaps the long-term significance of the Internet is that it will increasingly allow contacts among individuals with unconventional viewpoints who are geographically dispersed and might otherwise be unaware of the existence of others who share their views. In the mid-1990s, Internet newsgroups have played a role in the mobilization of "antigovernment" fringe groups.

The same principle seems to hold for another form of discussion on the Internet, known as a chat room. Chat rooms are on-line forums in which anonymous individuals form groups spontaneously and converse with one another. The topics change often as participants leave and are replaced by newcomers. Although chat rooms sometimes are the scenes of angry arguments, for the most part the groups that congregate in these on-line forums seem to share similar views. On a recent day, "rooms" in America Online's popular chat area included "From the Left," where liberal views were discussed, and "From the Right," where the discussion revolved around more conservative opinions. In the conservative chat room, participants discussed tax credits and conservative politicians. All the participants favored more tax credits to promote business activity. Several felt that Republican House Speaker Newt Gingrich had become too liberal. Not a single participant questioned the conservative climate of opinion in the room. In the liberal chat room, on this same day, participants were concerned with what many saw as the undue political influence of business and "big money" in the political process. Not a single participant in this chat group presented views that might have been considered conservative. Thus, like newsgroups, chat rooms seem to function as opinion enclaves where like-minded individuals from across the nation can congregate and reinforce one another's views.

REGULATION OF THE BROADCAST MEDIA

In some countries, the government controls media content. In other countries, the government owns the broadcast media (e.g., the BBC in Britain) but it does not tell the media what to say. In the United States, the government neither owns nor controls the communications networks, but it does regulate the broadcast media.

American radio and television are regulated by the Federal Communications Commission (FCC), an independent regulatory agency established in 1934. Radio and TV stations must have FCC licenses that must be renewed every five years. Licensing provides a mechanism for allocating radio and TV frequencies to prevent broadcasts from interfering with and garbling one another. License renewals are almost always granted automatically by the FCC. Indeed, renewal requests are now filed by postcard.

For more than sixty years, the broadcast media was subject to the control of the FCC, but in 1996 Congress passed the Telecommunications Act, a broad effort to do away with most regulations in effect since 1934. The act loosened restrictions on media ownership and allowed for telephone companies, cable television providers, and broadcasters to compete with one another for telecommunication services. Following the passage of the act, several mergers between telephone and cable companies and between different segments of the entertainment media produced an even greater concentration of media ownership.

The Telecommunications Act of 1996 also included an attempt to regulate the content of material transmitted over the Internet. This law, known as the Communications Decency Act, made it illegal to make "indecent" sexual material on the Internet accessible to those under eighteen years old. The act was immediately denounced by civil libertarians and brought to court as an infringement of free speech. The case reached the Supreme Court in 1997 and the act was ruled an unconstitutional infringement of the First Amendment's right to freedom of speech (see Chapter 5).

Although the government's ability to regulate the content of the electronic media on the Internet has been questioned, the federal government has used its licensing power to impose several regulations that can affect the political content of radio and TV broadcasts. The first of these is the **equal time rule,** under which broadcasters must provide candidates for the same political office equal opportunities to communicate their messages to the public. If, for example, a television station sells commercial time to a state's Republican gubernatorial candidate, it may not refuse to sell time to the Democratic candidate for the same position.

The second regulation affecting the content of broadcasts is the **right of rebuttal,** which requires that individuals be given the opportunity to respond to personal attacks. In the 1969 case of *Red Lion Broadcasting Company v. FCC,* for example, the U.S. Supreme Court upheld the FCC's determination that a radio station was required to provide a liberal author with an opportunity to respond to an attack from a conservative commentator that the station had aired.[12]

For many years, a third important federal regulation was the **fairness doctrine.** Under this doctrine, broadcasters who aired programs on controversial issues were required to provide time for opposing views. In 1985, however, the FCC stopped enforcing the fairness doctrine on the grounds that there were so many radio and television stations—to say nothing of newspapers and newsmagazines—that in all likelihood many different viewpoints were already being presented without having to require each station to try to present all sides of an argument. Critics of this FCC decision charge that in many media markets the number of competing viewpoints is small. Nevertheless, a congressional effort to require the FCC to enforce the fairness doctrine was blocked by the Reagan administration in 1987.

equal time rule

the requirement that broadcasters provide candidates for the same political office an equal opportunity to communicate their messages to the public

right of rebuttal

a Federal Communications Commission regulation giving individuals the right to have the opportunity to respond to personal attacks made on a radio or television broadcast

fairness doctrine

a Federal Communications Commission (FCC) requirement for broadcasters who air programs on controversial issues to provide time for opposing views. The FCC ceased enforcing this doctrine in 1985

POLICY DEBATE

Internet Regulation: The Communications Decency Act

When Congress, with the support of President Clinton, passed the Communications Decency Act (CDA) as one part of the Telecommunications Act of 1996, it sought to regulate the spread of indecent materials on the Internet—the vast electronic communications network now available to millions of Americans through computers and telephone transmission lines. The CDA sought to bar the transmission of obscene or indecent communications to anyone under the age of eighteen. The constitutionality of the CDA was immediately challenged by Internet service providers and civil liberties groups as an improper infringement of First Amendment liberties. In a sweeping 1997 decision, the Supreme Court ruled in *Reno v. American Civil Liberties Union* that such regulations are a violation of the First Amendment. More important, the Court established that the Internet is a form of communication entitled to the maximum degree of constitutional protection, analogous to newspapers, books, and magazines (electronic media, such as television and radio, may be more strictly regulated by the government). Yet this ruling has not ended the dispute between those favoring and opposing stricter Internet controls.

Supporters of Internet regulation argue that children must be protected from the vast amount of offensive material to be found on the Internet. More than 10,000 web sites are devoted to some form of pornography. Given the proliferation of obscene materials and sites, and given that the Internet is unregulated, government must be able to intervene to protect children. Despite the Supreme Court's ruling, the Internet is very different from newspapers and other printed media, in that there are no reporters, editors, publishers, or others who control the content of Internet communications.

Even more alarming, sexual predators have used Internet connections not only to expose children to obscene material, but to lure children to dangerous in-person meetings. For example, a California man was convicted of luring a thirteen-year-old girl from Kentucky to a meeting with him, the purpose of which was illegal sexual conduct. From 1995 to 1997, the FBI arrested thirty-five adults seeking to solicit sex from minors via the Internet. Apart from barring children from all Internet use, parents find themselves nearly powerless to protect their children, who often possess far more knowledge of computer technologies than their parents. Some limitation on liberty is necessary to protect America's children.

Those who oppose Internet regulation argue that the total harm done by regulations like the CDA far outweighs the benefits. In constitutional terms, the Internet

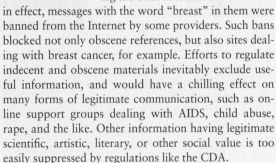

is a vast electronic forum for speech, expression, and education. Although some harm is likely to accompany the unfettered expression of thoughts and ideas, such expression is central to a democracy and to the fundamental liberties of its citizens. Efforts to regulate Internet content in the name of protecting children too easily restrict legitimate expression. For example, during the brief time that the CDA was in effect, messages with the word "breast" in them were banned from the Internet by some providers. Such bans blocked not only obscene references, but also sites dealing with breast cancer, for example. Efforts to regulate indecent and obscene materials inevitably exclude useful information, and would have a chilling effect on many forms of legitimate communication, such as online support groups dealing with AIDS, child abuse, rape, and the like. Other information having legitimate scientific, artistic, literary, or other social value is too easily suppressed by regulations like the CDA.

Concerned parents can always monitor Internet use by their children. They can obtain software that filters out objectionable materials. Above all, parents should have primary control over what their children do and do not see.

SOURCE: Amy Harmon, "Ruling Leaves Vexing Burden for Parents." *New York Times*, June 27, 1997.

THE MINNESOTA RAG AND PRESS FREEDOM

Few people liked Jay Near. A freelance reporter who wrote when and where he could find a job, Near eked out a living with stories that were usually scandalous and sometimes malicious. In the 1920s and 1930s, reporters like Near could find many small-time magazines and newspapers for which to write, as long as the stories were sensational enough. But Near brought his own personal hatreds into his writing; he was unapologetically anti-Semitic, anti-Catholic, antilabor, and antiblack. And he was not reluctant to express his views in his articles, often using the most offensive racial slurs when referring to individuals and groups. In short, Near was the kind of reporter who gave reporting a bad name.

With the help of an associate, Near began to publish his own weekly scandal sheet in the Minneapolis–St. Paul, Minnesota, area. He called his paper the *Saturday Press*. The life span of the *Press* consisted of nine issues published in the fall of 1927. Yet even before the first issue hit the streets, local authorities moved to stop publication of this odious rag, not only because it was racist and jingoist, but also because of allegations that Near printed of collusion between organized crime figures and local public officials. Coming during the era of alcohol prohibition in America, when bootlegging and related crimes led to widespread corruption among government officials, these allegations were at least partly true.

Authorities obtained a restraining order barring Near and his associates from publishing any present or future issues of the *Press*. The legal basis for this ruling was a Minnesota state law enacted in 1925 called the Public Nuisance Bill, also known as the "gag law." This law made illegal the production, publication, circulation, or possession of any publication found to be "obscene, lewd and lascivious" or "malicious, scandalous and defamatory." At first the restraining order was applied temporarily, but it was later made permanent. The *Saturday Press*

FREEDOM OF THE PRESS

prior restraint

an effort by a governmental agency to block the publication of material it deems libelous or harmful in some other way; censorship. In the United States, the courts forbid prior restraint except under the most extraordinary circumstances

Unlike the broadcast media, the print media are not subject to federal regulation. Indeed, the great principle underlying the federal government's relationship with the press is the doctrine against **prior restraint.** Beginning with the landmark 1931 case of *Near v. Minnesota*, the U.S. Supreme Court has held that, except under the most extraordinary circumstances, the First Amendment of the Constitution prohibits government agencies from seeking to prevent newspapers or magazines from publishing whatever they wish.[13] Indeed, in the case of *New York Times v. U.S.,* the so-called *Pentagon Papers* case, the Supreme Court ruled that the government could not even block publication of secret Defense Department documents furnished to the *New York Times* by an opponent of the Vietnam War who had obtained the documents illegally.[14] In a 1990 case, however, the Supreme Court upheld a lower-court order restraining Cable News Network (CNN) from broadcasting tapes of conversations between former Panamanian dictator Manuel Noriega and his lawyer, supposedly recorded by the U.S. government. By a vote of 7 to 2, the Court held that CNN could be restrained from broadcasting the tapes until the trial court in the Noriega case had listened to the tapes and had decided whether their broadcast would violate Noriega's right to a fair trial. This case would seem to weaken the "no prior restraint" doctrine. But whether the same standard will

was shut down; moreover, Near was barred from practicing his profession. Despite having little money and even fewer friends, Near appealed his conviction, which was upheld by Minnesota's highest court. Because of his dire financial and legal situation, Near appealed for help to the prominent publisher of the *Chicago Tribune*, Col. Robert R. McCormick. McCormick had no particular interest in helping Near, but he realized that the actions taken by the state of Minnesota against Near could also be applied to his newspaper by politicians in Illinois who would have gleefully put McCormick out of business because of his scorching criticisms of many prominent political figures. A new organization, formed to help average people protect their rights—the American Civil Liberties Union (ACLU)—also joined to help Near. The ACLU also realized that if a state could impose such a "prior restraint" on a publication, it could effectively exercise censorship, which would render meaningless the freedom of the press protected by the First Amendment.

At the time the Supreme Court agreed to hear Near's appeal, the right of American citizens to claim free press protection under the First Amendment had not yet been established (free speech had just been extended to all citizens by the Supreme Court in 1925). In a 5-to-4 decision handed down in 1931, the Court ruled in *Near v. Minnesota* that the Minnesota law was unconstitutional. The Court pointed out that the ability of the press to uncover scandal and wrongdoing could occur only by defaming the corrupt. Those who were legitimately wronged in the press have recourse through libel actions, the Court said, but the right to publish itself cannot be protected unless the right to publish scandalous and even defamatory stories is also protected. As Chief Justice Charles Evans Hughes wrote in the majority opinion, "The fact that the liberty of the press may be abused by miscreant purveyors of scandal does not make any the less necessary the immunity of the press from previous restraint in dealing with official misconduct."

Near himself was mostly forgotten after his brief fame. He died in poverty and obscurity in 1936. Yet because of this hate-monger, press freedom was given the special protection it rightly deserved.

SOURCE: Fred W. Friendly, *Minnesota Rag* (New York: Vintage, 1981).

The Saturday Press

Vol. 1, No. 4   Minneapolis, Minn., Oct. 15, 1927   Price 3 Cents

A Direct Challenge to Police Chief Brunskill

The Chief, in Banning This Paper from News Stands, Definitely Aligns Himself With Gangland, Violates the Law He Is Sworn to Uphold, When He Tries to Suppress This Publication. The Only Paper in the City That Dares Expose the Gang's Deadly Grip on Minneapolis. A Plain Statement of Facts and a Warning of Legal Action.

Respectfully Submitted

---

apply to the print media has yet to be tested in the courts. In 1994, the Supreme Court ruled that cable television systems were entitled to essentially the same First Amendment protections as the print media.[15]

Even though newspapers may not be restrained from publishing whatever they want, they may be subject to sanctions after the fact. Historically, newspapers were subject to the law of libel, which provided that newspapers that printed false and malicious stories could be compelled to pay damages to those they defamed. In recent years, however, American courts have greatly narrowed the meaning of libel. The most important case on this topic is the 1964 U.S. Supreme Court case of *New York Times v. Sullivan,* in which the Court held that to be deemed libelous a story about a public official not only had to be untrue, but had to result from "actual malice" or "reckless disregard" for the truth.[16] In other words, the newspaper had to deliberately print false and malicious material. In practice, it is nearly impossible to prove that a paper has deliberately printed false and damaging information and, as conservatives discovered in the 1980s, it is very difficult for a politician or other public figure to win a libel case. Libel suits against CBS News by General William Westmoreland and against *Time* magazine by Israeli general Ariel Sharon, both financed by conservative legal foundations that hoped to embarrass the media, were both defeated in court because they failed to show "actual malice." In the 1991 case of *Masson v. New Yorker Magazine,* this tradition was again affirmed when the Court held that fabricated quotations attributed to a public figure were libelous only if the fabricated account "materially changed" the meaning of what the person actually said.[17] For all intents and purposes, the print media can publish anything they want about a public figure.

★ News Coverage

▶ How are media content, news coverage, and bias affected by the producers, subjects, and consumers of the news?

Because of the important role the media can play in national politics, it is vitally important to understand the factors that affect media coverage.[18] What accounts for the media's agenda of issues and topics? What explains the character of coverage—why does a politician receive good or bad press? What factors determine the interpretation or "spin" that a particular story will receive? Although a host of minor factors plays a role, three major factors are important: (1) the journalists, or producers of the news; (2) the sources or topics of the news; and (3) the audience for the news.

JOURNALISTS

Media content and news coverage are inevitably affected by the views, ideals, and interests of those who seek out, write, and produce news and other stories. At one time, newspaper publishers exercised a great deal of influence over their papers' news content. Publishers such as William Randolph Hearst and Joseph Pulitzer became political powers through their manipulation of news coverage. Hearst, for example, almost single-handedly pushed the United States into war with Spain in 1898 through his newspapers' relentless coverage of the alleged brutality employed by Spain in its efforts to suppress a rebellion in Cuba, at that time a Spanish colony. The sinking of the American battleship *Maine* in Havana harbor under mysterious circumstances gave Hearst the ammunition he needed to force a reluctant President McKinley to lead the nation into war. Today, few publishers have that kind of power. Most publishers are concerned more with the business operations of their newspapers than with editorial content, although a few continue to impose their interests and tastes on the news.

More important than publishers, for the most part, are the reporters. Those who cover the news for the national media generally have a good deal of discretion or freedom to interpret stories and, as a result, have an opportunity to interject their views and ideals into news stories. For example, the personal friendship and respect that some reporters felt for Franklin Roosevelt or John Kennedy helped to generate more favorable news coverage for these presidents. Likewise, the dislike and distrust felt by many reporters for Richard Nixon was also communicated to the public. In the case of Ronald Reagan, the disdain that many journalists felt for the president was communicated in stories suggesting that he was often asleep or inattentive when important deci-

DESTRUCTION OF THE WAR SHIP MAINE WAS THE WORK OF AN ENEMY.

$50,000!

$50,000 REWARD!
For the Detection of the
Perpetrator of
the Maine Outrage!

Assistant Secretary Roosevelt
Convinced the Explosion of
the War Ship Was Not
an Accident.

The Journal Offers $50,000 Reward for the
Conviction of the Criminals Who Sent
258 American Sailors to Their Death.
Naval Officers Unanimous That
the Ship Was Destroyed
on Purpose.

$50,000!

$50,000 REWARD!
For the Detection of the
Perpetrator of
the Maine Outrage!

NAVAL OFFICERS THINK THE MAINE WAS DESTROYED BY A SPANISH MINE.

Hidden Mine or a Sunken Torpedo Believed to Have Been the Weapon Used Against the American Man-of-War—Officers
and Men Tell Thrilling Stories of Being Blown Into the Air Amid a Mass of Shattered Steel and Exploding
Shells—Survivors Brought to Key West Scout the Idea of Accident—Spanish Officials Pro-
test Too Much—Our Cabinet Orders a Searching Inquiry—Journal Sends
Divers to Havana to Report Upon the Condition of the Wreck.
Was the Vessel Anchored Over a Mine?

BY CAPTAIN E. L. ZALINSKI, U.S.A.

The *New York Journal*'s sensationalistic coverage of the sinking of the *Maine* in Havana harbor inflamed the American public and edged the United States toward war with Spain.

sions were made. One of the major reasons that Republican presidential candidate Bob Dole chose Jack Kemp as his running mate in 1996 was Kemp's popularity with the Washington press corps. Although Dole and Kemp had long disagreed on many substantive issues, Dole strategists calculated that Kemp's presence on the ticket would result in more positive media coverage. Conservatives have long charged that the liberal biases of reporters and journalists result in distorted news coverage. In an editorial in the *Wall Street Journal,* CBS news correspondent Bernard Goldberg agreed with conservative critics. According to Goldberg, "The old argument that the networks and other media elites have a liberal bias is so blatantly true, it's hardly worth discussing anymore." Goldberg's comments were criticized by CBS news anchor Dan Rather and by Jeff Fager, executive producer of the *CBS Evening News.* ABC correspondent David Brinkley, however, called Goldberg's assertion "probably true."[19]

A 1996 survey of Washington newspaper bureau chiefs and correspondents seems to support Goldberg's assertion.[20] The study, conducted by the Roper Center and the Freedom Forum, a conservative foundation, found that 61 percent of the bureau chiefs and correspondents polled called themselves "liberal" or "liberal to moderate." Only 9 percent called themselves "conservative" or "conservative to moderate." In a similar vein, 89 percent said they

Students and Politics

Sarah Gordon was looking for the best way to integrate two of her strongest interests: writing and a poignant, liberal viewpoint. "I always felt like a spectator while growing up," says the Harvard senior. "I just wasn't in a political environment." When she started college, though, she found opportunities to become active, first at Greenpeace, then at the campus liberal publication *Prospective,* and finally at the *Nation,* one of the country's most well known liberal magazines, where she worked for a semester as an assistant to investigative journalist Russ Baker on several stories, including one exposing the fund-raising methods of Republican candidates. "Writing is incendiary," she says, "and writing is a form of activism."

SOURCE: Sarah Gordon, interview by author, February 6, 1998.

had voted for Bill Clinton in 1992, while only 7 percent indicated that they had voted for George Bush. Fifty percent said they were Democrats, and only 4 percent claimed to be Republicans.[21]

This confluence of interests was in evidence during the 1996 presidential campaign. Most journalists endeavored to be evenhanded in their coverage of the candidates, subjecting all the major campaigns to regular scrutiny and criticism. As several studies have since indicated, however, during the course of the campaign the media tended to be more critical of Dole and more supportive of Clinton. Republican economic proposals were generally dismissed by the media as gimmickry. Republican efforts to question President Clinton's ethics—a topic the media had enjoyed probing during his first term—were rejected as inappropriate for a serious national campaign. Even the Republican National Convention was dismissed as a staged event not worthy of much news coverage. A major network news program, *Nightline,* showed its disdain for the GOP's convention by leaving before the convention ended, with anchorman Ted Koppel proclaiming, "Nothing surprising has happened."[22] One British observer wrote in reaction to these events, "Dole got his most sympathetic and in-depth coverage when he fell off the stage in Chico, California."[23] This biased coverage was an almost inevitable outgrowth of the de facto alliance that has developed over a number of years between the media and liberal forces. Like any long-standing relationship, this one tends to shape the attitudes and perceptions of the participants. Without any need for overt bias or sinister conspiracy, journalists tend naturally to provide more favorable coverage to liberal politicians and causes.

The linkage between substantial segments of the media and liberal interest groups is by no means absolute. Indeed, over the past several years a conservative media complex has emerged in opposition to the liberal media. This complex includes two major newspapers, the *Wall Street Journal* and the *Washington Times,* several magazines such as the *American Spectator,* and a host of conservative radio and television talk programs. These radio programs, in particular, helped Republicans win races in the 1994 and 1996 congressional elections. Conservative religious leaders like Rev. Jerry Falwell and Pat Robertson, founder of the Christian Coalition, have used their television shows to attack President Clinton's programs and to mount biting personal attacks on both Clinton and his wife. Other conservative groups not associated with the religious Right have also launched sharp assaults against the president. Nationally syndicated talk show host Rush Limbaugh, for example, is a constant critic of the administration.

The emergence of this conservative media complex has meant that liberal policies and politicians are virtually certain to come under attack even when the "liberal media" are sympathetic to them. For example, charges that President Clinton and his wife were involved in financial improprieties as partners in the Whitewater Development Corporation, as well as allegations that, while governor, Clinton had sexually harassed an Arkansas state employee, Paula Jones, were first publicized by the conservative press. Only after these stories had received a good deal of coverage in the *Washington Times* and the *American Spectator* did the mainstream "liberal" media begin to highlight them. Of course, once the stories broke, the *Washington Post,* the *New York Times,* and the major television networks devoted substantial investigative resources and time to them. In due course, the "liberal" media probably gave the Whitewater and Jones charges just as much play as the "conservative" media, often with just as little regard for evidence.[24]

Clinton's opponents later were able to gather evidence suggesting that the president may have had an affair with a White House intern named Monica Lewinsky. Once again, the "liberal" media gave the story enormous play. Interestingly, however, liberal news organizations made certain to point out that the story originated with Clinton's right-wing foes. For example, in its front-page coverage on January 24, 1998, the *Washington Post* revealed that the initial effort to gather evidence against Clinton had been the brainchild of a conservative activist and ardent foe of the president.[25] In this way, the *Post* appeared to be deflecting attention away from the allegations and toward the tactics of Clinton's enemies. Most journalists, however, deny that their political outlooks result in biased reporting.[26]

Probably more important than ideological bias is a selection bias in favor of news that the media view as having a great deal of audience appeal because of its dramatic or entertainment value. In practice, this bias often results in news coverage that focuses on crimes and scandals, especially those involving prominent individuals. For example, even though most journalists may be Democrats, this partisan predisposition did not prevent an enormous media frenzy in January 1998 when reports surfaced that President Clinton may have had an affair with White House intern Lewinsky. Once a hint of blood appeared in the water, partisanship and ideology were swept away by the piranhalike instincts often manifested by journalists.

SOURCES OF THE NEWS

News coverage is also influenced by the individuals or groups who are subjects of the news or whose interests and activities are actual or potential news topics. All politicians, for example, seek to shape or manipulate their media images by cultivating good relations with reporters as well as through news leaks and staged news events. Some politicians become extremely adept image makers—or at least skilled at hiring publicists who are skillful image makers.

Furthermore, political candidates often endeavor to tailor their images for specific audiences. For example, to cultivate a favorable image among younger voters during his 1992 campaign, Bill Clinton made several appearances on MTV, and he continued to grant interviews to MTV after his election. His

Students and Politics

Sam Dealey had not always held views on the Right of the American ideological spectrum. But when he arrived at Cornell University, he says, "I had not really thought out what I believed. I took some courses in college and proceeded to become a raving libertarian." Dealey's activism started when he worked on political campaigns in his native Texas, including that of Senator Kay Bailey Hutchison in 1993. In 1996, Dealey's interest in politics peaked as he interned with the *National Review,* a conservative political magazine that focuses on investigative journalism. While there, he wrote an article titled "New Girls' Network," about the alleged liberal bias of the Department of Housing and Urban Development in awarding contracts, and which caused a stir in Washington. Currently, Dealey works as assistant managing editor at the *American Spectator,* another major right-of-center political magazine.

SOURCE: Sam Dealey, interview by author, February 12, 1998.

Perspectives on Politics

SOURCES OF NEWS

What are your regular news sources?
The percentage of eighteen- to twenty-nine-year-olds who get their news from the following sources:

ELECTRONIC MEDIA
Television

Local news about your viewing area	69.9
National network news on CBS, ABC, or NBC	45.6
CNN	31.6
MacNeil/Lehrer	2.9
C-SPAN	10.1
Sunday morning news shows (such as *Meet the Press* or *Face the Nation*)	7.4
Newsmagazine shows (such as *60 Minutes* or *20/20*)	36.1
Talk shows (such as *Oprah, Donahue,* or *Geraldo*)	34.6

Radio

Programs on National Public Radio such as *Morning Edition* or *All Things Considered*	13.0
Call-in talk shows	12.4

PRINT MEDIA
Newspapers

Daily newspaper	56.5

Magazines

News (such as *Time, US News & World Report,* or *Newsweek*)	18.8
Personality (such as *People* or *US*)	16.0

SOURCE: 1993 Times Mirror poll, reported in Susan A. MacManus, *Young v. Old: Generational Combat in the 21st Century* (Boulder, CO: Westview, 1996), p. 54.

MTV forays came to an end, however, when he was severely criticized for discussing his preferred type of underwear with members of an MTV audience. Apparently undeterred by Clinton's experience, Republican presidential candidate Bob Dole sought to polish his image among younger voters in 1996 by also appearing on MTV. Dole's advisers hoped that the seventy-two-year-old candidate could use MTV to reach out to younger voters, but most observers thought Dole appeared out of place on the youth-oriented network.

By using media consultants and "issues managers," many social, economic, and political groups also vigorously promote their ideas and interests through speeches, articles, books, news releases, research reports, and other mechanisms designed to attract favorable media coverage. Typically, competing forces seek to present—and to persuade the media to present—their interests as more general or "public" interests. In recent years, for example, liberals have been very successful in inducing the media to present their environmental, consumer, and political reform proposals as matters of the public interest. Indeed, the advocates of these goals are organized in "public interest" groups (see Chapter 11). Seldom do the national media ever question a public interest group's equation of its goals with the general interest of all.

Occasionally, a clever ploy may allow a group completely to shape the news. In September 1996, for example, opponents of California's Proposition 209, which banned all gender and race preferences from state government and universities, were able to create a story that for a time completely discredited the proposition's supporters. Student opponents of the proposition at California State University at Northridge invited David Duke, a former Louisiana legislator and Ku Klux Klan leader, to speak in favor of ending racial and gender preferences at a campus forum. As his hosts had anticipated, Duke's presence on the Cal State campus sparked a riot that produced statewide news coverage linking the Klansman to Proposition 209. Duke's apparent association with the proposal silenced many of its legitimate supporters who feared being tainted by any connection to Duke.[27]

The capacity of news sources and subjects to influence the news is hardly unlimited. Media consultants and issues managers may shape the news for a time, but it is generally not difficult for the media to penetrate the smoke screens thrown up by news sources if they have a reason to do so. That reason is sometimes supplied by the third and most important factor influencing news content—the audience.

THE POWER OF CONSUMERS

The print and broadcast media are businesses that, in general, seek to show a profit. This means that like any other business, they must cater to the preferences of consumers. This has very important consequences for the content and character of the news media.

Catering to the Upscale Audience   In general, and especially in the political realm, the print and broadcast media and the publishing industry are not only responsive to the interests of consumers generally, but they are particularly responsive to the interests and views of the more "upscale" segments of their audience. The preferences of these audience segments have a profound effect on

Entertainment shows have become a popular means for candidates to reach the public. For instance, 1996 presidential hopeful Bob Dole appeared on David Letterman's late-night talk show. During that campaign, candidates also appeared on MTV and on the *Tonight Show*, hosted by Jay Leno.

the content and orientation of the press, of radio and television programming, and of books, especially in the areas of news and public affairs.[28]

Newspapers, magazines, and the broadcast media depend primarily upon advertising revenues for their profits. These revenues, in turn, depend upon the character and size of the audience that they are able to provide to advertisers for their product displays and promotional efforts. From the perspective of most advertisers and especially those whose products are relatively expensive, the most desirable audiences for their ads and commercials consist of younger, upscale consumers. What makes these individuals an especially desirable consumer audience is, of course, their affluence and their spending habits. Although they represent only a small percentage of the population, individuals under the age of fifty whose family income is in the eightieth percentile or better account for nearly 50 percent of the retail dollars spent on consumer goods in the United States. To reach this audience, advertisers are particularly anxious to promote their products in the periodicals and newspapers and on the radio and television broadcasts that are known or believed to attract upscale patronage. Thus, advertisers flock to magazines like the *New Yorker, Fortune, Forbes, Architectural Digest,* and *Time*. Similarly, the pages of elite newspapers like the *New York Times* and the *Washington Post* are usually packed with advertisements for clothing, autos, computer equipment, stereo equipment, furs, jewelry, resorts and vacations, and the entire range of products and services that are such integral parts of the lifestyles of the well-to-do business and professional strata.

Although affluent consumers do watch television programs and read periodicals whose contents are designed simply to amuse or entertain, the one area that most directly appeals to the upscale audience is that of news and

The O. J. Simpson trial received overwhelming media attention. Tabloid newspapers like those pictured here presented pages and pages of articles on the trial each day.

public affairs. The affluent—who are also typically well educated—are the core audience of newsmagazines, journals of opinion, books dealing with public affairs, such newspapers as the *New York Times* and the *Washington Post,* and broadcast news and weekend and evening public-affairs programs. Although other segments of the public also read newspapers and watch television news, their level of interest in world events, national political issues, and the like is closely related to their level of education. As a result, upscale Americans are overrepresented in the news and public-affairs audience. The concentration of these strata in the audience makes news, politics, and public affairs potentially very attractive topics to advertisers, publishers, radio broadcasters, and television executives.

Not surprisingly, given their general market power, it is the upper- and middle-class segments of the audience whose interests and tastes especially influence the media's news, public affairs, and political coverage. This is evident from the topics covered, the style of coverage, and in the case of network television, the types of reporters and newscasters who appear on the screen. First, the political and social topics given most extensive attention by the national media are mainly, albeit not exclusively, topics that appeal to the interests of well-educated professionals, executives, and intellectuals. In recent years, these topics have included the ecological and environmental matters, budgetary and fiscal questions, regulation of business and the economy, political changes in Russia, attacks on Americans and American interests by terrorists, and, of course, the fluctuations of the stock market, interest rates, the value of the dollar, the price of precious metals, and the cost of real estate. Although many of these topics may indeed be of general importance and concern, most are of more interest to upscale segments of the audience than to lower-middle- or working-class groups.

While these matters of concern to the upscale audience receive extensive media coverage, there are entire categories of events, issues, and phenomena of interest to lower-middle- and working-class Americans that receive scant attention from the national print and broadcast media. For example, trade-union news and events are discussed only in the context of major strikes or revelations of corruption. No network or national periodical routinely covers labor organizations. Religious and church affairs receive little coverage. The activities of veterans', fraternal, ethnic, and patriotic organizations are also generally ignored. Certainly, interpretations of economic events tend to reveal a class bias. For example, an increase in airline fares—a cost borne primarily by upper-income travelers—is usually presented as a negative development. Higher prices for commodities heavily used by the poor, such as alcohol and cigarettes, on the other hand, are generally presented as morally justified.

The upscale character of the national media's coverage stands in sharp contrast to the topics discussed by radio and television talk shows and the small number of news tabloids and major daily newspapers that seek to reach a blue-collar audience. These periodicals and programs feature some of the same events described by the national media. But from the perspective of these outlets and their viewers and readers, "public affairs" includes healthy doses of celebrity gossip, crime news, discussions of the occult, and sightings of UFOs. Also featured are ethnic, fraternal, patriotic, and religious affairs and even demolition derbies. Executives, intellectuals, and professionals, as well as the journalists and writers who serve them, may sneer at this blue-collar version of the news, but after all, are the stories of UFOs presented by the decidedly downscale *New York Post* any more peculiar than the stories of the UN told by the almighty *New York Times?*

The Media and Protest While the media respond most to the upscale audience, groups who cannot afford the services of media consultants and issues managers can publicize their views and interests through protest. Frequently, the media are accused of encouraging protest and even violence as a result of the fact that they are instantly available to cover it, providing protesters with the publicity they crave. Clearly, protest and even violence can be important vehicles for attracting the attention and interest of the media, and thus may provide an opportunity for media attention to groups otherwise lacking the financial or organizational resources to broadcast their views. During the

While demonstrating in Birmingham, Alabama, civil rights protesters were sprayed with fire hoses by the order of Police Commissioner Bull Conner. Images like this one were seen around the world and helped increase pressure on the United States to uphold its claims of being a nation of "liberty and justice for all."

1960s, for example, the media coverage given to civil rights demonstrators and particularly to the violence that southern law enforcement officers in cities such as Selma and Birmingham directed against peaceful black demonstrators at least temporarily increased white sympathy for the civil rights cause. This was, of course, one of the chief aims of Dr. Martin Luther King's strategy of nonviolence.[29] In subsequent years, the media turned their attention to antiwar demonstrations and, more recently, to antiabortion demonstrations, antinuclear demonstrations, and even to acts of international terrorism designed specifically to induce the Western media to publicize the terrorists' causes. But while protest, disorder, and even terrorism can succeed in drawing media attention, these methods ultimately do not allow groups from the bottom of the social ladder to compete effectively in the media.

The chief problem with protest as a media technique is that, in general, the media upon which the protesters depend have considerable discretion in reporting and interpreting the events they cover. This means that media interpretation of protest activities is more a reflection of the views of the groups and forces to which the media are responsive—as we have seen, usually segments of the upper-middle class—than a function of the wishes of the protesters themselves. It is worth noting that civil rights protesters received their most favorable media coverage when a segment of the white, upper-middle class saw blacks as potential political allies within the Democratic Party.

Thus, the effectiveness of protest as a media strategy depends, in large measure, on the character of national political alignments and coalitions. If protesters are aligned with or potentially useful to more powerful forces, then protest can be an effective mechanism for the communication of the ideas and interests of the lower classes. If, on the other hand, the social forces to which the media are most responsive are not sympathetic to the protesters or their views, then protest is likely to be defined by the print and broadcast media as mindless and purposeless violence. For example, the media have generally treated the white, working-class "militia" movement as a dangerous and irrational development while continuing to show a measure of sympathy and understanding for upper-middle-class animal-rights activists, even when the latter have engaged in violent and disruptive behavior. And in general, the media have been unsympathetic to antiabortion protesters, who tend to be drawn from the lower-middle class.

Typically, upper-class protesters—student demonstrators and the like—have little difficulty securing favorable publicity for themselves and their causes. Upper-class protesters are often more skilled than their lower-class counterparts in the techniques of media manipulation. That is, they typically have a better sense—often as a result of formal courses on the subject—of how to package messages for media consumption. For example, it is important to know what time of day a protest should occur if it is to be carried on the evening news. Similarly, the setting, definition of the issues, character of the rhetoric used, and so on, all help to determine whether a protest will receive favorable media coverage, unfavorable coverage, or no coverage at all. Moreover, upper-middle-class protesters can often produce their own media coverage through "underground" newspapers, college papers, student radio and television stations, and, now, over the Internet. The same resources and skills that generally allow upper-middle-class people to publicize their ideas are usually not left behind when segments of this class choose to engage in disruptive forms of political action.

★ Media Power in American Politics

▶ How do the media shape public perceptions of events, issues, and institutions?

▶ What are the sources of media power?

The content and character of news and public affairs programming—what the media choose to present and how they present it—can have far-reaching political consequences. Media disclosures can greatly enhance—or fatally damage—the careers of public officials. Media coverage can rally support for—or intensify opposition to—national policies. The media can shape and modify, if not fully form, public perceptions of events, issues, and institutions.

SHAPING EVENTS

In recent American political history, the media have played a central role in at least three major events. First, the media were a critically important factor in the civil rights movement of the 1950s and 1960s. Television photos showing peaceful civil rights marchers attacked by club-swinging police helped to generate sympathy among northern whites for the civil rights struggle and greatly increased the pressure on Congress to bring an end to segregation.[30] Second, the media were instrumental in compelling the Nixon administration to negotiate an end to American involvement in the Vietnam War. Beginning in 1967, the national media portrayed the war as misguided and unwinnable and, as a

Media images of the Vietnam War were seen by millions of Americans and helped turn public sentiment against U.S. involvement in the war. In this famous photo, terrified children flee from a Napalm bomb attack.

result, helped to turn popular sentiment against continued American involvement.[31] So strong was the effect of the media, in fact, that when Walter Cronkite told television news viewers that the war was unwinnable, Johnson himself was reported to have said, "If I've lost Walter, then it's over. I've lost Mr. Average Citizen."[32]

Finally, the media were central actors in the Watergate affair, which ultimately forced President Richard Nixon, landslide victor in the 1972 presidential election, to resign from office in disgrace. It was the relentless series of investigations launched by the *Washington Post,* the *New York Times,* and the television networks that led to the disclosures of the various abuses of which Nixon was guilty and ultimately forced Nixon to choose between resignation and almost certain impeachment.

THE SOURCES OF MEDIA POWER

Agenda Setting   The power of the media stems from several sources. The first is **agenda setting,** which means that the media help to set the agenda for political discussion. Groups and forces that wish to bring their ideas before the public in order to generate support for policy proposals or political candidacies must somehow secure media coverage. If the media are persuaded that an idea is newsworthy, then they may declare it an "issue" that must be confronted or a "problem" to be solved, thus clearing the first hurdle in the policy-making process. On the other hand, if an idea lacks or loses media appeal, its chance of resulting in new programs or policies is diminished. Some ideas seem to surface, gain media support for a time, lose media appeal, and then resurface. Examples include repair of the "infrastructure," a topic that surfaced in the early 1980s, disappeared after 1983, and then reemerged in the press in the 1992 presidential campaign. Similarly, national health insurance excited media attention in the 1970s, all but disappeared during the 1980s, and became a major topic again after 1992.

In most instances, the media serve as conduits for agenda-setting efforts by competing groups and forces. Occasionally, however, journalists themselves play an important role in setting the agenda of political discussion. For example, whereas many of the scandals and investigations surrounding President Clinton were initiated by his political opponents, the Watergate scandal that destroyed Nixon's presidency was in some measure initiated and driven by the *Washington Post* and the national television networks.

Framing   A second source of the media's power, known as **framing,** is their power to decide how political events and results are interpreted by the American people. For example, during the 1995–96 struggle between President Clinton and congressional Republicans over the nation's budget—a struggle that led to several partial shutdowns of the federal government—the media's interpretation of events forced the Republicans to back down and agree to a budget on Clinton's terms. At the beginning of the crisis, congressional Republicans, led by House Speaker Newt Gingrich, were confident that they could compel Clinton to accept their budget, which called for substantial cuts in domestic social programs. Republicans calculated that Clinton would fear being blamed for lengthy government shutdowns and would quickly accede to their demands, and that once Americans saw that life went on with government agen-

agenda setting

the power of the media to bring public attention to particular issues and problems

framing

the power of the media to influence how events and issues are interpreted

The shutdown of the federal government in 1995–96 closed all national parks and tourist sites, including the Washington Monument. The media helped direct popular opinion against the Republican-controlled Congress during the budget impasse that led to the shutdown.

cies closed, they would support the Republicans in asserting that the United States could get along with less government.

For the most part, however, the media did not cooperate with the GOP's plans. Media coverage of the several government shutdowns during this period emphasized the hardships imposed upon federal workers who were being furloughed in the weeks before Christmas. Indeed, Speaker Gingrich, who was generally portrayed as the villain who caused the crisis, came to be called the "Gin*grinch*" who stole Christmas from the children of hundreds of thousands of federal workers. Rather than suggest that the shutdown demonstrated that America could carry on with less government, media accounts focused on the difficulties encountered by Washington tourists unable to visit the capital's monuments, museums, and galleries. The woes of American travelers whose passports were delayed were given considerable attention. This sort of coverage eventually convinced most Americans that the government shutdown was bad for the country. In the end, Gingrich and the congressional Republicans were forced to surrender and to accept a new budget reflecting many of Clinton's priorities. The Republicans' defeat in the budget showdown contributed to the unraveling of the GOP's legislative program and, ultimately, to the Republicans' poor showing in the 1996 presidential elections. The character of media coverage of an event thus had enormous repercussions for how Americans interpreted it.

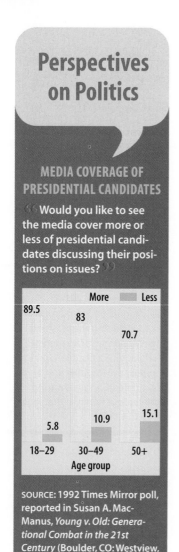

Perspectives on Politics

MEDIA COVERAGE OF PRESIDENTIAL CANDIDATES

" Would you like to see the media cover more or less of presidential candidates discussing their positions on issues? "

	More	Less

- 89.5
- 83
- 70.7
- 5.8
- 10.9
- 15.1

18–29   30–49   50+

Age group

SOURCE: 1992 Times Mirror poll, reported in Susan A. MacManus, *Young v. Old: Generational Combat in the 21st Century* (Boulder, CO: Westview, 1996), p. 86.

Media Coverage of Elections and Government   The media's agenda-setting and framing powers may often determine how people perceive an election's outcome. In 1968, despite the growing strength of the opposition to his Vietnam War policies, the incumbent president, Lyndon Johnson, won two-thirds of the votes cast in New Hampshire's Democratic presidential primary. His rival, Senator Eugene McCarthy, received less than one-third. The broadcast media, however, declared the outcome to have been a great victory for McCarthy, who was said to have done much better than "expected" (or at least expected by the media). His "defeat" in New Hampshire was one of the factors that persuaded Johnson to withdraw from the 1968 presidential race.

The media also have a good deal of power to shape popular perceptions of politicians and political leaders. Most citizens will never meet Bill Clinton or Al Gore or Newt Gingrich. Popular perceptions and evaluations of these individuals are often based solely upon their media images. Obviously, through public relations and other techniques, politicians seek to cultivate favorable media images. But the media have a good deal of discretion over how individuals are portrayed or how they are allowed to portray themselves.

In the case of political candidates, the media have considerable influence over whether or not a particular individual will receive public attention, whether or not a particular individual will be taken seriously as a viable contender, and whether the public will perceive a candidate's performance favorably. Thus, if the media find a candidate interesting, they may treat him or her as a serious contender even though the facts of the matter seem to suggest otherwise. In a similar vein, the media may declare that a candidate has "momentum," a mythical property that the media confer upon candidates they admire. Momentum has no substantive meaning—it is simply a media prediction that a particular candidate will do even better in the future than in the past. Such media prophecies can become self-fulfilling as contributors and supporters jump on the bandwagon of the candidate possessing this "momentum." In 1992, when Bill Clinton's poll standings surged in the wake of the Democratic

Politicians rely on the media for an inexpensive way to convey messages to the public. On NBC's *Meet the Press,* House Speaker Newt Gingrich presented his views to a national audience.

National Convention, the media determined that Clinton had enormous momentum. In fact, nothing that happened during the remainder of the race led the media to change its collective judgment. Even when George Bush's poll standing began to improve, many news stories pointed to Bush's inability to gain momentum. Although there is no way to ascertain what impact this coverage had on the race, at the very least, Republican contributors and activists must have been discouraged by the constant portrayal of their candidate as lacking—and the opposition as possessing—this magical "momentum." In 1996, the national media portrayed Bob Dole's candidacy as hopeless almost from the very beginning. Coverage of the Republican convention and the presidential debates emphasized Clinton's "insurmountable" lead. The media's coverage of Dole's campaign became a self-fulfilling prophesy of his defeat.

Media power to shape images is not absolute. Many journalists are dependent upon government officials as sources for the news, which gives these sources tremendous control over what is reported. Other image makers compete with and indeed do manipulate the media by planting stories and rumors and staging news events. Some politicians are so adept at communicating with the public and shaping their own images that the media seem to have little effect upon them. During the 1992 presidential campaign, candidates developed a number of techniques designed to take control of the image-making process away from journalists and media executives. Among the most important of these techniques were the many town meetings and television talk and entertainment show appearances that all the major candidates made. Frequent exposure on such programs as *Larry King Live* and *Today* gave candidates an opportunity to shape and focus their own media images and to overwhelm any negative image that might be projected by the media. Members of the national news media responded by aggressively investigating and refuting many of the candidates' claims. Each of the major television networks, for example, aired regular critical analyses of the candidates' speeches, television commercials, and talk show appearances. In 1996, the media subjected Bob Dole's tax cut proposal to intensive scrutiny, suggesting that it was based on faulty economic assumptions.

Some media commentators challenged the validity of the entire town meeting format, claiming that members of the general public—as distinguished from journalists—are not adequately prepared to confront the president. Commentators called for more events dominated by the media, such as press conferences, and fewer events like town meetings in which the role of the media is reduced.[33] This type of critical political coverage serves the public interest by subjecting candidates' claims to scrutiny and refuting errors and distortions. At the same time, such critical coverage serves the interests of the news media by enhancing their own control over political imagery and perceptions and, thus, the power of the media vis-à-vis other political actors and institutions in the United States. We shall examine this topic in the next section, as we consider the development and significance of adversarial journalism.

After his election, President Clinton returned to the town meeting and talk show formats that had served him well during the campaign as a way of reaching the public without media intervention. The national media, however, were not prepared to accept the president's efforts to circumvent them and moved to reassert their own political "spin" control. For example, following Clinton's February 10, 1993, nationally televised town meeting on the economy, many

SOURCES OF MEDIA POWER

Setting the Agenda for Political Discussion

Groups wishing to generate support for policy proposals or political candidacies must secure media coverage. The media must be persuaded that an item is newsworthy.

Framing

The media's interpretation or evaluation of an event or political action can sometimes determine how people perceive the event or result.

Shaping Perceptions of Leaders

Most citizens will never meet their political leaders, but will base opinions of these leaders on their media images. The media has a great deal of control over how a person is portrayed or whether an individual even receives public attention. The media are also able to shape how a policy issue is perceived by the public.

AMERICAN POLITICAL CULTURE

Comic Books

After television, the first mass medium that millions of young Americans become truly familiar with is comic books. Comic books come in all guises, from simply written juvenile stories to ambitious and complex narratives such as Harvey Pekar's brooding American Splendor series and Art Spiegelman's brilliant, Pulitzer Prize–winning Maus books. But the comic books with the widest audiences—the true mass media of the comic world—are superhero comics. At first, it might not seem that with their simple, repetitive plots of clashes between superheroes and supervillains, these comic books do much to shape Americans' cultural and political awareness. But precisely because superhero comic books describe endless variations on the battle between good and evil, they cannot entirely evade broader moral questions—in particular, questions about the relationship between the heroes and the society and government within which, or against which, they act. Over the last half-century, while the basic comic book conflict between heroes and villains has remained the same, the political and cultural backdrop has darkened, and faith in government has largely given way to cynicism.

The comic books that popularized the genre more than fifty years ago were staunchly patriotic. Superman was sworn to uphold "truth, justice, and the American way." Batman, the caped crusader, was allied with Gotham City's police department. Captain America, created by the government-sponsored Project Super Soldier during World War II, spent his first years helping American soldiers fight fascism. After Senate investigations in 1954 into the supposed link between the violence and immorality in comics and juvenile delinquency, however, superhero comic books went into decline. As they regained popularity at the end of the 1950s and into the 1960s, they continued to put forward a largely positive view of government. The characters in the X-men, for instance, one of the most popular and durable of the 1960s comic series, at first worked with the FBI.

But in the late 1960s and the early 1970s, superhero comics, mirroring broader changes in American culture, began to treat government less as an ally and more as part of the problem, and even on occasion as the enemy. In the years after the Watergate scandal, Captain America fought against a corrupt White House. The most acclaimed superhero comic of the 1980s, the Dark Knight series, cast the once pro-establishment Batman as "an embittered and misunderstood anti-hero hunted by . . . [a] Big Brotherish government, which has outlawed all superheros except for a subservient version of Superman."[1]

In recent years, overt political messages have tended to recede from comic-book story lines. But an underlying baseline of cynicism and skepticism seems to have been established. One of the more popular comic book series in the 1990s is Team Youngblood, about a band of young superheroes who must battle not only the usual assortment of menacing villains, but also a corrupt White House trying to exploit them. The twenty-eight-year-old creator of Team Youngblood explains how his depiction of the government arose: "I grew up watching the end of the Vietnam War, Watergate, the Iran-Contra affair. Now that the Soviets are gone, the biggest, most terrifying thing out there is the U.S. government."[2]

[1]David Segal, "Pow! Wham! Take That, Uncle Sam; In Today's Comic Book Culture, the Arch-Villain Is the Government," *Washington Post,* December 11, 1994, p. C3.
[2]Quoted in Segal, "Pow! Wham!"

major newspapers were sharply critical of the president's responses to questions posed by members of a Michigan studio audience and a group of callers from across the country. Clinton was accused both of giving inadequate answers to questions and of screening participants to exclude hostile questioners.

Indeed, President Bill Clinton has been one of the few politicians in recent American history who has been able to survive repeated media attacks. Clinton and his advisers crafted what the *Washington Post* called a "toolkit" for dealing with potentially damaging media revelations. This toolkit included techniques such as chiding the press, browbeating reporters, referring inquiries to lawyers who would not comment, and acting quickly to change the agenda.[34] All these techniques helped Clinton to weather repeated revelations of sexual improprieties, financial irregularities, and campaign funding illegalities.

THE RISE OF ADVERSARIAL JOURNALISM

The political power of the news media vis-à-vis the government has greatly increased in recent years through the growing prominence of "adversarial journalism"—a form of reporting in which the media adopt a hostile posture toward the government and public officials.

During the nineteenth century, American newspapers were completely subordinate to the political parties. Newspapers depended upon official patronage—legal notice and party subsidies—for their financial survival and were controlled by party leaders. (A vestige of that era survived into the twentieth century in such newspaper names as the *Springfield Republican* and the *St. Louis Globe-Democrat*.) At the turn of the century, with the development of commercial advertising, newspapers became financially independent. This made possible the emergence of a formally nonpartisan press.

Presidents were the first national officials to see the opportunities in this development. By communicating directly to the electorate through newspapers

Franklin Delano Roosevelt used radio addresses, called "fireside chats," to reach millions of listeners and build support for his New Deal programs.

and magazines, Theodore Roosevelt and Woodrow Wilson established political constituencies for themselves, independent of party organizations, and strengthened their own power relative to Congress. President Franklin Roosevelt used the radio, most notably in his famous fireside chats, to reach out to voters throughout the nation and to make himself the center of American politics. FDR was also adept at developing close personal relationships with reporters that enabled him to obtain favorable news coverage despite the fact that in his day a majority of newspaper owners and publishers were staunch conservatives. Following Roosevelt's example, subsequent presidents have all sought to use the media to enhance their popularity and power. For example, through televised news conferences, President John F. Kennedy mobilized public support for his domestic and foreign policy initiatives.

During the 1950s and early 1960s, a few members of Congress also made successful use of the media—especially television—to mobilize national support for their causes. Senator Estes Kefauver of Tennessee became a major contender for the presidency and won a place on the 1956 Democratic national ticket as a result of his dramatic televised hearings on organized crime. Senator Joseph McCarthy of Wisconsin made himself a powerful national figure through his well-publicized investigations of alleged communist infiltration of key American institutions. These senators, however, were more exceptional than typical. Through the mid-1960s, the executive branch continued to generate the bulk of news coverage, and the media served as a cornerstone of presidential power.

The Vietnam War shattered this relationship between the press and the presidency. During the early stages of U.S. involvement, American officials in Vietnam who disapproved of the way the war was being conducted leaked information critical of administrative policy to reporters. Publication of this material infuriated the White House, which pressured publishers to block its release—on one occasion, President Kennedy went so far as to ask the *New York Times* to reassign its Saigon correspondent. However, the national print and broadcast media—the network news divisions, the national newsweeklies, the *Washington Post,* and the *New York Times*—discovered that there was an audience for critical coverage among segments of the public skeptical of administration policy. As the Vietnam conflict dragged on, critical media coverage fanned antiwar sentiment. Moreover, growing opposition to the war among liberals encouraged some members of Congress, most notably Senator J. William Fulbright, chair of the Senate Foreign Relations Committee, to break with the president. In turn, these shifts in popular and congressional sentiment emboldened journalists and publishers to continue to present critical news reports. Through this process, journalists developed a commitment to "investigative reporting," or adversarial journalism, while a constituency emerged that would rally to the defense of the media when it came under White House attack.

This pattern, established during the Vietnam War, endured through the 1970s and into the 1980s. Political forces opposed to presidential policies, many members of Congress, and the national news media began to find that their interests often overlapped. Liberal opponents of the Nixon, Carter, Reagan, and Bush administrations welcomed news accounts critical of the conduct of executive agencies and officials in foreign affairs and in such domestic areas as race relations, the environment, and regulatory policy. In addition, many senators and representatives found it politically advantageous to champion causes favored by

Washington Post reporters Robert Woodward and Carl Bernstein played an important role in uncovering the Watergate conspiracy, which eventually led to the resignation of President Richard M. Nixon.

the antiwar, consumer, or environmental movements because, by conducting televised hearings on such issues, they were able to mobilize national constituencies, to become national figures, and in a number of instances to become serious contenders for their party's presidential nomination.

For their part, aggressive use of the techniques of investigation, publicity, and exposure allowed the national media to enhance their autonomy and carve out a prominent place for themselves in American government and politics. Increasingly, media coverage has come to influence politicians' careers, the mobilization of political constituencies, and the fate of issues and causes. Inasmuch as members of Congress and groups opposed to presidential policies in the 1970s and 1980s benefited from the growing influence of the press, they were prepared to rush to its defense when it came under attack. This constituency could be counted upon to denounce any move by the White House or its supporters to curb media influence as an illegitimate effort to manage the news, chill free speech, and undermine the First Amendment. It was the emergence of these overlapping interests, more than an ideological bias, that often led to a de facto alliance between liberal political forces and the national news media.

★ Media Power and Democracy

▶ Are the media too powerful and thus in need of restriction, or are a free media necessary for democracy?

The free media are an institution absolutely essential to democratic government. Ordinary citizens depend upon the media to investigate wrongdoing, to publicize and explain governmental actions, to evaluate programs and

Students and Politics

In 1995 Philip Lefebvre founded America the Younger, an organization devoted to finding and publicizing nonviolent forms of protest. The group evolved from an idea, to a producer of venues at which youth leaders were brought together to discuss ideas, and finally to a publication, the *Compass,* a monthly journal that allows contributors to discuss a given issue each week from the perspective of the younger generation. Recent issues have focused on youth in politics and women's rights. "It only takes me about twenty hours each week," says Lefebvre. The *Compass* started as a shoestring operation: "It was pretty modest," says the editor-in-chief, publisher, and production manager. "A circulation of two hundred, and most of that was at local coffee shops and campuses. It's still small, but it's a good starting point for me, with lofty goals: we intend nothing less than the complete reversal of how our generation is perceived."

SOURCE: Philip Lefebvre, interview by author, January 30, 1998.

politicians, and to bring to light matters that might otherwise be known to only a handful of governmental insiders. In short, without free and active media, popular government would be virtually impossible. Citizens would have few means through which to know or assess the government's actions—other than the claims or pronouncements of the government itself. Moreover, without active—indeed, aggressive—media, citizens would be hard-pressed to make informed choices among competing candidates at the polls. Often enough, the media reveal discrepancies between candidates' claims and their actual records, and between the images that candidates seek to project and the underlying realities. Of course, by continually emphasizing deceptions and wrongdoing on the part of political figures, the media encourage the public to become cynical and distrustful, not only of the people in office, but of the government and political process themselves. A widespread sense that all politics is corrupt or deceptive can easily lead to a sense that nothing can be done. In this way, the media's adversarial posture may contribute to the low levels of political participation seen in America today.

At the same time, the declining power of party organizations (as we will see in Chapter 9) has made politicians ever more dependent upon favorable media coverage. National political leaders and journalists have had symbiotic relationships, at least since FDR's presidency, but initially politicians were the senior partners. They benefited from media publicity, but they were not totally dependent upon it as long as they could still rely upon party organizations to mobilize votes. Journalists, on the other hand, depended upon their relationships with politicians for access to information and would hesitate to report stories that might antagonize valuable sources for fear of being excluded from the flow of information in retaliation. Thus, for example, reporters did not publicize potentially embarrassing information, widely known in Washington, about the personal lives of such figures as Franklin Roosevelt and John F. Kennedy.

With the decline of party organizations, the balance of power between politicians and journalists has been reversed. Now that politicians have become heavily dependent upon the media to reach their constituents, journalists no longer need fear that their access to information can be restricted in retaliation for negative coverage.

Such freedom gives the media enormous power. The media can make or break reputations, help to launch or to destroy political careers, and build support for or rally opposition to programs and institutions.[35] Wherever there is so much power, there exists at least the potential for its abuse or overly zealous use. All things considered, free media are so critically important to the maintenance of a democratic society that Americans must be prepared to take the risk that the media will occasionally abuse their power. The forms of governmental control that would prevent the media from misusing their power would also certainly destroy freedom.

★ The Citizen's Role

In their relationship to the media, most Americans adopt a passive stance. They read, they watch, or they listen to media accounts of events. However, it is relatively easy to become an active rather than a passive media user. One way to become an active media user is through letter-writing. Every newspaper and newsmagazine, and some television programs as well, provides a forum for citizen commentary. Letter writers have an opportunity to object to editorials with which they disagree, correct errors in news coverage, and even respond to other letter writers.

On one particular day, for example, the *New York Times* published eleven letters from readers. Several objected to the paper's editorial views, two asserted that news stories published in the paper had misrepresented important facts, and others commented on issues discussed in the paper. On the same day, the *Washington Post* published three long letters objecting to facts alleged in prior *Post* stories on German politics and on the problem of global warming. Obviously, a small number of letters cannot completely counterbalance all the errors or biases that may affect a newspaper's coverage. But if a newspaper or magazine were truly biased, it probably would not publish letters pointing out its biases.

Most newspapers and magazines feel some obligation to publish letters critical of their published materials. Even more important, letters can make editors aware of significant errors and omissions in the paper's coverage, perhaps leading them to admonish or reassign the journalists responsible. Letters to the editor can even compel college newspapers to correct errors in news coverage. In November 1997, for example, the University of Buffalo's student newspaper published an apology and retraction after letter writers pointed out significant errors in a news story.[36] This seems to be a far better approach than stealing the newspaper! Letters can also indicate to a newspaper or television station that its viewers are unhappy. As commercial enterprises, the media are very eager to maintain a high level of customer satisfaction.

Citizens must also learn to be critical consumers of the media. It is very important to be alert to the possible biases or hidden messages in any news story. First, when watching the news or reading a story, be alert to the author or reporter's implicit assumptions. For example, the media tend to be naive about the motives of any group claiming to work on behalf of the "public interest" or "citizens" and to take the claims of such groups at face value, especially if the group is criticizing business or the government. You should think carefully about the claims and facts being presented. Second, watch for stereotypes. Most newspapers and radio and television stations make an effort to avoid the racial and gender stereotypes that were once common. However, many other stereotypes are prevalent in the news. For example, some government programs such as the space program enjoy "good press" and generally receive positive coverage despite the often dubious claims made by their backers. Other programs, such as public-assistance programs and the highway program, are treated as "wasteful" or "pork-barrel projects," despite the good they may do. Critical consumers need to make up their own minds rather than allow media stereotypes to color their judgment.

STUDENTS AND POLITICS

Third, take note of news sources. Very often, reporters rely upon the views of a small number of top officials or influential figures who make it their business to cultivate journalists. When Henry Kissinger was secretary of state, he was such a successful manipulator of the media that most news about American foreign policy reflected his views. Often, politicians and interest groups retain public relations firms to contact journalists and disseminate their views. Always ask yourself whose interests might be served by a particular story. Often, those interests turn out to be the source of the story.

Finally, it is important to rely upon more than one source of news. The best approach is to make use of news sources with disparate ideological perspectives. For example, residents of Washington, D.C., sometimes read both the liberal *Washington Post* and the conservative *Washington Times.* Anyone can subscribe to both a liberal magazine, such as *The Public Interest,* and a conservative one, such as the *Weekly Standard,* that often cover the same topics. The importance of using such disparate news sources is to obtain different perspectives on the same events. This, in turn, will help you see more than one possibility and, ultimately, to make up your own mind.[37]

Summary

The American news media are among the world's most free. The print and broadcast media regularly present information and opinions critical of the government, political leaders, and policies.

The media help to determine the agenda or focus of political debate in the United States, to shape popular understanding of political events and results, and to influence popular judgments of politicians and leaders.

Over the past century, the media have helped to nationalize American political perspectives. Media coverage is influenced by the perspectives of journalists, the activities of news sources, and, most important, by the media's need to appeal to upscale audiences. The attention that the media give to protest and disruptive activities is also a function of audience factors.

Free media are an essential ingredient of popular government.

FOR FURTHER READING

Ansolabehere, Stephen, and Shanto Iyengar. *Going Negative: How Attack Ads Shrink and Polarize the Electorate.* New York: Free Press, 1995.

Bagdikian, Ben. *The Media Monopoly.* 4th ed. Boston: Beacon, 1992.

Cook, Timothy. *Making Laws and Making News: Media Strategies in the House of Representatives.* Washington, DC: Brookings, 1989.

Graber, Doris. *Mass Media and American Politics.* 4th ed. Washington, DC: Congressional Quarterly Press, 1992.

Hallin, Daniel C. *The Uncensored War.* Berkeley and Los Angeles: University of California Press, 1986.

Hart, Roderick. *Seducing America: How Television Charms the Modern Voter.* New York: Oxford University Press, 1994.

Hess, Stephen. *Live From Capitol Hill: Studies of Congress and the Media.* Washington, DC: Brookings, 1991.

Linsky, Martin. *Impact: How the Press Affects Federal Policymaking.* New York: Norton, 1986.

Owen, Diana. *Media Messages in American Presidential Elections.* Westport, CT: Greenwood, 1991.

Spitzer, Robert J., ed. *Media and Public Policy.* Westport, CT: Praeger, 1993.

West, Darrell. *Air Wars: Television Advertising in Election Campaigns, 1952–1992.* Washington, DC: Congressional Quarterly Press, 1993.

Winfield, Betty Houchin. *FDR and the News Media.* Urbana: University of Illinois Press, 1990.

STUDY OUTLINE

The Media Industry and Government

1. Americans obtain their news from radio, television, newspapers, magazines, and the Internet. Even though television news reaches more Americans than any other single news source, the print media are still important because they often set the agenda for the broadcast media and because they reach a more influential audience.

2. Since the passage of the Telecommunications Act of 1996, a wave of mergers and consolidations in the media industry has reduced the number of independent media in the United States.

3. The nationalization of the American news media, through which a relatively uniform picture of events, issues, and problems is presented to the entire nation, has contributed greatly to the nationalization of politics and of political perspectives in the United States.

4. Despite the widespread nationalization of news in America, news enclaves exist in which some demographic and ideological groups receive alternative news coverage.

5. Part of the Telecommunications Act of 1996, known as the Communications Decency Act, attempted to regulate the content of material transmitted over the Internet, but the law was overruled by the Supreme Court in the 1997 case *Reno v. American Civil Liberties Union.*

6. Under federal regulations, broadcasters must provide candidates seeking the same political office equal time to communicate their messages to the public.

7. Regulations also require that individuals be granted the right to rebut personal attacks.

8. Although recently diminished in importance, the fairness doctrine for many years required that broadcasters who aired programs on controversial issues provide time for opposing views.

9. Freedom of the press guarantees that the print media, unlike the broadcast media, are not subject to federal regulation, although they may be held responsible for libelous action.

News Coverage

1. Media content and news coverage are inevitably affected by the views, ideals, and interests of the journalists who seek out, write, and produce news stories.

2. News coverage is also influenced by the individuals or groups who are subjects of the news or whose interests and activities are actual or potential news topics.

3. Because the print and broadcast media are businesses that generally seek to show a profit, they must cater to the preferences of consumers.

4. The print and broadcast media, as well as the publishing industry, are particularly responsive to the interests and views of the upscale segments of their audiences.

5. Protest is one way that groups who cannot afford the services of media consultants and "issues managers" can publicize their views and interests.

Media Power in American Politics

1. In recent political history, the media have played a central role in the civil rights movement, the ending of American involvement in the Vietnam War, and in the Watergate investigation.

2. The power of the media stems from several sources, all of which contribute to the media's great influence in setting the political agenda, shaping electoral outcomes, and interpreting events and political results.

3. The political power of the news media has greatly increased in recent years through the growing prominence of investigative reporting.

Media Power and Democracy

1. Because the media provide the information citizens need for meaningful participation in the political process, they are essential to democratic government.

2. The decline of political parties has given the media enormous power, which creates a great potential for abuse.

PRACTICE QUIZ

1. The nationalization of the news has been influenced by which of the following trends in ownership of the media?
   a) the purchase of influential newspapers by foreign corporations
   b) the fragmentation of ownership of all media in the United States
   c) the wave of mergers and consolidations following the passage of the 1996 Telecommunications Act
   d) the purchase of the major news networks by the national government

2. Which of the following best describes national news in the United States?
   a) fragmented and localized
   b) nationalized and centralized
   c) centralized but still localized
   d) none of the above

3. Which of the following Supreme Court cases overruled the government's attempt to regulate the content of the Internet?
   a) *Near v. Minnesota*
   b) *New York Times v. United States*
   c) *Red Lion Broadcasting Company v. FCC*
   d) *Reno v. American Civil Liberties Union*

4. How do journalists compare to the general public in their political attitudes?
   a) Journalists are more conservative than the general public.
   b) The two groups' views are about the same.
   c) Journalists are more liberal than the general public.
   d) Journalists tend to be more Republican than the general public.

5. Which of the following have an impact on the nature of media coverage of politics?
   a) reporters
   b) political actors
   c) news consumers
   d) all of the above

6. Which of the following is a strategy available to poor people to increase their coverage by the news media?
   a) protest
   b) media consultants
   c) television advertising
   d) newspaper advertising "time sharing"

7. The media's powers to determine what becomes a part of the political discussion and to shape how political events are interpreted by the American people are known as
   a) issue definition and protest power.
   b) agenda setting and framing.
   c) the illusion of saliency and the bandwagon effect.
   d) the equal time rule and the right of rebuttal.

8. Which of the following can be considered an example of a news enclave?
   a) Internet chat groups
   b) letters to the editor
   c) readers of the *New York Times*
   d) people who watch CNN

9. Which of the following exemplifies the liberal bias in the news media?
   a) talk radio programs
   b) the *Wall Street Journal*
   c) the *American Spectator*
   d) none of the above

10. The newspaper publisher William Randolph Hearst was responsible for encouraging U.S. involvement in which war?
    a) the Spanish-American War
    b) the Vietnam War
    c) the U.S. war with Mexico
    d) the Gulf War

CRITICAL THINKING QUESTIONS

1. If the public receives most of its information about politics from the media, how accurate is its knowledge of government and politics? How does the media itself distort political reality? How do politicians use the media for their own purposes? What are the consequences for American democracy when the electorate is informed through such a filter? How might the quality of political information in America be improved?

2. There is a great deal of talk about the liberal bias of the media in American politics. To what extent is the media liberal? To what extent, do you think, is it biased? Considering the growing importance of conservative talk radio and news enclaves that support conservative causes, describe the ways in which discussions of a liberal bias in the media should be qualified. What other factors might mitigate the liberalism of the media?

KEY TERMS

agenda setting (p. 298)

equal time rule (p. 284)

fairness doctrine (p. 284)

framing (p. 298)

news enclave (p. 282)

prior restraint (p. 286)

right of rebuttal (p. 284)

9 Political Parties

STUDENTS AND POLITICS

I N many parts of the world, college students are associated with the most radical political parties and often spearhead riots, demonstrations, and other forms of political violence. In the Persian Gulf kingdom of Bahrain, for example, thousands of Shiite Muslim students clashed in late 1994 with police as part of a Shiite-supported party's effort to overthrow the Bahraini government. A number of police officers and students were killed.[1] In Bangladesh, a national student party led a general strike against the government. During the course of their protest, student demonstrators had a violent clash with police that led to more than eighty-five casualties.[2]

In the United States, by contrast, relatively few students belong to any political party, much less radical parties. During the 1960s, the Democratic Party appealed for the support of politically active students by sponsoring the Twenty-sixth Amendment, which lowered the voting age to eighteen. The Democrats also gave students an opportunity to play a greater role in party affairs by requiring state-level party organizations to make certain that young people were represented throughout the presidential nominating process, including in the state's delegation to the national presidential convention. These efforts do not seem to have borne much fruit, however. To be sure, young people (eighteen- to twenty-nine-year-olds) are slightly more likely to identify with the Democratic Party than with the Republicans. The strength of their attachment to the Democrats (or any other party), however, is generally weak, and many young people believe that candidates should run for office as individuals rather than as members of political parties.[3]

When American students engage in protest activities, they seem to focus more on matters of immediate concern or interest than on larger political or social issues. For example, in 1997, Utah State University students protested cuts in the university's athletic budget. Students at Los Angeles's Mission College protested financial aid cuts. Students at the University of Alabama's New College protested an administration move to merge their college with the university's College of Arts and Sciences. Stanford University students called for a boycott of *U.S. News and World Report* after their school had dropped one notch in that magazine's annual college ratings. A student at Moravian College in Pennsylvania handcuffed himself to the door of the administration building to protest his school's physical education requirement.

One major reason that American college students are less inclined toward radical politics is the relationship between education and access in American society. Higher education is probably the most important route of access to economic success and social status in the United States. Although a college or postgraduate degree is not an absolute guarantee of affluence, for the most part, graduates of American colleges and universities can look forward to

Perspectives on Politics

STRENGTH OF PARTY IDENTIFICATION

Percentage of Americans responding yes to the question,

" Do you feel a strong attachment to either the Democratic or Republican parties? "

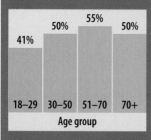

Age group	18–29	30–50	51–70	70+
	41%	50%	55%	50%

SOURCE: Adapted from American National Election Studies data reported in Jack Dennis and Diana Owen, "The Partisanship Puzzle: Identification and Attitudes of Generation X," in *After the Boom: The Politics of Generation X,* ed. Stephen C. Craig and Stephen Earl Bennett (Lanham, MD: Rowman and Littlefield, 1997), p. 46.

meaningful careers in which they will have the opportunity to use and profit from their academic credentials. This expectation, as much as anything else, works against political militancy on the part of American college and university students. Why would students participate in radical attacks upon a political and social order that promises to reward them?

Today's generation of young Americans is little different from earlier ones, which were also relatively indifferent to party politics. Over time, earlier generations began to recognize how differences between the two major parties affected their interests and began to show a greater interest in party politics. Today's generation will likely do the same.

The relationship between political parties and constituent social groups is never simple. Groups that in one social setting or time period are associated with radical parties may, in another place and time, be pillars of conservatism. Groups initially mobilized by one party may shift their allegiance to another as circumstances change. As we will see later in this chapter, during periods of electoral realignment in the United States, enormous blocs of voters have migrated from one party to the other, with major consequences for public policy and political power.

At the same time, the role of parties in political processes is more complex than we sometimes think. In modern history, political parties have been the chief points of contact between governments, on the one side, and groups and forces in society, on the other. In organized political parties, social forces can gain some control over governmental policies and personnel. Simultaneously, governments often seek to organize and influence important groups in society through political parties. All political parties have this dual character: they are instruments through which citizens and governments attempt to influence one another. In some nations, such as the People's Republic of China, the leading political party serves primarily the interests of the government. In others, such as the United States, political parties force the government to concern itself with the needs of its citizens.

The idea of political parties was not always accepted in the United States. In the early years of the Republic, parties were seen as threats to the social order. In his 1796 "Farewell Address," President George Washington warned his countrymen to shun partisan politics:

> Let me warn you in the most solemn manner against the baneful effects of the spirit of party generally. This spirit exists under different shapes in all government, more or less stifled, controlled, or repressed, but in those of the popular form it is seen in its greater rankness and is truly their worst enemy.

Often, those in power viewed the formation of political parties by their opponents as acts of treason that merited severe punishment. Thus, in 1798, the Federalist Party, which controlled the national government, in effect sought to outlaw its Jeffersonian Republican opponents through the infamous Alien and Sedition Acts, which, among other things, made it a crime to publish or say anything that might tend to defame or bring into disrepute either the president or the Congress. Under this law, fifteen individuals—including several Republican newspaper editors—were arrested and convicted.[4]

Obviously, over the past two hundred years, Americans' conception of political parties has changed considerably—from subversive organizations to bulwarks of democracy. In this chapter, we will examine the realities underlying these changing conceptions.

- ■ *We begin by explaining why political parties exist.* In answering this, we will see that parties play a significant role in key aspects of the political process.
- ■ *We then examine the history of the American two-party system.* As we will see, the history of parties has followed an interesting pattern that has had important consequences for governance.
- ■ *In the next three sections, we look at parties as organizations, parties in the electorate, and the role of parties in the campaign process.* We will see that although party organizations remain strong, the electorate's identification with parties and the role of parties in the electoral process have been declining in recent decades.
- ■ *We then assess the impact of parties on government and the policymaking process.* We will see that the differences between the two major parties can and do have an effect on policy.
- ■ *Finally, we conclude with an evaluation of the importance of political parties to democracy.* Healthy political parties are extremely important for maintaining American political values.

★ What Are Political Parties?

▶ How have political parties developed in the United States?

Political parties, like interest groups, are organizations seeking influence over government. Ordinarily, they can be distinguished from interest groups on the basis of their orientation. A party seeks to control the entire government by electing its members to office and thereby controlling the government's personnel. Interest groups usually accept government and its personnel as a given and try to influence government policies through them.

political parties
organized groups that attempt to influence the government by electing their members to important government offices

OUTGROWTHS OF THE ELECTORAL PROCESS

Political parties as they are known today developed along with the expansion of suffrage and can be understood only in the context of elections. The two are so intertwined that American parties actually take their structure from the electoral process. The shape of party organization in the United States has followed a simple rule: for every district where an election is held, there should be some kind of party unit. Republicans failed to maintain units in most counties of the southern states between 1900 and 1952; Democrats were similarly unsuccessful in many areas of New England. But for most of the history of the United States, two major parties have had enough of an organized presence to oppose each other in elections in most of the nation's towns, cities, and counties. This makes the American party system one of the oldest political institutions in the history of democracy.

Compared with political parties in Europe, parties in the United States have always seemed weak. They have no criteria for party membership—no cards for their members to carry, no obligatory participation in any activity, no notion of exclusiveness. Today, they seem weaker than ever; they inspire less loyalty and are less able to control nominations. Some people are even talking about a "crisis of political parties," as though party politics were being abandoned. But there continues to be at least some substance to party organizations in the United States.

OUTGROWTHS OF THE POLICYMAKING PROCESS

Political parties are also essential elements in the process of making policy. Within the government, parties are coalitions of individuals with shared or overlapping interests who, as a rule, will support one another's programs and initiatives. Even though there may be areas of disagreement within each party, a common party label in and of itself gives party members a reason to cooperate. Because they are permanent coalitions, parties greatly facilitate the policymaking process. If alliances had to be formed from scratch for each legislative proposal, the business of government would slow to a crawl or halt altogether. Parties create a basis for coalition and thus sharply reduce the time, energy, and effort needed to advance a legislative proposal. For example, in January 1998 when President Bill Clinton considered a series of new policy initiatives, he met first with the House and Senate leaders of the Democratic Party. Although some congressional Democrats disagreed with the president's approach to a number of issues, all felt they had a stake in cooperating with Clinton to burnish the party's image in preparation for the next round of national elections. Without the support of a party, the president would be compelled to undertake the daunting and probably impossible task of forming a completely new coalition for each and every policy proposal—a virtually impossible task.

The Two-Party System in America

▶ How do parties form? What are the historical origins of today's Democratic and Republican parties?

▶ What is the history of party politics in America?

▶ What has been the historical role of third parties in the United States?

two-party system

a political system in which only two parties have a realistic opportunity to compete effectively for control

Although George Washington, and in fact many other leaders of his time, deplored partisan politics, the **two-party system** emerged early in the history of the new Republic. Beginning with the Federalists and the Jeffersonian Republicans in the late 1780s, two major parties would dominate national politics, although which particular two parties they were would change with the times and issues. This two-party system has culminated in today's Democrats and Republicans (see Figure 9.1).

HOW THE PARTY SYSTEM EVOLVED

Figure 9.1

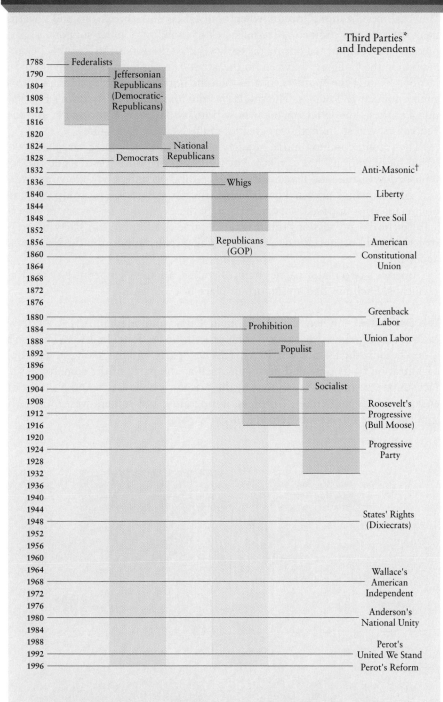

*Or in some cases, fourth party; most of these parties lasted through only one term.
†The Anti-Masonics had the distinction not only of being the first third party, they were also the first party to hold a national nominating convention and the first to announce a party platform.

HISTORICAL ORIGINS

Historically, parties form in one of two ways. The first, which could be called "internal mobilization," occurs when political conflicts break out and government officials and competing factions seek to mobilize popular support. This is precisely what happened during the early years of the American Republic. Competition in the Congress between northeastern mercantile and southern agrarian factions led first the southerners and then the northeasterners to attempt to organize popular followings. The result was the foundation of America's first national parties—the Jeffersonians, whose primary base was in the South, and the Federalists, whose strength was greatest in the New England states.

The second common mode of party formation, which could be called "external mobilization," takes place when a group of politicians outside the established governmental framework develops and organizes popular support to win governmental power. For example, during the 1850s, a group of state politicians who opposed slavery, especially the expansion of slavery in America's territorial possessions, built what became the Republican Party by constructing party organizations and mobilizing popular support in the Northeast and West.

America's two major parties now, of course, are the Democrats and the Republicans. Each has had an important place in U.S. history.

The Democrats   When the Jeffersonian Party splintered in 1824, Andrew Jackson emerged as the leader of one of its four factions. In 1830, Jackson's group became the Democratic Party. This new party had the strongest national organization of its time and presented itself as the party of the common man. Jacksonians supported reductions in the price of public lands and a policy of cheaper money and credit. Laborers, immigrants, and settlers west of the Alleghenies were quickly attracted to this new party.

Andrew Jackson's election to the presidency in 1828 was considered a victory for the common people and for the Democratic Party. Jackson's inauguration celebration on the White House lawn lasted several days. This engraving satirized Jackson's popular following.

From 1828, when Jackson was elected president, to 1860, the Democratic Party was the dominant force in American politics. For all but eight of those years, the Democrats held the White House. In addition, a Democratic majority controlled the Senate for twenty-six years and the House for twenty-four years during the same time period. These nineteenth-century Democrats emphasized the importance of interpreting the Constitution literally, upholding states' rights, and limiting federal spending.

In 1860, the issue of slavery split the Democrats along geographic lines. In the South, many Democrats served in the Confederate government. In the North, one faction of the party (the Copperheads) opposed the war and advocated negotiating a peace with the South. Thus, for years after the war, Republicans denounced the Democrats as the "party of treason."

The Democratic Party was not fully able to regain its political strength until the Great Depression. In 1933, Democrat Franklin D. Roosevelt entered the White House and the Democrats won control of Congress as well. Roosevelt's New Deal coalition, composed of Catholics, Jews, blacks, farmers, intellectuals, and members of organized labor, dominated American politics until the 1970s and served as the basis for the party's expansion of federal power and efforts to remedy social problems.

The Democrats were never fully united. In Congress, southern Democrats often aligned with Republicans in the "conservative coalition" rather than with members of their own party. But the Democratic Party remained America's majority party, usually controlling both Congress and the White House, for nearly four decades after 1932. By the 1980s, the Democratic coalition faced serious problems. The once-Solid South often voted for the Republicans, along with many white, blue-collar northern voters. On the other hand, the Democrats increased their strength among African American voters and women. The Democrats maintained a strong base in the bureaucracies of the federal government and the states, in labor unions, and in the not-for-profit sector of the economy. During the 1980s and 1990s, moderate Democrats were able to take control of the party nominating process and sought to broaden middle-class support for the Democrats. This helped the Democrats elect a president in 1992. In 1994, however, growing Republican strength in the South led to the loss of the Democrats' control of both houses of Congress for the first time since 1946. Although President Clinton, a Democrat, was able to win re-election to the White House in 1996 over the weak opposition of Republican Bob Dole, Democrats were unable to recapture control of either house of Congress. Some Democrats argued that the party needed to move even further to the political right and abandon its traditional support for social programs and affirmative action. Others argued that the party should redouble its efforts to appeal to poor and working-class Americans. In his 1998 legislative proposals to expand the government's social service programs, Clinton seemed to adopt the latter course.

Students and Politics

As president of the National College Democrats, Molly Morrison, a senior at Trinity College in New Jersey, coordinates a web of student party members that has ballooned to more than three hundred chapters in a period of six months. Morrison organizes events (such as numerous protests against Proposition 209 in California), ensures attendance and helps to set the agenda at the national student convention, and acts as a spokesperson for the organization. She says that she has seen a real difference with the rise of the College Democrats nationally, from successfully campaigning door-to-door for state assembly candidates to registering voters on campuses across the nation. "[Active] students can and do have a profound effect," she says, "not only in numbers, but in influence."

SOURCE: Molly Morrison, interview with author, February 19, 1998.

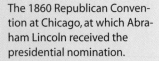

The Religious Right is an important part of the conservative coalition and is closely identified with Republicans. Former Christian Coalition executive director Ralph Reed is shown here addressing a Young Republicans' convention.

The 1860 Republican Convention at Chicago, at which Abraham Lincoln received the presidential nomination.

The Republicans The 1854 Kansas-Nebraska Act overturned the Missouri Compromise of 1820 and the Compromise of 1850, which had barred the expansion of slavery in the American territories. The Kansas-Nebraska Act gave each territory the right to decide whether or not to permit slavery. Opposition to this policy galvanized antislavery groups and led them to create a new party, the Republicans. It drew its membership from existing political groups—former Whigs, Know-Nothings, Free Soilers, and antislavery Democrats. In 1856, the party's first presidential candidate, John C. Fremont, won one-third of the popular vote and carried eleven states.

The early Republican platforms appealed to commercial as well as antislavery interests. The Republicans favored homesteading, internal improvements, the construction of a transcontinental railroad, and protective tariffs, as well as the containment of slavery. In 1858, the Republican Party won control of the House of Representatives; in 1860, the Republican presidential candidate, Abraham Lincoln, was victorious in a four-way race.

For almost seventy-five years after the North's victory in the Civil War, the Republicans were America's dominant political party, especially after 1896. Between 1860 and 1932, Republicans occupied the White House for fifty-six years, controlled the Senate for sixty years, and the House for fifty. During these years, the Republicans came to be closely associated with big business. The party of Lincoln became the party of Wall Street.

The Great Depression ended Republican hegemony, however. The voters held President Herbert Hoover responsible for the economic catastrophe, and by 1936, the party's popularity was so low that Republicans won only eighty-nine seats in the House and seventeen in the Senate. The Republican presidential candidate in 1936, Governor Alfred M. Landon of Kansas, carried only two states. The Republicans won only four presidential elections between 1932 and 1980, and they controlled Congress for only four of those years (1947–49 and 1953–55).

The Republican Party has widened its appeal over the last four decades. Groups previously associated with the Democratic Party—particularly white, blue-collar workers and white southern Democrats—have been increasingly attracted to Republican presidential candidates (for example, Dwight D. Eisenhower, Richard Nixon, Ronald Reagan, and George Bush). Yet Republicans generally did not do as well at the state and local levels and, until recently, had little chance of capturing a majority in either the House or the Senate. In 1994, however, the Republican Party finally won a majority in both houses of Congress, in large part because of the party's growing strength in the South.

During the 1990s, conservative religious groups, who had been attracted to the Republican camp by its opposition to abortion and support for school prayer, made a concerted effort to expand their influence within the party. This effort led to conflict between these members of the "religious Right" and more traditional "country-club" Republicans, whose major concerns were matters such as taxes and federal regulation of business. The coalition between these two wings won control of both houses of Congress in 1994 and was able to retain control of both houses in 1996, despite President Clinton's re-election. In 1997, however, severe strains began to show in the GOP coalition. Republican unity in Congress was weakened by an unsuccessful effort by some party members to oust House Speaker Newt Gingrich. In the 1998 elections, Republicans lost five House seats and remained even in the Senate. Even though they maintained a slight majority in both houses of Congress, it remains to be seen how long the Republicans can maintain a united front against the Democrats.

Students and Politics

The College Republicans (CR) at the University of Texas at Austin have been a bastion of conservatism at a vocally liberal campus. CR chair Michael Scaljon joined the organization in 1996 as a freshman, after realizing that "there were a lot more conservatives at [the university] than were speaking out. It's a chance to get people to be active . . . to get them to see both sides of issues." CR holds weekly meetings about campus and national issues, conducts debates, hosts speakers, registers students to vote, provides volunteers for national and local campaigns, and helps its members land jobs and internships with prominent politicians. Scaljon worked for the Texas lieutenant governor during the summer of 1997, organizing meetings and fielding phone calls from constituents. In 1996, CR became involved in a heavily publicized debate over the elimination of affirmative action at the University of Texas, after students who had been rejected by the law school had sued the University for its discriminatory policies.

SOURCE: Michael Scaljon, interview with author, January 5, 1998.

ELECTORAL ALIGNMENTS AND REALIGNMENTS

American party history has followed a fascinating pattern (see Figure 9.2). Typically, the national electoral arena has been dominated by one party for a period of roughly thirty years. At the conclusion of this period, the dominant party has been supplanted by a new party in what political scientists call an **electoral realignment.** The realignment is typically followed by a long period in which the new party is the dominant political force in the United States—not necessarily winning every election but generally maintaining control of the Congress and usually of the White House as well.[5]

Although there are some disputes among scholars about the precise timing of these critical realignments, there is general agreement that at least five have occurred since the Founding. The first took place around 1800 when the Jeffersonian Republicans defeated the Federalists and became the dominant force in American politics. The second realignment occurred in about 1828, when the Jacksonian Democrats took control of the White House and the Congress. The third period of realignment centered on 1860. During this period, the

electoral realignment

the point in history when a new party supplants the ruling party, becoming in turn the dominant political force. In the United States, this has tended to occur roughly every thirty years

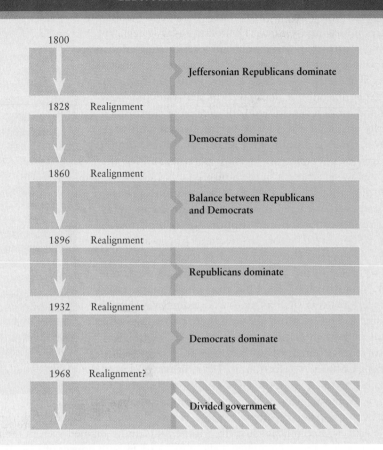

Figure 9.2

ELECTORAL REALIGNMENTS

1800
Jeffersonian Republicans dominate

1828 Realignment
Democrats dominate

1860 Realignment
Balance between Republicans and Democrats

1896 Realignment
Republicans dominate

1932 Realignment
Democrats dominate

1968 Realignment?
Divided government

Political scientists disagree over whether electoral alignments occurred in 1968, because no one party clearly dominated the national government after that election.

divided government

the condition in American government wherein the presidency is controlled by one party while the opposing party controls one or both houses of Congress

newly founded Republican Party led by Abraham Lincoln won power, in the process destroying the Whig Party, which had been one of the nation's two major parties since the 1830s. During the fourth critical period, centered on the election of 1896, the Republicans reasserted their dominance of the national government, which had been weakening since the 1880s. The fifth realignment took place during the period 1932–36, when the Democrats, led by Franklin Delano Roosevelt, took control of the White House and Congress and, despite sporadic interruptions, maintained control of both through the 1960s. Since that time, American party politics has been characterized primarily by **divided government,** wherein the presidency is controlled by one party while the other party controls one or both houses of Congress.

Historically, realignments occur when new issues combined with economic or political crises mobilize new voters and persuade large numbers of voters to reexamine their traditional partisan loyalties and permanently shift their support from one party to another. For example, during the 1850s, diverse regional, income, and business groups supported one of the two major parties, the Democrats or the Whigs, on the basis of their positions on various economic issues, such as internal improvements, the tariff, monetary policy, and banking. This economic alignment was shattered during the 1850s. The newly formed Republican Party campaigned on the basis of opposition to slavery and, in particular, opposition to the expansion of slavery into the territories. The issues of slavery and sectionalism produced divisions within both the Democratic and the Whig parties, ultimately leading to the dissolution of the latter, and these issues compelled voters to reexamine their partisan allegiances. Many northern voters who had supported the Whigs or the Democrats on the basis of their economic stands shifted their support to the Republicans as slavery replaced tariffs and economic concerns as the central item on the nation's political agenda. Many southern Whigs shifted their support to the Democrats. The new sectional alignment of forces that emerged was solidified by the trauma of the Civil War and persisted almost to the turn of the century.

In 1896, this sectional alignment was at least partially supplanted by an alignment of political forces based on economic and cultural factors. During the economic crises of the 1880s and 1890s, the Democrats forged a coalition consisting of economically hard-pressed midwestern and southern farmers, as well as small-town and rural economic interests. These groups tended to be native-stock, fundamentalist Protestants. The Republicans, on the other hand, put together a coalition comprising most of the business community, industrial workers, and city dwellers. In the election of 1896, Republican candidate William McKinley, emphasizing business, industry, and urban interests, defeated Democrat William Jennings Bryan, who spoke for sectional interests, farmers, and fundamentalism. Republican dominance lasted until 1932.

Such periods of party realignment in American politics have had extremely important institutional and policy results. Realignments occur when new issue concerns coupled with economic or political crises weaken the established political elite and permit new groups of politicians to create coalitions of forces capable of capturing and holding the reins of governmental power. The construction of new governing coalitions during these realigning periods has effected major changes in American governmental institutions and policies. Each period of realignment represents a turning point in American politics. The choices made by the national electorate during these periods have helped shape the course of American political history for a generation.[6]

AMERICAN THIRD PARTIES

Although the United States is said to possess a two-party system, the country has always had more than two parties. Typically, **third parties** in the United States have represented social and economic interests that, for one or another reason, were not given voice by the two major parties.[7] Such parties have had a good deal of influence on ideas and elections in the United States. The Populists, a party centered in the rural areas of the West and Midwest, and the Progressives, spokesmen for the urban middle classes in the late nineteenth and early

Students and Politics

Ross Perot's Reform Party, in both 1992 and 1996, relied heavily on grassroots campaigning. This effort has expanded into colleges and universities, including Rutgers University in New Jersey, where Scott Sanders has spearheaded efforts to promote the Reform Party's message of change. Sanders worked for the party as an intern in 1995, gradually progressing from answering telephones to presenting Perot with a "broom of cleaning government" at a party function. Today, Sanders participates in promoting the party on campus, including registering voters and conducting telephone drives to increase the vote. He also helps other colleges start their own party organizations.

SOURCE: Scott Sanders, interview with author, January 29, 1998.

third parties

parties that organize to compete against the two major American political parties

twentieth centuries, are the most important examples in the past hundred years. More recently, Ross Perot, who ran in 1992 as an independent and in 1996 as the Reform Party's nominee, impressed voters with his folksy style; he garnered almost 19 percent of the votes cast in the 1992 presidential election. Table 9.1 shows a listing of all the parties that offered candidates in one or more states in the presidential elections of 1996, as well as independent candidates who ran. With the exception of Ross Perot, the third-party and independent candidates together polled only 1.5 million votes. They gained no electoral votes for president, and most of them disappeared immediately after the presidential election. The significance of Table 9.1 is that it demonstrates the large number of third parties running candidates and appealing to voters.

Although the Republican Party was only the third American political party ever to make itself permanent (by replacing the Whigs), other third parties have enjoyed an influence far beyond their electoral size. This was because large parts of their programs were adopted by one or both of the major par-

Table 9.1	PARTIES AND CANDIDATES IN 1996		
Candidate	**Party**	**Vote total***[*]	**Percentage of vote***[*]
Bill Clinton	Democratic	45,628,667	49.16%
Bob Dole	Republican	37,869,435	40.80
Ross Perot	Reform	7,874,283	8.48
Ralph Nader	Green	580,627	.63
Harry Browne	Libertarian	470,818	.51
Howard Phillips	U.S. Taxpayers	178,779	.19
John Hagelin	Natural Law	110,194	.12
Monica Moorehead	Workers World	29,118	.03
Marsha Feinland	Peace and Freedom	22,593	.02
James Harris	Socialist Workers	11,513	.01
Charles Collins	Independent	7,234	.00
Dennis Peron	Grassroots	5,503	.00
Mary Hollis	Socialist	3,376	.00
Jerry White	Socialist Equality	2,752	.00
Diane Templin	Independent American	1,875	.00
Earl Dodge	Independent	1,198	.00
Peter Crane	Independent	1,105	.00
Ralph Forbes	Independent	861	.00
John Birrenbach	Independent Grassroots	760	.00
Isabell Masters	Independent	737	.00
Steve Michael	Independent	407	.00
Other candidates	—	5,575	.00
TOTAL		92,807,410	100.0%

*With 99 percent of votes tallied.
SOURCE: *USA Today,* November 8–10, 1996, p. 8A.

In the 1996 presidential election, in addition to the Democratic and Republican nominees, at least nineteen candidates appeared on the ballot in one or more states. Ross Perot came the closest to challenging the major-party candidates with more than 8 percent of the popular vote. The remaining eighteen candidates shared 1.56 percent of the votes cast with numerous write-ins.

ties, who sought to appeal to the voters mobilized by the new party, and so to expand their own electoral strength. The Democratic Party, for example, became a great deal more liberal when it adopted most of the Progressive program early in the twentieth century. Many Socialists felt that President Roosevelt's New Deal had adopted most of their party's program, including old-age pensions, unemployment compensation, an agricultural marketing program, and laws guaranteeing workers the right to organize into unions.

This kind of influence explains the short lives of third parties. Their causes are usually eliminated by the ability of the major parties to absorb their programs and to draw their supporters into the mainstream. There are, of course, additional reasons for the short duration of most third parties. One is the usual limitation of their electoral support to one or two regions. Populist support, for example, was primarily midwestern. The 1948 Progressive Party, with Henry Wallace as its candidate, drew nearly half its votes from the state of New York. The American Independent Party polled nearly 10 million popular votes and 45 electoral votes for George Wallace in 1968—the most electoral votes ever polled by a third-party candidate. But all of Wallace's electoral votes and the majority of his popular vote came from the states of the Deep South.

Americans usually assume that only the candidates nominated by one of the two major parties have any chance of winning an election. Thus, a vote cast for a third-party or independent candidate is often seen as a vote wasted. Voters who would prefer a third-party candidate may feel compelled to vote for the major-party candidate whom they regard as the "lesser of two evils" to avoid wasting their vote in a futile gesture. Third-party candidates must struggle—usually without success—to overcome the perception that they cannot win. Thus, in 1996, many voters who favored Ross Perot gave their votes to Bob Dole or Bill Clinton on the presumption that Perot was not really electable.

As many scholars have pointed out, third-party prospects are also hampered by America's **single-member-district** plurality election system. In many other nations, several individuals can be elected to represent each legislative district. This is called a system of **multiple-member districts.** With this type of system, the candidates of weaker parties have a better chance of winning at

single-member district

an electorate that is allowed to select only one representative from each district; the normal method of representation in the United States

multiple-member district

an electorate that selects all candidates at large from the whole district; each voter is given the number of votes equivalent to the number of seats to be filled

least some seats. For their part, voters are less concerned about wasting ballots and usually more willing to support minor-party candidates.

Reinforcing the effects of the single-member district, the **plurality system** of voting (see Chapter 10) generally has the effect of setting what could be called a high threshold for victory. To win a plurality race, candidates usually must secure many more votes than they would need under most European systems of **proportional representation.** For example, to win an American plurality election in a single-member district where there are only two candidates, a politician must win more than 50 percent of the votes cast. To win a seat from a European multiple-member district under proportional rules, a candidate may need to win only 15 or 20 percent of the votes cast. This high American threshold discourages minor parties and encourages the various political factions that might otherwise form minor parties to minimize their differences and remain within the major-party coalitions.[8]

It would nevertheless be incorrect to assert (as some scholars have maintained) that America's single-member plurality election system is the major cause of its historical two-party pattern. All that can be said is that American election law depresses the number of parties likely to survive over long periods of time in the United States. There is nothing magical about two. Indeed, the single-member plurality system of election can also discourage second parties. After all, if one party consistently receives a large plurality of the vote, people may eventually come to see their vote *even for the second party* as a wasted effort. This happened to the Republican Party in the Deep South before World War II.

★ Party Organization

▶ How are political parties organized? At what levels are they organized?

In the United States, **party organizations** exist at virtually every level of government (see Figure 9.3). These organizations are usually committees made up of a number of active party members. State law and party rules prescribe how such committees are constituted. Usually, committee members are elected at local party meetings—called **caucuses**—or as part of the regular primary election. The best known examples of these committees are at the national level—the Democratic National Committee and the Republican National Committee.

NATIONAL CONVENTION

At the national level, the party's most important institution is the quadrennial **national convention.** The convention is attended by delegates from each of the states; as a group, they nominate the party's presidential and vice presidential candidates, draft the party's campaign platform for the presidential race, and approve changes in the rules and regulations governing party procedures. Before World War II, presidential nominations occupied most of the time, energy, and effort expended at the national convention. The nomination process required days of negotiation and compromise among state party leaders and

---

plurality system

a type of electoral system in which, to win a seat in the parliament or other representative body, a candidate need only receive the most votes in the election, not necessarily a majority of votes cast

proportional representation

a multiple-member district system that allows each political party representation in proportion to its percentage of the total vote

party organization

the formal structure of a political party, including its leadership, election committees, active members, and paid staff

caucus (political)

a normally closed meeting of a political or legislative group to select candidates, plan strategy, or make decisions regarding legislative matters

national convention

a national party political institution that serves to nominate the party's presidential and vice presidential candidates, establish party rules, and write and ratify the party's platform

HOW AMERICAN PARTIES ARE ORGANIZED   Figure 9.3

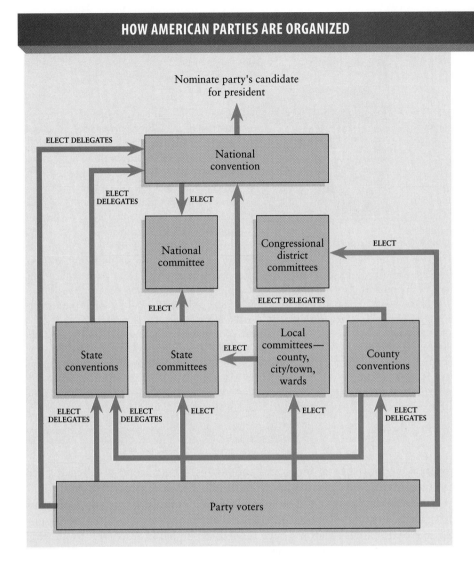

often required many ballots before a nominee was selected. In recent years, however, presidential candidates have essentially nominated themselves by winning enough delegate support in primary elections to win the official nomination on the first ballot. The actual convention has played little or no role in selecting the candidates.

The convention's other two tasks, determining the party's rules and its platform, remain important. Party rules can determine the relative influence of competing factions within the party and can also increase or decrease the party's chances for electoral success. In 1972, for example, the Democratic National Convention adopted a new set of rules favored by the party's liberal wing. Under these rules, state delegations to the Democratic convention were required to include women and members of minority groups in rough proportion to those groups' representation among the party's membership in that state. Liberals correctly calculated that women and African Americans would

We the People

THE PROHIBITION PARTY

From colonial crusades against the harmful effects of demon rum to the successful effort to raise the drinking age nationwide from eighteen to twenty-one in the late 1980s, the battle against alcohol has been one of America's most enduring social and moral crusades. The terrible social consequences of excessive alcohol consumption have been and continue to be widely and deeply felt throughout American society. The persistence of the temperance movement is epitomized by America's third oldest (and oldest third) political party, the Prohibition Party.

The party can be traced back to several separate state parties in Maine, New York, and Pennsylvania that formed in the 1850s. Many of the leaders of these parties were also prominent in the antislavery and women's suffrage movements—issues that also combined moral and social concerns. The resolution of the slavery issue with the Civil War prompted prohibitionists to turn their full attention to temperance. Despite early links with the Republican Party, neither of the major parties took much interest in the temperance cause. Worse, many states repealed prohibition measures after the Civil War, and others ceased enforcement. President Ulysses S. Grant, who was widely popular, embodied the turn toward liquor, as his partiality for strong spirits was widely known.

The first national Prohibition Party convention was held in 1869. Its first presidential nominating convention came three years later. The party's presidential candidate, James Black (a co-founder of the Republican Party in the 1850s), garnered a paltry 5,607 votes, but the party's early efforts revealed a profound and widespread concern for societal decline in morality and the need for a national "spiritual awakening." "A Christian lacking commitment to prohibition," asserted the party, was "no Christian at all."[1] In addition, the party in its formative years advocated such progressive political reforms as women's suffrage, civil service reform, inheri-

generally support liberal ideas and candidates. The rules also called for the use of proportional representation—a voting system liberals thought would give them an advantage by allowing the election of more women and minority delegates. (Although Republican rules do not require proportional representation, some state legislatures have moved to compel both parties to use this system in their presidential primaries.)

The convention also approves the party **platform.** Platforms are often dismissed as documents filled with platitudes that are seldom read by voters. To some extent this criticism is well founded. Not one voter in a thousand so much as glances at the party platform, and even the news media pay little attention to the documents. Furthermore, the parties' presidential candidates make little use of the platforms in their campaigns; usually they prefer to develop and promote their own themes. Nonetheless, the platform can be an important document. The platform should be understood as a contract in which the various party factions attending the convention state their terms for supporting the ticket. For one faction, welfare reform may be a key issue. For another faction, tax reduction may be more important. For a third, the critical issue might be deficit reduction. When one of these "planks" is included in the platform, its promoters are asserting that this is what they want in exchange for their support for the ticket, while other party factions are agreeing that the position seems reasonable and appropriate. Thus, party platforms should be seen more as internal party documents than as public pledges.

platform

a party document, written at a national convention, that contains party philosophy, principles, and positions on issues

tance and income tax legislation, child labor laws, and pensions for the elderly.

The party's high-water mark was reached in 1892, when its presidential candidate received 2.25 percent of the presidential vote. By the end of the decade, however, two forces undercut the party's growth and influence. First, those in the party who wanted it to focus solely on the alcohol issue gained control over those who advocated a more broad and progressive social and political agenda. This shift led to a contraction of the party's base of support. Second, the prohibition movement shifted away from party politics and toward two other groups, the Anti-Saloon League (ASL) and the Women's Christian Temperance Union (WCTU). The great political success of the temperance movement—the adoption of the Eighteenth Amendment to the Constitution in 1919—was the result of a pressure politics approach adopted by the ASL and the WCTU and applied to both major political parties. The Prohibition Party survived, but it viewed other temperance groups with suspicion because of the willingness of the ASL and the WCTU to bargain and seek compromise with others in the political process. The Prohibition Party considered issue purity to be more important, a fact that guaranteed that the party would remain small.

With the repeal of the prohibition amendment in 1933 (by passage of the Twenty-first Amendment), the Prohibition Party again assumed a prominent role in temperance politics. Yet from that time to the present, it has been a far more conservative and elitist movement, building its appeal on states' rights, distrust of the national government, international isolationism, and economic laissez-faire. Even though the Prohibition Party survives to the present, its narrow modern form all but prevents it from tapping into national grassroots concerns for alcohol abuse and moral crisis that fuel other contemporary political and social movements.

SOURCE: Norman Clark, *Deliver Us from Evil: An Interpretation of American Prohibition* (New York: Norton, 1976).
[1]Jack S. Blocker, Jr., *Retreat From Reform* (Westport, CT: Greenwood, 1976), p. 131.

NATIONAL COMMITTEE

Between conventions, each national political party is technically headed by its national committee. For the Democrats and Republicans, these are called the Democratic National Committee (DNC) and the Republican National Committee (RNC), respectively. These national committees raise campaign funds, head off factional disputes within the party, and endeavor to enhance the party's media image. The actual work of each national committee is overseen by its chairperson. Other committee members are generally major party contributors or fund-raisers and serve in a largely ceremonial capacity. In 1997, Senate hearings on campaign financing pointed to the importance of the national committees as fund-raising agencies. The DNC and RNC had each raised tens of millions of dollars for the 1996 national election campaigns.

For whichever party controls the White House, the party's national committee chair is appointed by the president. Typically, this means that that party's national committee becomes little more than an adjunct to the White House staff. For a first-term president, the committee devotes the bulk of its energy to the re-election campaign. The national committee chair of the party not in control of the White House is selected by the committee itself and usually takes a broader view of the party's needs, raising money and performing other activities on behalf of the party's members in Congress and in the state legislatures. Thus, after Bill Clinton took office in 1992, former DNC chairs

David Wilhelm and Christopher Dodd focused their efforts almost exclusively on Clinton's re-election. In both 1992 and 1996, former RNC chair Haley Barbour not only worked to put a Republican in the White House, but also sought to strengthen the Republican Party at the congressional and local levels by recruiting strong candidates and raising money for their campaigns. Barbour has been credited as the mastermind behind the GOP's 1996 congressional victory. In 1997, Colorado land developer Jim Nicholson replaced Barbour as head of the RNC while Colorado governor Roy Romer was named to lead the DNC. Day-to-day DNC operations are handled by Steve Grossman, a Massachusetts business executive.

CONGRESSIONAL CAMPAIGN COMMITTEES

Each party also forms House and Senate campaign committees to raise funds for House and Senate election campaigns. Their efforts may or may not be coordinated with the activities of the national committees. For the party that controls the White House, the national committee and the congressional campaign committees are often rivals, since both groups are seeking donations from the same people but for different candidates: the national committee seeks funds for the presidential race while the congressional campaign committees approach the same contributors for support for the congressional contests. In recent years, the Republican Party has attempted to coordinate the fund-raising activities of all its committees. Republicans have sought to give the GOP's national institutions the capacity to invest funds in those close congressional, state, and local races where they can do the most good. The Democrats have been slower to coordinate their various committee activities, and this may have placed them at a disadvantage in recent congressional and local races.

STATE AND LOCAL PARTY ORGANIZATIONS

Each of the two major parties has a central committee in each state. The parties traditionally also have county committees and, in some instances, state

The parties' national committees seek publicity whenever possible. Republican National Committee Chair Jim Nicholson, left, welcomes media opportunities such as appearances on NBC's *Meet the Press*, where he debated with Democratic National Committee Chair Roy Romer over campaign fund-raising issues.

senate district committees, judicial district committees, and in the case of larger cities, citywide party committees and local assembly district "ward" committees as well. Congressional districts also may have party committees.

Some cities also have precinct committees. Precincts are not districts from which any representative is elected but instead are legally defined subdivisions of wards that are used to register voters and set up ballot boxes or voting machines. A precinct is typically composed of three hundred to six hundred voters. Well-organized political parties—especially the famous old machines of New York, Chicago, and Boston—provided for "precinct captains" and a fairly tight group of party members around them. Precinct captains were usually members of long standing in neighborhood party clubhouses, which were important social centers as well as places for distributing favors to constituents.[9]

In the nineteenth and early twentieth centuries, many cities and counties and even a few states upon occasion have had such well-organized parties that they were called **machines** and their leaders were called "bosses." Some of the great reform movements in American history were motivated by the excessive powers and abuses of these machines and their bosses. But few, if any, machines are left today. Traditional party machines depended heavily upon **patronage,** their power to control government jobs. With thousands of jobs to dispense, party bosses were able to recruit armies of political workers who, in turn, mobilized millions of voters. Today, because of civil service reform, party leaders no longer control many positions. Nevertheless, state and local party organizations are very active in recruiting candidates, conducting voter registration drives, and providing financial assistance to candidates. In many respects, federal election law has given state and local party organizations new life. Under current law, state and local party organizations can spend unlimited amounts of money on "party-building" activities such as voter registration and get-out-the-vote drives (see Chapter 10). As a result, the national party organizations, which have enormous fund-raising abilities but are limited by law in how much they can spend on candidates, each year transfer millions of dollars to the state and local organizations. The state and local parties, in turn, spend these funds, sometimes called **"soft money,"** to promote the candidacies of national, as well as state and local, candidates. In this process,

machines

strong party organizations in late-nineteenth- and early-twentieth-century American cities. These machines were led by "bosses" who controlled party nominations and patronage

patronage

the resources available to higher officials, usually opportunities to make partisan appointments to offices and to confer grants, licenses, or special favors to supporters

soft money

money contributed directly to political parties for voter registration and organization

as local organizations have become linked financially to the national parties, American political parties have become somewhat more integrated and nationalized than ever before. At the same time, the state and local party organizations have come to control large financial resources and play important roles in elections despite the collapse of the old patronage machines.[10]

★ Parties and the Electorate

▶ What ties do people have to political parties?

party identification

an individual voter's psychological ties to one party or another

Party organizations are more than just organizations; they are made up of millions of rank-and-file members. Individual voters tend to develop **party identification** with one of the political parties. Although it is a psychological tie, party identification also has a rational component. Voters generally form attachments to parties that reflect their views and interests. Once those attachments are formed, however, they are likely to persist and even to be handed down to children, unless some very strong factors convince individuals that their party is no longer an appropriate object for their affections. In some sense, party identification is similar to brand loyalty in the marketplace: consumers choose a brand of automobile for its appearance or mechanical characteristics and stick with it out of loyalty, habit, and unwillingness to constantly reexamine their choices, but they may eventually change if the old brand no longer serves their interests.

Although the strength of partisan ties in the United States has declined in recent years, most Americans continue to identify with either the Republican Party or the Democratic Party (see Figure 9.4). Party identification gives citi-

These James Madison University students were activists for Oliver North's candidacy for the U.S. Senate in 1994.

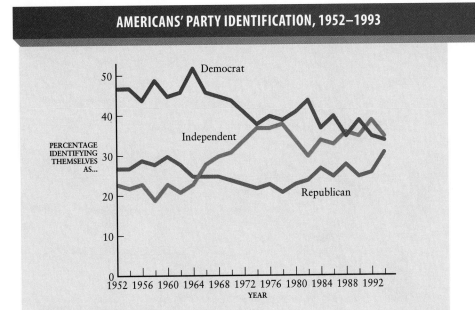

AMERICANS' PARTY IDENTIFICATION, 1952–1993   **Figure 9.4**

SOURCE: Harold W. Stanley and Richard G. Niemi, *Vital Statistics on American Politics,* 5th ed. (Washington, DC: Congressional Quarterly Press, 1995), p. 146.

zens a stake in election outcomes that goes beyond the particular race at hand. This is why strong party identifiers are more likely than other Americans to go to the polls and, of course, are more likely than others to support the party with which they identify. **Party activists** are drawn from the ranks of the strong identifiers. Activists are those who not only vote but also contribute their time, energy, and effort to party affairs. Activists ring doorbells, stuff envelopes, attend meetings, and contribute money to the party cause. No party could succeed without the thousands of volunteers who undertake the mundane tasks needed to keep the organization going.

party activists

partisans who contribute time, energy, and effort to support their party and its candidates

GROUP AFFILIATIONS

The Democratic and Republican parties are America's only national parties. They are the only political organizations that draw support from most regions of the country and from Americans of every racial, economic, religious, and ethnic group. The two parties do not draw equal support from members of every social stratum, however. When we refer to the Democratic or Republican "coalition," we mean the groups that generally support one or the other party. In the United States today, a variety of group characteristics are associated with party identification. These include race and ethnicity, gender, religion, class, ideology, and region.

Race and Ethnicity   Since the 1930s and Franklin Roosevelt's New Deal, African Americans have been overwhelmingly Democratic in their party identification. More than 90 percent of African Americans describe themselves as Democrats and support Democratic candidates in national, state, and local

Bill Clinton received strong support from women who are pro-choice, a core constituency of the Democratic Party.

elections. Approximately 25 percent of the Democratic Party's support in presidential races comes from African American voters.

Latino voters do not form a monolithic bloc, by contrast. Cuban Americans are generally Republican in their party affiliations, whereas Mexican Americans favor the Democrats by a small margin. Other Latino voters, including those from Puerto Rico, are overwhelmingly Democratic. Asian Americans tend to be divided as well, but along class lines. The Asian American community's influential business and professional stratum identifies with the Republicans, but less-affluent Asian Americans tend to support the Democrats.

Gender Women are somewhat more likely to support Democrats, and men somewhat more likely to support Republicans, in surveys of party affiliation. This difference is known as the **gender gap**. In the 1992 presidential election, women gave Bill Clinton 47 percent of their votes, while only 41 percent of the men who voted supported Clinton. In 1996, the gender gap was even more pronounced: women voted for Clinton 54 percent of the time, while only 43 percent of voting men did so.

Religion Jews are among the Democratic Party's most loyal constituent groups and have been since the New Deal. Nearly 90 percent of all Jewish Americans describe themselves as Democrats. Catholics were also once a strongly pro-Democratic group but have been shifting toward the Republican Party since the 1970s, when the GOP began to focus on abortion and other social issues deemed to be important to Catholics. Protestants are more likely to

gender gap

a distinctive pattern of voting behavior reflecting the differences in views between men and women identify with the Republicans than with the Democrats. Protestant fundamentalists, in particular, have been drawn to the GOP's conservative stands on social issues, such as school prayer and abortion.

Class   Upper-income Americans are considerably more likely to affiliate with the Republicans, whereas lower-income Americans are far more likely to identify with the Democrats. This divide is reflected and reinforced by the differences between the two parties on economic issues. In general, the Republicans support cutting taxes and social spending—positions that reflect the interests of the wealthy. The Democrats, on the other hand, favor increasing social spending, even if this requires increasing taxes—a position consistent with the interests of less-affluent Americans. One important exception to this principle is that relatively affluent individuals who work in the public sector or such related institutions as foundations and universities also tend to affiliate with the Democrats. Such individuals are likely to appreciate the Democratic Party's support for an expanded governmental role and high levels of public spending.

Ideology   Ideology and party identification are very closely linked. Most individuals who describe themselves as conservatives identify with the Republican Party, whereas most who call themselves liberals support the Democrats. This division has increased in recent years as the two parties have taken very different positions on social and economic issues. Before the 1970s, when party differences were more blurred, it was not uncommon to find Democratic conservatives and Republican liberals. Both these species are rare today.

Region   Between the Civil War and the 1960s, the "Solid South" was a Democratic bastion. Today, the South is becoming solidly Republican, as is much of the West and Southwest. The area of greatest Democratic Party strength is the Northeast. The Midwest is a battleground, more or less evenly divided between the two parties.

The explanations for these regional variations are complex. Southern Republicanism has come about because conservative white southerners identify the Democratic Party with the civil rights movement and with liberal positions on abortion, school prayer, and other social issues. Republican strength in the South and in the West is also related to the weakness of organized labor in these regions, as well as to the dependence of the two regions upon military programs supported by the Republicans. Democratic strength in the Northeast is a function of the continuing influence of organized labor in the large cities of this region, as well as of the region's large population of minority and elderly voters, who benefit from Democratic social programs.

Figure 9.5 indicates the relationship between party identification and a number of social criteria. Race, religion, and income seem to have the greatest influence on Americans' party affiliations. None of these social characteristics are inevitably linked to partisan identification, however. There are black Republicans, southern white Democrats, Jewish Republicans, and even an occasional conservative Democrat. The general party identifications just discussed are broad tendencies that both reflect and reinforce the issue and policy positions the two parties take in the national and local political arenas.

Figure 9.5   PARTY IDENTIFICATION BY SOCIAL GROUPS, 1995

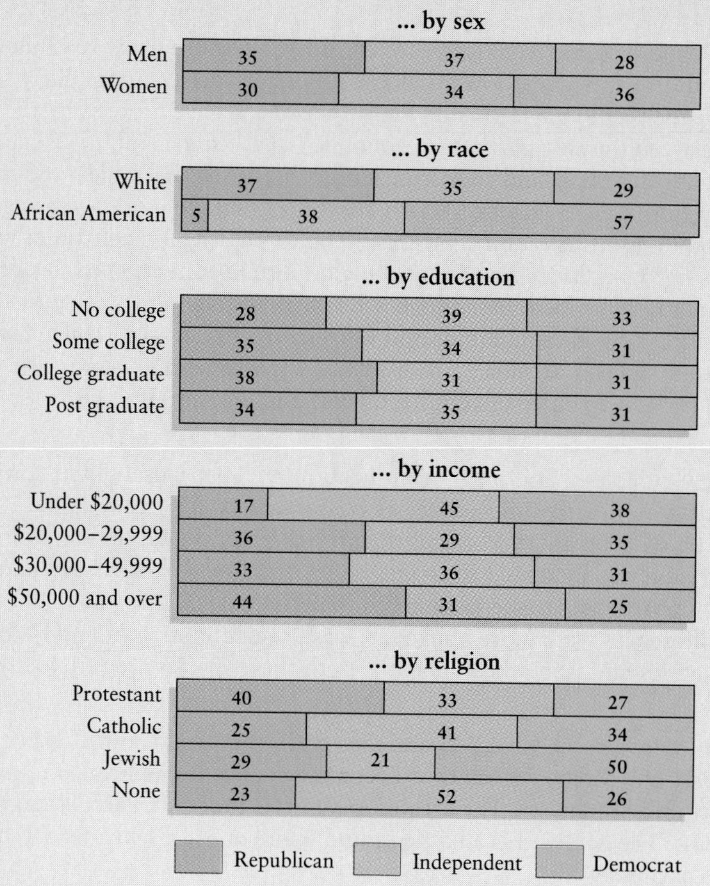

... by sex

	Republican	Independent	Democrat
Men	35	37	28
Women	30	34	36

... by race

	Republican	Independent	Democrat
White	37	35	29
African American	5	38	57

... by education

	Republican	Independent	Democrat
No college	28	39	33
Some college	35	34	31
College graduate	38	31	31
Post graduate	34	35	31

... by income

	Republican	Independent	Democrat
Under $20,000	17	45	38
$20,000–29,999	36	29	35
$30,000–49,999	33	36	31
$50,000 and over	44	31	25

... by religion

	Republican	Independent	Democrat
Protestant	40	33	27
Catholic	25	41	34
Jewish	29	21	50
None	23	52	26

☐ Republican   ☐ Independent   ☐ Democrat

SOURCE: Harold W. Stanley and Richard G. Niemi, *Vital Statistics on American Politics,* 5th ed. (Washington, DC: Congressional Quarterly Press, 1995), p. 149.

Parties and Elections

▶ What are the important electoral functions of parties? How has the role of political parties in electoral campaigns been transformed in recent decades?

Parties play an important role in the electoral process. They provide the candidates for office, get out the vote, and facilitate mass electoral choice. In recent decades, however, the role of the parties in the campaign process has been changed dramatically by the introduction of various high-tech campaign techniques.

RECRUITING CANDIDATES

One of the most important but least noticed party activities is the recruitment of candidates for local, state, and national office. Each election year, candidates must be found for thousands of state and local offices as well as congressional seats. Where they do not have an incumbent running for re-election, party leaders attempt to identify strong candidates and to interest them in entering the campaign.

An ideal candidate will have an unblemished record and the capacity to raise enough money to mount a serious campaign. Party leaders are usually not willing to provide financial backing to candidates who are unable to raise substantial funds on their own. For a House seat this can mean several hundred thousand dollars; for a Senate seat a serious candidate must be able to raise several million dollars. Often, party leaders have difficulty finding attractive candidates and persuading them to run. In 1998, for example, Democratic leaders in Kansas and Washington reported difficulties in recruiting congressional candidates. A number of potential candidates reportedly were reluctant to leave their homes and families for the hectic life of a member of Congress. GOP leaders in Washington and Massachusetts have had similar problems finding candidates to oppose popular Democratic incumbents.[11] Candidate recruitment has become particularly difficult in an era when political campaigns often involve mudslinging and candidates must assume that their personal lives will be intensely scrutinized in the press.[12]

NOMINATIONS

Article I, Section 4, of the Constitution makes only a few provisions for elections. It delegates to the states the power to set the "times, places, and manner" of holding elections, even for U.S. senators and representatives. It does, however, reserve to Congress the power to make such laws if it chooses to do so. The Constitution has been amended from time to time to expand the right to participate in elections. Congress has also occasionally passed laws about elections, congressional districting, and campaign practices. But the Constitution and the laws are almost completely silent on nominations, setting only citizenship and age requirements for candidates. The president must be at least thirty-five years of age, a natural-born citizen, and a resident of the United States for fourteen years. A senator must be at least thirty, a U.S. citizen for at least nine years, and a resident of the state he or she represents. A member of the House must be at least twenty-five, a U.S. citizen for seven years, and a resident of the state he or she represents.

Nomination is the process by which a party selects a single candidate to run for each elective office. The nominating process can precede the election by many months, as it does when the many candidates for the presidency are eliminated from consideration through a grueling series of debates and state primaries until there is only one survivor in each party—the party's nominee.

Nomination is the parties' most serious and difficult business. When more than one person aspires to an office, the choice can divide friends and associates. In comparison to such an internal dispute, the electoral campaign against the opposition is almost fun, because there the fight is against the declared adversaries.

Perspectives on Politics

YOUNG AMERICANS' VIEWS ON PARTY CANDIDATES

Responses of eighteen- to twenty-nine-year-olds to the question, Which party do you think selects good candidates for office?

Republicans 49%
Democrats 34%
Neither 9%
Both 5%

SOURCE: July 1994 poll reported in Susan A. MacManus, *Young v. Old: Generational Combat in the 21st Century* (Boulder, CO: Westview, 1996), p. 102.

nomination

the process through which political parties select their candidates for election to public office

Parties are responsible for nominating candidates to run for office. Here, the 1996 Republican hopefuls get ready for a public forum prior to the Iowa caucuses.

CAMPAIGNS AND HIGH-TECH POLITICS

The actual election period begins immediately after the nominations. Historically, this has been a time of glory for the political parties, whose popular base of support is fully displayed at election time. All the paraphernalia of party committees and all the committee members are activated into local party workforces.

In the nineteenth and early twentieth centuries, political campaigns were waged by the parties' enormous armies of patronage workers. Throughout the year, party workers cultivated the support of voters by helping them with legal problems, helping them find jobs, and serving as liaisons with local, state, and federal agencies. On election day throughout the nation hundreds of thousands of party workers marched from house to house reminding their supporters to vote, helping the aged and infirm to reach the polls, and calling in the favors they had accrued during the year. Campaigns resembled the maneuvers of huge infantries vying for victory. Historians have, in fact, referred to this traditional style of party campaigning as "militarist."

Contemporary political campaigns rely less on infantries and more on "air power." That is, rather than deploy huge armies of workers, contemporary campaigns make use of a number of communications techniques to reach voters and bid for their support. Five techniques are especially important.

Polling   Surveys of voter opinion provide the information that candidates and their staffs use to craft campaign strategies. Candidates employ polls to select issues, to assess their own strengths and weaknesses (as well as those of the opposition), to check voter response to the campaign, and to determine the degree to which various constituent groups are susceptible to campaign appeals. Virtually all contemporary campaigns for national and statewide office as well as many local campaigns make extensive use of opinion polling. As we

"Honest Graft"

Political wisdom is by no means the sole province of philosophers. Or, to be more precise, not all philosophers "is bookworms." This fact was confirmed by a Tammany Hall political leader and resident sage of the late 1800s and early 1900s, George Washington Plunkitt.

Born in a poor area of Manhattan called Nanny Goat Hill in 1842, Plunkitt extricated himself from poverty by rising in the ranks of the Democratic Party machine that dominated New York politics during his lifetime—the Tammany Machine. Organized originally as a nonpolitical social club in 1789, the Society of Saint Tammany (named after a legendary Delaware Indian chief) slowly became politicized as its ranks filled with the city's prominent Democrats. By the 1850s, it had sufficient clout to elect the city's mayor.

Plunkitt's rise in Tammany paralleled that of the organization. A district leader and office-holder, he became a millionaire through what he labeled "honest graft." By this, Plunkitt meant that he used inside knowledge of impending city deals (for example, where the city planned to build some large public structure) to buy cheap land that gained value after city plans were announced and then to sell it at a substantial profit. In Plunkitt's words. "Ain't it perfectly honest to charge a good price and make a profit on my investment and foresight? Of course, it is. Well, that's honest graft." Plunkitt distinguished between this and "dishonest graft"—"blackmailin' gamblers, saloonkeepers, disorderly people, etc." He also justified his behavior by differentiating between "political looters" and politicians who profit from politics: "The looter goes in for himself alone without considerin' his organization or his city. The politician looks after his own interests, the organization's interests, and the city's interests all at the same time."

On statesmanship, Plunkitt had simple advice. He disdained those who would "cram their heads with all sorts of college rot" as a means of preparing for politics. Instead, he said, "I got a marketable commodity—one vote." He then built on the number of votes he could deliver to Tammany, "and so it went like a snowball rollin' down hill."

Plunkitt used his common touch to build support for the Democratic Party to high levels, often combining personal intervention with the might of the party dollar. "What tells in holdin' your grip on your district is to go right down among the poor families and help them in different ways they need help," he said. "I've got a regular system for this. If there is a fire in Ninth, Tenth, or Eleventh Avenue, for example, any hour of the day or night, I'm usually there with some of my election district captains as soon as the fire engines."

He also used his position to help supporters, cementing his dominant position within the party. "The books are always all right," he said. "All they can show is that the Tammany heads of department looked after their friends, within the law, and gave them what opportunities they could to make honest graft." These "friends," in turn, helped the Democrats win elections.

Plunkitt had nothing but contempt for civil service, branding it "the curse of the nation." He considered the spoils system—jobs and other concrete rewards meted out to the party faithful—to be "patriotic." He argued with some acumen that the country was built by political parties, that the parties needed such patronage to operate and thrive, and that if patronage was withdrawn, the parties would "go to pieces" (as indeed they have)—and there goes democracy.

Plunkitt knew the importance of the common touch. Beyond that, he grasped a simple, central fact. To retain political influence, said Plunkitt, "you must study human nature and act accordin'." Plunkitt was a man who "seen his opportunities, and took 'em."

SOURCE: William Riordan, *Plunkitt of Tammany Hall* (New York: E. P. Dutton, 1963).

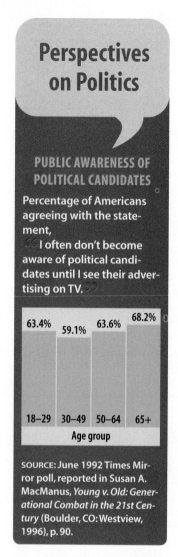

saw in Chapter 7, President Clinton made extensive use of polling data both during and after the 1996 presidential election to shape his rhetoric and guide his policy initiatives.

The Broadcast Media Extensive use of the electronic media, television in particular, has become the hallmark of the modern political campaign. Generally, media campaigns attempt to follow the guidelines indicated by a candidate's polls, emphasizing issues and personal characteristics that appear important in the poll data. The broadcast media are now so central to modern campaigns that most candidates' activities are tied to their media strategies.[13] Candidate activities are designed expressly to stimulate television news coverage. For instance, members of Congress running for re-election or for president almost always sponsor committee or subcommittee hearings to generate publicity.

Phone Banks Through the broadcast media, candidates communicate with voters en masse and impersonally. Phone banks, on the other hand, allow campaign workers to make personal contact with hundreds of thousands of voters. Personal contacts of this sort are thought to be extremely effective. Again, polling data serve to identify the groups that will be targeted for phone calls. Computers select phone numbers from areas in which members of these groups are concentrated. Staffs of paid or volunteer callers, using computer-assisted dialing systems and prepared scripts, then place calls to deliver the candidate's message. The targeted groups are generally those identified by polls as either uncommitted or weakly committed, as well as strong supporters of the candidate who are contacted simply to encourage them to vote.

Direct Mail Direct mail serves both as a vehicle for communicating with voters and as a mechanism for raising funds. The first step in a direct-mail campaign is the purchase or rental of a computerized mailing list of voters deemed to have some particular perspective or social characteristic. Often sets of magazine subscription lists or lists of donors to various causes are employed. For example, a candidate interested in reaching conservative voters might rent subscription lists from the *National Review, Human Events,* or *Conservative Digest;* a candidate interested in appealing to liberals might rent subscription lists from the *New York Review of Books* or the *New Republic.* Considerable fine-tuning is possible. After obtaining the appropriate mailing lists, candidates usually send pamphlets, letters, and brochures describing themselves and their views to voters believed to be sympathetic. Different types of mail appeals are made to different electoral subgroups. Often the letters sent to voters are personalized. The recipient is addressed by name in the text and the letter appears actually to have been signed by the candidate. Of course, these "personal" letters are written and even signed by a computer.

In addition to its use as a political advertising medium, direct mail has also become an important source of campaign funds. Computerized mailing lists permit campaign strategists to pinpoint individuals whose interests, background, and activities suggest that they may be potential donors to the campaign. Letters of solicitation are sent to these potential donors. Some of the money raised is then used to purchase additional mailing lists. Direct-mail solicitation can be enormously effective.[14]

Professional Public Relations   Modern campaigns and the complex technology upon which they rely are typically directed by professional public relations consultants. Virtually all serious contenders for national and statewide office retain the services of professional campaign consultants. Increasingly, candidates for local office, too, have come to rely upon professional campaign managers. Consultants offer candidates the expertise necessary to conduct accurate opinion polls, produce television commercials, organize direct-mail campaigns, and make use of sophisticated computer analyses.

The number of technologically oriented campaigns increased greatly after 1971. The Federal Election Campaign Act of 1971 prompted the creation of large numbers of political action committees (PACs) by a host of corporate and ideological groups. This development increased the availability of funds to political candidates—conservative candidates in particular—which meant in turn that the new technology could be used more extensively. Initially, the new techniques were employed mainly by individual candidates who often made little or no effort to coordinate their campaigns with those of other political aspirants sharing the same party label. For this reason, campaigns employing new technology sometimes came to be called "candidate-centered" efforts, as distinguished from the traditional party-coordinated campaign. Nothing about the new technology, however, precluded its use by political party leaders seeking to coordinate a number of campaigns. In recent years, party leaders—Republicans in particular—have learned to make good use of modern campaign technology. The difference between the old and new political methods is not that the latter are inherently candidate-centered while the former are strictly a party tool; it is a matter of the types of political resources upon which each method depends.

FROM LABOR-INTENSIVE TO CAPITAL-INTENSIVE POLITICS

The displacement of organizational methods by the new political technology is, in essence, a shift from labor-intensive to capital-intensive competitive electoral practices. Campaign tasks that were once performed by masses of party workers with some cash now require fewer personnel but a great deal more money, for the new political style depends on polls, computers, and other electronic paraphernalia. Of course, even when workers and organization were the key electoral tools, money had considerable political significance. Nevertheless, during the nineteenth century, national political campaigns in the United States employed millions of people. Indeed, as many as 2.5 million individuals did political work during the 1880s.[15] The direct cost of campaigns, therefore, was relatively low. For example, in 1860, Abraham Lincoln spent only $100,000—which was approximately twice the amount spent by his chief opponent, Stephen Douglas.

Modern campaigns depend heavily on money. Each element of the new political technology is enormously expensive. A sixty-second spot announcement on prime-time network television costs hundreds of thousands of dollars each time it is aired. Opinion surveys can be quite expensive; polling costs in a statewide race can easily reach or exceed the six-figure mark. Campaign consultants can charge substantial fees. A direct-mail campaign can eventually become an important source of funds but is very expensive to initiate. The inauguration of a serious national direct-mail effort requires at least $1 million

Campaign Finance Reform and Soft Money

Americans have long favored campaign finance reform, but the 1996 elections intensified cries for reform as never before. Chief among critics' complaints was the proliferation of "soft money"—money raised and spent by political parties. Unlike "hard money"—funds raised and spent directly on behalf of a candidate, subject to federal spending limits and other regulations spelled out in the Federal Election Campaign Act—soft money falls outside of federal regulations, as long as the funds are raised and spent by political parties or independent groups that have no formal affiliation with a candidate's campaign. Such spending is unregulated and subject only to limited disclosure. Although soft money made up a small percentage of all campaign spending up until 1992, it exploded in 1996. Aside from alarm over the sheer amount of money involved, some of the money apparently came from abroad, inviting charges that foreign governments were trying to shape American elections for their own benefit. Yet not all agree that the campaign finance system needs an overhaul.

Supporters of campaign finance reform argue that democratic values are subverted when a few wealthy, special interests dominate the campaign process. It is all but inevitable that candidates for office, as well as incumbents, will feel an obligation to those who expend thousands or millions of dollars on their behalf. More importantly, current campaign spending patterns overwhelmingly favor incumbents, making it even more difficult for challengers to vie for office. In 1992, incumbent senators spent on average about $4.2 million, whereas their challengers spent an average of $1.8 million. In 1994, incumbents seeking re-election to the House of Representatives outspent their challengers by an average ratio of 2.6 to 1.

The particular evil posed by soft money is that it represents a throwback to an earlier time when campaign spending was unregulated. The current system of regulated hard money spending and unregulated soft money spending invites an intolerable situation: the buying and selling of American elections to the highest bidder. Ideas for reform are abundant. The only question is whether

political leaders have the will to follow strong public support for real reform.

Opponents of campaign finance reform argue that most people misunderstand how and why campaigns operate as they do. Reform opponents point out that every attempt at campaign finance reform has been nothing short of disastrous. The last wave of reform laws, enacted in the 1970s, produced the current system, including the explosion of soft money spending. As several court decisions have suggested, tight limits on campaign spending may violate First Amendment rights and have a chilling effect on local political activities. To those who argue that too much is spent on campaigns, critics argue that, if anything, too little is spent on campaigns. In 1994, for example, Americans spent more than twice as much money on potato chips than they spent on all congressional elections. The momentous decision concerning who shall govern the country is surely more important than the level of money currently being spent. Moreover, research has demonstrated that voters are better informed in elections where more money is spent.

Contrary to popular impression, there is no simple connection between money spent and success at the polls. While money is obviously important, incumbents receive more money simply because it is well understood that incumbents are more likely to win. After all, they are more well known than their challengers, have more experience, and are knowledgeable about their jobs and how to keep them. Further, the idea that big money runs elections more than in the past is, good or bad, not new. Because of our relatively open democratic system, the vast majority of campaign money in the last century has always come from large corporations and the wealthy. Indeed, the 10 percent of citizens who give money to campaigns represents an increase in the percentage of Americans who gave in earlier times.

SOURCE: Bradley A. Smith, "Campaign Finance Regulation: Faulty Assumptions and Undemocratic Consequences," Cato Institute Policy Analysis 238, Washington, DC, September 13, 1995.

in "front-end cash" to pay for mailing lists, brochures, letters, envelopes, and postage.[16] Although the cost of televised debates is covered by the sponsoring organizations and the television stations and is therefore free to the candidates, even debate preparation requires substantial staff work, research, and, of course, money. It is the expense of the new technology that accounts for the enormous cost of recent American national elections (a topic we will explore further in Chapter 10).

Certainly "people power" is not irrelevant to modern political campaigns. Candidates continue to utilize the political services of tens of thousands of volunteer workers. Nevertheless, in the contemporary era, even the recruitment of campaign workers has become a matter of electronic technology. Employing a technique called "instant organization," paid telephone callers use phone banks to contact individuals in areas targeted by a computer (which they do when contacting potential voters, as we discussed before). Volunteer workers are recruited from among these individuals. A number of campaigns—Richard Nixon's 1968 presidential campaign was the first—have successfully used this technique.

The displacement of organizational methods by the new political technology has the most far-reaching implications for the balance of power among contending political groups. Labor-intensive organizational tactics allowed parties whose chief support came from groups nearer the bottom of the social scale to use the numerical superiority of their forces as a partial counterweight to the institutional and economic resources more readily available to the opposition. The capital-intensive technological format, by contrast, has given a major boost to the political fortunes of those forces whose sympathizers are better able to furnish the large sums now needed to compete effectively.[17] Indeed, the new technology permits financial resources to be more effectively harnessed and exploited than was ever before possible.

Dominated by the new technology, electoral politics has become a contest in which the wealthy and powerful have a decided advantage. Furthermore, both political parties are compelled to rely heavily on the support of well-funded special interests—a situation that has become clear in the fund-raising scandals that have plagued both parties in recent years. We shall return to this topic in Chapter 10.

★ Parties and Government

▶ How do the differences between Democrats and Republicans affect Congress, the president, and the policymaking process?

When the dust of the campaign has settled, does it matter which party has won? It can.

PARTIES AND POLICY

One of the most familiar observations about American politics is that the two major parties try to be all things to all people and are therefore indistinguishable

Perspectives on Politics

PARTIES' CONCERN FOR YOUNG AMERICANS

Responses of eighteen- to twenty-nine-year-olds to the question,
Which party is concerned with the needs of people like me?

Democrats	Republicans	Neither	Both
48%	38%	7%	3%

SOURCE: July 1994 poll reported in Susan A. MacManus, *Young v. Old: Generational Combat in the 21st Century* (Boulder, CO: Westview, 1996), p. 104.

policy entrepreneur

an individual who identifies a problem as a political issue and brings a policy proposal into the political agenda

from each other. Data and experience give some support to this observation. Parties in the United States are not programmatic or ideological, as they have sometimes been in Britain or other parts of Europe. But this does not mean there are no differences between them. During the Reagan era, important differences emerged between the positions of Democratic and Republican party leaders on a number of key issues, and these differences are still apparent today. For example, the national leadership of the Republican Party supports maintaining high levels of military spending, cuts in social programs, tax relief for middle- and upper-income voters, tax incentives to businesses, and the "social agenda" backed by members of conservative religious denominations. The national Democratic leadership, on the other hand, supports expanded social welfare spending, cuts in military spending, increased regulation of business, and a variety of consumer and environmental programs.

These differences reflect differences in philosophy as well as differences in the core constituencies to which the parties seek to appeal. The Democratic Party at the national level seeks to unite organized labor, the poor, members of racial minorities, and liberal upper-middle-class professionals. The Republicans, by contrast, appeal to business, upper-middle- and upper-class groups in the private sector, and social conservatives. Often, party leaders will seek to develop issues they hope will add new groups to their party's constituent base. During the 1980s, for example, under the leadership of Ronald Reagan, the Republicans devised a series of "social issues," including support for school prayer, opposition to abortion, and opposition to affirmative action, designed to cultivate the support of white southerners. This effort was extremely successful in increasing Republican strength in the once solidly Democratic South. In the 1990s, under the leadership of Bill Clinton, who called himself a "new Democrat," the Democratic Party has sought to develop new social programs designed to solidify the party's base among working-class and poor voters, and new, somewhat more conservative economic programs aimed at attracting the votes of middle- and upper-middle-class voters.

As these examples suggest, parties do not always support policies because they are favored by their constituents. Instead, party leaders can play the role of **policy entrepreneurs,** seeking ideas and programs that will expand their party's base of support while eroding that of the opposition. It is one of the essential characteristics of party politics in America that a party's programs and policies often lead, rather than follow, public opinion. Like their counterparts in the business world, party leaders seek to identify and develop "products" (programs and policies) that will appeal to the public. The public, of course, has the ultimate voice. With its votes it decides whether or not to "buy" new policy offerings.

Through members elected to office, both parties have made efforts to translate their general goals into concrete policies. Republicans, for example, implemented tax cuts, increased defense spending, cut social spending, and enacted restrictions on abortion during the 1980s and 1990s. Democrats were able to defend consumer and environmental programs against GOP attacks and sought to expand domestic social programs in the late 1990s. Both parties, of course, have been hampered by internal divisions and the recurrent pattern of divided control of Congress and the executive branch that has characterized American politics for the past two decades.

PARTIES IN CONGRESS

The ultimate test of the party system is its relationship to and influence on the institutions of government. Congress, in particular, depends more on the party system than is generally recognized. For one thing, the speakership of the House is essentially a party office. All the members of the House take part in the election of the Speaker. But the actual selection is made by the **majority party,** that is, the party that holds a majority of seats in the House. (The other party is known as the **minority party.**) When the majority party caucus presents a nominee to the entire House, its choice is then invariably ratified in a straight vote along party lines.

The committee system of both houses of Congress is also a product of the two-party system. Although the rules organizing committees and the rules defining the jurisdiction of each are adopted like ordinary legislation by the whole membership, all other features of the committees are shaped by parties. For example, each party is assigned a quota of members for each committee, depending upon the percentage of total seats held by the party. On the rare occasions when an independent or third-party candidate is elected, the leaders of the two parties must agree against whose quota this member's committee assignments will count. Presumably the member will not be able to serve on any committee until the question of quota is settled.

As we shall see in Chapter 12, the assignment of individual members to committees is a party decision. Each party has a "committee on committees" to make such decisions. Permission to transfer to another committee is also a party decision. Moreover, advancement up the committee ladder toward the chair is a party decision. Since the late nineteenth century, most advancements have been automatic—based upon the length of continual service on the committee. This seniority system has existed only because of the support of the two parties, however, and either party can depart from it by a simple vote. During the 1970s, both parties reinstituted the practice of reviewing each chair—voting anew every two years on whether each committee's chair would continue to be held by the same person. Few chairpersons actually have been removed, but notice has been served that the seniority system is no longer automatic, thereby reminding everyone that all committee assignments are party decisions. Thus, although party leaders no longer can control the votes of many members, the party system itself remains an important factor.

The continuing importance of parties in Congress became especially evident after the Republicans won control of Congress in 1994. During the first few months of the 104th Congress, the Republican leadership was able to maintain nearly unanimous support among party members on vote after vote as it sought to implement the GOP's legislative agenda. By the end of 1995, however, splits within the party began to surface over issues such as welfare reform and balancing the budget. This legislative struggle will be discussed further in Chapter 12.

PRESIDENT AND PARTY

As we saw earlier, the party that wins the White House is always led, in title anyway, by the president. The president normally depends upon fellow party

majority party
the party that holds the majority of legislative seats in either the House or the Senate

minority party
the party that holds a minority of legislative seats in either the House or the Senate

quite mundane. Thousands of envelopes are filled and sealed. A seemingly infinite number of postage stamps are licked. Many meetings are held. Politics at the "grass roots" is not very glamorous. However, if politics were only glamorous it could not be democratic. Grassroots party activity helps to ensure that the more glamorous world of Washington remains tied and responsive to Bozeman, Long Beach, Raleigh, and Utica. State and even national party leaders pay close attention to the views of local party organizations and activists. They depend upon these local organizations for ideas, for campaign workers, and often, for candidates. Many prominent politicians, including President Clinton, were themselves once young volunteers in a local party organization.

★ Summary

Political parties seek to control government by controlling its personnel. Elections are one means to this end. Thus, parties take shape from the electoral process.

The two-party system dominates U.S. politics. During the course of American history, the government has generally been dominated by one or the other party for long periods of time. This is generally followed by a period of realignment during which new groups attempt to seize power and the previously dominant party may be displaced by its rival. There have been five electoral realignments in American political history.

Third parties are short-lived for several reasons. They have limited electoral support, the tradition of the two-party system is strong, and a major party often adopts the platform of a third party. Single-member districts with two competing parties also discourage third parties.

Party organizations exist at every level of American government. The national party organizations are generally less important than the state and local party units. Each party's national committee and congressional campaign committees help to recruit candidates and raise money. The national conventions have, for the most part, lost their nominating functions, but still play an important role in determining party rules and party platforms.

Parties influence voting through the ties of party identification, particularly the strong ties formed with party activists. A variety of group characteristics can influence party identification, including race and ethnicity, gender, religion, class, ideology, and region.

Nominating and electing are the basic functions of parties. Parties are critical for getting out the vote, recruiting candidates, facilitating popular choice, and organizing the government. Strong parties are essential to the continuing vitality of American democracy.

FOR FURTHER READING

Aldrich, John H. *Why Parties? The Origin and Transformation of Political Parties in America*. Chicago: University of Chicago Press, 1995.

Andersen, Kristi. *After Suffrage: Women in Partisan and Electoral Politics before the New Deal*. Chicago: University of Chicago Press, 1996.

Baer, Denise L. *Elite Cadres and Party Coalitions: Representing the Public in Party Politics.* New York: Greenwood, 1988.

Beck, Paul A., and Frank J. Sorauf. *Party Politics in America.* 7th ed. New York: HarperCollins, 1991.

Carmines, Edward G., and James A. Stimson. *Issue Evolution: Race and the Transformation of American Politics.* Princeton, NJ: Princeton University Press, 1989.

Edsall, Thomas Byrne, and Mary D. Edsall. *Chain Reaction: The Impact of Race, Rights, and Taxes on American Politics.* New York: Norton, 1993.

Gilmour, John B. *Strategic Disagreement: Stalemate in American Politics.* Pittsburgh, PA: University of Pittsburgh Press, 1995.

Green, John C., and Daniel M. Shea, eds. *The State of the Parties: The Changing Role of Contemporary Parties.* 2d ed. Lanham, MD: Rowman and Littlefield, 1996.

Grimshaw, William J. *Bitter Fruit: Black Politics and the Chicago Machine, 1931–1991.* Chicago: University of Chicago Press, 1992.

Lawson, Kay, and Peter Merkl. *When Parties Fail: Emerging Alternative Organizations.* Princeton, NJ: Princeton University Press, 1988.

Milkis, Sidney. *The President and the Parties: The Transformation of the American Party System since the New Deal.* New York: Oxford University Press, 1993.

Phillips, Kevin. *Boiling Point: Democrats, Republicans, and the Decline of Middle Class Prosperity.* New York: Random House, 1993.

Shefter, Martin. *Political Parties and the State: The American Historical Experience.* Princeton, NJ: Princeton University Press, 1994.

STUDY OUTLINE

1. In modern history, political parties have been the chief points of contact between governments and groups and forces in society. By organizing political parties, social forces attempt to gain some control over government policies and personnel.

What Are Political Parties?

1. Political parties as they are known today developed along with the expansion of suffrage, and actually took their shape from the electoral process.
2. Political parties, as coalitions of those with similar interests, are also important parts of the policy-making process.

The Two-Party System in America

1. Historically, parties originate through either internal or external mobilization by those seeking to win governmental power.
2. The Democratic Party originated through a process of internal mobilization, as the Jeffersonian Party splintered into four factions in 1824, and Andrew Jackson emerged as the leader of one of these four groups.
3. The Republican Party grew through a process of external mobilization as antislavery groups formed a new party to oppose the 1854 Kansas-Nebraska Act.
4. The United States has experienced five realigning eras, which occur when the established political elite weakens sufficiently to permit the creation of new coalitions of forces capable of capturing and holding the reins of government.
5. American third parties have always represented social and economic protests ignored by the other parties, despite the fact that the United States is said to have a two-party system.

Party Organization

1. Party organizations exist at virtually every level of American government—usually taking the form of committees made up of active party members.
2. Although national party conventions no longer have the power to nominate presidential candidates, they are still important in determining the party's rules and platform.
3. The national committee and the congressional campaign committees play important roles in recruiting candidates and raising money.

Parties and the Electorate

1. Individuals tend to form psychological ties with parties; these ties are called "party identification." This identification often follows demographic, ideological, and regional lines.

Parties and Elections

1. Parties are important in the electoral process for recruiting and nominating candidates for office.
2. In recent years, the role of the parties during the general campaign has been transformed by the introduction of high-tech campaign techniques, including polls, using the broadcast media, phone banks, direct mail, and professional public relations.
3. The expense of these new campaign techniques means that modern campaigns depend heavily upon money.

Parties and Government

1. The differences between the two parties reflects a general difference in philosophy but also an attempt to appeal to core constituencies. These differences are often reflected in the policy agenda that party leaders adopt.
2. Political parties help to organize Congress. Congressional leadership and the committee system are both products of the two-party system.
3. The president serves as an informal party head by seeking support from congressional members of the party and by supporting their bids for re-election.

Parties and Democracy

1. Democracy has always depended upon strong parties, which promote electoral competition and voter turnout and make governance possible through their organizations in Congress.
2. The ties that parties have to the electorate are historically weak; the resulting "candidate-centered" politics has some negative consequences, including lower voter turnout, increased influence of interest groups, and a lack of effective decision making by elected leaders.
3. Parties could be strengthened through effective campaign finance reform.

PRACTICE QUIZ

1. A political party is different from an interest group in that a political party
   a) seeks to control the entire government by electing its members to office and thereby controlling the government's personnel.
   b) seeks to control only limited, very specific, functions of government.
   c) is entirely nonprofit.
   d) has a much smaller membership.

2. The periodic episodes in American history in which an "old" dominant political party is replaced by a "new" dominant political party are called
   a) constitutional revolutions.
   b) party turnovers.
   c) presidential elections.
   d) electoral realignments.

3. Through which mechanism did Boss Tweed and other party leaders in the late nineteenth and early twentieth centuries maintain their control?
   a) civil service reform
   b) soft money contributions
   c) machine politics
   d) electoral reform

4. Political parties in America are organized on what level?
   a) national
   b) state
   c) county
   d) all of the above

5. Contemporary national party conventions are important because they
   a) decide who will be the party's presidential candidate.
   b) determine the party's rules and platform.

   c) both a and b are correct.
   d) neither a nor b is correct.

6. Which party was founded as a political expression of the antislavery movement?
   a) American Independent
   b) Prohibition
   c) Republican
   d) Democratic

7. Historically, when do realignments occur?
   a) typically, every twenty years
   b) whenever a minority party takes over Congress
   c) when large numbers of voters permanently shift their support from one party to another
   d) in odd-numbered years

8. Parties today are most important in the electoral process in
   a) recruiting and nominating candidates for office.
   b) financing all of the campaign's spending.
   c) providing millions of volunteers to mobilize voters.
   d) creating a responsible party government.

9. What role do parties play in Congress?
   a) They select leaders, such as the Speaker of the House.
   b) They assign members to committees.
   c) Both a and b are correct.
   d) Parties play no role in Congress.

10. In general, parties are important in a democracy because they
    a) encourage electoral competition.
    b) promote voter turnout.
    c) make governance possible by organizing elected leaders into governing coalitions.
    d) all of the above.

CRITICAL THINKING QUESTIONS

1. Describe the factors that have contributed to the overall weakening of political parties in America. How are parties weaker? How do they remain important? What are the advantages of a political system with weak political parties? What are the disadvantages?

2. Historically, third parties have developed in American history when certain issues or constituencies have been ignored by the existing parties. Considering the similarities and differences between the Democratic and Republican parties, where might a budding third party find a constituency? What issues might it adopt? Finally, what structural and ideological obstacles might that third party face?

KEY TERMS

caucus (political) (p. 326)
divided government (p. 322)
electoral realignment (p. 321)
gender gap (p. 334)
machines (p. 331)
majority party (p. 345)
minority party (p. 345)
multiple-member district (p. 325)
national convention (p. 326)

nomination (p. 337)
party activists (p. 333)
party identification (p. 332)
party organization (p. 326)
patronage (p. 331)
platform (p. 328)
plurality system (p. 326)
policy entrepreneur (p. 344)

political parties (p. 315)
proportional representation (p. 326)
responsible party government (p. 348)
single-member district (p. 325)
soft money (p. 331)
third parties (p. 324)
two-party system (p. 316)

10 Campaigns

★ **Elections in America**

What is the history of the suffrage in the United States? What factors influence how many voters participate?

What different types of elections are held in the United States? What rules determine who wins elections?

How does the government determine the boundaries of electoral districts? How is the ballot determined?

★ **Election Campaigns**

What are the steps in a successful election campaign?

★ **Presidential Elections**

How is the president elected?

What factors have the greatest impact on a general election campaign?

★ **Money and Politics**

How do candidates raise and spend campaign funds? How does the government regulate campaign spending?

How does money affect how certain social groups achieve electoral success?

★ **How Voters Decide**

What are the primary influences on voters' decisions?

★ **The Decline of Voting**

Why is political participation relatively low in the United States? Have attempts to increase participation succeeded? Why or why not? What are the implications for democracy?

and Elections

OVER the past two centuries, elections have come to play a significant role in the political processes of most nations. The forms that elections take and the purposes they serve, however, vary greatly from nation to nation. The most important difference among national electoral systems is that some provide the opportunity for opposition while others do not. Democratic electoral systems, such as those that have evolved in the United States and western Europe, allow opposing forces to compete against and even to replace current officeholders. Authoritarian electoral systems, by contrast, do not allow the defeat of those in power. In the authoritarian context, elections are used primarily to mobilize popular enthusiasm for the government, to provide an outlet for popular discontent, and to persuade foreigners that the regime is legitimate—i.e., that it has the support of the people. In the former Soviet Union, for example, citizens were required to vote even though no opposition to Communist Party candidates was allowed.

In democracies, elections can also serve as institutions of legitimation and as safety valves for social discontent. But beyond these functions, democratic elections facilitate popular influence, promote leadership accountability, and offer groups in society a measure of protection from the abuse of governmental power. Citizens exercise influence through elections by determining who should control the government. The chance to decide who will govern serves as an opportunity for ordinary citizens to make choices about the policies, programs, and directions of government action. In the United States, for example, recent Democratic and Republican candidates have differed significantly on issues of taxing, social spending, and governmental regulation. As American voters have chosen between the two parties' candidates, they have also made choices about these issues.

Elections promote leadership accountability because the threat of defeat at the polls exerts pressure on those in power to conduct themselves in a responsible manner and to take account of popular interests and wishes when they make their decisions. As James Madison observed in the Federalist Papers, elected leaders are "compelled to anticipate the moment when their power is to cease, when their exercise of it is to be reviewed, and when they must descend to the level from which they were raised, there forever to remain unless a faithful discharge of their trust shall have established their title to a renewal of it."[1] It is because of this need to anticipate the dissatisfaction of their constituents that elected officials constantly monitor public opinion polls as they decide what positions to take on policy issues.

Finally, the right to vote, or **suffrage,** can serve as an important source of protection for groups in American society. The passage of the 1965 Voting Rights Act, for example, enfranchised millions of African Americans in the

suffrage

the right to vote; also called franchise

355

South, paving the way for the election of thousands of new black public officials at the local, state, and national levels and ensuring that white politicians could no longer ignore the views and needs of African Americans. The Voting Rights Act was one of the chief spurs for the elimination of many overt forms of racial discrimination as well as for the diminution of racist rhetoric in American public life.

■ *In this chapter, we shall examine the place of elections in American political life. We will first examine some of the formal aspects of electoral participation in the United States.* These include voting rights, registration requirements, types of elections, the ways that election winners are determined, electoral districts, the ballot, and the electoral college. As we shall see, all of these factors affect the type and level of influence that citizens have through the electoral process.

■ *In the next two sections, we will see how election campaigns are conducted in the United States.* The campaign for any political office consists of a number of steps. Election campaigns are also becoming increasingly expensive to wage.

■ *We then turn to the broader issue of money and elections.* Raising campaign funds is now a crucial factor for winning. Although attempts to reform campaign finance have been made, the money keeps pouring in. As we will see, this development has important consequences for democracy.

■ *Next, we assess the various factors that influence voters' decisions.* Despite the growing importance of money to elections, it is still voters who decide the outcomes.

■ *Finally, we will evaluate what we find to be a disturbing trend: the decreasing levels of participation in elections by American voters.* As we will argue, this trend has important consequences for the values of liberty, equality, and democracy in the United States.

★ Elections in America

▶ What is the history of the suffrage in the United States? What factors influence how many voters participate?

▶ What different types of elections are held in the United States? What rules determine who wins elections?

▶ How does the government determine the boundaries of electoral districts? How is the ballot determined?

In the United States, elections are held at regular intervals. National presidential elections take place every four years, on the first Tuesday in November;

congressional elections are held every two years on the same Tuesday. (Congressional elections that do not coincide with a presidential election are sometimes called **midterm elections.**) Elections for state and local office also often coincide with national elections. Some states and municipalities, however, prefer to schedule their local elections for times that do not coincide with national contests to ensure that local results will not be affected by national trends.

In the American federal system, the responsibility for organizing elections rests largely with state and local governments. State laws specify how elections are to be administered, determine the boundaries of electoral districts, and specify candidate and voter qualifications. Elections are administered by state, county, and municipal election boards that are responsible for establishing and staffing polling places and verifying the eligibility of individuals who come to vote.

VOTING RIGHTS

In principle, states determine who is eligible to vote. During the nineteenth and early twentieth centuries, voter eligibility requirements often varied greatly from state to state. Some states openly abridged the right to vote on the basis of race; others did not. Some states imposed property restrictions on voting; others had no such restrictions. Most states mandated lengthy residency requirements, which meant that persons moving from one state to another sometimes lost their right to vote for as much as a year. In more recent years, however, constitutional amendments, federal statutes, and federal court decisions have limited states' discretion in the area of voting rights. Individual states may establish brief residency requirements, generally fifteen days, for record-keeping purposes. Beyond this, states have little or no power to regulate suffrage.

Today in the United States, all native-born or naturalized citizens over the age of eighteen, with the exception of convicted felons, have the right to vote. During the colonial and early national periods of American history, the right to vote was generally restricted to white males over the age of twenty-one. Many states also limited voting to those who owned property or paid more than a specified amount of annual tax. Property and tax requirements began to be rescinded during the 1820s, however, and had generally disappeared by the end of the Civil War.

By the time of the Civil War, blacks had won the right to vote in most northern states. In the South, black voting rights were established by the Fifteenth Amendment, ratified in 1870, which prohibited denial of the right to vote on the basis of race. Despite the Fifteenth Amendment, the voting rights of African Americans were effectively rescinded during the 1880s by the states of the former Confederacy. During this period, the southern states created what was called the "Jim Crow" system of racial segregation. As part of this system, a variety of devices, such as **poll taxes** and literacy tests, were used to prevent virtually all blacks from voting. During the 1950s and 1960s, through the civil rights movement led by Dr. Martin Luther King, Jr., and others, African Americans demanded the restoration of their voting rights. Their goal was accomplished through the enactment of the 1965 Voting Rights Act, which provided for the federal government to register voters in states that discriminated against minority citizens. The result was the reenfranchisement of southern blacks for the first time since the 1860s.

midterm elections

congressional elections that do not coincide with a presidential election; also called off-year elections

After passage of the Voting Rights Act of 1965, the national government intervened in areas where African Americans were denied the right to vote. As a result, thousands of new black voters were registered.

poll tax

a state-imposed tax upon voters as a prerequisite for registration. Poll taxes were rendered unconstitutional in national elections by the Twenty-fourth Amendment, and in state elections by the Supreme Court in 1966

We The People

SENECA FALLS, 1848

The quiet upstate New York town of Seneca Falls played host to what would later come to be known as the starting point of the modern women's movement. Convened in July 1848, and organized by activists Elizabeth Cady Stanton (who lived in Seneca Falls) and Lucretia Mott, the Seneca Falls Convention drew three hundred delegates to discuss and formulate plans to advance the political and social rights of women.

The centerpiece of the convention was its Declaration of Sentiments and Resolutions. Patterned after the Declaration of Independence, the Seneca Falls document declared, "We hold these truths to be self-evident: that all men and women are created equal," and "The history of mankind is a history of repeated injuries and usurpations on the part of man toward woman, having in direct object the establishment of an absolute tyranny over her." The most controversial provision of the declaration, nearly rejected as too radical, was the call for the right to vote for women. Although most of the delegates were women, about forty men participated, including the renowned abolitionist Frederick Douglass.

The link to the antislavery movement was not new. Stanton and Mott had attended the World Anti-slavery Convention in London in 1840, but had been denied delegate seats because of their sex. This rebuke helped precipitate the 1848 convention. The movements for abolition of slavery and women's rights were also closely linked with the temperance movement (because alcohol abuse was closely linked to male abuses of women). The convergence of the antislavery, temperance, and suffrage movements was reflected in the views and actions of other women's movement leaders, such as Susan B. Anthony.

The convention and its participants were subjected to widespread ridicule, but similar conventions were organized in other states, and in the same year, New York State

Women won the right to vote in 1920, with the adoption of the Nineteenth Amendment. This amendment resulted primarily from the activities of the women's suffrage movement, led by Elizabeth Cady Stanton, Susan B. Anthony, and Carrie Chapman Catt during the late nineteenth and early twentieth centuries. The "suffragettes," as they were called, held rallies, demonstrations, and protest marches for more than half a century before achieving their goal. The cause of women's suffrage was ultimately advanced by World War I. President Woodrow Wilson and members of Congress were convinced that women would be more likely to support the war effort if they were granted the right to vote. For this same reason, women were given the right to vote in Great Britain and Canada during the First World War.

The most recent expansion of the suffrage in the United States took place in 1971, during the Vietnam War, when the Twenty-sixth Amendment was ratified, lowering the voting age from twenty-one to eighteen. Unlike black suffrage and women's suffrage, which came about in part because of the demands of groups that had been deprived of the right to vote, the Twenty-sixth Amendment was not a response to the demands of young people to be given the right to vote. Instead, many policy makers hoped that the right to vote would channel the disruptive protest activities of students involved in the anti–Vietnam War movement into peaceful participation at the ballot box.

passed the Married Women's Property Act in order to re-store the right of a married woman to own property. Frustration with the general failure to win reforms in other states accelerated suffrage activism after the Civil War. In 1872, Anthony and several other women were arrested in Rochester, New York, for illegally registering and voting in that year's national election. (The men who allowed the women to register and vote were also indicted; Anthony paid their expenses, and eventually won presidential pardons for them.) At her trial, Judge Ward Hunt ordered the jury to find her guilty without deliberation. Yet Anthony was allowed to address the court, saying, "Your denial of my citizen's right to vote is the denial of my right of consent as one of the governed, the denial of my right of representation as one of the taxed, the denial of my right to a trial of my peers as an offender against the law."[1] Hunt assessed Anthony a fine of $100, but did not sentence her to jail. Anthony refused to pay the fine.

The following decade, suffragists used the occasion of the Constitution's centennial to protest the continued denial of their rights. For these women, the centennial represented "a century of injustice." The unveiling of the Statue of Liberty, depicting liberty as a woman, in New York Harbor, in 1886, prompted women's rights advocates to call it "the greatest hypocrisy of the nineteenth century," in that "not one single woman throughout the length and breadth of the Land is as yet in possession of political Liberty."[2]

The climactic movement toward suffrage was formally launched in 1878 with the introduction of a proposed constitutional amendment in Congress. Parallel efforts were made in the states. The Nineteenth Amendment, granting women the right to vote, was finally adopted in 1920, after most of the movement's original leaders had died.

SOURCE: Miriam Gurko, *The Ladies of Seneca Falls: The Birth of the Women's Rights Movement* (New York: Macmillan, 1974).
[1]Jill Dupont, "Susan B. Anthony," *New York Notes* (Albany, NY: New York State Commission on the Bicentennial of the U.S. Constitution, 1988), p. 3.
[2]Dupont, "Susan B. Anthony," p. 4.

VOTER PARTICIPATION

Although the United States has developed a system of universal suffrage, America's rate of voter participation, or **turnout,** is very low. About 50 percent of those eligible participate in national presidential elections, while barely one-third of eligible voters take part in midterm congressional elections (see Figure 10.1). Turnout in state and local races that do not coincide with national contests is typically even lower. In European countries, by contrast, national voter turnout is usually between 80 and 90 percent.[2]

The difference between American and European levels of turnout has much to do with registration rules and party strength. In the United States, individuals who are eligible to vote must register with the state election board before they are actually allowed to vote. Registration requirements were introduced at the end of the nineteenth century in response to the demands of the Progressive movement. Progressives hoped to make voting more difficult both to reduce multiple voting and other forms of corruption and to discourage immigrant and working-class voters from going to the polls. When first introduced, registration was extremely difficult and, in some states, reduced voter turnout by as much as 50 percent.

Registration requirements particularly depress the participation of those

turnout

the percentage of eligible individuals who actually vote

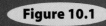

Figure 10.1

VOTER TURNOUT IN PRESIDENTIAL AND MIDTERM ELECTIONS, 1892–1996

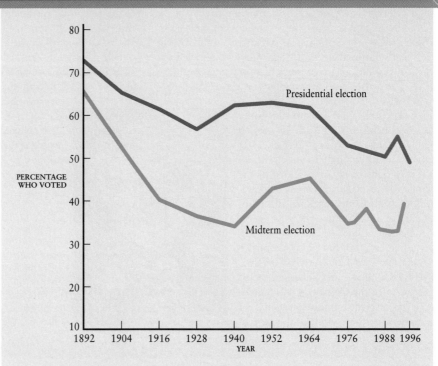

SOURCES: 1892–1958: Erik Austin and Jerome Clubb, *Political Facts of the United States since 1789* (New York: Columbia University Press, 1986), pp. 378–79; 1960–96. U.S. Bureau of the Census, *Statistical Abstract of the United States: 1997* (Washington, DC: Government Printing Office, 1997), p. 289.

More Americans tend to vote in presidential election years than in years when only congressional and local elections are held.

with little education and low incomes because registration requires a greater degree of political involvement and interest than does the act of voting itself. To vote, a person need be concerned only with the particular election campaign at hand. Requiring individuals to register before the next election forces them to make a decision to participate on the basis of an abstract interest in the electoral process rather than a simple concern with a specific campaign. Such an abstract interest in electoral politics is largely a product of education. Those with relatively little education may become interested in political events once the issues of a particular campaign become salient, but by that time it may be too late to register. Young people tend to assign a low priority to registration even if they are well educated. As a result, personal registration requirements not only diminish the size of the electorate but also tend to create an electorate that is, on average, better educated, higher in income and social status, and composed of fewer young people, African Americans, and other minorities than the citizenry as a whole (see Figure 10.2).

Over the years, voter registration restrictions have been modified somewhat to make registration easier. In most states, an eligible individual may register to vote simply by mailing a postcard to the state election board. In 1993, Congress approved and President Clinton signed the Motor Voter bill to ease voter registration by allowing individuals to register when they apply for driver's licenses, as well as in public assistance and military recruitment offices.[3] In Europe, there is typically no registration burden on the individual voter; voter registration is handled automatically by the government. This is one reason that voter turnout rates in Europe are higher than those in the United States.

The second factor explaining low rates of voter turnout in the United States is the weakness of the American party system. As we saw in Chapter 9, during the nineteenth century, American political party machines employed hundreds of thousands of workers to organize and mobilize voters and bring them to the polls. The result was an extremely high rate of turnout, typically more than 90 percent of eligible voters.[4] But political party machines began to

DIFFERENCES IN VOTER REGISTRATION RATES BY SOCIAL GROUP, 1996

Figure 10.2

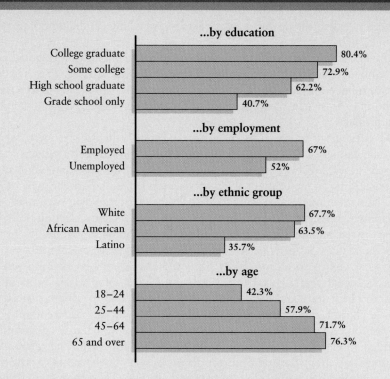

...by education

College graduate	80.4%
Some college	72.9%
High school graduate	62.2%
Grade school only	40.7%

...by employment

Employed	67%
Unemployed	52%

...by ethnic group

White	67.7%
African American	63.5%
Latino	35.7%

...by age

18–24	42.3%
25–44	57.9%
45–64	71.7%
65 and over	76.3%

SOURCES: U.S. Bureau of the Census, *Statistical Abstract of the United States: 1995* (Washington, DC: Government Printing Office, 1995), p. 289; and http://www.census.gov/population/socdemo/voting/history/vot23.txt.

The percentage of Americans who are registered to vote varies according to education level, employment status, ethnic group, and age.

decline in strength in the early twentieth century and by now have largely disappeared. Without party workers to encourage them to go to the polls and even to bring them there if necessary, many eligible voters will not participate. In the absence of strong parties, participation rates drop the most among poorer and less-educated citizens. Because of the absence of strong political parties, the American electorate is smaller and skewed more toward the middle class than the population of all those potentially eligible to vote.

TYPES OF ELECTIONS

Three types of elections are held in the United States: primary elections, general elections, and runoff elections. Americans occasionally also participate in a fourth voting process, the referendum, but the referendum is not actually an election.

Primary elections are used to select each party's candidates for the general election. In the case of local and statewide offices, the winners of primary elections face one another as their parties' nominees in the general election. At the presidential level, however, primary elections are indirect; they are used to select state delegates to the national nominating conventions, at which the major party presidential candidates are chosen. America is one of the only nations in the world to use primary elections. In most countries, nominations are controlled by party officials, as they once were in the United States. The primary system was introduced at the turn of the century by Progressive reformers who hoped to weaken the power of party leaders by taking candidate nominations out of their hands.

Under the laws of some states, only registered members of a political party may vote in a primary election to select that party's candidates. This is called a **closed primary.** Other states allow all registered voters to decide on the day of the primary in which party's primary they will participate. This is called an **open primary.**

The primary is followed by the general election—the decisive electoral contest. The winner of the general election is elected to office for a specified term. In some states, however, mainly in the southeast, if no candidate wins an absolute majority in the primary, a runoff election is held before the general election. This situation is most likely to arise if there are more than two candidates, none of whom receives a majority of the votes cast. A runoff election is held between the two candidates who received the largest number of votes.

Some states also provide for referendum voting. The **referendum** process allows citizens to vote directly on proposed laws or other governmental actions. In recent years, voters in several states have voted to set limits on tax rates, to block state and local spending proposals, and to prohibit social services for illegal immigrants. Although it involves voting, a referendum is not an election. The election is an institution of representative government. Through an election, voters choose officials to act for them. The referendum, by contrast, is an institution of direct democracy; it allows voters to govern directly without intervention by government officials. The validity of referenda results, however, are subject to judicial action. If a court finds that a referendum outcome violates the state or national constitution, it can overturn the result. This happened in the case of a 1995 California referendum curtailing social services to illegal aliens.[5]

primary elections

elections used to select a party's candidate for the general election

closed primary

a primary election in which voters can participate in the nomination of candidates, but only of the party in which they are enrolled for a period of time prior to primary day

open primary

a primary election in which the voter can wait until the day of the primary to choose which party to enroll in to select candidates for the general election

referendum

the practice of referring a measure proposed or passed by a legislature to the vote of the electorate for approval or rejection

THE CRITERIA FOR WINNING

In some countries, to win a seat in the parliament or other governing body, a candidate must receive an absolute majority (50% + 1) of all the votes cast in the relevant district. This type of electoral system is called a **majority system** and, in the United States, is used in primary elections by some southern states. Majority systems usually include a provision for a runoff election between the two top candidates, because if the initial race draws several candidates, there is little chance that any one will receive a majority.

In other nations, candidates for office need not win an absolute majority of the votes cast to win an election. Instead, victory is awarded to the candidate who receives the most votes, regardless of the actual percentage this represents. A candidate receiving 50 percent, 30 percent, or 20 percent of the vote can win if no other candidate received more votes. This type of electoral system is called a **plurality system** and is used in virtually all general elections in the United States.

Most European nations employ a third type of electoral system, called **proportional representation.** Under proportional rules, competing political parties are awarded legislative seats in rough proportion to the percentage of the popular votes cast that each party won. A party that wins 30 percent of the vote will receive roughly 30 percent of the seats in the parliament or other representative body. In the United States, proportional representation is used by many states in presidential primary elections.

In general, proportional representation works to the advantage of smaller or weaker groups in society, whereas plurality and majority rules tend to help larger and more powerful forces. Proportional representation benefits smaller or weaker groups because it usually allows a party to win legislative seats with fewer votes than would be required under a majority or plurality system. In Europe, for example, a party that wins 10 percent of the national vote might win 10 percent of the parliamentary seats. In the United States, by contrast, a party that wins 10 percent of the vote would probably win no seats in Congress. Because they give small parties little chance of success, plurality and majority systems tend to reduce the number of competitive political parties. Proportional representation, on the other hand, tends to increase the number of parties. It is in part because of its use of plurality elections that the United States has usually had only two significant political parties, while with proportional representation, many European countries have developed multiparty systems.

ELECTORAL DISTRICTS

The boundaries for congressional and state legislative districts in the United States are redrawn by the states every ten years in response to population changes determined by the decennial census. The character of district boundaries is influenced by several factors. Some of the most important influences have been federal court decisions. In the 1963 case of *Gray v. Sanders,* and in the 1964 cases of *Wesberry v. Sanders* and *Reynolds v. Sims,* the Supreme Court held that legislative districts within a state must include roughly equal populations, so as to accord with the principle of "one person, one vote."[6] During the 1980s, the Supreme Court also declared that legislative districts

majority system
a type of electoral system in which, to win a seat in the parliament or other representative body, a candidate must receive a majority of all the votes cast in the relevant district

plurality system
a type of electoral system in which, to win a seat in the parliament or other representative body, a candidate need only receive the most votes in the election, not necessarily a majority of votes cast

proportional representation
a multiple-member district system that allows each political party representation in proportion to its percentage of the total vote

gerrymandering

apportionment of voters in districts in such a way as to give unfair advantage to one racial or ethnic group or political party

benign gerrymandering

attempts to draw district boundaries so as to create districts made up primarily of disadvantaged or underrepresented minorities

minority district

a gerrymandered voting district that improves the chances of minority candidates by making selected minority groups the majority within the district

should, insofar as possible, be contiguous, compact, and consistent with existing political subdivisions.[7]

Despite judicial intervention, state legislators routinely seek to influence electoral outcomes by manipulating the organization of electoral districts. This strategy is called **gerrymandering**, in honor of a nineteenth-century Massachusetts governor, Elbridge Gerry, who was alleged to have designed a district in the shape of a salamander to promote his party's interests. The principle of gerrymandering is simple: different distributions of voters among districts can produce different electoral results. For example, by dispersing the members of a particular group across two or more districts, state legislators can dilute their voting power and prevent them from electing a representative in any district. Alternatively, by concentrating the members of a group or the adherents of the opposing party in as few districts as possible, state legislators can try to ensure that their opponents will elect as few representatives as possible. In recent years, the federal government has supported what is sometimes called **benign gerrymandering** through the creation of congressional districts made up primarily of minority group members. This practice was intended to increase the number of African Americans elected to public office (see Figure 10.3). The Supreme Court has viewed this effort as constitutionally dubious, however. Beginning with the 1993 case of *Shaw v. Reno*, the Court has undermined efforts to create such **minority districts**.[8]

THE BALLOT

Prior to the 1890s, voters cast ballots according to political parties. Each party printed its own ballots, listed only its own candidates for each office, and em-

Figure 10.3   **ELECTORAL GERRYMANDERING**

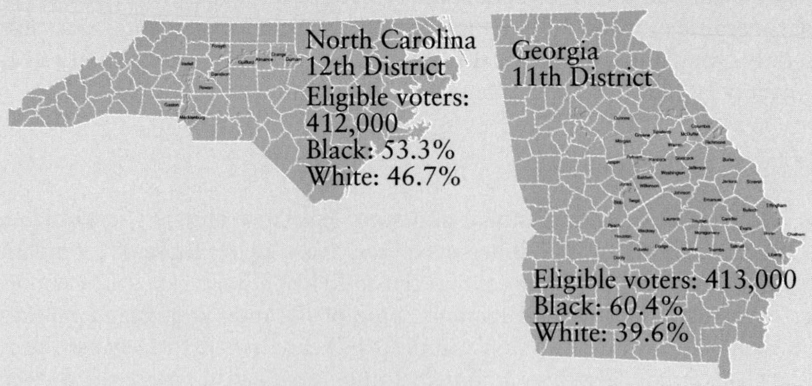

North Carolina's 12th Congressional District and Georgia's 11th Congressional District were drawn in unusual shapes in an attempt to create minority election districts and encourage the election of minority representatives to Congress. Both these districts have been ruled unconstitutional by the U.S. Supreme Court.

SOURCE: David Van Biema, "Snakes or Ladders?" *Time*, July 12, 1993, pp. 30–31. Reprinted with permission.

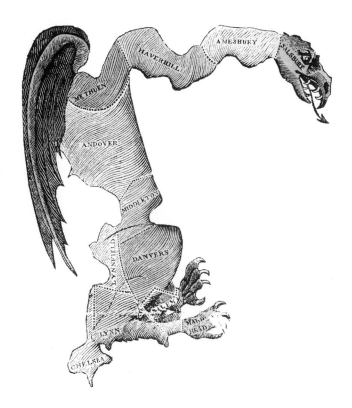

A cartoon of the original gerrymandered district in Massachusetts.

ployed party workers to distribute its ballots at the polls. Because only one party's candidates appeared on any ballot, it was very difficult for a voter to cast anything other than a straight party vote.

The advent of a new, neutral ballot represented a significant change in electoral procedure. The new ballot was prepared and administered by the state rather than the parties. Each ballot was identical and included the names of all candidates for office. This ballot reform made it possible for voters to make their choices on the basis of the individual rather than the collective merits of a party's candidates. Because all candidates for the same office now appeared on the same ballot, voters were no longer forced to choose a straight party ticket. This gave rise to the phenomenon of split-ticket voting in American elections.

If a voter supports candidates from more than one party in the same election, he or she is said to be casting a **split-ticket vote.** Voters who support only one party's candidates are casting a **straight-ticket vote.** Straight-ticket voting occurs most often when a voter casts a ballot for a party's presidential candidate and then "automatically" votes for the rest of that party's candidates. The result of this voting pattern is known as the **coattail effect.**

Prior to the reform of the ballot, it was not uncommon for an entire incumbent administration to be swept from office and replaced by an entirely new set of officials. In the absence of a real possibility of split-ticket voting, any desire on the part of the electorate for change could be expressed only as a vote against all candidates of the party in power. Because of this, there always

split-ticket voting

the practice of casting ballots for the candidates of at least two different political parties in the same election

straight-ticket voting

the practice of casting ballots for candidates of only one party

coattail effect

the result of voters casting their ballot for president or governor and "automatically" voting for the remainder of the party's ticket

Electoral Redistricting and Race

The process of redrawing election districts to take account of population shifts is both necessary and controversial. America's two major political parties have always vied to obtain political advantage through redistricting in the hope that redrawn district lines will help their candidates, or hurt the opposing candidates. Yet redistricting has also been used as a weapon to minimize the electoral influence of selected groups, especially African Americans, a process many consider an undemocratic denial of equality. To remedy this problem, Congress amended the 1965 Voting Rights Act in 1982 to compel states with significant African American and Latino populations to redraw district lines in such a way as to make more likely the election of representatives from these groups. This redistricting was carried out in thirteen states after the 1990 census, and it produced the desired effect. Before the 1990 reapportionment, the House of Representatives had a record-high 25 African American members (5.7 percent of members). After the reapportionment, which included the creation of districts having black majorities, 39 African Americans were elected (9 percent of the House); Latino representatives increased from 10 to 17. Yet many of these race-based reapportionment schemes were challenged in court.

Supporters of race-based redistricting argue that such drastic measures are necessary to overcome traditional white dominance. Southern blacks, in particular, traditionally have been frozen out of public office, since most American elections follow the winner-take-all system, meaning that election districts with substantial nonwhite populations could always be outvoted by a white majority. Indeed, studies have shown that race matters to voters. In a study from the 1980s, more than 80 percent of white North Carolina voters reported that they would not vote for an African American candidate, even if there was no other choice on the ballot. North Carolina did not elect an African American to Congress in the twentieth century until after the 1990 reapportionment, despite the fact that between one-fifth and one-third of the state's population was black.

Although race-based redistricting has produced some odd-shaped congressional districts, it increased not only the number of nonwhite representatives in Congress, but also increased their political voice and clout. This larger number of representatives has exerted more influence over national policymaking in such areas as crime and gun control. It also has increased the pool of potential office-seekers. The persistence of racism, and the resistance of institutions to change, has made such "minority" districts necessary.

Critics have argued that race-based redistricting is nothing more than racial gerrymandering, and that it perpetuates the very problem it claims to solve. While the number of minority representatives in Congress has increased, race-based reapportionment has also purged surrounding districts of nonwhite voters, transforming many of these districts from racially and politically competitive to uniformly white and Republican, a fact reflected in the shift of 12 seats to Republican candidates in the 13 states where these changes took place (because of the shifting of Democratic-voting blacks from these formerly competitive districts). Thus, black voters have been walled off from more conservative white voters.

The shoestring shape of many of these districts—some portions of some districts are no wider than an interstate highway—reveals their blatant gerrymandering. Even though the purpose of providing more representation for African Americans and Latinos may be praiseworthy, the method violates the principle of equal protection, as the Supreme Court has noted in recent decisions. Winner-take-all elections do often disguise the preferences of minority groups, but the remedy is stronger electoral competition and greater pressure from constituent groups. Reapportionment based on race is unacceptable, regardless of which race benefits.

SOURCE: Lani Guinier, "Don't Scapegoat the Gerrymander," *New York Times Magazine*, January 8, 1995.

existed the possibility, particularly at the state and local levels, that an insurgent slate committed to policy change could be swept into power. The party ballot thus increased the potential impact of elections upon the government's composition. Although this potential may not always have been realized, the party ballot at least increased the chance that electoral decisions could lead to policy changes. By contrast, because it permitted choice on the basis of candidates' individual appeals, ticket splitting led to increasingly divided partisan control of government.

THE ELECTORAL COLLEGE

In the early history of popular voting, nations often made use of indirect elections. In these elections, voters would choose the members of an intermediate body. These members would, in turn, select public officials. The assumption underlying such processes was that ordinary citizens were not really qualified to choose their leaders and could not be trusted to do so directly. The last vestige of this procedure in America is the **electoral college,** the group of electors who formally select the president and vice president of the United States.

electoral college

the presidential electors from each state who meet after the popular election to cast ballots for president and vice president

When Americans go to the polls on election day, they are technically not voting directly for presidential candidates. Instead, voters within each state are choosing among slates of electors selected by each state's party leadership and pledged, if elected, to support that party's presidential candidate. In each state, the slate that wins casts all the state's electoral votes for its party's candidate. Each state is entitled to a number of electoral votes equal to the number of the state's senators and representatives combined, for a total of 535 electoral votes for the fifty states. Occasionally, an elector will break his or her pledge and votes for the other party's candidate. For example, in 1976, when the Republicans carried the state of Washington, one Republican elector from that state refused to vote for Gerald Ford, the Republican presidential nominee. Many states have now enacted statutes formally binding electors to their pledges, but some constitutional authorities doubt whether such statutes are enforceable.

In each state, the electors whose slate has won proceed to the state's capital on the Monday following the second Wednesday in December and formally cast their ballots. These are sent to Washington, tallied by the Congress in January, and the name of the winner is formally announced. If no candidate receives a majority of all electoral votes, the names of the top three candidates would be submitted to the House, where each state would be able to cast one vote. Whether a state's vote would be decided by a majority, plurality, or some other fraction of the state's delegates would be determined under rules established by the House.

In 1800 and 1824, the electoral college failed to produce a majority for any candidate. In the election of 1800, Thomas Jefferson, the Jeffersonian Republican Party's presidential candidate, and Aaron Burr, that party's vice presidential candidate, received an equal number of votes in the electoral college, throwing the election into the House of Representatives. (The Constitution at that time made no distinction between presidential and vice presidential candidates, specifying only that the individual receiving a majority of electoral votes would be named president.) Some members of the Federalist Party in Congress suggested that they should seize the opportunity to damage the Republican cause by supporting Burr and denying Jefferson the presidency. Federalist leader Alexander Hamilton put a stop to this mischievous notion, however, and made certain that his party supported Jefferson. Hamilton's actions enraged Burr and helped lead to the infamous duel between the two men, in which Hamilton was killed. The Twelfth Amendment, ratified in 1804, was designed to prevent a repetition of such an inconclusive election by providing for separate electoral college votes for president and vice president.

In the 1824 election, four candidates—John Quincy Adams, Andrew Jackson, Henry Clay, and William H. Crawford—divided the electoral vote; no one of them received a majority. The House of Representatives eventually chose Adams over the others, even though Jackson had won more electoral and popular votes. After 1824, the two major political parties had begun to dominate presidential politics to such an extent that by December of each election year, only two candidates remained for the electors to choose between, thus ensuring that one would receive a majority. This freed the parties and the candidates from having to plan their campaigns to culminate in Congress, and Congress very quickly ceased to dominate the presidential selection process.

On all but two occasions since 1824, the electoral vote has simply ratified the nationwide popular vote. Since electoral votes are won on a state-by-state basis, it is mathematically possible for a candidate who receives a nationwide popular plurality to fail to carry states whose electoral votes would add up to a majority. Thus, in 1876, Rutherford B. Hayes was the winner in the electoral college despite receiving fewer popular votes than his rival, Samuel Tilden. In 1888, Grover Cleveland received more popular votes than Benjamin Harrison, but received fewer electoral votes.

The possibility that in some future election the electoral college will, once again, produce an outcome that is inconsistent with the popular vote has led to many calls for the abolition of this institution and the introduction of some form of direct popular election of the president. Ross Perot's 1992 candidacy, for example, at one point opened the possibility of a discrepancy between the popular and electoral totals, and even raised the specter of an election decided in the House of Representatives. Efforts to introduce such a reform, however, are usually blocked by political forces that believe they benefit from the present

Bob Dole's campaign staff surrounds him before he goes on stage for a debate during the 1996 New Hampshire primary.

system. For example, minority groups that are influential in large urban states with many electoral votes feel that their voting strength would be diminished in a direct, nationwide, popular election. At the same time, some Republicans believe that their party's usual presidential strength in the South and the West gives them a distinct advantage in the electoral college. There is little doubt, however, that an election resulting in a discrepancy between the electoral and popular outcomes would create irresistible political pressure to eliminate the electoral college and introduce direct popular election of the president.

★ Election Campaigns

▶ What are the steps in a successful election campaign?

A **campaign** is an effort by political candidates and their supporters to win the backing of donors, political activists, and voters in their quest for political office. Campaigns precede every primary and general election. Because of the complexity of the campaign process, and because of the amount of money that candidates must raise, presidential campaigns usually begin almost two years before the November presidential elections. The campaign for any office consists of a number of steps. Candidates must first organize groups of supporters who will help them raise funds and bring their name to the attention of the media and potential donors. This step is relatively easy for a candidate currently in the office. The current officeholder is called an **incumbent**. Incumbents usually are already well known and have little difficulty attracting supporters and contributors, unless of course they have been subject to damaging publicity while in office.

ADVISERS

The next step in a typical campaign involves recruiting advisers and creating a formal campaign organization (see Figure 10.4). Most candidates, especially for national or statewide office, will need a campaign manager, a media consultant, a pollster, a financial adviser, and a press spokesperson, as well as a staff director to coordinate the activities of volunteer and paid workers. For a local campaign, candidates generally need hundreds of workers. State-level campaigns call for thousands of workers, and presidential campaigns require tens of thousands of workers throughout the nation.

Professional campaign workers, including the managers, consultants, and pollsters required in a modern campaign, prefer to work for candidates who seem to have a reasonable chance of winning. For individuals like James Carville, who helped manage Bill Clinton's 1992 campaign; Dick Morris, credited as the mastermind behind Clinton's 1996 victory; or Republican strategists Roger Ailes and Bob Teeter, politics is a profession, and repeated associations with winning campaigns are the route to professional success. Candidates seen as having little chance of winning often have difficulty hiring the most experienced professional consultants. Professional political consultants have taken the place of the old-time party bosses who once controlled political

campaign

an effort by political candidates and their staffs to win the backing of donors, political activists, and voters in the quest for political office

incumbent

a candidate running for a position that he or she already holds

Figure 10.4   THE TYPICAL ORGANIZATION OF A NATIONAL POLITICAL CAMPAIGN

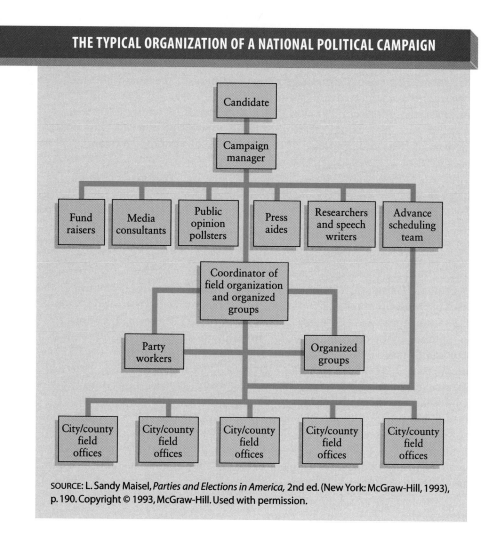

SOURCE: L. Sandy Maisel, *Parties and Elections in America,* 2nd ed. (New York: McGraw-Hill, 1993), p. 190. Copyright © 1993, McGraw-Hill. Used with permission.

campaigns. Most consultants who direct campaigns specialize in politics, although some are drawn from the ranks of corporate advertising and may work with commercial clients in addition to politicians. Campaign consultants conduct public opinion polls, produce television commercials, organize direct-mail campaigns, and develop the issues and advertising messages the candidate will use to mobilize support.

Together with their advisers, candidates must begin serious fund-raising efforts at an early stage in the campaign. To have a reasonable chance of winning a seat in the House of Representatives, a candidate may need to raise more than $500,000. To win a Senate seat, a candidate may need ten times that much. Candidates generally begin raising funds long before they face an election. For example, a year prior to the 1998 congressional elections, New York's Republican senator, Alfonse D'Amato, had already raised $9.7 million, nearly as much as he spent in his successful 1992 campaign. Throughout 1996 and 1997, D'Amato had raised money from the banking, insurance, real estate, and construction businesses that come under the jurisdiction of the Senate Banking,

Race and Representation

"No taxation without representation!" From the Boston Tea Party forward, the demand for political representation has been at the heart of American ideals of democratic governance. Every major advance of American democracy—Andrew Jackson's overthrow of the "King Caucus," the Fifteenth Amendment guaranteeing blacks the right to vote, the Nineteenth Amendment extending the right to vote to women—has also broadened the range of interests able to seek just representation. But what is "just" representation? In a political system based on majority rule, how can a minority be assured that its views will be listened to? And how can efforts to accommodate minorities be reconciled with the need to protect the no-less-important rights of majorities?

Tension between majorities and minorities over how to achieve fair representation in American government is as old as the Republic. Today Americans take for granted the compromises hammered out at the constitutional convention in Philadelphia. But it is important to realize that this solution to the problem of representation in the national legislature was a political compromise rather than the fulfillment of some ideal of perfect representation. In fact, every actual scheme of translating citizens' wishes into electoral outcomes distorts those wishes, emphasizing some and silencing others. It is in this context that we should understand contemporary debates about race and representation in America.

The century-long legacy of the abandonment of Reconstruction after the Civil War was the disenfranchisement of African Americans in the South. Finally, with the Voting Rights Act of 1965, the federal government took a major step to increase African Americans' electoral representation. The act's two major provisions prohibited states from denying anyone the right to vote on the basis of race, and required southern states to gain approval from the federal government before making any changes in voting procedures or electoral districts. The act's constitutionality was immediately challenged; in finding it constitutional in 1966, Supreme Court Chief Justice Earl Warren defended it but acknowledged the controversy over its intrusive means: "The Court has recognized that exceptional conditions can justify legislative measures not otherwise appropriate."[1]

Since 1965, the issue of how the federal government should protect the voting rights of African Americans has become more complex. The heart of the matter is that the more African Americans' voting power is concentrated in particular electoral districts, the less they are represented in other districts. Is a system that gives minorities a few token seats in the legislature, but denies them a significant role in affecting most elections, fair? No clear principles have emerged about what "fair" means when it comes to representation for minorities in America. Traditionalists argue that all concessions to racial-bloc voting threaten to fragment a system based on local, geographically distinct majorities. Critics of traditional voting methods argue that some form of proportional representation is the only fair way to give minorities an adequate voice in legislatures.

Current law exacerbates the widespread confusion. A 1982 amendment to the Voting Rights Act removed the need to prove deliberate discrimination in order to find a scheme of representation unfair, but also said that the law could not be read as guaranteeing a right to proportional representation. The Supreme Court, despite repeated rulings in voting rights cases, has yet to clarify the standards that should guide efforts to achieve just representation. Today it is clear what most Americans want: just representation, but also a move away from acknowledging race as a politically relevant fact. Can both be attained at the same time? Is the present widespread desire for color-blind representation a fulfillment, at last, of American ideals—or an abandonment by an arrogant majority of the push for equality?

[1]*South Carolina v. Katzenbach,* 383 U.S. 301 (1966).

Students and Politics

Life for a campaign worker can be difficult. Take the case of Jee Heng Lee, a Boston University graduate who worked on many campaigns for the Democratic Party while in college. Lee started as an intern for Massachusetts senator John Kerry's campaign for president in 1991. "[Campaign managers] expect you to be there a lot," he says. "They know that you have classes and things, but when it gets to early November, everyone is doing all they can around the clock." On the other hand, he says, working on the campaign provides an unparalleled opportunity for excitement. "Everything's moving so rapidly. As the election draws closer, everything becomes more energized and tense. You can see that the issues you believe in are really at stake. You think of this when you sleep eight hours over a weekend, or you don't receive your minimum-wage paycheck for over a month."

Lee sought to work for candidates who took strong stands on issues he was concerned with, such as abortion rights and the rights of Asian Americans. These interests led him to work in politics in his home district in San Jose, California, where Democrat Jerry Estruth and Republican Tom Campell were vying to succeed Norman Mineta, a powerful Korean American representative who had resigned. While working for Estruth, Lee realized what it took to succeed as a campaign worker: "People respect hard work and loyalty. . . . Basically, in campaigns, you build trust through other campaigns and hard work. People hire who they know and who they trust. It's a hard life, and it's not for everyone, but it can be an adrenaline rush."

SOURCE: Jee Heng Lee, interview with author, May 2, 1998.

Housing, and Urban Affairs Committee, which he chairs. A professional staff of fund-raisers, headed by long-term D'Amato consultant Arthur Finkelstein, labored full-time on the senator's behalf. For his efforts, Finkelstein earned nearly $100,000 during the second half of 1996 alone. In many states, an incumbent able to raise as much money as D'Amato might be able to frighten away most potential challengers. In New York, however, Democratic candidates can count on the support of some of the party's wealthiest contributors; Democratic senatorial candidate and congressman Charles Schumer of Brooklyn was expected to raise nearly as much money as D'Amato. We will look in more detail at political campaign financing later in this chapter.

POLLING

Another important element of a campaign is public-opinion polling. To be competitive, a candidate must collect voting and poll data to assess the electorate's needs, hopes, fears, and past behavior. Polls are conducted throughout most political campaigns. Surveys of voter opinion provide the basic information that candidates and their staffs use to craft campaign strategies—i.e., to select issues, to assess their own strengths and weaknesses as well as those of the opposition, to check voter response to the campaign, and to measure the degree to which various constituent groups may be responsive to campaign appeals. The themes, issues, and messages that candidates present during a campaign are generally based upon polls and smaller face-to-face sessions with voters, called "focus groups." In the 1992 presidential campaign, Bill Clinton's emphasis on the economy, exemplified by the campaign staff's slogan "It's the economy, stupid," was based on the view that the economy was the chief concern among American voters. In preparation for the 1996 campaign, Clinton adopted a strategy of "triangulation" based upon consultant Richard Morris's interpretation of poll data. Morris advised Clinton that he would win the most votes by positioning himself between liberal Democrats and conservative Republicans, in a sense forming the apex of a triangle.[9] In recent years, pollsters have become central figures in most national campaigns and some have continued as advisers to their clients after they win the election.

THE PRIMARIES

For many candidates, the next step in a campaign is the primary election. In the case of all offices but the presidency, state and local primary elections determine which candidates will receive the major parties' official nominations. Of course, candidates can run for office without the Democratic or Republican nomination. In most states, however, independent and third-party candidates must obtain many thousands of petition signatures to qualify for the general election ballot. This requirement alone discourages most independent and third-party bids. More important, most Americans are reluctant to vote for candidates other than those nominated by the two major parties. Thus most of the time, a major party nomination is a necessary condition for electoral success. Some popular incumbents coast to victory without having to face a serious challenge. In most major races, however, candidates can expect to compete in a primary election.

There are essentially two types of primary contests: the personality clash and the ideological, or factional, struggle. In the first category are primaries that simply represent competing efforts by ambitious individuals to secure election to office. In 1994, for example, six Republicans vied for the Republican Party's nomination for governor of Tennessee. All six candidates claimed to be conservative, and they had similar positions on most issues. The race was eventually won by Bill Frist, who went on to victory in the November election. This type of primary can be very healthy for a political party because it can enhance interest in the campaign and can produce a nominee with the ability to win the general election.

The second type of primary—the ideological struggle—can have different consequences. Ideological struggles usually occur when one wing of a party decides that an incumbent is too willing to compromise or too moderate in his or her political views. For example, in 1992, President George Bush was challenged for the Republican presidential nomination by conservative columnist Pat Buchanan. Buchanan charged Bush with being too willing to compromise conservative principles. Such ideological challenges not only reveal rifts within a party coalition, but the friction and resentment they cause can undermine a party's general election chances. In 1968, for example, primary struggles between liberal and moderate Democrats left such a bitter taste that many liberals sat out the general election, thus helping to ensure the victory of the Republican candidate, Richard Nixon.

Caucus chairperson Charles Richardson gathers ballots from Republican Party members in Runnells, Iowa, during the 1996 caucus.

Ideological struggles can also produce candidates who are too liberal or too conservative to win the general election. Primary electorates are much smaller and tend to be ideologically more extreme than the general electorate: Democratic primary voters are somewhat more liberal than the general electorate, and Republican primary voters are typically more conservative than the general electorate. Thus, the winner of an intraparty ideological struggle may prove too extreme for the general election. In 1994, for example, arch-conservative Oliver North won the Virginia Republican senatorial primary over a moderate opponent, but was drubbed in the general election. Many moderate Republicans, including Virginia's other senator, John Warner, refused to support North.

★ Presidential Elections

▶ How is the president elected?
▶ What factors have the greatest impact on a general election campaign?

Although they also involve primary elections, the major party presidential nominations follow a pattern that is quite different from the nominating process employed for other political offices. In some years, particularly when an incumbent president is running for re-election, one party's nomination may not be contested. If, however, the Democratic or Republican presidential nomination is contested, candidates typically compete in primaries or presidential nominating caucuses in all fifty states, attempting to capture national convention delegates. Most states use primary elections to choose the delegates for national conventions. A few states use the **caucus,** a nominating process that begins with precinct-level meetings throughout the state. Some caucuses, called **open caucuses,** are open to anyone wishing to attend. Other states use **closed caucuses,** open only to registered party members. Citizens attending the caucuses typically elect delegates to statewide conventions at which delegates to the national party conventions are chosen.

The primaries and caucuses usually begin in February of a presidential election year and end in June (see Figure 10.5). The early ones are most important because they can help front-running candidates secure media attention and financial support. Gradually, the primary and caucus process has become "front loaded," with states vying with one another to increase their political influence by holding their nominating processes first. Traditionally, the New Hampshire primary and the Iowa caucuses are considered the most important of the early events, and candidates spend months courting voter support in these two states. A candidate who performs well in Iowa and New Hampshire will usually be able to secure support and better media coverage for subsequent races. A candidate who fares badly in these two states may be written off as a loser.

As noted in Chapter 9, the Democratic Party requires that state presidential primaries allocate delegates on the basis of proportional representation; Democratic candidates win delegates in rough proportion to their percentage

caucus (political)

a normally closed meeting of a political or legislative group to select candidates, plan strategy, or make decisions regarding legislative matters

open caucus

a presidential nominating caucus open to anyone who wishes to attend

closed caucus

a presidential nominating caucus open only to registered party members

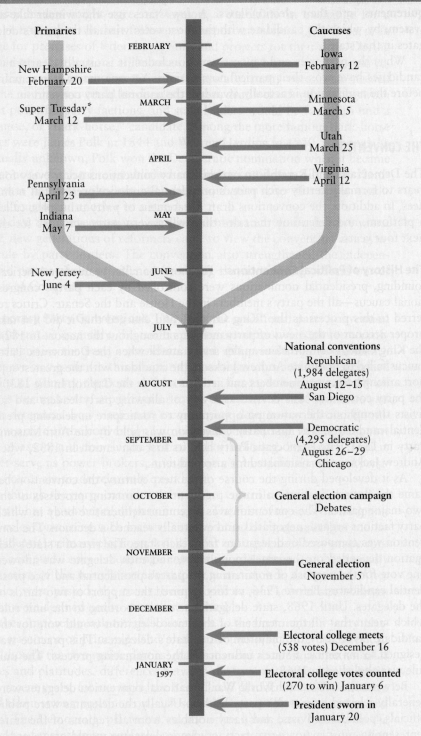

THE 1996 PRESIDENTIAL ELECTION SEASON

Figure 10.5

Primaries

FEBRUARY

New Hampshire
February 20

MARCH

Super Tuesday*
March 12

APRIL

Pennsylvania
April 23

Indiana
May 7

MAY

New Jersey
June 4

JUNE

JULY

AUGUST

SEPTEMBER

OCTOBER

NOVEMBER

DECEMBER

JANUARY
1997

Caucuses

Iowa
February 12

Minnesota
March 5

Utah
March 25

Virginia
April 12

National conventions
Republican
(1,984 delegates)
August 12–15
San Diego

Democratic
(4,295 delegates)
August 26–29
Chicago

General election campaign
Debates

General election
November 5

Electoral college meets
(538 votes) December 16

Electoral college votes counted
(270 to win) January 6

President sworn in
January 20

*Primaries or caucuses held in Texas, Florida, Tennessee, Louisiana, Oregon, Mississippi, Oklahoma, and Hawaii.

contrast, those earning more than $75,000 gave Dole their support by a 50-to-42 percent margin. Eighty-three percent of African Americans voted for Clinton. Those voters who call themselves liberals gave Clinton 78 percent of their votes. Americans who said Medicare and Social Security were their major concerns gave Clinton 67 percent of their votes. Finally, as has been the case in most recent elections, the 1996 results showed a significant "gender gap": 54 percent of women voted for Clinton, but only 44 percent of men did so.[10]

Despite Clinton's solid victory, Democratic Senate and House candidates did not fare especially well in 1996. Republicans actually gained two Senate seats to give the GOP a 55-to-45 majority in the upper chamber. In the House, Republicans maintained a large majority in the 105th Congress.

Poll data suggest that some voters deliberately split their tickets in order to prevent either political party from fully controlling the government. Ironically, many voters chose Clinton in part as a reaction to House Speaker Newt Gingrich and the Republican-led 104th Congress. Having decided to vote for Clinton, however, some of these individuals voted for Republican congressional candidates because they feared that a Democratic president plus a Democratic Congress would mean the enactment of expensive new federal programs.[11] Nearly one in seven, or more than 6 million voters who supported Clinton simultaneously gave their vote to a Republican congressional candidate.

Continuing Republican control of Congress after 1996 ensured that the work of the independent counsel investigating President Clinton's activities would continue. By 1997, independent counsel Kenneth Starr had acquired evidence indicating that Clinton had engaged in a sexual relationship with White House intern Monica Lewinsky and lied in a legal deposition about the matter. In September 1998, the president was compelled to admit publicly his affair with Lewinsky, sending shock waves through the nation. In response to Starr's findings, congressional Republicans launched an impeachment inquiry and eagerly looked forward to the 1998 elections. They assumed that voter disgust with Clinton's actions would give Republican candidates an edge in elections for House and Senate seats. Republican predictions were proven wrong, however. Most voters did not see Clinton's character as the central issue of the campaign. Moreover, as the GOP focused on Clinton's misdeeds, the party's leadership appeared to ignore other national issues. This provided Democratic candidates an opportunity to emphasize issues that voters cared about, such as education and Social Security. The results of the 1998 elections were a rebuke to the Republicans. In most midterm elections, the president's party loses seats in Congress; in 1998, however, the Democrats more than held their ground. In the House, Democrats posted a net gain of five seats, leaving the Republicans with a razor-thin 223-to-211 majority. In the Senate, the party balance remained unchanged at 55 to 45.

The 1998 elections seemed to have three major consequences. First, by strengthening Democratic forces in Congress, the election results probably saved Clinton from a lengthy impeachment hearing. Second, the elections sapped Republicans' confidence in their own congressional leadership. Third, the elections seemed to strengthen the positions of Vice President Al Gore, a Democratic presidential hopeful in 2000, and Texas governor George Bush, Jr., expected to be a frontrunner for the Republican presidential nomination in 2000 (Bush won an overwhelming victory in his gubernatorial re-election effort). Thus, the 1998 elections perpetuated the political struggle between and within the nation's two major parties.

★ Money and Politics

▶ How do candidates raise and spend campaign funds? How does the government regulate campaign spending?

▶ How does money affect how certain social groups achieve electoral success?

Modern national political campaigns are fueled by enormous amounts of money. In a national race, millions of dollars are spent on media time, as well as on public opinion polls and media consultants. In 1996, political candidates spent a total of more than $1 billion on election campaigns. The average winning candidate in a campaign for a seat in the House of Representatives spent more than $500,000; the average winner in a senatorial campaign spent $4 million.[12] The 1996 Democratic and Republican presidential candidates each received $75 million in public funds to run their campaigns.[13] Each presidential candidate was also helped by tens of millions of dollars in so-called independent expenditures on the part of corporate and ideological "political action committees." As long as such political expenditures are not formally coordinated with a candidate's campaign, they are considered to be constitutionally protected free speech and are not subject to legal limitation or even reporting requirements. Likewise, independent **soft money** spending by political parties is also considered to be an expression of free speech.[14]

soft money
money contributed directly to political parties for voter registration and organization

SOURCES OF CAMPAIGN FUNDS

Federal Election Commission data suggest that approximately one-fourth of the private funds spent on political campaigns in the United States is raised through small, direct-mail contributions; about one-fourth is provided by large, individual gifts; and another fourth comes from contributions from PACs. The remaining fourth is drawn from the political parties and from candidates' personal or family resources.[15]

Direct Mail Direct mail serves both as a vehicle for communicating with voters and as a mechanism for raising funds. Direct-mail fund-raising efforts begin with the purchase or rental of computerized mailing lists of voters deemed likely to support the candidate because of their partisan ties, interests, or ideology. Candidates send out pamphlets, letters, and brochures describing their views and appealing for funds. Tens of millions of dollars are raised by national, state, and local candidates through direct mail each year, usually in $25 and $50 contributions.[16]

Political Action Committees Political action committees (PACs) are organizations established by corporations, labor unions, or interest groups to channel the contributions of their members into political campaigns. Under the terms of the 1971 Federal Elections Campaign Act, which governs campaign finance in the United States, PACs are permitted to make larger contributions

political action committee (PAC)
a private group that raises and distributes funds for use in election campaigns

Box 10.1   FEDERAL CAMPAIGN FINANCE REGULATION

Campaign Contributions

No individual may contribute more than $1,000 to any one candidate in any single election. Individuals may contribute as much as $20,000 to a national party committee and up to $5,000 to a political action committee. Full disclosure is required by candidates of all contributions over $100. Candidates may not accept cash contributions over $100.

Political Action Committees

Any corporation, labor union, trade association, or other organization may establish a political action committee (PAC). PACs must contribute to the campaigns of at least five different candidates and may contribute as much as $5,000 per candidate in any given election.

Presidential Elections

Candidates in presidential primaries may receive federal matching funds if they raise at least $5,000 in each of twenty states. The money raised must come in contributions of $250 or less. The amount raised by candidates in this way is matched by the federal government, dollar for dollar, up to a limit of $5 million. In the general election, major-party candidates' campaigns are fully funded by the federal government. Candidates may spend no money beyond their federal funding. Independent groups may spend money on behalf of a candidate so long as their efforts are not directly tied to the official campaign. Minor-party candidates may get partial federal funding.

Federal Election Commission (FEC)

The six-member FEC supervises federal elections, collects and publicizes campaign finance records, and investigates violations of federal campaign finance law.

to any given candidate than individuals are allowed to make (see Box 10.1). Individuals may donate a maximum of $1,000 to any single candidate, but a PAC may donate as much as $5,000 to each candidate. Moreover, allied or related PACs often coordinate their campaign contributions, greatly increasing the amount of money a candidate actually receives from the same interest group. As a result, PACs have become central to campaign finance in the United States. Many critics assert that PACs corrupt the political process by allowing corporations and other interests to influence politicians with large contributions. It is by no means clear, however, that PACs corrupt the political process any more than large, individual contributions.

The United States is one of the few advanced industrial nations that permit individual candidates to accept large private contributions from individual or corporate donors. Most mandate either public funding of campaigns or, as in the case of Britain, require that large private donations be made to political parties rather than to individual candidates. The logic of such a requirement is that a contribution that might seem very large to an individual candidate would weigh much less heavily if made to a national party. Thus, the chance that a donor could buy influence would be reduced.

The Candidates   On the basis of the Supreme Court's 1976 decision in *Buckley v. Valeo,* the right of individuals to spend their *own* money to campaign for office is a constitutionally protected matter of free speech and is not subject to limitation. Thus, extremely wealthy candidates often contribute millions of dollars to their own campaigns. Michael Huffington, for example, spent approximately $20 million of his own funds in an unsuccessful California Senate bid in 1994. As was noted above, "independent" spending is also free from regulation; private groups, political parties, and wealthy individuals may spend as much as they wish to help elect one candidate or defeat another, as long as these expenditures are not coordinated with any political campaign. Many business and ideological groups engage in such activities, but since they are not subject to reporting requirements, the full extent of independent spending is not known.

Parties and Soft Money   State and local party organizations use soft money for get-out-the-vote drives and voter education and registration efforts. These are the party-building activities for which soft-money contributions are nominally made. Most soft-money dollars, however, are spent to assist candidates' re-election efforts in the form of "issue campaigns," campaigns on behalf of a particular candidate thinly disguised as mere advocacy of particular issues. For example, in 1996, issue advocacy commercials sponsored by state Democratic Party organizations looked just like commercials for Clinton. The issue commercials praised the president's stand on major issues and criticized the GOP's positions. The only difference was that the issue ads did not specifically call for the re-election of President Clinton. Critics contend that soft money is less a vehicle for building parties than it is a mechanism for circumventing federal election laws.

In some instances, large donors to the Democratic and Republican parties do not want to be publicly identified. To accommodate these "stealth donors," both parties have created sham nonprofit groups to serve as the nominal recipients of the gifts. For example, the Democratic Party established an organization

Bob Dole at a fund-raising event in New York City, part of a nationwide tour to raise money for his 1996 presidential campaign.

POLITICS ON THE WEB

If the Internet can change American democracy, it can do so most profoundly in the arena of elections. The convenience of Internet-based communication could make registering to vote, casting a ballot, and reporting vote tallies dramatically easier. Once citizens can fill out and submit voter registration forms electronically, at any hour of the day, the barriers to registration will be substantially reduced. Already, a site called "Rock the Ages," cosponsored by MTV's Rock the Vote, MCI, and the American Association of Retired Persons, will submit completed voter registration forms based on information entered via the Internet. In the future, citizens will cast ballots electronically from their home or workplace, significantly reducing the costs of voting and thereby increasing political participation. Although these possibilities pose serious challenges in guarding against fraud and protecting the integrity of the electoral process, the Internet clearly has tremendous potential to expand the pool of citizens participating in American elections.

www.wwnorton.com/wtp2e

called "Vote Now '96," which ostensibly worked to increase voter turnout. This organization received several million dollars in donations that were used on behalf of the Clinton-Gore re-election effort. For their part, Republicans created two nonprofit groups that took in more than $3 million.[17]

Public Funding　The Federal Elections Campaign Act also provides for public funding of presidential campaigns. As they seek a major party presidential nomination, candidates become eligible for public funds by raising at least $5,000 in individual contributions of $250 or less in each of twenty states. Candidates who reach this threshold may apply for federal funds to match, on a dollar-for-dollar basis, all individual contributions of $250 or less they receive. The funds are drawn from the Presidential Election Campaign Fund. Taxpayers can contribute $1 to this fund, at no additional cost to themselves, by checking a box on the first page of their federal income tax returns. Major party presidential candidates receive a lump sum (currently nearly $75 million) during the summer prior to the general election. They must meet all their general expenses from this money. Third-party candidates are eligible for public funding only if they received at least 5 percent of the vote in the previous presidential race. This stipulation effectively blocks preelection funding for third-party or independent candidates, although a third party that wins more than 5 percent of the vote can receive public funding after the election. In 1980, John Anderson convinced banks to loan him money for an independent candidacy on the strength of poll data showing that he would receive more than 5 percent of the vote and thus would obtain public funds with which to repay the loans. Under current law, no candidate is required to accept public funding for either the nominating races or general presidential election. Candidates who do not accept public funding are not affected by any expenditure limits. Thus, in 1992 Ross Perot financed his own presidential bid and was not bound by the $55 million limit to which the Democratic and Republican candidates were held that year. Perot accepted public funding in 1996.

CAMPAIGN FINANCE REFORM

Over the past several years, a number of pieces of legislation have proposed additional restrictions on the private funding of campaigns. Political reform has been blocked, however, because the two major parties disagree over the form it should take. The Republicans have developed a very efficient direct-mail apparatus and would be willing to place limits on the role of PACs. The Democrats, by contrast, depend more heavily on PACs and fear that limiting their role would hurt the party's electoral chances.

In the aftermath of the 1996 national elections, the role of soft money came under intense scrutiny. Both political parties raised and spent tens of millions of dollars in soft money to help their presidential candidates, congressional candidates, and candidates for state and local offices. The Democratic Party, for example, conducted a $45 million advertising campaign in key states during the summer of 1996. The campaign, which promoted Clinton's record while attacking Bob Dole's, was nominally not coordinated with the Clinton campaign and was thus not subject to federal regulation. However, former Clinton staffers have acknowledged that the White House was effectively in control of the ads.[18] Indeed, many of the questionable fund-raising practices.

attributed to the president and vice president by congressional probers involved efforts to raise the money needed for this huge campaign effort.

In response to the success of Democratic television ads, the Republicans launched their own soft-money advertising campaign on behalf of Bob Dole later in the summer of 1996. The GOP, however, reserved much of its soft money for use in congressional and local races. Some $30 million in national party funds helped Republicans to retain control of Congress and to strengthen their positions at the state and local levels.

In addition to the unregulated "soft money" spent by the two parties, political candidates in 1996 benefited from large expenditures by individuals and interest groups engaging in what is called **issues advocacy.** As a matter of constitutionally protected free speech, anyone may advocate any position during a political campaign without being subject to federal regulation, so long as they are not explicitly tied to or coordinated with any candidate's campaign organization. Some estimates suggest that groups and individuals spent as much as $150 million on issues advocacy—generally through television advertising—during the 1996 elections.[19]

Some groups are careful not to mention particular candidates in their issues ads to avoid any suggestion that they might merely be fronts for a candidate's campaign committee. Most issues ads, however, are attacks on the opposing candidate's record or character. Organized labor spent more than $35 million in 1996 to attack a number of Republican candidates for the House of Representatives. Business groups launched their own multimillion-dollar issues campaign to defend the GOP House members targeted by labor.[20]

In some instances, issues campaigns seem to violate federal election law by actually being coordinated with candidate or party committees. Democrats, for example, have charged that a 1996 issues campaign nominally run by Americans for Tax Reform, a conservative nonprofit group, was actually controlled by the Republican National Committee. Americans for Tax Reform spent roughly $4 million in 1996 on an issues campaign supporting Republican candidates in 150 House districts. The campaign was directed by a former RNC official. The RNC admits that it donated $4.6 million to the group, but denies any further involvement with the antitax group's efforts.[21]

In 1996, 1997, and 1998, Senators John McCain and Russell Feingold initiated an effort to pass legislation to restrict both soft-money contributions and issues advocacy. A combination of partisan and constitutional concerns, however, repeatedly doomed the McCain-Feingold initiative to defeat.

In general, efforts to change the rules governing campaign expenditures are undermined by constitutional issues or by the fact that one political party fears that change would help its opponent. Thus, for example, Democrats are more dependent upon PACs than are Republicans and are, as a result, suspicious about efforts to diminish PAC spending. The GOP, on the other hand, is generally able to raise more money than the Democrats and is, as a result, dubious about calls for limits on soft-money spending.

IMPLICATIONS FOR DEMOCRACY

The important role played by private funds in American politics affects the balance of power among contending social groups. Politicians need large amounts of money to campaign successfully for major offices. This fact inevitably ties

issues advocacy

independent spending by individuals or interest groups on a campaign issue but not directly tied to a particular candidate

Ellen Malcolm, president of EMILY's List, at a fund-raising event for the group.

their interests to the interests of the groups and forces that can provide this money. In a nation as large and diverse as the United States, to be sure, campaign contributors represent many different groups and often represent clashing interests. Business groups, labor groups, environmental groups, and pro-choice and right-to-life forces all contribute millions of dollars to political campaigns. Through such PACs as EMILY's List, women's groups contribute millions of dollars to women running for political office. One set of trade associations may contribute millions to win politicians' support for telecommunications reform, while another set may contribute just as much to block the same reform efforts. Insurance companies may contribute millions of dollars to Democrats to win their support for changes in the health care system, while physicians may contribute equal amounts to prevent the same changes from becoming law.

Despite this diversity of contributors, however, not all interests play a role in financing political campaigns. Only those interests that have a good deal of money to spend can make their interests known in this way. These interests are not monolithic, but they do not completely reflect the diversity of American society. The poor, the destitute, and the downtrodden also live in America and have an interest in the outcome of political campaigns. Who is to speak for them?

How Voters Decide

▶ What are the primary influences on voters' decisions?

Whatever the capacity of those with the money and power to influence the electoral process, it is the millions of individual decisions on election day that ultimately determine electoral outcomes. Sooner or later the choices of voters weigh more heavily than the schemes of campaign advisers or the leverage of interest groups.

Three types of factors influence voters' decisions at the polls: partisan loyalty, issue and policy concerns, and candidate characteristics.

PARTISAN LOYALTY

Many studies have shown that most Americans identify more or less strongly with one or the other of the two major political parties. Partisan loyalty was considerably stronger during the 1940s and 1950s than it is today. But even now most voters feel a certain sense of identification or kinship with the Democratic or Republican party. This sense of identification is often handed down from parents to children and is reinforced by social and cultural ties. Partisan identification predisposes voters in favor of their party's candidates and against those of the opposing party (see Figure 10.7). At the level of the presidential contest, issues and candidate personalities may become very important, although even here many Americans supported Bob Dole or Bill Clinton in the 1996 race only because of partisan loyalty. But partisanship is more likely to assert itself in the less-visible races, where issues and the candidates are not as

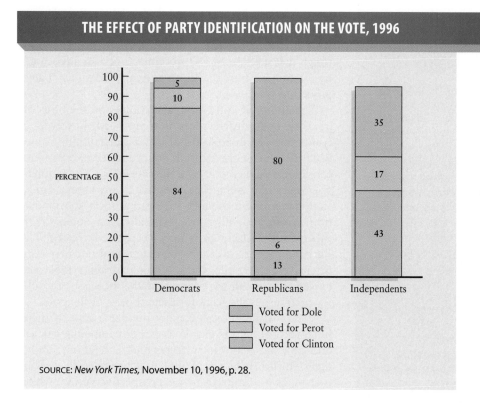

THE EFFECT OF PARTY IDENTIFICATION ON THE VOTE, 1996   Figure 10.7

PERCENTAGE

Democrats: 5, 10, 84
Republicans: 80, 6, 13
Independents: 35, 17, 43

Voted for Dole
Voted for Perot
Voted for Clinton

SOURCE: *New York Times,* November 10, 1996, p. 28.

well known. State legislative races, for example, are often decided by voters' party ties. Once formed, voters' partisan loyalties seldom change. Voters tend to keep their party affiliations unless some crisis causes them to reexamine the bases of their loyalties and to conclude that they have not given their support to the appropriate party. During these relatively infrequent periods of electoral change, millions of voters can change their party ties. For example, at the beginning of the New Deal era, between 1932 and 1936, millions of former Republicans transferred their allegiance to Franklin Roosevelt and the Democrats.

ISSUES

Issues and policy preferences are a second factor influencing voters' choices at the polls. Voters may cast their ballots for the candidate whose position on economic issues they believe to be closest to their own. Similarly, they may select the candidate who has what they believe to be the best record on foreign policy. Issues are more important in some races than others. If candidates actually "take issue" with one another, that is, articulate and publicize very different positions on important public questions, then voters are more likely to be able to identify and act on whatever policy preferences they may have. The 1992 election emphasized economic issues. Voters concerned with America's continuing economic recession and long-term economic prospects gave their support to Bill Clinton, who called for an end to "Reaganomics." Efforts by Bush to inject other issues, such as "family values," into the race

Students and Politics

As a member of the Council on Environmental Quality, Rutgers senior Heather Zichal meets weekly with Vice President Al Gore on some of the nation's most pressing environmental issues. Her introduction to political activism was not nearly so grand. Zichal attends college in New Jersey, a small state caught in a battle between industry and the environment. At Rutgers, Zichal founded the Sierra Student Coalition (SSC), an organization that, among other things, helped promote a "green" vote on campus by publishing a voter's guide to environmental issues and reminding students to vote in the 1997 election. The Sierra Club was happy to lend its support to Zichal's efforts; Sierra Club vice president Robby Cox visited the SSC in an effort to encourage grassroots organizing. The Center for Environmental Citizenship (CEC) of Washington, D.C., provided the students with information, including voting records, to arm the activists; the SSC was responsible for organizing and publicizing support for candidates taking environment-friendly positions. Their efforts helped lead many of the supported candidates into office; of the winners of the twenty-one statewide elected offices, nineteen were supported by the SSC. Zichal's work with the CEC helped her land a prized internship in the White House, but she doesn't necessarily want to continue in public policy. "I just want to work in an environmental community," she says. "I'm not doing this to be on the fast track to public policy."

SOURCE: Heather Zichal, interview with author, February 18, 1998.

proved generally unsuccessful. In 1996, Bob Dole's major issue was a pledge to cut federal income taxes. Bill Clinton called for a "middle-class bill of rights" and tough measures to deal with crime, and also advocated the "family values" that Bush had unsuccessfully championed in 1992.

The ability of voters to make choices on the basis of issue or policy preferences is diminished, however, if competing candidates do not differ substantially or do not focus their campaigns on policy matters. Very often, candidates deliberately take the safe course and emphasize topics that will not be offensive to any voters. Thus, candidates often trumpet their opposition to corruption, crime, and inflation. Presumably, few voters favor these things. Although it may be perfectly reasonable for candidates to take the safe course and remain as inoffensive as possible, this candidate strategy makes it extremely difficult for voters to make their issue or policy preferences the basis for their choices at the polls.

Voters' issue choices usually involve a mix of their judgments about the past behavior of competing parties and candidates and their hopes and fears about candidates' future behavior. Political scientists call choices that focus on future behavior **prospective voting,** while those based on past performance are called **retrospective voting.** To some extent, whether prospective or retrospective evaluation is more important in a particular election depends on the strategies of competing candidates. Candidates always endeavor to define the issues of an election in terms that will serve their interests. Incumbents running during a period of prosperity will seek to take credit for the economy's happy state and define the election as revolving around their record of success. This strategy encourages voters to make retrospective judgments. By contrast, an insurgent running during a period of economic uncertainty will tell voters it is time for a change and ask them to make prospective judgments. Thus, Bill Clinton focused on change in 1992 and prosperity in 1996, and through well-crafted media campaigns was able to define voters' agenda of choices.

prospective voting

voting based on the imagined future performance of a candidate

retrospective voting

voting based on the past performance of a candidate

CANDIDATE CHARACTERISTICS

Candidates' personal attributes always influence voters' decisions. Some analysts claim that voters prefer tall candidates to short ones, candidates with shorter names to candidates with longer names, and candidates with lighter hair to candidates with darker hair. Perhaps these rather frivolous criteria do play some role. But the more important candidate characteristics that affect voters' choices are race, ethnicity, religion, gender, geography, and social background. In general, voters prefer candidates who are closer to themselves in terms of these categories; voters presume that such candidates are likely to have views and perspectives close to their own. Moreover, they may be proud to see someone of their ethnic, religious, or geographic background in a position of leadership. This is why, for many years, politicians sought to "balance the ticket," making certain that their party's ticket included members of as many important groups as possible.

Just as a candidate's personal characteristics may attract some voters, they may repel others. Many voters are prejudiced against candidates of certain ethnic, racial, or religious groups. And for many years voters were reluctant to support the political candidacies of women, although this appears to be changing.

Voters also pay attention to candidates' personality characteristics, such as "decisiveness," "honesty," and "vigor." In recent years, integrity has become a key election issue. During the 1992 campaign, George Bush accused Bill Clinton of seeking to mislead voters about his anti–Vietnam War activities and his efforts to avoid the draft during the 1960s. This, Bush said, revealed that Clinton lacked the integrity required of a president. Clinton, in turn, accused Bush of resorting to mudslinging because of his poor standing in the polls—an indication of Bush's own character deficiencies. In 1996, Bob Dole sought to make "character" an issue in his campaign against Clinton. But Dole was not comfortable with something that might be called a "smear campaign" and did not press the character issue as vigorously as some of his advisers suggested.

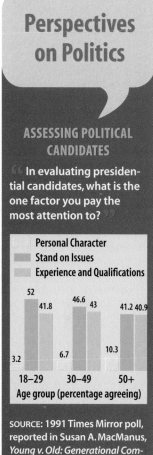

Perspectives on Politics

ASSESSING POLITICAL CANDIDATES

" In evaluating presidential candidates, what is the one factor you pay the most attention to? "

Personal Character
Stand on Issues
Experience and Qualifications

18–29: 3.2, 52, 41.8
30–49: 6.7, 46.6, 43
50+: 10.3, 41.2, 40.9

Age group (percentage agreeing)

SOURCE: 1991 Times Mirror poll, reported in Susan A. MacManus, *Young v. Old: Generational Combat in the 21st Century* (Boulder, CO: Westview, 1996), p. 87.

★ The Decline of Voting

▶ Why is political participation relatively low in the United States? Have attempts to increase participation succeeded? Why or why not? What are the implications for democracy?

Despite the sound and fury of contemporary American politics, one very important fact stands out: participation in the American political process is abysmally low. Politicians in recent years have been locked in intense struggles. Nevertheless, millions of citizens have remained uninvolved. For every American who voted in the bitterly fought 1994 congressional races, for example, two stayed home.[22]

This lack of popular involvement is sometimes attributed to the shortcomings of American citizens—many millions do not go to the trouble of registering and voting. In actuality, however, low levels of popular participation in American politics are as much (or more) the fault of politicians as of voters. Even with America's personal registration rules, higher levels of political participation could be achieved if competing political forces made a serious effort to mobilize voters. Unfortunately, however, contending political forces in the United States have found ways of attacking their opponents that do not require them to engage in voter mobilization, and many prefer to use these methods than to endeavor to bring more voters to the polls. The low levels of popular

Students and Politics

"With the support of musical artists such as Madonna, Queen Latifah, R.E.M., and Sheryl Crow—and with donated airtime on MTV for public service announcements—Rock the Vote is perhaps the most well known of young voter programs. In 1992, the organization helped to turn out a record number of young people following its unprecedented and much-publicized campaign. [In 1996] Rock the Vote [was] back in force, with PSAs [public service announcements] running on MTV and other stations, an interactive Web site where young people [could] register to vote on-line, a [toll-free] phone number for voter registration, and a lively presence at both the Democratic and Republican national conventions.

"According to [Rock the Vote organizer] Mark Strama, in the first four weeks of a [1996] register-by-phone campaign, Rock the Vote received 75,000 phone calls on its [toll-free] number. The organization also registered 10,000 young people at the Lollapalooza concert over the summer—bringing its total to more than 100,000 voters registered this year. And both parties' youth contingents are doing their share to inspire young voters, with a College Democrats' bus touring the country and the Young Republicans' Victory Train running from Iowa to New Mexico."

SOURCE: Joshua Wolf Shenk, "What Youth Politics?" *Who Cares* (Fall 1996), pp. 25–26. Reprinted with permission.

mobilization that are typical of contemporary American politics are very much a function of the way that politics is conducted in the United States today.

For most of U.S. history, elections were the main arenas of political combat. In recent years, however, elections have become less effective as ways of resolving political conflicts in the United States. Today's political struggles are frequently waged elsewhere, and crucial policy choices tend to be made outside the electoral realm. Rather than engage voters directly, contending political forces rely on such weapons of institutional combat as congressional investigations, media revelations, and judicial proceedings. In contemporary America, electoral success often fails to confer the capacity to govern, and political forces, even if they lose at the polls or do not even compete in the electoral arena, have been able to exercise considerable power.

ELECTIONS AND DEMOCRACY

During the political struggles of the past decades, politicians have sought to disgrace one another on national television, force their competitors to resign from office, and, in a number of cases, send their opponents to prison. Remarkably, one tactic that has not been so widely used is the mobilization of the electorate. Of course, Democrats and Republicans have contested each other and continue to contest each other in national elections. However, neither side has made much effort to mobilize *new* voters, to create strong local party organizations, or in general, to make full use of the electoral arena to defeat its enemies.

The 1993 Motor Voter bill was, at best, a very hesitant step in the direction of expanded voter participation. This act requires all states to allow voters to register by mail when they renew their driver's licenses (twenty-eight states already had similar mail-in procedures) and provides for the placement of voter registration forms in motor vehicle, public assistance, and military recruitment offices. This type of passive approach to registration still places the burden of action on the individual citizen and is not likely to result in many new voters, especially among the poor and uneducated. Since 1993, the National Voter Registration Act, as the Motor Voter bill is formally called, has added nearly five million new registrants to the voting rolls across the nation. Though this is a positive step, barely 10 percent of these new registrants have actually voted.[23] Mobilization requires more than the distribution of forms.[24]

It is certainly not true that politicians don't know how to mobilize new voters and expand electoral competition. Voter mobilization is hardly a mysterious process. It entails an investment of funds and organizational effort to register voters actively and bring them to the polls on election day. Occasionally, politicians demonstrate that they *do* know how to mobilize voters if they have a strong enough incentive. For example, a massive get-out-the-vote effort by Democrats to defeat neo-Nazi David Duke in the 1991 Louisiana gubernatorial election led to a voter turnout of over 80 percent of those eligible—twice the normal turnout level for a Louisiana election. And in the 1990s it was the GOP, through its alliance with conservative religious leaders, that made the more concerted effort to bring new voters into the electorate. This effort was limited in scope, but it played an important part in the Republican Party's capture of both houses of Congress in 1994. The GOP's gains from this limited strategy of mobilization demonstrate what could be achieved from a fuller mobilization of the national electorate. In 1996, many conservative Republican activists were unhappy with Bob Dole and did not vigorously mobilize their followers. As a result, turnout fell below 50 percent.

How extraordinary, then, that politicians stop short of attempting to expand the electorate to overwhelm their foes in competitive elections. Why is this? A large part of the answer to this question is that the decline of political party organizations over the past several decades strengthened politicians in both camps who were linked with and supported by the middle and upper-middle classes. Recall from Chapter 9 that party organization is an especially important instrument for enhancing the political influence of groups at the bottom of the social hierarchy—groups whose major political resource is numbers. Parties allowed politicians to organize the energies of large numbers of individuals from the lower classes to counter the superior financial and institutional resources available to those from the middle and upper classes.

The decline of party organization that resulted, in large measure, from the efforts of upper- and middle-class "reformers" over the years has undermined politicians such as union officials and Democratic and Republican "machine" leaders who had a stake in popular mobilization, while it has strengthened politicians with an upper-middle- or upper-class base. Recall the effects of registration laws that were discussed earlier in this chapter. As a result of these reforms, today's Democratic and Republican parties are dominated by different segments of the American upper-middle class. For the most part, contemporary Republicans speak for business and professionals from the private sector, while Democratic politicians and political activists are drawn from and speak for upper-middle-class professionals in the public and not-for-profit sectors.

Both sides give lip service to the idea of fuller popular participation in political life. Politicians and their upper-middle-class constituents in both camps, however, have access to a variety of different political resources—the news media, the courts, universities, and interest groups, to say nothing of substantial financial resources. As a result, neither side has much need for or interest in political tactics that might, in effect, stir up trouble from below. Both sides prefer to compete for power without engaging in full-scale popular mobilization. Without mobilization drives that might encourage low-income citizens or minorities to register and actually to vote, the population that does vote tends to be wealthier, whiter, and better educated than the population as a whole. Figure 10.8 shows the marked differences in voter turnout linked to ethnic group, education level, and employment status. This trend has created a political process whose class bias is so obvious and egregious that, if it continues, Americans may have to begin adding a qualifier when they describe their politics

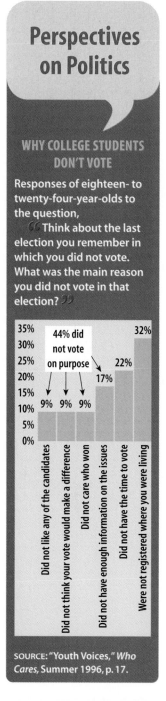

Perspectives on Politics

WHY COLLEGE STUDENTS DON'T VOTE

Responses of eighteen- to twenty-four-year-olds to the question, "Think about the last election you remember in which you did not vote. What was the main reason you did not vote in that election?"

44% did not vote on purpose

Did not like any of the candidates	Did not think your vote would make a difference	Did not care who won	Did not have enough information on the issues	Did not have the time to vote	Were not registered where you were living
9%	9%	9%	17%	22%	32%

SOURCE: "Youth Voices," *Who Cares,* Summer 1996, p. 17.

Figure 10.8   THE PERCENTAGE OF AMERICANS WHO VOTED, 1976–96

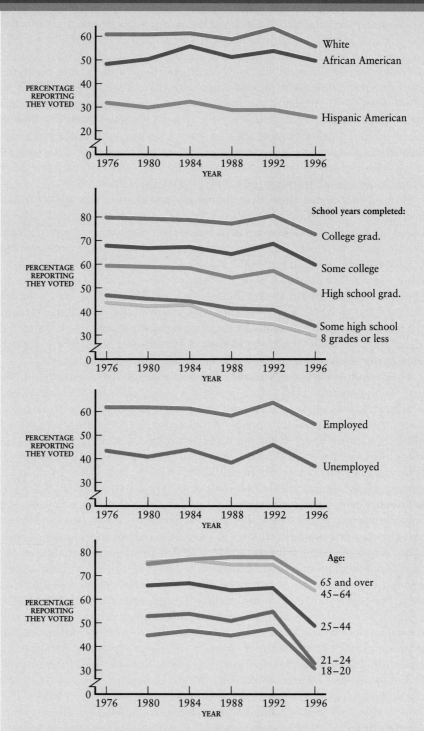

SOURCES: U.S. Bureau of the Census, *Statistical Abstract of the United States: 1994* (Washington, DC: Government Printing Office, 1994), p. 283; and http://www.census.gov/population/socdemo/voting/history/vot23.txt.

Whether or not Americans are likely to vote depends in part on their ethnic group, education level, employment status, and age.

as democratic. Perhaps the terms "semidemocratic," "quasidemocratic," or "neodemocratic" are in order to describe a political process in which ordinary voters have as little influence as they do in contemporary America.

ELECTIONS AND EQUALITY

In a quasidemocratic political process, those who do not participate are inherently unequal. It is because of the quasidemocratic character of American politics that both political parties today focus more on the middle-class concerns of deficits and taxes and far less on the working-class concern of unemployment. Is it not because of these quasidemocratic politics that the two parties argue about how much to cut social programs to balance the budget while barely mentioning the various tax deductions enjoyed by upper-middle-income voters?

ELECTIONS AND LIBERTY

Even a quasidemocratic process is better than none. Despite its imperfections, the electoral process remains an essential bulwark of liberty. The need to campaign for office and the fear of defeat is very much on the minds of politicians. After all, this is why they go to enormous lengths to raise the huge amounts of money needed for modern campaigns. Moreover, the fact that voters can remove officials who abuse their power and betray the public trust gives Americans, even in these quasidemocratic times, something akin to the right of revolution that political philosophers such as John Locke saw as an essential safeguard of liberty.

★ The Citizen's Role

In a sense, the role of the citizen in a democracy is obvious. Citizens have a right to vote. If citizens do not vote, then liberty, equality, and democracy become meaningless terms. To make democracy more vital and effective, however, citizens need to do more than vote. There are many opportunities for citizens, including college students, to become actively involved in the political process. Political parties and political campaigns are eager to sign on volunteer workers. Usually, the addresses and phone numbers of campaign offices are well publicized before elections. In addition, information about how to become involved with campaigns is available on the Internet from candidates' web sites. Political work can be fun and rewarding. Campaign workers can make a real difference in bolstering voter turnout and even in persuading undecided voters one way or the other.

College students can be extremely effective campaigners. For example, Jonathan Sweeney, an Arizona State University student from Boston, Massachusetts, worked as a student campaigner for the Clinton-Gore ticket in 1992. Sweeney was credited with helping to register more than 5,000 new Democratic voters in the Tempe, Arizona, area. He received an invitation to the Clinton inaugural ball in Washington for his efforts.[25]

> STUDENTS AND POLITICS

Sometimes students do even more than work in campaigns: sometimes they run for, and win, public office. Paul Soglin, the former mayor of Madison, Wisconsin, was a University of Wisconsin undergraduate when he began running for office. Similarly, Cornell University student David Lytell was for several years an important Ithaca, New York, alderman. After Lytell left Cornell, he went to work as a White House staffer, where he helped to design the White House web page.

As these examples suggest, significant opportunities exist for citizen involvement in American electoral politics. The contemporary political process may be quasidemocratic, but it need not remain so.

★ Summary

At the time of America's founding, the right to vote was generally limited to white males over the age of twenty-one. Many states also limited voting rights to those who owned property. Over the years, voting rights were expanded to give all adult Americans the right to participate in elections. Despite this, only about half of all American citizens over the age of eighteen actually vote in presidential elections. Turnout is limited by America's voter registration requirements and the absence of a strong party system to "get out the vote."

Three types of elections are held in the United States: general elections, primary elections, and runoff elections. In most contests, the candidate winning a plurality of the vote is the victor. In some contests, however, victory requires a majority of the votes cast, while others rely on proportional representation. State legislatures draw the boundaries of electoral districts. Often, political forces use a redistricting technique called gerrymandering to attempt to gain political advantage. Presidential elections are different from other American electoral contests. The president is elected indirectly through the electoral college.

Election campaigns are directed by candidates and their advisers. Candidates must secure endorsements, construct an organization, and raise money for both the primary and the general elections. Funds are raised from individuals and from political action committees. Presidential candidates must campaign in a series of statewide primaries and caucuses that lead up to the national party conventions, where the formal Democratic and Republican nominations take place. In addition to candidates' efforts, election outcomes are decided by partisan loyalty, voter response to issues, and voter response to candidates' personalities and qualifications.

The fact that many Americans do not vote gives the American political process a quasidemocratic character. Nonvoters tend to be drawn from low-income, low-education, and minority groups. Neither political party has shown much interest in vigorously promoting voter participation.

FOR FURTHER READING

Black, Earl, and Merle Black. *The Vital South: How Presidents Are Elected*. Cambridge, MA: Harvard University Press, 1992.

Carmines, Edward G., and James Stimson. *Issue Evolution: The Racial Transformation of American Politics*. Princeton, NJ: Princeton University Press, 1988.

Fowler, Linda, and Robert D. McClure. *Political Ambition: Who Decides to Run for Congress.* New Haven, CT: Yale University Press, 1989.

Ginsberg, Benjamin, and Martin Shefter. *Politics by Other Means: Institutional Conflict and the Declining Significance of Elections in America.* New York: Norton, 1999.

Piven, Frances Fox, and Richard A. Cloward. *Why Americans Don't Vote.* New York: Pantheon, 1988.

Sorauf, Frank. *Inside Campaign Finance: Myths and Realities.* New Haven, CT: Yale University Press, 1992.

Tate, Katherine. *From Protest to Politics: The New Black Voters in American Elections.* Cambridge, MA: Harvard University Press, 1994.

Wilcox, Clyde. *God's Warriors: The Christian Right in Twentieth-Century America.* Baltimore: Johns Hopkins University Press, 1991.

Witt, Linda, Karen Paget, and Glenna Matthews. *Running as a Woman: Gender and Power in American Politics.* New York: Free Press, 1994.

STUDY OUTLINE

Elections in America

1. In Democratic systems, elections can be used to replace current officeholders as well as to serve as institutions of legitimation.
2. Elections also help to promote government accountability and serve as a source of protection for groups in society.
3. In the American federal system, the responsibility for organizing elections rests largely with state and local governments.
4. Throughout American history, there has been a progressive, if uneven, expansion of suffrage to groups such as African Americans, women, and youths.
5. Though the United States now has a system of universal suffrage, voter turnout continues to be low.
6. State legislators routinely seek to influence electoral outcomes by manipulating the organization of electoral districts.
7. Prior to the 1890s, voters cast ballots according to political parties. The advent of the neutral ballot allowed voters to choose individual candidates rather than a political party as a whole.
8. Americans do not vote directly for presidential candidates. Rather, they choose electors who are pledged to support a party's presidential candidate.

Election Campaigns

1. The first step in campaigning involves the organization of supporters to help the candidate raise funds and create public name recognition.
2. The next steps of campaigning involve hiring experts—campaign managers, media consultants, pollsters, etc.—to aid in developing issues and a message and communicating them to the public.
3. Because most of the time a major party nomination is necessary for electoral success, candidates must seek a party's nomination in primary elections.

Presidential Elections

1. Presidential candidates secure a party's nomination by running in state party primaries and caucuses.
2. Nominations of presidential candidates were first made in caucuses of a party's members of Congress. This system was replaced, in the 1830s, by nominating conventions, which were designed to be a more democratic, deliberative method of nominating candidates.
3. Contemporary conventions merely ratify a party's presidential and vice presidential nominations, although conventions still draft the party platform and adopt rules governing the party and its future conventions.
4. General elections in local races involve labor-intensive campaigns, whereas general elections in statewide and national campaigns are more capital-intensive.
5. In capital-intensive campaigns, the main technique is to use the broadcast media to present the electorate with themes and issues that will induce them to support one candidate over another.

Money and Politics

1. Campaign funds in the United States are provided by small, direct-mail contributions, large gifts, PACs, political parties, candidates' personal resources, and public funding. In 1996, some candidates also benefited from issues advocacy.
2. Campaign finance is regulated by the Federal Elections Campaign Act of 1971. Following the 1996 elections, the role of soft money was scrutinized. The McCain-Feingold bill, a bipartisan attempt to restrict soft money contributions and issues advocacy, failed in consecutive years to gain support in Congress.
3. The role played by private money in American politics affects the relative power of social groups. As a result, less affluent groups have considerably less power in the political system.

How Voters Decide

1. Three factors influence voters' decisions at the polls: partisan loyalty, issues, and candidate characteristics.
2. Partisan loyalty predisposes voters in favor of their party's candidates and against those of the opposing party.
3. The impact of issues and policy preferences on electoral choice is diminished if competing candidates do not differ substantially or do not focus their campaigns on policy matters.
4. Candidates' attributes and personality characteristics always influence voters' decisions.
5. The salience of these three bases of electoral choice varies from contest to contest and from voter to voter.

The Decline of Voting

1. Participation in elections in the United States is low and relatively little effort has been made to mobilize voters because contending political forces rely less on elections to resolve political conflicts.
2. The Motor Voter bill was a hesitant step toward expanding voter participation.
3. The decline of political parties has strengthened the ties between elected leaders and members of the upper and middle classes, who tend to vote more regularly.
4. The quasidemocratic features of the American electoral system reveal its inherent inequality.

PRACTICE QUIZ

1. What is the most important difference between democratic and authoritarian electoral systems?
   a) The latter do not allow the defeat of those in power.
   b) There are no elections in authoritarian systems.
   c) Democratic systems use elections as a safety valve for social discontent.
   d) Authoritarian elections are not organized by party.

2. The neutral ballot made it possible for voters to
   a) vote the party line.
   b) split-ticket vote.
   c) send clear mandates for policy change.
   d) both a and b

3. Which of the following best describes the electorate in the United States prior to the 1820s?
   a) landowning white males over the age of 21
   b) all white males
   c) all literate males
   d) "universal suffrage"

4. Which of the following negatively impacts voter turnout in the United States?
   a) registration requirements
   b) weak parties
   c) neither a nor b
   d) both a and b

5. What is the difference between an open and a closed primary?
   a) You must pay a poll tax to vote in a closed primary.
   b) Open primaries allow voters to split the ticket.
   c) In closed primaries, only registered members of a political party may vote to select that party's candidates.
   d) They are fundamentally the same thing.

6. What are the potential consequences of ideological struggles in primary contests?
   a) General election chances may be undermined.
   b) Party extremists may win the nomination.
   c) Typical party supporters may refuse to support the party's nominee.
   d) all of the above

7. What is the most fundamental change in national conventions in the twentieth century?
   a) They no longer nominate presidential candidates.
   b) Now party platforms are written at the convention.
   c) The participation of electoral officials in conventions has continued to decline.
   d) none of the above

8. Which of the following is not an example of a media technique introduced in the 1992 presidential campaign?
   a) the spot advertisement
   b) the town meeting
   c) the infomercial
   d) a, b, and c were all introduced in 1992.

9. In *Buckley v. Valeo,* the Supreme Court ruled that
   a) PAC donations to campaigns are constitutionally protected.
   b) The right of individuals to spend their own money to campaign is constitutionally protected.
   c) The political system is corrupt.
   d) The Federal Elections Campaign Act is unconstitutional.

10. Partisan loyalty
    a) is often handed down from parents to children.
    b) changes frequently.
    c) has little impact on electoral choice.
    d) is mandated in states with closed primaries.

CRITICAL THINKING QUESTIONS

1. Describe the expansion of suffrage in the United States since the Founding. Why might the government have denied participation to so many for so long? What forces have influenced the eventual expansion of voting rights? What impact has the expansion of suffrage had on political parties, elections, and governance in the United States?

2. What are the sources of campaign money in American politics? Why do candidates for public office need to raise so much money? How has the government sought to balance the competing ideals of free expression and equal representation in regard to campaign financing? Is this yet another example of a conflict between liberty and democracy?

KEY TERMS

benign gerrymandering (p. 364)
campaign (p. 369)
caucus (political) (p. 374)
closed caucus (p. 374)
closed primary (p. 362)
coattail effect (p. 365)
delegates (p. 378)
electoral college (p. 367)
gerrymandering (p. 364)
incumbent (p. 369)
infomercial (p. 381)
issues advocacy (p. 387)
majority system (p. 363)

midterm elections (p. 357)
minority district (p. 364)
open caucus (p. 374)
open primary (p. 362)
platform (p. 376)
plurality system (p. 363)
political action committee (PAC) (p. 383)
poll tax (p. 357)
primary elections (p. 362)
proportional representation (p. 363)
prospective voting (p. 390)
referendum (p. 362)

retrospective voting (p. 390)
soft money (p. 383)
split-ticket voting (p. 365)
spot advertisement (p. 380)
straight-ticket voting (p. 365)
suffrage (p. 355)
superdelegate (p. 378)
town meeting (p. 380)
turnout (p. 359)
unit rule (p. 376)
winner-take-all system (p. 376)

11

Groups and

Interests

IN March 1995, about midway into the first one hundred days of the Republican-led 104th Congress, seven college students from Oregon met with Oregon senator Mark Hatfield, chairman of the powerful Senate Appropriations Committee, to persuade him to oppose cuts in the budget for student aid programs. Senator Hatfield, a long-standing member of the liberal wing of the Republican Party, cordially endorsed the students' goals but warned them that since the majority of Republicans in Congress were so strongly committed to the goals expressed in the Republican Contract with America and to the hundreds of billions of dollars of cuts that would be required to balance the federal budget by 2002, that the only way to protect the student aid program from complete elimination was to lobby mightily in favor of the program but to be ready to accept severe cuts in its funding. Few of the students' many sympathizers in Congress were going to be willing to go any further than that.

Meanwhile, student rallies were held on a number of East Coast campuses. These efforts generated letters and telephone calls estimated in the thousands.[1] An entirely new group was formed, the National Association of Students in Higher Education (NASHE), to concentrate exclusively on student aid, supplementing the efforts of the established general student interest group, the United States Students Association, which was involved in a variety of policy issues apart from student aid, and which also had a reputation for being too liberal for the Republican majority in the Congress. After four years of effort, NASHE is still small, but in conjunction with state-level student groups is beginning to offer testimony on Capitol Hill on issues relating to financial aid and the rising cost of higher education. Communication among the organizers and potential affiliates takes place over the Internet. Could this be a modern version of the "committees of correspondence" that helped mobilize colonial opposition to British rule in the years prior to the Revolution?

It is not an exaggeration to compare the 1995 student effort to citizen activities that had so impressed Alexis de Tocqueville in the 1830s. In Tocqueville's view, the genius of American democracy lay in "voluntary association." Tocqueville observed that Americans were not particularly civic-minded most of the time and were happy to go their individual ways seeking their fortunes as opportunity and imagination drove them. But, like the Minutemen of the Revolution, when a threat to their community or way of life was perceived, Americans mobilized into "voluntary associations" to engage in politics long enough to put things right.[2]

Thus our comparison is most appropriate. A few hundred college students, feeling the threat of discontinued federal assistance, set aside their books and laptop computers and formed a voluntary association to engage in politics

Students and Politics

The oldest national student advocacy group, the United States Student Association (USSA), uses its grassroots support to maintain a paid staff of recent college graduates in Washington, including a full-time lobbyist. The USSA fights for issues such as minimizing student fare increases on public transportation and maintaining affirmative action in higher education. Though many believe that the USSA's liberal positions are not representative of the full range of students' opinions, the organization continues to have a large support base and has helped win several legislative victories in Congress on matters of affirmative action and student financial aid, including increasing Pell grants and blocking legislation that would have prohibited consideration of gender, race, or national origin in admissions at universities that receive federal funds. The organization has gained a strong trust from its membership, due to its obvious influence on powerful members of both parties, including Senator Barbara Boxer of California, who has called USSA "an effective and forceful voice for students on Capitol Hill."

long enough to put their demands on the government agenda. In Tocqueville's day, such a voluntary association would have focused on local and state governments. Today the focus of group activity includes the national government as well, because groups go wherever power is. The fact that the NASHE was still a small group after four years of organizing does not negate the comparison—it makes it more realistic, demonstrating that in our time, and probably in the 1830s, it is simply not easy to get people to invest time and money into organization, even when ample threat or incentive is present.

As long as freedom exists, groups will organize and attempt to exert their influence over the political process. And groups will form wherever power exists. It should therefore be no surprise that the most impressive growth in the number and scale of interest groups has been at the national level since the 1930s. But even as the growth of the national government leveled off in the 1970s and 1980s, and actually declined in the late 1980s and 1990s, the spread of interest groups continued. It is no longer just the expansion of the national government that spawns interest groups, but the *existence* of that government with all the power it possesses. As long as there is a powerful government in the United States, there will be a large network of interest groups around it.

The framers of the American Constitution feared the power that could be wielded by organized interests. Yet they believed that interest groups thrived because of liberty—the freedom that all Americans enjoyed to organize and express their views. If the government were given the power to regulate or in any way to forbid efforts by organized interests to interfere in the political process, the government would in effect have the power to suppress liberty. The solution to this dilemma was presented by James Madison:

> Take in a greater variety of parties and interest [and] you make it less probable that a majority of the whole will have a common motive to invade the rights of other citizens. . . . [Hence the advantage] enjoyed by a large over a small republic.[3]

According to the Madisonian theory, a good constitution encourages multitudes of interests so that no single interest, which he called a "faction," can ever tyrannize the others. The basic assumption is that competition among interests will produce balance, with all the interests regulating each other.[4] Today, this Madisonian principle of regulation is called **pluralism**. According to pluralist theory, all interests are and should be free to compete for influence in the United States. Moreover, according to a pluralist doctrine, the outcome of this competition is compromise and moderation, since no group is likely to be able to achieve any of its goals without accommodating itself to some of the views of its many competitors.[5]

pluralism

the theory that all interests are and should be free to compete for influence in the government. The outcome of this competition is compromise and moderation

Tens of thousands of organized groups have formed in the United States, ranging from civic associations to huge nationwide groups like the National Rifle Association, whose chief cause is opposition to restrictions on gun own-

The NRA attempted to deflect some liberal criticism by starting a publicity campaign for gun safety, symbolized by mascot Eddie the Eagle.

ership, or Common Cause, a public-interest group that advocates a variety of liberal political reforms. Despite the array of interest groups in American politics, however, we can be sure neither that all interests are represented equally nor that the results of this group competition are consistent with the common good. One criticism of interest-group pluralism is its class bias in favor of those with greater financial resources. As one critic put it, "The flaw in the pluralist heaven is that the heavenly chorus sings with a strong upper-class accent."[6] Another assumption of pluralism is that all groups have equal access to the political process and that achieving an outcome favorable to a particular group depends only upon that group's strength and resources, not upon biases inherent in the political system. But, as we shall see, group politics is a political format that has worked and continues to work more to the advantage of some types of interests than others.

- **■ *In this chapter, we will examine some of the antecedents and consequences of interest-group politics in the United States. We will first seek to understand the character of interest groups.*** We will look at types of interests, the organizational components of groups, and the characteristics of members. We will also examine the important question of why people join interest groups.

- **■ *Second, we will assess the growth of interest-group activity in recent American political history.*** The number of interest groups has proliferated in recent years and we will examine the reasons why.

- **■ *Third, we will review and evaluate the strategies that competing groups use in their struggles for influence.*** The quest for political influence takes many forms.

- **■ *We conclude by evaluating some of the potential problems in trying to reduce the influence of interest groups in the political process.*** Interest-group politics is biased in favor of the most wealthy and powerful, but attempts to limit this influence are limits on liberty itself.

Student Perspectives

POLICY CHALLENGES FACING AMERICA

In their book *Revolution X*, Rob Nelson and Jon Cowan, founders of the interest group Lead or Leave, contend that "our political leaders have run up tremendous debts—economic, social and environmental burdens that our generation and generations to come must confront." Lead or Leave tried to mobilize young Americans through voter education and registration strategies with a focus on thirteen policy challenges for the future:

1. create good jobs
2. protect the planet
3. control crime
4. prevent AIDS
5. reinvent Social Security
6. design a post–Cold War military
7. make education affordable
8. give equal rights to gays
9. help end homelessness
10. guarantee freedom of choice
11. trim America's budget
12. win affordable health care
13. reform American politics.

SOURCE: Rob Nelson and Jon Cowan, *Revolution X: A Survival Guide for Our Generation* (New York: Penguin, 1994), pp. xvii, 107.

The Character of Interest Groups

▶ Why do interest groups form?

▶ What interests are represented by these groups?

▶ What are the organizational components of interest groups?

▶ What are the benefits of interest-group membership?

▶ What are the characteristics of interest-group members?

Individuals form groups in order to increase the chance that their views will be heard and their interests treated favorably by the government. Interest groups are organized to influence governmental decisions. There are an enormous number of interest groups in the United States, and millions of Americans are members of one or more groups, at least to the extent of paying dues or attending an occasional meeting.

By representing the interests of such large numbers of people and encouraging political participation, organized groups can and do enhance American democracy. Organized groups educate their members about issues that affect them. Groups lobby members of Congress and the executive, engage in litigation, and generally represent their members' interests in the political arena. Groups mobilize their members for elections and grassroots lobbying efforts, thus encouraging participation. Interest groups also monitor government programs to make certain that their members are not adversely affected. In all these ways, organized interests can be said to promote democratic politics. But because not all interests are represented equally, interest-group politics works to the advantage of some and the disadvantage of others.

WHAT INTERESTS ARE REPRESENTED?

Business and Agricultural Groups   Interest groups come in as many shapes and sizes as the interests they represent. When most people think about interest groups, they immediately think of groups with a direct economic interest in governmental actions. These groups are generally supported by groups of producers or manufacturers in a particular economic sector. Examples of this type of group include the National Petroleum Refiners Association and the American Farm Bureau Federation. At the same time that broadly representative groups such as these are active in Washington, specific companies, such as Shell Oil, International Business Machines, and General Motors, may be active on certain issues that are of particular concern to them.

Labor Groups   Labor organizations are equally active lobbyists. The AFL-CIO, the United Mine Workers, and the Teamsters are all groups that lobby on behalf of organized labor. In recent years, groups have arisen to further the interests of public employees, the most significant among these being the American Federation of State, County, and Municipal Employees.

Professional Associations   Professional lobbies like the American Bar Association and the American Medical Association have been particularly successful in furthering their members' interests in state and federal legislatures. Financial institutions, represented by organizations such as the American Bankers Association and the National Savings & Loan League, although often less visible than other lobbies, also play an important role in shaping legislative policy.

Public Interest Groups   Recent years have witnessed the growth of a powerful "public interest" lobby, purporting to represent interests whose concerns are not addressed by traditional lobbies. These groups have been most visible in the consumer protection and environmental policy areas, although public interest groups cover a broad range of issues. The National Resources Defense Council, the Sierra Club, the Union of Concerned Scientists, and Common Cause are all examples of public interest groups.

Ideological Groups   Closely related to and overlapping public interest groups are ideological groups, organized in support of a particular political or philosophical perspective. People for the American Way, for example, promotes liberal values, whereas the Christian Coalition focuses on conservative social goals and the National Taxpayers Union campaigns to reduce the size of the federal government.

Public-Sector Groups   The perceived need for representation on Capitol Hill has generated a public-sector lobby in the past several years, including the National League of Cities and the "research" lobby. The latter group comprises think tanks and universities that have an interest in obtaining government funds for research and support, and it includes such institutions as Harvard University, the Brookings Institution, and the American Enterprise Institute. Indeed, universities have expanded their lobbying efforts even as they have reduced faculty positions and course offerings.[7]

ORGANIZATIONAL COMPONENTS

Although there are many interest groups, most share certain key organizational components. These include leadership, money, an agency or office, and members.

First, every group must have a leadership and decision-making structure. For some groups, this structure is very simple. For others, it can be quite elaborate and involve hundreds of local chapters that are melded into a national apparatus. Interest-group leadership is, in some respects, analogous to business leadership. Many interest groups are initially organized by political entrepreneurs with a strong commitment to a particular set of goals. Such entrepreneurs see the formation of a group as a means both for achieving those goals and for enhancing their own influence in the political process. Just as is true in the business world, however, successful groups often become bureaucratized; the initial entrepreneurial leadership is replaced by a paid professional staff. In the 1960s, for example, Ralph Nader led a loosely organized band of consumer advocates ("Nader's Raiders") in a crusade for product safety that resulted in the enactment of a number of pieces of legislation and numerous regulations, such as the requirement that all new cars be equipped with air bags. Today, Nader remains active in the consumer movement, and his ragtag band of raiders has been transformed into a well-organized and

President Bill Clinton greets members of the American Federation of State, County, and Municipal Employees.

Consumer activist Ralph Nader, shown here at a demonstration in support of mandatory air bags in cars, founded a network of consumer advocacy groups.

Members and supporters of the National Organization for Women regularly participate in rallies organized by the group. This rally was held on the Mall in Washington in 1995.

well-financed phalanx of interlocked groups, including Public Citizen, the Center for the Study of Responsive Law, and the Center for Science in the Public Interest, all led by professional staffs.

Second, every interest group must build a financial structure capable of sustaining an organization and funding the group's activities. Most interest groups rely on membership dues and voluntary contributions from sympathizers. Many also sell some ancillary services to members, such as insurance and vacation tours. Third, most groups establish an agency that actually carries out the group's tasks. This may be a research organization, a public relations office, or a lobbying office in Washington or a state capital.

Finally, all interest groups must attract and keep members. Somehow, groups must persuade individuals to invest the money, time, energy, or effort required to take part in the group's activities. Members play a larger role in some groups than in others. In **membership associations,** group members actually serve on committees and engage in projects. In the case of labor unions, members may march on picket lines, and in the case of political or ideological groups, members may participate in demonstrations and protests. In another set of groups, **"staff organizations,"** a professional staff conducts most of the group's activities; members are called upon only to pay dues and make other contributions. Among the well-known public interest groups, some, such as the National Organization for Women (NOW), are membership groups, whereas others, such as Defenders of Wildlife and the Children's Defense Fund, are staff organizations.

The "Free Rider" Problem Whether they need individuals to volunteer or merely to write checks, both types of groups need to recruit and retain mem-

membership association

an organized group in which members actually play a substantial role, sitting on committees and engaging in group projects

staff organization

a type of membership group in which a professional staff conducts most of the group's activities

bers. Yet many groups find this task difficult, even when it comes to recruiting members who agree strongly with the group's goals. Why? As economist Mancur Olson explains, the benefits of a group's success are often broadly available and cannot be denied to nonmembers.[8] Such benefits can be called **collective goods.** This term is usually associated with certain government benefits, but it can also be applied to beneficial outcomes of interest-group activity. Following Olson's own example, suppose a number of private property owners live near a mosquito-infested swamp. Each owner wants this swamp cleared. But if one or a few of the owners were to clear the swamp alone, their actions would benefit all the other owners as well, without any effort on the part of those other owners. Each of the inactive owners would be a **free rider** on the efforts of the ones who cleared the swamp. Thus, there is a disincentive for any of the owners to undertake the job alone.

Since the number of concerned owners is small in this particular case, they might eventually be able to organize themselves to share the costs as well as enjoy the benefits of clearing the swamp. But suppose the numbers of interested people are increased. Suppose the common concern is not the neighborhood swamp but polluted air or groundwater involving thousands of residents in a region, or in fact millions of residents in a whole nation. National defense is the most obvious collective good whose benefits are shared by every resident, regardless of the taxes they pay or the support they provide. As the number of involved persons increases, or as the size of the group increases, the free rider phenomenon becomes more of a problem. Individuals do not have much incentive to become active members and supporters of a group that is already working more or less on their behalf. The group would no doubt be more influential if all concerned individuals were active members—if there were no free riders. But groups will not reduce their efforts just because free riders get the same benefits as dues-paying activists. In fact, groups may try even harder precisely because there are free riders, with the hope that the free riders will be encouraged to join in.

Why Join? Despite the free rider problem, interest groups offer numerous incentives to join. Most importantly, they make various "selective benefits" available only to group members. These benefits can be information-related, material, solidary, or purposive. Table 11.1 gives some examples of the range of benefits in each of these categories.

Informational benefits are the most widespread and important category of selective benefits offered to group members. Information is provided through conferences, training programs, and newsletters and other periodicals sent automatically to those who have paid membership dues.

Material benefits include anything that can be measured monetarily, such as special services, goods, and even money. A broad range of material benefits can be offered by groups to attract members. These benefits often include discount purchasing, shared advertising, and, perhaps most valuable of all, health and retirement insurance.

Another option identified on Table 11.1 is that of **solidary benefits.** The most notable of this class of benefits are the friendship and "networking" opportunities that membership provides. Another benefit that has become extremely important to many of the newer nonprofit and citizen groups is what has come to be called "consciousness-raising." One example of this can be

---

collective goods

benefits, sought by groups, that are broadly available and cannot be denied to nonmembers

free riders

those who enjoy the benefits of collective goods but did not participate in acquiring them

material benefits

special goods, services, or money provided to members of groups to entice others to join

solidary benefits

selective benefits of group membership that emphasize friendship, networking, and consciousness-raising

Table 11.1	SELECTIVE BENEFITS OF INTEREST GROUP MEMBERSHIP

Category	Benefits
Informational benefits	Conferences
	Professional contacts
	Training programs
	Publications
	Coordination among organizations
	Research
	Legal help
	Professional codes
	Collective bargaining
Material benefits	Travel packages
	Insurance
	Discounts on consumer goods
Solidary benefits	Friendship
	Networking opportunities
Purposive benefits	Advocacy
	Representation before government
	Participation in public affairs

SOURCE: Adapted from Jack Walker, Jr., *Mobilizing Interest Groups in America: Patrons, Professions, and Social Movements* (Ann Arbor: University of Michigan Press, 1991), p. 86.

purposive benefits

selective benefits of group membership that emphasize the purpose and accomplishments of the group

seen in the claims of many women's organizations that active participation conveys to each female member of the organization an enhanced sense of her own value and a stronger ability to advance individual as well as collective civil rights. A similar solidary or psychological benefit has been the mainstay of the appeal of group membership to discouraged and disillusioned African Americans since their emergence as a constitutionally free and equal people.

A fourth type of benefit involves the appeal of the purpose of an interest group. The benefits of religious interest groups provide us with the best examples of such **purposive benefits.** The Christian Right is a powerful movement made up of a number of interest groups that offer virtually no material benefits to their members. The growth and success of these groups depends upon the religious identifications and affirmations of their members. Many such religiously based interest groups have arisen, especially at state and local levels, throughout American history. For example, both the abolition and the prohibition movements were driven by religious interest groups whose main attractions were nonmaterial benefits.

Ideology itself, or the sharing of a commonly developed ideology, is another important nonmaterial benefit. Many of the most successful interest groups of the past twenty years have been citizen groups or public interest groups, whose members are brought together largely around shared ideological goals, including government reform, election and campaign reform, civil rights, economic equality, "family values," or even opposition to government itself.

The AARP and the Benefits of Membership One group that has been extremely successful in recruiting members and mobilizing them for political action is the American Association of Retired Persons (AARP). The AARP was founded in 1958 as a result of the efforts of a retired California high school principal, Ethel Percy Andrus, to find affordable health insurance for herself and for the thousands of members of the National Retired Teachers Association (NRTA). In 1955 she found an insurer who was willing to give NRTA members a low, group rate. In 1958, partly at the urging of the insurer (who found that insuring the elderly was quite profitable), Andrus founded the AARP. For the insurer it provided an expanded market; for Andrus it was a way to serve the ever-growing elderly population, whose problems and needs were expanding along with their numbers and their life expectancy.

Today, the AARP is a large and powerful organization with an annual income of $382 million. In addition, the organization receives $86 million in federal grants. Its national headquarters in Washington, D.C., staffed by 1,750 full-time employees, is so large that it has its own zip code. Its monthly periodical, *Modern Maturity,* has a circulation larger than the combined circulations of *Time, Newsweek,* and *US News and World Report.*[9]

How did this large organization overcome the free rider problem and recruit thirty-three million older people as members? First, no other organization on earth has ever provided more successfully the selective benefits necessary to overcome the free rider problem. It helps that the AARP began as an organization to provide affordable health insurance for aging members rather than as an organization to influence public policy. But that fact only strengthens the argument that members need short-term individual benefits if they are to invest effort in a longer-term and less concrete set of benefits. As the AARP evolved into a political interest group, its leadership also added more selective benefits for individual members. They provided guidance against consumer fraud, offered low-interest credit cards, evaluated and endorsed products that were deemed of best value to members, and provided auto insurance and a discounted mail-order pharmacy.

In a group as large as the AARP, members are bound to disagree on particular subjects, often creating serious factional disputes. But the resources of the AARP are so extensive that its leadership has been able to mobilize itself for each issue of importance to the group. One of its most successful methods of mobilization for political action is the "telephone tree," with which AARP leaders can quickly mobilize thousands of members for and against proposals that affect Social Security, Medicare, and other questions of security for the aging. A "telephone tree" in each state enables the state AARP chair to phone all of the AARP district directors, who then can phone the presidents of the dozens of local chapters, who can call their local officers and individual members. Within twenty-four hours, thousands of individual AARP members can be contacting local, state, and national officials to express their opposition to proposed legislation. It is no wonder that the AARP is respected and feared throughout Washington, D.C.

THE CHARACTERISTICS OF MEMBERS

Membership in interest groups is not randomly distributed in the population. People with higher incomes, higher levels of education, and management or professional occupations are much more likely to become members of groups than those who occupy the lower rungs on the socioeconomic ladder (see

A subscription to Modern Maturity is one of the selective benefits of membership in the AARP.

The political power of a group as large and well organized as the AARP is tremendous. AARP members can be counted on to protest whenever programs benefiting the elderly are threatened.

Figure 11.1   **INTEREST GROUP MEMBERSHIP BY INCOME LEVEL**

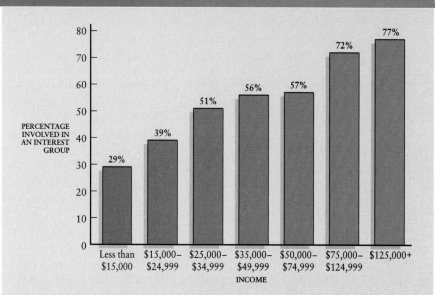

SOURCE: Kay Lehman Scholzman, "Voluntary Organizations in Politics: Who Gets Involved?" in *Representing Interests and Interest Group Representation,* ed. William Crotty, Mildred A. Schwartz, and John C. Green (Lanham, MD: University Press of America, 1994), p. 76.

The percentage of Americans who report that they are involved in an organization that takes a stand on political issues increases with income level.

Figure 11.1).[10] Well-educated, upper-income business and professional people are more likely to have the time and the money and to have acquired through the educational process the concerns and skills needed to play a role in a group or association. Moreover, for business and professional people, group membership may provide personal contacts and access to information that can help advance their careers. At the same time, of course, corporate entities—businesses and the like—usually have ample resources to form or participate in groups that seek to advance their causes.

The result is that interest-group politics in the United States tends to have a very pronounced upper-class bias. Certainly, there are many interest groups and political associations that have a working-class or lower-class membership—labor organizations or welfare-rights organizations, for example—but the great majority of interest groups and their members are drawn from the middle and upper-middle classes. In general, the "interests" served by interest groups are the interests of society's "haves." Even when interest groups take opposing positions on issues and policies, the conflicting positions they espouse usually reflect divisions among upper-income strata rather than conflicts between the upper and lower classes.

In general, to obtain adequate political representation, forces from the bottom rungs of the socioeconomic ladder must be organized on the massive scale associated with political parties. Parties can organize and mobilize the collective energies of large numbers of people who, as individuals, may have very limited resources. Interest groups, on the other hand, generally organize smaller numbers of the better-to-do. Thus, the relative importance of political parties and interest groups in American politics has far-ranging implications for the distribution of political power in the United States. As we saw in Chapter 9, political parties have declined in influence in recent years. Interest groups, on the other hand, as we shall see in the next section, have become much more numerous, more active, and more influential in American politics.

The Proliferation of Groups

▶ Why has the number of interest groups grown in recent years?
▶ What is the "New Politics" movement?

Over the past twenty-five years, there has been an enormous increase both in the number of interest groups seeking to play a role in the American political process and in the extent of their opportunity to influence that process. This explosion of interest-group activity has three basic origins—first, the expansion of the role of government during this period; second, the coming of age of a new and dynamic set of political forces in the United States—a set of forces that have relied heavily on "public interest" groups to advance their causes; and third, a surge explosion in the number and political vitality of grassroots and conservative groups.

THE EXPANSION OF GOVERNMENT

Modern governments' extensive economic and social programs have powerful politicizing effects, often sparking the organization of new groups and interests. The activities of organized groups are usually viewed in terms of their effects upon governmental action. But interest-group activity is often as much a consequence as an antecedent of governmental programs. Even when national policies are initially responses to the appeals of pressure groups, government involvement in any area can be a powerful stimulus for political organization and action by those whose interests are affected. For example, during the 1970s, expanded federal regulation of the automobile, oil, gas, education, and health care industries impelled each of these interests to increase substantially its efforts to influence the government's behavior. These efforts, in turn, spurred the organization of other groups to augment or counter the activities of the first.[11] Similarly, federal social programs have occasionally sparked political organization and action on the part of clientele groups seeking to influence the distribution of benefits and, in turn, the organization of groups opposed to the programs or their cost. For example, federal programs and court decisions in such areas as abortion and school prayer were the stimuli for political action and organization by fundamentalist religious groups. Thus, the expansion of government in recent decades has also stimulated increased group activity and organization.

One contemporary example of a proposed government program that sparked intensive organization and political action by affected interests is the case of regulating the tobacco industry. In 1997, an enormous lobbying battle broke out in Washington, D.C., over a proposed agreement regarding the liability of tobacco companies for tobacco-related illnesses. This agreement, reached between tobacco companies, state governments, trial lawyers (representing individuals and groups suing tobacco companies), and antismoking groups, called for the tobacco industry to pay the states and the trial lawyers nearly $400 billion over the next twenty-five years. In exchange the industry would receive protection from much of the litigation with which it is currently plagued. The settlement as negotiated would have required congressional and presidential approval.

After the settlement was proposed in June 1997, both the White House and some members of Congress began raising objections. Because of the enormous amounts of money involved, all the interested parties began intensive lobbying efforts aimed at both Congress and the executive branch. The tobacco industry retained nearly thirty lobbying firms at an initial cost of nearly $10 million to press its claims. During the first six months of 1997, the tobacco industry also contributed more than $2.5 million to political parties and candidates whom the industry thought could be helpful to its cause. One Washington lobbying firm, Verner, Liipfert, Bernhard, McPherson, and Hand, alone received nearly $5 million in fees from the four leading cigarette makers. The firm assigned a number of well-connected lobbyists, including former Texas governor Ann Richards, to press its clients' cause. Verner, Liipfert also hired pollsters, public relations firms, and economists to convince the public and the Washington establishment that the tobacco settlement made good sense.[12] Despite these efforts, the proposed tobacco settlement had not obtained congressional approval by mid-1998. Many Republicans feared that President Clinton would use the proceeds from the settlement to expand social programs, while some Democrats thought that tobacco companies were not being adequately punished.

THE NEW POLITICS MOVEMENT AND PUBLIC INTEREST GROUPS

The second factor accounting for the explosion of interest-group activity in recent years has been the emergence of a new set of forces in American politics that can collectively be called the "New Politics" movement.

The **New Politics movement** is made up of upper-middle-class professionals and intellectuals for whom the civil rights and antiwar movements were formative experiences, just as the Great Depression and World War II had been for their parents. The crusade against racial discrimination and the Vietnam War led these young men and women to see themselves as a political force in opposition to the public policies and politicians associated with the nation's postwar regime. In more recent years, the forces of New Politics have focused their attention on such issues as environmental protection, women's rights, and nuclear disarmament.

Members of the New Politics movement constructed or strengthened public interest groups such as Common Cause, the Sierra Club, the Environmental Defense Fund, Physicians for Social Responsibility, the National Organization for Women, and the various organizations formed by consumer activist Ralph Nader. Through these groups, New Politics forces were able to influence the media, Congress, and even the judiciary and enjoyed a remarkable degree of success during the late 1960s and early 1970s in securing the enactment of policies they favored. New Politics activists also played a major role in secur-

New Politics movement

a political movement that began in the 1960s and 1970s, made up of professionals and intellectuals for whom the civil rights and antiwar movements were formative experiences. The New Politics movement strengthened public interest groups

ing the enactment of environmental, consumer, and occupational health and safety legislation.

New Politics groups sought to distinguish themselves from other interest groups—business groups, in particular—by styling themselves as **public interest groups,** terminology which suggests that they served the general good rather than their own selfish interest. These groups' claims to represent *only* the public interest should be viewed with caution, however. Quite often, goals that are said to be in the general or public interest are also or indeed primarily in the particular interest of those who espouse them. It is not uncommon to find decidedly private interests seeking to hide behind the term "public interest." For example, in 1996, the *Washington Post* looked into the finances of one self-styled public interest group, "Contributions Watch." This group, presenting itself as an independent and nonpartisan organization working for campaign finance reform, released a study purporting to detail millions of dollars in political contributions to Democratic candidates by trial lawyers. The implication was that the lawyers' groups had made the contributions as part of their effort to defeat Republican reform proposals. The *Post*'s investigation revealed that Contributions Watch was created by a professional lobbying firm, State Affairs Co., which had been retained by a major Washington law firm, Covington and Burling, on behalf of its client, Philip Morris Tobacco. The giant tobacco company had sought the cover of "public interest" to mask an attack on its enemies, trial lawyers who are presently bringing or have already brought billions of dollars in damage suits against the tobacco companies.[13] Contributions Watch insisted that its report was accurate.

In recent years, the "squeaky-clean" reputation of public interest groups has been sullied by the questionable fund-raising practices of several groups. One important liberal public interest group, Citizen Action, which claims a nationwide membership of more than two million, was forced to close its national offices and dismiss its twenty national staff members after federal prosecutors charged that the group had been involved in an illegal financial arrangement with the Teamsters union. According to court papers filed in 1997, Citizens Action accepted contributions from the union and then made contributions to the 1996 re-election campaign of Teamsters president Ron Carey. In effect, Citizen Action served as a conduit for the illegal transfer of Teamsters funds into Carey's campaign. Before its demise, Citizen Action specialized in "issue campaigns" aimed at exposing lies and hypocrisy on the part of conservative politicians. While Citizen Action was foundering, a federal grand jury was looking into the fund-raising relationships between the Republican National Committee (RNC) and several Republican public interest groups, as part of an investigation of allegations that the RNC used these groups as conduits for political contributions from foreign business interests.[14]

These examples of the involvement of "public-interest" groups in what amounts to money laundering suggest that the term *public interest* should be used cautiously. Claims that a group and its programs serve only some abstract public interest should be treated with a healthy measure of skepticism.

CONSERVATIVE INTEREST GROUPS

The third factor associated with the expansion of interest-group politics in contemporary America has been an explosion of grassroots conservative activ-

public interest groups

groups that claim they serve the general good rather than their own particular interest

Many groups regularly demonstrate at the U.S. Capitol building. Members of Greenpeace, an environmental group, are shown here protesting against proposed environmental deregulation.

Students and Politics

While writing for her high school and college papers in South Carolina, Lori Cole experienced the bias of the media against her conservative ideas. "My high school advisor was supportive," she says. But when she arrived at the University of South Carolina, the campus paper was not so open-minded. "I had a problem getting my work published," reports Cole. "When I did, they changed the direction of the article in the name of space. They completely re-worded it, and I looked bad." Cole interned with an organization more sympathetic to her beliefs: the Eagle Forum, a conservative public interest group concentrating on education. While there, Cole assisted in several research and lobbying projects, including working against Title X, an appropriation for family planning, and spoke with several leading conservatives including former California representative Robert Dornan and Oklahoma representative J. C. Watts. After graduating, Cole returned to work for the Eagle Forum as director of their college outreach program. Cole says that her experience at the Eagle Forum helped to solidify her ideas, and taught her that breaking into politics works. "Don't be afraid of internships," she advises. "Meet people; you have to network. And stay strong in your beliefs."

SOURCE: Lori Cole, interview with author, Febuary 19, 1998.

ity. For example, the Christian Coalition, whose major focus is opposition to abortion, has nearly two million active members organized in local chapters in every state. Twenty of its state chapters have full-time staff and fifteen have annual budgets of over $200,000.[15] The National Taxpayers Union has several hundred local chapters. The National Federation of Independent Business (NFIB) has hundreds of active local chapters throughout the nation, particularly in the Midwest and Southeast. Associations dedicated to defending "property rights" exist at the local level throughout the West. Right-to-life groups are organized in virtually every U.S. congressional district. Even proponents of the rather exotic principle of "home schooling" are organized through the Home School Legal Defense Association (HSLDA), which has seventy-five regional chapters that, in turn, are linked to more than 3,000 local support groups.

These local conservative organizations were energized by the political struggles that have marked Bill Clinton's two terms. For example, battles over the restrictions on gun ownership in the Clinton administration's 1993 crime bill helped the National Rifle Association (NRA) energize local gun owners' groups throughout the country. The struggle over a proposed amendment to the 1993 education bill, which would have placed additional restrictions on home schooling, helped the HSLDA enroll thousands of active new members in its regional and local chapters. After an intense campaign, HSLDA succeeded in both defeating the amendment and enhancing the political awareness and activism of its formerly quiescent members. And, of course, the ongoing struggles over abortion and school prayer have helped the Christian Coalition, the Family Research Council, and other organizations that make up the Christian Right to expand the membership rolls of their state and local organizations. Antiabortion forces, in particular, are organized at the local level throughout the United States, ready to participate in political campaigns and legislative battles.

This extensive organization has meant that conservatives not only have been able to pressure the national government, but also have become a real presence in the corridors of state capitols, county seats, and city halls. For example, spurred by conservative groups and radio programs, legislators in all fifty states have introduced property rights legislation. Eighteen states have already enacted laws requiring a "takings impact analysis" before any new government regulation affecting property can go into effect.[16] Such legislation is designed to diminish the ability of state and local governments to enact restrictions on land use. Similarly, seventeen states, pressed by local conservative groups, have recently enacted legislation protecting or expanding the rights of gun owners.[17]

Christian groups have succeeded in large part because of their strong grassroots participation. This group in South Carolina is listening to Governor David Beasley during a "Traditional Family Values Rally."

Strategies: The Quest for Political Power

▶ What are some of the strategies interest groups use to gain influence?
▶ What are the purposes of these strategies?

As we have seen, people form interest groups in order to improve the probability that they and their interests will be heard and treated favorably by the government. The quest for political influence or power takes many forms, but among the most frequently used strategies are lobbying, establishing access to key decision makers, using the courts, going public, using electoral politics, and using bribery. These strategies do not exhaust all the possibilities, but they paint a broad picture of groups competing for power through the maximum utilization of their resources (see Figure 11.2).

LOBBYING

Lobbying is an attempt by an individual or a group to influence the passage of legislation by exerting direct pressure on members of the legislature. The person doing the lobbying is called a lobbyist. The First Amendment to the Constitution provides for the right to "petition the Government for a redress of grievances." But as early as the 1870s, "lobbying" became the common term for petitioning—and it is not an inaccurate one. Petitioning cannot take place on the floor of the House or Senate. Therefore, petitioners must confront members of Congress in the lobbies of the legislative chamber; this activity gave rise to the term "lobbying."

The Federal Regulation of Lobbying Act defines a lobbyist as "any person who shall engage himself for pay or any consideration for the purpose of

lobbying

a strategy by which organized interests seek to influence the passage of legislation by exerting direct pressure on members of the legislature

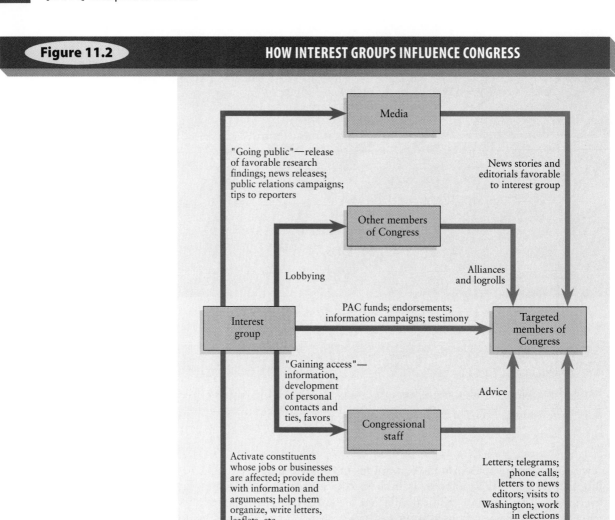

Figure 11.2

HOW INTEREST GROUPS INFLUENCE CONGRESS

attempting to influence the passage or defeat of any legislation of the Congress of the United States." Each lobbyist must register with the clerk of the House and the secretary of the Senate. Further legislation enacted in December 1995 requires all individuals lobbying the national government to register and disclose whom they represent, whom they lobby, what they are lobbying for, and how much they are paid. It is estimated currently that fewer than one-third of Washington's professional lobbyists are registered. The new law also prohibits certain types of nonprofit organizations that receive federal grants or contracts from using public funds for the purpose of lobbying the government. This portion of the law was intended by Republicans to dampen the lobbying activities of liberal public interest groups.

Lobbying involves a great deal of activity on the part of someone speaking for an interest. Lobbyists badger and buttonhole legislators, administrators, and committee staff members with facts about pertinent issues and facts or claims about public support of certain issues or facts.[18] Lobbyists can serve a useful purpose in the legislative and administrative processes by providing this kind of information. In 1978, during debate on a bill to expand the requirement for lobbying disclosures, Democratic senators Edward Kennedy of Massachusetts and Dick Clark of Iowa joined with Republican senator Robert Stafford of Vermont to issue the following statement: "Government without lobbying could not function. The flow of information to Congress and to every federal agency is a vital part of our democratic system."[19] But they also added that there is a darker side to lobbying—one that requires regulation.

Types of Lobbyists   The business of lobbying is uneven and unstable. Some groups send their own loyal members to Washington to lobby for them. These representatives usually possess a lot of knowledge about a particular issue and the group's position on it, but they have little knowledge about or experience in Washington or national politics. They tend not to remain in Washington beyond the campaign for their issue.

These lobbyists are waiting for members of Congress outside the House Ways and Means Committee room, in anticipation of arguing for their clients' interests.

Other groups select lobbyists with a considerable amount of Washington experience. During the battle over the 1996 federal budget, for example, medical specialists seeking favorable treatment under Medicare reimbursement rules retained a lobbying team that included former Minnesota Republican congressman Vin Weber, former New York Democratic congressman Tom Downey, and former Clinton chief legislative aide Patrick Griffin. Former Senate Finance Commitee chair Robert Packwood was retained by lumber mills and other small businesses to secure a cut in the estate tax. Similarly, in a fight between major airlines and regional carriers over airline taxes, the major airlines hired former transportation secretary James Burnley, former deputy Federal Aviation Administration administrator Linda Daschle (whose husband, Tom, is the Senate minority leader), former Reagan chief of staff Ken Duberstein, and former RNC chair Haley Barbour. The regional carriers retained former members of Congress Tom Downey and Rod Chandler, as well as a former top Senate Finance Committee staff member, Joseph O'Neil. In this battle of the titans, the major airlines ultimately prevailed.[20]

A third type of lobbyist—the staff lobbyist—is clearly distinguishable from the amateur and from the paid professional. Staff lobbyists are usually professionals who work full-time for a particular interest group. They have a number of duties, including part-time or full-time efforts to influence the drafting or enactment of legislation.

The Lobbying Industry   The lobbying industry in Washington is growing. At least eighteen hundred associations employing more than forty thousand persons are located in Washington. New groups are moving in all the time, relocating from Los Angeles, Chicago, and other important cities. More than two thousand individuals are registered with Congress as lobbyists, and many local observers estimate that the actual number of people engaged in significant lobbying (part-time or full-time) is closer to fifteen thousand. In addition to the various unions, commodity groups, and trade associations, many important business corporations keep their own representatives in Washington.

Many groups—even those with reputations for being powerful—are constantly forming and reforming lobby coalitions in order to improve their effectiveness with Congress and with government agencies. The AFL and the CIO, for example, merged in 1955, largely for political advantage, despite many economic disagreements between them. In the 1970s, the venerable National Association of Manufacturers (NAM) tried vainly to work out a merger with the Chamber of Commerce of the United States. During that same period, more than two hundred top executives of some of America's leading business corporations—including AT&T, Boeing, Du Pont, General Motors, Mobil Oil, and General Electric—joined in Washington to form a business roundtable, hoping to coordinate their lobbying efforts on certain issues. In subsequent years, the roundtable worked effectively to promote business interests on issues such as labor law reform, tax policy, and consumer protection.

cross-lobbying

a term to describe lobbyists lobbying one another

On some occasions, lobbies lobby one another. What is referred to as **cross-lobbying** came to play a major role in the struggle over health care reform. At one point, the tireless small-business lobbyists of the National Federation of Independent Business (NFIB), which opposed health care reform, lobbied the American Medical Association (AMA) to drop its support for the employer mandate opposed by small businesses. The AMA did so in exchange for an NFIB agreement to oppose controls on physicians' fees. Similarly, the pharmaceutical industry has vigorously, but unsuccessfully, courted the AARP to support its position on drug prices.[21]

reverse lobbying

a strategy by which members of Congress bring pressure to bear on lobby groups to support particular courses of action

Closely related to cross-lobbying is what might be called **reverse lobbying**, which refers to efforts by members of Congress to pressure lobby groups to support particular courses of action. For example, in 1993 and 1994, the Conservative Opportunity Society (COS), an organization comprising the most conservative Republican members of the House of Representatives, brought intense pressure to bear upon the U.S. Chamber of Commerce to oppose the Clinton administration's policy initiatives. The Chamber of Commerce, one of the nation's leading business lobbies, has traditionally been aligned with the Republican Party. In 1993, however, one of the organization's vice presidents, William Archey, decided that it might be worthwhile to cooperate with the Democratic administration. Outraged congressional Republicans mobilized the Chamber's members to oppose this apparent shift in the organization's stance. Republicans feared that any weakening of the Chamber's opposition to the Democrats would undermine their efforts to defeat President Clinton's major policy initiatives. After a struggle, Archey was compelled to resign and the Chamber returned to its traditional posture of support for the Republicans and opposition to the Democrats.[22] In a similar vein, Republican members of Congress sought to pressure the AMA to oppose President Clinton's health care initiatives.

In 1993, Clinton proposed that companies employing lobbyists be prohibited from deducting lobbying costs as business expenses from their federal taxes. This would, in effect, make it more difficult and costly for firms to employ lobbyists on behalf of their concerns. Not surprisingly, this proposal was bitterly resented by the lobbying industry, which saw it as a mortal threat to its own business interests. How did lobbying firms respond? By lobbying, of course. The American League of Lobbyists, a trade group representing the lobbying industry, quickly mobilized its members to conduct a vigorous campaign to defeat the proposal. One worried Washington lobbyist, however, observed, "This seems so self-serving, you wonder who is going to listen to us anyway."[23]

Clinton's proposal would have potentially reduced the influence of business groups in the policy process. This would, of course, work to the advantage of liberal public interest groups linked to the Democratic Party. For this reason, a variety of business groups joined forces with the lobbying industry to

POLICY DEBATE

Regulating Smoking and Tobacco

*R*oughly forty-five million Americans use a substance that is both highly addictive and lethal: tobacco. The fact that cigarettes are so abundant and available reflects the virtual absence of government regulation of tobacco products. This fact, in turn, reflects the political muscle of the giant tobacco industry. By pouring billions of dollars into lobbying, research, litigation, and advertising, tobacco interests have staved off most efforts to regulate their products. In fact, tobacco producers have benefited from Department of Agriculture price supports and rules that limit the amount that one tobacco company can produce. Powerful members of Congress from some of the twenty-two states that produce tobacco, anxious to protect jobs in and revenues from the industry, have successfully fought nearly every effort to regulate tobacco.

In 1997, however, lawsuits brought against cigarette makers by attorneys general of forty states resulted in a historic agreement. This watershed proposal called for the cigarette companies to pay $368 billion to the states over a twenty-five year period, to compensate the states for the costs of treating smoking-related illnesses, such as cancer and emphysema, for Medicaid patients. Furthermore, the tobacco companies would stop most forms of tobacco advertising, pay for antismoking advertising, and admit that smoking is both addictive and lethal.

Supporters of this "global tobacco settlement" have hailed its historic nature. For the first time, the industry was prepared to concede the direct adverse health consequences of its products. The proposed cash settlement was not sufficient to bankrupt the industry, so it would not disrupt local tobacco economies. The increased price to be paid for tobacco products under the settlement would both provide needed money to the states and discourage cigarette purchases (since consumption drops as prices increase). More important, the agreement to end most tobacco advertising breaks the key link between the industry and young people, because the vast majority of smokers begin their addictions during their teenage years, and most tobacco advertising has been aimed at young people, who are most vulnerable to advertising pressure. The tobacco companies would have to demonstrate the effectiveness of antismoking efforts, meeting goals of a 30 percent reduction in teen smoking within five years, a 50 percent reduction in seven years, and a 60 percent reduction in ten years.

Aside from the particular details of the plan, no agreement can occur until the plan is approved by Congress. This will provide the government, and the country, ample opportunity to debate and analyze the proposal's strengths and weaknesses. Despite the limitations of this proposed agreement, its sheer size and scope represent an unprecedented regulation of tobacco power.

Opponents of the tobacco settlement argue that the proposal gives more than it gets. The financial settlement is too small to place any dent in tobacco company operations. Most of the costs would be tax-deductible for the tobacco companies, meaning that taxpayers would, in effect, be subsidizing the industry's financial penalty. Worse, the agreement would shield the industry from potentially ruinous lawsuits by exempting them from future legal liability and capping possible settlement costs. It also limited document disclosure, a crucial basis of evidence for determining industry wrongdoing. While the Food and Drug Administration would be allowed to regulate tobacco, it could not ban nicotine for twelve years, and would have to follow a far more difficult procedure for doing so. Furthermore, the tobacco industry's track record has been so filled with deceit and the use of raw power that most critics assume that the industry will find ways around the advertising ban. The two most important weapons to use against the tobacco industry—product liability actions and FDA regulation of nicotine as a drug—are severely restricted under the proposed settlement. Worse, the prospect of congressional review and approval invites the tobacco industry to exert maximum lobbying pressure on Congress, where it has scored numerous successes over many decades. In short, the proposed settlement would strengthen, rather than weaken, the political hand of big tobacco.

oppose the administration's efforts. In 1994, Congress first passed and then rejected legislation requiring disclosure of lobbying activities and prohibiting lobbyists from giving gifts worth more than twenty dollars to members.[24] Such lobbying-reform legislation could force interest groups to rely even more heavily upon grassroots campaigns and less heavily upon "buying access."

GAINING ACCESS

access

the actual involvement of interest groups in the decision-making process

Lobbying is an effort by outsiders to exert influence on Congress or government agencies by providing them with information about issues, support, and even threats of retaliation. **Access** is actual involvement in the decision-making process. It may be the outcome of long years of lobbying, but it should not be confused with lobbying. If lobbying has to do with "influence on" a government, access has to do with "influence within" it. Many interest groups resort to lobbying because they have insufficient access or insufficient time to develop it. Access is usually a result of time and effort spent cultivating a position within the inner councils of government. This method of gaining access often requires the sacrifice of short-run influence.

iron triangle

the stable, cooperative relationship that often develops between a congressional committee, an administrative agency, and one or more supportive interest groups

Figure 11.3 illustrates one of the most important access patterns in recent American political history: that of the defense industry. Each such pattern, or **iron triangle,** is almost literally a triangular shape, with one point in an executive branch program, another point in a Senate or House legislative committee or

---

Figure 11.3   THE IRON TRIANGLE IN THE DEFENSE SECTOR

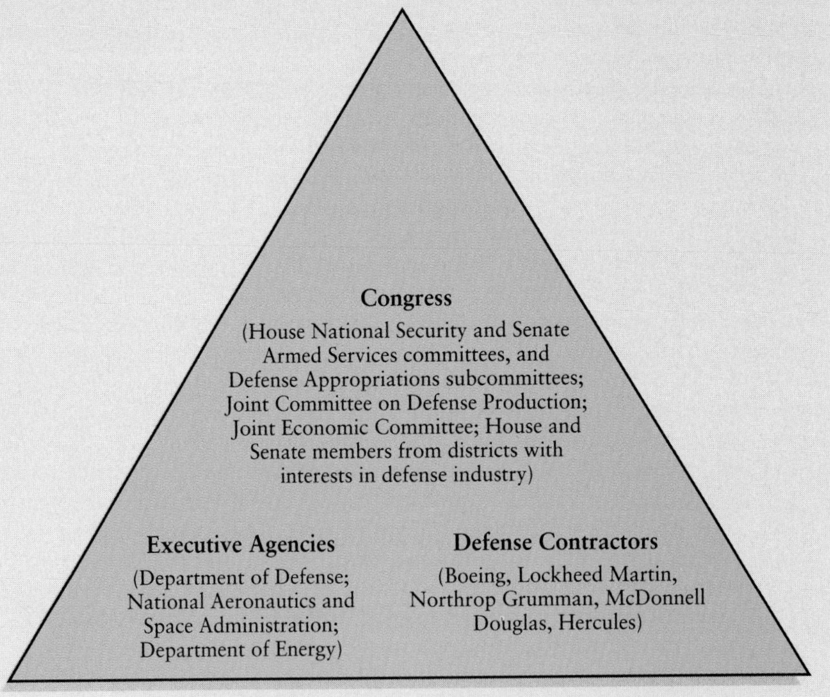

Defense contractors are powerful actors in shaping defense policy; they act in concert with defense committees and subcommittees in Congress and executive agencies concerned with defense.

Congress
(House National Security and Senate Armed Services committees, and Defense Appropriations subcommittees; Joint Committee on Defense Production; Joint Economic Committee; House and Senate members from districts with interests in defense industry)

Executive Agencies
(Department of Defense; National Aeronautics and Space Administration; Department of Energy)

Defense Contractors
(Boeing, Lockheed Martin, Northrop Grumman, McDonnell Douglas, Hercules)

subcommittee, and a third point in some highly stable and well-organized interest group. The points in the triangular relationship are mutually supporting; they count as access only if they last over a long period of time. For example, access to a legislative committee or subcommittee requires that at least one member of it support the interest group in question. This member also must have built up considerable seniority in Congress. An interest cannot feel comfortable about its access to Congress until it has one or more of its "own" people with ten or more years of continuous service on the relevant committee or subcommittee.

A number of important policy domains, such as the environmental and welfare arenas, are controlled, not by highly structured and unified iron triangles, but by rival **issue networks**. These networks consist of like-minded politicians, consultants, public officials, political activists, and interest groups who have some concern with the issue in question. Activists and interest groups recognized as being involved in the area are sometimes called "stakeholders," and are customarily invited to testify before congressional committees or give their views to government agencies considering action in their domain.

Corridoring: Gaining Access to the Bureaucracy   A bureaucratic agency is the third point in the iron triangle, and thus access to it is essential to the success of an interest group. Working to gain influence in an executive agency is sometimes called **corridoring**—the equivalent of lobbying in the executive branch. Even when an interest group is very successful at getting its bill passed by Congress and signed by the president, the prospect of full and faithful implementation of that law is not guaranteed. Often, a group and its allies do not pack up and go home as soon as the president turns their lobbied-for new law over to the appropriate agency. Agencies, too, can fall under the influence of or be **captured** by an interest group or a coalition of well-organized groups.[25] Granted, agencies are not passive and can do a good bit of capturing themselves. The point is that those groups that ignore the role of the agency in implementing legislation are simply not going to have any role in the outcome of agency decisions.

One lawyer for an important public interest group gave an unusually frank assessment of the need of an interest group to persist in its efforts to influence the agency: "You can't be successful at a regulatory agency unless you have the financial resources to sue their asses off."[26] That may be a self-serving overstatement, but it should not be discounted. One of the most thorough studies of interest-group activity reported that an average of 40 percent of all of the group representatives surveyed "regularly contacted" both legislative *and* executive branch organizations; while only 13 percent and 16 percent, respectively, regularly contacted only the legislature or only the executive branch.[27] Of course, few of these contacts with agencies actually involve the threat to sue. But that possibility is not something an agency can take lightly; some groups do use the lawsuit—a most formal technique of influence—to stop an agency from taking an action. Some use lawsuits to gain a more favorable interpretation of a rule. And some—most particularly women's groups, certain other civil rights groups, and a number of environmental groups—use lawsuits to get an agency to act more vigorously, as we shall see later in this chapter. This last category is an important aspect of the New Politics movement.

A slightly less formal method of influence occurs when an interest group participates in the regular decision-making processes of an agency. For example,

issue network

a loose network of elected leaders, public officials, activists, and interest groups drawn together by a specific policy issue

corridoring

working to gain influence in an executive agency

capture

an interest's acquisition of substantial influence over the government agency charged with regulating its activities

A Federal Drug Administration advisory committee hearing to debate the use of RU-486, popularly known as the abortion pill.

many agencies hold public hearings prior to taking an action—especially if the action involves taking over property for building a road or some other public work, or intervening against a company's or community's action that would violate some environmental protection law.[28] But unfortunately, hearings involving high-stakes local decisions to be made by a federal or state administrative agency can end up in highly heated and often stalemated and inconclusive sessions involving individuals and interest groups pleading "NIMBY"—not in my backyard.

So broad is the discretion granted to agencies by Congress, and so eager are agencies to gain the support and cooperation of the people they are regulating or serving, that virtually all agencies join in the trumpet call to kindle the spirit of participation. Some even refer to participation in agency decisions as "participatory democracy." Moreover, the broad discretion delegated to agencies in the laws passed by Congress gives all activist interest groups the unprecedented hope that the efforts made on behalf of their members will pay off where it counts—in implementation. These conditions have produced an explosive growth not only of interest groups in general but of public interest groups in particular.

Influence Peddling   The personnel interchange approach of many businesses is not the only way to engage in access politics. It is possible, although not easy, to buy access by securing the services of certain important Washington lawyers and lobbyists. These people can, for proper consideration, provide real access, not merely the more impersonal representation of the lobbyist. "Influence peddling" is the negative term for this sale or rental of access that goes on openly in Washington. For example, before joining President Clinton's cabinet as commerce secretary, the late Ron Brown was an important Washington lawyer and lobbyist, earning nearly one million dollars annually for his services to corporate clients and foreign governments. Brown's ties to a variety of corporate interests raised many questions about Clinton's wisdom in appointing him—questions that Brown and his supporters angrily rebutted.[29]

One way in which lobbying firms gain access is to hire former members of Congress. Former Republican Senate Finance Committee Chair Bob Packwood, shown here meeting with Bob Dole, opened his own lobbying firm after resigning from the Senate.

Many retired or defeated members of Congress join or form Washington law firms and spend all their time either lobbying or funneling access. An even larger number of former government officials and congressional staff members remain in Washington in order to make a living from their expertise and their access. (Laws that limit the freedom of former government employees to take jobs in directly related private companies do not apply to former employees of congressional committees.) The senior partnerships of Washington's top law firms are heavily populated with these former officials and staffers, and they practice law before the very commissions and committees on which they once served. There's an old saying about members of Congress—"they never go back to Pocatello"—and it is as true today as when it was coined.

Influence can be expensive. In 1996, for example, wealthy donors, including representatives of foreign business interests, paid thousands of dollars each to have lunch or coffee with the president and vice president. Some of the most generous donors were invited to spend the night in the White House's Lincoln Bedroom. Despite the criticism engendered by these practices, President Clinton felt compelled to resume this form of fund-raising in 1997 to help pay the Democratic Party's enormous debt from the 1996 campaigns. Thus, in October 1997, the Democratic Party invited donors to pay $50,000 each to participate in a Florida weekend retreat with the president, vice president, several members of Congress, and a number of administration officials. During the same month, while criticizing Clinton for his practices, Republicans invited donors to pay $10,000 apiece to have lunch with Senate Majority Leader Trent Lott. Donors are willing to contribute these large sums because they hope to benefit from rubbing shoulders with political leaders who are in a position to advance their economic interests or social concerns.[30]

USING THE COURTS (LITIGATION)

Interest groups sometimes turn to litigation when they lack access or when they are dissatisfied with government in general or with a specific government program and feel they have insufficient influence to change the situation. Interest groups can use the courts to affect public policy in at least three ways: (1) by bringing suit directly on behalf of the group itself, (2) by financing suits brought by individuals, or (3) by filing a companion brief as *"amicus curiae"* (literally "friend of the court") to an existing court case (see Chapter 15 for a discussion of *amicus curiae* briefs).

Among the most significant modern illustrations of the use of the courts as a strategy for political influence are those that accompanied the "sexual revolution" of the 1960s and the emergence of the movement for women's rights.

The 1973 Supreme Court case of *Roe v. Wade,* which made it illegal for states to ban abortions, sparked a controversy that brought conservatives to the fore on a national level.[31] These conservative groups made extensive use of the courts to whittle away the scope of the privacy doctrine. They obtained rulings, for example, that prohibit the use of federal funds to pay for voluntary abortions. And in 1989, right-to-life groups were able to use a strategy of litigation that significantly undermined the *Roe v. Wade* decision, namely in the case of *Webster v. Reproductive Health Services* (see Chapter 5), which restored the right of states to place restrictions on abortion.[32] The *Webster* case

Elaine Jones (right), director of the NAACP Legal Defense Fund, spoke with reporters outside the Supreme Court after the Court struck down redistricting plans in Texas and North Carolina.

brought more than three hundred interest groups on both sides of the abortion issue to the Supreme Court's door (see Table 11.2).

Another extremely significant set of contemporary illustrations of the use of the courts as a strategy for political influence are those found in the history of the NAACP. The most important of these court cases was, of course, *Brown v. Board of Education of Topeka, Kansas,* in which the U.S. Supreme Court held that legal segregation of the schools was unconstitutional.[33]

Business groups are also frequent users of the courts because of the number of government programs applied to them. Litigation involving large businesses is most mountainous in such areas as taxation, antitrust, interstate transportation, patents, and product quality and standardization. Often a business is brought to litigation against its will by virtue of initiatives taken against it by other businesses or by government agencies. But many individual businesses bring suit themselves in order to influence government policy. Major corporations and their trade associations pay tremendous amounts of money each year in fees to the most prestigious Washington law firms. Some of this money is expended in gaining access. A great proportion of it, however, is used to keep the best and most experienced lawyers prepared to represent the corporations in court or before administrative agencies when necessary.

New Politics forces made significant use of the courts during the 1970s and 1980s, and judicial decisions were instrumental in advancing their goals. Facilitated by changes in the rules governing access to the courts (standing is discussed in Chapter 15), the New Politics agenda was clearly visible in court decisions handed down in several key policy areas. In the environmental policy area, New Politics groups were able to force federal agencies to pay attention to environmental issues, even when the agency was not directly involved in activities related to environmental quality. For example, the Federal Trade Commission (FTC) became very responsive to the demands of New Politics activists during the 1970s and 1980s. The FTC stepped up its activities considerably, litigating a series of claims arising under regulations prohibiting deceptive advertising in cases ranging from false claims for over-the-counter drugs to inflated claims about the nutritional value of children's cereal.

And while feminists and equal rights activists enjoyed enormous success in litigating discrimination claims under Title VII of the Civil Rights Act of 1964, anti–nuclear power activists succeeded in virtually shutting down the nuclear power industry. Despite significant defeats, challenges to power plant siting and licensing regulations were instrumental in discouraging energy companies from pursuing nuclear projects over the long term.[34]

GOING PUBLIC

going public

a strategy that attempts to mobilize the widest and most favorable climate of public opinion

Going public is a strategy that attempts to mobilize the widest and most favorable climate of opinion. Many groups consider it imperative to maintain this climate at all times, even when they have no issue to fight about. An increased use of this kind of strategy is usually associated with modern advertising. As early as the 1930s, political analysts were distinguishing between the "old lobby" of direct group representation before Congress and the "new lobby" of public relations professionals addressing the public at large to reach Congress.[35]

institutional advertising

advertising designed to create a positive image of an organization

Institutional Advertising   One of the best known ways of going public is the use of **institutional advertising**. A casual scanning of important mass circula-

INTEREST GROUPS INVOLVED IN THE *WEBSTER* CASE

Table 11.2

Supporting restrictions on abortion rights

Alabama Lawyers for Unborn Children
American Collegians for Life
American Family Association
American Life League
Baptists for Life
Birthright
Catholics United for Life
Christian Action Council
Doctors for Life
Feminists for Life of America
Focus on the Family
Knights of Columbus
Lawyers for Life
Let Me Live
Missouri Catholic Conference
Missouri Citizens for Life
National Association of Evangelicals
National Right-to-Life Committee
Presbyterians Pro-Life
Right-to-Life Advocates
Southern Baptists for Life
United States Catholic Conference
Value of Life Committee
Women Exploited by Abortion of Greater Kansas City

Opposing restrictions on abortion rights

A Woman's Place
Abortion Rights Council
Abortion Rights Mobilization
Abuse and Rape Crisis Center
Alliance Against Women's Oppression
American Association of University Women
American Civil Liberties Union
American College of Obstetricians and Gynecologists
American Medical Association
American Nurses Association
Bioethicists for Privacy
Brooklyn Women's Martial Arts
California Republicans for Choice
Canadian Women's Organizations
Catholics for a Free Choice
CHOICE
Coalition of Labor Union Women
D.C. Rape Crisis Center
Episcopal Women's Caucus
Equal Rights Advocates
Federally Employed Women
Feminist Women's Health Center
Gay Men's Health Crisis
Hawaii Women Lawyers
International Women's Health Organizations
League of Women Voters of the United States
Mexican American Women's National Association
My Sister's Place
National Abortion Rights Action League
National Black Women's Health Project
National Family Planning and Reproductive Health Association
National Organization for Women
National Women's Political Caucus
Organization of Asian Women
Presbyterian Church
Religious Coalition for Abortion Rights
St. Louis Catholics for Choice
Sierra Club
Students and Youth Against Racism
United Electrical, Radio, and Machine Workers of America
Voters for Choice
Women for Racial and Economic Equality
Women of All Red Nations
Women's Action Alliance
Women's Equal Rights Legal Defense and Education Fund
Women's Equity Action League
Women's Rights Coalition
Women's Studies Program, Hunter College
Worldwatch Institute
YWCA of the U.S.A.
Zero Population Growth

SOURCE: Barbara Craig and David M. O'Brien, *Abortion and American Politics* (Chatham, N.J.: Chatham House, 1993), pp. 205, 214–18.

Listeners applaud Dr. Martin Luther King, Jr., during his speech at the 1963 March on Washington.

grassroots lobbying

a lobbying campaign in which a group mobilizes its membership to contact government officials in support of the group's position

tion magazines and newspapers will provide numerous examples of expensive and well designed ads by the major oil companies, automobile and steel companies, other large corporations, and trade associations. The ads show how much these organizations are doing for the country, for the protection of the environment, or for the defense of the American way of life. Their purpose is to create and maintain a strongly positive association between the organization and the community at large, in the hope that these favorable feelings can be drawn on as needed for specific political campaigns later on.

Social Movements Going public is not limited to businesses or to groups of upper-income professionals. Many groups resort to it because they lack the resources, the contacts, or the experience to use other political strategies. The sponsorship of boycotts, sit-ins, mass rallies, and marches by Martin Luther King's Southern Christian Leadership Conference (SCLC) and related organizations in the 1950s and 1960s is one of the most significant and successful cases of going public to create a more favorable climate of opinion by calling attention to abuses. The success of these events inspired similar efforts on the part of women. Organizations such as the National Organization for Women (NOW) used public strategies in their drive for legislation and in their efforts to gain ratification of the Equal Rights Amendment. In 1993, gay rights groups organized a mass rally as part of their effort to eliminate restrictions on military service and other forms of discrimination based on individuals' sexual preferences. Gay rights leaders met with President Clinton in mid-April 1993 and were assured of his support for a demonstration in Washington to be held at the end of the month.[36] Although President Clinton had campaigned actively for gay and lesbian support during the election, he did not attend the march for fear of offending religious conservatives.

Grassroots Mobilization Another form of going public is **grassroots lobbying**. In such a campaign, a lobby group mobilizes its members and their families throughout the country to write to their elected representatives in support of the group's position. For example, in 1993, lobbyists for the Nissan Motor Company sought to organize a "grassroots" effort to prevent President Clinton from raising tariffs on imported minivans, including Nissan's Pathfinder model. Nissan's twelve hundred dealers across the nation, as well as those dealers' employees and family members, were urged to dial a toll-free number that would automatically generate a prepared mailgram opposing the tariff to be sent to the president and each dealer's senators. The mailgram warned that the proposed tariff increase would hurt middle-class auto purchasers and small businesses, such as the dealerships.[37] During his 1992 presidential campaign, Ross Perot showed how effectively television can be used to carry one's message to the grass roots.

Among the most effective users of the grassroots lobby effort in contemporary American politics is the religious Right. Networks of evangelical churches have the capacity to generate hundreds of thousands of letters and phone calls to Congress and the White House. For example, the religious Right was outraged when President Clinton announced soon after taking office that he planned to end the military's ban on gay and lesbian soldiers. The Rev. Jerry Falwell, an evangelical leader, called upon viewers of his television program to

Losing Money Left and Right?

How did Coors do it? How did this large brewing company, which has annual sales of more than $1.5 billion, manage to provoke simultaneous calls for boycotts from opposite ends of the ideological spectrum—from gay and lesbian groups *and* from Christian and conservative groups? In the words of a Coors spokesperson, "We are caught between a rock and a hard place."[1] The case of the rival Coors boycotts reveals how intertwined politics, culture, and business are in American society.

The current boycott by gay and lesbian activist groups is due in part to the prominent role the Coors family has played in conservative politics. Jeffrey Coors, the nephew of the company's chairperson and brother of its chief executive officer, heads the Free Congress Foundation, a conservative group that opposes legislative efforts to define and protect the rights of homosexuals. But the gay and lesbian boycott can be traced back even further, to the 1980s, when Coors, because of its anti-union stance, was the object of a nationwide labor boycott. Many groups on the political left joined this labor boycott. Even after the labor boycott officially ended in 1987, many gay and lesbian activists refused to purchase Coors products. Despite efforts to win back their business by contributing money for AIDS research and gay community projects and conferences, Coors has remained an unpopular name in the gay community. Coors concedes it has suffered from the hostility of many gays and lesbians. "We can't tell you how much we've lost," says a Coors spokesperson, "but we know it has had an impact."

Against this background, in 1995 Coors became one of the first corporations in America to extend health care insurance and other benefits to the partners of its homosexual employees. Coors contends

that this "domestic partners program" is not an attempt to win back gays and lesbians by supporting gay rights, but is instead a reflection of the company's commitment to providing equitable benefits for all its employees. Gay and lesbian groups have reacted cautiously to the company's efforts. "We are always pleased to see any company make a step in the right direction, but we have to be careful shoppers and look at the big picture," said a spokesperson for one gay rights group.

But some conservative and Christian groups have responded to Coors's policy with fury. A conservative Kansas minister trying to organize an anti-Coors campaign sent faxes to churches around the country: "The Coors family of hypocrites claim to fear God, but sponsor filthy fags!" The press secretary for Concerned Women of America, a conservative organization with more than 600,000 members, said that Coors's new domestic-partners program "legitimizes the homosexual lifestyle"—a policy anathema to the values of conservative Americans.

Can corporations like Coors avoid triggering controversies as they navigate the complex terrain of American political culture in the 1990s? Probably not. Americans are sharply divided over community moral standards, over the "right" and "wrong" of how people should live their lives. And in a capitalist economy, how people live depends in large part on the salary and benefits they derive from their jobs. Thus cultural arguments about the values that shape Americans' lives spill over, inevitably, into arguments about how corporations ought to behave.

[1]Quoted in Jay Mathews, "At Coors, A Brewing Dilemma over Gay Rights," *Washington Post,* September 16, 1995, p. A1, from which all quotations herein are taken.

THE CHRISTIAN COALITION

ssues involving morality have received increasing public attention in recent years, and many interest groups have sought to promote their vision of the proper role of government in areas where politics and morality collide. One of the most prominent of these interest groups is the Christian Coalition.

Founded by television evangelist and 1988 Republican presidential aspirant Pat Robertson in 1989, the Christian Coalition drew initial strength from Robertson's presidential campaign apparatus and from followers of his evangelical television program, *The 700 Club*. The Christian Coalition first pursued a narrow strategy, opposing abortion, pornography, and homosexuality, and supporting school prayer and other "pro-family" issues. According to the coalition's former executive director, Ralph Reed, the organization's purpose is to "take back this country, one precinct at a time," in order to "see a country once again governed by Christians . . . and Christian values."[1]

Claiming about 1.7 million members, the coalition's strength derives mostly from evangelical Christians, who profess to have been "born again." Most of the leaders of the coalition are drawn from the Pentecostal sect. The largest Pentecostal church, the Assemblies of God, provided primary resources and personnel for Robertson's 1988 presidential bid.

The coalition has become an important force within the Republican Party, although it has some Democratic adherents as well. In 1992, incumbent presidential candidate George Bush gave coalition leaders and supporters control over the Republican Party platform in exchange for their support. The party's platform proved to be too extreme for many, however, and some analysts contended that the extremism demonstrated at the 1992 Republican National Convention contributed to Bush's defeat.

In an effort to broaden and soften the coalition's appeal, Reed pushed to widen and diversify the organization's concerns. In a 1993 interview, for example, Reed emphasized the importance of such issues as tax relief, increasing the standard income-tax deduction for children, a balanced budget amendment, and health care reform.[2] The organiza-

dial a telephone number that would add their names to a petition urging Clinton to retain the ban on gays in the military. Within a few hours, 24,000 people had called to support the petition.[38]

Grassroots lobbying campaigns have been so effective in recent years that a number of Washington consulting firms have begun to specialize in this area. Firms such as Bonner and Associates, for example, will work to generate grassroots telephone campaigns on behalf of or in opposition to important legislative proposals. Such efforts can be very expensive. Reportedly, one trade association recently paid the Bonner firm three million dollars to generate and sustain a grassroots effort to defeat a bill on the Senate floor.[39]

Has grassroots campaigning been overutilized? One story in the *New York Times* forces us to ask that question. Ten giant companies in the financial services, manufacturing, and high-tech industries began a grassroots campaign in 1992 and spent millions of dollars over the next three years to influence a decision in Congress to limit the ability of investors to sue for fraud. Retaining an expensive consulting firm, these corporations paid for the use of specialized computer software to persuade Congress that there was "an outpouring of popular support for the proposal." Thousands of letters from individuals flooded Capitol Hill. Many of those letters were written and sent by people who sincerely believed that investor lawsuits are often frivolous and should be

tion began to pay more attention to such issues as crime and education. In addition, Reed sought greater flexibility by encouraging the coalition to tone down its rhetoric and seek coalitions with other, more mainstream conservative groups. Thus members have been advised to be less abrasive and less strident. Reed also launched a campaign to broaden the group's support base, notably by seeking to recruit among religiously oriented blacks, Latinos, and Catholics. These tactics have met with limited success so far, but coalition leaders are confident that many Americans share the views of the Christian Coalition. According to Reed, the coalition needed to broaden its appeal because "we have allowed ourselves to be ghettoized by a narrow band of issues like abortion, homosexual rights and prayer in school."[3]

At the local level, the Christian Coalition has labored to elect school board members and win control of local party organizations around the country. As many as a dozen state-level Republican Party organizations are now significantly influenced by coalition adherents. To the dismay of critics, coalition members have often won elections by fielding so-called stealth candidates who conceal their affiliation with the coalition until after winning election. This sub-

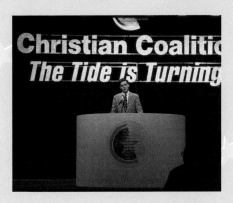

terfuge was pursued because of the coalition's reputation for taking a narrow, extremist, and exclusionary approach to politics. Reed encountered some criticism for bragging about the success of the organization's stealth tactics.[4]

Despite these criticisms, the coalition's influence in the Republican Party is reflected by the fact that, in 1996, nearly all of the party's contenders for the presidency spoke at the coalition's annual conventions and took other actions to court the support of coalition members. Although its size may remain limited, the Christian Coalition has played the interest-group politics game with remarkable skill and sophistication.

SOURCE: Allen D. Hertzke, *Echoes of Discontent: Jesse Jackson, Pat Robertson, and the Resurgence of Populism* (Washington, DC: Congressional Quarterly Press, 1993).
[1] James M. Perry, "The Christian Coalition Crusades to Broaden Rightist Political Base," *Wall Street Journal*, July 19, 1994, p. 1.
[2] "Mobilizing the Christian Right," *Campaigns and Elections*, October/November 1993, pp. 33–36.
[3] Laurence I. Barrett, "Fighting for God and the Right Wing," *Time*, September 13, 1993, p. 58.
[4] Barrett, "Fighting for God," p. 58.

curtailed. But much of the mail was phony, generated by the Washington-based campaign consultants; the letters came from people who had no strong feelings or even no opinion at all about the issue. More and more people, including leading members of Congress, are becoming quite skeptical of such methods, charging that these are not genuine grassroots campaigns but instead represent **"Astroturf lobbying"** (a play on the name of an artificial grass used on many sports fields). Such Astroturf campaigns have increased in frequency in recent years as members of Congress have grown more and more skeptical of Washington lobbyists and far more concerned about demonstrations of support for a particular issue by their constituents. But after the firms mentioned above spent millions of dollars and generated thousands of letters to members of Congress, they came to the somber conclusion that "it's more effective to have 100 letters from your district where constituents took the time to write and understand the issue," because "Congress is sophisticated enough to know the difference."[40]

Astroturf lobbying
a negative term used to describe group-directed and exaggerated grassroots lobbying

USING ELECTORAL POLITICS

Many interest groups decide that it is far more effective to elect the right legislators than to try to influence the incumbents through lobbying or through a

Students and Politics

In 1996, in response to predictions of an unfunded Social Security system within twenty-five years, American University student Mike Panetta founded X-PAC, a political action committee that promotes and publicizes the interests and views of Generation X-ers on Social Security reform. By working only ten hours a week on the X-PAC web page and a few publicity projects, Panetta has generated considerable support for his organization and greater interest among his generation in the issue, especially since merging with College of William and Mary student Christian Klein's PAC 20/20, which has solicited money for pro–Social Security reform candidates and held events such as the Easter fund-raiser at William and Mary. Klein and Panetta admit to fearing that the Social Security system will lose large amounts of money once the baby boomer generation retires: PAC 20/20 was named not as a reference to perfect vision on the issue, but for the year that the government program will go bankrupt. "Anyone can start an interest group or a PAC," says Panetta. "Just stick to your guns and keep your eye on the target. Some people will try to bring you down, but with a little homework and a good idea, you can be a player and make a difference."

SOURCE: Mike Panetta, interview with author, January 8, 1998.

political action committee (PAC)

a private group that raises and distributes funds for use in election campaigns

changed or mobilized mass opinion. Interest groups can influence elections by two means: financial support funded through political action committees, and campaign activism.

Political Action Committees By far the most common electoral strategy employed by interest groups is that of giving financial support to the parties or to particular candidates. But such support can easily cross the threshold into outright bribery. Therefore, Congress has occasionally made an effort to regulate this strategy. Congress's most recent effort was the Federal Election Campaign Act of 1971 (amended in 1974). This act limits campaign contributions and requires that each candidate or campaign committee itemize the full name and address, occupation, and principal business of each person who contributes more than $100. These provisions have been effective up to a point, considering the rather large number of embarrassments, indictments, resignations, and criminal convictions in the aftermath of the Watergate scandal.

The Watergate scandal was triggered by the illegal entry of Republican workers into the office of the Democratic National Committee in the Watergate apartment building. But an investigation quickly revealed numerous violations of campaign finance laws, involving millions of dollars in unregistered cash from corporate executives to President Nixon's re-election committee. Many of these revelations were made by the famous Ervin Committee, whose official name and jurisdiction was the Senate Select Committee to Investigate the 1972 Presidential Campaign Activities.

Reaction to Watergate produced further legislation on campaign finance in 1974 and 1976, but the effect has been to restrict individual rather than interest-group campaign activity. Individuals may now contribute no more than $1,000 to any candidate for federal office in any primary or general election. A **political action committee** (PAC), however, can contribute $5,000, provided it contributes to at least five different federal candidates each year. Beyond this, the laws permit corporations, unions, and other interest groups to form PACs and to pay the costs of soliciting funds from private citizens for the PACs.

Electoral spending by interest groups has been increasing steadily despite the flurry of reform following Watergate. Table 11.3 presents a dramatic picture of the growth of PACs as the source of campaign contributions. The dollar amounts for each year reveal the growth in electoral spending. The number of PACs has also increased significantly—from 480 in 1972 to more than 4,000 in 1992 (see Figure 11.4). Although the reform legislation of the early and mid-1970s attempted to reduce the influence that special interests have over elections, the effect has been almost the exact opposite. Opportunities for legally influencing campaigns are now widespread.

Indeed, PACs and campaign contributions provide organized interests with such a useful tool for gaining access to the political process that interests of all

PAC SPENDING, 1977–96		Table 11.3

Years	Contributions
1977–78 (est.)	$ 77,800,000
1979–80	131,153,384
1981–82	190,173,539
1983–84	266,822,476
1985–86	339,954,416
1987–88	364,201,275
1989–90	372,100,000
1991–92	402,300,000
1993–94	387,400,000
1995–96	467,000,000

SOURCE: Federal Election Commission.

political stripes are now willing to suspend their conflicts and rally to the defense of PACs when they come under attack. This support has helped to make the present campaign funding system highly resistant to reform. As we saw in Chapter 10, in May 1996, the Senate considered a bipartisan campaign

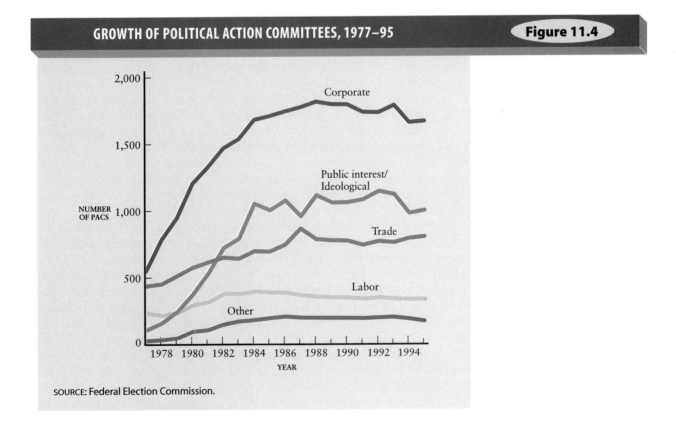

GROWTH OF POLITICAL ACTION COMMITTEES, 1977–95   Figure 11.4

SOURCE: Federal Election Commission.

Senators John McCain, left, and Russell Feingold, right, led a bipartisan effort to pass a campaign-finance reform bill in the 105th Congress.

finance bill sponsored by Senators John McCain, Russell Feingold, and Fred Thompson, which would have abolished PACs. The bill was staunchly opposed by a coalition of business groups, labor unions, liberal groups like EMILY's List, and conservative groups like Americans for Tax Reform. Though these groups disagree on many substantive matters, they agreed on the principle that abolition of PACs would "diminish the ability of average citizens to join together to have their voices heard." A less positive interpretation was offered by Common Cause president Ann McBride, a proponent of abolishing PACs, who characterized the pro-PAC alliance as an example of "labor and business coming together and agreeing on the one thing that they can agree on, which is maintaining the status quo and their ability to use money to buy outcomes on Capitol Hill[41]

Given the enormous costs of television commercials, polls, computers, and other elements of the new political technology (see Chapter 10), most politicians are eager to receive PAC contributions and are at least willing to give a friendly hearing to the needs and interests of contributors. It is probably not the case that most politicians simply sell their services to the interests that fund their campaigns. But there is considerable evidence to support the contention that interest groups' campaign contributions do influence the overall pattern of political behavior in Congress and in the state legislatures.

During the 1996 national election campaign, for example, thousands of special interest groups donated more than $1.5 billion to political parties and candidates at the national, state, and local levels. Business groups raised $242 million, mainly for Republicans, while organized labor donated $35 million to Democratic candidates and spent another $35 million directly to campaign for Democrats.[42] In response to charges that both he and President Bill Clinton were allowing major campaign contributors—including foreign firms—too much influence in the political process, Republican presidential candidate Bob Dole called for new campaign spending rules that would abolish large private contributions and prohibit noncitizens from contributing money to American political candidates.[43] Democrats immediately questioned Dole's sincerity, noting that the former Senate majority leader had personally raised some $100

John Huang, shown here with President Clinton, was accused in 1998 of soliciting illegal foreign donations to the Democratic National Committee.

million in campaign funds during the course of his long political career. While the two parties traded charges, Democratic fund-raiser John Huang was being forced to resign from the Democratic National Committee campaign staff amid allegations that he funneled millions of dollars in contributions from a wealthy Indonesian family into Democratic campaign coffers.[44]

In 1997, Vice President Al Gore was stung by charges that he had helped win federal contracts for a Massachusetts hazardous-waste disposal firm whose officers contributed heavily to the Clinton-Gore re-election effort. After officers of Molten Metal Technology, Inc., contributed generously to the Clinton-Gore campaign, the firm received millions of dollars in Department of Energy contracts. The firm's chief Washington lobbyist, Peter Knight, is also Gore's former chief of staff and a former chair of the Clinton-Gore re-election committee. Knight was able to arrange a visit by the vice president to Molten's plant to mark Earth Day. Gore, Knight, and Molten executives deny that there is any connection between the firm's campaign contributions and the contracts subsequently awarded to it by the federal government.[45]

PACs provide more than just the financial support that individual candidates receive. Under present federal law, there is no restriction on the amount that individuals and interests can contribute directly to the parties for voter registration, grassroots organizing, and other party activities not directly linked to a particular candidate's campaign. Such contributions, called **soft money**, allow individuals and interest groups to circumvent restrictions on campaign contributions. Critics argue that soft money contributions allow wealthy donors to have unfair influence in the political process. Perhaps this potential does exist. However, soft money also provides the national and state parties with the means to engage in voter registration and turnout drives. In 1996, the Supreme Court ruled in the case of *Colorado Republican Party v. Federal Election Commission* that the government could not restrict political parties' use of soft money.[46] In 1997, legislation designed to circumvent the Court's ruling and reduce the role of soft money was introduced by Senators McCain and Feingold, but was blocked by a Senate filibuster.

Often, the campaign spending of activist groups is carefully kept separate from party and candidate organizations in order to avoid the restrictions of federal campaign finance laws. So long as a group's campaign expenditures are not coordinated with those of a candidate's own campaign, the group is free to spend as much money as it wishes. Such expenditures are viewed as "issues advocacy" and are protected by the First Amendment and thus not subject to statutory limitation.[47]

In 1996, organized labor budgeted $35 million for independent efforts to elect prounion congressional candidates. At the same time, business groups sought to coordinate their activities through an alliance informally known as "the coalition." Prominent members of the coalition included the Chamber of Commerce, the National Federation of Independent Business (NFIB), the National Association of Manufacturers, the National Association of Wholesale Distributors, and the National Restaurant Association. Coalition members spent tens of millions of dollars on radio and television advertising in support of conservative congressional candidates.

Campaign Activism Financial support is not the only way that organized groups seek influence through electoral politics. Sometimes, activism can be

soft money
money contributed directly to political parties for voter registration and organization

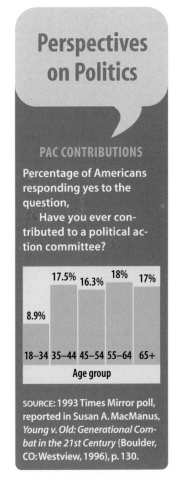

Perspectives on Politics

PAC CONTRIBUTIONS
Percentage of Americans responding yes to the question,
Have you ever contributed to a political action committee?

Age group				
8.9%	17.5%	16.3%	18%	17%
18–34	35–44	45–54	55–64	65+

SOURCE: 1993 Times Mirror poll, reported in Susan A. MacManus, *Young v. Old: Generational Combat in the 21st Century* (Boulder, CO: Westview, 1996), p. 130.

even more important than campaign contributions. Campaign activism on the part of conservative groups played a very important role in bringing about the Republican capture of both houses of Congress in the 1994 congressional elections. For example, Christian Coalition activists played a role in many races, including ones in which Republican candidates were not overly identified with the religious Right. One postelection study suggested that more than 60 percent of the more than 600 candidates supported by the Christian Right were successful in state, local, and congressional races in 1994.[48] The efforts of conservative Republican activists to bring voters to the polls is one major reason that turnout among Republicans exceeded Democratic turnout in a midterm election for the first time since 1970. This increased turnout was especially marked in the South, where the Christian Coalition was most active. In many Congressional districts, Christian Coalition efforts on behalf of the Republicans were augmented by grassroots campaigns launched by the NRA and the NFIB. The NRA had been outraged by Democratic support for gun control legislation, while the NFIB had been energized by its campaign against employer mandates in the failed Clinton health care reform initiative. Both groups are well organized at the local level and were able to mobilize their members across the country to participate in congressional races.

In 1996, by contrast, it was the Democrats who benefited from campaign activism. Organized labor made a major effort to mobilize its members for the campaign. Conservative activists, on the other hand, were not enthusiastic about GOP presidential candidate Bob Dole or his running mate Jack Kemp and failed to mobilize their forces for a maximum campaign effort. Dole belatedly recognized his need for the support of these activists, but was never able to energize them in sufficient numbers to affect the outcome of the election.[49]

Gaining the support of organized labor was an important part of Bill Clinton's strategy in the 1996 presidential campaign.

INTEREST GROUP STRATEGIES   Box 11.1

Going Public
Especially via advertising; also through boycotts, strikes, rallies, marches, and sit-ins, generating positive news coverage

Lobbying
Influencing the passage or defeat of legislation

Three types of lobbyists:

Amateur—loyal members of a group seeking passage of legislation that is currently under scrutiny

Paid—often lawyers or professionals without a personal interest in the legislation who are not full-time lobbyists

Staff—employed by a specific interest group full-time for the express purpose of influencing or drafting legislation

Access
Development of close ties to decision makers on Capitol Hill or in the executive branch

Litigation
Taking action through the courts, usually in one of three ways:

Filing suit against a specific government agency or program

Financing suits brought against the government by individuals

Filing companion briefs as *amicus curiae* (friend of the court) to existing court cases

Partisan Politics
Giving financial support to a particular party or candidate

Congress passed the Federal Election Campaign Act of 1971 to try to regulate this practice by limiting the amount of funding interest groups can contribute to campaigns

One remarkable fact about the political activity of interest groups is how infrequently major interest groups have tried to form their own party. The fact that they have rarely done so is to a large extent attributable to the strength of the two-party tradition in the United States. But there is also a significant negative influence: the barriers erected by state laws regarding the formation of new political parties. As a consequence, significant interests such as "the working class," women, and African Americans have not been able to find clear expression in the electoral process. Their interests are always being adulterated by other interests within their chosen party. Yet this situation has a positive side: the two-party system has—unintentionally—softened social demarcations by cutting across classes, races, and other fundamental interests that deeply divide people. These interests are adulterated and softened, subduing what might otherwise become the kind of class conflict that we see so often in European history, where class, race, and ethnic interests have become radicalized when they are not forced to reconcile themselves with other interests in a broad political party.[50]

POLITICS ON THE WEB

The Internet provides interest groups with an inexpensive means to recruit new members and reach their current membership. In addition to keeping members continuously informed of a group's actions and relevant policy decisions, a website can help build the kind of "grassroots" lobbying so important to modern interest-group strategies. For example, on the Greenpeace website one can find information on the group's activities, the progress of environmental legislation, the group's mission statement, and a history of the organization. The National Rifle Association maintains an active website, monitoring current legislation, recommending books and articles, and publicizing local courses in safe gun usage. Not surprisingly, these sites also give interest groups the opportunity to recruit new members. With all of the money that they save on mail and recruitment costs, groups have more money to directly influence the decisions of policy makers. And money is what interest-group politics in the United States is all about.

www.wwnorton.com/wtp2e.

Groups and Interests: The Dilemma

▶ What are the problems involved in curbing the influence of interest groups?

James Madison wrote that "liberty is to faction as air is to fire."[51] By this he meant that the organization and proliferation of interests was inevitable in a free society. To seek to place limits on the organization of interests, in Madison's view, would be to limit liberty itself. Madison believed that interests should be permitted to regulate themselves by competing with one another. So long as competition among different interests was free, open, and vigorous—that is, so long as pluralism thrives—there would be some balance of power among them and no one interest would be able to dominate the political or governmental process.

There is considerable competition among organized groups in the United States. As we saw, tobacco interests, consumer groups, and trial lawyers fought each other to a standstill in 1998. Similarly, prochoice and antiabortion forces continue to be locked in a bitter struggle. Nevertheless, interest-group politics is not as free of bias as Madisonian theory might suggest. Although the weak and poor do occasionally become organized to assert their rights, interest-group politics is generally a form of political competition in which the wealthy and powerful are best able to engage. In the realm of group politics, liberty seems inconsistent with equality.

Moreover, although groups sometimes organize to promote broad public concerns, interest groups more often represent relatively narrow, selfish interests. Small, self-interested groups can be organized much more easily than large and more diffuse collectives. For one thing, the members of a relatively small group—say, bankers or hunting enthusiasts—are usually able to recognize their shared interests and the need to pursue them in the political arena. Members of large and more diffuse groups—say, consumers or potential victims of firearms—often find it difficult to recognize their shared interests or the need to engage in collective action to achieve them.[52] This is why causes presented as public interests by their proponents often turn out, upon examination, to be private interests wrapped in a public mantle. Thus, group politics often appears to be inconsistent with democracy.

To make matters still more complicated, group politics seems to go hand-in-hand with government. As we saw earlier, government programs often lead to a proliferation of interest groups as competing forces mobilize to support, oppose, or take advantage of the government's actions. Often, the government explicitly encourages the formation of interest groups. From the perspective of a government agency, nothing is more useful than a well-organized constituency for its programs. Agencies such as the Department of Veterans Affairs, the Social Security Administration, and the Department of Agriculture devote a great deal of energy to the organization and mobilization of groups of "stakeholders" to support the agencies and their efforts. This strategy, a variant of what is sometimes called "interest-group liberalism," can be very effective. One reason that the Social Security program is considered politically invulnerable despite its fiscal shortcomings is that it is so strongly supported by a powerful group—the AARP. Significantly, the Social Security Administration played an important early role in the formation of the AARP, precisely because agency executives realized that this group could become a useful ally.

The responsiveness of government agencies to interest groups is a challenge to democracy. Groups seem to have a greater impact than voters upon the government's policies and programs. Yet, before we decide that we should do away with interest groups, we should think carefully: if there were no organized interests, would the government pay more attention to ordinary voters, or would the government simply pay no attention to anyone? In his great work *Democracy in America*, Alexis de Tocqueville argued that the proliferation of groups promoted democracy by encouraging governmental responsiveness. Does group politics foster democracy or impede democracy? It does both.

Thus, we have dilemmas for which there is no ideal answer. To regulate interest-group politics is, as Madison warned, to limit freedom and to expand governmental power. Not to regulate interest-group politics, on the other hand, may be to ignore equality and democracy. Those who believe that there are simple solutions to the issues of political life would do well to ponder this problem.

⋆ The Citizen's Role

The dilemmas posed by group politics raise questions for citizens, as well. If you can't beat them, should you join them?

Like political parties, interest groups are always looking for volunteers and members. Given the enormous number of groups in America today, every student should be able to find several whose causes seem worthwhile. One useful way to become involved in the world of group politics is to secure an internship in Washington with the national office of a public interest group. Washington is the home of groups from every part of the political spectrum, espousing every known cause from the defense of wildlife through the defense of upper-middle-class taxpayers. National, state, and local groups employ tens of thousands of college students every year. Student interns can become important staff members of a public interest group. Student interns research, attend congressional or state legislative hearings, communicate with citizens, and even help develop strategies. Working for an interest group can be one of the most effective ways of participating in politics.

While Steve Ma was growing up in suburban New Jersey, he didn't realize that his home state ranked last in the nation in industry compliance with clean water legislation. The extent of the problem and his ability to act became clear, however, when in high school he happened upon a protest over the Exxon Valdez oil spill. Concerned that government was taking inadequate action both in environmental legislation and in promoting citizen awareness, Ma began to search for a venue to make his voice heard. He found the place in the Student Public Interest Research Group (PIRG) of New Jersey at Rutgers University.

STUDENTS AND POLITICS

PIRGs exist in numerous states to promote various consumer rights, including minimizing student tuition increases, protecting the environment, and fighting homelessness. One of Ma's first activities with PIRG was to publish a guide to the goods and services available in New Brunswick, N.J., including critiques of landlords and apartment buildings, restaurant recommendations, and ratings of bookstores that paid for returned textbooks. As the year progressed, he worked on larger projects: he and his chapter worked with local businesses to find cost-effective ways to reduce pollution emissions, saving both the environment and the money necessary to clean contaminated areas. He also worked as an intern at New Jersey PIRG, researching and helping to write a report on the failed implementation of the New Jersey Motor Voter Bill, which required the state's Department of Motor Vehicles to distribute voter registration information to customers.

Over the next year, New Jersey PIRG lobbied heavily for the Clean Water Enforcement Act, a bill that would make New Jersey's clean water laws the most stringent in the nation. "We did so much against millions of dollars of industry lobbying," says Ma. "I actually lobbied the governor himself."[53] The bill passed by a close vote. Since then, New Jersey's compliance with water regulations has increased from last in the nation to fifteenth.

New Jersey PIRG next worked to pass a federal bill that would give redemption value to all recycled cans and bottles. As part of the campaign, Ma led an effort to collect aluminum cans, clean them, and mail them to the White House with stickers stating an individual's support for the bill. "I was literally climbing in dumpsters," he says, "retrieving cans and bottles people had thrown away."[54] PIRG ultimately failed in its efforts to pass the bill, but did create enough publicity for a hearing on the matter in a congressional committee.

After graduating with a B.S. in human ecology, Ma enrolled at Indiana University for his masters in public affairs. As part of his graduate work, he helped to organize a new PIRG in Indiana. After earning his degree, he began work as a full-time grassroots organizer at the California PIRG in Sacramento. "There is really an opportunity at the state level to create the issue," says Ma. "It sounds clichéd, but states are the laboratories of democracy. We were really effective; we had our heads on straight, an eye on the future, and an incredible ability to organize. Classrooms are good, but good internships in which you can do things like lobby the governor and organize meetings are invaluable."[55]

But what about the Madisonian dilemma? Should you become involved in group politics? Would you be contributing to the solution or exacerbating the problem?

★ Summary

Interest groups are pervasive in America. James Madison predicted that special interest groups would proliferate in a free society, but that competition among them would lead to moderation and compromise. Today, this theory is called pluralism. Individuals join or form groups to enhance their influence. To succeed, groups need leadership, a financial base, and active members. Recruiting new members can be difficult because of the "free rider" problem. Interest groups overcome this problem by offering selective benefits to members only. These include information, material benefits, solidary benefits, or purposive benefits.

The number of interest groups in America has increased because of the expansion of the government into new areas. This increase has included not only economic interests, but also "public interest" groups whose members do not seek economic gain. Both economic and public interest groups seek influence through a variety of techniques.

Lobbying is the act of petitioning legislators. Lobbyists—individuals who receive some form of compensation for lobbying—are required to register with the House and Senate. In spite of an undeserved reputation for corruption, lobbyists serve a useful function, providing members of Congress with a vital flow of information.

Access is participation in government. Groups with access have less need for lobbying. Most groups build up access over time through great effort. They work years to get their members into positions of influence on congressional committees. Means of gaining access include corridoring in the bureaucracy, grassroots approaches, and influence peddling.

Litigation sometimes serves interest groups when other strategies fail. Groups may bring suit on their own behalf, finance suits brought by individuals, or file *amicus curiae* briefs.

Going public is an effort to mobilize the widest and most favorable climate of opinion. Advertising is a common technique in this strategy. Other techniques are boycotts, strikes, rallies, and marches.

Groups engage in electoral politics either by embracing one of the major parties, usually through financial support, or through a nonpartisan strategy. Interest groups' campaign contributions now seem to be flowing into the coffers of candidates at a faster rate than ever before.

FOR FURTHER READING

Cigler, Allan J., and Burdett A. Loomis, eds. *Interest Group Politics*. Washington, DC: Congressional Quarterly Press, 1983.

Clawson, Dan, Alan Neustadtl, and Denise Scott. *Money Talks: Corporate PACs and Political Influence*. New York: Basic Books, 1992.

Costain, Anne. *Inviting Women's Rebellion: A Political Process Interpretation of the Women's Movement*. Baltimore, MD: Johns Hopkins University Press, 1992.

Day, Christine. *What Older Americans Think: Interest Groups and Aging Policy*. Princeton, NJ: Princeton University Press, 1990.

Goldfield, Michael. *The Decline of Organized Labor in the United States*. Chicago: University of Chicago Press, 1987.

Hansen, John Mark. *Gaining Access: Congress and the Farm Lobby, 1919–1981*. Chicago: University of Chicago Press, 1991.

Heinz, John P., Edward O. Laumann, Robert L. Nelson, and Robert H. Salisbury. *The Hollow Core: Private Interests in National Policy Making*. Cambridge, MA: Harvard University Press, 1993.

Lowi, Theodore J. *The End of Liberalism*. New York: Norton, 1979.

Moe, Terry M. *The Organization of Interests*. Chicago: University of Chicago Press, 1980.

Olson, Mancur, Jr. *The Logic of Collective Action: Public Goods and the Theory of Groups*. Cambridge, MA: Harvard University Press, 1971.

Olzak, Susan. *The Dynamics of Ethnic Competition and Conflict*. Stanford, CA: Stanford University Press, 1992.

Paige, Connie. *The Right-to-Lifers*. New York: Summit, 1983.

Petracca, Mark, ed. *The Politics of Interests: Interest Groups Transformed*. Boulder, CO: Westview, 1992.

Pope, Jacqueline. *Biting the Hand that Feeds Them: Women on Welfare at the Grass Roots Level*. New York: Praeger, 1989.

Schlozman, Kay Lehman, and John T. Tierney. *Organized Interests and American Democracy*. New York: Harper & Row, 1986.

Staggenborg, Suzanne. *The Pro-Choice Movement: Organization and Activism in the Abortion Conflict*. New York: Oxford University Press, 1991.

Truman, David. *The Governmental Process: Political Interests and Public Opinion*. New York: Knopf, 1951.

Vogel, David. *Fluctuating Fortunes*. New York: Basic Books, 1989.

STUDY OUTLINE

The Character of Interest Groups

1. An enormous number of diverse interest groups exists in the United States.
2. Most interest groups share key organizational components, such as mechanisms for member recruitment, financial and decision-making processes, and agencies that actually carry out group goals.
3. Interest-group politics in the United States tends to have a pronounced upper-class bias because of the characteristics of interest-group members.
4. Because of natural disincentives to join interest groups, groups offer material, solidary, and purposive benefits to entice people to join.

The Proliferation of Groups

1. The modern expansion of governmental economic and social programs has contributed to the enormous increase in the number of groups seeking to influence the American political system.
2. The second factor accounting for the explosion of interest-group activity in recent years was the emergence of a new set of forces in American politics: the New Politics movement.

Strategies: The Quest for Political Power

1. Lobbying is an effort by outsiders to influence Congress or government agencies by providing them with information about issues, giving them support, and even threatening them with retaliation.
2. Access is actual involvement and influence in the decision-making process.
3. Interest groups often turn to litigation when they lack access or feel they have insufficient influence over the formulation and implementation of public policy.
4. Going public is a strategy that attempts to mobilize the widest and most favorable climate of opinion.
5. Many groups use a nonpartisan strategy in electoral politics to avoid giving up access to one party by embracing the other.

Groups and Interests: The Dilemma

1. The organization of private interests into groups to advance their own views is a necessary and intrinsic element of the liberty of citizens to pursue their private lives, and to express their views, individually and collectively.
2. The organization of private interests into groups is biased in favor of the wealthy and the powerful, who have superior knowledge, opportunity, and resources with which to organize.

PRACTICE QUIZ

1. The theory that competition among organized interests will produce balance with all the interests regulating one another is
   a) pluralism.
   b) elite power politics.
   c) democracy.
   d) socialism.

2. To overcome the free rider problem, groups
   a) provide general benefits.
   b) litigate.
   c) go public.
   d) provide selective benefits.

3. Politically organized religious groups often make use of
   a) material benefits.
   b) solidary benefits.
   c) purposive benefits.
   d) none of the above.

4. Which of the following best describes the reputation of the AARP in the Washington community?

   a) It is respected and feared.
   b) It is supported and well liked by all political forces.
   c) It is believed to be ineffective.
   d) It wins the political battles it fights.

5. Which types of interest groups are most often associated with the New Politics movement?
   a) public interest groups
   b) professional associations
   c) government groups
   d) labor groups

6. Access politics, exemplified by defense contractors acting in concert with congressional committees and executive agencies, is an example of
   a) campaign activism.
   b) public interest politics.
   c) an iron triangle.
   d) the role of conservative interest groups.

7. "Corridoring" refers to
   a) lobbying the corridors of Congress.

b) a litigation technique.
c) lobbying the president and the White House staff.
d) lobbying an executive agency.

8. In which of the following ways do interest groups use the courts to affect public policy?
   a) filing *amicus* briefs
   b) bringing lawsuits
   c) financing those bringing suit
   d) all of the above

9. According to this text, what is the limit a PAC can contribute to a primary or general election campaign?
   a) $1,000
   b) $5,000
   c) $10,000
   d) $50,000

10. Which of the following is not an activity in which interest groups frequently engage?
    a) starting their own political party
    b) litigation
    c) lobbying
    d) contributing to campaigns

CRITICAL THINKING QUESTIONS

1. A dilemma is presented by the values of liberty and equality in regard to interest-group activity. On the one hand, individuals should have the liberty to organize themselves politically in order to express their views. On the other hand, there is a strong class bias in the politics of organized interests. How has the U.S. government sought to regulate group activity in order to balance these competing values? What else might government do to make group politics less biased? What are the potential consequences—both good and bad—of the actions you suggest?

2. Describe the different techniques of influence used by organized interests. When is one technique preferable to another? With the rise of the New Politics movement, different techniques are now used more frequently. Which ones? Why, do you think, are these techniques so well suited to New Politics?

KEY TERMS

access (p. 420)
Astroturf lobbying (p. 429)
capture (p. 421)
collective goods (p. 407)
corridoring (p. 421)
cross-lobbying (p. 418)
free riders (p. 407)
going public (p. 424)
grassroots lobbying (p. 426)

institutional advertising (p. 424)
iron triangle (p. 420)
issue network (p. 421)
lobbying (p. 415)
material benefits (p. 407)
membership association (p. 406)
New Politics movement (p. 412)
pluralism (p. 402)

political action committee (PAC) (p. 430)
public interest groups (p. 413)
purposive benefits (p. 408)
reverse lobbying (p. 418)
soft money (p. 433)
solidary benefits (p. 407)
staff organization (p. 406)

Institutions

12

Congress

I F you want to find out what your congressional representative or senator has been doing lately, there are many ways to do so. You can watch your mailbox—most congressional offices send newsletters to constituents to report the office's activities. You can find your representative's home page on the World Wide Web. To get a sense of what is happening in Congress you can tune your television to C-SPAN; chances are that some congressional debate or committee hearing will be in progress. If you want to make your views known to your congressional representative, that is also pretty easy. You can send a postcard or a letter—the address of your representative can usually be found in the blue pages of your local telephone book. You can also call or fax his or her Washington office. The number isn't hard to get; consult your local phone book or call Washington, D.C., directory information.

Many citizens have kept up with new technologies, weaving them into their efforts to influence Congress. Small groups with limited funding now find it easier to contact potential supporters and make their voices heard on Capitol Hill. Groups representing young people and students, such as the National Association of Twentysomethings and the Generation X Coalition, rely on the Internet to publicize their views and to attract support for their lobbying efforts in Congress. Groups also continue to use more old-fashioned methods—such as face-to-face contact—to influence Congress. The United States Student Association, a fifty-year-old organization, sponsors an annual national student lobby day, in which students come to Washington to learn about the legislative process and to lobby their state congressional delegations about issues that concern them, such as educational loans and grants.[1]

Despite these many different ways people can learn about Congress and contact their representatives and senators, citizens regularly complain that Congress is "out of touch." In a recent poll, only 12 percent of Americans said they believed that congressional representatives "pay a good deal of attention to the people who elect them when deciding what to do in Congress." Eighty percent felt that members of Congress lost touch with their constituents soon after being elected.[2] Many Americans believe there is something about politics in Washington that is corrupting. One voter described what happens to members of Congress in this way: "You find so many good people going in and the next thing you know they're corrupted."[3] Congress seems to be the least trusted of America's national institutions.

What is puzzling is that these feelings of distrust and alienation from Congress have grown stronger precisely as access to Congress and its members has increased. Most of the proceedings of Congress have been open to the public since the passage of numerous "sunshine reforms" in the 1970s; today Congress conducts very few secret hearings. Public opinion polls taken before

Congress became more accessible and open showed higher levels of trust and a greater belief that citizens could influence their representatives' decisions. Why has trust in Congress dropped rather than increased as new forms of access and increased openness have been put into place?

One answer to this puzzle is the growing professionalization of Congress as an institution. Professionalization means that Congress has grown more complex as an institution, with more powerful committees, longer terms for members, larger staffs, and higher salaries.[4] In many ways, professionalization makes Congress more capable of reaching informed decisions and makes it easier for members of Congress to serve their constituents. But professionalization also has a downside. It enhances the independence of individual congressional members, often making it harder for the institution as a whole to reach decisions. Moreover, as Congress has professionalized, narrowly focused, well-funded professional interest groups have formed to influence Congress. The growth and sophistication of these groups has made many ordinary citizens feel shut out, canceling out the positive side of the new openness and professionalization of Congress in the public mind. The public feeling of distance from Congress is compounded by the decline of political parties among the electorate. A crucial link that once connected Congress with voters has been severed.

In this chapter we will try to understand the relationship between Congress and the American people. Congress is central to American democracy because it serves as the voice of the people and because it controls a formidable battery of powers that it uses to shape policies.

- **To understand the pivotal role that Congress plays in American democracy, we will first examine the concept of representation.** We will look closely at what it means to say that Congress represents the people. We will also look at how members of Congress act on behalf of their constituents and how the electoral process affects the relationship between Congress and the people.

- **Next, we will discuss the legislative process.** We will study the building blocks of congressional organization, including political parties, the committee system, congressional staff, and caucuses. We then turn to the rules of congressional procedure, through which laws are formulated.

- **We then look at congressional decision making, examining the influences on the legislation that Congress produces.** The complex legislative process is subject to a variety of influences from inside and outside government, including constituencies, interest groups, and party leaders.

- **We next turn to other powers that allow Congress to influence the process of government.** In addition to the power to make law, Congress has an array of instruments to use in its relationship with the president and the executive branch.

- **We conclude by taking a closer look at Congress and democracy.** In assessing whether Congress fulfills democratic principles, we raise the question "why do ordinary people feel so distant from Congress and how can they exercise more influence over Congress?"

★ Congress: Representing the American People

▶ How does Congress represent the United States as a whole? In what ways is it not representative?

▶ In what specific ways do members of Congress act as agents for their constituencies?

▶ In what ways does the electoral system determine who is elected to Congress?

Assemblies and the idea of representation have been around in one form or another for centuries. But until the eighteenth century—with the American and French Revolutions—assemblies were usually means used by monarchs to gain or regain the support of local leaders. Eventually, regional lords and lesser barons, joined by the rising merchant classes, began to see the assembly as a place where they could state their case against the monarch, rather than merely receive his messages to take back to their regions. Through their efforts, the assembly was slowly converted from part of the monarch's regime to an institution that could be used against the monarchy and, later, used by the middle classes against the aristocracy. But the original function of the assembly—getting obedience through consent—never disappeared. It was simply joined by new functions. Once the assembly had evolved into a place where demands could be made, it became a "parliament"—a place where people could come together to talk. ("Parliament" is derived from the French *parler*—to talk.) The French and many other Europeans gave their national assemblies the name "parliament" because they felt that talk was the essential feature of these bodies. Although the U.S. Congress does not share that name, talk is still one of its essential ingredients, built into its very structure. Talk is facilitated by the fact that each member of the House and Senate is, in principle, equal to all the other members. Although the committee structure of Congress gives some members more power than others, a measure of equality in Congress exists by virtue of the fact that membership is determined entirely by election from districts defined as absolutely equal. Each member's primary responsibility is to the district, to his or her **constituency,** not to the congressional leadership, a party, or even Congress itself.

constituency

the district comprising the area from which an official is elected

HOUSE AND SENATE: DIFFERENCES IN REPRESENTATION

The framers of the Constitution provided for a **bicameral** legislature—that is, a legislative body consisting of two chambers. As we saw in Chapter 3, the framers intended each of these chambers, the House and Senate, to serve a different constituency. Members of the Senate, appointed by state legislatures for six-year terms, were to represent the elite members of society and to be more attuned to the interests of property than of population. Today, members of the House and Senate are elected directly by the people. The 435 members of the House are elected from districts apportioned according to population; the 100 members of the Senate are elected by state, with 2 senators from each. Senators continue to have much longer terms in office and usually represent much larger and more diverse constituencies than do their counterparts in the House (see Table 12.1).

bicameral

having a legislative assembly composed of two chambers or houses; opposite of unicameral

Table 12.1	DIFFERENCES BETWEEN THE HOUSE AND THE SENATE	

	House	Senate
Minimum age of member	25 years	30 years
U.S. citizenship	at least 7 years	at least 9 years
Length of term	2 years	6 years
Number per state	Depends on population: 1 per 30,000 in 1789; now 1 per 550,000	2 per state
Constituency	Tends to be local	Both local and national

The House and Senate play different roles in the legislative process. In essence, the Senate is the more deliberative of the two bodies—the forum in which any and all ideas can receive a thorough public airing. The House is the more centralized and organized of the two bodies—better equipped to play a routine role in the governmental process. In part, this difference stems from the different rules governing the two bodies. These rules give House leaders more control over the legislative process and provide for House members to specialize in certain legislative areas. The rules of the much-smaller Senate give its leadership relatively little power and discourage specialization.

Both formal and informal factors contribute to differences between the two chambers of Congress. Differences in the length of terms and requirements for holding office specified by the Constitution in turn generate differences in how members of each body develop their constituencies and exercise their powers of office. The result is that members of the House most effectively and frequently serve as the agents of well-organized local interests with specific legislative agendas—for instance, used-car dealers seeking relief from regulation, labor unions seeking more favorable legislation, or farmers looking for higher subsidies. The small size and relative homogeneity of their constituencies and the frequency with which they must seek re-election make House members more attuned to the legislative needs of local interest groups.

Senators, on the other hand, serve larger and more heterogeneous constituencies. As a result, they are somewhat better able than members of the House to serve as the agents for groups and interests organized on a statewide or national basis. Moreover, with longer terms in office, senators have the luxury of considering "new ideas" or seeking to bring together new coalitions of interests, rather than simply serving existing ones.

SOCIOLOGICAL VS. AGENCY REPRESENTATION

We have become so accustomed to the idea of representative government that we tend to forget what a peculiar concept representation really is. A representative claims to act or speak for some other person or group. But how can one person be trusted to speak for another? How do we know that those who call themselves our representatives are actually speaking on our behalf, rather than simply pursuing their own interests?

There are two circumstances under which one person reasonably might be trusted to speak for another. The first of these occurs if the two individuals are so similar in background, character, interests, and perspectives that anything said by one would very likely reflect the views of the other as well. This principle is at the heart of what is sometimes called **sociological representation**—the sort of representation that takes place when representatives have the same racial, ethnic, religious, or educational backgrounds as their constituents. The assumption is that sociological similarity helps to promote good representation; thus, the composition of a properly constituted representative assembly should mirror the composition of society.

The second circumstance under which one person might be trusted to speak for another occurs if the two are formally bound together so that the representative is in some way accountable to those he or she purports to represent. If representatives can somehow be punished or held to account for failing to speak properly for their constituents, then we know they have an incentive to provide good representation even if their own personal backgrounds, views, and interests differ from those they represent. This principle is called **agency representation**—the sort of representation that takes place when constituents have the power to hire and fire their representatives.

Both sociological and agency representation play a role in the relationship between members of Congress and their constituencies.

The Social Composition of the U.S. Congress   The extent to which the U.S. Congress is representative of the American people in a sociological sense can be seen by examining the distribution of important social characteristics in the House and Senate today. It comes as no surprise that the religious affiliations of members of both the House and Senate are overwhelmingly Protestant—the distribution is very close to the proportion in the population at large—although the Protestant category is composed of more than fifteen denominations. Catholics are the second largest category of religious affiliation, and Jews a much smaller third category.[5] Religious affiliations directly affect congressional debate on a limited range of issues where different moral views are at stake, such as abortion.

Statistics on ethnic or national background are difficult to get and generally unreliable. Individual members of Congress may make a point of their ethnic backgrounds, but an actual count has not been done. Occasionally, an issue like support for Israel or for the Greek community in Cyprus may activate members of Congress along religious or ethnic lines. But these exceptions actually underscore the essentially symbolic nature of these social characteristics.

African Americans, women, Hispanic Americans, and Asian Americans have increased their congressional representation somewhat in the past two decades (see Figure 12.1). In 1999, fifty-six women served in the House of Representatives (up from only twenty-nine in 1990). Nine women now serve in the Senate. However, the representation of women and minorities in Congress is still not comparable to their proportions in the general population. Since many important contemporary national issues do cut along racial and gender lines, a considerable amount of clamor for reform in the representative process is likely to continue until these groups are fully represented.

sociological representation

a type of representation in which representatives have the same racial, ethnic, religious, or educational backgrounds as their constituents. It is based on the principle that if two individuals are similar in background, character, interests, and perspectives, then one could correctly represent the other's views

agency representation

the type of representation by which representatives are held accountable to their constituency if they fail to represent that constituency properly. This is the incentive for good representation when the personal backgrounds, views, and interests of the representative differ from those of his or her constituency

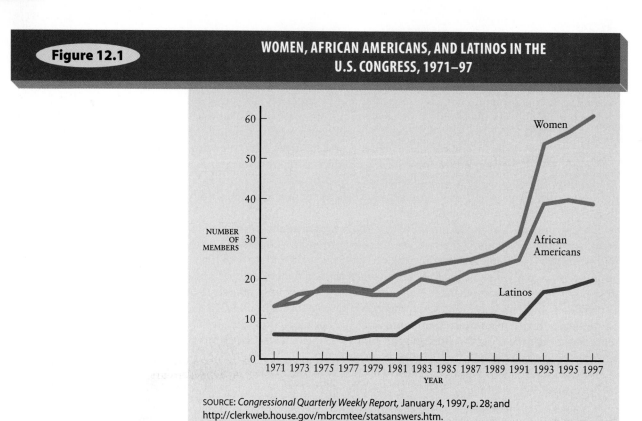

Figure 12.1

WOMEN, AFRICAN AMERICANS, AND LATINOS IN THE U.S. CONGRESS, 1971–97

SOURCE: *Congressional Quarterly Weekly Report,* January 4, 1997, p. 28; and http://clerkweb.house.gov/mbrcmtee/statsanswers.htm.

The occupational backgrounds of members of Congress have always been a matter of interest because so many issues cut along economic lines that are relevant to occupations and industries. The legal profession is the dominant career of most members of Congress prior to their election. Public service or politics is also a significant background. In addition, many members of Congress also have important ties to business and industry.[6] One composite portrait of a typical member of Congress has been that of "a middle-aged male lawyer whose father was of the professional or managerial class; a native-born 'white,' or—if he cannot avoid being an immigrant—a product of northwestern or central Europe or Canada, rather than of eastern or southern Europe, Latin America, Africa or Asia."[7] This is not a portrait of the U.S. population. Congress is not a sociological microcosm of American society, and it probably can never become one. One obvious reason is that the skills and resources needed to achieve political success in the United States are much more likely to be found among well-educated and relatively well-to-do Americans than among members of minority groups and the poor. Take money, for example. As we saw in Chapter 10, successful congressional candidates must be able to raise hundreds of thousands of dollars to finance their campaigns. Poor people from the inner city are much less likely to be able to convince corporate political action committees to provide them with these funds.

Is Congress still able to legislate fairly or to take account of a diversity of views and interests if it is not a sociologically representative assembly? The task is certainly much more difficult. Yet there is reason to believe it can. Representatives, as we shall see shortly, can serve as the agents of their constituents, even if they do not precisely mirror their sociological attributes. Yet, sociological representation is a matter of some importance, even if it is not an absolute prerequisite for fair legislation on the part of members of the House and Senate. At the least, the social composition of a representative assembly is important for symbolic purposes—to demonstrate to groups in the population that they are taken seriously by the government. Concern about the proportion of women, African Americans, and ethnic minorities in Congress and elsewhere in government would exist whether or not these social characteristics influenced the outcomes of laws and policies. It is rare to find a social group whose members do not feel shortchanged if someone like themselves is not a member of the assembly. Thus, the symbolic composition of Congress is ultimately important for the political stability of the United States. If Congress is not representative symbolically, then its own authority and indeed that of the entire government would be reduced.[8]

Representatives as Agents   A good deal of evidence indicates that whether or not members of Congress share their constituents' sociological characteristics, they *do* work very hard to speak for their constituents' views and serve their constituents' interests in the governmental process. The idea of representative as agent is similar to the relationship of lawyer and client. True, the relationship between the member of Congress and as many as 550,000 "clients" in the district, or the senator and millions of "clients" in the state, is very different from that of the lawyer and client. But the criteria of performance are comparable. One expects at the very least that each representative will constantly be seeking to discover the interests of the constituency and will be speaking for those interests in Congress and in other centers of government.[9]

There is constant communication between constituents and congressional offices. For example, each year the House and Senate post offices handle nearly 100 million pieces of incoming mail, and in recent years, members of Congress have spent $75 million annually to send out 400 million pieces of mail.[10]

The seriousness with which members of the House attempt to behave as representatives can be seen in the amount of time spent on behalf of their constituents. Well over a quarter of their time and nearly two-thirds of the time of their staff members is devoted to constituency service (called "case work"). This service is not merely a matter of writing and mailing letters. It includes talking to constituents, providing them with minor services, presenting special bills for them, and attempting to influence decisions by regulatory commissions on their behalf.[11]

Although no members of Congress are above constituency pressures (and they would not want to be), on many issues constituents do not have very strong views and representatives are free to act as they think best. Foreign policy issues often fall into this category. But in many districts there are two or three issues on which constituents have such pronounced opinions that representatives feel they have little freedom of choice. For example, representatives from districts that grow wheat, cotton, or tobacco probably will not want to exercise a great deal of independence on relevant agricultural legislation. In the oil-rich states (such as Oklahoma, Texas, and California), senators and members of the House are likely to be leading advocates of oil interests. For

A few of the fifty-seven women who served in the 104th Congress (1995–96), who introduced to Congress issues ranging from women's health to gun control. Shown here, from left to right, are Senators Nancy Kassebaum, Carol Moseley-Braun, Barbara Boxer, Barbara Mikulski, Kay Bailey Hutchison, Dianne Feinstein, and Patty Murray.

Members of Congress can reach out to their constituents by mailing thousands of newsletters free of charge.

Student Perspectives

ELECTING YOUNGER PEOPLE TO PUBLIC OFFICE

According to a 1996 "Youth Voices" survey and focus groups of 1,200 eighteen- to twenty-four-year-old college students, today's younger generation believes they are misunderstood by older political leaders, who do not share their priorities or understand their lives. Sixty-one percent believe that "politicians have failed my generation." What do these students think is the solution? Electing more younger people to public office. If that were to happen, many claim that they would more likely get involved in politics.

Responses of eighteen- to twenty-four-year-olds to the question,

" How important is it to you that we elect more people to public office who are younger—that is, who are in their twenties or thirties? "

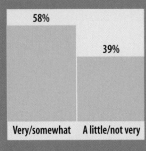

58%

39%

Very/somewhat   A little/not very

one thing, representatives are probably fearful of voting against their district interests; for another, the districts are unlikely to have elected representatives who would *want* to vote against them.

The influence of constituencies is so pervasive that both parties have strongly embraced the informal rule that nothing should be done to endanger the re-election chances of any member. Party leaders obey this rule fairly consistently by not asking any member to vote in a way that might conflict with a district interest.

THE ELECTORAL CONNECTION

The sociological composition of Congress and the activities of representatives once they are in office are very much influenced by electoral considerations. Three factors related to the U.S. electoral system affect who gets elected and what they do once in office. The first set of issues concerns who decides to run for office and which candidates have an edge over others. The second issue is that of incumbency advantage. Finally, the way congressional district lines are drawn can greatly affect the outcome of an election. Let us examine more closely the impact that these considerations have on representation.

Voters' choices are restricted from the start by who decides to run for office. In the past, decisions about who would run for a particular elected office were made by local party officials. A person who had a record of service to the party, or who was owed a favor, or whose "turn" had come up might be nominated by party leaders for an office. Today, few party organizations have the power to slate candidates in that way. Instead, the decision to run for Congress is a more personal choice. One of the most important factors determining who runs for office is a candidate's individual ambition.[12] A potential candidate may also assess whether he or she can attract enough money to mount a credible campaign. The ability to raise money depends on connections with other politicians, interest groups, and national party organizations. In the past, the difficulty of raising campaign funds posed a disadvantage to female candidates. Since the 1980s, however, a number of powerful **political action committees** (PACs) have emerged to recruit women and fund their campaigns. The largest of them, EMILY's List, has become one of the most powerful fund-raisers of all PACs. Recent research shows that money is no longer the barrier it once was to women running for office.[13]

Features distinctive to each congressional district also affect the field of candidates. Among them are the range of other political opportunities that may lure potential candidates away. In addition, the way the congressional district overlaps with state legislative boundaries may affect a candidate's decision to run. A state-level representative or senator who is considering running for the U.S. Congress is more likely to assess his or her prospects favorably if his or her state district coincides with the congressional district (because the voters will already know him or her). And for any candidate, decisions about running must be made early, because once money has been committed to already-declared candidates, it is harder for new candidates to break into a race. Thus, the outcome of a November election is partially determined many months earlier, when decisions to run are finalized.

Incumbency plays a very important role in the American electoral system and in the kind of representation citizens get in Washington. Once in office, members of Congress possess an array of tools that they can use to stack the deck in favor of their re-election. The most important of these is constituency service: taking care of the problems and requests of individual voters. Through such services and through regular newsletter mailings, the incumbent seeks to establish a "personal" relationship with his or her constituents. The success of this strategy is evident in the high rates of re-election for congressional incumbents: as high as 94 percent for House members and 96 percent for members of the Senate in recent years (see Figure 12.2). It is also evident in what is called "sophomore surge"—the tendency for candidates to win a higher percentage of the vote when seeking future terms in office.

Incumbency can also help a candidate by scaring off potential challengers. In many races, potential candidates may decide not to run because they fear that the incumbent simply has too much money or is too well liked or too well known. Potentially strong challengers may also decide that a district's partisan leanings are too unfavorable. The experience of Republican representative Dan Miller in Florida is instructive. When Miller first ran in 1992, he faced five opponents in the Republican primary and a bruising campaign against his Democratic opponent in the general election. In the 1994 election, by contrast, Miller faced only nominal opposition in the Republican primary, winning 81 percent of the vote. In the general election, the strongest potential challenger from the Democratic Party decided not to run; the combination of the incumbency advantage with the strongly Republican leanings of the district gave the Democrats little chance of winning. Miller was re-elected without a challenge.[14]

The advantage of incumbency thus tends to preserve the status quo in Congress. This fact has implications for the social composition of Congress. For example, incumbency advantage makes it harder for women to increase their numbers in Congress because most incumbents are men. Women who run for

political action committee (PAC)

a private group that raises and distributes funds for use in election campaigns

incumbency

holding a political office for which one is running

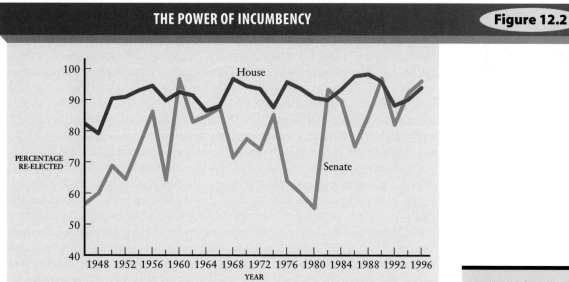

THE POWER OF INCUMBENCY

Figure 12.2

SOURCE: Norman J. Ornstein et al., eds., *Vital Statistics on Congress, 1995–1996* (Washington, DC: Congressional Quarterly Press, 1996), pp. 60–61; and authors' tabulation.

Members of Congress who run for re-election have a very good chance of winning.

Students and Politics

Have you ever wondered how money influences members of Congress? Allan Shuldiner did, and his curiosity led him to employment at the Center for Responsive Politics (CRP). After graduating from Claremont McKenna College in California with a degree in government, Allan parlayed summer internships with Senator Barbara Boxer and Representative Jane Harmon into work with this Washington, D.C., nonprofit organization that tracks money in politics. As the CRP's lobbying specialist, Allan tracks the money spent by special interests on lobbying Congress and ensures the information reaches the public through press releases and published reports. The CRP attempts to show the influence of the dollar on politics in general terms, and allows news agencies to use its information free of charge in news analysis. Occasionally a congressional staff member will call and complain about an unflattering report featuring campaign money. "It's a mix of grunt work, reporting, and analysis," Shuldiner says. "It can be tedious at times, but the information that we find out about Congress and its benefactors can be mind-blowing."

SOURCE: Allan Shuldiner, interview with author, January 22, 1998.

term limits

legally prescribed limits on the number of terms an elected official can serve

redistricting

the process of redrawing election districts and redistributing legislative representatives. This happens every ten years to reflect shifts in population or in response to legal challenges to existing districts

open seats (for which there are no incumbents) are just as likely to win as male candidates.[15] Supporters of **term limits** argue that such limits are the only way to get new faces into Congress. They believe that incumbency advantage and the tendency of many legislators to view politics as a career mean that very little turnover will occur in Congress unless limits are imposed on the number of terms a legislator can serve.

But the tendency toward the status quo is not absolute. In recent years, political observers have suggested that the incumbency advantage may be declining. In the 1992 and 1994 elections, for example, voters expressed considerable anger and dissatisfaction with incumbents, producing a 25 percent turnover in the House in 1992 and a 20 percent turnover in 1994. Yet the defeat of incumbents was not the main factor at work in either of these elections; 88.3 percent of House incumbents were re-elected in 1992, and 90.2 percent won re-election in 1994. In 1992, an exceptionally high retirement rate (20 percent, as opposed to the norm of 10 percent) among members of Congress created more open seats, which brought new faces into Congress. In 1994, a large number of open seats combined with an unprecedented mobilization of Republican voters to shift control of Congress to the Republican Party. Incumbents fared better in 1996 and 1998, when 95 and 98 percent of incumbents were re-elected, respectively.[16]

The final factor that affects who wins a seat in Congress is the way congressional districts are drawn. Every ten years, state legislatures must redraw congressional districts to reflect population changes. This is a highly political process: districts are shaped to create an advantage for the majority party in the state legislature, which controls the **redistricting** process. In this complex process, those charged with drawing districts use sophisticated computer technologies to come up with the most favorable district boundaries. Redistricting can create open seats and pit incumbents of the same party against one another, ensuring that one of them will lose. Redistricting can also give an advantage to one party by clustering voters with some ideological or sociological characteristics in a single district, or by separating those voters into two or more districts.

As we saw in Chapter 10, since the passage of the 1982 amendments to the 1964 Civil Rights Act, race has become a major—and controversial—consideration in drawing voting districts. These amendments, which encouraged the creation of districts in which members of racial minorities have decisive majorities, have greatly increased the number of minority representatives in Congress. After the 1991–92 redistricting, the number of predominantly minority districts doubled, rising from twenty-six to fifty-two. Among the most fervent supporters of the new minority districts were white Republicans, who used the opportunity to create more districts dominated by white Republican voters. These developments raise thorny questions about representation. Some analysts argue that the system may grant minorities greater sociological represen-

Representative Cynthia McKinney, a Democrat from Georgia, holds maps of her Congressional district (right) and the 6th District of Texas. In 1995, the Supreme Court held that McKinney's district, which was 64 percent African American, was unfairly based on race. No challenge was made to Texas's 6th District, which was predominantly white. McKinney handily won re-election in 1996 even though her district had been redrawn to include more white voters.

tation, but it has made it more difficult for minorities to win substantive policy goals. This was a common argument after the sweeping Republican victories in the 1994 congressional elections. Others dispute this argument, noting that the strong surge of Republican voters was more significant than any losses due to racial redistricting.[17]

In 1995, the Supreme Court limited racial redistricting in *Miller v. Johnson,* in which the Court stated that race could not be the predominant factor in creating electoral districts.[18] Yet concerns about redistricting and representation have not disappeared. The distinction between race being a "predominant" factor and its being one factor among many is very hazy. Because the drawing of district boundaries affects incumbents as well as the field of candidates who decide to run for office, it continues to be a key battleground on which political parties fight about the meaning of representation.

DIRECT PATRONAGE

As we saw in the preceding discussion, members of Congress often have an opportunity to provide direct benefits, or **patronage,** for their constituents. The most important of these opportunities for direct patronage is in legislation that has been described half-jokingly as the **pork barrel.** This type of legislation specifies a project to be funded or other authorizations, as well as the location of the project within a particular district. Many observers of Congress argue that pork-barrel bills are the only ones that some members are serious about

patronage

the resources available to higher officials, usually opportunities to make partisan appointments to offices and to confer grants, licenses, or special favors to supporters

pork barrel

appropriations made by legislative bodies for local projects that are often not needed but that are created so that local representatives can win re-election in their home districts

The building of dams is a classic example of pork-barrel spending.

line-item veto

the power of the executive to veto specific provisions (lines) of a bill passed by the legislature

private bill

a proposal in Congress to provide a specific person with some kind of relief, such as a special exemption from immigration quotas

moving toward actual passage, because they are seen as so important to members' re-election bids.

A common form of pork barreling is the "earmark," the practice through which members of Congress insert into otherwise pork-free bills language that provides special benefits for their own constituents. For example, in 1991, Representative Paul Kanjorski (D-Pa.) was able to insert into a section of the Pentagon's budget two paragraphs earmarking $20 million to create "an advanced technology demonstration facility for environmental technology," and stipulating further that "these funds are to be provided only to the organization known as 'Earth Conservancy' in Hanover Township, Pennsylvania." This organization was not only in Kanjorski's district, but was also headed by his brother.[19]

Often, congressional leaders will use pork-barrel projects in exchange for votes on other matters. For example, while serving as Senate majority leader in 1957, Lyndon Johnson won crucial support for civil rights legislation by awarding water projects to Senators Margaret Chase Smith of Maine and Frank Church of Idaho. The most important rule of pork-barreling is that any member of Congress whose district receives a project as part of a bill must support all the other projects on the bill. This cuts across party and ideological lines. Thus, the same 1984 appropriations bill that was supported by conservative Republican senator Ted Stevens of Alaska because it provided funds for Blackhawk helicopters for the Alaska National Guard was also supported by liberal Democrat Ted Kennedy, who had won a provision for $2 million for a lighthouse at Nantucket.

In 1996, as part of the Republicans' Contract with America, Congress granted the president a **line-item veto,** which allows the president to eliminate such earmarks from bills presented to the White House for signature. Republican leaders were willing to risk giving such a powerful tool to a Democratic president because they calculated that, over the decades of Democratic congresses, the GOP had learned to live without much pork, while Democrats had become dependent upon pork to solidify their electoral support. Republican leaders also hoped that a future Republican president, wielding the line-item veto, would be able to further undermine Democratic political strength. President Clinton used the line-item veto eleven times, eliminating 82 individual spending items. But in 1998 the Supreme Court struck down the line-item veto on the grounds that the Constitution does not give the president the power to amend or repeal parts of statutes.[20]

A limited amount of other direct patronage also exists (see Figure 12.3). One important form of constituency service is intervention with federal administrative agencies on behalf of constituents. Members of the House and Senate and their staff members spend a great deal of time on the telephone and in administrative offices seeking to secure favorable treatment for constituents and supporters. A small but related form of patronage is getting an appointment to one of the military academies for the child of a constituent. Traditionally, these appointments are allocated one to a district.

A different form of patronage is the **private bill**—a proposal to grant some kind of relief, special privilege, or exemption to the person named in the bill. The private bill is a type of legislation, but it is distinguished from a public bill, which is supposed to deal with general rules and categories of behavior, people, and institutions. As many as 75 percent of all private bills introduced (and one-third of the ones that pass) are concerned with providing relief for foreign

HOW MEMBERS OF CONGRESS REPRESENT THEIR DISTRICTS

Figure 12.3

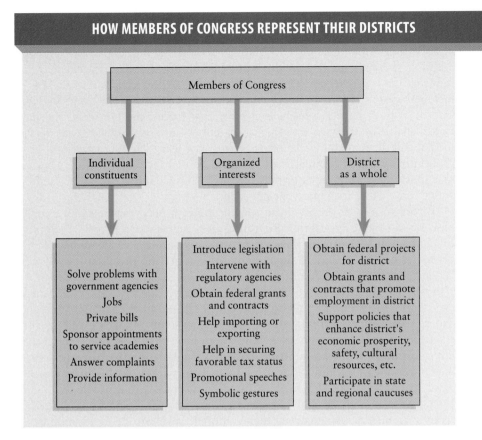

Members of Congress

Individual constituents	Organized interests	District as a whole
Solve problems with government agencies	Introduce legislation	Obtain federal projects for district
Jobs	Intervene with regulatory agencies	Obtain grants and contracts that promote employment in district
Private bills	Obtain federal grants and contracts	Support policies that enhance district's economic prosperity, safety, cultural resources, etc.
Sponsor appointments to service academies	Help importing or exporting	
Answer complaints	Help in securing favorable tax status	
Provide information	Promotional speeches	Participate in state and regional caucuses
	Symbolic gestures	

nationals who cannot get permanent visas to the United States because the immigration quota for their country is filled or because of something unusual about their particular situation.[21]

Private legislation is a congressional privilege that is often abused, but it is impossible to imagine members of Congress giving it up completely. It is one of the easiest, cheapest, and most effective forms of patronage available to each member. It can be defended as an indispensable part of the process by which members of Congress seek to fulfill their role as representatives. And obviously they like the privilege because it helps them win re-election.

The Organization of Congress

▶ What are the basic building blocks of congressional organization? What is the role of each in forming legislation?

The United States Congress is not only a representative assembly. It is also a legislative body. For Americans, representation and legislation go hand in hand. As we saw earlier, however, many parliamentary bodies are representative without the power to legislate. It is no small achievement that the U.S. Congress both represents *and* governs.

It is extraordinarily difficult for a large, representative assembly to formulate, enact, and implement laws. The internal complexities of conducting business within Congress—the legislative process—alone are daunting. In addition, there are many individuals and institutions that have the capacity to influence the legislative process. For example, legislation to raise the salaries of members of the House of Representatives received input from congressional leaders of both parties, special legislative task forces, the president, the national chairs of the two major parties, public interest lobbyists, the news media, and the mass public before it became law in 1989. Since successful legislation requires the confluence of so many distinct factors, it is little wonder that most of the thousands of bills considered by Congress each year are defeated long before they reach the president.

Before an idea or proposal can become a law, it must pass through a complex set of organizations and procedures in Congress. Collectively, these are called the policy-making process, or the legislative process. Understanding this process is central to understanding why some ideas and proposals eventually become law while most do not.

Over its more than two-hundred-year history, Congress has established procedures for creating a division of labor, setting an agenda, maintaining order through rules and procedures, and placing limits on debate and discussion. Still, congressional policy making often is an unwieldy process and the often torturous deliberation affects the kind of legislation that Congress ultimately produces. To win support for their ideas within this complex framework, sponsors of legislation must build compromises that accommodate a broad range of interests. As a consequence, it is far easier to pass bills that represent incremental change rather than comprehensive reform. In addition, legislation often resembles a Christmas tree—festooned with a variety of measures added on by individual congressional representatives. Although such measures may have little to do with the policy under consideration, they are needed to build majority support in Congress.

To exercise its power to make the law, Congress must first bring about something close to an organizational miracle. The building blocks of congressional organization include the political parties, the committee system, congressional staff, the caucuses, and the parliamentary rules of the House and Senate. Each of these factors plays a key role in the organization of Congress and in the process through which Congress formulates and enacts laws.

PARTY LEADERSHIP IN THE HOUSE AND THE SENATE

Every two years, at the beginning of a new Congress, the members of each party gather to elect their House leaders. This gathering is traditionally called the **conference** (House Democrats call theirs the **caucus**). The elected leader of the majority party is later proposed to the whole House and is automatically elected to the position of **Speaker of the House,** with voting along straight party lines. The House majority conference or caucus then also elects a **majority leader.** The minority party goes through the same process and selects the **minority leader.** Both parties also elect whips to line up party members on important votes and to relay voting information to the leaders.

Next in line of importance for each party after the Speaker and majority or minority leader is its Committee on Committees (called the Steering and Policy

---

conference

a gathering of House Republicans every two years to elect their House leaders. Democrats call their gathering the caucus

caucus (political)

a normally closed meeting of a political or legislative group to select candidates, plan strategy, or make decisions regarding legislative matters

Speaker of the House

the chief presiding officer of the House of Representatives. The Speaker is elected at the beginning of every Congress on a straight party vote. The Speaker is the most important party and House leader, and can influence the legislative agenda, the fate of individual pieces of legislation, and members' positions within the House

majority leader

the elected leader of the majority party in the House of Representatives or in the Senate. In the House, the majority leader is subordinate in the party hierarchy to the Speaker of the House

minority leader

the elected leader of the minority party in the House or Senate

The Values of Newt Gingrich

"America is an idea, the most idea-based civilization in history. To be an American is to embrace a set of values. . . ."[1] The writer of these words is Newt Gingrich, one of the most influential and important American politicians today. Gingrich, the fifty-five-year-old Speaker of the House, spearheaded the Republican takeover of Congress in 1994, in part by successfully casting the elections as a national referendum on "values." But what are the values that Newt Gingrich professes? Are those who embrace different values, or express ambivalence about them, not really Americans?

In his book *To Renew America,* Gingrich lists five values that "form the heart of [American] civilization."[2] They so deeply define an American identity, he says, that an immigrant who accepts them is as fully "American" as a Boston Brahmin whose ancestors arrived on the Mayflower. According to Gingrich, these core American values are, first, a common understanding of national identity and origin, an understanding based on religious faith: "In America, power comes from God to the individual and is loaned to the state."[3] The other American values according to Gingrich are an ethic of individual responsibility, a spirit of entrepreneurial free enterprise, the spirit of invention and discovery, and pragmatism and the concern for craft and excellence.

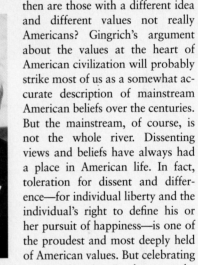

By portraying "the heart of our civilization" as agreement on certain values, Gingrich suggests that consensus is the normal mode of American life, and that conflict represents an aberration in that pattern. Such a "consensus model" was the dominant view of American historians in the 1950s and early 1960s, the years when Gingrich's intellectual orientation was formed and to which he constantly appeals as a high-water mark of American values: "If you want a sense of the personal values we should be communicating to children, get the Boy Scout or Girl Scout handbook. Or go and look at *Reader's Digest* and *The Saturday* *Evening Post* from around 1955."[4] The consensus model lost favor during the 1960s, first with the civil rights struggle in the South, and then with the disillusionment surrounding the Vietnam War. It is significant that Gingrich has little to say about this period as reflective of American values, although surely the mass political protests of that time drew deeply on a tradition of American idealism.

If "America is an idea," as Newt Gingrich says, and if that idea is represented by the values he professes, then are those with a different idea and different values not really Americans? Gingrich's argument about the values at the heart of American civilization will probably strike most of us as a somewhat accurate description of mainstream American beliefs over the centuries. But the mainstream, of course, is not the whole river. Dissenting views and beliefs have always had a place in American life. In fact, toleration for dissent and difference—for individual liberty and the individual's right to define his or her pursuit of happiness—is one of the proudest and most deeply held of American values. But celebrating certain "American" values runs the risk of turning difference into disloyalty, and politics from a civil struggle between honorably differing factions into a kind of holy war to preserve American culture. Such an impulse once drove Newt Gingrich to call President Clinton and his wife "the enemies of normal Americans." Are they? Or are they, and other political opponents of Newt Gingrich, as "normal" and "American" as he is, despite their different ideas?

[1] Newt Gingrich, *To Renew America* (New York: Harper-Collins, 1995), p. 30. All quotations herein are taken from this book.
[2] p. 32.
[3] p. 34.
[4] p. 78.

House Minority Leader Richard Gephardt, left, awards the Speaker's gavel to Newt Gingrich. At the beginning of each congress, the Speaker of the House is elected by a floor vote along party lines.

Committee by the Democrats), whose tasks are to assign new legislators to committees and to deal with the requests of incumbent members for transfers from one committee to another. Currently, the Speaker serves as chair of the Republican Committee on Committees, while the minority leader chairs the Democratic Steering and Policy Committee. (The Republicans have a separate Policy Committee.) At one time, party leaders strictly controlled committee assignments, using them to enforce party discipline. Today, in principle, representatives receive the assignments they want. But assignments on the most important committees are often sought by several individuals, which gives the leadership an opportunity to cement alliances (and, perhaps, make enemies) as it resolves conflicting requests.

Generally, representatives seek assignments that will allow them to influence decisions of special importance to their districts. Representatives from farm districts, for example, may request seats on the Agriculture Committee.[22] Seats on powerful committees such as Ways and Means, which is responsible for tax legislation, and Appropriations are especially popular.

Within the Senate, the president pro tempore exercises primarily ceremonial leadership. Usually, the majority party designates a member with the greatest seniority to serve in this capacity. Real power is in the hands of the majority leader and minority leader, each elected by party conference. Together they control the Senate's calendar, or agenda for legislation. In addition, the senators from each party elect a whip. Each party also elects a Policy Committee, which advises the leadership on legislative priorities.

The structure of majority party leadership in the House and the Senate is shown in Figures 12.4 and 12.5.

In addition to these tasks of organization, congressional party leaders may also seek to establish a legislative agenda. Since the New Deal, presidents have taken the lead in creating legislative agendas (this trend will be discussed in the

MAJORITY PARTY STRUCTURE IN THE HOUSE OF REPRESENTATIVES

Figure 12.4

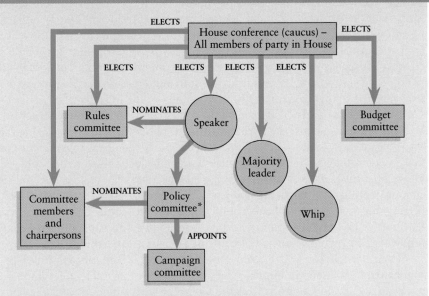

*Includes Speaker (chair), majority leader, chief and deputy whips, caucus chair, four members appointed by the Speaker, and twelve members elected by regional caucuses.

MAJORITY PARTY STRUCTURE IN THE SENATE

Figure 12.5

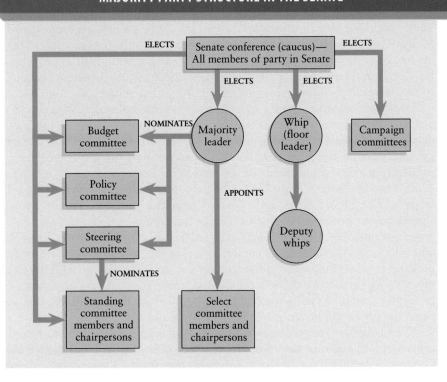

next chapter). But in recent years congressional leaders, facing a White House controlled by the opposing party, have attempted to devise their own agendas. Democratic leaders of Congress sought to create a common Democratic perspective in 1981 when Ronald Reagan became president. The Republican Congress elected in 1994 expanded on this idea, calling its agenda the "Contract with America." In both cases, the majority party leadership has sought to create a consensus among its congressional members around an overall vision to guide legislative activity and to make individual pieces of legislation part of a bigger picture that is distinct from the agenda of the president.

Congressional party leaders have used various strategies to construct such agendas and build consensus around them. Democratic leaders staged an annual Democratic Issues Conference to bring party members together to consider a common agenda. Ongoing task forces produced issue handbooks that highlighted the party's distinctive policy perspectives. These activities did not commit members to particular policies, but instead served to educate members, giving them a shared background on important issues.[23] But these efforts fell short of creating a common agenda. Committee and subcommittee chairs followed their own priorities, not those of the party leadership.

When Bill Clinton was elected president in 1992, Republicans followed a similar strategy, using an annual issues conference to promote a common Republican agenda in Congress. But the Contract with America went further in seeking party unity on policy. With much public fanfare Republican candidates signed the contract, promising to promote its objectives once they were elected. This device no doubt served to promote the unusual coherence and loyalty to the leadership agenda displayed by House Republicans in 1995.

THE COMMITTEE SYSTEM: THE CORE OF CONGRESS

The committee system is central to the operation of Congress. At each stage of the legislative process, Congress relies on committees and subcommittees to do the hard work of sorting through alternatives and writing legislation. There are several different kinds of congressional committees; these include standing committees, select committees, joint committees, and conference committees.

standing committee

a permanent committee with the power to propose and write legislation that covers a particular subject, such as finance or appropriations

Standing committees are the most important arenas of congressional policy making. These committees continue in existence from congress to congress; they have the power to propose and write legislation. The jurisdiction of each standing committee covers a particular subject matter, which in most cases parallels the major departments or agencies in the executive branch (see Table 12.2). Among the most important standing committees are those in charge of finances. The House Ways and Means Committee and the Senate Finance Committee are powerful because of their jurisdiction over taxes, trade, and expensive entitlement programs such as Social Security and Medicare. The Senate and House Appropriations committees also play important ongoing roles because they decide how much funding various programs will actually receive; they also determine exactly how the money will be spent. A seat on an appropriations committee allows a member the opportunity to direct funds to a favored program—perhaps one in his or her home district.

Except for the House Rules Committee, all standing committees receive proposals for legislation and process them into official bills. The House Rules Committee decides the order in which bills come up for a vote on the House

PERMANENT COMMITTEES OF CONGRESS

Table 12.2

House committees

Agriculture	National Security
Appropriations	Resources
Banking and Financial Services	Rules
Budget	Science
Commerce	Select Intelligence
Education and the Workforce	Small Business
Government Reform and Oversight	Standards of Official Conduct*
House Oversight	Transportation and Infrastructure
International Relations	Veterans' Affairs
Judiciary	Ways and Means

Senate committees

Agriculture, Nutrition, and Forestry	Finance
Appropriations	Foreign Relations
Armed Services	Governmental Affairs
Banking, Housing, and Urban Affairs	Judiciary
Budget	Labor and Human Resources
Commerce, Science, and Transportation	Rules and Administration
Energy and Natural Resources	Select Intelligence
Environment and Public Works	Small Business
	Veterans' Affairs

*Temporarily suspended at the start of the 105th Congress (1997).

floor and determines the specific rules that govern the length of debate and opportunity for amendments. The Senate, which has less formal organization and fewer rules, does not have a rules committee.

Select committees are usually not permanent and usually do not have the power to report legislation. (The House and Senate Select Intelligence committees are permanent, however, and do have the power to report legislation.) These committees may hold hearings and serve as focal points for the issues they are charged with considering. Congressional leaders form select committees when they want to take up issues that fall between the jurisdictions of existing committees, to highlight an issue, or to investigate a particular problem. Examples of select committees investigating political scandals include the Senate Watergate Committee of 1973, the committees set up in 1987 to investigate the Iran-Contra affair, and the Whitewater Committee of 1995–96. Select committees set up to highlight ongoing issues have included the House Select Committee on Hunger, established in 1984, and the House Select Narcotics Committee. A few select committees have remained in existence for many years, such as the select committees on aging; hunger; children, youth, and families; and narcotics abuse and control. In 1995, however, congressional Republicans abolished most of these select committees, both to streamline operations and to remove a forum used primarily by Democratic representatives and their allies.

select committee

a (usually) temporary legislative committee set up to highlight or investigate a particular issue or address an issue not within the jurisdiction of existing committees

joint committee

a legislative committee formed of members of both the House and the Senate

conference committee

a joint committee created to work out a compromise on House and Senate versions of a piece of legislation

seniority

priority or status ranking given to an individual on the basis of length of continuous service on a committee in Congress

Select committees are sometimes convened to investigate government abuses. Former national security adviser Robert C. McFarlane testified before a joint House-Senate Select Committee about his role in the Iran-Contra affair.

Joint committees involve members from both the Senate and the House. There are four such committees: economic, taxation, library, and printing. These joint committees are permanent, but they do not have the power to report legislation. The Joint Economic Committee and the Joint Taxation Committee have often played important roles in collecting information and holding hearings on economic and financial issues.

Finally, **conference committees** are temporary committees whose members are appointed by the Speaker of the House and the presiding officer of the Senate. These committees are charged with reaching a compromise on legislation once it has been passed by the House and the Senate. Conference committees play an extremely important role in determining what laws are actually passed, because they must reconcile any differences in the legislation passed by the House and Senate.

Assignments to standing committees are made by a "committee on committees" appointed by the leadership of each party in each chamber of Congress. For the most part, these committees try to accommodate the requests of individual members for assignments. The decision about which committee seats to pursue is the most important choice an incoming member of Congress faces. Members are guided by different considerations in requesting committee assignments, but most prominent are serving constituent interests, making good public policy, and winning more influence in Congress.[24]

Within each committee, hierarchy is based on seniority. **Seniority** is determined by years of continuous service on a particular committee, not years of service in the House or Senate. In general, each committee is chaired by the most senior member of the majority party. But the principle of seniority is not absolute. Both Democrats and Republicans have violated it on occasion. At the start of the 104th Congress in 1995, House Republicans violated the principle of seniority in the selection of a number of key committee chairs, for example.

Over the years, Congress has reformed its organizational structure and operating procedures. Most changes have been made to improve efficiency, but some reforms have also represented a response to political considerations. In the 1970s, for example, a series of reforms substantially altered the organization of power in Congress. Among the most important changes put into place at that time were an increase in the number of subcommittees; greater autonomy for subcommittee chairs; the opening of most committee deliberations to the public; and a system of multiple referral of bills, which allowed several committees to consider one bill at the same time. One of the driving impulses behind these reforms was an effort to reduce the power of committee chairs. In the past, committee chairs exercised considerable power; they determined hearing schedules, selected subcommittee members, and appointed committee staff. Some chairs used their power to block consideration of bills they opposed. Because of the seniority system, many of the key committees were chaired by southern Democrats who stymied liberal legislation throughout the 1960s and early 1970s. By enhancing subcommittee power and allowing more members to chair subcommittees and appoint subcommittee staff, the reforms undercut the power of committee chairs.

Yet the reforms of the 1970s created new problems for Congress. As a consequence of the reforms, power has become more fragmented, making it harder to reach agreement on legislation. With power dissipated over a large number of committees and subcommittees, members spend more time in unproductive "turf battles." In addition, as committees expanded in size, members found they had so many committee responsibilities that they had to run from meeting to meeting. Thus their ability to specialize in a particular policy area has diminished as their responsibilities have increased.[25] The Republican leadership of the 104th Congress (1995–96) sought to reverse the fragmentation of congressional power and concentrate more authority in the party leadership. One of the ways the House achieved this was by violating the principle of seniority in the selection of a number of committee chairs. This move tied committee chairs more closely to the leadership. In addition, the Republican leadership eliminated 25 of the House's 115 subcommittees and gave committee chairs more power over their subcommittees. The result was an unusually cohesive congressional majority, which pushed forward a common agenda. This unity came at a cost, however. Committees in the 104th Congress were far less likely to engage in deliberation, and the quickened pace of the legislative process meant that committee members often did not know the content of the bills they were considering.[26]

THE STAFF SYSTEM: STAFFERS AND AGENCIES

A congressional institution second in importance only to the committee system is the staff system. Every member of Congress employs a large number of staff members, whose tasks include handling constituency requests and, to a large and growing extent, dealing with legislative details and the activities of administrative agencies. Increasingly, staffers bear the primary responsibility for formulating and drafting proposals, organizing hearings, dealing with administrative agencies, and negotiating with lobbyists. Indeed, legislators typically deal with one another through staff, rather than through direct, personal contact. Representatives and senators together employ nearly eleven thousand staffers in their Washington and home offices. Today, staffers even develop policy ideas, draft legislation, and in some instances, have a good deal of influence over the legislative process.

In addition to the personal staffs of individual senators and representatives, Congress also employs roughly two thousand committee staffers. These individuals make up the permanent staff, who stay attached to every House and Senate committee regardless of turnover in Congress and who are responsible for organizing and administering the committee's work, including research, scheduling, organizing hearings, and drafting legislation. Committee staffers can come to play key roles in the legislative process. One example of the importance of committee staffers is the so-called Gephardt health care reform bill, named for the then–House majority leader, Richard Gephardt of

Students and Politics

Alisa Wrase, a student at Florida Atlantic University, interning in the office of Senator Bob Graham (D-Fl.): "While I have had an interest in politics for a few years, I never thought that I could have a voice or act in a way that could affect decision making. By taking this internship, I have realized that it is not only our elected officials who have the say in the decisions, but also the staff that keeps these officials updated and ready for new issues.... I have been able to help write a floor speech, research various topics of interest to the senator and myself, and help constituents with any problems or concerns of their own.

"Through my two months of legislative exposure, I have been able to see and do more than I ever thought possible. My supervisors have expected me to conduct meetings, update and edit constituent letters, and research issues that the senator has requested information about. Besides these tasks, I have been able to give the senator information about a bill that he chose, upon my recommendation, to cosponsor. With my research and interest, I was able to have the senator be the original Democratic cosponsor of the Internet Gambling Prohibition Act of 1997, introduced to the Senate on Wednesday, March 19th. This bill is especially exciting because of its bipartisan effort to correct a source of addiction without taking any power away from the states. Without my memos and work on the bill, the senator would probably never have even known that this bill was going to be introduced, much less cosponsor it and put in a floor statement for the *Congressional Record*."

SOURCE: The Washington Center for Internships and Academic Seminars, in agreement with W. W. Norton.

Representative Connie Morella meets with staff in her Capitol Hill office. Staffers typically perform routine office work and deal with requests from constituents, but some also help in developing new policy initiatives and drafting legislation.

Missouri, and introduced in August 1994. Though the bill bore Gephardt's name, it was actually crafted by a small group of staff members of the House Ways and Means Committee. These aides, under the direction of David Abernathy, the staff's leading health care specialist, debated methods of cost control, service delivery, the role of the insurance industry, and the needs of patients, and listened to hundreds of lobbyists before drafting the complex Gephardt bill.[27]

As Figure 12.6 shows, the number of congressional staff members grew rapidly during the 1960s and 1970s, leveled off in the 1980s, and decreased dramatically in 1995. This sudden drop fulfilled the Republican congressional candidates' campaign promise to reduce the size of committee staffs.

Not only does Congress employ personal and committee staff, but it has also established **staff agencies** designed to provide the legislative branch with resources and expertise independent of the executive branch. These agencies enhance Congress's capacity to oversee administrative agencies and to evaluate presidential programs and proposals. They include the Congressional Research Service, which performs research for legislators who wish to know the facts and competing arguments relevant to policy proposals or other legislative business; the General Accounting Office, through which Congress can investigate the financial and administrative affairs of any government agency or program; and the Congressional Budget Office, which assesses the economic implications and likely costs of proposed federal programs, such as health care reform proposals. A fourth agency, the Office of Technology Assessment, which provided Congress with analyses of scientific or technical issues, was abolished in 1995.

staff agency

a legislative support agency responsible for policy analysis

caucus (congressional)

an association of members of Congress based on party, interest, or social group, such as gender or race

INFORMAL ORGANIZATION: THE CAUCUSES

In addition to the official organization of Congress, there also exists an unofficial organizational structure—the caucuses. **Caucuses** are groups of senators

THE GROWTH OF CONGRESSIONAL STAFFS, 1930–95

Figure 12.6

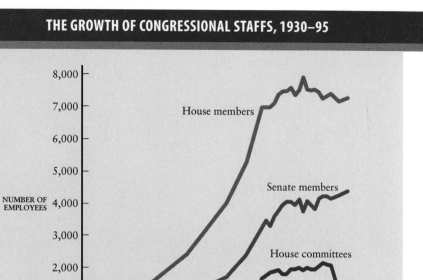

SOURCE: Norman J. Ornstein et al., eds., *Vital Statistics on Congress, 1997–1998* (Washington, DC: Congressional Quarterly Press, 1998), p. 201.

or representatives who share certain opinions, interests, or social characteristics. They include ideological caucuses such as the liberal Democratic Study Group, the conservative Democratic Forum (popularly known as the "boll weevils"), and the moderate Republican Wednesday Group. At the same time, there are a large number of caucuses composed of legislators representing particular economic or policy interests, such as the Travel and Tourism Caucus, the Steel Caucus, the Mushroom Caucus, and Concerned Senators for the Arts. Legislators who share common backgrounds or social characteristics have organized caucuses such as the Congressional Black Caucus, the Congressional Caucus for Women's Issues, and the Hispanic Caucus. All these caucuses seek to advance the interests of the groups they represent by promoting legislation, encouraging Congress to hold hearings, and pressing administrative agencies for favorable treatment. The Congressional Black Caucus, for example, which in 1996 included forty representatives and one senator, has played an active role in Congress since 1970.

Before 1995, many of the largest and most effective caucuses were registered as Legislative Service Organizations (LSOs). LSOs were allotted office space in congressional buildings and congressional members were allowed to transfer some of their own budgets to the LSO. Several of the most effective LSOs, including the Black Caucus, the Hispanic Caucus, and the Women's Caucus, were closely tied to the Democratic Party. One LSO, the Democratic Study Group (DSG), once employed eighteen full-time analysts to help congressional Democrats evaluate proposed and pending legislation. In 1995, the

The Black Caucus, gathered here to publicize its position on a sexual harassment case, has been a powerful force in American politics since 1970.

Republican leadership of the 104th Congress took away the budgets, staffs, and offices of all LSOs, in part because of these LSOs' links to the Democrats.[28] But most caucuses continued their activities, and new ones were created after this change. Of course, some of the larger caucuses found it harder to coordinate their activities and provide information to their members after they lost their status as LSOs, but caucuses continue to be an important part of congressional organization.[29]

Rules of Lawmaking: How a Bill Becomes a Law

▶ How do the rules of congressional procedure influence the fate of legislation as well as determine the distribution of power in Congress?

The institutional structure of Congress is one key factor that helps to shape the legislative process. A second and equally important set of factors is the rules of congressional procedure. These rules govern everything from the introduction of a **bill** through its submission to the president for signing (see Figure 12.7). Not only do these regulations influence the fate of each and every bill, they also help to determine the distribution of power in the Congress.

COMMITTEE DELIBERATION

Even if a member of Congress, the White House, or a federal agency has spent months developing and drafting a piece of legislation, it does not become a bill

bill

a proposed law that has been sponsored by a member of Congress and submitted to the clerk of the House or Senate

HOW A BILL BECOMES A LAW

Figure 12.7

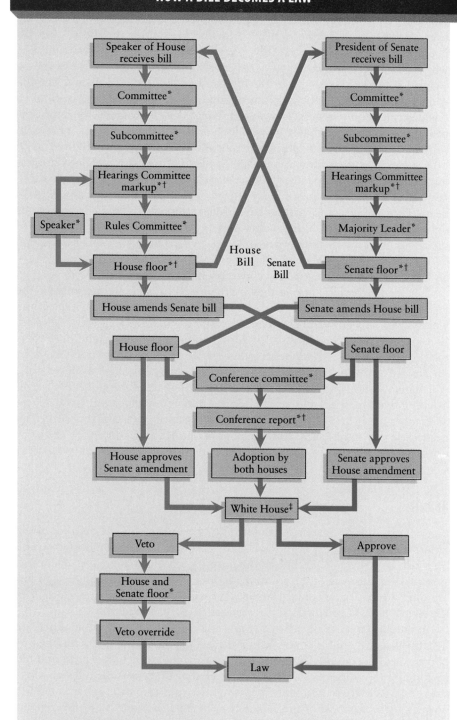

*Points at which a bill can be amended.
†Points at which a bill can die.
‡If the president neither signs nor vetoes a bill within ten days, it automatically becomes law.

until it is submitted officially by a senator or representative to the clerk of the House or Senate and referred to the appropriate committee for deliberation. No floor action on any bill can take place until the committee with jurisdiction over it has taken all the time it needs to deliberate. During the course of its deliberations, the committee typically refers the bill to one of its subcommittees, which may hold hearings, listen to expert testimony, and amend the proposed legislation before referring it to the full committee for consideration. The full committee may accept the recommendation of the subcommittee or hold its own hearings and prepare its own amendments. Or, even more frequently, the committee and subcommittee may do little or nothing with a bill that has been submitted to them. Many bills are simply allowed to "die in committee" with little or no serious consideration given to them. Often, members of Congress introduce legislation that they neither expect nor desire to see enacted into law, merely to please a constituency group. These bills die a quick and painless death. Other pieces of legislation have ardent supporters and die in committee only after a long battle. But, in either case, most bills are never reported out of the committees to which they are assigned. In a typical congressional session, 95 percent of the roughly eight thousand bills introduced die in committee—an indication of the power of the congressional committee system.

The relative handful of bills that are reported out of committee must, in the House, pass one additional hurdle within the committee system—the Rules Committee. This powerful committee determines the rules that will govern action on the bill on the House floor. In particular, the Rules Committee allots the time for debate and decides to what extent amendments to the bill can be proposed from the floor. A bill's supporters generally prefer a **closed rule,** which puts severe limits on floor debate and amendments. Opponents of a bill usually prefer an **open rule,** which permits potentially damaging floor debate and makes it easier to add amendments that may cripple the bill or weaken its chances for passage. Thus, the outcome of the Rules Committee's deliberations can be extremely important and the committee's hearings can be an occasion for sharp conflict.

DEBATE

Party control of the agenda is reinforced by the rule giving the Speaker of the House and the president of the Senate the power of recognition during debate on a bill. Usually the chair knows the purpose for which a member intends to speak well in advance of the occasion. Spontaneous efforts to gain recognition are often foiled. For example, the Speaker may ask, "For what purpose does the member rise?" before deciding whether to grant recognition.

In the House, virtually all of the time allotted by the Rules Committee for debate on a given bill is controlled by the bill's sponsor and by its leading opponent. In almost every case, these two people are the committee chair and the ranking minority member of the committee that processed the bill—or those they designate. These two participants are, by rule and tradition, granted the power to allocate most of the debate time in small amounts to members who are seeking to speak for or against the measure. Preference in the allocation of time goes to the members of the committee whose jurisdiction covers the bill.

In the Senate, the leadership has much less control over floor debate. Indeed, the Senate is unique among the world's legislative bodies for its commit-

closed rule

a provision by the House Rules Committee limiting or prohibiting the introduction of amendments during debate

open rule

a provision by the House Rules Committee that permits floor debate and the addition of new amendments to a bill

ment to unlimited debate. Once given the floor, a senator may speak as long as he or she wishes. On a number of memorable occasions, senators have used this right to prevent action on legislation that they opposed. Through this tactic, called the **filibuster,** small minorities or even one individual in the Senate can force the majority to give in. During the 1950s and 1960s, for example, opponents of civil rights legislation often sought to block its passage by staging a filibuster. The votes of three-fifths of the Senate, or sixty votes, are needed to end a filibuster. This procedure is called **cloture.**

Whereas the filibuster was once an extraordinary tactic used only on rare occasions, in recent years it has been used increasingly often. In 1994, the filibuster was used by Republicans and some Democrats to defeat legislation that would have prohibited employers from permanently replacing striking workers. Later, Republicans threatened to filibuster health care reform legislation. Some Democrats argued that Senate Republicans had begun to use the filibuster as a routine instrument of legislative obstructionism to make up for their minority status in Congress, and proposed rule changes that would make filibustering more difficult. One of the most senior Democrats in the Senate, however, former majority leader Robert Byrd of West Virginia, warned against limiting the filibuster, saying, "The minority can be right, and on many occasions in this country's history, the minority was right."[30] After the GOP won control of the Senate in 1994, many Democrats began to agree with Senator Byrd. They used the filibuster to block Republican initiatives on environmental and social policy. A Democratic-led filibuster in 1996, for example, halted Republican efforts to open up large areas of protected federal land in Utah for development.

Although it is the best known, the filibuster is not the only technique used to block Senate debate. Under Senate rules, members have a virtually unlimited ability to propose amendments to a pending bill. Each amendment must be voted on before the bill can come to a final vote. The introduction of new amendments can be stopped only by unanimous consent. This, in effect, can permit a determined minority to filibuster-by-amendment, indefinitely delaying the passage of a bill. This tactic was briefly used by Republicans in 1994 to delay the administration's health care initiative. Senators can also place "holds," or stalling devices, on bills to delay debate. Senators place holds on bills when they fear that openly opposing them will be unpopular. Because holds are kept secret, the senators placing the holds do not have to take public responsibility for their actions. Such holds blocked bipartisan efforts to enact popular health insurance reforms for much of 1996. In 1997, opponents of this practice introduced an amendment that would have required publicizing the identity of the senator putting a bill on hold. But when the Senate voted on the measure, the proposal to end the practice of anonymous holds had "mysteriously disappeared."[31] Although no one took credit for killing the measure, it was evident that the majority of senators wanted to maintain the practice.

Once a bill is debated on the floor of the House and the Senate, the leaders schedule it for a vote on the floor of each chamber. By this time, congressional leaders know what the vote will be; leaders do not bring legislation to the floor unless they are fairly certain it is going to pass. As a consequence, it is unusual for the leadership to lose a bill on the floor. On rare occasions, the last moments of the floor vote can be very dramatic, as each party's leadership puts its whip organization into action to make sure that wavering members vote with the party.

filibuster

a tactic used by members of the Senate to prevent action on legislation they oppose by continuously holding the floor and speaking until the majority backs down. Once given the floor, senators have unlimited time to speak, and it requires a vote of three-fifths of the Senate to end a filibuster

cloture

a rule allowing a majority of two-thirds or three-fifths of the members in a legislative body to set a time limit on debate over a given bill

Senator Strom Thurmond of South Carolina leaving the Senate chamber after delivering a twenty-four-hour, nineteen-minute filibuster against a civil rights bill in 1957.

CONFERENCE COMMITTEE: RECONCILING HOUSE AND SENATE VERSIONS OF LEGISLATION

Getting a bill out of committee and through one of the houses of Congress is no guarantee that a bill will be enacted into law. Frequently, bills that began with similar provisions in both chambers emerge with little resemblance to each other. Alternatively, a bill may be passed by one chamber but undergo substantial revision in the other chamber. In such cases, a conference committee composed of the senior members of the committees or subcommittees that initiated the bills may be required to iron out differences between the two pieces of legislation. Sometimes members or leaders will let objectionable provisions pass on the floor with the idea that they will get the change they want in conference. Usually, conference committees meet behind closed doors. Agreement requires a majority of each of the two delegations. Legislation that emerges successfully from a conference committee is more often a compromise than a clear victory of one set of forces over another.

When a bill comes out of conference, it faces one more hurdle. Before a bill can be sent to the president for signing, the House-Senate conference committee's version of the bill must be approved on the floor of each chamber. Usually such approval is given quickly. Occasionally, however, a bill's opponents use this round of approval as one last opportunity to defeat a piece of legislation.

PRESIDENTIAL ACTION

veto

the president's constitutional power to turn down acts of Congress. A presidential veto may be overriden by a two-thirds vote of each house of Congress

Once adopted by the House and Senate, a bill goes to the president, who may choose to sign the bill into law or **veto** it. The veto is the president's constitutional power to reject a piece of legislation. To veto a bill, the president returns it unsigned within ten days to the house of Congress in which it originated. If Congress adjourns during the ten-day period, and the president has taken no action, the bill is also considered to be vetoed. This latter method is known as

This conference committee is meeting to reconcile the differences between House and Senate versions of a budget bill.

the **pocket veto.** The possibility of a presidential veto affects how willing members of Congress are to push for different pieces of legislation at different times. If they think a proposal is likely to be vetoed they might shelve it for a later time.

A presidential veto may be overridden by a two-thirds vote in both the House and Senate. A veto override says much about the support that a president can expect from Congress, and it can deliver a stinging blow to the executive branch. President George Bush used his veto power on forty-six occasions during his four years in office and in all but one instance was able to defeat or avoid a congressional override of his action. Bush's frequent resort to the veto power was one indicator of the struggle between the White House and the Congress over domestic and foreign policy that took place during his term. Similarly, President Clinton used the veto to block many Republican programs in 1995.

pocket veto

a presidential veto that is automatically triggered if the president does not act on a given piece of legislation passed during the final ten days of a legislative session

How Congress Decides

▶ What sorts of influences inside and outside of government determine how members of Congress vote on legislation? How do these influences vary according to the type of issue?

What determines the kinds of legislation that Congress ultimately produces? According to the most simple theories of representation, members of Congress would respond to the views of their constituents. In fact, the process of creating a legislative agenda, drawing up a list of possible measures, and deciding among them is a very complex process, in which a variety of influences from inside and outside government play important roles. External influences include a legislator's constituency and various interest groups. Influences from inside government include party leadership, congressional colleagues, and the president. Let us examine each of these influences individually and then consider how they interact to produce congressional policy decisions.

Representative John Conyers meets with constituents in his Capitol Hill office.

CONSTITUENCY

Because members of Congress, for the most part, want to be re-elected, we would expect the views of their constituents to be a primary influence on the decisions that legislators make. Yet constituency influence is not so straightforward. In fact, most constituents do not even know what policies their representatives support. The number of citizens who *do* pay attention to such matters—the attentive public—is usually very small. Nonetheless, members of Congress spend a lot of time worrying about what their constituents think, because these representatives realize that the choices they make may be scrutinized in a future election and used as ammunition by an opposing candidate. Because of this possibility, members of Congress try to anticipate their constituents' policy views.[32] Legislators are more likely to act in accordance with those views if they think that voters will take them into account during

Students and Politics

The national student lobby has grown increasingly powerful over the last few years, thanks in part to the United States Student Association (USSA), which conducts annual clinics to train students from around the nation how to lobby their senators and representatives—then provides them with the opportunity to do so. Sarita Gupta of Mount Holyoke College participated in USSA's National Lobbying Day in 1996, and was not disappointed. "Most students feel that they can only influence local politics," she says. "This day is an empowering experience for a lot of people." The three-day training course in Washington, D.C., offers participants two types of workshops: one on educational issues, and one on the skills needed to lobby successfully. After the workshops, USSA organizes the students into lobbying teams. Gupta lobbied her senators from New York, Alfonse D'Amato and Daniel Patrick Moynihan, on increasing federal grants to students in need, maintaining equitable financial aid for legal residents, and keeping interest rates on students loans to a minimum. "As students, we have the ability to lobby effectively, but are usually not put in the position to do so. With twenty minutes to a half hour, we could say, 'Yes, we are your constituents, too, and you have to listen to us.'"

SOURCE: Sarita Gupta, interview with author, April 28, 1998.

elections. In October 1998, for example, thirty-one House Democrats broke party ranks and voted in favor of an impeachment inquiry against President Clinton because they believed a "no" vote could cost them re-election that November. In this way, constituents may affect congressional policy choices even when there is little direct evidence of their influence.

INTEREST GROUPS

Interest groups are another important external influence on the policies that Congress produces. When members of Congress are making voting decisions, those interest groups that have some connection to constituents in particular members' districts are most likely to be influential. For this reason, interest groups with the ability to mobilize followers in many congressional districts may be especially influential in Congress. In recent years, Washington-based interest groups with little grassroots strength have recognized the importance of locally generated activity. They have, accordingly, sought to simulate grassroots pressure, using a strategy that has been nicknamed "Astroturf lobbying." Such campaigns encourage constituents to sign form letters or postcards, which are then sent to congressional representatives. Sophisticated "grassroots" campaigns set up toll-free telephone numbers for a system in which simply reporting your name and address to the listening computer will generate a letter to your congressional representative. One Senate office estimated that such organized campaigns to demonstrate "grassroots" support account for two-thirds of the mail the office received. As such campaigns increase, however, they may become less influential, because members of Congress are aware of how rare actual constituent interest actually is.[33]

Interest groups also have substantial influence in setting the legislative agenda and in helping to craft specific language in legislation. Today, sophisticated lobbyists win influence by providing information about policies to busy members of Congress. As one lobbyist noted, "You can't get access without knowledge. . . . I can go in to see [former Energy and Commerce Committee chair] John Dingell, but if I have nothing to offer or nothing to say, he's not going to want to see me."[34] In recent years, interest groups have also begun to build broader coalitions and comprehensive campaigns around particular policy issues. These coalitions do not rise from the grass roots, but instead are put together by Washington lobbyists who launch comprehensive lobbying campaigns that combine simulated grassroots activity with information and campaign funding for members of Congress. In 1995, the Republican congressional leadership worked so closely with lobbyists that critics charged that the boundaries between lobbyists and legislators had been erased, and that lobbyists had become "adjunct staff to the Republican leadership."[35]

POLICY DEBATE

Tax Cuts vs. Social Welfare Spending

Since the start of the 1980s, a more conservative national mood has supported reductions in the size and cost of the federal government. While most citizens continue to favor most government spending programs, from Social Security to national defense, a new generation of conservative leaders has championed the popular cause of lower taxes and smaller government. Republicans who have long supported such reductions in the name of individual liberty, such as Speaker of the House Newt Gingrich, have been joined by Democrats—most notably by President Bill Clinton, who proclaimed in 1996 that "the era of big government is over." Acknowledging that few citizens enjoy paying taxes, critics of tax-cut enthusiasts have argued that the real agenda behind the tax-cut chant is a backdoor effort to cut popular and necessary government programs that conservatives have failed to cut through the regular political process.

Supporters of reduced taxes and smaller government point out that the government itself has grown out of control. For instance, from 1789 to 1980, the total accumulated federal debt stood at $1 trillion. Between 1980 and 1992, however, the total federal debt ballooned to over $4 trillion, a clear indication that government spending has spiraled out of control. At the same time, public opinion polls show that Americans have less and less trust in their government to spend tax dollars wisely or well. A family that spends irresponsibly and beyond its means must learn to tighten its belt, spend less, and aim to balance its checkbook. The government, most citizens agree, must do the same. By reducing taxes, the government can turn over to citizens more control over their own spending and wealth. As it is, the average family spends more on taxes than on food, shelter, and clothing combined. Two wage earners have become necessary for most families to make ends meet. By cutting taxes, citizens can direct more of their own resources

toward home purchases, saving for college, or other family priorities. Such an approach is an economical substitute for large, inefficient government programs designed to serve the same purposes. In short, citizens have made their preferences for the end of big government clear. Tax relief provides the avenue to achieve that end.

Opponents of big tax cuts argue that the conservative agenda offers a false promise—that citizens can continue to have the programs and services they favor while also getting big tax cuts. The ballooning deficits of the 1980s did indeed sound an alarm, but the crisis was not big government out of control. Rather, it was conservatives who cynically cut taxes and actually increased spending in areas like national defense, knowing that large deficits would be the result. Rather than take the blame, conservatives pointed their fingers at social welfare and other domestic spending programs. Large and expensive government programs like Social Security, Medicare, Medicaid, and national defense remained mostly untouched. Instead, public anger was directed at programs like Aid to Families with Dependent Children (AFDC), child nutrition programs, education, and environmental programs, which constitute less than 10 percent of the federal budget. Thus, the tax-cut mantra was a political gimmick to slash social programs despised by conservatives.

For all the criticism of tax rates, Americans pay a smaller proportion of income in taxes than citizens of most other Western nations. Surveys consistently show that, despite general cynicism about government—a cynicism fed in part by the drumbeat of tax-cut advocates—most Americans support reasonable domestic welfare and related expenditures. Social programs have already suffered successive cuts, and in the 1990s, the federal deficit has been brought under control, in both absolute dollars and as a percentage of the gross domestic product (GDP). For better and worse, taxes are the price we pay to have our government and our society.

We the People

THE AARP: GRAY POWER

America's elderly population has been growing at an ever-increasing rate. Advances in health care and quality of life for the nation's senior citizens have meant longer, fuller lives. As this population and its resources have grown, so has its political power.

In recent decades, many of the government's most important, large-scale programs have been aimed at the elderly population. Such landmark programs as Social Security, designed to provide a national, guaranteed retirement pension program, and Medicare, which provides health care to millions of senior citizens, have consumed a greater percentage of federal resources. As a consequence, these "entitlement" programs have come under close scrutiny by budget cutters looking for a way to reduce federal spending.

Yet no important changes in such programs are likely to occur without the approval of the American Association of Retired Persons (AARP). Arguably the most powerful and feared interest group in the country, the AARP was founded in 1958, partly in response to the unwillingness of private insurance companies to offer insurance protection for the elderly (a need that was filled with the creation of Medicare in 1965). The AARP at first had relatively little involvement in politics, but by the 1970s, its growing membership base became more politicized as tightening budget pressures squeezed entitlement programs.

In recent years, the AARP has grown by leaps and bounds; it now claims 33 million members. In 1994, it generated $382 million in revenues. In addition, it received another $86 million in federal grants. Almost half of its operating money comes from the sale of various products and services to its members; advertising in its publications, including the magazine *Modern Maturity,* generates about 12 percent of the organization's revenues. Annual member-

PARTY DISCIPLINE

party vote

a roll-call vote in the House or Senate in which at least 50 percent of the members of one party take a particular position and are opposed by at least 50 percent of the members of the other party. Party votes are rare today, although they were fairly common in the nineteenth century

roll-call vote

a vote in which each legislator's yes or no vote is recorded as the clerk calls the names of the members alphabetically

In both the House and Senate, party leaders have a good deal of influence over the behavior of their party members. This influence, sometimes called "party discipline," was once so powerful that it dominated the lawmaking process. At the turn of the century, party leaders could often command the allegiance of more than 90 percent of their members. A vote on which 50 percent or more of the members of one party take one position while at least 50 percent of the members of the other party take the opposing position is called a **party vote.** At the beginning of the twentieth century, nearly half of all **roll-call votes** in the House of Representatives were party votes. Today, this type of party-line voting is rare in Congress. It is, however, fairly common to find at least a majority of the Democrats opposing a majority of the Republicans on any given issue.

Typically, party unity is greater in the House than in the Senate. House rules grant greater procedural control of business to the majority party leaders, which gives them more influence over House members. In the Senate, however, the leadership has few sanctions over its members. Senate minority leader Tom Daschle once observed that a Senate leader seeking to influence other senators has as incentives "a bushel full of carrots and a few twigs."[36]

Party unity has increased in recent sessions of Congress as a result of the intense partisan struggles during the Reagan and Bush years (see Figure 12.8).

ship dues of $8 per year generate almost 40 percent of AARP revenues. AARP membership is attractive not only because of its low cost, but also because members have access to a wide array of discounted services and programs, including insurance, a mail-order prescription drug supply, and mutual funds. The only requirement for joining is that members be at least 50 years old.

The AARP's size and resources make it a powerful force in Washington politics, and one that few members of Congress have wanted to challenge. In addition, its vast membership base is composed of people who have a lifetime's accumulation of experience and knowledge that can be put to political purposes, and who also are more likely to have the time to devote to political activities precisely because many of them no longer work. Furthermore, although some elderly live on the edge of poverty, the average wealth of the elderly population is second only to that of the age group just below retirement age.

Yet the AARP's intensive and mostly effective lobbying efforts have come under political fire in recent years because the organization receives tax-exempt status by virtue of its status as a private social welfare organization. It thus pays no income taxes, and also receives federal grants and reduced postal rates. Critics in Congress have questioned whether the AARP should be engaged in political lobbying while receiving so many government benefits and breaks.

In 1995, legislation was introduced in Congress to prevent politically active groups such as the AARP from receiving federal grant money. In addition, both the Internal Revenue Service and the U.S. Postal Service have challenged some of the AARP's special breaks. Nevertheless, the movement of America's population patterns toward an ever-older society, combined with escalating pressures to reduce government spending and entitlement programs, all but guarantee that the AARP will continue to be a formidable force in Washington. Few elected officials can dismiss the weight of 33 million citizens.

SOURCE: Henry J. Pratt, *The Gray Lobby* (Chicago: University of Chicago Press, 1976).

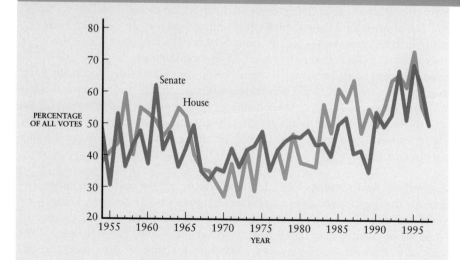

PARTY UNITY SCORES BY CHAMBER

Figure 12.8

PERCENTAGE OF ALL VOTES

Senate

House

YEAR

SOURCE: *Congressional Quarterly Weekly Report,* January 3, 1998, p. 18.

The party unity score is the percentage of times that members voted with the majority of their party on votes on which a majority of one party voted against the majority of the other party.

Although party voting continued briefly in the 103rd Congress (1993–94) following Bill Clinton's election in 1992, the situation soon gave way to the many long-term factors working against party discipline in the United States.[37]

Democratic disunity was especially evident on President Clinton's health care reform proposal. While Democrats divided in both the House and Senate, Republicans were virtually unanimous in their opposition to Clinton's proposals. House Republicans in particular, led by Newt Gingrich, worked hard to defeat the president's plan. The defeat of health care reform helped to undermine the Clinton presidency, and so helped to pave the way for the GOP's triumph in the 1994 elections.

After being named Speaker of the House, Gingrich sought to maintain Republican party unity behind a series of legislative proposals, the Contract with America. Among other things, this contract called for tax and spending cuts, a balanced budget amendment, civil litigation reforms, and congressional term limits. In 1995, at the beginning of the first session of the 104th Congress, Gingrich was able to secure the support of virtually all House Republicans for elements of the contract. As the session wore on, party unity diminished, particularly on the issue of tax cuts, which divided Republican "deficit hawks" from more moderate Republicans.

The GOP's offensive against social programs initially produced high levels of Democratic party unity in both the House and Senate. By March 1995, however, some conservative Democrats had begun to break ranks. On the whole, there was more party unity in the House during 1995 than in any year since 1954. But by 1996, the level of party unity was back to average. The Republicans who were newly elected in 1994 voted in near lock-step during 1995, but in 1996 they faced re-election and an electorate angry about the partisan gridlock that had produced a partial shutdown of the federal government at the end of 1995. The Republicans' caution resulted in a decline in party unity, which persisted into the 105th Congress in 1997.

To some extent, party unity is based on ideology and background. Republican members of Congress are more likely than Democrats to be drawn from rural or suburban areas. Democrats are likely to be more liberal on economic and social questions than their Republican colleagues. These differences certainly help to explain roll-call divisions between the two parties. Ideology and background, however, are only part of the explanation of party unity. The other part has to do with party organization and leadership. Although party organization has weakened since the turn of the century, today's party leaders still have some resources at their disposal: (1) committee assignments, (2) access to the floor, (3) the whip system, (4) logrolling, and (5) the presidency. These resources are regularly used and are often effective in securing the support of party members.

Committee Assignments Leaders can create debts among members by helping them get favorable committee assignments. These assignments are made early in the congressional careers of most members and cannot be taken from them if they later balk at party discipline. Nevertheless, if the leadership goes out of its way to get the right assignment for a member, this effort is likely to create a bond of obligation that can be called upon without any other payments or favors. This is one reason the Republican leadership gave freshmen favorable assignments when the Republicans took over Congress in 1995.

Access to the Floor The most important everyday resource available to the parties is control over access to the floor. With thousands of bills awaiting passage and most members clamoring for access in order to influence a bill or to publicize themselves, floor time is precious. In the Senate, the leadership allows ranking committee members to influence the allocation of floor time—who will speak for how long; in the House, the Speaker, as head of the majority party (in consultation with the minority leader), allocates large blocks of floor time. Thus, floor time is allocated in both houses of Congress by the majority and minority leaders. More importantly, the Speaker of the House and the majority leader in the Senate possess the power of recognition. Although this power may not appear to be substantial, it is a formidable authority and can be used to stymie a piece of legislation completely or to frustrate a member's attempts to speak on a particular issue. Because the power is significant, members of Congress usually attempt to stay on good terms with the Speaker and the majority leader in order to ensure that they will continue to be recognized.

Some House members, Republicans in particular, have also taken advantage of "special orders," under which members can address the floor after the close of business. These addresses are typically made to an empty chamber, but are usually carried live by C-SPAN, a cable television channel. Before 1995, when Democrats controlled the House floor, Republicans often were forced to use special orders to present their views effectively to national audiences. Representative Newt Gingrich, for example, launched a televised after-hours attack on Democratic House Speaker Jim Wright in 1988 that ultimately led to Wright's resignation.

The Whip System Some influence accrues to party leaders through the **whip system,** which is primarily a communications network. Between twelve and twenty assistant and regional whips are selected to operate at the direction of the majority or minority leader and the whip. They take polls of all the members in order to learn their intentions on specific bills. This enables the leaders to know if they have enough support to allow a vote as well as whether the vote is so close that they need to put pressure on a few undecided members. Leaders also use the whip system to convey their wishes and plans to the members, but only in very close votes do they actually exert pressure on a member. In those instances, the Speaker or a lieutenant will go to a few party members who have indicated they will switch if their vote is essential. The whip system helps the leaders limit pressuring members to a few times per session.

The whip system helps maintain party unity in both houses of Congress, but it is particularly critical in the House of Representatives because of the large number of legislators whose positions and votes must be accounted for. The majority and minority whips and their assistants must be adept at inducing compromise among legislators who hold widely differing viewpoints. The whips' personal styles and their perception of their function significantly affect the development of legislative coalitions and influence the compromises that emerge.

Logrolling An agreement between two or more members of Congress who have nothing in common except the need for support is called **logrolling.** The agreement states, in effect, "You support me on bill X and I'll support you on another bill of your choice." Since party leaders are the center of the communications networks in the two chambers, they can help members create large

PARTY DISCIPLINE

Party discipline is maintained through a number of sources:

Committee assignments: by giving favorable committee assignments to members, party leaders create a sense of debt.
Access to the floor: ranking committee members in the Senate, and the Speaker of the House, control the allocation of floor time, so House and Senate members want to stay on good terms with these party leaders in order that their bills get time on the floor.
Whip system: party leaders use whips to track how many votes they have for a given piece of legislation; if the vote is close, they can try to influence members to switch sides.
Logrolling: members who may have nothing in common can agree to support one another's legislation because each needs the other's vote.
Presidency: the president's legislative proposals are often the most important part of Congress's agenda. Party leaders use the president's support to rally members.

whip system

a communications network in each house of Congress; whips take polls of the membership in order to learn their intentions on specific legislative issues and to assist the majority and minority leaders in various tasks

logrolling

a legislative practice wherein agreements are made between legislators in voting for or against a bill. Unlike bargaining, logrolling parties have nothing in common but their desire to exchange support

logrolling coalitions. Hundreds of logrolling deals are made each year, and although there are no official record-keeping books, it would be a poor party leader whose whips did not know who owed what to whom. In some instances, logrolling produces strange alliances. A seemingly unlikely alliance emerged in Congress in June 1994, when 119 mainly conservative senators and representatives from oil-producing states met with President Clinton to suggest that they might be willing to support the president's health care proposals in exchange for his support for a number of tax breaks for the oil industry. Senator J. Bennett Johnston of Louisiana, a leader of the oil-state representatives, contended that the issues of health care and oil production were closely related since both "affected the long-term economic security of the nation." Ironically, the oil-producing groups that promoted this alliance are generally among the most conservative forces in the nation. When asked what he personally thought of the president's health care proposal, George Alcorn, a leading industry lobbyist involved in the logrolling effort, dismissed Clinton's plan as "socialized medicine." Good logrolling, it would seem, is not hampered by minor ideological concerns.[38]

The Presidency   Of all the influences that maintain the clarity of party lines in Congress, the influence of the presidency is probably the most important. Indeed, the office is a touchstone of party discipline in Congress. Since the late 1940s, under President Harry Truman, presidents each year have identified a number of bills to be considered part of their administration's program. By the mid-1950s, both parties in Congress began to look to the president for these proposals, which became the most significant part of Congress's agenda. The president's support is a criterion for party loyalty, and party leaders are able to use it to rally some members.

WEIGHING DIVERSE INFLUENCES

Clearly, many different factors affect congressional decisions. But at various points in the decision-making process, some factors are likely to be more influential than others. For example, interest groups may be more effective at the committee stage, when their expertise is especially valued and their visibility is less obvious. Because committees play a key role in deciding what legislation actually reaches the floor of the House or Senate, interest groups can often put a halt to bills they dislike, or they can ensure that the options that do reach the floor are those that the group's members support.

Once legislation reaches the floor and members of Congress are deciding among alternatives, constituent opinion will become more important. Legislators are also influenced very much by other legislators: many of their assessments about the substance and politics of legislation come from fellow members of Congress.

The influence of the external and internal forces described in the preceding section also varies according to the kind of issue being considered. On policies of great importance to powerful interest groups—farm subsidies, for example—those groups are likely to have considerable influence. On other issues, members of Congress may be less attentive to narrow interest groups and more willing to consider what they see as the general interest.

Finally, the mix of influences varies according to the historical moment. The 1994 electoral victory of Republicans allowed their party to control both houses of Congress for the first time in forty years. That fact, combined with an unusually assertive Republican leadership, meant that party leaders became especially important in decision making. The willingness of moderate Republicans to support measures they had once opposed indicated the unusual importance of party leadership in this period. As House minority leader Richard Gephardt put it, "When you've been in the desert 40 years, your instinct is to help Moses."[39]

Beyond Legislation: Other Congressional Powers

▶ Besides the power to pass legislation, what other powers allow Congress to influence the process of government?

In addition to the power to make the law, Congress has at its disposal an array of other instruments through which to influence the process of government. The Constitution gives the Senate the power to approve treaties and appointments. And Congress has a number of other powers through which it can share with the other branches the capacity to administer the laws.

OVERSIGHT

Oversight, as applied to Congress, refers not to something neglected, but to the effort to oversee or to supervise how legislation is carried out by the executive branch. Oversight is carried out by committees or subcommittees of the Senate or the House, which conduct hearings and investigations in order to analyze and evaluate bureaucratic agencies and the effectiveness of their programs. Their purpose may be to locate inefficiencies or abuses of power, to explore the relationship between what an agency does and what a law intended, or to change or abolish a program. Most programs and agencies are subject to some oversight every year during the course of hearings on **appropriations,** that is, the funding of agencies and government programs.

Committees or subcommittees have the power to subpoena witnesses, take oaths, cross-examine, compel testimony, and bring criminal charges for contempt (refusing to cooperate) and perjury (lying). Hearings and investigations resemble each other in many ways, but they differ on one fundamental point. A hearing is usually held on a specific bill, and the questions asked there are usually intended to build a record with regard to that bill. In an investigation, the committee or subcommittee does not begin with a particular bill, but examines a broad area or problem and then concludes its investigation with one or more proposed bills. One example of an investigation is the congressional inquiry into the Reagan administration's shipment of arms to the government of Iran.

ADVICE AND CONSENT: SPECIAL SENATE POWERS

The Constitution has given the Senate a special power, one that is not based on lawmaking. The president has the power to make treaties and to appoint top

oversight

the effort by Congress, through hearings, investigations, and other techniques, to exercise control over the activities of executive agencies

appropriations

the amounts of money approved by Congress in statutes (bills) that each unit or agency of government can spend

executive officers, ambassadors, and federal judges—but only "with the Advice and Consent of the Senate" (Article II, Section 2). For treaties, two-thirds of those present must concur; for appointments, a simple majority is required.

The power to approve or reject presidential requests also involves the power to set conditions. The Senate only occasionally exercises its power to reject treaties and appointments, and usually that is when opposite parties control the Senate and the White House. During the final two years of President Reagan's term, for example, Senate Democrats rejected Judge Robert Bork's Supreme Court nomination and gave clear indications that they would reject a second Reagan nominee, Judge Douglas Ginsburg, who withdrew his nomination before the Senate could act. These instances, however, actually underscore the restraint with which the Senate usually uses its power to reject presidential requests. For example, only nine judicial nominees have been rejected by the Senate during the past century, whereas hundreds have been approved.

executive agreement

an agreement, made between the president and another country, that has the force of a treaty but does not require the Senate's "advice and consent"

Most presidents make every effort to take potential Senate opposition into account in treaty negotiations and will frequently resort to **executive agreements** with foreign powers instead of treaties. The Supreme Court has held that such agreements are equivalent to treaties, but they do not need Senate approval.[40] In the past, presidents sometimes concluded secret agreements without informing Congress of the agreements' contents, or even their existence. For example, American involvement in the Vietnam War grew in part out of a series of secret arrangements made between American presidents and the South Vietnamese during the 1950s and 1960s. Congress did not even learn of the existence of these agreements until 1969. In 1972, Congress passed the Case Act, which requires that the president inform Congress of any executive agreement within sixty days of its having been reached. This provides Congress with the opportunity to cancel agreements that it opposes. In addition, Congress can limit the president's ability to conduct foreign policy through executive agreement by refusing to appropriate the funds needed to implement an agreement. In this way, for example, executive agreements to provide American economic or military assistance to foreign governments can be modified or even canceled by Congress.

IMPEACHMENT

impeachment

the formal charge by the House of Representatives that a government official has committed "Treason, Bribery, or other high Crimes and Misdemeanors."

The Constitution also grants Congress the power of **impeachment** over the president, vice president, and other executive officials. Impeachment means to charge a government official (president or otherwise) with "Treason, Bribery, or other high Crimes and Misdemeanors" and bring them before Congress to determine their guilt. Impeachment is thus like a criminal indictment in which the House of Representatives acts like a grand jury, voting (by simple majority) on whether the accused ought to be impeached. If a majority of the House votes to impeach, the impeachment trial moves to the Senate, which acts like a trial jury by voting whether to convict and forcibly remove the person from office (this vote requires a two-thirds majority of the Senate).

Controversy over Congress's impeachment power has arisen over the grounds for impeachment, especially the meaning of "high Crimes and Misdemeanors." A strict reading of the Constitution suggests that the only impeachable offense is an actual crime. But a more commonly agreed upon definition is that "an impeachable offense is whatever the majority of the House of Representatives considers it to be at a given moment in history."[41] In other words, impeachment, especially impeachment of a president, is a political decision.

The closest that the United States has come to impeaching and convicting a president came in 1867. President Andrew Johnson, a southern Democrat who had battled a congressional Republican majority over Reconstruction, was impeached by the House but saved from conviction by one vote in the Senate. At the height of the Watergate scandal in 1974, the House started impeachment proceedings against President Richard M. Nixon, but Nixon resigned before the House could proceed. The possibility of impeachment arose again in 1998 when President Clinton was accused of lying under oath and obstructing justice in the investigation into his sexual affair with White House intern Monica Lewinsky. In October 1998, the House voted to open an impeachment inquiry against President Clinton.

The impeachment power is a considerable one; its very existence in the hands of Congress is a highly effective safeguard against the executive tyranny so greatly feared by the framers of the Constitution.

★ Congress and Democracy

▶ How do the institutional features of Congress affect meaningful representation?

▶ What can Congress and citizens do to bring Congress closer to the American people?

Much of this chapter has described the major institutional components of Congress and has shown how they work as Congress makes policy. But what do these institutional features mean for how Congress represents the American public? If the chief complaint of many Americans is that Congress is out of touch with ordinary people, what can Congress do—and what can citizens do—to bring Congress closer to the people?

As we noted at the beginning of this chapter, Congress instituted a number of reforms in the 1970s to make itself looser and more accessible. These reforms sought to respond to public views that Congress had become a stodgy institution ruled by a powerful elite that made decisions in private. We have seen that these reforms increased the number of subcommittees, prohibited most secret hearings, and increased the staff support for Congress. These reforms spread power more evenly throughout the institution and opened new avenues for the public to contact and influence Congress.

But the opening of Congress seemed only to spark more discontent. In fact the congressional reforms enacted in the 1970s actually made Congress less effective and, ironically, more permeable to special interests. The fragmentation of power in Congress has made it harder for members to reach decisions. "Turf battles"—struggles over who should take charge of what—often take more congressional energy than deliberations over policy. The decentralization of power in Congress has made each member more of an independent operator. Members are now less willing to compromise and more eager to take

POLITICS ON THE WEB

The Internet has altered the relationship between members of Congress and the public. For citizens, the Internet allows more access to information about politics and about specific members of Congress—how they voted on every bill, speeches they have made, and even from whom they have received campaign contributions. In addition, Internet E-mail allows citizens to contact their members of Congress with little effort and cost. Of course, there is a downside to such enhanced participation: our representatives could easily be inundated with constituent messages, increasing their already tremendous workload.

For members of Congress, the Internet provides a practically free way to advertise their positions on key issues, which in re-election campaigns could save a lot of money. This, in turn, could undercut the impact of special interests, PACs, wealthy supporters, and the "conventional" media. Thus the Internet could give poorly financed challengers a more equal voice in a campaign.
www.wwnorton.com/wtp2e

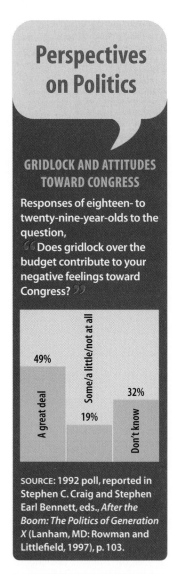

SOURCE: 1992 poll, reported in Stephen C. Craig and Stephen Earl Bennett, eds., *After the Boom: The Politics of Generation X* (Lanham, MD: Rowman and Littlefield, 1997), p. 103.

delegate

the role of a representative who votes according to the preferences of his or her constituency

trustee

the role of a representative who votes based on what he or she thinks is best for his or her constituency

positions that benefit them individually, even if they undermine possibilities for enacting policy. These circumstances have created a Congress that sometimes seems to spend endless hours in increasingly negative debates that do not produce results. The public, therefore, has come to view Congress as a group of privileged elites concerned only about their own prerogatives. The word "gridlock" seems to sum up the state of congressional decision making.

Ironically, the measures that sought to ensure more public access to Congress have increased the access of interest groups. Open committee meetings have made it possible for sophisticated interest groups to monitor and influence every aspect of developing legislation. The narrow perspective put forth by an interest group makes it difficult for members of Congress to keep their eyes on the big picture of what it wants to achieve. Hundreds of amendments can undermine the overall thrust of legislation. Open meetings also deprive members of Congress of the political "cover" often necessary to make compromises. Worried that particular actions could be used against them in a future election, members of Congress have become very risk-averse. In this sense, too much accountability can paralyze the institution.

The very strong role of the Republican congressional leadership elected in 1995 only temporarily quieted complaints about congressional gridlock. Doubts about congressional effectiveness and representativeness remain. The reforms of the 1970s, intended to distribute power more equally inside Congress in order to provide more equal representation to all constituents, instead made it more difficult for members to build coalitions and for legislators to become experts in particular policy areas. The unanticipated, negative consequences of these reforms have highlighted the trade-off between representation and effectiveness in Congress.[42] Americans are becoming increasingly aware that greater individual access to Congress and more symbolic representation do not add up to more power. The results have increased public cynicism and apathy. Rebuilding public faith in Congress may require yet another round of institutional reform, as well as efforts to organize and mobilize broad social interests to achieve meaningful representation.

But what does "meaningful representation" entail? A member of Congress can interpret his or her job as representative in two different ways: as a delegate or as a trustee. As a **delegate,** a member of Congress acts on the express preferences of his or her constituents; as a **trustee,** the member is more loosely tied to constituents and makes the decisions he or she thinks best. The delegate role appears to be the most democratic because it forces the representative to heed the desires of his or her constituents. But this requires the representative to be in constant touch with constituents; it also requires constituents to follow each policy issue very closely. The problem with this form of representation is that most people do not follow every issue so carefully; instead they focus only on extremely important issues or issues of particular interest to them. Many people are too busy to get the information necessary to make informed judgments even on issues they care about. Thus, adhering to the delegate form of representation risks that the voices of only a few active and informed constituents get heard. Although it seems more democratic at first glance, the delegate form of representation may actually open Congress up even more to the influence of the voices of special interests.

If a congressional member acts as a trustee, on the other hand, there is a danger that he or she will not pay sufficient attention to the wishes of constituents. In this scenario, the only way the public can exercise influence is by voting every two years for representatives or every six years for senators. Yet, most members of Congress take this electoral check very seriously. They try to anticipate the wishes of their constituents even when they don't know exactly what those interests are, because they know that unpopular decisions can be used against them in the coming election.

The public understands the trade-offs entailed in these different forms of representation and is, in fact, divided on how members of Congress should represent it. One poll found that 49 percent of the public thought that members of Congress "should do what their district wants them to do even if they think it is a bad idea." But 41 percent disagreed, and 10 percent were unsure about how Congress should best represent them.[43]

What the public dislikes most about Congress stems from suspicions that Congress acts as neither a trustee nor a delegate of the broad public interest, but instead is swayed by narrow special interests with lots of money.[44] Indeed, there is plenty of reason for the public to worry about the power of such groups: lobbying groups have continually adjusted their tactics to increase their ability to influence Congress. As reporter Jeffrey H. Birnbaum notes, lobbyists no longer fit the old caricature of "fat, cigar-smoking men who [shoved] hundred-dollar bills into the pockets of lawmakers."[45] Their tactics have grown much more sophisticated. Interest groups have used "Astroturf" lobbying to simulate a surge of grassroots interest on the part of constituents. More recently, as Congress has come to discount such influence as not really representing its constituents, lobbyists have changed tactics: they now concentrate on "grasstops" organizing, in which they mobilize important friends or associates of the representative or senator to present information favorable to the interest group's perspective. This new strategy is more subtle and may be more effective because it relies on a previous relationship of trust.

Moreover, many of the new technologies that make Congress more open have been used most effectively by special-interest groups. One professional consulting organization has created a subsidiary called NetRoots, which creates web sites for lobbying campaigns, helping interest groups mimic grassroots influence through the Internet. A web site for companies that oppose President Clinton's stands on global warming, for example, provides different, predrafted e-mails that sound as though they were written by senior citizens, small businesses, or other concerned individuals. These letters "can be launched directly to congressional representatives with the click of a mouse."[46]

The Citizen's Role

Are ordinary citizens powerless in the face of such activity by special-interest groups? The changing tactics of interest-group politics suggest that citizens, when they are organized and active, can greatly influence representatives. After all, what the most sophisticated interest groups are doing today is trying to convince members of Congress that there is genuine widespread grassroots support for their cause. This reflects the belief—rooted in long experience—that

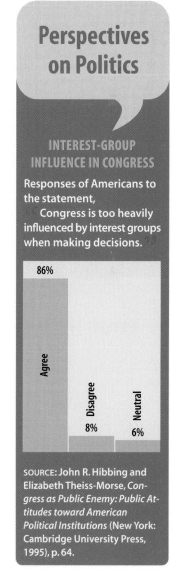

Perspectives on Politics

INTEREST-GROUP INFLUENCE IN CONGRESS

Responses of Americans to the statement,
Congress is too heavily influenced by interest groups when making decisions.

86% Agree
8% Disagree
6% Neutral

SOURCE: John R. Hibbing and Elizabeth Theiss-Morse, *Congress as Public Enemy: Public Attitudes toward American Political Institutions* (New York: Cambridge University Press, 1995), p. 64.

Students and Politics

Andy Pederson, a student at the University of Wisconsin at Milwaukee, interning at the Children's Rights Council:

"I have participated in the legislative process through lobbying and advocating issues before Congress. Congress has increasingly begun to deal with issues regarding family structure and child support. In advocating an issue, we obtain and evaluate legislation and then inform staff members and legislators on new ideas or proposals to reform existing ideas. Providing information, statistics and knowledge to congressional staffs is invaluable in the legislative process.

"Another way of advocating an issue is through grassroots mobilization. This is primarily achieved through keeping the members of the Children's Rights Council informed through newsletters and mailings that keep them up to date on pending legislation. Individuals also call the Council seeking help on specific issues or situations, and we are able to offer them resources. Most often, people want to become involved; they just don't know how to or what is at stake.

"The political process can be long and tiresome. Results are rarely seen immediately. But through this internship I have learned that individual citizens can make a difference if they participate in the process."

SOURCE: The Washington Center for Internships and Academic Seminars, in agreement with W. W. Norton.

what really sways representatives most is evidence that their constituents care about particular issues. To influence all of Congress, it is particularly important to build grassroots organization that is geographically broad. If members of Congress from many parts of the country are getting the same message from their constituents, there is a greater chance of successfully influencing policy.

The experience of some groups that have organized such broad-based grassroots activity indicates that ordinary citizens can affect what Congress does. In recent years, significant grassroots activism has emerged to influence government spending for research on diseases. The striking success of AIDS activists in dramatically increasing funding for AIDS research has inspired other groups to try similar strategies. One example is the National Breast Cancer Coalition, which represents 350 separate organizations around the country. Its aim has been to increase expenditures for federally sponsored research on breast cancer. When the coalition formed in 1991, the federal government spent $90 million a year on breast cancer research; by 1997 that amount had increased to $509 million.[47] Building on its grassroots strength and borrowing tactics from highly successful AIDS activists, the coalition sent six hundred thousand letters to Congress and to the White House in its first year alone. Initially told that the National Cancer Institute's priorities could not be changed so easily, they turned to the Defense Department, which had already spent some funds for breast cancer research. Today, the Defense Department is the second largest funder of breast cancer research, and citizens can monitor and affect its agenda through an independent panel overseeing the program. Both the increased expenditures and the ongoing public influence over the research agenda were a direct result of the grassroots activity of these local groups organized into a national coalition.

Organizing such grassroots groups takes time, expertise, and some resources. But the example of such groups as the Breast Cancer Coalition and AIDS activists indicate that, when organized, ordinary citizens can be effective. It is important for individuals who feel that Congress is out of touch to recognize that the path of influence may require considerable effort, but that it is available. In addition, ordinary citizens who may not want to participate so actively need to remember that they can influence their congressional representatives indirectly by voting. One of the first breaks in the unity of congressional Republicans in 1995 came from a moderate Republican from New York who knew that the voters in her district would not support the loosening of environmental regulations proposed by the Republican leadership. Her decision to break with her Republican colleagues indicates the power of the electoral threat in making representatives attentive to the views of their constituents.

★ Summary

The U.S. Congress plays a vital role in American democracy. It is both the key national representative body and the focal point for decision making in Washington, D.C. Throughout American history, Congress has sought to combine representation and power as it made policy. In recent years, however, many Americans have become disillusioned with the ability of Congress to represent fairly and to exercise power responsibly.

Both sociological and agency representation play a role in the relationship between members of Congress and their constituencies. However, Congress is not fully representative because it is not a sociological microcosm of the United States. Members of Congress do seek to act as agents for their constituents by representing the views and interests of those constituents in the governmental process.

The activities of members of Congress are strongly influenced by electoral considerations. Who gets elected to Congress is influenced by who runs for office, the power of incumbency, and the way congressional districts are drawn. In order to assist their chances of re-election, members of Congress provide services and patronage to their constituents.

In order to make policy, Congress depends on a complex internal organization. Six basic dimensions of Congress affect the legislative process: (1) the parties, (2) the committees, (3) the staff, (4) the caucuses, (5) the rules, and (6) the presidency.

Since the Constitution provides only for a presiding officer in each house, some method had to be devised for conducting business. Parties quickly assumed the responsibility for this. In the House, the majority party elects a leader every two years. This individual becomes Speaker. In addition, a majority leader and a minority leader (from the minority party) and party whips are elected. Each party has a committee whose job it is to make committee assignments. Party structure in the Senate is similar, except that the vice president of the United States is the Senate president.

The committee system surpasses the party system in its importance in Congress. In the early nineteenth century, standing committees became a fundamental aspect of Congress. They have, for the most part, evolved to correspond to executive branch departments or programs and thus reflect and maintain the separation of powers.

Congress also establishes rules of procedure to guide policy making. The Senate has a tradition of unlimited debate, on which the various cloture rules it has passed have had little effect. Filibusters still occur. The rules of the House, on the other hand, restrict talk and support committees; deliberation is recognized as committee business. The House Rules Committee has the power to control debate and floor amendments. The rules prescribe the formal procedure through which bills become law. Generally, the parties control scheduling and agenda, but the committees determine action on the floor. Committees, seniority, and rules all limit the ability of members to represent their constituents. Yet, these factors enable Congress to maintain its role as a major participant in government.

Perspectives on Politics

CONTACTING YOUR MEMBER OF CONGRESS

Percentage of Americans agreeing with the statement, ❝You have called or sent a letter to your congressional representative.❞

Age group	18–34	35–44	45–54	55–64	65+
Percentage	23.5%	42.9%	48.0%	50.1%	53.9%

SOURCE: 1993 Times-Mirror poll, reported in Susan A. MacManus, *Young v. Old: Generational Combat in the 21st Century* (Boulder, CO: Westview, 1996), p 141.

Many different factors affect how Congress ultimately decides on legislation. Among the most important influences are constituency preferences, interest group pressures, and party discipline. Typically party discipline is stronger in the House than in the Senate. Parties have several means of maintaining discipline: (1) favorable committee assignments create obligations; (2) floor time in the debate on one bill can be allocated in exchange for a specific vote on another; (3) the whip system allows party leaders to assess support for a bill and convey their wishes to members; (4) party leaders can help members create large logrolling coalitions; and (5) the president can champion certain pieces of legislation and thereby muster support along party lines. In most cases, party leaders accept constituency obligations as a valid reason for voting against the party position.

In addition to the power to make law, Congress possesses other formidable powers in its relationship with the executive branch. Among these are oversight, advice and consent on treaties and appointments, and the power to impeach executive officials. In spite of its array of powers, Congress is often accused of being ineffective and out of touch with the American people. At the heart of these criticisms lies the debate over whether members of Congress should act more as delegates or as trustees. An even more important concern facing Congress is whether it has become beholden to special interests and has, in effect, shut ordinary citizens out of the political process.

FOR FURTHER READING

Berg, John C., *Class, Gender, Race, and Power in the U.S. Congress*. Boulder, CO: Westview, 1994.

Burrell, Barbara C., *A Woman's Place Is in the House: Campaigning for Congress in the Feminist Era*. Ann Arbor: University of Michigan Press, 1994.

Cook, Elizabeth Adell, Sue Thomas, and Clyde Wilcox, eds. *The Year of the Woman: Myth and Reality*. Boulder, CO: Westview, 1994.

Davidson, Roger H., ed. *The Postreform Congress*. New York: St. Martin's, 1991.

Dodd, Lawrence, and Bruce I. Oppenheimer, eds. *Congress Reconsidered*. 5th ed. Washington, DC: Congressional Quarterly Press, 1993.

Fenno, Richard F. *Congressmen in Committees*. Boston: Little, Brown, 1973.

Fenno, Richard F. *Homestyle: House Members in Their Districts*. Boston: Little, Brown, 1978.

Fiorina, Morris. *Congress: Keystone of the Washington Establishment*. 2nd ed. New Haven, CT: Yale University Press, 1989.

Fowler, Linda, and Robert McClure. *Political Ambition: Who Decides to Run for Congress?* New Haven, CT: Yale University Press, 1989.

Light, Paul. *Forging Legislation*. New York: Norton, 1991.

Mayhew, David R. *Congress: The Electoral Connection*. New Haven, CT: Yale University Press, 1974.

Sinclair, Barbara. *The Transformation of the U.S. Senate*. Baltimore: Johns Hopkins University Press, 1989.

Smith, Steven S., and Christopher Deering. *Committees in Congress*. 2nd ed. Washington, DC: Congressional Quarterly Press, 1990.

Thomas, Sue. *How Women Legislate*. New York: Oxford University Press, 1994.

STUDY OUTLINE

Congress: Representing the American People

1. The House and Senate play different roles in the legislative process. The Senate is more deliberative, whereas the House is characterized by greater centralization and organization.

2. House members are more attuned to localized narrow interests in society, whereas senators are more able

than House members to represent statewide or national interests.

3. In recent years, the House has exhibited more partisanship and ideological division than the Senate.

4. Congress is not fully representative because it is not a sociological microcosm of American society.

5. Members of Congress frequently communicate with constituents and devote a great deal of staff time to constituency service.

6. Electoral motivations have a strong impact on both sociological and agency representation in Congress.

7. Incumbency affords members of Congress resources such as constituency service and mailing to help secure re-election.

8. In recent years, turnover rates in Congress have increased, although this is due more to incumbent retirement than to the defeat of incumbents in elections.

9. Members of Congress can supply benefits to constituents by passing pork-barrel legislation. Pork-barrel votes are exchanged by members of Congress for votes on other issues.

The Organization of Congress

1. At the beginning of each Congress, Democrats and Republicans gather to select their leaders. The leader of the majority party in the House of Representatives is elected Speaker of the House by a strict party-line vote.

2. In the Senate, the president pro tempore serves as the presiding officer, although the majority and minority leaders control the calendar and agenda of the Senate.

3. The committee system provides Congress with a second organizational structure that is more a division of labor than the party-based hierarchies of power.

4. With specific jurisdiction over certain policy areas and the task of processing proposals of legislation into bills for floor consideration, standing committees are the most important arenas of congressional policy making.

5. Power within committees is based on seniority, although the seniority principle is not absolute.

6. In the 1970s, reforms fragmented power in Congress—the committee system, specifically—by increasing both the number of subcommittees and the autonomy of subcommittee chairpersons.

7. Each member of Congress has a personal staff that deals with constituency requests and, increasingly, with the details of legislative and administrative oversight.

8. Groups of senators or representatives who share certain opinions, interests, or social characteristics form informal organizations called caucuses.

Rules of Lawmaking: How a Bill Becomes a Law

1. Committee deliberation is necessary before floor action on any bill.

2. Many bills receive little or no committee or subcommittee action; they are allowed to "die in committee."

3. Bills reported out of committee in the House must go through the House Rules Committee before they can be debated on the floor. The Rules Committee allots the time for floor debate on a bill and the conditions under which a bill may (or may not) be amended.

4. In the Senate, rules of debate are much less rigid. In fact, senators may delay Senate action on legislation by refusing to yield the floor; this is known as a filibuster.

5. Conference committees are often required to reconcile House and Senate versions of bills that began with similar provisions but emerged with significant differences.

6. After being adopted by the House and the Senate, a bill is sent to the president, who may choose to sign the bill or veto it. Congress can override a president's veto by a two-thirds vote in both the House and the Senate.

How Congress Decides

1. Creating a legislative agenda, drawing up a list of possible measures, and deciding among them is a complex process in which a variety of influences from inside and outside government play important roles.

2. Interest groups can influence congressional decision making by mobilizing followers in congressional districts, setting the agenda, or writing legislative language.

3. Party discipline is still an important factor in congressional voting, despite its decline throughout the twentieth century.

4. Party unity is typically greater in the House than in the Senate. Party unity on roll-call votes has increased in recent sessions of Congress.

5. Party unity is a result of a combination of the ideology and background of individual members and the resources party leaders have at their disposal.

6. The influence of the presidency is probably the most important of all the resources that maintain party discipline in Congress.

Beyond Legislation: Other Congressional Powers

1. Congress has increasingly relied on legislative oversight of administrators.

2. The Senate also has the power of approving or rejecting presidential treaties and appointments.

3. Congress has the power to impeach executive officials.

Congress and Democracy

1. Congressional reforms of the 1970s fragmented power in Congress and made it more open to special interests.

2. What the public dislikes most about Congress stems from suspicions that Congress does not act as a trustee or as a delegate of any broad interest but that it is swayed by narrow special interests with money.

PRACTICE QUIZ

1. Members of Congress can work as agents of their constituents by
   a) providing direct patronage.
   b) taking part in a party vote.
   c) joining a caucus.
   d) supporting term limits.

2. Why has public approval of Congress as an institution declined since the 1970s?
   a) Constituents don't like their own representatives in Congress.
   b) Congress has become increasingly inaccessible to the public since the 1970s.
   c) Citizens can now see members of Congress on television every night.
   d) Congress has increasingly opened itself up to the control of special interests.

3. Because they have larger and more heterogeneous constituencies, senators
   a) are more attuned to the needs of localized interest groups.
   b) care more about re-election than House members.
   c) can better represent the national interest.
   d) face less competition in elections than House members.

4. Sociological representation is important in understanding the U.S. Congress because
   a) members often vote based on their religion.
   b) Congress is a microcosm of American society.
   c) the symbolic composition of Congress is important for the political stability of the United States.
   d) there is a distinct "congressional sociology."

5. What type of representation is described when constituents have the power to hire and fire their representative?
   a) agency representation
   b) sociological representation
   c) democratic representation
   d) trustee representation

6. Incumbency is an important factor in deciding who is elected to Congress because
   a) incumbents have tools they can use to help ensure re-election.
   b) potentially strong challengers may be dissuaded from running because of the strength of the incumbent.
   c) Both a and b are true.
   d) Neither a nor b is true.

7. Some have argued that the creation of minority congressional districts has
   a) lessened the sociological representation of minorities in Congress.
   b) made it more difficult for minorities to win substantive policy goals.
   c) been a result of the media's impact on state legislative politics.
   d) lessened the problem of "pork barrel" politics.

8. Which of the following is *not* an important influence on how members of Congress vote on legislation?
   a) the media
   b) constituency
   c) interest groups
   d) party leaders

9. Which of the following types of committees does *not* include members of both the House and the Senate?
   a) standing committee
   b) joint committee
   c) conference committee
   d) No committees include both House members and senators.

10. An agreement between members of Congress to trade support for each other's bill is known as
    a) oversight.
    b) filibuster.
    c) logrolling
    d) patronage.

CRITICAL THINKING QUESTIONS

1. Two of Congress's chief responsibilities are representation and lawmaking. Describe the ways in which these two responsibilities might conflict with one another. How do these responsibilities support and reinforce one another? What would Congress be like if its sole function were representative? What would it be like if it were solely legislative?

2. Describe the process by which a bill becomes a law. At the various stages of this process, assess who—both within government and outside of government—makes and influences decisions. Are there stages at which the process is more democratic than it is at others? Are there stages at which the people have less influence? In your judgment, is the overall process democratic?

KEY TERMS

agency representation (p. 449)
appropriations (p. 481)
bicameral (p. 447)
bill (p. 468)
caucus (congressional) (p. 466)
caucus (political) (p. 458)
closed rule (p. 470)
cloture (p. 471)
conference (p. 458)
conference committee (p. 464)
constituency (p. 447)
delegate (p. 484)
executive agreement (p. 482)
filibuster (p. 471)

impeachment (p. 482)
incumbency (p. 453)
joint committee (p. 464)
line-item veto (p. 456)
logrolling (p. 479)
majority leader (p. 458)
minority leader (p. 458)
open rule (p. 470)
oversight (p. 481)
party vote (p. 476)
patronage (p. 455)
pocket veto (p. 473)
political action committee (PAC)
  (p. 453)

pork barrel (p. 455)
private bill (p. 456)
redistricting (p. 454)
roll-call vote (p. 476)
select committee (p. 463)
seniority (p. 464)
sociological representation (p. 449)
Speaker of the House (p. 458)
staff agency (p. 466)
standing committee (p. 462)
term limits (p. 454)
trustee (p. 484)
veto (p. 472)
whip system (p. 479)

13 The Presidency

★ **The Constitutional Powers of the Presidency**

What powers does the Constitution provide to the president as head of state? Have presidents used these powers to make the presidency too powerful or even imperial?

What powers does the Constitution provide to the president as head of government?

★ **Institutional Resources of Presidential Power**

What institutional resources does the president use to manage the executive branch?

Which of these resources have presidents increasingly relied on?

★ **Political Resources of Presidential Power**

What political resources can the president draw on in exercising the powers of the presidency? Which of these resources is a potential liability? Why?

★ **The Presidency and Democracy**

How did the presidency develop into a truly democratic institution?

How did the development of a mass presidential constituency contribute to the rise of presidential government?

N early 1998, the presidency appeared to be in crisis. President Bill Clinton had just been cleared of accusations that he was involved with illegal fundraising during the 1996 campaign, but he was still defending himself against two sets of charges. The first involved a sexual harassment suit by Paula Jones, a former employee of the state of Arkansas (of which Clinton was governor before his election to the presidency). The second charge, being investigated by independent counsel Kenneth Starr, focused on Clinton's alleged involvement with illegal real-estate speculation as part of the Whitewater Development Corporation. In seeking to prove that Clinton made a practice of seeking sexual favors from employees, Paula Jones's lawyers issued a subpoena to a former White House intern, Monica Lewinsky. It was alleged that Clinton and Lewinsky had had a sexual affair and that Clinton had urged Lewinsky to perjure herself by denying the accusation in a sworn deposition. Inconsistencies in Lewinsky's various accounts of her relationship with the president threw Clinton into the fight of his life. Although sexual misconduct of this kind has no legal significance, the charges against Clinton involved serious criminal charges of obstruction of justice. President Clinton was in trouble. What about the office of the presidency?

Public opinion about the President's affair with Lewinsky sheds light on the nature of the presidency today. When asked if they thought Clinton was engaged in a cover-up, 51 percent of respondents said yes. When asked if Clinton should be removed from office if he lied under oath about the affair, 55 percent said yes. When asked if he should be removed from office if he had encouraged Lewinsky to lie while under oath, 63 percent said yes. But when asked whether they approved or disapproved of the way President Clinton was handling his job, a whopping 68 percent said they approved, giving Clinton his highest approval rating up to that time.[1] Although the results of these polls may appear confusing at first glance, they confirm one important fact: the presidency has a dual nature, which Americans sense and act upon. The power that President Clinton exercises and the approval he seemed to gain following this setback are based more in the institution of the presidency than in the person of the president. In other words, Americans respect the presidency as an institution and all of its capabilities for governance, even if they don't approve of the individual in the office. It's the office that wields great power, not necessarily the person.

This duality does not mean that the presidency is more monarchy than democracy. The American president is the most democratized leader among all modern democracies. The presidential selection process, from the announcement of candidacies to their nomination to the election of a president, is the most open, participatory, and democratic of all elective offices around the world. Access to the president by the media is more extensive in the United States than anywhere else in the world. Through public opinion polls and through political parties, Americans also have more direct access to their president than do citizens of other democracies.

The influence of the American people on the president can be manifested in ways other than their responses to polls or the political party that they support. For example, in February 1998 President Clinton sent his three top foreign-policy aides into the American heartland to build support for a possible military attack on Iraq. A town meeting held at Ohio State University to discuss Americans' views on Iraq was broadcast nationally by CNN and covered extensively by all the other major television networks. During the town meeting, some heckling and shouts of protest were heard in the crowd, but the greatest influence on the issue came from the thoughtful and respectful questions posed by ordinary citizens in the audience, including some active-duty military personnel. These questions implied that although Americans would support a war with Iraq if it were to occur, they had many misgivings about its necessity and its probability of success. President Clinton was so moved by these views that he held an emergency press conference the following morning and ordered his foreign policy advisers to reconvene in Washington.

Of course, we cannot sentimentalize this event nor jump to dramatic conclusions about the political influence of each American citizen. Access to the president is not equal, as we saw during the 1996 presidential campaign when President Clinton sponsored White House "coffees" where, for a donation of ten thousand dollars or more to his campaign, one could meet with the president for a short time and express one's political concerns. Larger donors to Clinton's re-election campaign were also given the privilege of spending the night in the Lincoln Bedroom at the White House. These opportunities are not available to everyone. But given the proper forum, the average citizen can exercise some influence. The role of the citizen is to recognize one's capability and act on it when necessary.

The modern American presidency is the most powerful democratically elected political office in the world. But it is also one of the most frustrating and vulnerable. The very forces that can catapult a relative political unknown like Bill Clinton into the presidency can, once he is in office, rob him of much of his power and leave him responding to, rather than shaping, events. The president, more than any member of Congress, represents and articulates the will of the people. But the people's will can be a fickle and unreliable political resource—as Bill Clinton and all of his recent predecessors have learned. For with power comes vulnerability.

Our task is to explain how the presidency gained so much power and why this power leaves the president so vulnerable to the popular will. Why did the presidency not only become stronger but also displace Congress as the center, in a new system that we call presidential government? Why did that strong presidency become the center of a new, mass popular democracy with a single, national constituency? And why, as the power of the presidency has increased, have popular expectations of and popular influences on presidential performance increased at an even faster rate?

Critics charged the Clinton administration with selling access to the president by inviting donors to "coffees" at the White House.

■ *Our focus in the first three parts of this chapter is to explore the resources of presidential power, which we will divide into three categories: constitutional, institutional, and political.* The Constitution provides an array of powers to the president as head of state and as head of government. Although we give these two categories separate treatment, the presidency can be understood only as a combination of the two.

■ *We turn next to the institutional resources that presidents use as tools of management.* Without these resources, such as the Cabinet, presidents would be unable to use the powers provided by the Constitution.

■ *We will then examine the political resources of presidential power.* Presidents rely on their party, interest groups, the media, and public opinion in order to build support for their programs and persuade Congress to cooperate. These resources offer great strength to the president but, as we will see, can also be a great liability.

■ *We conclude by assessing the presidency as an institution of democracy.* The presidency has developed into a democratic institution with a mass constituency so great that we now have a "presidential government." We will explain how this development occurred.

The Constitutional Powers of the Presidency

▶ What powers does the Constitution provide to the president as head of state? Have presidents used these powers to make the presidency too powerful or even imperial?

▶ What powers does the Constitution provide to the president as head of government?

Article II of the Constitution, which establishes the presidency and defines a small number of expressed powers of the office, does not solve the dilemma of power. Although Article II has been called "the most loosely drawn chapter of the Constitution,"[2] the framers were neither indecisive nor confused. They held profoundly conflicting views of the executive branch, and Article II was probably the best compromise they could make. The formulation the framers agreed upon is magnificent in its ambiguity: "The executive Power shall be vested in a President of the United States of America" (Article II, Section 1, first sentence). The meaning of "executive power," however, is not defined except indirectly in the very last sentence of Section 3, which provides that the president "shall take Care that the Laws be faithfully executed."

One very important conclusion can be drawn from these two provisions: The office of the president was to be an office of **delegated powers**. Since, as we have already seen, all of the powers of the national government are defined as

delegated powers

constitutional powers that are assigned to one governmental agency but that are exercised by another agency with the express permission of the first

powers of Congress and are incorporated into Article I, Section 8, then the "executive power" of Article II, Section 3, must be understood to be defined as the power to execute faithfully the laws *as they are adopted by Congress.* This does not doom the presidency to weakness. Presumably, Congress can pass laws delegating almost any of its powers to the president. But presidents are not free to discover sources of executive power completely independent of the laws as passed by Congress. In 1890, the Supreme Court did hold that the president could be bold and expansive in the inferences drawn from the Constitution as to "the rights, duties and obligations" of the presidency, but the **inherent powers** of the president would have to be inferred from the Constitution, not from some independent or absolute idea of executive power.[3]

Immediately following the first sentence of Section 1, Article II defines the manner in which the president is to be chosen. This is a very odd sequence, but it does say something about the struggle the delegates were having over how to provide great power of action or energy to the executive and at the same time to balance that power with limitations. The struggle was between those delegates who wanted the president to be selected by, and thus responsible to, Congress and those delegates who preferred that the president be elected directly by the people. Direct popular election would create a more independent and more powerful presidency. With the adoption of a scheme of indirect election through an electoral college in which the electors would be selected by the state legislatures (and close elections would be resolved in the House of Representatives), the framers hoped to achieve a "republican" solution: a strong president responsible to state and national legislators rather than directly to the electorate. This indirect method of electing the president probably did dampen the power of most presidents in the nineteenth century. This conclusion is supported by the fact that, as we shall see below, presidential power increased as the president developed a closer and more direct relationship to a mass electorate.

The heart of presidential power as defined by the Constitution is found in Sections 2 and 3, where the several clauses define the presidency in two dimensions: the president as head of state and the president as head of government. Although these will be given separate treatment here, the presidency can be understood only by the combination of the two.

THE PRESIDENT AS HEAD OF STATE: SOME IMPERIAL QUALITIES

The constitutional position of the president as head of state is defined by three constitutional provisions, which are the source of some of the most important powers on which presidents can draw. The areas can be classified as follows:

1. *Military.* Article II, Section 2, provides for the power as "Commander in Chief of the Army and Navy of the United States, and of the Militia of the several States, when called in to the actual Service of the United States."
2. *Judicial.* Article II, Section 2, also provides the power to "grant Reprieves and Pardons for Offences against the United States, except in Cases of Impeachment."
3. *Diplomatic.* Article II, Section 3, provides the power to "receive Ambassadors and other public Ministers."

---

inherent powers

powers claimed by a president that are not expressed in the Constitution, but are inferred from it

Even though the presidency is an office of delegated powers, for a century and a half after the Founding, many feared that the president's power could become dictatorial. This political cartoon criticized President Andrew Jackson's use of the veto power.

BORN TO COMMAND.

OF VETO MEMORY.

HAD I BEEN CONSULTED.

KING ANDREW THE FIRST.

P. 0318 CARTOON BRANDING ANDREW JACKSON AS A DICTATOR.

Military First, the position of **commander in chief** makes the president the highest military authority in the United States, with control of the entire defense establishment. No American president, however, would dare put on a military uniform for a state function—not even a former general like Eisenhower—even though the president is the highest military officer in war and in peace. The president is also head of the secret intelligence network, which includes not only the Central Intelligence Agency (CIA) but also the National Security Council (NSC), the National Security Agency (NSA), the Federal Bureau of Investigation (FBI), and a host of less well known but very powerful international and domestic security agencies. But these impressive powers must be read in the context of Article I, wherein seven of the eighteen clauses of Section 8 provide particular military and foreign policy powers to Congress, including the power to declare wars for which presidents are responsible. Presidents have tried to evade this at their peril. In full awareness of the woe visited upon President Lyndon Johnson for evading and misleading Congress at the outset of the Vietnam War, President Bush sought explicit congressional authorization for the Gulf War in January 1991.

Judicial The presidential power to grant reprieves, pardons, and amnesties involves the power of life and death over all individuals who may be a threat to the security of the United States. Presidents may use this power on behalf of a particular individual, as did Gerald Ford when he pardoned Richard Nixon in 1974 "for all offenses against the United States which he . . . has committed or may have committed." Or they may use it on a large scale, as did President Andrew Johnson in 1868, when he gave full amnesty to all southerners who had participated in the "Late Rebellion," and President Carter in 1977, when he declared an amnesty for all the draft evaders of the Vietnam War. This power of life and death over others helped elevate the president to the level of earlier conquerors and kings by establishing him as the person before whom supplicants might come to make their pleas for mercy.

Diplomatic When President Washington received Edmond Genêt ("Citizen Genêt") as the formal emissary of the revolutionary government of France in 1793 and had his cabinet officers and Congress back his decision, he established a greatly expanded interpretation of the power to "receive Ambassadors and other public Ministers," extending it to the power to "recognize" other countries. That power gives the president the almost unconditional authority to review the claims of any new ruling groups to determine if they indeed control the territory and population of their country, so that they can

commander in chief

the power of the president as commander of the national military and the state national guard units (when called into service)

Students and Politics

In February 1998, a confrontation loomed between the United States and Iraq over the composition and powers of the United Nations weapons-inspection team that was to search Iraq for "weapons of mass destruction." In an attempt to determine and muster public support for a military strike, the Clinton administration held a town meeting at Ohio State University in Columbus. Secretary of State Madeleine Albright, Defense Secretary William Cohen, and National Security Adviser Sandy Berger spoke and fielded questions during the nationally televised forum.

Students—both for and against military intervention—attended the meeting and made their presence felt. Several loud student protesters gained admittance to the forum and attempted to disrupt the telecast with chants that depicted a military strike against Iraq as racist and implausible. Others protested against the repercussions that the use of force would have on Iraq's civilian population. "We're so concerned with justice, democracy, and freedom and we forget that humanity is what we need to be concerned about," said Ohio State sophomore Jaime Radich, who distributed fliers with photos of sick Iraqi children before the event.[1] Others, such as Miami University graduate John Strange, felt that the government held the meeting to further its own agenda, rather than determine the public mood: "I think they were looking for a pep rally, not a town meeting," he said. Others disapproved of the often rowdy student protesters. "It was good to have differing opinions, but it could have been done in a more respectful manner," said Ohio State junior Jonathan Rapp.[2]

[1]"Muslim Students, Others Object to U.S. Military Action," *Lantern* (Ohio State University), February 19, 1998.
[2]"OSU Students React to Protesters and Speakers at Town Hall Meeting," *Lantern* (Ohio State University), February 19, 1998.

commit it to treaties and other agreements. Critics may have questioned the wisdom of President Nixon's recognition of the People's Republic of China and of President Carter's recognition of the Sandinista government in Nicaragua. But they did not question the president's authority to make such decisions. Because the breakup of the Soviet bloc was generally perceived as a positive event, no one criticized President Bush for his quick recognition of the several former Soviet and Yugoslav republics as soon as they declared themselves independent states.

The Imperial Presidency?   Have presidents used these three constitutional powers—military, judicial, and diplomatic—to make the presidency too powerful, indeed "imperial?"[4] Debate over the answer to this question has produced an unusual lineup, with presidents and the Supreme Court on one side and Congress on the other. In 1936, the Supreme Court supported the expansive view of the presidency by holding that Congress may delegate a degree of discretion to the president in foreign affairs that might violate the separation of powers if it were in a domestic arena.[5] The Supreme Court also upheld the president's power to use executive agreements to conduct foreign policy.[6] An **executive agreement** is exactly like a treaty because it is a contract between two countries, but an executive agreement does not require a two-thirds vote of approval by the Senate. Ordinarily, executive agreements are used to carry out commitments already made in treaties, or to arrange for matters well below the level of policy. But when presidents have found it expedient to use an executive agreement in place of a treaty, the Court has gone along. This verges on an imperial power.

Many recent presidents have even gone beyond formal executive agreements to engage in what amounts to unilateral action. They may seek formal congressional authorization, as in 1964 when President Lyndon Johnson convinced Congress to adopt the Gulf of Tonkin Resolution authorizing him to expand the American military presence in Vietnam. Johnson interpreted the resolution as a delegation of discretion to use any and all national resources according to his own judgment. Others may not even bother with the authorization but merely assume it, as President Nixon did when he claimed to need no congressional authorization to continue or to expand the Vietnam War.

executive agreement

an agreement, made between the president and another country, that has the force of a treaty but does not require the Senate's "advice and consent"

President Lyndon B. Johnson pressured Congress to pass the Gulf of Tonkin resolution, which he quickly signed into law. Johnson interpreted the measure as a congressional declaration of war and used it as justification for escalating America's involvement in Vietnam.

PRESIDENTIAL ACTIONS TAKEN IN VIOLATION OF THE WAR POWERS ACT

Table 13.1

President	Presidential action	Date of action
Ford	Sent troops into Cambodia to rescue crew of the *Mayaguez,* which had been captured by Cambodian forces	May 1975
Carter	Sent troops into Iran in failed attempt to rescue American hostages	May 1980
Reagan	Stationed troops in Beirut with redefined mission of supporting the Lebanese government; 230 troops died	October 1983
Reagan	Sent troops to invade Grenada, with ostensible purpose of rescuing American students	October 1983
Reagan	Diverted profits from illegal arms sales to Iran to finance (illegally) the Contra rebels in Nicaragua	1985–86
Reagan	Ordered surprise bombing of Libya by U.S. planes overflying several European countries	April 1986
Bush	Ordered military invasion of Panama, ending in arrest of Panamanian president Manuel Noriega	December 1989
Bush	Stationed U.S. troops in Somalia to restore order and protect food deliveries	1992–93
Clinton	Ordered launch of 23 Tomahawk missiles against Iraqi intelligence headquarters	June 1993
Clinton	Ordered military intervention in Haiti	September 1994
Clinton	Ordered American planes to bomb Serbian positions in Bosnia	August 1995
Clinton	Committed American troops to maintain peace in Bosnia	December 1995

These presidential claims and actions led to a congressional reaction, however. In 1973, Congress passed the **War Powers Resolution** over President Nixon's veto. This resolution asserted that the president could send American troops into action abroad only in the event of a declaration of war or other statutory authorization by Congress, or if American troops were attacked or directly endangered. This was an obvious effort to revive the principle that the presidency is an office of delegated powers—that is, powers granted by Congress—and that there is no blanket prerogative.

Nevertheless, this resolution has not prevented presidents from using force when they have deemed it necessary (see Table 13.1). President Reagan took at least four military actions that could be seen as violations of the War Powers Resolution. President Bush disregarded Congress in the invasion of Panama but was fortunate in bringing the affair to a successful conclusion quite quickly. In contrast, once he saw that the situation in Kuwait in 1990 was tending toward protracted military involvement, he submitted the issue to Congress.

Although President Clinton appeared at first to be reluctant to take bold international initiatives, he did not hesitate to use direct action when events seemed to threaten his own position or his view of the national interest.

War Powers Resolution

a resolution of Congress that the president can send troops into action abroad only by authorization of Congress, or if American troops are already under attack or serious threat

Clinton's series of unilateral actions in Bosnia dramatically tested his independence from Congress. First, Clinton unilaterally approved the use of American planes to bomb Serbian strategic positions in the late summer of 1995 (which pressured the Serbs to participate in peace negotiations with Croats and Bosnian Muslims). Second, to make the peace negotiations succeed, Clinton unilaterally pledged the American military to monitor the implementation of the agreement, including committing twenty thousand U.S. troops to monitor the agreement on the ground. With U.S. forces already in Bosnia, all Congress could do was pass a resolution in December 1995, after a long debate, to authorize financial support for the troops but also to disapprove of Clinton's actions and to demand further reporting to Congress in the future.

THE DOMESTIC PRESIDENCY: THE PRESIDENT AS HEAD OF GOVERNMENT

The constitutional basis of the domestic presidency also has three parts. And here again, although real power grows out of the combination of the parts, the analysis is greatly aided by examining the parts separately:

1. *Executive.* The "executive power" is vested in the president by Article II, Section 1, to see that all the laws are faithfully executed (Section 3), and to appoint, remove, and supervise all executive officers and to appoint all federal judges (Section 2).
2. *Military.* This power is derived from Article IV, Section 4, which stipulates that the president has the power to protect every state "against Invasion; and . . . against domestic Violence."
3. *Legislative.* The president is given the power under various provisions to participate effectively and authoritatively in the legislative process.

Executive Power   The most important basis of the president's power as chief executive is to be found in Article II, Section 3, which stipulates that the president must see that all the laws are faithfully executed, and Section 2, which provides that the president will appoint, remove, and supervise all executive officers, and appoint all federal judges. The power to appoint the principal executive officers and to require each of them to report to the president on subjects relating to the duties of their departments makes the president the true chief executive officer (CEO) of the nation. In this manner, the Constitution focuses executive power and legal responsibility upon the president. The famous sign on President Truman's desk, "The buck stops here," was not merely an assertion of Truman's personal sense of responsibility but was in fact recognition by him of the legal and constitutional responsibility of the president. The president is subject to some limitations, because the appointment of all such officers, including ambassadors, ministers, and federal judges, is subject to a majority approval by the Senate. But these appointments are at the discretion of the president, and the loyalty and the responsibility of each appointment are presumed to be directed toward the president. Although the United States has no cabinet in the parliamentary sense of a collective decision-making body or board of directors with collective responsibilities, the Constitution nevertheless recognizes departments with department heads, and that recognition establishes the lines of legal responsibility up and down the executive hierarchy, culminating in the presidency (see Figure 13.1).

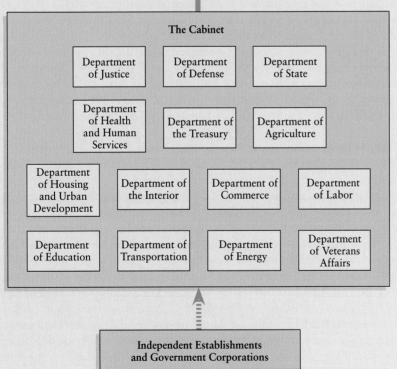

THE INSTITUTIONAL PRESIDENCY

Figure 13.1

The President

White House staff

Executive Office of the President

White House Office	Office of the U.S. Trade Representative
Office of Management and Budget	Council on Environmental Quality
Council of Economic Advisers	Office of Science and Technology Policy
National Security Council	Office of Policy Development
Office of National Drug Control Policy	Office of Administration
	Vice President

The Cabinet

Department of Justice

Department of Defense

Department of State

Department of Health and Human Services

Department of the Treasury

Department of Agriculture

Department of Housing and Urban Development

Department of the Interior

Department of Commerce

Department of Labor

Department of Education

Department of Transportation

Department of Energy

Department of Veterans Affairs

Independent Establishments and Government Corporations

SOURCE: Office of the Federal Register, National Archives and Records Administration, *The United States Government Manual, 1995–96* (Washington, DC: Government Printing Office, 1995), p. 22.

President Clinton tried to invoke executive privilege to prevent independent counsel Kenneth Starr from interviewing White House aides during Starr's investigation of charges that the president had committed perjury and obstructed justice.

Bearing the tremendous responsibilities implied in "the buck stops here," presidents have consistently resented and opposed efforts by Congress and the courts to break the "chain of command," even amid serious charges of wrongdoing. The infamous 1973 "Saturday Night Massacre" brought the whole issue dramatically into focus. In that incident the attorney general and the deputy attorney general both resigned rather than follow President Nixon's order to fire Archibald Cox, the special prosecutor appointed to investigate charges rising out of the Watergate affair. This led Congress to pass the independent counsel law, which provides that once the attorney general has appointed an **independent counsel,** that person can be removed only "for cause." This is certainly an infringement on the president's appointment power, but it was upheld by the Supreme Court.[7]

Nixon was also the first president to focus attention on "**executive privilege,**" the notion that the president has constitutional authority to withhold information from Congress and the judiciary in matters deemed to be of critical concern to the nation. But executive privilege is not as established an idea as the president's other powers. Raoul Berger, the most widely recognized expert on the subject, claims the whole notion of executive privilege is a myth, first articulated as a response to congressional investigations of alleged communists during the early 1950s.[8] The Supreme Court acknowledged its existence in the famous *U.S. v. Nixon* case in 1974, but ruled that the president has only *limited* executive privilege, covering confidentiality of executive communications if the disclosure would compromise the national interest. If the materials in question were required for a criminal trial, however, it would then be up to the trial judge to examine in secret the material to determine if military or diplomatic secrets would be compromised. This unanimous decision in the *Nixon* case provides for a very limited executive privilege.[9] For example, it encompassed efforts by President Clinton to excuse himself and his legal counsel and other confidential staff from giving testimony regarding perjury and obstruction of justice in the Monica Lewinsky scandal that erupted in 1998.

Military Sources of Domestic Presidential Power   Although Article IV, Section 4, provides that the "United States shall [protect] every State . . . against Invasion . . . and . . . domestic Violence," Congress has made this an explicit presidential power through statutes directing the president as commander in chief to discharge these obligations.[10] The Constitution restrains the president's use of domestic force by providing that a state legislature (or governor when the legislature is not in session) must request federal troops before the president can send them into the state to provide public order. Yet this proviso is not absolute. First, presidents are not obligated to deploy national troops merely because the state legislature or governor makes such a request. And more important, the president may deploy troops in a state or city without a specific request from the state legislature or governor if the president considers it necessary in order to maintain an essential national service during an emergency, in order to enforce a federal judicial order, or in order to protect federally guaranteed civil rights.

One historic example of the unilateral use of presidential emergency power to protect the states against domestic disorder, even when the states don't request it, was the decision by President Dwight Eisenhower in 1957 to send troops into Little Rock, Arkansas, literally against the wishes of the state of

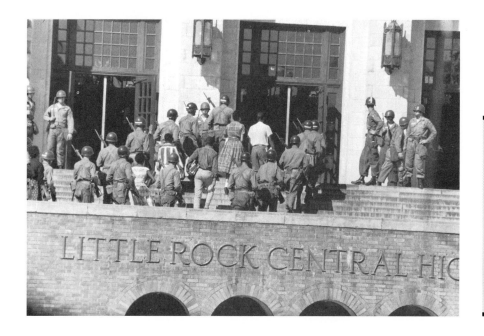

In 1957, Arkansas governor Orval Faubus ignored a federal court order and used the state's National Guard to prevent nine black students from attending Little Rock's Central High School. President Dwight Eisenhower was forced to send a thousand soldiers to protect the black students. The troops stayed for the entire school year.

Arkansas, to enforce court orders to integrate Little Rock's Central High School. The governor of Arkansas, Orval Faubus, had actually posted the Arkansas National Guard at the entrance of Central High School to prevent the court-ordered admission of nine black students. After an effort to negotiate with Governor Faubus failed, President Eisenhower reluctantly sent a thousand paratroopers to Little Rock, who stood watch while the black students took their places in the all-white classrooms. This case makes quite clear that the president does not have to wait for a request by a state legislature or governor before acting as a domestic commander in chief.[11]

However, in most instances of domestic disorder—whether from human or from natural causes—presidents tend to exercise unilateral power by declaring a "state of emergency," thereby making available federal grants, insurance, and direct assistance. In 1992, in the aftermath of the devastating riots in Los Angeles and the hurricanes in Florida, American troops were very much in evidence, sent in by the president, but in the role more of Good Samaritans than of military police.

The President's Legislative Power   The president plays a role not only in the administration of government but also in the legislative process. Two constitutional provisions are the primary sources of the president's power in the legislative arena. The first of these is the provision in Article II, Section 3, providing that the president "shall from time to time give to the Congress Information of the State of the Union, and recommend to their Consideration such Measures as he shall judge necessary and expedient." The second of the president's legislative powers is of course the veto power assigned by Article I, Section 7.[12]

Delivering a "State of the Union" address does not at first appear to be of any great import. It is a mere obligation on the part of the president to make recommendations for Congress's consideration. But as political and social conditions began to favor an increasingly prominent role for presidents, each

veto

the president's constitutional power to turn down acts of Congress. A presidential veto may be overridden by a two-thirds vote of each house of Congress

pocket veto

a presidential veto that is automatically triggered if the president does not act on a given piece of legislation passed during the final ten days of a legislative session

president, especially since Franklin Delano Roosevelt, began to rely on this provision to become the primary initiator of proposals for legislative action in Congress and the principal source for public awareness of national issues, as well as the most important single individual participant in legislative decisions. Few today doubt that the president and the executive branch together are the primary source for many important congressional actions.[13]

The **veto** power is the president's constitutional power to turn down acts of Congress (see Figure 13.2). This power alone makes the president the most important single legislative leader.[14] No bill vetoed by the president can become law unless both the House and Senate override the veto by a two-thirds vote. In the case of a **pocket veto**, Congress does not even have the option of overriding the veto, but must reintroduce the bill in the next session. A pocket veto

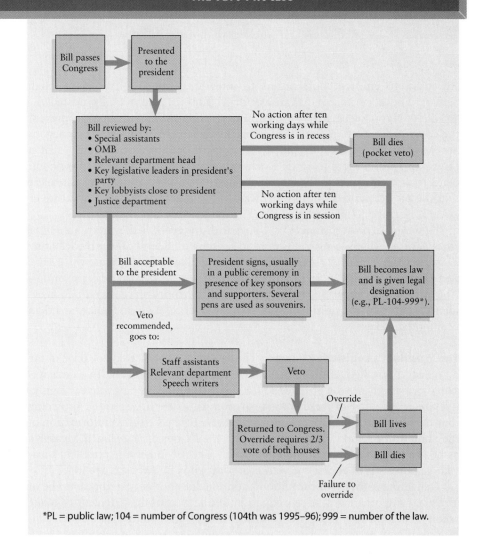

Figure 13.2 — THE VETO PROCESS

*PL = public law; 104 = number of Congress (104th was 1995–96); 999 = number of the law.

The Line-Item Veto

*I*n 1996, Congress passed a bill giving the president a limited version of a power that presidents have sought since the administration of Ulysses S. Grant. The line-item veto power, first used by President Bill Clinton, allows the president to selectively return to Congress portions of appropriations bills, items found within direct spending bills, and certain limited tax benefits. Each item disapproved by the president is returned separately to Congress, which may then pass the item again, if it chooses, by majority vote. The president then formally vetoes the items, returns them to Congress, where they can be overridden by a two-thirds vote. (This complicated procedure is actually "enhanced rescission" authority, but it operates as a line-item veto.)

Supporters of the line-item veto hail it as a targeted method for presidents to reduce wasteful, unnecessary, or pork-barrel spending, and to help balance the budget. The fact that a Republican-controlled Congress approved the power for a Democratic president underscores the need felt for better and tighter control over government spending. Members of Congress have always included in spending bills special items that provide jobs, money, or other concessions that benefit their districts or states. Presidents possessing only the regular veto could not discriminate among the parts of a bill, and would be faced with the unhappy choice of vetoing an entire bill because of a few objectionable items, or signing an entire bill, accepting the bad with the good. With the line-item veto, portions of spending bills of dubious value can now be eliminated by the president. In the fall of 1997, for example, President Clinton used the line-item veto to block $458 million in spending he considered unnecessary.

The line-item veto power, even in its limited form, is admittedly a departure from the intention of the Constitution's framers. On the other hand, the federal budget has become vast and complicated over the past two centuries; these changed circumstances call for added executive authority, supporters argue. Moreover, they point out, forty-three of the fifty state governors possess some form of line-item veto, ample precedent for a similar presidential power.

Opponents of the line-item veto power note that the positive effects of such a power have been, and continue to be, vastly overstated. Even a broader line-item veto power is not likely to appreciably reduce spending waste; the idea that presidents are uninterested in pork-barrel spending is a myth. Presidents seek to reward political friends, and punish political opponents, with pork-barrel spending. This pattern is especially apparent during presidential election years. Moreover, the president can exercise considerable influence over the legislative process at virtually every step, from the introduction of a bill, to its debate and passage, to a regular veto. Presidents thus have many opportunities to shape legislation aside from a line-item veto.

As for the current line-item veto, the actual amount of spending stemmed by the power is minuscule. The $458 million in spending blocked by President Clinton in 1997 was only 1.5 percent of the total of $291 billion in spending. The budget will not be balanced by the line-item veto.

Instead, the main effect of the line-item veto is political, say opponents. Special interests and members of Congress who support items vulnerable to the line-item veto now intensively lobby the president in addition to key members of Congress. The end product is more, rather than less, political deal-making. The president's greater power over the budget means that the modern strong president has yet another power to wield over Congress. While some may consider this a good development, the American government is based on a three-branch system of separation of powers. Further weakening of the hand of Congress weakens our constitutional system, as well. As for the model of state governors, their powers are designed to be far greater than those of the president. And studies of gubernatorial line-item vetoes show that they do not produce effective spending reductions.

Finally, the Constitution's framers understood, and consciously accepted, an all-or-nothing veto power for the president. Had they wanted presidents to have vastly greater powers over spending and legislation, they would have provided such power in the Constitution. In 1998, the Supreme Court agreed that the Constitution does not give the president this power.

can occur when the president is presented with a bill during the last ten days of a legislative session. Usually, if a president does not sign a bill within ten days, it automatically becomes law. But this is true only while Congress is in session. If a president chooses not to sign a bill presented within the last ten days that Congress is in session, then the ten-day limit does not expire until Congress is out of session, and instead of becoming law, the bill is vetoed. In 1996 a new power was added to the president's lineup—the **line-item veto**—giving the president power to strike specific spending items from appropriations bills passed by Congress, unless reenacted by a two-thirds vote of both House and Senate. In 1997, President Clinton used this power eleven times to strike eighty-two items from the federal budget. But, as we saw in Chapter 12, in 1998 the Supreme Court ruled that the Constitution does not authorize the line-item veto power. Only a constitutional amendment would restore this power to the president.

Figure 13.3 reveals the widely different uses presidents have made of their veto power. Use of the veto varies according to the political situation that each president confronts. Franklin D. Roosevelt, even with his own party in control of Congress, used the veto power extensively as an exercise of presidential leadership. As we shall see later in this chapter, FDR's time in office (1933–45) established the presidency as the center of the national government. Harry S. Truman (1945–53) and Dwight D. Eisenhower (1953–61) faced Congresses controlled by the opposition party and used the veto power vigorously to confront their opponents. During Bill Clinton's first two years in office, when Democrats controlled both houses of Congress, he vetoed no bills. Following the congressional elections of 1994, however, Clinton confronted a Republican-controlled Congress with a definite agenda, and he too began to use his veto power more vigorously. In the process, Clinton recaptured some of the national spotlight that had seemingly shifted to the Speaker of the House, Newt Gingrich.

Clinton also recaptured some of his leadership by finding the path of legislative initiative that he had lost with the Republican takeover of the House and Senate after the 1994 congressional elections. Although not explicitly stated, the Constitution provides the president with the power of **legislative initiative**. To "initiate" means to originate, and in government that can mean power. The framers of the Constitution clearly saw legislative initiative as one of the keys to executive power. Initiative obviously implies the ability to formulate proposals for important policies, and the president, as an individual with a great deal of staff assistance, is able to initiate decisive action more frequently than Congress, with its large assemblies that have to deliberate and debate before taking action. But Clinton, confronting Republican majorities in both chambers of Congress, had to adjust to the realities of **divided government**: he took up the legislative habit of "thinking small." Even in his fifth State of the Union Address, in January 1997, following his resoundingly strong re-election in 1996, was a shopping list of small state and local government proposals that sounded more like being "governor of the United States" than president of the United States.[16] One commentator observed that "the president seems to have over-learned the lesson of his first-term health fiasco. Instead of grand policy schemes, he has shifted to the other extreme: a laundry list of risk-free initiatives."[17] Yet there is power in initiative, even when the initiative is a thousand small steps rather than a few large ones.

line-item veto
the power of the executive to veto specific provisions (lines) of a bill passed by the legislature

legislative initiative
the president's inherent power to bring a legislative agenda before Congress

divided government
the condition in American government wherein the presidency is controlled by one party while the opposing party controls one or both houses of Congress

PRESIDENTIAL VETOES, 1789–1997

Figure 13.3

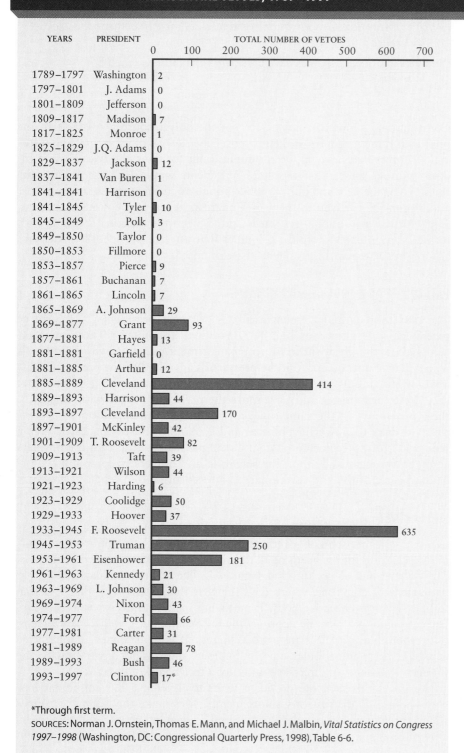

YEARS	PRESIDENT	TOTAL NUMBER OF VETOES
1789–1797	Washington	2
1797–1801	J. Adams	0
1801–1809	Jefferson	0
1809–1817	Madison	7
1817–1825	Monroe	1
1825–1829	J.Q. Adams	0
1829–1837	Jackson	12
1837–1841	Van Buren	1
1841–1841	Harrison	0
1841–1845	Tyler	10
1845–1849	Polk	3
1849–1850	Taylor	0
1850–1853	Fillmore	0
1853–1857	Pierce	9
1857–1861	Buchanan	7
1861–1865	Lincoln	7
1865–1869	A. Johnson	29
1869–1877	Grant	93
1877–1881	Hayes	13
1881–1881	Garfield	0
1881–1885	Arthur	12
1885–1889	Cleveland	414
1889–1893	Harrison	44
1893–1897	Cleveland	170
1897–1901	McKinley	42
1901–1909	T. Roosevelt	82
1909–1913	Taft	39
1913–1921	Wilson	44
1921–1923	Harding	6
1923–1929	Coolidge	50
1929–1933	Hoover	37
1933–1945	F. Roosevelt	635
1945–1953	Truman	250
1953–1961	Eisenhower	181
1961–1963	Kennedy	21
1963–1969	L. Johnson	30
1969–1974	Nixon	43
1974–1977	Ford	66
1977–1981	Carter	31
1981–1989	Reagan	78
1989–1993	Bush	46
1993–1997	Clinton	17*

*Through first term.

SOURCES: Norman J. Ornstein, Thomas E. Mann, and Michael J. Malbin, *Vital Statistics on Congress 1997–1998* (Washington, DC: Congressional Quarterly Press, 1998), Table 6-6.

★ Institutional Resources of Presidential Power

▶ What institutional resources does the president use to manage the executive branch?

▶ Which of these resources have presidents increasingly relied on?

Constitutional sources of power are not the only resources available to the president. Presidents have at their disposal a variety of other formal and informal resources that have important implications for their ability to govern. Indeed, without these other resources, presidents would lack the ability—the tools of management and public mobilization—to make much use of the power and responsibility given to them by Congress. Let us first consider the president's formal institutional resources and then, in the section following, turn to the more informal political resources that affect a president's capacity to govern, in particular the president's base of popular support.

PATRONAGE AS A TOOL OF MANAGEMENT

patronage

the resources available to higher officials, usually opportunities to make partisan appointments to offices and to confer grants, licenses, or special favors to supporters

The first tool of management available to most presidents is a form of **patronage**—the choice of high-level political appointees. These appointments allow the president to fill top management positions with individuals who will attempt to carry out the president's agenda. But the president must appoint individuals who have experience and interest in the programs that they are to administer and who share the president's goals with respect to these programs. At the same time, presidents use the appointment process to build links to powerful political and economic constituencies by giving representation to important state political party organizations, the business community, organized labor, the scientific and university communities, organized agriculture, and certain large and well-organized religious groups.

THE CABINET

Cabinet

the secretaries, or chief administrators, of the major departments of the federal government. Cabinet secretaries are appointed by the president with the consent of the Senate

In the American system of government, the **Cabinet** is the traditional but informal designation for the heads of all the major federal government departments. The Cabinet has no constitutional status. Unlike in England and many other parliamentary countries, where the cabinet *is* the government, the American Cabinet is not a collective body. It meets but makes no decisions as a group. Each appointment must be approved by the Senate, but Cabinet members are not responsible to the Senate or to Congress at large. Cabinet appointments help build party and popular support, but the Cabinet is not a party organ. The Cabinet is made up of directors, but is not a true board of directors.

National Security Council (NSC)

a presidential foreign policy advisory council composed of the president; the vice president; the secretaries of state, defense, and the treasury; the attorney general; and other officials invited by the president

Aware of this fact, the president tends to develop a burning impatience with and a mild distrust of Cabinet members; to make the Cabinet a rubber stamp for actions already decided on; and to demand results, or the appearance of results, more immediately and more frequently than most department heads can provide. Since Cabinet appointees generally have not shared political careers with the president or with each other, and since they may meet literally for the first time after their selection, the formation of an effective governing group out of this motley collection of appointments is unlikely. Although President Clinton's insistence on a Cabinet diverse enough to resemble American society could be considered an act of political wisdom, it virtually guaranteed that few of his appointees had ever spent much time working together or even knew the policy positions or beliefs of the other appointees.[18]

Some presidents have relied more heavily on an "inner Cabinet," the **National Security Council** (NSC). The NSC, established by law in 1947, is composed of the president, the vice president, the secretaries of state, defense, and the treasury, the attorney general, and other officials invited by the president. It has its own staff of foreign-policy specialists run by the special assistant to the president for national security affairs. For these highest appointments, presidents turn to people from outside Washington, usually longtime associates. A counterpart, the Domestic Council, was created by law in 1970, but no specific members were designated for it. President Clinton hit upon his own version of the Domestic Council, called the National Economic Council, which shares competing functions with the Council of Economic Advisers.

Presidents have obviously been uneven and unpredictable in their reliance on the NSC and other subcabinet bodies, because executive management is inherently a personal matter. Despite all the personal variations, however, one generalization can be made: Presidents have increasingly preferred the White House staff instead of the cabinet as their means of managing the gigantic executive branch.

THE WHITE HOUSE STAFF

The **White House staff** is composed mainly of analysts and advisers.[19] Although many of the top White House staff members are given the title "special assistant" for a particular task or sector, the types of judgments they are expected to make and the kinds of advice they are supposed to give are a good deal broader and more generally political than those coming from the Executive Office of the President or from the cabinet departments. The members of the White House staff also tend to be more closely associated with the president than other presidentially appointed officials.

From an informal group of fewer than a dozen people (popularly called the **Kitchen Cabinet**), and no more than four dozen at the height of the domestic Roosevelt presidency in 1937, the White House staff has grown substantially with each successive president (see Figure 13.4).[20] Richard Nixon employed 550 people in 1972. President Carter, who found so many of the requirements of presidential power distasteful, and who publicly vowed to keep his staff small and decentralized, built an even larger and more centralized staff. President Clinton promised during the campaign to reduce the White House staff by 25 percent, but there is no indication he sustained this effort. A large White House staff has become essential.

The biggest variation among presidential management practices lies not in the size of the White House staff but in its organization. President Reagan went to the extreme in delegating important management powers to his chief of staff, and he elevated his budget director to an unprecedented level of power in *policy* making rather than merely *budget* making. President Bush centralized his staff even more under chief of staff John Sununu. At the same

THE CABINET DEPARTMENTS

Department	Year created
State	1789
Treasury	1789
Defense*	1947
Justice	1789
Interior†	1849
Agriculture	1889
Commerce	1913
Labor	1913
Health and Human Services††	1953
Housing and Urban Development	1965
Transportation	1966
Energy	1977
Education	1979
Veterans Affairs	1989

*Formerly the War and Navy Departments, created in 1789 and 1798, respectively.

†Created in 1862; made part of Cabinet in 1889.

††Formerly Health, Education, and Welfare; reorganized in 1979 (when separate Department of Education was created).

White House staff

analysts and advisers to the president, often given the title "special assistant"

Kitchen Cabinet

an informal group of advisers to whom the president turns for counsel and guidance. Members of the official Cabinet may or may not also be members of the Kitchen Cabinet

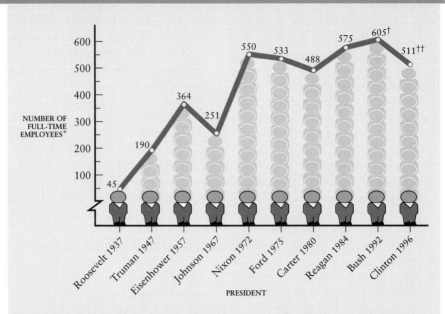

THE EXPANDING WHITE HOUSE STAFF, 1937–96

*These figures do not include the employees temporarily detailed to the White House from outside agencies (about 50–75 in 1992 and 1996).

†The vice president employs more than 20 people, and there are at least 100 people on the staff of the National Security Council. These people work in the White House and the Executive Office buildings, but are not included in these totals, except where noted.

††These figures include the staffs of the Office of the President, the Executive Residence, and the Office of the Vice President.

SOURCES: 1937–84: Thomas E. Cronin, "The Swelling of the Presidency: Can Anyone Reverse the Tide?" in *American Government: Readings and Cases*, 8th ed., ed. Peter Woll (Boston: Little, Brown, 1984), p. 347; 1992 and 1996: provided by the Office of Management and Budget and the White House.

time, Bush continued to deal directly with his Cabinet heads, the press, and key members of Congress. President Clinton showed a definite preference for competition among equals in his cabinet and among senior White House officials, obviously liking competition and conflict among staff members, for which FDR's staff was also famous. But the troubles Clinton has had in turning this conflict and competition into coherent policies and well-articulated messages suggests that he might have done better to emulate his immediate predecessors in their preference for hierarchy and centralization.[21]

THE EXECUTIVE OFFICE OF THE PRESIDENT

The development of the White House staff can be appreciated only in its relation to the still-larger **Executive Office of the President** (EOP). Created in 1939, the EOP is a major part of what is often called the "institutional presidency"—the permanent agencies that perform defined management tasks for the president (see Figure 13.5). The most important and the largest EOP

Executive Office of the President (EOP)

the permanent agencies that perform defined management tasks for the president. Created in 1939, the EOP includes the Office of Management and Budget, the Council of Economic Advisers, the National Security Council, and other agencies

agency is the Office of Management and Budget (OMB). Its roles in preparing the national budget, designing the president's program, reporting on agency activities, and overseeing regulatory proposals make OMB personnel part of virtually every conceivable presidential responsibility. The status and power of the OMB has grown in importance with each successive president. The process of budgeting at one time was a "bottom-up" procedure, with expenditure and program requests passing from the lowest bureaus through the departments to "clearance" in OMB and hence to Congress, where each agency could be called in to reveal what its "original request" had been before OMB revised it. Now the budgeting process is a "top-down"; OMB sets the terms of discourse for agencies as well as for Congress. The director of OMB is now one of the most powerful officials in Washington.

THE EXECUTIVE OFFICE OF THE PRESIDENT   Figure 13.5

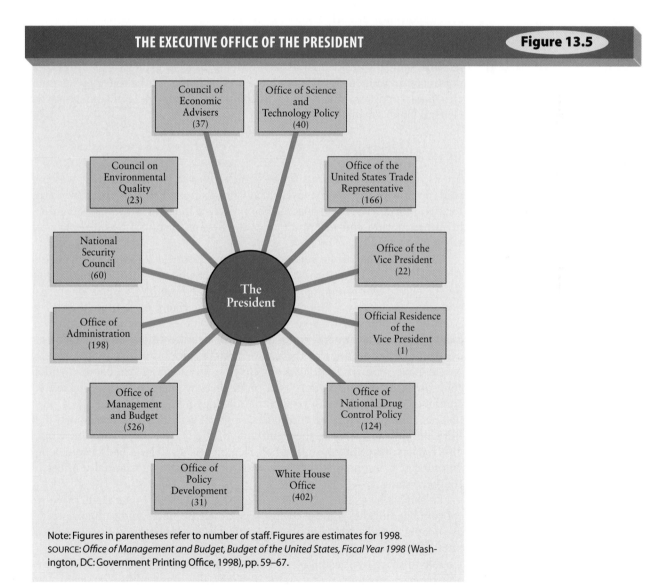

Note: Figures in parentheses refer to number of staff. Figures are estimates for 1998.
SOURCE: *Office of Management and Budget, Budget of the United States, Fiscal Year 1998* (Washington, DC: Government Printing Office, 1998), pp. 59–67.

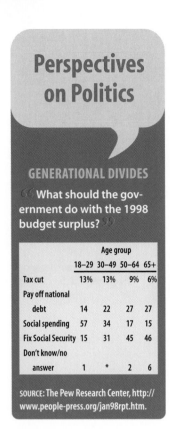

Perspectives on Politics

GENERATIONAL DIVIDES

"What should the government do with the 1998 budget surplus?"

	Age group			
	18–29	30–49	50–64	65+
Tax cut	13%	13%	9%	6%
Pay off national debt	14	22	27	27
Social spending	57	34	17	15
Fix Social Security	15	31	45	46
Don't know/no answer	1	*	2	6

SOURCE: The Pew Research Center, http://www.people-press.org/jan98rpt.htm.

The staff of the Council of Economic Advisers (CEA) constantly analyzes the economy and economic trends and attempts to give the president the ability to anticipate events rather than to wait and react to events. The Council on Environmental Quality was designed to do the same for environmental issues as the CEA does for economic issues. The National Security Council (NSC) is composed of designated cabinet officials who meet regularly with the president to give advice on the large national security picture. The staff of the NSC assimilates and analyzes data from all intelligence-gathering agencies (CIA, etc.). Other EOP agencies perform more specialized tasks.

Somewhere between fifteen hundred and two thousand highly specialized people work for EOP agencies.[22] Figure 13.5 shows the official numbers of employees in each agency of the EOP. However, these numbers do not include a substantial but variable number of key specialists detailed to EOP agencies from outside agencies, especially from the Pentagon to the staff of the NSC. The importance of each agency in the EOP varies according to the personal orientation of each president. For example, the NSC staff was of immense importance under President Nixon, especially because it served essentially as the personal staff of presidential assistant Henry Kissinger. But it was of less importance to President Bush, who looked outside the EOP altogether for military policy matters, much more to the Joint Chiefs of Staff and its chair, General Colin Powell.

THE VICE PRESIDENCY

The vice presidency is a constitutional anomaly even though the office was created along with the presidency by the Constitution. The vice president exists for two purposes only: to succeed the president in case of death, resignation, or incapacitation and to preside over the Senate, casting a tie-breaking vote when necessary.[23]

The main value of the vice presidency as a political resource for the president is electoral. Traditionally, a presidential candidate's most important rule for the choice of a running mate is that he or she bring the support of at least one state (preferably a large one) not otherwise likely to support the ticket. Another rule holds that the vice presidential nominee should provide some regional balance and, wherever possible, some balance among various ideological or ethnic subsections of the party. It is very doubtful that John Kennedy would have won in 1960 without his vice presidential candidate, Lyndon Johnson, and the contribution Johnson made to winning in Texas. Bill Clinton combined considerations of region and ideology in his selection of a vice presidential running mate. The choice of Tennessee senator Al Gore signaled that Bill Clinton was solidly in the right wing of the Democratic Party and would also remain steadfastly a southerner. Democratic strategists had become convinced that Clinton could not win without carrying a substantial number of southern states.

Presidents have constantly promised to give their vice presidents more responsibility, but they almost always break their promises, indicating that they are unable to utilize the vice presidency as a management or political resource after the election. No one can explain exactly why. Perhaps it is just too much trouble to share responsibility. Perhaps the president as head of state feels unable to share any part of that status. Perhaps, like many adult Americans who do not draw up their wills, presidents may simply dread contemplating their

Vice President Al Gore promoted his plan to "reinvent" government on David Letterman's television show, where he railed against the government's procurement requirements, which even specified the number of pieces into which a government ashtray may shatter.

own death. But management style is certainly a factor. George Bush, as vice president, was "kept within the loop" of decision making because President Reagan delegated so much power. A copy of virtually everything made for Reagan was made for Bush, especially during the first term, when Bush's close friend James Baker was chief of staff. President Bush did not take such pains to keep Dan Quayle "in the loop," but President Clinton has relied greatly on his vice president, Al Gore, and Gore has emerged as one of the most trusted and effective figures in the Clinton White House.

Vice President Gore's enhanced status was signaled early on, when President Clinton kept him visibly present at all public appearances during the transition and during the vital public and private efforts to present and campaign for the president's program early in 1993. Since then, he has remained one of the most consistently praised members of the administration. Gore's most important task has been to oversee the National Performance Review (NPR), an ambitious program to "reinvent" the way the federal government conducts its affairs. The NPR was initially dismissed as show rather than substance, but even the administration's toughest critics have had to admit that Gore has led the drive to streamline the federal government with energy and effectiveness.

THE FIRST LADY

The president serves as both chief executive and chief of state—the equivalent of Great Britain's prime minister and king rolled into one, simultaneously leading the government and serving as a symbol of the nation at official ceremonies and functions. For their part, most first ladies (all presidents so far have been men) limit their activities to the ceremonial portion of the presidency. First ladies greet foreign dignitaries, visit other countries, attend important national ceremonies, and otherwise act as America's "queen" when the president is called upon to serve in a kingly capacity.

Because the first lady is generally associated exclusively with the head of state aspect of America's presidency, she is usually not subject to the same sort of media scrutiny or partisan attack as that aimed at the president. The first lady is generally a symbol of the nation rather than of a partisan perspective or

First Lady Hillary Rodham Clinton played a prominent role in President Clinton's 1993 health care reform plan.

policy position. It is generally deemed inappropriate to attack her, much as it would be considered unseemly to launch an attack on the Statue of Liberty or the Washington Monument. Thus, even during the heat of the Watergate affair, no newspaper or politician attacked President Richard Nixon's wife, Pat.

Some first ladies have not resigned themselves to purely symbolic roles in the administration, however. Hillary Rodham Clinton initially played an important political and policy role in her husband's administration. During the 1992 campaign, Bill Clinton often intimated that she would be active in the policy realm by joking that the voters would get "two for the price of one" if they cast their ballots for him. After the election, Hillary took a leading role in a number of policy areas, most notably in crafting the health care reform proposals that were expected to be the centerpiece of Bill Clinton's first term.

At first, Hillary Rodham Clinton was an effective political operative precisely because the media and opposing politicians were reluctant to attack a first lady. In due course, however, she came to be seen less as a national symbol and more as a politician, and she, too, became vulnerable to the intensive media scrutiny and partisan attack that is the norm in American politics today. Opponents accused her of profiting from shady commodities trades, planning the firing of members of the White House travel office to make room for presidential cronies, and, of course, involvement in the Whitewater affair, a set of shady Arkansas real estate deals to which the president's foes sought to connect him. By 1995, Hillary Clinton was forced to withdraw to the more traditional role of a first lady, but she continued to draw the fire of the administration's opponents.

⭐ Political Resources of Presidential Power

▶ What political resources can the president draw on in exercising the powers of the presidency? Which of these resources is a potential liability? Why?

All presidents come to office with great strength. The Constitution and the institutional resources of presidential power that presidents accrue make this certain. Yet as Richard Neustadt argued in his book *Presidential Power,* a president's formal institutional resources of power are not the most important ones. Other political institutions such as Congress also possess formidable powers. As Neustadt put it simply, "presidential power is the power to persuade."[24] But presidents have varied in their abilities to "persuade" and thus exercise the powers of the office. The capacity to exercise these powers and govern effectively is affected by a number of political resources that presidents have grown to rely on, foremost among them the American people. These resources are a source of great strength but also, as we shall see, a potential source of weakness.

ELECTIONS AS A RESOURCE

Any ordinary citizen, legitimately placed in office, would be a very powerful president. Yet there is no denying that a decisive presidential election translates into a more effective presidency. Some presidents claim that a landslide election gives them a **mandate,** by which they mean that the electorate approved the programs offered in the campaign and that Congress ought therefore to go along. And Congress is not unmoved by such an appeal. The electoral landslides of 1964 and 1980 gave Presidents Johnson and Reagan real strength during their "honeymoon" years. In contrast, the close elections of Kennedy in 1960, Nixon in 1968, and Carter in 1976 seriously hampered those presidents' effectiveness. Although Bush was elected decisively in 1988, he had no legislative commitments that would have profited from any claim to an electoral mandate.

President Clinton, an action-oriented president, was nevertheless seriously hampered by having been elected in 1992 by a minority of the popular vote, a mere 43 percent. Clinton was re-elected in 1996 with 49 percent of the vote, a larger percentage of the electorate, but still a minority. His appeals to bipartisanship in 1997 reflected his lack of a mandate from the electorate.

mandate

a claim by a victorious candidate that the electorate has given him or her special authority to carry out promises made during the campaign

PARTY AS A PRESIDENTIAL RESOURCE

Although on the decline, the president's party is far from insignificant as a political resource (see also Chapter 9). Figure 13.6 dramatically demonstrates the point with a forty-three-year history of the presidential "batting average" in Congress—the percentage of winning roll-call votes in Congress on bills publicly supported by the president. Bill Clinton, in his first two years in office, enjoyed high averages of legislative success—86 percent in both 1993 and 1994—but that figure dropped dramatically to 35 percent in 1995 following the Republican takeover of Congress in the 1994 elections.

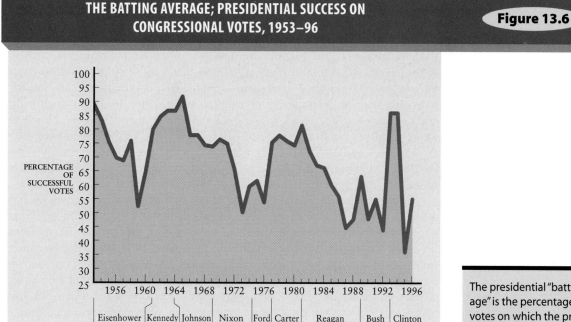

THE BATTING AVERAGE; PRESIDENTIAL SUCCESS ON CONGRESSIONAL VOTES, 1953–96

Figure 13.6

PERCENTAGE OF SUCCESSFUL VOTES

Eisenhower | Kennedy | Johnson | Nixon | Ford | Carter | Reagan | Bush | Clinton

SOURCE: *Congressional Quarterly Weekly Report,* December 21, 1996.

The presidential "batting average" is the percentage of votes on which the president took a position and that position was successful.

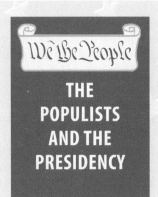

We the People

THE POPULISTS AND THE PRESIDENCY

The Populist Party of the late nineteenth century was the first third party to seriously challenge the dominance of the Republican and Democratic parties. More significantly, the populist movement from which the party arose was in every sense a grassroots movement, made up of average working people, that profoundly altered the course of American politics.

The Populists were composed of farmers and residents of small towns, mostly from the South, the Midwest, and the far West, who valued the agrarian life that was buffeted by harsh economic forces and was fast being eclipsed in America by the growth of urban areas and the rise of industrialization. Despite their loathing for corporate power and urban, monied interests, poor farmers sought alliances with two disparate and disaffected groups: urban workers and southern blacks. This alliance of America's downtrodden and underpaid workers emerged, according to historian Eric F. Goldman, "bursting up from the bottom [of society]."[1]

Meeting in 1892 in Omaha, Nebraska, the Populist Party (also called the People's Party) adopted a platform that shook much of the American establishment. Central to populist doctrine was the idea that the country was divided into producers and nonproducers. Producers were Americans who worked with their hands to create products and commodities that generated wealth. Because of their importance, producers (i.e., average workers) should exercise national political control, the Populists said. Nonproducers, such as bankers and financiers, were those who simply manipulated the wealth generated by producers; their power should be curtailed. To that end, the Populists proposed such radical ideas as the progressive income tax, federal ownership of public services such as the railroads and the telephone and telegraph systems, low-interest government-backed loan

---

The relatively low batting averages for Republican presidents such as Nixon, Ford, Reagan, and Bush are clearly attributable to the political party as a presidential resource. Democrats support Democratic presidents and Republicans support Republican presidents. Since, prior to 1995, during the years included in Figure 13.6, Democrats held the majority in the House of Representatives for all but the 1952–54 Congress and in the Senate except for the 1952–54 and 1980–86 Congresses, it is to be expected that the averages for Democratic presidents would be higher than they would be for Republican presidents. As Figure 13.6 shows clearly, the political party is the key factor.

Another indication of the influence of political parties is not shown on Figure 13.6 but is related to it: regardless of presidential batting average, legislative output was at a record low in 1995. Only eighty-eight bills were enacted during the entire session—the lowest legislative output since 1933, when the Twentieth Amendment abolished the "lame duck" session and moved the starting date of congressional sessions from March to early January (and thus cut two entire months off the length of the Congress that was in session at the time). This low output in 1995 was not due solely to the fact that Washington was in a state of divided government. When government is divided with Democrats controlling Congress and Republicans controlling the White House (as was the case during the George Bush administration, for example), legislative output remains rela-

programs for farmers, free coinage of silver, and such procedural reforms as the secret ballot, direct election of U.S. senators, and the initiative (the ability to turn an elected official out of office by a special vote) and the referendum.

In the 1892 elections, Populists elected five U.S. senators, ten members of the House of Representatives, three state governors, and over fifteen hundred state and local officials around the country. Populist presidential candidate James B. Weaver won electoral votes from six states and took over 8 percent of the popular vote. But Populist thunder was stolen in 1896 by the Democratic Party, which nominated for the presidency a young, fiery Populist midwesterner, William Jennings Bryan (shown in photo). Most Populists accepted a union with the Democrats, but Bryan failed to stir eastern urban workers, and he lost to Republican William McKinley.

In areas where Populists gained control, they succeeded in enacting meaningful reforms. In North Carolina, for example, a Populist-Republican coalition increased funding for public schools and advanced several economic reforms. Kansas Populists reformed banking and railroad regulations. Yet the failure of the altruistic effort by the Populists and Bryan to attract significant urban worker support doomed the movement, especially since the nation was shifting from a rural to an urban base.

This grassroots people's movement was prescient in its platform, in that most of the Populists' "radical" proposals eventually became law. The Populist effort to unite poor white farmers and urban workers with poor black farmers cost Populists key southern support. Nevertheless, populist efforts to unite poor whites and blacks reflected a nobility of sentiment not to be seen again until the civil rights movement of the 1950s and 1960s.

SOURCE: Lawrence Goodwyn, *The Populist Movement in America: A Short History of Agrarian Revolt in America* (New York: Oxford University Press, 1978).
[1]Eric F. Goldman, "A Least Common Denominator," in *Populism*, ed. Theodore Saloutos (New York: Holt, Rinehart, and Winston, 1968), p. 9.

tively high. But when divided government puts the Republicans in control of Congress, as in 1995, legislative output drops tremendously.[25]

At the same time, party has its limitations as a resource. The more unified the president's party is behind legislative requests from the White House, the more unified the opposition party is also likely to be. Unless the president's party majority is very large, appeals must also be made to the opposition to make up for the inevitable defectors within the ranks of the president's own party. Consequently, the president often poses as being above partisanship in order to win "bipartisan" support in Congress. But in pursuing a bipartisan strategy, a president cannot concentrate solely on building the party loyalty and party discipline that would maximize the value of the party's support in Congress. This is a dilemma for all presidents, particularly those faced with an opposition-controlled Congress.

Partisan opposition in Congress proved so strong that President Clinton was unable even to bring the centerpieces of his legislative agenda—health care and welfare reform—to votes during the years in which he enjoyed majorities in Congress. This helps explain the paradox of Clinton's legislative scorecard: high batting averages but failures on key issues. Clinton had a different kind of problem in 1997, one indicative of the vital role of the parties, even though in this case he was opposed by his own party. Clinton made a concerted effort throughout 1997 to restore "fast-track" authority to negotiate trade agreements that would get expedited review and yes-or-no votes in Congress, without the usual amendments that could substantially alter the agreement. Clinton feared he would lose in the House because of opposition by a large faction of his own party. So he turned to the Senate, even though the Constitution requires that such bills must originate in the House because they raise or lower revenues (in this case tariffs). He figured that a strong show of support in the Senate would influence the House. He even got the cooperation of Republican majority leader Senator Trent Lott in this flanking attack. The Senate action was not enough, however. The House leadership tabled the presidentially supported bill because of continued opposition by House Democrats, and the bill never even came to a vote. Clinton's difficulties in maintaining Democratic support in Congress were also evident from the October 1998 House vote in favor of investigating Clinton's possible impeachment. In the days leading up to the vote, Clinton and his staff lobbied House Democrats behind the scenes. Nonetheless, thirty-one Democrats broke ranks and voted in favor of the investigation. House Republicans, for their part, were united in favor of the impeachment inquiry.

GROUPS AS A PRESIDENTIAL RESOURCE

New Deal coalition

the coalition of northern urban liberals, southern white conservatives, organized labor, and blacks that dominated national politics until the 1960s

The classic case in modern times of groups as a resource for the presidency is the Roosevelt or **New Deal coalition**.[26] The New Deal coalition was composed of an inconsistent, indeed contradictory, set of interests. Some of these interests were not organized interest groups, but were regional interests, such as southern whites, or residents of large cities in the industrial Northeast and Midwest, or blacks who later succeeded in organizing as an interest group. In addition to these sectional interests that were drawn to the New Deal, the coalition included several large, self-consciously organized interest groups. The most important in the New Deal coalition were organized labor, agriculture, and the financial community.[27] All of the parts were held together by a

President Bill Clinton and Vice President Al Gore meet with auto executives from General Motors, Ford, and Chrysler. During his first term, Clinton courted big business in order to solidify his electoral base.

judicious use of patronage—not merely patronage in jobs but patronage in policies. Many of the groups were permitted virtually to write their own legislation. In exchange, the groups supported President Roosevelt and his successors in their battles with opposing politicians.

Republican presidents have had their group coalition base also. The most important segments of organized business have tended to support Republican presidents. They have most often been joined by upper-income groups, as well as by some ethnic groups. In recent years, Republican presidents have expanded their interest coalition base. President Reagan, for example, won the support of traditionally Democratic southern white and northern blue-collar voters. This expanded base of support served him well in his struggles with Congress. When the Reagan/Republican coalition began to loosen toward the end of the Bush administration, the astute Bill Clinton was quick to sense it. His 1992 campaign succeeded in part because he brought back together many of the original interests that had made up the New Deal coalition. But he attempted to go even beyond those interests by holding an unprecedented "economic summit" in Little Rock, Arkansas, less than a month after his election. It was a very public meeting of some three hundred bankers, corporate executives, interest-group representatives, prominent economists, and a sprinkling of average citizens—with Clinton himself presiding for almost the entire forty-eight hours of speech-making and serious discussion. It was indeed an extraordinary effort to expand the president's coalition base.

PRESIDENTIAL USE OF THE MEDIA

While the media have grown increasingly important during presidential campaigns (see Chapter 10), their importance is even greater during a president's term in office. Twentieth-century presidents have sought a more direct relationship with the public and have used the media to achieve this end. Modern presidents have learned that they can use their relationship with the media to mobilize popular support for their programs and to attempt to force Congress to follow their lead.

The president is able to take full advantage of access to the communications media mainly because of the legal and constitutional bases of initiative. In the media, reporting on what is new sells newspapers. The president has at hand the thousands of policy proposals that come up to the White House through the administrative agencies; these can be fed to the media as newsworthy initiatives. Consequently, virtually all newspapers and television networks habitually look to the White House as the chief source of news about public policy. They tend to assign one of their most skillful reporters to the White House "beat." And since news is money, they need the president as much as the president needs them in order to meet their mutual need to make news. Presidents have successfully gotten from Congress significant additions to their staff to take care of press releases and other forms of communication. In this manner, the formal and the informal aspects of initiative tend to reinforce each other: the formal resources put the president at the center of policy formulation; this becomes the center of gravity for all buyers and sellers of news, which in turn requires the president to provide easy access to this news. Members of Congress, especially senators, are also key sources of news. But Congress is an anarchy of sources. The White House has more control over what and when, which is what political initiative is all about.

Perspectives on Politics

THE MEDIA AND MONICA LEWINSKY: EVALUATING MEDIA COVERAGE OF THE SCANDAL

Percentage of respondents approving/disapproving of media coverage in certain areas.

	Excellent/ Good	Only fair/ Poor
How well is the media doing at…		
Checking facts before reporting	31%	65%
Being objective	36	60
Providing public with information it needs	45	52
Providing right amount of coverage	43	54

SOURCE: The Pew Research Center, http://www.people-press.org/feb98rpt.htm.

Teddy Roosevelt used the presidency as a "bully pulpit" to promote his vision of America.

Presidential personalities make a difference in how these informal factors are used. Different presidents use the media in quite different ways. One of the first presidents to use the media was Theodore Roosevelt, who referred to the presidency as a "bully pulpit" because its visibility allowed him to preach to the nation and bring popular pressure to bear against his opponents in Congress. But the first president to try to reach the public directly through the media was Franklin Roosevelt. During the 1930s, FDR used radio broadcasts known as "fireside chats," press conferences, speeches, and movie newsreels to rally support for his New Deal programs and, later, to build popular support for American rearmament in the face of the growing danger in Europe and the Far East. FDR also cultivated strong relationships with national news correspondents to ensure favorable publicity for his programs. FDR's efforts to reach out to the American people and mobilize their support were among the factors that made him one of the strongest presidents in American history. His appeals to the American people allowed FDR to "reach over the heads" of congressional opponents and force them to follow his lead because their constituents demanded it.

A president's personality also affects how the press conference is used. Since 1961, the presidential press conference has been a distinctive institution, available whenever the president wants to dominate the news. Between 300 and 400 certified reporters attend and file their accounts within minutes of the concluding words, "Thank you, Mr. President." But despite the importance of the press conference, its value to each president has varied. President Reagan held only seven press conferences during his entire first year in office and held them only sporadically thereafter. In great contrast, President Bush held more

During the 1992 presidential campaign, Bill Clinton appeared on MTV to court the votes of young Americans. Clinton answered questions about his vision for America but also about his personal life, including whether he would inhale if he smoked marijuana and what type of underwear he wears (boxers).

conferences during his first seventeen months than Reagan held in eight years. Bush also shifted them from elaborate prime-time television affairs in the ornate East Room to less formal gatherings in the White House briefing room. Fewer reporters and more time for follow-up questions permitted media representatives to "concentrate on information for their stories, rather than getting attention for themselves."[28] President Clinton has tended to take both Reagan and Bush approaches, combining Reagan's high profile—elaborate press conferences and prime-time broadcasts—with the more personal one-on-one approach generally preferred by Bush. There is now a third approach, for which President Clinton has shown a certain aptitude: the informal and basically nonpolitical talk shows, such as those of Larry King and Oprah Winfrey. Such an informal approach has its risks, however: President Clinton is widely perceived as lacking the gravity a president is expected to possess. It is hard to argue with this conclusion when one considers that he is the first president to have answered a question (on MTV) about what kind of underwear he wears.

Of course, in addition to the presidential press conference there are other routes from the White House to news prominence.[29] For example, President Nixon preferred direct television addresses, and President Carter tried to make initiatives more homey with a television adaptation of President Roosevelt's "fireside chats." President Reagan made unusually good use of prime-time television addresses and also instituted more informal but regular Saturday afternoon radio broadcasts, a tradition that President Clinton has continued.

PUBLIC OPINION

Most Americans feel that presidents should follow public opinion. Interestingly, however, many of the most successful presidents have been public opinion leaders rather than followers.

In 1963, President John Kennedy signed a nuclear test ban treaty with the Soviet Union, even though public opinion polls seemed to show that most Americans thought the treaty was a bad idea. Kennedy believed that the treaty served the national interest and that most Americans did not know enough about the issue at stake to have fixed views on the topic. He assured his nervous advisers that, since most Americans lacked strong views on the topic, they would assume that the president's actions were correct. Kennedy was right: after he signed the treaty, polls showed that most Americans supported his decision.

President George Bush used the same logic during the Persian Gulf crisis that followed the Iraqi invasion of Kuwait. At the time, opinion was divided both within Congress and among the broader public. Congressional leaders tried to constrain the president's ability to use forces in combat, urging him instead to rely on diplomacy and economic sanctions to compel Iraq's withdrawal. Congressional criticism, especially televised Senate hearings, helped erode Bush's popular standing and almost undermined his power to act. In January 1991, however, Bush sought and narrowly received congressional approval to use force against Iraq. The overwhelming success of the American military effort produced a surge of popular support for Bush; his approval rating rose to over 90 percent.

Presidents who devote too much of their time to the vicissitudes of public opinion polls often discover that they are several steps behind shifts in

The Clinton administration has used the Internet aggressively to advance its political agenda. Most of the White House website is devoted to political information, such as news releases, government statistics, and the president's current activities (although it does include a page devoted to Socks the Cat!). The site also includes an archive where one can find speeches, search White House documents, and view photos. Finally, the site provides citizen's resources—how to contact federal agencies, find out about veterans and Social Security benefits, and other "casework" information.

E-mail access is another change instituted by the Clinton White House. Although it is unlikely that the president sits by the computer and answers all or any of his own E-mail, this ability to contact our highest public official with a few clicks of a mouse can have beneficial results. Just the ability to express an opinion and interact with governmental officials might increase the public's faith and trust in governmental institutions.

www.wwnorton.com/wtp2e

Students and Politics

For six days in 1997, Laura Jackson slept an average of three hours each night. Jackson, a student at the University of Akron in Ohio, worked with President Clinton's preparation team for the December 1997 town meeting on race relations, racing from venue to venue to ensure that all tickets were distributed, all panels were assembled, and the immense technical efforts needed to host a president were completed. "The discussions went really well," she says. "Lots of times they were really heated." The panels consisted of several groups, including community leaders, students, and authors, all holding diverse views. "I wanted to be a lawyer when I first got to school," says Jackson, "but now I want to work behind the scenes in politics." She anticipates an internship in Columbus after the school year ends. "I didn't know what to do with myself," she says, referring to the doldrums after the president had left. "My normal life seemed boring."

SOURCE: Laura Jackson, interview with author, February 19, 1998.

opinion, for polls tell politicians what the public wanted yesterday, not what it will think tomorrow. This was certainly President Clinton's experience in 1993–94 with the issue of health care reform. Administration polls continually showed public support for the president's policy initiatives—until opponents of his efforts began getting their own message through. Using several highly effective media campaigns, Clinton's opponents convinced millions of Americans that the president's program was too complex and that it would reduce access to health care. The president was left promoting an unpopular program.

Bill Clinton relied heavily on public opinion in formulating and presenting many of his administration's programs. Several members of his staff were hired specifically to shape and influence public opinion. Clinton was heavily criticized for hiring David Gergen, who had previously worked for Ronald Reagan. This crossover raised important questions about the integrity of "spinmeisters" such as Gergen, who seem to care more about the influence they have with the public than about the policies they are hired to promote.

Politicians are generally better off if they try to do what they believe is best and then hope that the public will come to agree with them. Most politicians, however, are afraid to use such a simple approach.

MASS POPULARITY AS A RESOURCE (AND A LIABILITY)

In addition to utilizing the media and public opinion polls, recent presidents, particularly Bill Clinton, have reached out directly to the American public to gain its approval. President Clinton's enormously high public profile, as is indicated by the number of public appearances he makes (see Figure 13.7), is only the most recent dramatic expression of the presidency as a **"permanent campaign"** for re-election. A study by political scientist Charles O. Jones shows that President Clinton engaged in campaignlike activity throughout his presidency and is proving to be the most-traveled American president in history. In his first twenty months in office, he made 203 appearances outside of Washington, compared with 178 for George Bush and 58 for Ronald Reagan. Clinton's tendency to go around rather than through party organizations is reflected in the fact that while Presidents Bush and Reagan devoted about 25 percent of their appearances to party functions, Clinton's comparable figure is only 8 percent.[30] Throughout the controversy over campaign-finance abuses during 1997, President Clinton attended numerous fund-raising events to raise enough money to pay off the $30 million or more of debt from the 1996 presidential campaign. In fact, during the most intense moments of the Monica Lewinsky scandal of early 1998, Clinton continued his fund raising, and the Democratic National Committee had to add staff to answer all the telephone calls and mail that were responding positively to President Clinton's appeals. This is the essence of the permanent campaign.

permanent campaign

description of presidential politics in which all presidential actions are taken with re-election in mind

PUBLIC APPEARANCES BY PRESIDENTS, 1929–95

Figure 13.7

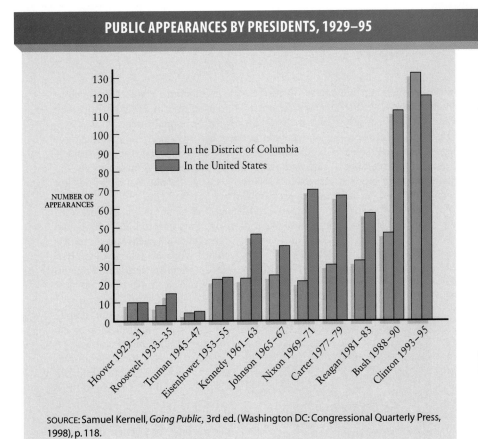

NUMBER OF APPEARANCES

In the District of Columbia
In the United States

Hoover 1929–31, Roosevelt 1933–35, Truman 1945–47, Eisenhower 1953–55, Kennedy 1961–63, Johnson 1965–67, Nixon 1969–71, Carter 1977–79, Reagan 1981–83, Bush 1988–90, Clinton 1993–95

SOURCE: Samuel Kernell, *Going Public*, 3rd ed. (Washington DC: Congressional Quarterly Press, 1998), p. 118.

President Bill Clinton made more public appearances in his first three years in office than any of his predecessors did in their first three years.

President Clinton uses his weekly radio address to help shape public opinion. Here, posing with young people, he speaks about penalizing tobacco companies for targeting children in marketing campaigns.

Harry S. Truman

Harry S. Truman, the thirty-third president of the United States, is as close to a folk hero as exists among modern presidents. Truman is often held up as a rebuke to today's politicians, a genuine, plain-spoken man whose favorite sayings—"The buck stops here" and "If you can't stand the heat, you better get out of the kitchen"—bespoke a personal integrity largely vanished from the field of politics. But the truth is far more complex. Truman, like any other person who rises to be president, was a consummate politician: shrewd, calculating, and self-interested. But he believed that politics could be a noble calling and that it was not dishonorable to further one's own ambition, if one did not lose sight of the true end of politics—the common good.

Love of politics was in Truman's blood. He grew up in Independence, Missouri, an avid reader of history. Among his family's favorite annual events were the Democratic picnics every August at Lone Jack, Missouri. The Truman family would arrive in a wagon laden with food and settle down for hours of listening to orations from politicians and would-be politicians. In the summer of 1900, when Truman was sixteen years old, his father took him to the Democratic National Convention in Kansas City, at which William Jennings Bryan, the candidate of the common man, was renominated to run against William McKinley. The half-hour of tumultuous cheering after Bryan was chosen was one of the most stirring things young Truman had ever witnessed.[1]

But Truman did not sentimentalize politics. In a letter he wrote as a young man he said, "Politics sure is the ruination of many a good man. . . . To succeed politically he must be an egoist or a fool or a ward boss tool."[2] (Ironically, the greatest obstacle Truman faced later in his career was the widespread perception that he was merely a "ward boss tool.") He entered politics in 1922 as a candidate for county judge, or administrator, picked by the powerful Kansas City political machine headed by Tom Pendergast. From the beginning, Truman combined two seemingly contradictory mo-

tives: loyalty to the Democratic Pendergast machine (and later on, as a senator, also to Franklin Roosevelt and the New Deal), with personal integrity and devotion to public service. In 1939, after FBI investigations exposed massive voting and financial fraud by Pendergast and many of his lieutenants, Truman wryly observed in a letter to his wife, "Looks like everybody got rich in Jackson County but me."[3]

Truman's combination of political loyalty and rectitude was one that many in his time did not believe, and one that many today cannot understand. When he assumed the presidency after the death of Franklin Roosevelt in April 1945, he portrayed himself as the executor of Roosevelt's programs. But despite his deep and evident loyalty to the memory of FDR, he was too savvy a politician to let it threaten his own term in office. He mistrusted the Cabinet he had inherited from Roosevelt: "There was not a man on the list who would talk frankly at a Cabinet meeting! The honest ones were afraid to and the others wanted to fool me anyhow."[4] Within four months, all but two members of Roosevelt's Cabinet had been replaced.

Truman was an intelligent, savvy man, not afraid to take steps he deemed necessary for his political ends. But he was never merely a politician in the commonest and worst sense of the word. A scholar speaking at a 1995 conference honoring the fiftieth anniversary of the Truman presidency deftly summed up Harry S. Truman's feelings about his life's work: "He was proud to be a politician. Imagine that."[5]

[1]David McCullough, *Truman* (New York: Simon & Schuster, 1992), p. 63.
[2]Quoted in ibid., pp. 89–90.
[3]Quoted in ibid., p. 240.
[4]Quoted in William E. Leuchtenberg, *In the Shadow of FDR: Harry Truman to Bill Clinton,* 2nd ed. revised (Ithaca, N.Y.: Cornell University Press, 1993), pp. 14–15.
[5]Betty Houchin Winfield, quoted in Charlotte Grimes, "This Politician Was Very Proud of What He Did," *St. Louis Post-Dispatch,* April 13, 1995, p. 5B.

Even with the help of all other institutional and political resources, successful presidents have to be able to mobilize mass opinion in their favor in order to keep Congress in line. But as we shall see, each president tends to *use up* mass resources. Virtually everyone is aware that presidents are constantly making appeals to the public over the heads of Congress and the Washington community. But the mass public does not turn out to be made up of fools. The American people react to presidential actions rather than mere speeches or other image-making devices.

The public's sensitivity to presidential actions can be seen in the tendency of all presidents to lose popular support. Despite the twists and turns shown on Figure 13.8, the percentage of positive responses to "Do you approve of the way the president is handling his job?" starts out at a level significantly higher than the percentage of votes the president got in the previous national election and then declines over the next four years. Though the shape of the line differs, the destination is the same.

PRESIDENTIAL PERFORMANCE RATINGS FROM KENNEDY TO CLINTON

Figure 13.8

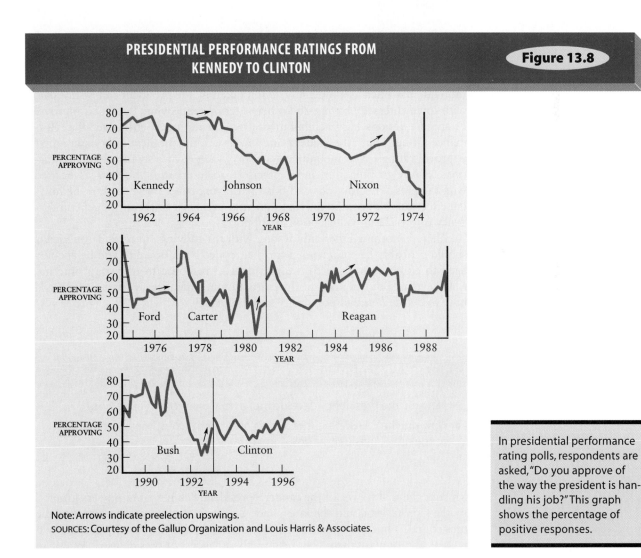

Note: Arrows indicate preelection upswings.
SOURCES: Courtesy of the Gallup Organization and Louis Harris & Associates.

In presidential performance rating polls, respondents are asked, "Do you approve of the way the president is handling his job?" This graph shows the percentage of positive responses.

Defense Secretary William Cohen, center, answers questions during a town meeting on Iraq. The State Department held the forum to gauge public support of a proposed military strike against Iraq for violation of United Nations sanctions.

rallying effect

the generally favorable reaction of the public to presidential actions taken in foreign policy, or more precisely, to decisions made during international crises

This general downward tendency is to be expected if American voters are rational, inasmuch as almost any action taken by the president can be divisive, with some voters approving and other voters disapproving. Public disapproval of specific actions has a cumulative effect on the president's overall performance rating. Thus all presidents are faced with the problem of boosting their approval ratings. And the public generally reacts favorably to presidential actions in foreign policy or, more precisely, to international events associated with the president. Analysts call this the **rallying effect.** Nevertheless the rallying effect turns out to be only a momentary reversal of the more general tendency of presidents to lose popular support.

There is nothing inherently wrong with the rallying effect, and Americans should probably be commended for their collective rationality and be encouraged to continue to rally to the president in response to important international events. But it is not a healthy situation in a democracy for a president to have to decide *between* popularity and diplomacy.

★ The Presidency and Democracy

▶ How did the presidency develop into a truly democratic institution?

▶ How did the development of a mass presidential constituency contribute to the rise of presidential government?

Most of the real power of the modern presidency comes from powers granted by the Constitution and the laws made by Congress delegating powers to the president.[31] Thus, any person properly elected and sworn in as president will possess almost all of the power held by the strongest of presidents in American history. Even a "lame duck" president (a sitting president who loses the election in November, but who does not leave office until January) still possesses all of the power of the office. For example, during the weeks after his electoral defeat in 1992, President Bush committed troops to Somalia and conducted a series of air strikes against Iraq.

The presidency has become a genuinely democratic institution, and its mass popular base is respected by Congress and by all of the social forces and organized interests that seek to influence the national government. But we must recognize an extremely important fact about the presidency: the popular base of the presidency is important less because it gives the president power, and more because it gives the president *consent to use* all of the power already vested in the presidency by the Constitution and by Congress. The other formal and informal resources lodged in the presidency—the resources we have studied throughout this chapter—are just that: resources. But resources are not power; they must be converted into power. Democratization, more than the Constitution and laws, is responsible for the enormous expansion of real presidential power in the twentieth century. The formal resources of the presidency have remained about the same for two hundred years. Democratization combined with these formal powers to give us presidential government.

THE LEGISLATIVE EPOCH, 1800–1933

In 1885, an obscure political science professor named Woodrow Wilson entitled his general textbook *Congressional Government* because American government was just that, "congressional government." This characterization seemed to fly in the face of the separation of powers principle that the three separate branches were and ought to be equal. Nevertheless, there is ample evidence that Wilson's description of the national government was consistent not only with nineteenth-century reality but also with the intentions of the framers. Within the system of three separate and competing powers, the clear intent of the Constitution was for *legislative supremacy.*

Another provision of the Constitution also portended a presidency that was secondary to the legislature: *indirect election.* Because of the mechanism of the electoral college and the prospect (strong in the nineteenth century) of presidential elections being settled in Congress, the presidency did not develop a large, popular constituency and was not closely linked to major national political and social forces.

The presidency was strengthened somewhat in the 1830s with the introduction of the national convention system of nominating presidential candidates. Until then, presidential candidates had been nominated by their party's congressional delegates. This was the **caucus** system of nominating candidates, and it was derisively called "King Caucus" because any candidate for president had to be beholden to the party's leaders in Congress in order to get the party's nomination and the support of the party's congressional delegation in the presidential election. The national nominating convention arose outside Congress in order to provide some representation for a party's voters who lived in districts where they weren't numerous enough to elect a member of Congress. The political party in each state made its own provisions for selecting delegates to attend the presidential nominating convention, and in virtually all states the selection was dominated by the party leaders (called "bosses"

caucus (political)

a normally closed meeting of a political or legislative group to select candidates, plan strategy, or make decisions regarding legislative matters

by the opposition party). Only in recent decades have state laws intervened to regularize the selection process and to provide (in all but a few instances) for open election of delegates. The convention system quickly became the most popular method of nominating candidates for all elective offices and remained so until well into the twentieth century, when it succumbed to the criticism that it was a nondemocratic method dominated by a few leaders in a "smoke-filled room." But in the nineteenth century, it was seen as a victory for democracy against the congressional elite. And the national convention gave the presidency a base of power independent of Congress.

This additional independence did not immediately transform the presidency into the office we recognize today, but the national convention did begin to open the presidency to larger social forces and newly organized interests in society. In other words, it gave the presidency a mass popular base that would eventually support and demand increased presidential power. Improvements in telephone, telegraph, and other forms of mass communication allowed individuals to share their complaints and allowed national leaders—especially presidents and presidential candidates—to reach out directly to people to ally themselves with, and even sometimes to create, popular groups and forces. Eventually, though more slowly, the presidential selection process began to be further democratized, with the adoption of primary elections through which millions of ordinary citizens were given an opportunity to take part in the presidential nominating process by popular selection of convention delegates.

But despite political and social conditions favoring the enhancement of the presidency, the development of presidential government as we know it today did not mature until the middle of the twentieth century. For a long period, even as the national government began to grow, Congress was careful to keep tight reins on the president's power. The real turning point in the history of American national government came during the administration of Franklin Delano Roosevelt. The New Deal was a response to political forces that had been gathering national strength and focus for fifty years. What is remarkable is not that they gathered but that they took so long to gain influence in Washington—and even then it took the Great Depression to bring about the new national government.

THE NEW DEAL AND THE PRESIDENCY

The "First Hundred Days" of the Roosevelt administration in 1933 had no parallel in U.S. history. But this period was only the beginning. The policies proposed by President Roosevelt and adopted by Congress during the first thousand days of his administration so changed the size and character of the national government that they constitute a moment in American history equivalent to the Founding or to the Civil War. The legislation creating those programs also directly and deliberately expanded presidential power. This expanded presidential power was both a response and a direct contributor to a vastly expanded presidential constituency. All of these changes deserve some discussion.

New Programs Expand the Role of National Government Many of the New Deal programs were extensions of the traditional national government approach, which was described already in Chapter 4 (see especially Table 4.1). But the New Deal went well beyond the traditional approach, adopting types

Franklin Delano Roosevelt signing the Social Security bill of 1935, one of the most significant pieces of legislation to come out of the New Deal.

of policies never before tried on a large scale by the national government; it began intervening in economic life in ways that had hitherto been reserved to the states. In other words, the national government discovered that it, too, had "the power" to directly regulate individuals as well as provide roads and other services.

Delegation of Power   The most important constitutional effect of Congress's actions during the New Deal was the enhancement of presidential power. Most major acts of Congress in this period involved significant exercises of control over the economy. But few programs specified the actual controls to be used. Instead, Congress authorized the president, or, in some cases, a new agency—to determine what the controls would be. Some of the new agencies were independent commissions responsible to Congress. But most of the new agencies and programs of the New Deal were placed in the executive branch directly under presidential authority.

Technically, this form of congressional act is called the "delegation of power." In theory, the delegation of power works as follows: (1) Congress recognizes a problem; (2) Congress acknowledges that it has neither the time nor the expertise to deal with the problem; and (3) Congress therefore sets the basic policies and then delegates to an agency the power to "fill in the details." But in practice, Congress was delegating not merely the power to "fill in the details," but actual and real policy-making powers, that is, real legislative powers, to the executive branch. During the 1930s, the growth of the national government through acts delegating legislative power tilted the American national structure away from a Congress-centered government toward a president-centered government.[32]

A Presidential Constituency: Citizens and the President

In the United States, as a general rule, democratization follows power. As already observed, many larger social forces were gathering around the presidency and looking to the presidency even before the New Deal and the rise of presidential government. But these social forces did not begin to come together as a discernible constituency or a presidential support structure until the New Deal. Relations between the presidency and this larger constituency did not become institutionalized until even later. Institutionalized relations bring close and constant communication with party, interest groups, polls, the media, and the other segments of political society that we have discussed in this and other chapters. This presidential constituency varies between Democratic and Republican administrations; it is more working class, elderly, urban, ethnic, and intellectual during Democratic administrations and more rural, suburban, middle and professional class, wealthy, and "higher" ethnic status during Republican administrations. In either case, however, it is a popular and democratized constituency. In sum, presidential power is democratized power, and democratization has made the presidency far more powerful. Yet we must not forget the duality of the presidency discussed at the beginning of this chapter:

President Clinton is shown here meeting with important donors to the Democratic Party. Many criticize the need for financial backing as creating too great an opportunity for wealthy interests to influence presidential decisions.

the presidency may be more powerful, but it is also more vulnerable. The dark side of presidential vulnerability is weakness, indecision, deceit, and fear of governing. The bright side of presidential vulnerability is energy, openness, vigor, and, above all, accountability to the people. Would we have it any other way? The epoch of presidential government continues today, and it is a people's epoch, for better or for worse.

★ Summary

The foundations for presidential government were laid in the Constitution, which provides for a unitary executive who is head of state as well as head of government. The first section of this chapter reviewed the powers of each: the head of state with its military, judicial, and diplomatic powers; the head of government with its executive, military, and legislative powers.

The second and third sections of this chapter focused on the president's institutional and political resources. The Cabinet, the other top appointments, the White House staff, and the Executive Office of the President are some of the impressive institutional resources of presidential power. The president's political party, the supportive group coalitions, and access to the media and, through that, access to the millions of Americans who make up the general public are formidable political resources that can be used to bolster a president's power. But these resources are not cost- or risk-free. A direct relationship with the mass public is the president's most potent modern resource, but it is also the most problematic.

The final section of this chapter traced the rise of modern presidential government after the much longer period of congressional dominance. There is no mystery in the shift to government centered on the presidency. Congress built the modern presidency by delegating to it not only the power to implement the vast new programs of the 1930s but also by delegating its own legislative power to make the policies themselves. Presidential government is now an established fact of American politics.

FOR FURTHER READING

Barber, James David. *The Presidential Character*. Englewood Cliffs, NJ: Prentice-Hall, 1985.

Drew, Elizabeth. *On the Edge: The Clinton Presidency*. New York: Simon & Schuster, 1994.

Hart, John. *The Presidential Branch: From Washington to Clinton*. Chatham, NJ: Chatham House, 1995.

Hinckley, Barbara, and Paul Brace. *Follow the Leader: Opinion Polls and Modern Presidents*. New York: Basic Books, 1992.

Kernell, Samuel. *Going Public: New Strategies of Presidential Leadership*. Washington, DC: Congressional Quarterly Press, 1986.

Lowi, Theodore J. *The Personal President: Power Invested, Promise Unfulfilled*. Ithaca, NY: Cornell University Press, 1985.

Milkis, Sidney M. *The President and the Parties: The Transformation of the American Party System since the New Deal*. New York: Oxford University Press, 1993.

Nelson, Michael, ed. *The Presidency and the Political System*. 4th ed. Washington, DC: Congressional Quarterly Press, 1994.

Neustadt, Richard E. *Presidential Power: The Politics of Leadership from Roosevelt to Reagan*. Rev. ed. New York: Free Press, 1990.

Pfiffner, James P. *The Modern Presidency*. New York: St. Martin's, 1994.

Skowronek, Stephen. *The Politics Presidents Make: Presidential Leadership from John Adams to George Bush*. Cambridge, MA: Harvard University Press, 1993.

Spitzer, Robert. *The Presidential Veto: Touchstone of the American Presidency*. Albany, NY: SUNY Press, 1988.

Tulis, Jeffrey. *The Rhetorical Presidency*. Princeton, NJ: Princeton University Press, 1987.

Watson, Richard A., and Norman Thomas. *The Politics of the Presidency*. Washington, DC: Congressional Quarterly Press, 1988.

STUDY OUTLINE

The Constitutional Powers of the Presidency

1. The president as head of state is defined by three constitutional provisions—military, judicial, and diplomatic—that are the source of some of the most important powers on which the president can draw.

2. The position of commander in chief makes the president the highest military authority in the United States, with control of the entire military establishment.

3. The presidential power to grant reprieves, pardons, and amnesties allows the president to choose freedom or confinement, and even life or death for all individuals who have violated, or are suspected of having violated, federal laws, including people who directly threaten the security of the United States.

4. The power to receive representatives of foreign countries allows the president almost unconditional authority to determine whether a new ruling group can indeed commit its country to treaties and other agreements.

5. The president's role as head of government rests on a constitutional foundation consisting of three principal sources: executive power, domestic military authority, and legislative power.

6. The Constitution delegated to the president, as commander in chief, the obligation to protect every state against invasion and domestic violence.

7. The president's legislative power consists of the obligation to make recommendations for consideration by Congress and the ability to veto legislation.

Institutional Resources of Presidential Power

1. Presidents have at their disposal a variety of institutional resources—such as the power to fill high-level political positions—that directly affect a president's ability to govern.

2. Presidents increasingly have preferred the White House staff to the Cabinet as a tool for managing the gigantic executive branch.

3. The White House staff, which is composed primarily of analysts and advisers, has grown from an informal group of fewer than a dozen people to a new presidential bureaucracy.

4. The Executive Office of the President, often called the institutional presidency, is larger than the White House staff, and comprises the president's permanent management agencies.

Political Resources of Presidential Power

1. The president also has political resources on which to draw in exercising the powers of office.

2. Presidents often use their electoral victories to increase their power by claiming the election was a mandate for a certain course of action.

3. Although its traditional influence is on the decline, the president's party is still significant as a means of achieving legislative success.

4. Interest groups and coalitions supportive of the president's agenda are also a dependable resource for presidential government.

5. Over the past half-century, the American executive branch has harnessed mass popularity successfully as a political resource.

The Presidency and Democracy

1. American government was dominated by Congress between 1800 and 1933; during that time the executive office played the secondary role anticipated by the framers of the Constitution.

2. During the New Deal, Congress shifted the balance in favor of the executive office by delegating vast discretionary power to the president for the implementation of policy.

3. Many New Deal programs expanded the traditional role of national government by allowing it to intervene in economic life in ways that previously had been reserved to the states.

4. Presidential power was enhanced by the New Deal's placement of new agencies and programs in the executive branch directly under presidential authority.

PRACTICE QUIZ

1. Which article of the Constitution established the presidency?
   a) Article I
   b) Article II
   c) Article III
   d) none of the above

2. Which of the following does not represent a classification of a constitutional provision designating the president as head of state?
   a) legislative
   b) military
   c) judicial
   d) diplomatic

3. Which of the following does not require the advice and consent of the Senate?
   a) an executive agreement
   b) a treaty
   c) Supreme Court nominations
   d) All of the above require the advice and consent of the Senate.

4. Which of the following terms has been used to describe the presidency as it has used constitutional and other powers to make itself more powerful?
   a) "the delegated presidency"
   b) "the imperial presidency"
   c) "the personal presidency"
   d) "the preemptive presidency"

5. By what process can Congress reject a presidential veto?
   a) veto override
   b) pocket veto
   c) executive delegation
   d) impeachment

6. Which of the following describes the presidential foreign policy advisory council composed of the president; the vice president; the secretaries of state, defense, and the treasury; the attorney general; and others?
   a) the "Inner Cabinet"
   b) the National Security Council
   c) both a and b
   d) neither a nor b

7. The Office of Management and Budget is part of
   a) the Executive Office of the President.
   b) the White House staff.
   c) the Kitchen Cabinet.
   d) both a and b.

8. In what book did Woodrow Wilson describe American government in 1885?
   a) *A Separated System*
   b) *Checks and Balances*
   c) *Presidential Government*
   d) *Congressional Government*

9. Which twentieth-century presidency transformed the American system of government from a Congress-centered to a president-centered system?
   a) Woodrow Wilson's
   b) Franklin Roosevelt's
   c) Richard Nixon's
   d) Jimmy Carter's

10. How many people work for agencies within the Executive Office of the President?
    a) 25 to 50
    b) 700 to 1,000
    c) 1,500 to 2,000
    d) 4,500 to 5,000

CRITICAL THINKING QUESTIONS

1. At times, the Congress has been the dominant branch of government. At other times, the presidency has predominated. Describe the changes in the relationship between the presidency and the Congress throughout American history. What factors contributed to the dominance of Congress? What factors contributed to the resurgence of the presidency? Which branch of government dominates now? Why do you think so?

2. Presidents have constitutional, institutional, and political sources of power. Which of the three do you think most accounts for the powers of the presidency? Is it, in fact, possible to discern among these the true source of presidential power? Select a president and discuss the ways in which that particular president used each source of power to succeed in the presidency.

KEY TERMS

Cabinet (p. 508)
caucus (political) (p. 527)
commander in chief (p. 497)
delegated powers (p. 495)
divided government (p. 506)
executive agreement (p. 498)
Executive Office of the President (EOP) (p. 510)
executive privilege (p. 502)

independent counsel (p. 502)
inherent powers (p. 496)
Kitchen Cabinet (p. 509)
legislative initiative (p. 506)
line-item veto (p. 506)
mandate (p. 515)
National Security Council (NSC) (p. 508)
New Deal coalition (p. 518)

patronage (p. 508)
permanent campaign (p. 522)
pocket veto (p. 504)
rallying effect (p. 526)
veto (p. 504)
War Powers Resolution (p. 499)
White House staff (p. 509)

14 Bureaucracy in

★ **Bureaucracy and Bureaucrats**

Why do bureaucracies exist? Why are they needed?

Has the federal bureaucracy grown too large?

What roles do government bureaucrats perform? What types of access do citizens have to the bureaucracy?

Is the federal bureaucracy representative?

★ **The Organization of the Executive Branch**

What are the agencies that make up the executive branch?

How can one classify these agencies according to their missions?

★ **Can the Bureaucracy Be Reduced?**

What methods have been used to reduce the size and the role of the federal bureaucracy?

How effective can efforts to reduce the bureaucracy be?

★ **Can Bureaucracy Be Controlled?**

How can bureaucracy and democracy coexist? What popular controls over the bureaucracy exist?

How do the president and Congress manage and oversee the bureaucracy?

What is the most effective means to guarantee a responsible bureaucracy?

a Democracy

THE "real world" that college students are told they are preparing for is largely a world of work—of earning a living by collaborating in the production of goods and services for which other people are willing to pay. For most students, college is an opportunity to improve their employment prospects. And with the exception of a few who will own and operate small businesses or independent medical or law practices or who will be self-supporting artists or musicians, most college graduates will go from a bachelor's, graduate, or professional degree directly to salaried employment in a private company or a public organization of a hundred or more employees. In other words, most college graduates will work for somebody else. The source of income for most will be a salary, which will come from an employer who makes the job possible.

That job will typically consist of a set of responsibilities and tasks defined by the employer to meet the needs of the organization. Specific assignments come from the employee's immediate superior. Often a new employee's real work begins after weeks or months of on-the-job training. This is true even for many who have advanced degrees or significant experience, because the organization—whether a private company or a government agency—will need to accustom the new employee to the special way the organization operates. To gain maximum efficiency, the employer provides a salary sufficient to get each employee to contribute precisely to the mission of the organization—whether the output of the organization is computers, television programs, welfare services, or environmental regulations. The organization has a mission defined by its output, and all of the jobs within that organization serve that mission.

In the course of a career, the average person will make two or three job changes. But with the exception of the few who will have enough capital to form a private practice or establish an independently owned company, the job changes will be from one position to another—one with more responsibility and higher pay—within one relatively large organization or from one large organization to another. For most people this will be the very definition of a career—moving upward, step by step, to higher levels of responsibility in return for higher salary and more privileges. Success in one's career is typically defined by the size of one's salary and other benefits, by titles that convey the level of responsibility one holds, and by certain additional titles and prizes that convey recognition for meritorious contributions.

Turn now to Table 14.1, which identifies the basic characteristics of bureaucracy. These characteristics are found in virtually *all* organizations, whether public or private, military or religious, for profit or nonprofit, producers of goods or providers of services. Most organizations are bureaucracies, and most of their employees are bureaucrats.

| Table 14.1 | THE SIX PRIMARY CHARACTERISTICS OF BUREAUCRACY |

Characteristic	Explanation
Division of labor	Workers are specialized. Each worker develops a skill in a particular job and performs the job routinely and repetitively, thereby increasing productivity.
Allocation of functions	Each task is assigned. No one makes a whole product; each worker depends on the output of other workers.
Allocation of responsibility	Each task becomes a personal responsibility—a contractual obligation. No task can be changed without permission.
Supervision	Some workers are assigned the special task of watching over other workers rather than contributing directly to the creation of the product. Each supervisor watches over a few workers (a situation known as "span of control"), and communications between workers or between levels move in a prescribed fashion (known as "chain of command").
Purchase of full-time employment	The organization controls all the time the worker is on the job, so each worker can be assigned and held to a task. Some part-time and contracted work is tolerated, but it is held to a minimum.
Identification of career within the organization	Workers come to identify with the organization as a way of life. Seniority, pension rights, and promotions are geared to this relationship.

But if bureaucracy is so common in the workplace, why have "bureaucracy" and "bureaucrat" become such negative words? Why has "bureaucracy" come to mean only government, when in fact it is a universal phenomenon? Why do we call government activity we don't like "bureaucracy" and government activity we approve of "administration"? Why do we reserve the term "bureaucrat" for people whose work we don't like when as a matter of fact most of us are or will be bureaucrats ourselves?

■ **We begin this chapter by clarifying what we mean by "bureaucracy."** Before we can understand the nature and character of the executive branch of the U.S. government, we must first examine why bureaucracy is necessary. From there, we then turn to the size, role, functions, and characteristics of the federal bureaucracy and bureaucrats.

■ **We next examine the organization of the executive branch as a whole, looking at the Cabinet departments, agencies, and bureaus that make up its operating parts.** Since the executive branch is vast and there are far too many agencies for us to identify here, we will instead evaluate the different broad purposes that federal agencies serve.

◼ ***We next turn to ways in which the size and role of the federal bureaucracy can be reduced.*** Although efforts to downsize government have been popular in recent years, we question whether these attempts are effective or even address the most pressing problem regarding the control of the federal bureaucracy

◼ ***We conclude this chapter by asking whether bureaucracy and democracy are contradictory.*** The bureaucracy is intended to be accountable to the president and Congress and through them to the American people. We will examine the ways in which the president and Congress have tried to manage the bureaucracy and hold it accountable and whether these management techniques have been effective. We conclude by reviewing the role of the average citizen in holding bureaucracy accountable.

Bureaucracy and Bureaucrats

▶ Why do bureaucracies exist? Why are they needed?

▶ Has the federal bureaucracy grown too large?

▶ What roles do government bureaucrats perform? What types of access do citizens have to the bureaucracy?

▶ Is the federal bureaucracy representative?

Bureaucracy is nothing more nor less than a form of organization, as defined by the attributes in Table 14.1. To gain some objectivity, and to appreciate the universality of bureaucracy, let us take the word and break it into its two main parts—*bureau* and *cracy*. *Bureau,* a French word, can mean either "office" or "desk." *Cracy* is the Greek word for "rule" or "form of rule." For example, "democracy" means rule by the people *(demos),* a form of government in which the people prevail. "Theocracy" refers to rule by clergy or churches. "Gerontocracy" would describe a system ruled by the elders of the community. Putting *bureau* and *cracy* back together produces a very interesting definition: **Bureaucracy** is a form of rule by offices and desks. Each member of an organization has an office, meaning a place as well as a set of responsibilities. That is, each "office" comprises a set of tasks that are specialized to the needs of the organization, and the person holding that office (or position) performs those specialized tasks. Specialization and repetition are essential to the efficiency of any organization. Therefore, when an organization is inefficient, it is almost certainly because it is not bureaucratized enough!

Since it is absolutely essential for any large organization to be run as efficiently as possible, organizations from every part of social life have made major contributions to the advancement of bureaucracy. For example, one of

bureaucracy

the complex structure of offices, tasks, rules, and principles of organization that are employed by all large-scale institutions to coordinate effectively the work of their personnel

Government bureaucracy performs many important tasks. For example, government bureaucrats in the Federal Emergency Management Agency (left) coordinate relief efforts to areas devastated by natural disasters. These soldiers (right), for instance, were sent to Florida to work in areas damaged by a hurricane.

the most widely used terms for a member of an organization is not "bureaucrat" but "clerk." It may come as something of a surprise that the origin of the world "clerk" is "cleric," which indicates that religious organizations, especially the Roman Catholic Church, have made major contributions to the advancement of bureaucracy, or what we now call "organization theory" or "management science." The Roman Catholic Church was also instrumental in the development of budgeting and accounting, without which no large organization, private or public, would be able to sustain itself.

Armies have also been great innovators in the advancement of bureaucracy. The use of the terms "line" and "staff" in organizations comes from military usage, indicating a strict specialization of function between the line units, which deal directly with the enemy, and the staff units, which support the line units. This distinction is just the beginning of the tremendous specialization of functions in any large military organization.

This line/staff distinction has spread to all sorts of organizations beyond the military. Private corporations have in some areas been even more inventive in the advancement of the principles of bureaucracy. The formal process of projecting goals and ways to meet them, something we call "planning," came not from governments but from large corporations. Industrial giants like the Ford Motor Company were the first organizations to prove that efficiency could be gained by careful study of every task until it could be reduced to its narrowest, most specialized, and most repetitive movements in order to "fine-tune" production for maximum output. Later on, when many reformers began to argue that governments should be run more like businesses, this efficiency and specialization is precisely what they meant: that government should be *more* bureaucratized.

The scientific study of organizational efficiency is called business administration and public administration, and there are advanced degree programs for the purpose, the master's of public administration (MPA) and the master's of business administration (MBA). Although "administration" more specifically refers to the processes of an organization, whereas "bureaucracy" refers to the structure of the organization, "administration" is often used to refer to a bureaucracy. (Imagine how popular the graduate studies programs would be if they awarded master's of public bureaucracy and master's of business bureaucracy!)

THE SIZE OF THE FEDERAL SERVICE

In his State of the Union address in 1996, President Bill Clinton declared that "the era of big government is over." With his re-election campaign looming, Clinton was capitalizing on popular sentiment that the federal government had grown too large. Despite fears of bureaucratic growth getting out of hand, however, the federal service has hardly grown at all during the past twenty-five years; it reached its peak postwar level in 1968 with 2.9 million civilian employees plus an additional 3.6 million military personnel (a figure swollen by Vietnam). The number of civilian federal employees has since fallen to approximately 2.7 million in 1996; the number of military personnel totals only 1.5 million.[1]

The growth of the federal service is even less imposing when placed in the context of the total workforce and when compared to the size of state and local public employment. Figure 14.1 indicates that, since 1950, the ratio of

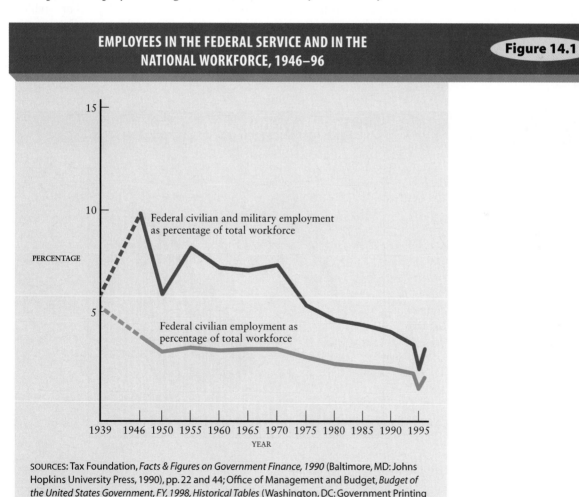

EMPLOYEES IN THE FEDERAL SERVICE AND IN THE NATIONAL WORKFORCE, 1946–96

Figure 14.1

Federal civilian and military employment as percentage of total workforce

Federal civilian employment as percentage of total workforce

PERCENTAGE

YEAR

SOURCES: Tax Foundation, *Facts & Figures on Government Finance, 1990* (Baltimore, MD: Johns Hopkins University Press, 1990), pp. 22 and 44; Office of Management and Budget, *Budget of the United States Government, FY, 1998, Historical Tables* (Washington, DC: Government Printing Office, 1997), p. 271, and U.S. Department of Labor, Bureau of Labor Statistics, *Employment and Earnings* (monthly).

federal employment to the total workforce has been steady, and in fact has *declined* slightly in the past fifteen years. In 1950, there were 4.3 million state and local civil service employees (about 6.5 percent of the country's workforce). In 1978, there were 12.7 million (nearly 15 percent of the workforce), and the ratio remained about the same for the ensuing decade. Federal employment, in contrast, exceeded 5 percent of the workforce only during World War II (not shown), and almost all of that momentary growth was military. After the demobilization, which continued until 1950 (as shown in Figure 14.1), the federal service has tended to grow at a rate that keeps pace with the economy and society. That is demonstrated by the lower line on Figure 14.1, which shows a constant relation between federal civilian employment and the size of the U.S. workforce. Variations in federal employment since 1946 have been in the military and are directly related to war and the cold war (as shown by the top line on Figure 14.1).

Another useful comparison is to be found in Figure 14.2. Although the dollar increase in federal spending shown by the bars looks impressive, the trend line indicating the relation of federal spending to the Gross Domestic Product (GDP) has moved in thirty-five years from 18 percent to 21 percent—which suggests that the national government has grown just a bit more than necessary to keep pace with the growth of the economy.

In sum, the national government is indeed "very large," but it has not been growing any faster than the economy or the society. The same is roughly true

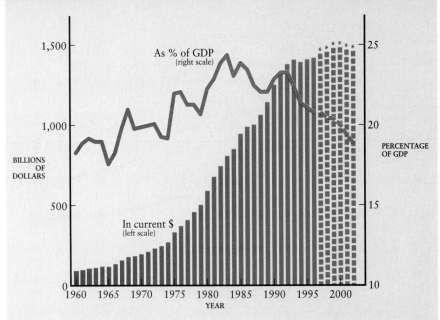

Figure 14.2   ANNUAL FEDERAL OUTLAYS, 1960–2002

*Data from 1997–2002 are estimated.
SOURCE: Office of Management and Budget, *Budget of the United States Government, Fiscal Year 1998, Historical Tables* (Washington, DC: Government Printing Office, 1997), Tables 8.2 and 8.4.

of the growth pattern of state and local public personnel. Bureaucracy keeps pace with society, despite people's seeming dislike for it, because the control towers, the prisons, the Social Security system, and other essential elements cannot be operated without bureaucracy. The United States certainly could not have conducted a successful war in the Persian Gulf without a gigantic military bureaucracy.

Although the federal executive branch is large and complex, everything about it is commonplace. Bureaucracies are commonplace because they touch so many aspects of daily life. Government bureaucracies implement the decisions made by the political process. Bureaucracies are full of routine because that assures the regular delivery of services and ensures that each agency fulfills its mandate. Public bureaucracies are powerful because legislatures and chief executives, and indeed the people, delegate to them vast power to make sure a particular job is done—enabling citizens to be more free to pursue their private ends. Citizens appreciate this fact even when they profess to be anti–big government. For example, when Housing and Urban Development (HUD) Secretary Andrew Cuomo announced plans in June 1997 to eliminate twenty-two federal employees in its Oklahoma City branch, Republican member of Congress Frank Lucas raised a loud public protest on behalf of his Oklahoma City constituents. His claim was that twenty-one of the twenty-two were survivors of the Alfred P. Murrah Federal Building bombing and that "some anonymous bureaucrat in Washington" was responsible (somehow markedly different from the "bureaucrats" in Oklahoma City he was defending). Yet the same vociferous representatives will argue that bureaucracies are a threat to freedom, because their size, their momentum, and the interests of the civil servants themselves in keeping their jobs impel bureaucracies and bureaucrats to resist any change of direction.

BUREAUCRATS

"Government by offices and desks" conveys to most people a picture of hundreds of office workers shuffling millions of pieces of paper. There is a lot of truth in that image, but we have to look more closely at what papers are being shuffled and why. More than seventy years ago, an astute observer defined bureaucracy as "continuous routine business."[2] As we saw at the beginning of this chapter, almost any organization succeeds by reducing its work to routines, with each routine being given to a different specialist. But specialization separates people from each other; one worker's output becomes another worker's input. The timing of such relationships is essential, and this requires that these workers stay in communication with each other. Communication is the key. In fact, bureaucracy was the first information network. Routine came first; voluminous routine came as bureaucracies grew and specialized.

What Do Bureaucrats Do? Bureaucrats, whether in public or in private organizations, first communicate with each other in order to coordinate all the specializations within their organization. All the shuffling of paper we associate with bureaucracy is a product of the second task of bureaucrats: the need to maintain a **"paper trail,"** which is a routinized means of ensuring that individuals' responsibilities are met. If a process breaks down, if there is a failure, if there is a loss of profit in a private company or a rising dissatisfaction among

Perspectives on Politics

Percentage of respondents reporting a favorable impression of certain federal departments and agencies.

Postal Service	89%
Park Service	85%
Centers for Disease Control	79%
Defense	76%
FDA	75%
NASA	73%
Federal Aviation Administration	70%
EPA	69%
Agriculture	68%
FBI	67%
SSA	62%
Education	61%
Veterans Administration	59%
Commerce	58%
Justice	56%
FTC	53%
HUD	51%
CIA	51%
IRS	38%

SOURCE: The Pew Research Center, http://www.people-press.org/trusttab.htm.

paper trail

written accounts by which the process of decision making and the participants in a decision can, if desired, be later reconstructed. Often called red tape clients of public agencies, the paper trail provides a means of determining who was responsible, who was at fault, and where routines ought to be improved.

One of the major reasons why there may be more paper shuffling in public agencies than in private agencies is the need to establish responsibility. As long as Americans want the agencies in the government bureaucracy to be maximally responsible (**accountable**) to the people—directly and through Congress and the chief executive—there must be dependable and thorough means of determining responsibility and blame. "Red tape" is the almost universal cry of citizens against all the numbered forms and required signatures that bureaucracies generate.[3] Yet many of the same people who complain about red tape are the first to demand subpoenas requiring delivery of every conceivable document that may have some bearing on an alleged error of an agency or of individuals in an agency. What if the issue is the tragic explosion of the *Challenger* space shuttle or a gigantic overrun of expenditures for a new missile system for the Air Force? The bureaucrats in the National Aeronautics and Space Administration (NASA) or in the Air Force are required to create the record by which their own performances will later be judged.[4] And since Americans are more fearful of public bureaucracies and are therefore more likely to demand their accountability, public bureaucracies are likely to produce a great deal more paper than private bureaucracies.

Those first two activities of bureaucrats—communicating with each other and keeping copies of all those communications to maintain a paper trail—add up to a third: **implementation,** that is, implementing the objectives of the organization as laid down by its board of directors (if a private company) or by law (if a public agency). In government, the "bosses" are ultimately the legislature and the elected chief executive.

When the bosses—Congress, in particular, when it is making the law—are clear in their instructions to bureaucrats, implementation is a fairly straightforward process. Bureaucrats translate the law into specific routines for each of the employees of an agency. But what happens to routine administrative implementation when there are several bosses who disagree as to what the instructions ought to be? This requires yet a fourth job for bureaucrats: interpretation. Interpretation is a form of implementation, in that the bureaucrats still have to carry out what they believe to be the intentions of their superiors. But when bureaucrats have to interpret a law before implementing it, they are in effect engaging in *lawmaking*. Congress often deliberately delegates to an administrative agency the responsibility of lawmaking. Members of Congress often conclude that some area of industry needs regulating or some area of the environment needs protection, but they are unwilling or unable to specify just how that should be done. In such situations, Congress delegates to the appropriate agency a broad authority within which the bureaucrats have to make law, through the procedures of **rulemaking** and **administrative adjudication.** Rulemaking is exactly the same as legislation; in fact it is often referred to as "quasi-legislation." Administrative adjudication is very similar to what the judiciary ordinarily does: applying rules and precedents to specific cases in order to settle disputes. Equally often, agencies engage in a combination of the two.

A good case study of the role agencies can play is the story of how ordinary federal bureaucrats created the Internet. Yes, it's true: what became the Internet was developed largely by the U.S. Department of Defense, and defense considerations still shape the basic structure of the Internet. In 1957, immedi-

---

accountability

the obligation to justify the discharge of duties in the fulfillment of responsibilities to a person or persons in higher authority, and to be answerable to that authority for failing to fulfill the assigned duties and responsibilities.

implementation

the efforts of departments and agencies to translate laws into specific bureaucratic routines

rulemaking

a quasi-legislative administrative process that produces regulations by government agencies

administrative adjudication

applying rules and precedents to specific cases to settle disputes with regulated parties

ately following the profound American embarrassment over the Soviet Union's launching of *Sputnik,* Congress authorized the establishment of the Advanced Research Projects Agency (ARPA) to develop, among other things, a means of maintaining communications in the event the existing telecommunications network (the telephone system) was disabled by a strategic attack. Since the telephone network was highly centralized and therefore could have been completely disabled by a single attack, ARPA developed a decentralized, highly redundant network. Redundancy in this case improved the probability of functioning after an attack. The full design, called by the pet name of Arpanet, took almost a decade to create. By 1971, around twenty universities were connected to the Arpanet. The forerunner to the Internet was born.[5]

Government bureaucrats do essentially the same things that bureaucrats in large private organizations do, and neither type deserves the disrespect embodied in the term "bureaucrat." But because of the authoritative, coercive nature of government, far more constraints are imposed on public bureaucrats than on private bureaucrats, even when their jobs are the same. During the 1970s and 1980s, the length of time required to develop an administrative rule from a proposal to actual publication in the *Federal Register* (when it takes on full legal status) grew from an average of 15 months to an average of 35 to 40 months. Inefficiency? No. Most of the increased time is attributable to new procedures requiring more public notice, more public hearings, more hearings held out in the field rather than in Washington, more cost-benefit analysis, and stronger legal obligations to prepare "environmental impact statements" demonstrating that the proposed rule or agency action will not have an unacceptably large negative impact on the human or physical environment.[6] Thus, a great deal of what is popularly paraded as the lower efficiency of public agencies can be attributed to the political, judicial, legal, and public-opinion restraints and extraordinarily high expectations imposed on public bureaucrats.

We will have more to say at the end of this chapter about bureaucratic accountability and the potential role of citizens in it. Suffice it to say here that if a private company such as Microsoft were required to open up all its decision processes and management practices to full view by the media, their competitors, and all interested citizens, Microsoft—despite its profit motive and the pressure of competition—would be far less efficient, perhaps no more efficient than public bureaucracies.

Buried in red tape? This Food and Drug Administration reviewer now works on a laptop computer. The FDA is striving to computerize its operations and reduce agency review time.

The Merit System: How to Become a Bureaucrat In return for all these inconveniences, public bureaucrats are rewarded in part with greater job security than employees of most private organizations enjoy. More than a century ago, the federal government attempted to imitate business by passing the Civil Service Act of 1883, which was followed by almost universal adoption of equivalent laws in state and local governments. These laws required that appointees to public office be qualified for the job to which they are appointed. This policy came to be called the **merit system;** its ideal was not merely to put an end to political appointments under the "spoils system" but also to require adequate preparation for every job by holding competitive examinations through which the very best candidates were to be hired.

As a further safeguard against political interference (and to compensate for the lower-than-average pay given to public employees), merit system employees—genuine civil servants—were given a form of tenure: legal protection

merit system

a product of civil service reform, in which appointees to positions in public bureaucracies must objectively be deemed qualified for the position

We the People

THE 1883 CIVIL SERVICE REFORM

Early in the history of the United States, the selection of those few employees hired by the government was based on competence and nonpartisanship. But beginning with the presidency of Andrew Jackson, the selection of government employees became partisan, with Jackson and subsequent presidents basing job decisions primarily on a person's party loyalty and his or her record of past political service. This practice, dubbed "the spoils system," degraded the quality and efficiency of government service to such an extent that in 1853 Congress instituted an examination system for departmental clerks. Yet the effort to improve and professionalize the governmental service requirements for the growing ranks of nonelective employees won little support until after the Civil War.

At the state and local levels, the awarding of government jobs to political friends was widespread. Indeed, it was a primary means by which local political organizations built their bases of strength. Such patronage practices still exist to a limited extent in state and local governments. At the national level, however, the patronage system was broken with the Pendleton (Civil Service Reform) Act of 1883.

The drive toward merit-based civil service was led by a member of Congress from Rhode Island, Thomas Jenckes, who proposed a set of competitive examinations (a system used by the military) as the basis for selecting government employees. In addition, he proposed that government employees be allowed to maintain their jobs as long as they performed satisfactorily; they would not need to fear the loss of their job at the whim of a political leader.

This system was proposed as a way to enhance the government's performance and to stem the growing tide of office-seekers whose demands diverted time and effort away from the task of governing. A merit-based system, argued reformers, would improve government efficiency by emphasizing skill over political connections and by ending the frequent replacement of employees each time a new election was held; it would also encourage the

against being fired without a show of cause. Reasonable people may disagree about the value of job tenure and how far it should extend in the civil service, but the justifiable objective of tenure—cleansing bureaucracy of political interference while upgrading performance—cannot be disputed.

Who Are the Bureaucrats?   To what extent does the American bureaucracy look like the American people? To what extent is it a microcosm of American society? Civil servants are not average Americans, but they are, in some respects, what most Americans would like to be and what most Americans would like the rest of the world to believe about them. As one expert appraisal put it, "While the popular image of the civil service is one of acres of clerks processing mountains of forms, in fact the activities and structure of the [federal civilian] workforce . . . now resemble those of a research-and-development company."[7] Nearly 65 percent of permanent civilian white-collar federal workers have had some college education; over 35 percent have a bachelor's degree or higher; about 7 percent have a master's degree; and about 2 percent have a Ph.D. This compares quite favorably with the general population. According to the 1990 census, for example, 13 percent of all persons 25 years or older held a bachelor's degree, and 7 percent held a graduate or professional degree. Moreover,

brightest and ablest young workers to join the federal service. In addition, the spoils system was morally corrupting in the eyes of reformers. As one noted, "the theory which regards places in the public service as prizes to be distributed after an election, like plunder after a battle . . . necessarily ruins the self-respect of public employees, . . . prostitutes elections into a desperate strife for personal profit, and degrades the national character by lowering the moral tone and standard of the country."[1]

Although the spoils system provided benefits to the winning political party, victorious presidents buckled under the weight of having to select so many employees. By the early 1880s, presidents filled up to two hundred thousand federal jobs with political friends and supporters. In 1881, President James Garfield wrote that "my day is frittered away with the personal seeking of people when it ought to be given to the great problems which concern the whole country."[2] Similar problems plagued members of Congress. Senator Henry Cabot Lodge complained that "the system of patronage . . . has converted Congress into a machine for the division of offices, for which it was never intended."[3] Ironi-

cally, the final political push that resulted in the enactment of civil service reform occurred when a frustrated office-seeker tracked down President James Garfield in a Baltimore train station and shot him in 1881.

The enactment of civil service reform did not need the connection between patronage and politics. Even today, presidents and members of Congress award jobs to the faithful. But with a federal bureaucracy of nearly three million employees, the number of politically appointed jobs amounts to a small percentage of the total—in the case of those appointed by the president, for example, to only a few thousand.

The change to the merit system was one applauded by most. But it had at least one unanticipated and probably undesirable consequence, in that it deprived political parties of a key resource—jobs—used to build party strength and support. Thus, civil service reform hastened the decline of political parties.

SOURCE: Leonard D. White, *The Republican Era* (New York: Free Press, 1958).
[1] Leonard D. White, *The Republican Era* (New York: Free Press, 1958), p. 298.
[2] Ibid., p. 6.
[3] Ibid., p. 300.

the infusion of technological skills into the federal civil service has occurred far faster and to a far greater extent than in the American workforce at large. For example, the number of engineers in the federal civil service increased by more than 50 percent between the early 1970s and the early 1990s; the number of computer specialists increased by more than 600 percent. Not counting occupations within the U.S. Postal Service, the occupational groups in the government that are expanding fastest today are legal and legal-related occupations, medical and other health groups, biological sciences, and social sciences.[8]

The image projected by the composition of the federal civil service is not quite as positive when we turn to an examination of its social characteristics other than education and training. This is precisely because, in the matter of the representation of women and minorities, the federal service resembles the workforce at large: women and minorities are not represented in the workforce in proportion to their representation in the population at large. But even so, the federal civil service is making more progress toward equal representation than is the case in the national workforce at large. For example, in 1965, women constituted 34 percent of the federal civilian workforce. But by 1985, women had moved up to 41 percent of the workforce, and by 1990, to 43 percent.[9] In 1965, African Americans constituted 13 percent of the federal civilian workforce; as of 1996, they constituted 17 percent. This compares to 10.8 percent in the civilian labor force at large (see Figure 14.3). Thus, blacks might even be said to be "overrepresented" in the federal bureaucracy.[10] The same is not the case for Hispanics, Asian Americans, and Native Americans, who tend to be slightly underrepresented in the federal civil service.

This picture of the civil service changes in an interesting way when federal employees are broken down according to salary, or "GS level."[11] As Figure 14.4 shows, each minority group is overrepresented in the lowest pay categories, but this success drops off as the pay scale goes up. Nevertheless, the representation of minority groups in the highest categories—GS 15 and the Senior Executive Service—is much better than in the past. Thus, although the picture is mixed, "it appears that the federal bureaucracy . . . is more open to minority employment than the private sector, which bodes well for an improvement in the way minorities are treated by the government."[12]

Even though opportunities at the very highest levels of public administration are still constricted for women and minorities, the "glass ceilings" and other artificial barriers of prejudice have been breaking down, and opportunities for women and minorities in the public service will continue to improve, not only because Americans at large are more receptive but also because affirmative action is still pursued more earnestly in the federal service than in any other occupational universe in the United States. Even the average income for

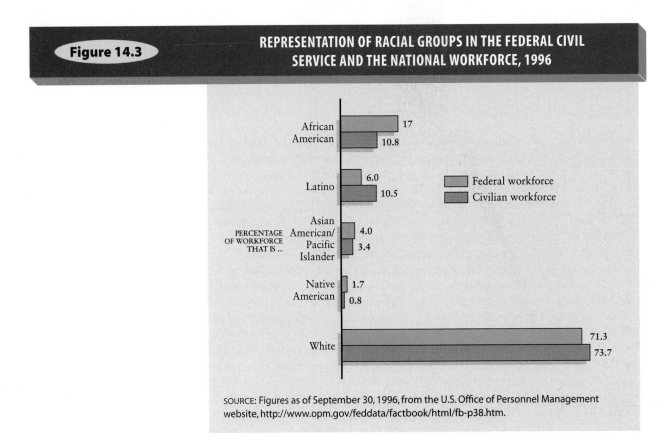

Figure 14.3

REPRESENTATION OF RACIAL GROUPS IN THE FEDERAL CIVIL SERVICE AND THE NATIONAL WORKFORCE, 1996

PERCENTAGE OF WORKFORCE THAT IS ...

African American: 17 / 10.8
Latino: 6.0 / 10.5
Asian American/ Pacific Islander: 4.0 / 3.4
Native American: 1.7 / 0.8
White: 71.3 / 73.7

Federal workforce
Civilian workforce

SOURCE: Figures as of September 30, 1996, from the U.S. Office of Personnel Management website, http://www.opm.gov/feddata/factbook/html/fb-p38.htm.

ETHNIC WORKERS IN THE FEDERAL WORKFORCE

Figure 14.4

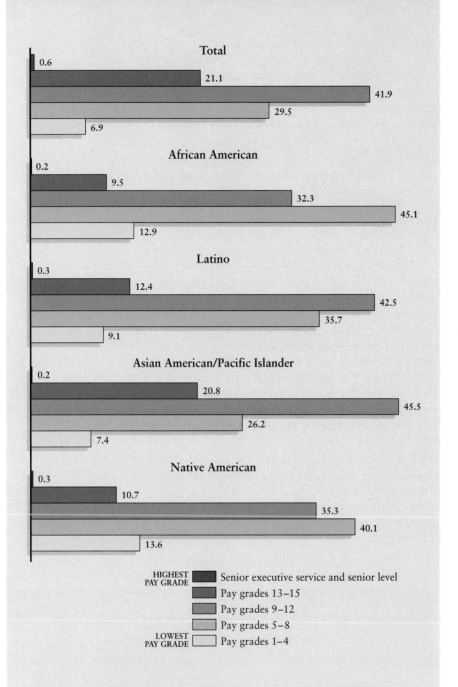

Total
- 0.6
- 21.1
- 41.9
- 29.5
- 6.9

African American
- 0.2
- 9.5
- 32.3
- 45.1
- 12.9

Latino
- 0.3
- 12.4
- 42.5
- 35.7
- 9.1

Asian American/Pacific Islander
- 0.2
- 20.8
- 45.5
- 26.2
- 7.4

Native American
- 0.3
- 10.7
- 35.3
- 40.1
- 13.6

HIGHEST PAY GRADE	Senior executive service and senior level
	Pay grades 13–15
	Pay grades 9–12
	Pay grades 5–8
LOWEST PAY GRADE	Pay grades 1–4

SOURCE: Figures as of September 30, 1994, from U.S. Office of Personnel Management, *Annual Report to Congress on the Federal Equal Opportunity Recruitment Program, Fiscal Year 1994* (Washington, DC: Career Entry Group, Office of Affirmative Recruiting and Employment, U.S. Office of Personnel Management, April 1995), Tables 13, 15, 17, and 19.

Most of the low-ranking IRS employees who process tax forms by hand are women, predominantly from minority groups.

civil servants has drawn closer and closer to that of equivalent jobs in the private sector—except for a rigid ceiling on the salaries payable to top administrators (including Cabinet-level officials), which is set and maintained by a long tradition that civil servants should receive salaries no higher than those received by senators and members of the House.[13]

During his 1992 presidential campaign, Bill Clinton expressed his desire for an administration that "looked like America"; he wanted to improve the administration's sociological representation. One appraisal of Clinton's Cabinet choices concluded that "Clinton succeeded . . . in naming a cabinet that is probably more diverse in background than any in history. His choice of six women, four blacks, and two Hispanics to 23 top-tier posts eclipsed Jimmy Carter's previous standard for slighting white males.[14] Following his re-election in 1996, Clinton named five women, two blacks, and two Hispanics to top posts, including the first female secretary of state, Madeleine Albright. But making the bureaucracy truly look like America will require decades and will happen only when American values wholly embrace such a goal. Even so, turning around an institution comprising nearly 3 million civilian and 1.5 million military employees is akin to turning around a large battleship with a few dozen oars.

★ The Organization of the Executive Branch

▶ What are the agencies that make up the executive branch?
▶ How can one classify these agencies according to their missions?

department

the largest subunit of the executive branch. The secretaries of the fourteen departments form the Cabinet

Cabinet departments, agencies, and bureaus are the operating parts of the bureaucratic whole. Figure 14.5 is an organizational chart of one of the largest and most important of the fourteen **departments,** the Department of Agriculture. At the top is the head of the department, who in the United States is

ORGANIZATIONAL CHART OF THE DEPARTMENT OF AGRICULTURE, 1998

Figure 14.5

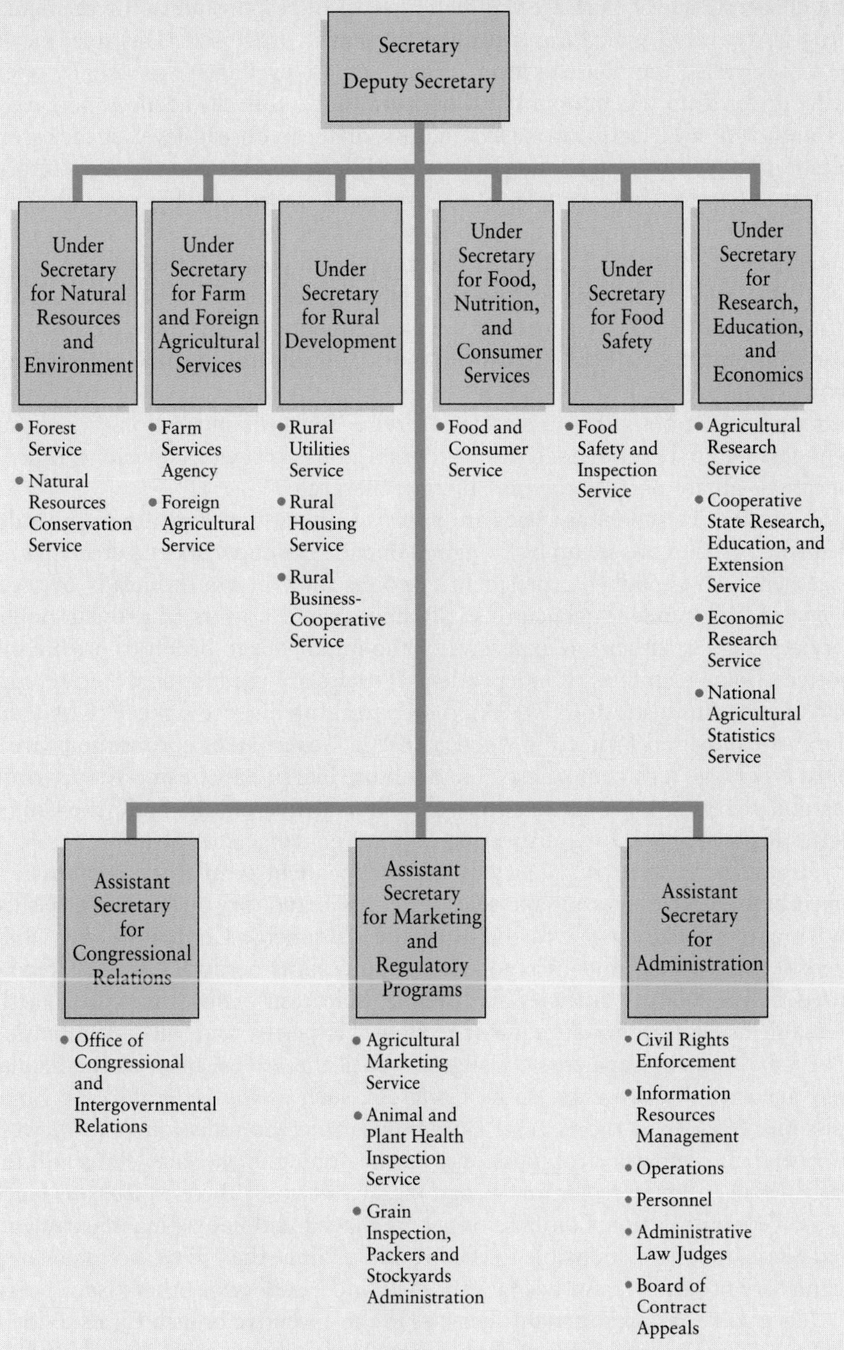

Secretary
Deputy Secretary

Under Secretary for Natural Resources and Environment
- Forest Service
- Natural Resources Conservation Service

Under Secretary for Farm and Foreign Agricultural Services
- Farm Services Agency
- Foreign Agricultural Service

Under Secretary for Rural Development
- Rural Utilities Service
- Rural Housing Service
- Rural Business-Cooperative Service

Under Secretary for Food, Nutrition, and Consumer Services
- Food and Consumer Service

Under Secretary for Food Safety
- Food Safety and Inspection Service

Under Secretary for Research, Education, and Economics
- Agricultural Research Service
- Cooperative State Research, Education, and Extension Service
- Economic Research Service
- National Agricultural Statistics Service

Assistant Secretary for Congressional Relations
- Office of Congressional and Intergovernmental Relations

Assistant Secretary for Marketing and Regulatory Programs
- Agricultural Marketing Service
- Animal and Plant Health Inspection Service
- Grain Inspection, Packers and Stockyards Administration

Assistant Secretary for Administration
- Civil Rights Enforcement
- Information Resources Management
- Operations
- Personnel
- Administrative Law Judges
- Board of Contract Appeals

SOURCE: U.S. Department of Agriculture World Wide Web home page, http://www.usda.gov/agencies/agchart.htm (accessed 5/11/98).

called the "secretary" of the department.[15] Below the secretary and the deputy secretary is a second tier of "undersecretaries" who have management responsibilities for one or more operating agencies, shown in the smaller print directly below each undersecretary. Those operating agencies are the third tier of the department, yet they are the highest level of responsibility for the actual programs around which the entire department is organized. This third tier is generally called the "bureau level." Each bureau-level agency is usually operating under a statute, adopted by Congress, that set up the agency and gave it its authority and jurisdiction. The names of these bureau-level agencies are often quite well known to the public—the Forest Service and the Agricultural Research Service, for example. These are the so-called line agencies, or agencies that deal directly with the public. (Recall the military origin of the term "line agency," discussed earlier in this chapter.) Sometimes these agencies are officially called "bureaus," as in the Federal Bureau of Investigation (FBI), which is a part of the third tier of the Department of Justice. But "bureau" is also the conventional term for this level of administrative agency, even though many agencies or their supporters have preferred over the years to adopt a more palatable designation, such as "service" or "administration." Each bureau is, of course, subdivided into still other units, known as divisions, offices, or units—all are parts of the bureaucratic hierarchy.

independent agency

an agency that is not part of a Cabinet department

Not all government agencies are part of Cabinet departments. Some **independent agencies** are set up by Congress outside the departmental structure altogether, even though the president appoints and directs the heads of these agencies. Independent agencies usually have broad powers to provide public services that are either too expensive or too important to be left to private initiatives. Some examples of independent agencies are the National Aeronautics and Space Administration (NASA), the Central Intelligence Agency (CIA), and the Environmental Protection Agency (EPA). **Government corporations** are a third type of government agency, but are more like private businesses performing and charging for a market service, such as delivering the mail (the United States Postal Service) or transporting railroad passengers (Amtrak).

government corporation

a government agency that performs a service normally provided by the private sector

Yet a fourth type of agency is the independent regulatory commission, given broad discretion to make rules. The first regulatory agencies established by Congress, beginning with the Interstate Commerce Commission in 1888, were set up as independent regulatory commissions because Congress recognized that regulatory agencies are "minilegislatures," whose rules are exactly the same as legislation but require the kind of expertise and full-time attention that is beyond the capacity of Congress. Until the 1960s, most of the regulatory agencies that were set up by Congress, such as the Federal Trade Commission (1914) and the Federal Communications Commission (1934), were independent regulatory commissions. But beginning in the late 1960s and the early 1970s, all new regulatory programs, with two or three exceptions (such as the Federal Election Commission), were placed within existing departments and made directly responsible to the president. Since the 1970s, no major new regulatory programs have been established, independent or otherwise.

Since there are far too many agencies in the executive branch for us to identify and discuss each in this chapter, a simple classification of agencies will be helpful. This classification is organized by the mission of each agency, as defined by the statute that gave the agency its jurisdiction in the first place: clientele agencies, agencies for maintenance of the Union, regulatory agencies, and redistributive agencies. Each type will be briefly evaluated in the following sections.

THE CLIENTELE AGENCIES

Although all administrative agencies have clientele, certain agencies are specifically called **clientele agencies** because they are directed by law to foster and promote the interests of a particular group or segment of American society. The first clientele department was the Department of Agriculture, established in 1862 to promote the interests of farmers. The departments of Commerce and Labor were founded in 1903 as a single department "to foster, promote and develop the foreign and domestic commerce, the mining, the manufacturing, the shipping, and fishing industries, and the transportation facilities of the United States."[16] They remained a single department until 1913, when Congress separated them into two departments, Commerce and Labor, with each directed to support and foster their respective clienteles.[17] Other clientele agencies include the four most recently established Cabinet departments: Housing and Urban Development (HUD), Transportation (DOT), Energy (DOE), and Education (ED). Two others are not strictly clientele departments but contain many agencies that are focused on a particular clientele: Interior, and Health and Human Services (HHS).[18]

Since clientele agencies exist to foster the interests of their clients, it is no wonder that clients organize to support the agency, especially when it is in jeopardy of being abolished, reorganized, or cut back. Figure 14.6 is a representation of the type of politics that tends to form around clientele agencies. This configuration is known as an **iron triangle,** a pattern of stable relationships between an agency in the executive branch, a congressional committee or subcommittee, and one or more organized groups of agency clientele. (Iron triangles were discussed in detail in Chapter 11.) Such mutually supportive relationships can be found in agencies that are not clientele agencies, but they are most likely to be found among clientele agencies. These relationships are highly successful in fighting off opposition, as the following brief case studies illustrate.

During his 1980 campaign, Ronald Reagan promised to dismantle the departments of Energy and Education as part of his commitment to get the government "off people's backs." After his election, President Reagan even appointed as the secretaries of these two departments individuals publicly committed to eliminating their departments and therefore their own jobs. Yet by the end of the Reagan administration in 1988, the Department of Education and the Department of Energy were still very much alive. Another ten years later they still have not been eliminated. Even though the "revolutionary" Republican 104th Congress pledged to kill these two departments as well as a third, the Department of Commerce, they did not fulfill this pledge. In fact, the House Republicans in 1995 called for the elimination of nearly three hundred programs but succeeded in killing only thirty. For the rest, they had to be

clientele agencies

departments or bureaus of government whose mission is to promote, serve, or represent a particular interest or a particular segment or geographical area of the country

Students and Politics

In 1997, President Clinton announced his "America Reads" initiative, a series of programs administered by the Department of Education designed to increase the reading levels of first- and second-grade students who have fallen behind their classmates. To this end, Congress increased federal work-study grants to colleges, with the requirement that colleges would use some of this money to provide student tutors to local schools for individualized lessons. Jane No, a senior at Portland State University in Oregon, heard of the program through her work-study counselor and decided to work two days each week at nearby Creston Elementary School through a program designed to bring students up to speed in four weeks. "I didn't know what to expect," she says. "The teacher I worked for was really nice and encouraging, but I had to learn a lot just by doing. It's a good thing kids are so accepting." Most of No's students reached grade-level reading comprehension while working in a one-on-one environment. "The work allowed for a flexible schedule," she says. "That—at least as much as the money— allowed me to do this." Since beginning to teach, No has thought about teaching as a career. The influence of her instruction had amazed her. "I was really surprised that they expected these kids to catch up in four weeks, but they actually do make it. It's just about getting to them while they're young, and devoting the attention and encouragement to help."

SOURCE: Jane No, interview with author, May 21, 1998.

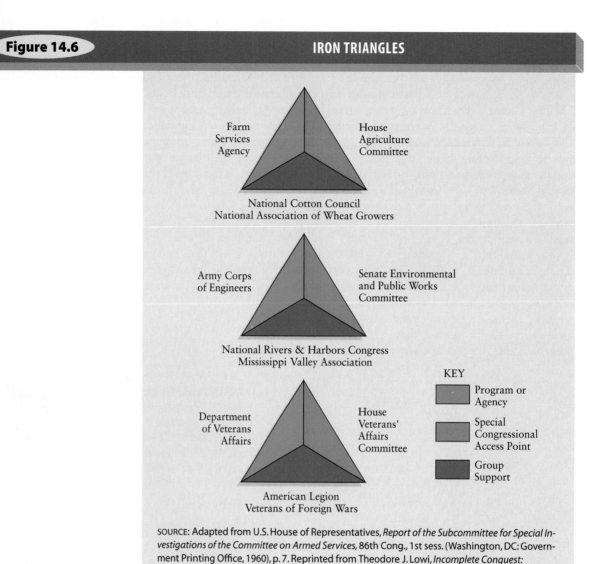

SOURCE: Adapted from U.S. House of Representatives, *Report of the Subcommittee for Special Investigations of the Committee on Armed Services,* 86th Cong., 1st sess. (Washington, DC: Government Printing Office, 1960), p. 7. Reprinted from Theodore J. Lowi, *Incomplete Conquest: Governing America,* 2nd ed. (New York: Holt, Rinehart and Winston, 1981), p. 139.

iron triangle

the stable, cooperative relationships that often develop between a congressional committee, an administrative agency, and one or more supportive interest groups. Not all of these relationships are triangular, but the iron triangle is the most typical

content with "squeezing budgets without eliminating functions . . . to deliver on every promise ever made with less and less money."[19]

Unless a president or congressional committee wants to drop everything else and concentrate entirely on eliminating one or two departments, the constituency of a clientele department is too strong to be battled on a part-time basis. The supportive constituency of the Department of Education includes the departments of education in all fifty states, all the school boards and school systems in the thousands of counties and cities across the country, the major unions of secondary-school teachers, and a large proportion of the teachers' colleges in the country. One of the most formidable lobbies in the United States is the National Education Association (NEA), which has a chapter in every state in the country. It was the NEA and its access to President Carter that led to the creation of the Department of Education in the first place. The constituency supporting the Department of Energy includes the major utilities and other power-generating industries, the major research universities, and the several states that produce oil and gas or that are home to atomic energy or other power plants that produce large amounts of energy.

Another factor that adds to the endurance of the clientele agencies is the fact that a large proportion of their employees work far from Washington, D.C. People may still believe that most federal bureaucrats live and work in the District of Columbia, but in fact nearly 90 percent of federal employees work elsewhere in the country, and a substantial number work abroad. The presence of so many federal employees in local areas works to the particular advantage of clientele agencies, because these employees are able to establish friendly and mutually supportive relationships with local businesses and other organized groups looking for help from the clientele departments. This adds weight to the third corner of the iron triangle, which is usually ready to come to the aid of the department or agencies in trouble.[20]

AGENCIES FOR MAINTENANCE OF THE UNION

One of the remarkable features of American federalism is that the most vital agencies for the maintenance of the Union are located in state and local governments—namely, the police. But some agencies vital to maintaining national integration do exist in the national government, and they can be grouped for convenience into three categories: (1) agencies for control of the sources of federal government revenue, (2) agencies for control of conduct defined as a threat to internal national security, and (3) agencies for defending American security from external threats. The departments of greatest concern in these three areas are, respectively, Treasury, Justice, and Defense and State.

Revenue Agencies   One of the first actions of Congress under President George Washington was to create the Department of the Treasury, and probably its oldest function is the collection of taxes on imports, called tariffs. Now housed in the United States Customs Service, federal customs agents are located at every U.S. seaport and international airport to oversee the collection of tariffs. But far and away the most important of the **revenue agencies** is the Internal Revenue Service (IRS). The Customs Service and the IRS are two of at least twelve bureaus within the Treasury Department. The IRS will be our single case study in this section.

The IRS is not unresponsive to political influences, especially given the fact that it must maintain cooperative relationships with the two oldest and most important congressional committees, the House Ways and Means Committee and the Senate Finance Committee. Nevertheless, the political patterns of the IRS are virtually the opposite of those of a clientele agency. As one expert put it, "probably no organization in the country, public or private, creates as much clientele *dis*favor as the Internal Revenue Service. The very nature of its work brings it into an adversary relationship with vast numbers of Americans every year."[21] Yet few scandals have soiled its record. Complaints against the IRS have cascaded during the past few years, particularly since 1996 presidential candidate Steve Forbes staged his entire campaign on the need to abolish the IRS and the income tax itself. But aside from the principle of the income tax,

President Clinton addressing the 1996 convention of the National Education Association. The teachers' lobby is an important constituency for the Democratic Party.

revenue agencies

agencies responsible for collecting taxes. Examples include the Internal Revenue Service for income taxes, the U.S. Customs Service for tariffs and other taxes on imported goods, and the Bureau of Alcohol, Tobacco, and Firearms for collection of taxes on the sales of those particular products

Students and Politics

"University student employees [enrolled at least half-time] are exempt from paying social security taxes, according to an [Internal Revenue Service] ruling in January 1998.

"The decision affects all higher learning institutions by more clearly defining a provision in the federal tax code. The provision exempts students employed by the college they attend from paying Federal Insurance Contributions Act (FICA) taxes, as long as they are enrolled half-time.

"'Well, it sounds like a good idea to me,' said Kevin Kolb, a freshman in the [University of Minnesota] College of Liberal Arts who also works for University Food Services.

"Students who are 'career employees,' defined as those eligible to receive retirement benefits, do not qualify for the exemption....

"Savings to the students are also significant, [a university administrator] said. 'A few dollars here or there to a student can be a pretty big deal, too,' she said.

"Previously, the IRS exempted students who were enrolled and regularly attending classes, but did not define how many credits a student had to take to qualify. Some schools took the definition to mean students taking at least one class.

"The new provision defines half-time students as those students taking half of a college's full-time requirement, as long as that requirement was comparable to the federal Department of Education's definition of half-time.

"The IRS also required students to work less than 20 hours a week to be exempt. The new rules do not have guidelines for number of hours worked....

"[A university administrator] credits the IRS for addressing and acting on the issue. 'This is one manifestation of a kinder, gentler IRS,' she said. 'I do have to give the IRS credit for being responsive.'"

SOURCE: Josh L. Dickey, "IRS Offers New Tax Exemptions for Students," *Minnesota Daily*, January 21, 1998; reprinted on UWire, http://www.uwire.com/uwire/98/l/news01219801.chtml.

all the other complaints against the IRS are against its needless complexity, its lack of sensitivity and responsiveness to individual taxpayers, and its overall lack of efficiency. As one of its critics put it, "Imagine a company that's owed $216 billion plus interest, a company with a 22-percent error rate. A company that spent $4 billion to update a computer system—with little success. It all describes the Internal Revenue Service."[22] Again leaving aside the issue of the income tax itself, all the other complaints amount to just one big complaint: the IRS is not bureaucratic enough; it needs more bureaucratization. It needs to succeed with its new computer processing system; it needs vast improvement in its "customer services"; it needs long-term budgeting and other management control; and it needs to borrow more management and technology expertise from the private sector.

The politics of the IRS is most interesting, because, although thousands upon thousands of individual corporations and wealthy individuals have a strong and active interest in American tax policy, key taxation decisions are not governed by iron triangles. They are in fact set by agreements between the president, the Treasury Department, and the leading members of the two tax committees in Congress. External influence is not spread throughout the fifty states, but instead is much more centralized in the majority political party, a few key figures in Congress, and a handful of professional lobbyists. Suspicions of unfair exemptions and of favoritism are widespread, and they do exist, but these exemptions come largely from Congress, *not* from the IRS itself.

Agencies for Internal Security   As long as the country is not in a state of insurrection, most of the task of maintaining the Union takes the form of legal work, and the primary responsibility for that lies in the Department of Justice. It is indeed a luxury, and rare in the world, when national unity can be maintained by routines of civil law with an army of lawyers, instead of martial law imposed by a real army with guns.

The largest and most important unit of the Justice Department is the Criminal Division. Lawyers in the Criminal Division represent the United States government when it is the plaintiff enforcing the federal criminal laws, except for those cases (about 25 percent) specifically assigned to other divisions or agencies. Criminal litigation is handled by U.S. attorneys, who are appointed by the president. There is one U.S. attorney in each of the ninety-four federal judicial districts; he or she supervises the work of a number of assistant U.S. attorneys.

The Civil Division of the Justice Department deals with litigation in which the United States is the defendant being sued for injury and damages allegedly

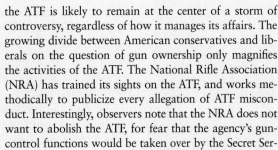

Storm over the ATF

The conflict between public power and private interest can be seen clearly in the activities of what has come to be the most unpopular agency of the 1990s: the Bureau of Alcohol, Tobacco, and Firearms (ATF). Charged with regulating the trade and use of liquor, cigarettes, and guns—three products especially dear to many Americans—the ATF carries out its mandate in an atmosphere of mistrust, violence, and accusations of misconduct. In 1995 such accusations resulted in congressional hearings into ATF operations and the validity of the charges against it.

Congressional investigations of the ATF are not new; as a consequence of investigations in 1979, Congress cut the agency's budget and prohibited it from computerizing its records (a prohibition that still stands).

The recent charges against the ATF arise in part from its involvement in the standoff at the Branch Davidian compound in Waco, Texas. The siege began on February 28, 1993, when, as part of a firearms investigation, ATF agents tried to serve a search warrant at the compound of a small religious community called the Branch Davidians. The heavily armed Davidians resisted the warrant, and in the ensuing shoot-out, four ATF agents and six Davidians were killed. (The FBI then took over the case, and was responsible for launching the tear-gas attack two months later that led to the fiery deaths of about eighty Davidians.) Critics charged that the ATF ignored warnings that the Davidians would respond to a show of force with violence and that the agency planned the operation, in which seventy armed agents took part, without informing senior officials who were supposed to oversee ATF activities. A subsequent Treasury Department review assailed the ATF for inaccurate information, poor plans, and subsequent lies by ATF officials to deflect blame onto subordinates.

At congressional hearings in the fall of 1995, senior ATF officials defended the agency by saying that it had made and was continuing to make significant reforms. But because of its frontline police and regulatory functions, especially on the hot-button issue of gun control,

the ATF is likely to remain at the center of a storm of controversy, regardless of how it manages its affairs. The growing divide between American conservatives and liberals on the question of gun ownership only magnifies the activities of the ATF. The National Rifle Association (NRA) has trained its sights on the ATF, and works methodically to publicize every allegation of ATF misconduct. Interestingly, observers note that the NRA does not want to abolish the ATF, for fear that the agency's gun-control functions would be taken over by the Secret Service and the FBI, which have sophisticated computer systems. Instead, in the words of one official, the NRA wants "a cowed and chastened ATF."[1] To that end, it has launched savage attacks on the agency, including a notorious 1995 fund-raising letter likening federal agents to Nazi storm troopers, which prompted former president George Bush to renounce his lifetime membership in the NRA.

The firestorm surrounding the ATF may have already radicalized some Americans. Timothy McVeigh, the man accused of the bombing of a federal office building in Oklahoma City, is said to have been driven to the deed by his rage over the Waco tragedy. And according to police officers, members of one paramilitary group, the Michigan Militia, "have been found with the names and addresses of ATF agents, as well as the addresses of their children's schools."[2] The spread of violence and the polarization of public opinion have put the ATF at the center of a storm—but its very functions create that storm. As long as there are laws concerning guns, alcohol, tobacco, or any other goods that are wanted by substantial numbers of people but are considered immoral or dangerous by others, there will be federal agencies that must apply and enforce those laws—and life-and-death disputes will play themselves out, on the boundary between private life and public order.

[1] Quoted in John Mintz, "A Way of Life for ATF: Fending Off Gun Lobby Efforts to Kill It," *Washington Post,* July 24, 1995, p. A4.
[2] Ibid.

J. Edgar Hoover built the FBI into one of the most famous and most feared government agencies in American history.

inflicted by a government official. The missions of the other divisions of the Justice Department—Antitrust, Civil Rights, Environment and Natural Resources, and Tax—are described by their names.

The best known bureau of the Justice Department is the Federal Bureau of Investigation (FBI). The FBI handles no litigation but instead serves as the principal information-gathering agency for the department and for the president. Established in 1908, the FBI expanded and advanced in stature during the 1920s and 1930s under the direction of J. Edgar Hoover. Although it is only one of the many bureaus and divisions in the Department of Justice, and although it officially has no higher status than any of the others, it is politically the most significant.

Despite its professionalism and its fierce pride in its autonomy, the FBI has not been unresponsive to the partisan commitments of Democratic and Republican administrations. Although the FBI has always achieved its best publicity from the spectacular apprehension of famous criminals, such as John Dillinger, George "Machine Gun" Kelly, and Bonnie and Clyde,[23] it has followed the president's direction in focusing on particular crime problems. Thus it has infiltrated Nazi and Mafia organizations; it operates the vast loyalty and security investigation programs covering all federal employees since the Truman presidency; it monitored and infiltrated the Ku Klux Klan and the civil rights movement in the 1950s and 1960s; and it has infiltrated radical political groups and extreme religious cults and survivalist militias in the 1980s and 1990s.

Agencies for External National Security   Two departments occupy center stage in maintaining national security: the departments of State and Defense.

Although diplomacy is generally considered the primary task of the State Department, diplomatic missions are only one of its organizational dimensions. As of 1996, the State Department comprised nineteen bureau-level units, each under the direction of an assistant secretary. Six of these are geographic or regional bureaus concerned with all problems within a defined region of the world; nine are "functional" bureaus, handling such things as economic and business affairs, intelligence and research, and international organizations. Four are bureaus of internal affairs, which handle such areas as security, finance and management, and legal issues.

These bureaus support the responsibilities of the elite of foreign affairs, the foreign service officers (FSOs), who staff U.S. embassies around the world and who hold almost all of the most powerful positions in the department below the rank of ambassador.[24] The ambassadorial positions, especially the plum positions in the major capitals of the world, are filled by presidential appointees, many of whom get their positions by having been important donors to the victorious political campaign.

Despite the importance of the State Department in foreign affairs, fewer than 20 percent of all U.S. government employees working abroad are directly under its authority. By far the largest number of career government professionals working abroad are under the authority of the Defense Department.

The creation of the Department of Defense by legislation between 1947 and 1949 was an effort to unify the two historic military departments, the War Department and the Navy Department, and to integrate them with a new department, the Air Force. Real unification, however, did not occur. The Defense Department simply added more pluralism to an already pluralistic national security establishment.

The American military, following worldwide military tradition, is organized according to a "chain of command"—a tight hierarchy of clear responsibility and rank, made clearer by uniforms, special insignia, and detailed organizational charts and rules of order and etiquette. The "line agencies" in the Department of Defense are the military commands, distributed geographically by divisions and fleets to deal with current or potential enemies. The "staff agencies," such as logistics, intelligence, personnel, research and development, quartermaster, and engineering, exist to serve the "line agencies." At the top of the military chain of command are chiefs of staff (called chief of naval operations in the Navy, and commandant in the Marines). These chiefs of staff also constitute the membership of the Joint Chiefs of Staff—the center of military policy and management.

America's primary political problem with its military has not been the historic one of how to keep the military out of politics (which is a perennial problem in many of the world's countries), but how to keep politics out of the military. In the heat of the 1992 presidential campaign, for example, President Bush made a stop in Fort Worth, Texas, where he announced his approval of the sale to Taiwan of up to 150 new F-16 fighter planes. It was no coincidence that the manufacture of military planes is an important part of the Fort Worth economy; Bush's decision saved an estimated 11,000 jobs. Bush's later decision to sell F-15 fighter planes to Saudi Arabia violated his own policy against the proliferation of high-tech weapons, but promised to save jobs in the St. Louis economy. Bush broke his reduced-spending pledge in Michigan, where "$9 billion in pork went out the window in one campaign week" with his renewal of M-1 tank production. As one senior member of the Senate Armed Services Committee asserted, "We already have more tanks than we will ever need."[25] President Clinton's long list of proposed military base closings, a major part of his budget-cutting drive for 1993, caused a firestorm of opposition even within his own party, including a number of members of Congress who were otherwise prominently in favor of significant reductions in the Pentagon budget.

Politicians' emphasis on jobs rather than on strategy and policy when dealing with military funding is a clear signal of the use of the military for political purposes. The 1995 Republican commitment to increase the amount of defense spending, coupled with President Clinton's willingness to cooperate by seeking an additional $25 billion increase in the Pentagon budget for 1995, had more to do with the domestic pressures of employment in defense and defense industries than with military necessity in the post–cold war era. The iron triangle of defense plays clientele agency politics inside the establishment that is responsible for the security of the entire nation.

THE REGULATORY AGENCIES

The United States has no "Department of Regulation" but has many **regulatory agencies.** Some of these are bureaus within departments, such as the Food and Drug Administration (FDA) in the Department of Health and Human Services, the Occupational Safety and Health Administration (OSHA) in the Department of Labor, and the Animal and Plant Health Inspection Service (APHIS) in the Department of Agriculture. As we saw earlier, other regulatory agencies are independent regulatory commissions, such as the Federal Communications Commission (FCC). But whether departmental or independent,

regulatory agencies

departments, bureaus, or independent agencies whose primary mission is to impose limits, restrictions, or other obligations on the conduct of individuals or companies in the private sector

FEDERAL GRAIN
INSPECTION SERVICE

STATE DEPARTMENT OF
AGRICULTURE INSPECTION
DIVISIONS

CENTER FOR FOOD SAFETY
AND APPLIED NUTRITION
(FDA)

PLANT PROTECTION
AND QUARANTINE

FOOD SAFETY AND
INSPECTION SERVICE

DAIRY DIVISION
(USDA)

COUNTY BOARD
OF HEALTH

USDA ANIMAL
PLANT HEALTH
INSPECTION SERVICE

STATE DEPARTMENT
OF HEALTH

ENVIRONMENTAL
PROTECTION AGENCY

AGRICULTURAL MARKETING
SERVICE

FRUIT AND VEGETABLE
QUALITY DIVISION (USDA)

Regulatory agencies have a strong presence in the lives of all Americans. For instance, the foods we eat are subject to myriad regulations from federal, state, and local agencies.

an agency or commission is regulatory if Congress delegates to it relatively broad powers over a sector of the economy or a type of commercial activity and authorizes it to make rules restricting the conduct of people and businesses within that jurisdiction. Rules made by regulatory agencies have the force and effect of law. And when these agencies make decisions or issue orders settling disputes between parties or between the government and a party, they are acting like courts. It is no wonder that we wonder whether such agencies are more accountable when they are within departments or when they are independent and therefore accountable directly to Congress.

AGENCIES FOR REDISTRIBUTION

Fiscal (or monetary) agencies and welfare agencies seem at first to be too far apart to belong to the same category, but they are related in a very special way. Both types are responsible for the transfer of hundreds of billions of dollars annually between the public and the private spheres. Through such transfers, these agencies influence how people and corporations spend and invest trillions of dollars each year. We call these types of agencies **redistributive agencies** because they influence the amount of money in the economy and because they directly influence who has money, who has credit, and whether people will want to invest or save their money rather than spend it.

Fiscal and Monetary Agencies   The best term for government activity affecting or relating to money is **fiscal policy**. The *fisc* was the Roman imperial treasury; "fiscal" can refer to anything and everything having to do with public finance. However, we in the United States choose to make a further distinction, reserving "fiscal" for taxing and spending policies and using "monetary" for policies having to do with banks, credit, and currency. Yet a third term, "welfare," deserves to be treated as an equal member of this redistributive category.[26]

redistributive agencies

a general category of agencies including fiscal agencies, monetary agencies, and welfare agencies, whose net effect is to shift large aggregates of wealth from rich to poor, young to old, etc.

fiscal policy

the use of taxing, monetary, and spending powers to manipulate the economy

The administration of fiscal policy occurs primarily in the Treasury Department. It is no contradiction to include the Treasury here as well as with the agencies for maintenance of the Union. This duplication indicates two things: first, that the Treasury is a complex department that performs more than one function of government; and second, that traditional controls have had to adapt to modern economic conditions and new technologies.

Today, in addition to collecting income, corporate, and other taxes, the Treasury is also responsible for managing the enormous national debt—$5.18 trillion in 1996. (The national debt was a mere $914 billion in 1980.)[27] Debt is not simply something the country owes; it is something a country has to manage and administer. The debt is also a fiscal instrument in the hands of the federal government that can be used—through manipulation of interest rates and through the buying and selling of government bonds—to slow down or to speed up the activity of the entire national economy, as well as to defend the value of the dollar in international trade.

The Treasury Department is also responsible for printing the U.S. currency, but currency represents only a tiny proportion of the entire money economy. Most of the trillions of dollars used in the transactions of the private and public sectors of the U.S. economy exist in computerized accounts, not in currency.

Another important fiscal agency (although for technical reasons it is called an agency of monetary policy) is the **Federal Reserve System,** which is headed by the Federal Reserve Board. The Federal Reserve System (called simply the Fed) has authority over the interest rates and lending activities of the nation's most important banks. Congress established the Fed in 1913 as a clearinghouse responsible for adjusting the supply of money and credit to the needs of commerce and industry in different regions of the country. The Fed is also responsible for ensuring that banks do not overextend themselves, a policy that guards against a chain of bank failures during a sudden economic scare, such as occurred in 1929. The Federal Reserve Board directs the operations of the twelve district Federal Reserve Banks, which are essentially "bankers' banks," serving the monetary needs of the hundreds of member banks in the national banking system.[28]

Welfare Agencies Welfare agencies seem at first glance to be just another set of clientele agencies, with dependent people as their clientele. But there is a big difference between welfare agencies and other clientele agencies: Welfare agencies operate under laws that discriminate between rich and poor, old and young. Access to welfare agencies is restricted to those individuals who fall within particular legally defined categories. Those who fall outside the relevant legal category would not be entitled to access even if they were to seek it. In contrast, people come under the jurisdiction of traditional clientele agencies (such as the Department of Agriculture) either through self-selection or by coincidence. Access to a genuine clientele agency is open to almost anyone.

The most important and expensive of the welfare programs are the insurance programs, traditionally called Social Security, to which all employed persons contribute through taxes during their working years and from which they receive benefits as a matter of right when in need.[29] Two other programs come closer to the popular understanding of welfare—Temporary Assistance to Needy Families (TANF) and Supplemental Security Income (SSI). No contributions are required for access to these programs, each of which is **means tested**—that is, applicants for benefits must demonstrate that their total annual cash earnings fall below the officially defined poverty line.

Federal Reserve System

a system of twelve Federal Reserve Banks that facilitates exchanges of cash, checks, and credit; regulates member banks; and uses monetary policies to fight inflation and deflation

means testing

a procedure by which potential beneficiaries of a public assistance program establish their eligibility by demonstrating a genuine need for the assistance

There is a third category of welfare, called "in-kind programs," which includes food stamps and Medicaid. These two programs are also means tested; people who fall below the minimum income qualify for the noncash benefits of food stamps and the noncash Medicaid services of hospitals and doctors. Cash is involved in the Medicaid program, but it does not go directly to the person receiving benefits; the government pays the doctor or hospital directly for the services rendered. Another welfare program with very large fiscal significance is Medicare, a health insurance program for the elderly, which is not means tested.

There is no single government department responsible for all of the programs that comprise the "Social Security system" or the "welfare state." The largest of all the agencies in this field is the Social Security Administration (SSA), an independent federal agency that manages Social Security and SSI. The Department of Health and Human Services administers the TANF, Medicare, and Medicaid programs. The Department of Agriculture is responsible for the food stamp program.

The entire welfare system is in trouble today. Welfare state programs redistribute a measurable amount of wealth from those who work to those who do not and from the young to the elderly. Since these programs were started, the redistribution of wealth has become legitimate in the United States, and even popular. But during the sixty-year history of the welfare state, the ratio of those in the workforce (being taxed) to those outside the workforce (dependent on assistance) has dropped from 18:1 to 4:1. It is therefore no wonder that a Democratic candidate for president in 1992 could campaign successfully on a pledge "to end welfare as we know it." In 1994, President Bill Clinton proposed reforming welfare to require that welfare recipients born after 1971 find work within two years of accepting welfare support for themselves and their children. The Republican Congress took a much more radical step in 1995: the Senate passed a bill to terminate entitlement programs for the poor and "devolve" all federal funding for such programs to the states, to use at their discretion. This convinced President Clinton that the time had finally come "to end welfare as we know it," and in 1996 he signed into law an even more radical bill to eliminate the federal guarantee of cash assistance to the needy, to authorize the states to run their own welfare programs, to put a lifetime limit of five years on benefits paid to any family, and to require work within two years of receipt of welfare assistance. Accountability in welfare agencies will be the key domestic political issue of the coming years.

★ Can the Bureaucracy Be Reduced?

▶ What methods have been used to reduce the size and the role of the federal bureaucracy?

▶ How effective can efforts to reduce the bureaucracy be?

Some Americans would argue that bureaucracy is always too big and that it always should be reduced. In the 1990s Americans seem particularly enthusiastic about reducing (or to use the popular contemporary word, "downsizing") the federal bureaucracy. This downsizing could be achieved in at least three ways: termination, devolution, or privatization.

Selecting locations for military bases is a classic example of clientele agency politics. As a result, the process of closing bases has been difficult. Members of Congress used to try to overturn decisions to close bases in their districts. Because that is no longer possible, members of Congress such as Senator Diane Feinstein of California have sought to convert military bases for other government purposes. Critics say this isn't reducing bureaucracy, just shifting it around.

TERMINATION

The only *certain* way to reduce the size of the bureaucracy is to eliminate programs. Variations in the levels of federal personnel and expenditures (as was shown in Figures 14.1 and 14.2) demonstrate the futility of trying to make permanent cuts in existing agencies. Furthermore, most agencies have a supportive constituency that will fight to reinstate any cuts that are made. Termination is the only way to ensure an agency's reduction and it is a rare occurrence, even with the Reagan and Bush administrations, both of which proclaimed a strong commitment to the reduction of the national government. In fact, not a single national government agency or program was terminated during the twelve years of Reagan and Bush.

The Republican-led 104th Congress (1995–96) was even more committed to the termination of programs. Newt Gingrich, Speaker of the House, took Congress by storm with his promises of a virtual revolution in government. But when the dust had settled at the end of the first session of the first Gingrich-led Congress, no significant progress had been made toward downsizing through termination of agencies and programs.[30] This lack of success is a reflection of Americans' love/hate relationship with the national government. As antagonistic as Americans may be toward bureaucracy in general, they grow attached to the services being rendered and protections being offered by particular bureaucratic agencies; that is, they fiercely defend their favorite agencies while perceiving no inconsistency between that defense and their antagonistic attitude toward the bureaucracy in general. A good case in point is the agonizing problem of closing military bases in the wake of the end of the cold war with the former Soviet Union, when the United States no longer needs so many bases. Since every base is in some congressional member's district, it proved impossible for Congress to decide to close any of them. Consequently, between 1988 and 1990, Congress established a Defense Base Closure and Realignment Commission to decide on base closings, taking the matter out of Congress's hands altogether.[31] And even so, the process has been slow and agonizing.

Elected leaders have come to rely on a more incremental approach to downsizing the bureaucracy. Much has been done by budgetary means, reducing the budgets of all agencies across the board by small percentages, and cutting some less-supported agencies by larger amounts. Yet these changes are still incremental, leaving the existence of agencies unaddressed.

An additional approach has been taken to thwart the highly unpopular regulatory agencies, which are so small (relatively) that cutting their budgets contributes virtually nothing to reducing the deficit. This approach is called **deregulation,** simply defined as a reduction in the number of rules promulgated by regulatory agencies. President Reagan used this strategy successfully and was very proud of it. Presidents Bush and Clinton have proudly followed Reagan's lead. But deregulation by rule reduction is still incremental and has certainly not satisfied the hunger of the American public in general and Washington representatives in particular for a genuine reduction of bureaucracy.

DEVOLUTION

The next best approach to genuine reduction of the size of the bureaucracy is **devolution**—downsizing the federal bureaucracy by delegating the implementation of programs to state and local governments. In some instances this may amount to genuine termination of certain programs, because some states will choose not to have the program at all, if the federal laws provide that much discretion to the states. In fact, many politicians favor devolution precisely because they see it as a politically safer way to terminate programs. But the problem that arises with devolution is that programs that were once uniform across the country (because they were the national government's responsibility) can become highly variable, with some states providing benefits not available in other states. To a point, variation can be considered one of the virtues of federalism. But there are dangers inherent in large variations and inequalities in the provision of services and benefits in a democracy. For example, since the Food and Drug Administration (FDA) has been under attack in recent years, could the problem be solved by devolving its regulatory tasks to the states? Would people care if drugs would require "caution" labels in some states and not in others? Would Americans want each state to set its own air and water pollution control policies without regard to the fact that pollution flows across state boundaries? Devolution, as attractive as it may be, is not an approach that can be applied across the board without analyzing carefully the nature of the program and of the problems it is designed to solve. Even the capacity of states to handle "devolved" programs will vary. According to the Washington research organization the Brookings Institution, the level of state and local government employment varies from state to state—from a low of 400 per 10,000 residents in some states to a high of 700 per 10,000 in others. "Such administrative diversity is bound to mediate the course and consequences of any substantial devolution of federal responsibility; no one-size-fits-all devolution [from federal to state and local government] can work."[32]

deregulation

a policy of reducing or eliminating regulatory restraints on the conduct of individuals or private institutions

devolution

a policy to remove a program from one level of government by delegating it or passing it down to a lower level of government, such as from the national government to the state and local governments

privatization

removing all or part of a program from the public sector to the private sector

PRIVATIZATION

Privatization seems like a synonym for termination, but that is true only at the extreme. Most of what is called "privatization" is not termination at all but the provision of government goods and services by private contractors under direct government supervision. Except for top-secret strategic materials, virtually all of the production of military hardware, from boats to bullets, is done on a privatized basis by private contractors. Billions of dollars of research services are bought under contract by governments; these private contractors are universities as well as ordinary industrial corporations and private "think tanks." **Privatization** simply means that a formerly public activity is picked up under contract by a private company or companies. But such programs are still very much government programs; they are paid for by government and supervised by government. Privatization downsizes the government only in that the workers providing the service are no longer counted as part of the government bureaucracy.

None of this analysis and criticism is intended to discourage efforts to downsize the government bureaucracies. But in the process of trying to downsize the government, two fundamental points ought to be kept clearly in mind. First, the federal bureaucracy is here to stay, and even if so-called revolutionary campaigns to downsize the government are completely successful, they will not reduce the federal bureaucracy by very much. Second, government must therefore concentrate on a much older but now much more pressing problem: how to make the bureaucracy that exists more compatible with the democracy the American people desire.

★ Can Bureaucracy Be Controlled?

▶ How can bureaucracy and democracy coexist? What popular controls over the bureaucracy exist?

▶ How do the president and Congress manage and oversee the bureaucracy?

▶ What is the most effective means to guarantee a responsible bureaucracy?

The title of this chapter, "Bureaucracy in a Democracy," is intended to convey the sense that the two are contradictory.[33] Americans cannot live with bureaucracy, but they also cannot live without it. The task is neither to retreat from bureaucracy nor to attack it, but to take advantage of its strengths while making it more accountable to the demands of democratic politics and representative government. This task will be the focus of the remainder of this chapter.

Two hundred years, millions of employees, and trillions of dollars after the Founding, we must return to James Madison's observation, "You must first enable the government to control the governed; and in the next place oblige it to control itself."[34] Today the problem is the same, only now the process has a name: administrative accountability. Accountability implies that there is some higher authority by which the actions of the bureaucracy will be guided and judged. The highest authority in a democracy is *demos*—the people—and the guidance for bureaucratic action is the popular will. But that ideal of account-ability must be translated into practical terms by the president and Congress. (The federal courts translate as well; they will be discussed in the next chapter.)

THE PRESIDENT AS CHIEF EXECUTIVE

In 1937, President Franklin Roosevelt's Committee on Administrative Man-agement gave official sanction to an idea that had been growing increasingly urgent: "The president needs help." The national government had grown rapidly during the preceding twenty-five years, but the structures and proce-dures necessary to manage the burgeoning executive branch had not yet been established. The response to the call for "help" for the president initially took the form of three management policies: (1) All communications and decisions that related to executive policy decisions must pass through the White House; (2) In order to cope with such a flow, the White House must have adequate staffs of specialists in research, analysis, legislative and legal writing, and pub-lic affairs; and (3) The White House must have additional staff to follow through on presidential decisions—to ensure that those decisions are made, communicated to Congress, and carried out by the appropriate agency.

Making the Managerial Presidency   Establishing a management capacity for the presidency began in earnest with FDR, but it did not stop there.[35] The story of the modern presidency can be told largely as a series of responses to the plea for managerial help. Indeed, each expansion of the national govern-ment into new policies and programs in the twentieth century has been accom-panied by a parallel expansion of the president's management authority. This pattern began even before FDR's presidency, with the policy innovations of President Woodrow Wilson between 1913 and 1920. Congress responded to Wilson's policies with the 1921 Budget and Accounting Act, which turned over the prime legislative power of budgeting to the White House. Each suc-cessive president has continued this pattern, creating what we now know as the "managerial presidency."

Presidents John Kennedy and Lyndon Johnson were committed both to government expansion and to management expansion, in the spirit of their party's hero, FDR. President Nixon also strengthened and enlarged the man-agerial presidency, but for somewhat different reasons. He sought the strongest possible managerial hand because he had to assume that the overwhelming ma-jority of federal employees had sympathies with the Democratic Party, which had controlled the White House and had sponsored governmental growth for twenty-eight of the previous thirty-six years.[36]

President Jimmy Carter was probably more preoccupied with administra-tive reform and reorganization than any other president in this century. His re-organization of the civil service will long be recognized as one of the most significant contributions of his presidency. The Civil Service Reform Act of 1978 was the first major revamping of the federal civil service since its creation in 1883. The 1978 act abolished the century-old Civil Service Commission (CSC) and replaced it with three agencies, each designed to handle one of the CSC's functions on the theory that the competing demands of these functions had given the CSC an "identity crisis." The Merit Systems Protection Board

(MSPB) was created to defend competitive merit recruitment and promotion from political encroachment. A separate Federal Labor Relations Authority (FLRA) was set up to administer collective bargaining and individual personnel grievances. The third new agency, the Office of Personnel Management (OPM), was created to manage recruiting, testing, training, and the retirement system. The Senior Executive Service was also created at this time to recognize and foster "public management" as a profession and to facilitate the movement of top, "supergrade" career officials across agencies and departments.[37]

Carter also tried to impose a stringent budgetary process on all executive agencies. Called "zero-base budgeting," it was a method of budgeting from the bottom up, wherein each agency was required to rejustify its entire mission rather than merely its next year's increase. Zero-base budgeting did not succeed, but the effort was not lost on President Reagan. Although Reagan gave the impression of being a laid-back president, he actually centralized management to an unprecedented degree. From Carter's "bottom-up" approach, Reagan went to a "top-down" approach, whereby the initial budgetary decisions would be made in the White House and the agencies would be required to fit within those decisions. This process converted the Office of Management and Budget (OMB) into an agency of policy determination and presidential management.[38] President Bush took Reagan's centralization strategy even further in using the White House staff instead of Cabinet secretaries for managing the executive branch.[39]

President Clinton engaged in the most systematic effort to "change the way the government does business," a phrase he used often to describe the goal of his National Performance Review (NPR), one of the most important administrative reform efforts of the twentieth century. In September 1993, he launched the NPR, based on a set of 384 proposals drafted by a panel headed by Vice President Al Gore. The avowed goal of the NPR was to "reinvent government"—to make the federal bureaucracy more efficient, accountable, and effective. But this is little more than new language for the same management goal held by each of his predecessors.

Virtually all observers agree that the NPR has made substantial progress. Its original goal was to save more than $100 billion over five years, in large part by cutting the federal workforce by 12 percent (more than 270,000 jobs) by the end of 1999. Actually, by the end of 1997, $111.8 billion in savings were already assured through legislative or administrative action. Another $18.1 billion in savings were contained in legislation pending before Congress as the second session of the 105th Congress began in 1998. The administration, under the leadership of Vice President Gore, claims that still another $24.8 billion in savings can be realized by acting on recommendations through the year 2000[40].

The NPR has also focused on cutting red tape, streamlining procurement (how the government purchases goods and services), improving the coordination of federal management, and simplifying federal rules. For instance, the OMB abolished the notorious ten-thousand-page Federal Personnel Manual and the Standard Form 171, the government's lengthy job application form. Another example is even more revealing of the nature of the NPR's work: the Defense Department's method for reimbursing its employees' travel expenses used to take seventeen steps and two months; an employee-designed reform encouraged by the NPR streamlined this to a four-step, computer-based

Downsizing Government: The National Performance Review

With the growth of the modern federal bureaucracy came the escalation of reformist cries. In the 1930s, a report by a committee charged with evaluating the growth of the national government called for a larger and more diversified bureaucracy to aid the president. But by the 1980s, reformers were calling for a smaller, less expensive bureaucracy with reduced powers that was also more compatible with democratic values of accountability. The Clinton administration, too, embraced the call for smaller government. In its National Performance Review (NPR), headed by Vice President Al Gore, a wide variety of recommendations were offered to make government work better at lower cost. The initial report, presented in September 1993, made 384 recommendations, incorporating 1,250 specific actions designed to save over $100 billion over five years. In the next two years, many of the report's recommendations were implemented by presidential directive, congressional enactment, and agency agreement.

Supporters of the effort have applauded the downsizing project. While smaller and less expensive government has been its primary goal, the NPR has also sought to encourage initiative within agencies and make them more responsive to citizens and others they serve. For example, the Food and Drug Administration (FDA) had been criticized for taking too long to approve new drugs and therapies for such illnesses as cancer and AIDS. Under NPR guidelines, the FDA announced in 1996 that it would accelerate the approval process for new cancer therapies. It also agreed to make promising but not yet fully approved cancer therapies available to patients lacking other treatment possibilities. And it pledged to be more responsive to the perspectives of cancer patients and others affected by FDA rulings.

By the end of 1995, agencies had implemented about 400 specific recommendations, producing $58 billion in savings. An additional $28 billion in annual reductions were also announced, as well as the elimination of 16,000 pages of regulations. Efforts to democratize the enforcement of regulations were also announced, designed to improve relations between regulatory agencies and those being regulated. As part of the NPR effort, President Clinton's 1997 budget proposed a 22 percent, six-year reduction in the overall size of domestic agencies. Congress proposed an even greater reduction. Efforts to reduce the size of the bureaucracy, while making it more efficient and responsive, will continue because of bipartisan agreement and public support.

Critics of the NPR point out its goals have more to do with politics than good policy. The image of a Washington-centered bureaucracy dominated by career civil servants contradicts the facts: 90 percent of all federal employees work outside of the Washington, D.C., area; the only part of the bureaucracy that has grown in size in the last thirty years is the number of political appointees; the federal civilian workforce of 2.1 million employees is actually smaller than it was in 1960, despite the fact that the government does more today; and major domestic social programs are carried out by state and local governments or private contractors, not by federal employees.

Given these facts, the main reason for the NPR, according to critics, has been political—to appeal to voters who supported Ross Perot's 1992 and 1996 presidential campaigns, which criticized government waste. The underlying concept of the NPR, to develop a bureaucracy that costs less but also works better, is contradictory. Government workers have pointed out that they have suffered from more than a decade of budget cuts, and that further cuts would simply result in doing less with less. Although the NPR did produce some initial savings, most of the proposed savings were difficult to implement, much less measure. For example, some early savings were reported by the administration to be $6 billion. But a review by the Congressional Budget Office reported that these savings were actually only $2.5 billion.

In sum, the NPR, according to critics, is just one more politically inspired pseudo-reform that will pass into history when a new presidential administration takes over.

procedure taking less than fifteen minutes, with an anticipated savings of $1 billion over five years.

One potentially significant weakness of the NPR noted by critics is that it has no strategy for dealing with congressional opposition to certain bureaucratic reforms. Donald Kettl, a respected reform advocate, warned that "virtually no reform that really matters can be achieved without at least implicit congressional support. The NPR has not yet developed a full strategy for winning that support."[41] One consequence, for instance, is that in 1994 Congress voted to exempt the Department of Veterans Affairs from the personnel reductions imposed by the NPR, a development that could make attainment of the NPR's goals impossible. A good way to fight such congressional actions is with publicity, but it is a troubling sign for the NPR's long-term prospects (and for President Clinton's standing) that national polls say two-thirds of Americans either have never heard of the NPR or believe the federal government is continuing to grow.[42] Another problem within the NPR is that continuing pressure to cut appropriations for agencies "has put a premium on preserving particular programs, projects, and activities from Executive Branch as well as congressional action." It also contributes to a climate in which agencies are afraid to take risks and be creative.[43]

The overall accomplishment of President Clinton and the NPR has certainly been respectable, even in the eyes of the Republican opposition. But despite this accomplishment and the optimism about further reform, a certain humility is in order when we think about "reinventing" the federal civil service. To make incremental changes in bureaucracies, even valuable ones, is possible; to change the very nature of bureaucracy is not.

The Problem of Management Control by the White House Staff   The Cabinet's inability to perform as a board of directors (see Chapter 13), and the inability of any other agency to perform that function have left a management vacuum in the U.S. government. OMB has met part of the need, and indeed the management power of the director of OMB seems to increase with each new president. But the need for executive management control goes far beyond what even the boldest of OMB directors can achieve. The White House staff has filled this vacuum to a certain extent precisely because, in the past thirty years, the "special assistants to the president" have been given relatively specialized jurisdictions over one or more departments or strategic issues. These staffers have additional power and credibility beyond their access to the president because they also have access to confidential information. Since information is the most important bureaucratic resource, White House staff members gain management power by having access to the CIA for international intelligence and the FBI and Treasury for knowledge about the personal life of every government official (since each government employee has to go through a rigorous FBI security clearance procedure prior to being appointed and promoted).

Responsible bureaucracy, however, is not going to come simply from more presidential power, more administrative staff, and more management control. All this was inadequate to the task of keeping the National Security Council staff from seizing the initiative to run its own policies toward Iran and Nicaragua for at least two years (1985–86) after Congress had explicitly restricted activities toward Nicaragua and the president had forbidden negotiations

In 1987, Oliver North, an aide to President Reagan's National Security Council, testified before a joint congressional committee investigating the Iran-Contra affair. Such congressional investigations are a classic example of oversight.

oversight

the effort by Congress, through hearings, investigations, and other techniques, to exercise control over the activities of executive agencies

with Iran. The Tower Commission, appointed to investigate the Iran-Contra affair, concluded that although there was nothing fundamentally wrong with the institutions involved in foreign-policy making—the Department of State, the Department of Defense, the White House, and Congress—there had been a "flawed process," "a failure of responsibility," and a thinness of the president's personal engagement in the issues. The Tower Commission found that "at no time did [President Reagan] insist upon accountability and performance review."[44]

No particular management style is guaranteed to work. Each White House management innovation, from one president to the next, shows only the inadequacy of the approaches of previous presidents. And as the White House and the Executive Office of the President grow, the management bureaucracy itself becomes a management problem. Something more and different is obviously needed.

CONGRESS AND RESPONSIBLE BUREAUCRACY

Congress is constitutionally essential to responsible bureaucracy because ultimately the key to bureaucratic responsibility is legislation. When a law is passed and its intent is clear, the accountability for implementation of that law is also clear. Then the president knows what to "faithfully execute," and the responsible agency understands what is expected of it. But when Congress enacts vague legislation, agencies must resort to their own interpretations. The president and the federal courts often step in to tell agencies what the legislation intended. And so do the most intensely interested groups. Yet when everybody, from president to courts to interest groups, gets involved in the actual interpretation of legislative intent, to whom and to what is the agency accountable? Even when the agency wants to behave responsibly, how shall accountability be accomplished?

Congress's answer is **oversight.** The more power Congress has delegated to the executive, the more it has sought to reinvolve itself in directing the interpretation of laws through committee and subcommittee oversight of each agency. The standing committee system in Congress is well suited for oversight, inasmuch as most of the congressional committees and subcommittees have jurisdictions roughly parallel to one or more departments and agencies, and members of Congress who sit on these committees can develop expertise equal to that of the bureaucrats. Appropriations committees as well as authorization committees have oversight powers—as do their respective subcommittees. In addition to these, the Government Reform and Oversight Committee in the House and the Governmental Affairs Committee in the Senate have oversight powers not limited by departmental jurisdiction.

The best indication of Congress's oversight efforts is the use of public hearings, before which bureaucrats and other witnesses are summoned to discuss and defend agency budgets and past decisions. The data drawn from systematic studies of congressional committee and subcommittee hearings and meetings show quite dramatically that Congress has tried through oversight to keep pace with the expansion of the executive branch. Between 1950 and 1980, for example, the annual number of committee and subcommittee meetings in the House of Representatives rose steadily from 3,210 to 7,022; in the Senate, the number of such meetings rose from 2,607 to 4,265 (in 1975–76).

Beginning in 1980 in the House and 1978 in the Senate, the number of committee and subcommittee hearings and meetings slowly began to decline, reaching 4,222 in the House and 2,597 in the Senate by the mid-1980s. This pattern of rise and decline in committee and subcommittee oversight activity strongly suggests that congressional vigilance toward the executive branch is responsive more to long-term growth in government than to yearly activity or to partisan considerations.[45] This is one of the best and most reassuring indications that Congress is committed to keeping the bureaucracy accountable.

Although congressional oversight is potent because of Congress's power to make, and therefore to change, the law, often the most effective and influential lever over bureaucratic accountability is "the power of the purse"—the ability of the House and Senate committees and subcommittees on appropriations to look at agency performance through the microscope of the annual appropriations process (see Chapter 12). A trenchant evaluation of oversight through the appropriations process is provided by the foremost student of the whole budgetary process, the late Aaron Wildavsky:

> The process of annually appropriating funds for federal agencies is intended to enforce dependence upon Congress of those agencies' officers. Unless an agency justifies itself each year, it risks losing funding. If the agency behaves in ways that upset Congress, [Congress] has an annual opportunity to bring the agency into line through threats or actual changes of appropriations. . . . We may ask why budget oversight . . . is not left to the authorizing committees . . . which write the legislation that creates, and gives power to, the agencies. The answer is that they do not have budget powers because Congress does not trust them to control themselves. [Members of] Congress . . . believe that members of the authorizing committees have very strong incentives to ally with the agencies they authorize. . . . [I]ntensive review enables members and staff of the appropriate . . . subcommittee to judge whether an agency is using the money as Congress intended, or as its members intend, rather than in the political interests of the current administration or the desires of administrators.[46]

In a public hearing before a House subcommittee, Kimberly Bergalis, who contracted AIDS from her dentist and later died from the disease, urged the subcommittee to enact legislation to make AIDS testing mandatory for health care workers.

POLITICS ON THE WEB

Can the Internet assist in efforts to "reinvent" government? In the long run it could, by helping to streamline agencies, publicize decisions, and improve communication. More importantly, the Internet can make a tremendous difference in the public's trust in government. In recent years federal agencies have used the Internet to help dispel negative public perceptions. For example, the Internal Revenue Service has made all tax forms available on the Web; soon you will be able to submit your taxes electronically, increasing accuracy and speeding refunds. Detailed data from the Census Bureau, campaign spending reports, and national and world economic statistics are also easily accessible on the Web. Even the Central Intelligence Agency, long suspicious of publicity, has developed a popular "kid secret zone" on its website. The hope is that these and similar efforts will counter the hostility and distrust that Americans have shown toward government, particularly the bureaucracy.
www.wwnorton.com/wtp2e

A more recent evaluation of the budget and appropriations process by the NPR is in full accord with Wildavsky's assessment but expresses one serious concern about oversight through appropriation: pressure to cut appropriations "has put a premium on preserving particular programs, projects, and activities from Executive Branch as well as congressional action."[47] This may be another explanation for why there may be some downsizing but almost no terminations of federal agencies.

Oversight can also be carried out by individual members of Congress. Such inquiries addressed to bureaucrats are considered standard congressional "case work" and can turn up significant questions of public responsibility even when the motivation is only to meet the demand of an individual constituent. Oversight also takes place through communications between congressional staff and agency staff. The number of congressional staff has been enlarged tremendously since the Legislative Reorganization Act of 1946, and the legislative staff, especially the staff of the committees, is just as professionalized and specialized as the staff of executive agencies. In addition, Congress has created for itself three large agencies whose obligations are to engage in constant research on problems taking place in or confronted by the executive branch. These are the General Accounting Office (GAO), the Congressional Research Service (CRS), and the Congressional Budget Office (CBO). Each of these agencies is designed to give Congress information independent of the information it can get directly from the executive branch through hearings and other communications.[48] Another source of information for oversight is direct from citizens through the Freedom of Information Act (FOIA), which gives ordinary citizens the right of access to agency files and agency data to determine whether derogatory information exists in the file about the citizens themselves and to learn about what the agency is doing in general. Nevertheless, the information gained by citizens through FOIA can be effective only through the institutionalized channels of congressional committees and, on a few occasions, through public-interest litigation in the federal courts.

Citizens and Bureaucracy

In France, citizens are called *administrés* by officials, meaning "administered persons"; this implies that citizens are expected to allow themselves to be administered, to be dealt with as part of continuous, routine business. Americans, too, believe that being a good citizen includes cooperation with the authorities and appreciation of the necessity for orderly conduct of public business. This is sometimes referred to as "civic duty" or "civic responsibility."

But good citizenship does not mean acceptance of powerlessness and resignation to one's fate without a whimper. Citizens are not powerless in the face of government bureaucracy. To have a healthy and effective relationship with bureaucracies, citizens must know their rights, and they must also know something about the agency or agencies of their concern. Whether it has to do with taxes and the IRS, or passports and the State Department, or the motor vehicles agency or absentee voting or traffic cops at the state and local levels, citizens have more tools available to them than they may think.

In the first place, as suggested earlier, public bureaucrats are subject to a great deal more access from the public than are private bureaucrats. They are required to maintain a far more thorough paper trail. People often complain about "red tape," implying that bureaucrats maintain bothersome procedures, require too many forms, and spend too much of their time exchanging memoranda. But as soon as there is an accident, such as the explosion of the *Challenger* or an airplane crash, everybody, not only the victims and their families, wants to know "who's to blame?" All that red tape becomes important, and citizens want to know and have a right to know.

Public access to the workings of bureaucracies has been vastly facilitated in the past thirty years, in large part due to FOIA, which was enacted in 1966. Under FOIA, ordinary citizens can request documents from any government agency; even CIA and FBI files are available under certain conditions. It takes a lot of time and effort to get such files, but it can be done. The news media can (and do) also use FOIA, which is why newspapers and their reporters have so much more access to public bureaucracies than they ever had before. The public in general and interested citizens in particular gain from this access. Moreover, although general newspapers have limited space and resources for reporting on all agencies, specialized newspapers are actively involved in investigating and reporting on agency activities. This textbook regularly cites the *Congressional Quarterly,* which reports regularly on the activities of the legislative branch but which often has good materials on agencies in the executive branch, as well. The *National Journal* also reports extensively on government agencies. Innumerable trade magazines, whose subscribers are largely the companies and individuals whose livings are earned in a particular trade or sector of the economy, perform superbly as critics and exposers of the agencies and decisions within their area of concern.

Michael Ravnitsky with some of the 900 FBI files he has requested under the Freedom of Information Act.

The activities of important "think tanks" (independently financed policy-research organizations in Washington, D.C., and elsewhere around the country) revolve around the formation and implementation of public policy. The Brookings Institution, for example, has been studying government policies and agencies for more than six decades, and, although considered more favorably disposed toward Democratic administrations, it is widely respected in all quarters. The same might be said of the best-known conservative-leaning think thank, the American Enterprise Institute, which has been a particularly important source of analysis and criticism of policies and agencies for the past twenty years.

Many of these information sources are already on the Internet. The same is true for a wide variety of government-provided publications of information on agencies and policies. Fortunately, virtually every college and university in the United States provides access to the Internet.

The bad news is that, although citizen influence on bureaucracy is definitely possible, it is expensive—in time and money. This gives it an upper-middle-class bias. The poor and uneducated lack virtually all the resources necessary to use the channels and opportunities available. But this class bias exists in all endeavors and walks of life; it is not particularly worse in the realm of bureaucracy. In fact, in many respects, now that political parties play less of a role in running the government, interaction with federal, state, and local agencies may be less daunting and discouraging than trying to influence legislatures.

In the final analysis, the best approach for citizens to take in trying to influence bureaucracy is to insist on clear rules and laws, maximum openness in agency decisions, clear rationales for those decisions, and accessible means for questioning and appealing those decisions. These methods are equally applicable to Congress as to the bureaucracy. The very best approach for Congress to ensure accountability of the bureaucracy is for Congress to spend more time clarifying its legislative intent and less time on oversight. Bureaucrats are more responsive to clear legislative guidance than to anything else, and when Congress and the president are at odds about the interpretation of laws, bureaucrats can evade responsibility by playing off one branch against another. If Congress's intent in its laws is made more clear, it could then defer far more to presidential management and presidential maintenance of bureaucratic accountability. Moreover, clearer laws from Congress and clearer rules and decisions made by administrative agencies would reduce the need for courts to review those laws and decisions; judicial approaches to administrative accountability are the most expensive and time consuming, and therefore the least available to individual citizens.

Bureaucracy and democracy can be more comfortable allies rather than warring adversaries. Make no mistake about it, however: bureaucracy is here to stay. No reinvention of government, or radical decentralization of power, or substantial budget-cutting, or reductions in personnel can alter the basic fact of bureaucracy or resolve the problem of reconciling bureaucracy with democracy. As is true of all complex social and political problems, the solution of the conflict between bureaucracy and democracy lies in a sober awareness of the nature of the problem.

★ Summary

Bureaucracy is a universal form of organization, found in businesses, churches, foundations, and universities, as well as in the public sphere. All essential government services and regulations are carried out by bureaucracies—specifically, by administrative agencies. Bureaucrats are appointed to their offices based on the "merit system." Federal bureaucrats are generally better educated than the U.S. population as a whole. Women and African Americans are also well represented, although they tend to be concentrated at the lower pay levels.

The agencies of the executive branch can be grouped into four categories: (1) clientele agencies, (2) agencies for maintaining the Union, (3) regulatory agencies, and (4) agencies for redistribution. All of these agencies are alike in that they are all bureaucratic. These agencies differ in the way they are organized, in the way they participate in the political process, and in their levels of responsiveness to political authority. In recent years, attempts have been made to reduce or "downsize" the bureaucracy by termination, devolution, and privatization. Although these efforts are popular with the American people, they cannot reduce the size of the federal bureaucracy by much.

The executive and the legislative branches do the toughest job any government is called on to do: making the bureaucracy accountable to the people. Democratizing bureaucracy is the unending task of politics in a democracy.

FOR FURTHER READING

Arnold, Peri E. *Making the Managerial Presidency: Comprehensive Organization Planning.* Princeton: Princeton University Press, 1986.

Fesler, James W., and Donald F. Kettl. *The Politics of the Administrative Process.* Chatham, NJ: Chatham House, 1991.

Skowronek, Stephen. *Building a New American State: The Expansion of National Administrative Capacities,* 1877–1920. New York: Cambridge University Press, 1982.

Wildavsky, Aaron. *The New Politics of the Budget Process.* 2nd ed. New York: HarperCollins, 1992.

Wilson, James Q. *Bureaucracy: What Government Agencies Do and Why They Do It.* New York: Basic Books, 1989.

Wood, Dan B. *Bureaucratic Dynamics: The Role of Bureaucracy in a Democracy.* Boulder, CO: Westview, 1994.

STUDY OUTLINE

Bureaucracy and Bureaucrats

1. Bureaucracy is simply a form of organization. Specialization and repetition are essential to the efficiency of any organization.
2. Despite fears of bureaucratic growth, the federal service has grown little during the past twenty-five years. The national government is large, but the federal service has not been growing any faster than the economy or the society.
3. Bureaucratic communication leaves a paper trail which, although unpopular, provides a means of holding bureaucrats responsible and accountable.
4. Because statutes and executive orders often provide only vague instructions, one important job of the bureaucrat is to interpret the intentions of Congress and the president prior to implementation of orders.
5. The lower efficiency of public agencies can be attributed to the added constraints put on them, as compared to those put on private agencies.
6. Through civil service reform, national and state governments have attempted to reduce political interference in public bureaucracies by granting certain public bureaucrats legal protection from being fired without a show of cause.
7. In terms of the hiring of various demographic groups, the federal civil service—like the rest of society—has problems, but it has been improving.

The Organization of the Executive Branch

1. One type of executive agency—the clientele agency—exists to foster the interests of a specific group in society. In turn, that group works to support its agency when it is in jeopardy.
2. America's chief revenue agency, the Internal Revenue Service, engenders hostility rather than clientele support among groups and individual citizens. For the most part, American tax-policy making is centralized; agreements are struck between the president, the Treasury Department, and the leading members of the two tax committees in Congress.
3. Political considerations have frequently had an impact both on agencies for internal security and on agencies for external national security.
4. Regulatory agencies in the United States are given the authority to regulate various industries; these agencies often act like courts when making decisions or settling disputes.
5. Agencies of redistribution influence the amount of money in the economy and directly influence who has money, who has credit, and whether people will want to invest or spend.

Can the Bureaucracy Be Reduced?

1. The bureaucracy can be reduced in three ways: termination, devolution, and privatization.

Can Bureaucracy Be Controlled?

1. Each expansion of the national government in the twentieth century has been accompanied by a parallel expansion of presidential management authority, but the expansion of presidential power cannot guarantee responsible bureaucracy.
2. Although Congress attempts to control the bureaucracy through oversight, a more effective way to ensure accountability may be to clarify legislative intent.

PRACTICE QUIZ

1. Which of the following best describes the growth of the federal service in the past twenty-five years?
   a) rampant, exponential growth
   b) little growth at all
   c) decrease in the total number of federal employees.
   d) vast, compared to the growth of the economy and the society

2. A means by which bureaucrats are regularly held accountable is
   a) media scrutiny.
   b) presidential site visits.
   c) the paper trail.
   d) none of the above

3. What task must bureaucrats perform if Congress charges them with enforcing a law through explicit directions?
   a) implementation
   b) interpretation
   c) lawmaking
   d) quasi-judicial decision making

4. Which of the following was *not* a component of the 1978 civil service reforms?
   a) the merit system
   b) a type of tenure system
   c) a spoils system
   d) All of the above were associated with the 1978 civil service reforms.

5. Which of the following terms best characterizes the representation of African Americans in the federal workforce?
   a) overrepresentation
   b) underrepresentation
   c) nonexistent
   d) bifurcated

6. Which of the following is a way in which the bureaucracy might be reduced?
   a) devolution
   b) termination
   c) privatization
   d) all of the above

7. Which of the following is *not* an example of a clientele agency?
   a) Department of Justice
   b) Department of Commerce
   c) Department of Agriculture
   d) Department of Housing and Urban Development

8. What explains the FBI's political significance as compared to the other divisions and bureaus within the Department of Justice?
   a) the FBI's higher legal status
   b) the leadership of J. Edgar Hoover in the 1920s and 1930s
   c) the FBI's clientele nature
   d) the FBI's relationship to the CIA

9. The concept of oversight refers to the effort made by
   a) Congress to make executive agencies accountable for their actions.
   b) the president to make Congress accountable for its actions.
   c) the courts to make executive agencies responsible for their actions.
   d) the states to make the executive branch accountable for its actions.

10. Which president instituted the stringent budgetary process known as "zero-base budgeting"?
    a) Richard Nixon
    b) Lyndon Johnson
    c) Jimmy Carter
    d) Ronald Reagan

CRITICAL THINKING QUESTIONS

1. Often the efficiency of public bureaucracies is judged in terms of the efficiency of private business and other organizations. In many instances, government has been expected to do things that businesses in the marketplace have chosen not to do or have found unprofitable. Might the tasks that government is asked to perform be more prone to inefficiency? Think about the ways in which business might be able to perform some tasks that government currently performs. Would business necessarily perform these tasks more efficiently? Should efficiency be the only priority in the public enterprise?

2. Describe the ways in which the public controls its bureaucracy. How much and what kind of control should the public exercise? Through elected officials—i.e., the president and the Congress—the public can achieve some control over the bureaucracy. What are the relative advantages and disadvantages of presidential and congressional control of the bureaucracy?

KEY TERMS

accountability (p. 542)
administrative adjudication (p. 542)
bureaucracy (p. 537)
clientele agencies (p. 551)
department (p. 548)
deregulation (p. 562)
devolution (p. 562)
Federal Reserve System (p. 559)

fiscal policy (p. 558)
government corporation (p. 550)
implementation (p. 542)
independent agency (p. 550)
iron triangle (p. 552)
means testing (p. 559)
merit system (p. 543)
oversight (p. 568)

paper trail (p. 541)
privatization (p. 562)
redistributive agencies (p. 558)
regulatory agencies (p. 557)
revenue agencies (p. 553)
rulemaking (p. 542)

15

The Federal

Courts

I N recent years, colleges and universities have seen a flood of civil and criminal litigation. Faculty members denied promotion or tenure have brought suits charging that their school's action was biased. Although the most familiar bias complaints involve allegations of discrimination against women or African Americans, it is becoming increasingly common for white male professors to charge that they, too, are the victims of prejudice. In one recent case, for example, a white male job applicant sued the College of Charleston in South Carolina, alleging that he had been denied a tenure-track position in the college's religious studies department because he was a devout Christian. The college denied the allegation, asserting that it had offered the position to the best qualified person from among nearly three hundred applicants—this individual happened to be Jewish. The judge who heard the case ruled in favor of the college.[1] In another recent federal court case, a white Duke University professor charged that he had been denied tenure simply because his department wished to fire a black professor and feared that it would be charged with racial bias if it did not also fire a white professor.[2]

In other instances, students may become involved in legal disputes. During the 1960s, of course, litigation initiated by African American students compelled many all-white universities in the South, such as the University of Mississippi and the University of Alabama, to admit black students. More recently, the battle for integration has broadened to include issues of gender as well as race. In 1994 and 1996, for example, the Supreme Court ordered the Citadel and the Virginia Military Institute, both all-male military colleges, to accept women who wished to attend. The Court reasoned that since these colleges were supported by public funds, they were prohibited by federal civil rights law from discriminating on the basis of gender in their admissions policies.[3] Another area of litigation at universities involves tuition. In 1997, a University of North Carolina graduate sued the school, asserting that he was overcharged for tuition during his senior year. Although the student was not a North Carolina resident when he arrived at Chapel Hill as a freshman, he asserts that after three years of residence at the university he should have been eligible for the lower in-state tuition charge.[4]

Gender discrimination has been the issue in a number of court cases arising from Title IX of the federal Higher Education Act. Title IX, among other things, requires colleges and universities to spend substantially equal amounts of money on men's and women's athletic programs. This requirement was resisted by a number of universities until female athletes began to secure federal court orders compelling schools to comply with the law. One university that has taken Title IX seriously is the University of Connecticut, which saw its men's and women's basketball teams ranked first in the nation in 1995.

Students and Politics

Clashes between university administrations and students with strong religious views have become more pronounced since the 1995 *Rosenberger v. University of Virginia* decision. In a 1997 suit filed in U.S. District Court in Connecticut, four students at Yale University sued the school over the requirement that all students live on campus during their freshman and sophomore years. The plaintiffs, dubbed the "Yale Four," claimed that such a requirement discriminates against their religion, Orthodox Judaism, which requires modesty in interactions with the opposite sex. (Yale dormitories frequently have coed floors and bathrooms.) The administration held that living on campus and exposure to students of different backgrounds and beliefs is integral to the learning experience at Yale. "We believe the undergraduate experience is more than just the classroom," says Richard Levin, Yale's president. "And we believe these aren't just dormitories, but communities.... These students want the education, but they don't want the encounter." But Batsheva Greer, one of the plaintiffs, could not reconcile religion and university policy. "It's not like I was debating the issue," she said of her decision to join the lawsuit. "It was definite in my mind. There was just no question that I would be sacrificing my religious upbringing to live on campus.... We're not out to change the university. We're just trying to live in accordance with Judaism."

SOURCE: Samuel G. Freedman, "Yeshivish at Yale," *New York Times Magazine,* May 24, 1998, p. 23.

Still another area of litigation pits students against faculty members and faculty against their universities: sexual harassment. Over the past several years, most schools have adopted rules and administrative procedures designed to protect students from inappropriate sexual overtures on the part of faculty and staff members. Until recently, students who were the victims of such harassment were often discouraged from making complaints. Today, however, most schools encourage students to bring complaints to administrative and faculty committees that investigate and punish violations of sexual conduct rules. Procedures for bringing charges are now widely publicized on most campuses. As a result, sexual harassment complaints have become more common at many schools.

Some college faculty members have charged that the rules governing sexual harassment are vaguely drawn and that the committees charged with investigating complaints are often biased against the accused. Several professors found guilty by college officials of harassment have filed suit in the federal courts to have these findings reversed. In one recent case that arose at the University of New Hampshire, for example, an English professor was disciplined and suspended because of sexual references he allegedly made during his class lectures. In 1994, a federal judge, asserting that the professor's comments fell well within the area of speech protected by the First Amendment, ordered the university to reinstate the professor and pay him nearly a quarter of a million dollars in back pay, damages, and legal fees.[5]

This sea of litigation is hardly unique to academe. University students and faculty are no more litigious than other Americans. Every year nearly twenty-five million cases are tried in American courts and one American in every nine is directly involved in litigation. Cases can arise from disputes between citizens, from efforts by government agencies to punish wrongdoing, or from citizens' efforts to prove that a right provided them by law has been infringed upon as a result of government action—or inaction. Many critics of the U.S. legal system assert that Americans have become much too litigious (ready to use the courts for all purposes), and perhaps that is true. But the heavy use that Americans make of the courts is also an indication of the extent of conflict in American society. And given the existence of social conflict, it is far better that Americans seek to settle their differences through the courts rather than by fighting or feuding.

The framers of the American Constitution called the Supreme Court the "least dangerous branch" of American government. Today, it is not unusual to hear friends *and* foes of the Court refer to it as the "imperial judiciary."[6] Before we can understand this transformation and its consequences, however, we must look in some detail at America's judicial process.

- *In this chapter we will first examine the legal system, including the types of cases that the federal courts consider and the types of law with which they deal.*

- *Second, we will assess the organization and structure of the federal court system as well as the flow of cases through the courts.*

- *Third, we will consider judicial review and how it makes the Supreme Court a "lawmaking body."* We will also analyze the procedures of and influences on the Supreme Court.

- *Finally, we will consider the role and power of the federal courts in the American political process, looking in particular at the growth of judicial power in the United States.* We conclude by looking at how this changing role affects liberty and democracy.

Some critics contend that American society has become too litigious, citing an increase in the number of "frivolous lawsuits" filed each year, such as the one filed by this homeless man against the Morristown Public Library, which had ejected him for offensive personal hygiene.

★ The Legal System

▶ Within what broad categories of law do cases arise?

▶ How is the U.S. court system structured?

Originally, a "court" was the place where a sovereign ruled—where the king and his entourage governed. Settling disputes between citizens was part of governing. According to the Bible, King Solomon had to settle the dispute between two women over which of them was the mother of the child both claimed. Judging is the settling of disputes, a function that was slowly separated from the king and the king's court and made into a separate institution of government. Courts have taken over from kings the power to settle controversies by hearing the facts on both sides and deciding which side possesses the greater merit. But since judges are not kings, they must have a basis for their authority. That basis in the United States is the Constitution and the law. Courts decide cases by hearing the facts on both sides of a dispute and applying the relevant law or principle to the facts.

CASES AND THE LAW

Court cases in the United States proceed under three broad categories of law: criminal law, civil law, and public law (see Table 15.1).

Cases of **criminal law** are those in which the government charges an individual with violating a statute that has been enacted to protect the public health, safety, morals, or welfare. In criminal cases, the government is always the **plaintiff** (the party that brings charges) and alleges that a criminal violation has been committed by a named **defendant.** Most criminal cases arise in state and municipal courts and involve matters ranging from traffic offenses through robbery and murder. Another large and growing body of federal criminal law

criminal law

the branch of law that deals with disputes or actions involving criminal penalties (as opposed to civil law); it regulates the conduct of individuals, defines crimes, and provides punishment for criminal acts

plaintiff

the individual or organization who brings a complaint in court

defendant

the one against whom a complaint is brought in a criminal or civil case

Table 15.1	TYPES OF LAWS AND DISPUTES	
Type of law	**Type of case or dispute**	**Form of case**
Criminal law	Cases arising out of actions that violate laws protecting the health, safety, and morals of the community. The government is always the plaintiff.	*U.S. (or state) v. Jones* *Jones v. U.S. (or state)*, if Jones lost and is appealing
Civil law	"Private law," involving disputes between citizens or between government and citizen where no crime is alleged. Two general types are contract and tort. *Contract cases* are disputes that arise over voluntary actions. *Tort cases* are disputes that arise out of obligations inherent in social life. Negligence and slander are examples of torts.	*Smith v. Jones* *New York v. Jones* *U.S. v. Jones* *Jones v. New York*
Public law	All cases where the powers of government or the rights of citizens are involved. The government is the defendant. *Constitutional law* involves judicial review of the basis of a government's action in relation to specific clauses of the Constitution as interpreted in Supreme Court cases. *Administrative law* involves disputes over the statutory authority, jurisdiction, or procedures of administrative agencies.	*Jones v. U.S. (or state)* *In re Jones* *Smith v. Jones*, if a license or statute is at issue in their private dispute

civil law

a system of jurisprudence, including private law and governmental actions, to settle disputes that do not involve criminal penalties

deals with such matters as tax evasion, mail fraud, and the sale of narcotics. Defendants found guilty of criminal violations may be fined or sent to prison.

Cases of **civil law** involve disputes among individuals or between individuals and the government where no criminal violation is charged. Unlike criminal cases, the losers in civil cases cannot be fined or sent to prison, although they may be required to pay monetary damages for their actions. In a civil case, the one who brings a complaint is the plaintiff and the one against whom the complaint is brought is the defendant. The two most common types of civil cases involve contracts and torts. In a typical contract case, an individual or corporation charges that it has suffered because of another's violation of a specific agreement between the two. For example, the Smith Manufacturing Corporation may charge that Jones Distributors failed to honor an agreement to deliver raw materials at a specified time, causing Smith to lose business. Smith asks the court to order Jones to compensate it for the damage allegedly suffered. In a typical tort case, one individual charges that he or she has been injured by another's negligence or malfeasance. Medical malpractice suits are one example of tort cases.

In deciding civil cases, courts apply statutes (laws) and legal **precedent** (prior decisions). State and federal statutes, for example, often govern the conditions under which contracts are and are not legally binding. Jones Distributors might argue that it was not obliged to fulfill its contract with the Smith Corporation because actions by Smith, such as the failure to make promised payments, constituted fraud under state law. Attorneys for a physician being sued for malpractice, on the other hand, may search for prior instances in which courts ruled that actions similar to those of their client did not constitute negligence. Such precedents are applied under the doctrine of *stare decisis,* a Latin phrase meaning "let the decision stand."

A case becomes a matter of the third category, **public law,** when a plaintiff or defendant in a civil or criminal case seeks to show that their case involves the powers of government or rights of citizens as defined under the Constitution or by statute. One major form of public law is constitutional law, under which a court will examine the government's actions to see if they conform to the Constitution as it has been interpreted by the judiciary. Thus, what began as an ordinary criminal case may enter the realm of public law if a defendant claims that his or her constitutional rights were violated by the police. Another important arena of public law is administrative law, which involves disputes over the jurisdiction, procedures, or authority of administrative agencies. Under this type of law, civil litigation between an individual and the government may become a matter of public law if the individual asserts that the government is violating a statute or abusing its power under the Constitution. For example, landowners have asserted that federal and state restrictions on land use constitute violations of the Fifth Amendment's restrictions on the government's ability to confiscate private property. Recently, the Supreme Court has been very sympathetic to such claims, which effectively transform an ordinary civil dispute into a major issue of public law.

Most of the important Supreme Court cases we will examine in this chapter involve judgments concerning the constitutional or statutory basis of the actions of government agencies. As we shall see, it is in this arena of public law that the Supreme Court's decisions can have significant consequences for American politics and society.

TYPES OF COURTS

In the United States, systems of courts have been established both by the federal government and by the governments of the individual states. Both systems have several levels, as shown in Figure 15.1. More than 99 percent of all court cases in the United States are heard in state courts. The overwhelming majority of criminal cases, for example, involve violations of state laws prohibiting such actions as murder, robbery, fraud, theft, and assault. If such a case is brought to trial, it will be heard in a state **trial court,** in front of a judge and sometimes a jury, who will determine whether the defendant violated state law. If the defendant is convicted, he or she may appeal the conviction to a higher court, such as a state **appellate court,** and from there to a state's **supreme court.** Similarly, in civil cases, most litigation is brought in the courts established by the state in which the activity in question took place. For example, a patient bringing suit

---

precedents

prior cases whose principles are used by judges as the bases for their decisions in present cases

stare decisis

literally, "let the decision stand." The doctrine that a previous decision by a court applies as a precedent in similar cases until that decision is overruled

public law

cases in private law, civil law, or criminal law in which one party to the dispute argues that a license is unfair, a law is inequitable or unconstitutional, or an agency has acted unfairly, violated a procedure, or gone beyond its jurisdiction

trial court

the first court to hear a criminal or civil case

appellate court

a court that hears the appeals of trial court decisions

supreme court

the highest court in a particular state or in the United States. This court primarily serves an appellate function

Figure 15.1   THE U.S. COURT SYSTEM

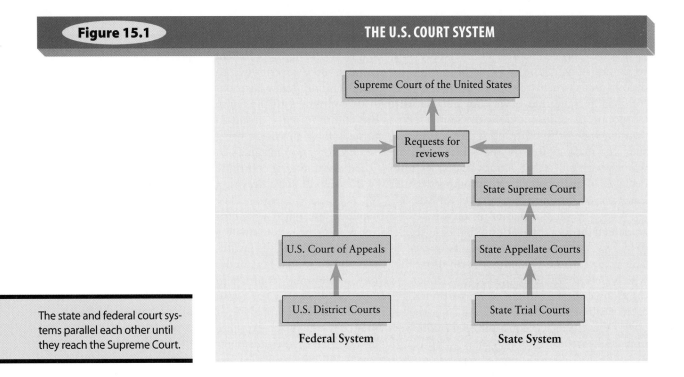

The state and federal court systems parallel each other until they reach the Supreme Court.

against a physician for malpractice would file the suit in the appropriate court in the state where the alleged malpractice occurred. The judge hearing the case would apply state law and state precedent to the matter at hand. (It should be noted that in both criminal and civil matters, most cases are settled before trial through negotiated agreements between the parties. In criminal cases these agreements are called **plea bargains.**)

Although each state has its own set of laws, these laws have much in common from state to state. Murder and robbery, obviously, are illegal in all states, although the range of possible punishments for those crimes varies from state to state. Some states, for example, provide for capital punishment (the death penalty) for murder and other serious offenses; other states do not. As we saw in Chapter 4, however, some acts that are criminal offenses in one state may be legal in another state. Prostitution, for example, is legal in some Nevada counties, although it is outlawed in all other states. Considerable similarity among the states is also found in the realm of civil law. In the case of contract law, most states have adopted the **Uniform Commercial Code** in order to reduce interstate differences. In areas such as family law, however, which covers such matters as divorce and child custody arrangements, state laws vary greatly.

Cases are heard in the federal courts if they involve federal laws, treaties with other nations, or the U.S. Constitution; these areas are the official **jurisdiction** of the federal courts. In addition, any case in which the U.S. government is a party is heard in the federal courts. If, for example, an individual is charged with violating a federal criminal statute, such as evading the payment of income taxes, charges would be brought before a federal judge by a federal prosecutor. Civil cases involving the citizens of more than one state and in which

plea bargains

negotiated agreements in criminal cases in which a defendant agrees to plead guilty in return for the state's agreement to reduce the severity of the criminal charge the defendant is facing

Uniform Commercial Code

code used in many states in the area of contract law to reduce interstate differences in judicial decisions

jurisdiction

the sphere of a court's power and authority

more than fifty thousand dollars is at stake may be heard in either the federal or the state courts, usually depending on the preference of the plaintiff.

Federal courts serve another purpose in addition to trying cases within their jurisdiction: that of hearing appeals from state-level courts. Individuals found guilty of breaking a state criminal law, for example, can appeal their convictions to a federal court by raising a constitutional issue and asking a federal court to determine whether the state's actions were consistent with the requirements of the U.S. Constitution. An appellant might assert, for example, that the state court denied him or her the right to counsel, imposed excessive bail, or otherwise denied the appellant **due process.** Under such circumstances, an appellant can ask the federal court to overturn his or her conviction. Federal courts are not obligated to accept such appeals and will do so only if they feel that the issues raised have considerable merit and if the appellant has exhausted all possible remedies within the state courts. (This procedure is discussed in more detail later in this chapter.) The decisions of state supreme courts may also be appealed to the U.S. Supreme Court if the state court's decision has conflicted with prior U.S. Supreme Court rulings or has raised some important question of federal law. Such appeals are accepted by the U.S. Supreme Court at its discretion.

Although the federal courts hear only a small fraction of all the civil and criminal cases decided each year in the United States, their decisions are extremely important. It is in the federal courts that the Constitution and federal laws that govern all Americans are interpreted and their meaning and significance established. Moreover, it is in the federal courts that the powers and limitations of the increasingly powerful national government are tested. Finally, through their power to review the decisions of the state courts, it is ultimately the federal courts that dominate the American judicial system.

due process of law
the right of every citizen against arbitrary action by national or state governments

★ Federal Jurisdiction

▶ What is the importance of the federal court system?

▶ What factors play a role in the appointment of federal judges?

▶ What shapes the flow of cases through the Supreme Court?

Of all the cases heard in the United States in 1993, federal district courts (the lowest federal level) received 274,000. Although this number is up substantially from the 87,000 cases heard in 1961, it still constitutes under 1 percent of the judiciary's business. The federal courts of appeal listened to 49,770 cases in 1993, and the U.S. Supreme Court reviewed 7,245 in its 1992–93 term. Only 83 cases were given full-dress Supreme Court review (the nine justices actually sitting *en banc*—in full court—and hearing the lawyers argue the case).[7]

THE LOWER FEDERAL COURTS

Most of the cases of original federal jurisdiction are handled by the federal district courts. Courts of **original jurisdiction** are the courts that are responsible

original jurisdiction
the authority to initially consider a case. Distinguished from appellate jurisdiction, which is the authority to hear appeals from a lower court's decision

for discovering the facts in a controversy and creating the record on which a judgment is based. Although the Constitution gives the Supreme Court original jurisdiction in several types of cases, such as those affecting ambassadors and those in which a state is one of the parties, most original jurisdiction goes to the lowest courts—the trial courts. (In courts that have appellate jurisdiction, judges receive cases after the factual record is established by the trial court. Ordinarily, new facts cannot be presented before appellate courts.)

There are eighty-nine district courts in the fifty states, plus one in the District of Columbia and one in Puerto Rico, and three territorial courts. These courts are staffed by 610 federal district judges. District judges are assigned to district courts according to the workload; the busiest of these courts may have as many as twenty-eight judges. Only one judge is assigned to each case, except where statutes provide for three-judge courts to deal with special issues. The routines and procedures of the federal district courts are essentially the same as those of the lower state courts, except that federal procedural requirements tend to be stricter. States, for example, do not have to provide a grand jury, a twelve-member trial jury, or a unanimous jury verdict. Federal courts must provide all these things.

The Supreme Court building in Washington, D.C.

THE APPELLATE COURTS

Roughly 10 percent of all lower court and federal agency cases are accepted for review by the federal appeals courts and by the Supreme Court in its capacity as an appellate court. The country is divided into twelve judicial circuits, each of which has a U.S. Court of Appeals. Every state, the District of Columbia, and each of the territories is assigned to the circuit in the continental United States that is closest to it.

Except for cases selected for review by the Supreme Court, decisions made by the appeals courts are final. Because of this finality, certain safeguards have been built into the system. The most important is the provision of more than one judge for every appeals case. Each court of appeals has from six to twenty-eight permanent judgeships, depending on the workload of the circuit. Although normally three judges hear appealed cases, in some instances a larger number of judges sit together *en banc*.

Another safeguard is provided by the assignment of a Supreme Court justice as the circuit justice for each of the twelve circuits. Since the creation of the appeals court in 1891, the circuit justice's primary duty has been to review appeals arising in the circuit in order to expedite Supreme Court action. The most frequent and best-known action of circuit justices is that of reviewing requests for stays of execution when the full Court is unable to do so—primarily during the summer, when the Court is in recess.

THE SUPREME COURT

chief justice

justice on the Supreme Court who presides over the Court's public sessions

The Supreme Court is America's highest court. Article III of the Constitution vests "the judicial power of the United States" in the Supreme Court, and this court is supreme in fact as well as form. The Supreme Court is made up of a chief justice and eight associate justices. The **chief justice** presides over the Court's public sessions and conferences. In the Court's actual deliberations and decisions, however, the chief justice has no more authority than his col-

The members of the Supreme Court in 1998 (from left to right): Antonin Scalia, Ruth Bader Ginsburg, John Paul Stevens, David Souter, Chief Justice William Rehnquist, Clarence Thomas, Sandra Day O'Connor, Stephen Breyer, and Anthony Kennedy.

leagues. Each justice casts one vote. To some extent, the influence of the chief justice is a function of his or her own leadership ability. Some chief justices, such as the late Earl Warren, have been able to lead the court in a new direction. In other instances, forceful associate justices, such as the late Felix Frankfurter, are the dominant figures on the Court.

The Constitution does not specify the number of justices that should sit on the Supreme Court; Congress has the authority to change the Court's size. In the early nineteenth century, there were six Supreme Court justices; later there were seven. Congress set the number of justices at nine in 1869, and the Court has remained that size ever since. In 1937, President Franklin D. Roosevelt, infuriated by several Supreme Court decisions that struck down New Deal programs, asked Congress to enlarge the Court so that he could add a few sympathetic justices to the bench. Although Congress balked at Roosevelt's "court packing" plan, the Court gave in to FDR's pressure and began to take a more favorable view of his policy initiatives. The president, in turn, dropped his efforts to enlarge the Court. The Court's surrender to FDR came to be known as "the switch in time that saved nine."

HOW JUDGES ARE APPOINTED

Federal judges are appointed by the president and are generally selected from among the more prominent or politically active members of the legal profession. Many federal judges previously served as state court judges or state or local prosecutors. In an informal nominating process, candidates for vacancies on the U.S. District Court are generally suggested to the president by a U.S. senator from the president's own party who represents the state in which the vacancy has occurred. Senators often see such a nomination as a way to reward important allies and contributors in their states. If the state has no senator from the president's party, the governor or members of the state's House delegation may make suggestions. In general, presidents endeavor to appoint judges who possess legal experience and good character and whose partisan and ideological views are similar to the president's own. During the presidencies of Ronald Reagan and George Bush, most federal judicial appointees were conservative Republicans. Bush established an advisory committee to screen judicial nominees in order to make certain that their legal and political philosophies were sufficiently conservative. Bill Clinton's appointees to the federal bench, on the other hand, have tended to be liberal Democrats. Clinton has also made a major effort to appoint women and African Americans to the federal courts. Nearly half of his nominees have been drawn from these groups.

Once the president has formally nominated an individual, the nominee must be considered by the Senate Judiciary Committee and confirmed by a majority vote in the full Senate. Before the president makes a formal nomination, however, the senators from the candidate's own state must indicate that they support the nominee. This is an informal but seldom violated practice called **senatorial courtesy.** Because the Senate will rarely approve a nominee opposed by a senator from his or her own state, the president will usually not bother to present such a nomination to the Senate. Through this arrangement, senators are able to exercise veto power over appointments to the federal bench in their own states. In recent years, the Senate Judiciary Committee has also sought to signal the president when it has had qualms about a judicial nomination. After the Republicans won control of the Senate in 1994, for example, Judiciary Committee chair Orrin Hatch of Utah let President Clinton know that he considered two of Clinton's nominees to be too liberal. The president withdrew the nominations.

Federal appeals court nominations follow much the same pattern. Since appeals court judges preside over jurisdictions that include several states, however, senators do not have as strong a role in proposing potential candidates. Instead, potential appeals court candidates are generally suggested to the president by the Justice Department or by important members of the administration. The senators from the nominee's own state are still consulted before the president will formally act.

If political factors play an important role in the selection of district and appellate court judges, they are decisive when it comes to Supreme Court appointments. Because the high court has so much influence over American law and politics, virtually all presidents have made an effort to select justices who share their own political philosophies. Presidents Ronald Reagan and George Bush, for example, appointed five justices whom they believed to have conservative perspectives: Justices Sandra Day O'Connor, Antonin Scalia, Anthony Kennedy, David Souter, and Clarence Thomas. Reagan also elevated William Rehnquist to the position of chief justice. Reagan and Bush sought appointees who believed in reducing government intervention in the economy and who supported the moral positions taken by the Republican Party in recent years, particularly opposition to abortion. However, not all the Reagan and Bush appointees have fulfilled their sponsors' expectations. Bush appointee David Souter, for example, has been attacked by conservatives as a turncoat for his decisions on school prayer and abortion rights. Nevertheless, through their appointments, Reagan and Bush were able to create a far more conservative Supreme Court. For his part, President Bill Clinton has endeavored to appoint liberal justices. Clinton named Ruth Bader Ginsburg and Stephen Breyer to the Court, hoping to counteract the influence of the Reagan and Bush appointees. (Table 15.2 shows information about the current Supreme Court justices.)

senatorial courtesy

the practice whereby the president, before formally nominating a person for a federal judgeship, seeks the indication that senators from the candidate's own state support the nomination

SUPREME COURT JUSTICES, 1998 (IN ORDER OF SENIORITY)   Table 15.2

Name	Year of birth	Prior experience	Appointed by	Year of appointment
William H. Rehnquist *Chief Justice*	1924	Assistant attorney general	Nixon*	1972
John Paul Stevens	1920	Federal judge	Ford	1975
Sandra Day O'Connor	1930	State judge	Reagan	1981
Antonin Scalia	1936	Law professor, federal judge	Reagan	1986
Anthony Kennedy	1936	Federal judge	Reagan	1988
David Souter	1939	Federal judge	Bush	1990
Clarence Thomas	1948	Federal judge	Bush	1991
Ruth Bader Ginsburg	1933	Federal judge	Clinton	1993
Stephen Breyer	1938	Federal judge	Clinton	1994

*Appointed chief justice by Reagan in 1986.

In recent years, Supreme Court nominations have come to involve intense partisan struggle. Typically, after the president has named a nominee, interest groups opposed to the nomination have mobilized opposition in the media, the public, and the Senate. When President Bush proposed conservative judge Clarence Thomas for the Court, for example, liberal groups launched a campaign to discredit Thomas. After extensive research into his background, opponents of the nomination were able to produce evidence suggesting that Thomas had sexually harassed a former subordinate, Anita Hill. Thomas denied the charge. After contentious Senate Judiciary Committee hearings, highlighted by testimony from both Thomas and Hill, Thomas narrowly won confirmation.

In testimony before the Senate Judiciary Committee, Anita Hill alleged that Supreme Court nominee Clarence Thomas had sexually harassed her. Hill's testimony brought nationwide attention to the nomination hearings. The Senate subsequently approved Thomas by the narrowest ratification margin in history, 52 to 48.

Likewise, conservative interest groups carefully scrutinized Bill Clinton's liberal nominees, hoping to find information about them that would sabotage their appointments. During his two opportunities to name Supreme Court justices, Clinton was compelled to drop several potential appointees because of information unearthed by political opponents.

These struggles over judicial appointments indicate the growing intensity of partisan struggle in the United States today. They also indicate how much importance competing political forces attach to Supreme Court appointments. Because these contending forces see the outcome as critical, they are willing to engage in a fierce struggle when Supreme Court appointments are at stake.

CONTROLLING THE FLOW OF CASES

In addition to the judges themselves, three other agencies or groups play an important role in shaping the flow of cases through the federal courts: the solicitor general, the Federal Bureau of Investigation, and federal law clerks.

solicitor general

the top government lawyer in all cases before the Supreme Court where the government is a party

The Solicitor General If any single person has greater influence than individual judges over the federal courts, it is the **solicitor general** of the United States. The solicitor general is the third-ranking official in the Justice Department (below the attorney general and the deputy attorney general) but is the top government lawyer in virtually all cases before the Supreme Court where the government is a party. The solicitor general has the greatest control over the flow of cases; his or her actions are not reviewed by any higher authority in the executive branch. More than half the Supreme Court's total workload consists of cases under the direct charge of the solicitor general.

The solicitor general exercises especially strong influence by screening cases before any agency of the federal government can appeal them to the Supreme Court; indeed, the justices rely on the solicitor general to "screen out undeserving litigation and furnish them with an agenda to government cases that deserve serious consideration."[8] Typically, more requests for appeals are rejected than are accepted by the solicitor general. Agency heads may lobby the president or otherwise try to circumvent the solicitor general, and a few of the independent agencies have a statutory right to make direct appeals, but these are almost inevitably doomed to *per curiam* rejection—rejection through a brief, unsigned opinion by the whole Court—if the solicitor general refuses to participate. Congress has given only a few agencies, including the Federal Communications Commission, the Federal Maritime Commission, and in some cases, the Department of Agriculture (even though it is not an independent agency), the right to appeal directly to the Supreme Court without going through the solicitor general.

per curiam

decision by an appellate court, without a written opinion, that refuses to review the decision of a lower court; amounts to a reaffirmation of the lower court's opinion

The solicitor general can enter a case even when the federal government is not a direct litigant by writing an *amicus curiae* ("friend of the court") brief. A "friend of the court" is not a direct party to a case but has a vital interest in its outcome. Thus, when the government has such an interest, the solicitor general can file as *amicus curiae*, or a federal court can invite such a brief because it wants an opinion in writing. The solicitor general also has the power to invite others to enter cases as *amici curiae*.

amicus curiae

literally, "friend of the court"; individuals or groups who are not parties to a lawsuit but who seek to assist the Supreme Court in reaching a decision by presenting additional briefs

In addition to exercising substantial control over the flow of cases, the solicitor general can shape the arguments used before the federal courts. Indeed, the Supreme Court tends to give special attention to the way the solicitor general characterizes the issues. The solicitor general is the person appearing most frequently before the Court and, theoretically at least, is the most disinterested. The credibility of the solicitor general is not hurt when several times each year he or she comes to the Court to withdraw a case with the admission that the government has made an error.

The solicitor general's sway over the flow of cases does not, however, entirely overshadow the influence of the other agencies and divisions in the Department of Justice. The solicitor general is counsel for the major divisions in the department, including the Antitrust, Tax, Civil Rights, and Criminal divisions. Their activities generate a great part of the solicitor general's agenda. This is particularly true of the Criminal Division, whose cases are appealed every day. These cases are generated by initiatives taken by the United States attorneys and the district judges before whom they practice.

The FBI Another important influence on the flow of cases through the federal appellate judiciary comes from the Federal Bureau of Investigation (FBI), one of the bureaus of the Department of Justice. Its work provides data for numerous government cases against businesses, individual citizens, and state and local government officials. Its data are the most vital source of material for cases in the areas of national security and organized crime.

The FBI also has the important function of linking the Justice Department very closely to cases being brought by state and local government officials. Since the FBI has a long history of cooperation with state and local police forces, the solicitor general often joins (as *amicus curiae*) appeals involving state criminal cases.

Law Clerks Every federal judge employs law clerks to research legal issues and assist with the preparation of opinions. Each Supreme Court justice is assigned four clerks. The clerks are almost always honors graduates of the nation's most

Law clerks play an important role in the Supreme Court justices' decisions to accept cases, in researching the backgrounds of cases that are accepted, and in drafting opinions. Here, Chief Justice Rehnquist meets with his law clerks.

prestigious law schools. A clerkship with a Supreme Court justice is a great honor and generally indicates that the fortunate individual is likely to reach the very top of the legal profession. The work of the Supreme Court clerks is a closely guarded secret, but it is likely that some justices rely heavily upon their clerks for advice in writing opinions and in deciding whether an individual case ought to be heard by the Court. In a recent book, a former law clerk to retired justice Harry Blackmun charged that Supreme Court justices yielded "excessive power to immature, ideologically driven clerks, who in turn use that power to manipulate their bosses."[9]

judicial review

the power of the courts to declare actions of the legislative and executive branches invalid or unconstitutional. The Supreme Court asserted this power in *Marbury v. Madison*

★ The Power of the Supreme Court: Judicial Review

▶ What is the basis for the Supreme Court's power of judicial review?

▶ How does the power of judicial review make the Supreme Court a lawmaking body?

▶ How does a case reach the Supreme Court? Once accepted, how does a case proceed?

▶ What factors influence the judicial philosophy of the Supreme Court?

One of the most important powers of the Supreme Court is the power of **judicial review**—the authority and the obligation to review any lower court decision where a substantial issue of public law is involved. The disputes can be over the constitutionality of federal or state laws, over the propriety or constitutionality of the court procedures followed, or over whether public officers are exceeding their authority. The Supreme Court's power of judicial review has come to mean review not only of lower court decisions but also of state legislation and acts of Congress. For this reason, if for no other, the Supreme Court is more than a judicial agency—it is a major lawmaking body.

The Supreme Court's power of judicial review over lower court decisions has never been at issue. Nor has there been any serious quibble over the power of the federal courts to review administrative agencies in order to determine whether their actions and decisions are within the powers delegated to them by Congress. There has, however, been a great deal of controversy occasioned by the Supreme Court's efforts to review acts of Congress and the decisions of state courts and legislatures.

JUDICIAL REVIEW OF ACTS OF CONGRESS

Since the Constitution does not give the Supreme Court the power of judicial review of congressional enactments, the Court's exercise of it is something of a usurpation. It is not known whether the framers of the Constitution opposed judicial review, but "if they intended to provide for it in the Constitution, they did so in a most obscure fashion."[10] Disputes over the intentions of the framers were settled in 1803 in the case of *Marbury v. Madison*.[11] Although Congress and the president have often been at odds with the Court, its legal power to re-

Chief Justice John Marshall established the Supreme Court's power to rule on the constitutionality of federal and state laws.

view acts of Congress has not been seriously questioned since 1803. One reason is that judicial power has been accepted as natural, if not intended. Another reason is that the Supreme Court has rarely reviewed the constitutionality of acts of Congress, especially in the past fifty years. When such acts do come up for review, the Court makes a self-conscious effort to give them an interpretation that will make them constitutional. In some instances, however, the Court reaches the conclusion that a congressional enactment directly violates the Constitution. For example, in 1998, the Court invalidated a statute through which Congress had given the president the authority to reject specific projects contained in spending bills. The Court ruled that this "line-item veto" power violated the constitutionally mandated separation of powers.[12]

JUDICIAL REVIEW OF STATE ACTIONS

The power of the Supreme Court to review state legislation or other state action and to determine its constitutionality is neither granted by the Constitution nor inherent in the federal system. But the logic of the **supremacy clause** of Article VI of the Constitution, which declares it and laws made under its authority to be the supreme law of the land, is very strong. Furthermore, in the Judiciary Act of 1789, Congress conferred on the Supreme Court the power to reverse state constitutions and laws whenever they are clearly in conflict with the U.S. Constitution, federal laws, or treaties.[13] This power gives the Supreme Court appellate jurisdiction over all of the millions of cases handled by American courts each year.

The supremacy clause of the Constitution not only established the federal Constitution, statutes, and treaties as the "supreme law of the land," but also provided that "the Judges in every State shall be bound thereby, any Thing in the Constitution or Laws of the State to the Contrary notwithstanding." Under this

supremacy clause

Article VI of the Constitution, which states that laws passed by the national government and all treaties are the supreme law of the land and superior to all laws adopted by any state or any subdivision

The Supreme Court has the power to overturn state laws. In 1996, the Supreme Court found unconstitutional a Rhode Island law that had prohibited the advertising of prices of alcoholic beverages. The Court claimed that the Rhode Island law had violated the First Amendment right of free speech.

authority, the Supreme Court has frequently overturned state constitutional provisions or statutes and state court decisions it deems to contravene rights or privileges guaranteed under the federal Constitution or federal statutes.

The civil rights area abounds with examples of state laws that were overturned because the statutes violated guarantees of due process and equal protection contained in the Fourteenth Amendment to the Constitution. For example, in the 1954 case of *Brown v. Board of Education,* the Court overturned statutes from Kansas, South Carolina, Virginia, and Delaware that either required or permitted segregated public schools, on the basis that such statutes denied black schoolchildren equal protection of the law. In 1967, in *Loving v. Virginia,* the Court invalidated a Virginia statute prohibiting interracial marriages.[14]

State statutes in other subject matter areas are equally subject to challenge. In *Griswold v. Connecticut,* the Court invalidated a Connecticut statute prohibiting the general distribution of contraceptives to married couples on the basis that the statute violated the couples' rights to marital privacy.[15] In *Brandenburg v. Ohio,* the Court overturned an Ohio statute forbidding any person from urging criminal acts as a means of inducing political reform or from joining any association that advocated such activities on the grounds that the statute punished "mere advocacy" and therefore violated the free speech provisions of the Constitution.[16]

JUDICIAL REVIEW AND LAWMAKING

When courts of original jurisdiction apply existing statutes or past cases directly to citizens, the effect is the same as legislation. Lawyers study judicial decisions in order to discover underlying principles, and they advise their clients accordingly. Often the process is nothing more than reasoning by analogy: the facts in a particular case are so close to those in one or more previous cases that the same decision should be handed down. Such judge-made law is called common law.

The appellate courts, however, are in another realm. Their rulings can be considered laws, but they are laws governing the behavior only of the judiciary. They influence citizens' conduct only because, in the words of Justice Oliver Wendell Holmes, who served on the Supreme Court from 1900 to 1932, lawyers make "prophecies of what the courts will do in fact."[17]

The written opinion of an appellate court is about halfway between common law and statutory law. It is judge-made and draws heavily on the precedents of previous cases. But it tries to articulate the rule of law controlling the case in question and future cases like it. In this respect, it is like a statute. But it differs from a statute in that a statute addresses itself to the future conduct of citizens, whereas a written opinion addresses itself mainly to the willingness or ability of courts in the future to take cases and render favorable opinions. Decisions by appellate courts affect citizens by giving them a cause of action or by taking it away from them. That is, they open or close access to the courts.

A specific case may help clarify the distinction. Before the Second World War, one of the most insidious forms of racial discrimination was the "restrictive covenant," a clause in a contract whereby the purchasers of a house agreed that if they later decided to sell it, they would sell only to a Caucasian. When a test case finally reached the Supreme Court in 1948, the Court ruled unanimously that citizens had a right to discriminate with restrictive covenants in their sales contracts but that the courts could not enforce these contracts. Its argument was that enforcement would constitute violation of the Fourteenth Amendment provision that no state shall "deny to any person within its jurisdiction equal protection under the law."[18] The Court was thereby predicting what it would and would not do in future cases of this sort. Most states have now enacted statutes that forbid homeowners to place such covenants in sales contracts.

The 1963 case *Gideon v. Wainwright* extends the point. When the Supreme Court ordered a new trial for Clarence Earl Gideon because he had been denied the right to legal counsel,[19] it said to all trial judges and prosecutors that henceforth they would be wasting their time if they cut corners in trials of indigent defendants. It also invited thousands of prisoners to appeal their convictions. (See Chapter 5 for a further discussion of this case.)

Many areas of civil law have been constructed in the same way—by judicial messages to other judges, some of which are codified eventually into legislative enactments. An example of great concern to employees and employers is that of liability for injuries sustained at work. Courts have sided with employees so often that it has become virtually useless for employers to fight injury cases. It has become "the law" that employers are liable for such injuries, without regard to negligence. But the law in this instance is simply a series of messages to lawyers that they should advise their corporate clients not to appeal injury decisions. In recent years, the Supreme Court has also been developing law in the realm of sexual harassment in the workplace. In one 1998 case, for example, the Court ruled that an employer can be held responsible if one of its employees is sexually harassed by a supervisor, even if the company was unaware of the supervisor's specific behavior.[20]

The appellate courts cannot decide what types of behavior will henceforth be a crime. They cannot directly prevent the police from forcing confessions from suspects or intimidating witnesses. In other words, they cannot directly change the behavior of citizens or eliminate abuses of government power. What they can do, however, is make it easier for mistreated persons to gain redress.

Students and Politics

"[In a decision announced in October 1997,] the Supreme Court chose not to hear a case against Indiana University challenging the use of religion in college graduation.... Alex Tanford, a law professor at Indiana University, had legally challenged the use of prayer in the school's commencements since 1995. Joseph Urbanski, a former student at Indiana, had also participated in the case against the university. They argued ... that the prayers violated the constitutional requirement of separation between church and state.

"After rulings in favor of the university by the district court and the U.S. Court of Appeals for the Seventh Circuit, Tanford and lawyers from the American Civil Liberties Union sought a hearing by the U.S. Supreme Court. The Court announced earlier this week that it would not hear the case, upholding the decisions of the lower courts. Tanford said that the decision is not surprising. 'Our timing, among other things, was particularly bad,' Tanford said. 'Our appeal is most likely the first to bring up religious activities at the college level.'

"Tanford believes that it is not likely that the Supreme Court will hear a case concerning prayer in college commencements until several more appeals are made by others. 'The Supreme Court has no reason to get involved because this may have been the first case like this to come before them concerning prayer at college commencements,' he said.

"Stan Fickle, an attorney for the Barnes and Thorburg law firm, defended Indiana in the case. Fickle said that he never expected the case to be heard by the Supreme Court.... 'You have to look at two things: Is anyone being coerced by the prayer, and is this practice being used to further religion?' Fickle said that he didn't see any evidence of either coercion by the prayer, or furthering of religion by the practice of it at the commencement.

"Despite being unsuccessful in trying to stop prayer in commencements at Indiana University, Tanford still questions the inclusion of it in the graduation process.... [He] said that prayer in commencement only serves to offend graduates who are not religious or not affiliated with the religion which the prayer is performed in."

SOURCE: Charles Robinson, "Supreme Court Refuses to Hear College Commencement Prayer Case," *State News* (Michigan State University), October 8, 1997; reprinted on UWire, http://www.uwire.com/uwire/97/10/news10089701.chtml.

In redressing wrongs, the appellate courts—and even the Supreme Court itself—often call for a radical change in legal principle. Changes in race relations, for example, would probably have taken a great deal longer if the Supreme Court had not rendered the 1954 decision *Brown v. Board of Education* that redefined the rights of African Americans.

Similarly, the Supreme Court interpreted the doctrine of the separation of church and state so as to alter significantly the practice of religion in public institutions. For example, in a 1962 case, *Engel v. Vitale*, the Court declared that a once widely observed ritual—the recitation of a prayer by students in a public school—was unconstitutional under the establishment clause of the First Amendment. Almost all the dramatic changes in the treatment of criminals and of persons accused of crimes have been made by the appellate courts, especially the Supreme Court. The Supreme Court brought about a veritable revolution in the criminal process with three cases over less than five years: *Gideon v. Wainwright*, in 1963, was just discussed. *Escobedo v. Illinois*, in 1964, gave suspects the right to remain silent and the right to have counsel present during questioning. But the *Escobedo* decision left confusions that allowed differing decisions to be made by lower courts. In *Miranda v. Arizona*, in 1966, the Supreme Court cleared up these confusions by setting forth what is known as the ***Miranda* rule**: arrested people have the right to remain silent, the right to be informed that anything they say can be held against them, and the right to counsel before and during police interrogation (see Chapter 5).[21]

One of the most significant changes brought about by the Supreme Court was the revolution in legislative representation unleashed by the 1962 case of *Baker v. Carr*.[22] In this landmark case, the Supreme Court held that it could no longer avoid reviewing complaints about the apportionment of seats in state legislatures. Following that decision, the federal courts went on to force reapportionment of all state, county, and local legislatures in the country.

HOW CASES REACH THE SUPREME COURT

Given the millions of disputes that arise every year, the job of the Supreme Court would be impossible if it were not able to control the flow of cases and its own caseload. Its original jurisdiction is only a minor problem. The original jurisdiction includes (1) cases between the United States and one of the fifty states, (2) cases between two or more states, (3) cases involving foreign ambassadors or other ministers, and (4) cases brought by one state against citizens of another state or against a foreign country. The most important of these cases are disputes between states over land, water, or old debts. Generally, the Supreme Court deals with these cases by appointing a "special master," usually a retired judge, to actually hear the case and present a report. The Supreme Court then allows the states involved in the dispute to present arguments for or against the master's opinion.[23]

Rules of Access   Over the years, the courts have developed specific rules that govern which cases within their jurisdiction they will and will not hear. In order to have access to the courts, cases must meet certain criteria. These rules of access can be broken down into three major categories: case or controversy, standing, and mootness.

Miranda rule

the requirement, articulated by the Supreme Court in *Miranda v. Arizona*, that persons under arrest must be informed prior to police interrogation of their rights to remain silent and to have the benefit of legal counsel

POLICY DEBATE

The Right to Privacy and Abortion

Although the word "privacy" does not appear in the Bill of Rights, the courts have agreed that such a fundamental right exists. They disagree, however, about exactly from where the protection arises and about how far it should be applied. Nowhere is this disagreement more protracted than for the issue of abortion.

Since its 1973 landmark ruling in *Roe v. Wade*, the Supreme Court has repeatedly found that the right to privacy protects the right of a woman to end a pregnancy via abortion, subject to some court-approved restrictions. Abortion opponents, of course, have rejected the premise of *Roe* that privacy protects an act they consider murder. For example, members of Congress who oppose abortion have succeeded in restricting federal Medicaid funding for abortions. Today's more conservative Supreme Court has allowed states to impose restrictions such as parental notification for minors and twenty-four-hour waiting periods for those seeking abortions.

Supporters of privacy-based protection for abortion argue that, as a matter of law and tradition, a developing fetus cannot be accorded the same legal status as the woman carrying a fetus. If privacy means anything, it must extend to the right of a woman to decide, at least during the early months of pregnancy (when the vast majority of abortions are performed, and before the point of viability, when the fetus can live outside of the woman), whether or not to have an abortion. For the government to require women to carry most or all pregnancies to term represents extreme government intrusion into the innately personal decision over procreation. The principle of individual liberty must allow women to make such fundamental decisions themselves.

Further, the idea that all abortions are murder means that a fertilized egg does and should possess the same traits as a full-term baby, an idea that is rejected by medical science, most Americans, and many religions. For example, when a spontaneous abortion occurs early in a pregnancy, it is called a "miscarriage," for which funeral services are not held. A late-term spontaneous abortion, called a "stillbirth," evokes a different and more complex response, reflecting the evident difference in development. Abortion laws properly reflect these differences. Finally, the Constitution speaks to the issue by noting that citizenship, and therefore the rights stemming from it, begins at birth.

Opponents of abortion argue that the relative differences observed in fetal development do not obviate the fact that, by genetic makeup, even a fertilized egg is a person. The right to privacy does not and cannot provide an excuse for murder. The absence of birth does not, in and of itself, mean that a fetus is without rights. Even if the Constitution's framers had all agreed that the Bill of Rights protected the liberty associated with privacy, there is no reason to believe that they would have countenanced its extension to abortion. Furthermore, to say that such matters are purely a matter of personal choice is to turn a blind eye to the sort of evil that government has every right to regulate or prohibit. And while pregnancy is a developmental process for the fetus, it is precisely because there is no magic, agreed-upon point at which a fetus becomes a person that the fetus must be protected as a person at all stages.

Women who become pregnant, whether by accident or intent, assume a special obligation to the innocent life they carry. Although some who oppose abortions are willing to allow exceptions for cases of rape or incest, such cases account for only a tiny percentage of all abortions. Legal abortion is harmful in other respects. It demeans respect for life by allowing, even encouraging, abortion as a means of birth control. If later-term abortions are allowed because of, say, fetal defect, it is a short step to euthanasia (so-called mercy killing) of living persons. Above all, the right of a fetus to live must supersede the privacy rights, however defined, of pregnant women.

Article III of the Constitution and Supreme Court decisions define judicial power as extending only to "cases and controversies." This means that the case before a court must be an actual controversy, not a hypothetical one, with two truly adversarial parties. The courts have interpreted this language to mean that they do not have the power to render advisory opinions to legislatures or agencies about the constitutionality of proposed laws or regulations. Furthermore, even after a law is enacted, the courts will generally refuse to consider its constitutionality until it is actually applied.

standing

the right of an individual or organization to initiate a court case

Parties to a case must also have **standing,** that is, they must show that they have a substantial stake in the outcome of the case. The traditional requirement for standing has been to show injury to oneself; that injury can be personal, economic, or even aesthetic, for example. In order for a group or class of people to have standing (as in class action suits), each member must show specific injury. This means that a general interest in the environment, for instance, does not provide a group with sufficient basis for standing.

mootness

a criterion used by courts to screen cases that no longer require resolution.

The Supreme Court also uses a third criterion in determining whether it will hear a case: that of **mootness.** In theory, this requirement disqualifies cases that are brought too late—after the relevant facts have changed or the problem has been resolved by other means. The criterion of mootness, however, is subject to the discretion of the courts, which have begun to relax the rules of mootness, particularly in cases where a situation that has been resolved is likely to come up again. In the abortion case *Roe v. Wade,* for example, the Supreme Court rejected the lower court's argument that because the pregnancy had already come to term, the case was moot. The Court agreed to hear the case because no pregnancy was likely to outlast the lengthy appeals process.

Putting aside the formal criteria, the Supreme Court is most likely to accept cases that involve conflicting decisions by the federal circuit courts, cases that present important questions of civil rights or civil liberties, and cases in which the federal government is the appellant. Ultimately, however, the question of which cases to accept can come down to the preferences and priorities of the justices. If a group of justices believes that the Court should intervene in a particular area of policy or politics, they are likely to look for a case or cases that will serve as vehicles for judicial intervention. For many years, for example, the Court was not interested in considering challenges to affirmative action or other programs designed to provide particular benefits to minorities. In recent years, however, several of the Court's more conservative justices have been eager to push back the limits of affirmative action and racial preference, and have therefore accepted a number of cases that would allow them to do so. In 1995, the Court's decisions in *Adarand Constructors v. Pena, Missouri v. Jenkins,* and *Miller v. Johnson* placed new restrictions on federal affirmative action programs, school desegregation efforts, and attempts to increase minority representation in Congress through the creation of "minority districts" (see Chapter 10).[24]

Writs Decisions handed down by lower courts can reach the Supreme Court in one of two ways: through a *writ of certiorari,* or, in the case of convicted state prisoners, through a writ of *habeas corpus.* A writ is a court document conveying an order of some sort. In recent years, an effort has been made to give the Court more discretion regarding the cases it chooses to hear. Before 1988, the Supreme Court was obligated to review cases on what was called a writ of appeal. This has since been eliminated, and the Court now has virtually complete discretion over what cases it will hear.

Most cases reach the Supreme Court through the **writ of *certiorari,*** which is granted whenever four of the nine justices agree to review a case. The Supreme Court was once so inundated with appeals that in 1925 Congress enacted laws giving it some control over its caseload with the power to issue writs of *certiorari*. Rule 10 of the Supreme Court's own rules of procedure defines *certiorari* as "not a matter of right, but of sound judicial discretion . . . granted only where there are special and important reasons therefor." The reasons provided for in Rule 10 are

1. Where a state has made a decision that conflicts with previous Supreme Court decisions;
2. Where a state court has come up with an entirely new federal question;
3. Where one court of appeals has rendered a decision in conflict with another;
4. Where there are other inconsistent rulings between two or more courts or states;
5. Where a single court of appeals has sanctioned too great a departure by a lower court from normal judicial proceedings (a reason rarely given).

The **writ of *habeas corpus*** is a fundamental safeguard of individual rights. Its historical purpose is to enable an accused person to challenge arbitrary detention and to force an open trial before a judge. But in 1867, Congress's distrust of southern courts led it to confer on federal courts the authority to issue writs of *habeas corpus* to prisoners already tried or being tried in state courts of proper jurisdiction where the constitutional rights of the prisoner were possibly being violated. This writ gives state prisoners a second channel toward Supreme Court review in case their direct appeal from the highest state court fails (see Figure 15.2). The writ of *habeas corpus* is discretionary; that is, the Court can decide which cases to review.

Lobbying for Access: Interests and the Court   At the same time that the Court exercises discretion over which cases it will review, groups and forces in society often seek to persuade the justices to listen to their problems. Interest groups use several different strategies to get the Court's attention. Lawyers representing these groups try to choose the proper client and the proper case, so that the issues in question are most dramatically and appropriately portrayed. They also have to pick the right district or jurisdiction in which to bring the case. Sometimes they even have to wait for an appropriate political climate.

Group litigants have to plan carefully when to use and when to avoid publicity. They must also attempt to develop a proper record at the trial court level, one that includes some constitutional arguments and even, when possible, errors on the part of the trial court. One of the most effective litigation strategies used in getting cases accepted for review by the appellate courts is bringing the same type of suit in more than one circuit (i.e., developing a "pattern of cases"), in the hope that inconsistent treatment by two different courts will improve the chance of a Supreme Court review.

Congress will sometimes provide interest groups with legislation designed to facilitate their use of litigation. One important recent example is the 1990

writ of *certiorari*

a decision of at least four of the nine Supreme Court justices to review a decision of a lower court; from the Latin "to make more certain"

writ of *habeas corpus*

a court order that the individual in custody be brought into court and shown the cause for detention. Habeas corpus is guaranteed by the Constitution and can be suspended only in cases of rebellion or invasion

Figure 15.2   HOW CASES REACH THE SUPREME COURT

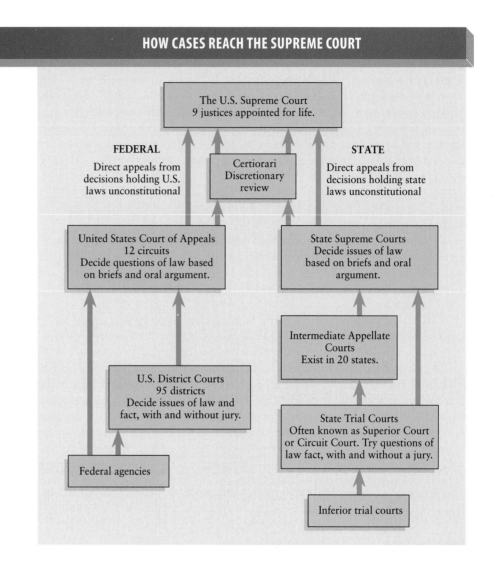

Americans with Disabilities Act (ADA), enacted after intense lobbying by public interest and advocacy groups. The ADA, in conjunction with the 1991 Civil Rights Act, opens the way for disabled individuals to make effective use of the courts to press their interests.

The two most notable users of the pattern of cases strategy in recent years have been the National Association for the Advancement of Colored People (NAACP) and the American Civil Liberties Union (ACLU). For many years, the NAACP (and its Defense Fund—now a separate group) has worked through local chapters and with many individuals to encourage litigation on issues of racial discrimination and segregation. Sometimes it distributes petitions to be signed by parents and filed with local school boards and courts, deliberately sowing the seeds of future litigation. The NAACP and the ACLU often encourage private parties to bring suit and then join the suit as *amici curiae*.

One illustration of an interest group employing a carefully crafted litigation strategy to pursue its goals through the judiciary was the Texas-based effort to establish a right to free public school education for children of illegal aliens. The issue arose in 1977 when the Texas state legislature, responding to a sudden public backlash against illegal immigration from Mexico, enacted a law permitting school districts to charge undocumented children hefty tuition for the privilege of attending public school. A public-interest law organization, the Mexican-American Legal Defense Fund, prepared to challenge the law in court after determining that public opposition precluded any chance of persuading the legislature to change its own law.

Part of the defense fund's litigation strategy was to bring a lawsuit in the northern section of Texas, far from the Mexican border, where illegal immigration would be at a minimum. Thus, in Tyler, Texas, where the complaint was initially filed, the trial court found only sixty undocumented alien students in a school district composed of 16,000. This strategy effectively contradicted the state's argument that the Texas law was necessary to reduce the burdens on educational resources created by masses of incoming aliens. Another useful litigation tactic was to select plaintiffs who, although illegal aliens, were nevertheless clearly planning to remain in Texas even without free public education for their children. Thus, all of the plaintiffs came from families that had already lived in Tyler for several years and included at least one child who was an American citizen by virtue of birth in the United States. By emphasizing the stability of such families, the defense fund argued convincingly that the Texas law would not motivate families to return to the poverty in Mexico from which they had fled, but would more likely result in the creation of a subclass of illiterate people who would add to the state's unemployment and crime rates. Five years after the lawsuit on behalf of the Tyler children began, the U.S. Supreme Court in the case of *Plyler v. Doe* held that

The Supreme Court is open to outside political influence. Interest groups lobby the Court formally by filing *amicus curiae* briefs, and informally through public opinion. In 1989, members of the National Organization for Women and the National Abortion Rights Action League gathered while the Court met to rule on *Webster v. Reproductive Health Services,* an important abortion rights case.

THE NAACP: USING THE LAW TO GET JUSTICE

*P*art of the white segregationist backlash that spread throughout the American South in the late 1800s and early 1900s was the enactment of the laws that mandated residential segregation by race. In the city of Louisville, Kentucky, the city council passed such an ordinance in 1914 in order to make sure that African Americans would not move into white-only portions of the city. This legal expression of racial hatred came under legal attack by a newly formed organization that had decided to devote its limited resources toward seeking legal remedies to racial discrimination.

The National Association for the Advancement of Colored People (NAACP) filed suit against Louisville's law. After they lost their case in state courts, the NAACP appealed the case to the Supreme Court. In 1917, the court struck down the segregationist law as a clear violation of the Fourteenth Amendment and of federal law granting blacks the same rights as whites to buy, sell, and own property.[1]

The NAACP's suit had struck down its first Jim Crow law.

By 1929, the NAACP had argued five cases before the Supreme Court, but its still-meager resources limited its ability to seek justice. But about this time, the fund of a wealthy philanthropist, Charles Garland, granted the organization $100,000 to conduct "a large-scale, widespread, dramatic campaign to give the Southern Negro his constitutional rights, his political and civil equality."[2] The NAACP drew up a detailed plan for challenging legalized segregation. Drawing on the brilliant legal skills of Charles Houston and his student from Howard University Law School, Thurgood Marshall, the group planned to attack the "separate but equal" doctrine established by *Plessy v. Ferguson* by first showing that facilities set aside for blacks were almost never equal. Their second step was to challenge the separate but equal doctrine directly as inconsistent with the principles embodied in the Constitution.

the Texas law was unconstitutional under the equal protection clause of the Fourteenth Amendment.[25]

In many states, it is considered unethical and illegal for attorneys to engage in "fomenting and soliciting legal business in which they are not parties and have no pecuniary right or liability." The NAACP was sued by the state of Virginia in the late 1950s in an attempt to restrict or eliminate its efforts to influence the pattern of cases. The Supreme Court reviewed the case in 1963, recognized that the strategy was being utilized, and held that it was protected by the First and Fourteenth Amendments, just as other forms of speech and petition are protected.[26]

Thus, many pathbreaking cases are eventually granted *certiorari* because continued refusal to review one or more of them would amount to a rule of law just as much as if the courts had handed down a written opinion. In this sense, the flow of cases, especially the pattern of significant cases, influences the behavior of the appellate judiciary.

THE SUPREME COURT'S PROCEDURES

The Supreme Court's decision to accept a case is the beginning of what can be a lengthy and complex process (see Figure 15.3). First, the attorneys on both

In the meantime, the NAACP challenged the legality of "kangaroo" courts that were used to convict innocent blacks, some of whom were sentenced to death by all-white juries without benefit of legal advice or a proper defense. In 1944, after three decades of lawsuits by the NAACP, the Supreme Court declared the southern "white primary" elections unconstitutional. Two years later, the NAACP won its first case against segregation in transportation when the Court struck down racial restrictions affecting buses. The NAACP also won victories on behalf of blacks seeking admission to state law schools.

A legal milestone was finally reached in 1954, when the Supreme Court unanimously overturned *Plessy v. Ferguson* and the principle of separate-but-equal, ordering segregated schools to begin the process of integration in *Brown v. Board of Education of Topeka, Kansas*. Thurgood Marshall, who led the legal charge in the *Brown* case, argued thirty-two civil rights cases for the NAACP, winning nearly all of them. In 1962, Marshall was appointed to the U.S court of appeals by President Kennedy. Five years later, he was elevated by President Johnson to the very court in which he had won so many battles for African Americans. As the first black to serve on the Supreme Court, Marshall continued to argue that, despite many legal victories, the structures of American society still protected racism.

Along with Marshall, many argue that racism was and is deeply embedded in the fabric of society. Indeed, the original Constitution not only acknowledged but condoned the subjugation of blacks through slavery. Even so, the NAACP was able to use the constitutional framework through the judicial branch to wipe away the most offensive structures of racism in America. The process took many decades, and it continues to the present.

SOURCE: Richard Kluger, *Simple Justice* (New York: Vintage, 1975).
[1]*Buchanan v. Warley,* 245 U.S. 60 (1917). The other cases discussed herein are *Smith v. Allwright,* 321 U.S. 649 (1944); *Plessy v. Ferguson,* 3 S.Ct. 18 (1896); *Morgan v. Virginia,* 328 U.S. 373 (1946); and *Brown v. Board of Education of Topeka, Kansas,* 74 S.Ct. 686 (1954).
[2]Richard Kluger, *Simple Justice* (New York: Vintage, 1975), p. 132.

sides must prepare **briefs**—written documents that may be several hundred pages long in which the attorneys explain why the Court should rule in favor of their client. Briefs are filled with referrals to precedents specifically chosen to show that other courts have frequently ruled in the same way that the Supreme Court is being asked to rule. The attorneys for both sides muster the most compelling precedents they can in support of their arguments.

As the attorneys prepare their briefs, they often ask sympathetic interest groups for their help. Groups are asked to file *amicus curiae* briefs that support the claims of one or the other litigant. In a case involving separation of church and state, for example, liberal groups such as the ACLU and Citizens for the American Way are likely to be asked to file *amicus* briefs in support of strict separation, whereas conservative religious groups are likely to file *amicus* briefs advocating increased public support for religious ideas. Often, dozens of briefs will be filed on each side of a major case. *Amicus* filings are one of the primary methods used by interest groups to lobby the Court. By filing these briefs, groups indicate to the Court where their group stands and signal to the justices that they believe the case to be an important one.

The next stage of a case is **oral argument,** in which attorneys for both sides appear before the Court to present their positions and answer the justices' questions. Each attorney has only a half hour to present his or her case, and

briefs

written documents in which attorneys explain, using case precedents, why the court should find in favor of their client

oral argument

stage in Supreme Court procedure in which attorneys for both sides appear before the Court to present their positions and answer questions posed by justices

Figure 15.3 — THE SUPREME COURT'S DECISION-MAKING PROCESS

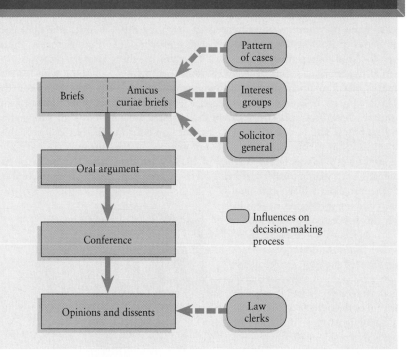

In addition to the individual justices who make up the Supreme Court, various groups and factors also may influence the Court's decision on any given case.

This 1935 photo is the only known photograph of the Supreme Court hearing oral arguments.

this time includes interruptions for questions. Certain members of the Court, such as Justice Antonin Scalia, are known to interrupt attorneys dozens of times. Others, such as Justice Clarence Thomas, seldom ask questions. For an attorney, the opportunity to argue a case before the Supreme Court is a singular honor and a mark of professional distinction. It can also be a harrowing experience, as justices interrupt a carefully prepared presentation to ask pointed questions. Oral argument can be very important to the outcome of a case. It allows justices to better understand the heart of the case and to raise questions that might not have been addressed in the opposing side's briefs. It is not uncommon for justices to go beyond the strictly legal issues and ask opposing counsel to discuss the implications of the case for the Court and the nation at large.

Following oral argument, the Court discusses the case in its Wednesday or Friday conference. The chief justice presides over the conference and speaks first; the other justices follow in order of seniority. The Court's conference is secret, and no outsiders are permitted to attend. The justices discuss the case and eventually reach a decision on the basis of a majority vote. If the Court is divided, a number of votes may be taken before a final decision is reached. As the case is discussed, justices may try to influence or change one another's opinions. At times, this may result in compromise decisions. On the current Court, for example, several justices, including Rehnquist, Scalia, and Thomas, are known to favor overturning the 1973 *Roe v. Wade* decision that prohibited the states from outlawing abortions. Other justices, including Souter, Breyer, and Ginsburg, are known to oppose such a course of action. This division has

"Our One Supreme Court": The Common-Law Court Movement

"I am a private party and not a subject of the United States nor subject to its jurisdiction, as it has no constitutional jurisdiction except in the District of Columbia and its possessions." With this statement, uttered in a common-law court, you can declare yourself a "freeman" and remove yourself from the duty to file income taxes, to obtain a driver's license, or indeed to be bound by any state or federal laws. Or so proponents of the common-law court movement argue.

The common-law movement arose in the West about twenty years ago. As environmental agents, sheriffs, IRS agents, and other government officials sought to foreclose or impose tax liens on property or investigate incidents of illegal hunting, many westerners felt the government had turned against them. One result was the common-law court movement.

Proponents trace the notion of common-law courts back to documents they believe are part of a western cultural tradition of individual liberty and sovereignty: the Bible, the Magna Carta, the U.S. Constitution, and certain state constitutions. So-called freemen begin with an idea that all Americans believe—that ultimate sovereignty rests in the hands of the people—but from this idea they draw a radical conclusion: that they can, as individuals, choose to repudiate all the powers of government. Freemen assert that the present forms of government in the United States, both state and national, are illegitimate and tyrannical; they often argue that the Constitution has been suspended since President Roosevelt declared emergency powers in 1933. Freemen portray themselves as committed to restoring American democracy and constitutional government.

Over the last twenty years the common-law movement has spread across the country. Today, thousands of Americans who consider themselves freemen meet in self-styled courts in places like Arlington, Texas; Columbus, Ohio; Franklin, Delaware; and Roundup, Montana. In a typical court, often called "Our One Supreme Court," a jury of twelve men is chosen (the common-

law movement discourages women from playing public roles). The jury is very important: jurors do not merely decide a case, they also act as judge and lawyers, asking questions, maintaining order, calling for documents, deliberating openly, and rendering a verdict.

Two kinds of cases heard in common-law courts are actions for "quiet title for person" and for "quiet title." A person claiming "quiet title for person" makes a statement like the one quoted at the beginning of this essay. With the jury's decision, the plaintiff is recognized as a freeman, no longer subject to the jurisdiction of the federal or state governments—even to the extent of rejecting ZIP codes and 911 emergency service. In a case for "quiet title," a plaintiff comes before the court to claim ownership of a plot of land, after having filed a public notice announcing the claim. Banks, corporations, and the government—the usual "owners" of the land in question—do not appear in "court" to contest the claim. In the absence of any contestation, the jury typically awards such plots of land to anyone who claims them.

Is there any common sense in the common-law movement? The logic of the common-law court movement is essentially anarchistic, as a common-law enthusiast makes plain: "Common law says the people have all the rights and the government can do nothing to infringe on the rights of the people."[1] Since most government action, by its very nature, represents a balance and compromise among the rights of groups or individuals, the logical conclusion is that there is very little of anything that government *can* do. Common-law advocates would enthusiastically endorse such a view. But in practice it would return us not to a once-upon-a-time America of small government and civic virtue, but to a land with no functioning governments at all, in which citizens would play out a radical version of self-reliance.

[1] Gene Schroder, quoted in Eileen Dempsey and Jim Woods, "Outside the System: An Uncommon Approach on Common Law," *Columbus Dispatch*, September 10, 1995, p. 1A.

resulted in several compromise decisions, in which the Court has allowed some state restriction of abortion but has not permitted states to outlaw abortion altogether.

Opinion Writing   After a decision has been reached, one of the members of the majority is assigned to write the **opinion**. This assignment is made by the chief justice, or by the most senior justice in the majority if the chief justice is on the losing side. The assignment of the opinion can make a significant difference to the interpretation of a decision. Every opinion of the Supreme Court sets a major precedent for future cases throughout the judicial system. Lawyers and judges in the lower courts will examine the opinion carefully to ascertain the Supreme Court's meaning. Differences in wording and emphasis can have important implications for future litigation. Once the majority opinion is drafted, it is circulated to the other justices. Some members of the majority may decide that they cannot accept all the language of the opinion and therefore write "concurring" opinions that support the decision but offer a somewhat different rationale or emphasis. In assigning an opinion, serious thought must be given to the impression the case will make on lawyers and on the public, as well as to the probability that one justice's opinion will be more widely accepted than another's.

One of the more dramatic instances of this tactical consideration occurred in 1944, when Chief Justice Harlan F. Stone chose Justice Felix Frankfurter to write the opinion in the "white primary" case *Smith v. Allwright*. The chief justice believed that this sensitive case, which overturned the southern practice of prohibiting black participation in nominating primaries, required the efforts of the most brilliant and scholarly jurist on the Court. But the day after Stone made the assignment, Justice Robert H. Jackson wrote a letter to Stone urging a change of assignment. In his letter, Jackson argued that Frankfurter, a foreign-born Jew from New England, would not win the South with his opinion, regardless of its brilliance. Stone accepted the advice and substituted Justice Stanley Reed, an American-born Protestant from Kentucky and a southern Democrat in good standing.[27]

Dissent   Justices who disagree with the majority decision of the Court may choose to publicize the character of their disagreement in the form of a **dissenting opinion**. Dissents can be used to express irritation with an outcome or to signal to defeated political forces in the nation that their position is supported by at least some members of the Court. Ironically, the most dependable way an individual justice can exercise a direct and clear influence on the Court is to write a dissent. Because there is no need to please a majority, dissenting opinions can be more eloquent and less guarded than majority opinions. Some of the greatest writing in the history of the Court is found in dissents, and some of the most famous justices, such as Oliver Wendell Holmes, Louis D. Brandeis, and William O. Douglas, were notable dissenters. In the single 1952–53 Court term, Douglas wrote thirty-five dissenting opinions. In the 1958–59 term, he wrote eleven dissents. During the latter term, Justices Frankfurter and Harlan wrote thirteen and nine dissents, respectively.

Dissent plays a special role in the work and impact of the Court because it amounts to an appeal to lawyers all over the country to keep bringing cases of the sort at issue. Therefore, an effective dissent influences the flow of cases

opinion

the written explanation of the Supreme Court's decision in a particular case

dissenting opinion

a decision written by a justice in the minority in a particular case in which the justice wishes to express his or her reasoning in the case

Oliver Wendell Holmes, Jr., the "great dissenter."

through the Court as well as the arguments that will be used by lawyers in later cases. Even more important, dissent emphasizes the fact that, although the Court speaks with a single opinion, it is the opinion only of the majority—and one day the majority might go the other way.

EXPLAINING SUPREME COURT DECISIONS

The Supreme Court explains its decisions in terms of law and precedent. But although law and precedent do have an effect on the Court's deliberations and eventual decisions, it is the Supreme Court that decides what laws actually mean and what importance precedent will actually have. Throughout its history, the Court has shaped and reshaped the law. In the late nineteenth and early twentieth centuries, for example, the Supreme Court held that the Constitution, law, and precedent permitted racial segregation in the United States. Beginning in the late 1950s, however, the Court found that the Constitution prohibited segregation on the basis of race and indicated that the use of racial categories in legislation was always suspect. By the 1970s and 1980s, the Court once again held that the Constitution permitted the use of racial categories—when such categories were needed to help members of minority groups achieve full participation in American society. In the 1990s, the Court began to retreat from this position, too, indicating that governmental efforts to provide extra help to racial minorities could represent an unconstitutional infringement on the rights of the majority.

Harry Blackmun, author of the Supreme Court's decision in *Roe v. Wade.*

Although it is not the only relevant factor, the prime explanation for these movements is shifts in judicial philosophy. These shifts, in turn, result from changes in the Court's composition as justices retire and are replaced by new justices who, as we saw earlier, tend to share the philosophical outlook of the president who appointed them.

Activism and Restraint   One element of judicial philosophy is the issue of activism versus restraint. Over the years, some justices have believed that courts should interpret the Constitution according to the stated intentions of its framers and defer to the views of Congress when interpreting federal statutes. The late justice Felix Frankfurter, for example, advocated judicial deference to legislative bodies and avoidance of the "political thicket," in which the Court would entangle itself by deciding questions that were essentially political rather than legal in character. Advocates of **judicial restraint** are sometimes called "strict constructionists," because they look strictly to the words of the Constitution in interpreting its meaning.

The alternative to restraint is **judicial activism.** Activist judges such as the former chief justice Earl Warren and two of the leading members of his Court, Justices Hugo Black and William O. Douglas, believed that the Court should go beyond the words of the Constitution or a statute to consider the broader societal implications of its decisions. Activist judges sometimes strike out in new directions, promulgating new interpretations or inventing new legal and constitutional concepts when they believe these to be socially desirable. For example, Justice Harry Blackmun's decision in *Roe v. Wade* was based on a constitutional right to privacy that is not found in the words of the Constitution. Blackmun and the other members of the majority in the *Roe* case argued that the right to privacy was implied by other constitutional provisions. In this

judicial restraint

judicial philosophy whose adherents refuse to go beyond the clear words of the Constitution in interpreting its meaning

judicial activism

judicial philosophy that posits that the Court should go beyond the words of the Constitution or a statute to consider the broader societal implications of its decisions

instance of judicial activism, the Court knew the result it wanted to achieve and was not afraid to make the law conform to the desired outcome.

Political Ideology The second component of judicial philosophy is political ideology. The liberal or conservative outlooks of justices play an important role in their decisions. Indeed, the philosophy of activism versus restraint is, to a large extent, a smokescreen for political ideology. For the most part, liberal judges have been activists, willing to use the law to achieve social and political change, whereas conservatives have been associated with judicial restraint. Interestingly, however, in recent years some conservative justices who have long called for restraint have actually become activists in seeking to undo some of the work of liberal jurists over the past three decades.

From the 1950s to the 1980s, the Supreme Court took an activist role in such areas as civil rights, civil liberties, abortion, voting rights, and police procedures. For example, the Supreme Court was more responsible than any other governmental institution for breaking down America's system of racial segregation. The Supreme Court virtually prohibited states from interfering with the right of a woman to seek an abortion and sharply curtailed state restrictions on voting rights. And it was the Supreme Court that placed restrictions on the behavior of local police and prosecutors in criminal cases. In a series of decisions between 1989 and 1997, however, the conservative justices appointed by Reagan and Bush were able to swing the Court to a more conservative position on civil rights, affirmative action, abortion rights, property rights, criminal procedure, voting rights, desegregation, and the power of the national government.

Yet the efforts by Reagan and Bush to reshape the federal judiciary were not fully successful. Often in American history, judges have surprised and disappointed the presidents who named them to the bench. Justice Souter, for example, has been far less conservative than President Bush and the Republicans who supported Souter's appointment thought he would be. Likewise, Justices O'Connor and Kennedy have disappointed conservatives by opposing limitations on abortion.

Nevertheless, with a combined total of twelve years in office, Reagan and Bush were also able to exercise a good deal of influence on the composition of the federal district and appellate courts. By the end of Bush's term, he and Reagan together had appointed nearly half of all federal judges. Thus, whatever impact Reagan and Bush ultimately have on the Supreme Court, their appointments will certainly influence the temperament and behavior of the district and circuit courts for years to come. One important example of the continuing legacy of Reagan and Bush came in November 1997, when the Court refused to hear a challenge to the constitutionality of California's Proposition 209 (see Chapter 6). This ballot measure, adopted by California's voters in 1996, abolished state programs of affirmative action in such realms as higher education and government hiring. By refusing to hear a challenge to the proposition, the Supreme Court, in effect, struck a blow at part of the civil rights legacy of the 1960s and 1970s. Critics charged that, coming on the heels of an earlier decision by the California Board of Regents to ban the use of race as a criterion for university admissions in California, the Court's refusal to listen to objections to Proposition 209 would inflame the state's already volatile racial climate.[28]

THE DIVERSITY OF FEDERAL COURT APPOINTEES FROM REAGAN TO CLINTON

Figure 15.4

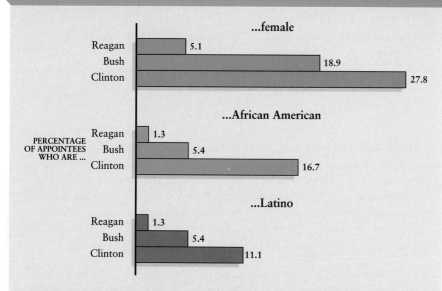

PERCENTAGE OF APPOINTEES WHO ARE ...

...female

Reagan	5.1
Bush	18.9
Clinton	27.8

...African American

Reagan	1.3
Bush	5.4
Clinton	16.7

...Latino

Reagan	1.3
Bush	5.4
Clinton	11.1

SOURCES: Harold W. Stanley and Richard G. Niemi, *Vital Statistics on American Politics,* 5th ed. (Washington, DC: Congressional Quarterly Press, 1995), pp. 268–69; Sheldon Goldman, "Bush's Judicial Legacy: The Final Imprint," *Judicature* 76 (April–May 1993), pp. 287, 293; and Sheldon Goldman, "Judicial Selection under Clinton: A Midterm Examination," *Judicature* 78 (May–June 1995), pp. 281, 287.

President Clinton promised to appoint more liberal jurists to the district and appellate courts, as well as to increase the number of women and minorities serving on the federal bench. During his first two years in office, Clinton held to this promise; more than 60 percent of his 128 judicial nominees were women or members of minority groups (see Figure 15.4).[29] A large number of judicial vacancies remained unfilled, however, when the Republicans took control of Congress at the end of 1994. Soon after the election, Senator Orrin Hatch of Utah, the new chair of the Senate Judiciary Committee, which confirms judicial nominations, indicated his intention to oppose any nominee whom he deemed to be too liberal. This prompted the Clinton White House to withdraw some nominations and to search for district and appellate nominees who would be more acceptable to the Republicans.[30]

The political struggles of the 1980s and 1990s amply illustrate the importance of judicial ideology. Is abortion a fundamental right or a criminal activity? How much separation must there be between church and state? Does the use of the Voting Rights Act to increase minority representation constitute a violation of the rights of whites? The answers to these and many other questions cannot be found in the words of the Constitution. They must be located, instead, in the hearts of the judges who interpret that text.

Judicial Power and Politics

▶ How has the power of the federal courts been limited throughout much of American history?

▶ How have the role and power of the federal courts been transformed over the last fifty years?

▶ How has the increase in the Supreme Court's power changed its role in the political process?

One of the most important institutional changes to occur in the United States during the past half-century has been the striking transformation of the role and power of the federal courts, and of the Supreme Court in particular. Understanding how this transformation came about is the key to understanding the contemporary role of the courts in America.

TRADITIONAL LIMITATIONS ON THE FEDERAL COURTS

For much of American history, the power of the federal courts was subject to five limitations.[31] First, courts were constrained by judicial rules of standing that limited access to the bench. Claimants who simply disagreed with governmental action or inaction could not obtain access. Access to the courts was limited to individuals who could show that they were particularly affected by the government's behavior in some area. This limitation on access to the courts diminished the judiciary's capacity to forge links with important political and social forces.

Second, courts were traditionally limited in the character of the relief they could provide. In general, courts acted only to offer relief or assistance to individuals and not to broad social classes, again inhibiting the formation of alliances between the courts and important social forces. Third, courts lacked enforcement powers of their own and were compelled to rely on executive or state agencies to ensure compliance with their edicts. If the executive or state agencies were unwilling to assist the courts, judicial enactments could go unheeded, as when President Andrew Jackson declined to enforce Chief Justice John Marshall's 1832 order to the state of Georgia to release two missionaries it had arrested on Cherokee lands. Marshall asserted that the state had no right to enter the Cherokee lands without their assent.[32] Jackson is reputed to have said, "John Marshall has made his decision, now let him enforce it."

Fourth, federal judges are, of course, appointed by the president (with the consent of the Senate). As a result, the president and Congress can shape the composition of the federal courts and ultimately, perhaps, the character of judicial decisions. Finally, Congress has the power to change both the size and jurisdiction of the Supreme Court and other federal courts. In many areas, federal courts obtain their jurisdiction not from the Constitution but from congressional statutes. On a number of occasions, Congress has threatened to take matters out of the Court's hands when it was unhappy with the Court's policies.[33] For example, in 1996 Congress enacted several pieces of legislation designed to curb the jurisdiction of the federal courts. One of these laws was the Prison Litigation Reform Act, which limits the ability of federal judges to issue "consent decrees" under which the judges could take control of state prison systems. Another jurisdictional curb was included in the Immigration Reform Act, which prohibited the federal courts from hearing class action suits against Immigration and Naturalization Service deportation orders. As to the size of the Court, on one memorable occasion, presidential and congressional threats to expand the size of the Supreme Court—Franklin Roosevelt's "court packing" plan—encouraged the justices to drop their opposition to New Deal programs.

As a result of these five limitations on judicial power, through much of their history the chief function of the federal courts was to provide judicial support for executive agencies and to legitimate acts of Congress by declaring them to be consistent with constitutional principles. Only on rare occasions have the federal courts actually dared to challenge Congress or the executive branch.[34]

TWO JUDICIAL REVOLUTIONS

Since the Second World War, however, the role of the federal judiciary has been strengthened and expanded. There have actually been two judicial revolutions in the United States since World War II. The first and most visible of these was the substantive revolution in judicial policy. As we saw earlier in this chapter and in Chapters 5 and 6, in policy areas, including school desegregation, legislative apportionment, and criminal procedure, as well as obscenity, abortion, and voting rights, the Supreme Court was at the forefront of a series of sweeping changes in the role of the U.S. government, and ultimately, in the character of American society.[35]

But at the same time that the courts were introducing important policy innovations, they were also bringing about a second, less visible revolution. During the 1960s and 1970s, the Supreme Court and other federal courts instituted a series of changes in judicial procedures that fundamentally expanded the power of the courts in the United States. First, the federal courts liberalized the concept of standing to permit almost any group that seeks to challenge the actions of an administrative agency to bring its case before the federal bench. In 1971, for example, the Supreme Court ruled that public interest groups could use the National Environmental Policy Act to challenge the actions of federal agencies by claiming that the agencies' activities might have adverse environmental consequences.[36]

Students and Politics

"Several students at public universities across the nation have followed the path blazed by [University of Wisconsin,] Madison, students, and filed suit against their universities claiming its mandatory student-fee systems are unconstitutional. Students of the University of Minnesota and Lane Community College in Oregon are currently suing their universities in federal court.... Jordan Lorence, the attorney representing students in the UW system lawsuit, is also representing the five University of Minnesota students in a similar case.

"Lorence said he believes lawsuits against the mandatory payment of fees by students to groups they object to is a national trend. 'The reason why these lawsuits are happening is because of the political activism of the funded groups is so extreme and so intense,' he said. 'If the fees only funded the ski club and the Chinese checkers society, there would be no lawsuits around the country.' ... Mark Gallagher, attorney for the Oregon students suing their community college, said the Supreme Court would likely hear one of the current cases. 'One of these cases will probably end up at the Supreme Court because three appellate courts have looked at the same issue and have all said different things about it,' Gallagher said. 'Each court has given different interpretations of the First Amendment and the Court would settle the dispute.'

"UW Associate Dean of Students Roger Howard said universities in Iowa, Illinois and Virginia have already voluntarily decided to refund segregated fees if students request a refund. However, Howard said the amount of refunds in these states were minimal.

"He said the current objection to mandatory fees at public universities is not merely 'child's play' on college campuses, but part of a broader political argument across the nation. 'It is a part of a larger argument in the U.S. and, in many ways, it goes beyond college campuses,' Howard said. 'It is an argument about how we tax ourselves, how we organize and how we make decisions in our communities.'"

SOURCE: Jason Moll, "Universities Across the U.S. Have Faced Similar Fee Issues," *Badger Herald*, April 3, 1998; reprinted on UWire, http://www.uwire.com/uwire/98/4/news04039809.chtml.

Congress helped to make it even easier for groups dissatisfied with government policies to bring their cases to the courts by adopting Section 1,983 of the U.S. Code, which permits the practice of "fee shifting"—that is, allowing citizens who successfully bring a suit against a public official for violating their constitutional rights to collect their attorneys' fees and costs from the government. Thus, Section 1,983 encourages individuals and groups to bring their problems to the courts rather than to Congress or the executive branch. These changes have given the courts a far greater role in the administrative process than ever before. Many federal judges are concerned that federal legislation in areas such as health care reform would create new rights and entitlements that would give rise to a deluge of court cases. "Any time you create a new right, you create a host of disputes and claims," warned Barbara Rothstein, chief judge of the federal district court in Seattle, Washington.[37]

Second, the federal courts broadened the scope of relief to permit themselves to act on behalf of broad categories or classes of persons in "class action" cases, rather than just on behalf of individuals.[38] A **class action suit** is a procedural device that permits large numbers of persons with common interests to join together under a representative party to bring or defend a lawsuit. One example of a class action suit is the case of *In re Agent Orange Product Liability Litigation,* in which a federal judge in New York certified Vietnam War veterans as a class with standing to sue a manufacturer of herbicides for damages allegedly incurred from exposure to the defendant's product while in Vietnam.[39] The class potentially numbered in the tens of thousands.

Third, the federal courts began to employ so-called structural remedies, in effect retaining jurisdiction of cases until the court's mandate had actually been implemented to its satisfaction.[40] The best known of these instances was Federal judge W. Arthur Garrity's effort to operate the Boston school system from his bench in order to ensure its desegregation. Between 1974 and 1985, Judge Garrity issued fourteen decisions relating to different aspects of the Boston school desegregation plan that had been developed under his authority and put into effect under his supervision.[41] In another recent case, Federal judge Leonard B. Sand imposed fines that would have forced the city of Yonkers, New York, into bankruptcy if it had refused to accept his plan to build public housing in white neighborhoods. After several days of fines, the city gave in to the judge's ruling.

Through these three judicial mechanisms, the federal courts paved the way for an unprecedented expansion of national judicial power. In essence, liberalization of the rules of standing and expansion of the scope of judicial relief drew the federal courts into linkages with important social interests and classes, while the introduction of structural remedies enhanced the courts' ability to serve these constituencies. Thus, during the 1960s and 1970s, the power of the federal courts expanded in the same way the power of the executive expanded during the 1930s—through links with constituencies, such as civil rights, consumer, environmental, and feminist groups, that staunchly defended the Supreme Court in its battles with Congress, the executive, or other interest groups.

THE JUDICIARY: LIBERTY AND DEMOCRACY

In the original conception of the framers, the judiciary was to be the institution that would protect individual liberty from the government. As we saw in

class action suit

a legal action by which a group or class of individuals with common interests can file a suit on behalf of everyone who shares that interest

Federal judge W. Arthur Garrity implemented the desegregation of the Boston public school system through a series of controversial court decisions.

Chapter 3, the framers believed that in a democracy the great danger was what they termed "tyranny of the majority"—the possibility that a popular majority, "united or actuated by some common impulse or passion," would "trample on the rules of justice."[42] The framers hoped that the courts would protect liberty from the potential excesses of democracy. And for most of American history, this was precisely the role played by the federal courts. The courts' most important decisions were those that protected the freedoms—to speak, worship, publish, vote, and attend school—of groups and individuals whose political views, religious beliefs, or racial or ethnic backgrounds made them unpopular.

In recent years, however, the courts have been changing their role in the political process. Rather than serve simply as a bastion of individual liberty against the excessive power of the majority, the judiciary has tried to play an active role in helping groups and forces in American society bring about social and political change in the fight for equality. In a sense, the judiciary has entered the political process and has begun to behave more like the democratic institutions whose sometimes misdirected impulses toward tyranny the courts were supposed to keep in check. This change poses a basic dilemma for students of American government. If the courts have become simply one more part of the democratic political process, then who is left to protect the liberty of individuals?

★ The Citizen's Role

The framers of the Constitution deliberately designed the judiciary to be independent of the ebb and flow of public sentiment. For this reason, federal judges are appointed for life. In many states, judges are appointed or elected for long terms. Citizen participation in the judicial process is, by design, limited.

One area, however, in which tens of thousands of citizens participate in the judicial process every year is through jury service. Citizens serve on grand juries, which are the bodies that conduct inquiries and hand down indictments, and trial juries. Trial juries decide the guilt or innocence of defendants in criminal cases and determine which side will prevail in civil cases. Juries have enormous power. In most instances, their findings of facts are final, and in most instances a jury verdict of "innocent" in a criminal case is conclusive. Although juries are formally bound to administer the law as presented to them by the judge, juries often stray from the letter of the law, and there is little that can be done to stop them. Some "antigovernment" groups are fond of arguing that juries should determine what the law is regardless of the judge's instructions.

As we have seen, the role of the courts has increased in the United States over the past several decades. This, in turn, has increased the importance of the jury. In recent years, juries have made decisions with important political consequences. For example, in 1996, a jury took less than two hours to acquit the head of the White House travel office, Billy Dale, of charges that he misused travel funds. Some critics believed that the Clinton administration had brought charges against Dale primarily to divert attention from the fact that the president had fired all the travel office's employees in order to give their

Outside the Los Angeles federal courthouse, women suffering the effects of defective silicone breast implants protested Dow Chemical's failure to pay the settlement of a class action suit. Federal courts have been the site of numerous class action suits in recent decades.

In the future, the Internet will greatly improve communications between the judiciary and the general public by dramatically increasing the speed and ease with which information is available. Already, the LEXIS on-line service has revolutionized legal research in this country, making statutes and opinions from hundreds of state and federal court cases available to subscribers in their homes or offices, as well as in law school and university libraries. Supreme Court decisions on important issues from abortion to civil rights to criminal justice will be available almost instantly to interested citizens. The courts have even begun posting audio content, such as oral arguments from the Supreme Court case *Clinton v. Jones.* In addition, the filing of court documents and *amicus curiae* briefs could become dramatically easier, as electronic submission makes the cumbersome rules of paper filing obsolete. The Internet shifts tremendous power— the power of information— to the legal consumer. Thus, the Internet has the potential to significantly streamline the conduct of judicial business in the United States.
www.wwnorton.com/wtp2e

jobs to cronies and relatives. The jury's actions caused considerable embarrassment to the president and saved Dale from what appeared to be a form of political persecution.

In hundreds of other cases, jury findings in liability cases have forced corporations to change the design of products, or the ways in which they deal with employees. A California jury's $15 million award to the parents of a child killed in a 1993 automobile accident compelled automakers to redesign their seat belt systems.[43] A leading antinausea drug was withdrawn from the market in 1994 after a jury found that it had extremely serious side effects and awarded $19 million to a plaintiff who claimed to have been harmed by the drug.[44] After a jury ordered Ortho Biotech, Inc., to pay several million dollars for failing to respond to an employee who claimed to have been sexually harassed by a manager, a number of corporations developed new guidelines for dealing with sexual harassment allegations.[45]

Thus, citizens can play an enormously important role in the judicial process. Jury pools are typically drawn from lists of registered voters and licensed drivers within each jurisdiction. In many jurisdictions, college students are summoned for jury duty. One Kansas State University philosophy major who served on a trial jury said, "There are real people on juries, and, in the end, I feel juries do reach the correct verdicts, and justice does prevail."[46]

★ Summary

Millions of cases come to trial every year in the United States. The great majority—nearly 99 percent—are tried in state and local courts. The types of law are common law, civil law, criminal law, and public law.

Three kinds of cases fall under federal jurisdiction: (1) civil cases involving citizens from different states, (2) civil cases where a federal agency is seeking to enforce federal laws that provide for civil penalties, and (3) cases involving federal criminal statutes or where state criminal cases have been made issues of public law. Judicial power extends only to cases and controversies. Litigants must have standing to sue, and courts neither hand down opinions on hypothetical issues nor take the initiative.

The organization of the federal judiciary provides for original jurisdiction in the federal district courts, the U.S. Court of Claims, the U.S. Tax Court, the Customs Court, and some federal agencies.

Each district court is in one of the twelve appellate districts, called circuits, presided over by a court of appeals. Appellate courts admit no new evidence; their rulings are based solely on the records of the court proceedings or agency hearings that led to the original decision. Appeals court rulings are final unless the Supreme Court chooses to review them. The Supreme Court has some original jurisdiction, but its major job is to review lower court decisions involving substantial issues of public law.

Federal judges are appointed by the president, subject to confirmation by the Senate. Presidents generally attempt to select judges whose political philosophy is similar to their own. Over time, presidents have been able to exert a great deal of influence over the federal courts through their appointments.

There is no explicit constitutional authority for the Supreme Court to review acts of Congress. Nonetheless, the 1803 case of *Marbury v. Madison* established the Court's right to review congressional acts. The supremacy clause of Article VI and the Judiciary Act of 1789 give the Court the power to review state constitutions and laws.

Both appellate and Supreme Court decisions, including the decision not to review a case, make law. The impact of such law usually favors the status quo. Yet, many revolutionary changes in the law have come about through appellate court and Supreme Court rulings—in the criminal process, in apportionment, and in civil rights. Judge-made law is like a statute in that it articulates the law as it relates to future controversies. It differs from a statute in that it is intended to guide judges rather than the citizenry in general.

Most cases reach the Supreme Court through a writ of *certiorari* or a writ of *habeas corpus*. Once the Court has accepted a case, attorneys for both sides prepare briefs and seek *amicus curiae* briefs from sympathetic groups. Cases are presented to the Court in oral argument, are discussed by the justices during the Court's conference, and are decided by a majority vote of the justices. The Court's opinion is written by a member of the majority. Members of the minority may write dissenting opinions, while other members of the majority may write concurring opinions.

The influence of any individual member of the Supreme Court is limited. Writing the majority opinion for a case is an opportunity for a justice to influence the judiciary. But the need to frame an opinion in such a way as to develop majority support on the Court may limit such opportunities. Dissenting opinions can have more impact than the majority opinion; they stimulate a continued flow of cases around an issue. The solicitor general is the most important single influence outside the Court itself because he or she controls the flow of cases brought by the Justice Department and also shapes the argument in those cases. But the flow of cases is a force in itself, which the Department of Justice cannot entirely control. Social problems give rise to similar cases that ultimately must be adjudicated and appealed. Some interest groups try to develop such case patterns as a means of gaining power through the courts.

In recent years, the importance of the federal judiciary—the Supreme Court in particular—has increased substantially as the courts have developed new tools of judicial power and forged alliances with important forces in American society.

FOR FURTHER READING

Abraham, Henry. *The Judicial Process.* 6th ed. New York: Oxford University Press, 1993.

Bryner, Gary, and Dennis L. Thompson. *The Constitution and the Regulation of Society.* Provo, UT: Brigham Young University, 1988.

Davis, Sue. *Justice Rehnquist and the Constitution.* Princeton: Princeton University Press, 1989.

Graber, Mark A. *Transforming Free Speech: The Ambiguous Legacy of Civil Libertarianism.* Berkeley: University of California Press, 1991.

Kahn, Ronald. *The Supreme Court and Constitutional Theory, 1953–1993.* Lawrence: University Press of Kansas, 1994.

McCann, Michael W. *Rights at Work.* Chicago: University of Chicago Press, 1994.

Mezey, Susan G. *No Longer Disabled: The Federal Courts and the Politics of Social Security Disability.* New York: Greenwood, 1988.

O'Brien, David M. *Storm Center: The Supreme Court in American Politics.* 4th ed. New York: Norton, 1996.

Rosenberg, Gerald. *The Hollow Hope: Can Courts Bring about Social Change?* Chicago: University of Chicago Press, 1991.

Rubin, Eva. *Abortion, Politics and the Courts.* Westport, CT: Greenwood Press, 1982.

Silverstein, Mark. *Judicious Choices: The New Politics of Supreme Court Confirmations.* New York: Norton, 1994.

STUDY OUTLINE

The Legal System

1. Court cases in the United States proceed under three categories of law: criminal, civil, and public.
2. In the area of criminal law, either a state government or the federal government is the plaintiff who alleges that someone has committed a crime.
3. Civil cases are those between individuals or between individuals and the government in which no criminal violation is charged. In deciding these cases, courts apply statutes and legal precedent.
4. Public law involves questions of whether the government has the constitutional or statutory authority to take action.
5. By far, most cases are heard by state courts.
6. Cases are heard in federal courts if the U.S. government is a party in the case or the case involves federal statutes, treaties with other nations, or the U.S. Constitution.
7. Although the federal courts hear only a fraction of all the cases decided every year in the United States, federal court decisions are extremely important.

Federal Jurisdiction

1. The eighty-nine federal district courts are trial courts of original jurisdiction and their cases are, in form, indistinguishable from cases in the state trial courts.
2. The twelve U.S. courts of appeals review and render decisions in approximately 10 percent of all lower-court and agency cases.
3. Federal judges are appointed by the president and confirmed by a majority vote of the full Senate.
4. The Supreme Court is the highest court in the country and has the power and the obligation to review any lower court decision involving a substantial issue of public law, state legislation, or act of Congress.
5. The Constitution does not specify the number of justices that should sit on the Supreme Court, although since 1869 there have been nine—one chief justice and eight associate justices.
6. The solicitor general can influence the Court by screening cases before they reach the Supreme Court, submitting *amicus* briefs, and shaping the arguments used before the Court.

The Power of the Supreme Court: Judicial Review

1. The Supreme Court's power to review acts of Congress, although accepted as natural and rarely challenged, is not specifically granted by the Constitution.
2. The Supreme Court's power to review state action or legislation derives from the Constitution's supremacy clause, although it is neither granted specifically by the Constitution nor inherent in the federal system.
3. Appeals of lower court decisions can reach the Supreme Court in one of two ways: through a writ of *certiorari,* or, in the case of convicted state prisoners, through a writ of *habeas corpus.*
4. Over the years, courts have developed specific rules that govern which cases within their jurisdiction they hear. These rules of access can be broken down into three categories: case or controversy, standing, and mootness.
5. Groups and forces in society attempt to influence justices' rulings on particular issues.
6. After filing written arguments, or briefs, attorneys present oral argument to the Supreme Court. After oral argument, the justices discuss the case and vote on a final decision.
7. The Supreme Court always explains its decisions in terms of law and precedent.
8. Despite the rule of precedent, the Court often reshapes law. Such changes in the interpretation of law can be explained, in part, by changes in the judicial philosophy of activism versus restraint and by changes in political ideology.

Judicial Power and Politics

1. For much of American history, the power of the federal courts was subject to five limitations: standing, the limited relief courts could provide, the lack of enforcement powers, political appointment, and the power of Congress to change the size and jurisdiction of federal courts.
2. The role of the federal judiciary has been strengthened since World War II by two judicial revolutions. The first revolution was a substantive revolution in several policy areas. The second revolution involved changes in judicial procedures that lessened traditional limitations on the courts.

PRACTICE QUIZ

1. Which of the following is a brief submitted to the Supreme Court by someone other than one of the parties in the case?
   a) *amicus curiae*
   b) *habeas corpus*
   c) solicitor general
   d) *ex post* brief

2. By what term is the practice of the courts to uphold precedent known?
   a) *certiorari*
   b) *stare decisis*
   c) rule of four
   d) senatorial courtesy

3. Which government official is responsible for arguing the federal government's position in cases before the Supreme Court?
   a) the vice president
   b) the attorney general
   c) the U.S. district attorney
   d) the solicitor general

4. Which of the following helps to explain the expanded power of the judiciary since World War II?
   a) changes in judicial procedure
   b) changes in judicial policy areas
   c) Neither a nor b is correct.
   d) Both a and b are correct.

5. What is the name for the body of law that involves disputes between private parties?
   a) civil law
   b) privacy law
   c) household law
   d) common law

6. Under what authority is the number of Supreme Court justices decided?
   a) the president
   b) the chief justice
   c) Congress
   d) the Constitution

7. Which of the following does not influence the flow of cases heard by the Supreme Court?
   a) the Supreme Court itself
   b) the solicitor general
   c) the attorney general
   d) the FBI

8. Which of the following cases involved the "right to privacy?"
   a) *Griswold v. Connecticut*
   b) *Brown v. Board of Education*
   c) *Schneckloth v. Bustamante*
   d) *Marbury v. Madison*

9. Which of the following Supreme Court cases from the 1960s involved the rights of criminal suspects?
   a) *Gideon v. Wainwright*
   b) *Miranda v. Arizona*
   c) *Escobedo v. Illinois*
   d) all of the above

10. Where do most trials in America take place?
    a) state and local courts
    b) appellate courts
    c) federal courts
    d) the Supreme Court

CRITICAL THINKING QUESTIONS

1. Judicial philosophies of activism and restraint are often confused with the political ideologies of liberalism and conservatism in the courts. What do you think the roots of this confusion are? To what extent is the common understanding correct? To what extent is it incorrect? Are there ways in which conservatives have been or could be activists in the courts? Are there ways in which liberals have exercised or could exercise judicial restraint?

2. In many ways, courts are expected to be apolitical institutions of government. In what ways are courts, judges, and justices shielded from politics and political pressure? In what ways are they vulnerable to political pressure? Are the courts an appropriate place for politics? What is the danger of having too much or too little political accountability in judicial decision making?

KEY TERMS

amicus curiae (p. 588)
appellate court (p. 581)
briefs (p. 601)
chief justice (p. 584)
civil law (p. 580)
class action suit (p. 610)
criminal law (p. 579)
defendant (p. 579)
dissenting opinion (p. 604)
due process of law (p. 583)
judicial activism (p. 605)
judicial restraint (p. 605)

judicial review (p. 590)
jurisdiction (p. 582)
Miranda rule (p. 594)
mootness (p. 596)
opinion (p. 604)
oral argument (p. 601)
original jurisdiction (p. 583)
per curiam (p. 588)
plaintiff (p. 579)
plea bargains (p. 582)
precedents (p. 581)
public law (p. 581)

senatorial courtesy (p. 586)
solicitor general (p. 588)
standing (p. 596)
stare decisis (p. 581)
supremacy clause (p. 591)
supreme court (p. 581)
trial court (p. 581)
Uniform Commercial Code (p. 582)
writ of *certiorari* (p. 597)
writ of *habeas corpus* (p. 597)

Appendix

The Declaration of Independence

In Congress, July 4, 1776

The unanimous Declaration of the thirteen united States of America,

When in the Course of human events, it becomes necessary for one people to dissolve the political bands which have connected them with another, and to assume among the powers of the earth, the separate and equal station to which the Laws of Nature and of Nature's God entitle them, a decent respect to the opinions of mankind requires that they should declare the causes which impel them to the separation.

We hold these truths to be self-evident, that all men are created equal, that they are endowed by their Creator with certain unalienable Rights, that among these are Life, Liberty and the pursuit of Happiness.—That to secure these rights, Governments are instituted among Men, deriving their just powers from the consent of the governed. —That whenever any Form of Government becomes destructive of these ends, it is the Right of the People to alter or to abolish it, and to institute new Government, laying its foundation on such principles and organizing its powers in such form, as to them shall seem most likely to effect their Safety and Happiness. Prudence, indeed, will dictate that Governments long established should not be changed for light and transient causes; and accordingly all experience hath shewn, that mankind are more disposed to suffer, while evils are sufferable, than to right themselves by abolishing the forms to which they are accustomed. But when a long train of abuses and usurpations, pursuing invariably the same Object evinces a design to reduce them under absolute Despotism, it is their right, it is their duty, to throw off such Government, and to provide new Guards for their future security.—Such has been the patient sufferance of these Colonies; and such is now the necessity which constrains them to alter their former Systems of Government. The history of the present King of Great Britain is a history of repeated injuries and usurpations, all having in direct object the establishment of an absolute Tyranny over these States. To prove this, let Facts be submitted to a candid world.

He has refused his Assent to Laws, the most wholesome and necessary for the public good.

He has forbidden his Governors to pass Laws of immediate and pressing importance, unless suspended in their operation till his Assent should be obtained; and when so suspended, he has utterly neglected to attend to them.

He has refused to pass other Laws for the accommodation of large districts of people, unless those people would relinquish the right of Representation in the Legislature, a right inestimable to them and formidable to tyrants only.

He has called together legislative bodies at places unusual, uncomfortable, and distant from the depository of their public Records, for the sole purpose of fatiguing them into compliance with his measures.

He has dissolved Representative Houses repeatedly, for opposing with manly firmness his invasions on the rights of the people.

He has refused for a long time, after such dissolutions, to cause others to be elected; whereby the Legislative powers, incapable of Annihilation, have returned to the People at large for their exercise; the State remaining in the mean time exposed to all the dangers of invasion from without, and convulsions within.

He has endeavoured to prevent the population of these States; for that purpose obstructing the Laws for Naturalization of Foreigners; refusing to pass others to encourage their migrations hither, and raising the conditions of new Appropriations of Lands.

He has obstructed the Administration of Justice, by refusing his Assent to Laws for establishing Judiciary powers.

He has made Judges dependent on his Will alone, for the tenure of their offices, and the amount and payment of their salaries.

He has erected a multitude of New Offices, and sent hither swarms of Officers to harrass our people, and eat out their substance.

He has kept among us, in times of peace, Standing Armies without the Consent of our legislatures.

He has affected to render the Military independent of and superior to the Civil power.

He has combined with others to subject us to a jurisdiction foreign to our constitution, and unacknowledged by our laws; giving his Assent to their Acts of pretended Legislation:

For Quartering large bodies of armed troops among us:

For protecting them, by a mock Trial, from punishment for any Murders which they should commit on the Inhabitants of these States:

For cutting off our Trade with all parts of the world:

For imposing Taxes on us without our Consent:

For depriving us in many cases, of the benefits of Trial by Jury:

For transporting us beyond Seas to be tried for pretended offences:

For abolishing the free System of English Laws in a neighboring Province, establishing therein an Arbitrary government, and enlarging its Boundaries so as to render it at once an example and fit instrument for introducing the same absolute rule into these Colonies:

For taking away our Charters, abolishing our most valuable Laws, and altering fundamentally the Forms of our Governments:

For suspending our own Legislatures, and declaring themselves invested with power to legislate for us in all cases whatsoever.

He has abdicated Government here, by declaring us out of his Protection and waging War against us.

He has plundered our seas, ravaged our Coasts, burnt our towns, and destroyed the lives of our people.

He is at this time transporting large Armies of foreign Mercenaries to compleat the works of death, desolation and tyranny, already begun with circumstances of Cruelty & perfidy scarcely parallelled in the most barbarous ages, and totally unworthy the Head of a civilized nation.

He has constrained our fellow Citizens taken Captive on the high Seas to bear Arms against their Country, to become the executioners of their friends and Brethren, or to fall themselves by their Hands.

He has excited domestic insurrections amongst us, and has endeavoured to bring on the inhabitants of our frontiers, the merciless Indian Savages, whose known rule of warfare, is an undistinguished destruction of all ages, sexes and conditions.

In every stage of these Oppressions We have Petitioned for Redress in the most humble terms: Our repeated Petitions have been answered only by repeated injury. A Prince whose character is thus marked by every act which may define a Tyrant, is unfit to be the ruler of a free people.

Nor have We been wanting in attentions to our Brittish brethren. We have warned them from time to time of attempts by their legislature to extend an unwarrantable jurisdiction over us. We have reminded them of the circumstances of our emigration and settlement here. We have appealed to their native justice and magnanimity, and we have conjured them by the ties of our common kindred to disavow these usurpations, which, would inevitably interrupt our connections and correspondence. They too have been deaf to the voice of justice and of consanguinity. We must, therefore, acquiesce in the necessity, which denounces our Separation, and hold them, as we hold the rest of mankind, Enemies in War, in Peace Friends.

We, Therefore, the Representatives of the United States of America, in General Congress, Assembled, appealing to the Supreme Judge of the world for the rectitude of our intentions, do, in the Name, and by Authority of the good People of these Colonies, solemnly publish and declare, That these United Colonies are, and of Right ought to be Free and Independent States; that they are Absolved from all Allegiance to the British Crown, and that all political connection between them and the State of Great Britain, is and ought to be totally dissolved; and that as Free and Independent States, they have full Power to levy War, conclude Peace, contract Alliances, establish Commerce, and to do all other Acts and Things which Independent States may of right do. And for the support of this Declaration, with a firm reliance on the protection of divine Providence, we mutually pledge to each other our Lives, our Fortunes and our sacred Honor.

The foregoing Declaration was, by order of Congress, engrossed, and signed by the following members:

John Hancock

NEW HAMPSHIRE
Josiah Bartlett
William Whipple
Matthew Thornton

MASSACHUSETTS BAY
Samuel Adams
John Adams
Robert Treat Paine
Elbridge Gerry

RHODE ISLAND
Stephen Hopkins
William Ellery

CONNECTICUT
Roger Sherman
Samuel Huntington
William Williams
Oliver Wolcott

NEW YORK
William Floyd
Philip Livingston
Francis Lewis
Lewis Morris

NEW JERSEY
Richard Stockton
John Witherspoon
Francis Hopkinson
John Hart
Abraham Clark

PENNSYLVANIA
Robert Morris
Benjamin Rush
Benjamin Franklin
John Morton
George Clymer
James Smith

George Taylor
James Wilson
George Ross

DELAWARE
Caesar Rodney
George Read
Thomas M'Kean

MARYLAND
Samuel Chase
William Paca
Thomas Stone
Charles Carroll,
* of Carrollton*

VIRGINIA
George Wythe
Richard Henry Lee
Thomas Jefferson

Benjamin Harrison
Thomas Nelson, Jr.
Francis Lightfoot Lee
Carter Braxton

NORTH CAROLINA
William Hooper
Joseph Hewes
John Penn

SOUTH CAROLINA
Edward Rutledge
Thomas Heyward, Jr.
Thomas Lynch, Jr.
Arthur Middleton

GEORGIA
Button Gwinnett
Lyman Hall
George Walton

Resolved, That copies of the Declaration be sent to the several assemblies, conventions, and committees, or councils of safety, and to the several commanding officers of the continental troops; that it be proclaimed in each of the United States, at the head of the army.

The Articles of Confederation

Agreed to by Congress November 15, 1777;
ratified and in force March 1, 1781

To all whom these Presents shall come, we the undersigned Delegates of the States affixed to our Names, send greeting. Whereas the Delegates of the United States of America, in Congress assembled, did, on the fifteenth day of November, in the Year of Our Lord One thousand Seven Hundred and Seventy seven, and in the Second Year of the Independence of America, agree to certain articles of Confederation and perpetual Union between the States of Newhampshire, Massachusetts-bay, Rhodeisland and Providence Plantations, Connecticut, New-York, New-Jersey, Pennsylvania, Delaware, Maryland, Virginia, North-Carolina, South-Carolina and Georgia in the words following, viz. "Articles of Confederation and perpetual Union between the states of Newhampshire, Massachusetts-bay, Rhodeisland and Providence Plantations, Connecticut, New-York, New-Jersey, Pennsylvania, Delaware, Maryland, Virginia, North-Carolina, South-Carolina and Georgia.

Art. I. The Stile of this confederacy shall be "The United States of America."

Art. II. Each state retains its sovereignty, freedom and independence, and every Power, Jurisdiction and right, which is not by this confederation expressly delegated to the United States, in Congress assembled.

Art. III. The said states hereby severally enter into a firm league of friendship with each other, for their common defence, the security of their Liberties, and their mutual and general welfare, binding themselves to assist each other, against all force offered to, or attacks made upon them, or any of them, on account of religion, sovereignty, trade, or any other pretence whatever.

Art. IV. The better to secure and perpetuate mutual friendship and intercourse among the people of the different states in this union, the free inhabitants of each of these states, paupers, vagabonds and fugitives from Justice excepted, shall be entitled to all privileges and immunities of free citizens in the several states; and the people of each state shall have free ingress and regress to and from any other state, and shall enjoy therein all the privileges of trade and commerce, subject to the same duties, impositions and restrictions as the inhabitants thereof respectively, provided that such restriction shall not extend so far as to prevent the removal of property imported into any state, to any other state, of which the Owner is an inhabitant; provided also that no imposition, duties or restriction shall be laid by any state, on the property of the united states, or either of them.

If any Person guilty of, or charged with treason, felony, or other high misdemeanor in any state, shall flee from Justice, and be found in any of the united states, he shall, upon demand of the Governor or executive power, of the state from which he fled, be delivered up and removed to the state having jurisdiction of his offence.

Full faith and credit shall be given in each of these states to the records, acts and judicial proceedings of the courts and magistrates of every other state.

Art. V. For the more convenient management of the general interests of the united states, delegates shall be annually appointed in such manner as the legislature of each state shall direct, to meet in Congress on the first Monday in November, in every year, with a power reserved to each state, to recall its delegates, or any of them, at any time within the year, and to send others in their stead, for the remainder of the Year.

No state shall be represented in Congress by less than two, nor by more than seven Members; and no person shall be capable of being a delegate for more than three years in any term of six years; nor shall any person, being a delegate, be capable of holding any office under the united states, for which he, or another for his benefit receives any salary, fees or emolument of any kind.

Each state shall maintain its own delegates in a meeting of the states, and while they act as members of the committee of the states.

In determining questions in the united states, in Congress assembled, each state shall have one vote.

Freedom of speech and debate in Congress shall not be

impeached or questioned in any Court, or place out of Congress, and the members of congress shall be protected in their persons from arrests and imprisonments, during the time of their going to and from, and attendance on congress, except for treason, felony, or breach of the peace.

Art. VI. No state without the Consent of the united states in congress assembled, shall send any embassy to, or receive any embassy from, or enter into any conference, agreement, or alliance or treaty with any King, prince or state; nor shall any person holding any office or profit or trust under the united states, or any of them, accept of any present, emolument, office or title of any kind whatever from any king, prince or foreign state; nor shall the united states in congress assembled, or any of them, grant any title of nobility.

No two or more states shall enter into any treaty, confederation or alliance whatever between them, without the consent of the united states in congress assembled, specifying accurately the purposes for which the same is to be entered into, and how long it shall continue.

No state shall lay any imposts or duties, which may interfere with any stipulations in treaties, entered into by the united states in congress assembled, with any king, prince or state, in pursuance of any treaties already proposed by congress, to the courts of France and Spain.

No vessels of war shall be kept up in time of peace by any state, except such number only, as shall be deemed necessary by the united states in congress assembled, for the defence of such state, or its trade; nor shall any body of forces be kept up by any state, in time of peace, except such number only, as in the judgment of the united states, in congress assembled, shall be deemed requisite to garrison the forts necessary for the defence of such state; but every state shall always keep up a well regulated and disciplined militia, sufficiently armed and accoutred, and shall provide and constantly have ready for use, in public stores, a due number of field pieces and tents, and a proper quantity of arms, ammunition and camp equipage.

No state shall engage in any war without the consent of the united states in congress assembled, unless such state be actually invaded by enemies, or shall have received certain advice of a resolution being formed by some nation of Indians to invade such state, and the danger is so imminent as not to admit of a delay, till the united states in congress asssembled can be consulted; nor shall any state grant commissions to any ships or vessels of war, nor letters of marque or reprisal, except it be after a declaration of war by the united states in congress assembled, and then only against the kingdom or state and the subjects thereof, against which war has been so declared, and under such regulations as shall be established by the united states in congress assembled, unless such state be infested by pirates; in which case vessels of war may be fitted out for that occasion, and kept so long as the danger shall continue, or until the united states in congress assembled shall determine otherwise.

Art. VII. When land-forces are raised by any state for the common defence, all officers of or under the rank of colonel, shall be appointed by the legislature of each state respectively, by whom such forces shall be raised, or in such manner as such state shall direct, and all vacancies shall be filled up by the state which first made the appointment.

Art. VIII. All charges of war, and all other expences that shall be incurred for the common defence or general welfare, and allowed by the united states in congress assembled, shall be defrayed out of a common treasury, which shall be supplied by the several states in proportion to the value of all land within each state, granted to or surveyed for any Person, as such land and the buildings and improvements thereon shall be estimated according to such mode as the united states in congress assembled, shall from time to time direct and appoint.

The taxes for paying that proportion shall be laid and levied by the authority and direction of the legislatures of the several states within the time agreed upon by the united states in congress assembled.

Art. IX. The united states in congress assembled, shall have the sole and exclusive right and power of determining on peace and war, except in the cases mentioned in the sixth article—of sending and receiving ambassadors—entering into treaties and alliances, provided that no treaty of commerce shall be made whereby the legislative power of the respective states shall be restrained from imposing such imposts and duties on foreigners, as their own people are subjected to, or from prohibiting the exportation of any species of goods or commodities whatsoever—of establishing rules for deciding in all cases, what captures on land or water shall be legal, and in what manner prizes taken by land or naval forces in the service of the united states shall be divided or appropriated—of granting letters of marque and reprisal in times of peace—appointing courts for the trial of piracies and felonies committed on the high seas and establishing courts for receiving and determining finally appeals in all cases of captures, provided that no member of congress shall be appointed a judge of any of the said courts.

The united states in congress assembled shall also be the last resort on appeal in all disputes and differences now subsisting or that hereafter may arise between two or more states concerning boundary, jurisdiction or any other cause whatever; which authority shall always be exercised in the manner following. Whenever the legislative or executive authority or lawful agent of any state in controversy with another shall present a petition to congress stating the matter in question and praying for a hearing, notice thereof shall be given by order of congress to the legislative or executive authority of the other state in controversy, and a day assigned for the appearance of the parties by their lawful agents, who shall then be directed to appoint by joint consent, commissioners or judges to constitute a court for hearing and determining the matter in question: but if they cannot agree, congress shall name three persons out of each of the united states, and from the list of such persons each party shall alternately strike out one, the petitioners beginning, until the number shall be reduced to thirteen; and from that number not less than seven, nor more than nine names as congress shall direct, shall in the presence of congress be drawn out by lot, and the persons whose names shall be so drawn or any five of them, shall be commissioners or judges, to hear and finally determine the controversy, so always as a major part of the judges who shall hear the cause shall agree in the determination: and if either party shall neglect to attend at the day appointed, without shewing reasons, which congress shall judge sufficient, or being present shall refuse to strike, the congress shall proceed to nominate three persons out of each state, and the secretary of congress shall strike in behalf of such party absent or refusing; and the judgment and sentence of the court to be appointed, in the manner before prescribed, shall be final and conclusive; and if any of the parties shall refuse to submit to the authority of such court, or to appear to defend their claim or cause, the court shall nevertheless proceed to pronounce sentence, or judgment, which shall in like manner be final and decisive, the judgment or sentence and other proceedings being in either case transmitted to congress, and lodged among the acts of congress for the security of the parties concerned: provided that every commissioner, before he sits in judgment, shall take an oath to be administered by one of the judges of the supreme or superior court of the state, where the cause shall be tried, "well and truly to hear and determine the matter in question, according to the best of his judgment, without favour, affection or hope of reward:" provided also, that no state shall be deprived of territory for the benefit of the united states.

All controversies concerning the private right of soil claimed under different grants of two or more states, whose jurisdictions as they may respect such lands, and the states which passed such grants are adjusted, the said grants or either of them being at the same time claimed to have originated antecedent to such settlement of jurisdiction, shall on the petition of either party to the congress of the united states, be finally determined as near as may be in the same manner as is before prescribed for deciding disputes respecting territorial jurisdiction between different states.

The united states in congress assembled shall also have the sole and exclusive right and power of regulating the alloy and value of coin struck by their own authority, or by that of the respective states—fixing the standard of weights and measures throughout the united states—regulating the trade and managing all affairs with the Indians, not members of any of the states, provided that the legislative right of any state within its own limits be not infringed or violated—establishing and regulating post-offices from one state to another, throughout all the united states, and exacting such postage on the papers passing thro' the same as may be requisite to defray the expences of the said office—appointing all officers of the land forces, in the service of the united states, excepting regimental officers—appointing all the officers of the naval forces, and commissioning all officers whatever in the service of the united states—making rules for the government and regulation of the said land and naval forces, and directing their operations.

The united states in congress assembled shall have authority to appoint a committee, to sit in the recess of congress, to be denominated "A Committee of the States," and to consist of one delegate from each state; and to appoint such other committees and civil officers as may be necessary for managing the general affairs of the united states under their direction—to appoint one of their number to preside, provided that no person be allowed to serve in the office of president more than one year in any term of three years; to ascertain the necessary sums of Money to be raised for the service of the united states, and to appropriate and apply the same for defraying the public expenses—to borrow money, or emit bills on the credit of the united states, transmitting every half year to the respective states an account of the sums of money so borrowed or emitted,—to build and equip a navy—to agree upon the number of land forces, and to make requisitions from each state for its quota, in proportion to the number of white inhabitants in such state; which requisition shall be binding, and thereupon the legislature of each state shall appoint the regimental officers, raise the men and cloath, arm and equip then in a soldier like manner, at the expense of the united states; and the officers and men so cloathed, armed and equipped shall march to the place appointed, and within the time agreed on by the united states in congress assembled: But if the united states in congress assembled shall, on consideration of circumstances judge proper that any state should not raise men, or should raise a smaller number than its quota, and that any other state should raise a greater number of men than the quota thereof, such extra number shall be raised, officered, cloathed, armed and equipped in the same manner as the quota of such state, unless the legislature of such state shall judge that such extra number cannot be safely spared out of the same, in which case they shall raise officer, cloath, arm and equip as many of such extra number as they judge can be safely spared. And the officers and men so cloathed, armed and equipped, shall march to the place appointed, and within the time agreed on by the united states in congress assembled.

The united states in congress assembled shall never engage in a war, nor grant letters of marque and reprisal in time of peace, nor enter into any treaties or alliances, nor coin money, nor regulate the value thereof, nor ascertain the sums and expenses necessary for the defence and welfare of the united states, or any of them, nor emit bills, nor borrow money on the credit of the united states, nor appropriate money, nor agree upon the number of vessels of war, to be built or purchased, or the number of land or sea forces to be raised, nor appoint a commander in chief of the army or navy, unless nine states assent to the same: nor shall a question on any other point, except for adjourning from day to day be determined, unless by the votes of a majority of the united states in congress assembled.

The congress of the united states shall have power to adjourn to any time within the year, and to any place within the united states, so that no period of adjournment be for a longer duration than the space of six Months, and shall publish the Journal of their proceedings monthly, except such parts thereof relating to treaties, alliances or military operations, as in their judgment require secrecy; and the yeas and nays of the delegates of each state on any question shall be entered on the Journal, when it is desired by any delegate; and the delegates of a state, or any of them, at his or their request shall be furnished with a transcript of the said Journal, except such parts as are above excepted, to lay before the legislatures of the several states.

Art. X. The committee of the states, or any nine of them, shall be authorised to execute, in the recess of congress, such of the powers of congress as the united states in congress assembled, by the consent of nine states, shall from time to time think expedient to vest them with; provided that no power be delegated to the said committee, for the exercise of which, by the articles of confederation, the voice of nine states in the congress of the united states assembled is requisite.

Art. XI. Canada acceding to this confederation, and joining in the measures of the united states, shall be admitted into, and entitled to all the advantages of this union: but no other colony shall be admitted into the same, unless such admission be agreed to by nine states.

Art. XII. All bills of credit emitted, monies borrowed and debts contracted by, or under the authority of congress, before the assembling of the united states, in pursuance of the present confederation, shall be deemed and considered as a charge against the united states, for payment and satisfaction whereof the said united states and the public faith are hereby solemnly pledged.

Art. XIII. Every state shall abide by the determinations of the united states in congress assembled, on all questions which by this confederation are submitted to them. And the Articles of this confederation shall be inviolably observed by every state, and the union shall be perpetual; nor shall any alteration at any time hereafter be made in any of them; unless such alteration be agreed to in a congress of the united states, and be afterwards confirmed by the legislatures of every state.

And Whereas it hath pleased the Great Governor of the World to incline the hearts of the legislatures we respectively represent in congress, to approve of, and to authorize us to ratify the said articles of confederation and perpetual union. Know Ye that we the undersigned delegates, by virtue of the power and authority to us given for that purpose, do by these presents, in the name and in behalf of our respective constituents, fully and entirely ratify and confirm each and every of the said articles of confederation and perpetual union, and all and singular the matters and things therein contained: And we do further solemnly plight and engage the faith of our respective constituents, that they shall abide by the determinations of the united states in congress assembled, on all questions, which by the said confederation are submitted to them. And that the articles thereof shall be inviolably observed by the states we respectively represent, and that the union shall be perpetual. In Witness whereof we have hereunto set our hands in Congress. Done at Philadelphia in the state of Pennsylvania the ninth day of July, in the Year of our Lord one Thousand seven Hundred and Seventy-eight, and in the third year of the independence of America.

The Constitution of the United States of America

[PREAMBLE]

We the People of the United States, in Order to form a more perfect Union, establish Justice, insure domestic Tranquility, provide for the common defence, promote the general Welfare, and secure the Blessings of Liberty to ourselves and our Posterity, do ordain and establish this Constitution for the United States of America.

ARTICLE I

Section 1

[LEGISLATIVE POWERS]

All legislative Powers herein granted shall be vested in a Congress of the United States, which shall consist of a Senate and House of Representatives.

Section 2

[HOUSE OF REPRESENTATIVES, HOW CONSTITUTED, POWER OF IMPEACHMENT]

The House of Representatives shall be composed of Members chosen every second Year by the People of the several States, and the Electors in each State shall have the Qualifications requisite for Electors of the most numerous Branch of the State Legislature.

No Person shall be a Representative who shall not have attained to the Age of twenty five Years, and been seven Years a Citizen of the United States, and who shall not, when elected, be an Inhabitant of that State in which he shall be chosen.

Representatives and *direct Taxes*[1] shall be apportioned among the several States which may be included within this Union, according to their respective Numbers, *which shall be determined by adding to the whole Number of free Persons, including those bound to Service for a Term of Years, and excluding Indians not taxed, three fifths of all other Persons.*[2] The actual Enumeration shall be made within three Years after the first Meeting of the Congress of the United States, and within every subsequent Term of ten Years, in such Manner as they shall by Law direct. The Number of Representatives shall not exceed one for every thirty Thousand, but each State shall have at Least one Representative; *and until such enumeration shall be made, the State of New Hampshire shall be entitled to chuse three, Massachusetts eight, Rhode-Island and Providence Plantations one, Connecticut five, New-York six, New Jersey four, Pennsylvania eight, Delaware one, Maryland six, Virginia ten, North Carolina five, South Carolina five, and Georgia three.*[3]

When vacancies happen in the Representation from any State, the Executive Authority thereof shall issue Writs of Election to fill such Vacancies.

The House of Representatives shall chuse their Speaker and other Officers; and shall have the sole Power of Impeachment.

Section 3

[THE SENATE, HOW CONSTITUTED, IMPEACHMENT TRIALS]

The Senate of the United States shall be composed of two Senators from each State, *chosen by the Legislature thereof,*[4] for six Years; and each Senator shall have one Vote.

---

[1]Modified by Sixteenth Amendment.

[2]Modified by Fourteenth Amendment.

[3]Temporary provision.

[4]Modified by Seventeenth Amendment.

Immediately after they shall be assembled in Consequence of the first Election, they shall be divided as equally as may be into three Classes. The Seats of the Senators of the first Class shall be vacated at the Expiration of the second Year, of the second Class at the Expiration of the fourth Year, and of the third Class at the Expiration of the sixth Year, so that one third may be chosen every second Year; *and if Vacancies happen by Resignation, or otherwise, during the Recess of the Legislature of any State, the Executive thereof may make temporary Appointments until the next Meeting of the Legislature, which shall then fill such Vacancies.*[5]

No Person shall be a Senator who shall not have attained to the Age of thirty Years, and been nine Years a Citizen of the United States, and who shall not, when elected, be an Inhabitant of that State for which he shall be chosen.

The Vice President of the United States shall be President of the Senate, but shall have no Vote, unless they be equally divided.

The Senate shall chuse their other Officers, and also a President pro tempore, in the Absence of the Vice President, or when he shall exercise the Office of President of the United States.

The Senate shall have the sole Power to try all Impeachments. When sitting for that Purpose, they shall be on Oath or Affirmation. When the President of the United States is tried, the Chief Justice shall preside: And no Person shall be convicted without the Concurrence of two thirds of the Members present.

Judgment in Cases of Impeachment shall not extend further than to removal from Office, and disqualification to hold and enjoy any Office of honor, Trust or Profit under the United States: but the Party convicted shall nevertheless be liable and subject to Indictment, Trial, Judgment and Punishment, according to Law.

Section 4

[ELECTION OF SENATORS AND REPRESENTATIVES]

The Times, Places and Manner of holding Elections for Senators and Representatives, shall be prescribed in each State by the Legislature thereof; but the Congress may at any time by Law make or alter such Regulations, except as to the Places of chusing Senators.

The Congress shall assemble at least once in every Year, and such Meeting shall be on the first Monday in December, unless they shall by Law appoint a different Day.[6]

---

[5]Modified by Seventeenth Amendment.
[6]Modified by Twentieth Amendment.

Section 5

[QUORUM, JOURNALS, MEETINGS, ADJOURNMENTS]

Each House shall be the Judge of the Elections, Returns and Qualifications of its own Members, and a Majority of each shall constitute a Quorum to do Business; but a smaller Number may adjourn from day to day, and may be authorized to compel the Attendance of absent Members, in such Manner, and under such Penalties as each House may provide.

Each House may determine the Rules of its Proceedings, punish its Members for disorderly Behaviour, and, with the Concurrence of two thirds, expel a Member.

Each House shall keep a Journal of its Proceedings, and from time to time publish the same, excepting such Parts as may in their Judgment require Secrecy; and the Yeas and Nays of the Members of either House on any questions shall, at the Desire of one fifth of those Present, be entered on the Journal.

Neither House, during the Session of Congress, shall, without the Consent of the other, adjourn for more than three days, nor to any other Place than that in which the two Houses shall be sitting.

Section 6

[COMPENSATION, PRIVILEGES, DISABILITIES]

The Senators and Representatives shall receive a Compensation for their Services, to be ascertained by Law, and paid out of the Treasury of the United States. They shall in all Cases, except Treason, Felony and Breach of the Peace, be privileged from Arrest during their Attendance at the Session of their respective Houses, and in going to and returning from the same; and for any Speech or Debate in either House, they shall not be questioned in any other Place.

No Senator or Representative shall, during the Time for which he was elected, be appointed to any civil Office under the Authority of the United States, which shall have been created, or the Emoluments whereof shall have been increased during such time; and no Person holding any Office under the United States, shall be a Member of either House during his Continuance in Office.

Section 7

[PROCEDURE IN PASSING BILLS AND RESOLUTIONS]

All Bills for raising Revenue shall originate in the House of Representatives; but the Senate may propose or concur with Amendments as on other Bills.

Every Bill which shall have passed the House of Representatives and the Senate, shall, before it become a Law, be presented to the President of the United States: If he approve he shall sign it, but if not he shall return it, with his Objections to that House in which it shall have originated, who shall enter the Objections at large on their Journal, and proceed to reconsider it. If after such Reconsideration two thirds of that House shall agree to pass the Bill, it shall be sent, together with the Objections, to the other House, by which it shall likewise be reconsidered, and if approved by two thirds of that House, it shall become a Law. But in all such Cases the Votes of both Houses shall be determined by yeas and Nays, and the Names of the Persons voting for and against the Bill shall be entered on the Journal of each House respectively. If any Bill shall not be returned by the President within ten Days (Sundays excepted) after it shall have been presented to him, the Same shall be a Law, in like Manner as if he had signed it, unless the Congress by their Adjournment prevent its Return, in which Case it shall not be a Law.

Every Order, Resolution, or Vote to which the Concurrence of the Senate and House of Representatives may be necessary (except on a question of Adjournment) shall be presented to the President of the United States; and before the Same shall take Effect, shall be approved by him, or being disapproved by him, shall be repassed by two thirds of the Senate and House of Representatives, according to the Rules and Limitations prescribed in the Case of a Bill.

Section 8

[POWERS OF CONGRESS]

The Congress shall have Power

To lay and collect Taxes, Duties, Imposts and Excises, to pay the Debts and provide for the common Defence and general Welfare of the United States; but all Duties, Imposts and Excises shall be uniform throughout the United States;

To borrow Money on the credit of the United States;

To regulate Commerce with foreign Nations, and among the several States, and with the Indian Tribes;

To establish an uniform Rule of Naturalization, and uniform Laws on the subject of Bankruptcies throughout the United States;

To coin Money, regulate the Value thereof, and of foreign Coin, and fix the Standard of Weights and Measures;

To provide for the Punishment of counterfeiting the Securities and current Coin of the United States;

To establish Post Offices and post Roads;

To promote the Progress of Science and useful Arts, by securing for limited Times to Authors and Inventors the exclusive Right to their respective Writings and Discoveries;

To constitute Tribunals inferior to the supreme Court;

To define and punish Piracies and Felonies committed on the high Seas, and Offences against the Law of Nations;

To declare War, grant Letters of Marque and Reprisal, and make Rules concerning Captures on Land and Water;

To raise and support Armies, but no Appropriation of Money to that Use shall be for a longer Term than two Years;

To provide and maintain a Navy;

To make Rules for the Government and Regulation of the land and naval Forces;

To provide for calling forth the Militia to execute the Laws of the Union, suppress Insurrections and repel Invasions;

To provide for organizing, arming, and disciplining, the Militia, and for governing such Part of them as may be employed in the Service of the United States, reserving to the States respectively, the Appointment of the Officers, and the Authority of training the Militia according to the discipline prescribed by Congress;

To exercise exclusive Legislation in all Cases whatsoever, over such District (not exceeding ten Miles square) as may, by Cession of particular States, and the Acceptance of Congress, become the Seat of the Government of the United States, and to exercise like Authority over all Places purchased by the Consent of the Legislature of the State in which the Same shall be, for the Erection of Forts, Magazines, Arsenals, dock-Yards, and other needful Buildings;—And

To make all Laws which shall be necessary and proper for carrying into Execution the foregoing Powers, and all other Powers vested by this Constitution in the Government of the United States, or in any Department or Officer thereof.

Section 9

[SOME RESTRICTIONS ON FEDERAL POWER]

The Migration or Importation of such Persons as any of the States now existing shall think proper to admit, shall not be prohibited by the Congress prior to the Year one thousand eight hundred and eight, but a Tax or duty may be imposed on such Importation, not exceeding ten dollars for each Person.[7]

The Privilege of the Writ of Habeas Corpus shall not be suspended, unless when in Cases of Rebellion or Invasion the public Safety may require it.

No Bill of Attainder or ex post facto Law shall be passed.

No Capitation, or other direct, Tax shall be laid, unless in Proportion to the Census or Enumeration herein before directed to be taken.[8]

No Tax or Duty shall be laid on Articles exported from any State.

No Preference shall be given by any Regulation of Commerce or Revenue to the Ports of one State over those of another; nor shall Vessels bound to, or from, one State, be obliged to enter, clear, or pay Duties in another.

[7]Temporary provision.

[8]Modified by Sixteenth Amendment.

No Money shall be drawn from the Treasury, but in Consequence of Appropriations made by Law; and a regular Statement and Account of the Receipts and Expenditures of all public Money shall be published from time to time.

No Title of Nobility shall be granted by the United States: And no Person holding any Office of Profit or Trust under them, shall, without the Consent of the Congress, accept of any present, Emolument, Office, or Title, of any kind whatever, from any King, Prince, or foreign State.

Section 10

[RESTRICTIONS UPON POWERS OF STATES]

No State shall enter into any Treaty, Alliance, or Confederation; grant Letters of Marque and Reprisal; coin Money; emit Bills of Credit; make any Thing but gold and silver Coin a Tender in Payment of Debts; pass any Bill of Attainder, ex post facto Law, or Law impairing the Obligation of Contracts, or grant any Title of Nobility.

No State shall, without the Consent of the Congress, lay any Imposts or Duties on Imports or Exports, except what may be absolutely necessary for executing it's inspection Laws: and the net Produce of all Duties and Imposts, laid by any State on Imports or Exports, shall be for the Use of the Treasury of the United States; and all such Laws shall be subject to the Revision and Controul of the Congress.

No State shall, without the Consent of Congress, lay any Duty of Tonnage, keep Troops, or Ships of War in time of Peace, enter into any Agreement or Compact with another State, or with a foreign Power, or engage in War, unless actually invaded, or in such imminent Danger as will not admit of delay.

ARTICLE II

Section 1

[EXECUTIVE POWER, ELECTION, QUALIFICATIONS OF THE PRESIDENT]

The executive Power shall be vested in a President of the United States of America. *He shall hold his Office during the Term of four Years, and, together with the Vice President, chosen for the same Term, be elected, as follows*[9]

Each State shall appoint, in such Manner as the Legislature thereof may direct, a Number of Electors, equal to the whole Number of Senators and Representatives to which the State may be entitled in the Congress: but no Senator or Representative, or Person holding an Office of Trust or Profit under the United States, shall be appointed an Elector.

The electors shall meet in their respective States, and vote by ballot for two Persons, of whom one at least shall not be an Inhabitant of the same State with themselves. And they shall make a List of all the Persons voted for, and of the Number of Votes for each; which List they shall sign and certify, and transmit sealed to the Seat of the Government of the United States, directed to the President of the Senate. The President of the Senate shall, in the Presence of the Senate and House of Representatives, open all the Certificates, and the Votes shall then be counted. The Person having the greatest Number of Votes shall be the President, if such Number be a Majority of the whole Number of Electors appointed; and if there be more than one who have such Majority, and have an equal Number of Votes, then the House of Representatives shall immediately chuse by Ballot one of them for President; and if no Person have a Majority, then from the five highest on the List the said House shall in like Manner chuse the President. But in chusing the President, the Votes shall be taken by States, the Representation from each State having one Vote; A quorum for this Purpose shall consist of a Member or Members from two thirds of the States, and a Majority of all the States shall be necessary to a Choice. In every Case, after the Choice of the President, the person having the greatest Number of Votes of the Electors shall be the Vice President. But if there should remain two or more who have equal Votes, the Senate shall chuse from them by Ballot the Vice President.[10]

The Congress may determine the Time of chusing the Electors, and the Day on which they shall give their Votes; which Day shall be the same throughout the United States.

No Person except a natural born Citizen, or a Citizen of the United States, at the time of the Adoption of this Constitution, shall be eligible to the Office of President; neither shall any Person be eligible to that Office who shall not have attained to the Age of thirty five Years, and been fourteen Years a Resident within the United States.

In Case of the Removal of the President from Office, or his Death, Resignation, or Inability to discharge the Powers and Duties of the said Office, the Same shall devolve on the Vice President, and the Congress may by Law provide for the Case of Removal, Death, Resignation or Inability, both of the President and Vice President, declaring what Officer shall then act as President, and such Officer shall act accordingly, until the Disability be removed, or a President shall be elected.

The President shall, at stated Times, receive for his Services, a Compensation, which shall neither be increased nor diminished during the Period for which he shall have been elected, and he shall not receive within that Period any other Emolument from the United States, or any of them.

---

[9]Number of terms limited to two by Twenty-second Amendment.

[10]Modified by Twelfth and Twentieth Amendments.

Before he enter on the Execution of his Office, he shall take the following Oath or Affirmation:—"I do solemnly swear (or affirm) that I will faithfully execute the Office of President of the United States, and will to the best of my Ability, preserve, protect and defend the Constitution of the United States."

Section 2

[POWERS OF THE PRESIDENT]

The President shall be Commander in Chief of the Army and Navy of the United States, and of the Militia of the several States, when called into the actual Service of the United States; he may require the Opinion, in writing, of the principal Officer in each of the executive Departments, upon any Subject relating to the Duties of their respective Offices, and he shall have Power to grant Reprieves and Pardons for Offences against the United States, except in Cases of Impeachment.

He shall have Power, by and with the Advice and Consent of the Senate, to make Treaties, provided two thirds of the Senators present concur; and he shall nominate, and by and with the Advice and Consent of the Senate, shall appoint Ambassadors, other public Ministers and Consuls, Judges of the supreme Court, and all other Officers of the United States, whose Appointments are not herein otherwise provided for, and which shall be established by Law: but the Congress may by Law vest the Appointment of such inferior Officers, as they think proper, in the President alone, in the Courts of Law, or in the Heads of Departments.

The President shall have Power to fill up all Vacancies that may happen during the Recess of the Senate, by granting Commissions which shall expire at the End of their next Session.

Section 3

[POWERS AND DUTIES OF THE PRESIDENT]

He shall from time to time give to the Congress Information of the State of the Union, and recommend to their Consideration such Measures as he shall judge necessary and expedient; he may, on extraordinary Occasions, convene both Houses, or either of them, and in Case of Disagreement between them, with Respect to the Time of Adjournment, he may adjourn them to such Time as he shall think proper; he shall receive Ambassadors and other public Ministers; he shall take Care that the Laws be faithfully executed, and shall Commission all the Officers of the United States.

Section 4

[IMPEACHMENT]

The President, Vice President and all civil Officers of the United States, shall be removed from Office on Im-

peachment for, and Conviction of, Treason, Bribery, or other high Crimes and Misdemeanors.

ARTICLE III

Section 1

[JUDICIAL POWER, TENURE OF OFFICE]

The judicial Power of the United States, shall be vested in one supreme Court, and in such inferior Courts as the Congress may from time to time ordain and establish. The Judges, both of the supreme and inferior Courts, shall hold their Offices during good Behaviour, and shall, at stated Times, receive for their Services, a Compensation, which shall not be diminished during their Continuance in Office.

Section 2

[JURISDICTION]

The judicial Power shall extend to all Cases, in Law and Equity, arising under this Constitution, the Laws of the United States, and Treaties made, or which shall be made, under their Authority;—to all Cases affecting Ambassadors, other public Ministers and Consuls;—to all Cases of admiralty and maritime Jurisdiction;—to Controversies to which the United States shall be a Party;—to Controversies between two or more States;—*between a State and Citizens of another State;*—between Citizens of different States,—between Citizens of the same State claiming Lands under Grants of different States, *and between a State,* or the Citizens thereof, *and foreign States, Citizens or Subjects.*[11]

In all Cases affecting Ambassadors, other public Ministers and Consuls, and those in which a State shall be Party, the supreme Court shall have original Jurisdiction. In all the other Cases before mentioned, the supreme Court shall have appellate Jurisdiction, both as to Law and Fact, with such Exceptions, and under such Regulations as the Congress shall make.

The Trial of all Crimes, except in Cases of Impeachment, shall be by Jury; and such Trial shall be held in the State where the said Crimes shall have been committed; but when not committed within any State, the Trial shall be at such Place or Places as the Congress may by Law have directed.

Section 3

[TREASON, PROOF, AND PUNISHMENT]

Treason against the United States, shall consist only in levying War against them, or in adhering to their Enemies, giving them Aid and Comfort. No Person shall be con-

---

[11]Modified by Eleventh Amendment.

victed of Treason unless on the Testimony of two Witnesses to the same overt Act, or on Confession in open Court.

The Congress shall have Power to declare the Punishment of Treason, but no Attainder of Treason shall work Corruption of Blood, or Forfeiture except during the Life of the Person attainted.

ARTICLE IV

Section 1

[FAITH AND CREDIT AMONG STATES]

Full Faith and Credit shall be given in each State to the public Acts, Records, and judicial Proceedings of every other State. And the Congress may by general Laws prescribe the Manner in which such Acts, Records and Proceedings shall be proved, and the Effect thereof.

Section 2

[PRIVILEGES AND IMMUNITIES, FUGITIVES]

The Citizens of each State shall be entitled to all Privileges and Immunities of Citizens in the several States.

A Person charged in any State with Treason, Felony or other Crime, who shall flee from Justice, and be found in another State, shall on Demand of the executive Authority of the State from which he fled, be delivered up, to be removed to the State having Jurisdiction of the Crime.

No person held to Service or Labour in one State, under the Laws thereof, escaping into another, shall, in Consequence of any Law or Regulation therein, be discharged from such Service or Labour, but shall be delivered up on Claim of the Party to whom such Service or Labour may be due.[12]

Section 3

[ADMISSION OF NEW STATES]

New States may be admitted by the Congress into this Union; but no new State shall be formed or erected within the Jurisdiction of any other State; nor any State be formed by the Junction of two or more States, or Parts of States, without the Consent of the Legislatures of the States concerned as well as of the Congress.

The Congress shall have Power to dispose of and make all needful Rules and Regulations respecting the Territory or other Property belonging to the United States; and nothing in this Constitution shall be so construed as to Prejudice any Claims of the United States, or of any particular State.

Section 4

[GUARANTEE OF REPUBLICAN GOVERNMENT]

The United States shall guarantee to every State in this Union a Republican Form of Government, and shall protect each of them against Invasion; and on Application of the Legislature, or of the Executive (when the Legislature cannot be convened), against domestic Violence.

ARTICLE V

[AMENDMENT OF THE CONSTITUTION]

The Congress, whenever two thirds of both Houses shall deem it necessary, shall propose Amendments to this Constitution, or, on the Application of the Legislatures of two thirds of the several States, shall call a Convention for proposing Amendments, which, in either Case, shall be valid to all Intents and Purposes, as Part of this Constitution, when ratified by the Legislatures of three fourths of the several States, or by Conventions in three fourths thereof, as the one or the other Mode of Ratification may be proposed by the Congress; *Provided that no Amendment which may be made prior to the Year One thousand eight hundred and eight shall in any Manner affect the first and fourth Clauses in the Ninth Section of the first Article;*[13] and that no State, without its Consent, shall be deprived of its equal Suffrage in the Senate.

ARTICLE VI

[DEBTS, SUPREMACY, OATH]

All Debts contracted and Engagements entered into, before the Adoption of this Constitution, shall be as valid against the United States under this Constitution, as under the Confederation.

This Constitution, and the Laws of the United States which shall be made in Pursuance thereof; and all Treaties made, or which shall be made, under the Authority of the United States, shall be the supreme Law of the Land; and the Judges in every State shall be bound thereby, any Thing in the Constitution or Laws of any State to the Contrary notwithstanding.

The Senators and Representatives before mentioned, and the Members of the several State Legislatures, and all executive and judicial Officers, both of the United States and of the several States, shall be bound by Oath or Affirmation, to support this Constitution; but no religious Test shall be required as a Qualification to any Office or public Trust under the United States.

---

[12]Repealed by the Thirteenth Amendment.

[13]Temporary provision.

ARTICLE VII

[RATIFICATION AND ESTABLISHMENT]

The Ratification of the Conventions of nine States, shall be sufficient for the Establishment of this Constitution between the States so ratifying the Same.[14]

Done in Convention by the Unanimous Consent of the States present the Seventeenth Day of September in the Year of our Lord one thousand seven hundred and Eighty seven and of the Independence of the United States of America the Twelfth. *In Witness* whereof We have hereunto subscribed our Names,

G:[0] WASHINGTON—
Presidt. and deputy from Virginia

NEW HAMPSHIRE
John Langdon
Nicholas Gilman

MASSACHUSETTS
Nathaniel Gorham
Rufus King

CONNECTICUT
Wm. Saml. Johnson
Roger Sherman

NEW YORK
Alexander Hamilton

NEW JERSEY
Wil: Livingston

David Brearley
Wm. Paterson
Jona: Dayton

PENNSYLVANIA
B Franklin
Thomas Mifflin
Robt. Morris
Geo. Clymer
Thos. FitzSimons
Jared Ingersoll
James Wilson
Gouv Morris

DELAWARE
Geo: Read
Gunning Bedford jun
John Dickinson
Richard Bassett
Jaco: Broom

MARYLAND
James McHenry
Dan of St Thos. Jenifer
Danl. Carroll

VIRGINIA
John Blair—
James Madison Jr.

NORTH CAROLINA
Wm. Blount
Richd. Dobbs Spaight
Hu Williamson

SOUTH CAROLINA
J. Rutledge
Charles Cotesworth
  Pinckney
Charles Pinckney
Pierce Butler

GEORGIA
William Few
Abr Baldwin

[14]The Constitution was submitted on September 17, 1787, by the Constitutional Convention, was ratified by the conventions of several states at various dates up to May 29, 1790, and became effective on March 4, 1789.

Amendments to the Constitution

Proposed by Congress and Ratified by the Legislatures of the Several States, Pursuant to Article V of the Original Constitution.

Amendments I-X, known as the Bill of Rights, were proposed by Congress on September 25, 1789, and ratified on December 15, 1791.

AMENDMENT I

[FREEDOM OF RELIGION, OF SPEECH, AND OF THE PRESS]

Congress shall make no law respecting an establishment of religion, or prohibiting the free exercise thereof; or abridging the freedom of speech, or of the press; or the right of the people peaceably to assemble, and to petition the Government for a redress of grievances.

AMENDMENT II

[RIGHT TO KEEP AND BEAR ARMS]

A well regulated Militia, being necessary to the security of a free State, the right of the people to keep and bear Arms, shall not be infringed.

AMENDMENT III

[QUARTERING OF SOLDIERS]

No Soldier shall, in time of peace be quartered in any house, without the consent of the Owner, nor in time of war, but in a manner to be prescribed by law.

AMENDMENT IV

[SECURITY FROM UNWARRANTABLE SEARCH AND SEIZURE]

The right of the people to be secure in their persons, houses, papers, and effects, against unreasonable searches and seizures, shall not be violated, and no Warrants shall issue, but upon probable cause, supported by Oath or affirmation, and particularly describing the place to be searched, and the persons or things to be seized.

AMENDMENT V

[RIGHTS OF ACCUSED PERSONS IN CRIMINAL PROCEEDINGS]

No person shall be held to answer for a capital, or otherwise infamous crime, unless on a presentment or indictment of a Grand Jury, except in cases arising in the land or naval forces, or in the Militia, when in actual service in time of War or in public danger; nor shall any person be subject for the same offence to be twice put in jeopardy of life or limb; nor shall be compelled in any criminal case to be a witness against himself, nor be deprived of life, liberty, or property, without due process of law; nor shall private property be taken for public use, without just compensation.

AMENDMENT VI

[RIGHT TO SPEEDY TRIAL, WITNESSES, ETC.]

In all criminal prosecutions, the accused shall enjoy the right to a speedy and public trial, by an impartial jury of the State and district wherein the crime shall have been committed, which district shall have been previously ascertained by law, and to be informed of the nature and cause of the accusation; to be confronted with the witnesses against him; to have compulsory process for obtaining witnesses in his favor, and to have the Assistance of Counsel for his defence.

AMENDMENT VII

[TRIAL BY JURY IN CIVIL CASES]

In suits at common law, where the value in controversy shall exceed twenty dollars, the right of trial by jury shall be preserved, and no fact tried by a jury, shall be otherwise reexamined in any Court of the United States, than according to the rules of the common law.

AMENDMENT VIII

[BAILS, FINES, PUNISHMENTS]

Excessive bail shall not be required, nor excessive fines imposed, nor cruel and unusual punishments inflicted.

AMENDMENT IX

[RESERVATION OF RIGHTS OF PEOPLE]

The enumeration in the Constitution, of certain rights, shall not be construed to deny or disparage others retained by the people.

AMENDMENT X

[POWERS RESERVED TO STATES OR PEOPLE]

The powers not delegated to the United States by the Constitution, nor prohibited by it to the States, are reserved to the States respectively, or to the people.

AMENDMENT XI

[Proposed by Congress on March 4, 1794; declared ratified on January 8, 1798.]

[RESTRICTION OF JUDICIAL POWER]

The Judicial power of the United States shall not be construed to extend to any suit in law or equity, commenced or prosecuted against one of the United States by Citizens of another State, or by Citizens or Subjects of any Foreign State.

AMENDMENT XII

[Proposed by Congress on December 9, 1803; declared ratified on September 25, 1804.]

[ELECTION OF PRESIDENT AND VICE PRESIDENT]

The Electors shall meet in their respective states and vote by ballot for President and Vice-President, one of whom, at least, shall not be an inhabitant of the same state with themselves; they shall name in their ballots the person voted for as President, and in distinct ballots the person voted for as Vice-President, and they shall make distinct lists of all persons voted for as President, and of all persons voted for as Vice-President, and of the number of votes for each, which lists they shall sign and certify, and transmit sealed to the seat of the government of the United States, directed to the President of the Senate;—the President of the Senate shall, in presence of the Senate and House of Representatives, open all the certificates and the votes shall then be counted;—The person having the greatest number of votes for President, shall be the President, if such number be a majority of the whole number of Electors appointed; and if no person have such majority, then from the persons having the highest numbers not exceeding three on the list of those voted for as President, the House of Representatives shall choose immediately, by ballot, the President. But in choosing the President, the votes shall be taken by states, the representation from each state having one vote; a quorum for this purpose shall consist of a member or members from two-thirds of the states, and a majority of all the states shall be necessary to a choice. And if the House of Representatives shall not choose a President whenever the right of choice shall devolve upon them, before the fourth day of March next following, then the Vice-President shall act as President, as in the case of the death or other constitutional disability of the President.—The person having the greatest number of votes as Vice-President, shall be the Vice-President, if such number be a majority of the whole number of Electors appointed, and if no person have a majority, then from the two highest numbers on the list, the Senate shall choose the Vice-President; a quorum for the purpose shall consist of two-thirds of the whole number of Senators, and a majority of the whole number shall be necessary to a choice. But no person constitutionally ineligible to the office of President shall be eligible to that of Vice-President of the United States.

AMENDMENT XIII

[Proposed by Congress on January 31, 1865; declared ratified on December 18, 1865.]

Section 1

[ABOLITION OF SLAVERY]

Neither slavery nor involuntary servitude, except as a punishment for crime whereof the party shall have been duly convicted, shall exist within the United States, or any place subject to their jurisdiction.

Section 2

[POWER TO ENFORCE THIS ARTICLE]

Congress shall have power to enforce this article by appropriate legislation.

AMENDMENT XIV

[Proposed by Congress on June 13, 1866, declared ratified on July 28, 1868.]

Section 1

[CITIZENSHIP RIGHTS NOT TO BE ABRIDGED BY STATES]

All persons born or naturalized in the United States, and subject to the jurisdiction thereof, are citizens of the United States and of the State wherein they reside. No State shall make or enforce any law which shall abridge the privileges or immunities of citizens of the United States; nor shall any State deprive any person of life, liberty, or property, without due process of law; nor deny to any person within its jurisdiction the equal protection of the laws.

Section 2

[APPORTIONMENT OF REPRESENTATIVES IN CONGRESS]

Representatives shall be apportioned among the several States according to their respective numbers, counting the whole number of persons in each State, excluding Indians not taxed. But when the right to vote at any election for the choice of electors for President and Vice- President of the United States, Representatives in Congress, the Executive and Judicial officers of a State, or the members of the Legislature thereof, is denied to any of the male inhabitants of such State, being twenty-one years of age, and citizens of the United States, or in any way abridged, except for participation in rebellion, or other crime, the basis of representation therein shall be reduced in the proportion which the number of such male citizens shall bear to the whole number of male citizens twenty-one years of age in such State.

Section 3

[PERSONS DISQUALIFIED FROM HOLDING OFFICE]

No person shall be a Senator or Representative in Congress, or elector of President and Vice-President, or hold any office, civil or military, under the United States, or under any State, who, having previously taken an oath, as a member of Congress, or as an officer of the United States, or as a member of any State legislature, or as an executive or judicial officer of any State, to support the Constitution of the United States, shall have engaged in insurrection or rebellion against the same, or given aid or comfort to the enemies thereof. But Congress may by a vote of two-thirds of each House, remove such disability.

Section 4

[WHAT PUBLIC DEBTS ARE VALID]

The validity of the public debt of the United States, authorized by law, including debts incurred for payment of pensions and bounties for services in suppressing insurrection or rebellion, shall not be questioned. But neither the United States nor any State shall assume or pay any debt or obligation incurred in aid of insurrection or rebellion against the United States, or any claim for the loss or emancipation of any slave; but all such debts, obligations and claims shall be held illegal and void.

Section 5

[POWER TO ENFORCE THIS ARTICLE]

The Congress shall have power to enforce, by appropriate legislation, the provisions of this article.

AMENDMENT XV

[Proposed by Congress on February 26, 1869; declared ratified on March 30, 1870.]

Section 1

[NEGRO SUFFRAGE]

The right of citizens of the United States to vote shall not be denied or abridged by the United States or by any State on account of race, color, or previous condition of servitude.

Section 2

[POWER TO ENFORCE THIS ARTICLE]

The Congress shall have power to enforce this article by appropriate legislation.

AMENDMENT XVI

[Proposed by Congress on July 2, 1909; declared ratified on February 25, 1913.]

[AUTHORIZING INCOME TAXES]

The Congress shall have power to lay and collect taxes on incomes, from whatever source derived, without apportionment among the several States, and without regard to any census or enumeration.

AMENDMENT XVII

[Proposed by Congress on May 13, 1912; declared ratified on May 31, 1913.]

[POPULAR ELECTION OF SENATORS]

The Senate of the United States shall be composed of two Senators from each State, elected by the people thereof, for six years; and each Senator shall have one vote. The electors in each State shall have the qualifications requisite for electors of the most numerous branch of the State legislatures.

When vacancies happen in the representation of any State in the Senate, the executive authority of such State shall issue writs of election to fill such vacancies: *Provided,* That the legislature of any State may empower the executive thereof to make temporary appointments until the people fill the vacancies by election as the legislature may direct.

This amendment shall not be so construed as to affect the election or term of any Senator chosen before it becomes valid as part of the Constitution.

AMENDMENT XVIII

[Proposed by Congress December 18, 1917; declared ratified on January 29, 1919.]

Section 1

[NATIONAL LIQUOR PROHIBITION]

After one year from the ratification of this article the manufacture, sale, or transportation of intoxicating liquors within, the importation thereof into, or the exportation thereof from the United States and all territory subject to the jurisdiction thereof for beverage purposes is hereby prohibited.

Section 2

[POWER TO ENFORCE THIS ARTICLE]

The Congress and the several States shall have concurrent power to enforce this article by appropriate legislation.

Section 3

[RATIFICATION WITHIN SEVEN YEARS]

This article shall be inoperative unless it shall have been ratified as an amendment to the Constitution by the legislatures of the several States, as provided in the Consti-

tution, within seven years from the date of the submission hereof to the States by the Congress.[1]

AMENDMENT XIX

[Proposed by Congress on June 4, 1919; declared ratified on August 26, 1920.]

[WOMAN SUFFRAGE]

The right of citizens of the United States to vote shall not be denied or abridged by the United States or by any State on account of sex.

Congress shall have power to enforce this article by appropriate legislation.

AMENDMENT XX

[Proposed by Congress on March 2, 1932; declared ratified on February 6, 1933.]

Section 1

[TERMS OF OFFICE]

The terms of the President and Vice President shall end at noon on the 20th day of January, and the terms of Senators and Representatives at noon on the 3d day of January, of the years in which such terms would have ended if this article had not been ratified; and the terms of their successors shall then begin.

Section 2

[TIME OF CONVENING CONGRESS]

The Congress shall assemble at least once in every year, and such meeting shall begin at noon on the 3d day of January, unless they shall by law appoint a different day.

Section 3

[DEATH OF PRESIDENT-ELECT]

If, at the time fixed for the beginning of the term of the President, the President elect shall have died, the Vice President elect shall become President. If a President shall not have been chosen before the time fixed for the beginning of his term, or if the President elect shall have failed to qualify, then the Vice President elect shall act as President until a President shall have qualified; and the Congress may by law provide for the case wherein neither

---

[1]Repealed by the Twenty-first Amendment

a President elect nor a Vice President elect shall have qualified, declaring who shall then act as President, or the manner in which one who is to act shall be selected, and such person shall act accordingly until a President or Vice President shall have qualified.

Section 4

[ELECTION OF THE PRESIDENT]

The Congress may by law provide for the case of the death of any of the persons from whom the House of Representatives may choose a President whenever the right of choice shall have devolved upon them, and for the case of the death of any of the persons from whom the Senate may choose a Vice President whenever the right of choice shall have devolved upon them.

Section 5

[AMENDMENT TAKES EFFECT]

Sections 1 and 2 shall take effect on the 15th day of October following the ratification of this article.

Section 6

[RATIFICATION WITHIN SEVEN YEARS]

This article shall be inoperative unless it shall have been ratified as an amendment to the Constitution by the legislatures of three-fourths of the several States within seven years from the date of its submission.

AMENDMENT XXI

[Proposed by Congress on February 20, 1933; declared ratified on December 5, 1933.]

Section 1

[NATIONAL LIQUOR PROHIBITION REPEALED]

The eighteenth article of amendment to the Constitution of the United States is hereby repealed.

Section 2

[TRANSPORTATION OF LIQUOR INTO "DRY" STATES]

The transportation or importation into any State, Territory, or Possession of the United States for delivery or use therein of intoxicating liquors, in violation of the laws thereof, is hereby prohibited.

Section 3

[RATIFICATION WITHIN SEVEN YEARS]

This article shall be inoperative unless it shall have

been ratified as an amendment to the Constitution by conventions in the several States, as provided in the Constitution, within seven years from the date of the submission hereof to the States by the Congress.

AMENDMENT XXII

[Proposed by Congress on March 21, 1947; declared ratified on February 27, 1951.]

Section 1

[TENURE OF PRESIDENT LIMITED]

No person shall be elected to the office of President more than twice, and no person who has held the office of President or acted as President, for more than two years of a term to which some other person was elected President shall be elected to the office of the President more than once. But this Article shall not apply to any person holding the office of President when this Article was proposed by the Congress, and shall not prevent any person who may be holding the office of President, or acting as President, during the term within which this Article becomes operative from holding the office of President or acting as President during the remainder of such term.

Section 2

[RATIFICATION WITHIN SEVEN YEARS]

This article shall be inoperative unless it shall have been ratified as an amendment to the Constitution by the legislatures of three-fourths of the several States within seven years from the date of its submission to the States by the Congress.

AMENDMENT XXIII

[Proposed by Congress on June 16, 1960; declared ratified on March 29, 1961.]

Section 1

[ELECTORAL COLLEGE VOTES FOR THE DISTRICT OF COLUMBIA]

The District constituting the seat of Government of the United States shall appoint in such manner as the Congress may direct:

A number of electors of President and Vice President equal to the whole number of Senators and Representatives in Congress to which the District would be entitled if it were a State, but in no event more than the least populous State; they shall be in addition to those appointed by the

States, but they shall be considered, for the purposes of the election of President and Vice President, to be electors appointed by a State; and they shall meet in the District and perform such duties as provided by the twelfth article of amendment.

Section 2

[POWER TO ENFORCE THIS ARTICLE]

The Congress shall have power to enforce this article by appropriate legislation.

AMENDMENT XXIV

[Proposed by Congress on August 27, 1962; declared ratified on January 23, 1964.]

Section 1

[ANTI-POLL TAX]

The right of citizens of the United States to vote in any primary or other election for President or Vice President, for electors for President or Vice President, or for Senator or Representative of Congress, shall not be denied or abridged by the United States or any State by reason of failure to pay any poll tax or other tax.

Section 2

[POWER TO ENFORCE THIS ARTICLE]

The Congress shall have power to enforce this article by appropriate legislation.

AMENDMENT XXV

[Proposed by Congress on July 6, 1965; declared ratified on February 10, 1967.]

Section 1

[VICE PRESIDENT TO BECOME PRESIDENT]

In case of the removal of the President from office or his death or resignation, the Vice President shall become President.

Section 2

[CHOICE OF A NEW VICE PRESIDENT]

Whenever there is a vacancy in the office of the Vice President, the President shall nominate a Vice President who shall take the office upon confirmation by a majority vote of both houses of Congress.

Section 3

[PRESIDENT MAY DECLARE OWN DISABILITY]

Whenever the President transmits to the President pro tempore of the Senate and the Speaker of the House of Representatives his written declaration that he is unable to discharge the powers and duties of his office, and until he transmits to them a written declaration to the contrary, such powers and duties shall be discharged by the Vice President as Acting President.

Section 4

[ALTERNATE PROCEDURES TO DECLARE AND TO END PRESIDENTIAL DISABILITY]

Whenever the Vice President and a majority of either the principal officers of the executive departments, or of such other body as Congress may by law provide, transmit to the President pro tempore of the Senate and the Speaker of the House of Representatives their written declaration that the President is unable to discharge the powers and duties of his office, the Vice President shall immediately assume the powers and duties of the office as Acting President.

Thereafter, when the President transmits to the President pro tempore of the Senate and the Speaker of the House of Representatives his written declaration that no inability exists, he shall resume the powers and duties of his office unless the Vice President and a majority of either the principal officers of the executive department, or of such other body as Congress may by law provide, transmit within four days to the President pro tempore of the Senate and the Speaker of the House of Representatives their written declaration that the President is unable to discharge the powers and duties of his office. Thereupon Congress shall decide the issue, assembling within forty eight hours for that purpose if not in session. If the Congress, within twenty one days after receipt of the latter written declaration, or, if Congress is not in session, within twenty one days after Congress is required to assemble, determines by two-thirds vote of both Houses that the President is unable to discharge the powers and duties of his office, the Vice President shall continue to discharge the same as Acting President; otherwise, the President shall resume the powers and duties of his office.

AMENDMENT **XXVI**

[Proposed by Congress on March 23, 1971; declared ratified on July 1, 1971.]

Section 1

[EIGHTEEN-YEAR-OLD VOTE]

The right of citizens of the United States, who are eighteen years of age or older, to vote shall not be denied or abridged by the United States or by any State on account of age.

Section 2

[POWER TO ENFORCE THIS ARTICLE]

The Congress shall have power to enforce this article by appropriate legislation.

AMENDMENT **XXVII**

[Proposed by Congress on September 25, 1789; declared ratified on May 8, 1992.]

[CONGRESS CANNOT RAISE ITS OWN PAY]

No law varying the compensation for the services of the Senators and Representatives, shall take effect, until an election of representatives shall have intervened.

The Federalist Papers

No. 10: Madison

Among the numerous advantages promised by a well constructed Union, none deserves to be more accurately developed than its tendency to break and control the violence of faction. The friend of popular governments never finds himself so much alarmed for their character and fate, as when he contemplates their propensity to this dangerous vice. He will not fail therefore to set a due value on any plan which, without violating the principles to which he is attached, provides a proper cure for it. The instability, injustice, and confusion introduced into the public councils have, in truth, been the mortal diseases under which popular governments have everywhere perished, as they continue to be the favorite and fruitful topics from which the adversaries to liberty derive their most specious declamations. The valuable improvements made by the American constitutions on the popular models, both ancient and modern, cannot certainly be too much admired; but it would be an unwarrantable partiality to contend that they have as effectually obviated the danger on this side, as was wished and expected. Complaints are everywhere heard from our most considerate and virtuous citizens, equally the friends of public and private faith and of public and personal liberty, that our governments are too unstable, that the public good is disregarded in the conflicts of rival parties, and that measures are too often decided, not according to the rules of justice and the rights of the minor party, but by the superior force of an interested and overbearing majority. However anxiously we may wish that these complaints had no foundation, the evidence of known facts will not permit us to deny that they are in some degree true. It will be found, indeed, on a candid review of our situation, that some of the distresses under which we labor have been erroneously charged on the operation of our governments; but it will be found, at the same time, that other causes will not alone account for many of our heaviest misfortunes; and, particularly, for that prevailing and increasing distrust of public engagements and alarm for private rights which are echoed from one end of the continent to the other. These must be chiefly, if not wholly, effects of the unsteadiness and injustice with which a factious spirit has tainted our public administration.

By a faction I understand a number of citizens, whether amounting to a majority or minority of the whole, who are united and actuated by some common impulse of passion, or of interest, adverse to the rights of other citizens, or to the permanent and aggregate interests of the community.

There are two methods of curing the mischiefs of faction: the one, by removing its causes; the other, by controlling its effects.

There are again two methods of removing the causes of faction: the one, by destroying the liberty which is essential to its existence; the other, by giving to every citizen the same opinions, the same passions, and the same interests.

It could never be more truly said than of the first remedy, that it is worse than the disease. Liberty is to faction what air is to fire, an aliment without which it instantly expires. But it could not be a less folly to abolish liberty, which is essential to political life, because it nourishes faction, than it would be to wish the annihilation of air, which is essential to animal life, because it imparts to fire its destructive agency.

The second expedient is as impracticable, as the first would be unwise. As long as the reason of man continues fallible, and he is at liberty to exercise it, different opinions will be formed. As long as the connection subsists between his reason and his self-love, his opinions and his passions will have a reciprocal influence on each other; and the former will be objects to which the latter will attach themselves. The diversity in the faculties of men, from which the rights of property originate, is not less an insuperable obstacle to a uniformity of interests. The protection of these faculties is the first object of Government. From the protection of different and unequal faculties of acquiring property, the possession of different degrees and kinds of property immediately results; and from the influence of these on the sentiments and views of the respective proprietors, ensues a division of the society into different interests and parties.

The latent causes of faction are thus sown in the nature of man; and we see them everywhere brought into different degrees of activity, according to the different circumstances of civil society. A zeal for different opinions concerning religion, concerning Government, and many other points, as well of speculation as of practice; an attachment to different leaders ambitiously contending for pre-eminence and power; or to persons of other descriptions whose fortunes have been interesting to the human passions, have in turn divided mankind into parties, inflamed them with mutual animosity, and rendered them much more disposed to vex and oppress each other, than to co-operate for their common good. So strong is this propensity of mankind to fall into mutual animosities, that where no substantial occasion presents itself, the most frivolous and fanciful distinctions have been sufficient to kindle their unfriendly passions, and excite their most violent conflicts. But the most common and durable source of factions has been the various and unequal distribution of property. Those who hold and those who are without property have ever formed distinct interests in society. Those who are creditors, and those who are debtors, fall under a like discrimination. A landed interest, a manufacturing interest, a mercantile interest, a moneyed interest, with many lesser interests, grow up of necessity in civilized nations, and divide them into different classes, actuated by different sentiments and views. The regulation of these various and interfering interests forms the principal task of modern Legislation, and involves the spirit of party and faction in the necessary and ordinary operations of Government.

No man is allowed to be judge in his own cause, because his interest would certainly bias his judgment and, not improbably, corrupt his integrity. With equal, nay with greater reason, a body of men are unfit to be both judges and parties at the same time; yet what are many of the most important acts of legislation but so many judicial determinations, not indeed concerning the rights of single persons, but concerning the rights of large bodies of citizens; and what are the different classes of legislators but advocates and parties to the causes which they determine? Is a law proposed concerning private debts? It is a question to which the creditors are parties on one side and the debtors on the other. Justice ought to hold the balance between them. Yet the parties are, and must be, themselves the judges; and the most numerous party, or in other words, the most powerful faction must be expected to prevail. Shall domestic manufacturers be encouraged, and in what degree, by restrictions on foreign manufacturers? are questions which would be differently decided by the landed

and the manufacturing classes, and probably by neither with a sole regard to justice and the public good. The apportionment of taxes on the various descriptions of property is an act which seems to require the most exact impartiality; yet there is, perhaps, no legislative act in which greater opportunity and temptation are given to a predominant party to trample on the rules of justice. Every shilling with which they overburden the inferior number is a shilling saved to their own pockets.

It is in vain to say that enlightened statesmen will be able to adjust these clashing interests and render them all subservient to the public good. Enlightened statesmen will not always be at the helm. Nor, in many cases, can such an adjustment be made at all without taking into view indirect and remote considerations, which will rarely prevail over the immediate interest which one party may find in disregarding the rights of another or the good of the whole.

The inference to which we are brought is that the *causes* of faction cannot be removed and that relief is only to be sought in the means of controlling its *effects*.

If a faction consists of less than a majority, relief is supplied by the republican principle, which enables the majority to defeat its sinister views by regular vote. It may clog the administration, it may convulse the society; but it will be unable to execute and mask its violence under the forms of the Constitution. When a majority is included in a faction, the form of popular government, on the other hand, enables it to sacrifice to its ruling passion or interest both the public good and the rights of other citizens. To secure the public good and private rights against the danger of such a faction, and at the same time to preserve the spirit and the form of popular government, is then the great object to which our enquiries are directed. Let me add that it is the great desideratum by which alone this form of government can be rescued from the opprobrium under which it has so long labored and be recommended to the esteem and adoption of mankind.

By what means is this object attainable? Evidently by one of two only. Either the existence of the same passion or interest in a majority at the same time must be prevented, or the majority, having such co-existent passion or interest, must be rendered, by their number and local situation, unable to concert and carry into effect schemes of oppression. If the impulse and the opportunity be suffered to coincide, we well know that neither moral nor religious motives can be relied on as an adequate control. They are not found to be such on the injustice and violence of individuals, and lose their efficacy in proportion to the number combined together, that is, in proportion as their efficacy becomes needful.

From this view of the subject it may be concluded that a pure Democracy, by which I mean a Society consisting of a small number of citizens, who assemble and administer the Government in person, can admit of no cure for the mischiefs of faction. A common passion or interest will, in almost every case, be felt by a majority of the whole; a communication and concert results from the form of Government itself; and there is nothing to check the inducements to sacrifice the weaker party or an obnoxious individual. Hence it is that such Democracies have ever been spectacles of turbulence and contention; have ever been found incompatible with personal security or the rights of property; and have in general been as short in their lives as they have been violent in their deaths. Theoretic politicians, who have patronized this species of Government, have erroneously supposed that by reducing mankind to a perfect equality in their political rights, they would at the same time be perfectly equalized and assimilated in their possessions, their opinions, and their passions.

A Republic, by which I mean a Government in which the scheme of representation takes place, opens a different prospect and promises the cure for which we are seeking. Let us examine the points in which it varies from pure Democracy, and we shall comprehend both the nature of the cure and the efficacy which it must derive from the Union.

The two great points of difference between a Democracy and a Republic are: first, the delegation of the Government, in the latter, to a small number of citizens elected by the rest; secondly, the greater number of citizens and greater sphere of country over which the latter may be extended.

The effect of the first difference is, on the one hand, to refine and enlarge the public views by passing them through the medium of a chosen body of citizens, whose wisdom may best discern the true interest of their country and whose patriotism and love of justice will be least likely to sacrifice it to temporary or partial considerations. Under such a regulation it may well happen that the public voice, pronounced by the representatives of the people, will be more consonant to the public good than if pronounced by the people themselves, convened for the purpose. On the other hand, the effect may be inverted. Men of factious tempers, of local prejudices, or of sinister designs, may, by intrigue, by corruption, or by other means, first obtain the suffrages, and then betray the interests of the people. The question resulting is, whether small or extensive Republics are most favorable to the election of proper guardians of the public weal; and it is clearly decided in favor of the latter by two obvious considerations.

In the first place it is to be remarked that however small the Republic may be, the Representatives must be raised to a certain number in order to guard against the cabals of a few; and that however large it may be they must be limited to a certain number in order to guard against the confusion of a multitude. Hence, the number of Representatives in the two cases not being in proportion to that of the Constituents, and being proportionally greatest in the small Republic, it follows that if the proportion of fit characters be not less in the large than in the small Republic, the former will present a greater option, and consequently a greater probability of a fit choice.

In the next place, as each Representative will be chosen by a greater number of citizens in the large than in the small Republic, it will be more difficult for unworthy candidates to practise with success the vicious arts by which elections are too often carried; and the suffrages of the people being more free, will be more likely to centre on men who possess the most attractive merit and the most diffusive and established characters.

It must be confessed that in this, as in most other cases, there is a mean, on both sides of which inconveniencies will be found to lie. By enlarging too much the number of electors, you render the representative too little acquainted with all their local circumstances and lesser interests; as by reducing it too much, you render him unduly attached to these, and too little fit to comprehend and pursue great and national objects. The Federal Constitution forms a happy combination in this respect; the great and aggregate interests being referred to the national, the local and particular to the State legislatures.

The other point of difference is the greater number of citizens and extent of territory which may be brought within the compass of Republican than of Democratic Government; and it is this circumstance principally which renders factious combinations less to be dreaded in the former than in the latter. The smaller the society, the fewer probably will be the distinct parties and interests composing it; the fewer the distinct parties and interests, the more frequently will a majority be found of the same party; and the smaller the number of individuals composing a majority, and the smaller the compass within which they are placed, the more easily will they concert and execute their plans of oppression. Extend the sphere and you take in a greater variety of parties and interests; you make it less probable that a majority of the whole will have a common motive to invade the rights of other citizens; or if such a common motive exists, it will be more difficult for all who feel it to discover their own strength and to act in unison with each other. Besides other impediments, it may be remarked, that where there is a consciousness of unjust or dishonorable purposes, communication is always checked by distrust in proportion to the number whose concurrence is necessary.

Hence, it clearly appears that the same advantage which a Republic has over a Democracy in controlling the effects of faction is enjoyed by a large over a small republic—is enjoyed by the Union over the States composing it. Does this advantage consist in the substitution of representatives whose enlightened views and virtuous sentiments render them superior to local prejudices and to schemes of injustice? It will not be denied that the representation of the Union will be most likely to possess these requisite endowments. Does it consist in the greater security afforded by a greater variety of parties, against the event of any one party being able to outnumber and oppress the rest? In an equal degree does the increased variety of parties comprised within the Union increase this security? Does it, in fine, consist in the greater obstacles opposed to the concert and accomplishment of the secret wishes of an unjust and interested majority? Here again the extent of the Union gives it the most palpable advantage.

The influence of factious leaders may kindle a flame within their particular States but will be unable to spread a general conflagration through the other States: a religious sect may degenerate into a political faction in a part of the Confederacy; but the variety of sects dispersed over the entire face of it must secure the national Councils against any danger from that source: a rage for paper money, for an abolition of debts, for an equal division of property, or for any other improper or wicked project, will be less apt to pervade the whole body of the Union than a particular member of it; in the same proportion as such a malady is more likely to taint a particular county or district than an entire State.

In the extent and proper structure of the Union, therefore, we behold a republican remedy for the diseases most incident to Republican Government. And according to the degree of pleasure and pride we feel in being republicans ought to be our zeal in cherishing the spirit and supporting the character of federalist.

PUBLIUS

No. 51: MADISON

To what expedient, then, shall we finally resort, for maintaining in practice the necessary partition of power among the several departments as laid down in the constitution? The only answer that can be given is that as all these exterior provisions are found to be inadequate the defect must be supplied, by so contriving the interior structure of the government as that its several constituent parts may, by their mutual relations, be the means of keeping each other in their proper places. Without presuming to undertake a full development of this important idea I will hazard a few general observations which may perhaps place it in a clearer light, and enable us to form a more correct judgment of the principles and structure of the government planned by the convention.

In order to lay a due foundation for that separate and distinct exercise of the different powers of government, which to a certain extent is admitted on all hands to be essential to the preservation of liberty, it is evident that each department should have a will of its own; and consequently should be so constituted that the members of each should have as little agency as possible in the appointment of the members of the others. Were this principle rigorously adhered to, it would require that all the appointments for the supreme executive, legislative, and judiciary magistracies should be drawn from the same fountain of authority, the people, through channels having no communication whatever with one another. Perhaps such a plan of constructing the several departments would be less difficult in practice than it may in contemplation appear. Some difficulties, however, and some additional expense would attend the execution of it. Some deviations, therefore, from the principle must be admitted. In the constitution of the judiciary department in particular, it might be inexpedient to insist rigorously on the principle: first, because peculiar qualifications being essential in the members, the primary consideration ought to be to select that mode of choice which best secures these qualifications; second, because the permanent tenure by which the appointments are held in that department must soon destroy all sense of dependence on the authority conferring them.

It is equally evident that the members of each department should be as little dependent as possible on those of the others for the emoluments annexed to their offices. Were the executive magistrate, or the judges, not independent of the legislature in this particular, their independence in every other would be merely nominal.

But the great security against a gradual concentration of the several powers in the same department consists in giving to those who administer each department the necessary constitutional means and personal motives to resist encroachments of the others. The provision for defence must in this, as in all other cases, be made commensurate to the danger of attack. Ambition must be made to counteract ambition. The interest of the man must be connected with the constitutional rights of the place. It may be a reflection on human nature that such devices should be necessary to control the abuses of government. But what is government itself but the greatest of all reflections on human nature? If men were angels, no government would be necessary. If angels were to govern men, neither external nor internal controls on government would be necessary. In framing a government which is to be administered by men over men, the great difficulty lies in this: You must first enable the government to control the governed; and in the next place oblige it to control itself. A dependence on the people is, no doubt, the primary control on the government; but experience has taught mankind the necessity of auxiliary precautions.

This policy of supplying, by opposite and rival interests, the defect of better motives, might be traced through the whole system of human affairs, private as well as public. We see it particularly displayed in all the subordinate distributions of power, where the constant aim is to divide and arrange the several offices in such a manner as that each may be a check on the other; that the private interest of every individual may be a sentinel over the public rights. These inventions of prudence cannot be less requisite in the distribution of the supreme powers of the State.

But it is not possible to give to each department an equal power of self-defense. In republican government, the legislative authority necessarily predominates. The remedy for this inconveniency is to divide the legislature into different branches; and to render them, by different modes of election and different principles of action, as little connected with each other as the nature of their common functions and their common dependence on the society will admit. It may even be necessary to guard against dangerous encroachments by still further precautions. As the weight of the legislative authority requires that it should be thus divided, the weakness of the executive may require, on the other hand, that it should be fortified. An absolute negative on the legislature appears, at first view, to be the natural defense with which the executive magistrate should be armed. But perhaps it would be neither altogether safe nor alone sufficient. On ordinary occasions it might not be exerted with the requisite firmness, and on extraordinary occasions it might be perfidiously abused. May not this defect of an absolute negative be supplied by some qualified connection between this weaker branch of the stronger department, by which the latter may be led to support the constitutional rights of the former, without being too much detached from the rights of its own department?

If the principles on which these observations are founded be just, as I persuade myself they are, and they be applied as a criterion to the several State constitutions, and to the federal Constitution, it will be found that if the latter does not perfectly correspond with them, the former are infinitely less able to bear such a test.

There are, moreover, two considerations particularly applicable to the federal system of America, which place that system in a very interesting point of view.

First. In a single republic, all the power surrendered by the people is submitted to the administration of a single government; and usurpations are guarded against by a division of the government into distinct and separate departments. In the compound republic of America, the power

surrendered by the people is first divided between two distinct governments, and then the portion allotted to each subdivided among distinct and separate departments. Hence a double security arises to the rights of the people. The different governments will control each other, at the same time that each will be controlled by itself.

Second. It is of great importance in a republic not only to guard the society against the oppression of its rulers, but to guard one part of the society against the injustice of the other part. Different interests necessarily exist in different classes of citizens. If a majority be united by a common interest, the rights of the minority will be insecure. There are but two methods of providing against this evil: The one by creating a will in the community independent of the majority—that is, of the society itself; the other, by comprehending in the society so many separate descriptions of citizens as will render an unjust combination of a majority of the whole very improbable, if not impracticable. The first method prevails in all governments possessing an hereditary or self-appointed authority. This, at best, is but a precarious security; because a power independent of the society may as well espouse the unjust views of the major as the rightful interests of the minor party, and may possibly be turned against both parties. The second method will be exemplified in the federal republic of the United States. Whilst all authority in it will be derived from and dependent on the society, the society itself will be broken into so many parts, interests and classes of citizens, that the rights of individuals, or of the minority, will be in little danger from interested combinations of the majority. In a free government the security for civil rights must be the same as that for religious rights. It consists in the one case in the multiplicity of interests, and in the other in the multiplicity of sects. The degree of security in both cases will depend on the number of interests and sects; and this may be presumed to depend on the extent of country and number of people comprehended under the same government. This view of the subject must particularly recommend a proper federal system to all the sincere and considerate friends of republican government: Since it shows that in exact proportion as the territory of the Union may be formed into more circumscribed Confederacies, or States, oppressive combinations of a majority will be facilitated; the best security, under the republican form, for the rights of every class of citizens, will be diminished; and consequently the stability and independence of some member of the government, the only other security, must be proportionally increased. Justice is the end of government. It is the end of civil society. It ever has been and ever will be pursued until it be obtained, or until liberty be lost in the pursuit. In a society under the forms of which the stronger faction can readily unite and oppress the weaker, anarchy may as truly be said to reign as in a state of nature, where the weaker individual is not secured against the violence of the stronger: And as, in the latter state, even the stronger individuals are prompted, by the uncertainty of their condition, to submit to a government which may protect the weak as well as themselves: So, in the former state, will the more powerful factions or parties be gradually induced, by a like motive, to wish for a government which will protect all parties, the weaker as well as the more powerful. It can be little doubted that if the State of Rhode Island was separated from the Confederacy and left to itself, the insecurity of rights under the popular form of government within such narrow limits would be displayed by such reiterated oppressions of factious majorities that some power altogether independent of the people would soon be called for by the voice of the very factions whose misrule had proved the necessity of it. In the extended republic of the United States, and among the great variety of interests, parties, and sects which it embraces, a coalition of a majority of the whole society could seldom take place on any other principles than those of justice and the general good; and there being thus less danger to a minor from the will of the major party, there must be less pretext, also, to provide for the security of the former, by introducing into the government a will not dependent on the latter, or, in other words, a will independent of the society itself. It is no less certain than it is important, notwithstanding the contrary opinions which have been entertained, that the larger the society, provided it lie within a practicable sphere, the more duly capable it will be of self-government. And happily for the *republican cause,* the practicable sphere may be carried to a very great extent by a judicious modification and mixture of the *federal principle.*

PUBLIUS

IMMIGRATION TO THE UNITED STATES BY PLACE OF ORIGIN, 1820–1989 (continued)

Region and Country of Last Residence[1]	1911–20	1921–30	1931–40	1941–50	1951–60	1961–70	1971–80	1981–89	Total 180 Years 1820–1989
All countries	5,735,811	4,107,209	528,431	1,035,039	2,515,479	3,321,677	4,493,314	5,801,579	55,457,531
Europe	4,321,887	2,463,194	347,566	621,147	1,325,727	1,123,492	800,368	637,524	36,977,034
Austria-Hungary	896,342[23]	63,548	11,424	28,329	103,743	26,022	16,028	20,152	4,338,049
Austria	453,649	32,868	3,563[24]	24,860[24]	67,106	20,621	9,478	14,566	1,825,172[3]
Hungary	442,693	30,680	7,861	3,469	36,637	5,401	6,550	5,586	1,666,801[3]
Belgium	33,746	15,846	4,817	12,189	18,575	9,192	5,329	6,239	209,729
Czechoslovakia	3,426[4]	102,194	14,393	8,347	918	3,273	6,023	6,649	145,223
Denmark	41,983	32,430	2,559	5,393	10,984	9,201	4,439	4,696	369,738
France	61,897	49,610	12,623	38,809	51,121	45,237	25,069	28,088	783,322
Germany	143,945[23]	412,202	114,058[24]	226,578[24]	477,765	190,796	74,414	79,809	7,071,313
Greece	184,201	51,084	9,119	8,973	47,608	85,969	92,369	34,490	700,017
Ireland[5]	146,181	211,234	10,973	19,789	48,362	32,966	11,490	22,229	4,715,393
Italy	1,109,524	455,315	68,028	57,661	185,491	214,111	129,368	51,008	5,356,862
Netherlands	43,718	26,948	7,150	14,860	52,277	30,606	10,492	10,723	372,717
Norway-Sweden	161,469	165,780	8,700	20,765	44,632	32,600	10,472	13,252	2,144,024
Norway	66,395	68,531	4,740	10,100	22,935	15,484	3,941	3,612	800,672[6]
Sweden	95,074	97,249	3,960	10,665	21,697	17,116	6,531	9,640	1,283,097[6]
Poland	4,813[23]	227,734	17,026	7,571	9,985	53,539	37,234	64,888	597,972
Portugal	89,732	29,994	3,329	7,423	19,588	76,065	101,710	36,365	497,195
Romania	13,311	67,646	3,871	1,076	1,039	2,531	12,393	27,361	201,345
Soviet Union	921,201[23]	61,742	1,370	571	671	2,465	38,961	42,898	3,428,927
Spain	68,611	28,958	3,258	2,898	7,894	44,659	39,141	17,689	282,404
Switzerland	23,091	29,676	5,512	10,547	17,675	18,453	8,235	7,561	358,151
United Kingdom[5, 8]	341,408	339,570	31,572	139,306	202,824	213,822	137,374	140,119	5,100,096
Yugoslavia	1,888[9]	49,064	5,835	1,576	8,225	20,381	30,540	15,984	133,493
Other Europe	31,400	42,619	11,949	8,486	16,350	11,604	9,287	7,324	181,064
Asia	247,236	112,059	16,595	37,028	153,249	427,642	1,588,178	2,416,278	5,697,301
China[10]	21,278	29,907	4,928	16,709	9,657	34,764	124,326	306,108	873,737
Hong Kong	—[11]	—[11]	—[11]	—[11]	15,541[11]	75,007	113,467	83,848	287,863[11]
India	2,082	1,886	496	1,761	1,973	27,189	164,134	221,977	426,907
Iran	—[12]	241[12]	195	1,380	3,388	10,339	45,136	101,267	161,946[12]
Israel	—[13]	—[13]	—[13]	476[13]	25,476	29,602	37,713	38,367	131,634[13]
Japan	83,837	33,462	1,948	1,555	46,250	39,988	49,775	40,654	455,813[14]
Korea	—[15]	—[15]	—[15]	107[15]	6,231	34,526	267,638	302,782	611,284[15]

Philippines	—[16]	—[16]	528	4,691	19,307	98,376	354,987	477,485	955,374[16]
Turkey	134,066	33,824	1,065	798	3,519	10,142	13,399	20,028	409,122
Vietnam	—[11]	—[11]	—[11]	—[11]	335[11]	4,340	172,820	266,027	443,522[11]
Other Asia	5,973	12,739	7,435	9,551	21,572	63,369	244,783	557,735	940,099
America	1,143,671	1,516,716	160,037	354,804	996,944	1,716,374	1,982,735	2,564,698	12,017,021
Canada & Newfoundland[17, 18]	742,185	924,515	108,527	171,718	377,952	413,310	169,939	132,296	4,270,943
Mexico[18]	219,004	459,287	22,319	60,589	299,811	453,937	640,294	975,657	3,208,543
Caribbean	123,424	74,899	15,502	49,725	123,091	470,213	741,126	759,416	2,590,542
Cuba	—[12]	15,901[12]	9,571	26,313	78,948	208,536	264,863	135,142	739,274[12]
Dominican Republic	—[20]	—[20]	1,150[20]	5,627	9,897	93,292	148,135	209,899	468,000[20]
Haiti	—[20]	—[20]	191[20]	911	4,442	34,499	56,335	118,510	214,888[20]
Jamaica	—[21]	—[21]	—[21]	—[21]	8,869[21]	74,906	137,577	184,481	405,833[21]
Other Caribbean	123,424	58,998	4,590	16,874	20,935[21]	58,980	134,216	111,384	762,547
Central America	17,159	15,769	5,861	21,665	44,751	101,330	134,640	321,845	673,385
El Salvador	—[20]	—[20]	673[20]	5,132	5,895	14,992	34,436	133,938	195,066[20]
Other Central America	17,159	15,769	5,188	16,533	38,856	86,338	100,204	187,907	478,319
South America	41,899	42,215	7,803	21,831	91,628	257,954	295,741	375,026	1,163,482
Argentina	—[20]	—[20]	1,349[20]	3,338	19,486	49,721	29,897	21,374	125,165[20]
Columbia	—[20]	—[20]	1,223[20]	3,858	18,048	72,028	77,347	99,066	271,570[20]
Ecuador	—[20]	—[20]	337[20]	2,417	9,841	36,780	50,077	43,841	143,293[20]
Other South America	41,899	42,215	4,894	12,218	44,253	99,425	138,420	210,745	623,454
Other America	—[22]	31[22]	25	29,276	59,711	19,630	995	458	110,126
Africa	8,443	6,286	1,750	7,367	14,092	28,954	80,779	144,096	301,348
Oceania	13,427	8,726	2,483	14,551	12,976	25,122	41,242	38,401	197,818
Not specified[22]	1,147	228	—	142	12,491	93	12	582	267,009

[15]Data not reported separately until 1948. [16]Prior to 1934, Philippines recorded as insular travel.
[17]Prior to 1920, Canada and Newfoundland recorded as British North America. From 1820–98, figures include all British North America possessions.
[18]Land arrivals not completely enumerated until 1908. [19]No data available for Mexico from 1886–93. [20]Data not reported separately until 1932.
[21]Data for Jamaica not collected until 1953. In prior years, consolidated under British West Indies, which is included in "Other Caribbean."
[22] "Other America" included in countries "Not specified" until 1925.
[23]From 1899–1919, data for Poland included in Austria-Hungary, Germany and the Soviet Union.
[24]From 1938–45, data for Austria included in Germany. [25]Includes 32,897 persons returning in 1906 to their homes in the United States.
— represents zero

NOTE: From 1820–67, figures represent alien passengers arrived at seaports; from 1868–91 and 1895–97, immigrant aliens arrived; from 1892–94 and 1898–1989, immigrant aliens admitted for permanent residence. From 1892–1903, aliens entering by cabin class were not counted as immigrants. Land arrivals were not completely enumerated until 1908. For this table, fiscal year 1843 covers 9 months ending September 1843; fiscal years 1832 and 1850 cover 15 months ending December 31 of the respective years; and fiscal year 1868 covers 6 months ending June 30, 1868.

SOURCE: U.S. Immigration and Naturalization Service, 1991.

Glossary

access the actual involvement of interest groups in the decision-making process (420)

accountability the obligation to justify the discharge of duties in the fulfillment of responsibilities to a person or persons in higher authority, and to be answerable to that authority for failing to fulfill the assigned duties and responsibilities (542)

administrative adjudication applying rules and precedents to specific cases to settle disputes with regulated parties (542)

administrative regulation rules made by regulatory agencies and commissions (626)

affirmative action government policies or programs that seek to address past injustices against specified groups by making special efforts to provide members of these groups with access to educational and employment opportunities (221)

agencies of socialization social institutions, including families and schools, that help to shape individuals' basic political beliefs and values (244)

agency representation the type of representation by which representatives are held accountable to their constituency if they fail to represent that constituency properly. This is the incentive for good representation when the personal backgrounds, views, and interests of the representative differ from those of his or her constituency (449)

agenda setting the power of the media to bring public attention to particular issues and problems (298)

Aid to Families with Dependent Children (AFDC) federal funds, administered by the states, for children living with parents or relatives who fall below state standards of need. Replaced in 1996 by TANF (666)

amendment a change added to a bill, law, or constitution (104)

American political community citizens who are eligible to vote and participate in American political life (36)

amicus curiae literally, "friend of the court"; individuals or groups who are not parties to a lawsuit but who seek to assist the Supreme Court in reaching a decision by presenting additional briefs (588)

Antifederalists those who favored strong state governments and a weak national government and who were opponents of the constitution proposed at the American Constitutional Convention of 1787 (100)

appellate court a court that hears the appeals of trial court decisions (581)

appropriations the amounts of money approved by Congress in statutes (bills) that each unit or agency of government can spend (481)

Articles of Confederation America's first written constitution; served as the basis for America's national government until 1789 (82)

Astroturf lobbying a negative term used to describe group-directed and exaggerated grassroots lobbying (429)

attitude (or opinion) a specific preference on a particular issue (238)

authoritarian government a system of rule in which the government recognizes no formal limits but may nevertheless be restrained by the power of other social institutions (16)

autocracy a form of government in which a single individual—a king, queen, or dictator—rules (16)

balance-of-power role the strategy whereby many countries from alliances with one or more other countries in order to counterbalance the behavior of other, usually more powerful, nation-states (724)

bandwagon effect a shift in electoral support to the candidate that public opinion polls report as the front-runner (267)

benign gerrymandering attempts to draw district boundaries so as to create districts made up primarily of disadvantaged or underrepresented minorities (364)

bicameral having a legislative assembly composed of two chambers or houses; opposite of unicameral (88, 447)

bilateral treaties treaties made between two nations (716)

bill a proposed law that has been sponsored by a member of Congress and submitted to the clerk of the House or Senate (468)

Bill of Rights the first ten amendments to the Constitution, which guarantee certain rights and liberties to the people (92, 151)

bills of attainder laws that decree a person guilty of a crime without a trial (154)

block grants federal grants-in-aid that allow states considerable discretion in how the funds should be spent (139)

briefs written documents in which attorneys explain, using case precedents, why the court should find in favor of their client (601)

Brown v. Board of Education the 1954 Supreme Court decision that struck down the "separate but equal" doctrine as fundamentally unequal. This case eliminated state power to use race as a criterion of discrimination in law and provided the national government with the power to intervene by exercising strict regulatory policies against discriminatory actions (201)

bureaucracy the complex structure of offices, tasks, rules, and principles of organization that are employed by all large-scale institutions to coordinate effectively the work of their personnel (537)

Cabinet the secretaries, or chief administrators, of the major departments of the federal government. Cabinet secretaries are appointed by the president with the consent of the Senate (508)

campaign an effort by political candidates and their staffs to win the backing of donors, political activists, and voters in the quest for political office (369)

capture an interest's acquisition of substantial influence over the government agency charged with regulating its activities (421)

categorical grants congressional grants given to states and localities on the condition that expenditures be limited to a problem or group specified by the law (133, 635)

caucus (congressional) an association of members of Congress based on party, interest, or social group such as gender or race (466)

caucus (political) a normally closed meeting of a political or legislative group to select candidates, plan strategy, or make decisions regarding legislative matters (326, 374, 458, 527)

checks and balances mechanisms through which each branch of government is able to participate in and influence the activities of the other branches. Major examples include the presidential veto power over congressional legislation, the power of the Senate to approve presidential appointments, and judicial review of congressional enactments (92)

chief justice justice on the Supreme Court who presides over the Court's public sessions (584)

citizenship informed and active membership in a political community (13)

civic engagement a sense of concern among members of the political community about public social and political life, expressed through participation in social and political organizations (63)

civil law a system of jurisprudence, including private law and governmental actions, to settle disputes that do not involve criminal penalties (580)

civil liberties areas of personal freedom with which governments are constrained from interfering (155)

civil penalties regulatory techniques in which fines or another form of material restitution is imposed for violating civil laws or common law principles, for example through negligence (625)

civil rights legal or moral claims that citizens are entitled to make upon government (156, 195)

class action suit a legal action by which a group or class of individuals with common interests can file a suit on behalf of everyone who shares that interest (610)

"clear and present danger" test test to determine whether speech is protected or unprotected, based on its capacity to present a "clear and present danger" to society (163)

clientele agencies departments or bureaus of government whose mission is to promote, serve, or represent a particular interest or a particular segment or geographical area of the country (551)

closed caucus a presidential nominating caucus open only to registered party members (374)

closed primary a primary election in which voters can participate in the nomination of candidates, but only of the party in which they are enrolled for a period of time prior to primary day (362)

closed rule a provision by the House Rules Committee limiting or prohibiting the introduction of amendments during debate (470)

cloture a rule allowing a majority of two-thirds or three-fifths of the members in a legislative body to set a time limit on debate over a given bill (471)

coalition a group in interests that join together for the purpose of influencing government (68)

coattail effect the result of voters casting their ballot for president or governor and "automatically" voting for the remainder of the party's ticket (365)

cold war the period of struggle between the United States and the former Soviet Union between the late 1940s and about 1990 (708)

collective goods benefits, sought by groups, that are broadly available and cannot be denied to nonmembers (407)

commander in chief the power of the president as commander of the national military and the state national guard units (when called into service) (497)

commerce clause Article I, Section 8, of the Constitution, which delegates to Congress the power "to regulate commerce with foreign nations, and among the several

States and with the Indian tribes." This clause was interpreted by the Supreme Court in favor of national power over the economy (127)

concurrent powers   authority possessed by both state and national governments, such as the power to levy taxes (120)

confederation   a system of government in which states retain sovereign authority except for the powers expressly delegated to the national government (83)

conference   a gathering of House Republicans every two years to elect their House leaders. Democrats call their gathering the caucus (458)

conference committee   a joint committee created to work out a compromise on House and Senate versions of a piece of legislation (464)

conservative   today this term refers to those who generally support the social and economic status quo and are suspicious of efforts to introduce new political formulae and economic arrangements. Conservatives believe that a large and powerful government poses a threat to citizens' freedom (254)

constituency   the district comprising the area from which an official is elected (447)

constitutional government   a system of rule in which formal and effective limits are placed on the powers of the government (16)

containment   the policy used by the United States during the cold war to restrict the expansion of communism and limit the influence of the Soviet Union (708)

contracting power   the power of government to set conditions on companies seeking to sell goods or services to government agencies (624)

contributory programs   social programs financed in whole or in part by taxation or other mandatory contributions by their present or future recipients. The most important example is Social Security, which is financed by a payroll tax (664)

cooperative federalism   a type of federalism existing since the New Deal era in which grants-in-aid have been used strategically to encourage states and localities (without commanding them) to pursue nationally defined goals. Also known as intergovernmental cooperation (134)

corridoring   working to gain influence in an executive agency (421)

cost of living adjustments (COLAs)   changes made to the level of benefits of a government program based on the rate of inflation (666)

criminal law   the branch of law that deals with disputes or actions involving criminal penalties (as opposed to civil law); it regulates the conduct of individuals, defines crimes, and provides punishment for criminal acts (579)

criminal penalties   regulatory techniques in which imprisonment or heavy fines and the loss of certain civil rights and liberties are imposed (625)

cross-lobbying   a term to describe lobbyists lobbying one another (418)

de facto   literally, "by fact"; practices that occur even when there is no legal enforcement, such as school segregation in much of the United States today (201)

de jure   literally, "by law"; legally enforced practices, such as school segregation in the South before the 1960s (201)

defendant   the one against whom a complaint is brought in a criminal or civil case (579)

delegate   the role of a representative who votes according to the preferences of his or her constituency (484)

delegated powers   constitutional powers that are assigned to one governmental agency but that are exercised by another agency with the express permission of the first (495)

delegates   political activists selected to vote at a party's national convention (378)

democracy   a system of rule that permits citizens to play a significant part in the governmental process, usually through the election of key public officials (16, 239)

department   the largest subunit of the executive branch. The secretaries of the fourteen departments form the Cabinet (548)

deregulation   a policy of reducing or eliminating regulatory restraints on the conduct of individuals or private institutions (562, 638)

deterrence   the development and maintenance of military strength as a means of discouraging attack (718)

devolution   a policy to remove a program from one level of government by delegating it or passing it down to a lower level of government, such as from the national government to the state and local governments (130, 562)

diplomacy   the representation of a government to other foreign governments (710)

direct democracy   a system of rule that permits citizens to vote directly on laws and policies (21)

direct-action politics   a form of politics, such as civil disobedience or revolutionary action, that takes place outside formal channels (21)

discount rate   the interest rate charged by the Federal Reserve System when commercial banks borrow in order to expand their lending operations; an effective tool of monetary policy (630)

discrimination   use of any unreasonable and unjust criterion of exclusion (197)

dissenting opinion   a decision written by a justice in the minority in a particular case in which the justice wishes to express his or her reasoning in the case (604)

divided government   the condition in American government wherein the presidency is controlled by one party while the opposing party controls one or both houses of Congress (322, 506)

double jeopardy   the Fifth Amendment right providing that a person cannot be tried twice for the same crime (179)

dual federalism the system of government that prevailed in the United States from 1789 to 1937, in which most fundamental governmental powers were shared between the federal and state governments (123)

due process of law the right of every citizen against arbitrary action by national or state governments (156, 583)

economic expansionist role the strategy often pursued by capitalist countries to adopt foreign policies that will maximize the success of domestic corporations in their dealings with other countries (724)

elastic clause Article I, Section 8, of the Constitution (also known as the necessary and proper clause), which enumerates the powers of Congress and provides Congress with the authority to make all laws "necessary and proper" to carry them out (94)

electoral college the presidential electors from each state who meet after the popular election to cast ballots for president and vice president (92, 367)

electoral realignment the point in history when a new party supplants the ruling party, becoming in turn the dominant political force. In the United States, this has tended to occur roughly every thirty years (321)

eminent domain the right of government to take private property for public use (180, 630)

entitlement eligibility for benefits by virtue of a category of benefits defined by legislation (668)

equal protection clause provision of the Fourteenth Amendment guaranteeing citizens "the equal protection of the laws." This clause has served as the basis for the civil rights of African Americans, women, and other groups (197)

equal time rule the requirement that broadcasters provide candidates for the same political office an equal opportunity to communicate their messages to the public (284)

equality of opportunity a widely shared American ideal that all people should have the freedom to use whatever talents and wealth they have to reach their fullest potential (23, 239, 659)

establishment clause the First Amendment clause that says that "Congress shall make no law respecting an establishment of religion." This law means that a "wall of separation" exists between church and state (159)

ex post facto laws laws that declare an action to be illegal after it has been committed (154)

exclusionary rule the ability of courts to exclude evidence obtained in violation of the Fourth Amendment (177)

executive agreement an agreement, made between the president and another country, that has the force of a treaty but does not require the Senate's "advice and consent" (482, 498, 702)

Executive Office of the President the permanent agencies that perform defined management tasks for the president. Created in 1939, the EOP includes the Office of Management and Budget, the Council of Economic Advisers, the National Security Council, and other agencies (510)

executive privilege the claim that confidential communications deemed vital to the national interest between the president and close advisers should not be revealed without the consent of the president (502)

expressed powers specific powers granted to Congress under Article I, Section 8, of the Constitution (94, 119)

expropriation confiscation of property with or without compensation (629)

fairness doctrine a Federal Communications Commission (FCC) requirement for broadcasters who air programs on controversial issues to provide time for opposing views. The FCC ceased enforcing this doctrine in 1985 (284)

federal funds rate the interest rate on loans between banks that the Federal Reserve Board influences by affecting the supply of money available (644)

Federal Reserve Board (Fed) the governing board of the Federal Reserve System, comprising a chair and six other members, all appointed by the president with the consent of the Senate (630)

Federal Reserve System a system of twelve Federal Reserve Banks that facilitates exchanges of cash, checks, and credit; regulates member banks; and uses monetary policies to fight inflation and deflation (559, 642)

federal system a system of government in which the national government shares power with lower levels of government, such as states (119)

federalism a system of government in which power is divided, by a constitution, between a central government and regional governments (92, 119)

Federalist Papers a series of essays written by James Madison, Alexander Hamilton, and John Jay supporting the ratification of the Constitution (101)

Federalists those who favored a strong national government and supported the constitution proposed at the American Constitutional Convention of 1787 (100)

fighting words speech that directly incites damaging conduct (170)

filibuster a tactic used by members of the Senate to prevent action on legislation they oppose by continuously holding the floor and speaking until the majority backs down. Once given the floor, senators have unlimited time to speak, and it requires a vote of three-fifths of the Senate to end a filibuster (471)

fiscal policy the use of taxing, monetary, and spending powers to manipulate the economy (558, 644)

food stamps coupons that can be exchanged for food at most grocery stores; the largest in-kind benefits program (667)

formula grants grants-in-aid in which a formula is used to determine the amount of federal funds a state or local government will receive (133)

framing   the power of the media to influence how events and issues are interpreted (298)

free exercise clause   the First Amendment clause that protects a citizen's right to believe and practice whatever religion he or she chooses (161)

free riders   those who enjoy the benefits of collective goods but did not participate in acquiring them (407)

full faith and credit clause   provision from Article IV, Section 1 of the Constitution, requiring that the states normally honor the public acts and judicial decisions that take place in another state (121)

gender gap   a distinctive pattern of voting behavior reflecting the differences in views between men and women (56, 247, 334)

gerrymandering   apportionment of voters in districts in such a way as to give unfair advantage to one racial or ethnic group or political party (213, 364)

going public   a strategy that attempts to mobilize the widest and most favorable climate of public opinion (424)

government   institutions and procedures through which a territory and its people are ruled (15)

government corporation   a government agency that performs a service normally provided by the private sector (530)

grand jury   jury that determines whether sufficient evidence is available to justify a trial; grand juries do not rule on the accused's guilt or innocence (178)

grants-in-aid   programs through which Congress provides money to state and local governments on the condition that the funds be employed for purposes defined by the federal government (132)

grassroots lobbying   a lobbying campaign in which a group mobilizes its membership to contact government officials in support of the group's position (426)

Great Compromise   the agreement reached at the Constitutional Convention of 1787 that gave each state an equal number of senators regardless of its population, but linked representation in the House of Representatives to population (88)

habeas corpus   a court order demanding that an individual in custody be brought into court and shown the cause for detention (154)

Holy Alliance role   a strategy pursued by a superpower to prevent any change in the existing distribution of power among nation-states, even if this requires intervention into the international affairs of another country in order to keep a ruler from being overturned (722)

home rule   power delegated by the state to a local unit of government to manage its own affairs (122)

illusion of saliency   the impression conveyed by polls that something is important to the public when actually it is not (266)

impeachment   the formal charge by the House of Representatives that a government official has committed "Treason, Bribery, or other high Crimes and Misdemeanors" (482)

implementation   the efforts of departments and agencies to translate laws into specific bureaucratic routines (542)

implied powers   powers derived from the "necessary and proper" clause of Article I, Section 8, of the Constitution. Such powers are not specifically expressed, but are implied through the expansive interpretation of delegated powers (120)

in-kind benefits   goods and services provided to needy individuals and families by the federal government (667)

incumbency   holding a political office for which one is running (453)

incumbent   a candidate running for a position that he or she already holds (369)

independent agency   an agency that is not part of a Cabinet department (550)

independent counsel   an official appointed to investigate criminal misconduct by members of the executive branch (502)

indexing   periodic process of adjusting social benefits or wages to account for increases in the cost of living (666)

inflation   a consistent increase in the general level of prices (630)

infomercial   a lengthy campaign advertisement on television (381)

inherent powers   powers claimed by a president that are not expressed in the Constitution, but are inferred from it (496)

institutional advertising   advertising designed to create a positive image of an organization (424)

intermediate scrutiny   test, used by the Supreme Court in gender discrimination cases, which places the burden of proof partially on the government and partially on the challengers to show that the law in question is constitutional (216)

International Monetary Fund (IMF)   an institution established in 1944 at Bretton Woods, New Hampshire, which provides loans and facilitates international monetary exchange (713)

iron triangle   the stable, cooperative relationships that often develop between a congressional committee, an administrative agency, and one or more supportive interest groups. Not all of these relationships are triangular, but the iron triangle is the most typical (420, 552)

issue network   a loose network of elected leaders, public officials, activists, and interest groups drawn together by a specific policy issue (421)

issues advocacy   independent spending by individuals or interest groups on a campaign issue but not directly tied to a particular candidate (382)

joint committee a legislative committee formed of members of both the House and the Senate (464)

judicial activism judicial philosophy that posits that the Court should go beyond the words of the Constitution or a statute to consider the broader societal implications of its decisions (605)

judicial restraint judicial philosophy whose adherents refuse to go beyond the clear words of the Constitution in interpreting its meaning (605)

judicial review the power of the courts to declare actions of the legislative and executive branches invalid or unconstitutional. The Supreme Court asserted this power in *Marbury v. Madison* (95, 590)

jurisdiction the sphere of a court's power and authority (581)

Kitchen Cabinet an informal group of advisers to whom the president turns for counsel and guidance. Members of the official Cabinet may or may not also be members of the Kitchen Cabinet (509)

laissez-faire capitalism an economic system in which the means of production and distribution are privately owned and operated for profit with minimal or no government interference (23)

legislative initiative the president's inherent power to bring a legislative agenda before Congress (506)

Lemon **test** a rule articulated in *Lemon v. Kurtzman* that government action toward religion is permissible if it is secular in purpose, does not lead to "excessive entanglement" with religion, and neither promotes nor inhibits the practice of religion (160)

libel a written statement made in "reckless disregard of the truth" that is considered damaging to a victim because it is "malicious, scandalous, and defamatory" (166)

liberal a liberal today generally supports political and social reform; extensive governmental intervention in the economy; the expansion of federal social services; more vigorous efforts on behalf of the poor, minorities, and women; and greater concern for consumers and the environment (253)

libertarian the political philosophy that is skeptical of any government intervention as a potential threat against individual liberty; libertarians believe that government has caused more problems than it has solved (689)

liberty freedom from government control (22, 238)

license permission to engage in some activity that is otherwise illegal, such as hunting or practicing medicine (625)

limited government a government whose powers are defined and limited by a constitution (22, 102)

line-item veto the power of the executive to veto specific provisions (lines) of a bill passed by the legislature (456, 506)

lobbying a strategy by which organized interests seek to influence the passage of legislation by exerting direct pressure on members of the legislature (415)

logrolling a legislative practice wherein agreements are made between legislators in voting for or against a bill. Unlike bargaining, parties to logrolling have nothing in common but their desire to exchange support (479)

loophole incentive to individuals and businesses to reduce their tax liabilities by investing their money in areas that the government designates (646)

machines strong party organizations in late-nineteenth- and early-twentieth-century American cities. These machines were led by "bosses" who controlled party nominations and patronage (331)

majority leader the elected leader of the majority party in the House of Representatives or in the Senate. In the House, the majority leader is subordinate in the party hierarchy to the Speaker of the House (458)

majority party the party that holds the majority of legislative seats in either the House or the Senate (345)

majority rule/minority rights the democratic principle that a government follows the preferences of the majority of voters but protects the interests of the minority (25)

majority system a type of electoral system in which, to win a seat in the parliament or other representative body, a candidate must receive a majority of all the votes cast in the relevant district (363)

mandate a claim by a victorious candidate that the electorate has given him or her special authority to carry out promises made during the campaign (515)

marketplace of ideas the public forum in which beliefs and ideas are exchanged and compete (258)

Marshall Plan the U.S. European Recovery Plan, in which over $34 billion was spent for the relief, reconstruction, and economic recovery of Western Europe after World War II (714)

material benefits special goods, services, or money provided to members of groups to entice others to join (407)

means testing a procedure by which potential beneficiaries of a public assistance program establish their eligibility by demonstrating a genuine need for the assistance (559, 666)

Medicaid a federally financed, state-operated program providing medical services to low-income people (666)

Medicare a form of national health insurance for the elderly and the disabled (665)

membership association an organized group in which members actually play a substantial role, sitting on committees and engaging in group projects (406)

merit system a product of civil service reform, in which appointees to positions in public bureaucracies must objectively be deemed qualified for the position (543)

midterm elections congressional elections that do not coincide with a presidential election; also called off-year elections (357)

minority district a gerrymandered voting district that improves the chances of minority candidates by making selected minority groups the majority within the district (364)

minority leader the elected leader of the minority party in the House or Senate (458)

minority party the party that holds a minority of legislative seats in either the House or the Senate (345)

Miranda **rule** the requirement, articulated by the Supreme Court in *Miranda v. Arizona*, that persons under arrest must be informed prior to police interrogation of their rights to remain silent and to have the benefit of legal counsel (180, 594)

mobilization the process by which large numbers of people are organized for a political activity (66)

monetary policies efforts to regulate the economy through manipulation of the supply of money and credit. America's most powerful institution in the area of monetary policy is the Federal Reserve Board (641)

monopoly the existence of a single firm in a market that controls all the goods and services of that market; absence of competition (626)

mootness a criterion used by courts to screen cases that no longer require resolution (596)

most favored nation status agreement to offer a trading partner the lowest tariff rate offered to other trading partners (649)

multilateralism a foreign policy that seeks to encourage the involvement of several nation-states in coordinated action, usually in relation to a common adversary, with terms and conditions usually specified in a multi-country treaty (708)

multiple-member district an electorate that selects all candidates at large from the whole district; each voter is given the number of votes equivalent to the number of seats to be filled (325)

Napoleonic role a strategy pursued by a powerful nation to prevent aggressive actions against themselves by improving the internal state of affairs of a particular country, even if this means encouraging revolution in that country (722)

nation-state a political entity consisting of a people with some common cultural experience (nation) who also share a common political authority (state), recognized by other sovereignties (nation-states) (710)

national convention a national party political institution that serves to nominate the party's presidential and vice presidential candidates, establish party rules, and write and ratify the party's platform (326)

National Security Council (NSC) a presidential foreign-policy advisory council composed of the president; the vice president; the secretaries of state, defense, and the treasury; the attorney general; and other officials invited by the president (508)

necessary and proper clause from Article I, Section 8 of the Constitution, it provides Congress with the authority to make all laws "necessary and proper" to carry out its expressed powers (120)

New Deal coalition the coalition of northern urban liberals, southern white conservatives, organized labor, and blacks that dominated national politics until the 1960s (518)

New Federalism attempts by Presidents Nixon and Reagan to return power to the states through block grants (139)

New Jersey Plan a framework for the Constitution, introduced by William Paterson, which called for equal state representation in the national legislature regardless of population (87)

New Politics movement a political movement that began in the 1960s and 1970s, made up of professionals and intellectuals for whom the civil rights and antiwar movements were formative experiences. The New Politics movement strengthened public-interest groups (412)

news enclave population subgroups that receive most of their political information from sources other than the major national news media (282)

nomination the process through which political parties select their candidates for election to public office (337)

noncontributory programs social programs that provide assistance to people based on demonstrated need rather than any contribution they have made (666)

North American Free Trade Agreement (NAFTA) trade treaty between the United States, Canada, and Mexico to lower and eliminate tariffs between the three countries (650, 703)

North Atlantic Treaty Organization (NATO) a treaty organization, comprising the United States, Canada, and most of western Europe, formed in 1948 to counter the perceived threat from the Soviet Union (708)

oligarchy a form of government in which a small group—landowners, military officers, or wealthy merchants—controls most of the governing decisions (16)

open caucus a presidential nominating caucus open to anyone who wishes to attend (374)

open market operations method by which the Open Market Committee of the Federal Reserve System buys and sells government securities, etc., to help finance government operations and to loosen or tighten the total amount of money circulating in the economy (643)

open primary a primary election in which the voter can wait until the day of the primary to choose which party to enroll in to select candidates for the general election (362)

open rule a provision by the House Rules Committee that permits floor debate and the addition of new amendments to a bill (470)

opinion the written explanation of the Supreme Court's decision in a particular case (604)

oral argument stage in Supreme Court procedure in which attorneys for both sides appear before the Court to present their positions and answer questions posed by justices (601)

original jurisdiction the authority to initially consider a case. Distinguished from appellate jurisdiction, which is the authority to hear appeals from a lower court's decision (583)

oversight the effort by Congress, through hearings, investigations, and other techniques, to exercise control over the activities of executive agencies (481, 568)

paper trail written accounts by which the process of decision making and the participants in decision can, if desired, be later reconstructed. Often called red tape (541)

party activists partisans who contribute time, energy, and effort to support their party and its candidates (333)

party identification an individual voter's psychological ties to one party or another (332)

party organization the formal structure of a political party, including its leadership, election committees, active members, and paid staff (326)

party vote a roll-call vote in the House or Senate in which at least 50 percent of the members of one party take a particular position and are opposed by at least 50 percent of the members of the other party. Party votes are rare today, although they were fairly common in the nineteenth century (476)

patronage the resources available to higher officials, usually opportunities to make partisan appointments to offices and to confer grants, licenses, or special favors to supporters (331, 455, 508)

per curiam decision by an appellate court, without a written opinion, that refuses to review the decision of a lower court; amounts to a reaffirmation of the lower court's opinion (588)

permanent campaign description of presidential politics in which all presidential actions are taken with re-election in mind (522)

plaintiff the individual or organization who brings a complaint in court (579)

platform a party document, written at a national convention, that contains party philosophy, principles, and positions on issues (328, 376)

plea bargains negotiated agreements in criminal cases in which a defendant agrees to plead guilty in return for the state's agreement to reduce the severity of the criminal charge the defendant is facing (582)

pluralism the theory that all interests are and should be free to compete for influence in the government. The outcome of this competition is compromise and moderation (21, 402)

plurality system a type of electoral system in which, to win a seat in the parliament or other representative body, a candidate need only receive the most votes in the election, not necessarily a majority of the votes cast (326, 363)

pocket veto a presidential veto that is automatically triggered if the president does not act on a given piece of legislation passed during the final ten days of a legislative session (473, 504)

police power power reserved to the government to regulate the health, safety, and morals of its citizens (120, 625)

policy entrepreneur an individual who identifies a problem as a political issue and brings a policy proposal into the political agenda (344)

policy of redistribution a policy whose objective is to tax or spend in such a way as to reduce the disparities of wealth between the lowest and the highest income brackets (645)

political action committee (PAC) a private group that raises and distributes funds for use in election campaigns (383, 430, 453)

political culture broadly shared values, beliefs, and attitudes about how the government should function. American political culture emphasizes the values of liberty, equality, and democracy (22)

political efficacy the ability to influence government and politics (10, 70, 257)

political equality the right to participate in politics equally, based on the principle of "one person, one vote" (23)

political ideology a cohesive set of beliefs that form a general philosophy about the role of government (238)

political institution an organization that connects people to politics, such as a political party, or a governmental organization, such as the Congress or the courts (66)

political machines local party organizations that controlled local politics in the late nineteenth and early twentieth centuries through patronage and control of nominations (38)

political participation political activities, such as voting, contacting political officials, volunteering for a campaign, or participating in a protest, whose purpose is to influence government (61)

political parties organized groups that attempt to influence the government by electing their members to important government offices (315)

political socialization the induction of individuals into the political culture; learning the underlying beliefs and values that the political system is based on (243)

politics conflict over the leadership, structure, and policies of governments (21)

poll tax a state-imposed tax upon voters as a prerequisite for registration. Poll taxes were rendered unconstitutional in national elections by the Twenty-fourth Amendment, and in state elections by the Supreme Court in 1966 (65, 357)

popular sovereignty a principle of democracy in which political authority rests ultimately in the hands of the people (34)

pork barrel appropriations made by legislative bodies for local projects that are often not needed but that are created so that local representatives can win re-election in their home districts (455)

power influence over a government's leadership, organization, or policies (21)

precedents prior cases whose principles are used by judges as the bases for their decisions in present cases (581)

preemption the principle that allows the national government to override state or local actions in certain policy areas (137)

primary elections elections used to select a party's candidate for the general election (362)

prior restraint an effort by a governmental agency to block the publication of material it deems libelous or harmful in some other way; censorship. In the United States, the courts forbid prior restraint except under the most extraordinary circumstances (286)

private bill a proposal in Congress to provide a specific person with some kind of relief, such as a special exemption from immigration quotas (456)

privatization removing all or part of a program from the public sector to the private sector (562)

privileges and immunities clause provision from Article IV, Section 2 of the Constitution, that a state cannot discriminate against someone from another state or give its own residents special privileges (122)

procedural liberties restraints on how the government is supposed to act; for example, citizens are guaranteed the due process of law (156)

progressive/regressive taxation taxation that hits the upper income brackets more heavily (progressive) or the lower income brackets more heavily (regressive) (644)

project grants grant programs in which state and local governments submit proposals to federal agencies and for which funding is provided on a competitive basis (133)

proportional representation a multiple-member district system that allows each political party representation in proportion to its percentage of the total vote (326, 363)

prospective voting voting based on the imagined future performance of a candidate (390)

public interest groups groups that claim they serve the general good rather than their own particular interest (413)

public law cases in private law, civil law, or criminal law in which one party to the dispute argues that a license is unfair, a law is inequitable or unconstitutional, or an agency has acted unfairly, violated a procedure, or gone beyond its jurisdiction (581)

public opinion citizens' attitudes about political issues, leaders, institutions, and events (238)

public opinion polls scientific instruments for measuring public opinion (263)

public policy a law, rule, statute, or edict that expresses the government's goals and provides for rewards and punishments to promote their attainment (620)

purposive benefits selective benefits of group membership that emphasize the purpose and accomplishments of the group (408)

push polling a polling technique in which the questions are designed to shape the respondent's opinion (267)

rallying effect the generally favorable reaction of the public to presidential actions taken in foreign policy, or more precisely, to decisions made during international crises (526)

redistributive agencies a general category of agencies including fiscal agencies, monetary agencies, and welfare agencies, whose net effect is to shift large aggregates of wealth from rich to poor, young to old, etc. (558)

redistributive programs economic policies designed to control the economy through taxing and spending, with the goal of benefiting the poor (141)

redistricting the process of redrawing election districts and redistributing legislative representatives. This happens every ten years to reflect shifts in population or in response to legal challenges to existing districts (454)

redlining a practice in which banks refuse to make loans to people living in certain geographic locations (214)

referendum the practice of referring a measure proposed or passed by a legislature to the vote of the electorate for approval or rejection (362)

regulated federalism a form of federalism in which Congress imposes legislation on states and localities, requiring them to meet national standards (136)

regulation a technique of control in which the government adopts rules imposing restrictions on the conduct of private citizens (625)

regulatory agencies departments, bureaus, or independent agencies whose primary mission is to impose limits, restrictions, or other obligations on the conduct of individuals or companies in the private sector (557)

regulatory tax a tax whose primary purpose is not to raise revenue but to influence conduct: e.g. a heavy tax on gasoline to discourage recreational driving (628)

representative democracy/republic a system of government in which the populace selects representatives, who play a significant role in governmental decision making (21)

reserve requirement the amount of liquid assets and ready cash that banks are required to hold to meet depositors' demands for their money (643)

reserved powers powers, derived from the Tenth Amendment to the Constitution, that are not specifically delegated to the national government or denied to the states (120)

responsible party government a set of principles that idealizes a strong role for parties in defining their stance on issues, mobilizing voters, and fulfilling their campaign promises once in office (348)

retrospective voting voting based on the past performance of a candidate (390)

revenue agencies agencies responsible for collecting taxes. Examples include the Internal Revenue Service for income taxes, the U.S. Customs Service for tariffs and other taxes on imported goods, and the Bureau of Alcohol, Tobacco, and Firearms for collection of taxes on the sales of those particular products (553)

revenue sharing the process by which one unit of government yields a portion of its tax income to another unit of government, according to an established formula. Revenue sharing typically involves the national government providing money to state governments (139)

reverse lobbying a strategy by which members of Congress bring pressure to bear on lobby groups to support particular courses of action (418)

right of rebuttal a Federal Communications Commission regulation giving individuals the right to have the opportunity to respond to personal attacks made on a radio or television broadcast (284)

right to privacy the right to be let alone, which has been interpreted by the Supreme Court to entail free access to birth control and abortions (184)

roll-call vote a vote in which each legislator's yes or no vote is recorded as the clerk calls the names of the members alphabetically (476)

rulemaking a quasi-legislative administrative process that produces regulations by government agencies (542)

salient interests attitudes and views that are especially important to the individual holding them (266)

sample a small group selected by researchers to represent the most important characteristics of an entire population (263)

select committee a (usually) temporary legislative committee set up to highlight or investigate a particular issue or address an issue not within the jurisdiction of existing committees (463)

selective incorporation the process by which different protections in the Bill of Rights were incorporated into the Fourteenth Amendment, thus guaranteeing citizens protection from state as well as national government (157)

senatorial courtesy the practice whereby the president, before formally nominating a person for a federal judgeship, seeks the indication that senators from the candidate's own state support the nomination (586)

seniority priority or status ranking given to an individual on the basis of length of continuous service on a committee in Congress (464)

separate but equal rule doctrine that public accommodations could be segregated by race but still be equal (198)

separation of powers the division of governmental power among several institutions that must cooperate in decision making (92)

shadow welfare state social benefits that private employers offer to their workers, such as medical insurance and pensions (674)

single-member district an electorate that is allowed to select only one representative from each district; the normal method of representation in the United States (328)

slander an oral statement, made in "reckless disregard of the truth," which is considered damaging to the victim because it is "malicious, scandalous, and defamatory" (166)

Social Security a contributory welfare program into which working Americans contribute a percentage of their wages, and from which they receive cash benefits after retirement (664)

socioeconomic status status in society based on level of education, income, and occupational prestige (63)

sociological representation a type of representation in which representatives have the same racial, ethnic, religious, or educational backgrounds as their constituents. It is based on the principle that if two individuals are similar in background, character, interests, and perspectives, then one could correctly represent the other's views (449)

soft money money contributed directly to political parties for voter registration and organization (331, 383, 433)

solicitor general the top government lawyer in all cases before the Supreme Court where the government is a party (588)

solidary benefits selective benefits of a group membership that emphasize friendship, networking, and consciousness-raising (407)

Speaker of the House the chief presiding officer of the House of Representatives. The Speaker is elected at the beginning of every Congress on a straight party vote. The Speaker is the most important party and House leader, and can influence the legislative agenda, the fate of individual pieces of legislation, and members' positions within the House (458)

speech-plus speech accompanied by conduct such as sit-ins, picketing, and demonstrations; protection of this form of speech under the First Amendment is conditional, and restrictions imposed by state or local authorities are acceptable if properly balanced by considerations of public order (165)

split-ticket voting the practice of casting ballots for the candidates of at least two different political parties in the same election (365)

spot advertisement a fifteen-, thirty-, or sixty-second television campaign commercial that permits a candidate's message to be delivered to a target audience (380)

staff agency a legislative support agency responsible for policy analysis (466)

staff organization a type of membership group in which a professional staff conducts most of the group's activities (406)

standing the right of an individual or organization to initiate a court case (596)

standing committee a permanent committee with the power to propose and write legislation that covers a particular subject, such as finance or appropriations (462)

stare decisis literally, "let the decision stand." The doctrine that a previous decision by a court applies as a precedent in similar cases until that decision is overruled (581)

states' rights the principle that the states should oppose the increasing authority of the national government. This principle was most popular in the period before the Civil War (129)

straight-ticket voting the practice of casting ballots for candidates of only one party (365)

strict scrutiny test, used by the Supreme Court in racial discrimination cases and other cases involving civil liberties and civil rights, which places the burden of proof on the government rather than on the challengers to show that the law in question is constitutional (162, 201)

subsidies government grants of cash or other valuable commodities such as land to individuals or organizations; used to promote activities desired by the government, to reward political support, or to buy off political opposition (623)

substantive liberties restraints on what the government shall and shall not have the power to do (155)

suffrage the right to vote; also called franchise (355)

superdelegate a convention delegate position, in Democratic conventions, reserved for party officials (378)

Supplemental Security Income (SSI) a program providing a minimum monthly income to people who pass a "means test" and who are sixty-five or older, blind, or disabled. Financed from general revenues rather than from Social Security contributions (667)

supremacy clause Article VI of the Constitution, which states that laws passed by the national government and all treaties are the supreme law of the land and superior to all laws adopted by any state or any subdivision (95, 591)

supreme court the highest court in a particular state or in the United States. This court primarily serves an appellate function (581)

tariff a tax on imported goods (644)

tax expenditures government subsidies provided to employers and employees through tax deductions for amounts spent on health insurance and other benefits; these represent one way the government helps to ensure the social welfare of the middle class (674)

Temporary Assistance to Needy Families (TANF) a fed-

eral block grant that replaced the AFDC program in 1996 (666)

term limits legally prescribed limits on the number of terms an elected official can serve (454)

third parties parties that organize to compete against the two major American political parties (324)

Three-fifths Compromise the agreement reached at the Constitutional Convention of 1787 that stipulated that for purposes of the apportionment of congressional seats, every slave would be counted as three-fifths of a person (89)

totalitarian government a system of rule in which the government recognizes no formal limits on its power and seeks to absorb or eliminate other social institutions that might challenge it (16)

town meeting a media format in which candidates meet with ordinary citizens. Allows candidates to deliver messages without the presence of journalists or commentators (380)

trial court the first court to hear a criminal or civil case (581)

trustee the role of a representative who votes based on what he or she thinks is best for his or her constituency (484)

turnout the percentage of eligible individuals who actually vote (359)

two-party system a political system in which only two parties have a realistic opportunity to compete effectively for control (316)

tyranny oppressive and unjust government that employs cruel and unjust use of power and authority (101)

uncontrollables budgetary items that are beyond the control of budgetary committees and can be controlled only by substantive legislative action in Congress. Some uncontrollables are beyond the power of Congress, because the terms of payments are set in contracts, such as interest on the debt (649)

unfunded mandates regulations or conditions for receiving grants that impose costs on state and local governments for which they are not reimbursed by the federal government (137)

Uniform Commercial Code code used in many states in the area of contract law to reduce interstate differences in judicial decisions (582)

unilateralism a foreign policy that seeks to avoid international alliances, entanglements, and permanent commitments in favor of independence, neutrality, and freedom of action (708)

unit rule the convention voting system under which a state delegation casts all of its votes for the candidate supported by the majority of the state's delegates (376)

unitary system a centralized government system in which lower levels of government have little power independent of the national government (119)

United Nations   an organization of nations founded in 1945 to serve as a channel for negotiation and a means of settling international disputes peaceably. The UN has had frequent successes in providing a forum for negotiation and on some occasions a means of preventing international conflicts from spreading. On a number of occasions, the UN has been a convenient cover for U.S. foreign policy goals (711)

values (or beliefs)   basic principles that shape a person's opinions about political issues and events (238)

veto   the president's constitutional power to turn down acts of Congress. A presidential veto may be overridden by a two-thirds vote of each house of Congress (472, 504)

Virginia Plan   a framework for the Constitution, introduced by Edmund Randolph, which called for representation in the national legislature based upon the population of each state (87)

War Powers Resolution   a resolution of Congress that the president can send troops into action abroad only by authorization of Congress, or if American troops are already under attack or serious threat (499)

whip system   a communications network in each house of Congress; whips take polls of the membership in order to learn their intentions on specific legislative issues and to assist the majority and minority leaders in various tasks (479)

white ethnics   white immigrants to the United States whose culture differs from that of WASPs (37)

White House staff   analysts and advisers to the president, often given the title "special assistant" (509)

white primary   primary election in which only white voters are eligible to participate (65)

winner-take-all system   a system in which all of a state's presidential nominating delegates are awarded to the candidate who wins the most votes, while runners-up receive no delegates (376)

writ of *certiorari*   a decision of at least four of the nine Supreme Court justices to review a decision of a lower court; from the Latin "to make more certain" (597)

writ of *habeas corpus*   a court order that the individual in custody be brought into court and shown the cause for detention. *Habeas corpus* is guaranteed by the Constitution and can be suspended only in cases of rebellion or invasion (597)

Endnotes

CHAPTER 1

1. Gary Orren, "Fall from Grace: The Public's Loss of Trust in Government," in *Why People Don't Trust Government,* ed. Joseph S. Nye, Jr., Philip D. Zelikow, and David C. King (Cambridge, MA: Harvard University Press, 1997), pp. 80–81.

2. Robert J. Blendon et al., "Changing Attitudes in America," in *Why People Don't Trust Government,* ed. Nye, Zelikow, and King, pp. 207–8.

3. Joseph S. Nye, Jr., "Introduction: The Decline of Confidence in Government," in *Why People Don't Trust Government,* ed. Nye, Zelikow, and King, p. 7.

4. Blendon et al., "Changing Attitudes in America," pp. 210–11.

5. On the role of the media see Orren, "Fall from Grace."

6. Richard Morin and Claudia Deane, "Poll Shows More Citizens Satisfied with Government," *Washington Post,* January 21, 1998, p. A6.

7. Diana Owen, "Mixed Signals: Generation X's Attitudes toward the Political System," in *After the Boom: The Politics of Generation X,* ed. Stephen C. Craig and Stephen Earl Bennett (Lanham, MD: Rowman and Littlefield, 1997), p. 95.

8. Nye, "Introduction," p. 4.

9. Orren, "Fall from Grace," p. 81.

10. Owen, "Mixed Signals," p. 98.

11. Michael Walzer, *Spheres of Justice* (New York: Basic Books, 1983), p. 304.

12. This definition is taken from Norman H. Nie, Jane Junn, and Kenneth Stehlik-Barry, *Education and Democratic Citizenship in America* (Chicago: University of Chicago Press, 1996).

13. See Eugen Weber, *Peasants into Frenchmen: The Modernization of Rural France, 1870–1914* (Stanford, CA: Stanford University Press, 1976), chap. 5.

14. See V. O. Key, *Politics, Parties, and Pressure Groups* (New York: Crowell, 1964), p. 201.

15. Harold Lasswell, *Politics: Who Gets What, When, How* (New York: Meridian Books, 1958).

16. Herbert McClosky and John Zaller, *The American Ethos: Public Attitudes toward Capitalism and Democracy* (Cambridge, MA: Harvard University Press, 1984), p. 19.

17. J. R. Pole, *The Pursuit of Equality in American History* (Berkeley: University of California Press, 1978), p. 3.

18. See Judith N. Shklar, *American Citizenship: The Quest for Inclusion* (Cambridge, MA: Harvard University Press, 1991).

19. Cindy Skrzycki, "OSHA Abandons Rules Effort on Repetitive Injury," *Washington Post,* June 13, 1995, p. D1.

20. See Rogers M. Smith, *Liberalism and American Constitutional Law* (Cambridge, MA: Harvard University Press, 1985), chap. 6.

21. The case was *San Antonio Independent School District v. Rodriguez,* 411 U.S. 1 (1973). See the discussion in Smith, *Liberalism and American Constitutional Law,* pp. 163–64.

22. See the discussion in Eileen McDonagh, "Gender Political Change," in *New Perspectives on American Politics,* ed. Lawrence C. Dodd and Calvin Jillson (Washington, DC: Congressional Quarterly Press, 1994), pp. 58–73. The argument for moving women's issues into the public sphere is made by Jean Bethke Elshtain, *Public Man, Private Woman* (Princeton, NJ: Princeton University Press, 1981).

23. On current differences in wealth, see Keith Bradsher, "Gap in Wealth in U.S. Called Widest in West," *New York Times,* April 17, 1995, p. A1; on income inequality, see Gary Burtless and Timothy Smeeding, "America's Tide Lifting the Yachts, Swamping the Rowboats," *Washington Post,* June 25, 1995, p. C3.

24. Kevin Phillips, *The Politics of Rich and Poor: Wealth and the American Electorate in the Reagan Aftermath* (New York: Random House, 1994); and Thomas Byrne Edsall, *The New Politics of Inequality* (New York: Norton, 1984).

25. Kevin Phillips, *Arrogant Capital: Washington, Wall Street, and the Frustration of American Politics* (Boston: Little, Brown, 1994).

CHAPTER 2

1. Only 11 million (42 percent) of eighteen- to twenty-year-olds actually registered to vote. See Congressional Quarterly, *Presidential Elections: 1789–1996* (Washington, DC: Congressional Quarterly Press, 1997), p. 80.

2. See Craig A. Rimmerman, *The New Citizenship: Unconventional Politics, Activism, and Service* (Boulder, CO: Westview, 1997), pp. 40–45.

3. Although we discuss each of these groups separately, it is important to note that these identities are not mutually exclusive. Members of different racial and ethnic groups also have class, gender, and religious allegiances. At times these overlapping affinities make it easier to reach consensus in politics because it means that individuals have cross-cutting identities; they can see much in common with many different people. In other cases, however, a single identity, such as race, can determine so much about a person's life that it draws a sharp line of difference.

4. Richard A. Easterlin, "Economic and Social Characteristics of the Immigrants," *Immigration,* ed. Richard A. Easterlin, David Ward, William S. Bernard, and Reed Ueda (Cambridge, MA: Harvard University Press, 1982), pp. 16–17.

5. It is important to note, however, that many European immigrants did not stay in the United States. Half of the southern Italians and over two-thirds of some groups from eastern Europe who came to the United States between 1890 and 1910 returned home. See Richard Oestreicher, "Urban Working-Class Political Behavior and Theories of American Electoral Behavior," *Journal of American History* 74 (March 1988), p. 1274. On naturalization and citizenship, see Reed Ueda, "Naturalization and Citizenship," *Immigration,* ed. Easterlin et al., pp. 106–54.

6. Reed Ueda, "Naturalization and Citizenship," p. 118.

7. Nathan Glazer and Daniel P. Moynihan, *Beyond the Melting Pot* (Cambridge, MA: MIT Press, 1970), pp. 301–10.

8. August Meier and Elliot Rudwick, *From Plantation to Ghetto* (New York: Hill and Wang, 1976), pp. 184–88.

9. On the growth of black political power and the more limited progress on social and economic change in the South after the civil rights movement, see James W. Button, *Blacks and Social Change: The Impact of the Civil Rights Movement in Southern Communities* (Princeton, NJ: Princeton University Press, 1993).

10. See William Julius Wilson, *The Truly Disadvantaged: The Inner City, the Underclass, and Public Policy* (Chicago: University of Chicago Press, 1987); and Douglas Massey and Nancy Denton, *American Apartheid: Segregation and the Making of the American Underclass* (Cambridge, MA: Harvard University Press, 1993).

11. See Michael C. Dawson, *Behind the Mule: Race and Class in African-American Politics* (Princeton, NJ: Princeton University Press, 1994), chaps. 5 and 6.

12. Ibid.

13. Patricia A. Montgomery, "The Hispanic Population in the United States: March 1993," *Current Population Reports,* P20-475 (Washington, DC: U.S. Government Printing Office, 1994).

14. New Mexico had a different history because not many Anglos settled there initially. ("Anglo" is the term for a non-Hispanic white generally of European background.) Mexican Americans had considerable power in territorial legislatures between 1865 and 1912. See Lawrence H. Fuchs, *The American Kaleidoscope* (Hanover, NH: University Press of New England, 1990), pp. 239–40.

15. On La Raza Unida Party, see "La Raza Unida Party and the Chicano Student Movement in California," in *Latinos in the American Political System,* ed. F. Chris Garcia (Notre Dame, IN: University of Notre Dame Press, 1988), pp. 213–35.

16. Glazer and Moynihan, *Beyond the Melting Pot,* p. 101.

17. U.S. House of Representatives, Committee on the Judiciary, Hearings on the Immigration and Nationality Act, 104th Cong., 1st sess. (May 1995), Serial no. 1, p. 596.

18. Rochelle L. Stanfield, "Cracking El Sistema," *National Journal,* June 1, 1991, pp. 1284–87.

19. *United States v. Wong Kim Ark,* 169 U.S. 649 (1898).

20. Only 1,428 Chinese were let in to the United States between 1944 and 1952. See Ronald Takaki, *A Different Mirror: A History of Multicultural America* (Boston: Little, Brown, 1993), p. 387.

21. U.S. House of Representatives, Committee on the Judiciary, Hearings on the Immigration and Nationality Act, 104th Cong., 1st sess. (May 1995), Serial no. 1, p. 596.

22. Ibid.

23. Jane Gross, "Diversity Hinders Asians' Power in the U.S.," *New York Times,* June 25, 1989, p. A22.

24. See Timothy P. Fong, *The First Suburban Chinatown* (Philadelphia: Temple University Press, 1994), pp. 153–56. Fong points out a persistent split among foreign-born and American-born Chinese.

25. Not all Indian tribes agreed with this, including the Navajos. See Takaki, *A Different Mirror,* pp. 238–45.

26. On the resurgence of Indian political activity, see Stephen Cornell, *The Return of the Native: American Indian Political Resurgence* (New York: Oxford University Press, 1990); and Dee Brown, *Bury My Heart at Wounded Knee* (New York: Holt, 1971).

27. Dirk Johnson, "Economic Pulse: Indian Country; Economics Come to Life on Indian Reservations," *New York Times,* July 3, 1994, p. 1.

28. Maria Puente, "The New Immigrants: Is the Latest Wave a Drain or Boon to Society?" *USA Today,* June 30, 1995, p. A1.

29. Cited in Maria Puente, "The New Immigrants."

30. See Robert Pear, "Deciding Who Gets What in America," *New York Times,* November 27, 1994, sec. 4, p. 5.

31. David Jackson, "Citizen Plan May Have Aided Felons; Proper Background Checks Not Done," *Chicago Tribune,* February 25, 1997, p. 3. On differences between immigration now and in the past see Nathan Glazer, "Immigration and the American Future," *Public Interest,* no. 118 (Winter 1995), pp. 45–60.

32. Maria Puente, "Immigrants Favor ID Card," *USA Today,* July 5, 1995, p. 1A.

33. In fact, some students of immigration worry that Americanization may be harmful to immigrants, especially for the children of nonwhite immigrants. These immigrants may find it difficult to enter middle-class white society; instead they may adopt values adversarial to the mainstream. In this case, remaining in immigrant circles may be the best strategy. See Alejandro Portes and Min Zhou, "Should Immigrants Assimilate?" *Public Interest,* no. 116 (Summer 1994), pp. 18–33.

34. On the Knights of Labor, see Leon Fink, *Workingmen's Democracy: The Knights of Labor and American Politics* (Urbana: University of Illinois Press, 1985).

35. Clay Chandler, "It's Getting Awfully Crowded in the Middle," *Washington Post,* December 18, 1994, p. H1.

36. See Edward N. Wolff, *Top Heavy: A Study of Increasing Inequality of Wealth in America* (New York: Twentieth Century Fund, 1995).

37. Cited in Benjamin DeMott, *The Imperial Middle: Why Americans Can't Think Straight about Class* (New York: Morrow, 1990), pp. 9–10.

38. On politics and women, see Paula Baker, "The Domestication of Politics: Women and American Political Society, 1780–1920," *American Historical Review* 89 (June 1984), pp. 620–47. On women's separate sphere, see Sheila M. Rothman, *Woman's Proper Place* (New York: Basic Books, 1978).

39. See Thomas B. Edsall, "Pollsters View Gender Gap as Political Fixture," *Washington Post,* August 15, 1995, p. A11.

40. Richard L. Berke, "Defections among Men to G.O.P. Helped Insure Rout of Democrats," *New York Times,* November 11, 1994, p. A1.

41. "Fact Sheet: Women in Elective Office," Center for the American Woman and Politics, Eagleton Institute of Politics, Rutgers University, May 1, 1995.

42. David S. Broder, "Key to Women's Political Parity: Running," *Washington Post,* September 8, 1994, p. A17.

43. "The Impact of Women in Public Office: Findings at a Glance," Center for the American Woman and Politics (New Brunswick, NJ: Rutgers University, n.d.).

44. Gwen Ifill, "The Louisiana Election; Female Lawmakers

Wrestle with New Public Attitudes on 'Women's' Issues," *New York Times,* November 18, 1991, p. B7.

45. *Engel v. Vitale,* 370 U.S. 421 (1962); *Abington School District v. Schempp,* 374 U.S. 203 (1963); *Roe v. Wade,* 410 U.S. 113 (1973).

46. David von Drehle, "Life of the Grand Old Party; Energized Coalition Enters Another Political Phase," *Washington Post,* August 14, 1994, p. A1.

47. For a discussion of the decline of voting turnout over time, see Ruy A. Teixeira, *The Disappearing American Voter* (Washington, DC: Brookings Institution Press, 1992). On the 1994 elections, see Paul Taylor, "Behind the Broom of '94: Wealthier, Educated Voters," *Washington Post,* June 8, 1995, p. A12.

48. Sidney Verba, Kay Lehman Schlozman, and Henry E. Brady, *Voice and Equality: Civic Voluntarism in American Politics* (Cambridge, MA: Harvard University Press, 1995), chap. 3, for kinds of participation, and pp. 66–67 for prevalence of local activity.

49. Verba, Schlozman, and Brady, *Voice and Equality,* p. 51.

50. Steven J. Rosenstone and John Mark Hansen, *Mobilization, Participation, and Democracy in America* (New York: Macmillan, 1993), chap. 3; and Verba, Schlozman, and Brady, *Voice and Equality,* pp. 71–74.

51. See Thomas B. Edsall, "Huge Gains in South Fueled GOP Vote in '94," *Washington Post,* September 27, 1995, p. A8.

52. See Richard A. Brody, "The Puzzle of Political Participation in America," in *The New American Political System,* ed. Anthony King (Washington, DC: American Enterprise Institute, 1978), chap. 8.

53. On the nineteenth century, see Michael E. McGerr, *The Decline of Popular Politics: The American North, 1865–1928* (New York: Oxford University Press, 1986).

54. Verba, Schlozman, and Brady, *Voice and Equality.*

55. See Alexis de Tocqueville, *Democracy in America* (New York: Vintage, 1945).

56. Robert D. Putnam, "Bowling Alone: America's Declining Social Capital," *Journal of Democracy* 6, no. 1 (January 1995), pp. 65–78.

57. On television see Robert D. Putnam, "Tuning In, Tuning Out: The Strange Disappearance of Social Capital in America," *PS: Political Science and Politics* 28, no. 4 (December 1995),

pp. 664–83; for a reply see Pippa Norris, "Does Television Erode Social Capital? A Reply to Putnam," *PS: Political Science and Politics* 29, no. 3 (September 1996), pp. 474–80.

58. Michael Schudson, "What If Civic Life Didn't Die?" *American Prospect* 25 (March–April, 1996), pp. 17–20.

59. Rosenstone and Hansen, *Mobilization, Participation, and Democracy in America,* p. 59.

60. Connie Cass, "'Motor Voter' Impact Slight," *Chattanooga News-Free Press,* June 20, 1997, p. A5. On the need to motivate voters see Marshall Ganz, "Motor Voter or Motivated Voter?" *American Prospect,* no. 28 (September–October 1996), pp. 41–49. On the hopes for Motor Voter see Frances Fox Piven and Richard A. Cloward, "Northern Bourbons: A Preliminary Report on the National Voter Registration Act," *PS: Political Science and Politics* 29, no. 1 (March 1996), pp. 39–42. On turnout in the 1996 election, see Barbara Vobejda, "Just under Half of Possible Voters Went to the Polls," *Washington Post,* November 7, 1996, p. A3.

61. Lawrence Bobo and Franklin D. Gilliam, "Race, Sociopolitical Participation, and Black Empowerment," *American Political Science Review* 24, no. 2 (June 1990), pp. 377–93.

62. Rosenstone and Hansen, *Mobilization, Participation, and Democracy in America,* p. 59.

63. Kenneth N. Weine, "Campaigns without a Human Face," *Washington Post,* October 27, 1996, p. C1.; see also Margaret Weir and Marshall Ganz, "Reconnecting People and Politics," *The New Majority: Toward Popular Progressive Politics,* ed. Stanley B. Greenberg and Theda Skocpol (New Haven: Yale University Press, 1997), pp. 149–71.

64. *Buckley v. Valeo,* 424 U.S. 1 (1976).

65. Schudson, "What If Civic Life Didn't Die?" p. 18.

66. See Christopher Lasch, *The Revolt of the Elites and the Betrayal of American Democracy* (New York: Norton, 1995). The idea of the "secession of the rich" comes from Robert Reich, *The Work of Nations* (New York: Knopf, 1991), chaps. 23 and 24.

67. Rene Sanchez, "Survey of College Freshmen Finds Rise in Volunteerism," *Washington Post,* January 13, 1997, p. A1.

68. See the discussion in Rimmerman, *The New Citizenship,* pp. 97–113.

69. Noah Bilenker, interview with the author, March 23, 1998.

CHAPTER 3

1. Herbert Storing, *What the Antifederalists Were For* (Chicago: University of Chicago Press, 1981).

2. The social makeup of colonial America and some of the social conflicts that divided colonial society are discussed in Jackson Turner Main, *The Social Structure of Revolutionary America* (Princeton, NJ: Princeton University Press, 1965).

3. George B. Tindall and David E. Shi, *America: A Narrative History,* 3rd ed. (New York: Norton, 1992), p. 194.

4. For a discussion of events leading up to the Revolution, see Charles M. Andrews, *The Colonial Background of the American Revolution* (New Haven, CT: Yale University Press, 1924).

5. See Carl Becker, *The Declaration of Independence* (New York: Knopf, 1942).

6. See Merrill Jensen, *The Articles of Confederation* (Madison: University of Wisconsin Press, 1970).

7. Reported in Samuel E. Morrison, Henry Steele Commager, and William Leuchtenberg, *The Growth of the American Republic,*

vol. 1 (New York: Oxford University Press, 1969), p. 244.

8. Quoted in Morrison et al., *The Growth of the American Republic,* vol. 1, p. 242.

9. Charles A. Beard, *An Economic Interpretation of the Constitution of the United States* (New York: Macmillan, 1913).

10. Madison's notes along with the somewhat less complete records kept by several other participants in the convention are available in a four-volume set. See Max Farrand, ed., *The Records of the Federal Convention of 1787,* 4 vols., rev. ed. (New Haven, CT: Yale University Press, 1966).

11. Farrand, ed., *The Records of the Federal Convention of 1787,* vol. 1, p. 476.

12. Farrand, ed., *The Records of the Federal Convention of 1787,* vol. 2, p. 10.

13. E. M. Earle, ed., *The Federalist* (New York: Modern Library, 1937), No. 71.

14. Earle, ed., *The Federalist,* No. 62.

15. Earle, ed., *The Federalist,* No. 70.

16. Max Farrand, *The Framing of the Constitution of the United States* (New Haven, CT: Yale University Press, 1962), p. 49.

17. Richard E. Neustadt, *Presidential Power* (New York: Wiley, 1960), p. 33.

18. Melancton Smith, quoted in Storing, *What the Anti-Federalists Were For,* p. 17.

19. "Essays of Brutus," No. 1, in Herbert Storing, ed., *The Complete Anti-Federalist* (Chicago: University of Chicago Press, 1981).

20. Earle, ed., *The Federalist,* No. 57.

21. "Essays of Brutus," No. 15, in Storing, ed., *The Complete Anti-Federalist.*

22. Earle, ed., *The Federalist,* No. 10

23. "Essays of Brutus," No. 7, in Storing, ed., *The Complete Anti-Federalist.*

24. "Essays of Brutus," No. 6, in Storing, ed., *The Complete Anti-Federalist.*

25. Storing, *What the Anti-Federalists, Were For,* p. 28.

26. Earle, ed., *The Federalist,* No. 51.

27. Quoted in Storing, *What the Anti-Federalists Were For,* p. 30.

28. Observation by Colonel George Mason, delegate from Virginia, early during the convention period. Quoted in Farrand, ed., *The Records of the Federal Convention of 1787,* vol. 1, pp. 202–3.

29. Clinton Rossiter, ed., *The Federalist Papers* (New York: New American Library, 1961), No. 43, p. 278.

30. See Marcia Lee, "The Equal Rights Amendment: Public Policy by Means of a Constitutional Amendment," in *The Politics of Policy-Making in America,* ed. David Caputo (San Francisco: Freeman, 1977); Jane Mansbridge, *Why We Lost the ERA* (Chicago: University of Chicago Press, 1986); and Donald Mathews and Jane Sherron DeHart, *Sex, Gender, and the Politics of the ERA* (New York: Oxford University Press, 1990).

31. The Fourteenth Amendment is included in this table as well as in Table 3.4 because it seeks not only to define citizenship but *seems* to intend also that this definition of citizenship included, along with the right to vote, all the rights of the Bill of Rights, regardless of the state in which the citizen resided. A great deal more will be said about this in Chapter 5.

32. Earle, ed., *The Federalist,* No. 10.

CHAPTER 4

1. Andre Henderson, "Cruise Control," *Governing,* February 1995, p. 39. Unemployment benefit figures are from U.S. House of Representatives, Committee on Ways and Means, *Where Your Money Goes: America's Entitlements: The 1994–95 Green Book* (Washington, DC: Brassey's, 1994), p. 276.

2. Ken I. Kersch, "Full Faith and Credit for Same-Sex Marriages?" *Political Science Quarterly,* no. 112 (Spring 1997), pp. 117–36; Joan Biskupic, "Once Unthinkable, Now Under Debate," *Washington Post,* September 3, 1996, p. A1.

3. Linda Greenhouse, "Supreme Court Weaves Legal Principles from a Tangle of Legislation," *New York Times,* June 30, 1988, p. A20.

4. *Hicklin v. Orbeck,* 437 U.S. 518 (1978).

5. *Sweeny v. Woodall,* 344 U.S. 86 (1953).

6. Marlise Simons, "France Won't Extradite American Convicted of Murder," *New York Times,* December 5, 1997, p. A9.

7. A good discussion of the constitutional position of local governments is in York Willbern, *The Withering Away of the City* (Bloomington: Indiana University Press, 1971). For more on the structure and theory of federalism, see Thomas R. Dye, *American Federalism: Competition among Governments* (Lexington, MA: Lexington Books, 1990), chap. 1; and Martha Derthick, "Up-to-Date in Kansas City: Reflections on American Federalism" (the 1992 John Gaus Lecture), *PS: Political Science & Politics* 25 (December 1992), pp. 671–75.

8. For a good treatment of the contrast between national political stability and social instability, see Samuel P. Huntington, *Political Order in Changing Societies* (New Haven, CT: Yale University Press, 1068), chap. 2.

9. *McCulloch v. Maryland,* 4 Wheaton 316 (1819).

10. *Gibbons v. Ogden,* 9 Wheaton 1 (1824).

11. The Sherman Antitrust Act, adopted in 1890, for example, was enacted not to restrict commerce, but rather to protect it from monopolies, or trusts, so as to prevent unfair trade practices, and to enable the market again to become self-regulating. Moreover, the Supreme Court sought to uphold liberty of contract to protect businesses. For example, in *Lochner v. New York,* 198 U.S. 45 (1905), the Court invalidated a New York law regulating the sanitary conditions and hours of labor of bakers on the grounds that the law interfered with liberty of contract.

12. The key case in this process of expanding the power of the national government is generally considered to be *NLRB v. Jones & Laughlin Steel Corporation,* 301 U.S. 1 (1937), in which the Supreme Court approved federal regulation of the workplace and thereby virtually eliminated interstate commerce as a limit on the national government's power.

13. *U.S. v. Darby Lumber Co.,* 312 U.S. 100 (1941).

14. W. John Moore, "Pleading the 10th," *National Journal,* July 29, 1995, p. 1940.

15. *Seminole Indian Tribe v. Florida,* 116 S.Ct. 1114 (1996).

16. *United States v. Lopez,* 115 S.Ct. 1624 (1995).

17. See the poll reported in Guy Gugliotta, "Scaling Down the American Dream," *Washington Post,* April 19, 1995, p. A21.

18. Kenneth T. Palmer, "The Evolution of Grant Policies," in *The Changing Politics of Federal Grants,* by Lawrence D. Brown, James W. Fossett, and Kenneth T. Palmer (Washington, DC: Brookings, 1984) p. 15.

19. Palmer, "The Evolution of Grant Policies," p. 6.

20. Morton Grozdins, *The American System,* ed. Daniel J. Elazar (Chicago: Rand McNally, 1966).

21. See Terry Sanford, *Storm Over the States* (New York: McGraw-Hill, 1967).

22. James L. Sundquist with David W. Davis, *Making Federalism Work* (Washington, DC: Brookings, 1969), p. 271. George Wallace was mistrusted by the architects of the War on Poverty because he was a strong proponent of racial segregation. He believed in "states' rights," which meant that states, not the federal government, should decide what liberty and equality meant.

23. See Don Kettl, *The Regulation of American Federalism* (Baton Rouge: Louisiana State University Press, 1983).

24. See Advisory Commission on Intergovernmental Relations, *Federal Regulation of State and Local Governments: The Mixed Record of the 1980s* (Washington, DC: Advisory Commission on Intergovernmental Relations, July 1993).

25. Advisory Commission on Intergovernmental Relations, *Federal Regulation of State and Local Governments,* p. iii.

26. Ann Devroy and Helen Dewar, "Hailing Bipartisanship, Clinton Signs Bill to Restrict Unfunded Mandates," *Washington Post,* March 23, 1995, p. A10.

27. Quoted in Timothy Conlon, *New Federalism: Intergovernmental Reform from Nixon to Reagan* (Washington, DC: Brookings, 1988), p. 25.

28. For the emergence of complaints about federal categorical grants, see Palmer, "The Evolution of Grant Policies," pp. 17–18. On the governors' efforts to gain more control over federal grants after the 1994 congressional elections, see Dan Balz, "GOP Governors Eager to Do Things Their Way," *Washington Post,* November 22, 1994, p. A4.

29. Advisory Commission on Intergovernmental Relations, *Federal Regulation of State and Local Governments,* p. 51.

30. Dan Balz, "Governors Press Congress for Power to Manage Programs at State Level," *Washington Post,* December 11, 1994, p. A6; Robert Pear, "Attention Is Turning Governors' Heads: But Some Still Worry that Congress Will Shift Burden to the States," *New York Times,* January 30, 1995, p. A14.

31. Robert Frank, "Proposed Block Grants Seen Unlikely to Cure Management Problems," *Wall Street Journal,* May 1, 1995, p. 1.

32. Judith Havemann, "Scholars Question Whether Welfare Shift Is Reform," *Washington Post,* April 20, 1995, p. A8.

33. Malcolm Gladwell, "Proposed Education Cuts Protested in New York," *Washington Post,* March 25, 1995, p. A4.

34. U.S. Committee on Federalism and National Purpose, *To Form a More Perfect Union* (Washington, DC: National Conference on Social Welfare, 1985). See also the discussion in Paul E. Peterson, *The Price of Federalism* (Washington, DC: Brookings, 1995), esp. chap. 8.

35. Malcolm Gladwell, "In States' Experiments, a Cutting Contest," *New York Times,* March 10, 1995, p. 6.

36. The phrase "laboratories of democracy" was coined by Supreme Court justice Louis Brandeis in his dissenting opinion in *New State Ice Co. v. Liebman,* 285 U.S. 262 (1932).

37. "Motor Vehicle Fatalities in 1996 were 12 Percent Higher on Interstates, Freeways in 12 States that Raised Speed Limits," Press Release of the Insurance Institute for Highway Safety, October 10, 1997.

38. See Stephen Barr, "Americans Gain a Small Measure of Confidence in Government," *Washington Post,* March 24, 1997, p. A17.

39. Sidney Verba, Kay Lehman Schlozman, and Henry E. Brady, *Voice and Equality: Civic Voluntarism in American Politics* (Cambridge, MA: Harvard University Press, 1995), pp. 66–67.

CHAPTER 5

1. *Reno, Attorney General of the United States, et al. v. American Civil Liberties Union et al.,* 117 S.Ct. 2329 (1997).

2. Amy Harmon, "Ideological Foes Meet on Web Decency," *New York Times,* December 1, 1997, p. D1.

3. Bennett Haselton, telephone interview by author, February 12, 1998; PEACEFIRE web site, http://www.peacefire.org.

4. Clinton Rossiter, ed., *The Federalist Papers* (New York: New American Library, 1961), No. 84, p. 513.

5. Rossiter, ed., *The Federalist Papers,* No. 84, p. 513.

6. Clinton Rossiter, *1787: The Grand Convention* (New York: Norton, 1987), p. 302.

7. Rossiter, *1787,* p. 303. Rossiter also reports that "in 1941 the States of Connecticut, Massachusetts and Georgia celebrated the sesquicentennial of the Bill of Rights by giving their hitherto withheld and unneeded assent,"

8. Let there be no confusion about the words "liberty" and "freedom." They are synonymous and interchangeable. "Freedom" comes from the German, *Freiheit.* "Liberty" is from the French, *liberté.* Although people sometimes try to make them appear to be different, both of them have equal concern with the absence of restraints on individual choices of action.

9. For some recent scholarship on the Bill of Rights and its development, see Geoffrey Stone, Richard Epstein, and Cass Sunstein, eds, *The Bill of Rights and the Modern State* (Chicago: University of Chicago Press, 1992); and Michael J. Meyer and William A. Parent, eds., *The Constitution of Rights* (Ithaca, NY: Cornell University Press, 1992).

10. *Barron v. Baltimore,* 7 Peters 243, 246 (1833).

11. The Fourteenth Amendment also seems designed to introduce civil rights. The final clause of the all-important Section 1 provides that no state can "deny to any person within its jurisdiction the equal protection of the laws." It is not unreasonable to conclude that the purpose of this provision was to obligate the state governments as well as the national government to take *positive* actions to protect citizens from arbitrary and discriminatory actions, at least those based on race. This will be explored in Chapter 6.

12. For example, *The Slaughterhouse Cases,* 16 Wallace 36 (1883).

13. *Chicago, Burlington and Quincy Railroad Company v. Chicago,* 166 U.S. 226 (1897).

14. *Gitlow v. New York,* 268 U.S. 652 (1925).

15. *Near v. Minnesota,* 283 U.S. 697 (1931); *Hague v. C.I.O.,* 307 U.S. 496 (1939).

16. *Palko v. Connecticut,* 302 U.S. 319 (1937).

17. All of these were implicitly included in the *Palko* case as "not incorporated" into the Fourteenth Amendment as limitations on the powers of the states.

18. There is one interesting exception, which involves the Sixth Amendment right to public trial. In the 1948 case *In re Oliver,* 33 U.S. 257, the right to the public trial was, in effect, incorporated as part of the Fourteenth Amendment. However, the issue in that case was put more generally as "due process," and public trial itself was not actually mentioned in so many words. Later opinions, such as *Duncan v. Louisiana,* 391 U.S. 145 (1968), cited the *Oliver* case as the precedent for more explicit incorporation of public trials as part of the Fourteenth Amendment.

19. For a lively and readable treatment of the possibilities of

restricting provisions of the Bill of Rights, without actually reversing prior decisions, see David G. Savage, *Turning Right: The Making of the Rehnquist Supreme Court* (New York: Wiley, 1992). For an indication that the Supreme Court in the 1990s may in fact be moving toward more restrictions on the Bill of Rights, see Richard Lacayo, "The Soul of a New Majority," *Time*, July 10, 1995, pp. 46–48.

20. *Abington School District v. Schempp,* 374 U.S. 203 (1963).

21. *Engel v. Vitale,* 370 U.S. 421 (1962).

22. *Wallace v. Jaffree,* 472 U.S. 38 (1985).

23. *Lynch v. Donnelly,* 465 U.S. 668 (1984).

24. *Lemon v. Kurtzman,* 403 U.S. 602 (1971). The *Lemon* test is still good law, but as recently as the 1994 Court term, four justices have urged that the *Lemon* test be abandoned. Here is a settled area of law that may soon become unsettled.

25. *Rosenberger v. Rector and Visitors of the University of Virginia,* 115 S.Ct. 2510 (1995).

26. *Agostini v. Felton,* 117 S.Ct. 1997 (1997). The case being overruled was *Aguilar v. Felton,* 473 U.S. 402 (1985).

27. *West Virginia State Board of Education v. Barnette,* 319 U.S. 624 (1943). The case it reversed was *Minersville School District v. Gobitis,* 310 U.S. 586 (1940).

28. *Employment Division, Department of Human Resources of Oregon v. Smith,* 494 U.S. 872 (1990).

29. *City of Boerne v. Flores,* 117 S.Ct. 293 (1996).

30. *Wisconsin v. Yoder,* 406 U.S. 205 (1972).

31. *U.S. v. Carolene Products Company,* 304 U.S. 144 (1938), note 4. This footnote is one of the Court's most important doctrines. See Alfred H. Kelly, Winfred A. Harbison, and Herman Belz, *The American Constitution: Its Origins and Development,* 7th ed. (New York: Norton, 1991), Vol. 2, pp. 519–23.

32. *Schenk v. U.S.,* 249 U.S. 47 (1919).

33. *Brandenburg v. Ohio,* 395 U.S. 444 (1969).

34. *Stromberg v. California,* 283, U.S. 359 (1931).

35. *Texas v. Johnson,* 488 U.S. 884 (1989).

36. *United States v. Eichman,* 496 U.S. 310 (1990).

37. For a good general discussion of "speech plus," see Louis Fisher, *American Constitutional Law* (New York: McGraw-Hill, 1990), pp. 544–46. The case upholding the buffer zone against the abortion protesters is *Madsen v. Women's Health Center,* 114 S.Ct. 2516 (1994).

38. *New York Times v. Sullivan,* 376 U.S. 254 (1964).

39. *Masson v. New Yorker Magazine,* 111 S.Ct. 2419 (1991).

40. *Hustler Magazine v. Falwell,* 108 S.Ct. 876 (1988).

41. *Roth v. US,* 354 U.S. 476 (1957).

42. Concurring opinion in *Jacobellis v. Ohio,* 378 U.S. 184 (1964).

43. *Miller v. California,* 413 U.S. 15 (1973).

44. See, for example, "Are Movies and Music Killing America's Soul?" *Time,* June 12, 1995.

45. Wray Herbert, "Is Porn Un-American?" *U.S. News and World Report,* July 3, 1995, pp. 51–54.

46. *Reno v. American Civil Liberties Union,* 117 S.Ct. 2329 (1997).

47. *Chaplinsky v. State of New Hampshire,* 315 U.S. 568 (1942).

48. *Dennis v. United States,* 341 U.S. 494 (1951), which upheld the infamous Smith Act of 1940, which provided criminal penalties for those who "willfully and knowingly conspire to teach

and advocate the forceful and violent overthrow and destruction of the government."

49. "The Penn File: An Update," *Wall Street Journal,* April 11, 1994, p. A14.

50. *Meritor Savings Bank, FBD v. Vinson,* 477 U.S. 57 (1986).

51. Charles Fried, "The New First Amendment Jurisprudence: A Threat to Liberty," in *The Bill of Rights and the Modern State,* ed. Stone, Epstein, and Sunstein, p. 249.

52. *Bethel School District No. 403 v. Fraser,* 478 U.S. 675 (1986).

53. *Hazelwood School District v. Kuhlmeier,* 108 S.Ct. 562 (1988).

54. *Broadcasting Company v. Acting Attorney General,* 405 U.S. 1000 (1972).

55. *Board of Trustees of the State University of New York v. Fox,* 109 S.Ct. 3028 (1989).

56. *City Council v. Taxpayers for Vincent,* 466 U.S. 789 (1984).

57. *Posadas de Puerto Rico Associates v. Tourism Company of Puerto Rico,* 479 U.S. 328 (1986).

58. Fisher, *American Constitutional Law,* p. 546.

59. *Bigelow v. Virginia,* 421 U.S. 809 (1975).

60. *Virginia State Board of Pharmacy v. Virginia Citizens Consumer Council,* 425 U.S. 748 (1976). Later cases restored the rights of lawyers to advertise their services.

61. *44 Liquormart, Inc. and Peoples Super Liquor Stores Inc., Petitioners v. Rhode Island and Rhode Island Liquor Stores Association,* 116 S.Ct. 1495 (1996).

62. *United States v. Miller,* 307 U.S. 174 (1939). A good, albeit brief, treatment of this will be found in Edward Corwin and J. W. Peltason, *Corwin & Peltason's Understanding the Constitution,* 13th ed. (Fort Worth, TX: Harcourt Brace, 1994), pp. 248–49.

63. *Printz v. United States,* 117 S.Ct. 2365 (1997), and *Mack v. United States,* 116 S.Ct. 2521 (1996).

64. The Supreme Court itself provides an intriguing suggestion for a criterion to distinguish between appropriate and inappropriate regulation of the right to bear arms. In 1939 the Supreme Court upheld a federal law making it a crime to ship sawed-off shotguns in interstate commerce, on the grounds that such weapons had no reasonable relationship "to the preservation or efficiency of a well-regulated militia." *U.S. v. Miller,* 307 U.S. 174 (1939). However, that does not make the current issues any easier to settle. The following are two treatments of the Second Amendment by two scholars who both favor handgun control but differ fundamentally on how to treat the issue and the general constitutional problem: Sanford Levinson, "The Embarrassing Second Amendment," *Yale Law Journal* 99 (1989), pp. 637–59; and Robert Spitzer, *The Politics of Gun Control* (Chatham, NJ: Chatham House, 1995).

65. See Corwin and Peltason, *Understanding the Constitution,* pp. 283–86.

66. *In re Winship,* 397 U.S. 361 (1970). An outstanding treatment of due process in issues involving the Fourth through Seventh Amendments will be found in Fisher, *American Constitutional Law,* chap. 13.

67. *Horton v. California,* 496 U.S. 128 (1990).

68. *Mapp v. Ohio,* 367 U.S. 643 (1961). Although Ms. Mapp went free in this case, she was later convicted in New York on nar-

cotics trafficking charges and served nine years of a twenty-year sentence.

69. For a good discussion of the issue, see Fisher, *American Constitutional Law*, pp. 884–89.

70. *National Treasury Employees Union v. Von Raab*, 39 U.S. 656 (1989).

71. *Skinner v. Railroad Labor Executives Association*, 489 U.S. 602 (1989).

72. *Vernonia School District 47J v. Acton*, 115 S.Ct. 2386 (1985).

73. See the discussion in David O'Brien, *Constitutional Law and Politics*, Vol. 2, (New York: Norton, 1995), pp. 840–57.

74. Corwin and Peltason, *Understanding the Constitution*, p. 286.

75. *Miranda v. Arizona*, 348 U.S. 436 (1966).

76. *Berman v. Parker*, 348 U.S. 26 (1954). For a thorough analysis of the case see Benjamin Ginsberg, *"Berman v. Parker: Congress, the Court, and the Public Purpose," Polity* 4 (1971), pp. 48–75. For a later application of the case that suggests that "just compensation"—defined as something approximating market value—is about all a property owner can hope for protection against a public taking of property, see Theodore Lowi et al., *Poliscide; Big Government, Big Science, Lilliputian Politics*, 2nd ed. (Lanham, MD: University Press of America, 1990), pp. 267–70.

77. *Gideon v. Wainwright*, 372 U.S. 335 (1963). For a full account of the story of the trial and release of Clarence Earl Gideon, see Anthony Lewis, *Gideon's Trumpet* (New York: Random House, 1964). See also David O'Brien, *Storm Center*, 2nd ed. (New York: Norton, 1990).

78. For further discussion of these issues, see Corwin and Peltason, *Understanding the Constitution*, pp. 319–23.

79. *Congressional Quarterly Weekly Report*, October 21, 1995, p. 3212.

80. *Furman v. Georgia*, 408 U.S. 238 (1972).

81. *Gregg v. Georgia*, 428 U.S. 153 (1976).

82. *Minerville School District v. Gobitis*, 310 U.S. 586 (1940).

83. *West Virginia State Board of Education v. Barnette*, 319 U.S. 624 (1943)

84. *NAACP v. Alabama ex rel. Patterson*, 357 U.S. 449 (1958).

85. *Griswold v. Connecticut*, 381 U.S. 479 (1965).

86. *Griswold v. Connecticut*, concurring opinion. In 1972, the Court extended the privacy right to unmarried women: *Eisenstadt v. Baird*, 405 U.S. 438 (1972).

87. *Roe v. Wade*, 410 U.S. 113 (1973).

88. See Paul Brest and Sanford Stevinson, *Processes of Constitutional Decision-Making: Cases and Materials*, 2nd ed. (Boston: Little, Brown, 1983), p. 660.

89. *Baker v. Carr*, 369 U.S. 186 (1962).

90. *Engle v. Vitale*, 370 U.S. 421 (1962), and the series of cases following on that case.

91. *Webster v. Reproductive Health Services*, 109 S.Ct. 3040 (1989), which upheld a Missouri law that restricted the use of public medical facilities for abortion. The decision opened the way for other states to limit the availability of abortion.

92. *Planned Parenthood of Southeastern Pennsylvania v. Casey*, 112 S.Ct. 2791 (1992).

93. Gayle Binion, "Under Burden? Government Now Has Wide Latitude to Restrict Abortions," *Santa Barbara News-Press*, July 5, 1992, p. A13.

94. *Bowers v. Hardwick*, 478 U.S. 186 (1986).

95. The dissenters were quoting an earlier case, *Olmstead v. United States*, 27 U.S. 438 (1928), to emphasize the nature of their disagreement with the majority in the Bowers *case*.

96. *Washington v. Glucksberg*, 117 S.Ct. 2258 (1997).

97. *Washington v. Glucksberg*.

98. *Washington v. Glucksberg*.

99. For an excellent discussion, see David M. O'Brien, *Supreme Court Watch 1997* (New York: Norton, 1998), pp. 117–30.

100. *Roe v. Wade*.

101. *Rosenberger v. University of Virginia*.

CHAPTER 6

1. William Booth, "U of Calif. Ends Racial Preferences," *Washington Post*, July 21, 1995, p. A1.

2. The *Slaughterhouse Cases*, 16 Wallace 36 (1873).

3. See *Civil Rights Cases*, 109 U.S. 3 (1883).

4. Anatole France, *Le lys rouge* (1984), chap. 7.

5. *Plessy v. Ferguson*, 163 U.S. 537 (1896).

6. The prospect of a Fair Employment Practices law tied to the commerce power produced the Dixiecrat break with the Democratic Party in 1948. The Democratic Party organization of the States of the Old Confederacy seceded from the national party and nominated its own candidate, the then-Democratic governor of South Carolina, Strom Thurmond, who is now a Republican senator. This almost cost President Truman the election.

7. This was based on the provision in Article VI of the Constitution that "all treaties made, . . . under the authority of the United States," shall be the "supreme law of the land." The committee recognized that if the U.S. Senate ratified the Human Rights Covenant of the United Nations—a treaty—then that power could be used as the constitutional umbrella for effective civil rights leg-

islation. The Supreme Court had recognized in *Missouri v. Holland*, 252 U.S. 416 (1920), that a treaty could enlarge federal power at the expense of the states.

8. *Missouri ex rel. Gaines v. Canada*, 305 U.S. 337 (1938).

9. *Sweatt v. Painter*, 339 U.S. 629 (1950).

10. *Smith v. Allwright*, 321 U.S. 649 (1944).

11. *Shelley v. Kraemer*, 334 U.S. 1 (1948).

12. Kermit L. Hall, *The Magic Mirror: Law in American History* (New York: Oxford University Press, 1989), pp. 322–24. See also Richard Kluger, *Simple Justice* (New York: Random House, Vintage Edition, 1977), pp. 530–37.

13. The District of Columbia case came up too, but since the District of Columbia is not a state, this case did not directly involve the Fourteenth Amendment and its "equal protection" clause. It confronted the Court on the same grounds, however—that segregation is inherently unequal. Its victory in effect was "incorporation in reverse," with equal protection moving from the Fourteenth Amendment to become part of the Bill of Rights. See *Bolling v. Sharpe*, 347 U.S. 497 (1954).

14. *Brown v. Board of Education of Topeka, Kansas,* 347 U.S. 483 (1954).

15. The Supreme Court first declared that race was a suspect classification requiring strict scrutiny in the decision *Korematsu v. United States,* 323 U.S. 214 (1944). In this case, the Court upheld President Roosevelt's executive order of 1941 allowing the military to exclude persons of Japanese ancestry from the West Coast and to place them in internment camps. It is one of the few cases in which classification based on race survived strict scrutiny.

16. The two most important cases were *Cooper v. Aaron,* 358 U.S. 1 (1958), which required Little Rock, Arkansas, to desegregate; and *Griffin v. Prince Edward County School Board,* 377 U.S. 218 (1964), which forced all the schools of that Virginia county to reopen after five years of closing to avoid desegregation.

17. In *Cooper v. Aaron,* the Supreme Court ordered immediate compliance with the lower court's desegregation order and went beyond that with a stern warning that it is "emphatically the province and duty of the judicial department to say what the law is."

18. *Shuttlesworth v. Birmingham Board of Education,* 358 U.S. 101 (1958), upheld a "pupil placement" plan purporting to assign pupils on various bases, with no mention of race. This case interpreted *Brown* to mean that school districts must stop explicit racial discrimination but were under no obligation to take positive steps to desegregate. For a while black parents were doomed to case-by-case approaches.

19. For good treatments of this long stretch of the struggle of the federal courts to integrate the schools, see Paul Brest and Sanford Levinson, *Processes of Constitutional Decision-Making: Cases and Materials,* 2nd ed. (Boston: Little, Brown, 1983), pp. 471–80; and Alfred Kelly et al., *The American Constitution: Its Origins and Development,* 6th ed. (New York: Norton, 1983), pp. 610–16.

20. Pierre Thomas, "Denny's to Settle Bias Cases," *Washington Post,* May 24, 1994, p. A1.

21. See Hamil Harris, "For Blacks, Cabs Can Be Hard to Get," *Washington Post,* July 21, 1994, p. J1.

22. For a thorough analysis of the Office for Civil Rights, see Jeremy Rabkin, "Office for Civil Rights," in *The Politics of Regulation,* ed. James Q. Wilson (New York: Basic Books, 1980).

23. This was an accepted way of using quotas or ratios to determine statistically that blacks or other minorities were being excluded from schools or jobs, and then on the basis of that statistical evidence to authorize the Justice Department to bring suits in individual cases and in "class action" suits as well. In most segregated situations outside the South, it is virtually impossible to identify and document an intent to discriminate.

24. *Swann v. Charlotte-Mecklenberg Board of Education,* 402 U.S. 1 (1971).

25. *Milliken v. Bradley,* 418 U.S. 717 (1974).

26. For a good evaluation of the Boston effort, see Gary Orfield, *Must We Bus? Segregated Schools and National Policy* (Washington: Brookings Institution, 1978), pp. 144–46. See also Bob Woodward and Scott Armstrong, *The Brethren: Inside the Supreme Court* (New York: Simon and Schuster, 1979), pp. 426–27; and J. Anthony Lukas, *Common Ground* (New York: Random House, 1986).

27. *Board of Education v. Dowell,* 498 U.S. 237 (1991).

28. *Missouri v. Jenkins,* 115 S.Ct. 2038 (1995).

29. See especially *Katzenbach v. McClung,* 379 U.S. 294 (1964). Almost immediately after passage of the Civil Rights Act of 1964, a case was brought challenging the validity of Title II, which covered discrimination in public accommodations. Ollie's Barbecue was a neighborhood restaurant in Birmingham, Alabama. It was located eleven blocks away from an interstate highway and even farther from railroad and bus stations. Its table service was for whites only; there was only a take-out service for blacks. The Supreme Court agreed that Ollie's was strictly an intrastate restaurant, but since a substantial proportion of its food and other supplies were bought from companies outside the state of Alabama, there was a sufficient connection to interstate commerce; therefore, racial discrimination at such restaurants would "impose commercial burdens of national magnitude upon interstate commerce." Although this case involved Title II, it had direct bearing on the constitutionality of Title VII.

30. *Griggs v. Duke Power Company,* 401 U.S. 24 (1971). See also Allan Sindler, *Bakke, DeFunis, and Minority Admissions* (New York: Longman, 1978), pp. 180–89.

31. For a good treatment of these issues, see Charles O. Gregory and Harold A. Katz, *Labor and the Law* (New York: Norton, 1979), chap. 17.

32. In 1970, this act was amended to outlaw for five years literacy tests as a condition for voting in all states.

33. Joint Center for Political Studies, *Black Elected Officials: A National Roster—1988* (Washington, DC: Joint Center for Political Studies Press, 1988), pp. 9–10. For a comprehensive analysis and evaluation of the Voting Rights Act, see Bernard Grofman and Chandler Davidson, eds., *Controversies in Minority Voting: The Voting Rights Act in Perspective* (Washington, DC: Brookings Institution, 1992).

34. See Douglas S. Massey and Nancy A. Denton, *American Apartheid: Segregation and the Making of the Underclass* (Cambridge, MA: Harvard University Press, 1993), chap. 7.

35. See Jane J. Mansbridge, *Why We Lost the ERA* (Chicago: University of Chicago Press, 1986); and Gilbert Steiner, *Constitutional Inequality* (Washington, DC: Brookings Institution, 1985).

36. *See Frontiero v. Richardson,* 411 U.S. 677 (1973).

37. See *Craig v. Boren,* 423 U.S. 1047 (1976).

38. *Franklin v. Gwinnett County Public Schools,* 503 U.S. 60 (1992).

39. Jennifer Halperin, "Women Step Up to Bat," *Illinois Issues* 21 (September 1995), pp. 11–14.

40. Joan Biskupic and David Nakamura, "Court Won't Review Sports Equity Ruling," *Washington Post,* April 22, 1997, p. A1.

41. *U.S. v. Virginia,* 116 S.Ct. 2264 (1996).

42. Judith Havemann, "Two Women Quit Citadel over Alleged Harassment," *Washington Post,* January 13, 1997, p. A1.

43. See Linda Greenhouse, "Court Spells out Rules for Finding Sex Harassment," *New York Times,* June 27, 1998, p. A1. The cases are *Burlington Industries v. Ellerth,* 97-569 (1998), and *Faragher v. City of Boca Raton,* 97-282 (1998).

44. *Lau v. Nichols,* 414 U.S. 563 (1974).

45. Dick Kirschten, "Not Black and White," *National Journal,* March 2, 1991, p. 497.

46. See the discussion in Robert A. Katzmann, *Institutional Disability: The Saga of Transportation Policy for the Disabled* (Washington, DC: Brookings Institution, 1986).

47. For example, after pressure from the Justice Department, one of the nation's largest rental-car companies agreed to make

special hand-controls available to any customer requesting them. See "Avis Agrees to Equip Cars for Disabled," *Los Angeles Times,* September 2, 1994, p. D1.

48. *Bowers v. Hardwick,* 478 U.S. 186 (1986).

49. Quoted in Joan Biskupic, "Gay Rights Activists Seek a Supreme Court Test Case," *Washington Post,* December 19, 1993, p. A1.

50. *Romer v. Evans,* 116 S.Ct. 1620 (1996).

51. From Lyndon B. Johnson, *The Vantage Point* (New York: Holt, Rinehart, and Winston, 1971), p. 166.

52. The Department of Health, Education, and Welfare (HEW) was the cabinet department charged with administering most federal social programs. In 1980, when education programs were transferred to the newly created Department of Education, HEW was renamed the Department of Health and Human Services.

53. *Regents of the University of California v. Bakke,* 438 U.S. 265 (1978).

54. See, for example, *United Steelworkers v. Weber,* 443 U.S. 193 (1979); and *Fullilove v. Klutznick,* 100 S.Ct. 2758 (1980).

55. *Ward's Cove v. Atonio,* 109 S.Ct. 2115 (1989).

56. *Griggs v. Duke Power Company,* 401 U.S. 24 (1971).

57. *Martin v. Wilks,* 109 S.Ct. 2180 (1989). In this case, some white firefighters in Birmingham challenged a consent decree mandating goals for hiring and promoting blacks. This was an affirmative action plan that had been worked out between the employer and aggrieved black employees and had been accepted by a federal court. Such agreements become "consent decrees" and are subject to enforcement. Chief Justice Rehnquist held that the white firefighters could challenge the legality of such programs, even though they had not been parties to the original litigation.

58. *St. Mary's Honor Center v. Hicks,* 113 S.Ct. 2742 (1993).

59. *Adarand Constructors v. Pena,* 115 S.Ct. 2097 (1995).

60. Ann Devroy, "Clinton Study Backs Affirmative Action," *Washington Post,* July 19, 1995, p. A1.

61. *Hopwood v. State of Texas,* 78 F3d 932 (5th Cir., 1996).

62. See Lydia Lum, "Applications by Minorities Down Sharply," *Houston Chronicle,* April 8, 1997, p. A1; R. G. Ratcliffe, "Senate Approves Bill Designed to Boost Minority Enrollments," *Houston Chronicle,* May 8, 1997, p. A1.

63. Linda Greenhouse, "Settlement Ends High Court Case on Preferences," *New York Times,* November 22, 1997, p. A1; Barry Bearak, "Rights Groups Ducked a Fight, Opponents Say," *New York Times,* November 22, 1997, p. A1.

64. Michael A. Fletcher, "Opponents of Affirmative Action Heartened by Court Decision," *Washington Post,* April 13, 1997, p. A21.

65. See Sam Howe Verhovek, "Houston Vote Underlined Complexity of Rights Issue," *New York Times,* November 6, 1997, p. A1.

66. There are still many genuine racists in America, but with the exception of a lunatic fringe, made up of neo-Nazis and members of the Ku Klux Klan, most racists are too ashamed or embarrassed to take part in normal political discourse. They are not included in either category here.

67. *Slaughterhouse Cases,* 16 Wallace 36 (1873).

68. See Paul M. Sniderman and Edward G. Carmines, *Reaching beyond Race* (Cambridge, MA: Harvard University Press, 1997).

CHAPTER 7

1. Alexander Astin et al., "The American Freshman: National Norms for Fall 1994," Cooperative Institutional Research Program of the American Council on Education and the Higher Education Research Institute of the University of California at Los Angeles, 1994.

2. Quoted in the *Tampa Tribune,* January 9, 1995, p. 1.

3. "UC Protest Rally Planned," *San Francisco Examiner,* July 23, 1995.

4. For a discussion of the political beliefs of Americans, see Harry Holloway and John George, *Public Opinion* (New York: St. Martin's, 1986). See also Paul R. Abramson, *Political Attitudes in America* (San Francisco: Freeman, 1983).

5. See Louis Hartz, *The Liberal Tradition in America* (New York: Harcourt, Brace, 1955).

6. See Paul M. Sniderman and Edward G. Carmines, *Reaching beyond Race* (Cambridge, MA: Harvard University Press, 1997).

7. Ben Gose, "Penn to Replace Controversial Speech Code; Will No Longer Punish Students for Insults," *Chronicle of Higher Education,* June 29, 1994, p. A30.

8. See Angus Campbell et al., *The American Voter* (New York: Wiley, 1960), p. 147.

9. Richard Morin, "Poll Reflects Division over Simpson Case," *Washington Post,* October 8, 1995, p. A31.

10. "Middle-Class Views in Black and White," *Washington Post,* October 9, 1995, p. A22.

11. For data see Rutgers University, Eagleton Institute of Poli-tics, Center for the American Woman in Politics, "Sex Differences in Voter Turnout," August 1994.

12. Pamela Johnston Conover, "The Role of Social Groups in Political Thinking," *British Journal of Political Science* 18 (1988), pp. 51–78.

13. See Michael C. Dawson, "Structure and Ideology: The Shaping of Black Opinion," paper presented to the 1995 annual meeting of the Midwest Political Science Association, Chicago, Illinois, April 7–9, 1995. See also Michael C. Dawson, *Behind the Mule: Race, Class, and African American Politics* (Princeton, NJ: Princeton University Press, 1994).

14. Elisabeth Noelle-Neumann, *The Spiral of Silence* (Chicago: University of Chicago Press, 1984).

15. Michael X. Delli Carpini and Scott Keeter, *What Americans Know about Politics and Why It Matters* (New Haven: Yale University Press, 1996).

16. Sniderman and Carmines, *Reaching beyond Race,* ch. 4.

17. For an interesting discussion of opinion formation, see John Zaller, *The Nature and Origins of Mass Opinion* (New York: Cambridge University Press, 1992).

18. Gerald F. Seib and Michael K. Frisby, "Selling Sacrifice," *Wall Street Journal,* February 5, 1993, p. 1.

19. Michael K. Frisby, "Clinton Seeks Strategic Edge with Opinion Polls," *Wall Street Journal,* June 24, 1996, p. A16.

20. James Carney, "Playing by the Numbers," *Time,* April 11, 1994, p. 40.

21. See Gillian Peele, *Revival and Reaction* (Oxford, U.K.: Clarendon, 1985). Also see Connie Paige, *The Right-to-Lifers* (New York: Summit, 1983).

22. See David Vogel, "The Power of Business in America: A Reappraisal," *British Journal of Political Science* 13 (January 1983), pp. 19–44.

23. See David Vogel, "The Public Interest Movement and the American Reform Tradition," *Political Science Quarterly* 96 (Winter 1980), pp. 607–27.

24. Jason DeParle, "The Clinton Welfare Bill Begins Trek in Congress," *New York Times*, July 15, 1994, p. 1.

25. Joe Queenan, "Birth of a Notion," *Washington Post*, September 20, 1992, p. C1.

26. Zaller, *The Nature and Origins of Mass Opinion.*

27. See Shanto Iyengar, *Is Anyone Responsible? How Television Frames Political Issues* (Chicago: University of Chicago Press, 1991); and Shanto Iyengar, *Do the Media Govern?* (Thousand Oaks, CA: Sage, 1997).

28. Michael Kagay and Janet Elder, "Numbers Are No Problem for Pollsters, Words Are," *New York Times*, August 9, 1992, p. E6.

29. See Richard Morin, "Is Bush's Bounce a Boom or a Bust?" *Washington Post National Weekly Edition*, August 31–September 6, 1992, p. 37.

30. See Thomas E. Mann and Gary Orren, eds., *Media Polls in American Politics* (Washington, DC: Brookings, 1992).

31. For an excellent and reflective discussion by a journalist, see Richard Morin, "Clinton Slide in Survey Shows Perils of Polling," *Washington Post*, August 29, 1992, p. A6.

32. See Michael Traugott, "The Impact of Media Polls on the Public," in *Media Polls in American Politics*, Mann and Orren, eds., pp. 125–49.

33. Michael Barone, "Why Opinion Polls Are Worth Less," *U.S. News and World Report*, December 9, 1996, p. 52.

34. Donn Tibbetts, "Draft Bill Requires Notice of Push Polling." *Manchester Union Leader*, October 3, 1996, p. A6.

35. "Dial S for Smear," *Memphis Commercial Appeal*, September 22, 1996, p. 6B.

36. Amy Keller, "Subcommittee Launches Investigation of Push Polls," *Roll Call*, October 3, 1996, p. 1.

37. For a discussion of the growing difficulty of persuading people to respond to surveys, see John Brehm, *Phantom Respondents* (Ann Arbor: University of Michigan Press, 1993).

38. For a fuller discussion of the uses of polling and the role of public opinion in American politics, see Benjamin Ginsberg, *The Captive Public* (New York: Basic Books, 1986).

39. Benjamin I. Page and Robert Y. Shapiro, "Effects of Public Opinion on Policy," *American Political Science Review* 77 (March 1983), pp. 175–90.

40. Robert A. Erikson, Gerald Wright, and John McIver, *Statehouse Democracy: Public Opinion and Democracy in the American States* (New York: Cambridge University Press, 1994).

41. The results of separate studies by the political scientists Lawrence Jacobs, Robert Shapiro, and Alan Monroe were reported by Richard Morin in "Which Comes First, the Politician or the Poll?" *Washington Post National Weekly Edition*, February 10, 1997, p. 35.

42. Delli Carpini and Keeter. *What Americans Know about Politics and Why It Matters.*

CHAPTER 8

1. Howard Kurtz, "A Trash Course in Free Speech; College Newspapers Pitched in Protests," *Washington Post*, July 29, 1993, p. C1.

2. Richard Daigle, "Collegiate Censorship by Theft," *Atlanta Journal and Constitution*, March 6, 1994, p. F1.

3. "Daily Cal Papers Stolen from Campus," *San Francisco Chronicle*, October 16, 1997, p. C14.

4. John O'Conner, "Wheatbread Editor Has Court Date with Dean," *Telegram and Gazette* (Worcester, MA), February 12, 1997, p. B8.

5. Daigle, "Collegiate Censorship by Theft."

6. Benjamin Ginsberg and Martin Shefter, *Politics by Other Means* (New York: Basic Books, 1990), p. 24.

7. U.S. Bureau of the Census, *Statistical Abstract of the United States: 1994* (Washington, DC: Department of Commerce, 1994), pp. 567, 576.

8. For a criticism of the increasing consolidation of the media, see the essays in Patricia Aufderheide et al., *Conglomerates and the Media* (New York: New Press, 1997).

9. See Leo Bogart, "Newspapers in Transition," *Wilson Quarterly*, special issue, 1982; and Richard Harwood, "The Golden Age of Press Diversity," *Washington Post*, July 22, 1994, p. A23.

10. See Benjamin Ginsberg, *The Captive Public* (New York: Basic Books, 1986).

11. Michael Dawson, "Structure and Ideology: The Shaping of Black Public Opinion," paper presented to the 1995 meeting of the Midwest Political Science Association, Chicago, Illinois, April 7, 1995.

12. *Red Lion Broadcasting Company v. FCC*, 395 U.S. 367 (1969).

13. *Near v. Minnesota*, 283 U.S. 697 (1931).

14. *New York Times v. U.S.*, 403 U.S. 731 (1971).

15. *Cable News Network v. Noriega*, 111 S.Ct. 451 (1990); *Turner Broadcasting System v. Federal Communications Commission*, 114 S.Ct. 2445 (1994).

16. *New York Times v. Sullivan*, 376 U.S. 254 (1964).

17. *Masson v. New Yorker Magazine*, 111 S.Ct. 2419 (1991).

18. See the discussions in Gary Paul Gates, *Air Time* (New York: Harper & Row, 1978); Edward Jay Epstein, *News from Nowhere* (New York: Random House, 1973); Michael Parenti, *Inventing Reality* (New York: St. Martin's, 1986); Herbert Gans, *Deciding What's News* (New York: Vintage, 1980); and W. Lance Bennett, *News: The Politics of Illusion* (New York: Longman, 1986).

19. Rowan Scarborough, "TV News Too Liberal, Says CBS Reporter," *Washington Times*, February 15, 1996, p. 1.

20. See Edith Efron, *The News Twisters* (Los Angeles: Nash Publishing, 1971).

21. Rowan Scarborough, "Leftist Press? Reporters Working

in Washington Acknowledge Liberal Leanings in Poll." *Washington Times,* April 18, 1996, p. 1.

22. Clarence Page, "Party, Media Get Their Chances," *Commercial Appeal* (Memphis), August 20, 1996, p. 8A.

23. Mark Steyn, "The Big Turn-Off," *Sunday Telegraph* (London), October 13, 1996, p. 36.

24. Howard Kurtz, "The Media and the Fiske Report," *Washington Post,* July 3, 1994, p. A4.

25. David Streitfeld and Howard Kurtz, "Literary Agent Was Behind Secret Tapes," *Washington Post,* January 24, 1988, p. 1.

26. Michael Kinsley, "Bias and Baloney," *Washington Post,* November 26, 1992, p. A29.

27. "Quota of Lies," *Detroit News,* September 28, 1996, p. C6.

28. See Tom Burnes, "The Organization of Public Opinion," in *Mass Communication and Society,* ed. James Curran (Beverly Hills, CA: Sage, 1979), pp. 44–230. See also David Altheide, Creating Reality (Beverly Hills, CA: Sage, 1976).

29. David Garrow, *Protest at Selma* (New Haven, CT: Yale University Press, 1978).

30. Garrow, *Protest at Selma.*

31. See Todd Gitlin, *The Whole World Is Watching* (Berkeley, CA: University of California Press, 1980).

32. Quoted in George Brown Tindall and David E. Shi, *America: A Narrative History,* 4th ed. (New York: Norton, 1996), p. 1429.

33. See Ann Devroy, "TV Public Puts Clinton on Defensive," *Washington Post,* February 11, 1993, p. 1. See also Howard Kurtz, "Inaugurating a Talk Show Presidency," *Washington Post,* February 12, 1993, p. A4.

34. Howard Kurtz, "One Too Many Revelations for the Masters of Spin," *Washington Post,* January 25, 1998, p. C1.

35. See Martin Linsky, *Impact: How the Press Affects Federal Policymaking* (New York: Norton, 1986).

36. Carl Allen, "UB Paper Prints Apology for Story on Student Poll," *Buffalo News,* November 15, 1997, p. 1B.

37. For a good discussion of how to evaluate media biases see Don Hazen and Julie Winokur, eds., *We the Media* (New York: New Press, 1997).

CHAPTER 9

1. Agence France Presse wire service report, December 20, 1994.

2. Pan Xiaozhu, Xinhua News Agency report, July 30, 1994.

3. Jack Dennis and Diana Owen, "The Partnership Puzzle: Identification and Attitudes of Generation X," in *After the Boom: The Politics of Generation X,* ed. Stephen C. Craig and Stephen E. Bennett (Lanham, MD: Rowman and Littlefield, 1997).

4. See Richard Hofstadter, *The Idea of a Party System* (Berkeley: University of California Press, 1969).

5. See Walter Dean Burnham, *Critical Elections and the Mainsprings of American Electoral Politics* (New York: Norton, 1970). See also James L. Sundquist, *Dynamics of the Party System* (Washington, D.C: Brookings, 1983).

6. Benjamin Ginsberg, *The Consequences of Consent* (New York: Random House, 1982), chap. 4.

7. For a discussion of third parties in the United States, see Daniel Mazmanian, *Third Parties in Presidential Election* (Washington, DC: Brookings, 1974).

8. See Maurice Duverger, *Political Parties* (New York: Wiley, 1954).

9. See Harold Gosnell, *Machine Politics Chicago Model,* rev. ed. (Chicago: University of Chicago Press, 1968).

10. For a useful discussion, see John Bibby and Thomas Holbrook, "Parties and Elections," in *Politics in the American States,* ed. Virginia Gray and Herbert Jacob (Washington, DC: Congressional Quarterly Press, 1996), pp. 78–121.

11. Alan Greenblatt, "With Major Issues Fading, Capitol Life Lures Fewer," *Congressional Quarterly Weekly Report,* October 25, 1997, p. 2625.

12. For an excellent analysis of the parties' role in recruitment, see Paul Herrnson, *Congressional Elections: Campaigning at Home and in Washington* (Washington, DC: Congressional Quarterly Press, 1995).

13. Larry J. Sabato, *The Rise of Political Consultants* (New York: Basic, 1981).

14. Larry J. Sabato, *The Rise of Political Consultants,* p. 250.

15. M. Ostrogorski, *Democracy and the Organization of Political Parties* (New York: Macmillan, 1902).

16. Timothy Clark, "The RNC Prospers, the DNC Struggles as They Face the 1980 Election," *National Journal,* October 27, 1980, p. 1619.

17. For discussions of the consequences, see Thomas Edsall, *The New Politics of Inequality* (New York: Norton, 1984). Also see Thomas Edsall, "Both Parties Get the Company's Money—But the Boss Backs the GOP," *Washington Post National Weekly Edition,* September 16, 1986, p. 14; and Benjamin Ginsberg, "Money and Power: The New Political Economy of American Elections," in *The Political Economy,* ed. Thomas Ferguson and Joel Rogers (Armonk, NY: M. E. Sharpe, 1984).

18. Duverger, *Political Parties,* p. 426.

19. Duverger, *Political Parties,* chap. 1.

20. Stanley Kelley, Jr., Richard E. Ayres, and William Bowen, "Registration and Voting: Putting First Things First," *American Political Science Review* 61 (June 1967), pp. 359–70.

21. David H. Fischer, *The Revolution of American Conservatism,* (New York: Harper & Row, 1965), p. 93.

22. Fischer, *The Revolution of American Conservatism,* p. 109.

23. Henry Jones Ford, *The Rise and Growth of American Politics* (New York: Da Capo Press, 1967 reprint of the 1898 edition), chap. 9.

24. Ford, *The Rise and Growth of American Politics,* p. 125.

25. Ford, *The Rise and Growth of American Politics,* p. 125.

26. Ford, *The Rise and Growth of American Politics,* p. 126.

27. Mark Barabak, "Los Angeles Times Interview: Cruz Bustamente: On Surviving a Bruising First Term as Assembly Speaker," *Los Angeles Times,* August 24, 1997, p. M3.

CHAPTER 10

1. Clinton Rossiter, ed., *The Federalist Papers* (New York: New American Library, 1961), No. 57, p. 352.

2. Robert Jackman, "Political Institutions and Voter Turnout in the Democracies," *American Political Science Review* 81 (June 1987), p. 420.

3. Helen Dewar, "'Motor Voter' Agreement Is Reached," *Washington Post,* April 28, 1993, p. A6.

4. Erik Austin and Jerome Chubb, *Political Facts of the United States since 1789* (New York: Columbia University Press, 1986), pp. 378–79.

5. *League of United Latin American Citizens v. Wilson,* CV-94-7569 (C.D. Calif.), 1995.

6. *Gray v. Sanders,* 372 U.S. 368 (1963); *Wesberry v. Sanders,* 376 U.S. 1 (1964); *Reynolds v. Sims,* 377 U.S. 533 (1964).

7. *Thornburg v. Gingles,* 478 U.S. 613 (1986).

8. *Shaw v. Reno,* 509 U.S. 113 (1993).

9. Mary McGrory, "The Lost Leader," *Washington Post,* October 26, 1995, p. A2.

10. Data are drawn from exit poll results reported in the *Washington Post,* November 6, 1996, p. B7.

11. See David Broder, "Parceling Out Power to Both Parties," *Washington Post,* November 6, 1996, p. B1.

12. Jonathan Salant, "Million-Dollar Campaigns Proliferate in 105th," *Congressional Quarterly Weekly Report,* December 21, 1996, pp. 3448–51.

13. U.S. Federal Election Commission, "Financing the 1996 Presidential Campaign," Internet Release, April 28, 1998.

14. *Buckley v. Valeo,* 424 U.S. 1 (1976); *Colorado Republican Party v. Federal Election Commission,* 64 U.S.L.W. 4663 (1996).

15. FEC reports.

16. FEC reports.

17. Jill Abramson and Leslie Wayne, "Nonprofit Groups Were Partners to Both Parties in Last Election," *New York Times,* October 24, 1997, p. 1.

18. Fred Wertheimer, "Clinton's Subterfuge Is No Technicality," *Washington Post,* November 9, 1997, p. C1.

19. David Broder and Ruth Marcus, "Wielding Third Force in Politics," *Washington Post,* September 20, 1997, p. 1.

20. Broder and Marcus, "Wielding Third Force in Politics."

21. Leslie Wayne, "Papers Detail GOP Ties to Tax Group," *New York Times,* November 10, 1997, p. A27.

22. *Congressional Research Report* 95–237, Government Information Access Company Newsletter Database, January 1, 1996.

23. See, for example, John Kennedy, "Will Florida's Drive Yield Turnout?" *Fort Lauderdale Sun-Sentinal,* December 18, 1995, p. 1A.

24. For an excellent discussion see Steven J. Rosenstone and John Mark Hansen, *Mobilization, Participation, and Democracy in America* (New York: Macmillan, 1993), chap. 8.

25. Andy Dabilis, "Two New Senators Begin Their Terms as Mavericks," *Boston Globe,* January 10, 1993, p. 2.

CHAPTER 11

1. Jim Zook, "Students Get a Crash Course in Lobbying Against Cuts to Federal Aid," *Chronicle of Higher Education,* March 31, 1995, p. A25.

2. Alexis de Tocqueville, *Democracy in America* (New York: Random House, 1955), vol. 1, chap. 12; vol. 2, chap. 5.

3. Clinton Rossiter, ed., *The Federalist Papers* (New York: New American Library, 1961), No. 10, p. 83.

4. Rossiter, ed., *Federalist Papers,* No. 10.

5. The best statement of the pluralist view is in David Truman, *The Governmental Process* (New York: Knopf, 1951), chap. 2.

6. E. E. Schattschneider, *The Semisovereign People* (New York: Holt, Rinehart, and Winston, 1960), p. 35.

7. Betsy Wagner and David Bowermaster, "B.S. Economics," *Washington Monthly,* November 1992, pp. 19–21.

8. Mancur Olson, *The Logic of Collective Action* (Cambridge, MA: Harvard University Press, 1965).

9. Timothy Penny and Steven Schier, *Payment Due: A Nation in Debt, A Generation in Trouble* (Boulder, CO: Westview, 1996), pp. 64–65.

10. Kay Lehman Schlozman and John T. Tierney, *Organized Interests and American Democracy* (New York: Harper & Row, 1986), p. 60.

11. John Herbers, "Special Interests Gaining Power as Voter Disillusionment Grows," *New York Times,* November 14, 1978.

12. Saundra Torry, "Army of Lobbyists Has Drawn $8 Million on Tobacco Fight," *Washington Post,* September 11, 1997, p. A4.

13. Ruth Marcus, "Tobacco Lobby Created Campaign 'Watchdog,'" *Washington Post,* September 30, 1996, p. 1.

14. Thomas B. Edsall, "Liberal Lobby Snared in Campaign Probes," *Washington Post,* November 3, 1997, p. A9.

15. Rich Lowry, "How the Right Rose," *National Review* 66 (December 11, 1995), pp. 64–76.

16. Neil Peirce, "Second Thoughts about Takings Measure," *Baltimore Sun,* December 18, 1995, p. 13A.

17. Chris Warden, "A GOP Revolution That Wasn't," *Investor's Daily,* January 2, 1996, p. A1.

18. For discussions of lobbying, see Allan J. Cigler and Burdett A. Loomis, eds., *Interest Group Politics* (Washington, DC: Congressional Quarterly Press, 1983). See also Jeffrey M. Berry, *Lobbying for the People* (Princeton, NJ: Princeton University Press, 1977).

19. "The Swarming Lobbyists," *Time,* August 7, 1978, p. 15.

20. Ruth Marcus, "Lobbying's Big Hitters Go to Bat," *Washington Post,* August 3, 1997, p. 1.

21. Michael Weisskopf, "Health Care Lobbies Lobby Each Other," *Washington Post,* March 1, 1994, p. A8.

22. Gregory B. Wilson, "A Congressional Lobbying Effort against the U.S. Chamber of Commerce," unpublished research paper, Johns Hopkins University, 1994.

23. Michael Weisskopf, "Lobbyists Rally around Their Own

Cause: Clinton Move to Eliminate Tax Break Sparks Intense Hill Campaign," *Washington Post,* May 14, 1993, p. A16.

24. Phil Kuntz, "Ticket to a Better Image?" *Congressional Quarterly Weekly Report,* May 7, 1994, p. 1105.

25. See especially Marver Bernstein, *Regulating Business by Independent Commission* (Princeton, NJ: Princeton University Press, 1955). See also George J. Stigler, "The Theory of Economic Regulation," *Bell Journal of Economics and Management Science* 2 (1971), pp. 3–21.

26. Quoted in John E. Chubb, *Interest Groups and the Bureaucracy: The Politics of Energy* (Stanford, CA: Stanford University Press, 1983).

27. John P. Heinz, Edward O. Laumann, Robert L. Nelson, and Robert H. Salisbury, *The Hollow Core: Private Interests in National Policy Making* (Cambridge, MA: Harvard University Press, 1993), p. 96. See also Schlozman and Tierney, *Organized Interests and American Democracy,* chap. 13.

28. The famous and prophetic movie *The China Syndrome* portrayed some dramatic moments at a public hearing involving an administrative agency's decision to build or expand an atomic energy plant.

29. William Raspberry, "Why Did Ron Brown Become a Target?" *Washington Post,* January 20, 1993, p. A21.

30. Ruth Marcus, "A $50,000 Weekend with Clinton, Gore," *Washington Post,* October 22, 1997, p. A4.

31. *Roe v. Wade,* 93 S.Ct. 705 (1973).

32. *Webster v. Reproductive Health Services,* 109 S.Ct. 3040 (1989)

33. *Brown v. Board of Education of Topeka, Kansas,* 74 S.Ct. 686 (1954).

34. See, for example, *Duke Power Co. v. Carolina Environmental Study Group,* 438 U.S. 59 (1978).

35. E. Pendleton Herring, *Group Representation before Congress* (New York: McGraw-Hill, 1936).

36. Ann Devroy, "Gay Rights Leaders Meet President in Oval Office: White House Tries to Play Down Session," *Washington Post,* April 17, 1993, p. 1.

37. Michael Weisskopf and Steven Mufson, "Lobbyists in Full Swing on Tax Plan," *Washington Post,* February 17, 1993, p. 1.

38. Michael Weisskopf, "Energized by Pulpit or Passion, the Public is Calling," *Washington Post,* February 1, 1993, p. 1.

39. Stephen Engelberg, "A New Breed of Hired Hands Cultivates Grass-Roots Anger," *New York Times,* March 17, 1993, p. A1.

40. Jane Fritsch, "The Grass Roots, Just a Free Phone Call Away," *New York Times,* June 23, 1995, pp. A1 and A22.

41. Ruth Marcus, "Campaign Finance Proposal Drawing Opposition from Diverse Groups," *Washington Post,* May 1, 1996, p. A12.

42. Leslie Wayne, "Business Is Biggest Campaign Spender, Study Says," *New York Times,* October 18, 1996, p. 1.

43. Thomas B. Edsall, "Dole Outlines Changes for Political Financing," *New York Times,* October 21, 1996, p. 1.

44. David Sanger and James Sterngold, "Fund Raiser for Democrats Now Faces Harsh Spotlight," *New York Times,* October 21, 1996, p. 1.

45. Guy Gugliotta and Edward Walsh, "House Fund-Raising Hearings Grow Stormy," *Washington Post,* November 8, 1997, p. A8.

46. Filed as *Colorado Republican Federal Campaign Committee v. Jones,* 95-489 (1996).

47. Ruth Marcus, "Outside Groups Pushing Election Laws into Irrelevance," *Washington Post,* August 8, 1996, p. A9.

48. Richard L. Burke, "Religious-Right Candidates Gain as GOP Turnout Rises," *New York Times,* November 12, 1994, p. 10.

49. John Harwood, "Dole Presses Hot-Button Issues to Try to Rouse GOP Activists Missing from Campaign So Far," *Wall Street Journal,* October 16, 1996, p. A22.

50. Some Americans and even more Europeans would stress only the negative aspect of the softening and adulterating effect of the two-party system on class and other basic subdivisions of society. For a discussion of how the working class was divided and softened, with native workers joining the Democratic Party and new immigrant workers becoming Republicans, see Gwendolyn Mink, *Old Labor and New Immigrants in American Political Development: Union, Party, and State, 1875–1920* (Ithaca, NY: Cornell University Press, 1986).

51. Rossiter, ed., *The Federalist Papers,* No. 10.

52. Olson, *The Logic of Collective Action.*

53. Steve Ma, telephone interview by author, February 12, 1998.

54. Steve Ma, interview, February 12, 1998.

55. Steve Ma, interview, February 12, 1998.

CHAPTER 12

1. See Cara Tanamachi, "Groups Give Voice to Generation X," *Austin-American Statesman,* October 22, 1996, p. A1.

2. Herb Asher and Mike Barr, "Popular Support for Congress and Its Members," and Karlyn Borman and Everett Carll Ladd, "Public Opinion toward Congress: A Historical Look," in *Congress, the Press, and the Public,* ed. Thomas E. Mann and Norman J. Ornstein (Washington DC: American Enterprise Institute and Brookings Institution, 1994), pp. 34, 51, 53.

3. John R. Hibbing and Elizabeth Theiss-Morse, *Congress as Public Enemy: Public Attitudes toward American Political Institutions* (New York: Cambridge University Press, 1995), p. 100.

4. This argument is developed in Hibbing and Theiss-Morse, *Congress as Public Enemy.* For more on the institutionalization of Congress, see Nelson Polsby, "The Institutionalization of the US House of Representatives," *American Political Science Review* 62 (1968): 144–68; on professionalization see Alan Ehrenhalt, *The United States of Ambition: Politicians, Power, and the Pursuit of Office* (New York: Times Books, 1991).

5. For data on religious affiliations of the members of the 105th Congress, see *Congressional Quarterly Weekly Report,* January 4, 1997.

6. For data on occupational backgrounds of the members of the 105th Congress, see *Congressional Quarterly Weekly Report,* January 4, 1997.

7. Marian D. Irish and James Prothro, *The Politics of American Democracy,* 5th ed. (Englewood Cliffs, NJ: Prentice-Hall, 1971), p. 352.

8. For a discussion, see Benjamin Ginsberg, *The Consequences of Consent* (New York: Random House, 1982), chap. 1.

9. For some interesting empirical evidence, see Angus Campbell, Philip Converse, Warren Miller, and Donald Stokes, *Elections and the Political Order* (New York: Wiley, 1966), chap. 11.

10. Congressional Quarterly, *Guide to the Congress of the United States,* 3rd ed. (Washington, DC: Congressional Quarterly Press, 1982), p. 599.

11. John S. Saloma, *Congress and the New Politics* (Boston: Little, Brown, 1969), pp. 184–85. A 1977 official report using less detailed categories came up with almost the same impression of Congress's workload. Commission on Administrative Review, *Administrative Reorganization and Legislative Management,* House Doc. #95-232 (September 28, 1977), vol. 2, especially pp. 17–19.

12. See Linda Fowler and Robert McClure, *Political Ambition: Who Decides to Run for Congress* (New Haven: Yale University Press, 1989); and Alan Ehrenhalt, *The United States of Ambition.*

13. See Barbara C. Burrell, *A Woman's Place Is in the House: Campaigning for Congress in the Feminist Era* (Ann Arbor: University of Michigan Press, 1994), chap. 6; and the essays in Elizabeth Adell Cook, Sue Thomas, and Clyde Wilcox, eds., *The Year of the Woman: Myths and Realities* (Boulder, CO: Westview, 1994).

14. Kevin Merida, "The 2nd Time Is Easy; Many House Freshmen Have Secured Seats," *Washington Post,* October 18, 1994, p. A1.

15. See Burrell, *A Woman's Place Is in the House;* and David Broder, "Key to Women's Political Parity: Running," *Washington Post,* September 8, 1994, p. A17.

16. Based on authors' tabulations.

17. "Did Redistricting Sink the Democrats?" *National Journal,* December 17, 1994, p. 2984.

18. *Miller v. Johnson,* 115 S.Ct. 2475 (1995).

19. Tim Weiner, "Sending Money to Home District: Earmarking and the Pork Barrel," *New York Times,* July 13, 1994, p. 1.

20. Robert Pear, "Justices, 6-3, Bar Veto of Line Items in Bills; See H.I.V. as Disability," *New York Times,* June 26, 1998, p. A1.

21. Congressional Quarterly, *Guide to the Congress of the United States,* 2nd ed. (Washington, DC: Congressional Quarterly Press, 1976), pp. 229–310.

22. Richard Fenno, Jr., *Home Style: House Members in Their Districts* (Boston: Little, Brown, 1978).

23. On the agenda activities of the Democratic leadership, see Paul S. Herrnson and Kelly D. Patterson. "Toward a More Programmatic Democratic Party? Agenda-Setting and Coalition-Building in the House of Representatives." *Polity* 27 (summer 1995) pp. 607–28.

24. Richard C. Fenno, *Congressmen in Committees* (Boston: Little, Brown, 1973), p. 1; Richard L. Hall, "Participation, Abdication, and Representation in Congressional Committees," in *Congress Reconsidered,* 5th ed., ed. Lawrence C. Dodd and Bruce I. Oppenheimer (Washington DC: Congressional Quarterly Press, 1993), p. 164.

25. See Thomas E. Mann and Norman J. Ornstein, *Renewing Congress: A First Report of the Renewing Congress Project* (Washington, DC: American Enterprise Institute and Brookings Institution, 1992). See also the essays in Roger H. Davidson, ed., *The Postreform Congress* (New York: St. Martin's, 1992).

26. Adam Clymer, "The House: Battlefield of Short-Tempered Partisanship," *New York Times,* July 16, 1995, p. 14; David S. Broder, "At 6 Months, House GOP Juggernaut Still Cohesive," *Washington Post,* July 17, 1995, p. A1.

27. Robert Pear, "With Long Hours and Little Fanfare, Staff Members Crafted a Health Bill," *New York Times,* August 6, 1994, p. 7.

28. Kenneth Cooper, "GOP Moves to Restrict Office Funds," *Washington Post,* December 7, 1994, p. 1.

29. Susan Webb Hammond, "Congressional Caucuses in the 104th Congress," in *Congress Reconsidered,* 6th ed., ed. Lawrence C. Dodd and Bruce I. Oppenheimer (Washington, DC: Congressional Quarterly Press, 1996).

30. Richard Sammon, "Panel Backs Senate Changes, But Fights Loom for Floor," *Congressional Quarterly Weekly Report,* June 18, 1994, pp. 1575–76.

31. See Robert Pear, "Senator X Kills Measure on Anonymity," *New York Times,* November 11, 1997, p. 12.

32. See John W. Kingdon, *Congressmen's Voting Decisions* (New York: Harper and Row, 1973), chap. 3; and R. Douglas Arnold, *The Logic of Congressional Action* (New Haven, CT: Yale University Press, 1990).

33. Jane Fritsch, "The Grass Roots, Just a Free Phone Call Away," *New York Times,* June 23, 1995, p. A1.

34. Daniel Franklin, "Tommy Boggs and the Death of Health Care Reform," *Washington Monthly,* April 1995, p. 36.

35. Peter H. Stone, "Follow the Leaders," *National Journal,* June 24, 1995, p. 1641.

36. Holly Idelson, "Signs Point to Greater Loyalty on Both Sides of the Aisle," *Congressional Quarterly Weekly Report,* December 19, 1992, p. 3849.

37. David Broder, "Hill Democrats Vote as One: New Era of Unity or Short-term Honeymoon?" *Washington Post,* March 14, 1993, p. A1. See also Adam Clymer, "All Aboard: Clinton's Plan Gets Moving," *New York Times,* March 21, 1993, sec. 4, p. 1.

38. Allen R. Meyerson, "Oil-Patch Congressmen Seek Deal With Clinton," *New York Times,* June 14, 1994, p. D2.

39. David Broder, "At 6 Months, House GOP Juggernaut still Cohesive."

40. *U.S. v. Pink,* 315 U.S. 203 (1942). For a good discussion of the problem, see James W. Davis, *The American Presidency* (New York: Harper & Row, 1987), chap. 8.

41. Carroll J. Doherty, "Impeachment: How It Would Work," *Congressional Quarterly Weekly Report,* January 31, 1998, p. 222.

42. See Kenneth A. Shepsle. "Representation and Governance: The Great Legislative Trade-off," *Political Science Quarterly* 103:3 (1988), pp. 461–84.

43. Hibbing and Theiss-Morse, *Congress as Public Enemy,* p. 66.

44. See Hibbing and Theiss-Morse, *Congress as Public Enemy,* p. 105.

45. Jeffrey H. Birnbaum, "Washington's Power 25," *Fortune,* December 8, 1997, p. 144.

46. Birnbaum, "Washington's Power 25."

47. Marilyn Werber Serafini, "Biomedical Warfare," *National Journal,* February 1, 1997, p. 220.

CHAPTER 13

1. CNN/*Time* polls, January 23 and 30, 1998.

2. E. S. Corwin, *The President: Office and Powers,* 3rd rev. ed. (New York: New York University Press, 1957), p. 2.

3. *In re Neagle,* 135 U.S. 1 (1890). Neagle, a deputy U.S. marshal, had been authorized by the president to protect a Supreme Court justice whose life had been threatened by an angry litigant. When the litigant attempted to carry out his threat, Neagle shot and killed him. Neagle was then arrested by the local authorities and tried for murder. His defense was that his act was "done in pursuance of a law of the United States." Although the law was not an act of Congress, the Supreme Court declared that it was an executive order of the president, and the protection of a federal judge was a reasonable extension of the president's power to "take care that the laws be faithfully executed."

4. Arthur Schlesinger, Jr., *The Imperial Presidency* (Boston: Houghton Mifflin, 1973).

5. *U.S. v. Curtiss-Wright Corp.,* 299 U.S. 304 (1936). In 1934, Congress passed a joint resolution authorizing the president to prohibit the sale of military supplies to Bolivia and Paraguay, who were at war, if the president determined that the prohibition would contribute to peace between the two countries. When prosecuted for violating the embargo order by President Roosevelt, the defendants argued that Congress could not constitutionally delegate such broad discretion to the president. The Supreme Court disagreed. Previously, however, the Court had rejected the National Industrial Recovery Act precisely because Congress had delegated too much discretion to the president in a domestic policy. See *Schechter Poultry Corp. v. U.S.,* 295 U.S. 495 (1935).

6. In *United States v. Pink,* 315 U.S. 203 (1942), the Supreme Court confirmed that an executive agreement is the legal equivalent of a treaty, despite the absence of Senate approval. This case approved the executive agreement that was used to establish diplomatic relations with the Soviet Union in 1933. An executive agreement, not a treaty, was used in 1940 to exchange "fifty overage destroyers" for ninety-nine-year leases on some important military bases.

7. *Morrison v. Olson,* 486 U.S. 654 (1988).

8. Raoul Berger, *Executive Privilege: A Constitutional Myth* (Cambridge, MA: Harvard University Press, 1974), p. vii.

9. *U.S. v. Nixon,* 418 U.S. 683 (1974).

10. These statutes are contained mainly in Title 10 of the United States Code, Sections 331, 332, and 333.

11. The best study covering all aspects of the domestic use of the military is that of Adam Yarmolinsky, *The Military Establishment* (New York: Harper & Row, 1971). Probably the most famous instance of a president's unilateral use of the power to protect a state "against domestic violence" was in dealing with the Pullman Strike of 1894. The famous Supreme Court case that ensued was *In re Debs,* 158 U.S. 564 (1895).

12. There is a third source of presidential power implied from the provision for "faithful execution of the laws." This is the president's power to impound funds—that is, to refuse to spend money Congress has appropriated for certain purposes. One author referred to this as a "retroactive veto power" (Robert E. Goosetree, "The Power of the President to Impound Appropriated Funds," *American University Law Review,* January 1962). This impoundment power was used freely and to considerable effect by many modern presidents, and Congress occasionally delegated such power to the president by statute. But in reaction to the Watergate scandal, Congress adopted the Budget and Impoundment Control Act of 1974 and designed this act to circumscribe the president's ability to impound funds by requiring that the president must spend all appropriated funds unless both houses of Congress consent to an impoundment within forty-five days of a presidential request. Therefore, since 1974, the use of impoundment has declined significantly. Presidents have either had to bite their tongues and accept unwanted appropriations or had to revert to the older and more dependable but politically limited method of vetoing the entire bill.

13. For a different perspective, see William F. Grover, *The President as Prisoner: A Structural Critique of the Carter and Reagan Years* (Albany: State University of New York Press, 1988).

14. For more on the veto, see Chapter 12 and Robert J. Spitzer, *The Presidential Veto: Touchstone of the American Presidency* (Albany: State University of New York Press, 1989).

15. *Raines v. Byrd,* 117 S.Ct. 2312 (1997).

16. David Broder, "Thinking Small," *Washington Post National Weekly Edition,* February 10, 1997, p. 4.

17. Richard Darman, "Zero-Risk Leadership," *New York Times,* February 9, 1997, p. D15. The examples he gave included $11 million more for food safety; 100,000 more master teachers, without specifying the appropriations necessary; and 500 more waste sites to be cleaned up. Other similar incremental initiatives proposed by the president for the 1997–98 agenda included support for school uniforms; commitment to finding reading tutors, largely volunteers, for hundreds of thousands of schoolchildren; and an order to the FBI to develop a national registry to track sex offenders and child molesters. Political scientist Charles O. Jones referred to all of this as "the trivialization of presidential power."

18. *New York Times,* December 23, 1992, p. 1.

19. A substantial portion of this section is taken from Theodore J. Lowi, *The Personal President* (Ithaca, NY: Cornell University Press, 1985), pp. 141–50.

20. All the figures since 1967, and probably 1957, are understated, because additional White House staff members were on "detail" service from the military and other departments (some secretly assigned) and are not counted here because they were not on the White House payroll.

21. See Donna K. H. Walters, "The Disarray at the White House Proves Clinton Wouldn't Last as a Fortune 500 CEO," *Plain Dealer,* July 10, 1994, p. 1C; and Paul Richter, "The Battle for Washington: Leon Panetta's Burden," *Los Angeles Times Sunday Magazine,* January 8, 1995, p. 16.

22. The actual number is difficult to estimate because, as with White House staff, some EOP personnel, especially in national security work, are detailed to EOP from outside agencies.

23. Article I, Section 3, provides that "The Vice-President . . . shall be President of the Senate, but shall have no Vote, unless they be equally divided." This is the only vote the vice president is allowed.

24. Richard Neustadt, *Presidential Power* (New York: Wiley, 1960), p. 26.

25. *Congressional Quarterly Weekly Report,* Vol. 54, no. 1 (1996), p. 7.

26. A wider range of group phenomena was covered in Chapter 11. In that chapter the focus was on the influence of groups *upon* the government and its policy-making processes. Here our concern is more with the relationship of groups to the presidency and the extent to which groups and coalitions of groups become a dependable resource for presidential government.

27. For a more detailed review of the New Deal coalition in comparison with later coalition, see Thomas Ferguson and Joel Rogers, *Right Turn: The Decline of the Democrats and the Future of American Politics* (New York: Hill & Wang, 1986), chap. 2. For updates on the group basis of presidential politics, see Thomas Ferguson, "Money and Politics," in *Handbooks to the Modern Worlds: The United States,* vol. 2, ed. Godfrey Hodgson (New York: Facts on File, 1992), pp. 1060–84; and Lucius J. Barker, ed., "Black Electoral Politics," *National Political Science Review,* vol. 2 (New Brunswick, NJ: Transaction Publishers, 1990).

28. David Broder, "Some Newsworthy Presidential CPR," *Washington Post National Weekly Edition,* June 4–10, 1990, p. 4.

29. See George Edwards III, *At the Margins: Presidential Leadership of Congress* (New Haven, CT: Yale University Press, 1989), chap. 7; and Robert Locander, "The President and the News Media," in *Dimensions of the Modern Presidency,* ed. Edward Kearney (St. Louis: Forum Press, 1981), pp. 49–52.

30. Study cited in Ann Devroy, "Despite Panetta Pep Talk, White House Aides See Daunting Task," *Washington Post,* January 8, 1995, p. A4.

31. This very useful distinction between power and powers is inspired by Richard Neustadt, *Presidential Power* (New York: Wiley, 1960), p. 28.

32. The Supreme Court did in fact disapprove broad delegations of legislative power by declaring the National Industrial Recovery Act of 1933 unconstitutional on the grounds that Congress did not accompany the broad delegations with sufficient standards or guidelines for presidential discretion (*Panama Refining Co. v. Ryan,* 293 U.S. 388[1935], and *Schechter Poultry Corp. v. United States,* 295 U.S. 495 [1935]). The Supreme Court has never reversed those two decisions, but it has also never really followed them. Thus, broad delegations of legislative power from Congress to the executive branch can be presumed to be constitutional.

CHAPTER 14

1. U.S. Bureau of the Census, *Statistical Abstract of the United States, 1997* (Washington, DC: U.S. Government Printing Office, 1997), pp. 348, 355.

2. Arnold Brecht and Comstock Glaser, *The Art and Techniques of Administration in German Ministries* (Cambridge, MA: Harvard University Press, 1940), p. 6.

3. "Red tape" actually refers to the traditional practice of tying up bundles of bureaucratic records before storing them somewhere.

4. The presidential commission that investigated the *Challenger* tragedy was able to pinpoint a single technical failure on the basis of the evidence—the paper trail—assembled. Analysts of the tragedy concluded that "the decision to launch the *Challenger* was flawed. Those who made the decision were unaware of the recent history of [technical] problems. . . . If the decision-makers had known all the facts it is highly unlikely that they would have decided to launch [the shuttle] on January 28, 1986." See Barbara S. Romzek and Melvin Dubnick, "Accountability in the Public Sector: Lessons from the *Challenger* Tragedy," in *Current Issues in Public Administration,* 5th ed., ed. Frederick S. Lane (New York: St. Martin's, 1994), pp. 158–59.

5. This account is drawn from Alan Stone, *How America Got On-Line: Politics, Markets, and the Revolution in Telecommunications* (Armonk, NY: M. E. Sharpe, 1997), pp. 184–87.

6. Gary Bryner, *Bureaucratic Discretion* (New York: Pergamon, 1987).

7. Charles H. Levine and Rosslyn S. Kleeman, "The Quiet Crisis in the American Public Service," in *Agenda for Excellence: Public Service in America,* ed. Patricia Ingraham and Donald Kettl (Chatham, NJ: Chatham House, 1992), p. 214.

8. Levine and Kleeman, "The Quiet Crisis," p. 214.

9. Levine and Kleeman, "The Quiet Crisis," p. 209.

10. Figures cited in Paula D. McClain and Joseph Stewart, Jr., *"Can't We All Get Along?" Racial and Ethnic Minorities in American Politics* (Boulder, CO: Westview, 1995), pp. 102–5.

11. "GS" refers to the general schedule, or chart, of salary levels for all federal civil service employees.

12. McClain and Stewart, *"Can't We All Get Along,"* p. 105.

13. As of 1998, salaries for GS-15 federal employees in Washington, D.C., could range from $77,798 to $101,142; salaries for the Senior Executive Service could range between $110,700 and $151,800 annually. Office of Personnel Management, Salaries and Wages web page, http://www.opm.gov/oca/payrates/index.htm (accessed 5/11/98).

14. Joel D. Aberbach, "The Federal Executive under Clinton," in *The Clinton Presidency: First Appraisals,* ed. Colin Campbell and Bert Rockman (Chatham, NJ: Chatham House, 1996), pp. 163–76.

15. There are historical reasons why American cabinet-level administrators are called "secretaries." During the Second Continental Congress and the subsequent confederal government, standing committees were formed to deal with executive functions related to foreign affairs, military and maritime issues, and public financing. The heads of those committees were called "secretaries" because their primary task was to handle all correspondence and documentation related to their areas of responsibility.

16. 32 Stat. 825; 15 U.S.C. 1501.

17. See Theodore J. Lowi, *The End of Liberalism* (New York: Norton, 1979), pp. 78–84.

18. There are other departments that are placed under different classifications but that possess a few clientele agencies, even though the entire department is not a clientele department.

19. "The Republican Congress—The Evolution of a Revolution," *Economist,* November 4, 1995, pp. 23–25.

20. For a good story on the difficulty of abolishing a clientele agency, see David E. Sanger, "GOP Finds Commerce Department Is Hard to Uproot," *New York Times,* September 19, 1995, p. 1.

21. George E. Berkley, *The Craft of Public Administration* (Boston: Allyn & Bacon, 1975), p. 417. Emphasis added.

22. Correspondent Kelli Arena, "Overhauling the IRS," CNN Financial Network, March 7, 1997.

23. See William Keller, *The Liberals and J. Edgar Hoover* (Princeton, NJ: Princeton University Press, 1989). See also Victor Navasky, *Kennedy Justice* (New York: Atheneum, 1971), chap. 2 and p. 8.

24. For more detail, consult John E. Harr, *The Professional Diplomat* (Princeton, NJ: Princeton University Press, 1972), p. 11; and Nicholas Horrock, "The CIA Has Neighbors in the 'Intelligence Community,'" *New York Times,* June 29, 1975, sec. 4, p. 2. See also Roger Hilsman, *The Politics of Policy Making in Defense and Foreign Affairs,* 3rd ed. (Englewood Cliffs, NJ: Prentice Hall, 1993).

25. William Safire, "Bush's Gamble," *New York Times Magazine,* October 18, 1992, p. 60.

26. See Paul Peterson, *The Price of Federalism* (Washington, DC: Brookings, 1995) for a recent argument that "redistribution" is the distinctive function of the national government in the American federal system.

27. *Budget of the United States Government, FY 1998: Analytical Perspectives* (Washington, DC: U.S. Government Printing Office, 1997), Table 12-2, p. 219.

28. For an excellent political analysis of the Fed, see Donald Kettl, *Leadership at the Fed* (New Haven, CT: Yale University Press, 1986).

29. These are called "insurance" because the Social Security tax is a kind of premium; however, the programs are not fully self-sustaining, and people do not receive benefits in proportion to the size of their premiums.

30. A thorough review of the first session of the 104th Congress will be found in "Republican's Hopes for 1996 Lie in Unfinished Business," *Congressional Quarterly Weekly Report,* January 6, 1996, pp. 6–18.

31. Public Law 101-510, Title XXIX, Sections 2,901 and 2,902 of Part A (Defense Base Closure and Realignment Commission).

32. Donald F. Kettl and John I. DiIulio, *Fine Print,* Center for Public Management Report no. 95-1 (Washington, DC: Brookings Institution, 1995).

33. The title was inspired by a book by Charles Hyneman, *Bureaucracy in a Democracy* (New York: Harper, 1950). For a more recent effort to describe the federal bureaucracy and to provide some guidelines for improvement, see Patricia W. Ingraham and Donald F. Kettl, eds., *Agenda for Excellence: Public Service in America* (Chatham, NJ: Chatham House, 1992).

34. Clinton Rossiter, ed., *The Federalist Papers* (New York: New American Library, 1961), No. 51, p. 322.

35. The title of this section was inspired by Peri Arnold, *Making the Managerial Presidency* (Princeton, NJ: Princeton University Press, 1986).

36. See Richard Nathan, *The Plot that Failed: Nixon and the Administrative Presidency* (New York: Wiley, 1975), pp. 68–76.

37. For more details and evaluations, see David Rosenbloom, *Public Administration* (New York: Random House, 1986), pp. 186–221; Levine and Kleeman, "The Quiet Crisis"; and Patricia Ingraham and David Rosenbloom, "The State of Merit in the Federal Government," in *Agenda for Excellence,* ed. Ingraham and Kettl.

38. Lester Salamon and Alan Abramson, "Governance: The Politics of Retrenchment," in *The Reagan Record,* ed. John Palmer and Isabel Sawhill (Cambridge, MA: Ballinger, 1984), p. 40.

39. Colin Campbell, "The White House and the Presidency under the 'Let's Deal' President," in *The Bush Presidency: First Appraisals,* ed. Colin Campbell and Bert A. Rockman (Chatham, NJ: Chatham House, 1991), pp. 185–222.

40. See National Performance Review Savings, http://www.npr.gov/library/review.html (accessed on October 15, 1997).

41. Quoted in Stephen Barr, "Midterm Exam for 'Reinvention'; Study Cites 'Impressive Results' But Calls for Strategy to Win Congressional Support," *Washington Post,* August 19, 1994, p. A25.

42. There are many other examples of the difficulty of succeeding at administrative reform, especially in the public opinion vacuum that appears to surround this area. One fascinating case study involves the General Services Administration (GSA), one of the most notoriously unwieldy bureaucracies. See Faye Fiore, "Exec's Baptism of Fire in D.C.; GSA Chief Roger Johnson Reflects on Frustrating First Year that Made Him Yearn for Home," *Los Angeles Times,* July 14, 1994, p. A1.

43. Quote from Irene S. Rubin, *The Politics of Public Budgeting: Getting and Spending, Borrowing and Balancing* (Chatham, NJ: Chatham House, 1997), pp. 250 and 278.

44. Quoted in I. M. Destler, "Reagan and the World: An 'Awesome Stubborness,'" in *The Reagan Legacy: Promise and Performance,* ed. Charles O. Jones (Chatham, NJ: Chatham House, 1988), pp. 244 and 257. The source of the quote is *Report of the President's Special Review Board* (Washington, DC: U.S. Government Printing Office, 1987).

45. Data from Norman Ornstein et al., *Vital Statistics on Congress, 1987–1988* (Washington, DC: Congressional Quarterly Press, 1987), pp. 161–62. See also Lawrence Dodd and Richard Schott, *Congress and the Administrative State* (New York: Wiley, 1979), p. 169. For a valuable and skeptical assessment of legislative oversight of administrations, see James W. Fesler and Donald F. Kettl, *The Politics of the Administrative Process* (Chatham, NJ: Chatham House, 1991), chap. 11.

46. Aaron Wildavsky, *The New Politics of the Budgetary Process,* 2d ed. (New York: HarperCollins, 1992), pp. 15–16.

47. National Performance Review, *From Red Tape to Results: Creating a Government That Works Better and Costs Less* (Washington, DC: U.S. Government Printing Office, 1993), p. 42.

48. The Office of Technology Assessment (OTA) was a fourth research agency serving Congress until 1995. It was one of the first agencies scheduled for elimination by the 104th Congress. Until 1983, Congress had still another tool of legislative oversight: the legislative veto. Each agency operating under such provisions was obliged to submit to Congress every proposed decision or rule, which would then lie before both chambers for thirty to sixty days. If Congress took no action by one-house or two-house resolution explicitly to veto the proposed measure during the prescribed period, it became law. The legislative veto was declared unconstitutional by the Supreme Court in 1983 on the grounds that it violated the separation of powers—the resolutions Congress passed to exercise its veto were not subject to presidential veto, as required by the Constitution. See *Immigration and Naturalization Service v. Chadha,* 462 U.S. 919 (1983).

CHAPTER 15

1. Carolyn J. Mooney, "Judge Finds No Anti-Christian Bias in Tenure Case," *Chronicle of Higher Education,* February 17, 1995, p. A18.

2. Peter Appelbome, "Goal Unmet, Duke Reveals Perils in Effort to Increase Black Faculty," *New York Times,* September 19, 1993, p. A1.

3. See Mike Clary, "The Citadel Surrenders Its All-Male Tradition," *Los Angeles Times,* August 13, 1995, p. A1; and *United States v. Virginia,* 518 U.S. 515 (1996).

4. Duncan Murrell, "UNC Graduate Fights Board's Fickle Tuition Ruling," *Chapel Hill Herald,* October 26, 1997, p. 1.

5. Richard Bernstein, "Guilty if Charged," *New York Review of Books,* January 13, 1994, p. 11.

6. See Richard Neely, *How Courts Govern America* (New Haven, CT: Yale University Press, 1981).

7. U.S. Bureau of the Census, *Statistical Abstract of the United States* (Washington, DC: Government Printing Office, 1995).

8. Robert Scigliano, *The Supreme Court and the Presidency* (New York: Free Press, 1971), p. 162. For an interesting critique of the solicitor general's role during the Reagan administration, see Lincoln Caplan, "Annals of the Law," *New Yorker,* August 17, 1987, pp. 30–62.

9. Edward Lazarus, *Closed Chambers* (New York: Times Books, 1998), p. 6.

10. C. Herman Pritchett, *The American Constitution* (New York: McGraw-Hill, 1959), p. 138.

11. *Marbury v. Madison,* 1 Cr. 137 (1803).

12. *Clinton v. City of New York,* 55 U.S.L.W. 4543 (1998).

13. This review power was affirmed by the Supreme Court in *Martin v. Hunter's Lessee,* 1 Wheat. 304 (1816).

14. *Brown v. Board of Education,* 347 U.S. 483 (1954); *Loving v. Virginia,* 388 U.S. 1 (1967).

15. *Griswold v. Connecticut,* 381 U.S. 479 (1965).

16. *Brandenburg v. Ohio,* 395 U.S. 444 (1969).

17. Oliver Wendell Holmes, Jr., "The Path of the Law," *Harvard Law Review* 10 (1897), p. 457.

18. *Shelley v. Kraemer,* 334 U.S. 1 (1948).

19. *Gideon v. Wainwright,* 372 U.S. 335 (1963).

20. *Burlington Industries v. Ellerth,* 97-569 (1998).

21. *Engel v. Vitale,* 370 U.S. 421 (1962); *Gideon v. Wainwright,* 372 U.S. 335 (1963); *Escobedo v. Illinois,* 378 U.S. 478 (1964); and *Miranda v. Arizona,* 384 U.S. 436 (1966).

22. *Baker v. Carr,* 369 U.S. 186 (1962).

23. Walter F. Murphy, "The Supreme Court of the United States," in *Encyclopedia of the American Judicial System,* ed. Robert J. Janosik (New York: Scribner's, 1987).

24. *Adarand Constructors v. Pena,* 115 S.Ct. 2097 (1995); *Missouri v. Jenkins,* 115 S.Ct. 2573 (1995); *Miller v. Johnson,* 115 S.Ct. 2475 (1995).

25. *Plyler v. Doe,* 457 U.S. 202 (1982).

26. *NAACP v. Button,* 371 U.S. 415 (1963). The quotation is from the opinion in this case.

27. *Smith v. Allwright,* 321 U.S. 649 (1994).

28. See John E. Morris, "Boalt Hall's Affirmative Action Dilemma," *American Lawyer,* November 1997, p. 4.

29. *Chicago Daily Law Bulletin,* October 5, 1994.

30. R. W. Apple, Jr., "A Divided Government Remains, and with It the Prospect of Further Combat," *New York Times,* November 7, 1996, p. B6.

31. For limits on judicial power, see Alexander Bickel, *The Least Dangerous Branch* (Indianapolis, IN: Bobbs-Merrill, 1962).

32. *Worcester v. Georgia,* 6 Pet. 515 (1832).

33. See Walter Murphy, *Congress and the Court* (Chicago: University of Chicago Press, 1962).

34. Robert Dahl, "The Supreme Court and National Policy Making," *Journal of Public Law* 6 (1958), p. 279.

35. Martin Shapiro, "The Supreme Court: From Warren to Burger," in *The New American Political System,* ed. Anthony King (Washington, DC: American Enterprise Institute, 1978).

36. *Citizens to Preserve Overton Park v. Volpe,* 401 U.S. 402 (1971).

37. Toni Locy, "Bracing for Health Care's Caseload," *Washington Post,* August 22, 1994, p. A15.

38. See "Developments in the Law—Class Actions," *Harvard Law Review* 89 (1976), p. 1318.

39. *In re Agent Orange Product Liability Litigation,* 100 F.R.D. 718 (D.C.N.Y. 1983).

40. See Donald Horowitz, *The Courts and Social Policy* (Washington, DC: Brookings Institution, 1977).

41. *Moran v. McDonough,* 540 F. 2nd 527 (1 Cir., 1976; *cert. denied* 429 U.S. 1042 [1977]).

42. Clinton Rossiter, ed., *The Federalist Papers* (New York: New American Library, 1961), No. 10, p. 78.

43. *Adam Ketchum, A Minor, et. al. v. Hyundai Motor Company,* Los Angeles County, CA, Case No. VC004170 (1993).

44. *Blum v. Merrell Dow Pharmaceuticals, Inc.,* Philadelphia County, PA, Case No. 82-09-1027 (1994).

45. *Michigan Employment Law Letter* 7:12 (February 1997), p. 1.

46. Bree Bisnette, "Students Fulfill Civic Duties, Serve Justice on Jury Duty," *Kansas State Collegian,* August 30, 1996, p. 5.

Illustration Credits

Answer Key

CHAPTER 1	CHAPTER 4	CHAPTER 7	CHAPTER 10	CHAPTER 13
1. d	1. b	1. c	1. a	1. b
2. b	2. c	2. a	2. b	2. a
3. c	3. d	3. d	3. a	3. a
4. c	4. c	4. c	4. d	4. b
5. b	5. c	5. d	5. c	5. a
6. d	6. b	6. b	6. d	6. c
7. d	7. a	7. d	7. a	7. a
8. a	8. d	8. b	8. a	8. d
9. a	9. a	9. a	9. b	9. b
10. a	10. d	10. b	10. a	10. c

CHAPTER 2	CHAPTER 5	CHAPTER 8	CHAPTER 11	CHAPTER 14
1. b	1. a	1. c	1. a	1. b
2. a	2. c	2. b	2. d	2. c
3. c	3. c	3. d	3. c	3. a
4. d	4. a	4. c	4. a	4. c
5. d	5. d	5. d	5. a	5. a
6. a	6. d	6. a	6. c	6. d
7. b	7. b	7. b	7. d	7. a
8. d	8. d	8. a	8. d	8. b
9. d	9. b	9. d	9. b	9. a
10. c	10. c	10. a	10. a	10. c

CHAPTER 3	CHAPTER 6	CHAPTER 9	CHAPTER 12	CHAPTER 15
1. b	1. b	1. a	1. a	1. a
2. b	2. a	2. d	2. d	2. b
3. b	3. b	3. c	3. c	3. d
4. b	4. b	4. d	4. c	4. d
5. c	5. c	5. b	5. a	5. a
6. c	6. b	6. c	6. c	6. c
7. d	7. d	7. c	7. b	7. c
8. d	8. d	8. a	8. a	8. a
9. d	9. d	9. c	9. a	9. d
10. a	10. a	10. d	10. c	10. a

Index